MISUSE OF DRUGS AND DRUG TRAFFICKING OFFENCES

AUSTRALIA
Law Book Co.
Sydney

CANADA AND USA
Carswell
Toronto

NEW ZEALAND
Brookers
Auckland

SINGAPORE and MALAYSIA
Sweet & Maxwell Asia
Singapore and Kuala Lumpur

Misuse of Drugs
and
Drug Trafficking Offences

Fourth edition

Rudi Fortson LL.B. (Lond.)
of the Middle Temple,
Barrister

London
Sweet & Maxwell
2002

First edition 1988
Second edition 1992
Third edition 1996
Fourth edition 2002

Published in 2002 by
Sweet & Maxwell Ltd., of
100 Avenue Road
London NW3 3PF
(http://www.sweetandmaxwell.co.uk)
Typeset by Wyvern 21, Bristol
Printed and bound in Great Britain
by Athenaeum Press

A CIP catalogue for this book is
available from the British Library

ISBN 0421 763 302

PREFACE

It has been five years since the last edition was published. Substantial changes to the law have forced a massive revision of the text for this edition. This is particularly true in respect of Chapter 13 (confiscation). Of necessity, that chapter has expanded to the extent that it now occupies almost 25 per cent of the book. The volume of confiscation case law is colossal; much of it is discussed in Chapter 13. Few practitioners relish confiscation proceedings. There are many pit-falls and the law is not straightforward. Confiscation cases, and family law cases, have at least one feature in common; they are rarely concluded. The parties often return to Court—perhaps years after the original order was made. Often there is much at stake. The provisions of the Drug Trafficking Act 1994 can bite hard—not just against the convicted defendant, but third parties too. Politicians loosely refer to confiscation as being the recovery of "ill-gotten gains" or "profit". That is to seriously understate the true position: confiscation under the Drug Trafficking Act relates to the recovery of the "proceeds" of drug trafficking. Depending on how "benefit" is calculated (there can be more than one correct way to calculate the "benefit" figure in each case) the value can sometimes be gigantic. Crime should not pay, but I venture to suggest that the State has a moral obligation to be realistic about the amounts recoverable under a confiscation order: see, for example, *Attorney General's Reference No. 25 Of 2001 (Moran)* [2001] EWCA Crim 1770, a decision under Part VI of the Criminal Justice Act 1988. Of Course, practitioners and the judiciary must grapple with the legislation as it stands. To that end, much of Chapter 13 is devoted to detailed commentary to the Drug Trafficking Act 1994. The chapter also includes three guides (i) a guide to the Drug Trafficking Act 1994, (ii) a guide to Part VI of the Criminal Justice Act 1988, and (iii) an outline of the Proceeds of Crime Bill 2001. The guides are a new feature of this edition. The revised text takes account of human rights jurisprudence, including *Phillips v. United Kingdom* (July 7, 2001; E.Crt.H.R.).

Parliament's output of legislation continues to be prolific. Quite apart from the Human Rights Act 1998, Parliament has enacted the *Criminal Justice and Public Order Act 1996, Crime (Sentences) Act 1997, Police Act 1997, Crime and Disorder Act 1998, Access to Justice Act 1999, Youth Justice and Criminal Evidence Act 1999, Powers of the Criminal Courts (Sentencing) Act 2000, Regulation of Investigatory Powers Act 2000, Postal Service Act 2000, Criminal Justice and Court Services Act 2000*, and the *Criminal Justice and Police Act 2001*. It is an exacting task to keep abreast of new legislation. It is an even more exacting task to be aware of statutory provisions currently in force. Unsurprisingly, some practitioners have been heard to say that, for a while at least, the "best change" might be "no change". This is not a statement to be taken literally—we all know that there will be change—but sometimes it does seem that Parliament legislates in haste, and repents almost as quickly by introducing amending legislation. By contrast, and to its credit, the Government is taking a great deal of time to consult in relation to its far-reaching proposals regarding the recovery of the proceeds of crime, and to tackle money laundering. The language is changing too: the key phrase is "asset recovery"—not merely confiscation following conviction, but also the recovery of property (without conviction) that probably represents the proceeds of crime. In February 2001, the Government printed the first draft of the Proceeds of Crime Bill, for consultation purposes. That document should read in conjunction with the Report of the Performance and Innovation Unit, *"Recovering the Proceeds of Crime"* (June 2000). The draft Bill has been revised several times. It is probable that a Proceeds of Crime Act will be enacted in 2002 but may not come into force until 20003. Much of Chapter 13 (confiscation) will continue to be relevant for the shelf life of this edition.

On July 5, 2001, the House of Lords delivered opinions in *Lambert* [2001] UKHL 37. It is a landmark decision on two points: first, as to whether the Human Rights Act 1998 is of retrospective application, and secondly, as to the construction of section 28 of the Misuse of Drugs Act 1971. That section created statutory defences which the defendant is required to prove. The inclusion in section 28, of the phrase "nor had reason to suspect", was bound to expose that section to a challenge under the Human Rights Act 1998. In order to keep section 28 convention-compliant, one option was to read-down that provision, by excluding the phrase. However, in *Lambert*, the majority of their Lorsdships went much further, and held (Lord Hutton dissenting) that after October 2, 2000, defendants would shoulder the *evidential* burden of proving a defence under section 28—and this despite the fact that section 28(2) includes the expression "it shall be . . . for the accused to prove . . ." and section 28(3)(b) says "if he proves". The decision of the majority is consistent with the views of the Criminal Law Revision Committee in its Eleventh Report (paragraph 140), but the reader should note that in 1985, the Law Commission did not follow the recommendations of the CLRC (Law Com. No. 143, chapter 6; and see Part 6 of the Law Commission Commentary on the Draft Criminal Code Bill; Law Com. No. 177).

There seems to be no doubt that Parliament intended that section 28 should place a persuasive burden on the accused—a point that troubled Michael Havers MP (as he then was; see Hansard, House of Commons, July 16, 1970; col. 1769), and Mr Crowder MP (Hansard, December 9, 1970, col. 616). The then Solicitor General told the House of Commons that the possession of certain drugs had been an absolute offence, and that:

"... the formulation which appears in the Bill is that approved and recommended by the Law Commission ... The view taken was that although it would be wrong to maintain an absolute offence, to put the burden of proving guilty knowledge in respect of all these offences on the prosecution would be to put too high a burden on it in respect of matters which are a cause of such concern and which need stringent measures to control and regulate them. A middle position has been arrived at."

[Hansard, December 9 1970, Misuse of Drugs Bill, col. 619]

It seems that the Bar Council made "strong representations to the Government" about section 28(2), but the Government relied on the speech of Lord Reid in *Warner v. Metropolitan Police Commissioners* [1969] 2 A.C. 256, in which he said:

"... in a case like this Parliament, if consulted, might think it right to transfer the onus of proof so that an accused would have to prove that he neither knew nor had any reason to suspect that he had a prohibited drug in his possession".

The Government won the day. *Lambert* may fuel the debate about the role of the Courts and the will of Parliament. That said, it seems likely that the decision (insofar as it relates to section 28 of the Misuse of Drugs Act) will be welcomed by most commentators. Despite the fears expressed by the Solicitor-General in 1970 (see above) it will usually not be difficult for the prosecution to negate a section 28 defence: the prosecution need only prove that the accused *did* have *reason to suspect* the existence of the relevant fact. What must an accused do to discharge the evidential burden? Is it enough for him/her to say, during a search, "I had no idea it was a controlled drug"? Doubtless, the topic will considered by an appellate Court before long.

There has also been a challenge under the Human Rights Act 1998 in respect of prosecutions for the posession of cannabis for personal use: *R v. Ham* (July 9, 2001, Southwark Crown Court, His Honour Judge Rivlin Q.C.). The result is discussed in Chapter 3, but suffice to say that the challenge failed. There are other similar cases pending before Crown Courts around the country (several internet websites provide a list of such cases), but it is unlikely that any of them will succeed if the main point is that a prosecution for the possession of cannabis for personal use, is a disproportionate response, and/or that such a prosecution violates article 8 of the Human Rights Act 1998/ECHR. In *Ham*, the defendant declined the offer of a caution. There may be cases where prosecution would not be in the public interest, or be more detrimental to the accused than the perceived or actual mischief. Each case will turn on its own facts, but it will be rare that discretion exercised by the police or by a prosecuting authority, as to how a case should proceed, is challengeable in the courts. It may be said that whereas it is permissible to exercise discretion on a case-by-case basis, a blanket policy to prosecute, or not to prosecute, is a different manner.

That may be so, but even here, the police have wide discretion as to how they allocate their resources, and the extent to which particular laws will be enforced. Discretion is playing an increasingly important role in the administration of justice (at all levels and stages). The "culture" of human rights will play a significant part in shaping rules regulating the exercise of discretion. Proportionality is an important concept but laypersons tend to interpret "proportionality" rather more broadly than lawyers do. Nevertheless, it is the layperson's construction that will usually determine how public authorities respond to events. It is highly desirable that discretion exercisable by public authorities (*e.g.* cautioning, informal warnings, criteria for prosecution) should be the subject of clear policy statements, which are kept under review, and accessible to members of the public.

This edition is published at a time when the so-called "drugs debate" has reached new heights. One of the stated aims of the *Police Foundation Independent Inquiry into the Misuse of Drugs Act 1971*, of which I was a member, was ". . . to raise the level of public understanding and debate about the effectiveness of the relevant legislation, and the efficiency of its enforcement in achieving the aim of curbing the misuse of controlled drugs" [Report March 2000; Chairman, Viscountess Runciman DBE]. That aim has certainly been achieved. The inquiry examined and explained the development of United Kingdom drug laws in an international, and domestic, context. It commissioned research, including a detailed comparative study of several other European countries' drug laws. The study shows that notwithstanding our international obligations, there exists room for manoeuvre, and that this "room" is being used. The study has now been published (*European Drug Laws: the Room for Manoeuvre*, 2001; DrugScope). The intensity of the drugs debate shows no signs of receding. However, the debate has sometimes been marred by the understandable, but casual, use of phrases such as "descriminalisation" and "legislation". Those two expressions (often used interchangeably) are a source of misunderstanding and confusion. It would be preferable for debaters and commentators to explain what *they* mean by those expressions. There is, I suggest, a difference between "legislation" and "decriminalisation"—a difference highlighted in the way offences are created under the Misuse of Drugs Act 1971. It will be seen that various sections make an acitivity unlawful (*e.g.* possession s.5(1)), and *then* proceed to make that activity a criminal offence (s.5(2)). Section 3 does not make it an offence to import or export a controlled drug, but it does prohibit both activities. It is the Customs and Excise Management Act 1979 that makes a breach of the prohibition "criminal". Savings exist by Regulations made under the Misuse of Drugs Act 1971. In theory, Parliament could make possession of particular drugs unlawful, but not criminal ("decriminalised"): sanctions might be civil rather than criminal. Again, it could go further, and make possession neither criminal ("decriminalised") nor unlawful ("legalised"). Even if the Misuse of Drugs Act 1971 was abolished, other enactments are likely to limit the free movement of drugs, and to continue to make certain acts "criminal" (e.g. under the Medicines Act 1968). The supply of intoxicating liquor has not been totally 'legalised' or 'decriminalised'. A more realistic approach is to focus on the *intensity of control*, and to recognise that regulatory controls are often enforced coercively, using the criminal law. The options for reform are not always as stark, or as clear, as some commentators suggest.

In preparing this edition, I have been greatly assisted by many individuals, Government Departments, private and public agencies, as well as law enforcement agencies (here and abroad). I have been impressed by the extent of their cooperation, frankness, and openness. I am not able to acknowledge them all by name, but needless to say, I am extremely grateful to them: my thanks (in alphabetical order) to the Association of Chief Police Officers; the Bar Council of England and Wales; DS Martin Cook; the Criminal Bar Association of England and Wales; the Drugs Directorate of the Metropolitan Police; DrugScope (formerly ISDD and SCODA); DC Steven Duce (South Yorkshire); Essex Police FIU; the European Criminal Defence Bar Associaiton; Sebastian Gardiner; Mike Goodman (Release); Hampshire Police FIU; the Institute for Public Policy Research; Paul Mendelle; DS Geoffrey Monaghan; John Perry Q.C.; the members and secretariat of the Police Foundation Independent Inquiry (experts in their own right, from whom I learnt a great deal); Beth Reilly; 'Release'; His Honour Judge Rivlin Q.C.; Dame Ruth Runciman; Dr Guy Stessens (University of Antwerp); members and clerks of the Chambers of Rock Tansey Q.C., and indeed to Rock Tansey Q.C., and to Tony White (formerly of the United Nations Supply Reduction Unit). I continue to learn a great deal from the enquiries that I receive each week, and many people are kind enough to forward judgements and materials to me: to all who have taken the trouble to contact me, very many thanks. I should also like to thank the person whose idea it was that I would write this book, Mr G. Eysling.

The publication of a book following submission of proofs from the author, is a highly skilled, labour intensive, task. The preparation of this edition has entailed a considerable amount of painstaking work on the part of many people within Sweet and Maxwell. As with all true experts, they make their work look easy: it is not. I am immensely grateful to all of them. If there are errors in the text, the fault is entirely mine.

Finally, there is one person who is to be afforded the highest praise: my wife. She has considerable patience (fortunately for me) and her support has been unfailing.

This edition is dedicated to my father.

Rudi F. Fortson

TABLE OF CONTENTS

Chapter 3 – Possession of Drugs

Chapter 4 – Possession with Intent to Supply

TABLE OF CASES

TABLE OF STATUTES

TABLE OF STATUTORY INSTRUMENTS

2001 Criminal Justice and Court Services Act 2000 (Commencement No. 7) Order (S.I. 2001 No. 2232) 15–63, 15–65, 15–66

TABLE OF CIVIL PROCEDURE RULES

Chapter 1
Introduction

A. AN HISTORICAL SKETCH OF DRUG MISUSE

Until the early 1960s Britain did not have a major social narcotics problem but by 1986, a survey carried out by the BBC "Drugwatch" team suggested that at least four million people in Britain had tried a controlled drug at some point in their life (Drugwatch, *Just Say No*, (1986)). Fourteen years later, the Police Foundation. Independent Inquiry into the Misuse of Drugs Act 1971, chaired by Viscountess Runciman DBE, conducted the most extensive review of drug distribution and use patterns, ever undertaken in this country, as well as a thorough examination of the United Kingdom's drug laws. In its Report (March, 2000), the Inquiry team was "forcibly struck" by the lack of research and weakness of the information base about drug use in the United Kingdom. The position is improving, and more long-term longitudinal studies/surveys are being conducted. 1–01

Between 1994 and 1998, on average 25 per cent of people between the ages of 16 to 29 admitted taking a controlled drug of some description "last year", whilst 15 per cent of that age group admitted taking a controlled drug "last month". Given that cannabis is by far the most popular drug of choice, it is estimated that two and a half million 16 to 29-year-olds in England and Wales used cannabis "last year", and one and a half million had done so "last month" (1998 British Crime Survey; and see Ch. 2, para. 22, of the Report). The findings of the Scottish Crime Surveys are similar (Anderson and Trischer).

Most users of controlled drugs are aged between 16 and 29 years. Drug use seems to decline after the age of 24 to 29, and it also appears to be that age group that is particularly responsive to treatment measures (including Community Rehabilitation Orders) and Drug Treatment and Testing Orders): see pages 11–22 of the Annual Report 2000 of the European Monitoring Centre for Drugs and Drug Addiction (EMCDDA). This may be explained on the basis that persons of that age range have obtained jobs and taken on responsibilities that force a change in attitudes, and perhaps lifestyle. However, an accurate assessment can only be determined with the assistance of longitudinal studies. About 50 per cent of people under the age of 24 years have never used a controlled drug, and a large proportion 1–02 of those that have do not repeat the experiment. It is not accurate to imagine that most young people are "drug users". Nevertheless it does seem that the incidence of drug-taking by persons aged between 16 and 39 is higher in the United Kingdom than in a number of other Western European countries although the statistics should be viewed with caution, partly because the information relates to a drug taken at any time in the last 12 months (which may not give a reliable picture of the numbers who regularly use drugs) and partly because the methods by which information is obtained and recorded varies between States.

The Inquiry noted that there has been a steady increase in "problem drug use", that is to say, "use whose features include dependence, regular excessive use, and serious health, and other social consequences" (overview, para. 5; and Ch. 2, para. 2).

1–03 The proportion of problem drug users injecting, fell from 65 per cent to 47 per cent between 1989 and 1996, and HIV prevalence among injecting drug users in the United Kingdom is lower than in any other Western Euro-

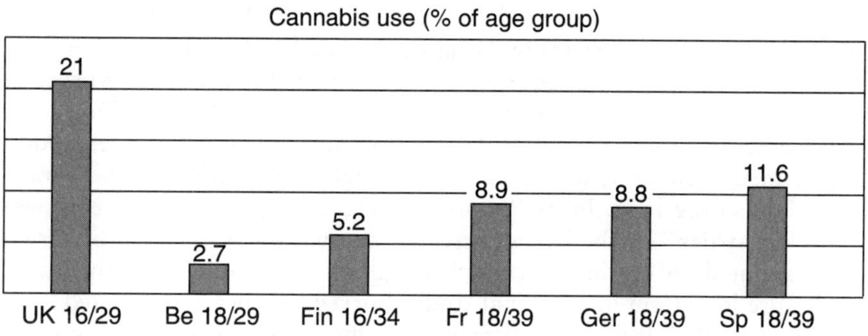

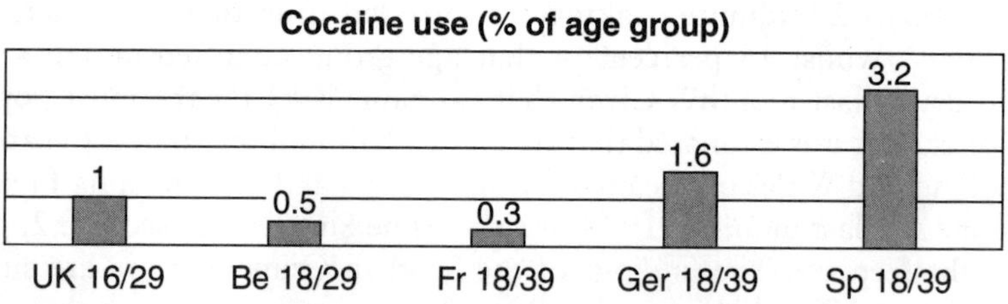

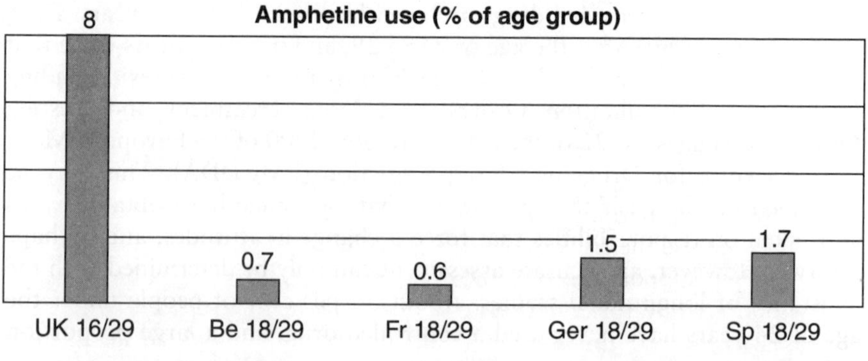

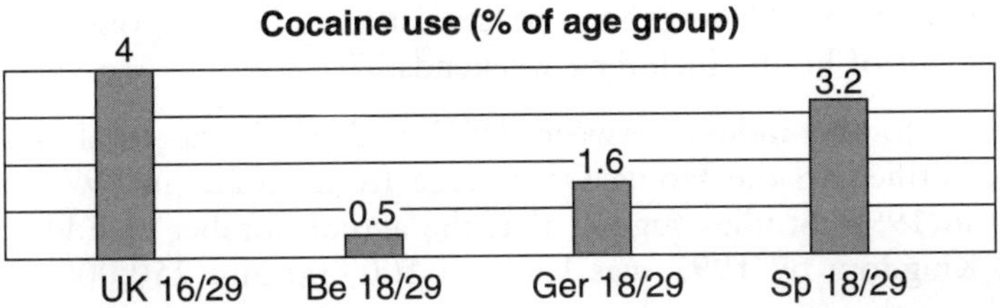

pean country of a similar size (Ch. 2, para. 4, and see the EMCDDA Report, p. 19). However, there are high levels of hepatitis C among problem drug users and there is evidence of a slight increase in the proportion of those who inject heroin and amphetamine. It would therefore seem that at least six per cent of the population of the United Kingdom (about three million people) take a controlled drug of some kind each year (see the Government's White Paper "*Tackling Drugs Together*" Cm 2846, 1995; Cm 2678, 1994).

These figures do not mean of course that there are three million addicts in this country nor does it follow that anything like this number persistently take illegal substances. It should also be emphasised that the Government's own finding is that, of those who take drugs more than once, "only a small proportion may move on to drugs such as heroin and cocaine" (para. A.13).

The "addicts index"

For obvious reasons, the incidence of drug addiction is always a matter of serious concern in any country. It is therefore surprising to discover that the quantity of accurate data as to the level of drug addiction in the United Kingdom is small. Between 1968 and 1997, there was a statutory duty on doctors to notify the Home Office of patients who were addicted to one or more class A drugs. That requirement no longer exists. Admittedly, the "addicts index" tended to understate the actual number of addicts in the United Kingdom (partly because many addicts did not seek treatment) but that does not mean the data was worthless. The Independent Inquiry's conclusion was that the ". . . abolition of the requirement for doctors to notify their addict patients to the Chief Medical Officer at the Home Office has created a new obstacle to responsible prescribing for problem drug users" (Ch. 8). It added: 1–04

> ". . . There is now no national information system to provide general practitioners and other prescribers with up-to-date information on prescribing, in particular of Class A drugs to problem drug users, so as to minimise the risks of double prescribing. This gap needs to be filled and we support the recommendation by the British Medical Association in 1997 for 'a national, comprehensive, confidential information system . . . to provide up-to-date prescribing information on indi-

viduals, accessible to general practitioners and other prescribers, available out-of-hours, including weekends.' "

According to the index, between 1973 and 1997 the total number of addicts notified to the Home Office rose from 3,022 (in 1973) to some 43,000 in 1996. Studies suggest that the actual number of addicts in the United Kingdom by 1997 was between 100,000 and 250,000. The data also tells us that more people are seeking treatment—and not just for class A drugs. There are a large number of "problem" benzodiazepine users who are seeking help. Cannabis is not harmless. Some persons report that their use of cannabis has become problematic but the majority of cannabis uses report no long-term effects (in any).

The estimated number of addicts (even when taken at its highest) falls far short of the number one might expect to find if the so-called "Gateway theory" is valid. However, a detailed discussion of that topic is beyond the scope of this book: suffice to say that the matter has been the subject of considerable analysis by many commentators: see D.B. Kandell, *Journal On Studies On Alcohol* (53) 1972, pp. 447–457, see also the Advisory Committee On Drug Dependence 1968; paragraph 6.3; and the Independent Inquiry Report, Chapter 7; paragraphs to 14–19. Much has been said, and written, about the extent to which there are causal links between drugs and crime. The issue is complex. There is no doubt that a number of problem drug users do commit acquisitive crimes to finance their level of drug use. However, such offenders may commit offences in large numbers. It does not follow that a problem user will commit acquisitive crimes. Measuring the proportion of offences that are drug-related is exceedingly difficult. Much work is being done on the complex issue of drugs and crime. Merely testing arrestees for the presence of controlled drugs and alcohol in their body is insufficient: there is a distinction to be drawn between offenders, whose drug-taking contributed to the commission of an offence, and those who take controlled drugs but offend for some other reason. What is a "drug-related offence"? It tends to mean an offence that is a consequence of a person's drug-taking. Some would therefore argue that it is not appropriate to describe the unlawful possession of a controlled drug as "drug-related". In 1998 drug possession offences accounted for between 83 and 90 per cent of offences committed under the Misuse of Drugs Act, and of those convicted of possession, some 70 per cent of cases related to cannabis. On the other hand, where a drug is supplied by a user, his supplying might be described as "drug-related".

1–05 Drug-related deaths might make headline news—particularly when the drug is ecstasy. Heroin-related deaths are scarcely reported in the media, no matter how young the user. The EMCDDA found that a "clear ageing trend is evident among drug-related deaths" but that such deaths have stabilised overall in the European Union although there are divergent trends in some countries (EMCDDA Report 2000, p. 18). Identifying the precise cause of death is often difficult. The Independent Inquiry found that drug-related deaths have "undoubtedly risen since the early 1980s" of which the use of heroin, methadone, and other opiates contributed to death. Recorded deaths per year average between 1,800 to 2,100 (see the office of national mortality statistics) of which ecstasy perhaps accounts for 10 to 12 deaths per year. It is beyond the scope of this book to analyse the magnitude of risk of death associated with the taking of controlled drugs. Suffice to say that the Independent Inquiry reviewed the current classification of drugs under the Misuse of Drugs Act having regard to the relative dangerousness of each drug (Ch. 3). Alcohol and tobacco are also dangerous substances.

Unfortunately, official statistics provided by the law enforcement agencies do not provide a true reflection of the pattern of drug distribution and use in this country. That is not a criticism of them. Drug markets are not fully understood. Both the police and the Customs and Excise are engaged in separate, as well as joint operations, to seize controlled drugs, and both agencies can properly claim success in seizing substantial amounts of illicit drugs. The following graphs (drawn by the author on the basis of information supplied by the Home Office) show a progressive increase in the quantities of the drugs that are most commonly used, being seized.

Since the enactment of the Misuse of Drugs Act, the number of persons 1–06 found guilty, or cautioned (fiscal fines in Scotland) or dealt with by the way of compounding, rose from nearly 12,000 to over 130,000 in 1998 but fell to about 120,000 in 1999. These figures do not of course take account of cases dealt with by way of a formal, or informal, warning. Between 83 and 90 per cent of drug offenders were dealt with for possession in 1998, of which cannabis possession accounted for some 71 per cent of cases under the Misuse of Drugs Act.

When compared with the number of persons estimated to be using controlled drugs each year, the number who enter the criminal justice process for possession offences is very low. More worryingly, the Independent Inquiry found "little evidence to indicate that enforcement efforts have led to increased prices, decreased availability, or decreased purity" (Ch. 2, paras 33 to 40). Some 2,341 kilograms of heroin were seized in 1999. Seizures of Ecstasy-type drugs rose to 6,323 doses in 1999.

The gulf between actual offending and detection is therefore obvious. Street-values of controlled drugs are a crude and unreliable means by which to gauge the level of drug use or the effectiveness of law enforcement agencies in stemming the lines of supply.

Cannabis is the most popular drug consumed in the United Kingdom. 1–07 Twenty-four per cent of persons aged between 16 and 29 years report long-term cannabis use, but the 1990s witnessed the introduction of Ecstasy into the drug culture and a revival of the use of LSD in doses much weaker than in the 1960s and early 1970s. According to a survey in 1994, three per cent of those aged between 16 to 19 years have tried LSD, nine per cent have tried Ecstasy and 11 per cent have taken amphetamines. A survey based on a sample of 80 offenders aged between 15 and 24 years, produced results that were even more dramatic. Seventy offenders had tried cannabis, 26 had taken LSD (17 of whom are now

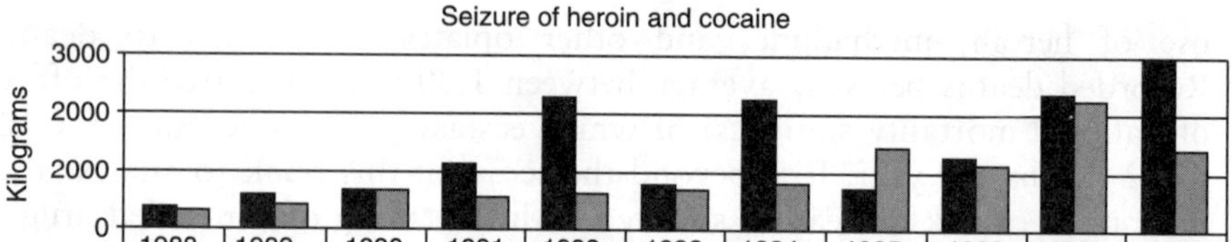

	1988	1989	1990	1991	1992	1993	1994	1995	1996	1997	1998
Cocaine	323	499	611	1078	2248	717	2262	672	1219	2350	2960
Heroin	236	351	603	493	547	656	744	1395	1070	2235	1345

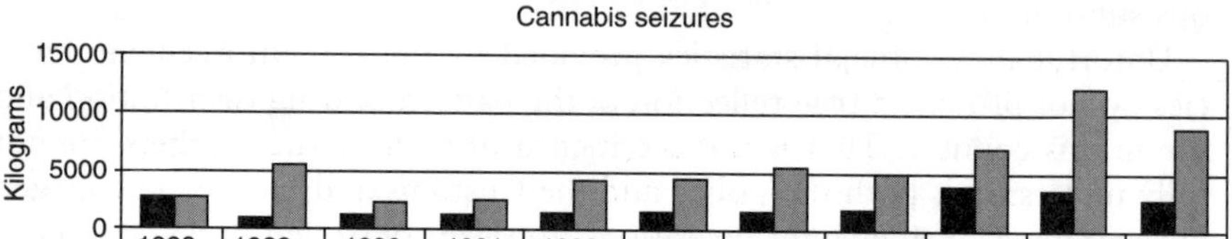

	1988	1989	1990	1991	1992	1993	1994	1995	1996	1997	1998
Herbal	24098	6781	9338	9525	11391	11976	11579	13872	34189	31120	21659
Resin	21365	52578	21550	22676	39705	41585	51430	44607	66937	118849	85823

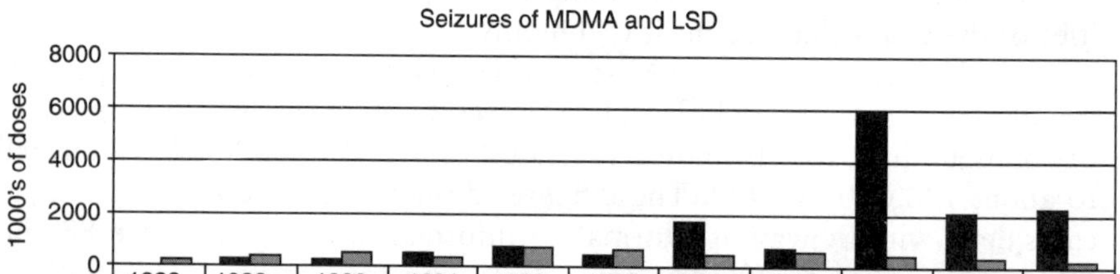

	1988	1989	1990	1991	1992	1993	1994	1995	1996	1997	1998
MDMA		39	44	365	554	302	1564	555	5798	1926	2095
LSD	63	147	295	170	544	454	214	382	216	164	38

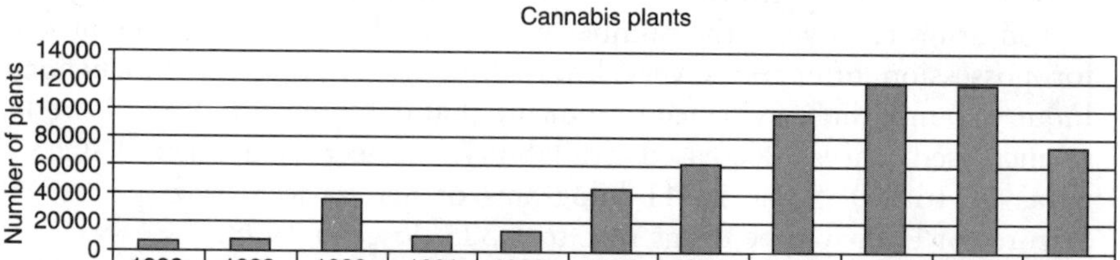

	1988	1989	1990	1991	1992	1993	1994	1995	1996	1997	1998
Plants	4762	6263	34299	8896	11839	40589	57846	94202	116218	114988	71970

regular users), 23 had tried heroin and 19 offenders had tried crack cocaine (Question Research and Marketing Strategists' Report, Police Review, March 1994). On the basis of information supplied to the author by drug users, LSD is often tried but seldom enjoyed and its use is not usually sustained, whereas Ecstasy produces an effect perceived as being much more pleasurable and the drug will sometimes be "stacked" (*i.e.* the dose is increased). Figures for deaths attributed to Ecstasy have ranged between 25 and 50 and it is estimated that the quantity of Ecstasy consumed per year averages 25 million tablets (*Heart of the Matter*, BBC, March 24, 1996). According to *The Economist* (November

13, 1993, p.38), some 500,000 people in the United Kingdom expended £700 million on the drug and approximately the same number of people use Ecstasy every week (see *The Guardian*, March 19, 1996).

Those statistics tend to be banded about as representing the current level of consumption: the actual figures might be very different. The purchase cost of any controlled drug will vary according to a number of factors. John Martin Corkery, at the Home Office, has included a very helpful table (table 2.8) in the 1999 *United Kingdom Drug Seizure and Offender Statistics* (March, 2001). The entire document is highly commended to the reader, and it contains useful analysis of the statistics.

The magnitude of risk to life in consuming Ecstasy is a topic very much in debate between experts as comparisons are made with deaths related to prescribed medicines (whether controlled under the Misuse of Drugs Act 1971 or not), or when compared with deaths attributed to alcoholic beverages and tobacco (and see Robson, *Forbidden Drugs*, (1994) p.107). What is frequently complained of, by users of Ecstasy, are the number of pills passed off as the drug but which, in reality, are a cocktail of undesired substances including amphetamine, LSD, and Ketamine (Ketalar). The latter is derived from phencyclidine ("Angel Dust") but Ketamine does have a legitimate use as an anaesthetic. It is sometimes used, as an alternative to Ecstasy but the side effects of abuse cannot be minimised. It is not a safe alternative.

Temazepam continues to pose a major social problem (when misused) 1–08
particularly it seems in Scotland, which has now resulted in further restrictions being imposed in respect of the importation, exportation, possession and distribution of that substance: see the Misuse of Drugs (Amendment) (No.2) Regulations 1995, S.I. 1995 No. 3244.

It is beyond the scope of this book to examine why drug-taking should have such a wide appeal. The reasons are intensely complicated and probably not fully understood but it should always be borne in mind that not all drug abuse is rooted in delinquency; drugs are often unwittingly misused as well. The familiar image of the physically sick addict ignores the fact that many drugs produce harmful effects even if they are not proved physically dangerous, *e.g.* psychological dependence or drug-related crime.

It is therefore with good reason that the legislature has moved away from narrow terms such as "dangerous drugs" and "poisons" and speaks instead of the "misuse" of drugs: hence the Misuse of Drugs Act 1971.

I. The Emergence of a Social Drug Problem

Drug misuse is an ancient problem. It is easy to overlook the fact that 1–09
probably the oldest drug is alcohol, which has been used and misused on an international scale since time immemorial. In the Far East and in Africa, opium and cannabis have been taken socially for thousands of years. The South Americans discovered that chewing coca-leaves stimulated the mind while the Greeks and Aztecs used hallucinogenic herbs and plants in some

of their religious ceremonies to create mystical effects. The Egyptians, too, compounded many mind-altering potions.

With the advent of the Industrial Revolution (1760–1840), the skills of chemistry and pharmacy were combined to form a powerful industry that made available a host of new drugs to meet a host of new demands.

1–10 Opium was principally used for the purposes of stupefaction but no restrictions were placed on its distribution and use until the Pharmacy Act 1868 regulated the sale of the drug. Nevertheless, the drug remained readily obtainable for many years thereafter. As early as 1803 morphine (an opiate) was developed and soon became recognised as a most powerful pain reliever. It was also highly addictive. Its widespread use to treat the wounded, both in wartime and in peacetime, unfortunately resulted in a large number of patients becoming opiate-dependent. Moreover, drugs such as opium and morphine found their way into many commercial substances and products that claimed to alleviate all kinds of ailments. Morphine, in turn, led to the discovery of another powerful drug, heroin, produced in London in 1874. Foolishly, this drug was also used in many commercial preparations. It was thought not to be addictive. It is, and it follows from the above that many opiate users became unwillingly addicted.

There were, of course, substances and products, which were wilfully (even fashionably) misused by the consumer. Thus, cocaine, formerly a popular local anaesthetic, appealed to an eccentric, middle-aged circle of the Victorian middle class, as a stimulant. Sir Arthur Conan Doyle mirrored that fact in his portrayal of the fictional character Sherlock Holmes as an occasional user of the drug. Interest in cocaine waned until the 1920s when, once again, a relatively well-heeled set in America, and in Europe, misused it.

1–11 Similarly, amphetamine was used to treat depression and narcolepsy, but its ability to stimulate the mind has, for decades, prompted people to use or abuse it. The drug was used by soldiers in the Spanish Civil War and indeed by British forces during the Second World War ("wakey-wakey" pills) and it is rumoured that Hitler was administered methylamphetamine (for a detailed history of this drug see Robson, *Forbidden Drugs* (1994) p.58). Drinamyl attained notoriety in the 1960s when it was widely misused by delinquent teenagers, by students revising for examinations and by performers in the entertainment industry. Better known as the "Purple Heart" this product accelerated legislation to control amphetamines.

Ritalin became popular with heroin addicts who used it to counteract some of the adverse effects experienced with heroin, *e.g.* depression. Other products contained active constituents (*e.g.* morphine or amphetamine) the effects of which were not fully understood until the manifestations of abuse or side effects were realised.

–12 It is sometimes said that major wars have contributed to the current drug problem but this superficial claim overlooks the fact that the majority of those currently abusing drugs have not seen National Service, let alone active service. Certainly major wars have significantly contributed to the development of new drugs and probably encouraged a much wider use of many dangerous substances such as morphine and other painkillers. As we have seen, amphetamines were regularly administered to servicemen, to keep them awake and alert during combat. Their use could not be sustained since they were addictive and capable of producing aggression, confusion and panic.

Significantly, in the West, relatively few drug abusers deliberately self-administered the first dose of a "hard drug", *e.g.* heroin, until the 1960s. By contrast, opium addiction in the Far East was a major concern of the world over 150 years ago.

Unfortunately, Britain played a major role in the highly profitable 1–13 "opium trade" of the Far East. In 1830, Britain declined to allow China to put a ban on opium and 1842 saw Britain's victory in the so-called "opium war". The resulting widespread abuse of opium generated international alarm, with calls for positive action to eradicate the problem. A series of conferences and treaties followed. Britain honoured its commitment by ratifying several treaties. The Pharmacy Act 1868 regulated the use and preparation of opium. Between 1868 and 1925, three further statutes were passed restricting the use of a number of other substances.

Cannabis ("Indian hemp") was further controlled by the Dangerous Drugs Act 1932 (c. 15) which also amended the 1920 Act by restricting the importation, exportation, manufacture and sale of any "extracts or tincture of Indian hemp" (s. 8(1)) and this provision was extended to preparations of the same substance.

There is some evidence that, after 1925, drug abuse in the United King- 1–14 dom (as small as it was) was in decline. Of course, domestic laws could have little effect on the drug problem overseas. Accordingly, the League of Nations, and later the United Nations, sought to prevent addiction and drug trafficking throughout the world. Their success has been limited and perhaps frustrated by a cumbersome bureaucratic method of control based on quantifying the amount of world production and consumption of dangerous drugs. "Taking stock" of drug production is largely dependant on relying on Member States submitting estimates of their own production of the relevant drug. Inevitably, the drug barons, carrying out illicit production and supplies, either furnish no particulars at all or falsify them. Member States whose "balance sheets" reveal a disturbing quantity of "lost drugs" may be asked to explain the loss, but efficiently policing drug production and supply, in this way and in accordance with international law, is virtually impossible.

For approximately 100 years between 1860 and 1960, the addict was seen as a person suffering from illness. In one sense, such a perception is justified if one looks purely at the effects various drugs may have on both the body and the mind, but drug abuse cannot be regarded as a disease, as it certainly was regarded in 1926, when the Departmental Committee on Morphine and Heroin Addiction (the "Rolleston Committee") published its Report (HMSO, 1926). Medical thinking had not significantly changed when the first Report of the Interdepartmental Committee on Drug Addiction (the ICDA) was published in 1961. Again, the suggestion was that drug addicts were "sick", suffering from a form of mental illness.

1–15 However, in the wake of rapid cultural changes, narcotic abuse became fashionable on an international scale. The second Report of the ICDA (HMSO, 1965) shows that the committee revised its thinking and directed its attack against the black market and doctors who over-prescribe.

In the treatment of addicts, the role of doctors complicates the picture. A doctor might, for example, prescribe the hard drug itself, or prescribe a substitute, *e.g.* methadone for heroin, or prescribe nothing at all and instead advise therapy. Often doctors prescribe controlled drugs privately. The pharmacist may charge a fee for encashing the prescription. From the addict's point of view the cost is cheaper than buying on the black market, but such a doctor was (and is) in danger of becoming an "easy touch", liable to attract many drug users. He may be encouraged to prescribe liberally, perhaps fearing that to turn users away empty-handed may force them to resort to the black market and probably to commit offences in order to pay the black market prices. The General Medical Council has considered many cases of doctors prescribing in this way. Some doctors were undoubtedly well-motivated while a few were unscrupulous and issued private prescriptions like confetti. Although the existence and enforcement of regulations may seriously reduce the range of drugs a doctor may administer, prescribe and supply, nevertheless the Regulations also serve to protect him from manipulative addicts.

The doctor was (and still is) liable to be the victim of another manipulation of the system, namely unwittingly prescribing controlled drugs to a drug user who is already registered with another doctor. The practice of "double-scripting" remains rife and not easy to detect. The addict having increased his supply of drugs through the comparatively cheap medium of the private or National Health Service might then sell his surplus stock on the black market at street level prices. The income enables the addict to pay his doctor's fees, allows him to buy other drugs and to pay the general household bills. It is partly with this practice in mind that the legislature has sought to enact a structured system of licensing, registration, recording and bookkeeping in order to monitor the distribution of controlled drugs.

II. Sketching the History of United Kingdom Drug Legislation

(a) International Agreements Mould United Kingdom Legislation

–16 Much of the legislative measures to curb drug consumption and drug trafficking are rooted in international obligations and treaties. The first significant development began with the signing of the International Opium Convention at The Hague in 1912 (105 State Papers, 490) and the effect of this Convention should not be underestimated because it established the principle of international co-operation in the campaign against the trafficking in narcotics as a matter of international law. The 1909 Shanghai Treaty resulted in an agreement that the use of opium should be limited to medical purposes. Other uses of that substance (*e.g.* industrial or research) was to be controlled by a system that involved *both* prohibition *and* regulation. The Shanghai Conference in 1909 was followed by the Hague Convention in 1912. The manufacture, trade and use of opiates were to be limited to medicinal use; opium dens were to be closed, and the possession, or sale, of opiates to unauthorised persons were to be punishable offences.

(b) Dangerous Drugs Act 1920

The Dangerous Drugs Act 1920 codified a number of wartime regulations that outlawed the possession of opium and cocaine for personal consumption as well as restricting the production, importation and exportation of those drugs. The Act enabled the United Kingdom to ratify the Hague Convention of 1912. Although principally concerned with opium, the Act placed controls on the importation, exportation, and manufacture of tinctures of cannabis and preparations containing dihydrocodeine. **1–17**

There is much in the drafting of the Dangerous Drugs Act 1920 (now repealed) that is mirrored in parts of the Misuse of Drugs Act 1971. Both Acts were drafted:

(i) to include restrictions on the importation and exportation of drugs specified by the statute;

(ii) to create an offence directed against occupiers and persons concerned in the management of premises to permit (now "permit or suffer") the smoking of prepared opium. Section 8 of the Misuse of Drugs Act is broader in that it extends to the smoking of cannabis on premises as well as permitting, or suffering, the production, or supply, of any controlled drug on premises.

(iii) To make it an offence to unlawfully possess prepared opium. The offence of possession under the Misuse of Drugs Act is of course now much broader.

(iv) To prohibit the possession of utensils for smoking opium and to make such an act an offence (consider now s.9 and s.9A of the Misuse of Drugs Act);

(v) To punish the performance of acts in this country that resulted in the commission of an offence contrary to a "corresponding law" abroad (see now s.20 of the Misuse of Drugs Act).

(c) Dangerous Drugs Act 1925

Following the Geneva International Opium Convention 1925 (Cm 3244), and in the light of strong representations made by the Egyptian Delegation, the use of cannabis for non-medicinal purposes was condemned. As a result, the Dangerous Drugs Act 1925 regulated the possession and use of that substance. The Act amended the Dangerous Drugs Act 1920 Act to restrict the importation and exportation of coca-leaf and cannabis into the United Kingdom. The 1925 Convention (and a further Convention in 1931, Cm 4413) **1–18** resulted in the setting up of two bodies: (i) the Permanent Central Opium Board (an independent body of experts to monitor and to advise on matters relating to opiate distribution and control), and (ii) the Drug Supervising Body. The International Narcotics Central Board replaced both bodies following the "Vienna Single Convention" in 1961. The 1925 Convention also created a system for reporting annually the level of drug stocks, the amount of narcotic substances manufactured, and shipped.

(d) Dangerous Drugs Act 1932

1–19 This Act enabled the United Kingdom to give effect to the 1931 International Convention for Limiting the Manufacture and Regulating the Distribution of Narcotic Drugs, which prohibited the trade in, and manufacture of, cocaine and opium for other than medical and scientific purposes. Under the terms of the Convention, Parties were required to furnish estimates of drug consumption and other statistics.

(e) Legislation Until 1951

1–20 The Convention for the Suppression of the Illicit Traffic in Dangerous Drugs of 1936 also aimed to limit the distribution of a number of drugs to medical and scientific purposes. The Geneva Protocol of 1946 transferred the functions of the League of Nations (of which the United States of America was not a member) to the United Nations. This event was marked in our legislation by the Dangerous Drugs (Amendment) Act 1950. The Paris Protocol of 1948 authorised the World Health Organisation to report and advise in relation to any substance capable of causing dependence and which might warrant international control.

(f) Dangerous Drugs Act 1951

1–21 The Acts of 1920, 1925 and 1932 were consolidated, without amendment, by the Dangerous Drugs Act 1951. At an international level, there was concern that the international system of drug control was complex and needed to be streamlined: Opium Protocol (New York, 1953). Accordingly, in July 1958, the United Nations proposed the adoption of a Single Convention On Narcotic Drugs to replace existing multilateral treaties and to reduce the number of international agencies that had been charged with the task of controlling the distribution of narcotic drugs.

(g) Dangerous Drugs Act 1964 and the Drugs (Prevention of Misuse) Act 1964

–22 It became an offence for an occupier to permit his premises to be used for the purpose of smoking cannabis (s. 9; see now s. 8, MDA 1971). It also became an offence to cultivate cannabis plants (s. 10; see now s. 6,

MDA 1971). The possession and importation of Lysergamide, and its derivatives were restricted by the Drugs (Prevention of Misuse) Act 1964 (c.64).

(h) Dangerous Drugs Act 1965

The Dangerous Drugs Acts of 1951 and 1964 were consolidated by the Dangerous Drugs Act 1965 (c.15) which, in turn, was repealed and replaced by the Misuse of Drugs Act 1971 (c.38). That Act also repealed the Drugs (Prevention of Misuse) Act 1964. 1–23

(i) The Future of U.K. Drug Legislation

Much controversy has arisen concerning the "drugs problem" and how to deal with it. Views range between demands for stern penal sanctions on the one hand, to calls for no action at all on the other. The former school advocates the need to deter others; the latter advocates that left alone the "practice" will burn out. It is not proposed to examine in this book the case for, and against, the 'legalisation' or 'decriminalisation' of any, or all, controlled drugs. The matter was considered in detail by the Independent Inquiry: there is of course a wealth of material devoted to this topic not least on the internet. However, the "debate" would undoubtedly be more fruitful if contributors define what *they* mean by "legalisation" or "decriminalisation". That tends not to happen. The debate becomes bogged down through misunderstanding and confusion. Frequently, the expressions "legalisation" and "decriminalisation" are used interchangeably. This is not a quibble because it will be seen that the Misuse of Drugs Act follows a two-stage approach in the creation of offences. First, certain activities are made "unlawful" (*e.g.* possession, s.5(2)). Secondly, the unlawful act is then made an offence (*e.g.* possession, s.5(3)) subject to certain exceptions or exemptions. It should be noted that the Misuse of Drugs Act is subject to the Misuse of Drugs Regulations 1985. The effect of those two instruments can be shortly stated: what the Misuse of Drugs Act prohibits, the Misuse of Drugs Regulations 1985 permits. When properly understood the Misuse of Drugs Act is capable of being a highly flexible instrument. It would be possible to devise a model (using the Misuse of Drugs Act) by which the distribution of particular controlled drugs remains unlawful (*i.e.* in that sense 'not legalised'), but the violation would not amount to a criminal offence (in effect "decriminalised"). Redress would be available in civil proceedings but a prosecution would not result. Those who support "decriminalisation" might not support "legalisation". Others would go further and argue that some acts should not be regulated at all (*e.g.* possession for personal use) *i.e.* "legalisation". Furthermore, those who argue for "legalisation" or "decriminalisation" often overlook that the law may exist in layers. Even if the Misuse of Drugs Act was swept away there might remain the Medicines Act 1968 and its numerous, bulky, schedules. That Act, too, creates a number of offences that might operate against a person engaged in the retail/supply of particular substances. 1–24

The laws of the United Kingdom do not exist in isolation. For decades, 1–2 this country's drug laws have had more than just an international dimension. Successive governments of the United Kingdom have been highly instrumental in securing international agreements on drug issues. That of course holds true for many other States. In many instances, such instruments have shaped domestic law: sometimes domestic law sets the pace for international change. There are powerful links between the legislative processes of the United Kingdom, the E.U., the United Nations, and of course agreements between States. It is important to be aware of current initiatives to improve co-operation and assistance between States: *e.g.* mutual recognition of decisions in civil and criminal matters, multi-lateral treaties, *corpus juris*, various E.U. initiatives (for example on money-laundering), increasing the jurisdiction of the International Court of Justice, and many other international developments and initiatives.

This country is not free to legislate entirely as it pleases by reason (among others) of the three main United Nations Conventions, namely, the Single Convention 1961; the 1971 U.N. Convention on Psychotropic Substances, and the 1988 Convention Against Illicit Traffic In Narcotics Drugs And Psychotropic Substances. Those three Conventions do not have direct application in English law: the terms of the Conventions must be incorporated or adopted in law by a statutory measure. That has largely happened.

1–26 The significance of all this was examined by the Independent Inquiry that commissioned a substantial comparative study of drug law in several E.U. countries, *Room to Manoeuvre* (see also the article by Neil Boister, "Decriminalising the personal use of cannabis in the United Kingdom: does international law leave room to manoeuvre?" [2001] Crim. L.R. 171). The structure of domestic and international politics is such that it is immensely difficult for one contracting State to unilaterally renege on a treaty that has secured the signatures of many other powerful nations. There are political and economic sanctions for non-compliance, as well as legal sanctions in some instances. Contracting States that violate or stray from any one of the three United Nations Conventions can be "named and shamed". With "shame", there might also be loss of political influence and credibility. However, the three United Nations Conventions leave more room for manoeuvre than might be supposed at first sight. Thus, the drafting of offences, the mental ingredient required to be proved by the prosecution, the classification of drugs, the penalties to be imposed on offenders (or even whether there should be a prosecution at all) are matters usually left to the discretion of Contracting States. The three United Nations Conventions focus on trafficking—particularly where there is a commercial element.

III. The Three United Nations Conventions

(a) The 1961 Single Convention

(1) *Classification of Narcotics Under the Single Convention*

1–27 Representatives of 73 States took part in the conference. The Convention is "single" in three dimensions. First, it consolidates earlier treaties and agreements in the field of narcotic control. Secondly, it secured the agreement of the Parties to be single-minded, *i.e.* to provide mutual co-operation and assistance. Thirdly, the Parties would pursue a single objective (subject to Arts 25 to 28 inclusive) namely, to limit "exclusively to medical and scientific purposes the production, manufacture, export, import, distribution of, trade in, use and possession of drugs" (see Art. 4(c)).

The 1961 Single Convention On Narcotics Drugs is unhappily phrased because a number of substances do not fall within the strict definition of a "narcotic": indeed "narcotic" is not defined in the Convention. Nevertheless, the aim of the Convention is to limit the drugs listed in its schedules, including cannabis and cannabis resin, to medical, scientific, and limited industrial purposes. The 1961 Convention has been ratified by a considerable number of States including the Netherlands.

The Single Convention contains four Schedules (I to IV) in which nar- 1–28
cotics are listed according to the intensity of controls that apply to drugs in a particular schedule. That may or may not say something about the perceived level of harm (in 1961) associated with the drugs listed in each schedule. However, not only does the Convention include some drugs that would not ordinarily be described as "narcotics"—a problem recognised by the Shafer Commission of 1970—but the basis for including a substance in one schedule, as opposed to another, is not explained in the Convention.

Drugs listed in Schedule IV also appear in Schedule I. They are subject to "special measures of control" (see Art. 2.5(a)) so that a Party may (actually *should*)—prohibit the production, manufacture, import, trade, possession and use of any such drug (see Art. 2.5(b)). It is often said that Schedule IV drugs have no medicinal or therapeutic value. That is an oversimplification of the position. The better explanation is that their potential for causing harm may exceed their therapeutic value. Thus, cannabis, cannabis resin and heroin appear in Schedule IV. Tighter controls apply to drugs in that schedule. Under Article 2.5(b) a Party is obliged to *prohibit* the possession and use of such drugs, except for amounts which may be necessary for medical and scientific research only, including clinical trials, if in that Party's opinion, such a prohibition is the most appropriate means of protecting public health and welfare. Note that Article 2.5(b) limits use to research purposes only: it does not extend to medicinal use. Note that it is arguable that Article 2.5(b) does not require Parties to "criminalise" violations of that prohibition.

(ii) *A summary of the principal obligations of the Single Convention*

The Single Convention lays down minimum obligations, leaving the Par- 1–29
ties free to impose a more restrictive/penal regime if they wish to do so (see Article 39).

The minimum obligations may be loosely classified as being of three types:

(i) *Mandatory obligations*: for example, that the trade in or distribution of drugs must be under licence: Article 30.

(ii) *Qualified obligations*: obligations that may be triggered upon the existence of a particular state of affairs (*e.g.* that a drug poses a threat to public health prompting a Party to prohibit particular activities in relation to that drug: see Article 22; and consider Article 26).

(iii) *Conditional obligations*: these are controls that a Party will be expected to introduce as part of their domestic law subject, for example, to a Party's Constitution or Bill of Rights (Art. 36.1(a)) or its legal system or domestic laws (see Art. 36.2).

(iii) *Limiting production and cultivation to Legitimate Uses*

1–30 The Single Convention imposes an obligation on all Parties to limit the production and importation of any Sched. I or II narcotic to the amount that will not exceed (i) the quantity estimated to be consumed for medical or scientific purposes or (ii) the quantity estimated to be used in the manufacture of other drugs including substances not covered by the Single Convention (see for example, Arts 21, 21bis, 23, and 24 in relation to opium, cannabis, and coca bush as the case may be).

There is no general obligation to prohibit the cultivation of cannabis, or coca bush or the opium poppy. Nevertheless, the language and structure of the Single Convention implies a presumption that such plants be prohibited, or at least that cultivation should be confined to as small an area as possible to prevent a risk to public health or the "diversion of drugs into illicit traffic" (see Art. 22). In countries where the cultivation of the opium poppy, or cannabis, or coca bush, is permitted, the Government must ensure that cultivation is under the control of a Government agency; that growers are licensed to operate in areas designated by the agency for the purpose of producing the final product (see Arts 23, (opium poppy), Art. 26 (coca-bush) and Art. 28 (cannabis)).

General obligations under the Single Convention

1–31 Article 4 of the Single Convention imposes a mandatory obligation on Parties to take "legislative and administrative measures as may be necessary" to limit the production, manufacture, export, import, distribution of, trade in, use and possession of drugs: see Article 4(c). By Article 33, Parties "shall not permit the possession of drugs except under legal authority".

Three points should be noted about this general statement of principle.

(i) the words "as *may* be necessary" mean that the Party is required to take preventative action to limit the activities mentioned in Article 4(c) in order to protect public health and welfare.

(ii) Article 4 does not mean *by itself* that Parties have to use the criminal justice process to achieve any of the objectives in Article 4(c). This is subject to a true construction of article 36, which is directly concerned with the creation of "punishable offences" and other penal measures (and see Art. 33).

(iii) Given that Article 33 obliges Parties not to permit the *possession* of drugs except under legal authority, the combined effect of Article 4 and Article 33 is that it is not open to a Party to totally "legalise" (as opposed to 'criminalise'), possession, or arguably use, of a narcotic (*e.g.* cannabis) for anything other than a "medical or scientific purpose": to do so would put that Party in breach of its international obligations under the Single Convention.

(iv) *Creating criminal offences under the Single Convention*

Although a Party may be required to prohibit or restrict an activity, the next question is whether that activity must also be a punishable offence? Article 36 of the Single Convention is relevant here. It requires the Parties to introduce punishable offences in respect of two sets of activities: (i) cultivation, production, distribution and (confusingly) possession, and (ii) "any other action which in the opinion of the Party may be contrary to the provisions of [the Single Convention]". 1–32

In the absence of an unambiguous provision, the second category seems to permit each Party to form its own view as to whether or not a provision is contrary to the Single Convention or not and to legislate accordingly.

(v) *Possession and Use—whether "punishable offences"?*

Articles 36 provides: 1–33

> "cultivation, production, manufacture, extraction, preparation, **possession**, offering . . . distribution . . . importation and exportation of drugs . . . shall be punishable offences when committed intentionally, and that serious offences shall be liable to adequate punishment particularly by imprisonment . . .". [emphasis added]

Article 33 also provides that States:

> "shall not permit the possession of drugs except under legal authority".

At first blush, Arts 36 and 33 seem to provide a blanket prohibition on possession, but it seems that the intended purpose of that provision was to outlaw possession for distribution rather than for personal use. It is probable that the Single Convention was not drafted to require States to prohibit the use of narcotics (see the Report prepared by the Secretariat for the 5th United Nations Congress on the *Prevention of Crime and the Treatment of Offenders* (A/Conf.56/10); and see the Report on the 11th *International Conference on International Law*, 1974; and Noll, *Drug Abuse and Penal Provisions of the International Drug Control Treaties*, Bulletin on Narcotics, Issue 4–003, 1977). The *Official Commentary to the Single Convention* is phrased in guarded tones and provides no easy answer. Indeed, it actually avoids providing an answer. It tells us what is obvious, namely, that some Governments consider that they are not required to punish the unauthorised possession of drugs by addicts for their personal use because of the narrow interpretation that those Governments place on the scope of Article 36.1. It then states that whatever the position taken by Govern- 1–34 ments in relation to "this question of penal sanctions" it does not affect the general obligation not to permit the unauthorised possession of drugs for personal consumption without legal authority.

Boister suggests that the Single Convention "does admit of interpretations permitting Parties to decriminalise the simple possession of cannabis and its cultivation for personal use" (p.174). There is force in that statement. The Convention does admit of "interpretations" to that effect. However, Conventions are not statutes: they embrace statements of ambition (not necessarily shared by all Parties) as well as agreed matters of principle. One suspects that some States were hotly opposed to moves to prohibit possession and cultivation of cannabis for personal use, while others were strongly in favour of prohibition and criminalisation of those activities. The trend has been for many States to restrict the use of, or to criminalise, the possession of many substances.

1–35 Some commentators might point to Article 36.1(b) of the Single Convention, which provides that when "abusers of drugs" have committed a punishable offence, the Party may impose measures of education or treatment, or rehabilitation on that person, and it may do so in addition to conviction or punishment or as an alternative to conviction or punishment. The argument might run that this provision only makes sense if "possession" in Article 36.1(a) includes possession for personal consumption.

However, as originally drafted, the Single Convention in 1961 did not include this provision. It was added by the 1972 Protocol. So, what is its purpose? The most logical answer is that it was designed to ensure that drug use is not seen as just a "crime" issue, but a health and education issue too. Similar provision exists in the 1971 Convention in respect of psychotropic substances. It therefore made good sense to make the Single Convention consistent in that regard (see Noll, *Drug Abuse and Penal Provisions of the International Drug Control Treaties*, Bulletin on Narcotics, Issue 4–003, 1977). It is arguable that Article 36.1(b) would only operate in respect of users of drugs if the Government penalised possession for personal consumption. Nevertheless, in cases where the Government has not done so, Article 38 of the Single Convention (which is broadly mirrored in Art. 20 of the 1971 Convention) places a responsibility on Governments to take practical measures for the prevention of drug abuse, and to advance rehabilitation and social reintegration.

(vi) *Constitutional Limitations*

1–36 Whether or not Article 36.1(a) includes possession for personal consumption, the obligation to make any of the activities or actions listed in that provision 'punishable offences', is subject to the "constitutional limitations" of the relevant Party. A contentious issue is whether this saving enables (or requires) a Party not to enact penal legislation to give effect to a Convention requirement, on the grounds of constitutional incompatibility. The official answer suggested by the Official Commentary to the Single Convention is "no", on the grounds that the Party is bound to obtain the necessary authority: but once obtained, the precise manner in which the offence is defined, or prosecuted, is largely a matter for each Party subject to its "legal system and domestic law" (see, in this context, Art. 36.2).

(b) The 1971 Convention on Psychotropic Substances

The 1971 Convention is more tightly drawn and much more restrictive than the Single Convention. Whereas the 1961 Single Convention is directed against "narcotic drugs" (or more precisely the drugs listed in Schedules I to IV) the 1971 Convention is directed against "psychotropic substances" whether natural or synthetic. The term 'psychotropic' is not defined. However, the substances listed include hallucinogens, stimulants and sedatives. Such drugs are listed in Schedules I to IV to that Convention. The four schedules group substances according to their potential for dependence and abuse, as well as their therapeutic value. 1–37

Schedule I drugs include LSD, MDMA, MDA, and DOB and tetrahydrocannabinol. Substances in Schedule 1 (including cannabinol but not now dronabinol) are prohibited from use except for "scientific and very limited medical purposes by duly authorised persons in medical or scientific establishments, which are directly under the control of their governments or specifically approved by them" (Art. 7 (a)). It is for that reason that cannabinols cannot be supplied on prescription (without violating Art. 7) whereas cannabis and cannabis resin are subject to the 1961 Single Convention and could be supplied on prescription, if Parliament considered it appropriate to do so.

A good example of how all this works in practice is Dronabinol (synthetic THC in sesame oil) that can alleviate some of the adverse effects of chemotherapy. That drug is licensed for use in the USA but not in the United Kingdom. It seems that the drug has to be imported for prescription on a "named patient basis" (see p.4, BMA Report, *Therapeutic Uses of Cannabis*). Dronabinol has been treated as a "cannabinol derivative" for the purposes of the MDA. "Cannabinol derivatives" are Class A drugs. They also appear in Schedule 1 of the M.D. Regulations 1985 (*i.e.* drugs that have little or no therapeutic value and which cannot be prescribed by doctors). However, following the advice of the World Health Organisation, the United Nations Commission on Narcotic Drugs amended the 1971 Convention in such a way that the U.K. Government was able to move Dronabinol from Schedule 1 to Schedule 2 of the M.D. Regulations 1985 (see the Misuse of Drugs (Amendment) Regulations 1995, S.I. 1995 No. 2048, para. 2(a) and (b)). This means that doctors can prescribe Dronabinol, albeit on a tightly controlled basis. 1–38

Schedule II of the 1971 Convention includes amphetamine, dronabinol (a synthetic cannabinol derivative), and methamphetamine. Schedule III includes cathine, flunitrazepam, and pentobarbital. Schedule IV contains diazepam, flurazepam, and temazepam. Drugs falling in Schedules II, III and IV (but not Sched. I) must, by Article 5.2, be limited to "scientific and medical purposes"—a phrase that also appears in the Single Convention—which would seem to include medically justified maintenance of drug addiction programmes (see Official Commentary on the 1971 United Nations Convention on Psychotropic Substances, para.2). The limitation applies whether the drugs are manufactured, exported, imported, or distributed. Similarly, the possession and use of such drugs, must also be limited to "medical and scientific purposes".

1–39 The aim of the Convention is to limit the application of psychotropic drugs to medical and scientific purposes. Accordingly, their quasi-medical or non-medical use (whether styled "recreational", "cultural", "traditional", or "casual") is not permitted, as a rule. The one exception relates to places where plants, in which a psychotropic substance naturally subsists, grow wild but are traditionally used "by a certain small, clearly determined group in magical or religious rites".

Like the procedure under the Single Convention, it is open to the INCB to name and shame those Parties that fail to meet their obligations under the Convention: see Article 13.3 of the Single Convention and Article 19.3 of the 1971 Convention. Once again, the 1971 Convention requires a Party to punish "any action" amounting to a violation of a Convention-obligation (Art. 22). In practice the offending action will be contrary to an existing law, or one that is created (in order to ratify the Convention) and which forms part of the domestic law of the relevant Party.

The 1971 Convention imposes controls on production and distribution that are similar to those under the Single Convention. The intensity of control will depend on the nature of the drug in question, its properties, the relative social or personal harm associated with the drug, and its medicinal or therapeutic benefits.

(i) *Must possession or use be made a criminal offence under the 1971 Convention?*

1–40 Article 5.2, by itself, does not require Governments to use the criminal justice system to give effect to the obligation that possession and use must be limited to medical and scientific purposes. But this is not a complete answer because by Article 22.1(a), *any action* contrary to the provision of the 1971 Convention should be dealt with as a "punishable offence" (in effect a criminal offence in the United Kingdom).

At first blush it might therefore be thought that the possession or use of a psychotropic drug in Schedules II, III or IV, for any purpose that is not a medical or scientific one, would be contrary to the 1971 Convention and thus would need to be dealt with as a criminal offence under the domestic law of the Parties (subject to its constitutional limitations). But this construction has often been disputed, mainly on the ground that both the 1961 and the 1971 Convention is aimed at illicit trafficking and not the personal use and consumption of drugs. On this reasoning, "possession" for the purposes of Article 5.2, concerns acts in pursuance of trafficking, so that *possession for consumption*, or "use", does not come within Article 5.2. This argument appears to have been based in part on a draft headed "measures against illicit traffickers" and used as a working document during the

Plenipotentiary Conference (and see the Official Commentary to the 1971 Convention, para.18.).

A second argument, often put forward, is that possession for personal use, and use, do not amount to "actions" under Article 22.1(a) (see the Commentary to the 1988 Convention, para.3.89). The validity of that argument may depend on whether the first argument is correct. 1–41

A third argument concerns the relationship between Article 5.2 and Article 5.3 of the 1971 Convention. Article 5.3 says that it is "desirable" that the Parties do not permit the possession of psychotropic drugs in Schedules II, III and IV, without legal authority. Desirable but not compulsory. Article 5.3 says nothing about "use". The argument runs that if there is no obligation under the 1971 Convention, to prohibit possession without legal authority, then the Convention cannot insist on making it a criminal offence to be in possession of such a substance without legal authority. The argument continues that Article 5.2 has to be interpreted in the context of Article 5.3.

One answer is that Article 5.2 and Article 5.3 are dealing with two different situations. The former is concerned with purpose. The latter is concerned with procedure, *i.e.* no possession without proper documentation even if a person intended to use the drug for a proper medical or scientific purpose. A second answer is to be found in the Official Commentary to the 1971 Convention. It states that "possession" in Article 5.3 means possession *for personal consumption*—even though Article 5.3 does not in fact include those three important qualifying words (see para.8 of the commentary). 1–42

Articles 5.2 and 5.3 may therefore be aimed at different goals but none of the Official Commentaries dismiss out-of-hand the argument that neither the 1961 nor the 1971 Convention oblige Parties to create criminal offences in respect of the possession or use of narcotic or psychotropic drugs for a non-medical or non-scientific purpose. However, the Commentaries also make it clear that not all Governments agree that the argument is correct.

(c) The 1988 United Nations Convention Against the Illicit Traffic of Narcotic Drugs and Psychotropic Substances

Purpose of the 1988 Convention

It was against that background that the 1988 Convention was convened. It is noteworthy that the Preamble records that the Parties recognise "the need to reinforce and supplement the measures provided in the Single Convention . . . as amended by the 1972 Protocol . . . and the 1971 Convention . . . in order to counter the magnitude and extent of illicit traffic and its grave consequences." 1–43

The 1988 Convention is, as its full title suggests, an instrument to tackle illicit traffic in narcotic drugs and psychotropic substances. Breaches of the Convention are to be punishable has criminal offences. It requires member States to legislate in respect of "precursor chemicals" and to create offences in respect of drug money laundering.

1–44 By its title, the 1988 Convention expressly relates to both narcotics (as defined by the Single Convention) and psychotropic substances (as defined by the 1971 Convention). Three objectives of the 1988 Convention are particularly relevant: (i) to clarify ambiguities in the 1961 and the 1971 Conventions, (ii) to strengthen obligations of mutual assistance and enforcement; (iii) *either*, depending on one's point of view, to introduce *new* obligations under the 1988 Convention, resulting (if necessary) in the creation of new offences under the domestic law, *or* to confirm and emphasise the *existence* of obligations under earlier Conventions, the meaning and scope of which had been misunderstood, *or* (arguably) both. The 1988 Convention requires each Party to take "legislative and administrative measures" in carrying out their obligations under the Convention but it also recognises that each Party is "equal" and "sovereign". Accordingly, the general obligation under Article 2 can be put no higher than that each Party must act in a manner that conforms with "the fundamental provisions of [the Parties] respective domestic legislative systems": Article 2.1 and Article 2.2.

(i) *Emphasis on illicit traffic*

1–45 It will be seen that the emphasis of the 1988 Convention is on "illicit traffic". Article 1 deals with definitions. Article 2 acknowledges the principles of sovereignty, equality and territorial integrity of States. Article 3 of the Convention details "offences and sanctions".

By article 3.2:

> "subject to its constitutional principles and the basic concepts of its legal system each Party shall adopt such measures as may be necessary to establish as a criminal offence under its domestic law, when committed intentionally, the *possession*, purchase or cultivation of narcotic drugs or psychotropic substances *for personal consumption* contrary to the provisions of the 1961 Convention, the 1961 Convention as amended or the 1971 Convention".

Does Article 3.2 require Parties to make possession for personal consumption a criminal offence? Does it also require Parties to make other activities, *e.g.* cultivation of one's own use a criminal offence?

1–46 It seems highly probable that both questions have to be answered in the affirmative. This is the view expressed in the commentary to the 1988 Convention. There is a saving where creating such offences " . . . would be contrary to the constitutional principles and basic concepts of their legal systems to do so" (para. 3.95 of the Official Commentary). The saving may apply where individuals are free to harm themselves but the saving is soon lost if the harmful effects extend to third parties. A series of cases await the decision of courts in the United Kingdom as to whether the laws relating to the possession and cultivation of cannabis for personal use amount to a violation of Human Rights Act 1998/ECHR. Those cases raise interesting issues but it is a bid, which the author predicts, is doomed to fail. Prosecution for possession of personal use (and cultivation of cannabis for personal use) is not inevitable: such cases usually attract a caution or warning (at least for the first violation). It seems that some of the defendants rejected a caution in order to be able to challenge the decision to prosecute them under the Human Rights Act. Since writing the above, H. H. Judge Rivlin Q.C. in *R. v. Ham* (July, 2001) ruled that the prosecution, on the facts of that case, was HRA 1998 compliant. (See para. 3–05 where that case is discussed in greater detail).

(d) Enforcing the Conventions

Enforcing the Single Convention (as well as the 1971 and 1988 Conventions) occurs on a horizontal and a vertical plane. Horizontally in the sense that once the Parties have in place measures that are convention-compliant, they may be enforced in a manner consistent with that Party's domestic law and constitutional limitations. All three Conventions give scope to the Parties—considerable scope—as to how violations of the domestic law are handled especially in relation to case disposal—*i.e.* whether by conviction and punishment, or by other means including (as an alternative to, or in addition to, conviction or punishment) measures of treatment, education, after care, rehabilitation and social integration (see for example, Art. 36). This aspect of all three Conventions has been much understated or perhaps just not fully understood. But enforcement also exists on a vertical plane, by which we mean that each Party to the Convention is accountable not only to other Parties to the Convention in question, but also to the United Nations itself through, as the first step, the International Narcotics Control Board set up under the terms of the Single Convention. The INCB has the right to open consultations with the relevant government if the INCB has reason to believe that the aims of the Convention are being "seriously endangered" or if there exists a "serious risk" that a Party may become an important centre of "traffic in or consumption of drugs" (see Article 14.1(a), UNC 1961). The INCB may call upon that Party to "adopt remedial measures" (Art. 14.1(b)) and where that fails, to seek "co-operative actions at the international level with a view to remedying "the situation (Art. 14.1(d)). In practice, of course, disputes are dealt with diplomatically. 1–47

(e) Room to manoeuvre

There are several key areas where, within the scope of the three main Conventions, there is considerable latitude for imaginative and appropriate use of the domestic law in the area of drug-control. 1–48

1. Classification of drugs, subject to control, is largely a matter of domestic law. The three Classes of drugs under the Misuse of Drugs Act should say something about relative harm, but they are certainly highly relevant to the maximum penalty that may be

imposed by the courts in respect of the commission of drug offences.

2. Secondly, some activities fall outside the Conventions. One example relates to section 8(c) and (d) by which it is an offence for occupiers or those concerned in the management of premises, to allow or to suffer the smoking of cannabis or prepared opium on premises. In assessing the need for such an offence, one must have regard to its impact on acts and schemes that have at their heart harm reduction or the promotion of public health and welfare. Similar considerations apply to the scope of offences relating to the provision of articles by responsible persons, for safer drug consumption.
3. Thirdly, there are actions that may properly be taken, within the terms of the Conventions, to divert persons away from conviction or punishment altogether. Such actions include cautions, warnings, reprimands, as well as courses of treatment, rehabilitation, education and social integration—many of which are *expressly* cited and permitted under the 1961 and 1971 U.N. Conventions.
4. There is considerable latitude for individual States to determine penalties or other methods of case disposal.

Recent Initiatives

1–49 Initially, the approach of the United Kingdom government and courts has been to attack drug trafficking at the points of demand and supply. This remains true but the intensity of control and enforcement is probably strongest in tackling the lines of supply. More recently, statutory powers of asset forfeiture backed up by offences directed against money laundering have been created. The aim is two-fold: first, to strip offenders of their ill-gotten proceeds (the Drug Trafficking Act 1994 is not concerned with profit) and secondly, to take out of circulation monies that could be used to finance further illegal activities. Such a scheme can only begin to work (even in theory) if there is a global commitment to it, coupled with mutual assistance in respect of the exchange of information and the enforcement of court orders, wherever they are made. Asset forfeiture is intended to be the means by which organisers of international crime can be reached by the courts, *i.e.* by confiscating the proceeds of drug trafficking received by a defendant irrespective of whether those proceeds were generated by the defendant, or anyone else, and irrespective of where they were generated. As we have seen, legislation has recently been enacted to recover the proceeds of drug trafficking, notably the Drug Trafficking Act 1994 (the DTOA 1986 will still apply in some cases), (or, in Scotland, the Proceeds of Crime (Scotland) Act 1995) and see the Criminal Law (Consolidation) (Scotland) Act 1995, Part V, (c. 39)). Although these statutes are not primarily directed at drug use, the Government clearly hopes that by stripping drug traffickers of their ill-gotten proceeds, others will be deterred from embarking upon drug trafficking (and see Teff, "The Development of Control" [1972] 35 M.L.R. 225). Note also that the Government has introduced a consultation draft of the Proceeds Of Crime Bill 2001—an measure designed to tighten still further rules relating to confiscation of the proceeds of drug trafficking and other criminal offences, as well as inducing confiscation without conviction ("asset recovery").

In the 1994 Report, by the Advisory Council on the Misuse of Drugs (Part II: Police, Drug Misusers and the Community), it is said that the elimination of drug misuse is "generally regarded as an unobtainable goal" (para. 1.1) and that containment, rather than elimination of drug misuse, is the more "realistic objective" (para. 4.1). The Council recommends the wider adoption of harm reduction principles in developing enforcement strategies that should have the following characteristics: 1–50

(i) where choices have to be made between enforcement operations against different kinds of drugs, the drug which causes most harm should be the principal target. It will not always be possible for policing strategies to target individual drugs, given the extent of polydrug misuse, but the enforcement process can consider this.
(ii) If possible, where choices have to be made between enforcement operations, priority should be given to early intervention to eliminate drug-dealing sites, particularly new locations, before these have the chance to establish and advertise themselves.
(iii) Enforcement should support the efforts of other agencies working to reduce the harm caused by drug misuse.
(iv) A recognition that harm reduction has a part to play in returning areas to normality through improvements to the environment, such as better street lighting, public buildings and amenities."

The Independent Inquiry went much further and made 81 recommendations. The report is available from the Police Foundation (not the "Police Federation") at 1 Glyn Street, Vauxhall, London, SE11 5RA.

B. DRUG CONTROL AND DRUG CLASSIFICATION

Introduction

For over 100 years attention was focused on those drugs considered "dangerous". In truth, little was known about the medical and social effects of many popular drugs from aspirin and Librium, to cannabis and cocaine. To control the use of some drugs and not others was unpopular in principle because legislation was thereby demonstrated to be arbitrary in its approach. Parliament ultimately endeavoured to search for a method of control that would be open-ended in its scope and reasonably subtle in its administration. The result was the Misuse of Drugs Act 1971. 1–51

The Misuse of Drugs Act 1971 (the "MDA") can be summarised as setting up six main objectives. First, to control the use, production and distribution of all drugs recognised as being medically or socially harmful. Secondly, to create a body (the Advisory Council) comprising of experts in the fields of science and social science to give to the government of the day sound professional advice. Thirdly, to promote a deeper understanding of the problem by undertaking research. Fourthly, to enforce the law by criminal sanctions if necessary. Fifthly, to facilitate the treatment of drug dependants and finally to educate the public.

I. Which Drugs are Liable to Control?

1–52 The *Oxford English Dictionary* defines a "drug" as being:

> "An original, simple, medicinal substance organic or inorganic used by itself or as an ingredient in medicine . . . a narcotic or opiate . . ."

The word "narcotic", by contrast has a much narrower meaning:

> " . . . a substance which when swallowed, inhaled or injected into the system induces drowsiness, sleep, stupefaction or insensibility".

Oddly, the Misuse of Drugs Act 1971 does not define the word "drug", preferring instead to merely list those "substances" which are "controlled" in their use. Note that "preparations" and "products", containing a controlled substance, will also be controlled for the purposes of the Misuse of Drugs Act.

Clearly all medicines are drugs but not all drugs are medicines. Scientists generally access a drug's level of safety by reference to its therapeutic index, being the ratio between the median effective dose as against the median toxic dose.

For present purposes drugs can be loosely grouped as follows:

- (i) substances either organic or inorganic, which are used in medicines;
- (ii) drugs present in naturally occurring substances, *e.g.* caffeine in tea and coffee, alcohol, nicotine in tobacco, THC in cannabis, psilocin (the "magic mushroom");
- (iii) narcotics contained in substances not naturally occurring, *e.g.* in solvent glues, nail varnishes, butane fuels;
- (iv) substances cultivated, extracted or created principally for narcotic abuse, *e.g.* LSD, 2C-B, DOB, MDMA (and other "ecstasy" type substances).

The Preamble to the MDA reads as follows:

> "An Act to make provision with respect to dangerous or otherwise harmful drugs . . ."

1–53 Hence certain drugs are "controlled" and listed as Class A, B or C type drugs depending on the magnitude of danger or harm attached to them: see section 2(1) MDA. Note that the practical significance of the three Classes is that different penalties attach to each Class. While it is not difficult to predict substances that would fall into the dangerous drugs category, being dangerous to one's health, physically or mentally, it is apparent that Parliament had in mind yet another category of drug which it sought to control, namely, those drugs that are described by the MDA as being " otherwise harmful". The problem is identifying those drugs that are liable to fall into this latter category. An indication is given in section 1(2) which imposes a duty on the Advisory Council to keep under review drugs "likely to be misused and of which the misuse is capable of having harmful effects to constitute a social problem" What then is meant by the phrase "a harmful effect" in the context of section 1(2) MDA? What type of problem is a "social" one?

(a) Harmful effects

The first point to note is that, unlike the Preamble to the Act, section 1(2) does not distinguish between "dangerous" drugs and those that are "otherwise harmful". Instead, the legislature preferred to rely on the phrase "harmful effects" as being all-embracing. Secondly, Parliament clearly intended to include drugs that were not only capable of causing physical or mental "harm" to the user, directly or indirectly, but also drugs which are capable of producing harmful results, or consequences, amounting to a "social problem". Accordingly, in this wider context, the "harm" encompasses sociological "damage", *e.g.* delinquency, or the emergence of a social group of users who are in danger of acquiring no more than psychological dependence to a certain drug, *e.g.* barbiturates. 1–54

The Government in their White Paper "Tackling Drugs Together" (1995; Cm 2846) suggest that drug misuse can damage communities in two main ways. First, the misuse may cause "under-achievement, ill-health, suffering and even death" and secondly, it may result in "lost productivity and particularly because of drug-related criminal activity and the fear that this causes" (para. A.8). As the White Paper made clear, there is no firm estimate of the value of drug related crime but one estimate suggests that heroin misuse in England and Wales could be as high as £864 million per annum, financed largely by so-called "acquisitive crime". This is a staggering sum and one that is impossible to verify. There are no statistics available which show the number of cases where injury or death has stemmed from the actual business of illicit drug-trafficking.

(b) Defining what is a social problem

Any irregular activity in the pattern of human behaviour in which some action is required to be carried out by and on behalf of the community in order to maintain harmonious co-existence, or to maintain the reciprocation of benefits, may be said to give rise to a social problem. Accordingly, drugs that cause an unacceptably high level of addiction and which place significant demands on the resources of the medical profession and the social sciences create a social problem. However, suppose the taking of a certain drug does no more than mark adolescent rebellion and causes no 1–55 physical or psychological harm at all. Such behaviour may be delinquent and therefore a "social problem" but it is also likely to be seen as a harmful effect of the drug misuse and the drug is liable to be controlled.

With the emphasis therefore being placed on the recognition of any drug-linked social problem (which need not be based on delinquency), it is evident that all drugs are capable of being controlled by the MDA even if they may not produce any physical or psychological harm (medically speaking). The consequential sociological problem is, in itself, one "harmful effect" of the abuse.

1–56 The Independent Inquiry adopted a more straightforward approach. The committee recommended that the main criterion should continue to be that of dangerousness—determined by a number of factors "some applying to the individual, others to society" [Ch. 3, para. 8]. It suggested that personal harm might be assessed based on four factors:

1. risks of the drug itself: acute (short-term) and chronic (long-term) toxicity;
2. risks due to the route of use;
3. extent to which the drug controls behaviour (addictiveness/dependency);
4. ease of stopping

1–57 Significantly, the Independent Inquiry considered that harm to the user was relevant because it is impossible to separate harm to users from harm to others (Ch. 3, para. 7]:

> "The relative dangerousness of drugs is determined by a number of factors, some applying to the individual, others to society. The main justification for controlling drugs lies in the harm that the use causes to society. However, we should make it clear that, as a matter of principle, it is right for the law to take into account harm the drugs cause to users themselves, as well as to other people affected by users or to the community at large. It is widely agreed that there are cases in which the law may properly try to protect people from harming themselves. These are cases—seat belts and motorcyclist's helmets are examples—in which the damage is serious, almost always comes about unintentionally, and is hard to reverse. This is the kind of risk that is associated in varying degrees with dangerous drugs, in the case is even stronger to the extent that they take away the power of choice. For these reasons, we think, as most people do, that the law should take into account the harms the drugs do to the people who use them. In any case, it is impossible in fact, to separate harms to users from harms to others; self-inflicted damage usually results in costs to others. The harm to the individual as a consequence of the pharmacological effect of the drug lends itself best to objective evaluation. Initially at least, this harm is likely to be the best indicator of how strictly a drug needs to be controlled."

The classes of controlled drugs are not closed, and consequently substances may be added to or removed from Schedule 2 by an Order in Council: section 2(2). A draft of that order must be laid before Parliament and approved by a resolution of each House: section 2(5). This is designed to give Parliament the opportunity of vetting any proposed changes to the law. It is also the probable reason why any radical alteration to Schedule 2 is unlikely to occur lest it should spark off a politically damaging response.

II. Practical Considerations of Drug Classification

(a) Flexibility

It is clearly desirable that the classes of controlled drugs should be kept open and that any alterations made to them are based on sound empirical research. Both the Advisory Council and the Secretary of State may initiate their own research to that end, but the Secretary of State cannot lay a draft order before Parliament without first consulting the Advisory Council: see section 2(5). Determining just how flexible the law really is can best be measured by noting the rate at which the law changes in response to the prevailing conditions and state of scientific opinion. 1–58

Since 1971 no less than 13 "Modification Orders" have been approved, the latest being S.I.1998 No. 750, (see also S.I. 1973 No. 771, S.I. 1975 No. 421, S.I. 1977 No. 1243, S.I. 1979 No. 299, S.I. 1983 No. 765, S.I. 1984 No. 859, S.I. 1985 No. 1995, S.I. 1986 No. 2230, S.I. 1989 No. 1340, S.I. 1990 No. 2589 and S.I. 1995 No. 1966, S.I. 1996 No. 1300.) In the majority of cases, the changes have not been particularly startling. But changes that are more sweeping have taken place in the last few years, including (after much pressure), controlling certain barbiturates and tranquillisers which have been deliberately misused or taken to excess for a considerable number of years.

However, as the Independent Inquiry discovered, transfers between classes of controlled drugs have occurred only twice, namely nicodicodine from Class A to Class B (1978) and methaqualone from Class C to Class B. Methaqualone was moved on the recommendation of the Advisory Council On The Misuse Of Drugs (1979) but another recommendation (that cannabis be moved from Class B to Class C) was rejected by the Government. It is well known that the Independent Inquiry was firmly of the view that cannabis is "wrongly placed" in Class B and should be transferred to Class C along with cannabinol and its derivatives: (Ch. 7; and Ch. 3, para. 28]. 1–59

A decade ago the policy seemed to be to select, with one hand, an increasing number of drugs for the purposes of classification so as to bring them within the control of the law but, using the other hand, to grant an extension of the general authority to possess and supply, a limited number of them; as well as making a number of other concessions. However, recent changes to the law suggest that a less flexible approach is being adopted towards drug use and drug distribution. It is important for the law to be flexible, but three other factors must be put into the equation. First, the law must strive to be certain. From the moment of manufacture, until the moment of consumption, a drug will change hands countless times. It may be imported or exported. It will be used for different purposes. Different considerations will inevitably apply at different stages, but the manufacturer and every other party in the chain must make his arrangements in accordance with the law, and he can only do so if he knows where he stands. Secondly, the law does not exist to make criminals out of people unnecessarily. The wider the net of the MDA is cast, the more likely it is that individuals and companies will fall foul of the law. Thirdly, consideration must also be given to the impact that such a restriction will have on innocent parties, including the drug manufacturers themselves who can suddenly experience administrative inconvenience, loss of income and possible legal action. The manufacturer may also be forced to litigate, at much expense, and challenge the classification of his drug as a "controlled" drug.

(b) Classification should not be arbitrary

1–60 This is particularly important where drugs are controlled on the basis that their misuse may have harmful effects sufficient to constitute a social problem. Drugs may or may not be fashionable to misuse. Those which are fashionable and meet the criteria, one would expect to see added to the list, and those ceasing to be so, deleted. Furthermore, it was presumably not the intention of the legislature to control drugs that demonstrably appealed only to an eccentric few and were likely to remain so. In those circumstances, the abuse is contained, limited to an isolated group, and therefore not likely to constitute a social problem. If flexibility is not maintained so that drugs are classified in keeping with current social and scientific opinion, then the courts are placed at a considerable disadvantage, at least on the question of sentence, believing the drugs in question to be more or less harmful than they really are.

(c) Challenging the classifications

1–61 Most people recognise certain drugs by their "brand name" but the Government designates a controlled drug by its chemical address, as it must do for clarity. Since drugs are controlled in this way it follows that many different brands can be affected even if it is, in truth, one brand name that seems to be the target of misuse. Furthermore, a drug, which produces an effect similar to the misused drug, might also find itself being controlled for that reason, even though the comparable substance has a different chemical make-up, and has no history of having been misused at all. The drug may also be controlled, not because it is inherently dangerous, but because its harmful effect is said to be rooted in a social problem.

What, then, can a company do about it? Its only recourse is to attempt to go behind the making of the Order in Council by ascertaining that the Secretary of State acted *ultra vires* and the designation was made on a misconceived basis. Such a company sets itself a most formidable task.

III. Exercising Control: Mapping the MDA 1971

Since the MDA is designed and intended to regulate the flow of drugs and their use, the following structure is enacted: 1–62

(i) Certain drugs are specified as being "controlled": see Schedule 2.
(ii) Generally, it is unlawful to:
  (a) import or export controlled drugs: section 3;
  (b) produce or supply controlled drugs: section 4;
  (c) possess controlled drugs: section 5;
  (d) cultivate the cannabis plant: section 6;
  (e) prepare or smoke opium: section 9;
  (f) permit premises to be used for the purposes listed above: section 8;
  (g) use utensils or allow others to use them in connection with the smoking of opium: section 9;
  (h) frequent opium "dens": section 9.
(iii) It is unlawful for a person in the United Kingdom to assist in or induce the commission of a "corresponding offence" abroad: section 20.
(iv) Companies may also be guilty of committing offences: section 21.
(v) However, the Government may create exceptions to the general rule and;
  (a) allow certain controlled drugs to be imported/exported, produced, supplied or possessed: section 7(1)(a);
  (b) allow certain persons to use controlled drugs under licence: section 7(1)(b) and section 7(2);
  (c) allow practitioners in the medical and veterinary professions to supply drugs: section 7(3)(a);
  (d) allow those practitioners to possess certain controlled drugs: section 7(3)(b); But :
(vi) The Government may:
  (a) restrict certain controlled drugs to research use only: section 7(4)(a);
  (b) require medical practitioners, etc., to hold a licence before supplying or possessing certain controlled drugs: section 7(4)(b).

IV. The Structure and Nature of the 1985 Regulations

The MDA provides the legal framework. However, it is the regulations that seek to administer its objectives. The combined effect of the Misuse of Drugs Act and the Misuse of Drugs Regulations 1985 is that a very flexible system of control (supported by coercive criminal law sanctions) has been introduced. In short: what the Misuse of Drugs Act prohibits, the Misuse of Drugs Regulations 1985 permit. 1–63

The bulk of the regulations are to be found in the Misuse of Drugs Regulations 1985 (S.I. 1985 No. 2066) (the M.D. Regulations as amended by S.I. 1986 No. 2330, S.I. 1988 No. 916, S.I. 1989 No. 1460, S.I. 1990 No. 2630, S.I. 1995 No. 2048 and S.I. 1995 No. 3244). The earlier Misuse of Drugs Regulations 1973 and its amending instruments have been revoked. Other regulations are considered separately in this work.

Many of the regulations and rules are designed to ensure that certain beneficial drugs remain in proper hands by requiring that drugs be kept secure; that documents are kept of drug transactions; that suitable records be maintained and furnished for possible inspection; that drugs are properly packed, labelled and safely transported; and that the issue of prescriptions be carefully regulated.

The M.D. Regulations 1985

1–64 1. Regulations made under the MDA fall into two groups:

(a) Regulations that permit or restrict activities, relating to controlled drugs, which would otherwise be unlawful under the MDA (s.7). Thus:

(i) The Secretary of State may make Regulations that *permit* the cultivation, production, supply, or possession of drugs. His permission may be conditional (*e.g.* a licence is required) or unconditional (in the case of some very weak preparations);

ii) The Secretary of State may *restrict* activities with respect to controlled drugs. He can achieve this result by transferring a drug (*e.g.* temazepam) from one schedule in the Regulations to another. Such a step can have dramatic consequences because a number of Regulations that did not apply to the substance in question are brought into operation. For example, a drug that had been in Sched. 4 to the Regulations (so that a prescription was not required to obtain it) but which was then transferred to Sched. 3, means that a prescription *would* be required under the MDA 1971 *unless* a specific exception is made. Such an exception occurred in respect of temazepam in 1995. That drug was transferred from Sched. 4 to Sched. 3 so, in the ordinary way, a prescription would have been necessary to obtain it. However, the heading to Sched. 3 was amended in 1995 to read "except Temazepam" in so far as that exception relates to the form of prescriptions. This area is separately examined in greater detail below;

(iii) The Secretary of State may at any time make activities *unlawful* with respect to specified controlled drugs by laying a Statutory Instrument before Parliament. Where the Secretary of State takes that step the Instrument is titled a "Designation Order".

(b) Regulations designed to prevent the misuse of controlled drugs by imposing administrative obligations or requirements, *e.g.* by regulating the issuing of prescriptions, record-keeping; rules relating to safe-custody of drugs etc.

2. Regulations were made in 1973 but revoked and replaced by the Misuse of Drugs Regulations 1985.
3. It should be noted that various factors determine the scope of an 1–65
exemption (or authorisation) under the Regulations, for example,
   - the degree of harm/risk associated with the drug/product (see below);
   - the category of person handling the substance (*e.g.* a police officer seizing heroin, a patient prescribed heroin);
   - the circumstances in which the drug is to be handled or used (*e.g.* a doctor who wishes to administer a drug to another; or where *any* person is asked to administer a drug under the directions of a doctor, *e.g.* at a road-side pile up);
   - international obligations;
   - the toxic effect versus therapeutic value of a substance, etc.
4. To give effect to the above, the Regulations contain *five* schedules. Each schedule takes into account the risk of harm, or degree of harm, associated with the drug in question (*or product* containing a controlled drug). However, the following points should be noted:
   (i) It would be an *error* to say that it is the level of "dangerousness" or "harmfulness" of a controlled drug that *always acts* as the primary, or deciding factor for the purpose of Schedules 1 to 5. This cannot be so because (i) Sched. 2 to the Regulations is the largest schedule and (ii) Sched. 2 contains Class A and B drugs.
   (ii) However, the intensity of control imposed by the Regulations on a person's ability to possess, supply, or import controlled drugs, is heavily *influenced* by the level of harm associated with the drug *or product* in question. The Regulations also take into account a person's qualifications/occupation to use a particular drug safely. Heroin can kill but used correctly and appropriately, it has medicinal uses. Note that a "product" is also a controlled drug if the substance contains a controlled *ingredient*. Thus, a preparation or product containing less than 0.1% cocaine is still a Class A drug but it appears in Schedule 5 of the Regulations as a substance that anyone may possess lawfully. There is no conflict or contradiction of approach here. *Prima facie* cocaine is potentially dangerous/harmful but at 0.1%, it is so weak as to be relatively harmless.
5. The Schedules primarily relate to *activities* that may be performed 1–66
by persons, or groups of persons, specified by the Secretary of State in the Regulations in connection with the drugs contained in the relevant schedule. Some persons (*e.g.* doctors) have greater

lawful authority to handle drugs than other persons do. *Each schedule may serve more than one function for the purpose of the MDA and the Regulations made under it.* Frequently the same persons will be able to perform the same conduct in respect of most of the drugs falling within Schedule 2 and Schedule 3, but more paper work, and tighter security precautions, are required in respect of Schedule 2 drugs than Schedule 3 drugs.

The Schedules to the 1985 Regulations

1–67 Sched. 1: Drugs that have little or no medicinal/therapeutic value but which may have research uses (*e.g.*, LSD, psilocin (found in so-called magic mushrooms) cannabis and cannabis resin). Medical practitioners cannot *prescribe* drugs in this Schedule. However, the Secretary of State may, by licence, authorise the production, supply, and possession of any controlled drug in accordance with the terms of the licence (Reg. 5). This provision is intended to facilitate research (including clinical trials). Accordingly, although a practitioner cannot "prescribe" a Sched. 1 drug, a researcher could supply the substance to another providing (i) he is in possession of a licence that permits clinical trials on humans in respect of that drug *and* (ii) the licence expressly permits the researcher to administer the drug to the subject.

- **Note** that all the drugs that appear in this Schedule *also* appear in yet another schedule annexed to the Misuse of Drugs (Designation) Order 1986, as amended. Designation Orders are made by the Secretary of State for the Home Office pursuant to section 7(4) of the MDA 1971. Their purpose is to specify those controlled drugs (*i.e.* Class A, B, or C drugs) that are not permitted to be used for medical purposes. It is not clear why the Legislature considers that it is necessary to specify the same drugs (that are deemed to have no medicinal value) in two separate Statutory Instruments (*i.e.* Sched. 1, 1985 Regulations, and in a Designation Order).
- In a recent television debate (Channel 5; *Legalising Cannabis*, September 27, 1998) a speaker stated that cannabis appears in Schedule 1 to the Regulations on the grounds that "it has no medicinal value". This assertion is made so often (and in many respected quarters) that it is assumed to be true (and see p. 3 of the BMA Report *Therapeutic Uses of Cannabis*). However, the following points may be of interest:
    - All drugs appearing in Schedule 1 are made under section 7(4) of the MDA 1971. Accordingly, doctors and pharmacists are prohibited from producing, supplying or possessing Schedule 1 drugs except under licence. One reasonable explanation is that Schedule 1 drugs have no medicinal value.

- However, until 1973 doctors were permitted to prescribe cannabis (cannabis often appeared as a tincture). The 1973 Regulations put an end to that (now see the 1985 Regulations, Sched. 1).
- There exists a passage in the Wootton Report which may in fact hold the real reason why cannabis appears in Schedule 1:
  "In 1961 new restrictions on cannabis and cannabis resin were introduced by the Single Convention . . . designed to impose much the same controls on production and distribution of these substances as are applicable to opium and other drugs and to bring to an end the non-medicinal use of the drug in certain Eastern countries. In addition, these drugs were separately scheduled [a reference to Schedule IV of the 1961 Convention] with others of special danger such as heroin, because in the opinion of the World Health Organisation none of these drugs had an **irreplaceable therapeutic value.**"
- The true position may be that the World Health Organisation did *not* say that cannabis had *no* therapeutic value, but merely that it should be possible to replace cannabis products with synthetic substitutes or provide alternative products, *e.g.* Nabilone ("Cesamet") and Dronabinol. It may be that the decision to place cannabis in Schedule 1 was therefore based on a belief that the drug (as a medicine) could be made redundant on the grounds that its "harmful effects" outweighed those associated with the synthetic alternatives.

Sched. 2: **Drugs that have a medicinal value but which are liable to be misused/abused.** This is the largest schedule in the Regulations. Most of the drugs are opiates and the major stimulants. Accordingly, drugs in this group include a number of Class A drugs, *e.g.* cocaine, and Class B substances, *e.g.* amphetamine. The activities permitted or restricted (*e.g.* possession or supply) in respect of the drugs listed in this schedule, as well as the documentation required to be kept, and the categories of persons who may handle the substances, are the same irrespective of whether the controlled drug is Class A or Class B. 1–68

The distribution and use of Sched. 2 drugs are tightly controlled by Regulations made under the MDA. Various Regulations ensure that only those persons who can be trusted to handle Sched. 2 drugs appropriately, do so—and only when they need to handle them. A doctor must act in his capacity as a doctor and a conveyor/courier of a Sched. 2 drug must deliver it to a person lawfully entitled to possess it. Records must be kept at every stage. A doctor can supply or administer a drug directly to the patient but additional records, prescriptions, and books must be kept if drugs are to be taken away from the hospital or surgery. Bottles of pills etc. must be labelled. Prescriptions must be written in indelible form recording the total quantity of the drug supplied (in words and figures), dosage units etc. Pharmacists can only supply on the back of a prescription issued by a practitioner. Special rules apply in situations where doctors or pharmacists may not be found, *e.g.* on a ship, oilrig, residential home (more paperwork).

1–69 Sched. 3: **Drugs that have a medicinal value but warrant fewer controls over their distribution.** Many of the drugs in Schedule 3 are barbiturates. The controls imposed under the 1985 Regulations are less onerous than drugs listed in Sched. 2 and the amount of paperwork is reduced. Temazepam is something of a special case in Sched. 3. Temazepam was supplied on prescription, but that obligation arose under the Medicines Act 1968 (and still does). Rules relating to the form of prescriptions under the MA 1968 are less onerous than those under the Misuse of Drugs Regulations 1985. Given the vast number of patients supplied with Temazepam, that drug (and only that drug in Sched. 3) is exempted from the prescription requirements under the MDA.

1–70 Sched. 4: **Drugs that may be lawfully exported or imported or which may be possessed lawfully.**

- **Note** that drugs falling within Schedules 4 and 5 of the Regulations are subject to *far fewer* administrative controls or criminal sanctions.
- Schedule 4 drugs may lawfully be possessed by anyone—provided they are in the form of "medicinal products".
- Schedule 4 (Part I) drugs may also be lawfully imported if they, too, are in the form of "medicinal products". Part I of Sched. 4, contains anabolic and androgenic steroids.
- Schedule 4 (Part II) drugs can be freely imported or exported whether they are "medicinal products" or not. Part II contains benzodiazepines.
- No prescription is necessary *under the MDA 1971* to possess a Sched. 4 drug or indeed a Sched. 5 drug. **Note** that many controlled drugs may also be "medicinal products" for the purposes of the Medicines Act 1968 and they will thus be subject to administrative controls imposed by that Act. The "labelling provisions" of the MDA do not apply to Sched. 4 or Sched. 5 drugs but labelling provisions under the MA 1968 may apply. Furthermore, the Medicines Act *has its own rules relating to the issuing of prescriptions in respect of specified "medicinal products"*, *e.g.* "Prescription Only Medicines". These are medicines that may only be sold or supplied by retail from pharmacies in accordance

with a prescription issued by a practitioner. This means that a Sched. 4 drug could be subject to a prescription requirement under the MA 1968. **Note** that the burden is on the person who *sells* (or who supplies a "medicinal product" *for retail*) to comply with the prescription requirements. The last point is important because a person found in possession of a Sched. 4 or Sched. 5 controlled drug (as a "medicinal product") without a prescription, does not mean that he/she was in unlawful possession of it *under the MDA*. This is because a prescription is not a precondition of lawful possession for the purposes of the Misuse of Drugs Act in respect of Sched. 4 or Sched. 5 drugs.

- There is no obligation under the MDA for Sched. 4 (or Sched. 5) drugs to be kept in a locked safe or in secured conditions to prevent unauthorised access to the products.
- Persons/groups who are authorised by the Secretary of State to supply drugs may be required to record the quantity of Sched. 4 drugs that they import or export.

Sched. 5: **Very weak preparations or products.** Drugs in this Schedule may be freely imported, exported, or possessed by anyone. Note that some products specified in this Schedule may contain one or more Class A drugs, *e.g.* cocaine (but the amount of cocaine must not exceed 0.1%). Note also the observations mentioned above in respect of Schedule 4 drugs. 1–71

Effect of Moving a Controlled Drug from Schedule 4 or 5 to Schedule 3 or Higher.

6. Drugs falling within Sched. 4 or Sched. 5 are subject to very few restrictions under the MDA. They are "controlled", but there are no restrictions on the *administration* of Sched. 5 drugs under the Misuse of Drugs Act (see para. 5 above for a discussion regarding the meaning of "administering" and "supplying"). Anyone may import, export, or possess a Sched. 5 drug. The possession of Sched. 4 drugs is lawful providing the substance is in the form of a medicinal product. The importation/exportation of drugs listed in Sched.4 (Part I) is lawful if they appear in the form of a "medicinal product". The importation or exportation of all Sched. 4 (Part II) drugs is lawful whether in the form of a "medicinal product" or not. In an emergency the patient may request, or the doctor may decide to administer, a supply of a sched.4 or sched.5 drug without contravening either the MDA or the Medicines Act 1968. The prescription requirements *imposed by the MDA* do not apply to Sched. 4 or Sched. 5 drugs and the safe custody requirements do not apply. 1–72
7. However, once a drug is transferred from Sched. 4 or Sched. 5 to say Sched. 3, then the freedoms and privileges mentioned above, 1–73

disappear. In 1985, when the 1985 Regulations were introduced, Temazepam appeared in Sched. 4 but in 1995 (following concerns about the misuse of that substance) the Government transferred Temazepam from Sched. 4 to Sched. 3. However, the draftsman was careful to amend Sched. 3 by stipulating that Regulation 15 does not apply to Temazepam. The effect is that a prescription is **not** required *under the MDA* for the supply or possession of Temazepam (see reg. 15(1) as amended). *Note that only Temazepam has been afforded this exemption in Sched. 3.* The reason would appear to be that the prescription requirements under the MDA (over and above the requirements imposed by the MA 1968) would have placed a colossal—and probably unacceptable burden on the medical profession given the amount of Temazepam that is supplied each week.

1–74 8. It does not follow that if other drugs were moved from Sched. 4 to Sched. 3 that a similar exemption would be made. Thus, Flunitrazepam (a benzodiazepine drug used to treat insomnia: trade name "Rohypnol") was a Sched. 4 (Part II) drug, until 1998. It was then taken out of that Schedule and moved to Sched. 3, (see S.I. 1998 No. 882), but the 'Temazepam exemption' does not apply to Flunitrazepam.

1–75 9. Note that the transfer of Flunitrazepam from Sched. 4 to Sched. 3 mirrors amendments made to the U.N. Conventions in respect of that substance. The social problem in relation to that drug existed abroad and not in the United Kingdom. The point merely serves to demonstrate, yet again, how our laws are tied in with our international obligations under the Conventions.

1–76 10. Note that usually a Sched. 3 drug (that is also a "medicinal product" and a Prescription Only Medicine) cannot be supplied by a retail pharmacy business without a MA 1968 prescription *even in an emergency*. This is not so in respect of Temazepam—the emergency provisions under the MA 1968 *do* apply in relation to Temazepam.

1–77 11. By transferring Temazepam and Flunitrazepam from Sched. 4 to Sched. 3, the two substances are subject to greater controls. It is now unlawful to import or to export Temazepam or Flunitrazepam other than by licence. It is also an offence to possess either drug unless the person in possession can prove that it was lawfully supplied to him. This he or she can do by showing for example (on a balance of probabilities) that the drug was supplied for medical purposes "in accordance with the directions of a practitioner" (See reg.10(2)). The existence of a prescription issued under the MA 1968 would be compelling evidence of that fact and it would be rare in the extreme if a doctor or a pharmacist did not supply the drug without some record being kept of the transaction.

1–78 12. A burden is placed on those who store Temazepam, and Flunitrazepam, to do so in secure conditions so as to prevent unauthorised access to the drug.

Summary of Controls

Controls under existing drug legislation operate as follows: 1–79

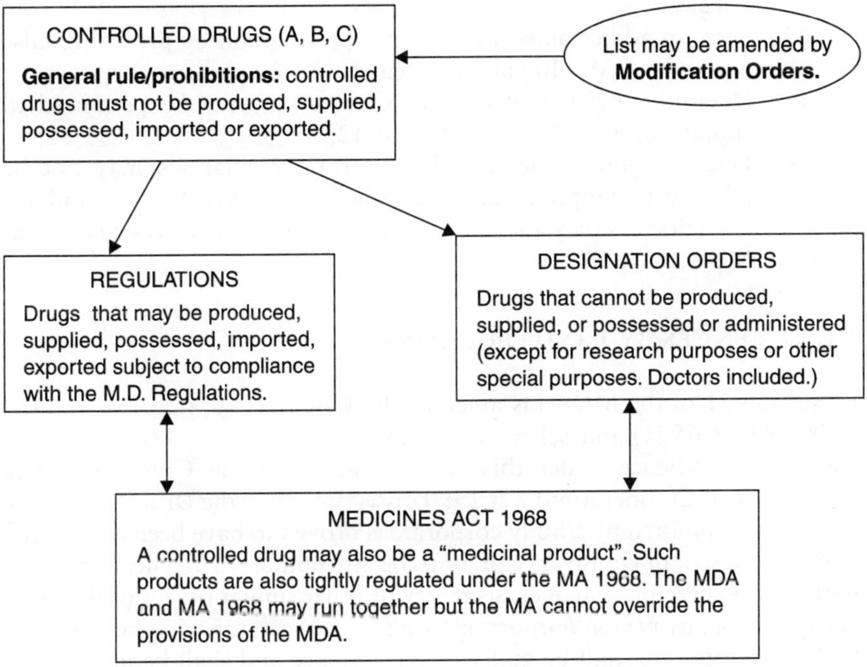

V. Controlling the Activities of Doctors/Pharmacists, etc

Again, the MDA seeks to provide a framework regulating the activities of patients, doctors and pharmacists. 1–80

Put in simplified terms the basic framework is as follows:

(i) A doctor may administer specified drugs: M.D. Regulations reg. 7(2).

(ii) Certain doctors may supply or offer to supply specified drugs to another: M.D. Regulations 8(4) and 9(4).

(iii) Prescriptions must meet certain conditions: M.D. Regulations regs 15 and 16.

(iv) A doctor who attends a person whom he suspects to be addicted to any drug must normally notify the Chief Medical Officer at the Home Office: section 10(h) MDA 1971 and S.I. 1973 No. 799, reg. 3(1).

(v) Only a licensed doctor may prescribe cocaine, heroin or dipipanone to addicts: S.I. 1973 No. 799, reg. 4(1)(b); MDA s.10 and reg. 5 of the MD Regulations

(vi) An addict lawfully entitled to drugs may administer them to himself and therefore be in possession of them: MDA, s.5 (1) and M.D. Regulations 10(2).

(vii) Such an addict must NOT "double-script": MD Regulations 10(2)(a).

(viii) Such an addict must not obtain a prescription by providing false particulars: MD Regulations reg. 10(2)(b).

(ix) Doctors convicted of certain offences may not be permitted to supply controlled drugs: MDA, s.12.

(x) Doctors who act in breach of certain regulations may not be allowed to supply certain controlled drugs: MDA, ss.13 and 14. Such doctors may also be committing criminal offences as a result: MDA, s.18.

VI. Offences by Corporations

1–81 By section 21 of the MDA (as amended by CJICA 1990, s.23 (3); and the DTA 1994, s.65 (1) and Sched. 1, para.3):
"Where any offence under this Act or Part II of the Criminal Justice (International Co-operation) Act 1990 or section 49 of the Drug Trafficking Act 1994 committed by a body corporate is proved to have been committed with the consent or connivance of, or to be attributable to any neglect on the part of, any director, manager, secretary or other similar officer of the body corporate, or any person purporting to act in any such capacity, he as well as the body corporate shall be guilty of that offence and shall be liable to be proceeded against accordingly." In *Boal* (1992) 95 Cr. App. R. 272, the Court of Appeal considered the expression "any director, manager, secretary or other similar officer of the body corporate" as it appears in section 23 of the Fire Precautions Act 1971. In the context of that Act, the Court held:

> "The intended scope of s.23 is, we accept, to fix with criminal liability only those who are in a position of real authority, the decision-makers within the company who have both the power and responsibility to decide corporate policy and strategy. It is to catch those responsible for putting proper procedures in place: it is not meant to strike at underlings."

Support for the above statement, was derived from a passage in the judgement of Blackburn J. in *Gibson v. Barton* (1875) L.R. 10, Q.B. 329, when he said that a manager would be "in ordinary talk" a person who has "the management of the whole affairs of the company" not an agent or a servant who is to obey orders "but a person who is entrusted with power to transact the whole of the affairs of the company."

Chapter 2
The Importation and Exportation of Controlled Drugs

A. THE IMPORTATION AND EXPORTATION OF CONTROLLED DRUGS

Of all narcotics appearing in Britain, the vast majority will have been imported, particularly those drugs which naturally subsist in plants and which cannot be successfully grown in this country. All heroin and cocaine must be imported. Cannabis can be home produced but only with varying degrees of success and subject to the skill of the grower using hydroponic methods. The home-grown plant tends to be less bushy than it would otherwise be if grown in warmer regions of the world. In regions, such as Morocco, Nigeria and Jamaica, the plant grows in such natural abundance that its harvesting, processing and exportation are remarkably inexpensive exercises. The British domestic market, however, accounts for only a part of all drug importations. Britain's geographical position makes it an ideal "staging post" for the onward transmission of narcotics to other countries. This is because many air routes converge in the United Kingdom making it one of the busiest "junctions" in the world. Some other European countries are also distribution points. A great deal of cannabis passes through Holland (*e.g.* through the port of Rotterdam) and Spain. 2–01

As we shall see, the movement of controlled drugs entering and leaving the country is heavily restricted or prohibited. It is therefore hardly surprising to discover that much court time is devoted to the disposal of cases involving the unlawful evasion of the prohibitions and/or the restrictions imposed.

The burden of "policing" the flow of imports and exports and prosecuting offenders, falls chiefly on the Commissioners of Customs and Excise whose existence, powers, rights and privileges are embodied in the Customs and Excise Management Act 1979 ("CEMA") which describes the duties to be performed by the Commissioners, and which are known as "assigned 2–02 matters" (see s.1 (1)). At one time it was not clear whether any of the provisions of the Drug Trafficking Offences Act 1986 ("DTOA") were "assigned matters" for the purposes of CEMA 1979, s.1. For reasons that are not entirely clear, the Home Office Working Party on Drug Trafficking thought that the answer was in the negative. However, in *Stafford Magistrates' Court, ex p. Commissioners of Customs & Excise* [1991] 2 Q.B. 339, the Divisional Court concluded, on the facts in that case, that an offence under section 24 of the DTOA (now s.50 of the DTA 1994) (assisting a drug trafficker to retain the proceeds of drug trafficking) was for all material purposes an "assigned matter", being a matter in relation to which the commissioners were required in pursuance of an enactment to perform any duties: *per* Watkins L.J. Now, all offences in connection with the proceeds of drug trafficking (*i.e.* under Pt III of the DTA 1994) are "assigned matters" for the purposes of the CEMA 1979: see s.60 (4) and (6) of the 1994 Act.

To increase resources, as circumstances demand, Parliament has imposed a duty on all constables, coast-guards and members of the armed forces, to assist in enforcing the law in respect of these matters; see section 11 of the CEMA.

2–03 Regulating the flow of goods into and out of this country cannot be viewed purely in terms of domestic policy because a variety of agreements and treaties relate to the movement of goods between nations. Any question as to the meaning or effect of any of the European Community Treaties is to be treated as a matter of law (s. 3(1), European Communities Act 1972) and by Article 30 of the EEC Treaty, qualitative restrictions on imports "shall . . . be prohibited between Member States" subject to other articles of that Treaty. Thus, Article 36 qualifies Article 30 by permitting Member States to impose prohibitions or restrictions on imports that are justified on grounds of "public policy or security": and see *Goldstein* [1983] 1 W.L.R. 151, HL. The prohibition on the importation or exportation of controlled drugs, imposed by section 3 of the MDA, could thus be justified under Article 36 of the Treaty.

There are a number of chemicals which have many legitimate uses but which are also used in the illicit production of controlled drugs. Many of these substances are precursor chemicals, *e.g.* solvents such as acetone (used in nail-varnish removers, and for dissolving polyester resins in glass-fibre work) or BMK (often used in the manufacture of amphetamine). Sections 12 and 13 of the Criminal Justice (International Co-operation) Act 1990 controls the manufacture, supply and distribution of some of these chemicals. The United Kingdom must therefore take care to ensure that restrictions on exports do not run contrary to our international obligations: see *Searle and KCS Products* [1966] Crim. LR 58. Various chemicals (that could be used in the illicit production of controlled drugs) have been made the subject of European Council Regulation (No. 3677/90) and this, in turn, has been given statutory effect by the Controlled Drugs (Substances Useful for Manufacture) Regulations 1991, S.I. 1991 No. 1285 as amended by S.I. 1992 No. 2914. The regulations give effect to Council Regulation

(EEC) No. 3677/90, which has its own list of "scheduled substances" that broadly follows the chemicals listed in CJICA 1990.

Not all controlled drugs are subject to a complete embargo on importation or exportation. For example, diamorphine (heroin) has legitimate medicinal uses and therefore diamorphine may be imported subject to the appropriate licences being obtained. Whether a licence should be granted (or in what circumstances) is not solely a matter for the Member State considering the grant of a licence, to decide. In *R. v. Secretary of State for the Home Department, ex p. Evans Medical Ltd* [1995] T.L.R. 271, the European Court of Justice held that a national practice of refusing licences for the importation of drugs from another Member State did not come within the derogation from Article 30 provided by Article 36, if it was based on the need to safeguard the commercial survival of a firm, or undertaking. 2–04

Every drug seized on the streets (and which must originally have been unlawfully imported) is of interest to customs officers, but in practice, offences committed at this stage will normally be a matter for the police to investigate pursuant to their powers under the MDA. The police try to avoid charging individuals with offences under the CEMA since all proceedings under that Act should be instituted by order of the Commissioners (s. 145). Conversely, the Commissioners of Customs and Excise prefer not to charge offenders with offences under the MDA if they can bring a prosecution under the CEMA. As a result, a defendant accused of drug smuggling is likely to find that he faces very different charges depending on which law-enforcement agency is investigating the matter. Clearly, this is not a satisfactory state of affairs. For example, in the case of a smuggler who imports a quantity of heroin which is wholly inconsistent with personal use, the police (if they are investigating the matter) are likely to charge the accused with the unlawful possession of drugs with intent to supply them contrary to section 5(3) of the MDA or, alternatively (if others are involved), with conspiracy to evade the prohibition on importation imposed by section 3(1) of the MDA (see *Whitehead* [1982] Q.B. 1272; and see *Keyes and others, The Times* April 5, 2000). The Commissioners of Customs and Excise would, by contrast, charge the accused with an "importation/exportation offence" under the CEMA, which is eminently more appropriate. It should also be borne in mind that defences available to an accused under one-enactment will not always be available to him under another enactment. Thus, section 28 of the MDA, as interpreted by the House of Lords in *Lambert* (July 5, 2001), will not apply to offences brought under the CEMA.

(a) General obligations on the part of travellers and powers of customs officers

By section 78 of CEMA, all persons entering or leaving the United Kingdom have certain obligations to declare goods subject to duty, and not to 2–05 import or to export goods subject to a prohibition or restriction otherwise than permitted by statute.

Thus, section 78 of CEMA (as amended by the Isle of Man Act 1979, s.13, Sched. 1; the CJA 1982, ss. 38, 46; the Finance (No. 2) Act 1992, s. 5; and the Customs and Excise (Single Market etc.) Regulations 1992 (S.I. 1992 No. 3095), reg. 3(10)) provides:

"78(1) Any person entering the United Kingdom shall, at such place and in such manner as the Commissioners may direct, declare any thing contained in his baggage or carried with him which—

(a) he has obtained outside the United Kingdom; or

(b) being dutiable goods or chargeable goods, he has obtained in the United Kingdom without payment of duty or tax,

and in respect of which he is not entitled to exemption from duty and tax by virtue of any order under section 13 of the Customs and Excise Duties (General Relief) Act 1979 (personal reliefs).

In this subsection 'chargeable goods' means goods on the importation of which value added tax is chargeable or goods obtained in the United Kingdom before 1st April 1973 which are chargeable goods within the meaning of the Purchase Tax Act 1963; and "tax" means value added tax or purchase tax.

(1A) Subsection (1) above does not apply to a person entering the United Kingdom from the Isle of Man as respects anything obtained by him in the Island unless it is chargeable there with duty or value added tax and he has obtained it without payment of the duty or tax.

(1B) Subsection (1) above does not apply to a person entering the United Kingdom from another member State, except—

(a) where he arrives at a customs and excise airport in an aircraft in which he began his journey in a place outside the member States; or

(b) as respects such of his baggage as—

(i) is carried in the hold of the aircraft in which he arrives at a customs and excise airport, and

(ii) notwithstanding that it was transferred on one or more occasions from aircraft to aircraft at an airport in a member State, began its journey by air from a place outside the member States.

(2) Any person entering or leaving the United Kingdom shall answer such questions as the proper officer may put to him with respect to his baggage and any thing contained therein or carried with him, and shall, if required by the proper officer, produce that baggage and any such thing for examination at such place as the Commissioners may direct.

(2A) Subject to subsection (IA) above, where the journey of a person arriving by air in the United Kingdom is continued or resumed by air to a destination in the United Kingdom which is not the place where he is regarded for the purposes of this section as entering the United Kingdom subsections (1) and (2) above shall apply in relation to that person on his arrival at that destination as they apply in relation to a person entering the United Kingdom.

(3) Any person falling to declare any thing or to produce any baggage or thing as required by this section shall be liable on summary conviction to a penalty of three times the value of the thing not declared or of the baggage or thing not produced, as the case may be, or level 3 on the standard scale whichever is the greater.

(4) Any thing chargeable with any duty or tax which is found concealed, or is not declared, and any thing which is being taken into or out of the United Kingdom contrary to any prohibition or restriction for the time being in force with respect thereto under or by virtue of any enactment, shall be liable to forfeiture."

The Channel Tunnel (Customs and Excise) Order 1990 (S.I. 1990 No. 2167), Sched., para. 17B (inserted by the Channel Tunnel (International Arrangements) Order 1993 (S.I. 1993 No. 1813), Sched. 5, para. 27), as amended by the Channel Tunnel (Miscellaneous Provisions) Order 1994 (S.I. 1994 No. 1405) provides that, for the purposes of section 78 of the 1979 Act: 2–06

(a) a person intending to travel to the United Kingdom through the tunnel who has entered a control zone in France or Belgium shall be treated as a person entering the United Kingdom,
(b) a person who has travelled from the United Kingdom through the tunnel and is in such a control zone shall be treated as still being a person leaving the United Kingdom, and
(c) concealment shall be taken to include concealment in such a control zone.

Note that by The Channel Tunnel (Customs and Excise) Order 1990 (S.I. 1990 No. 2167, Sched., para. 20A)—which was inserted by S.I. 1993 No. 1813, Sched. 5, para. 30—customs officers have power to seize or detain anything liable to forfeiture which shall be taken to include a power for any officer or constable to seize or detain any such thing in a control zone in France (s. 139(1), CEMA 1979, and in Belgium (December 1, 1997); and see the Channel Tunnel (Miscellaneous Provisions) Order 1994 (S.I. 1994 No. 1405), art. 8, Sched. 4, para. 7.

B. THE STATUTORY PROHIBITIONS

Section 3 of the MDA 1971 reads: 2–07

"(1) Subject to subsection (2) below
(a) the importation of a controlled drug; and
(b) the exportation of a controlled drug, are hereby prohibited.

(2) Subsection (1) above does not apply

(a) to the importation or exportation of a controlled drug which is for the time being excepted from paragraph (a) or, as the case may be, paragraph (b) of subsection (1) above by regulations under section 7 of this Act; or

(b) to the importation or exportation of a controlled drug under and in accordance with the terms of a licence issued by the Secretary of State and in compliance with any conditions attached thereto."

It will be seen that section 3(1) of the MDA merely establishes the existence of two separate prohibitions it does not, by itself, make it an offence to contravene either prohibition. The reason is that many enactments similarly prohibit or restrict the importation, exportation, or carriage coastwise, of many different goods, substances, or even wildlife (See *Sissen* (December, 8, 2000, CA). Thus, no "medical product" may be imported without a licence: section 7, Medicines Act 1968. The need for a licence is a restriction on importation; and see section 13(2) of the Criminal Justice (International Co-operation) Act 1990. Accordingly, for the purposes of the CEMA, the legislature aptly terms all such goods "prohibited or restricted goods" (see section 1(1) of the CEMA) and has created a mere handful of offences to punish an unlawful contravention of the relevant prohibition or restriction.

2–08 "Prohibited or restricted goods" must be carefully distinguished from "dutiable goods". Dutiable goods may be lawfully imported but customs "duty" or "excise" is payable before the goods may be cleared. The importance of making this distinction will become apparent see [2–17] and [2–25] *et seq*.

Given that section 3(1) of the MDA only imposes a prohibition on the exportation or importation of controlled drugs, it is necessary to look to the CEMA to find the offences arising out of a contravention of section 3(1). Broadly speaking, there are three offences. Section 50 punishes unlawful or improper importations; section 68 punishes unlawful exportations; and section 170 serves as a "mopping-up" provision, punishing ventures designed to evade the prohibitions. Each offence is widely drawn. Each section uses different language that inevitably creates problems of construction. In practice, offences under section 50 or section 68 are rarely charged whereas offences under section 170 are commonplace.

It follows that offences for the unlawful exportation or importation of controlled drugs arise by a combination of section 3(1) of the MDA and an offence created under the CEMA. As a matter of convenience the offence may be described, or even charged, as an offence under either or both enactments but the underlying offence undoubtedly exists under the CEMA. Accordingly, no proceedings for an offence arising out of a contravention of section 3(1) of the MDA may be instituted except by order of the Commissioners of Customs and Excise, unless they fall within section 145(6): see section 145(1) of the CEMA, *Menocal* [1980] A.C. 598 and *Whitehead* [1982] Q.B. 1272.

I. Instituting Proceedings

In the majority of cases, few problems are likely to be encountered, but the relevant provisions cannot always be applied literally. As a result, some difficulties of construction arise. If charges are brought then care must be taken to ensure that they are not bad for duplicity and one test to be applied is whether the criminal enterprise formed part of what was in reality one activity, and this is a question of fact and degree: *Fyffe and others* [1992] Crim. L.R. 442 and see *Wilson* (1979) 69 Cr.App.R. 83. 2–09

The basic restriction on the institution of proceedings appears in section 145 of the CEMA (as amended by the Police and Criminal Evidence Act 1984, s.114), which reads as follows:

"(1) Subject to the following provisions of this section, no proceedings for an offence under the customs and excise Acts or for condemnation under Schedule 3 to this Act shall be instituted except by order of the Commissioners.

(2) Subject to the following provisions of this section, any proceedings under the customs and excise Acts instituted in a magistrates' court, and any such proceedings instituted in a court of summary jurisdiction in Northern Ireland, shall be commenced in the name of an officer.

(3) Subsections (1) and (2) above shall not apply to proceedings on indictment in Scotland.

(4) In the case of the death, removal, discharge or absence of the officer in whose name any proceedings were commenced under subsection (2) above, those proceedings may be continued by any officer authorised on that behalf by the Commissioners.

(5) Nothing in the foregoing provisions of this section shall prevent the institution of proceedings for an offence under the customs and excise Acts by order and in the name of a law officer of the Crown in any case in which he thinks it proper that proceedings should be so instituted.

(6) Notwithstanding anything in the foregoing provisions of this section, where any person has been [arrested] for any offence for which he is liable to be [arrested] under the customs and excise Acts, any court before which he is brought may proceed to deal with the case although the proceedings have not been instituted by order of the Commissioners or have not been commenced in the name of an officer."

After some initial confusion it is now clear that the Commissioners of Customs and Excise are entitled to prosecute a defendant, in respect of a case investigated by the Commissioners, notwithstanding that the defendant was charged at a police station by a custody officer: see *R. v. Stafford J.J, ex p. Customs and Excise Commissioners* [1991] 2 Q.B. 339. The confusion arose following the decision of the Divisional Court in *R. v. Ealing Justices, ex p. Dixon* [1990] 2 Q.B. 91 which is no longer to be regarded as good law. Section 3(2)(a) of the Prosecution of Offences Act 1985 imposes a duty on the D.P.P. to "take over the conduct of all criminal proceedings . . . instituted on behalf of the police force". What, then, is 2–10 meant by the phrase "on behalf of the police"? Part of the answer is to be found in section 15(2) of the 1985 Act, which states that proceedings are instituted, *inter alia*, when a person "is charged with the offence after being taken into custody without a warrant". The duty of charging offenders (arrested without a warrant) rests solely with the custody officer at a police station: see section 37(1)(a) PACE. Although various provisions of PACE apply to customs officers, just as they do to the police, a customs officer is not permitted to charge a person with any offence (see Art. 3(1) and Art. 4 of the Police and Criminal Evidence Act 1984 (Application to Customs and Excise) Order 1985, S.I. 1985 No. 1800). This means that a defendant must be taken to a police station and presented before the custody officer who determines whether he has sufficient evidence to charge that person. *Dixon's case* held that the custody officer has no power to charge a person "on behalf of a private individual". This passage, when read in isolation, could be construed as limiting itself to prosecutions brought by individuals but the Divisional Court in *Stafford Justices* concluded that the effect of the reasoning in *Dixon's case* was, that as soon as the custody officer accepted a charge at the police station, he acted on behalf of the police force no matter who investigated the offence. In *Jackson* [1990] Crim. L.R. 55 his Honour Judge Laurie at Southwark Crown Court rejected a defence submission that the indictment should be quashed in circumstances where the committal for an offence under section 170(2)(a) CEMA 1979 was conducted by a customs officer even though the defendant had been charged by the custody officer at a police station. Judge Laurie ruled that "on behalf of" in section 3(2)(a) of the 1985 Act, means something like "in the interest of [the law enforcement agency]". The Divisional Court, in *Stafford Justices*, held that Judge Laurie reached the correct conclusion and that the charging process "is neutral in this context:" *Dixon's case* was held to be wrongly decided: and see *R. v. Croydon J.J, ex p. Holmberg* [1992] Crim. L.R. 892.

2–11 There is a peculiar conflict if it be a conflict between the effect of subsection (1) and subsection (6). On the one hand, proceedings can only be instituted by order of the Commissioners (subs. (1)) but on the other hand, no such order is required if the defendant is detained, or arrested, for a customs offence (subs. (6)). It is difficult to envisage many cases, involving the prosecution of a customs offence, which would not be satisfied by section 145(6), even if an order of the Commissioners is not obtained under subsection (1). One possible explanation for this curious state of affairs was given by Donaldson L.J. in *Whitehead* [1982] Q.B. 1272, when he said (at 1282 B):

> "the section is designed only to ensure that proceedings under [the CEMA] are not brought without the commissioners being aware of them. The commissioners will become aware of such proceedings if the proceedings are brought by their order. They should also become aware of them if the accused is detained by any offence under the Act.

In *Whitehead* [1982] Q.B. 1272 the appellants had been convicted of two counts of conspiracy to evade the prohibition imposed by section 3(1) of the MDA contrary to section 1(1) of the Criminal Law Act 1977. On appeal, it was contended that the proceedings were invalid on the grounds that: (a) section 3(1) merely imposed a prohibition on importation or exportation; (b) the offence of evading s. 3(1) existed under section 304 of the Customs and Excise Act 1952 (now s. 170 of the CEMA); (c) an order of the Commissioners was therefore required to institute proceedings under the Customs and Excise Acts (see s. 145(1), formerly s. 281(1) of the 1952 Act); (d) such an order was required for a conspiracy to commit the offence (see s. 4(3) of the Criminal Law Act 1977); and (e) no such consent had in fact been obtained.

The Court of Appeal dismissed the appeals but only after a non-literal application of section 145(6) (formerly s. 281(4) of the 1952 Act). The Court held, first, that the offence arose by a combination of section 3(1) of the MDA and what is now, section 170 of the CEMA: see *Menocal* [1980] A.C. 598 and *Williams* [1971] 1 W.L.R. 1029. Secondly, the underlying offence was an offence under the CEMA requiring an order of the commissioners to institute proceedings. Thirdly, that no such order was required if the appellants had been "detained" within the meaning of section 145(6) of the CEMA Finally, that the appellants had been so detained. Note that PACE 1984 substituted the word "arrested" for "detained". 2–12

By section 145(6) of the CEMA, an order is not required "where any person has been detained for any offence for which he is liable to be detained under the customs and excise Acts". (Note the words in italics.) A contravention of section 170 of the CEMA is one such offence, but in *Whitehead*, neither appellant had been charged with that or any other substantive offence, under the Act. A conspiracy to evade section 3(1) of the MDA is not, strictly speaking, an offence under the customs and excise Acts and therefore if section 145(6) is strictly applied such a conspirator is not a person "liable to be detained" under the Customs and Excise Acts. However, the Court of Appeal held that the words in section 281(4) now section 145(6) should read "where any person has been detained for conspiracy to commit any offence for which he would be liable to be detained under the customs and excise Acts".

On this basis, both appellants had been so detained and therefore section 145(6) of the CEMA should be construed as including cases of conspiracy to commit an offence for which an accused would be liable to be detained/arrested under the CEMA. 2–13

Section 4(3) of the Criminal Law Act 1977 provides, as far as it is material:

> "Any prohibition by or under any enactment on the institution of proceedings for any offence shall apply also in relation to proceedings under section 1 above for conspiracy to commit that offence."

Donaldson L.J. said, *obiter*, in *Whitehead* that section 4(3) confers authority on the Commissioners to make an order in relation to a statutory conspiracy to commit an offence under the Customs and Excise Acts. The matter was again considered in *Keyes and others, The Times*, April 5, 2000, and see Shotonwa (December 14, 1998, CA).

II. Lawful Shipments

2–14 Section 3(2) and section 7 of the MDA permit the Secretary of State to except any controlled drug from the relevant prohibitions. This he has done by virtue of regulation 4(1) of the Misuse of Drugs Regulations 1985, which provides that section 3(1) shall not have effect in relation to the drugs specified in Schedules 4 Part II, and 5 of the 1985 Regulations. The drugs listed in Schedule 4 Part II will be exempt if they are in the form of medicinal products. A "medicinal product" is defined by section 130 of the Medicines Act 1968. Note that the operation of section 3(1) of the Misuse of Drugs Act insofar as it creates an offence under section 50(1) to (4) and section 68(2) and (3) of CEMA, excludes any prohibition or restriction on importation of drugs specified in Part I to Schedule 4 of the Misuse of Drugs Regulations 1985 provided that they are in the form of a "medicinal product" and that they are intended for self-administration: Regulation 4(1A).

Other controlled drugs may only be imported or exported under and in accordance with the terms of a licence issued by the Secretary of State: see section 3(2)(b) of the MDA.

III. Defining the Moment of Importation or Exportation

2–15 This is dealt with in the CEMA, by section 5, as amended by the Customs and Excise (Single Market etc.) Regulations 1992 (S.I. 1992 No. 3095), reg. 10(1), Sched. 1, para. 3):

> "5(1) The provisions of this section shall have effect for the purposes of the customs and excise Acts.
>
> (2) Subject to subsections (3) and (6) below, the time of importation of any goods shall be deemed to be—
>
> (a) where the goods are brought by sea, the time when the ship carrying them comes within the limits of a port;
>
> (b) where the goods are brought by air, the time when the aircraft carrying them lands in the United Kingdom or the time when the goods are unloaded in the United Kingdom, whichever is the earlier;
>
> (c) where the goods are brought by land, the time when the goods are brought across the boundary into Northern Ireland.
>
> (3) In the case of goods brought by sea of which entry is not required under regulation 5 of the Customs Controls on Importation of Goods Regulations 1991, the time of importation shall be deemed to be the time

when the ship carrying them came within the limits of the port at which the goods are discharged.

(4) Subject to subsections (5) and (7) below, the time of exportation of any goods from the United Kingdom shall be deemed to be—

(a) where the goods are exported by sea or air, the time when the goods are shipped for exportation;

(b) where the goods are exported by land, the time when they are cleared by the proper officer at the last customs and excise station on their way to the boundary.

(5) In the case of goods of a class or description with respect to the exportation of which any prohibition or restriction is for the time being in force under or by virtue of any enactment which are exported by sea or air, the time of exportation shall be deemed to be the time when the exporting ship or aircraft departs from the last port or customs and excise airport at which it is cleared before departing for a destination outside the United Kingdom.

(6) Goods imported by means of a pipe-line shall be treated as imported at the time when they are brought within the limits of a port or brought across the boundary into Northern Ireland.

(7) Goods exported by means of a pipe-line shall be treated as exported at the time when they are charged into that pipe-line for exportation.

(8) A ship shall be deemed to have arrived at or departed from a port at the time when the ship comes within or, as the case may be. leaves the limits of that port."

A "port" means any port appointed by the Commissioners (under s. 19). 2–16
The Commissioners may also determine the "limits" of the port: see section 1(1). A large number of Statutory Instruments have ensured that the entire coastline has been embraced. It may happen, of course, that controlled drugs (destined for the United Kingdom) are, say, jettisoned at sea beyond the limits of a port and remain there. In those circumstances, no offence would be committed under CEMA 1979, section 50, nor would the full offence under section 170(2) be committed because the drugs remained beyond the limit of a port and there had not been an effective importation within the meaning of section 5 of the Act. The position would probably be different if the tide, for example, brought the drugs within the jurisdiction of this country: consider *Jakeman* (1983) 76 Cr.App.R. 223 and *Latif and Shahzad* [1996] 1 All E.R. 353, HL; and see *Panayi (No.2)* [1989] 1 W.L.R. 187.

In *MacNeill v. H.M. Advocate*, 1986 S.C.C.R. 288, the appellants carried 2–17
cannabis on board a vessel which because of bad weather entered the limits of a port in Northern Ireland for a short time before entering the Port of Strathclyde in order to refuel for a voyage in international waters. The jury were directed that the importation had taken place in the Port of Strathclyde. The court rejected the argument that the prosecution had to prove that an importation occurred within the limits of the first appointed port within which the vessel passed. Importation occurs at any port where the

goods are discovered and also at any port in the United Kingdom, which has been entered en route to that port. In any event a temporary stop-over, at a point identified as coming within the limits of a port for the purposes of sections 5 and 19 of the CEMA 1979, will not preclude a charge under section 50 or section 170 of the 1979 Act if the evidence discloses an "importation" at the port where the drugs are discovered: and see *De Sain v. H.M. Advocate*, 1993 G.W.D. 306. The term "ship" is broadly defined to include any boat or other vessel whatsoever: section 1(1).

It is not entirely clear why Parliament has provided that "prohibited goods" are deemed to be exported at the moment when the exporting ship or aircraft "departs from the last port or customs and excise airport at which it is cleared before departing for a destination outside the United Kingdom . . ." (s. 5(5)). If prohibited goods leave the United Kingdom from a place other than a recognised port or airport then, clearly, section 5(5) can have no application. In this event there is no reason why section 5(4)(a) should not prevail.

In *Sissen* (December 8, 2000, CA), S travelled to Yugoslavia and Slovakia to buy macaws subject to restrictions on importation into the European Union by Article 5(1) of E.C. Regulation 3626/82 (in respect of eight birds), and by Article 4(1) of E.C. Regulation 338/97 in respect of one bird. S smuggled the birds into the European Union and then into England. For the purposes of the appeal, the court proceeded on the basis that the point of entry of the birds was probably Austria, and not the United Kingdom. S contended that he could not be convicted of an offence under section 170(2)(b) of CEMA 1979 because the moment of importation was outside the United Kingdom. He contended that the offence was committed and triable in Austria, and he relied on *Air India v. Wiggins* [1980] 1 W.L.R. 815. However, section 170(2)(b) refers to "any prohibition or restriction" imposed by virtue of "any enactment". By section 2(1) of the European Communities Act 1972, restrictions arising under "the Treaties" are to be given legal effect. The Court of Appeal held that S's conviction was correct in law.

Sissen is a decision of some importance. It is all too easy to view the Customs and Excise Acts as being relevant only to goods entering or leaving the United Kingdom, whereas the legislation is also relevant to goods entering and leaving the European Community / European Union. The arguments advanced by the parties appear to have ranged widely, but it is not clear to what extent the court's attention was drawn to section 5 of CEMA 1979 (defining the moment of importation or exportation). It is submitted that the decision is perhaps best explained if the following points are considered. First, section 170(2)(b) of CEMA, refers to any prohibition or restriction "with respect to the goods". Usually, the prohibition / restriction will relate to goods entering or leaving the *United Kingdom*, but on a literal reading of section 170(2)(b), the prohibition or restriction might embrace a wider area—provided the measure exists "by virtue of any enactment". It may be significant that s.170(2)(b) does *not* actually say "any prohibition or restriction" *on importation*—which would engage section 5 of CEMA. Secondly, the birds entered the European Union contrary to a restriction imposed by virtue of an enactment (namely, ECA 1972 and related instruments). Thirdly, there was an evasion of the restriction imposed within the European Union, and that evasion continued as the birds made their way into England. Fourthly, S intended that the birds should be carried into England.

IV. Importation Through the Channel Tunnel

The Channel Tunnel (Customs and Excise) Order 1990 (S.I. 1990 No. 2–18
2167), Sched., para. 8, (as amended by the Channel Tunnel (International Arrangements) Order 1993 (S.I. 1993 No. 1813), Art. 8, and Sched. 5, para. 21; and the Channel Tunnel (Miscellaneous Provisions) Order 1994 (S.I. 1994 No. 1405), art. 8, and Sched. 4, para. 7) provides as follows:

> 8. Section 50(2) (penalty for improper importation of goods) shall have effect as if—
>
> (a) any person who unloads or assists or is otherwise concerned in the unloading of those goods mentioned in section 50(1) from any vehicle which has arrived from France through the tunnel, or who brings or assists or is otherwise concerned in the bringing of such goods into a control zone in France or Belgium, were a person who unships such goods in a port; and
>
> (b) any person who removes or assists or is otherwise concerned in the removal of such goods from any customs approved area were a person who removes such goods from an approved wharf."

The Commissioners may approve, for such periods and subject to such conditions and restrictions as they think fit, places in the United Kingdom, and in France in a control zone within the tunnel system, for the customs and excise control of persons, goods or vehicles in relation to the construction, operation or use of the tunnel or any part of it, and may also so approve all or any through trains while they are within any area in the United Kingdom specified in the approval or while they constitute a control zone, and any place or train so approved is referred to as a "customs approved area": S.I. 1990 No. 2167, as amended by S.I. 1993 No. 1813, art. 8, Sched. 5, para. 9.

(a) Time of importation for the purposes of Channel Tunnel importations

This is dealt with by S.I. 1990 No. 2167, of which article 5(1), (2) (as 2–19
amended by S.I. 1993 No. 1813, Sched. 5, Pt II, para. 10; and by S.I. 1994 No. 1405, Sched. 4, para. 6), provides:

> "5(1) The provisions of this article shall have effect for the purposes of the customs and excise Acts and of any enactment under or by virtue of which any prohibition or restriction with respect to the importation or exportation of any goods is for the time being in force.

(2) Goods intended to be brought into the United Kingdom through the tunnel shall be treated as being imported into the United Kingdom—

(a) in the case of goods intended to be carried in a shuttle train, when they are taken into a control zone in France within the tunnel system,

(b) in the case of goods carried, while the train constitutes a control zone in France or Belgium, in a through train carrying passengers on a journey intended to end at a place in Great Britain other than London, at the time when officers become authorised under Article 12 of the international Articles or, as the case may be, under Article 5 of the Part II provisions, to begin to carry out controls and

(c) in any other case, when they cross the frontier."

(i) *Exportation through the Channel Tunnel*

2–20 It is appropriate or at least convenient to deal with this issue at this stage. The Channel Tunnel (Customs and Excise) Order 1990 (S.I. 1990 No. 2167), art. 5(6) provides:

> "In the case of goods of a class or description with respect to the exportation of which any prohibition or restriction is for the time being in force under or by virtue of any enactment and which are exported by vehicle through the tunnel, the time of exportation shall be deemed to be the time when the exporting vehicle departs from the last customs approved area at which goods were loaded onto it for exportation."

As to the meaning of "customs approved area", see Archbold 2001, § 25–412.

V. Goods Sent By Post

2–21 Prior to the Postal Services Act 2000, section 16 of the Post Office Act 1953 (as amended) ensured that the provisions of CEMA applied to importations (and exportations) by post. The 1953 has now been repealed and replace by section 105 of the PSA 2000 which provides as follows:

> "105.—(1) Subject as follows, the enactments for the time being in force in relation to customs or excise shall apply in relation to goods contained in postal packets to which this section applies which are brought into or sent out of the United Kingdom by post from or to any place outside the United Kingdom as they apply in relation to goods otherwise imported, exported or removed into or out of the United Kingdom from or to any such place.
>
> (2) The Treasury, on the recommendation of the Commissioners of Customs and Excise and the Secretary of State, may make regulations for-
>
> (a) specifying the postal packets to which this section applies,

(b) making modifications or exceptions in the application of the enactments mentioned in subsection (1) to such packets,
(c) enabling persons engaged in the business of a postal operator to perform for the purposes of those enactments and otherwise all or any of the duties of the importer, exporter or person removing the goods,
(d) carrying into effect any arrangement with the government or postal administration of any country or territory outside the United Kingdom with respect to foreign postal packets,
(e) securing the observance of the enactments mentioned in subsection (1),
(f) without prejudice to any liability of any person under those enactments, punishing any contravention of the regulations."

Goods ordered and purchased via the internet (or by mail order) are not immune from the rules relating to prohibitions or restrictions on importation/exportation, and duties may be payable on imports too: 2–22

"(3) Duties (whether of customs or excise) charged on imported goods or other charges payable in respect of postal packets to which this section applies (whether payable to a postal operator or to a foreign administration) may be recovered by the postal operator concerned and in England and Wales and Northern Ireland may be so recovered as a civil debt due to him.

(4) In any proceedings for the recovery of any charges payable as mentioned in subsection (3), a certificate of the postal operator concerned of the amount of the charges shall be evidence (and, in Scotland, sufficient evidence) of that fact.

(5) In this section "foreign postal packet" means any postal packet either posted in the United Kingdom and sent to a place outside the United Kingdom, or posted in a place outside the United Kingdom and sent to a place within the United Kingdom, or in transit through the United Kingdom to a place outside the United Kingdom.

(a) Powers for postal operators

In the ordinary way, a 'postal operator' (defined by s. 125 of the Act) would not be entitled to interfere with private correspondence, but limited exceptions are made in respect of packages suspected to contain contraband. It is important to read the following provisions in conjunction with the Postal Packets (Customs and Excise) Regulations 1986, as amended by Postal Packets (Customs and Excise) (Amendment) Regulations 1992. 2–23

"106.—(1) A postal operator may—
(a) detain any postal packet if he suspects that it may contain relevant goods,
(b) forward any packet so detained to the Commissioners of Customs and Excise.

(2) In this section "relevant goods" means—

(a) any goods chargeable with any duty charged on imported goods (whether a customs or an excise duty) which has not been paid or secured, or

(b) any goods in the course of importation, exportation or removal into or out of the United Kingdom contrary to any prohibition or restriction for the time being in force by virtue of any enactment.

(3) Subsection (1) is without prejudice to section 105.

(4) The Commissioners may open and examine any postal packet forwarded to them under this section—

(a) in the presence of the person to whom the packet is addressed, or

(b) where the address on the packet is outside the United Kingdom or where subsection (5) applies, in the absence of that person.

(5) This subsection applies where—

(a) the Commissioners have

(i) left at the address on the packet notice requiring the attendance of the person concerned, or

(ii) forwarded such notice by post to that address, and

(b) the addressee fails to attend.

(6) If the Commissioners find any relevant goods on opening and examining a postal packet under this section, they may detain the packet and its contents for the purpose of taking proceedings in relation to them.

(7) If the Commissioners do not find any relevant goods on opening and examining a postal packet under this section, they shall

(a) deliver the packet to the addressee upon his paying any postage and other sums chargeable on it, or

(b) if he is absent, forward the packet to him by post."

C. IMPROPER IMPORTATION: SECTION 50 CEMA 1979

2–24 Section 50 of the CEMA (as amended by s. 114(1) PACE 1984) defines the offence arising out of an unlawful or improper importation as follows:

"(1) Subsection (2) applies to goods of the following descriptions, that is to say

(a) goods chargeable with a duty which has not been paid; and

(b) goods the importation, landing or unloading of which is for the time being prohibited or restricted by or under any enactment.

(2) If any person with intent to defraud Her Majesty of any such duty or to evade any such prohibition or restriction as is mentioned in subsection (1) above

(a) unships or lands in any port or unloads from any aircraft in the United Kingdom or from any vehicle in Northern Ireland any goods to which this subsection applies, or assists or is otherwise concerned in such unshipping, landing or unloading; or

(b) removes from their place of importation or from any approved wharf, examination station, transit shed or customs and excise station any goods at which this subsection applies or assists or is otherwise concerned in such removal,

he shall be guilty of an offence under this subsection and may be [arrested].

(3) If any person imports or is concerned in importing any goods contrary to any prohibition or restriction for the time being in force under or by virtue of any enactment with respect to those goods, whether or not the goods are unloaded, and does so with intent to evade the prohibition or restriction, he shall be guilty of an offence under this subsection and may be [arrested].

To seek to argue that no offence is committed under this section on the grounds that the accused was merely being used as an informer in an undercover operation, and thus should be afforded the protection of section 5(4) of the MDA 1971, would be fallacious because that section quite clearly only applies to an offence of possession: see *De Sain v. H.M. Advocate* 1993 G.W.D. 306.

I. The Ambit of Section 50(1)

Quite clearly the draftsman was careful to distinguish between "dutiable goods" (s.50(1)(a)) and "prohibited and restricted goods" (s.50(1)(b)): see *Superheater Co. Ltd v. Commissioners of Customs & Excise* [1969] 1 W.L.R. 858. At first blush, a problem of construction arises when the wording of section 50(1)(b) is examined. If (b) was merely concerned with the unlawful importation of prohibited goods, and nothing else, what then does the draftsman gain by adding the words "landing" or "unloading"? Although it may be tempting to argue that Parliament was merely describing or demonstrating an act of importation, this contention is soon defeated once it is remembered that "importation" is sufficiently defined under the Act by reference to the moment when goods are deemed to be imported under section 5. Therefore, goods may be imported (and the prohibitions against importation evaded) before the goods are even unloaded. However, the solution to the problem lies in recognising that each of the three words ("importation", "landing", and "unloading") may relate to a wholly separate and distinct prohibition, or restriction, which must be expressly imposed by the relevant enactment. Thus, for the purposes of section 3(1)(a) of the MDA the "importation" of controlled drugs is prohibited. Other statutes, for their respective purposes, prohibit or restrict the "landing" or "unloading" of certain goods but do not seek to prohibit 2–25 their actual importation: see section 13(2) Criminal Justice (International Co-operation) Act 1990 [and see the Medicines Act 1968].

The terms "goods imported" and "goods unloaded" are not mutually exclusive. In *Smith (Donald)* [1973] Q.B. 924, cannabis was sent by air from Nairobi to Bermuda via London. The drug was unloaded at London Airport, transferred to another aircraft and flown to Bermuda. S was convicted of fraudulently evading the prohibition against its importation (contrary to s. 304(b) of the Customs and Excise Act 1952) and its subsequent exportation (contrary to s. 56(2) of that Act). The appellant argued that reference to "goods unloaded" in section 45 of the 1952 Act (now s. 50) was excluded from the category of "goods imported" and therefore since S merely facilitated the unloading of goods he had therefore not imported them.

2–26 The Court of Appeal rejected that argument, concluding that section 45 of the old Act was concerned with the "improper importation" of goods. Willis J. said:

> "... it is to be observed that ss.44 and 45 are concerned with the improper importation of goods. It seems quite clear that the Act contemplates that goods can be imported before they are either landed from a ship or unloaded from an aircraft ... it would be strange indeed for Parliament to have excluded from the various categories of 'goods imported' a category of 'goods unloaded' without such an intention being precisely indicated. We cannot think ... that there can be a category of goods which are simply 'unloaded' and not 'imported' when they are taken off an aircraft ... until reloaded for onward transmission outside the country."

The result is patently right since to treat "imported goods" and "unloaded goods" as being mutually exclusive is to make a nonsense of the wording of the Act. It should be noted that the appellant was not charged with an offence under what is now section 50, but with the offence of being knowingly concerned in the fraudulent evasion of a prohibition against the importation of a controlled drug (*i.e.* what is now s.170(2)). When Willis J. described section 45 of the 1952 Act as being concerned with the "improper importation of goods" he was careful not to say that section 45 was concerned only with the unlawful importation of goods. He clearly recognised that goods might be lawfully imported but illegally unloaded or landed and he therefore described section 45 in neutral terms as being concerned with the "improper" importation of goods.

II. Section 50(2) Offences

2–27 It is clear that subsection (2) creates two sets of offences one in relation to "dutiable goods" and another in respect of "prohibited or restrictive goods". Therefore, a person arriving in the United Kingdom knowing that the goods he is carrying are subject to a prohibition against importation, will commit an offence contrary to section 50(2)(a) if he removes them from a ship in a port, or unloads them from any aircraft.

Whereas section 50(2)(a) applies to goods removed from any aircraft in the United Kingdom (whether or not the aircraft has landed at a recognised "Customs and Excise airport"), it seems that no offence is committed contrary to section 50(2)(a) if goods are unshipped from a vessel outside the limits of "a port" as defined by section 19(1) of the CEMA.

The words "with intent to defraud" are relevant in cases where duty has not been paid (see *Frailey v. Charlton* [1920] 1 K.B. 147). Those words have no relevance in a drug smuggling venture.

III. SECTION 50(3)

(a) "Concerned"

The actus reus of the offence is very narrow, particularly when it is compared with the much broader offence of "being knowingly concerned in the fraudulent evasion of the prohibition", against importation, contrary to section 170(2). In essence, section 50(3) is concerned solely with the single word "importation". Consequently, if the prosecution is to succeed under section 50(3), it must prove that the accused participated in the actual importation, *e.g.* by carrying the drug, or that he was at least in such a position as to be able to lend his assistance if required, in the smuggling operation. 2–28

Unlike section 170(2), the offence is not a continuing one, and cannot therefore include persons who subsequently handle the drug, even if they are aware of its origin, but who were not parties to the original importation.

Where more than one person is alleged to have been involved in the commission of the offence, it is at least arguable that the word 'concerned' (as it appears in s. 50(3)) makes it unnecessary for the court to apply the usual rules of joint enterprise. Indeed there may be no place for the application of those rules: see *H.M. Advocate v Hamill*, 1998 S.L.T. 1260, and see *Salmon v H.M. Advocate*, 1999 S.L.T. 169. It is submitted that section 50(3) makes it clear that the offence may be committed by the importer or by a person 'concerned' with the importation of the goods but in each case, he must have an intention to evade the prohibition or restriction.

(b) The mens rea

The intent required is an intent to evade the relevant prohibition. Section 50(3) is explicit as to the mental ingredient required to be proved by the prosecution, namely, the defendant himself must intend to evade the relevant prohibition or restriction. It is not enough to prove that the defendant took part in an enterprise (which someone else devised) to evade the relevant prohibition or restriction because section 50(3) uses the phrase "and 2–29 does so with intent" (*i.e.* imports or is concerned in importing goods). By contrast, an offence charged under section 170(2) is much broader in scope and catches persons who are knowingly concerned in another person's fraudulent evasion or attempted evasion irrespective as to whether the defendant personally intended to evade the prohibition or restriction or not.

In *Latif* [1996] 1 All E.R. 353, HL, a customs officer without a licence, but with the full knowledge of his superiors, carried heroin into the United Kingdom. Lord Steyn remarked that it was "common ground" in argument that the customs officer had committed an offence under section 50(3). Despite the requirement in section 50(3) of an "intent to evade", Lord Steyn inclined to the view that this concession was "rightly made". His lordship went on to assume without deciding the point that the officer was also guilty of an offence under section 170(2). Both the concession and the assumption made in *Latif* should be viewed with care. It should not be assumed that Lord Steyn was acknowledging that the concession was rightly made as being correct in law: concessions may be made because they are tactically prudent. As Staughton L.J. remarked "[it] is generally wise to concede that which one does not need to defend". ([1995] 1 Cr. App. R. 270, 274). The prosecution were prudent to make the concession because they wanted to prove, if they could, the full offence under section 170(2)(b). If the officer was guilty of the offence then the case against L and S was much easier to establish. The defence made the same concession, no doubt to support the argument that the proceedings should have been stayed as an abuse of process (or that items of evidence should have been excluded under PACE, s. 78) and to support a submission of no case to answer, made on behalf of S, on the grounds that S was not concerned in the officer's enterprise. Whatever the officer's position may have been, as far as an offence under section 170(2) is concerned, it is submitted that he could not have been guilty of an offence under section 50(3) because he did not intend to evade the prohibition on importation. *Latif* is considered in detail at para. 2–53.

2–30 Evidence of an intention to take the imported goods elsewhere without landing them, or that the accused intended to keep the vessel carrying the drug in an anchorage long enough to buy fuel for a voyage into international waters, is irrelevant once it is proved that the accused knew that the goods were being imported contrary to a prohibition on importation: *MacNeill v. H.M. Advocate*, 1986 S.C.C.R. 288.

Given that section 50(3) requires proof of an intention "to evade the prohibition", it is arguable that the actor must know the relevant prohibition he or she is evading. If that is the law then an importer of drugs commits no offence, under this subsection, if he genuinely believes that the drugs are not subject to a prohibition. Similarly, if an importer makes a complete mistake as to the nature of the goods imported, believing for example, that he has smuggled weapons (which he knows to be "prohibited goods") whereas he has unwittingly imported heroin, then no offence under section 50(3) has been committed since he does not intend to evade the prohibition imposed by section 3(1) of the MDA. However, a mistaken belief that he is importing cannabis whereas he is importing heroin, is no defence since both commodities are subject to the same prohibition.

It is not necessary for the prosecution to prove dishonesty on the part of the importer in the sense of practising a deceit on a customs officer in his or her presence. By "evade" Parliament meant no more than an intention on the part of the accused to "get around" the prohibition. "Evade", in this context, does not carry the connotation of fraud or dishonesty as it does in income tax law: see *Hurford-Jones* (1977) 65 Cr.App.R. 263. It follows that it would be no defence for a cannabis smuggler, knowing of the prohibition, to say that he considered he was doing nothing wrong, believing that the drug cured most ailments.

D. UNLAWFUL EXPORTATION: SECTION 68

Section 68(2) of the CEMA (as amended by the Forgery and Counterfeiting Act 1981, section 23(2) (insertion of subs. (4A)); the CJA 1982, ss.38, 46; the PACE Act 1984, s.114(1); and the Finance Act 1988, s.12(1)(a), (6) (substitution of "7 years" for "2 years" in subs. (3) (b)), provides that: 2–31

"68(1) If any goods are—

(a) exported or shipped as stores; or

(b) brought to any place in the United Kingdom for the purpose of being exported or shipped as stores,

and the exportation or shipment is or would be contrary to any prohibition or restriction for the time being in force with respect to those goods under or by virtue of any enactment, the goods shall be liable to forfeiture and the exporter or intending exporter of the goods and any agent of his concerned in the exportation or shipment or intended exportation or shipment shall each be liable on summary conviction to a penalty of three times the value of the goods or level 3 on the standard scale, whichever is the greater.

(2) Any person knowingly concerned in the exportation or shipment as stores, or in the attempted exportation or shipment as stores, of any goods with intent to evade any such prohibition or restriction as is mentioned in subsection (1) above shall be guilty of an offence under this subsection and may be arrested.

(3) [Identical to s.50(4) save that "(4) or (4A) replaces "(5) or (5A)" and the words "or (3)" do not appear]

(4) In the case of an offence under subsection (2) above in connection with a prohibition on exportation having effect by virtue of section 3 of the Misuse of Drugs Act 1971, subsection (3) above shall have effect subject to the modifications specified in Schedule 1 to this Act

(4A) [identical to s.50 (5A) except that "or (3)" do not appear and "21" replaces "20"]

(5) If by virtue of any such restriction as is mentioned in subsection (1) above any goods may be exported only when consigned to a particular place or person and any goods so consigned are delivered to some other place or person, the ship, aircraft or vehicle in which they were exported shall be liable to forfeiture unless it is proved to the satisfaction of the Commissioners that both the owner of the ship, aircraft or vehicle and the master of the ship, commander of the aircraft or person in charge of the vehicle—

(a) took all reasonable steps to secure that the goods were delivered to the particular place to which or person to whom they were consigned; and

(b) did not connive at or, except under duress, consent to the delivery of the goods to that other place or person.

(6) [Corresponds to s.50(7]"

2–32 It should be noted that where there is a contravention of the Controlled Drugs (Substances Useful for Manufacture) Regulations 1991 (S.I. 1991 No. 1285), then by way of regulation 6, section 68 will be read as if the expressions, set out below, were inserted into the section.

"(a) section 68(1) has effect as if after the word 'greater' there were added the words 'but not exceeding the statutory maximum';

(b) section 68(3)(a) has effect as if after the word 'greater' there were added the words 'but not exceeding the statutory maximum', and for the words '6 months' there were substituted the words '3 months'; and

(c) section 68(3) (b) has effect as if for the words '7 years' there were substituted the words '2 years'."

2–33 Oddly, the draftsman has adopted a formula of words in section 68(1) that is very different from section 50. It is difficult to see why there should be a difference. First, the use of the word "knowingly" appears to add nothing to the subsection since the prosecution is in any event required to prove that the accused intended to evade any prohibition or restriction in force with respect to those goods. Secondly, quite unlike section 50, the requirement that the prosecution must prove an intent "to evade any prohibition or restriction" is ambiguous; it may be sufficient for the prosecution merely to prove that the accused knew that the goods he was exporting were subject to some prohibition, albeit that he was unaware of the precise one. Thus, it would be no defence for an exporter to say that he believed he was exporting guns (knowing them to be subject to a prohibition on exportation) and not heroin. Nevertheless, if he believed that he was exporting brandy then it cannot be said that he intended to evade a prohibition on exportation because brandy does not come within the category of "prohibited goods or restricted goods" (see s. 1(1) of the CEMA) but "dutiable goods".

Note that there are a number of statutory provisions which deem a restriction to be imposed for the purposes of section 68 of the 1979 Act: see CJICA 1990 s.13(2) and see the Controlled Drugs (Substances Useful for Manufacture) Regulations 1991, S.I. 1991 No.1285, amended by S.I. 1992 No.2914 and the European Council Regulation No.3677/90.

If an exporter obtains a licence, to export the goods in question, care must be taken to ensure that its terms are complied with for otherwise the export (or an attempt to export) may be unlawful: see *R v. Redfern and Dunlop Ltd* [1993] Crim. L.R. 43.

E. FRAUDULENT EVASIONS: SECTION 170

Commercially motivated contraband smuggling almost always involves a high degree of planning and requires a team of participants to secure the distribution of smuggled goods and to prevent their confiscation by law enforcement officers. An evasion of a prohibition or restriction on the importation or exportation of goods is therefore a continuing process and not confined to the moment when the goods actually enter or leave the country. Accordingly, it is not surprising that statutory measures designed to combat smuggling cast a particularly wide net. The drawback is that some of these measures lack precision and create ambiguity and uncertainty as section 170 demonstrates. 2–34

(a) Subsection (1)

Section 170(1) (as amended by PACE 1984, s. 114(1) reads as follows: 2–35

"Without prejudice to any other provision of the Customs and Excise Acts 1979, if any person

(a) knowingly acquires possession of any of the following goods, that is to say
   (i) goods that have been unlawfully removed from a warehouse or Queen's warehouse;
   (ii) goods that are chargeable with a duty, which has not been paid;
   (iii) goods with respect to the importation or exportation of which any prohibition or restriction is for the time being in force under or by virtue of any enactment; or
(b) is in any way knowingly concerned in carrying, removing, depositing, harbouring, keeping or concealing or in any other manner dealing with any such goods,

and does so with intent to defraud Her Majesty of any duty payable on the goods or to evade any such prohibition or restriction with respect to the goods he shall be guilty of an offence under this section and may be [arrested]."

Note the words "acquires possession" in section 170(1)(a) and the activities required to be proved in section 170(1)(b). Note also that the relevant *mens rea*, in cases of drug smuggling, is an intention to "evade any such prohibition or restriction with respect to the goods" and note the observations made in respect of the wording of section 50(3) of the CEMA 1979 (see Ch. 2–28 *et seq.*).

(b) Subsection (2)

2–36 Now compare the above with the wording of subsection (2) set out below:

> "Without prejudice to any other provision of the Customs and Excise Acts 1979, if any person is, in relation to any goods, in any way knowingly concerned in any fraudulent evasion or attempt at evasion
> (a) of any duty chargeable on the goods;
> (b) of any prohibition or restriction for the time being in force with respect to the goods under or by virtue of any enactment; or
> (c) of any provision of the Customs and Excise Acts 1979 applicable to the goods,
> he shall be guilty of an offence under this section and may be [arrested]."

It will be seen that section 170(2) is very broadly drawn and it is worth emphasising at this stage that the heart of the offence is the concept of being knowingly concerned in a *fraudulent evasion* or attempt at evasion. A fraudulent evasion is therefore not to be equated with a fraudulent importation (by contrast see section 50(3) of the 1979 Act). Accordingly, an offence under section 170(2):

(a) may be committed if one or more persons intend to get around the prohibition or restriction on importation or exportation of the goods; but -
(b) it is submitted that the defendant need only be proved to have been concerned in the smuggling venture knowing what was afoot; see *Latif* [1996] 1 All E.R. 353, HL.
(c) in the light of (b) above, the prosecution is not required to prove that the defendant personally intended to evade the prohibition or restriction: and see *Att.-Gen. Reference (No. 1 of 1998)*, *The Times*,October 2, 1998, judgment August 10, 1998.
(d) the offence may be committed under section 170(2) either by fraudulently evading the prohibition, or by attempting to evade the prohibition. The difference is that a fraudulent evasion requires, for example, an importation of the offending goods whereas an attempted evasion does not: see *Latif* [1996] 1 All E.R. 353, HL, pp.365j–366b.

2–37 As far as point (d) is concerned, it follows that section 170(2) creates only one offence (albeit capable of being committed in one of two ways). It is therefore unnecessary to charge an attempted fraudulent evasion under the Criminal Attempts Act 1981 and indeed, in *Latif*, such a charge was withdrawn from the jury at the end of the prosecution case. Although it is desirable that the prosecution should describe the offence (if they can) as being either an evasion, or an attempted evasion, it will not be fatal to their case if they fail to do so or even if they misstate the category: see *Latif, per* Lord Steyn at pp.365j–366a. The point also arose in *Qadir and Khan* (July 25, 1997).

> Q and K were convicted of being knowingly concerned in the attempted fraudulent exportation of over 12 kilograms of heroin to the USA, contrary to section 170(2) of the Customs and Excise Act 1979. Q claimed that he acted at the request of his uncle who persuaded him that by assisting the law enforcement agencies to apprehend M, Q would be immune from prosecution. Q then worked for M. The defence argued that his acts were merely preparatory to the attempted evasion. The Court held that section 170(2) created a "compendious provision" that embraced an evasion or an attempted evasion. The *actus reus* was the attempt at fraudulent evasion, in which it was alleged Q, K, and M, were knowingly concerned and thus liable for the single offence. It was not clear whether the word "attempt" in section 170(2) was to be construed in the same way as under the Criminal Attempts Act 1981, but that did not need to be decided in this case: see *Gullefer*, 91 Cr.App.R. 356.

I. General Statement of the Law

Interpreting section 170 has become something of a judicial nightmare particularly in the last few years and it would be idle to pretend that considerable difficulties of reconciliation do not exist between the many cases, which have wrestled with drug-related importations. Nevertheless, it is clear that a set of rules is not only crystallising but is also displaying signs of durability. Accordingly, before examining the wording of section 170 and the relevant decisions, it may be of assistance to summarise the basic legal position at this stage. 2–38

If a charge is brought under section 170(1) then the prosecution must prove that:

(a) the accused either :
  (i) knowingly acquires possession of goods; or
  (ii) is "knowingly concerned" in carrying, removing, depositing, harbouring (see *Cohen* (1950) 34 Cr.App.R. 239), keeping or concealing, "or in any other manner" dealing with goods (see *Schneider v. Dawson* [1960] 2 Q.B. 106); and

(b) the goods in question are subject to a prohibition or restriction on importation in force under or by virtue of any enactment (and see *Sissen* (December 8, 2000, CA); and

(c) the accused intended to evade a prohibition or restriction imposed with respect to the goods.

If, however, the charge is brought under section 170(2) then the prosecution must prove that:

(a) the goods in question are subject to a prohibition or restriction under or by virtue of any enactment (see *Sissen* (December 8, 2000, (A) and para. 2–17); and
(b) a fraudulent evasion or attempted evasion of a prohibition or restriction has taken place in relation to those goods; and
(c) the accused is concerned in that fraudulent evasion; and
(d) the accused was concerned in that fraudulent evasion "knowingly" see *Latif and Shahzad* [1996] 1 All E.R. 353, H.L.

2–39 In respect of each subsection, the following propositions currently represent the law. Propositions referable to "importations" apply equally to "exportations" thus:

- There must be proof (at least for an evasion) that the goods were "imported": see *Watts* (1979) 70 Cr.App.R. 187 and see *Latif and Shahzad* [1996] 1 All E.R. 353, H.L.
- To be "knowingly concerned" it is not necessary for the accused to have taken steps to bring about the importation of the offending item: see *Att.-Gen. Reference (No. 1 of 1998), The Times*, October 2, 1998, and see *Neal* (1983) 77 Cr.App.R. 283.
- The prosecution must prove that the accused knew that the goods were prohibited or (as the case may be) restricted from importation.
- However, the prosecution does not have to prove that the accused knew:
  (a) the precise prohibition involved; or
  (b) the class of drug actually imported; or
  (c) the actual drug imported.

2–40 See *Hussain* [1969] 2 Q.B. 567; *Hennessey* (1978) 68 Cr.App.R. 419, CA; *Shivpuri* [1987] A.C. 1; *Ellis* (1987) 84 Cr.App.R. 235; *Forbes* [2001] 3 W.L.R. 428, HL; and, by way of a contrast, see *Daghir* [1994] Crim. L.R. 945.

- It is therefore a defence for the accused to say that he did not know that the goods imported were subject to any prohibition or restriction on importation.
- It is a defence for the accused to say that he believed he was importing goods not subject to a prohibition or restriction but that they came within some other category, for instance, "dutiable goods", *e.g.* brandy.
- It is a defence for the accused to say that he mistakenly believed that he was importing goods of a particular description (*e.g.* currency) which he believed to be prohibited from importation when, as a matter of law, they would not have been prohibited: see *Taaffe* [1984] A.C. 539.
- An offence may be committed by a person who is involved in the venture before or after the moment of importation of the goods into the

country: see *Mitchell* [1992] Crim. L.R. 594 and *Att.-Gen. Reference (No. 1 of 1998)* 163 J.P. 390.

- Acts committed abroad are nevertheless punishable in England if the prohibited goods are consequentially imported into that country: see *Wall* [1974] 2 All E.R. 245; and see *Latif and Shahzad* [1996] 1 All E.R. 353; and note *Jakeman* (1983) 76 Cr. App. R. 223.

II. Distinguishing Section 170(1) from Section 170(2)

In *Neal* (1983) 77 Cr.App.R. 283, Griffiths L.J. contrasted the language of subsections (1) and (2) and commented that: 2–41

> "The language of [subsection (1)] is so embracing and casts the net so wide that one is left to wonder what purpose is served by subsection (2) . . . We are satisfied that [subsection (2)] was inserted by the draftsman with the intention of casting his net as widely as words enabled him—note his language, 'if any person' and 'in any way'".

It follows that the accused need not perform steps to bring about the importation of the drugs in order to be guilty of an offence under section 170(2)(b): *Att.-Gen. Reference (No. 1 of 1998), The Times*, October 2, 1998. The Court remarked that the section ought to be given the widest possible interpretation. Certainly both subsections are very widely drawn and catch individuals who were not party to the original smuggling operation. A person who conceals drugs at a safe house, long after the moment of importation, is therefore caught by either subsection, provided that he intended to evade a prohibition against the importation of the goods.

However, there is in fact a significant distinction to be made between the scope of subsections (1) and (2). It will be seen that section 170(1)(a) makes it plain that an acquisition or possession of the goods is a necessary prerequisite for an offence under section 170(1)(a). Similarly, proof of custody or control over prohibited goods is implicitly required in respect of any of the activities referred to in section 170(1)(b) of the Act. By contrast, subsection (2) imposes no such restrictions. 2–42

Whereas section 170(1) expressly requires proof of an intention to evade the prohibition or restriction, section 170(2) is not so worded. The distinction requires clarification. For the purposes of section 170(1) the prosecution is required to prove that the accused performed one or more of the activities referred to in section 170(1)(a) or (b). It must also be proved that at the time the acts were done the defendant intended to defraud, or to evade a prohibition or restriction (as the case may be) with respect to the goods.

> In *Coghlan*, (May 12, 1997) C a diplomat shipped his belongings, including obscene videos, from Tokyo to Madrid via the United Kingdom. He was convicted of being concerned in importing indecent or obscene material. He completed a false C3 Customs form and the goods were to be stored until they could be shipped to Spain. C argued

> that that although the videos were prohibited goods, he had not been a party to their importation; the goods were innocently imported by the shippers. Held: in refusing leave to appeal against his conviction, the Court noted that section 170(2) of the Customs and Excise Management Act 1979 did not require an intent to "defraud", unlike subs. (1)(b) (*Neal* 77 Cr.App.R. 283). Evasion of a prohibition on importation was a continuous process, which was not limited to landing the goods.

It is submitted that where an offence under section 170(1) is charged jointly, and the goods in question are controlled drugs, each defendant must be proved to have had the intention to evade a prohibition on importation of the goods.

2–43 The next question is whether the accused must intend to evade the particular prohibition imposed in respect of the goods actually imported. Most of the authorities that deal with the issue of *mens rea* relate to charges under section 170(2) of the Act (or its forerunner *i.e.* s. 304(b) of the Customs and Excise Act 1952). However, the answer seems to be that irrespective as to whether the offence is charged under section 170(1), or under section 170(2), the accused need only know that the goods are subject to a prohibition on importation (any prohibition). Thus, for an offence of attempting to be knowingly concerned in dealing with or harbouring a controlled drug (contrary to s. 1(1) of the Criminal Attempts Act 1981 and s. 170(1)(b) of the 1979 Act) the House of Lords rejected the argument that the prosecution were required to prove, that the accused new that the goods were subject to a particular prohibited category: *Shivpuri* [1987] A.C.1. Also, note the words in section 170(1) "with intent to evade any such prohibition. . . ."

Section 170(2) is less straightforward but it may be summarised as follows. First, there must be a fraudulent evasion or an attempted fraudulent evasion. Fraudulent, in this context, means "dishonest conduct deliberately intended to evade the prohibition or restriction with respect to, or the duty chargeable on, goods as the case may be": *per* Lord Lane C.J. in *Att.-Gen.'s Ref. (No.1 of 1981)* [1982] Q.B. 848. "Fraudulent" does not mean a deception practised on the officers of customs and excise. *Borro and Abdullah* [1993] Crim. L.R. 513, CA, which asserted the contrary, is no longer good law. Secondly, the fraudulent evasion or attempted evasion may be committed by a person or persons other than the defendant on trial. The problem that arises is whether it is enough that the accused was concerned in a drug smuggling venture, knowing that another person intended to evade the prohibition or restriction on importation, even if the accused did not assent to the plan, and did not desire that the prohibition should be evaded. It was this issue that gave rise to difficulties in *Latif and Shahzad* [1996] 1 All E.R. 353. A customs officer imported heroin into the United Kingdom without a licence but with the full knowledge of his superiors. His purpose was law enforcement. Without deciding the point, the House of Lords was prepared to assume that the officer was guilty of an offence under section

170(2). The officer did not intend to evade the prohibition on importation but he was ostensibly acting on behalf of others who did have that intention. The House of Lords could see no justification for construing section 170(2) as if it read that the defendant must be "fraudulently and knowingly concerned" in an evasion, observing that such a construction "may cause practical difficulties in other cases". The circumstances in which a person may therefore be held liable under section 170(2) for a result, which they do not desire, nor intend to bring about, is considered in detail below.

Note that most statutory prohibitions relate to the importation or exportation of goods into the United Kingdom but that need not always be so: See *Sissen* (December 8, 2000, CA) and para. 2–17.

III. Evading the Prohibition or Restriction

(a) Evasion as a continuing state of affairs

The popular image of smuggling is a venture involving the surreptitious landing of contraband at an unofficial point of entry into a country. However, the "evasion" of "any prohibition or restriction on importation" as required by subsection (1) or (2), is wider than simply the single word "importation", as Kenneth Jones J. vividly illustrated in *Neal* (1983) 77 Cr.App.R. 283: 2–44

> "A boat arrives . . . in this country . . . and it has on board cannabis resin. One of the sailors . . . actually carries the cannabis resin ashore. He hands it over to another man . . . who loads it into a van. The van is driven off to some place where the drug is . . . stored . . . and at a later stage, it is transported to yet another building and is stored there and it may be . . . that behind all this operation . . . is some organising person. Now you see, of all those men . . . strictly speaking, only the sailor has imported the drugs into this country . . . and that is what importation means, but he and each of those other persons . . . have all taken a part in setting at nought the ban which the law imposes on the importation of the drug."

The illustration vividly demonstrates that the evasion of a prohibition is a continuing process rather than an isolated act, and accordingly offences under section 170 are continuing offences. It follows that arguments, that attempt to narrowly construe section 170, to include only those persons who were parties to the original smuggling operation, must be fallacious. The organiser who never makes an appearance at the moment of importation is as guilty as the sailor who brings the goods ashore is. Thus, in *Neal* (above) Griffiths L.J. said: 2–45

> "Subsection (1) clearly includes those who are not a part of the original smuggling team. For example, it includes anyone who acquires possession of goods unlawfully removed from a warehouse, or anyone who hides goods on which duty has not been paid, or anyone who carries

goods the importation of which is forbidden; and there can be no warrant for reading into the language of the subsection the qualification 'provided they are part of the original smuggling team' . . ."

2–46 As MacKenna J. pointed out in *Ardalan* [1972] 1 W.L.R. 463, s. 170(1)(a) (formerly section 304(a) of the 1952 Act) embraces an accused who "acquires possession" of prohibited goods. Obviously, he can only "acquire" goods after (or before) the moment of importation or exportation. Equally, the person who (contrary to s. 170(1)(b)) carries, removes or harbours prohibited goods, may do so before, or subsequent to, the moment of importation. In other words, the very language of section 170(1), itself proves that offences under that subsection are continuing. Since subsection (2) merely widens the scope of subsection (1) it follows that offences under subsection (2) must also be continuing. Persons who are therefore not parties to the actual importation may nevertheless join or leave the venture at any time until the goods cease to be prohibited and are therefore criminally liable for their acts under section 170. Thus in *Green* [1976] Q.B. 985, a crate containing cannabis arrived at Southampton and was placed in a shed. Customs officers removed the cannabis and substituted a quantity of peat. A month after the importation G rented a garage in a false name. The crate was delivered to the garage where it was stored. The Court of Appeal dismissed G's appeal against his conviction under what is now section 170(2) (formerly s. 304(b)). The offence was a continuing one and the evasion did not cease when the drugs were seized. Renting the garage, knowing that it was to be used to store cannabis that had been unlawfully imported, completed the offence.

Again, in *Neal* (above), the provision of a barn on a farm in which six hundredweight of cannabis was concealed behind a false wall was sufficient evidence of being concerned in the unlawful importation of drugs even though there was no evidence as to where, or how, the drugs had been imported.

2–47 It will be recalled that in *Green* (above) customs officers removed the drug shortly after it was imported and substituted a quantity of peat. Perhaps encouraged by this decision, it has long been the practice of customs officers to substitute an innocuous substance for the smuggled goods before allowing the container to be delivered to the consignee (see para. 2–81 below). Accordingly, where any person was "knowingly concerned" in the evasion of the prohibition on importation of a controlled drug (*i.e.* after the goods were imported and seized) he will still be guilty of an offence contrary to section 170(2) of the CEMA.

This startling result has been confirmed by the Court of Appeal in *Ciappara* [1988] Crim.L.R. 172.

> In Bolivia, C's sister addressed two packets containing cocaine to C. The packets were unsolicited by C. Customs officers intercepted the packets and substituted baking powder for the cocaine. Each packet consisted of a note (asking C for money) wrapped around a postcard to form a container for the drug. C threw away the note, and the

postcard, but kept the powder that he believed to be cocaine. He was convicted of an offence under section 170(2) in respect of one packet (which was sent to his place of work) but he was acquitted of a similar charge in respect of the other packet that had been sent to his home address. C's appeal against his conviction was dismissed.

C contended, on appeal, that (a) the packets were unsolicited, (b) the importation was complete by the time the packages were intercepted, (c) the drug had been removed before C received the packages and therefore, (d) C could not be said to be "knowingly concerned" with the importation of cocaine. The Court of Appeal rejected C's contention. There was no dispute that the packets were unsolicited and that the importation was complete by the time the packages were intercepted. However, section 170(2) did not exclude those whose only involvement arose after the importation, provided they knowingly participated. The Court's attention was drawn to *DPP v. Doot* [1973] A.C. 807, *Neal* (1983) 77 Cr.App.R. 283 and *Ardalan* [1972] 1 W.L.R. 463, but not it would seem to *Green* (above): but see now *Mitchell* [1992] Crim. L.R. 594.

The commentary to *Ciappara*, provided by Professor Sir John Smith Q.C., is thought provoking but (it is submitted) erroneous. Professor Smith remarked (at 173): 2–48

> "So he is convicted of being knowingly concerned in the fraudulent evasion of the prohibition on the importation of cocaine, although, in fact, the only substance he ever dealt with was baking powder! Surely that cannot be right. . . . How can a person properly be said to be concerned in evasion of a prohibition on importation when the importation is complete before he even knows anything about it. . . . .The onus should surely be on the prosecution to show that there are words justifying the remarkable wider meaning given to the section. It is like saying I am knowingly concerned in killing X if, after finding that X has been killed, I help to dispose of the body."

However, the definition of "murder", "manslaughter" (or even "killing") is very different to the wording of CEMA, s.170(2). A "killing" occupies a moment, and so does an "importation". However, it is not the fact of importation that is the continuing element of an offence under section 170(2). It is the evasion of a prohibition or restriction on importation that continues. Thus, the evasion continues until the goods cease to be prohibited or, possibly, until the goods are re-exported. The fact that they have been seized in the interim is irrelevant; *Cf. Mitchell* [1992] Crim.L.R. 594.

(b) Acts that bring about an importation of prohibited goods may be punishable

Applying the same reasoning, acts done before the moment of importation with the requisite *mens rea*, are punishable under section 170, even if the acts are performed abroad. So where, in *Wall* [1974] 1 W.L.R. 930, W 2–49 travelled to Afghanistan with others and handled packages of cannabis which were later shipped to the United Kingdom, it was held that he had been knowingly concerned in the fraudulent evasion.

The appellant contended that if he had done nothing on the day of importation, and if what he did do earlier was not done in England, then he should not have been convicted. This contention implied that the offence is not a continuing one and therefore overlooked the fact that the court was not restricted to focusing its attention on acts done in England when the goods were imported. There was a clear causal link between the defendants' activities abroad and the eventual arrival of the drug into England. If *Wall* had been decided differently, the ramifications would have been colossal. Organisers, operating abroad, who shipped vast quantities of drugs to England, could therefore never be convicted of an offence under section 170(2) because of their absence at the moment of importation.

2–50 The decision in *Wall* is, in fact, supported by a long line of authorities including *DPP v. Doot* [1973] A.C. 807, *Treacy v. DPP* [1971] A.C. 537, *Baxter* [1972] Q.B. 1 and *Millar* [1970] 2 Q.B. 54.

In *Smith (Donald)* [1973] Q.B. 924, Willis J. said:

> "It was quite unnecessary to prove that the applicant did anything to further the transaction in this country."

It follows that once steps are taken by an individual to bring about the fraudulent evasion of the prohibition, an act of remorse (even if coupled with a wish to abandon the enterprise) will not save that person from a conviction under section 170 if an importation in fact results.

> In *Jakeman* (1983) 76 Cr.App.R. 223, J was recruited to carry a case of cannabis from Ghana to Heathrow, via Paris. She withdrew from the enterprise in Paris by abandoning the suitcase at the airport. Baggage officials found the suitcase and believing it to have been misrouted, rushed it to London.
>
> *Held*: her appeal against conviction for an offence under section 170(2)(b) was dismissed. Her initial actions ultimately brought about the importation.

2–51 The result may seem harsh but it is consistent with the wording of section 170(2), under which *Jakeman* had been charged. As Wood J. observed in that case, the correct approach is to analyse the offence itself. At best, her withdrawal from the enterprise was good mitigation; but it was not a defence. It was ingeniously contended on the appellant's behalf that she should not be convicted unless her guilty state of mind subsisted at the time of importation. Once again, the argument assumed that the offence is only committed at the moment of importation which, clearly, it is not. It will be remembered that in *Neal*, the accused prepared a hiding place in a barn to store cannabis; he was recruited after the moment of importation and therefore his mind could not possibly have been a "guilty" one when the drugs were imported into the United Kingdom from the Lebanon. Nevertheless, he was guilty of an offence under section 170(2).

In *Jakeman*, Wood J. observed that:

> "What matters is the state of mind at the time the relevant acts are done, *i.e.* at the time the defendant is concerned in bringing about the importation. This accords with the general principles of common law. To stab a victim in a rage with the necessary intent for murder or manslaughter leads to criminal responsibility for the resulting death regardless of any repentance between the act of stabbing and the time of death, which may be hours or days later." [Emphasis added]

Although it is correct to say, as Wood J. effectively did on the facts of this particular case, that the applicant's initial actions ultimately brought about the importation, this is a feature that must not be taken too far. Wood J. went on to say: "[f]or guilt to be established the importation must, of course, result as a consequence, if only in part, of the activity of the accused". 2–52

Construed literally, those passages may be thought to suggest that in every case the prosecution must establish a chain of causation between the actions of the accused and the ultimate importation of the drug. This would obviously be impossible to prove in the case of a person who (not being a party to the original importation) committed acts in furtherance of the evasion after the drugs had been imported, yet such persons are caught by the section. Furthermore, construed literally, the words of Wood J. would mean that any act which breaks the chain of causation would provide a defence.

If causation does have a place in this area of the law, and if it could be established that the act of the baggage officials in re-directing the suitcase from Paris to London broke the chain of causation, then *Jakeman* should have been decided differently. So why was it not so decided?

(c) Causation and *Latif* and *Shahzad*

The principles referred to in *Jakeman* were considered by the House of Lords in *Latif and Shahzad* [1996] 1 All E.R. 353. The case gives rise to interesting but difficult points of law. 2–53

(i) *The facts*

> H was a law enforcement agent working in Pakistan. S was introduced to H. S said he wanted to export 20 kilograms of heroin to England. The customs and excise mounted an undercover operation. As part of that operation, H agreed with S that H would recruit an airline pilot to take the drug to England. The "pilot" was B a British customs officer. 20 kilograms of heroin was delivered by S to H. With the knowledge of the customs and excise, B brought the drug to England. H then came to England and persuaded S to travel there in order to take delivery of the drug. S entered the United Kingdom and went to an hotel with L. Officers delivered bags of what purported to be heroin but which in fact contained "Horlicks". S and L were arrested.

The House of Lords dismissed the appeals against conviction but departed from the reasoning of the Court of Appeal (1995) 1 Cr.App.R. 270.

2–54 Their lordships held that S was not guilty of the full offence under section 170(2) of CEMA 1979 because the importation had been performed by a customs officer who was not acting fraudulently and with full knowledge of his superiors. Their lordships also held that the customs officer did not act in concert with S—he acted for his own purpose, and that fact broke the chain of causation. However, S had committed two attempts at evasion, contrary to section 170(2): first in Pakistan, and the second in London, when he tried to collect the heroin from H.

S and L were charged with two offences namely, an offence committed under section 170(2) of the 1979 Act and an offence of attempting to evade the prohibition on importation contrary to section 1(1) of the Criminal Attempts Act 1981 and section 170(2) of the 1979 Act. The second charge was withdrawn at the end of the prosecution case.

2–55 Several points should be noted about these facts. First, the customs and excise knew of the plan from a very early stage if not from the outset. Secondly, the customs and excise controlled and monitored the progress of the shipment of the drug from Pakistan to England. Thirdly, there was an importation of the drug. The customs were not deceived by B's conduct. Fourth, S did plan the unlawful importation of a controlled drug into the United Kingdom. Fifth, the House of Lords was prepared to assume that the officer was guilty of an offence under section 170(2) of CEMA.

(ii) *The concessions and assumptions made in the appeal*

2–56 The parties to the appeal conceded that the officer, B, committed an offence under section 50(3) of the 1979 Act (*i.e.* improper importation). Lord Steyn was inclined "to the view" that despite the words "intent to evade" in section 50(3), this concession was "rightly made" (see 360c/d) but no reasons were given for that conclusion. Their lordships were also prepared to assume that the officer was guilty of an offence under section 170(2)(b). Both the concession and the assumption should be viewed with caution because there were sound tactical reasons for the concession being made.

From the appellant's point of view, it was tactically advantageous to make the concession in order to support a submission that the proceedings should be stayed as an abuse of process (or that items of evidence should be excluded under PACE 1984, s.78) as well as supporting the argument that S was not acting in concert with the officer because the officer was driven by motives of law enforcement. However, once those arguments failed, the concession became a weapon in the hands of the prosecutor who argued that even if the officer and the appellants had not acted in concert the appellants were nevertheless knowingly *concerned* in the officer's criminal act. This argument requires clarification. S, L and H agreed that a controlled drug should be imported into England but it was not H's intention to evade the prohibition, still less to evade it fraudulently. On the other hand, S, and L did intend to perpetrate a fraudulent evasion. S delivered the heroin to H with that intention. Accordingly, H, S and L, were not of like mind and to that extent they were not acting in concert. However, the offence is committed if a person is 'knowingly concerned' in a fraudulent evasion, and therefore, it was argued that H's motive was irrelevant. S and L were concerned in a plan to fraudulently evade the prohibition with full knowledge of what was afoot. It may be that the use of the word 'concerned' in section 170(2)(b) displaces the usual rules in relation to joint enterprise: see *Salmon v H.M. Advocate*, 1999 S.L.T. 169, and *H.M. Advocate v. Hamill*, 1998 S.C.C.R. 164. Similarly, if the officer was guilty of the section 170(2) offence, on the basis that he was concerned in another person's fraudulent evasion, and with knowledge of that fact, it follows that anyone else who concerned themselves in that venture (with knowledge of what was afoot) would be guilty of the same offence. S and L did have that degree of knowledge, and they too played a part in the fraudulent evasion. Accordingly, the assumption that the officer was guilty of the offence operated against S and L.

(iii) *Did the officer's acts amount to an offence under section 50(3)?*

It is difficult to see how the officer could be guilty of this offence because section 50(3) expressly requires that the person who imports prohibited goods (or is concerned in their importation) "does so with intent to evade the prohibition". The officer in *Latif* did not have that intent but acted with the full knowledge of his superiors in the customs and excise. Clearly, the officer acted contrary to the embargo imposed by section 3 of the MDA 1971 (his conduct was arguably unlawful as being contrary to section 3 of the Misuse of Drugs Act) but he did not intend to evade the prohibition for the purpose of section 50(3). 2–57

(iv) *Did the officer or the appellants commit an offence under section 170(2)(b)?*

This is much more difficult. The prosecution conceded that the officer was guilty of an offence under section 170(2) and the House of Lords assumed this to have been the case but the Court of Appeal did not make that assumption or decide the point. The section 170(2)(b) offence is wider in scope than the section 50(3) offence partly because the latter includes the words "with intent to evade the prohibition . . ." whereas section 170(2)(b) does not. Thus, on one interpretation of section 170(2), it is enough that a person is "knowingly concerned" in a fraudulent evasion devised by somebody else. S and L did intend to import heroin into England. The officer, B, did not deceive customs but as Staughton L.J. remarked a "successful deceit of a customs officer is certainly not an essential element of the offence. Sometimes the customs officer knows in advance that a passenger is smuggling" ([1995] 1 Cr.App.R. 270, 274G). The House of Lords declined to construe section 170(2) as if it read " fraudulently and knowingly concerned" because "such a construction may cause practical 2–58 difficulties in other cases" ([1996] 1 All E.R. at 360 e–f). However, the absence of those words in section 170(2) seems to reinforce the argument that the prosecution need only prove that the accused knew that what was afoot was the evasion of the ban on importation of the goods. The accused does not have to assent to the enterprise and he may not desire its commission but if he takes part in it with that knowledge, the offence is complete.

(v) *The nature of the section 170(2)(b) offence*

2–59 In *Latif*, the offence was described by the Court of Appeal as follows:

> "At first sight one might have thought that there had to be some fraudulent person bringing the goods into this country and deceiving the Customs and Excise in the process. If that be right there was no completed offence in this case, for even without a licence Mr. Bolton was not fraudulent and did not deceive anybody. His superiors knew what he was doing. Mr. Shahzad and Mr. Latif would not be guilty of the complete offence, but it is arguable they would be guilty of an attempt.
>
> Such a construction of section 170(2) is not, in our judgement, correct. It would not catch the man who organises an importation by an innocent courier. There would be no fraudulent evasion by anybody in such a case, and the organiser could not therefore be knowingly concerned in the fraudulent evasion. Mr. Bloom submitted that the organiser would be liable as the principal of the courier who acted as his agent. We do not find that suggestion of vicarious liability plausible.
>
> In our judgement the words 'fraudulent evasion' include a good deal more than merely entering the United Kingdom with goods concealed and no intention of declaring them. They extend to any conduct, which is directed and intended to lead to the importation of goods covertly in breach of a prohibition on import."; *per* Staughton LJ.

2–60 The House of Lords referred to this passage and said that the "foundation of the reasoning of the Court of Appeal was therefore wrong" (363 f–g) and pointed out that the prosecution did not try to support this reasoning. Professor Sir John Smith did not much care for this reasoning either (see [1994] Crim. LR. 750, 751). He suggested that the officer's actions amounted to a *novus actus interveniens* that broke the chain of causation. The House of Lords, as we shall see, similarly analysed the facts in *Latif* as a problem of causation and so practitioners will need to keep this principle in mind. However, although the decision of the House of Lords clearly represents the law it is worth examining in greater detail what it was that Staughton L.J. really said. Has that passage, to some extent, been misunderstood?

It is plain from the first paragraph of the above extract, that Staughton L.J. was rejecting (and rightly) any suggestion that a "fraudulent evasion" means there has to be "some fraudulent person bringing the goods into this country and deceiving the customs and excise in the process". Staughton

L.J. then explained what the consequences would be if that were to be the law . Thus, the appellants could not be guilty of the full offence because the officer was not acting fraudulently but they might be guilty of an attempt. Again, the man who organised the importation (using an innocent courier) would not be caught by section 170(2), because the courier was not acting fraudulently. If there is no fraudulent evasion then an organiser cannot logically be vicariously liable for an offence that was not committed. It is in this context that Staughton L.J. said that the suggestion of "vicarious liability" is not plausible.

However, Staughton L.J. went on to say that a "fraudulent evasion" extends to "any conduct, which is directed and intended to lead to the importation of goods covertly in breach of a prohibition on import". In the House of Lords it was said that this passage "went too far" (363 g–h) because: 2–61

> "It gave no effect to the fact that an evasion (as opposed to an attempted evasion) necessarily involves an importation. Moreover, this reasoning does not allow for the fact that section 170(2) in so far as it is directed at an attempted importation, already covers certain pre-importation acts. The reasoning of the Court of Appeal *seems to allow little or no scope for an attempted evasion* for which section 170(2) provides . . ." [emphasis added]

Taken literally, the words of Staughton L.J. are capable of meaning that all conduct that is *intended* to result in the importation of prohibited goods amounts to a fraudulent evasion, irrespective as to whether the goods have in fact been imported or not. That certainly would be going too far: it would mean that acts performed outside the United Kingdom in pursuance of an agreement / conspiracy to import prohibited goods into that State, would amount to a "fraudulent evasion" even if the goods were never imported. However, it is submitted that Staughton L.J. was in fact describing a situation where the prohibited goods had in fact been imported, albeit using, for example, an innocent agent. In such a case, persons concerned in the venture, knowing what was afoot, had taken part in a "fraudulent evasion" of the prohibition. Staughton L.J. merely made the point supported by ample authority that acts done before (or even after) the moment of importation, may amount to being "knowingly concerned" in the fraudulent evasion: see *Neal*, above. The case of *Jakeman* is a further illustration. It has already been said that the heart of the offence, under section 170(2)(b), is a "fraudulent evasion" not a "fraudulent importation" and therefore the offence is a continuing one.

The case of *Latif* highlights a further issue, namely, when is a prohibition evaded? At first sight, it may seem that if customs officers act on a tip-off and seize prohibited goods as soon as they are imported, then there has been no successful evasion of the prohibition, and D's acts amount to no more than an attempted evasion. Similarly, it may be thought that on every occasion a customs officer examines baggage, and discovers prohibited goods, that the facts disclose an attempted evasion rather than an actual 2–62 evasion. However, the cases of *Green* (above) and *Ciappara* (above), serve as a reminder that an evasion may continue after the goods have been seized. The evasion begins the moment the goods have been 'imported' (as defined by CEMA). It follows that the notion of a 'fraudulent evasion' casts a net over a very wide area indeed. But for the causation point, there is little doubt that the House of Lords in *Latif* would have held that there had been a fraudulent evasion (and not just an attempted evasion) if the officer acted in concert and not for his own purposes (whether lawful or to advance his own criminal ambitions).

(vi) *Causation.*

2–63 The House of Lords held that the problem posed by the facts of *Latif* was one of causation to which a general principle applied, namely:

> "that the free, deliberate and informed intervention of a second person, who intends to exploit the situation created by the first, but is not acting in concert with him, is held to relieve the first actor of criminal responsibility: see Hart and Honoré, *Causation in the Law*, 2nd ed., (1985) pp. 326 *et seq.*; Blackstone's Criminal Practice, (1995), pp.13–15."

This was also the view of Professor Sir John Smith in his commentary to the judgment of the Court of Appeal in *Latif.*

It is easy to see that if D1 intends to plant a bomb at a particular address, but D2 steals the bomb and (for his own purposes) uses it to blow up the same building, D1 should not be held responsible for the acts of D2. The chain of causation would have been broken: or simply stated, D2 went on a venture of his own. Lord Steyn remarked that:

> ". . . if a thief had stolen the heroin after Shahzad delivered it to Honi, and imported it into the United Kingdom, the chain of causation would plainly have been broken."

2–64 With due deference to others who clearly hold a different view, it is quite another thing to say that if D2 agreed with D1 to carry the bomb on the latter's behalf, that the chain of causation would be broken if D2 was in fact an undercover police officer and thus he did not act in concert with D1. Their lordships were prepared to assume that the customs officer committed an offence contrary to section 170(2)—presumably on the basis that he was concerned in the smuggling venture knowing what was afoot, albeit that he did not act fraudulently himself. If the concession was rightly made it is difficult to see how the officer was not acting "in concert" for the purposes of section 170(2). Motive and intention must not be confused. It is therefore not surprising that the prosecutor's argument was that an offence under section 170(2) extends to persons "knowingly concerned in the fraudulent evasion on importation. Although a "fraudulent evasion" requires an intention on somebody's part, to evade the prohibition, the actual importation of the goods can be performed by an innocent agent: see *Att.-Gen.'s Reference (No.1 of 1981)* [1982] Q.B. 848. Did it therefore matter whether the officer was guilty or innocent? As far as S was concerned, the officer was part of S's plan to evade the prohibition on importation. On this analysis, S had the intention to evade the prohibition the officer was merely the vehicle, or the agent, by which the drug was imported. Was it really necessary to embark on questions of causation?

It may be asked whether *Jakeman* remains good law. Presumably, it must be, because the House of Lords certainly did not suggest otherwise and the Court of Appeal placed reliance on that decision. There is a significant distinction to be drawn between the facts in *Jakeman* and *Latif* respectively. It could not be said that the baggage officials "intended to exploit the situation" created by *Jakeman* or that their intervention was "informed". Yet it seems that if Jakeman had been relieved of her suitcase by a thief, who nevertheless carried it to London, she would have been absolved of liability at least in respect of the full offence and she stood to be acquitted of an attempt if her actions were no more than merely preparatory to the commission of the so-called full offence (consider also the case of *Ahmed* [1990] Crim. L.R. 648: an offence under MDA, s.20).

A person who is not a party to the original smuggling operation will still commit an offence if he acts in joint enterprise with one or more persons to contravene section 170. A classic example of this situation is *Williams* [1971] 1 W.L.R. 1029: 2–65

> H, an Indian, asked W if he had contacts for selling cannabis as H was returning to India and could send on "samples". W gave H a forwarding address, occupied by X. H said he would send a letter to W informing him of an impending delivery at that address. X opened one such letter in error but decided to tell W that no letter had arrived. Customs officers discovered a parcel containing cannabis at that address shortly thereafter. W was convicted of an offence contrary to section 304(b) of the 1952 Act (now s.170(2)(b) of the CEMA). W contended that the offence had not been made out since an agreement to sell cannabis after it had been imported into the United Kingdom was not a sufficiently proximate act to the original importation to be guilty of the offence charged.
>
> *Held*: the appeal was dismissed. There may well have been a joint enterprise to unlawfully import but in any event, what W did was sufficiently proximate to make him guilty of the offence.

W was sufficiently proximate to the actual importation to make him guilty of the offence. It was not necessary for W to be present at the moment of importation, or to know when the illicit parcel was being posted, or to know that the parcel had in fact arrived in the United Kingdom; indeed it is not apparent from the report that there was any evidence that W did know that the cannabis had arrived in the United Kingdom. Even so, the interval of time between the defendant agreeing to receive the drugs, and the moment of importation, was not so great as to make him insufficiently proximate to the importation. Like *Jakeman* (1983) 76

Cr.App.R. 223, W's initial actions brought about the eventual importation of the drug.

(vii) *Drugs in transit*

2–66 It follows from the above that the fact that the drugs were merely in transit to another country will not protect the shipper once the goods are technically imported.

> In *Smith (Donald)* [1973] Q.B. 924, packets of cannabis were sent by air from Nairobi to Bermuda, via London. S was a party to the shipment and there was evidence that he knew of the likely route. S was convicted, *inter alia*, of being knowingly concerned in the fraudulent evasion of the prohibition on the importation of cannabis. S argued, on appeal, that he did nothing in this country to further the transaction.
>
> *Held*: the appeal would be dismissed. It was unnecessary for the prosecution to prove such an ingredient. The goods were deliberately "introduced" into this country and were therefore "imported".

A similar point was made in *Berner* (1953) 37 Cr.App.R. 113 where B took goods prohibited from exportation out of the United Kingdom with the intention that they be brought back in again. The fact that they were to be brought back did not mean that the exportation ceased to be prohibited.

2–67 In *MacNeill v. H.M. Advocate*, 1986 S.C.C.R. 288, it was held that to be concerned in the importation of goods, a person has to be involved in the enterprise in some way if only in the sense of having accepted a role to be performed if circumstances so required. It is not enough for the Crown to show merely that the accused was being kept informed of what others were doing. There must be evidence that the accused played or held himself available to play some role in furtherance of the smuggling venture.

The judgment in *MacNeill*, above, is also of interest as to the extent to which dissociation from the enterprise is a relevant consideration when a person has played some part in it.

(d) Exportation: acts done before or after that moment

2–68 There is clear authority for the proposition that acts done before the moment of exportation are caught by the section. Thus, where in *Garrett v. Arthur Churchill (Glass) Ltd* [1970] 1 Q.B. 92 the defendant handed goods over for export knowing that they were prohibited from exportation, he committed an offence contrary to section 170. There is no logical reason why the principles applicable to importations should not equally apply to exportations.

(e) At what point in time does an offence under section 170 cease?

2–69 How far removed from the original smuggling operation does a person have to be before he is no longer liable under section 170? The answer is of some importance because, in theory at least, a person arrested in London in possession of one gram of so-called "Lebanese Gold" (*i.e.* cannabis resin from the Lebanon) may be said to be evading the prohibition on importation of that drug by dealing with it unlawfully. Moreover, consider the case of a person in England, who plants cannabis seeds taken from a cannabis plant imported by another: is that person guilty of an offence under the same section?

In *Ardalan* [1972] 1 W.L.R. 463, A was recruited to collect packages, which contained drugs, long after they had arrived in the United Kingdom, Roskill L.J. observed that:

> "If once . . . there can be an offence committed at some point of time and at some place after importation . . . it is difficult to see why there should be any limit to that point of time or place provided always, of course, that the goods . . . are the subject of a prohibition . . . and with intent to evade that prohibition."

Logically, there can be no limit either as to time or as to place, before the offence is committed, providing (and this is the crucial point) that the acts are done with the intention of evading the relevant prohibition. It is when the prosecution ceases to be able to prove the requisite *mens rea* that the cut-off point is reached. In *Neal* (1983) 77 Cr.App.R. 283, Griffiths L.J. expressed the position thus: 2–70

> "If no more can be proved than that a piece of cannabis changed hands in Piccadilly Circus, no doubt it would be foolish of the prosecution to proceed under [s.170] of the Customs and Excise Management Act 1979 for it would be far-fetched to suggest that the real intent of such a transaction is to evade the prohibition on the import of cannabis."

The holder of a small piece of cannabis may know that the drug comes from the Lebanon but his intention is to use it either for his own or for another's benefit. He is unlikely to use the drug in a manner intended to avoid, or to get around, the ban on its importation.

In *Watts* (1979) 70 Cr.App.R. 187, S was arrested upon leaving a public house and found to be in possession of cocaine, scales and other drug paraphernalia. A large sum of money was found at an address which S had earlier visited and where W was arrested. Bridge L.J. said, *obiter*: 2–71

> "Merely to establish that there has been a dealing with the prohibited goods, and that by virtue of the presumptions [see now s.154(2)] they are presumed at some time in the infinite past to have been unlawfully imported, would not, in our judgment, ever justify, without anything further, inviting a jury to conclude that the evidence established an intent to evade the prohibition on importation."

Accordingly, Bridge L.J. reached the conclusion that:

> ". . . on a true construction of section 304(a) (now section 170(1)), in order to establish that any particular dealing with goods was done with intent to evade the relevant prohibition on importation, the onus

on the Crown to prove that intent must involve establishing a link or nexus between the actus reus of the offence and some prohibited importation". [emphasis added]

2–72 Just as one must be careful not to construe too literally the words of Wood J. in *Jakeman* (1983) 76 Cr.App.R. 223 when he said that the importation must result " . . . as a consequence, if only in part, of the activity of the accused . . . "so one must be careful not to treat references made by Bridge L.J. to a "link" or "nexus" as establishing hard and fast ingredients of the offence.

However, that said, there is a great deal of force in the dictum of Bridge L.J. in *Watts* which should not be overlooked. *Watts* was cited in *Neal* (1983) 77 Cr.App.R. 283 but most unfortunately, the head-note to *Neal* [as it appears in the Criminal Appeal Reports], states that the dictum of Bridge L.J. was "not applied". In fact, this is not so. It is important to emphasise that their Lordships adopted the dictum for the purpose of stressing the importance of the prosecution leading evidence to prove the necessary intent to evade the prohibition. What the Court of Appeal in *Neal* could not accept was that the words of Bridge L.J. had the meaning attached to them by Counsel for the appellants who argued that a "nexus between the *actus reus* of the offence and some prohibited importation" meant that offences under section 170 could only be committed by persons involved in the initial smuggling operation. Such a contention was clearly going too far since Bridge L.J. was careful to use the words "link" or "nexus" to indicate a point of involvement beyond the initial smuggling operation but not so far removed as to be unrealistic and incapable of proving intent.

2–73 The appellant's argument in *Neal* ignored the fact that Bridge L.J. was merely describing a method of proving *mens rea*. He was not, it is submitted, setting out to redefine the *actus reus* of the offence.

If Bridge L.J. really did intend to express the construction, for which the appellants in *Neal* contended, then such a dictum would at least be in conflict with *Ardalan* [1972] 1 W.L.R. 463. However, Bridge L.J. was careful to refer to *Ardalan*, and in any event, it was not the belief of their Lordships in *Neal* that Bridge L.J. intended any such conflict.

2–74 The decision in *Watts* (1979) 70 Cr.App.R. 187 is a revealing example of how easy it is to be misled by the sweeping words of section 170(1) and to ignore the essential ingredient that for the full offence under section 170(1) there must be an intent to evade the prohibition and that there must be proof that the goods were imported. In *Watts*, there was clear evidence that the accused dealt in cocaine but there was no evidence at all to show that they had imported the cocaine into the United Kingdom. The trial judge held that there was an evasion of a prohibition on importation of goods once goods of that description were shown to have been "dealt with" in the United Kingdom from which an intention to evade the prohibition could be inferred. Astonishing, perhaps, is the fact that the judge accepted the argument that the growing of cannabis plants in a back garden in England would be an evasion of the prohibition on the importation of cannabis, or that LSD manufactured in the United Kingdom, would similarly be an evasion of the prohibition on importation of LSD. In neither example could it be said that a prohibited importation had taken place. The absence of such a fact was fatal to the argument and accordingly, it was not advanced before the Court of Appeal.

The above examples pose very different situations to the facts in, say, *Neal*, where there was evidence that goods had been imported and the prohibition evaded although there was no evidence as to when or how that importation had taken place. The only issue was whether the defendant was a party to that evasion of the prohibition on importation.

IV. Proving the Importation

Arising out of the above, it follows that in every case of drug smuggling, charged under section 50(3) or the full offence under section 170(1) or (2) the prosecution is faced with the obvious practical problem of proving that the drug was in fact imported. This may not be very easy if there is no evidence as to the place or the time of importation of the goods. To circumvent this difficulty the Crown, in *Watts*, argued that section 154 of the Customs and Excise Management Act 1979 (as it now is) enacts a series of presumptions in favour of the Crown to place the burden of proving that there had been no importation on the defendant. The Court of Appeal did not find that contention attractive. Bridge L.J. said: 2–75

> "The Court feels grave doubt as to whether the opening words of [s. 154(2)] are apt to refer to an issue as to whether goods have been imported or not. We think it more probable that those words are directed to an issue, which may arise in determining at what rate import duty is to be levied, as to the country from which the imported goods have originated."

Nevertheless, the Court decided the appeal on the assumption that the contention was correct. The point is not straightforward. Section 154(2), insofar as it is material, provides that:

> "Where in any proceedings relating to customs and excise any question arises as to the place from which any goods have been brought or as to whether or not
> (a) any duty has been paid or secured in respect of any goods; or
> (b) any goods or other things whatsoever are of the description or nature alleged in the information, writ or other process; or
> (c) any goods have been lawfully imported or lawfully unloaded from any ship or aircraft; or
> (d) any goods have been lawfully loaded into any ship or aircraft or lawfully exported or were lawfully water-borne; or
> (e) any goods were lawfully brought to any place for the purpose of being loaded into any ship or aircraft or exported; or

(f) any goods are or were subject to any prohibition of or restriction on their importation or exportation then, where those proceedings are brought by the Commissioner the burden of proof shall lie upon the other party to the proceedings."

It is important to note that questions arising in connection with "the place from which any goods have been brought" (see the opening words of s. 154(2)) and questions arising as to any of the matters listed in section 154(2)(a) to (f), are separate and distinct.

2–76 To demonstrate how devastating these presumptions can be, consider *Mizel v. Warren* [1973] 1 W.L.R. 899. In 1962, M bought (in England) a second-hand bracelet from C. The bracelet was made of white gold and platinum. The bracelet was seized by Customs and Excise officers in 1970 on the basis that it was of Belgian manufacture and there was no evidence that duty had been paid on it when it had been imported. However, evidence adduced by M suggested that it could have been of English or foreign manufacture. The Crown Court preferred the evidence called by M. However, the prosecution relied on what is now section 154(2)(b), and argued that the place of manufacture formed part of the "description", and that the burden therefore fell on M to prove that the bracelet was manufactured in England. The Divisional Court agreed.

The repercussions of the decision in *Mizel v. Warren* are enormous. A person approached by a customs officer in connection with a camera in his possession may be faced with the task of proving that the camera was of British manufacture or, if he cannot do so, of proving that the duty was paid in respect of it, a task that is likely to be quite impossible to fulfil. Again, a person found in possession of cannabis may, likewise, be faced with the task of proving that the drug was grown in Britain.

2–77 It may be asked why the Court in *Mizel v. Warren* was so concerned with "description" and not with the opening words of section 154(2). Lord Widgery C.J. reflected on this aspect when he said:

> "Some time was spent in the Crown Court in considering the opening words of [section 154(2)] dealing with the place from which any goods have been brought; but it is obvious to me that that is not the point with which we are concerned. The argument is concerned with their place of manufacture so we are not interested in the place from whence the goods have been brought; we are very much concerned in whether they have been imported in the sense they began life in a foreign country."

There is, of course, force in this line of reasoning on the particular facts of that case. M did not "bring" the bracelet from any "place". In any event, the opening words of section 154(2) apply, for example, to cases where different rates of duty are payable on goods brought into the United Kingdom from countries outside the E.C., as opposed to payments on the same goods brought in from countries outside the E.C. In such cases, it is important to ascertain the place from which the goods were in fact brought. Identifying the exact country of origin was not relevant to the issue to be determined in *Mizel v. Warren*. It was not relevant to ascertain the actual place from which the bracelet was brought at all. It was only necessary to ascertain whether the bracelet was of "foreign manufacture" or not; if it was then it must have been imported. The court was therefore concerned with the description of the goods. "Havana cigars" or "Chinese silk" are clearly descriptions that include the country of origin. The fact that goods are said to be "foreign" is also part of the description.

Given the above, suppose D, an American tourist, is arrested in Piccadilly and found to be in possession of LSD. The prosecution alleges that the drug was manufactured in the United States of America and imported into this country by D. D is adamant that he bought the LSD in Piccadilly. On such facts, the country of origin is likely to be regarded as part of the description of the drugs and accordingly, the burden will be on D to prove that the substance was manufactured in the United Kingdom and therefore could not have been imported by him. 2–78

It is important to note that, for the purposes of section 154(2)(b), the presumption arises once it is alleged in the information, writ, or other process, that the goods are of a particular description. In *Mizel v. Warren*, it was alleged that the bracelet was of foreign manufacture. Evidence was called to support the allegation but the evidence does not appear to have been accepted by the Court as being convincing. Nevertheless, it was enough to bring the presumption into play in favour of the Commissioner of Customs and Excise.

V. Proving *Mens Rea* for an Offence Under Section 170(2)

In 1969, the Court of Appeal delivered judgment in *Hussain* (1969) 53 Cr.App.R. 448, a case, which has been the subject of much scrutiny both in the Court of Appeal and in the House of Lords, but it continues to be the leading authority on the *mens rea* required for an offence under section 170(2)(b) of the CEMA. The facts are as follows: 2–79

> A motor vessel arrived at Liverpool from Las Palmas. The vessel was boarded by an officer who entered a cabin occupied by H and two other crew members. The officer removed the bulkhead panel in the cabin and discovered some 10 packets of cannabis resin concealed behind it. H told customs officers that the second engineer and a carpenter (who carried a bucket containing the 10 packets) came into his cabin and put the packets behind the bulkhead. H was told he would have his throat cut if he said anything about it. H was charged with an offence under what is now section 170(2)(b). The chairman directed the jury in the following terms:
>
> "The question is; has it been proved that the defendant was knowingly concerned in that operation? 'Knowingly concerned in that operation' means co-operating with the smugglers and it does not

> matter if he did not know precisely the nature of the goods the smugglers were dealing with. He would be just as guilty if he had thought they were dealing with brandy, for instance, but what has to be proved is that he was knowingly and consciously and deliberately concerned in co-operating in what he must have known was an operation of smuggling or getting prohibited goods into this country."

Held: inter alia, that "knowingly" in s. 304(b) of the 1952 Act (now s. 170(2)(b)), is concerned with knowing that a fraudulent evasion in respect of goods is taking place. It is not necessary that the defendant should know the precise category of goods the importation of which has been prohibited.

2–80 In order to be able to follow the history of this case and to be able to understand the complaints that have been levelled against the decision, it is desirable that the reader should note the following features. First, on more than one occasion the chairman referred to "smugglers" and "smuggling" but on no occasion did he actually define those terms. This may seem a relatively unimportant omission until it is remembered that the CEMA applies not only to "prohibited goods" but also to other categories of goods including "dutiable goods". Secondly, the chairman said (by way of example) that it did not matter if Hussain thought he was importing brandy. However, brandy is a dutiable commodity: it is not prohibited or restricted from importation. Thirdly, although the chairman directed the jury that it did not matter whether Hussain knew precisely the "nature of the goods" being dealt with, there remained the question whether an accused need know the precise prohibition involved? It has to be noted that if Hussain did not know what was actually being imported, then he would not know which prohibition was being contravened.

As to the first point, the Court of Appeal rejected the complaint swiftly. The court took the view that there was no reason to suppose that the jury would associate the word "smugglers" solely with those who seek to evade customs duty. The second and third complaints posed considerable problems, however.

2–81 In *Hussain*, the Court of Appeal isolated the three essential elements of the *mens rea*, which the prosecution is required to prove against an accused, namely:

(a) knowledge that the goods which are being imported are subject to a prohibition; and
(b) knowledge that he is concerned in an operation designed to evade that prohibition; and
(c) knowledge that the prohibition is to be evaded fraudulently.

The burden of proving the above rests on the prosecution because nothing in the CEMA, or the MDA, suggests that section 170 or section 3(1) of the MDA is subject to section 28 of the MDA. Furthermore, none of the statutory presumptions listed in section 154 of the CEMA shifts the evidential burden onto the accused to rebut a presumption of knowledge of any of the three elements.

There must be evidence from which a reasonable jury, properly directed, may safely infer that a defendant knew that what was afoot was an unlawful evasion of the prohibition on the importation of prohibited goods. In practice, this means there must be sufficient evidence that the accused knew of the existence of the prohibited goods that were being smuggled. In *Suurmeijer* [1991] Crim.L.R. 773, S was the passenger in a car driven by H, which was stopped by customs officers in the "Nothing to Declare" channel at Sheerness. The petrol tank had been adapted to conceal 30.5 kilograms of cannabis. H hired the car and paid for the tickets on behalf of himself and S. The Court of Appeal quashed S's conviction in respect of the unlawful importation of drugs. The mere presence of S, in the company of H, in the car was insufficient. The Court said " . . . there was no evidence here upon which the jury could be sure that the appellant knew about the drugs in the petrol tank of the car": see also *Strong, The Times*, January 26, 1989, *Irala-Prevost* [1965] Crim.L.R. 606, *Berry* [1998] Crim. L.R., but see *Starch and others* (April 26, 1999, CA).

VI. Must an Accused Know the Precise Prohibition or Goods Involved?

In *Hussain* (para. 2–79 *et seq*., above), the appellant submitted that the prosecution was required to prove that the accused knew the precise nature of the goods that had actually been imported, namely, cannabis resin. This was a very bold submission since one might have anticipated the appellant to have conceded that there was a sufficient *mens rea* if the accused knew that goods of a type subject to a particular prohibition (*e.g.* controlled drugs) had been imported. It will be necessary to return to this point when we examine *Hussain* in the light of the decision of the House of Lords in *Courtie* [1984] A.C. 463. In the event, the Court of Appeal rejected the submission advanced on behalf of the appellant. Widgery L.J. said: 2–82

> "It seems perfectly clear that the word 'knowingly' in the section in question is concerned with knowing that a fraudulent evasion of a prohibition in respect of goods is taking place. If, therefore, the accused knows that what is afoot is the evasion of a prohibition against importation and he knowingly takes part in that operation, it is sufficient to justify his conviction, even if he does not know precisely what kind of goods are being imported."

Widgery L.J. made it clear that it is essential that the accused should know that the imported goods are subject to a prohibition on importation, but he added that "it is not necessary he should know the precise category of the goods the importation of which has been prohibited". Accordingly, by the jury's verdict, Hussain knew that the packages were being smuggled contrary to a prohibition against their importation and that he was a party to that operation. The fact that he did not know precisely what those packages contained was held to be irrelevant.

Hussain has been held to have been correctly decided in a number of subsequent cases and, notably, by the House of Lords in *Taaffe* [1984] A.C. 539 *Shivpuri* [1987] A.C. 1 and *Forbes* [2000] 1 W.L.R. 428.

2–83 If all that has to be proved is that an accused knew that the goods imported were subject to "a prohibition", does that include a belief (mistakenly but genuinely held) that he was importing goods of a different description (*e.g.* firearms instead of heroin) but which would, if true, also have been subject to a prohibition against importation? On a strict reading of the judgment in *Hussain*, the answer must be in the affirmative since it was said, in terms, that it is not necessary for the prosecution to prove that an accused knew the precise "category of goods" prohibited from importation.

An attempt was made in *Hennessey* (1978) 68 Cr.App.R. 419 to challenge directly the correctness of the decision in *Hussain* and to renew the submission, (rejected in *Hussain*) which the prosecution had to prove that the accused knew what the imported goods actually were. Thus:

> In *Hennessey*, stolen cars were adapted so that cannabis could be hidden in them and then used to bring the cannabis over to the United Kingdom from the Continent. H drove one such car to the Continent and returned to Dover some six days later. Customs officers found 28.14 kilograms of cannabis resin in the vehicle. H said that he believed he was importing pornography into the United Kingdom of a type, which would have been prohibited from importation.

Lawton L.J., giving judgment for the Court, followed *Hussain*, "for the best of reasons it was correctly decided", and added: "In plain English [Hennessey] was smuggling goods. It matters not for the purpose of conviction what the goods were as long as he knew that he was bringing into the United Kingdom goods which he should not have been bringing in."

2–84 The decisions of *Hussain* and *Hennessey* produce harsh results and pose special problems, not least on the issue of sentence. Different statutory prohibitions may attract different maximum penalties, but an accused's mistaken belief as to the goods he in fact imported affords him no defence. The sentencer is thus confronted with a difficult sentencing problem. On which basis does he sentence the accused? In *Hennessey*, an application for leave to appeal against sentence was made on the basis that he should not have been sentenced as a drug smuggler but as a smuggler of pornography. The Court of Appeal side-stepped that issue, claiming that H's story "was not credible anyway" and secondly, that "he was lucky to be sentenced as leniently as he was".

A second, but far more subtle, attack has been made on the correctness of *Hussain* and *Hennessey*, on the grounds that both cases have wrongly attributed the *mens rea* of one prohibition to offences requiring proof of a very different prohibition and required proof of a corresponding *mens rea*; see *Shivpuri* [1987] A.C. 1, considered later in this chapter. If the complaint is valid then the prosecution is put in the very difficult position of having to prove that the accused knew that the goods imported were at least subject to a particular prohibition. Many guilty persons, it is said, would slip through the net as a result.

One solution is to impose a presumption of knowledge on the accused and to shift the burden onto him to prove (on a balance of probabilities) that he neither knew, believed, suspected, nor had reason to suspect that the goods he was importing were the goods alleged, *i.e.* controlled drugs. In other words, one solution is to direct that section 28 of the MDA applies to drug-related importations. 2–85

In respect of offences created by sections 4, 5, 6 and 9 of the MDA, section 28(2) and (3) already applies to those offences. Obviously the reason why there is no corresponding provision for the purposes of section 3(1) of the MDA is that Parliament considered that such a course was unnecessary: the difficulty lies in understanding why Parliament took that view. The basic explanation favoured by many lawyers is that Parliament was satisfied that *Hussain* already governed the position and therefore statutory intervention was not required. The problem with that explanation is that lawyers have not been agreed on the true *ratio* of *Hussain*. For this reason two opposing theories are worth mentioning.

The first theory is that Parliament was not concerned as to whether or not an importer made a mistake about the goods actually imported. That is his problem. The relevant fact is that he knew he was smuggling prohibited goods, whatever their description and whatever the prohibition involved. *Hussain*, it is argued, is authority for that proposition. Since *Hussain* already governed the position, there was no need for Parliament to take any further action. The fact that an accused faces different penalties depending on the goods actually imported was not the legislature's concern but a matter for the sentencing court. Indeed, under the MDA different penalties apply to Class A, B and C drugs (see Schedule 4 of the MDA, as amended by the Controlled Drugs (Penalties) Act 1985). Nevertheless, section 28 makes it plain that it is no defence for a person to say "but I thought I was supplying methaqualone [now Class B, formerly Class C] and not heroin (Class A)". 2–86

The second theory, which advocates that *Hussain* should be narrowly construed, starts on the basis that Parliament accepted the principle that persons who believed they were dealing with substances other than controlled drugs should not be convicted of a drugs-related offence. Hence section 28, enacted in the light of *Warner v. MPC* [1969] 2 A.C. 256. This was so whether a person produced, possessed, supplied, or imported, a drug. It was not intended that a supplier should be more favourably treated than an importer. Once it was established that an accused knew that he was dealing with a drug, it really did not matter thereafter what he believed that drug to be. However, there was no need to extend section 28(3) to importation cases, because the burden of proving knowledge (according to *Hussain*) rests entirely on the Crown and that burden never shifts. Parliament's understanding in 1971 (so the argument runs), was that *Hussain* 2–87 did not establish the sweeping proposition that an accused need only be proved to have known that the goods were subject to any prohibition. That was not made clear until *Hennessey* was decided in 1978. The judgment in *Hussain* was understood to mean, in 1971, no more than that it did not matter whether an accused knew exactly what the imported goods were so long as he knew that they were of a type subject to the same prohibition. Thus, for example, an accused's belief that he was importing methaqualone (Class B) whereas he was importing heroin (Class A) was not fatal to a conviction under section 170(2) since he knew he was importing a controlled drug of some description. If Parliament knew in 1971, what it now knows, then section 28(3) would indeed have been expressed to apply to section 3(1).

It must be stressed that, for the moment at least, the position is that *Hussain* and *Hennessey* represent the law. *Forbes* is a very clear reminder of that fact. All that the prosecution need prove is that an accused knew the goods were prohibited from importation. He does not need to know the precise prohibition involved and still less does he need to know the class of drugs actually imported. However, it is a defence for him to say that he mistakenly believed that the goods imported were not subject to any prohibition and it is also a defence for him to say that he mistakenly believed he was importing goods subject to a prohibition when (as a matter of law) they would not have been; see *Taaffe* [1984] A.C. 539.

VII. An Historical Perspective of Drug Importation Offences

2–88 Section 304(b) of the Customs and Excise Act 1952 was the forerunner to section 170(2)(b) of the CEMA, and read:

> "... if any person; ... is, in relation to any goods, in any way knowingly concerned in any fraudulent evasion or attempt at evasion of any duty chargeable thereon or any such prohibition or restriction as aforesaid or of any provision of this Act applicable to those goods he may be detained and shall be liable to a penalty. ... "

When *Hussain* was decided in 1969, the relevant prohibition on the importation of various drugs was imposed by section 2 of the Dangerous Drugs Act 1965. Under the Customs and Excise Act 1952, the maximum penalty for contravening section 304 was two years' imprisonment unless a different penalty was expressly imposed by a different enactment. However, the Dangerous Drugs Act 1965 did not in fact provide a different penalty. Two years later, the Dangerous Drugs Act 1967 (s. 7) increased the maximum sentence for drug smuggling to 10 years' imprisonment. Thus, whether the drug imported was a Class A, B or C drug, the maximum penalty was the same. It was against this background that *Hussain* was decided.

2–89 Widgery L.J. said in *Hussain* (1969) 53 Cr.App.R. 448, 452, that it was essential that an accused should know that the goods which were being imported were subject to a prohibition but "it is not necessary he should know the precise category of the goods the importation of which has been prohibited".

It has been queried by some practitioners whether Widgery L.J. was saying that the *mens rea* for one prohibition would support an offence in connection with the importation of goods subject to another prohibition so that the accused only had to know that the goods were "prohibited goods". The fact that Widgery L.J. referred to "goods" and not to "drugs" is one indication that he was saying precisely that. His reference to knowledge of "a" prohibition (rather than "the" prohibition) is another indication. However, he went on to say that an accused must be proved to be engaged in an operation "designed to evade that prohibition" which might, on its own, suggest that proof of the specific prohibition was required.

The MDA swept away the Dangerous Drugs Acts of 1965 and 1967, as well as the Drugs (Prevention of Misuse) Act 1964. New offences were created under the MDA, the most important of which are subject to the statutory defences created by section 28. Parts of that section are reminiscent of the judgment of Lord Pearce in *Warner*. A smuggler, charged with offences under the MDA (*e.g.* possession with intent to supply) has a defence under section 28(3) of the MDA, which he does not have if he is charged under section 170 of the CEMA.

(a) The *Courtie* argument

In *Courtie* [1984] A.C. 463, the House of Lords held that the Sexual Offences Act 1967 created several different offences, given that proof of different factual ingredients attracted different penalties. Each offence would require the requisite *mens rea*. 2–90

Lord Diplock explained the position as follows (at 471):

> "Where it is provided by a statute that an accused person's liability to have inflicted upon him a maximum punishment which, if the prosecution are successful in establishing the existence in his case of a particular factual ingredient, is greater than the maximum punishment that could be inflicted on him if the existence of that particular factual ingredient were not established, it seems to me to be plain beyond argument that Parliament has thereby created two distinct offences, whether the statute by which they are created does so by using language which treats them as being different species of a single genus of offence, or by using language which treats them as separate offences unrelated to one another. . . . The statement of offence in the instant case may therefore just pass muster, provided that it is supplemented by adequate particulars of offence which give to Courtie reasonable information as to which of the particular species of offences falling within the genus buggery, was the offence with which he was charged."

2–91 In *Taaffe* [1984] 78 Cr.App.R. 301, a case involving a rather different point, Lord Scarman said (at 304), *obiter*, that:

> "While there can be no doubt that *Hussain* was correctly decided, it may be that *Hennessey* will have to be reconsidered in the light of the House's decision to-day in the case of *Courtie*. For the court in *Hennessey* appears to have paid no regard to the effect of section 26 of the Misuse of Drugs Act 1971 upon section 304 of the Customs and Excise Act 1952 . . . it would seem likely that these two sections (now consolidated into section 170 of the Act of 1979) have substituted several offences for one offence in relation to all prohibited imports which existed before the Misuse of Drugs Act 1971 was enacted. But the point does not arise and I therefore express no concluded opinion as to whether the decision in *Hennessey* can stand with . . . *Courtie*."

Those observations have resulted in two further cases reaching the appellate courts, namely, the House of Lords in *Shivpuri* [1987] A.C. 1 and more recently, the Court of Appeal in *Ellis* (1987) 84 Cr.App.R. 235. The background to these two decisions should now be explained.

2–92 In 1971, offences contrary to sections 4, 5, 6 and 9 generally attracted identical maximum penalties depending on the class of drug involved. Thus, Class A and B drugs attracted 14 years' imprisonment while a Class C drug attracted five years' imprisonment (lesser penalties were imposed for offences of simple possession). Offences committed under the Customs and Excise Act 1952 in respect of drug-smuggling attracted like penalties: see section 26 of the MDA.

Section 26 was repealed with the passing of the Customs and Excise Management Act 1979 but the same penalties were then re-enacted in Schedule 1, 2, 3 of that Act. However, under the Controlled Drugs (Penalties) Act 1985, the maximum penalty for offences involving a Class A drug was increased to life imprisonment. Accordingly, each class of controlled drug now attracted a different maximum penalty. Moreover, unlawfully importing or exporting other prohibited goods attracted a maximum of two years' imprisonment (unless a different penalty was stipulated by the relevant enactment).

2–93 In *Shivpuri*, Lord Bridge said, (at 15):

> "It follows from this, applying the reasoning in *Courtie* . . . that each of the three distinct offences has different ingredients and, leaving aside considerations of impossibility arising under the Criminal Attempts Act 1981, part of the actus reus of the offence which must be proved in each case is the importation, actual or attempted, of goods which were in fact of the appropriate category to sustain the offence charged. So far the argument (we interpose as in the instant case) seems to be irrefutable and is not challenged by the Crown."

Lord Bridge then proceeded to deal with the mental ingredient. He said, (at page 15):

"It is the next step in the argument which is the critical one. If each of the three offences involves proof of a different element as part of the actus reus, that is importation of the appropriate category of prohibited goods, it follows, so it is submitted, that 'knowingly' wherever it appears in section 170(1) and (2) of the Act of 1979 connotes a corresponding *mens rea*, that is knowledge of the importation of goods in the appropriate category. I recognise the force of this submission. The point may be put in the form of a rhetorical question. Can it be supposed that Parliament intended that the *mens rea* appropriate to an offence carrying a maximum sentence of two years' imprisonment should equally be sufficient to sustain a conviction for an offence carrying a maximum sentence of 14 years' imprisonment?"

The impact of *Courtie* [1984] A.C. 463 is now evident. If separate offences are created, because separate penalties arise out of different factual ingredients, which are required to be proved by the prosecution, then this means: 2–94

(a) that separate offences exist where goods are subject to different prohibitions attracting different penalties; and
(b) that, in the case of a drug-related importation, three separate offences exist in relation to Class A, B and C drugs because each class attracts a different penalty. In other words, if different offences are created under section 170 of the CEMA then, in the case of drug smuggling, the prosecution is required to prove as part of the *actus reus* that an accused imported or exported the appropriate class of controlled drug. That being so, is it not also incumbent on the prosecution to prove a corresponding *mens rea*? If the answer is "yes" then *Hennessey*, and possibly *Hussain*, were wrongly decided.

In *Shivpuri* [1987] A.C. 1, S believed he was importing a suitcase of cannabis whereas he actually imported harmless vegetable matter and was accordingly charged with attempting to contravene section 170(1)(b), contrary to section 1 of the Criminal Attempts Act 1981. The House of Lords feared that if the answer to the question posed above was in the affirmative, then "the task of the prosecution in proving an offence in relation to the importation of prohibited drugs would in many cases be rendered virtually impossible" (*per* Lord Bridge).

Their Lordships in *Shivpuri* recognised the force of the arguments based on *Courtie*. Lord Bridge traced the history of the legislation, with particular reference to section 28, pointing out that Parliament overcame the "almost insurmountable difficulty of proving the appropriate guilty knowledge" for the purposes of offences under the MDA by placing the burden of proving a lack of knowledge on the accused. Lord Bridge asked why section 28 did not apply to section 3(1) of the MDA, concluding that *Hussain* made such a provision unnecessary for the following reasons (at 996): 2–95

"Irrespective of the different penalties attached to offences in connection with the importation of different categories of prohibited goods, *Hussain* established that the only *mens rea* necessary for any such offence was knowledge that the goods were subject to a prohibition on importation."

It is to be noted that Lord Bridge referred to "goods", not "drugs", and also, that he, like Widgery L.J. in *Hussain*, referred to "a" prohibition, not "the" prohibition, Lord Bridge added (at 996): "Had [*Hussain*] been decided otherwise it is surely inconceivable that Parliament, in the 1971 Act, would not have made provision such as section 28(3) applicable to drug related offences connected with importation."

2–96 However, this observation is not, with respect, a complete answer because at that time, by section 28(3) of the MDA, it was for the accused to prove that he did not believe or suspect or had reason to suspect that the substance was a controlled drug at all. This is very different from the effect of *Hussain* and *Hennessey*, which affords a defendant, charged with an offence under section 170(2) no such defence. Note that the effect of the House of Lord's decision in *Lambert* (July 5, 2001) is that it is for the prosecution to rebut a defence under Section 28 if the defendant discharges the evidential burden on him.

Lord Bridge considered that the issue resolved itself once the history of the legislation was traced. Of course, that is to assume that Parliament had the foresight to anticipate the decision in *Courtie*, which is highly unlikely. Lord Bridge has bravely attempted to rationalise the relevant history and to the extent that it is capable of rationalisation, the broad construction of the ratio in *Hussain* is to be preferred. However, ultimately, rationalising the authorities has proved to be somewhat artificial, and perhaps unnecessary, because in the final analysis it is the wording of the relevant enactment that counts. No matter how hard one tries to scrutinise the decisions of the courts, the colossal difficulties of reconciliation remain. For the moment, *Hussain* and *Hennessey* remain the law. Suggestions that *Shivpuri* has not closed the doors to the argument that a mistaken belief that the goods were subject to a wholly different prohibition provided a defence are unfounded. In *Shivpuri* (para. 2–93 above) their Lordships did not expressly approve *Hennessey* and this may have generated confusion and the suspicion that the argument was still open so that a person who believes he is importing goods subject to one prohibition, when in fact he is importing goods subject to a different prohibition, does not have the requisite *mens rea*. It is submitted that this construction is a misreading of the opinions delivered in *Shivpuri*. Significantly, Lord Scarman who made the now famous remarks in *Taffe* (para. 2–93, above) concerning the implications of *Courtie* also heard the appeal in *Shivpuri*, but said no more in *Shivpuri* than that he agreed with the speech of Lord Bridge. It is not apparent why Lord Scarman in *Taffe* readily accepted that *Hussain* was rightly decided but queried the correctness only of *Hennessey*. This fuelled speculation in legal circles that the judgment in *Hussain* was to be narrowly construed speculation which was not only proved to be unfounded but which also might have ended with the decision in *Shivpuri*. However, in *Ellis* (1987) 84 Cr.App.R. 235, the appellants imported cannabis believing that they were importing pornography. The facts were therefore identical to *Hennessey*. The Court of Appeal was invited to rule that *Hennessey* was wrongly decided and could not stand with subsequent decisions of the House of Lords. The Court of Appeal had no difficulty in holding that the true *ratio* of *Hussain* is that it does not matter what a person believes the nature of the prohibition to be. In *Ellis*, the appellants contended that in *Hussain*, the defendant simply did not care what the material was, and accordingly, *Hussain* could be distinguished from *Hennessey*. However, by the jury's verdict, *Hussain* must have known as a fact that the goods were prohibited, even if he did not know of their actual description. O'Connor L.J. said: "if a man does not know what prohibited material is being imported but only knows that it is prohibited, it follows that he cannot know which prohibition is being broken".

In *Shivpuri* [1987] A.C. 1, Lord Bridge remarked that where the accused is charged with an attempt to contravene section 170 of the CEMA 1979 then to tell the jury that they may convict the accused if they are sure "that he knew or believed the substance was [a Class A drug] or [a Class B drug] or some other prohibited drug" included a misdirection, namely, the reference to "some other prohibited drug". 2–97

In *Ellis* (1986) 84 Cr.App.R. 234 O'Connor L.J. said *obiter*:

> "It is difficult to see why Lord Bridge thought it was a technical misdirection because Class C drugs are just as surely prohibited as A or B and on *Hussain* and certainly on *Hennessey*, a mistaken belief that it is a Class C drug would be no defence, and therefore no misdirection."

It should be borne in mind that at the time *Shivpuri* was tried, the maximum sentences imposed for the unlawful importation of Class A and B drugs were the same (14 years' imprisonment) and the observations of Lord Bridge were made with *Courtie* (above) in mind. Furthermore, the remarks of Lord Bridge were directed to cases where the accused was charged with an attempt and not the full offence. The *mens rea* for an attempt is an intention to commit the *actus reus* of the offence. As Professor Smith has pointed out ([1987] Crim.L.R. 47), if an accused is charged with attempting to import a Class A drug, his intention to import a Class C drug (being a different offence) will not support the conviction but in the light of *Shivpuri*, an accused may be convicted of attempting to import a Class C drug (intending to import a Class C drug) even if the drug actually imported is a Class A drug. The fact that the commission of the Class C offence is impossible is not defence under the Criminal Attempts Act 1981.

(b) Applying *Hussain* and *Hennessey*

Once it is proved first, that controlled drugs were imported contrary to section 3(1) of the MDA, secondly, that a prohibition was evaded fraudulently, thirdly, that the accused knew that the goods were subject to a pro- 2–98 hibition, and finally that the accused was concerned in that fraudulent evasion, then an offence under section 170(2) is made out.

However, a person is to be judged "against the facts as he believed them to be" (per Lord Lane C.J. in *Taaffe* [1983] 1 W.L.R. 627)

> In *Taaffe*, T drove his car through the green channel of the ferry terminal at Sheerness. The vehicle was stopped. Packets of cannabis resin were found in a tyre and more packets of cannabis were found on T's person. T maintained that he thought the packets contained currency. He mistakenly believed that currency was prohibited from importation.
>
> *Held*: if T's story was true he was entitled to be acquitted. Had T indeed imported currency then no offence would have been committed and T's mistake of law could not convert his reprehensible belief into a criminal offence.

2–99 The House of Lords in *Taaffe* [1984] A.C. 539 adopted the reasoning of Lord Lane C.J., which they found compelling, Lord Lane C.J. said ([1983] 2 All E.R. 626, 628h):

> "He is to be judged against the facts, as he believed them to be. Had this indeed been currency and not cannabis, no offence would have been committed. Does it make any difference that the appellant thought wrongly that by clandestinely importing currency he was committing an offence? Counsel for the Crown strongly submits that it does. He suggests that a man in his situation has to be judged according to the total mistake that he has made. . . . We think that that submission is wrong. It no doubt made his actions morally reprehensible. It did not . . . turn what he . . . believed to be the importation of currency into the commission of a criminal offence."

It may be said that the result in *Taaffe* is inconsistent with *Hussain* and *Hennessey* in that T was not judged on the facts as he believed them to be because T believed currency to be prohibited and that if his belief had been true then he would have had no defence. However, two points should be noted. First, that by the jury's verdict in *Hussain*, and by the defendant's admission in *Hennessey*, both defendants knew that the goods actually imported were subject to a prohibition. Secondly, when a person is judged against the facts, as he believes them to be, he is judged "according to law". Thus, in *Hennessey* (para. 2–83, above) H believed that he was importing pornography. The law states pornography is prohibited from importation and so too were the drugs actually imported. Hennessey's belief that the goods were prohibited would, if true, have been correct in law. However, in *Taaffe*, T made a mistake of law, which saved him. His views on the law were totally irrelevant.

It will be recalled that in *Hussain* the chairman directed the jury that it did not matter if the defendant did not know precisely what the imported goods were: "He would be just as guilty if he thought [the smugglers] were dealing in brandy". This, of course, was a misdirection since brandy is not prohibited from importation. Accordingly, if Hussain believed he was importing brandy then he would have had a defence for the reasons given in *Taaffe*. However, this was not a misdirection, which the court regarded as being fatal to the conviction.

(c) Meaning of the words "knowingly" and "fraudulently"

(i) *"Fraudulent"*

This does not mean that a deception must be practised on Customs and Excise officers, in their presence. It also does not mean that the deception must have been effective. If the position be otherwise, there could not be a fraudulent evasion in a case where officers act on a 'tip-off'. "Fraudulent" means a dishonest intention to evade the relevant prohibition or restriction; see the *Att.-Gen.'s Reference (No. 1 of 1981)* [1982] Q.B. 848. The decision of *Borro* [1973] Crim.L.R. 513 to the contrary, was decided *ex tempore* and was therefore not followed by the court. Lord Lane C.J. said (at 856): 2–100

> "the prosecution must prove fraudulent conduct in the sense of dishonest conduct deliberately intended to evade the prohibition or restriction with respect to, or the duty chargeable on, goods as the case may be."

The word "knowingly" in section 170 is explicit. It means that the prosecution must prove knowledge on the part of the accused of all the relevant elements of the offence. This would include knowledge that the goods imported were of a type prohibited from importation; and that he knew that what was afoot was the evasion of that prohibition. In *Warner v. Metropolitan Police Commissioner* [1969] 2 A.C. 256, Lord Reid seemed to equate knowledge with "wilfully shutting one's eyes to the truth". However, that was a case dealing with the elusive concept of possession in respect of which their lordships attempted to define the mental element required (see para. 3–27, below and *Lewis* (1988) 87 Cr.App.R. 270). There is now much authority to support the view that "wilful blindness" is a question of evidence not law and that what is required is proof of actual knowledge of the relevant elements of the offence: see *Panayi (No. 2)* [1989] 1 W.L.R. 187; *Grainge* [1974] 1 W.L.R. 619; *Griffiths* (1974) 60 Cr.App.R. 14; but see *Atwal v. Massey* (1971) 56 Cr.App.R. 6 D.C.

For the purpose of section 170 of the 1979 Act, the accused must intend 2–101
to take part in an enterprise, which he knows is designed to evade the prohibition or restriction imposed by the laws of this country. It follows that a person who genuinely believes that it is legal to import cannabis into this country commits no offence contrary to section 170 of the 1979 Act because such a person would not know that a fraudulent evasion in respect of the goods is taking place. Where an accused does not intend to import prohibited goods into this country but negligently or recklessly imports them (within the meaning of s. 5 of the Act) he commits no offence contrary to section 170: *Panayi (No.2)*.

In *Panayi (No. 2)* (above), P and K were arrested on board their yacht which had been intercepted inside British territorial waters 1.1 nautical miles off the Isle of Wight (within Port Solent for the purposes of CEMA 1979, s.5), 690 kilograms of cannabis resin were found on board. The drug had been loaded on board in Spain. The appellants contended that the drugs were intended for Holland and that their presence in the United Kingdom was the result of navigational errors and contrary tides.

Held: quashing the convictions, that the wording of s.170(2)(b) precluded a construction, which equated recklessness or negligence with knowledge.

The appellants' yacht was equipped with electronic navigational equipment but their intention was not to enter territorial waters of the United Kingdom. Bush J. said:

> "... they cannot be knowingly concerned in the fraudulent evasion unless they intend dishonestly to evade the restriction. They cannot knowingly be involved in the evasion if one of the essential ingredients, namely the fact that they are within territorial waters, is unknown to them; provided of course that they never had any intention of entering the United Kingdom territorial waters ... Though it is possible in some cases to equate recklessness with knowledge or general intent, this cannot be done in this kind of case where the specific intent is required of being knowingly concerned in any fraudulent evasion."

2–102 Two points should be noted in respect of the above passage of Bush J. First, although it is clear that there must be a venture designed to set at nought the ban on importation of the goods (see *Neal* (1983) 77 Cr. App. R. 283) it is less clear that the prosecution are required to prove that each person who played a part in that venture intended to dishonestly evade the prohibition: see *Latif* [1996] 1 All E.R. 353, HL. Certainly, those who desire and execute a plan to smuggle prohibited goods into this country, knowing of the prohibition, act dishonestly intending to evade the relevant enactment but in *Latif*, the question arose as to whether an undercover officer who imports controlled drugs in the interests of law enforcement, was nevertheless guilty of an offence under section 170 merely by concerning himself with an enterprise which somebody else intended should lead to a fraudulent evasion? The point remains open because their lordships assumed that the undercover officer in that case was guilty of an offence under both section 50(3) and section 170(2)(b) of the Act. Secondly, the reference to "territorial waters" is confusing because section 5 of the Act (which defines the moment of importation) does not refer to "territorial waters" at all. Goods brought by sea and which come within the "limits of a port" are deemed to be imported at that moment. The precise limits, seaward, are defined by the relevant statutory instrument.

In *Lewis* (Isleworth Crown Court, August 1992, unreported), L was charged with the unlawful importation of cannabis into the United Kingdom (contrary to s. 170(2)). L obtained the cannabis in Jamaica and he had carried the drug to New York where he was intercepted by an officer. Some cannabis was found in his shoes and his luggage was removed for further inspection. He was informed (according to L) that he could elect to be deported voluntarily or be taken before a court. L agreed to deportation and being a British national, he was deported to the United Kingdom with his luggage. Upon arrival at Heathrow airport, he was intercepted by a customs officer who found cannabis in his luggage, which had not been removed by the officials in New York. The question arose whether the facts disclosed a case to answer. The cases of *Panayi (No.2)* and *Jakeman* were considered by the court. The trial judge ruled that because L knew that the drugs were still in his luggage when he entered the United Kingdom and that he had attempted to mislead the officers in this country with a false story, this was sufficient evidence to establish a *prima facie* case that L was knowingly concerned in a plan to evade the prohibition on importation. It is submitted that even if L had not furnished a false story, but harboured an intention to evade the prohibition on importation (which might have been difficult to prove) the offence would still be made out because L elected deportation to the United Kingdom knowing that he was carrying goods prohibited from importation. The interception by officials in New York coupled with L's deportation could hardly be described as a *novus actus interveniens* that broke the chain of causation: and see *Latif*, above.

(d) When must the intent be formed?

In *Jakeman* (1983) 76 Cr.App.R. 223 it was held that what matters is the state of the accused's mind at the time the relevant acts were done, *e.g.* at the time when there was an intention to bring about an unlawful importation. Accordingly, where a courier of drugs abandoned her intention to carry her suitcase of cannabis into the United Kingdom in Paris, she could not escape conviction under section 170 once the cannabis arrived in the United Kingdom, albeit in an unexpected way. **2–103**

(e) Innocuous substitutes

Article 11 of the 1988 *Vienna Convention Against Illicit Traffic in Narcotic Drugs and Psychotropic Substances* provides "for the use of controlled deliveries at international level and paves the way for 'clean' deliveries". **2–104**

A "clean" delivery involves the substitution of an innocuous substance for the controlled drug in question. This technique is frequently employed in drug trafficking investigations and indeed this has been the case for many years: see *Green* [1976] Q.B. 985.

The "clean" delivery has the obvious advantage of removing the offending substance from circulation and preserving vital evidence whilst permitting the investigation to run its course without the risk of losing the drug if the trafficker secures an advantage over his investigator. The substitution normally takes place in the country where the offender is likely to be apprehended and tried. Technical difficulties might arise if the substitution were to take place abroad. It would mean, for example, that the substance actually imported into the United Kingdom was not a controlled drug at all whereas a charge under section 170(2) of the CEMA 1979 requires proof that prohibited, restricted, or dutiable goods have actually been imported. Accordingly, where the accused acts with others and the substitution takes place abroad, then the appropriate charge would be one of conspiracy to contravene section 170(2): see *Sansom* [1991] 2 All E.R. 145 and *Somchai Liangsiriprasert v. U.S. Government* [1990] 2 All E.R. 866. Note also the arguments in *Ciappara* (1988) 87 Cr.App.R. 316

2–105 The "clean" delivery is to be contrasted with a "controlled" delivery in which the law enforcement agency allows detected drugs to be moved down the chain of supply. Drugs detected in one country may be allowed to travel across national frontiers in order to identify and to obtain evidence against the participants in international drug trafficking. In 1986, the *Report of the Committee of Inquiry into the Drugs Problem in the Member States of the Community* (European Parliament, September 1986, p. 56) suggested that controlled deliveries were rarely used because of legal restrictions in some countries or rivalry or mistrust between law enforcement agencies. No doubt, it has been experienced that customs officials in one country will not permit a detected drug to be exported if a prosecution can be brought in that country. However, a substantial number of investigations depend on sound intelligence gathered at home and overseas and which, in turn, depend on detected drugs being shipped across several national frontiers. In its Seventh Report, *Drug Trafficking and Related Serious Crime* (Session 1988–89, paras 51 and 52), the Committee noted that since 1986 the "situation has improved".

VIII. Removing Goods in the Charge of Customs and Excise

2–106 Note that where goods imported are detained for examination (or other reasons) by customs officers, they must not be removed if the purpose in doing so is to evade any prohibition or restriction in relation to those goods, or with intent to defraud Her Majesty: section 159 of CEMA 1979:

> "... (5) If any imported goods which an officer has power under the Customs and Excise Acts 1979 to examine are without the authority of the proper officer removed from customs and excise charge before they have been examined, those goods shall be liable to forfeiture.
>
> (6) If any goods falling within subsection (5) above are removed by a person with intent to defraud Her Majesty of any duty chargeable thereon or to evade any prohibition or restriction for the time being in force with respect thereto under or by virtue of any enactment,

that person shall be guilty of an offence under this subsection and may be arrested.

(7) A person guilty of an offence under subsection (6) above shall be liable—

(a) on summary conviction, to a penalty of the prescribed sum or of three times the value of the goods, which ever is the greater, or to imprisonment for a term not exceeding 6 months, or to both; or

(b) on conviction on indictment, to a penalty of any amount, or to imprisonment for a term not exceeding 7 years, or to both."

IX. Offences Committed at Sea

(a) Drug trafficking offences committed on British ships

The definition of a "drug trafficking offence" appears in the Drug Trafficking Act 1994 (previously the Drug Trafficking Offences Act 1986) and the purpose of section 18 of Criminal Justice (International Co-operation) Act 1990 is to widen the jurisdiction of British courts in relation to drug trafficking offences committed on British ships. 2–107

"18. Anything which would constitute a drug trafficking offence if done on land in any part of the United Kingdom shall constitute that offence if done on a British ship."

By section 21(2) proceedings can only be commenced with the consent of the Director of Public Prosecutions.

(b) Ships used for drug trafficking

Following the 1988 Vienna Convention, and other high-level meetings, the United Kingdom Government enacted Criminal Justice (International Co-operation) Act 1990. Section 18 is dealt with above, but section 19 goes very much further, and empowers law enforcement agencies to combat drug trafficking that involves (i) a British ship, or (ii) a ship that is registered in another State but which is also a party to the 1988 Convention, or (iii) a ship that is not registered in any country or territory. 2–108

It will be seen that section 19(2)(a) penalises possession of any controlled drug on such a ship (whether for personal use or not), while section 19(b) makes it an offence for any person to be knowingly concerned in the carrying or concealing of a controlled drug on a ship (again whether for personal use or not). It will also be noted that the section applies to "any person"—whether a British national or not. The section will also be engaged whether the ship is in British territorial waters or not.

"19(1) This section applies to a British ship, a ship registered in a state other than the United Kingdom which is a party to the Vienna Convention (a "Convention state") and a ship not registered in any country or territory.

(2) A person is guilty of an offence if on a ship to which this section applies, wherever it may be, he—

(a) has a controlled drug in his possession; or
(b) is in anyway knowingly concerned in the carrying or concealing of a controlled drug on the ship,

knowing or having reasonable grounds to suspect that the drug is intended to be imported or has been exported contrary to section 3(1) of the Misuse of Drugs Act 1971 or the law of any state other than the United Kingdom.

(3) A certificate purporting to be issued by or on behalf of the government of any state to the effect that the importation or export of a controlled drug is prohibited by the law of that state shall be evidence, and in Scotland sufficient evidence, of the matters stated.

(4) A person guilty of an offence under this section is liable—

(a) in a case where the controlled drug is a Class A drug—
  (i) on summary conviction, to imprisonment for a term not exceeding six months or a fine not exceeding the statutory maximum or both;
  (ii) on conviction on indictment, to imprisonment for life or a fine or both;
(b) in a case where the controlled drug is a Class B drug—
  (i) on summary conviction, to imprisonment for a term not exceeding six months or a fine not exceeding the statutory maximum or both;
  (ii) on conviction on indictment, to imprisonment for a term not exceeding fourteen years or a fine or both;
(c) in a case where the controlled drug is a Class C drug—
  (i) on summary conviction, to imprisonment for a term not exceeding three months or a fine not exceeding the statutory maximum or both;
  (ii) on conviction on indictment, to imprisonment for a term not exceeding five years or a fine or both.

(5) In this section "a controlled drug" and the references to controlled drugs of a specified Class have the same meaning as in the said Act of 1971; and an offence under this section shall be included in the offences to which section 28 of that Act (defences) applies".

2–109 The object of sections 18 and 19 is obvious, but enforcing those two provisions is not straightforward. How, for example, is a ship (or a crew member) to be apprehended and brought to justice? How are these sections to be policed? Part of the answer is found in Article 17 of the 1988 Vienna Convention, which provides:

"1. The Parties shall cooperate to the fullest extent possible to suppress illicit traffic by sea, in conformity with the international law of the sea.
2. A Party which has reasonable grounds to suspect that a vessel flying

its flag or not displaying a flag or marks of registry is engaged in illicit traffic may request the assistance of other Parties in suppressing its use for that purpose. The Parties so requested shall render such assistance within the means available to them.

3.A Party which has reasonable grounds to suspect that a vessel exercising freedom of navigation in accordance with international law and flying the flag or displaying marks of registry of another Party is engaged in illicit traffic may so notify the flag State, request confirmation of registry and, if confirmed, request authorisation from the flag State to take appropriate action in regard to that vessel.

4. In accordance with paragraph 3 or in accordance with treaties in force between them or in accordance with any agreement or arrangement otherwise reached between those Parties, the flag State may authorise the requesting State to, *inter alia*:

(a) Board the vessel;
(b) Search the vessel;
(c) If evidence of involvement in illicit traffic is found, take appropriate action with respect to the vessel, persons and cargo on board.

9. The Parties shall consider entering into bilateral or regional agreements or arrangements to carry out, or to enhance the effectiveness of, the provisions of this article."

It was made clear in *Dean and Bolden* [1998] 2 Cr. App. R. 171, at 177 B/D, that it is for the prosecution to prove, to the criminal standard of proof, that the ship in question is one to which section 19 applies. The Court said that it is "sensible" to decide that issue at the outset of the trial rather than at the end of the prosecution case. On the facts of that particular case, the judge found that the ship was not registered anywhere and thus section 19 was engaged. 2–110

Dean and Bolden is of particular interest in relation to the interpretation of Article 17(4). It will be seen that the powers exercisable in that measure are subject to the Parties meeting one of three conditions set out in Article 17(4). If Article 17(3) does not apply, then authority to act in the manner permitted by Article 17(4)(a)–(c), must be derived from treaty or from an agreement. As Dyson J said in *Dean*, reference in Article 17(4) to "agreement" means something formal, at high level. It certainly does not mean an informal meeting of minds about a proposed action-plan arising out of a request for assistance in a given case coupled with a willingness to cooperate. Dyson J. expressed the position as follows:

"We now turn to the proper interpretation of Article 17(4). It defines the circumstances in which the flag State may authorise the requesting State to board the vessel etc. There are three: (i) in accordance with paragraph 3 (*i.e.* following confirmation of registry); (ii) in accordance with treaties in force; and (iii) in accordance with any agreement or arrangement otherwise reached between the parties. In our judgment, an "agreement or arrangement" must be something other than the agreement constituted by the particular request and authorisation themselves. The paragraph states that the flag State may authorise the requesting state "in accordance with" treaties in force between the parties or any agreement or arrangement otherwise reached between them. It does not simply say, as it might have done, that the flag State may authorise the requesting State to board the vessel etc. It might have made a provision which, *mutatis mutandis*, was similar to that contained in Article 17(2), namely that the requesting State may request authorisation to board the vessel etc., and the flag State may authorise the requesting State to act in accordance with the request."

2–111 Dyson J. then dealt with the crucial issue at to whether a mere request and authorisation is sufficient "agreement" for the purpose of Article 17(4):

> "It is, however, clear from the language of Article 17(4) that a request and authorisation, without more, are not sufficient. If (as in the present case) the request was not in accordance with Article 17(3), then the request and authorisation must be in accordance either with a treaty in force between the parties, or an agreement or arrangement otherwise reached between them. Whether the request and authorisation are in accordance with either of them will depend on the terms of the relevant treaty or agreement or arrangement (if any), and the terms in which the request and authorisation are expressed.
>
> In a sense, of course, a request and authorisation constitute an agreement or arrangement, and if made by officials who have been authorised by parties to the Vienna Convention to make them, then that agreement or arrangement can be said to have been made by those parties. In our view, however, it is plain from the language of Article 17(4) itself that such an agreement or arrangement is not one which comes within the meaning of that paragraph. We have already drawn attention to the words 'in accordance with'. The phrase "otherwise reached" is also of some significance . . . [counsel is right] . . . when he submits that *the agreement or arrangement contemplated is something formal, at high level, of general application and akin to a treaty*. It is straining language to regard an individual agreement comprised in the response by such an authority to a request as an agreement reached by the parties "otherwise than by a treaty.'" [emphasis added]

Note that offences under section 19 are subject to section 28 of the Misuse of Drugs Act 1971 (s. 19(5)). In relation to section 28, note the effect of the decision of the House of Lords in *Lambert* (July 5, 2001). A conviction under section 19 will also be a drug trafficking offence for the purposes of confiscation proceedings under the Drug Trafficking Act 1994. For cases that consider sentences under these provisions see *Wagenaar and Pronk* (1997) 1 Cr.App.R(S.) 178, CA, and *R. v. Maguire* (1997) 1 Cr.App.R. (S) 130, CA.

Enforcement power available to officers in respect of matters under s.18 and s.19

The following provisions are relevant to powers available to officers under sections 18 and 19. Note that section 20 is set out as amended by section 23(2)(a) of the Criminal Justice Act 1993: 2–112

"20(1) The powers conferred on an enforcement officer by Schedule 3 to this Act shall be exercisable in relation to any ship to which section 18 or 19 above applies for the purpose of detecting and the taking of appropriate action in respect of the offences mentioned in those sections.

(2) Those powers shall not be exercised outside the landward limits of the territorial sea of the United Kingdom in relation to a ship registered in a Convention state except with the authority of the Commissioners of Customs and Excise; and they shall not give their authority unless that state has in relation to that ship—

(a) requested the assistance of the United Kingdom for the purpose mentioned in subsection (1) above; or

(b) authorised the United Kingdom to act for that purpose.

(3) In giving their authority pursuant to a request for authorisation from a Convention state the Commissioners of Customs and Excise shall impose such conditions or limitations on the exercise of the powers as may be necessary to give effect to any conditions or limitations imposed by that state.

(4) The Commissioners of Customs and Excise may, either of their own motion or in response to a request from a Convention state, authorise a Convention state to exercise, in relation to a British ship, powers corresponding to those conferred on enforcement officers by Schedule 3 to this Act but subject to such conditions or limitations, if any, as they may impose.

(5) Subsection (4) above is without prejudice to any agreement made, or which may be made, on behalf of the United Kingdom whereby the United Kingdom undertakes not to object to the exercise by any other state in relation to a British ship of powers corresponding to those conferred by that Schedule.

(6) The powers conferred by that Schedule shall not be exercised in the territorial sea of any state other than the United Kingdom without the authority of the Commissioners of Customs and Excise and they shall, not give their authority unless that state has consented to the exercise of those powers."

Section 20 SCHEDULE 3 2–113

ENFORCEMENT POWERS IN RESPECT OF SHIPS

Preliminary

1.—(1) In this Schedule "an enforcement officer" means—

(a) a constable;
(b) an officer commissioned by the Commissioners of Customs and Excise under section 6(3) of the Customs and Excise Management Act 1979; and
(c) any other person of a description specified in an order made for the purposes of this Schedule by the Secretary of State

(2) (Procedure regarding sub-para. (1)(c).)

(3) In this Schedule "the ship" means the ship in relation to which the powers conferred by this Schedule are exercised.

Power to stop, board, divert and detain

2.—(1) An enforcement officer may stop the ship, board it and, if he thinks it necessary for the exercise of his functions, require it to be taken to a port in the United Kingdom and detain it there.

(2) Where an enforcement officer is exercising his powers with the authority of the Commissioners of Customs and Excise given under section 20(2) of this Act, the officer may require the ship to be taken to a port in the Convention state in question or, if that state has so requested, in any other country or territory willing to receive it.

(3) For any of those purposes he may require the master or any member of the crew to take such action as may be necessary.

(4) If an enforcement officer detains a vessel he shall serve on the master a notice in writing stating that it is to be detained until the notice is withdrawn by the service on him of a further notice in writing signed by an enforcement officer.

Power to search and obtain information

2–114 3.—(1) An enforcement officer may search the ship, anyone on it and anything on it including its cargo.

(2) An enforcement officer may require any person on the ship to give information concerning himself or anything on the ship.

(3) Without prejudice to the generality of those powers an enforcement officer may—
(a) open any containers;
(b) make tests and take samples of anything on the ship;
(c) require the production of documents, books or records relating to the ship or anything on it;
(d) make photographs or copies of anything whose production he has power to require.

Powers in respect of suspected offence

4. If an enforcement officer has reasonable grounds to suspect that an offence mentioned in section 18 or 19 of this Act has been committed on a ship to which that section applies he may—
(a) arrest without warrant anyone whom he has reasonable grounds for suspecting to be guilty of the offence; and
(b) seize and detain anything found on the ship which appears to him to be evidence of the offence.

Assistants

5.—(1) An enforcement officer may take with him, to assist him in exercising his powers— 2–115

(a) any other persons; and
(b) any equipment or materials.

(2) A person whom an enforcement officer takes with him to assist him may perform any of the officer's functions but only under the officer's supervision.

Use of reasonable force

6. An enforcement officer may use reasonable force, if necessary, in the performance of his functions.

Evidence of authority

7. An enforcement officer shall, if required, produce evidence of his authority. 2–116

Protection of officers

8. An enforcement officer shall not be liable in any civil or criminal proceedings for anything done in the purported performance of his functions under this Schedule if the court is satisfied that the act was done in good faith and that there were reasonable grounds for doing it.

Offences

9.—(1) A person is guilty of an offence if he— 2–117

(a) intentionally obstructs an enforcement officer in the performance of any of his functions under this Schedule;
(b) fails without reasonable excuse to comply with a requirement made by an enforcement officer in the performance of those functions; or
(c) in purporting to give information required by an officer for the performance of those functions—
   (i) makes a statement which he knows to be false in a material particular or recklessly makes a statement which is false in a material particular or
   (ii) intentionally fails to disclose any material particular.

(2) A person guilty of an offence under this paragraph is liable on summary conviction to a fine not exceeding level 5 on the standard scale.

(i) *Meaning of "Enforcement officer"*

Note: The Criminal Justice (International Co-operation) Act 1990 (Enforcement Officers) Order 1990 (S.I. 1992 No. 77) provides that the following persons, in addition to those specified in paragraph 1(a) and (b) shall be enforcement officers for the purposes of that Schedule— 2–118

(a) commissioned officers of any of Her Majesty's ships;
(b) officers of the sea-fishery inspectorate of the Minister of Agriculture, Fisheries and Food; and
(c) officers of the fishery protection service of the Secretary of State

for Scotland holding the rank of commander, first officer or second officer.)

(d) **Provisions relevant to jurisdiction and prosecutions:** s.21, as amended by the CJA 1993, s.23(2)(b)

2–119 "21—(1) Proceedings under this Part of this Act or Schedule 3 in respect of an offence on a ship may be taken, and the offence may for all incidental purposes be treated as having been committed, in any place in the United Kingdom.

(2) No such proceedings shall be instituted

(a) in England or Wales except by or with the consent of the Director of Public Prosecutions or the Commissioners of Customs and Excise;

(b) (N.I.)

(3) Without prejudice to subsection (2) above no proceedings for an offence under section 19 above alleged to have been committed outside the landward limits of the territorial sea of the United Kingdom on a ship registered in a Convention state shall be instituted except in pursuance of the exercise with the authority of the Commissioners of Customs and Excise of the powers conferred by Schedule 3 to this Act; and section 3 of the Territorial Waters Jurisdiction Act 1878 (consent of Secretary of State for certain prosecutions) shall not apply to those proceedings."

(e) **Interpretation of Part II**

2–120 24—(1) In this Part of this Act— "British ship" means a ship registered in the United Kingdom or a colony;

"Convention state" has the meaning given in section 19(1) above; "scheduled substance" has the meaning given in section 12(4) above; "ship" includes any vessel used in navigation;

"the territorial sea of the United Kingdom" includes the territorial sea adjacent to any of the Channel Islands, the Isle of Man or any colony;

"the Vienna Convention" means the United Nations Convention against Illicit Traffic in Narcotic Drugs and Psychotropic Substances which was signed in Vienna on 20th December 1988.

(2) Any expression used in this Part of this Act which is also used in the Drug Trafficking Act 1994 has the same meaning as in that Act.

(3) (Scotland)

(4) If in any proceedings under this Part of this Act any question arises whether any country or territory is a state or is a party to the Vienna Convention, a certificate issued by or under the authority of the Secretary of State shall be conclusive evidence on that question."

Chapter 3: Possession of Drugs

A. INTRODUCTION

Any person approaching the concept of possession for the first time could reasonably be forgiven if he expected the legal principles involved to be straightforward. They are not. He might expect to find, for example, that the ingredients of possession are encapsulated in a sentence or two, whereas the ingredients differ from one branch of the law to another. As a rule, a person has in his possession anything, which is in his physical custody, or under his control. Although this bald statement represents the law (see *DPP v. Brooks* [1974] A.C. 862, PC) it is a statement heavily peppered with qualifications and exceptions, notably in the field of criminal law, where a strict adherence to the rule would produce intolerably harsh results. The reason is that the fact of possession does not require the existence of a mental ingredient. For example, one would normally say that a person is in possession of items that he carries in the pockets of his clothing, and the fact that he has forgotten that some of the items are there makes no difference. However, when possession becomes an essential element of a criminal offence, other considerations become relevant. Is a person to be held criminally liable if he did not know of the existence of an article that he carried, or if he makes a mistake as to its quality? In order to avoid harsh/unjust results the seemingly simple definition of possession needs to be restated in terms that recognise the existence of a mental ingredient of some sort. The history of the law of possession, in the criminal law, is very much a history of the attempts made by the judges to explain what that mental ingredient is, and of course, to explain what the law means by 'custody' and 'control'. The Court of Appeal has now decided numerous cases on the meaning of "possession" in drug cases. A large number are cited in the following pages. A few are landmark decisions (such as *Warner v. Metropolitan Police Commissioner* [1969] 2 A.C. 256, *Lewis* (1988) 87 Cr. App. R. 270, *McNamara* (1988) 87 Cr.App.R. 246, 3–01

Boyesen [1982] 2 All E.R. 161, and *Watson* (October 19, 1995, unreported)). The majority are illustrative of general propositions, but for that reason, provide considerable assistance in serving to define difficult concepts, such as "control", by example.

3–02 Given that the definition of possession is elusive, it is unsurprising that the Misuse of Drugs Act 1971 (the MDA) does not provide a statutory definition of possession. Section 37(3) merely provides that: "... the things which a person has in his possession shall be taken to include anything subject to his control, which is in the custody of another". That at least tells us that possession includes constructive possession. A person who deposits a suitcase (knowing that it contains cannabis) in a left luggage office at a railway station, while retaining the keys, no longer has custody of the suitcase, but by section 37(3), he remains in possession of it because he retains control of the keys. The Act offers little more by way of assistance. In *Amato v. Walkinghsaw* 1989, S.C.C.R. 564, an envelope containing heroin was posted by the appellant to himself but it was received by another who intended to deliver it to the appellant. It seems that the appellant anticipated that the envelope would be received and held on his behalf. The appellant was therefore in possession and his appeal against conviction for unlawful possession was dismissed. It is important to remember that the Act is designed to regulate the flow and use of controlled drugs: it is not designed to outlaw the majority of them. It follows that the MDA must distinguish between persons who are lawfully entitled to possess controlled drugs but are merely restricted as to how they may use them, and those persons who are unlawfully in possession of them. Only the latter, of course, will be guilty of the offence of unlawful possession.

For ease of understanding, it may be helpful to approach the law of possession in the following stages. First, look briefly at the sections of the Act, which make possession of controlled drugs not only unlawful but also a criminal offence. Secondly, examine what may be lawfully possessed under the Act, and finally examine cases of unlawful possession.

B. MAKING POSSESSION UNLAWFUL

3–03 Section 5(1) is expressed as follows:

> "Subject to any regulations under section 7 of this Act . . . it shall not be lawful for a person to have a controlled drug in his possession."

Although section 5(1) establishes a general rule that it is unlawful to possess all controlled drugs, many exceptions are to be found in the Misuse of Drugs Regulations 1985. One must therefore look initially to the drugs listed in Schedule 2 to the MDA to see if the drug is controlled. If it is, one then turns to the various Schedules set out in the Regulations (which do not correspond to the Schedules in the MDA) to see if the drug in question comes within one of the exceptions.

Note that section 5(1) merely makes the possession of controlled drugs unlawful. The *offence*, of being in unlawful possession, is created by section 5(2) which provides:

> "Subject to section 28 of this Act and to subsection (4) below, it is an offence for a person to have a controlled drug in his possession in contravention of subsection (1) above."

Three ingredients are required to be proved, by the prosecution, before an offence under section 5(2) is committed: 3–04

(i) the item must be in the physical custody or control of the accused,

(ii) the accused must know, or at least could reasonably have known, of the existence of the item in question,

(iii) the item must be proved to be a controlled drug within the meaning of the Misuse of Drugs Act 1971 and see *Watson* (October 19, 1995, unreported).

Note that both section 28 and section 5(4) provide an accused with a variety of defences in narrowly defined circumstances, being defences, which, for the most part, did not exist before the Misuse of Drugs Act came into force. Both sections are examined in detail elsewhere but significantly, the statutory defences are all concerned with the state of mind of the person said (among other things) to be in unlawful possession of a controlled drug. Thus, by section 28 it is a defence for the accused to prove (an evidential burden) that he neither believed, suspected, nor had reason to suspect that what he had was a controlled drug, but it is no defence for him to say that he believed he had LSD whereas the drug turned out to be heroin: see *Lambert* (July 5, 2001, HL). Parliament was making it plain that section 5(2) does not create an absolute offence: unlawful possession requires proof of the requisite *mens rea* before an offence is committed under that section.

There have been many changes to the law since a number of cases were decided. Thus, in *Warner v. Metropolitan Police Commissioner* [1969] 2 A.C. 256, the House of Lords considered the meaning of "possession" but that was, of course, before the passing of the Misuse of Drugs Act and before the introduction of defences created by section 28 of the Misuse of Drugs Act. Not all the opinions expressed in *Warner* have the significance that they had in 1969: see, for example, *Lambert* (July 5, 2001, HL). It is, however, necessary to look at these authorities, since they affect the way in which a case of possession is to be approached, and they have a bearing on the terms in which a jury should be directed by the trial judge (and see Teff, "The Meaning of Possession in Drug Offences" [1971] 34 M.L.R. 582). 3–05

Many persons have queried whether the law relating to possession for personal use under the Misuse of Drugs Act 1971 is compatible with the European Convention on Human Rights. In *R. v. Ham* (July, 2000), a decision at first instance (Southwark Crown Court), an attempt was made to challenge the prosecution of a user of cannabis on the grounds that the decision to prosecute, and to proceed with the prosecution, violated H's Convention rights. The challenge failed, and H was convicted by a 10–2 majority verdict of the jury. Similar challenges are unlikely to succeed in all but the rarest of cases. There may be cases where a decision to prosecute is reviewable by a court—perhaps because the decision is unreasonable or because the decision to prosecute is not a proportionate response. In *Ham*, H rejected the offer of a caution in order to state his case, but that left the prosecuting agency with the option of either taking no further action at all or pursuing a prosecution. In some jurisdictions, the written constitution provides a limitation on prosecution if the acts in question are performed on the actor and no harm or injury is caused to third parties. No such protection expressly exists in the ECHR or in the Human Rights Act 1998. The jurisprudence of the Strasbourg Court has not yet developed to the point where it is realistically foreseeable that the ECHR would have that effect. The reason is that attitudes, towards the criminalisation and prosecution of users of particular substances, differ (sometimes markedly) in E.C. / E.U. States. In any event, the United Kingdom would need to be mindful of its wider international obligations—not least the three main United Nations Conventions (1961, 1971 and 1988). However, for the reasons given by the Police Foundation Independent Inquiry, there does exist considerable room for manoeuvre in the way the drug laws of the United Kingdom are shaped and used. The use of discretion in the criminal justice process is becoming increasingly important. It is here that society is likely to see significant changes in the way the law operates in practice.

I. Lawful Possession

3–06 If there were to be an absolute rule that nobody is entitled to possess any controlled drug, ridiculous results would follow. A police officer seizing a controlled drug from an addict would be guilty of unlawful possession. Accordingly, the Secretary of State, after consultation with the Advisory Council, may, by regulations, permit certain persons to possess particular controlled drugs, or he may make it lawful for individuals to do a number of things in relation to controlled drugs that would otherwise be unlawful for them to do: see section 7. To this end, the Secretary of State may also make different provisions in relation to different controlled drugs; he may affect different categories of persons, he may impose conditions on the right to possess particular drugs, or he may grant an authority to possess them contingent upon the happening of certain events.

The relevant provisions are mainly to be found in the Misuse of Drugs Regulations 1985 (S.I. 1985 No. 2066), which came into operation on April 1, 1986 (as amended by S.I. 1986 No. 2330, S.I. 1988 No. 916, S.I. 1989 No. 1460, S.I. 1990 No. 2589, S.I. 1990 No. 2630, S.I. 1995 No. 2048, S.I. 1995 No. 3244, S.I. 1996 No. 1597, S.I. 1998 No. 882, and S.I. 1999 No. 1404).

The Misuse of Drugs Regulations 1973 (S.I. 1973 No. 797) have been revoked, along with their amending Regulations, namely: S.I. 1974 No. 402, S.I. 1975 No. 499, S.I. 1977 No. 1380, S.I. 1979 No. 326, S.I. 1983 No. 788 and S.I. 1984 No. 1143.

By section 10 of the MDA 1971, the Secretary of State may also make regulations, as appears to him necessary or expedient, for preventing the misuse of controlled drugs. For example, the Secretary of State may require certain drugs to be kept in a locked safe or room, or in other secure conditions. The relevant regulations, made under section 10, are embodied in the Misuse of Drugs (Safe Custody) Regulations 1973 (S.I. 1973 No. 798) as amended by S.I. 1974 No. 1449, S.I. 1975 No. 294, S.I. 1983 No. 1909, S.I. 1984 No. 1146, S.I. 1985 No. 2067, S.I. 1986 No. 2332, S.I. 1995 No. 3244 and S.I. 1999 No. 1403.

The Secretary of State is empowered (by virtue of section 10 of the MDA 1971), to regulate (*inter alia*) the issue of prescriptions or the supply of controlled drugs to drug addicts. This he has done by the Misuse of Drugs (Notification and Supply to Addicts) Regulations 1973 (S.I. 1973 No. 799) as amended (most recently by S.I. 1997 No. 1001). 3–07

It should be noted that, for the purposes of the Misuse of Drugs Regulations 1985 (S.I. 1985 No. 2066), controlled drugs are listed in five Schedules. It is these Schedules that must be referred to when considering the extent of the exemptions from section 5(1) and other provisions of the MDA Schedules 1 to 5 have been amended by the Misuse of Drugs (Amendment) Regulations 1986 (S.I. 1986 No. 2330, and S.I. 1988 No. 916, S.I. 1989 No. 1460, S.I. 1990 No. 2589, S.I. 1990 No. 2630, S.I. 1995 No. 2048 and S.I. 1995 No. 3244, S.I. 1996 No. 1597, S.I. 1998 No.882, and S.I. 1999 No. 1404).

The major exemptions under the Misuse of Drugs Regulations 1985 are summarised and set out below. Note that the Schedules to the Regulations may contain different Classes of controlled drug.

(a) Persons who may possess any controlled drugs

There are two ways in which it is possible for a person to possess any controlled drug lawfully, no matter how dangerous it may be. The first protection is afforded by regulation 6(7), and the second is afforded by way of a licence issued by the Secretary of State. 3–08

(i) *Regulation 6(7)*

Regulation 6(7) provides six classes of persons with immunity from pro- 3–09 secution under section 5(1) when acting in the course of their respective duties, namely:

> "(a) a constable when acting in the course of his duty as such;
> (b) a person engaged in the business of a carrier when acting in the course of that business;
> (c) a person engaged in the business of the Post Office when acting in the course of that business;
> (d) an officer of customs and excise when acting in the course of his duty as such;
> (e) a person engaged in the work of any laboratory to which the drug has been sent for forensic examination when acting in the course of his duty as a person so engaged;
> (f) a person engaged in conveying the drug to a person who may lawfully have that drug in his possession."

The last category certainly protects those who convey drugs to one of the remaining five groups stated above but would seem, equally, to protect the person who, for example, collects controlled drugs from a pharmacist and delivers them to a person entitled to receive them under a prescription. Where a person acts outside the scope of his duties he will lose the protection of regulation 6(7) and so will be guilty of unlawful possession. Thus, a forensic laboratory technician would not be acting in the course of his duties if he took cannabis resin home to show his family what it looks like. Curiously, a disturbing omission from regulation 6(7) is any specific exemption for court staff, including counsel, jurors or members of the judiciary who frequently handle controlled drugs as court exhibits. Frankly, it is difficult to know by what authority court staff may lawfully handle such exhibits by virtue of any other provision of the MDA or the Regulations.

(ii) *Regulation 5*

3–10 Another method of securing protection is afforded by regulation 5 which enables the Secretary of State to issue a licence authorising any individual to possess any controlled drug: see *Ewens* [1966] 2 All E.R. 470 and *Scott* (1921) 86 J.P. 69. The licensee must abide by the terms and conditions attached to the licence. Failure to do so may amount to the commission of a separate offence (s. 18) but such a breach is unlikely to vitiate the effect of the licence. However, the Secretary of State is empowered to revoke or modify the licence at any time.

(b) Persons who may possess Schedule 2 drugs

3–11 The following substances and products, their salts and stereo isomeric forms, are included in Schedule 2 to the M.D. Regulations 1985 (as amended):

CONTROLLED DRUGS SUBJECT TO THE REQUIREMENTS OF REGULATIONS 14, 15, 16, 18, 19, 20, 21, 23, 25 AND 26

1. The following substances and products, namely—

Acetorphine
Alfentanil
Allylprodine
Alphacetylmethadol
Alphameprodine
Alphamethadol
Alphaprodine
Anileridine
Benzethidine
Benzylmorphine (3-benzylmorphine)
Betacetylmethadol
Betameprodine
Betamnethadol
Betaprodine
Bezitramide
Carfentanil
Clonitazene
Cocaine
Desomorphine
Dextromoramide
Diamorphine
Diampromide
Diethylthiambutene
Difenoxin
Dihydrocodeinone
Dihydromorphine
Dimenoxadole
Dimepheptanol
Dimethylthiambutene
Dioxaphetyl butyrate
Diphenoxylate
Dipipanone
Dronabinol[1]
Drotebanol
Ecgonine, and any derivative of ecgonine which is convertible to ecgonine or to cocaine
Ethylmethylthiambutene
Etonitazene
Etorphine
Etoxeridine
Fentanyl
Furethidine
Hydrocodone
Hydromorphinol
Hydromorphone
Hydroxypethidine
Isomethadone
Ketobemidoneacid
4-Cyano-2-dimethylamino-4, 4-diphenylbutane
4-Cyano-l-methyl4phenyl piperidine
Levomethorphan
Levomoramide
Levophenacylmorphan
Levorphanol
Lofentanil
Medicinal opium
Metazocine
Methadone
Methadyl acetate
Methyldesorphine
Methyldihydromorphine (6-methyldihydromorphine)
Metopon
Morpheridine
Morphine methobromide, morphine morphine derivativesMorphine
Myrophine
N-oxide & other pentavalent nitrogen
Nicomorphine
Noracymethadol
Norlevorphanol
Normethadone
Normorphine
Norpipanone
O-Carboxymethyloxime
Oxycodone
Oxymorphone
Pethidine

Phenadoxone
Phenampromide
Phenazocine
Phencyclidine
Phenomorphan
Phenoperidine
Piminodine
Piritramide
Proheptazine
Properidine
Racemethorphan
Racemoramide
Racemorphan
Sufentanil
Thebacon
Thebaine
Tilidate
Trimeperidine
2-Methyl-3-morpholino-1, 1-diphenylpropanecarboxylic
1-Methyl4phenylpiperidine-4–carboxylic acid
4-Phenylpiperidine-4-carboxylic acid ethyl ester
Zipeprol[2]

2. Any stereoisomeric form of a substance specified in paragraph 1 not being dextromethorphan or dextrorphan.

3. Any ester or ether of a substance specified in paragraph 1 or 2, not being a substance specified in paragraph 6.

4. Any salt of a substance specified in any of paragraphs 1 to 3.

5. Any preparation or other product containing a substance or product specified in any of paragraphs 1 to 4, not being a preparation specified in Schedule 5.

6. The following substances and products, namely—

Acetyldihydrocodeine
Amphetamine
Codeine
Dextropropoxyphene
Dihydrocodeine
Ethylmorphine (3-ethylmorphine)
Fenethyline
Glutethimide
Lefetamine
Mecloqualone
Methaqualone
Methylamphetamine
Methylphenidate
Nicocodine
Nicodicodine (6-nicotinoyldihydrocodeine)
Norcodeine
Phenmetrazine
Pholcodine
Propiram
Quinalbarbitone[3]

7. Any stereoisomeric form of a substance specified in paragraph 6.

8. Any salt of a substance specified in paragraph 6 or 7.

9. Any preparation or other product containing a substance or product specified in any of paragraphs 6 to 8, not being a preparation specified in Schedule 5.

[This Schedule is printed as amended by S.I. 1986 No. 2330, S.I. 1988 No. 916, S.I. 1995 No. 2048, and S.I. 1998 No. 882]

[1] Inserted by S.I. 1995 No. 2048
[2] Inserted by S.I. 1998 No. 882 [May 1, 1998]
[3] Inserted by S.I. 1988 No. 916

It will be seen that some of the drugs referred to in Schedule 2 to the 1985 Regulations include some of the most dangerous drugs, *e.g.* heroin, cocaine, dipipanone, methadone, medical opium, morphine, DF 118 and methaqualone. However, because such substances are also recognised as being a valuable contribution to medicine when properly and professionally administered, regulation 10(1)(a) provides that the following classes of persons (set out in regulation 8(2)) are entitled to possess Schedule 2 drugs (and to supply them) namely: 3–12

"(a) a practitioner;
(b) a pharmacist;
(c) a person lawfully conducting a retail pharmacy business;
(d) the person in charge or acting person in charge of a hospital or nursing home which is wholly or mainly maintained by a public authority out of public funds or by a charity or by voluntary subscriptions;
(e) in the case of such a drug supplied to her by a person responsible for the dispensing and supply of medicines at the hospital or nursing home, the sister or acting sister for the time being in charge of a ward, theatre or other department in such a hospital or nursing home as aforesaid;
(f) a person who is in charge of a laboratory the recognised activities of which consist in, or include, the conduct of scientific education or research and which is attached to a university, university college or such a hospital as aforesaid or to any other institution approved for the purpose under this sub-paragraph by the Secretary of State;
(g) a public analyst appointed under section 27 of the Food Act 1990 or section 27 of the Food and Drugs (Scotland) Act 1956;
(h) [repealed];
(i) a sampling officer within the meaning of Schedule 3 to the Medicines Act 1968;
(j) a person employed or engaged in connection with a scheme for testing the quality or amount of the drugs, preparations and appliances supplied under the National Health Service Act 1977 or the National Health Service (Scotland) Act 1978 and the Regulations made thereunder;
(k) a person authorised by the Pharmaceutical Society of Great Britain for the purposes of section 108 or 109 of the Medicines Act 1968,

[This part of the regulation is published as amended by the Food Safety Act 1990 Consequential Modifications (No. 2) (Great Britain) Order (S.I. 1990 No. 2487)]

A person who is an authorised member of a group may, in accordance with the terms of his group authority, have a Schedule 2 drug in his possession: see regulation 10(3).

A person receiving controlled drugs from a doctor, is entitled to possess them and to take them by reason of regulation 10(2) which provides:

> "Notwithstanding the provisions of section 5(1) of the Act, a person may have in his possession any drug specified in Schedule 2 or 3 for administration for medical, dental or veterinary purposes in accordance with the directions of a practitioner. . . . "

(c) Persons who may possess Schedule 3 and Schedule 4 drugs

3–13 The persons entitled to possess (and supply) these drugs include the following persons (see reg. 10(1)(b) in conjunction with reg. 9(2)):

"(a) a practitioner;
(b) a pharmacist;
(c) a person lawfully conducting a retail pharmacy business;
(d) a person in charge of a laboratory the recognised activities of which consist in, or include, the conduct of scientific education or research;
(e) a public analyst appointed under section 27 of the Food Act 1990 or section 27 of the Food and Drugs (Scotland) Act 1956;
(f) [repealed];
(g) a sampling officer within the meaning of Schedule 3 to the Medicines Act 1968;
(h) a person employed or engaged in connection with a scheme for testing the quality or amount of the drugs, preparations and appliances supplied under the National Health Service Act 1977 or the National Health Service (Scotland) Act 1978 and the Regulations made thereunder.
(i) a person authorised by the Pharmaceutical Society of Great Britain for the purposes of section 108 or 109 of the Medicines Act 1968 . . ."

[This part of the regulation is printed as amended by the Misuse of Drugs (Amendment) Regulations 1986 (S.I. 1986 No. 2330) and S.I. 1990 No. 2487]

3–14 By regulation 10(1)(c), (in conjunction with reg. 9(3)(b), (c) and 9(6) as amended by S.I. 1986 No. 2330), the following persons are also included and may therefore possess any Schedule 3 drug, namely:

(i) "a person in charge or acting person in charge of a hospital or nursing home": *per* regulation 9(3)(b) as amended by S.I. 1986 No. 2330;
(ii) "in the case of such a drug supplied to her by a person responsible for the dispensing and supply of medicines at the hospital or nursing home, the sister or acting sister for the time being in charge of a ward, theatre, or other department in such a hospital or nursing home": *per* regulation 9(3)(c) as amended by S.I. 1986 No. 2330;
(iii) a person in charge of a laboratory may possess (and supply or

offer to supply) any drug specified in Schedule 3 which is required for use as a buffering agent in chemical analysis: see regulation 9(6) inserted by S.I. 1986 No. 2330.

A person receiving controlled drugs from a doctor, is entitled to possess them and to take them by reason of regulation 10(2) which provides:

> "Notwithstanding the provisions of section 5(1) of the Act, a person may have in his possession any drug specified in Schedule 2 or 3 for administration for medical, dental or veterinary purposes in accordance with the directions of a practitioner. . . ."

(d) Schedule 3 drugs

The drugs in Schedule 3 are less dangerous than those in Schedules 1 and 2. They include the barbiturates, *e.g.* methylphenobarbitone. 3–15

CONTROLLED DRUGS SUBJECT TO THE REQUIREMENTS OF REGULATIONS 14, 15 (EXCEPT TEMAZEPAM),[1] 16, 18, 22, 23, 24, 25 AND 26.

1. The following substances, namely—

(a)
Benzphetamine	Mephentermine
Buprenorphine[2]	Meprobamate
Cathine	Methylphenobarbitone
Chlorphentermine	Methyprylone
Diethylpropion	Pentazocine
Ethchlorvynol	Phendimetrazine
Ethinamate	Phentermine
Flunitrazepam[3]	Pipradrol
Mazindol	Temazepam[4]

(b) any 5,5 disubstituted barbituric acid not being quinalbarbitone.[5]

2. Any stereoisomeric form of a substance specified in paragraph 1 not being phenylpropanolamine.

3. Any salt of a substance specified in paragraph 1 or 2.

4. Any preparation or other product containing a substance specified in any of paragraphs 1 to 3, not being a preparation specified in Schedule 5.

[This Schedule is printed as amended by S.I. 1986 No. 2330, S.I. 1988 No. 916, the Misuse of Drugs (Amendment) Regulations 1989 (S.1. 1989 No. 1460), S.I. 1995 No. 3244, and S.I. 1998 No. 882]

[1] Inserted by S.I. 1995 No. 3244
[2] Inserted by S.I. 1989 No. 1460
[3] Inserted by S.I. 1998 No. 882 [May 1, 1998]
[4] Inserted by S.I. 1995 No. 3244
[5] Inserted by S.I. 1988 No. 916

(e) **Schedule 4 drugs**

3–16 It will be seen that drugs that come within Schedule may be possessed (imported, or exported) by many persons on condition that the conditions set out in the Schedule are fulfilled.

Regulation 3

SCHEDULE 4
PART I[1]

CONTROLLED DRUGS EXCEPTED FROM THE PROHIBITION ON POSSESSION WHEN IN THE FORM OF A MEDICINAL PRODUCT, EXCLUDED FROM THE APPLICATION OF OFFENCES ARISING FROM IMPORTATION ON IMPORTATION AND EXPORTATION WHEN IMPORTED OR EXPORTED IN THE FORM OF A MEDICINAL PRODUCT BY ANY PERSON FOR ADMINISTRATION TO HIMSELF; AND SUBJECT TO THE REQUIREMENTS OF REGULATIONS 22, 23, 25 AND 26.[2]

1. The following substances, namely—

Atamestane
Bolandiol
Bolasterone
Bolazine
Boldenone
Bolenol
Bolmantalate
Calusterone
4-Chloromethandienone
Clostebol
Drostanolone
Enestebol
Epitiostanol
Ethyloestrenol
Fluoxymesterone
Formebolone
Furazabol
Mebolazine
Mepitiostane
Mesabolone
Mestanolone
Mesterolone
Methandienone
Methandriol
Methenolone
Methyltestosterone
Metribolone
Mibolerone
Nandrolone
Norboletone
Norclostebol
Norethandrolone
Ovandrotone
Oxabolone
Oxandrolone
Oxymesterone
Oxymetholone
Prasterone
Propetandrol
Quinbolone
Roxibolone
Silandrone
Stanolone
Stanozolol
Stenbolone
Testosterone
Thiomesterone
Trenbolone

2. Any compound (not being Trilostane or a compound for the time being specified in paragraph 1 of this Part of this Schedule) structurally derived from 17-hydroxyandros-tan-3-one or from 17-hydroxyestran-3-one by modification in any of the following ways, that is to say,

(a) by further substitution at position 17 by a methyl or ethyl group;
(b) by substitution to any extent at one or more of positions 1,2,4,6, 7,9,11 or 16, but at no other position;
(c) by unsaturation in the carbocyclic ring system to any extent, provided that there are no more than two ethylenic bonds in any one carbocyclic ring;
(d) by fusion of ring A with a heterocyclic system.

3. Any substance which is an ester or ether (or, where more than one hydroxyl function is available, both an ester and an ether) of a substance specified in paragraph 1 or described in paragraph 2 of this Part of this Schedule.

4. The following substances, namely—

Chorionic Gonadotrophin (HCG)
Clenbuterol
Non-human chorionic gonadotrophin
Somatotropin
Somatrem
Somatropin

5. Any stereoisomeric form of a substance specified or described in any of paragraphs 1 to 4 of this Part of this Schedule.

6. Any salt of a substance specified or described in any of paragraphs 1 to 5 of this Part of this Schedule.

7. Any preparation of other product containing a substance or product specified or described in any of paragraphs 1 to 6 of this Part of this Schedule, not being a preparation specified in Schedule 5.

PART II[3]

CONTROLLED DRUGS EXCEPTED FROM THE PROHIBITION ON IMPORTATION, EXPORTATION AND, WHEN IN THE FORM OF A MEDICINAL PRODUCT, POSSESSION AND SUBJECT TO THE REQUIREMENTS OF REGULATIONS 22, 23, 25 AND 26

1. The following substances and products, namely— 3–17

Alprazolam
Aminorex[4]
Bromazepam
Brotizolam[5]
Camazepam
Chlordiazepoxide
Clobazam
Clonazepam
Clorazepic acid
Clotiazepam
Cloxazolam
Delorazepam
Diazepam
Estazolam
Ethyl loflazepate
Fencamfin
Fenproporex
Fludiazepam
Flurazepam
Halazepam
Haloxazolam
Ketazolam
Loprazolam
Lorazepam
Lormetazepam
Medazepam
Mefenorex
Mesocarb[6]
Midazolam[7]
N-Ethylamphetamine
Nimetazepam
Nitrazepam

Nordazepam	Pyrovalerone
Oxazepam	Tetrazepam
Oxazolam	Triazolam
Pemoline[8]	[Flunitrazepam][9]
Pinazepam	[Propylhexedrine][10]
Prazepam	[Temazepam][11]

2. Any steroisomeric form of a substance specified in paragraph 1.

3. Any salt of a substance specified in paragraph 1 or 2.

4. Any preparation or other product containing a substance or product specified in and of paragraphs 1 to 3, not being a preparation specified in Schedule 5.

[This Schedule is printed as amended by S.I. 1986 No. 2330, S.I. 1989 No. 1460, S.I. 1990 No. 2630, S.I. 1995 No. 2048, S.I. 1995 No. 3244, S.I. 1996 No. 1597 (which, *inter alia*, inserted Part I as from September 1, 1996), and S.I. 1998 No. 882]

1 Inserted by S.I. 1996 No. 1597
2 Inserted by S.I. 1996 No. 1597
3 Inserted by S.I. 1996 No. 1597
4 S.I. 1998 No. 882
5 S.I. 1998 No. 882
6 Inserted by S.I. 1998 No. 882
7 Inserted by S.I. 1990 No. 2630
8 Inserted by S.I. 1989 No. 1460 (originally Part II was para.1 of Sched.4)
9 Deleted by S.I. 1998 No. 882.
10 Deleted by S.I. 1995 No. 2048
11 Deleted by S.I. 1995 No. 3244 and moved to Sched. 3, para.1(a).

(f) Persons who may possess drugs under a practitioner's control

3–18 A person receiving controlled drugs from a doctor, is entitled to possess them and to take them by reason of regulation 10(2) which provides:

> "Notwithstanding the provisions of section 5(1) of the Act, a person may have in his possession any drug specified in Schedule 2 or 3 for administration for medical, dental or veterinary purposes in accordance with the directions of a practitioner . . ."

Note that only Schedule 2 and 3 drugs are referred to. There was no point in the draftsman including Schedule 5 drugs since anybody may possess these (with or without the directions of a practitioner) by virtue of regulation 4(2)(b) which provides that:

> "Section 5(1) of the Act shall not have effect in relation to (b) the drugs specified in Schedule 5".

The same consideration applies to Schedule 4 drugs in medicinal form which are also excluded from section 5(1): see regulation 4(2)(a).

3–19 The reader may be wondering why none of the drugs listed under Schedule 1 are included under this heading. The reason is that Parliament has ensured that certain drugs are not supplied to any patient by any doctor, *e.g.* cannabis in all forms, coca leaf (but not cocaine), LSD, psilocin (extracted from the magic mushroom), or raw opium.

"Administration", within the meaning of regulation 10(2), clearly embraces persons who intend to administer drugs to themselves as well as to others; regulation 7(3) provides that:

> "Any person other than a doctor or dentist may administer to a patient any drug specified in Schedule 2, 3 or 4."

As regulation 7(3) gives the general right to administer such drugs, in accordance with the directions of a doctor or dentist, it makes obvious sense to give a corresponding right to possess the drug(s) in question, hence regulation 10(2).

In cases of self-administration, it is equally important that the drug should be used for the purpose for which it was intended and in a manner that will not cause harm to the user. Accordingly, regulation 10 requires that drugs be administered for "medical, dental or veterinary purposes in accordance with the directions of a practitioner".

Thus, an individual originally in lawful possession of barbiturates will lose the protection of regulation 10 if he uses a drug for a non-medicinal purpose (*e.g.* in an attempt to commit suicide) or if he displays mala fides by administering the drug in a way that does not accord with the directions of a practitioner.

In *Dunbar* [1981] 1 W.L.R. 1536, D was a registered medical practitioner who had no patients. He obtained heroin and pethidine for "professional purposes" and administered them to himself. D told police that he intended committing suicide, but at his trial stated that he wished to alleviate his depression. The trial judge ruled that D had no defence to a charge of unlawful possession of the drugs, contrary to section 5(1) MDA 1971, on the basis that regulation 10(2) had not been complied with since D had not acted "with the directions of a practitioner". 3–20

During the course of the appeal, the Crown argued that a doctor who has no patients is not acting in his capacity as a doctor. The Court of Appeal did not find that argument attractive and held that a doctor who bona fide prescribed a controlled drug for himself was acting in his capacity as a doctor even though he was the person receiving the benefit.

The decision is patently right. The definition of a doctor is not dependent on whether he has patients or not. Moreover, regulation 10(2) is designed to ensure the prudent use of controlled drugs (*e.g.* for medical purposes), when those drugs are in the hands of persons who are not medically qualified. A doctor treating himself, in a bona fide fashion, clearly meets the object of this provision. Like anyone else, a doctor who administers a drug to himself for a non-medical purpose, *e.g.* an attempt to commit suicide or simply to abuse the drug, cannot avail himself of the protection of regulation 10 and is accordingly guilty of an offence under section 5(2): see *Taylor* [1986] Crim.L.R. 680. 3–21

Regulation 10(2) is important for another but less obvious reason. One of the objects of the legislation is to ensure that those who require controlled substances for legitimate, medical, educational/research, or even industrial purposes, get them. There exists the obvious risk that controlled drugs will "leak" out of the category of persons entitled to possess them. The Regulations attempt to minimise that risk. Thus by Regulation 10(2), a patient should act in accordance with the "directions" of a practitioner. Often that will mean complying with the terms of a prescription. The expectation is that practitioners will be responsible to ensure that drugs are appropriately dispensed/prescribed by them, and that patients are indeed complying with their directions. The issuing of "repeat prescriptions" requires practitioners to be vigilant in ensuring that patient supervision is maintained, and that control is not lost.

(g) All persons may possess Schedule 5 drugs

3–22 By regulation 4(2)(b), all drugs specified in Schedule 5 to the 1985 Regulations are exempt from section 5(1) of the MDA. Accordingly, any person may possess such drugs.

Schedule 5 is set out below.

"Regulation 3 SCHEDULE 5

CONTROLLED DRUGS EXCEPTED FROM THE PROHIBITION ON IMPORTATION EXPORTATION AND POSSESSION AND SUBJECT TO THE REQUIREMENTS OF REGULATIONS 24 AND 25

1.—(1) Any preparation of one or more of the substances to which this paragraph 2 applies, not being a preparation designed for administration by injection, when compounded with one or more other active or inert ingredients and containing a total of not more than 100 milligrammes of the substance or substances (calculated as base) per dosage unit or with a total concentration of not more than 2.5 per cent (calculated as base) in undivided preparations.

(2) The substances to which this paragraph applies are acetylidhydrocodeine, codeine, dihydrocodeine, ethylmorphine, nicocodine, nicodicodine (6-nicotinoyldi-liydrocodeine), norcodeine, pholcodine, and their respective salts.

2. Any preparation of cocaine containing not more than 0.1 per cent of cocaine calculated as cocaine base, being a preparation compounded with one or more other active or inert ingredients in such a way that the cocaine cannot be recovered by readily applicable means or in a yield which would constitute a risk to health.

3. Any preparation of medicinal opium or of morphine containing (in either case) not more than 0.2 per cent of morphine calculated as anhydrous morphine base, being a preparation compounded with one or more other active inert ingredients in such a way that the opium or, as the case may be, the morphine, cannot be recovered by readily applicable means or in a yield which would constitute a risk to health.

4. Any preparation of dextropropoxyphene, being a preparation

designed for oral administration, containing not more than 135 milligrammes of dextropropoxyphene (calculated as base) per dosage unit or with a total concentration of not more than 2.5 per cent (calculated as base) in undivided preparations.

5. Any preparation of difenoxin containing, per dosage unit, not more than 0.5 milligrammes of difenoxin and a quantity of atropine sulphate equivalent to at least 5 per cent, of the dose of difenoxin.

6. Any preparation of diphenoxylate containing, per dosage unit, not more than 2.5 milligrammes of diphenoxylate calculated as base, and a quantity of atropine sulphate equivalent to at least 1 per cent of the dose of diphenoxylate.

7. Any preparation of propiram containing, per dosage unit, not more than 100 milligrammes of propiram calculated as base and compounded with at least the same amount (by weight) of methylcellulose.

8. Any powder of ipecacuanha and opium comprising—10 per cent opium, in powder, 10 per cent ipecacuanha root, in powder, well mixed with 80 per cent of any other powdered ingredient containing no controlled drug.

9. Any mixture containing one or more of the preparations specified in paragraphs 1 to 8, being a mixture of which none of the other ingredients is a controlled drug.

Duress of circumstances

There have been attempts to resist a conviction for possession of drugs (usually cannabis) on the basis that the defendant admits using the drug in order to treat a medical condition. The Independent Inquiry recommended that it should be a defence to possess cannabis for that purpose subject to certain conditions being met. At the moment, the defences to possession under the Misuse of Drugs Act are limited in scope, and therefore a number of defendants have sought to raise the defence of 'duress of circumstances' or 'necessity'. It is perhaps surprising that the Court of Appeal has not been asked to give a definitive judgment on the matter more than once, but the reason may be that juries often acquit such defendants where a serious medical condition does exist—although, it must be said, that such verdicts probably have more to say about compassion than applying the letter of the law. However, in *Huckell* (November 26, 1998), the Court of Appeal did make it clear that, in law, such a defence is not sustainable. 3–23

II. Unlawful Possession

(a) Two special cases of unlawful possession

At this stage, it is appropriate to look at two specific cases of unlawful possession. 3–24

(i) *"Double-scripting" nullifies lawful possession*

The purpose of the Regulations is to ensure that controlled drugs remain in the hands of those persons entitled to possess them and who will deal with them in a way that produces no harmful effects resulting in a social problem. Since regulation 10(2) gives all individuals the right to administer drugs specified in Schedule 2 and 3 in accordance with the directions of a practitioner, including controlled drugs supplied to them on prescription from a doctor, the object of the regulations would be defeated if users could simply increase their supply by obtaining prescriptions from more than one doctor at a time.

Accordingly, regulation 10(2) shall not have effect in the case of a person to whom the drug has been supplied by or on the prescription of a doctor if "(a) that person was then being supplied with any controlled drug by or on the prescription of another doctor and failed to disclose that fact to the first mentioned doctor before the supply by him or on his prescription". Thus, if A obtains drugs from Dr 1 and Dr 2, but fails to inform the latter of the prescription received from Dr 1, then A will be guilty of unlawfully possessing the drugs received from Dr 2. However, A will still be in lawful possession of the drugs received from Dr 1.

(ii) *Persons dishonestly obtaining drugs*

3–25 Furthermore, regulation 10(2) shall not have effect in the case of a person to whom the drug has been supplied by or on the prescription of a doctor if:

> "(b) that or any other person on his behalf made a declaration or statement which was false in any particular, for the purpose of obtaining the supply or prescription."

A person who falsely represents to a doctor that he is unable to sleep and needs a strong barbiturate, commits an offence contrary to section 5(1) if he obtains the drug to crush up and injects it for "kicks". The phrase "false in any particular" must refer to a material particular, the falsity of which was intended to induce the doctor to supply the controlled drug. Upon a literal construction of regulation 10(2)(b), the words " . . .for the purpose of obtaining . . ." mean that it is the intention of the recipient that is all-important. It would not be necessary to show that the doctor was in fact induced to supply the drug by the false particulars.

III. The General Principles of Possession

(a) The mental element of possession

3–26 Given that, in general terms, a person has in his possession whatever is in his physical custody or under his control, it may be thought that possession is a purely physical concept involving no mental ingredient at all whereas, in fact, the law separates the physical element of possession (the corpus) from the mental element (the *animus possidendi*), sometimes termed "the intention to possess". It must be emphasised that this does not mean that for the purposes of section 5 of the MDA, the prosecution must prove that the accused desired, wanted or assented to having a controlled drug in his custody or under his control. Once the prosecution have proved that the substance in question is a controlled drug, it is only necessary to prove that the accused knew of the existence of the article and that he exercised control over it: see *Lambert* (July 5, 2001, HL) in relation to defences under section 28 of the MDA.

In *Watson* (October 19, 1995, unreported) it was argued on behalf of the appellant that an intention to control the drugs was an essential ingredient of possession for the purposes of section 5. The Court of Appeal rejected this argument and the decision is explained in detail below. The *animus* is satisfied upon proof that the defendant has knowledge of the existence of the thing and that he is exercising control over it. "Control" means something more than mere acquiescence: there must be evidence of something positive, *e.g.* encouragement: see *Conway and Burkes* [1994] Crim. L.R. 826. As Professor Sir John Smith has pointed out in his commentary to this case the mental ingredient required to be proved in respect of an alleged secondary party may be different (and indeed more strict) than a principal charged with simple possession: note *Patel* [1970] Crim. L.R. 274 and *Fernandez* [1970] Crim. L.R. 277. It should be noted that it is not always necessary for the accused to know the quality of the thing that he has, or controls, in order to be in possession of it. For the purposes of the MDA 1971, the provisions of that Act make it plain that it is for the accused to discover for himself the nature of the substance, which he has. He will not be liable if he neither believed, nor suspected, nor had any reason to suspect that the substance was a controlled drug (s. 28(3)(b)(i)). By contrast, a mistake of fact as to the precise controlled drug possessed is no defence (see s. 28(3)(a)). However, since the provisions of the Act are superimposed on existing case law, it follows that the pre-Misuse of Drugs Act cases remain relevant. An examination of the earlier case law helps to explain the relationship between section 5 and section 28.

In *Warner v. Metropolitan Police Commissioner* [1969] 2 A.C. 256, W handled two boxes that he believed contained scent. In fact, one box contained amphetamine sulphate. W was charged with an offence under section 1 of the Drugs (Prevention of Misuse) Act 1964 (now repealed), which provided that "(1) . . . it shall not be lawful for a person to have in his possession a substance . . . specified in the Schedule to this Act . . .". The House of Lords held that the offence was absolute and did not require proof of *mens rea*. However, the prosecution was required to prove that the accused knew of the existence of the thing alleged, although a mistake as to its quality was generally no defence. Moreover, special considerations apply in connection with "container cases" and it was a defence for the accused to show that he believed the contents to be of a wholly different character. 3–27

Lord Reid observed (at 391) that:

> "As a legal term 'possession' is ambiguous at least to this extent: there

is no clear rule as to the nature of the mental element required. All are agreed that there must be some mental element in possession, but there is no agreement as to what precisely it must be. Indeed the view which prevailed in *R. v. Ashwell* (1885) 16 Q.B.D. 190, and was approved in *R. v. Hudson* [1943] 1 K.B. 458, went so far that a person who received a sovereign thinking it to be a shilling was held not to possess the sovereign until he discovered the mistake."

3–28 It will be observed from the above summary that four points emerge: (i) possession involves no *mens rea*, but (ii) knowledge of the existence of the thing is required, (iii) a mistake as to quality is no defence but (iv) belief that the contents of a container were of a wholly different character may be a defence. At first sight it may seem as if (i) and (ii) contradict each other, and that (iv) is an exception to the principle stated in (iii). However, it is important to emphasise that their lordships in relation to (ii) brought to the fore an essential legal component of possession, namely, the *animus* without adding any other mental ingredient except in relation to 'container' cases. In Lord Reid's example, a mistake was made as to the quality of the item—a mistake that, as we now know, would not usually result in a finding that the person holding the property was not in possession.

Lord Scarman remarked in *Boyesen* [1982] 2 All E.R. 161, 163g:

> "Possession is a deceptively simple concept. It denotes a physical control or custody of a thing plus knowledge that you have it in your custody or control. You may possess a thing without knowing or comprehending its nature; but you do not possess it unless you know you have it."

3–29 Lord Wilberforce in *Warner* referred to "the intention to possess"—a reference to the *animus possidendi* of possession. He then proceeded to give some guidance as to his definition of possession, and how a jury might be directed:

> ". . . the question, to which an answer is required, and in the end a jury must answer, is whether in the circumstances the accused should be held to have possession of the substance, rather than mere control. In order to decide between these two the jury should . . . be invited to consider all the circumstances—to use again the words of Pollock and Wright (*Possession In The Common Law*, p 119)—the 'modes or events' by which the custody commences the legal incident in which it is held. By these I mean, relating them to typical situations, that they must consider the manner and circumstances in which the substance, or something which contains it, has been received, what knowledge or means of knowledge or guilty knowledge as to the presence of the substance, or as to the nature of what has been received, the accused had at the time of receipt or thereafter up to the moment when he is found with it; his legal relation to the substance or package (including his right of access to it). On such matters as these (not exhaustively stated) they must make that the decision whether, in addition to phys-

ical control, he has, or all to have imputed to him, the intention to possess, or knowledge that he does possess, what is in fact a prohibited substance. If he has this intention or knowledge, it is not addition a necessary that he should know the nature of the substance."

Lord Morris in *Warner*, said the defendant must knowingly exercise control of the offending article (at 403–404; and see Professor Smith's commentary ([1988] Crim.L.R. 518)): 3–30

> "In my view in order to establish possession the prosecution must prove that an accused was knowingly in control of something in circumstances which showed that he was assenting to being in control of it; they need not prove that in fact he had actual knowledge of the nature of that which he had."

Lord Morris added, with particular relevance to container cases:

> ". . . there can be no rigid formula to be used in directing a jury. Varying sets of facts and circumstances will call for guidance on particular matters. The conception to be explained, however, will be that of being knowingly in control of the thing in circumstances which have involved an opportunity (whether availed of or not) to learn all to discover at least in a general way what the thing is."

Lord Pearce provided a description of possession ([1969] A.C. 256, at 305) that is perhaps the most satisfactory, and on which section 28 of the Misuse of Drugs Act was based: 3–31

> *"I think the term 'possession' is satisfied by knowledge only of the existence of the thing itself and not its qualities and that ignorance or mistake as to its qualities will not excuse. This would comply with a general understanding of the word 'possess'.* Though I reasonably believe the tablets which I possess to be aspirin, yet if they turn out to be heroin I am in possession of heroin tablets. This would be so, I think, even if I believe them to be sweets. It would be otherwise in I believe them to be something of a wholly different nature. At this point, a question of degree arises as to whether a difference in qualities amounts to a difference in kind. That is a matter for a jury who would probably decide it sensibly in favour of the genuinely innocent than against the guilty. The situation with regard to containers presents further problems. If a man is in possession of the contents of a package, prima facie his possession of the package leads to the strong inference that he is in possession of its contents. But can this be rebutted by evidence that he was mistaken as to its contents? As in the case of goods that have been 'planted' in his pocket without his knowledge, so I do not think that he is in possession of contents which are quite different in kind from what he believed." [emphasis added]

Accordingly, in *Warner*, the majority of their Lordships held that once possession is proved then the offence is absolute and no proof of *mens rea* is required. As we have seen, section 28 of the MDA now ameliorates some of the harshness of the decision in *Warner* by shifting the onus on to the accused to prove (evidential burden only: *Lambert*) that he did not believe, suspect or had reason to suspect that the substance in question was a controlled drug.

3–32 Lord Scarman, with whom their Lordships in that case concurred, adopted the description of possession given by Lord Wilberforce in *Warner v. M.P.C.* (who also heard *Boyesen*) when he said (at 310):

> "The question to which an answer is required . . . is whether in the circumstances the accused should be held to have possession of the substance rather than control. In order to decide between these two, the jury should, in my opinion, be invited to consider all the circumstances . . . the manner and circumstances in which the substance, or something which contains it, has been received. . . . On such matters as these (not exhaustively stated) they must make the decision whether, in addition to physical control, he has, *or ought to have imputed to him* the intention to possess, or knowledge that he does possess, what is in fact a prohibited substance. If he has this intention or knowledge, it is not additionally necessary that he should know the nature of the substance." [emphasis added]

As we shall see, Lord Reid's formulation of possession has proved problematic. There seems to be agreement that a person must know that he has the item in his custody or under his control, and the phrase "intention to possess" probably means no more than this. However, in what circumstances ought a person to have "imputed" to him that knowledge?

(b) The impact of section 28 of the Misuse of Drugs Act on the concept of possession

3–33 See Chapter 8 for a detailed explanation of section 28 and *Lambert* (July 5, 2001, HL).

In *Wright* (1975) 62 Cr.App.R. 169, CA the prosecution argued that the MDA redefined the word "possession", by virtue of the wording of section 28, to place the burden of proving a lack of knowledge firmly on the accused. The Court of Appeal did not think that the Crown's contention was correct but the Court was not prepared to make a decision on the point.

Section 28(2) reads as follows:

> "Subject to subsection (3) below, in any proceedings for an offence to which this section applies, it shall be a defence for the accused to prove that he neither knew of nor suspected nor had reason to suspect the existence of some fact alleged by the prosecution which it is necessary for the prosecution to prove if he is to be convicted of the offence charged."

3–34 The issue raised in *Wright* was whether an accused's knowledge of the existence of the offending article, is a "fact alleged by the prosecution which it is necessary for the prosecution to prove". If the answer is "no", then the burden of proving a lack of knowledge shifts to the accused by operation of section 28. The point was fully considered in *Ashton-Rickhardt* [1978] 1 All E.R. 173. The appellant was found asleep in his car. A cigarette, containing cannabis, was discovered in the vehicle. The trial judge directed the jury that "the burden of proof rests on the defendant . . . that he did not know it [the cigarette] was there". This was a clear misdirection in the light of *Warner* (and see *Smith* [1966] Crim.L.R. 588), but the Crown contended that section 28(2) altered the position. Roskill L.J., who delivered the judgment of the court, had no difficulty in rejecting the Crown's argument. He said (at 178d):

> "When one construes [sections 28(2) and (3)] in the 1971 Act together with section 5(1) and (2) and one realises that s.5(2) and indeed (3) are each made subject to s.28 of the Act, it is apparent that whatever the precise scope of the various subsections of s.28 may be, their manifest purpose is to afford a defence to an accused person where no defence had previously existed."

Section 28 provides shields. It does not lighten the burden carried by the 3–35
prosecution to prove the essential elements of possession.

The matter has also been concerned fairly recently in Scotland, where the judges in that jurisdiction have reached a similar view. The difference in Scotland relates to the application and scope of section 28 (considered in detail in a separate chapter). Thus, in *Salmon v. H.M. Advocate*, 1999 S.L.T. 169, at 175, the Lord Justice General reviewed the authorities and said:

> ". . . under the 1964 Act, on the other hand, there was never any doubt that the burden approving the necessary knowledge and control rested on the Crown. With the advent of section 28 of the 1971 Act, however, the Crown began to argue that the effect of section 28(2) had been to shift the onus in regard to proving the necessary knowledge from the Crown to the defence . . . not surprisingly, this kind of argument provoked a strong reaction from the courts, both in Scotland and in England. They rejected the arguments for the Crown and affirmed that section 28(2) did not shift the onus proving knowledge onto the defence (*Mackenzie v Skeen* 1983 S.L.T. 121, *per* the Lord Justice General (at 121)) in Scotland and *Ashton-Rickhardt*, *per* Roskill L.J. ((1977) 65 Cr.App.R. at 67) in England). The courts were plainly right to reject the Crown's argument: as Roskill L.J. pointed out, the manifest purpose of section 28 was not place a new onus on an accused person but 'to afford a defence to an accused person where no defence had previously existed'."

The Lord Justice General then went on to point out the divergence of 3–36
views held in England and Scotland respectively as to the effect of section 28:

> "... Unfortunately, having rejected the extreme argument advanced by the Crown as to the effect of section 28(2), the courts seem to have felt that there was no place left for that subsection in a system, such as they envisaged, where the burden of proving the necessary knowledge and control continued to rest on the Crown. Hence, subsection (2) disappeared from view. Once the proper but limited range of section 28(3) is appreciated, however, there is no inconsistency in holding both that the burden of proving the necessary knowledge and control rests on the Crown and the section 28(2) has a distinct role to play."

A little later, in the judgment of the Lord Justice General, he said this:

> "I consider that in *McNamara* the appellant required to bring himself within the scope of section 28(2) rather than of section 28(3)(b)(i). A similar approach has been adopted in Scotland. In a passage in his opinion in *Mackenzie v. Skeen* which is not reproduced in the Scots Law Times report, the Lord Justice General remarked: "in most cases possession of container will support the inference of possession of his actual contents but it must always be a question to be decided in the particular circumstances of the particular case"."

It will be seen in Chapter 8, dealing with section 28, that the analysis in the Scottish courts on the effect of that section is not without its problems.

(b) What the prosecution must prove

3–37 As we have noted, three ingredients are required to be proved, by the prosecution, before an offence under section 5(2) is made out:

- (i) the item must be in the physical custody or control of the accused (note the word "or": see *Pentecost* (March 10, 1998, CA);
- (ii) the accused must know, or at least could reasonably have known, of the existence of the item: see *Lewis* (1988) 87 Cr.App.R. 270; and
- (iii) the item must be a controlled drug.

Ideally, one would prefer to examine the authorities in respect of each ingredient in isolation, but this approach is not appropriate since the first two ingredients heavily overlap. For this reason (although it is essential to keep the three ingredients very much in the forefront of one's mind) a better approach is to examine seven typical situations, namely, where:

1. The defendant knows of the existence of the thing and he has the custody or control of it.
2. The defendant has no knowledge of the thing, or article, and therefore he is not in a position to exercise control over it.
3. The defendant has the custody of, or general control over, a number of articles but he does not know of the existence of the offending article.

(4) The defendant knows of the existence of the thing but he does not exert any control over it.
(5) The defendant knows of the existence of the thing and he has custody or control, but he makes a mistake as to its quality.
(6) The defendant has the custody, or control, of a container but he has no knowledge of its contents.
(7) The quantity is so minute that the presence of the drug indicates no more than previous possession.

(i) *Proof of knowledge and control*

Few problems are likely to be encountered in cases where an accused had custody of a controlled drug or exercised control over it. However, prosecutors have a duty to ensure that the accused is charged appropriately. Thus, in *Muir v. Smith* [1978] Crim.L.R. 293, DC, the defendant was charged with being in possession of "cannabis resin". Police searched the defendant's flat and found 20 micrograms of cannabis, which could have been herbal cannabis, or resin. There was no doubt that the defendant was in possession of some kind of cannabis. The Divisional Court held that the conviction had to be quashed because herbal cannabis and resin were two very different substances. 3–38

However, if the prosecutor had amended the charge to read "a quantity of cannabis or cannabis resin" then it is difficult to see what answer the defendant would have had to the charge. Indeed, in *Best* (1979) 70 Cr.App.R. 21, the Court of Appeal so held when dismissing appeals against conviction by five appellants who had been charged with possession of "cannabis or cannabis resin". The scientific evidence was that the drug found was either of those two substances. The charge was held not to be bad for duplicity and reliance on rule 7 of the Indictment Rules 1971 was not necessary.

The trial judge must ensure that when the jury are directed on the definition of possession that they be told that there are two very separate elements, namely, that there must be knowledge and control. The judge must also ensure that the directions in respect of these two elements are sufficient in the circumstances: *Martin v. H.M. Advocate* (1992) S.C.C.R. 356; *Martin v. H.M. Advocate*, 1989 S.C.C.R. 546 distinguished. 3–39

Knowledge and control may be inferred from the surrounding circumstances. Thus, in *McGill v. MacDougall*, 1993 G.W.D. 2456, the High Court held that both elements could be inferred from M's responses to police that he knew of the existence of cannabis resin in a drawer in M's kitchen and that M exercised control over the drug. M's answers were such that on his account only M or the police could have put the drug into the drawer: and see *Marshall (Tina)* (March 31, 1999), and *Reid v Buchanan*, 2000 S.C.C.R. 747, as other examples of knowledge and control.

In *McGill (David Alexander) v. H.M. Advocate*, 2000 S.C.C.R. 253, the Court dismissed M's appeal against his conviction for being concerned in the unlawful supply of drugs worth £67,000, that had been secreted behind the dashboard of M's car. M claimed that there was insufficient evidence to prove that he knew of the presence of the drug. The Court held that the evidence was capable of excluding the likelihood of anyone putting the drugs in the car before M obtained it. The previous owner denied that the drugs were his or that he put them behind the dashboard. M's reaction when stopped by police and his lack of surprise when they discovered the drugs, were significant and relevant. A police officer testified that it would be highly unusual for anyone to conceal drugs in another person's vehicle even if the car was not secured. It is perhaps surprising that the officer was permitted to give that evidence.

3–40 Again, in *McAllan v HM Advocate*, 1996 S.C.C.R. 899, the police discovered 100 amphetamine tablets in a cigarette packet in a car that had been driven by M some six days before the police searched the car. The car had been involved in an accident and taken to a compound for repairs. There was evidence that the compound was not totally secure as a small person was able to crawl under the gate and occasionally property had been stolen from cars kept there. However, the defendant's home address (which he shared with his girlfriend) was searched, and a large sum of money was found there. M's appeal against his conviction for being concerned in the supply of a controlled drug was dismissed on the grounds that M's case was fanciful and the prosecution were not required to call more evidence than did to rebut the defendant's explanation.

3–41 Again, in *Brown v. Neizer*, 1995 G.W.D. 118, it was held that sufficient evidence existed to establish joint possession against B and C in circumstances where the drugs were found on C but both men appeared nervous and looked furtively at each other. B was found in possession of cigarette papers marked with a cannabis motif and other drug paraphernalia. When questioned, B said "I know what you are talking about but it's nothing to do with me . . . I wasn't in control of it."

In *McTurk v. H.M. Advocate*, 1997 S.C.C.R. 1, it was held that there is no absolute rule that evidence of possession will be insufficient if more than one person had access to the premises or article in question where the drugs were found. Every case will turn on its own facts and much will depend on the nature and extent of any access by a third party. In that case the sheriff rejected a submission of no case to answer in respect of controlled drugs found in a purse belonging to the defendant. She had lost her purse at a nightclub, but the purse was handed in to the office by a member of staff, and the drugs, along with a large quantity of cash and credit cards, were found in the purse soon after the defendant claimed it as hers. It was contended that the prosecution could not prove that the defendant had the necessary knowledge and control to establish possession of the controlled drug on the basis that the purse might have been tampered with by a third party. This, in the Court's opinion, and was not a realistic suggestion.

(ii) *No knowledge of the thing*

3–42 Suppose D attends a party at which a number of guests are smoking cigarettes. The police raid the premises and a quantity of "joints" containing cannabis are found. If D does not know of the existence of the "joints", he cannot be said to be in possession of the drug contained in them. The position would be different if, upon the arrival of police, the accused unwittingly picked up the offending cigarettes in order to try to "tidy up". In the eyes of the law, D will now be in possession of the cigarettes including the drug. Accordingly, D's possession will be unlawful unless he can prove, under section 28, that he neither believed, suspected, nor had reason to suspect that the cigarettes contained a controlled drug. In *Searle v. Randolph* [1972] Crim.L.R. 779, DC, D picked up a number of cigarette ends in a tent used by a number of individuals. One cigarette contained cannabis. He was convicted on the basis that he had the drug in his custody and a mistake as to the quality of the substance was (at that time) no defence. Of course, he would now have a defence under section 28.

The crucial fact in *Searle v. Randolph* is that D knew of the existence of the articles, *i.e.* the cigarettes when he picked them up. Had he left them untouched, he would only have had a general interest in the contents of the tent, which would not have been sufficiently specific to amount to control.

Where *unsolicited* goods containing drugs are delivered to an individual's address, in the absence of the addressee, he is clearly not able to exercise control over them (by reason of his absence) and therefore he cannot be said to have custody or control over them until he returns and becomes aware of their existence. These principles are clearly demonstrated in *Cavendish* [1961] 1 W.L.R. 1083, a case involving the receipt of stolen property, in which it was held that in order to prove possession, something more must be proved in addition to the goods being found on the defendant's premises: namely, that upon his return he became aware of their presence and exercised some control over them, directly or indirectly. The point to note is that Cavendish was not responsible for the delivery of the goods. He was not exercising control. However, if goods are solicited, having been ordered by D, then the opposite is true and the fact that D is absent from the premises at the time of delivery can be no defence (and see *Murray v McPhail*, 1991 S.C.C.R. 245). D may not know of the time or the day of delivery, but it was he who ensured its delivery. He was in control. Accordingly, if the packet contains a controlled drug, D is guilty of unlawful possession, unless he can avail himself of a defence under section 28. 3–43

In *Peaston* (1978) 69 Cr.App.R. 203, P occupied a bed-sit in a house made up of such accommodation. He received through the post a package containing amphetamine that he had ordered. P was unaware of its arrival. Police arrived shortly after it was delivered and handed the package to P who then opened it. He was charged and convicted of being in unlawful possession of the drugs.

Held: the conviction was right. P had ordered the drugs.

(iii) *General control but no knowledge*

The prosecution must prove that the defendant knew of the existence of the offending article. Thus, in *Bath v. H.M. Advocate*, 1995 G.W.D. 642, 3–44 police found a Class A drug under a cover of the windscreen wiper of a motor vehicle that was kept for repair in a garage rented by B. Both B and his father were seen working in the garage. It could not be determined whether B or his father concealed the drug and accordingly there was insufficient evidence to show that B knew of the existence of the offending substance and B's conviction for unlawful possession was quashed (and see *McAllan v H.M. Advocate* 1996 S.C.C.R. 899.

There will often be cases where D exercises control over a considerable number of goods, not all of which he necessarily knows exist. In *Lockyer v. Gibb* [1967] 2 Q.B. 243, the defendant was stopped by police. She had in her possession a holdall containing many items including a paper bag that contained a bottle in which white tablets were visible. The tablets were morphine sulphate. The defendant knew of the existence of the tablets but there was a possibility that she did not know that the tablets contained a prohibited substance. Her conviction, for the unlawful possession of morphine, was upheld. D was clearly aware of the existence of the tablets. She therefore exercised clear control over them. Her mistake as to the nature of the tablets was purely a mistake as to quality, which, at that time, afforded D no defence. Now she would have a defence under section 28. However, Lord Parker C.J. remarked: "If something were slipped into your basket and you had not the vaguest notion it was there at all, you could not possibly be said to be in possession of it."

3–45 It is not difficult to see how such a set of facts might arise in practice. For example, D arrives in the United Kingdom, having travelled from Morocco by air. X, a passenger on the same flight, and fearing detection, slips two slabs of cannabis resin into D's wicker basket before D enters the "nothing to declare" channel. D certainly has control over the basket and has an interest in the contents. In the ordinary way, one would say that D "possesses" the contents. So why should D escape conviction under section 5(2)? The answer is that since possession requires an *animus* (see *Warner* and note *Watson*, October 19, 1995, unreported), it follows that custody or control is subject to the knowledge that one has something that is additional to those articles that one already knows to exist. Thus, in *Searle v. Randolph* the defendant knew of the existence of cigarette ends (the articles) but only made a mistake as to the quality of the "tobacco". However, in our example, D knew she possessed the wicker basket and certain contents but not the slabs of resin that another person had put there.

The same reasoning probably explains the decision in *Irving* [1970] Crim.L.R. 642, CA. The defendant was in possession of a bottle of stomach pills but one tablet was heroin. He said that his wife must have put it there. His conviction was quashed since there was no evidence that he knew of its existence. He knew of the existence of the bottle and the stomach pills but that was all.

3–46 The same principles apply to all situations in which an individual has general custody of a number of items, some of which he knows to exist and others, which he does not. In *Warner*, the House of Lords approved that part of the judgment of Lord Parker C.J., in *Lockyer v. Gibb*, when he said: it is quite clear that a person cannot be said to be in possession of some article which he or she does not realise is, or may be, in her handbag, in her room, or in some other place over which she had control.

The classic situation is a house used and occupied by a number of individuals.

> In *Smith* [1966] Crim.L.R. 588, CA, police found Indian hemp in a room at a house where S was arrested. The room was used in common by all the people living in the house but the judge directed the jury that they could convict if they concluded that "she did live in that room and had an interest in it so that she controlled all the things that were in it".
>
> *Held*: the direction was defective since it did not go far enough to demonstrate control and the judge had not dealt with the issue of knowledge at all. S had a general interest in the room but that was all.

Smith is therefore distinguishable from *Searle v. Randolph* (cigarette ends in a tent) where the defendant, in *Searle v. Randolph*, knew of the existence of the articles, *i.e.* the cigarettes, when he picked them up. There is, of course, an apparent conflict between the results in *Irving, Smith*, the *dictum* of Lord Parker C.J. in *Lockyer v. Gibb* on the one hand, and the result of *Searle v. Randolph* on the other hand. Thus, if Irving was not in possession of a tablet, which he did not know existed in the bottle, then why should D, in *Searle v. Randolph*, be in possession of the cannabis, which, again, he did not know existed in the cigarette? In both cases, the offending material was held in a container over which the accused exercised custody and/or control. Why, then, was there a different result? The admittedly subtle distinction is that if the drug and the remaining articles are blended to form one substance then that is the commodity over which control is exercised. If the accused therefore knows of the existence of the blend (albeit that he may not appreciate its real quality), then he will have the necessary knowledge to put him in possession of it. In *Irving*, and *Smith*, the drug had a separate and distinct existence from its neighbouring articles. The issue was whether the defendant knew of the existence of the thing that was, in fact, a controlled drug and, if he did do so, whether he exercised control over it. By contrast, in *Searle v. Randolph* the tobacco and cannabis were mixed to form (in reality) one substance. The distinction is capable of producing curious results. If D is given a parcel which, upon examination, is found to contain two bags, one containing flour and the other containing heroin, it seems that D will not be guilty of possessing the heroin if he only knows of the existence of the bag of flour. It is for the prosecution to prove that the defendant had the necessary *animus* in respect of each commodity. However, if both drugs had been blended and put into the parcel, D would be in possession of the blend even though he believed the entire substance to be flour: he made a mere mistake as to quality. In these circumstances the evidential burden would therefore be on the defendant to prove, under section 28, that he did not have reason to suspect that the substance included a controlled drug. 3–47

3–48 The point is again demonstrated in *Marriott* [1971] 1 W.L.R. 187:

> Police searched M's flat. M was found to be in possession of a pen-knife. On the blade, forensic scientists detected the presence of cannabis resin. The judge directed the jury that if M was in possession of the knife then even if he did not know of the existence of the material on the blade, he was guilty of possessing what turned out to be cannabis resin. The Court of Appeal held that the judge misdirected the jury. M had to be aware of the existence of some foreign matter on the knife. It was not enough for M to know of the existence of the knife, he also had to know of the existence of the extra substance as well. If he did know of its existence but simply thought that the substance was toffee, his mistake would merely be one of quality. Once again, by virtue of section 28, the evidential burden would now be on the accused to prove a lack of knowledge: see also *Coffey v. Douglas*, May 20, 1976, unreported.

3–49 **The problem of drug traces.** Section 5(1) makes it unlawful to possess "any controlled drug". Strictly interpreted, that phrase means that the actual quantity involved is irrelevant. Unfortunately, the courts became confused as to whether a person can properly be said to be in possession of a drug (for the purposes of section 5) if the quantity involved is so small that it cannot be seen with the naked eye or that it can only be detected by the use of precise scientific equipment. Alternatively, it has been queried whether a person can properly be said to be in possession if the drug is capable of being weighed or otherwise measured but is merely too small to be of any practical value to a drug abuser. In a bid to mitigate the strictness of section 5, some courts effectively attempted to add words to section 5(1) in order to give effect to the spirit of the MDA. Thus, in *Worsell* [1970] 1 W.L.R. 111:

> W was found in possession of a tube that was apparently empty. However, a few droplets of heroin were detected under a microscope.
>
> *Held*: that the tube was in reality empty and therefore the prosecution could not prove that there was any drug for the defendant to possess at the time of his arrest. However, there would have been no defence if the charge were amended to cover possession at an earlier stage.

The conclusion that the tube was in reality empty is, of course, a fiction since the drug exists as a trifling amount. The courts refined this approach until they developed a so-called "usability" test. By virtue of this test, a person could only be in possession of the drug if it was either usable or sufficiently great to amount to "something". The House of Lords in *Boyesen* [1982] A.C. 768 later rejected the usability test. There really was no need to create the fiction in the first instance. In cases where presence of the drug is so minute as to be unusable or even (following *Worsell*) practically "non-existent", the prosecution is unlikely to be able to prove that an accused knew of the existence of the drugs. It is the issue of knowledge that would normally be at the heart of the case. In *Worsell*, W knew of the existence of the tube but that was all. He could only be guilty if he knew that he had, or controlled, something else, *i.e.* some substance or matter that in fact turned out to be a controlled drug. However, he did not know any such thing. If a scientist would not have known of the presence of a drug without the use of special equipment, it is difficult to understand how it can be proved that the accused would have known of its existence.

Stinson J. upheld a submission of no case to answer in *Colyer* [1974] Crim.L.R. 243, where C possessed a pipe that was forensically examined. The scientist could not see anything in it but, by an elaborate process, approximately a millionth of an ounce of cannabis was found. There was no evidence that C knew of its existence albeit he exercised control of the pipe. 3–50

A similar submission was upheld in *Hieorowski* [1978] Crim.L.R. 563, where H admitted that three reefer ends were his. The presence of the drug was only detected by an elaborate chemical process. It could not be presumed that H would have been aware of such small amounts for had that been his state of mind, then he would probably have smoked the remainder.

One can only wonder whether the result in *Searle v. Randolph*, or *Muir v. Smith* [1978] Crim.L.R. 293, DC (20 micrograms of cannabis), would have been the same if a similar point had been taken on behalf of the defence.

Whether an amount is so small that the prosecution cannot establish a *prima facie* case of knowledge is a matter of degree and is to be determined by the trial judge: see *Webb* [1979] Crim.L.R. 462 (0.4 milligrams and 0.6 milligrams of cannabis not enough).

It may be thought that, by virtue of section 28, the burden is on the defendant to show that he had no reason to suspect the presence of the trace, but this is not so. It is for the prosecution to establish a prima facie case in respect of all three ingredients to prove possession. Only when the prosecution succeeds in so doing, does section 28 come into play.

Can possession be "lost" by forgetfulness? The point arose in the interesting case of *Buswell* [1972] 1 W.L.R. 64: 3–51

> B, a drug addict, was prescribed 70 amphetamine tablets by his doctor. He put the tablets in his jeans. His mother washed the jeans. B, assuming the tablets to have been washed away, obtained a second prescription. He later found the original tablets in a drawer. The police made a search of B's home and found the drugs.
>
> *Held*: *inter alia*, that where a person in lawful possession of the drugs forgot their existence, he remained in possession of them. They were still in his custody. B's conviction was quashed. The authorities of *Warner v. Metropolitan Police Commissioner* and *Lockyer v. Gibb* [1967] 2 Q.B. 213 were referred to in the judgment. Phillimore L.J. held that those two cases dealt with something "very different, *i.e.* the question whether an article ever came into the individual's possession at all". The example was given of the drug slipped into somebody's

> pocket without that person's knowledge. The Court distinguished that situation from *Buswell*'s case where the article was "undoubtedly in B's possession".

At this stage, it is worth bearing in mind that two separate considerations arose in *Buswell*. The first concerned the validity of the prescription, *i.e.* whether the legality of the original prescription was destroyed by the obtaining of a second prescription, and secondly, whether the accused continued to possess the drugs. If he did, and if the prescription was no longer valid, then his possession of the drugs would have been unlawful. In respect of the first point the Court found nothing to show that the prescription was not, as it were, still "lawful".

Accordingly, since B had originally been in lawful possession of the drugs because of the earlier prescription, his right to possess those drugs under the prescription was not lost by his forgetfulness, or his mistaken belief that they had been destroyed.

3–52 That leaves the second point. The prosecution had contended that B had "lost" his original possession when he believed that the drugs were destroyed. Phillimore L.J. questioned whether possession could have been in a state of limbo and added:

> ". . . it is idle to say that if mistakenly you think your mother has dissolved the tablets which you put in the pocket of your jeans, whereas in fact they are still in the drawer, they have in some way passed out of your possession. They have never left your care and control accordingly, you are in possession."

The Court of Appeal in *Martindale* [1986] 1 W.L.R. 1042 followed the reasoning in *Buswell*, holding that possession did not depend on the alleged possessor's power of memory. In *Martindale*, M was given a piece of cannabis, in Canada, in 1983. Two years later, he was arrested in the United Kingdom and searched by police. The officers discovered the cannabis in his wallet. M had forgotten all about it although he admitted that he had put it there some two years previously. Lord Lane C.J. delivered the judgment of the Court and said:

> "In our judgment, he remained in possession, even though his memory of the presence of the drug had faded or disappeared altogether. Possession does not depend on the alleged possessor's powers of memory. Nor does possession come and go as memory revives or fails. If it were to do so, a man with a poor memory would be acquitted, he with the good memory would be convicted."

3–53 The Court of Appeal had been referred to *Russell* (1985) 81 Cr.App.R. 315, which the court declined to follow and implied that *Russell* was wrongly decided. However, in *Russell*, the Court of Appeal was concerned with a charge of possession of an offensive weapon, namely a cosh, which was under the driver's seat of a car driven by the defendant. Jupp J. delivered the judgment of the Court in *Russell*, and said: "It would in our judgment be wrong to hold that a man knowingly has a weapon with him if his forgetfulness of its existence or presence in his car is so complete as to amount to ignorance that it is there at all."

In *Martindale*, the Court of Appeal had little doubt that if the court in *Russell* had been referred to *Buswell* the decision " would almost certainly have gone the other way". However, why should that have been the case? As the Court of Appeal pointed out in *McCalla* (1988) 87 Cr. App. R. 372, what is relevant to a charge under section 1(1) of the Prevention of Crimes Act 1953 (which, insofar as it is material, reads "any person who has with him any offensive weapon") is having the offensive weapon in a public place and to have something with one necessarily required closer contact than a person in possession of something. Nevertheless, in *McCalla*, the Court thought that in either case, considerations of forgetfulness and recollection were the same and held that *Russell* was decided *per incuriam*:

> "... once someone had or possessed something, be it offensive weapons or drugs he continued to have or possess it until something was done by him or another to rid him of it. Mere forgetting that one had possession, having once had possession knowingly, was not enough to prevent the state of possessing continuing" *per* May L.J. and see *Wright* [1992] Crim. L.R. 596.

In *Cugullere* [1961] 1 W.L.R. 858, it was held that the words of s.1(1) of the 1953 Act mean "knowingly has with him in any public place" and that it was for the prosecution to prove knowledge and see *Harrison* [1996] Crim. L.R. 200. "Knowingly", for the purposes of that statute means, it would seem, the first occasion on which the defendant knew he had the offensive weapon with him in a public place. In *McCalla*, the Court said that their reasoning did not detract at all from the decision in *Cugullere* that could be distinguished on its facts in that there was no knowledge of the offending article from the outset so that it was not a question of forgetting possession after obtaining it. It is debatable whether it was necessary for the Court to try to equate the concept of possession with the rather more immediate state of affairs associated with the phrase "[knowingly] has with him". Possession requires an *animus possidendi* (the intention to possess in the sense that one has knowledge of the existence of the thing) and once this intent is formed, it is easy to see how, logically, such a state of mind cannot be destroyed by merely forgetting that one has the thing in question. The reasoning of the Court of Appeal in *Martindale* was followed in *Gill v. Lockhart*, 1987 S.C.C.R. 599. In that case, police found a piece of cannabis resin wrapped in cling film in a pocket of a golf bag in the appellant's room. He had placed it in there some two years earlier and had forgotten about it. The Court held that the appellant had the necessary *mens rea*, which continued to be applied to the physical possession throughout the whole period. 3–54

Knowledge and imputed knowledge. The question that arises here is whether the accused must have actual knowledge of the existence of the 3–55 offending substance or whether there are circumstances, in which the requisite knowledge may be imputed. In *Warner v. Metropolitan Police Commissioner* [1969] 2 A.C. 256, Lord Reid said (at 279): "The object of the legislation is to penalise possession of certain drugs. . . . And it is a commonplace that, if the accused had a suspicion but deliberately shut his eyes, the court or jury is well entitled to hold him guilty." With respect, Lord Wilberforce's description of possession (although it seems currently to represent the law) goes much further than the description of possession expressed by Lord Morris and Lord Pearce. The speeches on this aspect are difficult if not impossible to reconcile. On what basis should a defendant have imputed to him an intention that he does not in fact have? Is "imputed intention" not a contradiction in terms? It may be that imputed knowledge means no more than wilfully shutting one's eyes to the obvious. It would be one way of proving knowledge.

In *Lewis*, L was the sole tenant of a house that was searched by police in L's absence. The police found 42.5 grams of amphetamine sulphate and one milligram of cannabis resin. L claimed that he never intended to live there and that he only went to the premises occasionally. He never looked in the cupboards and he never suspected the presence of drugs. The Court of Appeal held that it was not necessary to direct the jury that they had to be satisfied that the defendant had actual knowledge that the drugs were under his control before they could convict. The question is whether the defendant is proved to have, or ought to have imputed to him, either the intention to possess or the knowledge that he possessed what was in fact a prohibited substance. It is not necessary for the jury to be directed that they had to be satisfied that the defendant had actual knowledge that he had the drugs in question under his control before they could convict. Professor Sir John Smith has suggested that this conclusion was wrong (see [1994] Crim. L.R. 826). See also B. Boulter, "Possession of Drugs," L.S.Gaz., November 23, 1988, and *McKenzie v. Sheen*, 1983 S.L.T. 121, and *Bland* [1988] Crim.L.R. 41, para. 3–53, below.

3–56 In *Murray v. MacPhail* [1991] S.C.C.R. 245, the appellant agreed with his co-accused that the latter could conceal cannabis in the appellant's room while the appellant was on holiday. The appellant expected the cannabis to have been removed by the time he returned. The appellant returned as police were searching his room during the course of which 21 grams of cannabis were found under his bed. On appeal, it was not disputed that the appellant had control of the cannabis because it was in his room. The Court held that the element of knowledge was satisfied by the appellant's consent to the hiding of the drugs in his room. His consent imported the necessary knowledge.

It is submitted that this case is not straightforward and should be read with the case of *Lewis* (1988) 87 Cr.App.R. 270 in mind. The appellant was absent when the drugs were placed under the bed. The appellant's room had no lock and access could easily be gained. The Court concluded that the appellant had allowed the drugs to come into his possession, and control, by virtue of the standing arrangement he had with the co-accused.

Although such a "standing arrangement" may be evidence of control, it does not necessarily prove knowledge of the existence of the offending substance. The co-accused may change his mind and not take advantage of the standing arrangement. The defendant may or may not be mistaken in his belief that the co-accused has concealed drugs in accordance with the open-ended arrangement. The Court dismissed the appeal on the narrow basis that the cannabis had been put beneath his bed by the co-accused with the consent of the appellant. However, the appellant's state of mind was no more than merely anticipatory. There is a world of difference between a mere intention to possess and proof that the defendant had actual knowledge of the offending substance under his control before the Court can convict. If all that is required to be proved is an intention to possess then the result in *Murray v. MacPhail* (above) was a foregone conclusion. The appellant's consent to the hiding of drugs in his room amounted (at the very least) to an intention to possess.

The better view is that an accused must know of the existence of the thing which he controls, albeit that he may be mistaken as to its precise quality (see s. 28 of the MDA in this context). In so far as references, in *Warner*, to "imputed knowledge" have any place in this area of the law, they should be confined, it is submitted, to so-called "container cases" where it is presumed that a person in possession of a container may be presumed to possess the contents as well: see para. 3–68, *et seq*. Establishing what amounts to a "container" for this purpose may not always be straightforward and it may be that the Court in *Lewis* regarded the contents of a house as falling into that category. 3–57

In *Watson* (October 19, 1995, unreported) police officers found 28 grams of cannabis and 49 squares of LSD beneath a seat cushion of a chair in the living room. More cannabis was found in a jar in the kitchen. The house was occupied by W, his wife and their children. W looked embarrassed and uncomfortable when he was told that the police intended to search the premises. The Court held that possession exists if a defendant has knowledge and control. The Court pointed out that section 5 of the 1971 Act contains two defences (*i.e.* s. 5(4)), which the Act of 1964 did not contain when *Warner* was decided. Thus a person may take possession of drugs for the purpose of destroying them or giving them to, say, a police officer in order to prevent another from committing an offence (see s. 5(4)(a)) or in order to give the drugs to a person lawfully entitled to take custody of them (s. 5(4)(b)). Perhaps the thinking of the Court, in referring to section 5(4), was to demonstrate that but for the statutory protection, a person who took control over the substances knowing that they were controlled drugs would be guilty of an offence under section 5(2) of the 1971 Act. Section 5(4) merely adds defences that did not previously exist. That section, in common with section 28, does not alter in any way the definition of possession. The simple solution is to equate the phrase "an intention to possess" (*i.e.* the *animus*) with proof of knowledge of the existence of the thing which is under the control of the accused.

3–58 The Court did not refer to *Conway and Burkes* [1994] Crim. L.R. 826 or to *Lewis* (1988) 87 Cr. App. R. 270.

In *McNamara* (1988) 87 Cr.App.R. 246 it was said, correctly, that a person does not have possession of something that had been put into his pocket or house without his knowledge. That proposition is consistent with some of the speeches of their Lordships in *Warner* [1969] 2 A.C. 256, *per* Lord Pearce at 302 and Lord Morris at 283. However, Lord Wilberforce said that the jury "must make the decision whether, in addition to physical control [the defendant] has, or ought to have imputed to him, the intention to possess, or knowledge that he does possess, what is in fact a prohibited substance". This description of "possession" was adopted by Lord Scarman in *Boyesen* [1982] A.C. 768 and by the Court of Appeal in *Lewis* (1988) 87 Cr.App.R. 270.

3–59 **Further examples of control.** In *Feeney v. Jessop*, 1990 S.C.C.R. 565, F was convicted of possessing a small quantity of cannabis resin lying on his towel which was on a central heating pipe alongside the bed he was lying on. When charged, F said, "So it's my towel. I'm saying fuck all". The court held that the absence of any explanation from F was not evidence of knowledge, but that the place where the drugs were found coupled with the power F had to remove the drugs from the towel, and the relationship of the drug and towel to the place where the appellant was lying before the search began, was ample evidence of knowledge and control and therefore possession: see *Crowe v. MacPhail*, 1987 S.L.T. 316, *Mackay v. Hogg*, 1973 S.C.C.R. Supp. 41 and see *Douglas v. Normand*, 1994 G.W.D. 1108 where the Court held that there was ample evidence of knowledge and control to demonstrate possession of amphetamine found in a drawer containing female clothing in the sole bedroom of a house occupied by the female defendant.

Again, in *Davidson v. H.M. Advocate*, 1990 S.C.C.R. 699, police found cannabis under the bed of the co-defendant. Beside the bed, police found a set of electronic scales, which D had bought. D did not live in the co-defendant's house but he was in the bedroom when the police arrived and he had visited the premises in order to get cannabis. When the police entered the bedroom D climbed out of the window. The Court held that the facts amounted to sufficient evidence of possession to go before the jury. The evidence was the slightest but the High Court seem to have regarded the appellant's flight from the premises as being evidence from which the jury could infer control of the drug under the bed.

3–60 In *Hughes v. Guild*, 1990 S.L.T. 715, the two appellants were charged with the unlawful possession of cannabis resin contrary to section 5(2) of the MDA 1971. The appellants lived together and were the only persons to occupy a house searched by police in which two small pieces of cannabis resin were found on the mantelpiece in the living room, and traces of cannabis were found on a knife lying in front of the fireplace. Two torn packets of cigarette papers were found in the living room. The High Court held that there was sufficient evidence of possession and control because (i) all the relevant articles were lying in the open in their own living room; (ii) the appellants were the only persons occupying the house; and (iii) if they knew that the drugs were in their own room they could have picked them up and done with them what they wished. The High Court correctly observed that each case must be decided on its own facts but that cases of joint occupancy are no different from any other case in which the elements of knowledge and control must be established by inference. In some cases, it may be possible to distinguish the position of one occupier from another if drugs are concealed or if one occupier is absent at the crucial time, or where the fact that others have access to the premises makes it unreasonable to attribute knowledge or control to the occupiers.

Thus, *Hughes v. Guild* was distinguished in *Bain v. H.M. Advocate*, 1992 G.W.D. 1534, where B was a regular visitor to premises occupied by B's girlfriend and B's co-defendant S. B attended the premises at least once a week. Drugs were found in open view on a shelf in an alcove. The High Court held that B's involvement with the house was insufficient to enable the Court to draw the inference that B was equivalent to an occupier and thus in control of the premises or its contents, and see *Lustmann v. Stewart*, 1971 S.L.T. 58 and *Mingay v. Mackinnon*, 1980 J.C. 33.

(iv) *Knowledge of the substance but no control*

Mere knowledge of the presence of the offending substance is not enough because the person must be in a position to exercise practical control over it in some way: see *Black v. H.M. Advocate*, 1974 S.L.T. 247 and *Hughes v. Guild*, 1990 S.C.C.R. 527. **3–61**

Joint possession. So far, we have been looking at examples where only one person is said to be in physical custody or control of the drug. Not infrequently, the suggestion is that a number of people are in joint possession. A typical situation is that of a police raid at a dwelling house occupied by a number of residents and a quantity of a drug is found. The police may not be in a position to say to whom the drug belongs but they do find signs of communal living coupled with evidence of communal drug abuse. It may well be that all the residents know of the existence of the drug on the premises but only two or three of them are active users. **3–62**

In *Searle* [1971] Crim.L.R. 592, CA, drugs were found in a vehicle which was used by the defendants on a touring holiday. The prosecution could not say which defendant intended to benefit from each type of drug found. The case was based on the concept of joint enterprise. The judge told the jury "if they all knew that those drugs were then in the possession of other people and they knew they were drugs then you probably will not have any difficulty in deciding that they are guilty". It was held that the judge misdirected the jury by equating knowledge with possession. A direction that ought to have been given was to ask the jury to consider whether the drugs formed part of a common pool from which each defendant was entitled to draw.

It was unnecessary for the prosecution to assert joint enterprise. The **3–63** crucial feature in this case was that each defendant intended to draw from the common pool, each defendant exercised control over the pool and accordingly, each defendant was in possession of the drugs in question. To equate mere knowledge of the existence of the pool of drugs, however, was a clear misdirection since such knowledge could not itself be proof of control.

A similar problem occurred in *Tansley v. Painter* [1969] Crim.L.R. 139, DC, where two persons were seen sitting in a car but of whom only X sold drugs from the vehicle. The Divisional Court allowed D's appeal on the basis that mere knowledge that X was selling drugs was not evidence that he was in joint possession since, again, mere knowledge of the existence of the drugs could not be equated with custody or control.

3–64 Again, in *Irala-Prevost* [1965] Crim.L.R. 606, D was a passenger in a motor vehicle driven by D2 on a journey from North Africa to England. A large quantity of a drug was concealed in the vehicle. The judge directed the jury that if both defendants knew of the existence of the drug, and both intended that it should be taken along in the car, then both were guilty of possessing the drug. The Court of Appeal held that the judge had not said enough to make the jury realise the degree of control required. Properly directed, a jury would have had abundant evidence upon which to convict each defendant of possession. The point here is that the mere presence of the passenger in the car is insufficient evidence of control even if he knows of the existence of goods in the vehicle: see *Bland* [1988] Crim.L.R. 41 (below). In *Strong and Berry, The Times*, January 26, 1989, it was held that the evidence established only the presence of the passenger in the vehicle [S] and failed to establish his knowledge of the existence of the drug let alone control over it. The prosecution based their case on joint possession but that would entail that each party had the right to say what should be done with the drug and that presupposed that each person knew of the existence of the drug. That element had not been proved so far as S was concerned: he had been the rear seat passenger in a car in which drugs, digital kitchen scales and a plastic tray were found under the front passenger seat occupied by Budd. B. was the driver. Accordingly, S's appeal was allowed but B's appeal was dismissed because, on the facts, his position was "very different". He was the joint owner of the car with Budd and B claimed that the scales had come from his home address, which he shared with Budd. Both B and Budd were entitled to drive the car and given that B was driving the car, the facts appertaining to him would be a sufficient basis to enable a jury to infer control over the contents of the car and thus the drugs: see also *Suurmeijer* [1991] Crim.L.R. 773.

3–65 By contrast, in *Bath v. HM Advocate*, 1995 G.W.D. 642, police found a Class A drug under a cover of the windscreen wiper of a motor vehicle that was kept for repair in a garage rented by B. Both B and his father were seen working in the garage. It could not be determined whether B or his father concealed the drug and accordingly there was insufficient evidence to show that B knew of the existence of the offending substance and B's conviction for unlawful possession was quashed (and see *McAllan v. H.M. Advocate*, 1996 S.C.C.R. 899.

It should be noted that on the question of knowledge the prosecution is required to prove a stricter intent in the case of an aider or an abettor, namely that the accused knew that the principal was in possession of a controlled drug. It is not necessary that the prosecution prove the type of drug in question: see *Patel* [1970] Crim.L.R. 274 and *Fernandez* [1970] Crim.L.R. 277, CA.

However, there must be evidence of assistance, active or passive. Passive 3–66 assistance involves more than mere knowledge that the confederate possesses or supplies controlled drugs: it requires evidence of encouragement or some element of control. In *Bland* [1988] Crim.L.R. 41, CA, the appellant had been living with her co-accused, R, in one room of a house which was occupied by others. The police had been observing the house and had seen a number of people calling. Some of the visitors were stopped, questioned, and found to be in possession of drugs. A search warrant was executed and traces of drugs were found. The defendant denied knowledge of the presence of the drugs and said that she could not believe that R had either possessed or supplied drugs. She was charged with possession with intent to supply. The case against her rested solely on the fact that she was living with R at a time when he was undoubtedly dealing with drugs. Her conviction was quashed, the Court of Appeal ruling that the case should have been withdrawn from the jury at the close of the prosecution case. The fact that the appellant and R lived together in the same room was not sufficient evidence from which the jury could infer that she exercised custody or control. There was sufficient evidence to infer knowledge that R was dealing in drugs but no more: see also *Searle* [1971] Crim.L.R. 592, C.A. (para. 3–62, above) and see *Brown v. Neizer*, 1995, G.W.D. 118 and see *Watson*, October 19, 1995, unreported, and *Conway and Burkes* [1994] Crim. L.R. 826. On the facts in *Bland*, there was no evidence from which a jury could impute even an intention to possession: see *Lewis* (1988) 87 Cr.App.R. 270, *Hughes v. Guild*, 1990 S.L.T. 715 (para. 3–60, above) and *Allan v. Milne*, 1974 S.L.T. (Notes) 76.

(v) *Knowledge is proved but there is a mistake as to quality*

It will be remembered that in *Warner* it was held that ignorance or mis- 3–67 take as to the quality of a substance will not prevent the accused being in possession of it if that substance turns out to be a controlled drug. In *Lockyer v. Gibb* [1967] 2 Q.B. 243, L was found in possession of a bottle of morphine sulphate. There was doubt as to whether she knew of the nature of the substance. Nevertheless, even if she did not, she merely made a mistake as to quality, which afforded her no defence (and see, by analogy under the Firearms Act 1968, *Howells* [1977] Q.B. 614 and *Hussain* [1981] 1 W.L.R. 416). For the same reason, it would have made no difference in *Marriott* [1971] 1 W.L.R. 187 if M believed that the substance on the blade of the knife was toffee. Both cases were, of course, decided before the passing of the MDA. Both cases remain relevant to demonstrate when a person will be held to be in possession of the offending article, but the significant difference now is that the accused's possession will not be unlawful if he can bring himself within section 28, section 5(4), or one of the categories exempt from section 5. In *Leeson*, (transcript, August 5, 1999, CA) police searched L's flat where they found a quantity of cannabis, cocaine and amphetamine, three sets of scales, cling film, cellophane bags, and £355 cash. L claimed that eleven days before his arrest, he saw X (a drug dealer) leave his car unlocked and enter a public house. L saw a bag on the back seat of the car and stole the bag believing that it contained "smart clothes". At his home address, L removed the cannabis from the bag and found other substances that he thought was amphetamine. He denied knowing that the other powder was cocaine. At his trial, L attempted to rely on section 28(2) of the Misuse of Drugs Act (lack of knowledge of facts which the prosecution are required to prove) and s. 28(3)(b)(ii) of that Act (belief that substance is a controlled drug of a description which the accused could lawfully handle). The Court of Appeal dismissed the appeal. Even on L's account, he made a mistake as to the quality of the drug. The prosecution were required to prove that the drug was controlled. It was not necessary to a charge under section 5(3) (possession with intent to supply) that the drug had to be cocaine. Section 28(3) had no application either. In short, L's submissions were valiant, but misconceived. However, it is important for the reader to read Chapter 8 in relation to section 28. The case of *Leeson* is discussed in greater detail. The reasoning of the Court of Appeal is of considerable importance as to the application of that section.

(vi) *The "container" cases*

3–68 Is a person who knowingly exercises custody or control of a parcel, box or other container thereby deemed to be in possession of its contents, if he (a) has no idea what they are; (b) cannot see inside the container; (c) has no opportunity to examine it, or (d) has no authority to do so? These were the issues that confronted the House of Lords in *Warner* [1969] 2 A.C. 256:

W sold scent as a sideline. The proprietor of a cafe told W that two boxes, under the counter, were for him. One box contained scent but the other contained 20,000 tablets of amphetamine sulphate. W contended that he believed both boxes contained scent. He was convicted.

Held: W had a defence since he claimed that he believed the contents to be of a wholly different character, but the evidence against him was so strong that the appeal would be dismissed.

Before going further, consider some of the situations that might reasonably arise in respect of "container cases". First, a person in possession of a container may believe that it is empty: in fact, it contains drugs. Secondly, he may believe that it contains goods of a wholly different description, *e.g.* jewellery. Thirdly, he may believe that it contains one type of drug whereas, in fact, it contains another drug. Finally, he may believe that the container holds one commodity whereas he has been the victim of a trick, and drugs have been intermixed with innocent goods.

It has been asserted that section 28 (which permits a lack of knowledge to be a defence in certain cases) now governs each situation. This is not entirely correct. The first step is for the prosecution to prove that the accused was in possession of the drugs for the purposes of section 5. Only when it has done so does section 28 come into operation. Accordingly, the decision in *Warner* (and other container cases) is relevant in determining whether an accused ever came into possession of the container and its contents in the first place. Although in every case of possession there must be an *animus possidendi*, the question is whether it is sufficient that the accused has knowledge of the container and exercises control over it, or whether the accused must know of and exercise control over the drugs as well: and see *Watson* (October 19, 1995, unreported). Only if the accused is in possession of the container and its contents is it possible to consider whether a mistake of fact is a defence and, again, section 28 comes into play. 3–69

The present position may be summarised as follows. In the ordinary way, the fact that a person is in possession of a container will lead to a strong inference that he possessed the contents as well (and see *Leeson* (transcript, August 5, 1999). However, that presumption may be displaced if he shows either that he had no right to open the container and had no reason to suspect that its contents were drugs or were in any way illicit, or alternatively, that he could have opened the container if he so wanted, but he received it innocently, and did not have a reasonable opportunity to acquaint himself with the actual contents or to discover their illicit nature. At this stage, the only issue is whether the fact of possession is established against an accused. If it is, then one considers whether that possession is lawful or unlawful. When the above is compared with section 28 then an overlap does appear, but even so, section 28 does not replace the ingredients required to be proved for an offence under section 5.

It will be recalled that in *Warner* their Lordships were concerned with section 1(1) of the Drugs (Prevention of Misuse) Act 1964 which provided that "it shall not be lawful for a person to have in his possession [a prohibited substance]". Section 5(2) of the MDA is worded in similar terms except that it is subject to section 28. The opinions expressed in *Warner* are therefore still relevant and it is on those opinions that the above summary is based: see also *McNamara* (1988) 87 Cr.App.R. 246, below; *Lewis* (1988) 87 Cr.App.R. 270; *Bradish* [1990] 1 All E.R. 460; *Waller* [1991] Crim. L.R. 381; *Vann* [1996] Crim. L.R. 52 and note *Howells* [1977] Q.B. 614 and *Hussain* [1981] 1 W.L.R. 416. However, the opinions in *Warner* vary enormously. They are also difficult to reconcile in places and rely on decisions which themselves conflict. 3–70

Lord Reid found great difficulty in accepting that Parliament intended to create an absolute offence. However, knowing where to draw the line between *mens rea* and absolute liability proved an equally difficult task:

> "... suppose that an innkeeper is handed ... a box or package by a guest for safe-keeping.... I cannot agree with the contention that if

> the possessor of a box genuinely believes that there is nothing in the box then he is not in possession of the contents but . . . if he knows there is something in it he is in possession of the contents though they may turn out to be something quite unexpected."

3–71 In order to drive the point home Lord Reid added:

> "It would, I think, be absurd to say that the innkeeper is not guilty . . . if he genuinely believes that the box is empty but that he is guilty of an offence . . . if he truly believes that it contains jewellery, though it also contains some drugs secreted in it. If he is not guilty in the case where the box contains jewellery as well as drugs, on what rational ground can he become guilty if there is not jewellery in the box but only drugs."

By contrast Lord Guest felt that the words (in s. 1 of the 1964 Act) created an absolute offence, while Lord Morris of Borth-y-Guest walked a middle course, holding that possession was established if (a) the accused knew he controlled a container; (b) he had the opportunity to know or to discover the contents; and (c) that the contents were in fact controlled drugs.

3–72 However, Lord Pearce (with whom Lord Wilberforce and, reluctantly, Lord Reid concurred) indicated that an appropriate direction to juries would be as follows:

> "The Act forbids possession of these drugs . . . If a man has physical control or possession of a thing that is sufficient possession under the Act provided that he knows that he has the thing; but a man does not (within the meaning of the Act of 1964) possess things of whose existence he is unaware."

Accordingly, an accused is not in possession of the contents if he believes the container to be empty. Lord Pearce continued:

> "The prosecution has here proved that he possessed the parcel, but has it proved that he possessed its contents also? There is a very strong inference of fact in any normal case that a man who possesses a parcel also possesses its contents, an inference on which a jury would in a normal case be justified in finding possession."

Once that inference exists, it may be rebutted by the accused in the following way:

> ". . . by evidence that, although a man was in possession of a parcel, he was completely mistaken as to its contents and would not have accepted possession had he known what kind of thing the contents were. A mistake as to the qualities of the contents, however, does not negative possession. . . . If the accused knew that the contents were drugs or were tablets, he was in possession of them, though he was mistaken as to their qualities."

3–73 In other words, an accused must show that he believed the goods to be of a very different character. It is always a question of degree whether goods are of a similar character or not. In an earlier passage, Lord Pearce thought that sweets would be sufficiently similar, although it is difficult to see why. However, the matter is entirely one for the tribunal of fact to determine.

In *Lockyer v. Gibb*, Lord Parker C.J. considered that:

> ". . . while it is necessary to show that the appellant knew she had the articles which turned out to be a drug, it is not necessary that she should know that in fact it was a drug and a drug of a particular character."

This was not an approach that found favour with Lord Reid who thought that the distinction would not bear critical examination. Nevertheless, he recognised that the appeal in *Warner* would produce that result. It will be recalled that in *Lockyer v. Gibb*, L was found in possession of a bottle of morphine sulphate but she did not realise that the bottle contained that substance. She made a mere mistake as to its quality but it afforded her no defence. Today, she would still be held to be in possession of the contents, but she will not be criminally liable if she can establish a defence under, say, section 28 of the MDA.

Opportunity to examine the contents. On this aspect, the House of Lords in *Warner* made three observations. First, where a person is entitled to open a container, but did not do so at the first opportunity to ascertain the nature of the contents, then the "proper inference is that he was accepting possession of them" (*per* Lord Pearce). Secondly, that inference might not be appropriately drawn if he had no authority to open the container. Finally, if any person had cause to suspect that there was something wrong with the contents, it was his business to verify them and if he failed to do so, an adverse inference may be drawn that he was accepting possession of them. 3–74

Thus, it should not be inferred, in the case of a secretary who receives a bulky letter (containing cocaine) which is addressed to her employer and marked "strictly private and confidential", that she was accepting possession of the contents, providing she did not suspect that there was anything wrong with the letter. If she did, then it would be her responsibility to open it to verify the contents. Consider, on the other hand, the position of a left-luggage attendant, who accepts baggage on the strict understanding that he has a general right to examine it at his discretion. In such a situation, if he is so busy that he chooses not to examine baggage, is it to be inferred that he is accepting possession of the contents of an item of baggage, even if he is unaware that it holds cannabis? Such a conclusion would be unfair on the custodian. However, once he is given that right, such an inference is difficult to resist. In *Warner*, Lord Pearce said:

> ". . . a man takes over a package or suitcase at risk as to its contents being unlawful, if he does not immediately examine it (if he is entitled to do so). As soon as may be he should examine it and, if he finds the contents suspicious, reject possession by either throwing them away or by taking immediate sensible steps for their disposal."

Nevertheless, it is still open to him to rely on any defences available to him under section 28.

3–75 It is implicit in the decision in *Warner* that a person who fails to take the opportunity to ascertain the contents of a container, only accepts possession of those items that would be discovered by a reasonable examination of the container. Accordingly, if the drug was concealed, say in a false compartment of a suitcase, the attendant who failed to examine the case would not be accepting possession of the drug because (a) a reasonable examination would not have disclosed its existence in any event, and (b) even if he had done so there would be evidence that he knew of the existence of the case and of the visible contents but no evidence at all that he was aware of anything else (see *Irving* [1970] Crim.L.R. 642, CA).

The length of time a container remains in the hands of the recipient is also material. If the period of retention is so short that it prevented a reasonable examination of the contents then it could not be inferred that possession of the contents was accepted. In *Wright* (1975) 62 Cr.App.R. 169, CA, W was a passenger in a motor vehicle. A fellow passenger gave W a tin which he almost immediately threw out of the window, before he had any idea what it contained. It actually contained cannabis. He therefore had an insufficient opportunity to examine the contents and accordingly he was not in possession of the drug.

3–76 In *McNamara*, the Court of Appeal again wrestled with the concept of possession as far as that concept has been affected by the interplay between section 28 of the MDA and the seemingly conflicting opinions of their Lordships in *Warner*:

> M rode his motorcycle to an address occupied by a co-defendant. Police found a box containing cannabis resin on the back of the motorcycle. M denied that he knew the box contained drugs and insisted that he thought the box contained pornography or pirate videos. The trial judge directed the jury that if M was in possession of the box, and that he knew the box contained "something," then M had the burden of proving on a balance of probabilities that he did not know, or suspect, or had reason to suspect that the box contained a controlled drug.
>
> *Held*: the direction was correct.

Having regard to the aforementioned principles of law, it may be thought that the result in *McNamara* was inevitable. Nevertheless, the court took the opportunity to look again at the decision in *Warner* (in the light of s. 28) and extracted the following propositions:

(1) A man did not have possession of something that had been put into his pocket or house without his knowledge.
(2) A mere mistake as to the quality of a thing under the defendant's control was not enough to prevent his being in possession, *e.g.* being in possession of heroin, believing it to be cannabis or aspirin.

(3) If the defendant believed that the thing was of a wholly different nature from that which in fact it was, then to use the words of Lord Pearce, at 305 in *Warner*, "the result would be otherwise".
(4) In the case of a container, or box, the defendant's possession of it led to the strong inference that he was in possession of the contents. However, if the contents were quite different in kind from what he believed, he was not in possession of them.
(5) The draftsmen of the 1971 Act intended that the prosecution should have the initial burden of proving that the defendant had and knew that he had the box in his control and also that the box contained something.
(6) Thereafter, section 28(3) places the burden on the accused to prove that he neither believed, nor suspected, nor had reason to suspect that the thing in question was a controlled drug.

A similar approach was taken in *Matrix (Billy)* (August 4, 1997), the Court 3–77
of Appeal dismissed M's appeal against conviction for being in possession of indecent photographs of a child contrary to section 1(1) of the Protection Of Children Act 1978. The appellant was an assistant in a shop that sold adult videos among other things. It was submitted that the judge erred by equating possession with mere physical control. The Court held that on the facts of the case, and having regard to M's position in the shop, M was in possession of a video. The video was stored for distribution and in the circumstances, it was not necessary for the prosecution to prove that M new the precise content of the video: *McNamara* (1988) 87 Cr.App.R. 246, applied.

It must be emphasised that the above has been considered solely in the context of "possession" as that term appears in the MDA 1971. There are many authorities that seek to define, or to explain, the concept of possession in respect of other enactments but, although it is clearly prudent to compare one enactment with another, the authorities demonstrate one overriding point: that the courts will look to the purpose of the enactment in question and temper the definition of "possession" accordingly. In *Howells* [1977] Q.B. 614, H was charged with possessing a revolver without a firearms certificate contrary to section 1(1) of the Firearms Act 1968. H mistakenly believed the gun to be an antique and that he did not require a certificate. The Court of Appeal rejected a submission that H was not in possession because of his mistake. H had custody and control of the item but he made a mistake as to the quality of the item. *Howell* was not a "container" case unlike *Warner* and the result is consistent with *Lockyer v. Gibb* [1967] 2 Q.B. 243. The Court went on to hold that the offence under section 1(1) imposed strict liability, a view reinforced by the existence of statutory defences in the MDA and the absence of a provision similar to section 28 of that Act. A similar result followed in *Hussain* [1981] 1 W.L.R. 416 and *Bradish* [1990] 1 All E.R. 460, although in the latter case the appellant sought to argue that CS gas in a canister fell to be considered as a "container" case. The Court rejected that argument because section 5(1) of the 1968 Act prohibited possession of any "weapon" and that a mistake as to the quality of that item would not afford an accused a defence.

3–78 By contrast, *Waller* [1991] Crim. L.R. 381, *Steele* [1993] Crim. L.R. 298 and *Vann* [1996] Crim. L.R. 52 are truly "container" cases: a firearm was carried by each of the appellants in a bag. *Waller* decided that for the purposes of the firearms legislation, the "normal inference that a person who accepts possession of a parcel accepts possession of its contents can be shaken by evidence of mistake on the defendant's part as to the contents" did not apply. The decision was applied in *Steele*, and considered in *Vann*, but in the latter case, the charge alleged that V had the gun "with him" (see s. 19, FA 1968) and therefore *Vann* had to be considered in terms wider than if the issue was solely one of possession. *Harrison* [1996] Crim. L.R. 200, also concerned a charge under section 19 of the 1968 Act where H carried a loaded shotgun in a public place. He denied knowledge that the gun was loaded. The short report implies that the Court did not need to decide whether the gun amounted to a "container" because even if it was, H had no defence (*Waller*) and, if the gun was not a container, H made a mistake as to the quality of the thing and thus he still had no defence: *Howell* and *Bradish*, above. In *Afzal* (transcript, June 19, 2000), the police testified that as A and S stood next to each other, S bent down and picked something from the ground (said to be a cigarette packet that contained heroin). The police found the packet close to where the men were standing. Both men denied knowing of the existence of the packet and its contents. However, the police discovered two wraps of 'brown powder' in A's possession. The powder was heroin. The appellants were convicted of possessing the heroin with intent to supply. During the course of the trial, the question arose whether the defendants knew that the substance was heroin or just 'brown powder'. On appeal, it was argued that knowledge or belief that the substance was a 'non-specific brown powder' would afford a defence because such a powder (not believed to be a controlled drug) is wholly different in nature from heroin. It was also argued that the judge failed to direct the jury to the defence under section 28. The appeal was dismissed. The overall effect of the summing up left the jury in no doubt as to the task that they had to perform. The judge gave a direction very near to a section 28 direction, and which was more generous to the appellants than strictly warranted.

3–79 **Mixed drugs and goods.** A different problem arose in *Irving* [1970] Crim.L.R. 642, where "I" possessed a bottle containing stomach pills. Unbeknown to him one heroin tablet also found its way into the bottle. He contended that his wife must have put it there. His conviction was quashed. At first sight, the decision seems to be at variance with the principle that a mistake as to quality does not negative possession (subject to s. 28(3)), and seems not to accord with other "container cases", but the reasoning is sound. Irving admitted knowing of the existence of the bottle and the stomach pills. It was in respect of those pills that he intended to exercise control. However, he was not aware of the existence of a prohibited substance. The position is therefore identical to that of a lady carrying a wicker basket full of groceries, unaware of the fact that a slab of cannabis has been slipped into it. Only if the prosecution could prove that Irving knew of the existence of a thing in addition to the stomach pills would a mistake as to its quality not suffice: see *Searle v. Randolph* [1972] Crim.L.R. 779. The tenor of the opinions in *Warner* support the correctness of *Irving* although their Lordships were not then dealing specifically with a case involving a mixture of substances in one container of which only some were controlled drugs. Most interestingly, Lord Reid said:

> "I do not know what the result would be . . . if, in the present case, both the scent and the drugs had been in the same parcel. The appellant, if his story were accepted, would have rightly believed that the parcel contained scent, but would have been ignorant of the fact that drugs had been slipped in with the scent. Could it be right that if the appellant had taken possession of the parcel of scent and thereafter the drugs had been slipped in without his knowledge he would be innocent (which is Lord Parker's view), but that if the drugs had been slipped in without his knowledge before he took possession then he would be guilty? That seems to me to be quite unreasonable. . . . "

It may be that in *Irving*, I's wife put the drug into the bottle before I took hold of it but, if she did then, as Lord Reid pointed out, it would be unreasonable to distinguish between drugs slipped into a container prior to possession, and afterwards, if the defendant's state of mind is identical in both instances. 3–80

Finally, it may be asked what constitutes a container? In *Searle v. Randolph*, it was no defence for the accused to deny possession of cannabis in respect of cigarettes, which he had picked up, merely because he did not know that they contained the drug. The cigarette paper certainly sealed in the tobacco and cannabis. To that extent, the paper "tube" was a container. Nevertheless, the tobacco and cannabis were blended to form one substance. He knew of the existence of that substance (or thing) and therefore made a mere mistake as to quality.

(vii) *Quantity too minute to possess*

In *Worsell* [1970] 1 W.L.R. 111, referred to earlier, the Court of Appeal held that where the presence of a controlled drug is so minute that it cannot be seen with the naked eye, measured or poured, and amounted in reality to nothing, it could not be said that the accused was in possession of the drug. The evidence established no more than proof of an earlier possession. 3–81

The principle is, of course, a fiction because section 5(1) prohibits the possession of "any " controlled drug including, on a literal interpretation, a trace however slight. Undoubtedly, the principle is sensible, but the very words of section 5(1) indicate just how limited in scope the application of the principle must be. Over the years the courts have shifted their ground until eventually, in *Carver* [1978] Q.B. 472, they departed from the original point enunciated in *Worsell*. This shift can be clearly demonstrated by a brief chronological examination of the authorities. In *Hambleton v. Callinan* [1968] 2 Q.B. 427, C provided a urine sample in which was found a trace of "amphetamine powder". The justices held that C was not in possession because the powder, having been consumed, was now completely changed in its character. Lord Parker C.J. concluded that the justices were right and said:

> "It was contended by the prosecution . . . that a man can be in possession of a prohibited substance . . . if he has traces of it in his urine, in his intestines, or any other part of his body in which it can be found . . . once you had consumed something and its whole character had altered and no further use could be made of it . . . a man could not be said to be in possession of the prohibited substance."

3–82 It is significant that the emphasis was placed on the changed character of the substance. Clearly, in that event, it is impossible to hold that a person is in possession of the original controlled substance. The trace in the urine could only prove an earlier possession and the consumer should be charged accordingly. Lord Parker C.J. acknowledged that a person who swallows a diamond or a gold ring would still be in possession of it. That much is obvious because neither object would change character. Likewise, in *Worsell* (above) the Court was concerned with a minute quantity of a drug that, again, had not changed character. Even so, in *Worsell*, it was decided that the courts would equate minute quantities with "nothing". It was now that the fiction was created. How then was it to be determined whether a drug amounted to "something" or effectively "nothing"? One method is to adopt a principle akin to *de minimis non-curat lex*, but to do so would be to add words to section 5, which prohibit possession of "any" amount of a controlled drug. Another approach is to discover whether the trace is capable of being weighed, measured, poured or seen with the naked eye. Such tests could not be performed in *Worsell*. However, in *Graham* [1970] 1 W.L.R. 113, G had scrapings of cannabis taken out of his pocket; they were very small but were capable of being weighed and measured. Accordingly, it could not be said that the amounts were so small that they amounted to nothing because they had at least been measured.

In *Frederick* [1969] 3 All E.R. 804, police searched F's flat. Traces of cannabis were found on two pipes and a tobacco pouch. However, 307 grains of cannabis resin were found in a bag inside a television set. F denied knowledge of the cannabis. The judge directed the jury that if the jury were sure that F possessed the traces but not the 307 grains, then they should convict, and vice versa. The Court of Appeal held that there were logical difficulties in concluding that F was in possession of the traces alone, but the scientific evidence was not tested as to whether the traces were so small as to amount to nothing. Furthermore, the jury could infer from the existence of the traces that F was in possession of the 307 grains.

3–83 In *Bocking v. Roberts* [1974] Q.B. 307, Lord Widgery C.J. held that the *de minimis* rule did not apply to offences under section 5(1) but that slight traces merely indicated presence on an earlier occasion. Even 20 micrograms of cannabis resin, found in a pipe, had been measured and therefore amounted to something. Interestingly, the point does not appear to have been taken that the quantity was so small that there was no evidence that the accused knew of its existence, *i.e.* no *animus possidendi*.

A different conclusion was reached by Stinson J. in *Colyer* [1974] Crim.L.R. 243, who declined to follow *Bocking v. Roberts*, being, as it was, a decision of the Divisional Court. C was in possession of a pipe, which had traces of cannabis weighing 20 micrograms (one millionth of an ounce). Stinson J. held that to say this amount was "measurable", after a complicated process of extraction, was stretching the meaning of section 5(1). Alternatively, he held that there was no proof of knowledge. Likewise, in *Hierowski* [1978] Crim.L.R. 563, Edmonson J. upheld a submission of no case to answer when not less than 20 micrograms of resin was found by chemical analysis. The judge regarded the amount as being effectively nothing.

By 1977, the principle in *Worsell* had been thoroughly glossed. However, in *Bayliss and Oliver* [1978] Crim.L.R. 361, DC the courts went even further. The defendants were tried for possession of 0.011 grams and 0.083 grams of cannabis. The Crown had adduced no evidence that the drug was "usable". It was held that there was no evidence that the defendants were in possession of a usable quantity. The learned judge cited Salmon L.J. in *Worsell*, concluding that the appropriate test was one of "usability". 3–84

The judgment has two curious features. First, the principle in *Worsell* was not one of usability but whether the drug was capable of amounting to "something". In *Worsell*, the drug could not be weighed or measured. That certainly had been done in *Bayliss*. Secondly, the learned judge included an additional ingredient, which the prosecution had to prove, namely, that the drug was usable. Such an ingredient is not even implicit in the wording of section 5(1). It is true that one finds reference to the "use of the drug" in *Worsell* as one did in *Hambleton v. Callinan*, yet in neither case did the Court intend to establish a usability test.

However, in *Carver* [1978] Q.B. 472, the Court of Appeal did exactly that. The reasoning in *Bocking v. Roberts* was accepted but Michael Davies J. at 477 added: 3–85

> "... if the quantity of the drug found is so minute as to amount to nothing ... or *if the evidence be that it is not usable in any manner which the Misuse of Drugs Act 1971 was intended to prohibit*, then a conviction for being in possession ... would not be justified". (emphasis added.)

On that basis the "usability test" was no longer a mere guide to determine whether a drug amounted to something because, even if it did, it must be capable of being used "in any manner which the Misuse of Drugs Act 1971 was intended to prohibit". However, what exactly did the MDA intend to prohibit and, secondly, did the "use" of a drug imply obtaining the desired effect from it? These issues resulted in the appeal to the House of Lords in *Boyesen* [1982] A.C. 768.

In *Boyesen*, B carried a metal tin, which contained a polythene bag. Traces of cannabis resin were found in the bag. The traces were visible to the naked eye and weighed five milligrams. An expert said that it could be picked up and put into a pipe or cigarette.

3–86 Lord Scarman, with whom all their Lordships agreed, held that section 5(1) did not depend upon the test of "usability" but simply whether the drug amounted to something. *Carver* was overruled. *Bocking v. Roberts* was approved. Lord Scarman found himself entirely persuaded by the reasoning of the Lord Justice-Clerk (Wheatley) in *Keane v. Gallacher* (1980) J.C. 77, 81–82:

> "The decision in *R. v. Carver* seems to entail the importation into section 5(1) of a qualification to the term 'controlled drug', namely 'which is capable of being used'. If that be the case, it would add an additional onus on the prosecution to prove that fact. If Parliament had intended that such a qualification should be added it would have been simple to give express effect to it. . . . It is the possession of the controlled drug which is made punishable by section 5(1) and (2), not its use or potential use."

However, if the quantity of the drug involved is minute, *e.g.* it is invisible to the naked eye, it would be far-fetched to allege that the person in possession "knew" of the existence of the substance and was therefore in possession. To that extent, the quantity of the drug involved is an important factor when considering the accused's knowledge.

3–87 **Using traces to prove past possession.** Even if the prosecution fails to prove possession of the trace, for the purposes of section 5, it is always open to the prosecution to rely on the existence of the trace to show that the accused was in possession of a much larger quantity of the drug on an earlier occasion; see *Worsell* and *Graham* (above). This is so even if the prosecution cannot show how much of the drug was involved or when it was acquired. However, prosecutors must display wisdom and not act oppressively. The point is graphically demonstrated in *Pragliola* [1977] Crim.L.R. 612:

> A pipe belonging to P was taken by police in 1975 and found to contain traces of cannabis. He was not charged in relation to the traces and the pipe was returned to him. Much later P was charged with being in possession of the traces.
>
> *Held*: the charge was oppressive and could not be justified in the circumstances. Each case must be decided on its own facts.

IV. Statutory Defences Under Section 5(4)

3–88 In addition to any other defence open to an accused, the MDA provides two statutory defences to a charge of unlawful possession, notwithstanding that he knew or suspected the substance to be a controlled drug. In each case, the burden of proving the defence is on the accused. Section 5(4) provides:

> "In any proceedings for an offence under [section 5(2)] above in which it is proved that the accused had a controlled drug in his possession, it shall be a defence for him to prove—
>
> (a) that, knowing or suspecting it to be a controlled drug, he took possession of it for the purpose of preventing another from committing or continuing to commit an offence in connection with that drug and that as soon as possible after taking possession of it he took all such steps as were reasonably open to him to destroy the drug or to deliver it into the custody of a person lawfully entitled to take custody of it; or
>
> (b) that, knowing or suspecting it to be a controlled drug, he took possession of it for the purpose of delivering it into the custody of a person lawfully entitled to take custody of it and that as soon as possible after taking possession of it he took all such steps as were reasonably open to him to deliver it into the custody of such a person."

(a) Section 5(4)(a)

It follows that an accused must prove: 3–89

(i) that he took possession of the drug; and
(ii) that he did so for the purpose of preventing another committing or continuing to commit an offence in connection with that drug; and
(iii) that, as soon as possible, he took all reasonable steps to:
  (a) destroy the drug; or
  (b) deliver it into the custody of a person lawfully entitled to take custody of it.

The clearest example is that of a parent finding his son or daughter unlawfully possessing a controlled drug. The parent is entitled to take the drug and to destroy it or to hand it over to a person entitled to receive it, *e.g.* a police officer (by virtue of regulations 6(6) and (7) of the M.D. Regs. 1985).

The words "preventing another from committing an offence" would 3–90
include the parent who finds, in her child's absence, a cannabis plant growing in the bedroom and destroys the plant. However, it seems that no protection is afforded by section 5(4)(a) if no offence is being committed in relation to the drug in question. For example, if D finds a packet of heroin in a bedroom, occupied by a guest, D will not be protected under subsection (4)(a) if it turns out that the guest is a heroin addict lawfully prescribed the drug, and thus entitled to possess it. However, protection would have been afforded under subsection (4)(b) had the drug not been destroyed but given to the police instead.

It is therefore unfortunate that section 5(4)(a) does not protect a person who has reasonable cause to suspect that an offence is or may be being committed in relation to that drug.

It is important to note that the terms of section 5(4)(a) make it clear that the accused must take possession of the drug for the limited purpose afforded by the subsection. A drug which originally came into the hands of a person for an unlawful purpose (*e.g.* as a custodian) renders the possession of it unlawful and it does not become lawful merely because he decides not to supply the drug to another (*e.g.* by returning the drug) even if he destroys the substance or delivers it to a person entitled to take custody of it.

(b) Section 5(4)(b)

3–91 The accused must prove:

(i) that he took possession of the drug; and
(ii) that he did so for the purpose of delivering it into the custody of a person lawfully entitled to take custody of it; and
(iii) that, as soon as possible thereafter, he took all reasonable steps to deliver it into the custody of that person.

It will be noted that subsection (4)(b) is not dependent on preventing the commission of a crime and secondly, it is confined to delivery of the drug to a lawful custodian and it does not protect a person who destroys the drug.

> In *Dempsey* (1986) 82 Cr.App.R. 291, MD was a registered drug addict and lawfully entitled to possess ampoules of physeptone. His wife D, held some of the ampoules for safekeeping while MD went into a lavatory to inject himself with the remainder. It was held that D did not come within section 5(4)(b) because she took possession of the drugs in order to remove them from MD (albeit temporarily) and not for delivering them within the meaning of the sub-paragraph.

3–92 It is not clear whether a person "lawfully entitled to take custody" of a drug includes all persons who would be lawfully entitled to possess a controlled drug of a particular description or whether the category of persons is limited to those listed in regulations 6(6) and (7) of the M.D. Regs. 1985. Parliament's use of the phrase "to take custody" implies a very restricted class and therefore that latter construction was probably intended by Parliament.

Section 5(4) provides a defence only to a charge of possession. Thus, in *X* [1994] Crim. L.R. 827, X, a registered police informant, was arrested in possession of 1,121 tablets of amphetamine sulphate. His defence (to a charge of possessing the drug with intent to supply) was that he agreed with police to possess the drug and to give it to R so that the latter could attempt to sell the drug to an undercover officer and thus result in R's arrest. The trial judge ruled that section 5(4) had no application in those circumstances because the section was a defence only to possession *simpliciter*; and see *De Sain v. H.M. Advocate*, 1993 G.W.D. 306, where the Court held that section 5(4) could not apply to a charge under section 50 of the CEMA 1979.

Chapter 4
Possession With Intent To Supply

A. SECTION 5(3) possession with intent to supply

Section 5(3) of the MDA provides that: 4–01

> "Subject to section 28 of this Act, it is an offence for a person to have a controlled drug in his possession, whether lawfully or not, with intent to supply it to another in contravention of section 4(1) of this Act."

Section 4(1) makes it unlawful to supply or to offer to supply a controlled drug to another. It will be seen that "supplying", and "offering to supply" for the purposes of the MDA does not involve any commercial ingredient, a social supply is still a supply. A conviction, for the offence possessing a controlled drug with intent to supply contrary to section 5(3) of the MDA, is a "drug trafficking offence" for the purpose of the Drug Trafficking Act 1994: see section 1(3)(a).

It has been said that there is a logical difficulty inherent in the wording 4–02 of section 5(3) in that an intention to supply a controlled drug cannot make the possession of it lawful. (See Richard Lord, *Controlled Drugs, Law & Practice* (Butterworths, 1984).) If that is true then the words "whether lawfully or not" are redundant. However, there is no general proposition of law that possession is, or becomes, unlawful merely because the purpose for which the drug is intended to be used is unlawful. Therefore, where any person, by virtue of a prescription, lawfully and honestly obtains controlled drugs, which he subsequently intends to supply, then his simple possession of those drugs remains lawful, even though his subsequent intention now makes him guilty of an offence contrary to section 5(3). In other words, what is being punished in section 5(3) is the guilty intent and it therefore does not matter whether his possession of the drugs was either lawful or unlawful. It is true that *Dunbar* [1981] 1 W.L.R. 1536 and regulation 10(2) of the Misuse of Drugs Regulations 1985 are concerned with rendering unlawful the possession of drugs (which had originally been lawful) in cases of dishonest "double-scripting", or where drugs have been dishonestly obtained from a doctor on prescription. However, these are isolated examples expressly catered for by the Regulations.

B. PROVING THE OFFENCE

4–03 The prosecution must prove (subject to section 28) first, that the accused was in possession of drugs; secondly, that those drugs were controlled by the MDA; and thirdly; that the accused intended to supply the drugs to another. Unfortunately, the Act does not define the word "supply" other than to say that "supplying includes distributing": see section 37(1).

No difficulty arises in the classic and most obvious example of supplying, namely, where a person transfers both custody and total control of a controlled drug to another so that he may do with it as he pleases: see *Mills* [1963] 1 Q.B. 522. Obviously, a person cannot be supplied with what he already has. In *Harris* [1968] 1 W.L.R. 769, H injected F with F's own heroin. The Court of Appeal held that H was not supplying F since the heroin was already in F's possession and undoubtedly belonged to him. H did no more than to help F administer his own drug. Of course, H did exercise some control over the substance in the sense that she controlled the top of the syringe and thus forced the drug into F's body, but physical control of the drug had not been transferred to H.

4–04 Where more than one person has an "interest" in the drug, for example, where one person buys cannabis on behalf of a number of others, then each party exercises some degree of control over the substance once it is acquired by the agent. To that extent, each contributor may be said to be in possession of it. However, if the agent then allows each contributor to draw his share of the drugs from the pool or, if he distributes the drug to the contributors concerned, then he is supplying them because "supplying" is expressed by section 37(1) of the MDA to include "distributing".

A curious state of affairs arose in *Lockhart v. Hardie*, 1994 S.C.C.R. 722. H was charged with being in possession of cannabis resin with intent to supply "on the 9th June 1993, at the Marriott Hotel" and at the "Grampian Police Sub-division office". The charge specified two locations on the same day. Police arrested H at the hotel and conveyed him to the police station where he was found to be in possession of the drug. The Sheriff had little difficulty in deciding that H possessed an amount of the drug that was indicative of a "dealer's stock", but he "could not sensibly deduce that any sane person could have an intent to supply anyone when he was locked up in a police cell". Of course, it may be that once H was in police custody all notions of supplying the drug evaporated and it would be mere speculation to say that H lived in hope that he would be released in possession of the drug so that he could supply it. The High Court of Justiciary held that the Sheriff had been in error and said:

> "Intent to supply denotes supply taking place sometime in the future and we are certainly satisfied that there is no necessity for the Crown to prove that at the particular time when the accused is found to be in possession, he has some intent to make an immediate supply to some other person."

This, of course, is correct but the charge was equally valid if the case had been put on the basis of the defendant's state of mind before the police arrived. The Sheriff, for reasons that are not entirely clear, was not satisfied that H was in possession of the drug at all at the hotel.

I. "Distributing"

In common usage, "distributing", means to "deal out in portions or to share among others". In *Holmes v. Chief Constable of Merseyside* [1976] Crim.L.R. 125, the Divisional Court held that the word "supply" had to be given its ordinary everyday meaning, so that a person who bought drugs on behalf of himself and others is to be regarded as supplying those drugs if he thereafter "distributes" them or shares them out. In delivering the judgment of the court, the Lord Chief Justice said (as cited in the judgement of Lane L.J. (as he then was) in *Buckley and Lane* [1979] 69 Cr.App.R. 371, 374): 4–05

> ". . . the question of joint possession can become highly relevant on a charge of possessing, but I do not believe that the question of possession or no, is a satisfactory route to an answer in the type of case we are dealing with at the present time where the charge is of supplying or possession with intent to supply. Section 37 of the Misuse of Drugs Act 1971 in terms says 'supplying' includes distributing, and in my judgment when a court has to consider an allegation of supply under this Act it must give the word 'supply' its perfectly ordinary natural everyday meaning. I have no doubt at all that a man who goes to market shopping for drugs on behalf of himself and others will often properly be regarded as supplying those drugs when he brings them home and distributes them because distribution is by statute a form of supply and that in itself is enough to cover such a case."

In *Buckley and Lane* [1979] 69 Cr.App.R. 371 B and G agreed to buy cannabis resin in bulk by pooling their money and thereafter, to take their respective shares. B, having been put in funds, visited Lane who supplied B with one pound of cannabis. B gave G three-quarters of a pound of the resin, and retained the remainder for himself. At his trial, B pleaded guilty to a charge that he "lawfully supplied to [G] three-quarters of a pound of cannabis resin". Despite his plea of guilty, B appealed, contending that he was merely G's intermediary, and that G acquired ownership and possession of his share of the drug when B handed the money for the drug over to L. It was argued that B could not be said to be supplying G with what was already his. The Court of Appeal described the argument as "recon- 4–06 dite", but found a simple answer to the problem in section 37(1) of the MDA in that "supplying" is expressed to include "distributing". Lane L.J. remarked:

> "Whatever else Buckley may or may not have been doing when he divided up the cannabis and gave three-quarters of a pound to Gilchrist and kept the other quarter pound for himself, he was without any shadow of a doubt—it seems to us—distributing the cannabis whoever may have been the owner or the custodian or in possession of the drug."

As the Court in *Buckley and Lane* pointed out, had the appellant's contention been correct, any drug-pusher could effectively circumvent the provisions of section 4 by merely collecting monies in advance from all interested purchasers and then buying the controlled drugs so ordered. Such a conclusion would have made a mockery of section 4: see *Denslow* (February 6, 1998, CA) in which *Buckley and Lane* was approved and followed.

4–07 By contrast, in *Searle* [1971] Crim.L.R. 592, C.A., the defendants had been on a touring holiday. A motor vehicle used by them for that purpose was searched and controlled drugs were found. The drugs could not be attributed to any particular defendant. Accordingly, the Court of Appeal held that if the drugs represented a common pool from which the defendants were entitled to draw at will and if there was a joint enterprise to do so, then each defendant who is proved to be a party to that joint enterprise is to be regarded as being in possession of the drugs. Obviously, on the special facts in *Searle*, an intention to distribute drugs to the others could not be established against any of the defendants.

Consider the example of D providing a platter of "reefer" cigarettes for the enjoyment of guests at a party. On these facts D is clearly in possession of the cigarettes with intent to distribute them and thus to supply the drug which they contain.

4–08 A more complex problem, which has yet to be satisfactorily resolved by the courts, arises in connection with the smoking of a "reefer" cigarette, which is then passed round a circle of smokers. In *King* [1978] Crim.L.R. 288, K made reefer cigarettes in the presence of friends. The drug was taken from K's own supply. He passed the reefer round. Each person took it in turns to draw a puff from the reefer and then passed the reefer on. His Honour Judge Finlay Q.C. held that K was not guilty of possessing the reefer with intent to supply it, contrary to section 5(3), because the degree of control exercised by each person within the smoking circle was insufficient. The reasoning of the court was as follows:

> ". . . only taking a puff and passing it on does not constitute supplying the material in the cigarette as it exists. It is only a supply if at the beginning the defendant has the material in his possession and at the end it has come into the possession of another in the sense that the other can do with it as he wishes."

This passage is not easy to understand. One supposes that the contention was that only the smoke (a puff) was being supplied and not the drug itself.

Smoke was not the material in the cigarette "as it existed". Since only smoke was acquired at the beginning of the defendant's period of possession he did not, and could not, transfer it to another, which that other could do with as he wished. Meanwhile the maker of the reefer retained control of the drug."

The reasoning in *King* is ingenious but strained. It depends on drawing a distinction between the substance itself, and the vapour that will be produced, if the drug is smoked. There is no sound basis for the existence of such a distinction. What was being transferred was the control of the reefer. By drawing smoke, the user was effectively diminishing the drug-stock in the cigarette. Since the words, "supplying" and "distributing" must be given their everyday meaning it follows that the drug was being distributed for use within the circle of smokers. 4–09

> In *Moore* [1979] Crim.L.R. 789 M persuaded two girls to "go for a smoke". He rolled a reefer, which he intended to share with them. It was submitted to the trial judge that the offer was an offer to supply "smoke" rather than the material in the cigarette.
>
> *Held*: there was a supply. The court declined to follow King.

The Court accepted that what was being offered was not only smoke but also the custody and temporary control of the reefer from which the two girls could draw smoke. To that extent, there had been an offer to distribute the drug by sharing custody of the reefer. The fact that custody was retained for a very short period was irrelevant. It is also irrelevant that only a fraction of the drug would have been consumed. It is submitted that Moore is to be preferred and this would seem to be the current thinking of the Court of Appeal: *Chief Constable of Cheshire v. Hunt* (April 25, 1983; unreported).

II. The Problem of "Bailment"

So far, we have seen examples in which the intention has been to supply the drug for the use or for the benefit of another person. However, suppose A intends to give B drugs purely for safe-keeping. Does A intend to supply B contrary to section 5(3)? Furthermore, if B actually receives the drug from A, intending to restore it to A later, does B commit an offence contrary to section 5(3)? 4–10

On one interpretation of the term, "supplying" it may be thought that all that is required to be proved is a transfer of physical custody of the drug to another. On this basis it hardly matters whether A gives drugs to B for safe-keeping or not, either way physical custody has been transferred.

However, in order to avert conclusions which would either be regarded as an affront to common sense, or which would seriously weaken an ambition of the Act, the courts have attempted to define the concept of supplying in the context of the policy of the Act. As a result, various ingredients are said to exist which the prosecution may be required to prove in certain 4–11 drug-related cases, *e.g.* by requiring proof of an intention on the part of the transferor, to enable the transferee to use the drugs for his own purposes. Unfortunately, the efforts of the courts to produce a logical and consistently applied set of qualifications or refinements to the concept of supplying have largely failed, so that the law produces some strange results. For the moment the law states that a person who deposits drugs with a custodian for safe-keeping will not ordinarily be guilty of supplying, contrary to section 4 of the MDA, whereas the custodian will be guilty of supplying the depositor if he returns the drug to him! This is the effect of the decision of the House of Lords in *Maginnis* [1987] 1 All E.R. 907, approving *Delgado* [1984] 1 W.L.R. 89, and *Donnelly v. H.M. Advocate*, 1985 S.L.T. 243. The conclusion that the custodian is put in a worse position than the depositor is both startling and it is submitted, grossly illogical.

III. The Difficulty of Defining "Supply"

4–12 It is not always easy to state or to define the ordinary natural meaning of a word. "Supply" and "supplying" are two prime examples. Both expressions are not always used precisely and in any event, not everyone perceives an act of supply in the same terms. The Shorter Oxford English Dictionary devotes almost an entire column to the word "supply" defining it as "... fulfilling a want or demand to furnish with to satisfy the wants of provide for to use", and so on. Accordingly, different instances of supplying may, in fact, possess different characteristics but the existence (or absence) of a possible characteristic does not necessarily determine whether there has been a supply or not.

As the authorities are examined, it will be seen that different courts seem to focus on different characteristics and treat them as if they were conclusive of an act of supplying. Thus in *Dempsey* [1986] Crim.L.R. 171, the Court looked to see if the transfer was an act designed to benefit the transferee: but not every supply necessarily benefits the recipient. Again, in *Delgado*, (above), the court focused its attention on the passing of physical control of the article to another. However, in *Dempsey*, (paras. 4–10 and 4–11, below) there was a transfer of physical control of a drug and yet the conviction for supplying the drug was quashed.

(a) A delivers the drug to B

4–13 Assume that A's intention is that B should act as custodian of the drug so that, upon demand, the drug is returned to A.

> In *Dempsey* [1986] Crim.L.R. 171, D was a registered drug addict. He lawfully obtained 25 ampoules of physeptone. Maureen held some of the ampoules while D went into the lavatory to inject himself with the remainder. D pleaded guilty to supplying Maureen.
>
> *Held*: the conviction must be quashed. The mere deposit of an article for safe-keeping and return could not amount to an act of supply.

Lord Lane C.J., giving the judgment of the Court, referred to the word "supply" as it appears in the Shorter Oxford English Dictionary and noted that it seems to be an act designed to benefit the recipient, but he added:

> "It does not seem to us that it is apt to describe the deposit of an article with another person for safe keeping, as was the case here. The example was canvassed in argument of a person who hands his coat to a cloakroom attendant for safe keeping during the show in a theatre or cinema. It could scarcely be said that the person handing the coat supplies it to the cloakroom attendant. Nor do we think it makes any difference that the cloakroom attendant wishes in one sense to get his coat, thinking that he may get a tip at the end of the evening. That is not the sort of wish or need, which is envisaged by the definition of the offence."

Clearly, if the transfer of the drug to Maureen was to enable her to use the drug for her own purposes, then there would have been a supply of the drug to her.

The Court of Appeal added that the jury had to decide whether the drug was being supplied to Maureen for her own purposes, *e.g.* to hand on to someone else, or to use upon her own body, in which case there would have been a supply, or whether it was simply for safe-keeping and return to D "who was lawfully entitled to the drug". The words quoted are perhaps unnecessary and even a little misleading since they may be thought to imply that a depositor who is not lawfully entitled to possess the drug commits an offence of supplying if he deposits the drug with another for safe-keeping. However, this logically cannot be so. Custody and physical control of the drug was given to Maureen but ultimate control was nevertheless retained by D. In ordinary language, the drug "belonged" to D and it was not intended that Maureen could deal with it as she pleased. Whether D was lawfully entitled to the drug or not was irrelevant. 4–14

In *Maginnis* [1987] 1 All E.R. 907, HL (which is now the leading case on this aspect of the law) Lord Keith said (at 909 f-g): "The word 'supply', in its ordinary natural meaning, conveys the idea of furnishing or providing to another something which is wanted or required in order to meet the wants or requirements of that other."

The word "supply" does convey such ideas but it can also convey other ideas not dependent on what is either wanted or required by the recipient. Lord Keith, who delivered the majority opinion in the House of Lords, went on to say (at 909g): "It ['supply'] connotes more than the mere transfer of physical control of some chattel or object from one person to another. No one would ordinarily say that to hand over something to a mere custodian was to supply him with it." In so holding, their Lordships were clearly approving at least part of the reasoning in *Dempsey*.

(i) *Enabling the drug to be applied for the purposes desired by the recipient*

However, Lord Keith then dealt with an "additional concept" said to be involved in a supply, namely (at 909 g-h): ". . . that of enabling the recipi- 4–15 ent to apply the thing handed over to purposes for which he desires or has a duty to apply it".

This is not an easy concept to understand. Lord Keith may have meant no more than that a supply connotes the transfer of substantial or complete control in relation to the article handed over. However, construed literally, Lord Keith seems to be saying that the additional concept is satisfied once the recipient is given the opportunity of applying the thing to his own purposes if he so wishes or, if he is under a duty to apply it. However "enabling" is itself a broad concept. It is difficult to think of any physical transfer of goods to another, which does not tend to "enable" the recipient to deal with the goods as he wishes, whether he is entitled to do so or not, and irrespective of the transferor's intentions. On this basis the cloakroom attendant is enabled, or given the opportunity, to apply the patron's coat to the purposes for which he desires (lawfully or otherwise) but that fact does not convert the transfer of the coat to the cloakroom attendant into an act of supply.

Where a custodian is under a "duty to apply" the article in question then he may be said to have been supplied with it. For example, where B is given a power drill by A for safe-keeping (while A is on holiday) with a direction that B completes work on A's house in the meantime, then it is difficult to resist the view that B has been supplied with the drill. However, this is, of course, a very different case to the custodian who is merely asked to look after the article in question.

The concept of enabling the recipient to apply the thing for the purposes for which he desires to apply it is most likely to be encountered by practitioners as a live issue, in cases where a person holds the drug on behalf of another, intending that the latter should resume possession of it.

(b) B holds the drugs intending to return them to A

4–16 In *Maginnis* [1987] 1 All E.R. 907:

> A package of cannabis resin was found by police in M's motorcar. He claimed that the package had been left there by a friend who was to collect it from him. He pleaded guilty to an offence under section 5(3) after the trial judge had ruled that the intention to return the package constituted the requisite intent. The Court of Appeal allowed the appeal against that conviction. The Crown appealed to the House of Lords.
>
> *Held*: the Crown's appeal would be allowed. M intended to return the drug to his friend for that person's benefit.

The majority of their Lordships (Lord Goff dissented) analysed supply in the context of "enabling" the recipient to apply the thing for the recipient's own benefit. Thus, Lord Keith said (at 910i): "If on a later occasion the defendant had handed the drugs back to his friend, he would have done so in order to enable the friend to apply the drugs for the friend's own purposes."

Lord Keith examined earlier authorities and distinguished them by ascertaining whether the drugs were transferred "so as to enable those persons to apply the drugs to their own purposes". Of course, a person may, as a fact, enable another to apply the thing in question to his own purposes without actually intending to do so, but it is not clear whether the majority of their Lordships were in fact holding that such an intent is required. The tenor of the opinions delivered suggests that proof of such an intent is required although the certified question was amended by their Lordships to read only as follows: 4–17

> "Whether a person in unlawful possession of a controlled drug which has been deposited with him for safe-keeping has the intent to supply that drug to another if his intention is to return the drug to the person who deposited it with him."

The majority of their Lordships answered the amended question in the affirmative. Unfortunately, the certified question was not amended to include an intention, on the part of the transferor, to enable the transferee to apply the drugs for his own purposes. The amendment was considered necessary because the original question was said not to be "in all respects apt to raise the true issue in the case".

The legal position of a custodian, who merely intends to return the drugs to the person who deposited them, has posed a difficult analytical problem for the courts to resolve. The reason is that a custodian of controlled drugs must realise that, in almost every case, the depositor ultimately intends to either unlawfully use the drugs himself or to unlawfully pass them onto others. It is therefore tempting, for the purposes of section 5(3), to include an element that the person in possession must know that he is enabling the recipient to use the drugs for the latter's benefit. However, the issue is whether the inclusion of such an ingredient gives "supply" an artificial meaning. Take, for example, the cloakroom analogy. The patron who hands a coat to the attendant relinquishes, temporarily, the custody and physical control of the coat. However, it is not the attendant's coat to do with as he wishes, since ultimate control remains with the depositor. The latter may call for its return. Accordingly, when the attendant returns the coat, he does not as a matter of common sense, "supply" the depositor with it. He knows perfectly well that the coat will be used by the depositor for his own use and has enabled him to use it. But that fact does not, it is submitted, ordinarily convert a return of an article in those circumstances into an act of supply. There is a mere resumption of total possession. 4–18

However, a very different view was taken in *Delgado* [1984] 1 W.L.R. 89. In that case, the Court of Appeal analysed "supply" in the context of whether or not there had been a transfer of physical control.

> Police arrested D who was carrying 6.31 kilograms of cannabis in a holdall. He said that he was taking them to the persons who had given him the drugs for safe-keeping.
>
> *Held*: D intended to transfer the drug to another at an agreed time and place and had committed an offence contrary to section 5(3).

The Court held that section 5(3) covered a wide range of transactions and that a feature common to all of them is a transfer of physical control of a drug from one person to another. Skinner J. observed (at 179) that: "In our judgment questions of the transfer of ownership or legal possession of those drugs are irrelevant to the issue whether or not there was an intention to supply."

4–19 Obviously, every case of supplying involves a transfer of physical control but the converse is not always true. The fact that physical control has been transferred cannot, without more, establish an act of supplying. *Maginnis* is itself authority for that proposition. Yet, on the face of it *Delgado* appears to be establishing precisely that. By contrast, in *Dempsey* D gave ampoules (which belonged to him) to Maureen to hold temporarily. D therefore transferred physical control of the ampoules to Maureen, but the Court of Appeal held that D had not supplied her with the drug: something more was required, namely that there had to be a benefit transferred to the recipient as well.

Not surprisingly the Court of Appeal, in *Maginnis* [1986] 2 All E.R. 110, believed that a conflict existed between *Delgado* and *Dempsey*. Thus, Mann J., giving judgment for the court, said of those two decisions (at 113–114):

> "We find it impossible to reconcile the meaning put on the word 'supply' in *R. v. Delgado* with the meaning put on that word in *R. v. Dempsey*. The decision in *Delgado* is that the word is satisfied if there is a transfer of physical control of the drug in question. However, in *Dempsey* there was a transfer of physical control, yet the conviction was quashed In our judgement the meaning put on the word 'supply' in *Dempsey* is to be preferred."

4–20 The Court of Appeal could not accept that the word "supply", as a matter of ordinary language, is apt to mean merely the transfer of physical control. Mann J. said (at 113–114):

> "We agree with the view of the court in *Dempsey*, that for there to be a supply there must be a transfer of physical control which is for the benefit of the recipient of the article. Counsel for the Crown accepted that this was the correct formulation but agreed that the transferee obtains a benefit when he receives back an article which he has placed in the custody of another."

The only discernible benefit that the Court of Appeal in *Maginnis* could find was the resumption of actual possession that the Court could not accept was sufficient to amount to an act of supply.

However, when *Maginnis* went to the House of Lords ([1987] 1 All E.R. 907), their Lordships held that both *Dempsey* and *Delgado* are distinguishable on the facts. Lord Keith explained the distinction in the following terms (at 912d):

> "In *R. v. Delgado* a custodian was found to have the necessary intent

to supply because his intention was to hand back controlled drugs to the persons who had deposited them with him so as to enable those persons to apply the drugs to their own purposes, and thus put them back into circulation. In *R. v. Dempsey* there was a mere placing in temporary custody, and no intention of enabling the custodian to use the drugs for her own purposes."

The House of Lords held *Delgado* to have been rightly decided and applied it.

Their Lordships approved, for the most part, the decision of the High Court of Justiciary in Scotland, in *Donnelly v. H.M. Advocate*, 1985 S.L.T. 243. In that case, the appellant claimed that a quantity of controlled drugs found in her possession had been put there by another. The Court (approving *Delgado*) said, (at 244) "if the appellant intended to part with all or some of the drugs in her possession to Colin Stewart, even for his own use, she intended to supply Colin Stewart, and it matters not whether his intention was to use them himself or to supply others". 4–21

In *Maginnis*, their Lordships remarked that if this passage was intended to mean that a mere transfer of physical control of a drug from one person to another may constitute supply then this was not "entirely correct". It would therefore seem that the transferor must at least intend to release the reigns of possession unconditionally, but that it need not be proved that the transferor intended that the recipient should use the drug in a particular way. In other words, if Donnelly intended that Colin Stewart should have the drugs for a short time but that the drugs were to be given back to her, then Donnelly would not be parting with the drugs unconditionally, *i.e.* to enable Stewart to use them as he wished. On the other hand, if Donnelly gave the drugs to Stewart unconditionally, not caring whether he used them himself or sold them, then it is submitted there has been an act of supply by her.

If X stores drugs with D, and D permits X to draw on the store (even when D is not at the premises), then D may be held to be in possession with intent to supply those drugs: see *Pentecost* (March 10, 1998, CA).

(i) *Motive not to be confused with intention*

What would be the position if X said to Y: "take these drugs; give them to the police; I do not want them in my house"? It could be argued that X did not transfer possession unconditionally and that Y was not able to apply the drugs for the purposes he desired. It is submitted that, in the light of *Maginnis*, there would be a supply on these facts for the following reasons. First, as far as X is concerned, he would have parted with the drug unconditionally in the sense that he did not wish to have the drug at all. Secondly, it is what the recipient desires that matters, not what the transferor would like to see happening to the drug. Thirdly, X would be enabling Y to apply the drug for the purposes which Y desired because (i) Y may act according to X's wishes or (ii) he may choose to flout X's wishes and apply them in some other way. In other words, one must not confuse 4–22 motive with intention. The transferor may give drugs to another with the best of motives but the act may still be a supply for the purposes of the MDA. This may explain the decision in *X* ([1994] Crim. L.R. 827). X, a registered police informant, was arrested in possession of 1,121 tablets of amphetamine sulphate. His defence (to a charge of possessing the drug with intent to supply) was that he agreed with police to possess the drug and to give it to R so that the latter could attempt to sell the drug to an undercover officer and thus result in R's arrest. It was contended on behalf of the defendant that if his version might be true then the plan did not fall within the meaning of the word "supply" as interpreted by their Lordships in *Maginnis*, on the grounds that the purpose of the supply was not to enable R to apply the drug for his own purposes, but to trap him. The jury, by way of a rider said "Guilty, but defendant ultimately intended the drugs to get into police hands." The Court of Appeal dismissed X's appeal against conviction because X's contention confused motive with intention.

Clearly there is a difference between motive and intention. A person may take steps with the intention that another should import controlled drugs contrary to a prohibition but the motive is to enable officers to arrest the smuggler. On the facts, in *X*, the appellant was (on his own account) engaged in a plan whereby R would be given the drug in the hope that R would attempt to sell the drugs to an undercover officer. If true, then X acted in the belief that R desired to supply the drug to another and thus X (whether assisting the police or not) intended to enable R to have the drug for that purpose. In the light of *Maginnis*, even that analysis could be said to be generous to X because all that need be proved is that X intended to transfer the drug to R unconditionally. X did not want the drug back: he hoped the police would seize it upon R being arrested. It is difficult therefore, to see how, in the light of the decision in *Maginnis*, X had a defence to the charge. The trial judge (without criticism) directed the jury that "whether [X] is guilty or not depends upon the meaning you give the word 'supply'". It was a kindness to X that the judge left open the definition of "supply" to the jury because the definition of "supply" is a matter of law but whether there has been a supply (or an intention to supply) is a question of fact. In *Finch* (July 20, 1994, unreported) Lloyd L.J. said:

> "If a person acquires drugs with a view to supplying them, he is guilty of the offence and he would be guilty, notwithstanding that he intended to give the information, and no person is entitled to do this."

4–23 The reasoning of Lloyd L.J. is correct and it often happens that officers working covertly find themselves in situations where they must be careful to avoid committing a criminal offence themselves. Thus, customs officers pretending that they are postmen, would commit the offence of supplying a controlled drug if they handed a parcel, containing the offending substance, to the trafficker who had been awaiting its receipt. In order to prevent problems of this sort occurring, an inert material is often substituted for the drug; and see for example, *Yip Chiu-Cheung v. R* (1994) 99 Cr. App.R. 406, where it was held that where an undercover officer had the necessary *mens rea* for the offence of conspiracy, it followed that his co-conspirators could be convicted of a criminal conspiracy with him.

Occasionally, "controlled deliveries" are made by officers who monitor the movement of drugs from the original supplier, to others in the chain of distribution. The officers will not contravene the MDA providing nothing is done by them to aid, abet, counsel or procure the commission of any offence at any stage in the venture.

(ii) *The concept of "supply" and* Maginnis

The decision of the House of Lords in *Maginnis* is fraught with difficulty and throws up more issues than it settles. Whereas the Court of Appeal in that case looked to see what benefit was conferred on the recipient, the House of Lords by contrast, referred to the intention of the transferor to enable the transferee to use the drugs for his own purposes. The upshot is that the custodian will often be in a worse position than the depositor, as the custodian will know that he is enabling the depositor to use the drug, whereas the depositor does not intend the custodian to do likewise. Lord Goff of Chieveley (who dissented in *Maginnis*) was clearly concerned that the word "supply" would not be given a common sense interpretation if the majority of their Lordships were right. He found himself in agreement with the Court of Appeal in *Dempsey* but he regarded *Delgado* and *Donnelly v. H.M. Advocate* to be wrongly decided. 4–24

Lord Goff considered that the primary rule of construction is that the courts should attribute to words their natural and ordinary meaning unless the context otherwise requires but he hesitated to attempt a definition "especially as the word is not always very precisely used" and thus demonstrated how elusive the ordinary natural meaning of words, can be. However, Lord Goff observed (at 913f-g) that "the word [supply], as used in relation to goods, connotes the idea of making goods available to another from resources other than those of the recipient".

In other words, the act of making goods available to a recipient, when those goods already form part of the recipient's own resources, cannot amount to an act of supply. Put another way, a recipient cannot be given what he effectively already has. Thus, Lord Goff said (at 913j): "I would not describe the re-delivery by the depositee to the depositor as a supply of goods, because the goods are simply being returned to him, rather than being made available to him from resources other than his own." 4–25

Lord Goff agreed with that part of the judgment of Mann J. when he said ([1986] 2 All E.R. 110, 113–114; [1986] Q.B. 618, 624): "In ordinary language the cloakroom attendant, the left luggage officer, the warehouseman and the shoe mender do not 'supply' to their customers the articles which those customers have left with them."

However, Lord Keith pointed to the example of a storekeeper who provided equipment to employees out of the store (at 909h): 4–26

> ". . . if an employee draws from his employers store materials or equipment which he requires for purposes of his work, it involves no strain-

ing of language to say that the storekeeper supplies him with those materials or equipment, notwithstanding that they do not form part of the storekeeper's own resources and that he is merely the custodian of them. . . ."

In this example, however, it was not the employee who deposited the supplies or the equipment with the storekeeper in the first place. That is why the storekeeper could properly be described as a "distributor", and "supplying" of course includes "distributing". Lord Keith therefore gave the additional example of the owner of a business, who obtains tools and materials from his own storekeeper being articles that formed part of the owner's assets and concluded that the storekeeper "can be said to be supplying him what he needs" (at 909j). This was not an illustration that found favour with Lord Goff (see 914d-3) who did not think that it would be appropriate to use the word "supply" to describe this situation. He added:

> "Even if the word 'supply' were to be used in such a context, I would regard it as a loose or aberrant use of the word which should be regarded as providing any foundation for the proposition that the word can be appropriately used, or is normally used, in every case where a depositee returns the goods to a depositor."

4–27 Surprisingly, the majority of their Lordships, in *Maginnis* adopted a highly legalistic approach to justify answering the amended certified question in the affirmative. Lord Keith observed that in *Dempsey* there was no intention of enabling Maureen (the custodian) to use the drugs for her own purposes and accordingly, a transfer of the drugs to her in those circumstances could not amount to an act of supply. However, Lord Keith added (at 912e):

> "One who deposits controlled drugs of which he is in unlawful possession with a temporary custodian has no legal right to require the drugs to be handed back to him. Indeed, it is the duty of the custodian not to hand them back but to destroy them or to deliver them to a police officer so that they may be destroyed. The custodian in choosing to return the drugs to the depositor does something which he is not only not obliged to do, but which he has a duty not to do."

There seems to be no good reason for introducing such legalistic considerations into the concept of "supplying" for the purposes of the MDA. If a custodian may be compelled, as a matter of law, to return goods to the depositor, does that mean that the depositor has therefore not been "supplied" with those goods, but that if a custodian cannot be compelled in law to return goods (*e.g.* controlled drugs) then he is guilty of supplying them if they are returned?

Lord Goff tested the validity of that approach when he said (at 914):

> "Let us forget about controlled drugs for the moment; and let us suppose that, owing to some technical rule of law, a contract of deposit of goods is unenforceable. . . . But the depositee is an honourable man,

and returns the goods to the man who deposited them with him. Nobody would, I think, describe him in ordinary language as supplying the goods to the depositor, simply because he was not legally bound to return them. The fact is that the goods came from the depositor's own resources; and all the depositee was doing was returning them to him."

In *Carey* (1990) N.S.W.L.R. 292, the Court of Criminal Appeal (Australia) declined to follow *Maginnis*. The court was concerned with the construction of section 3 of the Drug Misuse and Trafficking Act 1985 (Australia). "Supply" is defined in section 3 of that Act to include "having in possession for supply". However, the court decided the case on the basis of the ordinary meaning of the word "supply" in circumstances where a person has possession of the drug but intends merely to transfer the physical control of it to its owner or the person reasonably believed to be such (*i.e.* the "custodian to depositor" situation). In *Carey*, a folded handkerchief containing 15 small packages containing substances from cocaine to cannabis was found in a chest beside the appellant's bed. The appellant said the drugs belonged to her sister which the appellant agreed to "mind" overnight and that the sister would collect the drugs the next day. The appellant's only intention as to the destination of the drugs was to return them to her sister. In delivering the judgment of the court, Hunt J. said: 4–28

"The word 'supply', however, retains its ordinary meaning as well as the extended meaning for which that inclusive definition [s.3] provides. The various dictionary meanings of the word are generally agreed as being to furnish or to provide something that is needed, wanted, or required by the person to whom it is given. They do not suggest that the use of the word is appropriate when that something is merely returned to its owner or the person reasonably believed to be its owner."

The Court referred to *O'Brien v. Smith* (May 9, 1986; unreported, Australia) in which Yeldham J. ruled that the word "supply" did not apply to the mere return of the drugs to their owner or to the person reasonably believed to be such. In discussing *Maginnis* [1987] 1 A.C. 303, *Dempsey* (1985) 82 Cr.App.R. 291 and *Delgado* [1984] 1 W.L.R. 89, Hunt J. observed that the ordinary meaning of any word may change according to the context in which it is used and that (in relation to *Maginnis*): 4–29

"... it must be that the special statutory context in which the word 'supply' was there used caused the House of Lords to give an extended meaning to the word which it does not bear in its ordinary use. The Misuse of Drugs Act 1971 which was there under consideration includes as a defence to one of the charges under section 5 ... that the accused, knowing the drug to be a controlled drug, took possession of it for the purpose of delivering it into the custody of a person lawfully entitled to take custody of it. It may be (I say no more) that in that context their Lordships were able to give an interpretation to the word

> 'supply' which appears on its face to go beyond the ordinary accepted meaning of the word."

Hunt J. agreed with the reasoning of Lord Goff in *Maginnis*. The court declined to follow *Maginnis*, and *Excell v. Dellaca* (1987) F.L.R. 157 in which Kelly J. found the reasoning of Lord Goff more attractive but felt constrained to follow the opinion of the majority in *Maginnis*.

4–30 In the opinion of Hunt J., the policy of the Drug Misuse and Trafficking Act 1985 (Australia) would not be thwarted by giving the word "supply" its ordinary accepted meaning:

> "Such a consequence will not open the floodgates. In many (if not in most) cases, the circumstances of the delivery would be such as to establish that the accused was an accessory of the person to whom the delivery was effected. The acts of a storeman to which Lord Keith referred in *Maginnis* (at 309) would clearly fall within the ordinary meaning of the word 'supply'."

There is much force in the reasoning of Hunt J. In *Carey* the case had to be decided on the narrow basis that the appellant's only intention was to return the drugs to her sister but in many cases, the evidence may disclose a joint venture (or a conspiracy) with the depositor to supply the drugs to a third party. Where A and B possess drugs intending to supply C then both A and B are guilty of an offence under section 5(3) of the MDA 1971 (or alternatively of a conspiracy to supply a controlled drug contrary to the Criminal Law Act 1977).

4–31 The Court went on to consider the situation where one person obtains drugs on behalf of a group of persons. The Court concluded that this situation is in no sense analogous to the "bailment" situation that would necessarily fall within the ordinary meaning of the word "supply". The reasoning of the court in Carey on this aspect is entirely consistent with the law in the United Kingdom under the Misuse of Drugs Act 1971: see *Buckley and Lane* (1979) 69 Cr.App.R. 371 and *Denslow* (February 6, 1998, CA), para. 4–06, above.

In *Panton* [2001] E.W.C.A. Crim 611, the Court of Appeal held that there was no distinction between a "voluntary" and "involuntary" custodian of drugs. It cannot be said that in the latter case there is, or would be, no supply to the person who deposited the drugs with the custodian when the latter retrieved them, or intended to do so. The issue as to whether the or not the custodian's possession of the drugs was voluntary or not was irrelevant. If possession was truly "involuntary", the accused would have a defence of duress.

(c) The special case of *Harris*

4–32 In *Harris* [1968] 1 W.L.R. 769:

> H and F were heroin addicts. H was registered as an addict whereas F was not. At Kingston railway station, H and F were seen sitting close

together in the waiting room. Sticking in F's arm was a syringe, containing F's heroin. H was seen injecting F's arm by pushing the top of the syringe. At the police station, H told police, "I didn't give him the jack, it was one of his own. I was only helping him".

Held: the conviction would be quashed. The jury should have been directed to be sure that the drug belonged to the appellant and that the drug administered to the co-defendant was not already his.

This case has sometimes been cited to support the contention that a transfer of custody or physical control of a drug cannot amount to a supply even if the transfer was for the benefit of the recipient. In fact, one should approach this case with caution since the Court of Appeal had to decide the appeal on the basis that the drug belonged to F and indeed, he pleaded guilty to possessing the drug. In allowing the appeal Lord Parker C.J. said: "If B has obtained in some way the possession of the heroin, and all that A is doing is to assist in injecting that heroin into B, then A is not supplying heroin contrary to the Regulation."

In ordinary language, the heroin "belonged" to F and as a matter of common sense, F could not be supplied with what he already had. It would not appear from the facts, as reported in *Harris*, that the defendant had been in possession of the drug (whether jointly or otherwise) moments before she injected F with "his" drug and again, there appears to have been no evidence that H inserted the needle into F's arm which would otherwise have meant that she had been in possession of the drug prior to administering it. If H was not in possession of the drug before, or at the moment of injection, then clearly there was nothing for H to supply. On one view of the facts F was administering his own drug H merely helped him. Accordingly, one may be compelled to treat *Harris* as having been decided on its own very special facts. In *Delgado* (1984) 78 Cr.App.R. 175 Skinner J. seems to have interpreted the facts in *Harris* in this way for he said (at 178): "The drugs which were injected never left the presence of the owner nor, as it was strongly argued, his physical control". 4–33

(d) B possesses drugs intending to act jointly with A

Again, in *Maginnis* [1987] 1 All E.R. 907, 909j Lord Keith said: 4–34

> "If a trafficker in controlled drugs sets up a store of these in the custody of a friend whom he thinks unlikely to attract the suspicions of the police and later draws on the store for the purposes of his trade, or for his own use, the custodier is in my opinion rightly to be regarded as supplying him with drugs."

In practice the prosecution may have no difficulties in proving that a custodian (in the circumstances described by Lord Keith) was acting in concert with the depositor and therefore both may be convicted of supplying a third party in accordance with the usual rules of joint enterprise. Thus, the facts of *Delgado* were capable of showing more than just an intention to return the drugs to his friends. There was at least a prima facie case that D was engaged in a joint venture (or a conspiracy) to supply persons unknown; a matter, which clearly loomed large during the course of the hearing of the appeal in that case.

4–35 However, even if the custodian intended to supply the depositor, knowing that the latter would supply the drug to others, that does not mean that the custodian possesses the drug intending to supply those third parties. Thus in *Greenfield* (1984) 78 Cr.App.R. 179, G was stopped by police in his car. Between the front seats was a plastic bag containing cannabis. G told police that a friend left the bag with him but he knew that his friend was a supplier of cannabis. The judge directed the jury principally on the basis that G held the drug for X knowing that X would supply it. Less emphasis was placed, by the judge in his summing-up, on the alternative case, namely, that G himself was engaged on a joint venture with X to supply. G's appeal against conviction for an offence under section 5(3) was allowed on the basis that the intent of somebody else to supply the drugs was not enough. "The words 'with intent to supply' predicate that it should be the intent on the part of the person who possesses to supply and not the intent of someone other than that who is in possession of drugs to supply."

A similar point arose in *Downes* [1984] Crim.L.R. 552, where the trial judge directed the jury that a defendant was guilty under section 5(3) if he knew full well that the depositor was ultimately going to supply the drugs to others even if he, personally, was not going to be involved in the supply. The Court of Appeal quashed the conviction. The prosecution must establish a joint venture with the requisite joint intention. *Greenfield* does not appear to have been cited in *Downes* but both decisions are clearly consistent: see also *Tansley v. Painter* [1969] Crim.L.R. 139, D.C.

(e) Meaning of "to another"

4–36 This matter is dealt with in greater detail in the next chapter. Having regard to a passage in the judgement of Griffiths L.J. in *Smith (Brian)* (February 14, 1983. unreported), it seems that it is permissible to charge two or more persons with a conspiracy to supply a controlled drug to another, even if that other is an alleged named co-conspirator, providing the prosecution make that fact clear in the particulars of the charge. This now appears to be the view of the Court of Appeal in *Drew* [2000] 1 Cr. App. R. 91, and *Jackson* [2000] 1 Cr. App. R. 97. In *Drew*, Waller LJ reviewed most, but not all, of the authorities and said:

> "It will be noted that the decision in the case [*i.e. Smith*] is confined to a ruling that the particulars of the offence were not of the offence on which the jury convicted. . . ."

The Court referred to the judgement of Mantell L.J. in *Barker* (March 27, 1988), who placed reliance on *Ferrara*, but the result in *Barker* was determined by the way the prosecution had put their case at trial.

Plea of Guilty Not Accepted by Prosecution

Where a defendant is faced with a charge that he was in possession of drugs with intent to supply them to another, but then purports to plead guilty to possession, that plea is not effective if the prosecution reject the plea and proceed to a trial on the more serious charge. If the defendant is acquitted of the more serious charge, it is not open to the court to sentence on the basis of the offered plea: *Yeardley (Peter)* [2000] 2 W.L.R. 366. Prosecutors should also be mindful of the observations of Mantell L.J. in *Denslow* (February 6, 1998, CA) in relation to cases where D buys a small quantity of a controlled drug on behalf of himself and another: 4–37

> "It was inevitable that the appellant would be dealt with at worst as though he were in possession of the drugs and . . . as though he were without any criminal responsibility for that particular part of the transaction. We are told that a plea had been offered to a charge of possession. It ought to have been accepted. We hope that those words will be borne in mind by prosecuting authorities in the future."

Chapter 5
Supplying Controlled Drugs

Section 4 of the Misuse of Drugs Act 1971 reads as follows: 5–01

"(1) Subject to any regulations under section 7 of this Act for the time being in force, it shall not be lawful for a person

(a) to produce a controlled drug; or

(b) to supply or offer to supply a controlled drug to another.

(2) Subject to section 28 of this Act, it is an offence for a person

(a) to produce a controlled drug in contravention of subsection (1) above; or

(b) to be concerned in the production of such a drug in contravention of that subsection by another.

(3) Subject to section 28 of this Act, it is an offence for a person

(a) to supply or offer to supply a controlled drug to another in contravention of subsection (1) above; or

(b) to be concerned in the supplying of such a drug to another in contravention of that subsection; or

(c) to be concerned in the making to another in contravention of that subsection of an offer to supply such a drug."

As obvious as the proposition may sound, the Court of Justice of the European Communities has held in two Dutch cases that Value Added Tax is not payable on the illegal sale of controlled substances because such conduct does not amount to an "economic activity" for the purposes of VAT collection and the illegal supply of drugs was wholly alien to the provisions of the "Sixth Directive": *Mol v. Inspecteur der Invoerrechten en Accijinzen* [1989] 3 C.M.L.R. 729; and see *Vereniging Happy Family Rustenburgerstrat v. Inspecteur der Omzetbelasting* [1989] 3 C.M.L.R. 743 and *Einberger v. Hauptzollamt Freiburg* [1984] E.C.R. 1177.

It will be seen that section 4(1) merely imposes prohibitions on the pro- 5–02
duction or supplying of controlled drugs (or against the making of an offer to supply such drugs) but offences, arising out of a contravention of any of the prohibitions, are created by subsections (2) and (3).

Unfortunately, the concept of supplying is not straightforward and the MDA offers little assistance. By section 37(1), "supplying" includes "distributing". There is no commercial element to definition of "supply" for the purposes of the MDA a social supply is still a supply but, whether the supply is social or not, a conviction for an offence contrary to section 4(2) or section 4(3) is a "drug trafficking offence" for the purposes of the Drug Trafficking Act 1994: see section 1(3) of that Act.

5–03 In *Mills* [1963] 1 Q.B. 522 it was suggested by the Court of Appeal that "supply" involves the passing of possession from one person to another. This statement is plainly an over-simplification and not apt to cover every situation. In the wake of the decision of the House of Lords in *Maginnis* [1987] 1 All E.R. 907 it is now more appropriate to view a supply in the context of a transfer of physical control of a controlled drug, to another, with the intention of enabling the recipient to use that drug for his own purposes. Although many cases of supply will involve the passing of a benefit, or reward, to the transferee, it is going too far to "gloss" the meaning of "supply" in those terms. So, where a chain of persons is involved in the distribution of controlled drugs, it follows that each member who transfers the drug to the next person in the chain will commit a separate act of supply, even if each distributor receives no discernible benefit or reward himself.

Many of the authorities which have considered the meaning of "supplying" and "distributing" are examined in Chapter 4 ("Possession With Intent To Supply") which the reader is strongly invited to read.

A. DRUGS THAT MAY LAWFULLY BE SUPPLIED

5–04 Bearing in mind that the object of the MDA is to regulate the flow of controlled drugs and their use, and that not all controlled drugs are equally dangerous to use, Parliament has endeavoured to introduce as flexible a system of distribution as it can under a statute. For this reason some drugs may be more freely supplied than others. Indeed, one substance, "Poppy-straw", is not subject to section 4(1) of the MDA at all (see reg. 4(3) of the Misuse of Drugs Regulations 1985). "Poppy-straw" is defined in Part IV of Schedule 2 to the MDA to mean "all parts, except the seeds, of the opium poppy, after mowing". The extent to which various classes of persons are permitted to supply specified controlled drugs are set out in the Misuse of Drugs Regulations 1985 (S.I. 1985 No. 2066), which came into operation on April 1, 1986 (as amended by S.I. 1986 No. 2330, S.I. 1988 No. 916, S.I. 1989 No. 1460, S.I. 1990 No. 2589, S.I. 1990 No. 2630, S.I. 1995 No. 2048, S.I. 1995 No. 3244, S.I. 1996 No.1597, S.I. 1998 No.882 and SI 1999 No.1404).

The Misuse of Drugs Regulations 1973 (S.I. 1973 No. 797) have been revoked, along with its amending Regulations have also been revoked, namely: S.I. 1974 No. 402, S.I. 1975 No. 499, S.I. 1977 No. 1380, S.I. 1979 No. 326, S.I. 1983 No. 788 and S.I. 1984 No. 1143.

B. PERSONS WHO MAY LAWFULLY SUPPLY ANY CONTROLLED DRUG

I. LICENSEES

Any person may supply any controlled drug if authorised by licence so to do: see regulation 5. The licence is issued by the Secretary of State. Obviously, any supply (or offer to supply) not in accordance with the terms and conditions attached to the licence will render such a supply (or offer to supply) unlawful, although it is unlikely to render the licence invalid. 5–05

II. GENERAL AUTHORITY TO SUPPLY

Regulation 6(1) provides that: 5–06

> "Notwithstanding the provisions of section 4(1)(b) of the Act, any person who is lawfully in possession of a controlled drug may supply that drug to the person from whom he obtained it."

Regulation 6(1) protects the person who, for example, is prescribed a course of controlled drugs and is therefore lawfully entitled to possess them but who then wishes to return all unused drugs to the prescribing doctor. Regulation 6(1) cannot be used to protect a "bailee" who is given controlled drugs for safe-keeping, which are then returned to the "bailor", if the bailee is not a person lawfully entitled to take possession of them in the first instance.

By virtue of regulation 6(5), and notwithstanding the provisions of section 4(1)(b) of the Act, "any of the persons specified in regulation 6(7) may supply any controlled drug to any person who may lawfully have that drug in his possession". The six classes of persons listed in regulation 6(7) are:

> "(a) a constable when acting in the course of his duty as such;
> (b) a person engaged in the business of a carrier when acting in the course of that business;
> (c) a person engaged in the business of the Post Office when acting in the course of that business;
> (d) an officer of customs and excise when acting in the course of his duty as such;
> (e) a person engaged in the work of any laboratory to which the drug has been sent for forensic examination when acting in the course of his duty as a person so engaged;
> (f) a person engaged in conveying the drug to a person who may lawfully have that drug in his possession.

III. Authority to Supply Schedule 2, 3, 4, & 5 Drugs

(a) Drugs returned by patient to practitioner

5–07 Regulation 6(2) provides that:

> "Notwithstanding the provisions of section 4(1)(b) of the Act, any person who has in his possession a drug specified in Schedule 2, 3, 4 or 5 which has been supplied by or on the prescription of a practitioner for the treatment of that person, or of a person whom he represents, may supply that drug to any doctor, dentist or pharmacist for the purpose of destruction."

Accordingly, a patient who has been supplied controlled drugs by a "practitioner", and who now wishes to see some or all of those drugs destroyed, may deliver (*i.e.* supply) those drugs to any doctor, dentist or pharmacist for that purpose. It is therefore not necessary to return the drugs only to the person who supplied them. Nor is it necessary for the patient, who was the original recipient, to deliver them up for destruction: he may appoint another person to perform that task. The latter will also be protected by regulation 6(7). The term "practitioner" is not defined by the Regulations, but is stated in section 37(1) of the 1971 Act to mean "a doctor, dentist, veterinary practitioner or veterinary surgeon".

(b) Drugs returned to veterinary practitioners

5–08 It is often forgotten that controlled drugs are also supplied, prescribed and administered in the treatment of animals as well as human beings. Accordingly, persons who have such drugs in their possession will be protected if they are supplied to them in a form authorised by the Regulations. Any person who intends to deliver them up for destruction will be protected by regulation 6(3) if certain conditions are fulfilled. Regulation 6(3) provides that:

> "Notwithstanding the provisions of section 4(1)(b) of the Act, any person who is lawfully in possession of a drug specified in Schedule 2, 3, 4 or 5 which has been supplied by or on the prescription of a veterinary practitioner or veterinary surgeon for the treatment of animals may supply that drug to any veterinary practitioner, veterinary surgeon or pharmacist for the purposes of destruction."

(c) Administration of drugs

5–09 Every act involving the administration of a controlled drug to another is an act of supply. In respect of drugs specified in Schedule 5 to the 1985 Regulations, any person may administer such drugs to anyone else (reg. 7(1)). Doctors and dentists may lawfully administer drugs listed in Schedules 2, 3, and 4, to a patient under regulation 7(2). Indeed, any person may administer such drugs to another providing that the drugs are administered in accordance with the directions of a doctor or a dentist: see regulation 7(3).

C. PERSONS WHO MAY SUPPLY SCHEDULE 2 OR 5 DRUGS

(a) Classes of persons lawfully entitled to supply Schedule 2 or 5 drugs

Notwithstanding the provisions of section 4(1) (b) of the Act, eleven categories of persons may, by regulation 8(2) (as amended by the Food Safety Act 1990 Consequential Modifications (No. 2) (Great Britain) Order (S.I. 1990 No. 2487)), lawfully supply or offer to supply Schedule 2 or 5 drugs to any person who may lawfully have that drug in his possession (but only when acting in his capacity as such) namely: 5–10

"(a) a practitioner;
(b) a pharmacist;
(c) a person lawfully conducting a retail pharmacy business;
(d) the person in charge or acting person in charge of a hospital or nursing home which is wholly or mainly maintained by a public authority out of public funds or by a charity or by voluntary subscriptions;
(e) in the case of such a drug supplied to her by a person responsible for the dispensing and supply of medicines at the hospital or nursing home, the sister or acting sister for the time being in charge of a ward, theatre or other department in such a hospital or nursing home as aforesaid;
(f) a person who is in charge of a laboratory the recognised activities of which consist in, or include, the conduct of scientific education or research and which is attached to a university, university college or such a hospital as aforesaid or to any other institution approved for the purpose under this sub-paragraph by the Secretary of State;
(g) a public analyst appointed under section 27 of the Food Act 1990 or section 27 of the Food and Drugs (Scotland) Act 1956;
(h) [repealed];
(i) a sampling officer within the meaning of Schedule 3 to the Medicines Act 1968;
(j) a person employed or engaged in connection with a scheme for testing the quality or amount of the drugs, preparations and appliances supplied under the National Health Service Act 1977 or the National Health Service (Scotland) Act 1978 and the Regulations made thereunder;
(k) a person authorised by the Pharmaceutical Society of Great Bri-

tain for the purposes of section 108 or 109 of the Medicines Act 1968."

5–11 In Regulation 8(2) provides two very important restrictions, namely, that:

"... nothing in this paragraph authorises—

(i) the person in charge or acting person in charge of a hospital or nursing home, *having a pharmacist responsible* for the dispensing and supply of medicines, to supply or offer to supply any drug;

(ii) a sister or acting sister for the time being in charge of a ward, theatre or other department to supply any drug *otherwise than for administration to a patient* in that ward, theatre or department *in accordance with the directions of a doctor or dentist.* [emphasis added]

Drugs listed in Schedule 2

CONTROLLED DRUGS SUBJECT TO THE REQUIREMENTS OF REGULATIONS 14, 15, 16, 18, 19, 20, 21, 23, 25 AND 26

5–12 1. The following substances and products, namely—

Acetorphine
Alfentanil
Allylprodine
Alphacetylmethadol
Alphameprodine
Alphamethadol
Alphaprodine
Anileridine
Benzethidine
Benzylmorphine (3-benzylmorphine)
Betacetylmethadol
Betameprodine
Betamnethadol
Betaprodine
Bezitramide
Carfentanil
Clonitazene
Cocaine
Desomorphine
Dextromoramide
Diamorphine
Diampromide
Diethylthiambutene
Difenoxin
Dihydrocodeinone
Dihydromorphine
Dimenoxadole
Dimepheptanol
Dimethylthiambutene
Dioxaphetyl butyrate
Diphenoxylate
Dipipanone
Dronabinol[1]
Drotebanol
Ecgonine, and any derivative of ecgonine which is convertible to ecgonine or to cocaine
Ethylmethylthiambutene
Etonitazene
Etorphine
Etoxeridine
Fentanyl
Furethidine
Hydrocodone
Hydromorphinol
Hydromorphone
Hydroxypethidine
Isomethadone

Ketobemidone
4-Cyano-2-dimethylamino-4,
4-diphenylbutane
4-Cyano-l-
methyl4phenylpiperidine
1-Methyl4phenylpiperidine-4-
carboxylic acid
Levomethorphan
Levomoramide
Levophenacylmorphan
Levorphanol
Lofentanil
Medicinal opium
Metazocine
Methadone
Methadyl acetate
Methyldesorphine
Methyldihydromorphine
(6-methyldihydromorphine)
Metopon
Morpheridine
Morphine methobromide, morphine
Morphine
Myrophine
N-oxide & other pentavalent
nitrogen morphine derivatives
Nicomorphine
Noracymethadol
Norlevorphanol
Normethadone
Normorphine
Norpipanone
O-Carboxymethyloxime
Oxycodone
Oxymorphone
Pethidine
Phenadoxone
Phenampromide
Phenazocine
Phencyclidine
Phenomorphan
Phenoperidine
Piminodine
Piritramide
Proheptazine
Properidine
Racemethorphan
Racemoramide
Racemorphan
Sufentanil
Thebacon
Thebaine
Tilidate
Trimeperidine
2-Methyl-3-morpholino-1,1-
diphenylpropanecarboxylic
acid
4-Phenylpiperidine-4-carboxylic
acid ethyl ester
Zipeprol[2]

2. Any stereoisomeric form of a substance specified in paragraph 1 not being dextromethorphan or dextrorphan.

3. Any ester or ether of a substance specified in paragraph 1 or 2, not being a substance specified in paragraph 6.

4. Any salt of a substance specified in any of paragraphs 1 to 3.

5. Any preparation or other product containing a substance or product specified in any of paragraphs 1 to 4, not being a preparation specified in Schedule 5.

6. The following substances and products, namely—

Acetyldihydrocodeine
Amphetamine
Codeine
Dextropropoxyphene
Dihydrocodeine
Ethylmorphine (3-ethylmorphine)
Fenethyline
Glutethimide
Lefetamine
Mecloqualone
Methaqualone
Methylamphetamine

Methylphenidate
Nicocodine
Nicodicodine
(6-nicotinoyldihydrocodeine)
Norcodeine
Phenmetrazine
Pholcodine
Propiram
Quinalbarbitone[3]

7. Any stereoisomeric form of a substance specified in paragraph 6.

8. Any salt of a substance specified in paragraph 6 or 7.

9. Any preparation or other product containing a substance or product specified in any of paragraphs 6 to 8, not being a preparation specified in Schedule 5.

[This Schedule is printed as amended by S.I. 1986 No. 2330, S.I. 1988 No. 916, S.I. 1995 No. 2048, and S.I. 1998 No. 882]

[1] Inserted by S.I. 1995 No. 2048
[2] Inserted by S.I. 1998 No. 882 [May 1, 1998]
[3] Inserted by S.I. 1988 No. 916

(c) Group authority

5–13 By regulation 8(3), persons who are members of a group, and where that group has written authority issued by the Secretary of State (sometimes styled "group authority"), may supply drugs in Schedule 2 or 5:

> "Notwithstanding the provisions of section 4(1) (b) of the Act, a person who is authorised as a member of a group may, under and in accordance with the terms of his group authority and in compliance with any conditions attached thereto, supply or offer to supply any drug specified in Schedule 2 or 5 to any person who may lawfully have that drug in his possession."

It will be seen from the above that members must comply (a) with the terms of his group authority, and (b) with any conditions attached to that authority.

By regulation 2(1), a person is "authorised as a member of a group" if he is:

> ". . . authorised by virtue of being a member of a class as respects which the Secretary of State has granted an authority under and for the purposes of Regulations 8(3), 9(3) or 10(3) which is in force, and 'his group authority', in relation to a person who is a member of such a class, means the authority so granted to that class;"

(d) Provisions applicable to non-doctors at sea

5–14 "(5) Notwithstanding the provisions of section 4(1) (b) of the Act—
(a) the owner of a ship, or the master of a ship which does not carry a doctor among the seamen employed in it;
(b) the installation manager of an offshore installation,
may supply or offer to supply any drug specified in Schedule 2 or 5—
(i) for the purpose of compliance with any of the provisions

specified in paragraph (6), to any person on that ship or installation;
(ii) to any person who may lawfully supply that drug to him;
(iii) to any constable for the purpose of the destruction of that drug"

"(6) The provisions referred to in paragraph (5) are any provision of, or of any instrument which is in force under—
(a) the Merchant Shipping Acts;
(b) the Mineral Workings (Offshore Installations) Act 1971; or
(c) the Health and Safety at Work etc. Act 1974."

D. PERSONS WHO MAY SUPPLY SCHEDULE 3 DRUGS

The drugs in Schedule 3 are less dangerous than those in Schedules 1 and 2. They include the barbiturates, *e.g.* methylphenobarbitone. 5–15

CONTROLLED DRUGS SUBJECT TO THE REQUIREMENTS OF REGULATIONS 14, 15 (EXCEPT TEMAZEPAM),[1] 16, 18, 22, 23, 24, 25 and 26.

1. The following substances, namely—

(a)	Benzphetamine	Mephentermine
	Buprenorphine[2]	Meprobamate
	Cathine	Methylphenobarbitone
	Chlorphentermine	Methyprylone
	Diethylpropion	Pentazocine
	Ethchlorvynol	Phendimetrazine
	Ethinamate	Phentermine
	Flunitrazepam[3]	Pipradrol
	Mazindol	Temazepam[4]

(b) any 5,5 disubstituted barbituric acid not being quinalbarbitone.[5]

2. Any stereoisomeric form of a substance specified in paragraph 1 not being phenylpropanolamine.

3. Any salt of a substance specified in paragraph 1 or 2.

4. Any preparation or other product containing a substance specified in any of paragraphs 1 to 3, not being a preparation specified in Schedule 5.

[This Schedule is printed as amended by S.I. 1986 No. 2330, S.I. 1988 No. 916, the Misuse of Drugs (Amendment) Regulations 1989 (S.1. 1989 No. 1460), S.I. 1995 No. 3244 and S.I. 1998 No. 882]

[1] Inserted by S.I. 1995 No. 3244
[2] Inserted by S.I. 1989 No.1460
[3] Inserted by S.I. 1998 No. 882 [May 1, 1998]
[4] Inserted by S.I. 1995 No. 3244
[5] Inserted by S.I. 1988 No.916

(a) Wildlife licensees

5–16 Subject to an appropriate licence being granted under section 16 of the Wildlife and Countryside Act 1981, it is not unlawful to supply or to offer to supply a controlled drug falling within Schedule 3: see regulation 6(4).

(b) Buffering agents in chemical analysis

5–17 It is often necessary for laboratory personnel to use a variety of chemicals (some of which may be controlled) in order to carry out chemical analysis. Limited protection is afforded by regulation 9(6) (as amended by the Misuse of Drugs (Amendment) Regulations 1986 (S.I. 1986 No. 2330) which provides:

> "Notwithstanding the provisions of section 4(1)(b) of the Act, a person in charge of a laboratory may, when acting in his capacity as such, supply or offer to supply any drug specified in Schedule 3 which is required for use as a buffering agent in chemical analysis to any person who may lawfully have that drug in his possession."

E. PERSONS WHO MAY SUPPLY SCHEDULE 3 OR 4 DRUGS

(a) Classes of persons lawfully entitled to supply others

5–18 The following nine classes of persons may, by regulation 9(2) (as amended by the Misuse of Drugs (Amendment) Regulations 1986 (S.I. 1986 No. 2330) and S.I. 1990 No. 2487), lawfully supply or offer to supply controlled drugs to any person lawfully entitled to have such drugs in his possession, namely:

> "(a) a practitioner;
> (b) a pharmacist;
> (c) a person lawfully conducting a retail pharmacy business;
> (d) a person in charge of a laboratory the recognised activities of which consist in, or include, the conduct of scientific education or research;
> (e) a public analyst appointed under section 27 of the Food Act 1990 or section 27 of the Food and Drugs (Scotland) Act 1956;
> (f) [repealed];
> (g) a sampling officer within the meaning of Schedule 3 to the Medicines Act 1968;
> (h) a person employed or engaged in connection with a scheme for testing the quality or amount of the drugs, preparations and appliances supplied under the National Health Service Act 1977 or the National Health Service (Scotland) Act 1978 and the Regulations made thereunder.

(i) a person authorised by the Pharmaceutical Society of Great Britain for the purposes of section 108 or 109 of the Medicines Act 1968. . . .”

The regulations also permit a retail pharmacist to supply what he is authorised to produce. Thus, by regulation 9(4)(b) “a person who is authorised under paragraph 9(1)(c) may supply or offer to supply any drug which he may, by virtue of being so authorised, lawfully produce to any person who may lawfully have that drug in his possession”.

On April 1, 1987, the Misuse of Drugs (Amendment) Regulations 1986 5–19
(S.I. 1986 No. 2330) substituted the following paragraph for regulation 9(3), which now reads:

“(3) Notwithstanding the provisions of section 4(1)(b) of the Act
(a) a person who is authorised as a member of a group, under and in accordance with the terms of his group authority and in compliance with any conditions attached thereto;
(b) the person in charge or acting person in charge of a hospital or nursing home;
(c) in the case of such a drug supplied to her by a person responsible for the dispensing and supply of medicines at that hospital or nursing home, the sister or acting sister for the time being in charge of a ward, theatre or other department in a hospital or nursing home,

may, when acting in his capacity as such, supply or offer to supply any drug specified in Schedule 3, or any drug specified in Schedule 4 which is contained in a medicinal product, to any person who may lawfully have that drug in his possession:

Provided that nothing in this paragraph authorises
(i) the person in charge or acting person in charge of a hospital or nursing home, having a pharmacist responsible for the dispensing and supply of medicines, to supply or offer to supply any drug;
(ii) a sister or acting sister for the time being in charge of a ward, theatre or other department to supply any drug otherwise than for administration to a patient in that ward, theatre or department in accordance with the directions of a doctor or dentist.”

(b) Provisions applicable to non-doctors at sea

By regulation 9(5): 5–20

“(a) . . . the owner of a ship, or the master of a ship which does not carry a doctor among the seamen employed in it;

(b) the installation manager of an offshore installation, may supply or offer to supply any drug specified in Schedule 3, or any drug specified in Schedule 4 which is contained in a medicinal product

(i) for the purpose of compliance with any of the provisions specified in Regulation 8(6), to any person on that ship or installation; or

(ii) to any person who may lawfully supply that drug to him."

(c) **Drugs listed in Schedule 4 of the 1985 Regulations**

SCHEDULE 4

PART I[1]

CONTROLLED DRUGS EXCEPTED FROM THE PROHIBITION ON POSSESSION WHEN IN THE FORM OF A MEDICINAL PRODUCT, EXCLUDED FROM THE APPLICATION OF OFFENCES ARISING FROM IMPORTATION ON IMPORTATION AND EXPORTATION WHEN IMPORTED OR EXPORTED IN THE FORM OF A MEDICINAL PRODUCT BY ANY PERSON FOR ADMINISTRATION TO HIMSELF; AND SUBJECT TO THE REQUIREMENTS OF REGULATIONS 22, 23, 25 AND 26.[2]

5–21 1. The following substances, namely—

Atamestane
Bolandiol
Bolasterone
Bolazine
Boldenone
Bolenol
Bolmantalate
Calusterone
4-Chloromethandienone
Drostanolone
Enestebol
Epitiostanol
Ethyloestrenol
Fluoxymesterone
Formebolone
Furazabol
Mebolazine
Mepitiostane
Mesabolone
Mestanolone
Mesterolone
Methandienone
Methandriol
Methenolone
Methyltestosterone
Metribolone
Mibolerone
Nandrolone
Norboletone
Norclostebol
Norethandrolone
Ovandrotone
Oxabolone
Oxandrolone
Oxymesterone
Oxymetholone
Prasterone
Propetandrol
Quinbolone
Roxibolone
Silandrone
Stanolone
Stanozolol
Stenbolone
Testosterone
Thiomesterone
Trenbolone

2. Any compound (not being Trilostane or a compound for the time being specified in paragraph 1 of this Part of this Schedule) structurally derived from 17-hydroxyandros-tan-3-one or from 17-hydroxyestran-3-one by modification in any of the following ways, that is to say,

(a) by further substitution at position 17 by a methyl or ethyl group;

(b) by substitution to any extent at one or more of positions 1,2,4,6, 7,9,11 or 16, but at no other position;

(c) by unsaturation in the carbocyclic ring system to any extent, provided that there are no more than two ethylenic bonds in any one carbocyclic ring;

(d) by fusion of ring A with a heterocyclic system.

3. Any substance which is an ester or ether (or, where more than one hydroxyl function is available, both an ester and an ether) of a substance specified in paragraph 1 or described in paragraph 2 of this Part of this Schedule.

4. The following substances, namely—

Chorionic Gonadotrophin (HCG)
Clenbuterol
Non-human chorionic gonadotrophin
Somatropin
Somatotropin
Somatrem

5. Any stereoisomeric form of a substance specified or described in any of paragraphs 1 to 4 of this Part of this Schedule.

6. Any salt of a substance specified or described in any of paragraphs 1 to 5 of this Part of this Schedule.

7. Any preparation of other product containing a substance or product specified or described in any of paragraphs 1 to 6 of this Part of this Schedule, not being a preparation specified in Schedule 5.

PART II[3]

CONTROLLED DRUGS EXCEPTED FROM THE PROHIBITION ON IMPORTATION, EXPORTATION AND, WHEN IN THE FORM OF A MEDICINAL PRODUCT, POSSESSION AND SUBJECT TO THE REQUIREMENTS OF REGULATIONS 22, 23, 25 AND 26

1. The following substances and products, namely— 5–22

Alprazolam
Aminorex[4]
Camazepam
Bromazepam
Brotizolam[5]
Chlordiazepoxide
Clobazam
Clonazepam
Clorazepic acid
Clotiazepam
Cloxazolam
Delorazepam
Diazepam
Estazolam
Ethyl loflazepate
Fencamfin
Fenproporex
Fludiazepam
Flurazepam
Halazepam
Haloxazolam
Ketazolam
Loprazolam
Lorazepam
Lormetazepam
Medazepam
Mefenorex
Mesocarb[6]
Midazolam[7]
N-Ethylamphetamine
Nimetazepam
Nitrazepam
Nordazepam
Oxazepam

Oxazolam
Pemoline[8]
Pinazepam
Prazepam
Pyrovalerone
Tetrazepam
Triazolam
[Flunitrazepam][9]
[Propylhexedrine][10]
[Temazepam][11]

2. Any steroisomeric form of a substance specified in paragraph 1.

3. Any salt of a substance specified in paragraph 1 or 2.

4. Any preparation or other product containing a substance or product specified in and of paragraphs 1 to 3, not being a preparation specified in Schedule 5.

[This Schedule is printed as amended by S.I. 1986 No. 2330, S.I. 1989 No. 1460, S.I. 1990 No. 2630, S.I. 1995 No. 2048, S.I. 1995 No. 3244, S.I. 1996 No. 1597 (which, *inter alia*, inserted Part I as from September 1, 1996), and S.I. 1998 No. 882]

1 Inserted by S.I. 1996 No. 1597
2 Inserted by S.I. 1996 No. 1597
3 Inserted by S.I. 1996 No. 1597
4 S.I. 1998 No. 882
5 S.I. 1998 No. 882
6 Inserted by S.I. 1998 No. 882
7 Inserted by S.I. 1990 No. 2630
8 Inserted by S.I. 1989 No. 1460 (originally Part II was para.1 of Sched. 4)
9 Deleted by S.I. 1998 No. 882.
10 Deleted by S.I. 1995 No. 2048
11 Deleted by S.I. 1995 No. 3244 and moved to Sch.3 Para.1(a)

F. PERSONS WHO MAY SUPPLY SCHEDULE 5 DRUGS

5–23 We have already seen that any person may administer to another a controlled drug providing that it is a drug specified in Schedule 5. The drugs coming within this category are as follows:

"Regulation 3 SCHEDULE 5

CONTROLLED DRUGS EXCEPTED FROM THE PROHIBITION ON IMPORTATION EXPORTATION AND POSSESSION AND SUBJECT TO THE REQUIREMENTS OF REGULATIONS 24 AND 25

1.—(1) Any preparation of one or more of the substances to which this paragraph 2 applies, not being a preparation designed for administration by injection, when compounded with one or more other active or inert ingredients and containing a total of not more than 100 milligrammes of the substance or substances (calculated as base) per dosage unit or with a total concentration of not more than 2.5 per cent (calculated as base) in undivided preparations.

(2) The substances to which this paragraph applies are acetylidhydrocodeine, codeine, dihydrocodeine, ethylmorphine, nicocodine, nicodicod-

ine (6-nicotinoyldi-liydrocodeine), norcodeine, pholcodine, and their respective salts.

2. Any preparation of cocaine containing not more than 0.1 per cent of cocaine calculated as cocaine base, being a preparation compounded with one or more other active or inert ingredients in such a way that the cocaine cannot be recovered by readily applicable means or in a yield which would constitute a risk to health.

3. Any preparation of medicinal opium or of morphine containing (in either case) not more than 0.2 per cent of morphine calculated as anhydrous morphine base, being a preparation compounded with one or more other active inert ingredients in such a way that the opium or, as the case may be, the morphine, cannot be recovered by readily applicable means or in a yield which would constitute a risk to health.

4. Any preparation of dextropropoxyphene, being a preparation designed for oral administration, containing not more than 135 milligrammes of dextropropoxyphene (calculated as base) per dosage unit or with a total concentration of not more than 2.5 per cent (calculated as base) in undivided preparations.

5. Any preparation of difenoxin containing, per dosage unit, not more than 0.5 milligrammes of difenoxin and a quantity of atropine sulphate equivalent to at least 5 per cent, of the dose of difenoxin.

6. Any preparation of diphenoxylate containing, per dosage unit, not more than 2.5 milligrammes of diphenoxylate calculated as base, and a quantity of atropine sulphate equivalent to at least 1 per cent of the dose of diphenoxylate.

7. Any preparation of propiram containing, per dosage unit, not more than 100 milligrammes of propiram calculated as base and compounded with at least the same amount (by weight) of methylcellulose.

8. Any powder of ipecacuanha and opium comprising—10 per cent opium, in powder, 10 per cent ipecacuanha root, in powder, well mixed with 80 per cent of any other powdered ingredient containing no controlled drug.

9. Any mixture containing one or more of the preparations specified in paragraphs 1 to 8, being a mixture of which none of the other ingredients is a controlled drug.

G. WRITTEN AUTHORITY TO SUPPLY

By regulation 8(4) it is possible for named individuals to supply a Schedule 5 drug where s/he has written authority to do so: 5–24

> "Notwithstanding the provisions of section 4(1)(b) of the Act, a person who is authorised by a written authority issued by the Secretary of State under and for the purposes of this paragraph and for the time being in force may, at the premises specified in that authority and in

compliance with any conditions so specified, supply, or offer to supply any drug specified in Schedule 5 to any person who may lawfully have that drug in his possession."

H. ISSUING A PRESCRIPTION NOT A "SUPPLY"

5–25 In *Taylor* [1986] Crim.L.R. 680 a general practitioner prescribed 70 people quantities of methadone, a Class A controlled drug. At the close of the prosecution case, it was successfully submitted on behalf of the defence that even assuming T acted unlawfully and in bad faith, the mere issuing of a prescription authorising a pharmacist to dispense a drug did not amount to "supplying" for the purposes of section 4 of the Misuse of Drugs Act 1971. In the judgment of His Honour Judge Hickman, "supplying" involves the physical transfer of the substance involved from the supplier to the supplied. The case of *Taylor* raises a number of interesting points. The doctor was not in possession of methadone and therefore, even if his intention had been to supply the drug to patients, he could not be convicted of an offence under section 5(3) of the 1971 Act. However, the pharmacist supplies patients with drugs once they are handed over to the patient. As Professor Sir John Smith has pointed out ([1986] Crim.L.R. 681) if the doctor was acting unlawfully and in bad faith, the "patient" was not entitled to have the drug and therefore the supply by the pharmacist was an *actus reus* and the defendant, with *mens rea*, had caused that *actus reus* to occur. Although the pharmacist is an innocent agent, he nevertheless acts on the directions and with the authority of the doctor: see *Cogan* [1976] Q.B. 217, CA.

I. THE UNLAWFUL SUPPLY OF CONTROLLED DRUGS

5–26 The unlawful supply of controlled drugs Offences arising out of a contravention of section 4(1)(b) appear in section 4(3) that reads:

Subject to section 28 of this Act, it is an offence for a person

(a) to supply or offer to supply a controlled drug to another in contravention of subsection (1); or
(b) to be concerned in the supplying of such a drug to another in contravention of that subsection; or
(c) to be concerned in the making to another in contravention of that subsection of an offer to supply such a drug."

Although the offences of supplying and offering to supply appear together in section 4(3)(a), they must be regarded as distinct offences so that charges or counts in the indictment must clearly specify which offence is being alleged.

It will be seen that section 4(3) creates four offences. The difference between (b) and (c) is that in (b) there must be an actual supply made by an accused, whereas in (c) the accused need only be concerned in making an offer to supply: see *Kerr v. H.M. Advocate*, 1986 S.C.C.R. 81, *Clements v. H.M.Advocate*, 1991 S.L.T. 388, *Dickinson v. H.M. Advocate*, 1995 S.L.T. 703 and para. 5-28, below. Again, in respect of both (b) and (c), the word "knowingly" does not appear since both offences are subject to section 28: see *DPP ex parte Bora*, (June 14, 1999), and *McAllan v. H.M. Advocate*, 1996 S.C.C.R. 899.

In *Hughes* (1985) 81 Cr.App.R. 344, the Court of Appeal listed the three elements, which the prosecution must prove for any offence under s.4(3), namely: 5–27

(1) the supply of a drug to another or, as the case may be, the making of an offer to supply the drug to another; and
(2) participation by the accused in an enterprise involving such a supply or, as the case may be, such an offer to supply; and
(3) knowledge by the accused of the nature of the enterprise; either knowledge that it is a venture to supply or to make an offer to supply the drug in question. It is not apparent from the report whether the court heard argument as to the effect of section 28 on section 4; and see *McCallum v. McKay*, G.W.D. September 19, 1997 for an example of knowledge being inferred from the defendants awareness of what cannabis resin looks like.

"Supplying" includes "distributing": see section 37(1). In *Holmes v. Chief Constable Merseyside Police* [1976] Crim.L.R. 125, counsel for the defence submitted that a person who held drugs on behalf of himself and others was in joint possession and that a subsequent division of the drugs could not amount to a supply. The Divisional Court rejected that submission, holding that the word "supply" had to be given its ordinary natural meaning (see also *Searle* [1971] Crim.L.R. 592).

> In *Buckley* (1979) 69 Cr.App.R. 371, B and G pooled their money intending to buy cannabis in bulk. B took the money to L, the supplier, and bought 1lb of cannabis resin. Thereafter, B gave 3/4 lb of the drug to G representing the latter's contribution to the purchase price. B argued that he could not "supply" to G what he already possessed.
>
> *Held*: B was guilty of supplying the drug because he distributed it. *Holmes v. Chief Constable Merseyside Police* applied.

In *Denslow* (February 6, 1998), the Court of Appeal applied *Buckley and Lane* and gave some guidance to prosecutors. As the law presently stands, there is a supply upon the transfer of custody and physical control of a controlled drug to another, to enable that other to benefit from its use: see *Maginnis* [1987] 1 All E.R. 907. Many of the authorities relevant to this topic have been considered in Chapter 4, entitled "Possession with Intent to Supply".

I. Making an Offer to Supply

5–28 Where an offer is made to supply a drug in the belief that it is one which is controlled under the Misuse of Drugs Act 1971. In *Morrison (Gerard) v. Normand*, 1997 S.C.C.R. 469, it was held that the offence of offering to supply a controlled drug did not require an accused to be physically in possession of a controlled drug. Accordingly, an offence is committed even though the substance sold is not the drug it was thought to be and was not even a controlled drug: see *Goodard* [1992] Crim.L.R. 588 and *Mitchell* (June 3, 1992, unreported). Similar considerations apply where the charge is a conspiracy to offer to supply controlled drugs (for a discussion on the preferring of conspiracy courts in respect of an offer to supply, see H. Keating, [1994] 110 L.Q.R. 373). In *Gill* (1993) 97 Cr.App.R. 215 the Court of Appeal regarded themselves bound by *Goodard* [1992] Crim.L.R. 588 and *Mitchell* (June 3, 1992).

> In *Haggard v. Mason* [1976] 1 W.L.R. 187, DC, M bought 1,000 tablets of what he believed to be lysergide (LSD), a Class A controlled drug, and sold some of the tablets to Heward. Heward similarly believed the substance to be LSD whereas, in fact, the substance was Bromo STP (another hallucinogenic drug, similar in effect and appearance to LSD but not then controlled under the 1971 Act). M was convicted of offering to supply a controlled drug to H contrary to s.4(3)(a) of the 1971 Act.
>
> *Held*: appeal dismissed *per* Lawson J. at 190: In my judgment, the offence was completed at the time when the appellant met Heward and offered to sell him a quantity of lysergide. It matters not in relation to the offence of offering to supply that what is in fact supplied pursuant to that offer, the offer having been accepted, is not in fact a controlled drug.

Section 4(3)(c) has been particularly widely drawn to involve people who may be at some distance from the actual making of the offer: see *Blake* (1979) 68 Cr.App.R. 1, CA and *Hughes* (1985) 81 Cr.App.R. 344, CA.

5–29 The decision of *Haggard v. Mason* (above) is of some importance. Three situations often fall to be considered in respect of charges under section 4(3)(a) and (c). The first is where the accused makes an offer to supply a controlled drug of one description (*e.g.* cocaine), which in fact turns out to be a controlled drug of a wholly different description. On these facts there exists no difficulty and section 28(3) affords no defence. The offence would seem to be in the making of the offer to supply a controlled drug. The fact that a different controlled drug is involved, is irrelevant.

The second situation is where an accused offers to supply what he believes to be a controlled drug, whereas the substance is in fact not controlled. This situation arose in *Haggard v. Mason*. That case makes it plain that the accused has no defence. The third situation is where an accused offers to supply a controlled drug that in fact, and to the knowledge or belief of the accused, is not controlled at all. The Divisional Court in *Haggard v. Mason* did not need to consider the state of mind of an accused falling into this latter category. If the offence is solely in the making of the offer then it is immaterial whether the representations made by the defendant are true or not: and see *Dhillon* (March 24, 2000) where the offer was for heroin, but in the event, only flour was supplied.

In *Goodard* [1992] Crim. L.R. 588, G admitted to police in interview that he offered to get cannabis for another upon payment of £30. G said that he had not intended to carry the offer into effect and that the offer was a "confidence trick". In dismissing an appeal against conviction for an offence under section 4(3), the Court said: 5–30

> "... it is quite plain that the offence is complete when the offer to supply a controlled drug is made, quite regardless of whether the offeror intends to carry the offer into effect by actually supplying the drug.... If a defendant having been convicted of this offence persuades a judge that it was not his intention to carry the deal into effect that may be a matter of mitigation but it cannot be a defence to the charge."

Again, in *Mitchell* (unreported, June 3, 1992, CA) M offered to supply cannabis to another and when M was searched, he was found in possession of a substance, which resembled herbal cannabis, but it was innocuous. In delivering the judgment of the court, Staughton L.J. said:

> "An offer may be by words or conduct. If it is by words, one has to judge from the words whether it is an offer to supply a controlled drug. If a person knowingly makes an offer to supply in words which have that effect, that is the offence. Of course if the offer was by conduct, such as holding a packet in one's hand and in the other hand a placard saying '£20', it might be another question; there it might be relevant whether what was in the packet was a controlled drug or not."

It is submitted that the only reason why it may be important to establish the true contents of the packet (in the example given) would be to prove the nature of the offer being made, *i.e.* an offer to supply a controlled drug. If that fact could be established by reference to all the surrounding circumstances of the case then, it is submitted, the exact identity of the substance is irrelevant (and see *Showers* [1995] Crim. L.R. 400). 5–31

Section 28 of the Act applies to offences under section 4(3). Construed literally it follows that section 28 extends to offences under section 4(3)(a) and (c). The question arises whether an accused falling within the third category, has a defence under section 28(3)(b)(i), *i.e.* that he neither believed nor suspected nor had reason to suspect that the substance was a controlled drug. However, section 28(3) only begins to come into play in cases where the prosecution are required to prove (and have proved) that the substance in question is a controlled drug. Section 28(3) therefore has no application where an offer to supply a controlled drug is made at least by words: see *Mitchell* [1992] Crim. L.R. 594.

Although, in the ordinary way, a person is entitled to be judged on the facts as he believed them to be (see *Taaffe* [1984] A.C. 539 and *DPP v. Nock* [1978] A.C. 979) it is submitted that the mischief which the legislature has sought to punish is the act of making an offer to supply a controlled drug, irrespective as to whether the offer was bogus in nature or not.

II. Being Concerned in the Supply of a Drug

(a) "Being concerned"

5–32 Where a prosecution is brought under section 4(3) (b) or (c), it is the duty of the trial judge to assist the jury as to the meaning of the word "concerned": see *Hughes* (above). A failure to do so may result in the conviction being quashed. Given that "concerned" involves some identifiable act of participation, it follows that the assistance given to the jury, by the judge, will vary from case to case. However, any direction must have regard to the relevant evidence of the accused's conduct in the transaction: see, for example, *Burton v. H.M. Advocate*, G.W.D. March 28, 1997, *McCreadie v. H.M. Advocate*, G.W.D. March 1, 1996, and *McQuinlan v. H.M. Advocate*, G.W.D. May 23, 1997.

Some guidance as to the meaning and scope of the phrase "being concerned in the supplying" of a controlled drug to another is to be found in a passage of Lord Hunter's opinion in *Kerr v. H.M. Advocate* 1986 S.C.C.R., when he said:

> "I consider s.4(3)(b) was purposely enacted in the widest terms and was intended to cover a great variety of activities at the centre and also on the fringes of dealing in controlled drugs. It would, for example, in appropriate circumstances include the activities of financiers, couriers and other go-betweens, look-outs, advertisers, agents and many links in the chain of distribution, it would certainly include the activities of persons who take part in the breaking up of bulk, the adulteration and reduction of purity, the separation and division into deals and the weighing and packaging of deals."

5–33 It will frequently happen that an accused is found in possession of a large quantity of controlled drugs and there may be evidence that he or she separated the quantity into "deals". Such evidence would be typical of a charge brought under section 5(3) of the MDA (*i.e.* possession with intent to supply) but, in the absence of evidence that the accused played some identifiable part in one or more acts of supply, it would not be sufficient to mount a charge under section 4(3)(b). As the court in *Dickinson v. H.M. Advocate*, 1995 S.L.T. 703 pointed out, the mere act of buying drugs and separating them into deals would probably not be enough to support a charge under section 4(3)(b). The court suggested that "something more, by way of involvement in other transactions is needed" and that typically such a charge would "involve some activities extending over a period of time". However, it is submitted that an offence under section 4(3)(b) is not complete without proof that the defendant was concerned in a particular transaction, that is to say that the defendant must at least have been aware of what was afoot and played some part with that knowledge: see *Duffin v. H.M. Advocate*, 2000 J.C. 316.

(b) Is a section 4(3)(b) offence an activity offence?

The point is not straightforward but it is submitted that the safest course is to treat each of the offences created by section 4(3) of the Misuse of Drugs Act as embracing single transactions only. As we have seen, notions of "supply" and "supplying" elude a clear definition apt to cover all situations. In everyday speech, both of those expressions are likely to cover single or multiple transactions. However, it is obviously important that the criminal law should strive to be clear and certain so that defendants know the case they have to meet, and sentencers are able to impose appropriate penalties. Parliament did not enact an offence of "dealing" specifically to embrace multiple acts of supply. The Independent Inquiry recommended that such an offence should exist—a recommendation rejected by the Government but not on the basis that section 4(3)(b) already covers the position. Where there is a course of dealing—particularly if committed over a long period of time—prosecutors will need to ensure that the indictment contains sufficient counts to enable the court to sentence adequately. For what the point may be worth, it is submitted that the language of section 4 tends to support the contention that section 4(3) was not drafted with multiple acts of supply in mind. Section 4(3)(a), for example, does not say that it is an offence to "supply a controlled drug to another or others in contravention of . . .". At the time section 4 was enacted, it was widely understood that sentencers did have power to sentence offenders on the basis of sample or specimen counts, and that there was no injustice in doing so provided it was clear that the prosecution were putting their case that way, and that the defendant would be sentenced on that basis if convicted. It is difficult to find the origin of the practice of drafting specimen counts let alone sentencing on that basis. By the mid 1980s there were signs that this approach might be inappropriate: see *Ayensu* (1982) 4 Cr. App. R.(S) 248 and *O'Connner* (1981) 3 Cr. App. R.(S) 225, but contrast with *Russen* (1981) 3 Cr. App. R.(S) 134. The catalyst for a major review of this topic was the Criminal Justice Act 1991. In *Barry* (unreported) the issue of sentencing on the basis of specimen counts was carefully considered by the Court of Appeal although the reasoning of that court was not followed in the decision of *Canavan and Kidd* [1998] 1 Cr. App. R.(S) 243 that soon followed it, and see now *Brown* [2000] 1 Cr. App. R.(S) 300, *Evans* [2000] 1 Cr. App. R.(S) 144, and *Twisse* (November 7, 2000). In *Brown*, B was 5–34 convicted of an offence under section 4(3)(b) on the basis—as it turned out—of one transaction. However, at the trial there appears to have been considerable uncertainty on the part of the parties to the proceedings, as to whether the offence was confined to a single act for the purpose of sentencing. The judge ruled that the offence was an "activity offence" that entitled him to look at the "wider picture". In the event B was sentenced in respect of a single transaction, and the Court of Appeal left open the question as to whether the offence is an activity offence. The question was also left open in *Levantiz* (November 5, 1998) although their lordships assumed "without investigating the matter in detail" that the count (charged under section 4(3)(b)) was indeed duplicitous in the form in which it was left to the jury. . . ."

5–35 A similar problem arose in *Martens and White* [1998] 2 Cr. App. R. 385, in relation to offences charged under section 170(2) of CEMA 1979. The Court of Appeal held that the offence in question was an activity offence. However, it should be carefully noted that the precise offence related to the unlawful evasion of the payment of duty and not to the unlawful evasion of a prohibition on importation of prohibited goods. The distinction may be important because in respect of the latter, determining whether there has been an "evasion" or an "attempted evasion", is determined by whether there had been an effective importation of the goods in question. There may be a number of reasons why goods are not imported and thus there will be no evasion in those circumstances: see *Latif and Shahzad* [1996] 2 Cr. App. R. 92.

Although the position is not entirely clear, it is submitted that a charge under section 4(3)(b) is apt to cover a single transaction only so that it is not appropriate to prefer one charge embracing a series of transactions (note the wording of s. 4(3)). In *Twisse* (November 7, 2000), it was suggested that if the prosecution can prove that a defendant has been acting as a supplier over a substantial period of time, it can put the court in a position to sentence properly by (i) charging a number of offences of supplying or possession of drugs at different dates; or (ii) by charging the defendant with conspiracy to supply over a prescribed period; or (iii) by charging him with being concerned in the supply of a controlled drug over a specified time, contrary to section 4(3)(b) of the Misuse of Drugs Act 1971. However, with respect, the third of those options may or may not be well founded. It seems that in Scotland the offence is treated as an activity offence: see for example, *Kearney v. H.M. Advocate*, 1998 S.C.C.R. 52, and *Hepplewhite v. Russell*, G.W.D. May 9, 1997. It is submitted that for the moment the wisest course is to treat the offence under section 4(3)(b) as being confined to a single transaction.

There will be cases when it will be appropriate to join a series of transactions on one indictment to show a course of conduct. In such a case it would be permissible for the prosecution to adduce evidence of drugs found in the possession of a defendant coupled with the seizure of drug paraphernalia, recorded transactions and money, in order to prove a series of counts on an indictment that corresponds to a series of transactions. Each case must of course be judged on its own facts but practitioners must be vigilant to ensure that evidence adduced by the prosecutor is properly admissible (*i.e.* relevant and probative) in respect of the charge which the tribunal of fact has to consider: see, for example, *Gordon* [1995] Cr. App. R. 61; *Halpin* [1996] Crim. L.R. 112; *Peters* [1995] 2 Cr. App.R. 77; see Chapter 11 of this work.

(c) Does "being concerned" replace notions of "aiding and abetting"?

There exists, at present, a rather speculative interpretation as to whether the use of the word "concerned" was intended by the legislature to replace the principles of aiding and abetting. If not then why did Parliament enact (b) and (c) at all? As Eveleigh L.J. said in *Blake* (1979) 68 Cr.App.L.R. 1, section 4(3)(c) is very widely drawn to include people "who may be at some distance from the actual making of the offer". In *Blake*, O made an offer to supply drugs to X in Piccadilly. B was not present but X and O went to B's flat to obtain the drugs. B's conviction for being concerned in the making of an offer to supply was upheld. In *H.M. Advocate v. Hamill*, 1998 S.C.C.R. 164, it was held that in Scottish law, the charge under section 4(3) was broad enough that there was no place for the application of the common law doctrine of concert: and see *Harrison v. H.M. Advocate*, 2000 S.L.T. 2. 5–36

In *Clements v. H.M. Advocate*, 1991 S.L.T. 388, the High Court of Justiciary had to consider whether acts done in England were triable in Scotland. In that case, the only evidence led by the Crown was to the effect that "X" and "Y" collected 7 kilograms of cannabis resin in London and gave it to a co-accused who had travelled from Scotland and then returned to Scotland by train. Both "X" and "Y" were convicted of an offence under section 4(3)(b). It was submitted on their behalf that nothing in the 1971 Act overcame the presumption that a criminal statute was not intended to have extra-territorial effect. In refusing the appeals, the Court held that the problem posed was as to territorial limitations between different jurisdictions within the United Kingdom. The answer depended on constitutional practice and not international comity. The 1971 Act created a statutory offence, which operates within the United Kingdom, and accordingly there was nothing in precedent, comity or good sense to inhibit the Scottish courts from treating as justiciable acts committed in another part of the United Kingdom, which formed part of the chain in supplying, controlled drugs to persons in Scotland. The Court distinguished *Somchai Liangsiripprasert v. Government of the United States of America* [1990] 3 W.L.L.R. 606.

(d) Supplying to "another"

If A supplies B with a controlled drug, is it permissible to charge them both on a single count, with an offence contrary to section 4, or is that course impermissible on the basis that B would in effect be charged with 5–37 supplying drugs to himself and not to "another"? The answer seemed to be the latter, based on the decision of the Court of Appeal in *Paolo Ferrara* (July 17, 1984, CA; unreported). In that case, F and S were tried on a charge that they, *together with* W, were concerned in supplying a controlled drug to "another". It seems that the case that was finally left to the jury whether F and/or S, supplied drugs to W. In quashing the conviction, the court held that the word "another" in the count, "in the context of the description of the offence is clearly used to denote somebody other than [F, S, and W]. The basis, therefore, on which the judge told the jury that they could convict was not the offence described in the particulars of offence."

Ferrara was based on another decision of the Court of Appeal in *Smith (Brian)* (February 14, 1983, unreported). It was alleged that S conspired with W to supply a controlled drug to "another". The case was thus one of conspiracy but it is submitted that that the principles are, or should be, the same whether the charge is conspiracy or a substantive charge under the Misuse of Drugs Act. The prosecution case was that the "another" was S. In quashing S's conviction, Griffiths L.J. said:

> "'Another' in the context of that description of the offence is clearly equivalent to somebody else Anybody reading those particulars of the offence would come prepared to meet a case in which what the prosecution were alleging was that Smith and Wilkins had come to an agreement together that they would supply cannabis to some third party. The prosecution did not come up to making out such a case. . . . The judge accepted the prosecution's submission that the word 'another' in the particulars of the offence could refer to Smith. This court is quite unable to accept that construction of the wording of the particulars of the offence. As a matter of ordinary usage of English 'another' clearly does not refer to Smith but refers to some other third party."

The upshot was that both those cases have been taken to be authority for the proposition that where two or more persons are charged on the same count with supplying drugs to "another", the "another" cannot be a person named in that count.

5–38 However, in *Smith*, Griffiths L.J. pointed out that the prosecution stated during the trial that their case was that W supplied S with a controlled drug, but the defence complained that "the prosecution had not charged the accused with that offence". Griffiths L.J. said:

> "That, of course, could have been charged as a conspiracy and would, of itself, have been an offence. . . ."

On that basis it seems that Griffiths L.J. was saying that it is permissible to charge two or more persons with a conspiracy to supply a controlled drug to another, even if that other is an alleged named co-conspirator, providing the prosecution make that fact clear in the particulars of the charge.

This now appears to be the view of the Court of Appeal in *Drew* [2000] 1 Cr. App. R. 91, and *Jackson* [2000] 1 Cr. App. R. 97. In *Drew*, Waller L.J. reviewed most, but not all, of the authorities and said:

> "It will be noted that the decision in the case [*i.e. Smith*] is confined to a ruling that the particulars of the offence were not of the offence on which the jury convicted. . . ."

The Court referred to the judgment of Mantell L.J. in *Barker* (March 27, 1988), who placed reliance on *Ferrara*, but the result in *Barker* was also determined by the way the prosecution had put their case at trial. See also *Gingell* (April 16, 1999, CA).

However, in *Adepoju* [1988] Crim.L.R. 378, CA the Court of Appeal appeared to hold that the "another", for the purposes of section 4, cannot be a person "in the indictment". This seemed to go a great deal further than the decision in *Ferrara* (as *Ferrara* was then generally understood). In *Adepoju*, A, L and a Carol Curmi were all charged with being concerned in the unlawful supply of heroin to another (*i.e.* to Curmi) contrary to section 4(3) of the MDA 1971. At the end of the prosecution case Curmi successfully submitted that there was no case for her to answer on the basis that she could not supply herself. The prosecutor successfully applied to the Court for leave to amend the indictment to delete Curmi as a defendant from that charge but to name her as the "another" to whom the supply was made. 5–39

That amendment prevented the appellants from successfully submitting that there was no case for them to answer on the basis that the prosecution had failed to prove that the appellants had supplied another. Even if supply to Carol Curmi could be established she was not "another" so long as she was included in the count on the indictment. The Court of Appeal held that the appellants had been entitled to a ruling in respect of their submission of no case to answer as the indictment stood "at the time". The judge had accordingly been wrong to allow the amendment. As the court remarked, "the trouble had arisen because of careless drafting of the indictment". That might now be said to be consistent with the reasoning of the Court of Appeal in *Drew* and *Jackson*. However, the Court concluded that "it was a matter of common sense that 'another' could not be a person in the indictment ".

It was most unfortunate that, in *Adepoju*, the Court throughout its judgment used the word "indictment", as opposed to "count", but the ambiguity was resolved by the Court of Appeal in *Connelly* [1992] Crim.L.R. 296, *The Times*, November 6, 1991. The Court explained *Adepoju* on the basis that, in strict law, each count was a separate indictment. The cases of *Smith* (above), *Ferrara* (above) and *Adepoju* (above) did not hold that the other person could not be somebody who was a defendant on the same indictment. However, according to the report of *Connelly* in *The Times*, the Court held that "where a defendant was charged with supplying a controlled drug to another, the 'another' referred to could be someone named in the same indictment although it could not be someone named in the 5–40 same count" and "that the reasoning behind all three decisions was that in plain English where A, B and C were charged with supplying another, that other could not be A, B or C".

In the commentary to that case Professor Smith said:

> "A single defendant, A, could not be guilty of supplying drugs to himself. If A, B and C are charged in a single count, only one offence, one act of supply, is alleged. A, B and C may have in fact been guilty of supplying drugs to one another but then there would be a series of offences which has not been charged. In the absence of a fourth person to whom they supplied drugs, they could no more be all guilty as principals in one offence of supplying than could the single defendant. If no fourth party is involved the only conceivable way in which A, B and C could be guilty of a single offence would be by holding one or two of them to be guilty as secondary parties to the supply of the goods by the other or others. For example, A asks B and C to supply him with drugs. B and C do so. B and C are principal offenders. A is guilty as a counsellor and procurer of the offence. This might perhaps be thought a devious way to proceed; but it seems right in principle."

(e) Can one supply to another outside the United Kingdom?

5–41 It has not been resolved by an appellate court whether an intention to supply a person abroad with a controlled drug is an offence under section 5(3) of the Act. It is submitted that it is not. This is because offences under the Act are local. Offences under section 20 fall into a very different category. It would not be an offence under section 4 for a person having travelled from England, on holiday in India, to supply a controlled drug to another person there. Again, a person who posts drugs to another abroad commits no offence under section 4 although he commits at least an exportation offence. Accordingly, a person who possesses a drug intending to "supply" a person abroad commits no offence under section 5(3) because the supply must be contrary to section 4.

(f) Need the transaction be complete?

5–42 For the purposes of section 4(3)(b) a person may be guilty of being concerned in the supplying of a controlled drug to another even if no supply actually took place: in *Kerr v. H.M. Advocate*, 1986 S.C.C.R. 81, Lord Hunter said:

> "Section 4(3)(b) covers the whole process of supplying to others, a process which may not be completed The provision is designed to catch any person who is concerned at any stage in the process of supplying to others from the beginning of that process to the end."

The Lord Justice Clerk said, by way of example, that if a man were to assist a drug user by introducing him to a supply of controlled drugs, that could involve the former being concerned in the supplying of a controlled drug to another even though no actual supply took place on the occasion in question (see 89).

(g) What must the accused intend?

In the third edition of this book, brief consideration was given as to the relationship between section 4(3)(b) and section 28. In the ordinary way, a person charged with an offence under section 4(3)(b), will find that the prosecution only have to prove that he supplied a thing that was in fact a controlled drug. Thereafter, it would be for him to establish a defence under section 28. The position is the same in England and in Scotland. Thus, in *Tudhope v. McKee*, 1987 S.C.C.R. 663, it was held that where the defendant is not acting in concert with another, the offence under section 4(3)(b) was one of strict liability subject only to section 28. A gloss appears to have been placed on this principle by the Court in *Robertson v. H.M. Advocate*, 1994 G.W.D. 468, where it was held that R was guilty of an being concerned in the supply of a Class A drug, contrary to section 4(3)(b), where he knew of the presence of cannabis in the car but did not know of the existence of LSD which was with it. This perhaps turns on whether or not the defendant could be said to be in possession of the LSD at all. 5–43

However, in *Rodden v. H.M. Advocate*, 1994 S.C.C.R. 841, the Court considered the position of persons acting in concert and held that where two or more persons are charged jointly with an offence under section 4(3)(b) of the MDA, the prosecution must prove that *each defendant* had knowledge that "drugs" were involved in the transaction. The author was critical of that decision because it put parties to a joint enterprise in a more favourable position that a person acting alone. The latter would have to avail himself of a defence under section 28 whereas, in the case of parties acting in concert, the prosecution would have to prove that each defendant (alleged to be acting in concert) knew that the supply related to controlled drugs. By section 28(3)(b)(i) it is a defence if the accused can prove that he "neither believed nor suspected nor had reason to suspect that the substance or product in question was a controlled drug" (in Scots law, s. 28(2), is the most significant provision but see *Lambert* (July 5, 2001, HL). If D2 hands a substance to X in the belief that he is supplying him with a "drug", which D2 mistakenly thinks is not controlled, then s.28(3)(b)(i) affords him a defence but the evidential burden is on him to prove it. However, it is clear that in *Rodden*, the Court was going very much further. The court purported to apply *McCadden v. H.M. Advocate*, 1986 S.C.C.R. 16.

In *Salmon v. H.M. Advocate*, 1999 SLT 169, at p. 178, the Lord Justice General said: 5–44

> "... the use of the words 'concerned in' in section 4(3)(b) shows that the accused person must have a degree of knowledge. One cannot be 'concerned in' supplying a controlled drug, if one is not aware of being

> involved in supplying. . . . Just as with possession, so also in section 4(3) cases, the question arises as to the degree of knowledge which the Crown must establish. In my view, by a parallel train of reasoning to that which applies in section 5 cases, the Crown must establish that the accused knew that he was involved in supplying something, and must prove that the thing which he was concerned in supplying was the controlled drug [alleged] in the charge. . . . The accused will then be convicted unless he can establish one of the defences in section 28."

The position was critically reviewed by the High Court of Justiciary in *Salmon v. H.M. Advocate*, 1999 S.L.T. 169. In short, the Court rejected the proposition that parties to a joint enterprise must be proved to have known that the supply involved a controlled drug. The Lord Justice General said (at 180):

> ". . . in some of the Scottish authorities there is an indication that, in cases where the Crown rely on concert to establish guilt of a section 4(3)(3) offence, the Crown must prove that the accused knew that they were concerned in supplying a controlled drug. This proposition first emerged in *McCadden v. H.M. Advocate*, 1986 S.C.C.R. 16 . . .in due course *McCadden* was cited to the court in *McKee* as support for a contention that, on a charge under section 4 (3) (b), the Crown had to prove that the accused knew that the subject of the supply was controlled drugs. . . . In *McKee* . . . the Lord Justice Clerk distinguished *McCadden* on the basis that the decision had depended on concert . . . 'he could not have been held to be engaged with others in the commission of a common criminal purpose in relation to supplying drugs unless he knew that the common criminal purpose related to controlled drugs'. In view of what is said in *Rodden v. H.M. Advocate*, 1995 S.L.T. 185 . . . it is worth noting that in this passage [*i.e.* in *McKee*] it was *only in the case of the accused who was to be convicted on the basis of concert that the Lord Justice Clerk stipulated that he required to know that the common purpose related to controlled drugs. . . .*" [italicised words added by the author]

5–45 The Court then went on to consider the case of *Rodden*:

> ". . . The Crown argued that being concerned in supplying a controlled drug was an offence of strict liability, subject only to section 28. . . . The court rejected that submission. Giving the opinion of the court, Lord Justice Clerk Ross stated: '. . . where two or more accused are charged with acting [in concert] in the contravention of section 4(3)(b) of the Act of 1971, it must be established by sufficient evidence that there was knowledge on the part of each accused that drugs were involved in the transaction in question'. . . . The general statement in the Lord Justice Clerk's opinion about the requisite knowledge in a case of concert goes further, however, than was necessary for the disposal of that case and it is accordingly obiter. . . . Neither *McCadden*

> nor *McKee* is authority for a statement of this breadth and in my view as a general proposition, it cannot be correct. . . ."

The Lord Justice General expressed the true position (at least insofar as it represents the law in Scotland) in the following terms:

> ". . . if the Crown establish that the packages contained controlled drugs and that the accused knew that he was involved in supplying the contents of the packages, they will be entitled to seek a conviction without proving that the accused knew that the packages contained controlled drugs—subject to any defence that the accused may put forward in terms of section 28."

III. INTOXICATING SUBSTANCES

So far, we have only been concerned with offences in connection with controlled drugs. However, by the Intoxicating Substances (Supply) Act 1985, Parliament made it an offence to supply or to offer to supply, to a person under 18 years of age, a substance other than a controlled drug, if he knows or has reasonable cause to believe that the substance is, or its fumes are, likely to be inhaled by the recipient for the purpose of intoxication: see section 1(1) of the Intoxicating Substances Act (Supply) 1985. 5–46

However, the substance must be supplied to a person who is under 18 years of age and whom the accused knows, or has reasonable cause to believe, to be under that age: see section 1(1)(a). Alternatively, the substance must be supplied or offered to a person who is acting on behalf of a person under 18 years of age, and whom he knows, or has reasonable cause to believe, to be so acting: see section 1(1)(b) of the Intoxicating Substances (Supply) Act 1985.

If the accused can prove (because the burden is on him) that he was under 18 years of age at the time when it is alleged that he contravened subsection (1), and that he was acting otherwise than in the course or furtherance of a business, he is entitled to be acquitted: see subsection (2). It follows that an accused aged 18 years or over commits an offence under the Act whether he supplies an intoxicating substance in the course of a business or not. The Act does not make it an offence for, say, a 17-year-old solvent abuser to supply the substance he is abusing to another 17-year-old. However, if a minor regularly sells part of his stock, he may (for the purposes of the Act) be engaged in a "business". 5–47

Chapter 6
The Manufacture and Production of Controlled Drugs

A. SUBSTANCES USEFUL FOR MANUFACTURE OF CONTROLLED DRUGS

The Criminal Justice (International Co-operation) Act 1990 received its Royal Assent on April 5, 1990, just a few days prior to the World Ministerial Summit to Reduce the Demand for Drugs and to Combat the Cocaine Trade was held in London, on April 9–11, 1990. 6–01

Part II of the Act was aimed at regulating the manufacture and supply of a variety of substances which may have a legitimate use in industry but which are also used in the unlawful production of controlled drugs. Enactment of Part II of the Act enables the Government to ratify the 1988 Vienna Convention against Illicit Traffic in Narcotic Drugs and Psychotropic Substances.

Sections 12 and 13 regulate and control the manufacture, transportation or distribution of substances listed in Schedule 2 of the Act to prevent their use for the unlawful production of a controlled drug (see Arts 3, 12 and 13 of the 1988 Vienna Convention).

By section 12 of CJICA 1990: 6–02

"12(1) It is an offence for a person—
(a) to manufacture a scheduled substance; or
(b) to supply such a substance to another person,
knowing or suspecting that the substance is to be used in or for the unlawful production of a controlled drug.

(1A) A person does not commit an offence under subsection (1) above if he manufactures or, as the case may be, supplies the scheduled substance with the express consent of a constable.

(2) A person guilty of an offence under subsection (1) above is liable—
(a) on summary conviction, to imprisonment for a term not

exceeding six months or a fine not exceeding the statutory maximum or both;

(b) on conviction on indictment, to imprisonment for a term not exceeding fourteen years or a fine or both.

(3) In this section 'a controlled drug' has the same meaning as in the Misuse of Drugs Act 1971 and 'unlawful production of a controlled drug' means the production of such a drug which is unlawful by virtue of section 4(1)(a) of that Act.

(4) In this section and elsewhere in this Part of this Act "a scheduled substance" means a substance for the time being specified in Schedule 2 to this Act.

(5) Her Majesty may by Order in Council amend that Schedule (whether by addition, deletion or transfer from one Table to the other) but—

(a) no such Order shall add any substance to the Schedule unless—
  (i) it appears to Her Majesty to be frequently used in or for the unlawful production of a controlled drug; or
  (ii) it has been added to the Annex to the Vienna Convention under Article 12 of that Convention; and

(b) no such Order shall be made unless a draft of it has been laid before and approved by a resolution of each House of Parliament."

(Subs. (1A) was inserted by the Criminal Justice (International Co-operation) (Amendment) Act 1998, s.1)

The substances (particularised in Schedule 2 to the 1990 Act as amended by the Criminal Justice (International Co-operation) Act 1990 (Modification) Order 1992, S.I. 1992 No. 2873) are set out in two distinct groups.

6–03 Table I lists "precursors", that is to say, chemicals that may have a legitimate use clinically or in the pharmaceutical industry but which are also used in the unlawful production of a controlled drug. Notification of the proposed exportation of the substances listed in Table I may be required by regulations made under section 13(1)(b) and section 13(2) of the Act. Thus:

N-Acetylanthranilic acid	
Ephedrine	(methamphetamine production)
Ergometrine	(LSD production)
Ergotamine	(LSD production)
Isosafrole	
Lysergic Acid	(LSD production)
3, 4-Methylene-Dioxyphenyl-2-Propanone	
1-Phenyl-2-Propanone	(amphetamine production)
Piperonal	
Pseudoephedrine	(amphetamine production)
Safrole	

The salts (if any) of the above are also included.

Table II lists those chemicals which also have a legitimate purpose in industry and commerce (or generally) but which may also be used as reagents or solvents in the production of a controlled drug. Thus: 6–04

Acetic Anhydride	(heroin and amphetamine production)
Acetone	(cocaine and heroin production)
Anthranilic Acid	(methaqualone production)
Ethyl Ether	(cocaine and heroin production)
Hydrochloric Acid	
Methyl Ethyl Ketone	
Phenylacetic Acid	(amphetamine production)
Piperidine	(phencyclidine production) ("Angel Dust")
Potassium Permanganate	
Sulphuric Acid	
Toulene	

Again, the salts (if any) of the above are included except in respect of hydrochloric acid and sulphuric acid whenever the existence of such salts is possible.

Note also the Commission Directive 2001/8 (February 8, 2001), which replaces Annex 1 to Council Directive 92/109 on the manufacture and placing on the market of various substances used in the illegal manufacture of narcotic and psychotropic substances [2000] O.J.L39/31. The purpose of the 1992 Council Directive (92/109/EEC, of December 14, 1992) is to establish intra-Community monitoring of certain substances frequently used for the illicit manufacture of narcotic drugs and psychotropic substances with a view to preventing the diversion of such substances: Article 1. 6–05

At the same time Commission Regulation (EC)No 260/2001 of February 8, 2001 replaces the Annex to Council Regulation (EEC)No 3677 /90 laying down measures to be taken to discourage the diversion of certain substances to the illicit manufacture of narcotic drugs and psychotropic substances, in this instance to give effect to the decision taken by the United Nations Commission on Narcotic Drugs in March 2000, to include norephedrine in Table I of the Annex to the 1988 U.N. Convention. In order to give effect to this decision, it was necessary to amend "category 1" of the Annex to Regulation (EEC) 3677/90. The Regulation came into force, by Article 2, on March 1, 2001, and shall be binding in its entirety and directly applicable in all Member States.

6–06

CATEGORY 1[1]

Substance	Designated name
1-Phenyl-2-propanone	Phenylacetone
N-acetylanthranilic acid	2-Acetamidobenzoic acid
Isosafrol (cis +trans)	
3,4-Methylenedioxyphenylpropane-2-one	1-(1,3-Benzodioxol-5-yl)propan-2-one
Piperonal	
Safrole	
Ephedrine	
Pseudoephedrine	
Norephedrine	
Ergometrine	
Ergotamine	
Lysergic acid	

(1) The salts of the substances listed in this category whenever the existence of such salts is possible.

(2) O.J. L278, 28.10.1999, p.1.

6–07

CATEGORY 2[1]

Acetic anhydride
Phenylacetic acid
Anthranilic acid
Piperidine

(1) The salts of the substances listed in this category whenever the existence of such salts is possible.

6–08

CATEGORY 3

Substance	Designated name
Hydrochloric acid	Hydrogen chloride
Sulphuric acid	
Potassium permanganate (*)	
Toluene (*)	
Ethyl ether (*)	Diethyl ether
Acetone (*)	
Methylethylketone (MEK)(*)	Butanone

(*) The salts of these substances whenever the existence of such salts is possible.

Section 13(1) of the CJICA 1990 empowers the Secretary of State to make regulations for the keeping of records and the furnishing of information in respect of those substances while regulations made under section 13(2) may require manufacturers and suppliers to give notification of any proposed exportation to any country specified in the regulations in respect of a scheduled substance. Where the requisite notice has not been given, the substance shall be deemed to be exported for the purposes of section 68 of the CEMA 1979 (offences relating to the exportation of prohibited or restricted goods): see section 13(2). 6–09

Given our special trading relationship with Europe and that many of the chemicals specified in CJICA 1990 do have legitimate uses, it has been necessary to make special provision in respect of various chemicals supplied to members of the European Market. Thus, Article 30 of the EEC Treaty provides:

> "Quantitative restrictions on imports and all measures having equivalent effect shall, without prejudice to the following provisions, be prohibited between Member States."

The ban imposed by Article 30 is not absolute because it is qualified by Article 36 which permits prohibitions or restrictions on imports "justified on grounds of . . . public policy or public security": *Goldstein* [1983] 1 W.L.R. 151. The substances specified in the 1990 Act could, perhaps, be justified on public policy grounds but the position is now covered by the Controlled Drug (Substances Useful of Manufacture) Regulations 1991 (S.I. 1991 No. 1285) as amended by S.I. 1992 No. 2914. The regulations give effect to Council Regulations (EEC) No. 3677/90, which has its own list of "scheduled substances" that broadly follows the chemicals listed in CJICA 1990. 6–10

For the purposes of section 68 of the CEMA (prohibited or restricted exportations) any substance listed in the European Council Regulation is deemed to be exported contrary to a restriction imposed by S.I. 1991 No. 1285 if it is exported without authorisation obtained under Article 5 of the European Regulations: see regulation 5A, S.I. 1991 No. 1285. It should be noted that the police may exercise their powers under section 23 of the MDA 1971 (but not s. 23(3)(a)) as if the words "scheduled substances" were substituted for "controlled drugs": see regulation 5C, S.I. 1991 No. 1285, as amended.

Parliament was concerned to ensure that nothing in sections 12 or 13 undermined the voluntary system (which has been in operation for a number of years) of passing information to law enforcement agencies by manufacturers and distributors of scheduled substances.

I. Offences in Respect of Section 13

Two offences (non-compliance with the regulations and furnishing false information) are created by CJICA 1990, s.13 (5) which provides: 6–11

> "Any person who fails to comply with any requirement imposed by the regulations or, in purported compliance with any such requirement, furnishes information which he knew to be false in a material particular is guilty of an offence."

It would seem that neither offence is extraditable since they are not specified as "drug trafficking offences" for the purposes of the DTA 1994 (and see s. 22 and Sched. 4 of the 1990 Act).

By section 13(2) a failure to give notification of the proposed exportation of a substance specified in Table I of Schedule 2 (required by regulations made under section 13(1)(b)) shall be deemed to be exported contrary to a restriction in force for the purposes of section 68 of the CEMA 1979 and note para. 6–02 above. A conviction under section 68 of the CEMA 1979 is a "drug trafficking offence" for the purposes of the DTA 1994 (s. 1(3)(c)(ii)) and is therefore extraditable: see section 22 of the CJICA 1990 and *Governor of Pentonville, ex p. Chinoy* [1992] 1 All E.R. 317.

B. THE PRODUCTION OF CONTROLLED DRUGS

6–12 Subject to any regulations which the Secretary of State may make pursuant to section 7 of the MDA, it is not lawful for any person to produce a controlled drug: see section 4(1)(a). Contravention of this subsection is made a criminal offence by section 4(2) of the MDA.

I. What is Meant by "Production of a Controlled Drug"?

6–13 According to MDA, s.37 (1), the legislature has defined the word "produce" to mean, "producing [a controlled drug] by manufacture, cultivation or any other method, and 'production' has a corresponding meaning".

It is worth pointing out at this stage that although "production" includes "cultivating", Parliament (by section 6(2) of the Act) makes it a distinct offence to cultivate plants of the genus cannabis, unless the grower is authorised to do so by a licence issued by the Secretary of State: see regulation 12 of the Misuse of Drugs Regulations 1985, which provides that:

> "Where any person is authorised by a licence of the Secretary of State issued under this Regulation and for the time being in force to cultivate plants of the genus cannabis, it shall not by virtue of section 6 of the Act be unlawful for that person to cultivate any such plant in accordance with the terms of the licence and in compliance with any conditions attached to the licence."

6–14 It is not immediately apparent why Parliament specifically created this separate offence until one gives "producing" and "production" a narrow meaning. It is clear from section 37(1) that what has to be produced is the controlled drug itself, *i.e.* as specified in Schedule II to the Misuse of Drugs Act 1971. Some drugs are produced by a process of synthesis, *e.g.* LSD and some are produced by cultivation, in the sense that penicillin, for example, is produced from the mould *Penicillium notatum*. Other drugs are produced after a process of extraction. Thus, cannabis resin is the resin separated from the cannabis plant.

The word "cultivation" certainly includes the act of nursing plants to fruition, but not every cultivated plant, in which a drug naturally subsists, is an act of "production", within the meaning of section 37(1), because what is physically produced is not the drug itself (that still subsists in the plant). In 1971, when the Misuse of Drugs Act was passed, "cannabis" was a controlled drug, but the definition of "cannabis" was restricted to the flowering and fruiting tops of the plant: see *Goodchild* [1977] 2 All E.R. 103, and *DPP v Goodchild* [1978] 2 All E.R. 161. Accordingly, in 1971, a cannabis plant that had not flowered, or produced fruiting tops, was not a controlled drug, even though the active ingredient subsisted in the plant. If the infant plant had been cultivated, it follows that a controlled drug had not, at that stage, been "produced" either. Accordingly, in order to prohibit persons growing the plant of the genus cannabis at all, Parliament enacted section 6.

By contrast, cocaine is a controlled drug, extracted from the coca-leaf. 6–15
Obviously, the process of extraction is an act of production. However, the coca-leaf itself, is a controlled drug, and may therefore be "produced" by growing it.

In 1977, the definition of "cannabis" as a controlled drug was extended to include virtually the entire plant (see Criminal Law Act 1977, s.52). As a result, there is now no reason at all why the act of growing the cannabis plant should not be regarded as an act of "production" for the purposes of section 4 of the MDA.

> In *Taylor v. Chief Constable of Kent* [1981] 1 W.L.R. 606 police found cannabis plants in T's premises but not in a room occupied by him. Nevertheless, T knew that the plants were there and that they had been cultivated by X who was convicted under section 6 for so doing. T was charged with permitting or suffering the "production" of the plants in the premises under section 8. The defence argued that the plants had not been produced but only cultivated which was not an activity included in section 8.
>
> *Held*: the appeal would be dismissed. The 1977 amendment of the term "cannabis", included virtually the whole plant, and now equated production with its cultivation.

So-called "magic mushrooms" have given rise to other problems. A number of species of mushroom contain psilocin, *e.g. Liberty Cap*. Psilocin is listed as a Class A controlled drug in Part I of Schedule 2 to the MDA but none of the species of mushroom that contain that psilocin, is specifically listed in that Schedule. It follows that none of the mushrooms are expressly controlled by the Act.

Therefore, merely to cultivate the mushroom cannot amount to producing the drug: see *Stevens* [1981] Crim.L.R. 568, *Cuncliffe* [1986] Crim.L.R. 547 and *Walker* [1987] Crim.L.R. 565, C.A.

6–16 However, that is not the end of the matter. The MDA 1971 also controls "preparations" containing a substance or product that is controlled by the Act. A "preparation" is any process that puts a substance or material into a form suitable for consumption. Thus, merely picking the mushrooms (*Walker* [1987] Crim. L.R. 565) or freezing them (*Hodder v. DPP* [1990] Crim. L.R. 261) are not acts of "preparation". *Hodder v. DPP* is consistent with *Murray v. MacNaughten*, 1984 S.C.C.R. 361 where it was held that magic mushrooms that had been picked and then kept in a bag did not amount to an act of "preparation". Deliberately drying the mushrooms would be sufficient (*Stevens* [1981] Crim. L.R. 568; *Cunliffe* [1986] Crim. L.R. 547; and see 10–04). In *Calabria v. The Queen* [1982] 151 Crim.L.R. 671 (Aus), it was said by the court that "prepare: is:

> "... a word in common use and means 'make ready' or 'to bring into proper state for use by some special or technical process' although it can also mean 'to manufacture, to make up or compound ... the process of drying may be called special even if it is not technical and it conforms to ordinary usage to say that person who dries, *e.g.* fish, or fruit or coffee, to bring it into a state in which it is fit for consumption in a particular way takes part in its preparation. Thus in the ordinary sense of the word, one who dries Indian hemp, in order to make it fit for use, 'prepares' it".

Previous editions of this work have suggested that an act of "preparation" may also amount to "production" for the purposes of section 4 of the Misuse of Drugs Act. This view is supported by the decision in *Calabria v. The Queen* (above), and by the decision of the Court of Appeal in *Harris and Cox* [1995] T.L.R. 455 where it was held that the stripping of cannabis plants after they have been cut and harvested is an act of production because the drug is prepared by discarding the unusable portions of the plant while retaining the useable parts. The statutory definition of "cannabis" excludes the seeds and stalks of the plant. Separating wheat from chaff is ordinarily regarded as an act of "production" and the term "production" is to be given its ordinary meaning. The reasoning of the Court of Appeal in *Harris and Cox* is therefore difficult to fault.

6–17 Not every act of preparation will be an act of production because what must be produced (having regard to s. 37(1)) is a drug controlled by the Act, *i.e.* that the substance can be identified in Schedule 2 by reference to its chemical address (*e.g.* psilocin) or by its description (*e.g.* cocoa-leaf). Accordingly, if the plant is not listed in Schedule 2 (*e.g.* Liberty Cap) albeit that a controlled drug subsists in that plant (psilocin) the plant is not a controlled drug. On the other hand, a controlled drug contained in any "preparation" is expressly caught by Schedule 2 and it is thus controlled by the Act. If the useable parts of the cannabis plant were to be blended with tobacco, the blend would be a "preparation" for the purposes of Schedule 2. If the blend was then packed, ready for sale, it seems likely that the courts (following *Hodder*) would conclude that the packages were "products" (see Sched. 2) and it is therefore difficult to see how the act of packaging can be described as anything other than "production". Converting a substance from one controlled drug to another is "production": see *Russell* (1992) 94 Cr. App. R. 351.

In *Hodder*, police searched premises occupied by H and another where they found bags of frozen magic mushrooms (containing psilocybin) in the freezer compartment of the refrigerator belonging to the defendants. The mushrooms had therefore been picked, packaged and frozen by the appellants.

Held: (1) There was no evidence that freezing the mushrooms brought them into a suitable state to be consumed. They could not be used until defrosted. The act of freezing the mushrooms was not an act of "preparation", but:

Held: (2) the act of picking, packaging and freezing the mushrooms was enough to bring them within the definition of "product" or "other product" in paragraph 5 of Schedule 2 to the Act and therefore the appeal would be dismissed.

The Court of Appeal, in *Hodder*, sought to place an ordinary and natural meaning to the word "product" as it appears in the Act. It is submitted that "product", "produce" and "production" have a corresponding meaning which involve putting the substance into a form ready and intended to be used as a drug controlled by Schedule 2 to the Act. It is a startling result that a person who picks and immediately consumes 10 magic mushrooms would not be in possession of a controlled drug, but if due to lack of appetite he packs and/or freezes them for later consumption, he is then said to be in possession of a controlled "product". If the Court of Appeal is right, then the consequence, in theory at least, is that he has also committed an offence of unlawfully producing a Class A drug (or, more accurately, producing a product containing psilocybin) contrary to section 4(2) of the Act. Nevertheless, it is submitted that prosecutors should charge wisely and not charge as "production" a case that the sentencer is likely to treat as one of possession. 6–18

In *Russell* (1992) 94 Cr.App.R. 351: The appellant's car was stopped and searched. He was found in possession of equipment used by the appellant for converting cocaine hydrochloride (a salt) into free base cocaine. Coca-leaf, cocaine and its salt are controlled as Class A drugs. It was conceded that the base and hydrochloride forms of cocaine are chemically different and have different properties. Paragraph 5 of Schedule 2 of the 1971 Act includes "preparation or other product containing a substance or product" specified in that Schedule.

Held: the conversion of one form of a Class A drug into another form of the same genus may be production. The conversion of the salt was production of a substance described in paragraph 5.

The Court of Appeal pointed out, correctly, that coca-leaf is also controlled as a Class A drug. Base cocaine may be converted into a salt by the addition of hydrochloric acid to produce cocaine hydrochloride. Such a conversion would amount to production.

6–19 The conversion of cocaine, from its salt form to base, involves adding an alkali (*e.g.* bicarbonate of soda) to a solution of the cocaine hydrochloride and water, which is then boiled. (Alternatively, the salt may be moistened, the soda added and heated in a microwave oven.) Either method involves a process. It is not artificial to describe that process as an act of "production".

But for the decision in *Greensmith* [1983] 3 All E.R. 444 it might not have been necessary to have relied on paragraph 5, because some analysts would say that the reference to "cocaine" in paragraph 1 of Schedule 2 to the Act, is in fact a reference to base cocaine ("crack" when dried). Paragraph 4 includes cocaine as a salt. However, in *Greensmith* it was held that whether the drug is the coca-leaf, in its base form or a salt, it is still "cocaine" generically speaking for the purposes of paragraph 1 of Schedule 2. See para. 11–14 and Chapter 16.

In the light of the above it follows that the definition of "preparation" or "product" might include a great deal more than something made commercially in a laboratory or factory. Khat is not yet a controlled drug but cathine and cathinone naturally subsists in the plant, and both of those substances are Class C drugs. Preparing tinctures from the plant by using a solvent to leech out the cathine, would render the tinctures a "preparation" or "product" for the purpose of the Misuse of Drugs Act. It is arguable that khat that is bundled and packaged for use or sale is also a "product"—if the decision in *Hodder* is correct.

II. Lawful Production

6–20 Since many controlled drugs have a medicinal value, the policy of the MDA and the Regulations is to restrict the category of persons who may lawfully produce controlled drugs so that their activities may be closely monitored and regulated.

Accordingly, if the Secretary of State is of the opinion that it is in the public interest (*inter alia*) for the production, supply and possession of specified controlled drugs to be either totally unlawful, or unlawful except for research purposes, or except under licence, then he may, by Regulation, "designate" the drugs as being so affected: see section 7(4) of the MDA 1971; and the Misuse of Drugs (Designation) Order 1986 (S.I. 1986 No. 2331 as amended by S.I. 1990 No. 2631) which, as from April 1, 1987, revoked earlier orders, namely S.I. 1977 No. 1379 and S.I. 1984 No. 1144.

6–21 The most important drugs which are thus subject to section 7(4) of the MDA appear in Part I of the Schedule to the 1986 Order, and include:

Cannabinol
Coca-leaf
Cannabinol derivatives
LSD
Cannabis
Psilocin
Cannabis resin
Raw Opium

Thus, regulation 8(1)(a) of the M.D. Regulations permits a practitioner or pharmacist to manufacture or compound any drug specified in Schedule 2 or Schedule 5 of the M.D. Regulations providing that they act in their respective capacities. Thus, a pharmacist cannot "produce" a controlled drug merely to demonstrate to family and friends how drugs are made.

Again, by regulation 8(1)(b) a person who lawfully conducts a retail pharmacy business may manufacture or compound controlled drugs provided (i) that he acts in his capacity as such and (ii) that the production is carried on at the business premises of the registered pharmacy. A person "lawfully conducting a retail pharmacy business" means, by section 37(1) of the MDA, (and subject to subsection (5)) "a person lawfully conducting such a business in accordance with section 69 of the Medicines Act 1968";

Section 37(5) qualifies the above in the following terms: 6–22

> "So long as sections 8 to 10 of the Pharmacy and Poisons Act 1933 remain in force, this Act in its application to Great Britain shall have effect as if for the definition of 'person lawfully conducting a retail pharmacy business' in subsection (1) above there were substituted—
>
> > 'a person lawfully conducting a retail pharmacy business' means an authorised seller of poisons within the meaning of the Pharmacy and Poisons Act 1933'."

A similar concession is given to the aforementioned persons in respect of drugs listed in Schedule 3 and Schedule 4 of the M.D. Regulations see regulation 9(1)(a) and regulation 9(1)(b). Because the controlled drugs in Schedules 3 and 4 are considered by the Legislature to be less dangerous to use, a further exemption is given to persons who hold a written authority to produce controlled drugs. Such written authority is granted by the Secretary of State, subject to any conditions which he may provide: see regulation 9(1)(c).

A 'written authority' is to be distinguished from a "licence to produce" which may be issued by the Secretary of State in respect of any controlled drug and subject to the terms and conditions attached to the licence: see regulation 5. However, where a person is authorised to produce drugs either by written authority or under licence, he will be obliged to keep a record of each quantity of drug produced by him: see regulation 22(1). Such a record must be preserved for a period of two years (reg. 23(2)).

6–23 In any event any producer of a Schedule 3 or 5 drug must keep every invoice (or similar record) in respect of any such drug which is either obtained by him for the purposes of that production or supplied by him: see regulation 24(1).

Clearly, it is important that the Secretary of State (or an authorised agent) is able to demand the production and inspection of records kept by a drug manufacturer. Such a power is afforded to him by regulation 25(1)(a).

For a multitude of reasons a person entitled to produce drugs under section 4(1)(a) may wish to destroy the end product, *e.g.* because they are not of the required standard or the stock is getting old. Nevertheless, to ensure that such controlled drugs do not fall into the wrong hands, Parliament has provided that drugs listed in Schedules 1 to 4 are destroyed only in the presence of an authorised person and in accordance with his directions: see regulation 26(1). The producer is obliged to keep a record of the date of destruction and the quantity of the drug destroyed: see regulation 26(3).

III. The Unlawful Production of Controlled Drugs

6–24 Although section 4(1)(a) of the Act imposes a general prohibition on the production of controlled drugs, it is section 4(2) which creates offences arising out of a contravention of subsection (1).

Thus, section 4(2) provides:

> "Subject to section 28 of this Act, it is an offence for a person
> (a) to produce a controlled drug in contravention of subsection (1) above; or
> (b) to be concerned in the production of such a drug in contravention of that subsection by another."

In respect of both sections 4(2)(a) and (b) the prosecution must prove that the accused played some identifiable part in the production process.

> In *Farr* [1982] Crim.L.R. 745 F admitted to police that on one occasion A and C arrived at his house, asking to use his kitchen, which he allowed. He knew that A and C produced "pink heroin" there. F was charged with an offence under section 4(2). He had not been charged with an offence of allowing his premises to be used for the production of a drug under section 8.
>
> *Held*: F's conviction would be quashed. He took no identifiable role in the production although he would have had no answer to a charge under section 8.

It will be noted that section 8 of the MDA prohibits an occupier to suffer or permit premises to be used for producing any controlled drug.

(a) Proving Participation in the Production

In *Farr* [1982] Crim.L.R. 745, the Court of Appeal held that there must be established some identifiable participation in the process of producing a controlled drug before a person can be convicted under section 4 of the 1971 Act. What that decision does not make clear (as reported) is whether sections 4(1) and (2) exclude the ordinary rules in respect of participation by secondary parties and thus restrict liability under section 4(2): see the commentary to that case ([1982] Crim.L.R.745). It is submitted that this is not what either Parliament or indeed the Court of Appeal in *Farr* intended. The full transcript of the judgment of that Court suggests that it is a case best seen as having been decided on its "unique" facts. The appellant, a heroin addict, was convicted of producing a controlled drug contrary to section 4(2)(a) of the Misuse of Drugs Act 1971. Adams and Childs arrived unannounced at premises occupied by the appellant and were admitted. Adams and Childs asked to use the kitchen, the appellant knowing that they were going to produce (as they did) pink heroin from morphine. The Court regarded as "relevant" the fact that there was no evidence that the appellant knew what Adams and Childs were going to do until after he had admitted them to his home. In quashing the conviction, the Court held that there was no evidence that "the Appellant did anything that could amount to participation, or that could be interpreted as an act of participation, in the manufacture of a controlled drug": *per* Purchas J. The Court examined the relationship between section 8 and section 4 and concluded that: 6–25

> "there must be some identifiable participation in the process of producing the drug, established before a person can be convicted as an aider and abettor under section 4. To take an example, if, by prior arrangement, the Appellant had come to an agreement with Adams and Childs that he would admit them to his premises and provide facilities, then another situation might well have arisen which would fall within section 4. In this case there is no doubt whatever that the facts established on the evidence would make this Appellant liable to conviction under section 8. But that is not the section with which he is charged. It is therefore necessary to see whether any evidence can be spelt out of the interview between the police officers and this Appellant, which would indicate significant participation. This must involve both the intention to participate and some actus reus in that direction, before there would be evidence which could be left to the jury."

The Court concluded that the evidence demonstrated only "passive presence" of the appellant at the premises and that what he was doing "was knowingly permitting or suffering the production, by Adams and Childs of this drug". The Court added that ". . . there may be many occasions upon which someone permits the production of a drug and also, at the same time, participates in its production. The two situations are not mutually exclusive. . . ."

6–26 In the commentary to *Farr* [1982] Crim.L.R. 745, the question is posed why the appellant, in allowing his kitchen to be used for the production of pink heroin, did not aid and abet production for the purposes of section 4. One suggested answer was that section 4(2) excludes the application of the ordinary law of aiding and abetting and, that support for such a construction, may be found in section 4(2)(b) on the grounds that "concerned in" embraces many instances of aiding and abetting so that "section 4(2) has a narrowing effect on liability". It is plain, from the transcript in *Farr*, that the appellant had argued that the ordinary rules of aiding and abetting did not apply not, however, on the basis of section 4(2)(b) but on the grounds that section 8 covered the case of a person who permits or suffers production on premises and, therefore, such facts cannot fall under section 4. However, the Court of Appeal rejected that argument saying:

> "There are sufficient areas upon which, taking various combinations of events, section 8 can impinge, without there being any conflict with an aiding and abetting under section 4 by making the premises available as a deliberate part of participation in the act of production of the controlled drug."

The case therefore seems to have been decided on a very slender distinction. If the appellant had known that Adams and Childs intended to produce heroin before he had admitted them, then this would have been some evidence of participation in the production by making the premises available for that purpose, but sufferance of that activity after they had been admitted was held not to be enough. It would therefore seem that the Court was not seeking to define the parameters of the offence under section 4 at all, but to decide whether the facts in *Farr* fell within the parameters of aiding and abetting in accordance with existing principles of law. *Farr* should therefore be read with care.

6–27 Sections 4 and 8 are not mutually exclusive since the premises could be made available as part of the act of production, *e.g.* by a pre-arrangement that the premises would be so used. This had not occurred in *Farr*. Passive conduct would not in itself be enough. It may be said that giving encouragement is a sufficient participation in accordance with the usual principles of aiding and abetting the commission of an offence. The difficulty is that section 4(b) also makes it an offence to be "concerned" in the production of a controlled drug. This implies that, once again, some identifiable part in the production of the drug is required and that, accordingly, there is no room for the application of the principles of aiding and abetting: see *Carmichael & Sons (Worcester) Ltd v. Cottle* [1971] R.T.R. 11 and *cf. Blake* (1979) 68 Cr.App.R. 1.

The word "concerned" in section 4(2)(b) is not qualified by the word "knowingly" for the simple reason that section 4(2)(b) is subject to section 28. The burden will therefore be on an accused to show that he did not believe, or suspect or have any reason to suspect that what was actually being produced was a controlled drug (s. 28(3)(b)(i)); or that he did not know, or suspect or have reason to suspect that what he was in fact concerned in was a production venture (section 28(2)).

For a definition of "production", see para. 6–13 above.

It will be seen that the offence of unlawfully producing a controlled drug is subject to the defences available under section 28 of the Misuse of Drugs Act 1971. Of course that provision does not apply where the defendants are charged with a conspiracy to produce controlled drugs. In such a case the reader should bear in mind the observations of the Court of Appeal in *Broad & Others* (April 25, 1997). 6–28

In *Broad and others*, B and others were convicted of conspiracy to produce a Class A drug (count 1) and conspiracy to produce a Class B drug (count 2). The defendants purchased chemicals, and equipment, and set up a laboratory at which traces of amphetamine were detected by police. There were also indications that precursors had been obtained from nutmeg oil for the purpose of producing MMDA, MDA and TMA. The judge directed the jury that, in relation to count one, the Crown did not have to prove that the drugs produced were in fact Class A drugs, or that the appellants knew that it was a criminal offence to manufacture them. The appellants complained that the judge misdirected the jury. In dismissing the appeals against conviction, the Court held that the prosecution had to prove participation in an agreement to produce an illicit controlled drug of Class A. The controlled drugs contemplated are all in Class A, namely, MMDA, MDA, and TMA. The appellants agreed to unlawfully produce controlled substances. The absence of belief that the drugs were in fact controlled was irrelevant: see *Patel* (August 11 1991), *Siracusa*, 90 Cr.App.R. 340, and *Churchill v. Walton* 2 A.C. 224.

C. THE CULTIVATION OF CANNABIS

Although the word "produce" for the purposes of section 4(1)(a) includes "cultivation" (see s. 37(1)), it is the drug which is to be cultivated and not simply the plant in which the drug naturally subsists unless that plant is itself listed as a controlled drug in the Schedules to the MDA. Thus, growing the magic mushroom is not an offence merely because a controlled drug (psilocin) naturally subsists within that plant. On the other hand, the entire cannabis plant is a controlled drug. Originally, only the flowering and fruiting tops of the plant were controlled by the MDA in 1971, hence the probable reason why section 6 was enacted. However, today there is no good reason why the cultivation of a cannabis plant should not be an offence under section 4(1)(a) production and section 6. It follows that an occupier, or manager of premises, who permits or suffers the "production" of cannabis will be guilty of an offence under section 8: see *Taylor v. Chief* 6–29

Constable of Kent [1981] 1 W.L.R. 606, the facts of which are given at para. 6–15, above. Both offences are subject to section 28.

Section 6 provides:

"(1) Subject to any regulation under section 7 of this Act for the time being in force, it shall not be lawful for a person to cultivate any plant of the genus Cannabis.

(2) Subject to section 28 of this Act, it is an offence to cultivate any such plant in contravention of subsection (1) above. The exception to section 6(1) is, in the case of plants cultivated under a licence issued by the Secretary of State, and subject to his terms and conditions endorsed on the licence: see regulation 12 of the M.D. Regulations. The principal reason for this exemption is to facilitate research into the drug."

6–30 An offence under section 6(2) is made out once the prosecution has proved, first, that the accused was cultivating a plant, and, secondly, that the plant was in fact a cannabis plant. It is not necessary for the prosecution to prove that the accused knew that what was being cultivated was in fact a cannabis plant: and see Chapter 7. Thus, in *Champ* (1981) 73 Cr.App.R. 367:

> C was a herbalist who cultivated a plant in a window box. She believed the plant to be hemp, which, according to an elderly gypsy, was good for various ailments. The plant was actually cannabis.
>
> *Held*: the burden was on C to prove, under section 28, that she did not know the plant to be cannabis.

Champ has the curious feature that the defendant believed the plant to be hemp: but hemp is another term for cannabis. However, the point does not seem to have been taken either by counsel or by the court.

An offence under section 6 is not absolute since it is expressed to be subject to section 28.

Chapter 7
Drug Activities on Premises

Policing and enforcing the prohibitions imposed by the MDA on the production, supply and use of controlled drugs is an expensive and difficult task, particularly since many offences are likely to be committed on premises which are owned, occupied or managed by persons who may not themselves be concerned in the commission of the offences. 7–01

They may be absent at the material time. Nevertheless, it was clearly Parliament's hope that obligations imposed on occupiers and managers not to permit, or suffer, a limited range of activities to take place on their premises, would encourage them to "police" the Act. Thus, by section 8:

> "A person commits an offence if, being the occupier or concerned in the management of any premises, he knowingly permits or suffers any of the following activities to take place on those premises, that is to say
> (a) producing or attempting to produce a controlled drug in contravention of section 4(1) of this Act;
> (b) supplying or attempting to supply a controlled drug to another in contravention of section 4(1) of this Act, or offering to supply a controlled drug to another in contravention of section 4(1);
> (c) preparing opium for smoking;
> (d) smoking cannabis, cannabis resin or prepared opium."

Note that by section 38 of the Criminal Justice and Police Act 2001, section 8 is likely to be amended by substituting a new 8(d) as follows:

> "administering or using a controlled drug which is unlawfully in any person's possession at or immediately before the time when it is administered or used."

This provision will not be brought into force without further consultation and (probably) without Home Office guidance to prosecutors. Concern has been expressed as to how this provision would work in practice and what adverse effect it might have on proper harm-reduction schemes. The amendment was sought to tackle so-called "crack houses" but the provision has a much greater reach.

As a piece of Parliamentary drafting, section 8 represents a quite extraordinary example, peppered, as it is, with a host of obvious anomalies. Thus, an occupier is forbidden to permit the smoking of cannabis or pre- 7–02 pared opium to take place on his premises, but not the smoking or injecting of heroin, the snorting of cocaine, the cooking of a "cannabis cake", or the growing of, for example, Liberty Cap (a "magic mushroom"), but permitting a person to deliberately dry out "magic mushrooms", probably would be embraced because "preparing" a drug can be an act of production: see *Hodder v. DPP* [1990] Crim.L.R. 261.

At first sight, the wording of section 8 is astonishing, or at least bewildering. What caused Parliament to legislate against some "use" activities, but not others? There seem to be a number of factors that have led to this result. First, section 8 differs from its forerunner in that section 8 forbids permitting certain activities to take place *on* premises, whereas section 5 of the Dangerous Drugs Act 1965 made it an offence to permit the premises *to be used for* prohibited purposes. It *may be* that Parliament did not wish to make the offence too wide. Secondly, how would occupiers and managers know that their premises were being used for the smoking of cannabis? The answer appears to be that cannabis, and its smoke, have a distinctive aroma, and should thus put a person (who knows what cannabis smells like) on enquiry. On the other hand, occupiers might not be able to tell one tablet, or powder, from another. Arguably, that reason becomes weaker as public awareness of drugs, and their use/misuse, becomes greater. Thirdly, making it an offence to "permit" or to "suffer" the use of controlled drugs raises difficult philosophical and jurisprudential questions about coercing amateurs to enforce a law not only against traffickers, but also against users (some countries recognise the right to self-harm). Fourthly, there are many points at which section 8, if too widely drawn, could adversely affect laudable harm reduction schemes. Fifthly, there are concerns (beyond the scope of this book) about the effectiveness of the offence: who should be targeted?

7–03 It will also be seen that Parliament did not attempt to define several key words and phrases, leaving it to the courts to perform that task. Thus, the terms "occupier" and persons "concerned in the management of premises" are not defined by the Act. A Report by Justice, *Drugs and the Law* (June 1991), recommended that the law be changed to embrace premises that are used for the "ingesting of any controlled drug" (para. 7.8) and that the definition of "premises" is clarified (para. 7.9). However, with the benefit of an additional ten years' experience, the Independent Inquiry (also entitled "*Drug and the Law*") reviewed the position and reached very different conclusions. It recommended the retention of section 8(a) and (b) (and that both should be "drug trafficking offences" for the purpose of the Drug Trafficking Act 1994, but the repeal of section 8(c) and (d).

Note that an offence under section 8 is not a "drug trafficking offence" for the purposes of the DTA 1994, s. 1(3). That will change under the proposed Proceeds of Crime Bill 2001.

Section 8 of the Misuse of Drugs Act has its origins in the Dangerous Drugs Act 1920. Section 5(d) of that Act made it an offence to be "concerned in the management of any premises" used for various purposes in connection with opium including the smoking of that drug. Section 5(c) made it an offence for an occupier to permit "those premises to be used *for the purpose of* the preparation of opium for smoking or the sale or smoking of prepared opium".

The offences in section 5(c) and (d) were replicated in section 6 of the 1951 Dangerous Drugs Act.

New offences were created under the Dangerous Drugs Act 1964 in connection with cannabis (previously known as "Indian hemp"), and section 9(a) of that Act, imposed an obligation on occupiers of premises, not to permit them to be used "for the purpose of smoking cannabis or cannabis resin or of dealing in cannabis or cannabis resin (whether by sale or otherwise) . . . ". By contrast, section 9(b) stated that if any person is "concerned in the management of any premises used for any such purpose" he too committed an offence. 7–04

It will be seen that there appears to have been a significant difference between the two provisions in the 1964 Act. In section 9(a) the occupier had to be proved to have *permitted* the offending activity to take place on premises, whereas section 9(b) included that element and therefore on a literal reading, section 9(b) gave rise to an offence of strict liability: see *Yeandel v. Fisher* [1965] 3 All E.R. 158.

Section 9(a) and (b) of the 1964 Act were replicated in section 5(a) and (b) of the Dangerous Drugs Act 1965. The House of Lords in *Sweet and Parsley* [1970] A.C. 132 examined whether section 5(b) really did create an offence of strict liability. Their lordships concluded that it did not. A person concerned in the management of premises must know what is occurring and that the unlawful purpose was in effect the purpose of the management. Sweet's conviction was quashed: her purpose was to obtain rent. As Lord Reid remarked, " . . . no doubt that greatly reduces the scope of this provision when applied to the use of cannabis . . .". 7–05

It will therefore be seen that section 8 of the Misuse of Drugs Act differs from section 5 of the 1965 Act in two significant respects. First, as to knowledge, both occupiers and those concerned in the management of premises must *knowingly* permit or suffer the offending activity to take place on the premises. Secondly, section 8 is broader than its predecessor because section 8 is directed against activities that take place *on premises*: it is no longer necessary for the premises to be used for *the purpose of* prohibited activities under the Act (*e.g.* as an opium "den").

A. PREMISES

Defining "premises" for the purpose of the MDA is not straightforward. Unfortunately, the draftsmen failed on this occasion to provide a "clarifying definition" a device to state expressly that certain matters are to be treated as coming within a definition. 7–06

In tort, we find that the word "premises" has been broadly construed to include real property; appliances and objects upon it, *e.g.* ships in dry dock

(*London Graving Dock v. Horton* [1951] A.C. 737); and also includes movables not in transit such as ships (see *Duncan v. Cammell Laird & Co.* [1946] A.C. 401); aircraft (see *Fosbroke-Hobbes v. Airwork Ltd* [1937] 1 All E.R. 108); or permanently moored house-boats (see *West Mersea Urban District Council v. Fraser* [1950] 2 K.B. 119). If these authorities can be relied upon as being definitive of the word "premises" for the purposes of section 8 then some curious results follow. Thus, on one view of the authorities it might be argued that the owner of a river cruiser, knowing that cannabis is being smoked on board while the vessel is in motion, will not be guilty of an offence contrary to section 8(d). However, in *Darby* (unreported, 1989; Southwark Crown Court) His Honour Judge Rivlin Q.C., ruled that a pleasure vessel cruising on the river Thames was "premises" within the meaning of section 8. The learned judge derived some support for his conclusions from the decisions of *Andrews v. Andrews and Mears* [1908] 2 K.B. 567 and *Gardiner v. Sevenoaks Rural District Council* [1950] 2 All E.R. 84. There is no logical reason for excluding movables from the scope of this section providing, of course, that the offence is committed within the jurisdiction of the courts.

7–07 There is abundant authority for the proposition that buildings (whether subject to a lease or not) are "premises", but mere land without structures upon it probably falls outside the definition of "premises": see *Bracey v. Read* [1963] Ch. 88. In *Brown* (unreported, 1991; Snaresbrook Crown Court) an "acid house" party was organised at which controlled drugs were consumed. The party was held within a marquee. Unhappily, the trial judge was not required to decide whether the marquee temporarily erected on land was "premises", but it is submitted that it was: see *Norton v. Knowles* (1969) 1 Q.B. 572; *Metropolitan Water Board v. Paine* (1907) 1 K.B. 285; *Field Place Caravan Park v. Harding* [1966] 2 Q.B. 484.

It will be noted, from the opening words of section 8, that the section is expressly directed against activities taking place "on" premises, *e.g.* in a house or dance hall. What is the position if drugs are being supplied from premises? It often happens that drugs are packaged and prepared for supply on premises occupied by the defendant but the actual transactions, and exchange of money for drugs, takes place a short distance away, *e.g.* by a staircase leading to a neighbouring block of flats. Unfortunately, there is as yet no authority directly on the point. It also remains to be decided whether the separation of drugs or packaging them, is an act of "production" for the purposes of section 4 and/or section 8: see *Hodder v. DPP* [1990] Crim. L.R. 261 and *Harris and Cox* [1995] T.L.R. 455.

B. WHO IS RESPONSIBLE?

7–08 Responsibility is clearly based on occupancy or control and not merely on ownership. Section 8 is expressly aimed at the occupiers or the managers of premises since it is they who may exercise immediate supervision over the activities carried on within them. As the Court of Appeal pointed out in *Tao* [1977] Q.B. 141 the fact that the term "occupier" was not defined in the Act suggests that the intention of the Legislature was to leave it to the tribunal of fact to decide whether an accused exercised "sufficient exclusivity of possession so that he can fairly be said to be 'the occupier'" (*per* Roskill L.J.).

The Court held that a common sense rather than a legalistic meaning should be given to the term "occupier" so that a person who was in a position to exercise a sufficient degree of control to exclude, say, a cannabis smoker was an occupier for the purposes of section 8.

> In *Read (Keith Paul) v. DPP* (June 20th, 1997) the divisional Court dismissed an appeal by way of case stated against R's conviction of being the occupier of premises in which he knowingly permitted or suffered the smoking of cannabis to take place contrary to section 8 (D) of the Misuse of Drugs Act 1971. R contended that he was not the occupier of the premises because the tenancy of the council house was in the name of his girlfriend with whom he had been cohabiting for some nine years. The court held that R was clearly an occupier and his claim to the contrary was unrealistic.
>
> In *Coid* (October 6, 1997), C was convicted of permitting or suffering premises to be used for supplying cannabis resin contrary to section 8 of the Misuse of Drugs Act 1971. C was the boyfriend of Miss M: he cohabited with her at the premises although she was the tenant. When she was away C would look after the premises. Drugs paraphernalia were found in the premises. When interviewed D gave the address as being his. C's defence was in part that he was not an occupier for the purpose of the Misuse of Drugs Act. The Court of Appeal held that Miss M's tenancy did not preclude C from being an occupier, which was a question of fact for the jury, and the judge gave a proper direction. The Court considered *Tao*, 63 Cr.App.R. 163, 165; and *Mogford*, 63 Cr.App.R. 168.
>
> In *Tao*, the accused, an undergraduate, occupied a room allocated to him by his college. He lived there and held the key to the room. Police found traces of cannabis resin and they smelled burning cannabis.
>
> *Held*: T had sufficient exclusivity of possession to be an occupier for the purposes of section 8 of the MDA. The argument advanced by the appellant was that a distinction had to be drawn between "an occupier" and "being in occupation".

There was force in T's argument. A number of persons may decide to occupy premises as "squatters". They are certainly in occupation but scarcely enjoy a legal exclusivity of possession. Can they therefore properly be said to be "occupiers"? Support for the argument was found in *Mogford* (1970) 63 Cr.App.R. 168, which was then concerned with the word "occupier" as it appeared in section 5 of the Dangerous Drugs Act 1965. On 7–09 that occasion, Neild J. held that it must be shown that an accused was in "legal possession" of the premises. He said (at 169):

> "... the word 'occupier' is not defined in this enactment ... it is a penal statute ... the provisions must be construed strictly and favourably to accused persons ... it seems quite impossible to say here that the word 'occupier' must mean 'owner' ... the word 'occupier' is used in this Act in its advisory sense in a context which shows clearly that the person ... is in legal occupation and in control of premises. ... "

Accordingly, where two sisters, aged 20 and 15 years, allowed cannabis to be smoked in their parents' house (while their parents were away on holiday), they were not to be regarded as occupiers since they were not in legal possession of the house and therefore, they committed no offence under section 5 of the 1965 Act.

7–10 In *Tao*, however, although the Court of Appeal approved the result in *Mogford*, the court did not approve of the reasoning. It was not entirely clear what Neild J., in *Mogford*, meant by "legal possession", given that an individual can be in legal possession of premises without being a tenant or having any estate in land; (see: *Errington v. Errington* [1952] 1 K.B. 290 and *cf. Heslop v. Burns* [1974] 1 W.L.R. 1241). Furthermore, it is not entirely clear from the report what the facts in *Mogford* really were. It may be that a jury would not have been able to say exactly what the nature of the arrangement was, to amount to occupation of those premises (a matter, which evidently troubled the court in *Campbell* [1982] Crim.L.R. 595). However, it is submitted that it is not necessary to embark on an enquiry to determine the exact nature of the proprietary rights (if any) of an accused. For the purposes of section 8, it is sufficient if the prosecution can show that the accused exercised control, or had the authority of another, to exclude persons from premises or to prohibit any of the activities referred to in section 8. On the facts of *Tao*, it was held to be enough that the accused had a contractual licence to use the room. He may not have been able to exclude college staff from entering his room but he could exclude cannabis smokers or, for that matter, any smoker. In other words, he was in a position to exercise control over the activities that took place there.

7–11 Both *Tao* and *Mogford* were considered by His Honour Judge Oddie in *Campbell* [1981] Crim.L.R. 595:

> S lived at his mother's address. With her approval, but in her absence, S held a party at the address. G, who lived elsewhere, attended. Following a police raid at the party, G and S were arrested and both accepted responsibility for the cannabis smoking by other guests at the party.
>
> *Held*: the facts were indistinguishable from *Mogford* and accordingly, G and S were not "occupiers" for the purposes of section 8.

The decision is of interest for several reasons but only a brief report of the case is available. As reported, the Court explained *Mogford* in the following terms:

> "Not every transient use of premises or physical ability to remove another from the premises would enable the court or jury to find the nature, extent and degree of possession sufficient for finding that the person was the occupier of premises."

The Court went on to point out that, in *Campbell*, the parents remained occupiers but had delegated to G and S the task of permitting the guests a licence to enter the premises for the purposes of the party while their parents were away overnight. For those reasons G and S were not occupiers. However, on its facts, *Campbell* poses a problem. S arranged the party, he organised it, he decided who should be invited and, no doubt, decided who should remain. In short, he was in control.

In *Mogford*, Neild J. observed that: 7–12

> "Upon the second aspect of the test, namely, control, it was no doubt open to these daughters to invite guests and indeed to exclude persons from their parents' house in the absence of those parents . . . but that does [not] amount to the nature and measure of control which is envisaged in the present statute."

Although the court in *Campbell* felt that the facts were indistinguishable from *Mogford*, in fact, the position in *Mogford* was very different an aspect which it is now necessary to examine.

The section then being considered was section 5 of the Dangerous Drugs Act 1965 which made it an offence to permit premises "to be used for the purpose of smoking cannabis". [Note the words "for the purpose of".] By contrast, section 8 refers to permitting the activity to take place "on those premises". Neild J. explained section 5 of the 1965 Act when he said that the words of that section "denote a purpose which is or has become a significant one or a recognised one though certainly not necessarily the only one".

Examples were given in *Mogford* of the bowling alley or a hairdressing salon or a café. Thus, for the purposes of the 1965 Act, "control" meant control over premises used for a primary purpose. However, in the 1971 Act, section 8 is drafted to include a temporary use of the premises for any of the activities referred to in that section.

Accordingly, the decision of *Campbell* should be viewed with caution. It is submitted that *Tao* establishes the correct test for the purposes of section 8 of the 1971 Act.

(a) Liability of one occupier for the acts of a co-occupier

A co-occupier who permits or suffers another co-occupier to do any of the activities referred to in section 8 commits an offence under that section as if the co-occupier had invited a friend to the premises and permitted him to perform the prohibited activity: *Ashdown* (1974) 59 Cr.App.R. 193. 7–13

In that case, four defendants were charged with an offence under section 5 of the Dangerous Drugs Act 1965 in the following terms, that "being the occupiers of premises", they "permitted those premises to be used for the purpose of smoking cannabis resin". All four defendants were co-tenants having jointly entered into a tenancy agreement. It was argued that it was not possible in law for one co-tenant knowingly to permit another co-tenant to smoke cannabis on the premises. The Court of Appeal held the argument to be fallacious. Roskill L.J. said (at 194):

> "The important point is that the essence of the offence is knowingly permitting that activity to be carried on why is there any privilege or immunity attaching to his position of co-tenant which would prevent him being guilty of an offence against what was section 5 of the 1965 Act merely because he happens to be one co-tenant and the offender who is in possession of the cannabis which he is unlawfully smoking is another co-tenant?"

For a further discussion of problems associated with controlled drugs on premises see Robert Shiels, "Controlled Drugs And Premises Of Multiple Occupancy" by Robert Shiels [1998] Crim L.R. 404.

C. PERSONS IN UNLAWFUL POSSESSION OF PREMISES

7–14 In *Tao* [1977] Q.B. 141 the court held that the person charged must be proved to have had, "whether lawfully or otherwise", sufficient exclusivity of possession of the premises to be an "occupier". There is no authority, specifically on the point, as to whether or not trespassers may nevertheless be "occupiers" for the purposes of section 8. In *Mogford* and *Tao* the Court was concerned with lawful possession or occupation. Indeed, in *Tao*, the Court went so far as to classify T's right to possession on the basis that he was a "contractual licensee", although Roskill L.J. commented that it would be "somewhat astonishing" if a squatter could not be an "occupier" under the Act. The matter is not free from difficulty but there exists no logical reason why "occupier" should be glossed to mean only a person in lawful possession of premises. One must also have regard to the mischief, which the Act seeks to prevent and, as the Court in *Tao* remarked, the concept of occupation and possession should not be construed too legalistically: see also para. 7–09, above.

D. PERSONS CONCERNED IN THE MANAGEMENT OF PREMISES

7–15 "Management" imports the notion of control over the running of the affairs of an enterprise, venture or business. If a person therefore controls premises by running, organising or planning them then he will be "managing" them: see *Josephs* (1977) 65 Cr.App.R. 253. In order to be concerned in the management, it is enough to share, or assist in, the running of the premises. However, there must be something more than the performance of purely menial or routine duties, see *Abbott v. Smith* [1965] 2 Q.B. 622. Thus, the cleaner of a nightclub would not be assisting in the management of that club even if he knew that the reason for its existence was primarily the smoking of cannabis.

Although many occupiers may also be concerned in the management of premises, the converse need not necessarily follow. Indeed, there is no reason why a manager should have any proprietary interest in the premises at all. Thus, in *Josephs* (above) the appellants were squatters on premises but ran a "card school" in the basement. They were convicted of being concerned in the management of premises upon which they knowingly permitted the supplying of cannabis, contrary to section 8. Their appeal against conviction was dismissed. They were managing premises and the fact that they were trespassers was irrelevant.

(a) Knowingly

In *Thomas* (1976) 63 Cr.App.R. 65 the Court was asked to consider whether the word "knowingly" in section 8 added anything to the section. The court held that it did not: the words "permitting" and "suffering" clearly implied knowledge of the relevant activity. 7–16

The point referred to in *Thomas* is hardly novel given the abundance of authority that exists in respect of similar phrases as they appear in other statutes (see: *Gray's Haulage Co. Ltd v. Arnold* [1966] 1 W.L.R. 534; *Taylor's Central Garages (Exeter) Ltd v. Roper* (1951) 2 W.N. 383; *Lucas v. Peek* [1947] 2 All E.R. 574).

In *Gray's Haulage*, Lord Parker C.J. said:

> "... knowledge is really of two kinds; actual knowledge and knowledge which arises either from shutting one's eyes to the obvious, or what is much the same thing put in another way, failing to do something or doing something not caring whether contravention takes place or not."

The next question is whether proof of knowledge necessarily implies permission or sufferance in respect of that activity. 7–17

In *Gray's Haulage*, Lord Parker C.J. said:

> "... Knowledge is not imputed by mere negligence but by something more than negligence, something which one can describe as reckless not caring what happens."

The Court of Appeal in *Thomas* (above) went a little further, observing that knowledge was not to be implied "from neglect to make such inquiries as a reasonable and prudent person would make, which, generally speaking, has no place in the criminal law".

Although section 8 requires proof of knowledge, that does not mean 7–18 that an occupier / manager must witness for himself the offending activity. Knowledge may be proved by demonstrating that the accused wilfully shut his eyes to the obvious. Section 8 does not impose a general duty on occupiers / managers to investigate what is taking place on the premises. However, an occupier / manager will be acting at his peril if he does not take reasonable and appropriate steps to investigate, and deal with, matters that have come to his attention or of which he should reasonably have known. The extent of an accused's knowledge of relevant facts, his actions and his credibility, are often the focus of critical examination at the investigative stage, and at trial, of any alleged contravention of section 8.

> In *Thomas* (above), police found cannabis and cannabis smoking equipment at T's home. T said that it belonged to a friend saying, "I have asked him not to smoke in my house but what can you do?"
>
> *Held*: that the jury were properly directed. Knowledge may include shutting one's eyes to the obvious. The appellant did little to prevent cannabis being smoked on his premises.

7–19 A very different conclusion was reached in *Souter* [1971] 1 W.L.R. 1187:

> S let rooms in his house to drug addicts, retaining the living room for his own occupation. He put a notice on the door of that room to the effect that the police would be called immediately if illegal drugs were found on the premises. On several occasions, S had turned away illegal drug users from his premises. There was evidence that cannabis had been unlawfully smoked on the premises.
>
> *Held*: S could do no more to stop the unlawful smoking (Court of Appeal).

Every case must, of course, be decided on its own facts. Merely putting up signs prohibiting acts contrary to the MDA taking place on the premises will not necessarily protect the occupier/manager from prosecution or conviction. Evidence as to what took place on premises may be proved by observation or even by expert evidence, but the evidence must be probative. Thus, in *Richards* [1967] Crim. L.R. 589, evidence that a girl attended premises "clad only in a wrap" and appeared "merry and unconcerned" was not probative that she displayed the manifestations of cannabis use and the evidence should not have been admitted: and see *Warner and Jones* (1993) 96 Cr. App. R. 324, and *Rothwell* (1994) 99 Cr. App. R. 388.

(b) "Permits or suffers"

7–20 In *Thomas*, it was said that the trial judge was right to direct the jury to disregard the phrase "or suffers" because "'permits' and 'suffers' mean the same thing". In most cases, there is no need to draw a distinction, but there is in fact a difference which is highlighted by the words of Lord Parker C.J. in *Gray's Haulage*. Thus, "to suffer" an activity involves a failure to act but knowing what is taking place. To "permit" an activity is to do something but not caring whether contravention takes place or not. The distinction is admittedly a fine one but it is safer not to regard these phrases as being synonymous.

In *Sweet v. Parsley* [1970] A.C. 132, Lord Diplock defined "permits" (albeit in the context of section 5 of the Dangerous Drugs Act 1965) as follows:

> "... the word 'permits' used to define the prohibited act, in itself connotes a mental element of the prohibited conduct knowledge *or grounds for reasonable suspicion* on the part of the occupier that the premises will be used by someone for that purpose and *an unwillingness on his part to take means available* to him to prevent it ... " [emphasis added]

Edmund Davies L.J. went on to say that:

> "the best indication of such unwillingness is proof of failure to take reasonable steps readily available to prevent the prohibited activity".

In *Brock and Wyner* (December 21, 2000), the Court of Appeal rejected the submission that "reasonable" has a subjective element. "A belief by a defendant that he has taken reasonable steps does not afford any defence. ... It is not for the defendant to judge his own conduct"; *per* Rose L.J. This is plainly correct. However, it should also be noted that Edmund Davies L.J. said that the "best indication" of unwillingness is failure to take reasonable steps. This is guidance on how the court might best approach the issue as to whether the defendant permitted the offending activity or not. Accordingly, in *Brock*, Rose L.J., said: 7–21

> "What the prosecution must prove to establish the offence of permitting under section 8(b) is (i) knowledge, actual or by closing eyes to the obvious, that heroin dealing is taking place; and (ii) unwillingness to prevent it, which can be inferred from failure to take reasonable steps readily available to prevent it".

It is submitted that a further factor for the Court to consider under (ii) above, is whether the defendant allowed the activity to go on "not caring whether an offence was committed or not": see Edmund Davies L.J. in *Souter*, who adopted the test of "permitting" as expressed by Lord Parker C.J. in *Gray's Haulage v. Arnold*:

> "Actual knowledge or knowledge of circumstances so that it could be said that they had *shut their eyes to the obvious*, or had allowed something to go on, *not caring whether an offence was committed or not*". [emphasis added]

Not caring whether a contravention of the prohibited activity takes place or not, was held to be a relevant feature of "permitting" in *James v. Smee* [1955] 1 Q.B. 89. A person who does not care whether drug supplying is taking place on premises or not can hardly be said to be willing to prevent it. It may be said that it is not helpful for a court to consider whether the accused cared whether the offending activity took 7–22 place on the premises or not, because this would introduce subjective considerations that might be difficult to apply in practice. This was not the view of the Independent Inquiry which recommended that section 8 should be made much clearer, and that 'permitting' should be qualified with the word 'wilful', that is to say, that the accused did not care whether the activity occurred or not. This would give statutory effect to the meaning of 'permitting' as explained by Lord Parker C.J. in *Gray's Haulage*. Caring, or not caring, is merely another factor to be taken into account. The manager of premises who knows that cannabis is being smoked on his premises, might indeed care about that fact and wish to do something about it. He could eject the offender, call the police, or shout commands to the offender to stop. He might also be inhibited at that time from doing any of those things (*e.g.* risk of public disorder) or his work is in the area of "harm-reduction" (not harm elimination) but he knows that he must act discreetly or tactfully. The existence and reach of section 8 has proved to be a difficult issue for policy-makers who strive to balance a number of factors and interests. It is the Government's intention to broaden the scope of section 8 to include the unlawful use of all controlled drugs (Criminal Justice and Police Act 2001, s. 38) and to make any conviction under section 8 a drug trafficking offence for the purpose of the Drug Trafficking Act 1994: see the Proceeds of Crime Bill 2001.

(c) Can managers have knowledge imputed to them?

7–23 There remains an interesting question as to whether an offence under section 8 can be committed by a person concerned in the management of premises, who was unaware of what was happening, but delegated tasks to others who did know of the offending activity. Can the knowledge of subordinates be imputed to the manager? One's instinct is to answer in the negative. However, in *Ferguson v. Weaving* [1951] K. B. 814, Lord Goddard C.J. said:

> "we will assume for the purpose of this case that the licensee had delegated to the waiters the conduct and management of the concert room, and if the [Licensing Act 1921] had made it an offence for a licensee knowingly to permit liquor to be consumed after hours, then the fact that she had delegated the management and control of the concert room to the waiters would have made their knowledge her knowledge." [Emphasis added]

The principle was said to be based "on the fact that the person who is responsible in law, as for example, a licensee under the Licensing Acts, has chosen to delegate his duties, powers and authority to another": *per* Lord Goddard C.J., *Linnet v. Metropolitan Police Commissioner* [1946] K. B. 290, cited in the judgment of *Ferguson v. Weaving* (above, at 821). However, on the facts in *Ferguson v. Weaving*, the relevant provisions in the Licensing Act 1921 did not create an offence of "knowingly permitting" drinking after hours, and the Court was not prepared to widen liability so as to convict a licensee of counselling and procuring on the basis of knowledge imputed to him.

Where does all this leave persons charged under section 8 who are concerned in the management of premises? *Ferguson v. Weaving* was cited in the judgment of the Court in *James v. Smee* but in the latter case, it was said that "knowledge . . . includes the state of mind of a man who shuts his eyes to the obvious or allows his servant to do something in the circumstances where a contravention is likely, not caring whether a contravention takes place or not": *per* Parker J. 7–24

This is much closer to the present position (see *Brock*) and see the opinion of Lord Diplock in *Sweet v. Parsley* [1970] A.C. 132 at 163.

It is submitted that for the purposes of section 8 of the Misuse Of Drugs Act, the preferred view is that knowledge of persons, to whom tasks were delegated by the accused, should not be imputed to him. The case of *Tuck v. Robson* [1970] 1 A.E.R. 1171 (which considered *Ferguson v. Weaving*) does not take the matter very much further.

(d) Must the defendant know the precise drug that is involved?

It is submitted that the answer depends on whether the offence concerns production or supply (s. 8(a) and (b)) or whether the offence relates to the preparation of opium for smoking (s. 8(c)) or the smoking of prepared opium, or cannabis, or cannabis resin (s. 8(d)). It is also submitted that, in the case of section 8(c) and section 8(d), it is for the prosecution to prove that the defendant knew the drug involved, but not in respect of the remaining provisions of section 8. The reasons for that are (i) that section 8 is not subject to section 28 because the offence includes the word "knowingly", (ii) Parliament deliberately limited the scope of section 8(c) and (d) to the *smoking* of cannabis, cannabis resin, and opium—for the reasons given in the introduction to this chapter. 7–25

In *Bett (Robert)* [1999] 1 Cr. App. R. 361, the Court of Appeal held that in respect section 8(b) of the Misuse of Drugs Act (supply), the accused is not required to know the identity of the substance supplied. It is respectfully submitted that this decision does not extend to prosecutions founded on a contravention of section 8(c) or (d). Indeed, in that case, Mantell L.J. was careful to point out that section 8(b) " . . . speaks only of controlled drugs as does 8(a) in relation to producing or attempting to produce a controlled drug. In that (a) and (b) are to be contrasted with (c) and (d) which nominate the particular drug to which the offence relates . . . ". The appeal concerned B's conviction on four counts of supplying cocaine, ecstasy, cannabis and cannabis resin, and amphetamine, respectively. The trial judge directed the jury that it was not necessary for the prosecution to prove that the defendant knew the particular identity and class of drug that was in fact being supplied before they could convict. B challenged the correctness of the directions to the jury by reference to the principle in *Courtie* (1984) 78 Cr.App.R. 292. Mantell L. J. said: 7–26

"... the appellant points out, the penalty may vary according to the classification of the drug involved: see section 25 and Schedule 4 to the 1971 Act. He submits, therefore that the naming of the particular drug is a necessary averment in the charge Though it is unnecessary for present purposes to pronounce on the matter, as counts 1–4 did indeed identify the particular drug, the submission would appear to have powerful support.

In *R. v. Courtie* (1984) 78 Cr.App.R. 292, A.C. 463 the House of Lords had to consider the framing of an indictment in a case of buggery where the prescribed punishment differed depending on the particular factual ingredients. It was put thus by Lord Diplock at page 298 and page 471:

> 'Where it is provided by a statute that an accused person's liability to have inflicted upon him a maximum punishment which, if the prosecution are successful in establishing the existence in his case of a particular factual ingredient, is greater than the maximum punishment that could be inflicted on him if the existence of that particular factual ingredient were not established, it seems to me to be plain beyond argument that Parliament has thereby created two distinct offences, whether the statute by which they are created does so by using language which treats them as being different species of a single genus of offence, or by using language which treats them as separate offences unrelated to one another.... The statement of offence in the instant case may therefore just pass muster, provided that it is supplemented by adequate particulars of offence which give to Courtie reasonable information as to which of the particular species of offences falling within the genus buggery, was the offence with which he was charged.'

Shivpuri was a case arising out of the importation of drugs in relation to which the maximum sentence varied according to the classification of the drugs involved. After pointing that out, Lord Bridge said at 184 and 15 respectively:

> 'It follows from this, applying the reasoning in *Courtie* (1984) 78 Cr.App.R. 292, (1984) A.C. 463 that each of the three distinct offences has different ingredients and, leaving aside considerations of impossibility arising under the Criminal Attempts Act 1981, part of the *actus reus* of the offence which must be proved in each case is the importation, actual or attempted, of goods which were in fact of the appropriate category to sustain the offence charged. So far the *actus reus* of the offence which must be proved in each case is the importation, actual or attempted, of goods which were in fact of the appropriate category to sustain the offence charged. So far the argument (We interpose as in the instant case) seems to be irrefutable and is not challenged by the Crown.'

So, [counsel] proceeds, if the nomination of the particular drug is a necessary factual ingredient of the offence so it must be that the prosecution have to prove that the appellant knew not only that controlled drugs were being supplied but also in relation to any particular count that it was the drug specified. In this he is rehearsing the argument advanced in *Shivpuri*. We return to Lord Bridge at pages 184 and 15:

> 'It is the next step in the argument which is the critical one. If each of the three offences involves proof of a different element as part of the *actus reus*, that is importation of the appropriate category of prohibited goods, it follows, so it is submitted, that "knowingly" wherever it appears in section 170(1) and (2) of the Act of 1979 connotes a corresponding *mens rea*, that is knowledge of the importation of goods in the appropriate category. I recognise the force of this submission. The point may be put in the form of a rhetorical question. Can it be supposed that Parliament intended that the *mens rea* appropriate to an offence carrying a maximum sentence of two years' imprisonment should equally be sufficient to sustain a conviction for an offence carrying a maximum sentence of 14 years' imprisonment?'

Mantell L. J. concluded:

> . . . .To our way of thinking neither argument is well founded. In the first place there are and have been many examples of offences where powers of sentence are linked to proof of some factual ingredient of which it is not necessary for the defendant to have knowledge. Examples may be found in certain sexual cases—see section 37(3) and Schedule 2, column 3 to the Sexual Offences Act 1956 and, if another is needed, *Shivpuri*'s case itself. As to the second argument we have no doubt that . . . the respondent is right in that section 28 in the 1971 Act is a direct response to the decision of the House of Lords in *Warner v. Metropolitan Police Commissioner* (1968) 52 Cr.App.R. 373. . . . "

It is submitted that the argument was not well founded for a further reason. In *Courtie*, separate offences were created by the existence of separate penalties in respect of different acts. The crucial point appears in the judgment of Lord Diplock, when he said " . . . where it is provided by a statute that *an accused person's liability to have inflicted upon him a maximum punishment which*, if the prosecution are successful in establishing the existence in his case of a particular factual ingredient, *is greater than the maximum punishment that could be inflicted on him if the existence of that particular factual ingredient were not established* . . ." [emphasis added]. The maximum sentence that a judge can impose for an offence of conspiracy is the maximum that may be imposed if the conduct was charged as a substantive offence. However, an offence under section 8 carries the same maximum term (14 years' imprisonment) irrespective as to whether a controlled drug of Class A, B or C was involved. 7–27

E. PROHIBITING OPIUM SMOKING

7–28 Prohibiting opium smoking, section 9(1), provides, *inter alia*:

"Subject to section 28 of this Act, it is an offence for a person
(a) to smoke or otherwise use prepared opium; or
(b) to frequent a place used for the purpose of opium smoking; or
(c) to have in his possession [certain equipment for use in connection with opium smoking] [Prepared opium is defined by section 37(1) to mean prepared for smoking and includes the dross and other residues after opium has been smoked.]"

Section 9(2) is considered separately in the next chapter concerning the provision of drug kits because of the addition of section 9A of the MDA as amended by the DTOA. 1986.

The section is largely self-explanatory. The words "otherwise use" in subsection (a) must, it is submitted, refer to other methods of consumption. If the allegation is that opium was being sold by an accused then the proper charge is one alleging the supplying of the drug, *e.g.* under section 4(1)(b) or a kindred offence.

Opium "dens" have a notorious history. Subsection (b) is intended to attack their survival by prohibiting opium smokers frequenting such premises. The prosecution must prove that the main use or recognised purpose of the premises is for smoking opium although, of course, that need not be its only one (see *Mogford* [1970] 1 W.L.R. 988).

The courts have not been asked to define the word "frequent" for the purpose of section 9.

7–29 As a matter of natural construction, the word "frequent", in this context, implies a regular course of conduct or, at least, conduct that is repeated more than once. In *Airton v. Scott* (1909) 25 T.L.R. 250, the appellant had attended an athletics ground for betting. Lord Alverstone C.J. observed at p.250 that: "As to the word 'frequent', it was plain that being long enough on the premises to effect the particular object aimed at was 'frequenting'."

However, in *Clark v. The Queen* (1884) 14 Q.B.D. 92 it was held that merely being in a public place does not amount to "frequenting" and in *Rawlings v. Smith* [1938] 1 K.B. 675, it was held that frequenting involved "the notion of something which to some degree is continuous or repeated" (*per* Lord Hewart C.J.). Both *Clark* and *Rawlings* were applied in *Nakhla v. The Queen* [1976] A.C. 1, a decision of the Privy Council. Lord Morris of Borth-y-Gest considered that "frequents" must be considered in its context, which may require an enquiry as to the reason why a person is at the premises, the nature of the place, the time spent on the premises, his movements and continuing or recurrent activities. It is submitted that a similar approach is likely to be adopted if the issue ever arose in section 9.

F. DRUG KITS AND ARTICLES FOR USE IN DRUG MISUSE

I. Articles for Opium Smoking

Section 9 of the MDA is directed entirely to prohibiting the possession of opium smoking equipment. Section 9 reads: 7–30

"Subject to section 28 of this Act, it is an offence for a person
- (a) to smoke or otherwise use prepared opium; or
- (b) to frequent a place used for the purpose of opium smoking; or
- (c) to have in his possession
  - (i) any pipes or other utensils made or adapted for use in connection with the smoking of opium, being pipes or utensils which have been used by him or with his knowledge and permission in that connection or which he intends to use or permit others to use in that connection; or
  - (ii) any utensils, which have been used by him or with his knowledge and permission in connection with the preparation of opium smoking."

Opium addiction, notably in the Far East, spans a period of history that is both well known and well recorded. It is therefore not at all surprising to discover that Parliament, for decades, has forbidden opium smoking in the United Kingdom and has sought to punish those who are in possession of opium smoking equipment. Section 9 of the MDA reflects that established policy. Broadly speaking, section 9(c)(i) makes it an offence to possess equipment used in connection with the smoking of opium, while section 9(c)(ii) is targeted against those persons who possess articles used in connection with the preparation of opium for smoking. It will therefore now be obvious that the ambit of section 9 is incredibly narrow and presents more interest in terms of what is glaringly omitted than what is actually included. Thus, Parliament has made no provision for the possession of equipment used in connection with opium taken other than by smoking. Furthermore, it is not an offence to possess articles used in the preparation or administration of other controlled drugs, *e.g.* hubble-bubble pipes used for smoking cannabis. Such omissions are all the more remarkable when it is remembered that the MDA was passed to combat a rising tide of drug abuse which then, and now, involves the misuse of many dangerous substances. Indeed, opium smoking now represents a very small part of the overall drug problem. Moreover, Parliament has not sought to broaden section 9. In the wake of public concern at the number of so-called "drug kits" hitting the market, Parliament inserted section 9A into the MDA in order to prohibit their sale: see section 34 of the Drug Trafficking Offences Act 1986. Although most of the 1986 Act was repealed by the DTA 1994, section 34 was not repealed (s. 67, Sched. 3, DTA). However, section 9A 7–31 is only concerned with the supply of articles used to unlawfully administer controlled drugs and makes no corresponding provision for being in possession of articles supplied in contravention of that section.

(a) Section 9(c)(i)

7–32 Section 9(c)(i) applies to "pipes or other utensils". It is not clear whether "pipes" includes any conduit used in connection with opium smoking or whether it is restricted to the complete smoking apparatus including the bowl. If the latter interpretation is to be preferred, then although various parts of the smoking apparatus such as the mouthpiece or the connecting tube would fall outside the definition of a "pipe", they may come within the word "utensils".

It is clear from section 9 that the words "pipes or other utensils" are qualified by the words "made or adapted for use in connection with the smoking of opium". A typical tobacco pipe could not be said to be "made" for opium smoking but can it be said to be "adapted for use", if it is in fact used for that purpose? Certainly, one would normally say that the word "adapt" imparts the requirement of change, adjustment or alteration, *e.g.* to the original article. Merely to adapt an article for a different purpose would not be sufficient. However, section 9(c) (i) refers to "pipes or utensils which have been used by him or which he intends to use in that connection".

7–33 There is therefore force in the view that those words embrace the adoption of a normally innocent piece of equipment, *e.g.* a tobacco pipe that has been used for the purposes of opium smoking.

Once it has been proved that the article is a "pipe" or "utensil" made or adapted for opium smoking, the prosecution must then prove that the article:

(1) was so used by the accused; or
(2) was so used with his knowledge and with his permission; or
(3) was intended to be so used by the accused, or (with his permission) by others.

It is not enough to prove the accused knew a pipe had been used by someone else. It must be proved that the accused went further and gave his permission for the article to be used in connection with opium smoking.

(b) Section 9(c)(ii)

7–34 It is not necessary for the prosecution to prove that the utensils have been made or adapted for use in connection with the preparation of opium for smoking. Any article, which has been used in that regard will come within section 9(c)(ii). However, articles merely intended by the accused to be so used fall outside the section.

Again, if the utensils have been used by a person other than the accused, the prosecution must prove that the accused knew of that other person's use of those items and that he permitted him to use them. Permission may be granted expressly or by implication, *e.g.* conduct.

II. Drug Administration Kits Generally

During the 1980s, the appearance of so-called "drug-kits" on the legitimate consumer market became prevalent. Some kits were elaborate and did little to hide the fact that they would be of particular interest to drug users but of limited interest to anyone else. Thus, pouches containing a small mirror, a knife, a broad tube, matches, etc., were handy "kits" for snorting cocaine or heroin. Other kits were far less elaborate and, indeed, many of the items sold could not even be described as "kits", *e.g.* the sale of a mirror and a packet of wide straws. To the ordinary bystander the sale looked innocent enough but to the retailer, it may have been apparent that he was selling articles to a drug user whom he believed would use them for that purpose. 7–35

To meet this situation, Parliament, by section 34A of the DTOA, inserted section 9A into the MDA, which provides:

"(1) A person who supplies or offers to supply any article which may be used or adapted to be used (whether by itself or in combination with another article or other articles) in the administration by any person of a controlled drug to himself or another, believing that the article (or the article as adapted) is to be so used in circumstances where the administration is unlawful, is guilty of an offence.

(2) It is not an offence under subsection (1) above to supply or offer to supply a hypodermic syringe, or any part of one.

(3) A person who supplies or offers to supply any article which may be used to prepare a controlled drug for administration by any person to himself or another believing that the article is to be so used in circumstances where the administration is unlawful is guilty of an offence.

(4) For the purposes of this section, any administration of a controlled drug is unlawful except—

(a) the administration by any person of a controlled drug to another in circumstances where the administration of the drug is not unlawful under section 4(1) of this Act, or

(b) the administration by any person of a controlled drug to himself in circumstances where having the controlled drug in his possession is not unlawful under section 5(1) of this Act.

(5) In this section, references to administration by any person of a controlled drug to himself include a reference to his administering it to himself with the assistance of another."

(a) Section 9A(1)

It should be made clear at this stage that section 9A is not concerned with kits sold to abusers of solvents. That matter is dealt with by the Intox- 7–36 icating Substances (Supply) Act 1985. Section 9A of the MDA is solely concerned with kits supplied in connection with the administration of controlled drugs: solvents are not controlled under the MDA.

Section 9A(1) is very widely drawn. Unlike section 9 which refers to "utensils", section 9A(1) applies to any article which "may be used" or which may be "adapted to be used" in the administration of a controlled drug. In other words, any article that has the capability of being used by another to abuse any controlled drug falls within this subsection. Parliament has been careful not to prohibit merely the supply of a collection of articles, which may be termed a "kit". Thus, even if only one article is supplied, which by itself could not be used to facilitate drug abuse but which, if combined with other articles, could be so used, then it falls within section 9A(1).

It is not necessary for the prosecution to prove that the article has been sold or supplied for any consideration or to prove that the article was supplied to a person who himself intended to use that article for drug abuse. It is enough that the supplier (or the offeror) believes that the article is to be used (not "may be used") "in circumstances where the administration is unlawful".

(i) Mens rea *under section 9A(1)*

7–37 Proof that the supplier *suspected* that the article would be used for the unlawful administration of a controlled drug is not enough. The prosecution need prove no more than that the accused *believed* that the article would be used "in circumstances where the administration is unlawful".

What is the position if the supplier's belief is, in fact, erroneous? It is submitted that his mistake affords him no defence. It seems that the supplier will be judged on the facts as he believed them to be. Section 9A(1) prohibits the supplying of (or an offer to supply) any article, which may be used or adapted to be used in the administration of a controlled drug. Presumably an accused's belief must be reasonably held having regard to all the circumstances of the case. Section 28 is not expressed to have any application. Therefore, a perfectly innocent mirror which is sold in the belief that it will be used in connection with the unlawful snorting of heroin or cocaine is an offence contrary to section 9A(1). Of course, some harsh results will flow if a mistaken belief affords the supplier of an article with no defence in circumstances where the recipient never actually intended to use the mirror for anything other than a lawful purpose. Suppose X supplies a box of wide straws to Y knowing that Y regularly snorts cocaine using straws and believes that all or some of the straws will be so used. In fact, Y never intended any such thing but planned to use them for milkshake consumption at a children's party. On a strict interpretation of section 9A(1), X is damned by his own mistaken belief.

Again, suppose Y (weeks later) does in fact use one of the remaining straws to snort cocaine. Is X's fate sealed? It is important that X has more than just a suspicion that the straws will be used for the administration of controlled drugs. However, nothing in section 9A prevents the supply or the offer to supply any article for use in connection with the administration of a controlled drug if the drug may be lawfully administered to another by the recipient or may be possessed by him for self-administration: see section 9A(4). The maximum sentence is six months' imprisonment and/or a financial penalty on level five.

(b) Section 9A(2)

It may seem surprising that hypodermic syringes are excluded from subsection (1). As a matter of logic, no doubt they ought to have been included, but as a matter of policy, one can see reasons why they are not. First, there is the quite considerable problem of regulating the distribution of such syringes if they were to be included. Secondly, and most importantly, it is now well known that serious disease can be readily spread by the use of contaminated needles. The distribution of clean needles and syringes even from dubious sources is a high health objective. 7–38

(c) Section 9A(3)

Not unlike section 9(c)(ii) of the MDA, section 9A(3) is concerned to prohibit the supply, or an offer to supply, any article which may be used to prepare any controlled drug for administration. Again, like section 9, it is not necessary for the prosecution to prove that the article had been "adapted" for use in the preparation of a controlled drug. 7–39

Chapter 8
Section 28 of the Misuse of Drugs Act 1971

A. SECTION 28

Section 28 of the Misuse of Drugs Act 1971 provides a number of statutory defences as follows: 8–01

"(1) This section applies to offences under any of the following provisions of this Act, that is to say section 4(2) and (3), section 5(2) and (3), section 6(2) and section 9.

(2) Subject to subsection (3) below, in any proceedings for an offence to which this section applies it shall be a defence for the accused to prove that he neither knew of nor suspected nor had reason to suspect the existence of some fact alleged by the prosecution which it is necessary for the prosecution to prove if he is to be convicted of the offence charged.

(3) Where in any proceedings for an offence to which this section applies it is necessary, if the accused is to be convicted of the offence charged, for the prosecution to prove that some substance or product involved in the alleged offence was the controlled drug which the prosecution alleges it to have been, and it is proved that the substance or product in question was that controlled drug, the accused

(a) shall not be acquitted of the offence charged by reason only of proving that he neither knew nor suspected nor had reason to suspect that the substance or product in question was the particular controlled drug alleged; but

(b) shall be acquitted thereof

(i) if he proves that he neither believed nor suspected nor had reason to suspect that the substance or product in question was a controlled drug; or

(ii) if he proves that he believed the substance or product in question to be a controlled drug, or a controlled drug of a description, such that, if it had in fact been that controlled drug or a controlled drug of that description, he would not at the material time have been committing any offence to which this section applies.

(4) Nothing in this section shall prejudice any defence which it is open to a person charged with an offence to which this section applies to raise apart from this section."

8–02 Without section 28, the offences to which this section relates, would lead to some very harsh results. As the Divisional Court remarked, in the *DPP, ex parte Bora* (June 14, 1999), section 28 is "clearly there to prevent injustice by allowing a defendant who would otherwise be convicted to demonstrate, if he can, sufficient ignorance of an essential part of the Crown's case to exculpatory him". Thus section 6(2) (cultivation of cannabis) would arguably be an absolute offence. The decision in *Warner v. Metropolitan Police Commissioner* [1969] 2 A.C. 256 produced an unhappy compromise between absolute liability and *mens rea* in cases of the alleged possession of prohibited drugs. Indeed, section 28 reflects many of the sentiments expressed by Lord Pearce in *Warner* and the reader is invited to read the speech of Lord Pearce in its entirety. However, section 28(4) makes it plain that nothing in this provision was intended to alter the earlier law but merely runs parallel to established principles. Furthermore, drug importations or exportations contrary to section 3(1) are not subject to this provision, perhaps for the reasons expressed by Lord Bridge in *Shivpuri* [1987] A.C. 1. Similarly, section 28 has no application in respect of a charge of conspiracy: *McGowan, The Times*, January 27, 1990.

8–03 Section 28 is not an easy section to understand, and indeed its existence is often overlooked, partly because the instinct of most criminal practitioners is to assume that the prosecution has the task of proving to the criminal standard of proof, every assertion that makes. Usually this is true but where it is alleged that the defendant was in possession of cocaine, it is necessary for the prosecution to prove the fact of possession, and that the substance was indeed a controlled drug, *e.g.* cocaine, but it will often not be necessary for the prosecution to prove that the defendant knew he possessed a controlled drug, still less that he knew the drug to be of a particular type. These principles are well established and reinforced by recent cases: see *Afzal and Shakiel* (June 19, 2000), and *Leeson*, August 5, 1999), and *DPP, ex parte Bora* (June 14, 1999.)

B. SECTION 28(2)

8–04 In respect of each charge to which section 28 applies, the prosecution is required to prove the existence of certain factual ingredients. Thus, for an offence under section 6(2), the prosecution is required to prove that the accused (i) cultivated a plant and (ii) that the plant cultivated was of the genus Cannabis. The prosecution is not required to prove that the plant was cannabis. However, by section 28(2), it is open to the accused to prove that he did not know, suspect, nor had reason to suspect that the plant was a cannabis plant (but note the House of Lords decision in Lambert (July 5, 2001)).

It is sometimes said that there exists a difficulty in understanding the relationship between subsections (2) and (3). The wording is certainly confusing and an overlap undoubtedly exists. Thus if X did not know that the plant was of the genus Cannabis, then he has a defence under section 28(3)(b)(i) as well as section 28(2).

> In *Champ* (1981) 73 Cr.App.R. 367, C had a window box which contained a cannabis plant. Her defence to a charge under section 6(2) was that she thought the plant was "hemp" which she believed was good for alleviating ailments. The trial judge ruled that the burden was on C to prove that she did not know the plant was cannabis.
>
> *Held*: the judge's ruling was correct. Section 28(2) was subject to subsection (3) "which is not relevant in this case" but subsection (2) placed the burden of proof on C.

The decision, when examined, highlights the confusion that can arise. 8–05
It is not clear why the Court thought that subsection (3) was not relevant, since one complaint made by the appellant was that the judge ruled that the burden of proof was on her that she did not know that the plant was cannabis by virtue of that very subsection. Another complaint was that the trial judge was wrong to rule that section 28(2) had no application to a charge under section 6(2): yet the court held that the judge directed the jury correctly. Clearly, the burden of proof was on the appellant by virtue of subsection (2) and/or (3)(b)(i). In any event, her defence was extraordinarily thin since "hemp" is regarded as another term for cannabis.

The point to note is that subsection (2) is "subject to" subsection (3), so that subsection (3) is solely concerned with the state of the accused's knowledge of the nature of the "substance or product" that he handled. There may of course be an overlap between those two subsections. Suppose an accused (X) is charged with frequenting premises used for the purposes of smoking opium (section 9(b)). The prosecution must prove (a) that the premises were being used for smoking; (b) that opium was being smoked on those premises; and (c) that the accused frequented those premises. If X does not know of the existence of (a) then section 28(2) gives X a defence, which he must prove. If X does know of fact "(a)", but not fact "(b)", then he has a defence under section 28(2) and section 28(3)(b)(i).

In *Salmon v. HM Advocate*, 1999 SLT 169, the High Court of Justiciary 8–06
gave detailed consideration of the application of section 28 including, the relationship between section 28(2) and section 28(3). In that case, *Salmon* was convicted of being concerned in the supply of cocaine contrary to section 4(3)(b) of the Misuse of Drugs Act 1971. The Lord Justice General (Rodger) complained that section 28(2) "has vanished into a legal black hole". It is difficult to do justice to the reasoning of the Court without

citing passages from the judgment in some detail. The Lord Justice General said:

> ". . . I start with the opening words of subsection (2), 'subject to subsection (3) below'. Those words immediately indicate that, although the scope of subsection (2) is wider than the scope of subsection (3), subsection (3) is designed to apply a special legislative regime to a particular situation which would otherwise fall within subsection (2) and be regulated by it. . . . It is significant that Parliament uses the words 'substance or product' rather than some general word such as 'article'. . . . "

8–07 The reason why the court thought it significant that Parliament uses the words "substance or product", rather than some general word such as "article", is because Schedule 2 to the Misuse of Drugs Act controls in three Classes (A, B, and C) "substances and products"—not "articles". It may be that Parliament thought that if an accused knew of the existence of the thing, which in fact is proved to be a controlled drug, but he mistakenly believed he was dealing with material of a wholly different character, then there would be no need to invoke section 28 at all: he would not be in possession of the drug, and for similar reasons he may be acquitted on a charge of supplying a drug. However, charges of being concerned in supplying a controlled drug, and producing a controlled drug, might be more problematic to resolve satisfactorily on that basis.

It is certainly true that section 28(2) is concerned with "some fact alleged by the prosecution which it is necessary for the prosecution to prove", whereas subsection (3) is concerned with cases where it is necessary for the prosecution to prove a particular fact, namely, "that some substance or product" is the controlled drug which the prosecution alleges it to have been". The Lord Justice General then said:

> "That meaning must be carried through to the remainder of the subsection [3] . . . Parliament is saying that an accused is to be acquitted if he proves that he neither believed nor suspected nor had reason to suspect that the *powder* or *tablets* in question were a controlled drug. . . . " [emphasis added]

8–08 It seems that the Court was of the view that the accused must at least be aware of the existence of the "substance or product" before section 28(3) is engaged. The subsection, in the opinion of the Court, is thus confined to the case where an accused admits that he knew of the existence of the substance, but he did not at the very least have reason to suspect that substance was a controlled drug of any description. This is not how the law has developed in England, as the Lord Justice General pointed out (173):

> "That being the scope of subsection (3), it is not apt to apply to the kind of case envisaged in *McNamara* where an accused says that he thought that the contents of a box on his motorcycle were porno-

graphic or pirate videos rather than cannabis resin. In such a case, the accused is not claiming that he did not know that the organic matter ('the substance or product in question') was a controlled drug. Rather, he is saying that he did not think that the cannabis resin was there at all: he thought that the box contained videos."

It will be seen that the Court regarded section 28(3) as being relevant to the form in which the substance appears. However, the form must, it seems, be a "substance or product" of a type that might be confused with a controlled drug, and not just an article. Therefore, knowledge of the existence of powder in a bag that the accused believed to be sherbert, but which was in fact high-grade cocaine hydrochloride, might afford him a defence under section 28(3). 8–09

"... 28(3) ... is therefore concerned with a situation where the Crown had to prove the existence of a particular fact, *viz.*, that the substance or product in question was a controlled drug. ... Therefore ... subsection (3) turns out to be simply a particular example of the wider class of situations covered by subsection (2) ... So, for instance, in *McNamara* it was necessary for the Crown to prove that there was organic matter in the box on the back of the appellant motorcycle and it was cannabis resin. The function of subsection (2) is to give an accused person in the position of McNamara a defence—which subsection (3) does not afford him—if he proves that he neither knew nor suspected nor had reason to suspect that the organic matter was in the box. ... A person in McNamara's position would have a defence, but the defence will arise, not—as the Court of Appeal thought—under section 28 (3), but rather under section 28(2) ..."

In order to explain the above, the Court provided the following example: 8–10

"To succeed in a particular prosecution the Crown must prove the charge which they bring. In particular where they have alleged, say, that the accused possessed ecstasy with intent to supply, they must prove that it was ecstasy, and not any other controlled drug, that the accused possessed ... At his trial the accused may say a number of things. First, he may say that he was completely unaware that the drugs were in the house ... alternatively, the accused may say that although he knew that the bag was in the house and contained something, ... nonetheless he did not know that it contained tablets ... The accused will therefore be convicted, unless he proves that he did not know nor suspected nor had reason to suspect that the tablets were in the bag. If he proves this, then even though he was in possession of the tablets, he must be acquitted in terms of section 28(2) ... Thirdly ... the accused may say that, although ... he knew [the bag] contained tablets, nonetheless he did not know that the tablets comprised ecstasy ... The accused the therefore be convicted unless he brings himself within the scope of the defences in section 28(3)."

Notwithstanding the care with which the court in *Salmon* explained their reasoning, it is submitted that subsection (3) was designed spell out the limits of the defence afforded by subsection (2)—hence the words "subject to subsection (3)" in that provision.

(a) When is proof that a substance is a particular controlled drug "necessary" to a conviction?

8–11 The reasoning of the Court in *Salmon* proceeds on the basis that a defence under section 28 may be available if "it is *necessary*" for the prosecution to prove that a particular "substance or product" was the controlled drug alleged "if [the accused] is to be convicted of the offence charged". Thus, the Lord Justice General said: "where [the prosecution] have alleged, say, that the accused possessed ecstasy with intent to supply, they must prove that it was ecstasy, and not any other controlled drug, that the accused possessed".

In *Leeson* (August 15, 1999) the Court of Appeal also considered the application and scope of section 28. The appellant testified that he had stolen a bag out of a motor vehicle initially believing that the bag of contained a quantity of "smart clothes". He later noticed that the bag contained powder that he thought was amphetamine but which was in fact cocaine. The appellant's submission was that his error afforded him a defence under section 28. The Court held that section 28(2) did not afford the appellant a defence because proof that he "neither knew of, nor suspected nor had reason to suspect" that a substance was cocaine, was not a lack of knowledge of the existence of a fact, alleged by the prosecution, which it was *necessary for the prosecution to prove* if he were to be convicted of the offence charged. The particulars of a count on an indictment, that identified a substance as a particular controlled drug, were not matters that the prosecution had to prove in order to obtain a conviction. The appellant also relied on section 28 (3)(b)(ii). Again, the Court held that this provision did not afford the appellant a defence because this was not a case where it was necessary, if the accused was to be convicted of the offence charged, for the prosecution to prove that some substance or product involved in the alleged offence was a controlled drug which the prosecution alleged it to have been. Roch L.J., in giving judgment for the Court, said:

> ". . . all that section 5(3) requires the prosecution to prove is that the accused is in possession of a controlled drug with intent to supply that drug to another. This is to be contrasted with the provision in section 9 where in order to obtain a conviction, the prosecution would have to establish that the substance in question was opium, as opposed to being simply a controlled drug. The same applies where the charge is made under section 6, where the prosecution had to prove that the person charged has been cultivating a plant of the genus cannabis. Moreover, even were the appellant to have proved that he believed the

substances found on him and in the bedroom were amphetamine, he would still at the material time have been committing an offence to which section 28 applied, namely an offence under section 5(3) of that act. This reading of the subsection is confirmed by the terms of subsection (3)(a) that the accused is not to be acquitted of the offence charged by reason only of proving that he neither knew nor suspected nor had reason to suspect that the substance or product in question was the particular controlled drug alleged. The opening words of section 28(3) mean that if the prosecution alleged that the substance or product in question is a controlled drug of a particular kind, for example opium, because the substance or product being opium as opposed to being simply a controlled drug is a matter which it is necessary for the prosecution to prove if the accused is to be convicted of the offence charged, then the remainder of the provisions in section 28(3) applied. That does not apply in this case. It was not necessary in order for the appellant to be convicted . . . for the prosecution to prove that the substance in the appellant possession was cocaine."

However, the Court added, "even if that were to be wrong, then under (a) the accused is not to be acquitted by reason only of proving that he neither knew nor suspected nor had reason to suspect that the substance or product in question was the particular controlled drug alleged". 8–12

It will be seen that in the opinion of the Court, section 28 is only engaged if it is necessary for the prosecution to prove an essential fact (for example that some substance or product in the alleged offence was the controlled drug alleged) in order for the accused to be convicted of the offence charged. If the Court of Appeal's analysis is correct then the scope of the defences available under section 28 is very much narrower than had previously been believed by many practitioners and judges. It is of course true that section 9 and section 6 require, as an essential ingredient of the offence, proof that the drug was opium (s. 9) and cannabis (s. 6). However the Court of Appeal's analysis would mean that in all other cases, where the chemical name of a controlled drug is not a material particular of the count on the indictment, section 28 would not apply even if the defendant had no reason to suspect that the substance was a controlled drug. It is respectfully submitted that this is not what Parliament had in mind when section 28 was enacted. That section provides defences where none had previously existed. In almost every case to which section 28 applies, the prosecution will need to prove that the substance in question was a controlled drug of some description. An exception relates to the offence of making an offer to supply a controlled drug. Such an offence may be committed even if the substance supplied, or to be supplied, is innocuous. Section 28(3)(b) has the effect of ensuring the person is not acquitted because he is indifferent as to whether the drug is controlled or not, but affords him a defence which he must prove in the circumstances set out in (3)(b)(i) and (ii).

C. DOES SECTION 28(2) ALTER THE DEFINITION OF POSSESSION?

8–13 Whereas, in *Warner*, the prosecution was held to be required to prove that an accused had the intention to possess the substance which was prohibited, the question arises whether this amounts to "some fact alleged by the prosecution which it is necessary for the prosecution to prove . . . " and therefore, by section 28(2), the onus is now on the accused to prove that he neither knew of, nor suspected, nor had reason to suspect, the existence of this fact.

In *Wright* (1975) 62 Cr.App.R. 169, the argument was raised but the Court of Appeal did not need to consider it. However, in *Ashton-Rickhardt* [1978] 1 W.L.R. 37:

> Police officers found the appellant asleep in his car. A cigarette, containing cannabis, was found in the pocket of the driver's door. The appellant denied knowledge of the reefer or that it contained cannabis. The judge directed the jury that the burden of proving a lack of knowledge fell on the appellant.
>
> *Held*: section 28(2) had not altered the burden of proof. The burden of proving knowledge of the article rested on the prosecution.

Accordingly, where drugs are planted on an accused, or added to the goods which he knows he controls (see *Irving* [1970] Crim.L.R. 642, CA) the onus of proving knowledge remains on the prosecution. Again, where the accused is in possession of a "trace" of a controlled drug the burden of proving knowledge of the trace falls on the prosecution (*per* Stinson J. in *Colyer* [1974] Crim.L.R. 243) and see the interesting and very helpful article by Ribeiro and Perry, "Possession and section 28 of the Misuse of Drugs Act 1971" [1979] Crim.L.R. 90.

8–14 The matter has also been considered recently in Scotland, where the judges in that jurisdiction have reached a similar view. Thus, in *Salmon v. H.M. Advocate* 1999 S.L.T. 169, at 175, the Lord Justice General reviewed the authorities and said:

> ". . . under the 1964 Act, on the other hand, there was never any doubt that the burden approving the necessary knowledge and control rested on the Crown. With the advent of section 28 of the 1971 Act, however, the Crown began to argue that the effect of section 28(2) had been to shift the onus in regard to proving the necessary knowledge from the Crown to the defence . . . not surprisingly, this kind of argument provoked a strong reaction from the courts, both in Scotland and in England. They rejected the arguments for the Crown and affirmed that section 28(2) did not shift the onus proving knowledge onto the defence (*Mackenzie v. Skeen*, 1983 S.L.T. 121, *per* the Lord Justice General (at 121)) in Scotland and *Ashton-Rickhardt, per* Roskill L.J. ((1977) 65 Cr.App.R. at 67) in England). The courts were plainly right

to reject the Crown's argument: as Roskill L.J. pointed out, the manifest purpose of section 28 was not to place a new onus on an accused person but 'to afford a defence to an accused person where no defence had previously existed.'"

The Lord Justice General then went on to point out the divergence of views held in England and Scotland respectively as to the scope of section 28: 8–15

> "... Unfortunately, having rejected the extreme argument advanced by the Crown as to the effect of section 28(2), the courts seem to have felt that there was no place left for that subsection in a system, such as they envisaged, where the burden of proving the necessary knowledge and control continued to rest on the Crown. Hence, subsection (2) disappeared from view. Once the proper but limited range of section 28(3) is appreciated, however, there is no inconsistency in holding both that the burden of proving the necessary knowledge and control rests on the Crown and the section 28(2) has a distinct role to play."

A little later, in the judgment of the Lord Justice General, he said this:

> "I consider that in *McNamara* the appellant required to bring himself within the scope of section 28(2) rather than of section 28(3)(b)(i). A similar approach has been adopted in Scotland. In a passage in his opinion in *Mackenzie v. Skeen* which is not reproduced in the Scots Law Times report, the Lord Justice General remarked: 'in most cases possession of container will support the inference of possession of his actual contents but it must always be a question to be decided in the particular circumstances of the particular case'."

D. WHAT IS TO BE PROVED BY THE ACCUSED?

Until the decision in the House of Lords in *Lambert* (July 5, 2001), it was settled law that the defendant shouldered the legal burden of proving a defence under section 28 of the Misuse of Drugs Act 1971. In *Rautamaki* [1993] Crim. L.R. 691: 8–16

> R was convicted of an offence of possessing Ecstasy with intent to supply. His case was that a passenger asked him to look after a carrier bag (which contained the drug) but he believed the bag contained steroids.
>
> *Held*: the burden was on the defendant to prove a lack of knowledge under section 28(3) but the summing up seemed to proceed on the assumption that the burden was on the prosecution to prove knowledge that he had a controlled drug in his possession.

The facts of that case were of the classic "container" type problem considered in *Warner v. Metropolitan Police Commissioner* [1969] 2 A.C. 256 and in *McNamara* (1988) 87 Cr. App. R. 246. Again, in *Hadley* (February 19, 1998), H was observed loading boxes into a motor vehicle driven by F. The boxes contained a substantial quantity of cannabis and cannabis resin. H denied knowledge of the existence of the cannabis and the jury was directed as to the defence available under section 28. In dismissing the appeal against conviction, the Court observed that the draughtsman of the Misuse of Drugs Act intended that the prosecution should have the initial burden of proving that the defendant had and knew that he had the boxes in his control and also that the boxes contained something. That, as the Court held, "... establishes the necessary possession. They must also of course prove that the box in fact contained the drug alleged, in this case cannabis resin. If any of those matters are unproved, there is no case to go to the jury." The burden was on the defendant to prove lack of knowledge of the terms set out in section 28.

(a) Does section 28(3)(b)(i) contain an objective element?

8–17 It will be appreciated that the defence in section 28(3)(b)(i) can be broken down into three components, namely, that the defendant must prove:

(i) that he did not know the existence of the relevant fact (subjective); and
(ii) that he did not suspect the existence of the same (again subjective); and
(iii) that he had no reason to suspect the existence of that fact (subjective or objective?).

The position has been the subject of dispute between writers but there has been remarkably little authority on the point.

The policy of the Misuse Of Drugs Act is to place a degree of responsibility on those who handle items, such as packages, to make some investigation as to their quality: see *Warner* [1969] 2 A.C. 256. It will frequently happen that an item is handled by a person in circumstances which, viewed subjectively, would not give rise to a suspicion that the thing was (or contained) a controlled drug. A person who picks up, from the floor, a long hand-rolled cigarette, which in fact turns out to be a reefer (containing cannabis), should not be convicted merely because he did not know what a reefer looks like, even if most people do know. On the other hand, must the reason always be "known to the defendant" (*per* Laws L.J. in *Rice*)?

8–18 In *Rice* (transcript, November 20, 2000), the Court of Appeal was clearly of the view that (iii) is subject to a subjective interpretation. R delivered packages on behalf of W to two undercover police officers. The packages contained controlled drugs. R testified that he was not engaged in the supply of controlled drugs at all, and that he had not looked into the packages to discover the contents. R contended that the words "nor had reason to suspect" are capable of two different interpretations: one subjective, one objective. The objective interpretation would arise if the words were taken to mean that the defendant could simply prove that there was not in existence any reason to suspect that the substance was a controlled drug. The subjective interpretation would arise if the words are taken to mean that the defendant must prove that his cards he was not aware of any reason to suspect that the substance or product was a controlled drug. The point was advanced in order to support a complaint that those words, if they gave rise to an objective test, contravened the Human Rights Act 1998/ECHR. In refusing leave to appeal, the Court of Appeal held that the test was in any event subjective:

> "we are not aware that the first of these possibilities, the so-called objective approach, has ever been suggested before in the context of this statute's construction. It seems to us quite plain that the statute is looking at the presence or absence of a reason known to the defendant. The words are 'if the defendant proves that he neither believed or suspected nor had reason to suspect', not 'if the defendant proves that there was no reason to suspect' . . . in those circumstances . . . the subjective interpretation is the right one. . . . "

Whilst the result in that case is to be welcomed it is a pity that the Court seems not have been aware of the case of *Young* [1984] 1 W.L.R. 654. Suppose D is too drunk to know the material circumstances, but should have known of them? This was the position in *Young* [1984] 1 W. L. R. 654. 8–19

> In *Young* Y, who was seriously affected by drink and was almost incapable, sold LSD to W. As Y was about to negotiate a further sale of the drug, he was arrested. Y was charged with possessing LSD intending to supply it contrary to section 5(3). Y relied on section 28(3)(b)(i). At a District Court-Martial, the assistant Judge Advocate General directed that the test to be applied under section 28(3)(b)(i) was that of an "ordinary, reasonable and sober man".
>
> *Held:* the appeal against conviction would be dismissed. Although it was unnecessary to gloss the direction by referring to the "reasonable, sober man", it was a correct direction since self-induced intoxication did not avail Y. The third limb of section 28(3)(b)(i) is objective.

The assistant Judge Advocate General was clearly influenced by *DPP v. Majewski* [1977] A.C. 443, HL, but the Courts-Martial Appeals Court had doubts as to whether the same criterion applies when knowledge (as distinct from intent) is under consideration.

In *Young*, Kilner Brown J., said: 8–20

> "for the appellant it is contended that 'had reason to suspect' . . . is not the same thing as 'reasonable grounds for belief'. Reliance is placed on the decision of the Divisional Court in *Jaggard v. Dickenson* [1980] 3 A.E.R. 716. That is authority not binding on this court, but neverthe-

less persuasive for the proposition that, where there is an exculpatory statutory defence of honest belief, self-induced intoxication is a factor which must be considered in the context of a subjective consideration of the individual state of mind. The objective test of a reasonable sober man is irrelevant. Accepting and applying this decision as we do, it would lead to the conclusion that, as far as the belief and suspicion are concerned, there would have been a misdirection in the instant case. But it leaves untouched the problem created by the introduction of the third limb, which is an integral part of the exculpatory defence. The remaining question is whether any reason is something entirely personal and individual, calling for an entirely subjective consideration, or involves the wider concept of an objective rationality. We are of the opinion that is the latter. It follows therefore that, in our judgment, it was a correct direction that the self-induced intoxication did not avail. Moreover, it was an unnecessary gloss to introduce a concept of the reasonable sober man. Nevertheless, this gloss did not vitiate the fundamental direction that the self-intoxication was no defence. The drunkenness relied on could not assist in considering whether or not the accused had no reason to suspect. The effect of this conclusion is that self-induced intoxication is not a relevant consideration in exercise of the statutory defence."

It is true that an objective interpretation of the words "nor had reason to suspect" could produce harsh results. A person might act in haste in accepting a package that contains a controlled drug, without being aware of certain facts that, with the benefit of hindsight, should have put him on inquiry as to the true nature of the contents. In 1984, Richard Lord (*Controlled Drugs, Law And Practice*) said:

"it very frequently occurs that D is in possession of a controlled drug without knowing the exact chemical name of the drug. D may be in possession of a substance he knows as 'acid' without knowing that he is in possession lysergide. He may be unaware that the substance is in fact a controlled drug. This ignorance will not give him any defence under section 28. However, in the following situation D would have a defence under section 28: D is in possession of a substance which he knows of as 'blues'. He thinks that the term 'blues' is common parlance for [a drug that is not controlled]. In fact the term 'blues is common parlance for amphetamine. The substance is in fact amphetamine. To borrow the terminology of a series of contract cases, D must be mistaken as to the identity of the substance and not merely its attributes (such as its name) in order to have a defence under section 28."

8–21 At first blush, it may be difficult to see why the result should be different in those two examples. However, it is submitted that in the first example, D would have no defence under section 28(3)(b)(i) because although D did not know the chemical name for the substance he possessed, he was aware of the qualities of the product, which he described as "acid". If D did not know that "acid"/LSD was a controlled drug, his ignorance of the law would afford him no defence or excuse. This, presumably, is what Mr Lord had in mind. In the second example, Mr Lord suggests that D would have a defence (viewed subjectively) because D made a complete mistaken as to the identity of the substance. One might add that D believed he possessed an article of a very different nature—*i.e.* a drug that was not controlled. However, it is at this point that a divergence of opinion has arisen as to what Parliament intended to achieve by adding the third limb to section 28(3)(b)(i). If Parliament did intend to restrict the scope of the defence by including an objective element, then D would face colossal difficulties in maintaining a defence under section 28, if the third limb does indeed involve the "wider concept of an objective rationality" (*per* Kilner Brown J. in *Young* (above)). Why would Parliament have wished to restrict the defence in this way? The answer might be twofold. First, section 28 creates defences that did not previously exist. Parliament wanted to reduce, but only to a very limited extent, the severity of the old legislation. Secondly, Parliament may have wished to ensure that those who come into possession of property, make some inquiry about its quality or its history. For example, the burden imposed on occupiers and persons concerned in the management of property not to permit or suffer certain activities to take place on their premises (s. 8), is a way of encouraging amateurs to police the legislation and to be responsible for their own affairs. On that basis, a phrase popularly used to describe a controlled drug is likely to be a sufficient reason to cause a person to suspect that the substance which he possesses, bearing that description, is in fact a controlled drug. As Robert Shiels has pointed out (*Controlled Drugs Statutes And Cases*, Sweet & Maxwell, 1991) "the objective nature of the last limb to section 28(3)(b)(i) means that there is a limit to the extent to which an accused can be judged on the facts as he believed them to be".

It remains to be seen whether in a subsequent decision, the court will be driven to add a proviso, namely, "or where the defendant ought to have been aware of reasons to suspect". That step might not be necessary if the view is taken that, in practice, an accused already faces an uphill challenge to prove a defence under section 28(3)(b)(i) even if the defence is entirely subjective: and see *Afzal* (June 19, 2000).

(b) If section 28(3)(b)(i) does contain an objective element, is it HRA/ECHR-compliant?

In *Rice* (transcript, November 20, 2000, above), R's primary complaint was that section 28(3) of the Misuse Of Drugs Act 1971 contravened Article 6(2) of the European Convention On Human Rights, on the grounds that section 28(3)(b)(i) was not Convention-compliant because it included an objective element, namely, "nor had reason to suspect". In refusing leave to appeal, the Court of Appeal held that the words were subject to a subjective interpretation but in any event, the provision was Convention- 8–22 compliant. The Court noted that the matter had already been considered by the court in *Lambert and others* (July 31, 2000) in which it was held that section 28 did comply with the Convention. The same point was taken, with the same result, in *Pegg* (transcript, October 3, 2000).

E. SECTION 28(3)(b)(ii)

8–23 As the MDA permits the Secretary of State, by regulations, to exempt certain controlled drugs from the activities prohibited by that Act, *e.g.* sections 4 and 5, it is conceivable that a person may deal with drug X (which is not exempt) while believing that he is dealing with drug Y (which is exempt). Thus, regulation 4(2) of the 1985 Regulations permits any person to possess drugs listed in Schedule 4 of those regulations (*e.g.* Lorazepam) notwithstanding section 5(1).

Accordingly, section 28(3)(b)(ii) affords a defence to an accused who in fact possesses heroin believing that the drug is Lorazepam. The test is entirely subjective.

Chapter 9
Offences Contrary to a Corresponding Law

A. GENERAL NOTE

Section 20 Misuse of Drugs Act 1971 provides that: 9–01

> "A person commits an offence if in the United Kingdom he assists in or induces the commission in any place outside the United Kingdom of an offence punishable under the provisions of a corresponding law in force in that place."

It is submitted that the following propositions represent the law:

(1) Section 20 creates a statutory offence punishable under the Act: the section does not merely give the courts of the United Kingdom jurisdiction to try offences that would otherwise be "local" to courts of foreign jurisdiction.

(2) To prove the full offence under section 20:
   (a) the "foreign offence" must actually have been committed: *Panayi (No. 1)* (1988) 86 Cr.App.R. 261;
   (b) the "foreign offence" must be punishable under the provisions of a "corresponding law"; see section 20 and section 36.

(3) Where the foreign offence has not been committed then:
   (a) a conspiracy to commit an offence under section 20 may lie if two or more persons agree to commit a foreign offence: *Vickers* (1975) 61 Cr.App.R. 48;
   (b) an attempt to commit a section 20 offence may lie if the accused performs acts in the United Kingdom (being more than merely preparatory) in an attempt to induce the commission of the "foreign offence". Note that an offence committed under section 20 is a "drug trafficking offence" for the purposes of the DTA 1994: section 1(3)(b)

B. WHAT IS CAPABLE OF AMOUNTING TO "ASSISTANCE"

9–02 In *Vickers* [1975] 1 W.L.R. 811, the Court of Appeal held that the words "assisting in or inducing the commission of" in section 20 were chosen by Parliament: "so as to leave to a jury the opportunity of exercising a common sense judgment on the facts of a particular case" (*per* Scarman L.J.).

> In *Vickers, ibid.*; V and J agreed in England and elsewhere that V would obtain a truck in London to collect and load, a number of speaker cabinets, which he would then deliver to Italy knowing (as was the case) that cannabis would be fitted into the cabinets and shipped to the United States of America. V performed his part of the agreement. He was convicted of conspiracy to contravene section 20 of the Misuse of Drugs Act 1971 by agreeing to assist in, or induce the commission in the United States of America of offences punishable under the United States Comprehensive Drug Abuse Prevention and Control Act 1970, "corresponding" to the United Kingdom law (namely section 3(1) of the MDA 1971 and what is now section 180 of the CEMA 1979).
>
> *Held*: V's acts in obtaining the truck and collecting the speakers were sufficient "assistance" within the United Kingdom for the purposes of section 20.

9–03 V contended that the words "assists in or induces the commission", as they appear in section 20 MDA must be narrowly construed as covering only acts directly concerned with the actual importation. Two arguments were advanced in support of this proposition. The first was that the offence was one of strict liability and therefore the words must be narrowly construed. This argument was swiftly rejected on the basis that "one who assists knows what he is doing and the purpose with which it is done" (*per* Scarman L.J. at 818): and see para., below. The second argument was founded on the wording of the previous legislation which, by section 13(d) of the Dangerous Drugs Act 1965, provided that:

> "A person . . .
> (d) who in the United Kingdom . . . does an act preparatory to, or in furtherance of, an act which if committed in the United Kingdom would constitute an offence against this Act; shall be guilty of an offence. . . . "

The wording of section 13(d) therefore embraced preparatory acts albeit that they fell short of an attempt to commit the full offence. By contrast, section 20 omits those words: see *Johnston*, March 22, 1974 (unreported, but summarised in *Evans* (1976) 64 Cr.App.R. 237).

9–04 In *Vickers*, the appellant argued that if preparatory acts now fall outside the scope of section 20 then Parliament must have intended to restrict the meaning of the phrase "assist in or induces the commission of . . . an offence" to acts directly concerned with the actual importation of the drug into the United States of America. Presumably, as part of that submission, the appellant also contended that if preparatory acts are excluded from section 20 then the answer should not be different merely because the accused is charged with conspiracy. The Court of Appeal rejected that argument on the straightforward basis that the offence under section 13(d) is abolished and what matters now is the construction of section 20 as a matter of plain English.

In order to understand the submissions made by the appellant in *Vickers*, it is helpful to look at the history of section 20.

Under the Single Convention on Narcotic Drugs 1961, to which the United Kingdom is a party, each Member State agreed to "assist each other in the campaign against the illicit traffic in narcotic drugs": Article 35(b). To that end, Article 36 provides that:

> "36.1. (a) Subject to its constitutional limitations each party shall adopt such measures as will ensure that cultivation, production, manufacture, extraction, preparation, possession, offering, offering for sale, distribution, purchase, sale, delivery on any terms whatsoever, brokerage, dispatch, dispatch in transit, transport, importation and exportation of drugs contrary to the provisions of the Convention . . . shall be punishable offences when committed intentionally.
>
> 36.2. (a) (i) Each of the offences enumerated in paragraph 1, if committed in different countries, shall be considered as a distinct offence;
>
> (ii) Intentional participation in, conspiracy to commit and attempts to commit, any of such offences, and preparatory acts and financial operations in connection with the offences referred to in this article, shall be punishable offences as provided in paragraph 1;"

It will be seen that Article 36(2)(a)(ii) embraces "preparatory acts". 9–05
Although at common law, the test of an attempt has been expressed differently over the years, the law recognised in essence that acts which are merely preparatory to the commission of an offence do not amount to an attempt to commit the full offence if the accused is not yet "on the job": *per* Rowlatt J. in *Osborn* (1919) 84 J.P. 63. See also *Gullefer* [1987] Crim.L.R. 195, CA.

Accordingly, ratification of Article 36(2)(a)(ii) necessitated a radical departure from the position at common law: hence section 13(d) of the Dangerous Drugs Act 1965, cited at para. 9–03, above.

Section 13(d) was concerned with two sets of offences. First, "aiding, abetting, counselling or procuring" the commission of a foreign offence. The foreign offence had actually to have been committed because one cannot otherwise aid or abet its commission: see *Panayi (No. 1)* (1988) 86 Cr.App.R. 261, 266, and see para. 9–07, below. The second set of offences concerned conspiracies, or preparatory acts falling short of an attempt, to commit an offence contrary to the 1965 Act. This included an offence punishable under a corresponding law in a foreign country, providing that the acts complained of would, if committed in the United Kingdom, constitute an offence under the 1965 Act: see *Johnston*, (March 22, 1974, unreported).

9–06 The Misuse of Drugs Act 1971 simplified this framework. It deleted any reference to preparatory acts but (for the purpose of s. 20 of the MDA 1971) it replaced the words "aids, abets, counsels or procures" as they appeared in section 13(d) with the broad words "assists in or induces the commission of".

The submission of the appellant in *Vickers* appears to have been that if section 20 now excludes acts which are merely preparatory, Parliament must have intended that the words "assists" in section 20, should be narrowly construed so as to relate to acts proximate to the moment of importation. The Court of Appeal rejected the argument founded on section 13(d) of the 1965 Act as being "beside the point" and that the meaning of the plain English words in a statute is a question of fact (see *Cozens v. Brutus* [1973] A.C. 854, 861).

In the view of the Court of Appeal in *Vickers*, Parliament chose the plain English phrase "assist in the commission of" so as to leave to a jury the opportunity of exercising a common-sense judgment on the facts of a particular case: *per* Scarman L.J. In this regard, the Court of Appeal was plainly right because there exists no logical reason why those words should be subject to an artificially restricted meaning.

9–07 All that need be proved, for the full offence, under section 20, is that a foreign offence was actually committed (whether that offence be substantive or inchoate: and see *Panayi (No. 1)* (1986) 86 Cr.App.R. 261) and that the defendant did acts within the United Kingdom which assisted or induced the commission of that offence.

> In *Panayi (No.1)* (1988) 86 Cr.App.R. 261, a yacht carrying 690 kilograms of cannabis worth £1.3 million from Spain to Holland sailed into British territorial waters within the limits of Port Solent (see s. 5 of the CEMA 1979) whereupon the appellants, who crewed the yacht, were arrested and charged on count 2 with an offence under section 20, that they assisted in the United Kingdom in the commission in the Netherlands of an offence punishable under the provisions of a corresponding law in force in the Netherlands.
>
> *Held*: the conviction would be quashed. The offence, said to be punishable under a corresponding law in the Netherlands, was not committed. In Panayi the "foreign offence" relied upon, appears to have been a substantive offence contrary to the laws of the Netherlands.

"Preparatory acts" are relevant if they provide evidence that the defendant assisted in, or induced, the commission of the foreign offence.

9–08 In cases where a foreign offence has not been committed, the prosecutor may wish to consider whether he can properly charge an attempt to induce the commission of the foreign offence contrary to section 20 of the MDA 1971 under section 1(1) and (4) of the Criminal Attempts Act 1981 or, to charge a conspiracy to contravene section 20. Indeed, where two or more persons are involved, the prosecution may find it easier to allege a conspiracy even if a foreign offence has been committed and this seems to have been the situation in *Vickers* itself.

Acts preparatory to the commission of an offence are insufficient to prove an attempt to commit that offence, but they may provide some evidence of an agreement to contravene section 20: see *Cooper and Compton* [1947] 2 All E.R. 701, *DPP v. Bhagwan* [1972] A.C. 60; *Knuller (Publishing, Printing and Promotions) Ltd. v. DPP* [1973] A.C. 435 and *Vickers*.

Suppose A and B agree in England to import cannabis into country X. 9–09
The drug is concealed in furniture and stored in London. Both A and B travel to country X to familiarise themselves with the airport: they return to England the following day. Assume that it is an offence in country X to attempt to import cannabis, and that the government of X certifies that the offence is punishable under a corresponding law for the purposes of section 36. On those facts A and B are guilty of the full offence under section 20. They are also guilty of conspiring to commit an "exportation offence" contrary to section 68 or section 170(2) of the CEMA 1979 and section 3 of the MDA 1971.

Furthermore, it would be open to the prosecution to charge A and B with a conspiracy to commit the section 20 offence on the basis that if the agreement had been carried out "in accordance with their intentions", the substantive offence (by the law of X) would have been committed: see section 1(1) of the Criminal Law Act 1977; and see *Vickers* (1975) 61 Cr.App.R. 48 where a conspiracy was charged. If the appellants in *Panayi* had been charged with a conspiracy to contravene section 20 itself (as opposed to a conspiracy to commit the foreign offence), by agreeing in the United Kingdom to assist in the commission of a substantive offence punishable under a corresponding law in the Netherlands, the result might have been different providing there was evidence that the appellants, whilst they were within British territorial waters, agreed to assist or to induce the commission of the "foreign offence". Panayi's defence appears to have been that he was asleep on board at the time the vessel entered British territorial waters. If true, it is difficult to see how he could be said to have formed an agreement with Karte to contravene section 20.

The cases of *Vickers* and *Panayi* (above) demonstrate the importance of identifying carefully the "foreign offence" alleged to have been committed and drafting an appropriate count to meet the facts of any given case: see *Mushtaq Ahmed* [1990] Crim.L.R. 648.

C. ASSISTING "IN THE UNITED KINGDOM"

Something must be done by the accused in the United Kingdom that 9–10
assisted or induced, the commission of an offence punishable under a corresponding law abroad must have been performed in the United Kingdom.

In *Evans* (1977) 64 Cr.App.R. 237, E agreed with J to go to Brussels, to pick up a parcel of cannabis, and to take it to Canada. E was provided with his airline ticket and met J at an hotel in Brussels where he was given a holdall containing the drug which E then took with him to Montreal and delivered the holdall to X, contrary to the Narcotic Control Act 1960 61 of Canada. On appeal, against his conviction under section 20 of the MDA 1971, E contended that he had done nothing in the United Kingdom, which was capable to amounting to "assisting" in the commission of the offence charged.

Held: dismissing the appeal, E's conduct in going to London airport and collecting his ticket, knowing the illicit purpose of his journey, was sufficient evidence of "assistance" to go to the jury.

See also *Coppack* (June 10, unreported, 1994,CA) where a similar point was taken.

D. "OFFENCE PUNISHABLE UNDER A CORRESPONDING LAW"

9–11 By section 36 of the MDA 1971:

"(1) In this Act the expression 'corresponding law' means a law stated in a certificate purporting to be issued by or on behalf of the government of a country outside the United Kingdom to be a law providing for the control and regulation in that country of the production, supply, use, export and import of drugs and other substances in accordance with the provisions of the Single Convention on Narcotic Drugs signed at New York on March 30th, 1961 or a law providing for the control and regulation in that country of the production, supply, use, export and import of dangerous or otherwise harmful drugs in pursuance of any treaty, convention or other agreement or arrangement to which the government of that country and Her Majesty's Government in the United Kingdom are for the time being parties.

(2) A statement in any such certificate as aforesaid to the effect that any facts constitute an offence against the law mentioned in the certificate shall be evidence, and in Scotland sufficient evidence, of the matters stated."

On a proper construction of section 20 a person cannot be guilty of committing an offence in a place outside the United Kingdom unless the offence outside the United Kingdom was in fact committed: see *Panayi (No.1)* (1986) 86 Cr.App.R. 261. The Court of Appeal reviewed the authorities of *Vickers* [1975] 1 W.L.R. 811 and *Evans* (1977) 64 Cr.App.R. 237 and said: "A whole series of acts might be done preparatory to the commission of an offence, but if no offence is in fact committed, it is difficult to see how you can assist in its commission": *per* O'Connor L.J.

E. IMPORTATION PERFORMED BY AN INNOCENT THIRD PARTY

In *Ahmed* [1990] Crim.L.R. 648: 9–12

> Cannabis concealed in a quantity of raisins was sent to Rotterdam but the goods were not collected there as intended. An innocent third party, employed by a firm of shipping agents, sent the goods to Belgium in the name of the consignee. Documents relating to the consignment were found at the appellant's address in the United Kingdom hidden behind a lavatory cistern. He had earlier visited Amsterdam to collect the shipping documents. He was also observed by officers meeting an accomplice named Bashir whom the appellant knew to be a drug smuggler.
>
> *Held*: on appeal, that "it was not necessary to prove that the appellant intended that the goods should be imported into Belgium. It was enough to prove that [the appellant] assisted in a course of business which had that result being well aware, as he was, that Bashir was involved in drug smuggling".

It is submitted that the position on this point is analogous to the 9–13
reasoning in *Jakeman* (1983) 76 Cr.App.R. 223: paras 2–38 and 2–80, above and contrast with *Latif and Shahzad* [1996] 1 All E.R. 353, HL. In each case, the accused brought about the *actus reus* of the offence in question. The accused must know, of course, what is afoot and what he is doing and the purpose with which he acts. However, whereas in *Jakeman* the defendant did intend to import the drugs into the United Kingdom before she abandoned the enterprise, in *Ahmed* the appellant did not intend to import the drug into Belgium: and see *Panayi (No. 2)* [1989] 1 W.L.R. 187 in this regard.

It is not necessary for the prosecution to identify the "principal offender": see *Ahmed*, *ibid*. In that case, the submission appears to have been that acts of assistance must relate to the activities of an identifiable principal offender (and not an innocent third party) who affected the actual importation. That submission, rejected by the Court of Appeal, overlooked the unique nature of the offence under section 20. The section is aimed at those who give assistance. For the purposes of that section, the persons who "assist" are the principal offenders. The person who effects the importation into a foreign country may not, in fact, be guilty of any offence contrary to English law at all. To seek to distinguish between so-called "principal offenders" and "assistances" as if they were mere accessories or secondary parties in these circumstances is, with respect, fallacious. It must, of course, be proved that somebody committed the offence: see *Panayi (No. 1)* (1988) 86 Cr.App.R. 261, above.

F. MENS REA FOR AN OFFENCE UNDER SECTION 20

9–14 In *Vickers* (above) V, knew the object of the venture but he did not know whether it would be carried out, or how, or by whom. To say (as was said in *Cozens v. Brutus*, para. 9–06 above, and by Scarman L.J. in *Vickers*), that the meaning of a plain English word is a question of fact, may be an over-simplification in the context of a statutory provision creating a criminal offence. In plain English, "assisting in" may or may not involve knowledge of the object or venture. This is not always an issue to be left to a jury to determine in a criminal case and indeed, in *Vickers*, Scarman L.J. answered that aspect when he said that "in ordinary English one who assists knows what he is doing and the purpose with which it is done; and this appellant was well aware of the purpose for which the containers he conveyed to Italy were wanted". To that extent the *mens rea* imported into the word "assists" as it appears in section 20, has been determined as a matter of law.

Chapter 10
Conspiracy and Attempt to Commit a Drug Offence

A. INTRODUCTION

In the last 20 years, the law of conspiracy and attempt has undergone much change; indeed the common law offences of conspiracy and attempt have been largely abolished by statute. Furthermore, the old offences of inciting the commission of, or attempting to commit, a conspiracy are also abolished (s. 5(7) of the Criminal Law Act 1977). 10–01

Instead, the Criminal Law Act 1977 now creates a statutory offence of conspiracy, which, by section 1(1) (as amended by s. 5 of the Criminal Attempts Act 1981) provides:

> "Subject to the following provisions of this Part of the Act, if a person agrees with any other person or persons that a course of conduct shall be pursued which, if the agreement is carried out in accordance with their intentions, either
>
> (a) will necessarily amount to or involve the commission of any offence or offences by one or more of the parties to the agreement, or
>
> (b) would do so but for the existence of facts which render the commission of the offence or any of the offences impossible,
>
> he is guilty of conspiracy to commit the offence or offences in question."

It follows that an agreement to do any of the acts prohibited by the Misuse of Drugs Act 1971 or the Customs and Excise Management Act 1979 may be charged as a statutory conspiracy.

To be guilty of a conspiracy, it is not necessary that the accused was a party to the original scheme. Conspirators may enter and leave a conspiracy at any time during its operation: see *Simmonds* [1969] 1 Q.B. 685. The role of each conspirator must be seen in the context of the concerted course of conduct: see *Ardalan* [1972] 1 W.L.R. 463 and *Bailey* (1913) 9 Cr.App.R. 94. 10–02

It used to be said that the essence of a conspiracy is the plotting by two or more persons to do an unlawful act, or to do a lawful act but by unlawful means, with the intention of carrying out the unlawful purpose: see *Thompson* [1966] 1 W.L.R. 405. However, this formulation may no longer be apt in the light of the terms of section 1 of the 1977 Act as interpreted by the House of Lords in *Anderson* (1985) 81 Cr.App.R. 253 but see *Yip Chiu-Cheung* (1994) 99 Cr. App. R. 406, PC. Indeed, in relation to conspiracies arising out of offences under the Misuse of Drugs Act 1971, the reader should have in mind the combined effect of *Anderson* (above); *Courtie* [1984] A.C. 463; *Siracusa* (1990) 90 Cr.App.R. 340; *Patel* (August 7, 1991, unreported); and see *Broad and Others* (April 25, 1997). The facts of *Siracusa* and *Patel* are summarised below.

10–03 It is submitted that the following propositions emerge from those authorities:

(1) The accused must agree to commit an unlawful object: *Walker* [1962] Crim.L.R. 458; *Yip Chiu-Cheung* (1994) 99 Cr. App. R. 406 but note *Anderson*, above;
(2) the accused must know, in general terms, that an offence will be committed if the agreed course of conduct is carried out: see *Siracusa, ibid.*, at 349 *per* O'Connor L.J.; and *Anderson* (1985) 81 Cr.App.R. 253, 258, *per* Lord Bridge;
(3) however, the accused need not know the name of the offence or the relevant provision which will be contravened: *per* O'Connor L.J. *Siracusa, ibid.*, at 349; and see Woolf L.J. in *Patel, ibid.*;
(4) the accused must intend to play some part in the agreed course of conduct in furtherance of the criminal purpose which the agreement was intended to achieve: *per* Lord Bridge in *Anderson, ibid.*, at 258 an undercover agent who has no intention of committing the crime lacks the necessary *mens rea* to be a conspirator": *per* Lord Griffiths, *Yip Chiu-Cheng*, PC, above.
(5) the prosecution must prove the terms of the agreement. "You do not prove an agreement to import heroin by proving an agreement to import cannabis": *per* O'Connor L.J. in *Siracusa, ibid.*, at 350; but:
    (a) a different penalty attaches to each Class of drug under Sched. 2 of the MDA 1971 and therefore each Class of drug creates a separate offence: *Courtie* (above) and *Shivpuri* [1987] A.C. 1. Therefore:
    (b) different answers may result depending on the accused's belief as to the nature of the drug he thought he was dealing with; and depending on whether the charge of conspiracy identifies the drug in question as part of the Particulars of Offence: see (6) and (7) below:
(6) the accused must know that the drugs to which the conspiracy relates were controlled drugs: see *Patel, per* Woolf L.J., at 17 D-E of the transcript;
(7) if the drug is identified in the Particulars of Offence then the accused is to be:

(a) *acquitted*, if he may have mistakenly believed that the conspiracy related to a different drug (*e.g.* cannabis, Class B) from that identified in the Particulars of Offence (*e.g.* heroin, Class A), provided that:
  (i) the "different drug" is in another Class and,
  (ii) that "other Class" attracts a lesser penalty than the Class of drug identified in the Particulars of Offence; see *Patel*, *ibid.*,

(b) *convicted*, if the accused believes he was dealing with a drug attracting a "higher" penalty (*i.e.* this is the converse of 7(a) above: see *Patel*, *per* Woolf L.J. at 18 A-C;

(c) *convicted*, if the accused believes the drug belonged to the same Class as the drug identified in the Particulars of Offence: *Patel*, *per* Woolf L.J. at 18 C-D;

(d) *convicted*, if the accused knows that controlled drugs are involved but he does not know what they are: *Patel*, *per* Woolf L.J. at 18E.

One implication of the decision in *Patel* is that the difficulties in *Siracusa* could be avoided if the Particulars of Offence did not specify any particular controlled drug. 10–04

In *Patel*, Woolf L.J. (at 16 B-F) regarded the name of the drug as a "material allegation", relevant to sentence, but he did not regard the name as a "material averment" so long as the defendant did not believe he was dealing with a drug in a different Class (*i.e.* the *Courtie* principle). Nevertheless, Woolf L.J. emphasised the desirability that the Particulars of Offence should identify the drug if the Crown is clear as to which drug was involved: see 18F.

Although Woolf L.J. thought that the name of the drug was relevant to sentence, this should not normally be the case since all drugs coming within a particular Class are subject to the same maximum penalty and therefore, in the ordinary way, they should all be treated similarly.

B. PROVING THE CONSPIRACY

The *actus reus* is the agreement to commit an unlawful object but the whole concept is heavily dependent on the mental element, namely, on the terms of the agreement and the beliefs held by each party to the agreement. 10–05

Considerations applicable in the civil law have little place in the construction of section 1 of the Criminal Law Act 1977.

In *Anderson* [1986] A.C. 27, the House of Lords explored the scope of section 1 of that Act.

> In *Anderson*, X and A shared a cell. A agreed to help X escape. A was bailed and received £2000 in order to buy equipment in order to facilitate X's escape. At his trial A claimed that he never actually intended

to take part in X's escape although he had planned to smuggle equipment into the prison. A's object was primarily to make money out of X.

The House of Lords held that the fact that A did not intend to participate any further in the escape bid, or that A believed the escape to be impossible, afforded A no defence (and see *Gortat and Pirog* [1973] Crim.L.R. 648).

10–06 There is little difficulty where the evidence shows that the parties to the conspiracy all intended to commit an unlawful object and acted in furtherance of that unlawful object "in accordance with their intentions": such an intent is joint. However, in *Anderson*, their Lordships were concerned to look at the position of those who are subordinates in a conspiracy (say C and D) who may or may not know the true objects of the conspiracy but which is well known to the prime movers (A and B). The point is graphically demonstrated in the case of an undercover officer who infiltrates a drug-trafficking ring. Such an officer may be a party to discussions (or even to an agreement) concerning the shipment of narcotics but he does not intend that the criminal enterprise should be successful nor does he necessarily intend to participate in the agreed course of conduct. Is he to be convicted in such circumstances merely by joining an agreement to be carried out in accordance with the intentions of the instigators? In other words, when section 1 refers to an agreement being carried out "in accordance with their intentions", must each party to the agreement have precisely the same intention? Is this another situation where intention must not be confused with motive? Regard must now be had to the opinion of Lord Bridge in *Anderson* and Lord Griffiths in *Yip Chiu-Cheung*.

10–07 In dealing with this issue, Lord Bridge in *Anderson* said (i) that the accused must enter into an *agreement* that a course of conduct be pursued, but (ii) it was not necessary to prove that the accused intended that the crime or crimes should in fact be committed. This last point has been forcefully criticised on the basis that if no intention need be proved in the case of one conspirator, then why should it be proved on the part of another, and yet, if it is not proved in respect of at least two persons, the upshot would be that a conspiracy exists that none of the conspirators intends to carry out! For a fuller analysis, see Smith and Hogan, *Criminal Law* (9th ed., Butterworths, p.275, 276). Professor Sir John Smith suggests that *Anderson* "should not be followed in this respect" and cites examples where the Court of Appeal has ignored the point: *Edwards* [1991] Crim.L.R. 45; *Ashton* [1992] Crim.L.R. 667; and *Harvey* [1999] Crim.L.R. 70. In practice, the position seems to be that once the conspiracy is proved to be "up and running", the prosecution does not need to prove that any subsequent party joining that conspiracy intended that the offence should be committed. An undercover police officer, engaged in a covert operation, would therefore not be protected on this basis. Their Lordships in *Anderson* had such officers well in mind when analysing the effect of section 1 of the 1977 Act which caused Lord Bridge to remark that "the *mens rea* implicit in the offence of statutory conspiracy must clearly be such as to recognise the innocence of such a person" who did not desire the performance of the object. How, logically, can this result be achieved? A result intended need not always be a result that is desired, and similar difficulties exist in relation to the substantive, but widely drawn offence under section 170(2) of CEMA 1979: see for example, *Latif* [1996] 1 All E.R. 353. In *Yip Chiu-Cheung*, above, a United States undercover drug enforcement officer, agreed with Y and others that five kilograms should be transported from Hong Kong and Australia. The officer kept the authorities in Hong Kong and Australia informed, and they agreed that he would not be prevented from carrying the heroin into Australia albeit that he did not have a licence for that purpose. Lord Griffiths accepted that the officer was acting "with the best of motives" but he added that:

> "The crime of conspiracy requires an agreement between two or more persons to commit an unlawful act with the intention of carrying it out. It is the intention to carry out the crime that constitutes the necessary *mens rea* for the offence."

The crucial phrase is "carry out the *crime*"—that is to say, an intention that the *actus reus* with the requisite *mens rea*, be performed. Although Lord Griffiths was not dealing with section 1 of the Criminal Law Act 1977 it is difficult to see why this reasoning should not also be valid for the purposes of that provision. Such a principle would be consistent with the words "in accordance with their intentions" as they appear in section 1 of the Act. The problem is that Lord Bridge in *Anderson* seemed to be saying the opposite. It is submitted that the law as stated by Lord Griffiths is correct but how is the difference between the opinions of Lord Griffiths and Lord Bridge to be reconciled? Lord Griffiths in *Yip Chiu-Cheung* suggests that there is not a difference of opinion only the facts are different in the two cases and therefore *Anderson* was to be distinguished because, as "Lord Bridge pointed out, an undercover agent who has no intention of committing the crime lacks the necessary *mens rea* to be a conspirator". It is debatable whether this really does represent what Lord Bridge was saying, particularly when the opinion is read as a whole, but Lord Griffiths may have had the following passage in mind: 10–08

> ". . . the necessary *mens rea* of the crime is established if, and only if, it is shown that the accused, when he entered into the agreement, intended to play some part in the agreed course of conduct *in furtherance of the criminal purpose which the agreed course of conduct was intended* to achieve": *per* Lord Bridge (at 39) [emphasis added]

How does all this stand with *El Ghazal* [1986] Crim.L.R. 52, decided before *Anderson* was heard (and see the commentary of Professor Sir John Smith in [1994] Crim. L.R. 825)? It is submitted that *El Ghazal* is reconcil able. 10–09

In *El Ghazal* [1986] Crim.L.R. 52, E, T and C were charged with a conspiracy to obtain cocaine. T asked E if he could arrange a meeting between T and C so that both T and C could "make a deal about cocaine". E arranged the meeting and attended it for a short period. E complained that the judge misdirected the jury by implying that an agreement to do acts that were merely preparatory to commit a crime amounted to a conspiracy under section 1(1).

Held: the appeal would be dismissed. If E introduced T to C, knowing of T's intention and knowing that one of them would seek to obtain cocaine, then that was the agreement for the purpose of section 1(1).

10–10 At first sight, the decision is a little difficult to understand since E, on one interpretation of the facts, seems to have done no more than to arrange a meeting between T and C so that a conspiracy to possess cocaine could take place. For this reason the decision, or at least the basis for attaching liability, has been criticised, notably by the learned commentator in the Criminal Law Review (see [1986] Crim.L.R. 52) and the reader is encouraged to consult this. However, it was the prosecution's case that E knew from the start that either T or C would obtain the cocaine and therefore E had conspired with T to obtain the drug. C only joined the conspiracy at a later stage. It is submitted that, if the jury reached the conclusion that E did know of the object of the meeting right from the start, then it was logical to hold that E conspired with T to obtain drugs. That was the conspiracy. The fact that C might have been a necessary link to complete performance (C not yet having been recruited) is not a relevant consideration.

To give a hypothetical example, even if it was not E's purpose that a controlled drug of any description should be supplied, and E was actually indifferent as to whether the transaction related to drugs or some other illicit activity, E intended that "the crime" should be carried out. The fact that E was present at the meeting, albeit for a short time, was capable of being evidence to support that inference.

10–11 The opinion of Lord Bridge that proof of conspiracy required evidence that the accused ". . . intended to play some part in the agreed course of conduct" has been described as "novel dictum" (Smith and Hogan, *Criminal Law*, 9th edition, p. 277). Given that the essence of conspiracy is the agreement to commit an unlawful object, it is unnecessary for a conspirator to intend to play any part in the venture. Clearly, the agreement, in order for a statutory conspiracy to be committed, envisages that someone will carry out the plan "in accordance with their intentions". Taken literally, Lord Bridge's "novel dictum" would mean that organisers of criminal enterprises, who played no part in the execution of the unlawful plan, could not be convicted of conspiracy. In *Siracusa* (1990) 90 Cr. App. R. 34, O'Connor L.J. made it plain that Lord Bridge did not intend his remarks to have that effect.

In *Siracusa* (1990) 90 Cr.App.R. 340, O'Connor L.J. observed that Lord Bridge did not intend to say that the organiser of a crime who recruited others to carry it out would not be guilty of conspiracy unless it could be proved that he intended to play some active part himself thereafter. In the judgment of the Court of Appeal in *Siracusa*, an intention to participate in the furtherance of the enterprise can be established by the accused's failure to stop the unlawful activity (*per* O'Connor L.J. at 349). This, of course, raises an interesting question as to when he should do so. To infer intention from such failure is a speculative concept. An undercover officer, for example, may wait until the very last moment before arrests are made and the venture is halted.

It should also be noted that a secret and uncommunicated intention to join in an illegal enterprise should the occasion arise is not by itself sufficient to make that person a party to a conspiracy: see *Scott (Valerie)* (1978) 68 Cr. App. R. 164.

I. Proving the Terms of the Agreement

The House of Lords in *Anderson* [1986] A.C. 27 did not resolve the question whether all the conspirators must be of one mind in respect of the course of conduct to be pursued but *Yip Chiu-Cheung* (1994) 99 Cr. App. R. 406, PC, seems to have done so (at least in terms of the offence or type of offence which the parties have in contemplation). However, to what extent must the parties be agreed as to details of the plan? 10–12

> In *Siracusa* (above) the appellants were convicted on two counts of conspiracy, one to import cannabis (count 1) and the other to import heroin (count 2). The cannabis was imported from India and the heroin from Thailand. Each drug arrived on different dates but each drug was concealed in furniture. Each count specified the drug imported and that, in essence, the appellants conspired to import that drug. The appellants contended that, as charged, the prosecution had to prove that each defendant knew the precise drug being imported.
>
> *Held*: the submissions were correct but the appeals against conviction would be dismissed on other grounds.

It is important to bear in mind that on each count the name of the drug had been particularised and the case was therefore decided on that basis. The Court referred to *Anderson* [1986] A.C. 27 but, in the final analysis, the point made was a short one: "you do not prove an agreement to import heroin by proving an agreement to import cannabis": *per* O'Connor L.J. at 350.

The result and the reasoning are plainly right. The prosecution had alleged an agreement on a narrow basis and they had to prove it. O'Connor L.J., as if to reinforce the point, said (at 350): 10–13

> "If the facts suggest that the agreement was to import prohibited drugs of more than one class, that can be appropriately laid because section 1(1) of the Criminal Law Act 1977 expressly provides for the agreed

> course of conduct to involve the commission of more than one offence."

On the facts in *Siracusa*, the two drugs (heroin and cannabis) fell into Classes A and B respectively. Different penalties attach to each of the three Classes of controlled drugs under Schedule 2 to the MDA 1971, and therefore create three separate offences: see *Courtie* [1984] A.C. 463 and *Shivpuri* [1987] A.C. 1.

10–14 In *Siracusa*, the Court did not need to consider whether the result would have been different if drugs of the same Class had been imported.

> In *Patel* (August 7, 1991, unreported), three men named Patel and two others operated a pharmacy, which supplied chemicals, used to manufacture amphetamine sulphate (Class B). They were convicted on two counts of conspiracy, one to produce amphetamine and the other to supply that drug. Each count named the drug in the Particulars of Offence. The Patels denied any knowledge that any drugs were being manufactured or supplied as alleged. The trial judge directed the jury that they had to decide in the case of each defendant whether "his knowledge of the scheme and the actual scheme was sufficiently close that it can properly be said that he attached himself to that scheme and not to something different".
>
> *Held*: the Patels were not prejudiced by the directions of the judge given their complete denial of the knowledge of the scheme. The naming of the drug was not a material averment but it was a material allegation relevant to sentence.

The narrow ground on which *Patel* was decided turned on the effect of the Patels' denials. In the opinion of the Court: "If they were not believed then they either did not know precisely what drugs were involved or they knew it was amphetamine sulphate." If they did not know which drugs were involved then this would span drugs falling into three Classes of drug and therefore (following *Courtie*) three categories of offence. The question was whether this made any difference.

10–15 In a lengthy judgment Woolf L.J. held that *Siracusa* was only authority for the proposition that:

> ". . . if a defendant joined a conspiracy believing it involved one Class of drug, he is not guilty of that conspiracy if he believes the drug involved is a drug which belongs to a lesser Class to that named The Court gave as its reason that "the conspiracy in which the defendant intended to become involved would then relate to a different and less serious offence ."

By a "different" offence, the Court meant that if a defendant believes he is dealing with cannabis (Class B) whereas it is alleged that he conspired to supply heroin (Class A), then the two drugs relate to two different offences (see *Courtie*). By "a less serious" offence, the Court was referring to what it understood to be the effect of the decision in *Courtie*.

If the Court in *Patel* is right, then where an accused believed he was dealing with heroin when in fact he was dealing with cannabis, he had no defence to a charge of conspiracy to supply cannabis because his mistaken belief went to a "graver offence": indeed this is precisely what Woolf L.J. suggests (at 18 B-C). It is respectfully submitted that this is not what *Courtie* decided when read in conjunction with *Shivpuri* (above): see also *Ellis* (1986) 84 Cr.App.R. 235. Each Class creates a separate offence. It is a startling conclusion (if correct) that a mistake as to the quality of the substance may be sufficient *mens rea* depending on the seriousness of his mistake.

There exists, however, a fundamental challenge to the correctness of *Patel*, based on a natural construction of the word "agree", as it appears in section 1(1) of the Criminal Law Act 1977. Put shortly, if the prosecution alleges by its Particulars of Offence an agreement based on one set of terms then either the defendant entered into that agreement or he did not. As Professor Smith remarked in his commentary to *Siracusa* [1989] Crim.L.R. 712, 713: "It is the defendant's belief as to the nature of the drug, not how it is classified by the law, that is relevant." 10–16

In *Daghir* [1994] Crim. L.R. 945 the appellants were charged with a conspiracy to export electronic goods to Iraq with intent to evade a prohibition on exportation imposed by the Export of Goods (Control) Order 1989. The Crown alleged that the appellants knew that the goods were intended to equip a nuclear weapon. The Court of Appeal held that the prosecution had to prove that the goods were prohibited from exportation and that the defendant knew, for the purposes of the 1989 Order, that the goods were intended for any "military use". However, the convictions were quashed because the case was charged as a conspiracy to evade the prohibition and the Crown's case was put on the narrow basis that the appellants agreed to export the electronic goods for use in a nuclear weapon. The jury should therefore have focused their attention on that narrow issue.

In *Patel*, the Court drew on the law which is undoubtedly relevant in respect of the *mens rea* of a substantive offence but, as O'Connor L.J. pointed out in *Siracusa* (1990) 90 Cr.App.R. 340, 350, the *mens rea* sufficient to support the commission of a substantive offence will not necessarily be sufficient to support an inchoate offence: and see section 19(2) of the 1977 Act. 10–17

The Court of Appeal in *Patel* advanced a number of other propositions, which should be carefully noted: see above.

The cases of *Patel* and *Siracusa* were again considered in *Broad and Others* (April 25, 1997).

> B and others were convicted of conspiracy to produce a Class A drug (count 1) and conspiracy to produce a Class B drug (count 2). The defendants purchased chemicals, and equipment, and set up a laboratory at which traces of amphetamine were found. There were also indications that precursors had been obtained from nutmeg oil for the purpose of producing MMDA, MDA and TMA. The judge directed

the jury that, in relation to count one, the Crown did not have to prove that the drugs produced were in fact Class A drugs, or that the appellants knew that it was a criminal offence to manufacture them. The appellants complained that the judge misdirected the jury. In dismissing the appeals against conviction, the Court held that the prosecution had to prove participation in an agreement to produce an illicit controlled drug of Class A. The controlled drugs contemplated are all in Class A, namely, MMDA, MDA, and TMA. The appellants agreed to unlawfully produce controlled substances. The absence of belief that the drugs were in fact controlled was irrelevant: see *Patel* (August 11 1991), *Siracusa*, 90 Cr.App.R. 340, and *Churchill v. Walton* 2 A.C. 224.

C. CONSPIRACIES FORMED ABROAD

10–18 Historically the jurisdiction to try criminal cases was summarised by the phrase "all crime is local" and by Lord Halsbury L.C. in *MacLeod v. Attorney-General for New South Wales* [1891] A.C. 455, 458 when he said: "The jurisdiction over the crime belongs to the country where the crime is committed." Accordingly, an agreement made in England to commit an unlawful act constitutes the crime of conspiracy only if the act is unlawful by the law of England and Wales. It is not enough that it is unlawful only by the law of the country in which the act is to be committed: *Board of Trade v. Owen* [1957] A.C. 602.

Where the agreement to commit an offence contrary to the law of the United Kingdom is made entirely abroad, one might have thought that such an agreement falls outside the jurisdiction of the courts of England and Wales and indeed this was the view of the Court of Appeal in *Doot* [1973] Q.B. 73. However, two cases of the Court of Appeal, following the decision of the Privy Council in *Somchai Liangsiriprasert v. Government of the United States of America* (1991) 92 Cr.App.R. 77, made it plain that an agreement made abroad to commit a crime in England is triable in the English courts even if nothing was done in England by the conspirators to further that agreement: see *Sansom* [1991] 2 Q.B. 130 and *Murchia* (December 20, 1991, unreported; 89/344/Y3). The principle enunciated in those cases goes further than the *ratio* of the House of Lords in *DPP v. Doot* [1973] A.C. 807, which confined itself to circumstances where acts in furtherance of the conspiracy (whether legal or illegal in themselves) were done in England. No distinction is to be made for these purposes between the position at common law and under the Criminal Law Act 1977: see *Sansom*, para. 10–23, below.

10–19 Although the House of Lords has yet to confirm that the decisions in *Somchai Liangsiriprasert* and *Sansom* are correct, it is submitted that they are sound and consistent with the dicta of a majority in the House of Lords in *Doot*. A brief historical sketch perhaps makes this clear.

In *Doot*, the appellants conspired in Belgium or Morocco to obtain cannabis resin in Morocco and to import it into the United States of America, having shipped it from England. In pursuance of the conspiracy, the appellants drove three specially adapted cars concealing the cannabis into Southampton whereupon the appellants were arrested. In holding that the conspiracy was not triable in England, it was central to the reasoning of the Court of Appeal that the offence of conspiracy was completed when the agreement was made.

In other words, the offence itself was said not to be continuous, having been completed when the agreement was made, although the effect of the agreement would endure until it was performed or terminated. There seemed to be some support for this proposition on one interpretation (not adopted in the House of Lords) of a passage in the judgment of Brett J.A. in *Aspinall* (1876) 2 Q.B.D. 48 when he said that the crime of conspiracy "was completed when they agreed".

In *Doot*, the Court of Appeal held that acts in performance of the agreement were evidence to prove the existence of the conspiracy that, on the facts in *Doot*, was made by the appellants in Morocco and therefore the offence was committed in Morocco. The conviction was quashed. The Court of Appeal took on board the fact that the charge was framed as a conspiracy to contravene section 304(b) of the Customs and Excise Act 1952 (now s. 170(2) of CEMA 1979) although, even on this point, the judgment suggests that there had been argument as to whether the substantive offence under that section was a continuing one, and if it was, whether that fact had any bearing on the ingredients of the charge. 10–20

On appeal, the House of Lords restored the conviction. Their Lordships held that the offence of conspiracy was continuing and, to that extent, the Court of Appeal had been in error. Viscount Dilhorne said that "a conspiracy does not end with the making of the agreement. It will continue so long as there are two or more parties to it intending to carry out the design." He was driven to conclude that:

> "If [conspiracy] is a continuing offence then the courts of England, in my view, have jurisdiction to try the offence if and only if, the evidence suffices to show that the conspiracy whenever or wherever it was formed was in existence when the accused were in England."

It is important to bear this passage in mind when considering the decisions of *Somchai Liangsiriprasert* and *Sansom*. In that particular passage, jurisdiction is not expressed as being dependant upon proof of overt acts in furtherance of the agreement being performed in England and it therefore seems that Viscount Dilhorne considered such an ingredient not to be essential to the question of jurisdiction. Not all of their Lordships were united on this aspect. By contrast, Lord Pearson (with whom Lord Wilberforce concurred) opined that "a conspiracy to commit in England an offence against English law ought to be triable in England if it has been wholly or partly performed in England". Lord Kilbrandon said no more, other than he would answer the certified question in the affirmative (a 10–21 question certified on the basis that the agreement was carried out by importing the drug into England), while Lord Salmon considered that a conspiracy entered into abroad was "certainly" triable in England if acts in furtherance of the conspiracy are done in this country but he left open "what the position might be if the conspirators came to England for an entirely innocent purpose".

The diversity of opinion, as to whether anything had to be done in England in pursuance of the agreement, reflects understandable anxiety as to the extent to which English courts may claim jurisdiction to try persons (who may not be British nationals) in respect of unperformed agreements made entirely abroad. If X and Y conspire in France to smuggle drugs into England, should that conspiracy be triable in England if X and/or Y arrive in England on holiday and not with an intention to do anything in pursuance of that conspiracy? Is the position any different if X or Y abandons performance of their agreement before their arrival or may they be tried because of their agreement at the time it was alive? (See the opinion and example given by Lord Salmon in *Doot* [1973] A.C. 807, 833F.)

10–22 If an agreement to commit a crime had been made in England then an English court would only be concerned with the nature of the agreement. It is not an essential element for a conspiracy made in England that anything overt should be done, beyond the agreement, in pursuance of the conspiracy (see *Aspinall* (1876) 2 Q.B.D. 48, 58–59) and it is no defence for a conspirator to say that he subsequently had second thoughts and withdrew from the criminal enterprise: see *Gortat* [1973] Crim.L.R. 648 and *Anderson* [1986] A.C. 27. Why, then, should different considerations apply merely because the agreement was made abroad? Both the Court of Appeal and the House of Lords in *Doot* attached much significance to the existence of overt acts performed in England and, in the opinions of Lord Wilberforce and Lord Pearson, regarded their existence as being necessary to found jurisdiction. However, why should this be so? The real significance of the existence of overt acts is evidential, namely, to prove (1) that an agreement had been made to commit a crime in England; (2) the terms of that agreement; and (3) that the agreement was alive at the time the acts were done. This accords with opinions expressed by their Lordships in *DPP v. Doot* [1973] A.C. 807. Lord Salmon observed (at 956h):

> "It was unusual until recently to have any direct evidence of conspiracy. Conspiracy was usually proved by what are called overt acts. . . . Today, however, it is possible to have direct evidence such as tape recordings or oral agreements."

It was against this background that *Somchai Liangsiriprasert* [1990] 3 W.L.R. 606 and *Sansom* (1991) 92 Cr.App.R. 115 were decided.

10–23 In *Somchai Liangsiriprasert*, the Privy Council was concerned with a conspiracy to import heroin into the United States of America from Thailand, the proceeds to be collected in Hong Kong. Lord Griffiths stated that in general terms the English criminal law does not concern itself with crimes abroad but added (at 620) that:

> "Their lordships can find nothing in precedent, comity or good sense that should inhibit the common law from regarding as justiciable in England inchoate crimes committed abroad which are intended to result in the commission of criminal offences in England."

In *Sansom*, the appellants agreed abroad to import half a ton of cannabis resin from Morocco into Belgium (according to the appellants) or England (according to the Crown). A vessel, commissioned by one conspirator (acting in England) to carry the drug was arrested in the English Channel. The appellants submitted that if the vessel had been arrested outside British territorial waters then no unlawful act had been performed in England in furtherance of the conspiracy. The Court of Appeal rejected the submission. First, an overt act had been performed in England when commissioning the vessel at a time when the agreement was still subsisting. Secondly, the principle propounded in *Somchai* by Lord Griffiths "should now be regarded as the law of England on this point" and the principle applies equally to common law conspiracies and extra-territorial conspiracies charged under the Criminal Law Act 1977: *per* Taylor L.J. (1991) 92 Cr.App.R. 115 (at 120).

The decisions of *Somchai Liangsiriprasert* and *Sansom* reflect the reality that crime is international and that much has been done between nations to improve mutual assistance and co-operation to combat it: see the Criminal Justice (International Co-operation) Act 1990; the Single Convention on Narcotic Drugs, 1961, Cmnd 2631; the European Convention on Mutual Assistance 1959; the Vienna Convention Against Illicit Traffic in Narcotic Drugs and Psychotropic Substances, 1988, Cmnd 804; and the Extradition Acts 1870 and 1989. 10–24

In *Borro and Abdullah* [1973] Crim.L.R. 513, the appellants agreed abroad to send cannabis from Beirut to Antigua via London. The appellants did no more than to stay overnight in a hotel in London while control over the baggage was retained by the airline. The Court of Appeal dismissed their appeals against their conviction and found no basis upon which *Doot* could be distinguished.

Where goods have been imported and thereafter two or more persons join the conspiracy to deal with the goods, knowing that the goods were prohibited from importation, a conspiracy to fraudulently evade the prohibition contrary to section 170(2) of the CEMA will lie against them because the section 170 offence is also a continuing one. In *Ardalan* [1972] 1 W.L.R. 463 drugs were posted from Beirut to London and, long after the moment of importation, A arranged to collect them. A's appeal against his conviction for a conspiracy to contravene what is now section 170, was dismissed.

The Court in *Ardalan* indicated that terms such as "wheels", "chains", "sub-conspiracies", etc., should be used with care, only to illustrate and to clarify the definition of conspiracy and for no other reason. 10–25

In every case, the facts must not disclose more than one conspiracy (see *Griffiths* (1965) 49 Cr.App.R. 279): if they do the count is bad and may be quashed: and see *Roberts and others* [1998] 1 Cr. App. R. 441. Alternatively, a submission of no case can only be upheld: by then, it may well be too late for the prosecution to amend the indictment.

D. CONSPIRACY TO DO THE PHYSICALLY IMPOSSIBLE

10–26 Section 1(1) of the Criminal Law Act 1977 (as amended) now overrules the decision in *DPP v. Nock* [1978] A.C. 979 in so far as section 1 applies to offences committed after August 1981. If two or more persons agree to pursue a course of conduct but, for reasons unknown to them, the object is incapable of performance, a statutory conspiracy will still be committed. In *Nock*, the defendants attempted to extract cocaine from powder, which was not capable of releasing cocaine, and so the object was incapable of performance. The House of Lords held that no offence had been committed. However, today section 1(1) covers the position. *Nock* was distinguished in *Harris (K.A.)* (1979) 69 Cr.App.R. 122:

> H and other persons attempted to make amphetamine. They had the correct formula but incompetently obtained the wrong ingredients and did not fully understand the process of production. They were convicted of conspiring to produce a controlled drug contrary to section 4(1) of the MDA.
>
> *Held*: the offence was capable of performance but merely ineptly carried out.

E. ATTEMPTING TO COMMIT A DRUG OFFENCE

10–27 It is important to note at the outset, that although the juridical basis of the law of attempt is similar (but not identical) in England, and in Scotland, the law is different. When the Misuse of Drugs Act 1971 was enacted, attempts to commit any offence under that Act was made a criminal offence by section 19 which read:

> "It is an offence for a person [*to attempt to commit an offence under any other provision of this Act*] or to incite [*or attempt to incite*] another to commit such an offence."

When the Criminal Attempts Act 1981 was enacted, a new statutory offence of attempting to commit a criminal offence was created:

> (1) If, with intent to commit an offence to which this section applies, a person does an act which is more than merely preparatory to the commission of the offence, he is guilty of attempting to commit the offence.

(2) A person may be guilty of attempting to commit an offence to which this section applies even though the facts are such that the commission of the offence is impossible.

(3) In any case where

(a) apart from this subsection a person's intention would not be regarded as having amounted to an intent to commit an offence; but

(b) if the facts of the case had been as he believed them to be, his intention would be so regarded,

then, for the purposes of subsection (1) above, he shall be regarded as having had an intent to commit that offence". The 1981 Act repealed that part of section 19 of the MDA, which was concerned with attempts to commit offences contrary to that Act. Section 19 is now only concerned with "inciting" the commission of any offence under the MDA. More radical still is the effect of section 6 of the 1981 Act, which abolished the offence of attempt at common law.

As a result, Parliament amended section 19 of the Misuse of Drugs Act 10–28
1971 by limiting that section to incitement only, and which now reads:

"It is an offence for a person to incite another to commit such an offence."

Unhappily, the amendment was flawed and section 19, read literally, does not make it clear what is meant by "such offence". The Court of Appeal decision in *Marlow* makes it plain that section 19 continues to make the incitement of any offence under the Misuse of Drugs Act an offence. However, both the amendment and the subsequent confusion caused by it, has no direct relevance to the law in Scotland because section 1 of the Criminal Attempts Act 1981 does not apply in Scotland. Section 19 remains intact in that jurisdiction, and section 61 of the Criminal Procedure (Scotland) Act 1887, ensures that an attempt to commit an indictable offence is itself an indictable offence.

However, some of the earlier authorities help to define the limits of the offence under the 1981 Act. Thus, an accused commits an offence contrary to section 1(1) if he does an act that is "more than merely preparatory" to the commission of the offence. The practical significance of these words is similar to the proximity test laid down in *Osborn* (1919) 84 J.P. 63, namely that the actor is effectively "on the job": *per* Rowlatt J. In *DPP v. Stonehouse* [1978] A.C. 55, Lord Diplock provided a neat test to be applied when determining whether or not the facts of a given case amount to an attempt or not, namely that "the offender must have crossed the Rubicon and burnt his boats." This test has since been criticised: see *Gullefer* [1987] Crim.L.R. 195, CA, but see *Widdowson* (1985) 82 Cr.App.R. 314 and commentary at [1986] Crim.L.R. 233.

Turner J. adopted a six-fold classification of attempts in *Donnelly* [1970] 10–29
N.Z.L.R. 980; thus an accused:

(1) may change his mind before committing any act sufficiently overt to amount to an attempt to commit the full offence;
(2) may change his mind, but too late to deny that he had got so far as an attempt;
(3) may be prevented from completing the offence by an outside agency, *e.g.* the arrival of police;
(4) may fail to complete the offence by ineptitude;
(5) may find that commission of the offence is impossible by virtue of some physical fact;
(6) may find that his course of conduct does not amount to an offence.

No offence is committed in case (1). An offence is clearly established in cases (2) and (3); and most probably established in case (4). What about cases (5) and (6)? At first sight, it may be thought that there is, in substance, no difference between (5) and (6). If D handles property in the belief that the goods were stolen, the fact that they were not stolen is as much a fact as any other. However, it is submitted that there is a material difference between (5) and (6). In relation to (6), a person who stabs a pillow or bolster with the *mens rea* to kill or to cause grievous bodily harm, would be guilty of attempted murder, or attempted grievous bodily harm: that is to say, by reason of section 1(1) of the Criminal Attempts Act 1981 (in England) and *Docherty v. Brown*, 1996 S.L.T. 325 (in Scotland). On the other hand, if as in *Taffe* [1983] 2 All E.R. 625, D believed that the money he imported was prohibited from importation, he would not be guilty of an attempt to contravene section 170(2) CEMA 1979 because D made a mistake *of law*: his knowledge of the law is irrelevant.

10–30 Prior to the 1981 Act being enacted, the effect of the decision of the House of Lords in *Haughton v. Smith* [1975] A.C. 476, was that acts falling within (5) are not, at common law, attempts to commit a criminal offence. When the Criminal Attempts Act 1981 was enacted, it was widely thought that statutory attempts reversed the effect of *Haughton v. Smith*. However, in *Anderton v. Ryan* [1985] A.C. 567, the House of Lords held that an accused who purchased a video recorder believing it to be stolen (when in fact it was not) was not guilty of an offence of attempting to handle stolen goods. The decision was overruled in *Shivpuri* [1987] A.C. 1:

> While in India, S was persuaded by D to receive a suitcase containing drugs, which a courier would give to him in Cambridge. S was to deliver the drugs in accordance with D's instructions to third parties. S believed the drugs to be cannabis or heroin but, upon analysis, the substance was found to be either snuff or some such vegetable matter.
>
> *Held*: a person was guilty of an offence under section 1(1) of the 1981 Act if the performed steps (that) were more than merely preparatory. The fact that such an offence was impossible to commit affords S with no defence.

In *Anderton v. Ryan*, the House of Lords had tried to distinguish between "guilty acts" and those acts that were "objectively innocent"; in the latter case the mind was said to be guilty but the act was actually innocent (*per* Lord Bridge).

In *Shivpuri*, however, Lord Bridge reflected on the distinction he drew in *Anderson v. Ryan* saying (at 21B): "If we fell into error, it is clear that our concern was to avoid convictions in situations which most people, as a matter of common sense, would not regard as involving criminality." Later Lord Bridge added (at 21G): 10–31

> "I am satisfied on further consideration that the concept of 'objective innocence' is incapable of sensible application in relation to the law of criminal attempts. The reason for this is that any attempt to commit an offence that involves an 'act, which is more than merely preparatory to the commission of the offence' and which for any reason fails, so that in the event no offence is committed, must ex hypothesi, be 'objectively innocent'. What turns what would otherwise . . . be an innocent act into a crime is the intent of the actor to commit an offence."

Arguably, every case where the offence is impossible to commit involves the taking of steps, which are merely preparatory to the commission of the offence. Accordingly, Lord Bridge considered that the distinction sought to be drawn in *Anderton v. Ryan* could not be maintained and that "there is no valid ground on which *Anderton v. Ryan* can be distinguished":

> "If I could extract from the speech of Lord Roskill or from my own speech a clear and coherent principle distinguishing those cases of attempting the impossible which amount to offences under the statute from those which do not, I should have to consider carefully on which side of the line the instant case fell. But I have to confess that I can find no such principle."

Their Lordships therefore overruled *Anderton v. Ryan* in accordance with the 1966 Practice Statement [1966] 3 All E.R. 77.

In Scotland, *H.M. Advocate v. Anderson* held that a charge of attempted abortion was bad because it was not alleged that the woman in question was pregnant. This case appeared to be authority for the proposition that a person cannot be convicted of attempting to commit the impossible. When the Scottish courts came to consider an "empty pocket" case, Lord Sands in *Lamont v. Strathern* 1933 S.L.T. 110 said: 10–32

> "I am not, I confess, impressed by the metaphysical argument that, whereas one cannot take what is not there, therefore one cannot attempt to take what is not there. I apprehend that, if men were charged with illegally attempting to take salmon with a net from a certain pool, contrary to any Act which declared any such attempt to be illegal, it would be a futile defence that, as they caught nothing, the pool proving to be empty, they did not attempt to take the salmon.

> Nor, I think, would it be reasonable to deny to Mother Hubbard the credit of an attempt to fetch a bone for her dog."

Lord Sands did not hold that *H.M. Advocate v. Anderson* was wrongly decided. Instead, he sought to explain the result in that case by distinguishing between cases where a particular fact is an integral condition or prerequisite of the offence (so that there is no attempt if that condition did not exist) and cases where no such conditions existed. Lord Sands said:

> "A charge of attempt at criminal abortion is a charge of an attempt to make a pregnant woman abort. A charge of attempt to steal is a charge of attempting to steal anything of value that might be found. The completed acts may be on the same footing. One cannot cause abortion if the womb be empty, or steal a valuable if the pocket be empty But the attempts may be on a different footing. As regards abortion, I understand that the view taken was that attempt to commit abortion must be an attempt to cause a pregnant woman to abort. A pregnant woman is a condition of the offence. On the other hand, in the case of attempted theft from a pocket, that is an attempt to steal whatever may be found there. A pocket which may contain something of value is the only condition."

10–33 This is a very slender distinction, which is difficult to understand, and difficult to apply in practice. It is doubtful that Lord Sands had in mind what English lawyers might style a "conditional intent" of a kind considered in *Husseyn* (1977) 67 Cr. App. R. 131, because that case relates to an intention to steal, but only if *what is found* is worth stealing. In *Lamont v. Strathern*, Lord Sands appears to have thought it sufficient that D intends to steal whatever *may* be found there, although in fact the packet or bag is empty. In any event, this is not a distinction that found favour with the Lord Justice Clerk (Ross) who said in *Docherty v. Brown*, 1996 S.L.T. 325:

> "Although *Lamont v. Strathern*, was, in my opinion, correctly decided, I am not persuaded that the approach favoured by Lord Sands towards the end of his opinion is well founded. He described a pocket, which may contain something of value as a condition of the offence which he was considering. In my opinion, that is not the proper approach. It is unnecessary to consider whether, as Lord Anderson thought, an allegation of pregnancy was an essential part of the charge, which he was considering, or, as Lord Sands thought, whether a pocket which might contain something of value, was a condition of the charge, which he had under review, and indeed such an approach is misleading. When considering whether a relevant charge of attempting to commit a crime has been laid, it is not necessary to consider whether or not it was impossible for the complete crime to be committed. All that the court requires to do is to consider whether the accused has the necessary *mens rea*, and has taken matters further by doing some positive act towards execution of his purpose."

It will be seen that the Lord Justice Clerk added: 10–34

> "In my opinion if it is impossible to commit the complete crime, it does not follow that an accused can carry out no acts which are perpetration or are acts proximate to the crime which is being attempted."

The position, in Scotland, is therefore very similar to the position in England pursuant to the Criminal Attempts Act 1981.

Is an accused's belief therefore wholly irrelevant? The answer in both jurisdictions is "no". As the Lord Justice Clerk in *Docherty*, made clear:

> "... where the accused knows of the impossibility of doing what he is attempting to do there can be no attempt. In a charge such as the present charge, the charge would be irrelevant unless it were libelled that the accused believed that the tablets of which he had taken possession contained controlled drugs. If he did not believe that, the charge of attempting to commit the crime could not, in the circumstances succeed."

This was also the conclusion of Lord Cameron of Lochbroom (at 340).

Both English law and Scots law now seem closer to the law as described 10–35
some 200 years ago by Lord Mansfield in *Scofield* (1784) Cald Mags Cas 397, when he said:

> "... the English approach appears to have been very similar to that described by Baron Hume for Scotland. In *R. v. Scofield*, Lord Mansfield said: 'So long as an act rests in bare intention it is not punished by our laws, but immediately when an act is done, the law judges, not only of the act done, but of the intent with which it is done, and if it is coupled with an unlawful and malicious intent, though the act itself would otherwise have been innocent, the intent being criminal, the act becomes criminal and punishable.'"

The current position is also broadly in line with Australian law. In *Britten v. Alpogut* [1987] VR 929, the appellant's mistaken belief that he had imported cannabis, when in fact he had imported an innocuous substance, afforded him no defence to a charge of attempting to contravene a prohibition on importation of cannabis. Murphy J. reviewed in detail the English authorities from *Scofield* to *Shivpuri*, and said:

> "... at common law a criminal attempt is committed if it is proven that the accused had at all material times the guilty intent to commit a recognised crime and it is proven that at the same time he did an act or acts (which in appropriate circumstances would include omissions which are seen to be sufficiently proximate to the commission of the said crime and are not seen to be merely preparatory to it. The 'objective innocence' or otherwise of those acts is irrelevant. Impossibility is also irrelevant, unless it be that the so-called crime intended is not a crime known to the law, in which case a criminal attempt to commit it cannot be made."

F. INCITEMENT TO COMMIT A MISUSE OF DRUGS ACT OFFENCE

10–36 Section 19 of the Misuse of Drugs Act (as amended) reads:

> "It is an offence for a person to incite another to commit such an offence."

However, as drafted, the original wording of the 1971 Act read very differently:

> "It is an offence for a person [*to attempt to commit an offence under any other provision of this Act*] or to incite [*or attempt to incite*] another to commit such an offence."

The words italicised, and within square parentheses, reflect the amendments made pursuant to Schedule I of the Criminal Attempts Act 1981. That Schedule provided for deletion of the words "to attempt to commit an offence under any other provision of the Act. . . ." It left in the words "or to incite" and then further deleted the words "or attempt to incite".

In *Marlow* [1997] Crim.L.R. 897 (judgment July 14, 1997):

> The appellant wrote and published a book relating to the cultivation of cannabis, which he advertised for sale and sold about 500 copies. The prosecution contended that the book amounted to an incitement of those who bought it to cultivate cannabis—an offence under section 4(2) (production) and section 6 of the Misuse of Drugs Act 1971. It was argued that the book was not a bona fide textbook. The defence contended that the book was a genuine contribution to the debate about legalisation of cannabis and it only contained general advice and information, which was freely available elsewhere. It was argued that the book was too remote from the actions of those reading it to constitute incitement. When interviewed, the appellant told the police that he had no intention of inciting people to do anything. He realised that incitement was illegal and supply was illegal. The book also contained a proposal to change the law. The judge directed the jury that they had to be sure that it was a book which *may* "encourage or persuade or . . . is capable of encouraging and persuading other people to produce the drug. M submitted that this was a misdirection as to the *actus reus* of the offence of incitement.
>
> *Held*: the judge should not have introduced the word "may". However, taken as a whole there was no misdirection, and the conviction was not unsafe (the court considered *Invicta Plastics Ltd v. Clare* R.T.R. 251; *R. v. Higgins* (1801) 2 East 5; *R. v. Nkosiyana* 1966 (4) S.A. 655, 688 (SA); and see the *Law Commission's Working Paper on Incitement* (1993)).

10–37 The Court of Appeal remarked that at common law the crime of incitement consists of inciting another to commit a *crime*: see *R. v. Higgins*

(1801) 2 East 5. The Court then referred to *Smith and Hogan's Criminal Law*, 8th edition, and quoted from the South African case of *Nkosiyana* 1966 (4) SA 655 at 688, as to the nature of an inciter, namely:

> "... one who reaches and seeks to influence the mind of another to the commission of a crime. The machinations of criminal ingenuity being legion, the approach to the other's mind may take various forms, such as suggestion, proposal, request, exhortation, gesture, argument, persuasion, inducement, goading or the arousal of cupidity."

The court said that—

> "... it is of interest that, whilst running a gamut of words appropriate to the concept of incitement, the passage omits the use of the word "encourages", which represents as well as any modern word can, the concept involved. As stated in *Blackstone's Criminal Practice* (1996) at paragraph A6.2 in relation to the *actus reus* of incitement:
>
> > 'A person incites another to commit an offence if he encourages that other to do what would be an offence if carried out by the person incited."'

In the 9th edition of his work, Professor Sir John Smith, replied: 10–38

> "In *Marlow* the court observed that this 'gamut of words' omits 'encourage' which, it thought, 'represents as well as any modern word can the concept involved'; but then added the proviso that it must be clear that the encouragement involved a positive step 'aimed at inciting another to commit a crime'. So, it is not every encouragement, which necessarily amounts to incitement. Perhaps the best word is 'incite' itself.
>
> A person may, however, incite another by threats or pressure as well as by persuasion [*Race Relations Board v. Applin* [1973] Q.B. 815, *per* Lord Denning M.R., at 827]. Incitement may be implied as well as express. To advertise an article for sale, representing its virtue to be that it may be used to do an act which is an offence, is an incitement to commit that offence [*Invicta Plastics*] even when accompanied by a warning that the act is an offence. But the mere intention to manufacture and sell wholesale a device which has no function other than one involving the commission of an offence is not an intention to incite the commission of that offence [*James and Ashford* (1985) 82 C.A.R. 226 at 232]."

There does not appear to be a real difference of opinion between the Court of Appeal in *Marlow* and Professor Sir John Smith as to the definition and scope of the offence of incitement. The Court in *Marlow* added: 10–39

> "Provided it is clear that the encouragement referred to involves words or actions amounting to a positive step or steps aimed at inciting another to commit a crime, that seems to be a satisfactory statement of the position. It makes clear that it is not necessary to a charge of

incitement to prove that the crime incited was actually carried out. At the same time, it makes clear that, whatever the intention of the inciter, if what is incited would, if done, not be a crime, then the offence of incitement has not been committed. The word 'encouraged' has a wide meaning, and it is legitimate, as well as desirable, for a judge directing a jury to use appropriate words of similar connotation to fit the facts and assist the jury in the circumstances of the case. That is because the concept of incitement can for instance include threats or pressure: see *Race Relation Board v. Applin* Q.B. 815 at 827, and judges frequently and properly refer to incitement as involving a suggestion, proposal, persuasion or inducement to commit an offence: see *Invicta Plastics Ltd v. Clare* R.T.R. 251, a decision of the Divisional Court. In that case, the Court upheld the finding of justices that a company which advertised a device which could detect police radar traps was properly convicted of inciting the readers of the advertisement to use unlicensed apparatus for wireless telegraphy, contrary to section 1(1) of the Wireless Telegraphy Act 1949. That was a case where the advertisement included a specific observation that:

> 'It is illegal to employ the Radatec specifically for the reception of, for instance, police radar transmissions.'

The Court held that:

> 'Looking at the pamphlet as a whole . . . it is plain that, from the words used, readers were being persuaded and incited to use the Radatec device.' That case illustrates the point that if justices or a jury before whom a charge of incitement is preferred are satisfied that, (a) taken as a whole, the words on which the charge is based amount to encouragement or persuasion of a person to whom they are directed to commit a crime, and (b) the author of the words in fact intended to encourage the commission of that crime, then the offence of incitement is established".

10–40 The appellant's submission in *Marlow* was that the section should now be construed as referring back, by the words "such offence", to section 18 only, in relation to which no evidence was called. The submission was a brave one but it stood no prospect of success. It is plain that there was a drafting error following the enactment of the Criminal Attempts Act 1981. It is significant that, in Scotland, section 19 applies in its original form because the Criminal Attempts Act 1981 does not apply there. It would be absurd if in Scotland section 19 (attempts and incitement) applies to *all* offences under the Misuse of Drugs Act, whilst in England, incitement (under s.19) would only apply to offences charged under section 18 of that Act. The Court rejected the appellant's argument:

> "This seems to us a point devoid of any legal merit whatever. It seems clear, as we have already indicated, that the obscurity of the phraseology arises through a draftsman's error.

However, there was plainly no intention to alter the terms or the extent of criminality provided for in the 1971 Act, save in relation to attempts. Thus, unless the alteration effective to the wording of section 19 compels us to hold otherwise, the presumed meaning must be that the word 'such' refers not only to section 18, which immediately precedes section 19, but to offences elsewhere in the Act. It seems to us that this view is supported by reference to a number of other provisions and sources."

Chapter 11
Evidence

A. PROOF THAT THE DRUG IS CONTROLLED AND PROHIBITED

All drugs controlled by the MDA are listed in Schedule 2 of the Act and fall into one of three Classes (*i.e.* Classes A to C in Parts I to III respectively of Schedule 2). Classification depends on the potential of the drugs for causing "harm" but the practical significance of the Schedules is that the Classes determine the maximum penalties that offences under the MDA attract. The list is not closed. The Secretary of State may, by an Order in Council, add other drugs to the list, re-classify existing controlled drugs or he may remove some or all of them from Schedule 2 completely. 11–01

Since the MDA was passed, Schedule 2 has been extensively modified by 13 "Modification Orders", the latest being S.I. 1998 No. 750, (see also S.I. 1973 No. 771, S.I. 1975 No. 421, S.I. 1977 No. 1243, S.I. 1979 No. 299, S.I. 1983 No. 765, S.I. 1984 No. 859, S.I. 1985 No. 1995, S.I. 1986 No. 2230, S.I. 1989 No. 1340, S.I. 1990 No. 2589, S.I. 1995 No. 1966 and S.I. 1996 No. 1300.)

It is important to note that the Act also controls (where appropriate) any stereoisomeric form of a controlled drug, any of their esters, ethers or salts or certain "preparations" which contain a controlled substance or product.

I. Determining Whether a Given Substance or Product is a Controlled Drug

In the ordinary way determining whether a substance or product is controlled or not, is a straightforward matter: one simply looks to see if the substance is listed in Schedule 2. However, the matter is only made straightforward because Parliament has been careful to ensure that the term "a controlled drug" is narrowly defined so that (except where expressly provided) it is the chemical, which is the controlled "substance" or "product" and nothing else. 11–02

Accordingly, a drug that naturally subsists in a plant or material and which has not been extracted is not a controlled drug unless that plant or substance has itself been expressly controlled by the Act. Thus, in *Goodchild (No. 2)* [1977] 1 W.L.R. 1213:

> G was charged with being in possession of cannabis resin after the police found four ounces of stalks and leaves of cannabis plants at G's address. At that time the stalks and leaves were not expressly controlled by the Act, just the flowering and fruiting tops of the plant. However, the scientific evidence was that the stalks and leaves would naturally contain cannabis resin. Hence the charge. However, section 37(1) defines "cannabis resin" as "separated resin obtained from [a cannabis plant]". This implied some form of extraction, which, on the facts, had not occurred. Accordingly, G's conviction had to be quashed.

11–03 The definition of cannabis has now been extended to include all of the plant except the mature stalk, fibre and the seeds.

Similarly, cocaine is extracted from the coca-leaf but without further provision, the coca-leaf itself would not be a controlled drug. Accordingly, Parliament specifically included the leaf as a Class A substance. "Poppy-straw" (Class A) is yet another example.

Note that the so-called "magic mushroom" (*e.g.* Liberty cap or psilocybe mexicana) is not controlled even though it contains psilocin, which is a controlled drug (Class A). Accordingly, it is therefore not unlawful to pick the mushroom, to possess it, or to supply it.

(a) Esters, salts and ethers are also controlled

11–04 As we have noted, any esters, ethers, salts or any stereoisomeric forms of drugs specified in Classes A, B and C are "controlled" substances. These are terms of science. Thus, a salt of diamorphine is still heroin (*cf. Greensmith* [1983] 1 W.L.R. 1124; and see *Russell* (1992) 94 Cr.App.R. 351).

(b) Meaning of "preparation"

11–05 "Preparation" is broadly defined by the Shorter Oxford English Dictionary to mean, *inter alia*, the "composition, manufacture of a chemical, medicinal, or other substance".

The appearance of the word "manufacture" in this definition is of particular interest since it is undoubtedly the case that "preparing" a drug may amount to an act of "production" for the purposes of section 4 of the MDA. However, much will depend on the facts of a given case. It would be unsafe to assume that every act of production amounts to an act of preparation or indeed, conversely, that every act of preparation amounts to an act of production. It is submitted that the MDA contemplates a subtle distinction, namely, that an act of "preparation" is calculated to convert a controlled drug into a form suitable for consumption, whereas "producing" a controlled drug is generally confined to the act of creating the drug. It must be remembered that many drugs are synthetically created in a laboratory, *e.g.* LSD. Steps taken to create such drugs are obviously steps taken to "produce" them. However, applying drops of LSD to sugar cubes for human consumption is an act of "preparation", not an act of production.

The distinction has practical significance in cases involving the so-called 11–06
"magic mushroom". The potency of psilocin (the drug that subsists in that particular mushroom) is considerably increased if the mushroom is dried. In *Stevens* [1981] Crim.L.R. 568, CA it was held that the term "preparation" had to be given its natural and ordinary meaning. It is not a term of art. So, where S dried magic mushrooms at a low heat, thereby converting them into a powder, he had accordingly made a "preparation" containing a controlled drug (psilocin). The mushrooms ceased to be in their natural growing state and were now "altered by the hand of man". The intervention of the "hand of man" is the crucial test.

Stevens was applied in *Cuncliffe* [1986] Crim.L.R. 547. In that case, C, by the jury's verdict, had subjected a quantity of magic mushrooms to sunlight so that they dried out. He had therefore "prepared" them and he was held to be rightly convicted of possessing a controlled drug.

There is clearly a mental element in the act of preparation, namely, an 11–07
intention to alter the condition of the thing coupled with an intention that the substance should serve as a drug in the future. Accordingly, no offence is committed if the mushrooms in D's possession had dried out of their own accord. The prosecution must show that someone deliberately brought about the change.

> In *Walker* [1987] Crim.L.R. 565, CA police found 1,000 to 2,000 dried magic mushrooms in a cupboard at W's premises. W said that they must have dried out of their own accord. Two-thirds of them had been seized by police in 1982 and then returned. The remainder he had since picked. The jury asked why the mushrooms were returned to W and were they then unlawful for him to possess. The judge directed the jury that they were unlawful to possess in 1982. During the appeal, the prosecution argued that picking the mushrooms amounted to an act of "preparation".
> *Held*: that the Court was not inclined to accept that merely picking the mushroom amounted to preparation. However, the jury's question, although difficult to understand, was answered incorrectly since it had to be proved that someone deliberately brought about a change in the condition of the mushrooms.

The Court was right not to hold that merely to pick the mushroom was an act of preparation because it does not follow that the mushroom will dehydrate as a result. It could not have been the intention of the legislature to include, for example, persons who innocently pick the mushrooms which then dry out of their own accord. Obviously, if the mushrooms are picked and are then deliberately kept in a dry environment so that they dry out, then a process is being adopted to alter the condition "by the hand of man". But deliberate conduct implies the existence of a mental ingredient.

However, the courts have not been asked to examine the nature or the limits of that mental ingredient.

11–08 Suppose, now, that a person picks a "magic mushroom" which is then deliberately allowed to dry out so that it may be preserved for botanical study. Is such a person now guilty of being in unlawful possession of psilocin? Such a harsh result could be avoided if "preparation" is construed to include a gloss to the mental element, namely, that the accused intended to put the thing into a form suitable for administration or consumption. It is submitted that such a construction is consistent with the ordinary natural meaning of the word "preparation" in the context of drug use and abuse; see *Hodder v. DPP* [1990] Crim.L.R. 261 and *Murray v. MacNaughton*, 1984 S.C.C.R. 361 (discussed above at para. 6–16 in relation to the production of controlled drugs and the reader is invited to refer to that section).

If a substance or product is not expressed in Schedule 2 of the MDA to be a controlled drug, and if the prosecution fails to prove that it amounts to a "preparation", then that substance or product cannot be regarded as a controlled drug. This may seem obvious but consider the case of a person who innocently picks magic mushrooms, which dry out naturally. He will not be guilty of unlawful possession if he subsequently learns that the powder is a narcotic and uses it as such. Moreover, if he then shares the substance with others, he cannot be guilty of unlawfully supplying it.

(c) Meaning of "product"

11–09 In *Hodder v. DPP* [1990] Crim.L.R. 261, it was held that the picking, packaging and freezing of several bags of magic mushrooms was a process which brought the mushrooms within the definition of a "product" for the purposes of the Act. This case, and its facts, are considered in relation to the production of controlled drugs (see Chapter 6).

In *Russell* (December 11, 1991, unreported) the Court of Appeal held that the conversion of cocaine hydrochloride (the salt) into cocaine base, was an act of production and so is the stripping of the leaves and flowering and fruiting tops of a cannabis plant from the stalk: see *Harris and Cox* [1995] T.L.R. 455 see paras 6–16 to 6–19, above.

(d) Definition of cannabis

11–10 Section 37(1) of the MDA as amended by section 52 of the Criminal Law Act 1977, defines cannabis as:

> "... any plant of the genus Cannabis or any part of such a plant (by whatever name designated) except that it does not include cannabis resin or any of the following products after separation from the rest of the plant, namely

(a) mature stalk of any such plant,
(b) fibre produced from mature stalk of any such plant, and
(c) seed of any such plant."

Cannabis resin means:

> "... the separated resin, whether crude or purified, obtained from any plant of the genus Cannabis".

Both cannabis (herbal) and cannabis resin are Class B drugs. However, cannabinol and cannabinol derivatives are Class A drugs since they are far more potent. Cannabinol is not further defined but cannabinol derivatives are defined in Part IV of Schedule 2 to mean:

> "... .the following substances, except where contained in cannabis or cannabis resin, namely tetrahydro derivatives of cannabinol and 3-alkyl homologues of cannabinol or of its tetrahydro derivatives."

Although all of the above are types of cannabis, it would not be right to regard them as generic for the purpose of drafting charges of indictments. Each drug is separately controlled and should be separately particularised in any charge: see *Muir v. Smith* [1978] Crim.L.R. 293; *cf. Best* (1979) 70 Cr.App.R. 21 and see *Mitchell* (June 3, 1992, unreported) and para. 3–38, above. 11–11

Since the seeds of the cannabis plant are not controlled, it follows that these may be lawfully possessed. But it is an offence to sow them and to cultivate the plant: see section 6 of the MDA 1971.

Although "cannabis resin" means resin that is separated from the plant, it does not mean that the prosecution has to show that the resin was separated to the extent that all the cannabis had been removed from the oil-bearing glandular trichomes, since resin includes "crude resin": see *Thomas* [1981] Crim.L.R. 496.

(i) *Cannabis oil*

It is not always a straightforward matter to determine whether "cannabis oil" (loosely so-called) is a Class A or a Class B drug. It is appropriate to examine this issue in stages. First, cannabis is a plant and therefore what is sometimes referred to as "liquid cannabis" is imprecise because that expression does not appear, in terms, in Schedule 2 to the MDA. Secondly, separated resin whether crude or purified is "cannabis resin": a Class B drug. Note that "cannabis" and "cannabis resin" are separate substances and each is controlled under the Act (Class B and see *Arnott v. MacFarlane* 1976 S.L.T. 39). Thirdly, when a solvent is applied to either cannabis or cannabis resin the product is a dark-coloured viscous liquid sometimes known as "liquid cannabis" or "hash oil. These labels can be misleading and a trap for the unwary because they beg the question whether the drug is Class A or B. Liquid cannabis, obtained by using a solvent, will contain a number of chemicals termed "cannabinoids" including tetrahydrocannabinol (*i.e.* THC, a derivative of cannabinol) and possibly 11–12 "cannabidiol". Fourthly, "cannabidiol" is found in liquid produced by solvent extraction of cannabis resin. Fifthly, "cannabidiol" is not found in liquid produced by solvent extraction of herbal cannabis and therefore cannot be regarded as purified cannabis resin. Accordingly, the liquid is not cannabis (because it is not a plant) and it is not resin. However, the liquid will also contain THC (a derivative of cannabinol). A cannabinol derivative is a Class A drug unless it is contained in cannabis (*i.e.* the plant) or cannabis resin (Pt IV, Sched. 2). Because this particular form of liquid is neither cannabis nor resin some experts conclude that the liquid is a "preparation" (containing a cannabinol derivative) and therefore a Class A drug.

The key to all of this is to focus on the presence (or otherwise) of cannabidiol. If it is present in the liquid then it should be treated as a purified form of cannabis resin (Class B). If it is not present in the liquid then the liquid was not obtained by solvent extraction of resin and the Court is likely to conclude that it is a Class A drug. This was the approach adopted by His Honour Judge May in *Carter* (December 16, 1992, Oxford Crown Court). The learned judge heard expert evidence called by the prosecution and the defence.

11–13 Obviously, the method by which the relevant chemicals are detected is of great importance. One of the issues, canvassed in *Carter*, is to what extent a lack of evidence for the presence of a chemical in a substance is sufficient to establish that it did not in fact exist. Much depends on the type of analysis carried out and the sensitivity of the equipment used to perform the tests, *e.g.* "thin layer" or "gas" chromatography. The result in *Carter* was also achieved by a process of elimination: if the liquid was not cannabis (as defined by s. 37(1)) and it was not cannabis resin, whether crude or purified, then it is a liquid which has been prepared and which contains a Class A drug and thus, because a "preparation" is controlled by Schedule 2 to the 1971 Act, the substance is to be regarded as a Class A drug. It is difficult to fault the reasoning but the difficulty is that one could also argue that Class B drugs similarly embrace "preparations" that contain herbal cannabis and therefore solvent extraction of herbal cannabis is a preparation falling within Class B! It is to be regretted that confusion over the classification of cannabis oil should exist. Sometimes a defendant will enter a plea of guilty on the strength of the finding of an expert that the drug is Class A and the judge is then asked to sentence on the basis that the defendant mistakenly believed he was dealing with a Class B substance. If there is an issue as to whether cannabis oil is Class A or B then that issue should be determined before a plea of guilty is entered and not left until a *Newton* hearing. This is because Class A, B and C drugs attract separate penalties and create separate offences (see *Courtie* [1984] 78 Cr. App. R. 292). Such a course may be considered to be largely academic at least from the defendant's point of view because, even if the judge concludes that the substance is Class A (whereas the defendant believed it to be Class B), the defendant's mistaken belief affords him no defence: see section 28 of the MDA 1971.

This is a difficult area and one where expert opinion is not agreed. It is important that each case be carefully considered because the Court of Appeal will not lightly interfere with a conviction based on forensic evidence which is unchallenged: see *Etrue* (August 21, 1998, CA).

(e) Meaning of "cocaine"

In *Greensmith* [1983] 1 W.L.R. 1124, 11–14

> G was convicted of possession of 9.04 grams of powder containing 40 per cent cocaine with intent to supply it. The prosecution called no evidence as to whether the drug was in fact cocaine, or a stereoisomeric form or a salt of cocaine. The expert said whatever it was "it was still cocaine".
>
> *Held*: G's appeal would be dismissed. "Cocaine" was generic in paragraph 1 of Part I of Schedule 2 and included a natural substance, *e.g.* coca-leaf or a substance resulting from a chemical transformation. Both are cocaine. There was no need for the prosecution to prove the exact form.

The Court attached importance to the words "any substance or product". The word "substance" has a wider meaning than "product". Lawton L.J. noted that "any kind of matter comes within 'substance,' whereas 'product' envisages the result of some kind of process".

Two Crown Court cases, *Leaman* (May 17, 1978; unreported; Maidstone Crown Court) and *Steeper* (September 27, 1979; unreported: Inner London Sessions), were referred to in the judgment of the Court of Appeal. Both cases held that the prosecution was bound to specify in the indictment whether the drug was of a form expressed in paragraph 1 of Schedule 2, Part I or whether it was an "ester, ether, salt etc". The Court of Appeal in *Greensmith* advised that both decisions should not be followed. This must be correct upon a literal reading of the MDA. Paragraph 1 of Part I indicates those substances and products which are controlled. It does not matter for present purposes that neither the word "substance" nor "product" is defined. What does matter, as a matter of science, is that a given substance or product referred to in Schedule 2 may have related to it certain stereoisomeric forms, esters, ethers, or salts. In other words, they are generic. Accordingly, the prosecution is not obliged to particularise which form the drug takes. It is still the same substance or product. See also *Watts* [1984] 1 W.L.R. 757. 11–15

In *Russell*, the Court of Appeal held that the conversion of cocaine hydrochloride to base cocaine was an act of production: see para. 6–18, above.

(f) Opiate-related definitions

"Raw opium" includes: 11–16

> "... powdered or granulated opium but does not include medicinal opium": see Part IV of Schedule 2."

"Medicinal opium " is defined in Part IV of Schedule 2 to mean:

> "... raw opium which has undergone the process necessary to adapt it for medicinal use in accordance with the requirements of the British Pharmacopoeia, whether it is in the form of powder or is granulated or is in any other form, and whether it is or is not mixed with neutral substances. . . . "

"Prepared opium", by section 37(1) of the MDA, means:

> "... opium prepared for smoking and includes dross and other residues remaining after opium has been smoked"

"Opium poppy" means "... the plant Papaver somniferum L"
"Poppy straw" means, by Part IV: "... all parts, except the seeds of the opium poppy, after mowing "
Concentrate of poppy straw" means, by Part IV:

> "... the material produced when poppy-straw has entered into a process for the concentration of its alkaloids"

(g) Amphetamine

11–17 In *Heywood v. Macrae*, 1987 S.C.C.R. 627 it was held that the sheriff erred in concluding that the prosecution must specify whether the substance in the possession of the accused was "amphetamine" or one of its salts: and see *Watts* [1984] 2 All E.R. 380.

(h) Ecstasy

11–18 The chemical term for "Ecstasy" is "3, 4 Methylene-dioxy-N- methyl-amphetamine:" (MDMA). References to "3, 4" and "N" are frequently omitted and therefore a charge or a count on an indictment, that describes the drug as "methylenedioxymethyl amphetamine" would not be defective on that ground.

However, one will also come across two other substances which are also popularly termed "Ecstasy" namely, "3,4 Methyene-Dioxy-Ethyl-Amphetamine" (MDEA) and "3, 4 Methylene-Dioxy-Amphetamine" (MDA). Note that capital letters and hyphens have been employed merely to indicate the main components of each substance.

11–19 Ecstasy has been controlled since 1977: see the MDA 1971 (Modification) Order 1977, S.I. 1977 No. 1243, which inserted sub-paragraph (c) to the list of Class A drugs in Part 1; paragraph 1 of Schedule 2 to the 1971 Act:

> "... any compound (not being methoxyphenamine or a compound for the time being specified in sub-paragraph (a) above) structurally derived from phenethylamine, an N-alkylphenethylamine, a-methylphenethylamine, an N-alkyl-a-methylphenethylamine, a-ethylphenethylamine, or an N-alkyl-a-ethylphenethylamine by substitution in the

ring to any extent with alkyl, alkoxy, alkylenedioxy or halide substituents, whether or not further substituted in the ring by one or more other univalent substituents". [emphasis added]

The words to note, in the aforementioned paragraph, are "structurally derived . . . by substitution in the ring. . . ." In *Couzens and Frankel* [1992] Crim. L.R. 822, powder was found in C's flat which contained MDMA and both C and F were charged with offences including producing that substance. The defence was that the powder did not come within sub-paragraph 1(c) of Part I to Schedule 2 to the 1971 Act because the method adopted by C to produce it did not involve a human process to achieve a "substitution into the ring . . . with alkylenedioxy" because the starting material (said to have been used by C) was isosafrole, a natural substance and alkylenedioxy was already present in isosafrole. C contended the phrase "the substitution in the ring" imported a positive human act into the process and that sub-paragraph (c) stipulates that MDMA, for example, should be produced in a particular way, *i.e.* "structurally derived" by "substitution in the ring" of the chemicals set out in the sub-paragraph.

The Court of Appeal rejected this argument. Sub-paragraph (c) had to 11–20 be given its ordinary and natural meaning as understood by a chemist. In this case the judge was entitled to accept the evidence of a chemist, that the whole family of hallucinatory substances (of which MDMA was one) was a Class A drug. The Court concluded that where there are two possible constructions, one of which gave a sensible result and one of which produced an absurdity, the Court was entitled, even obliged, to adopt the construction that would avoid the absurd result.

It should also be noted that there is nothing wrong with random sampling to determine purity of the drug in question. It is unnecessary to examine all the drugs. Random sampling will often be a cost-effective method of analysis. However, it is obviously important that such sampling should be sufficiently reliable to support the analyst's conclusions in his / her report, and to enable proper inferences to be drawn from that method of analysis: and see *Carnegie v. Findlay*, 2000 S.C.C.R. 873.

II. Using an Admission to Prove the Substance is a Drug

Usually, it is the result of scientific analysis, which will prove or disprove 11–21 that the substance is a controlled drug of a particular description. But, occasionally, an accused may also be in a position to express an expert opinion as to the nature of the substance he possesses. In *Bird v. Adams* [1972] Crim.L.R. 179, DC the defendant was found in possession of 15 tablets. He maintained that they contained LSD, and that he had been selling them. The prosecution called no scientific evidence. The Divisional Court held that (1) where an accused was not an expert then an "admission" was in reality no admission at all; and (2) an admission may be valueless where an accused could not have the necessary knowledge; but (3), on the facts, the defendant had sufficient knowledge, having peddled the drug, to make his admission a prima facie case against him.

Each case must of course be decided on its own facts, but a mere belief that a substance is a controlled drug is certainly not sufficient: *Mieras v. Rees* [1975] Crim.L.R. 224, CA.

By contrast, in *Wells* [1976] Crim.L.R. 518, CA, W admitted taking cannabis and amphetamine sulphate. She pleaded guilty to possessing those drugs. The Court of Appeal held that her pleas were good since "in the last analysis all evidence as to the nature of the substance was an expression of opinion, though scientists might be able to express more reliable opinions than others". The court distinguished *Mieras v. Rees* on the basis that there was a plea of not guilty in which the circumstances required proof of the nature of the substances.

11–22 To describe the results of chemical analysis as an expression of "opinion" is an understatement to say the least. However, most users will have their own method of ascertaining the nature of the substance they have acquired in order to avoid being deceived into receiving a substance of a very different description. Consuming the drug and noting its effects is one method. Once *Wells* had consumed the substance and thereafter pleaded guilty to possessing drugs of a type specified by the prosecution, the Court was entitled to act on the basis that she knew perfectly well what the drugs were. Her pleas were the best evidence: *cf. Porter* [1976] Crim.L.R. 58.

Again, a person who admits injecting himself with heroin but later retracts that admission by asserting that he in fact used flour has at least a case to answer: see *Chatwood* [1980] 1 All E.R. 467. The original admission is a declaration against interest in circumstances in which, as a user of the drug, he is likely to know the effects of heroin consumption. However, his subsequent assertion is self-serving; it does not neutralise the admission, still less does it prove innocence: see *Storey* (1968) 52 Cr.App.R. 334.

III. Analyst's Reports and the Decision in *Hunt*

(a) Proof that the drug is in prohibited form

11–23 It is for the Crown to prove that the substance in question is the controlled drug alleged but, in certain cases, it is also incumbent on the prosecution to prove that the drug had been in prohibited form at the material time. Thus, where (by virtue of the MDA and the Regulations) it is an offence to have a controlled substance in one form but it is not an offence to have that substance in another form, then it is for the prosecution to prove that the substance is in the prohibited form for otherwise no offence is established: *Hunt* [1987] A.C. 352, and see *Jones (Keith), The Times*, April 24, 1997 and *Squires v. CPS* (July 19, 1999).

(i) *Hunt: the facts*

One hundred and fifty-four milligrams of white powder was found in a packet at the appellant's home. H told the police that the powder was amphetamine sulphate. The analyst's statement, which was read to the jury, stated that, "This powder was found to contain morphine mixed with caffeine and atropine. Morphine is a controlled drug within the Misuse of Drugs Act 1971, Part I of Schedule 2 (Class A drugs). Caffeine and atropine are not controlled under the Misuse of Drugs Act 1971." 11–24

Counsel for the appellant unsuccessfully submitted that there was no case to answer, whereupon the appellant pleaded guilty.

By regulation 4 of and Schedule 1 to the Misuse of Drugs Regulations 1973 (S.I. 1973 No. 797) (now reg. 4(1) and (2) and Schedule 5 of the Misuse of Drugs Regulations 1985) the Secretary of State directed, pursuant to section 7 of the Misuse of Drugs Act 1971, that section 5(1) (dealing with possession) "shall not have effect in relation to" any preparation of morphine containing "not more than 0.2 per cent of morphine calculated as anhydrous morphine base being a preparation compounded with one or more other active or inert ingredients in such a way that the morphine cannot be recovered by readily applicable means". The Court of Appeal dismissed the appeal on the basis that although the regulation and the Schedule created an exception, the burden of proving the exception rested on the accused and, in this instance, the appellant had pleaded guilty. 11–25

On appeal to the House of Lords, their Lordships, in allowing the appeal held that (what is now reg. 4(1) and (2) and Schedule 5 of the M.D. Regulations 1985) "deals not with exceptions to what would otherwise be unlawful but with the definition of the essential ingredients of an offence" (*per* Lord Griffiths at 1130B) and that the burden was on the prosecution to prove that the morphine in the possession of the appellant had been in the prohibited form. The prosecution only tendered facts, which might or might not amount to an offence (under s. 5(2)) (*per* Lord Templeman at 1118G).

(ii) *An explanation of* Hunt

It is important to bear in mind that in *Hunt* the relevant regulation and Schedule were made pursuant to section 7(1)(a) of the Misuse of Drugs Act 1971. Whereas section 7(1)(a) empowers the Secretary of State to "except" a controlled drug from any of the prohibitions set out in the section, by contrast, section 7(1)(b) merely enables the Secretary of State to make lawful various activities which would "otherwise be unlawful" under sections 4, 5 and 6. In other words, regulations made under section 7(1)(a) go directly to the elements of the offence which must be proved, whereas regulations made under section 7(1)(b) give an immunity or provide a defence in cases where the offence is otherwise made out. 11–26

In *Hunt*, the effect of the analyst's ambiguous report meant that the accused may or may not have come within the exception. The question then arose as to whether the burden was on the prosecution to negate the possibility that he did, or whether it rested on the accused to prove that he came within the exception on a balance of probabilities. Both the Court of Appeal and the House of Lords accepted the fundamental rule that the prosecution must prove every element of the offence charged. But, in *Edwards* [1975] Q.B. 27 the Court of Appeal stated that there was an exception to this "fundamental rule" so as to shift the burden on the defendant to prove that he was entitled to do the "prohibited act" but this exception was "limited to offences arising under enactments which prohibit the doing of an act save in specified circumstances": *per* Lawton L.J. (at 39, 40). This, of course, begs the question. In *Hunt*, the "prohibited act" had yet to be established. Accordingly, the Court of Appeal held (in effect) that the principle in Edwards could have no application to "exceptions" made under section 7(1)(a). As if to underline the point, the Court of Appeal observed that by contrast, most, if not all of the remaining regulations (not made under s. 7(1)(a)) "must fall within the principle in *Edwards* [1975] Q.B. 27" (per Robert Goff L.J. at 233 G-H) because the effect of them is simply to make lawful (in specified circumstances) that which would otherwise be unlawful.

11–27 However, this did not dispose of the matter, because both the Court of Appeal and the House of Lords held that practical considerations may be taken into account when construing a particular piece of legislation, in order to determine upon whom the burden of proof rests. In this instance the Court of Appeal considered that only rarely would an accused wish to be brought within one of the exceptions whereas, if the burden rests on the prosecution, then in many cases it would be necessary "to produce evidence from an analyst" ([1986] 2 W.L.R. 225, 234). Furthermore, the Court of Appeal felt that the burden of proof in the regulations should be applied consistently (at 234 A-B).

The House of Lords, however, noted that in cases where the burden lies on the defendant, the burden can be easily discharged: *per* Lord Griffiths ([1987] A.C. 352, 365). Their Lordships did not share the "anxieties of the Court of Appeal" (at 1130 F, H) and accordingly held that the burden was on the prosecution to negate the possible application of the statutory exceptions. See also Patrick Healy, "Proof and Policy: No Golden Threads" [1987] Crim.L.R. 355.

(iii) *The importance of a precise analyst's report*

11–28 In *Hunt* Lord MacKay of Clashfern remarked (at 1131 G-H):

> "I consider that this case emphasises the need for absolute clarity in the terms of the analyst's certificate founded on by the prosecution in cases of this sort and, in my opinion, it would be wise where there is any possibility of one of the descriptions in the relevant Schedule applying . . . that the analyst should state expressly whether or not the substance falls within that description as well as stating whether or not it is a controlled drug within the meaning of the Act of 1971."

In *Jones (Keith), The Times*, April 24, 1997, J appealed against his conviction for possessing cocaine contending that the analyst's certificate was inadequate because it stated that the substance "appeared to contain cocaine of a high purity". The appeal was dismissed, and *Hunt* was distinguished, on the basis that the forensic evidence clearly established that the purity of the drug was above 0.1 per cent and therefore the substance was not excluded by the Misuse of Drugs Regulations 1985, Schedule 5, paragraph 2. Nevertheless, it was important that an analyst's certificate was absolutely clear.

In the ordinary way a report from an authorised analyst to the effect that the substance in question is the controlled drug alleged is sufficient evidence of the matters set out therein for the purposes of the MDA 1971 and there exists no burden on the Crown to exclude the possibility that the substance in question had been manufactured synthetically: *Guild v. Ogilvie*, 1986 S.C.C.R. 67. It is obviously essential that the evidence is sufficient to establish continuity or a link between what is found and the content of an analyst's report: *Allan v. Ingram*, 1995 G.W.D. 770. **11–29**

Note that a gaschromotography printout is not hearsay: see *Golizadeh* [1995] Crim. L.R. 232 in which it was held that in almost every case in which an expert gave evidence, he would rely on the work of assistants or on the result of machines. Where a machine is used so that an opinion is derived partly from the results of that equipment, the evidence is not hearsay because it still amounted to an expert opinion on data considered by the expert and by way of his expertise in interpreting the results of the analysis.

B. LETTERS; DOCUMENTS; BOOKS

I. Duty of the Prosecution

In the ordinary way, the prosecution is under a duty to disclose to the defence all probative evidence on which the prosecution intends to rely in support of the prosecution case. Duties and rules relating to disclosure are now largely set out in the Criminal Procedure and Investigations Act 1996. Frequently, documents are seized by police or customs officers during the course of a search, which are retained by them but not formally exhibited or identified. When the defendant comes to be cross-examined, prosecuting counsel may then seek to put to him material not previously disclosed in order to undermine or to rebut the defendant's evidence. Obviously, the prosecution is not obliged to overload its case by including every single article or document seized merely because it has some probative value. However, where the prosecution foresees an issue which is likely to form a rational basis for a plea of not guilty, then the prosecution should not wait until the defendant gives evidence before disclosing the relevant material to the defence. In *Phillipson* (1990) 91 Cr.App.R. 226 the Court of Appeal **11–30** quashed the appellant's conviction for an offence of being knowingly concerned in the prohibited importation of 350 grams of heroin concealed inside her body on the basis that the prosecution had been wrong not to disclose various letters in their possession which, prima facie, undermined the appellant's claim that she acted under duress.

> In *Phillipson*, P admitted that the heroin had been imported at the instigation of Icheke with whom P lived and who was the father of her baby. During her trial, she testified that Icheke frequently assaulted her. In cross-examination, the prosecution put to her letters written by Icheke to P as well as one letter written by P to Icheke and a photograph. The purpose of putting the letters to her was to demonstrate a loving relationship and to undermine her evidence that she acted under duress. There was no evidence as to where the letters had been found and the defence was not told of their existence.
>
> *Held*: on appeal, that the evidence of the letters and photograph should have been included as part of the prosecution case. The letters, written by a person not called as a witness (Icheke) were not evidence of the truth of the various statements contained in them. They could not therefore be evidence of the true reason why P had gone to Pakistan or of the true relationship between P and Icheke.

11–31 The Court recognised that by disclosing probative material in advance of trial, a defendant may be afforded the opportunity of trimming his evidence, but the rationale in favour of disclosure rested not on the view that the law wished to help liars to tell more convincing lies but because an accused needed to know in advance the case which would be made against him if he was to have a proper opportunity of giving his answers to the best of his ability. "It was better in the interests of justice that an accused was not induced, by thinking that he was safe is he did so, to exaggerate, or to embroider, or to lie": *per* Gibson L.J.

The importance of the principles referred to in *Phillipson* (1990) 91 Cr.App.R. 226 were repeated in *Sansom* (1991) 92 Cr.App.R. 115. In that case the Court of Appeal quashed the conviction of S in circumstances where documents were put to S in cross-examination, which had not previously been disclosed to the defence. The duty of the Crown is to disclose all the evidence upon which it proposes to rely by the end of the prosecution case: see also *Rice* [1963] 1 Q.B. 857, *Kane* (1977) 65 Cr.App.R. 270. If the prosecution decides not to rely on certain documents as part of their case, then they fall into the category of "unused material": note that the topic of disclosure is now so detailed that it is beyond the scope of this book to deal with it, however, the position is concisely dealt with in *Archbold Criminal Pleading, Evidence, and Practice*, Chapter 12. As to the extent to which it is permissible to cross-examine on matters not previously established in evidence, see Hill 96 Cr.App.R. 456 and *Tuegal* [2000] 2 All E.R. 872.

11–32 In *Sansom* (1991) 92 Cr.App.R. 115, the Court of Appeal emphasised that it is the duty of the prosecuting authority to sift and evaluate the material in its possession in good time. Unused material required to be disclosed under the Attorney-General's Guidelines should be disclosed at the proper time and in proper manner: *per* Taylor L.J. (at 123) but see the ruling of Henry J. in *Saunders* (September 29, 1990, unreported); *Ward* (1993) 96 Cr. App. R. 1; *Davis and Oths* (1993) 97 Cr. App. R. 110; *Keane* (1994) 99 Cr. App. R. 1; *Brown* [1995] 1 Cr. App. R. 191; *Thornton* [1995] 1 Cr. App. R. 578, and note *R. v. Horseferry Road Magistrates, ex. p. Bennett* [1994] Crim. L.R. 370.

A failure to disclose material that ought to be disclosed to the defence is capable of resulting in a conviction being quashed: see *Lawson* (1990) 90 Cr. App. R. 107 but the Court of Appeal declined to take this step in *Dye, Williamson and Davies* [1992] Crim. L.R. 449 where, to the knowledge of the prosecution, a television company filmed and interviewed a number of prosecution witnesses (including an accomplice) before the trial began. The defence were not informed of this fact until after the trial. However, the differences between what was said on the film and in evidence were not so great as to render the convictions unsafe or unsatisfactory.

On the other hand, the fact that relevant documents or items should have been delivered to the defence (or returned to the defendant) but which have been lost due to delay or negligent mishandling by agencies acting on behalf of the prosecution, will not necessarily result in a stay of proceedings on the grounds of abuse of process, or in a conviction being quashed: see *Smith (Alan McDonald)*, May 26, 2000 where information stored in a psion organiser, that had been seized by officers, was "lost".

(a) Establishing a nexus between the content of documents and the offence

The type of problem that is being considered under this heading relates to documents, which are found in the possession of the accused or the contents of which are relied upon by the prosecution as proving that he is guilty of the offence charged because the document in some way explains the defendant's conduct, or his state of mind: see *Cray* (February 26, 1993, unreported, CA) where a diary belonging to C was held to be properly admitted because "it went to the very root" of one of the matters the prosecution had to prove, namely the knowledge on the part of the accused: and see *Reeves, Togher and others* (December 4, 1998, CA). 11–33

A letter written by X to D which discusses the supplying of a controlled drug, may be sought to be admitted in evidence to support such a charge against D on a number of different grounds:

(i) that the document can be relied on as evidence of the truth of its contents by way of an exception to the hearsay rule, *e.g.* a business record; see s.24 of the C.J.A. 1988, and see *Murphy, Wiseman and Mason* [1992] Crim. L.R. 883;

(ii) that the document is not relied on as to the truth of its contents but that the document is itself circumstantial or real evidence in the case and therefore the hearsay rule does not apply: see *Subramaniam v. Public Prosecutor* [1956] 1 W.L.R. 965; and see *Cooper* (1986) 82 Cr.App.R. 74; *Lydon* (1987) 85 Cr.App. R. 221. Of particular relevance to this discussion see: *Horne* [1992] Crim. L.R. 304; *McIntosh* [1992] Crim. L.R. 651;

(iii) that the document is circumstantial evidence which discloses the commission of an offence by the defendant, other than the one with which he is charged, but is said to be admissible because it explains or rebuts assertions made by the defendant, *e.g.* that he was in innocent dupe to an importation of a controlled drug: see *Willis* (January 29, 1979); *Thrussell* (November 30, 1981); *Alexiou* (November 14, 1983); *Madden* [1986] Crim.L.R. 804 and *Bagga* (May 21, 1986); *Morgan* [1993] Crim. L.R. 56; *Peters* [1995] 2 Cr. App. R. 77; *Burrage*, January 27,1997; *Sabouri*, January 20, 1997; *Burley*, March 16, 1995; *Sanders*, February 25, 1997; *Yalman* (March 30, 1998); *Barner-Rajmussen* [1996] Crim.L.R. 497; *Groves* Crim. L.R. 200; *R. v. P* [1991] 2 A.C. 447, and see *Esmieu* (February 20, 1998) and *Dellaway* (April 7, 2000, CA).

11–34 It may well be the case that one or more of these categories will need to be considered when determining the admissibility of a document but it seems to be in the nature of things that issues of admissibility evolve in separate compartments without reference to other areas of evidence which involve similar or identical issues.

Thus, in *Horne* [1992] Crim. L.R. 304, H's conviction for an offence of being knowingly concerned in the fraudulent evasion of the prohibition on importation of cocaine, was quashed. Two pieces of paper, which had been found at the address of a co-defendant, were admitted in evidence against H and contained H's telephone number and calculations, which were alleged to be referable to the illegal venture. There was no evidence as to who the author was or that H even knew of their existence. The co-defendant had pleaded guilty and gave evidence against H. The fact that H had not seen the documents is not necessarily fatal to their admissibility because ultimately the test is whether the evidence is relevant to an issue. In this case, the evidential link could not be established because it does not seem to have been the co-defendant who wrote the documents and thus it would be difficult for the prosecution to rely on their compilation as acts done in furtherance of a joint venture. The content of the documents was not probative of knowledge as far as H was concerned.

11–35 A different result occurred in *McIntosh* [1992] Crim. L.R. 651. M was charged with the unlawful importation of cocaine. At an address, where M lived with his wife, pieces of paper were found concealed in the chimney. The writing on the papers was not M's but it referred to the price and weight of a consignment of drugs. In dismissing M's appeal against conviction, the Court held that the document did not offend the hearsay rule but was real evidence, which tended to connect M with the offence charged. It is difficult to avoid this result in cases where the defendant is in possession of a document, which is referable to the offence charged, and in circumstances where, for example, he has retained the document to assist him in the venture. The fact that he is not the author of the document is unimportant but the result in *McIntosh* would probably have been different if it could not be inferred that M knew of the existence of the papers and he could not be in possession of them without that knowledge.

In *Madden* [1986] Crim.L.R. 804, a trunk was sent from Jamaica to M's home address in England. Officers found cannabis concealed in the trunk and they found two letters in a chest of drawers, written by the father of some of the children. The letters were at least one year old. They referred to smuggling small amounts of cannabis into the United Kingdom in batteries and tapes and "the reasons why you didn't get any herbs is because the man didn't have much". The Court held that as the letters were addressed to M, which she clearly read, they were admissible to rebut the defence that the trunk was unsolicited and that she did not know of its contents. Although this case raised an additional point concerning the suggestion, implicit in the letters, that she had previously imported cannabis nevertheless both *Madden* and *McIntosh* demonstrate that evidence of documents may be admissible if relevant irrespective of whether the accused is the author of them or not.

II. Evidence as to "Other Misconduct" May Become Relevant

Evidence tending to show merely a propensity to commit the offence 11–36
charged is not admissible: but see *P* [1991] 2 A.C. 447, HL and *Sokialiois* [1993] Crim. L.R. 872. There does exist, however, a line of cases on which the prosecution has been held entitled to rely concerning the finding of drug-related material in the possession of the defendant in order to prove mens rea of the offence charged or to rebut a defence of innocent association or "plant": see *Willis* (January 29, 1979); *Thrussell* (November 30, 1981); *Alexiou* (November 14, 1983); *Madden* [1986] Crim.L.R. 804 and *Bagga* (May 21, 1986); *Morgan* [1993] Crim. L.R. 56; *Peters* [1995] 2 Cr. App. R. 77, *Esmieu* (February 20, 1998) and see *Dellaway* (April 7, 2000, CA)

As will be seen, these cases do not establish new law but they are increasingly relied upon by advocates appearing on behalf of the prosecution.

The general principle of law was stated by Lord Herschell in *Makin v.* 11–37
Attorney-General for New South Wales [1894] A.C. 57, when he said (at 65):

> "... the mere fact that the evidence adduced tends to show the commission of other crimes does not render it inadmissible if it be relevant to an issue before the jury, and it may be so relevant if it bears upon the question whether the acts alleged to constitute the crime charged in the indictment were designed or accidental, or to rebut a defence

which would otherwise be open to the accused. The statement of these general principles is easy, but it is obvious that it may often be very difficult to draw the line and decide whether a particular piece of evidence is on the one side or the other."

The principle in that case was fully discussed in *DPP v. Boardman* [1975] A.C. 421, and again in *P* (above). A similar principle operates in Scotland: see *Nelson v. H.M. Advocate*, 1994 S.L.T. 389.

11–38 The overriding consideration is whether the evidence is relevant and probative subject to the general discretion to exclude in cases where the prejudicial effect of the evidence outweighs its probative value (see ss. 78 and 82(3) of PACE 1984). In some of the cases, referred to below, the basis upon which the evidence was admitted seems strained (*e.g. Willis*) and in others briefly examined (*e.g. Madden*).

In *Willis* W arrived at Heathrow carrying her handbag and a suitcase. A photograph album found in her handbag contained 134.5 grams of opium. Another album in her suitcase contained 75 grams of heroin. From her home address was seized a spoon bearing traces of heroin and a box containing a folded piece of paper inside which was 80 milligrams of heroin. W was charged with the unlawful importation of the drugs found in her luggage under the forerunner to section 170, CEMA 1979 (Customs and Excise Act 1952, s.304). In interview, W had denied knowledge of the drugs in her luggage.

Held: the finding of the items at her flat showed that W was connected with heroin inside the United Kingdom. That fact, in the ordinary way, would not have been relevant but it became relevant in the light of her defence disclosed in the interviews.

11–39 The Court of Appeal stated as its reason that:

"... what the prosecution were doing was to show that her seeming possession in the United Kingdom of a small quantity of heroin was the odd coincidence in the case of a woman who was saying that she had no knowledge whatsoever that she was bringing dangerous drugs into the country. The jury was entitled to consider ... that coincidence."

During the course of argument the appellant contended that the finding of the items at the flat were not relevant to the offence charged. The Court of Appeal replied:

"Prima facie, that is so. The Court, however, has to look to see what was the defence which the appellant disclosed in the course of her interviews ... what she was saying was that she had no knowledge whatsoever of the fact that inside the albums there was opium in one and heroin in the other."

11–40 The approach, if not the result, is undoubtedly correct. The finding of articles, prima facie unconnected with the offence charged, may become relevant and admissible if they are probative of an issue in the case. The facts in *Thrussell*, below, provide a good example of this. However, the validity of the result in *Willis* is less certain. A person who imports prohibited goods may or may not be a victim of a trick, a "plant", or misinformation. Why a user of a particular drug should be less likely to be a "victim" is difficult to follow. The Court relied on what it described as the "odd coincidence" of the presence of heroin found at the premises and drugs found in the albums. However, was the coincidence "odd", or so odd as to be probative? A vast number of people abuse drugs in this country. Not every abuser is an importer nor is he to be assumed to be in a better position to know what he is carrying than anyone else is. There was the "coincidence" that heroin was carried in one album but the coincidence would have been much more cogent if opium had been found at the premises as well. Suppose the whole consignment had been opium or cannabis. Would the result have been different?

In *Thrussell* H and T travelled together on May 20, 1980 from London to Peru via Miami. On May 25, H returned to London. In a suitcase, which H carried, 2.93 kilograms of cocaine was discovered by customs officers. On May 26, T returned to London. T's home address was searched and the sum of $45,400 and a book entitled the Cocaine Consumer's Handbook were seized. The book described the methods of using cocaine; how to import it; the countries most suitable for export as well as data and advice on how the trade should be carried out. When asked about the cocaine in H's suitcase T replied, "Where would I get that sort of stuff?"

Held: the book was relevant and admissible to prove knowledge by T of the importation of the drug in respect of a charge under CEMA 1979, s.170.

The Court said that the book showed knowledge by the appellant of the drug trade. It may be questioned how the book (which was found in the possession of the courier) could be probative evidence against T that he knew importation of the drug by the courier. The answer to this question has to be seen in the light of the other evidence but it is submitted, that the decisive factor was the appellant's claim that he would not know where to get cocaine. The book was undoubtedly capable of rebutting that assertion. When coupled with the journey made by both defendants, and the circumstances in which the two men returned separately over two days, that was sufficient to render the book relevant, probative and admissible. As the Court remarked, the book was "the one piece of evidence which showed knowledge by the Appellant of the drug trade": *per* Waller L.J. 11–41

In *Alexiou*, 24 boxes arrived at Heathrow airport. The boxes contained chandeliers but their false bottoms concealed a total of 107.45 kilograms of cannabis resin. The boxes were loaded onto a van and taken to an address where the appellant was waiting and he helped to carry the boxes into the house. The appellant's own home was searched. A suitcase and scales were found. Both items had traces of cannabis on them. Officers also seized £600 in cash in a bread bin, and a diary containing calculations said to relate to drug dealings.

Held: that the evidence was admissible to rebut the defence that his presence at the premises to which the drugs were delivered was innocent.

11–42 The Court in *Alexiou* placed much reliance on the decision in *Willis*. Although the articles, found at the *Alexiou's* home, may have shown that he was connected with cannabis inside the United Kingdom, it is submitted that those items could not by themselves prove that the appellant knew the boxes contained cannabis. It may be that the Court was influenced by the fact that there was an abundance of other evidence, including articles found at the premises to which the boxes were delivered, that was admissible to prove *mens rea*. One such article was a jigsaw with traces of cannabis resin upon it: the invoice for the jigsaw being at the appellant's home address.

In *Madden*, a trunk was sent from Jamaica to England and the addressee was a child of M's. M arranged for the collection of the trunk. She paid some of the freight charges. Officers found the trunk at M's home address. Cannabis was found in the trunk. The officers also found two letters in a chest of drawers, written by the father of some of the children. The letters were at least one year old. They referred to smuggling small amounts of cannabis into the United Kingdom in batteries and tapes and "the reasons why you didn't get any herbs is because the man didn't have much".

Held: the letters were addressed to M, which she clearly read. They were admissible to rebut the defence that the trunk was unsolicited and that she did not know of its contents.

11–43 In dismissing the appeal, the Court referred to *Alexiou* and *Thrussell*. However, the decision in *Madden* is, with respect, not without difficulty. The letters were adduced to show that the appellant knew the trunk contained cannabis and that she solicited the trunk, but neither letter suggested any such delivery. The probative value of those letters therefore seems speculative. However, there was evidence before the Court that the appellant said to the disguised officer who delivered the trunk, "Now we can see what is in it. We know what is in it. We have been told." The true basis for the decision may be that her response showed a connection between the letters and the delivery of the trunk.

In *Bagga*, Mrs. R arrived at Heathrow airport with a suitcase found to contain 12.3 kilograms of heroin. She was met by her husband and B. Officers searched B's house. They found a briefcase and electronic scales capable of weighing in grams to an accuracy of two decimal points. Traces of heroin were found in the briefcase and on the scales. In interview, B asserted that his presence at the airport was innocent and that he had no knowledge of the presence of heroin carried by Mrs. R.

Held: the evidence of the traces found in the briefcase and on the scales was relevant and admissible.

The Court concluded that it was open to the prosecution to invite the jury to consider whether the evidence of prior unexplained handling of heroin by the appellant destroyed his defence of innocent and ignorant presence. Again, it was not explained by the court how this evidence would logically achieve that result. At first sight, the facts in *Bagga* were more strongly weighted in favour of admissibility than in the case of *Willis*. *Bagga* only came to be tried after the courier had been convicted and after her husband had been given immunity from prosecution: both then gave evidence against Bagga. If their evidence was true the jury had to consider whether Bagga's visit to the airport was innocent or part of a concerted plan to import heroin. The presence of the traces of heroin inside the briefcase and on the scales (consistent arguably with the acts of a dealer) went, it was said, to that issue. Curiously, the trial judge in *Bagga* withdrew from the jury a charge of conspiracy to supply heroin on the basis, *inter alia*, that the "possible findings in relation to importation might, despite the most careful direction as to propensity, be very damaging to the appellant". On appeal, it was contended that this reasoning justified the exclusion of the evidence in respect of the charge under section 170, CEMA 1979 as well. The Court of Appeal queried whether the conspiracy should have been withdrawn and cited, in support of its own reasoning, the judgment in *Willis*. 11–44

In *Morgan* [1993] Crim. L.R. 56, M arrived at Heathrow Airport carrying two boxes containing recording tapes, which concealed 227.6 grams of cocaine. M contended that she was an innocent dupe on whom the drugs had been planted. In an interview, M told officers that she smoked cocaine and allowed others to smoke cocaine at her premises. The prosecution contended that M's answers were relevant evidence to a charge of being knowingly concerned in the fraudulent evasion of the prohibition on the importation of a controlled drug because it showed that she had a link with cocaine and that it was a strange coincidence that of all the people coming in from Jamaica on a particular flight, it was M who had that link. M's appeal against her conviction was dismissed. The evidence was relevant and admissible. As Professor Smith has pointed out in his commentary to this case, who is to say how many passengers on this flight were carrying cocaine? This line of cases started with *Willis*, which regarded as a relevant consideration the "odd coincidence" of a person in possession of drugs who was saying that he had no knowledge whatsoever that he was bringing dangerous drugs into the country. An "odd coincidence" it may have been in 1979 (when *Willis* was decided) but what is so unique or "odd" about that feature now? Many knowing couriers are persons of previous good character who are recruited by unscrupulous organisers because they are less likely to attract suspicion. A person is surely no less likely to be a victim of a trick or a plant merely because they use a particular controlled drug or associate with one or more drug traffickers.

11–45 In *Peters* [1995] 2 Cr.App.R. 77, the Court of Appeal applied *Willis* but on somewhat stronger ground than was the case in Morgan. Peters was stopped by customs officers at Dover in which 2.58 kilograms of amphetamine sulphate was found. When questioned, Peters said that he did not know anything about the drugs but then added, "I don't know about drugs" and "I don't have any idea about anything like that". During the course of a search at P's home, a small amount of cannabis and drug-related equipment was found including a pipe all of which Peters admitted were his. As the Court of Appeal pointed out in Peters, the only knowledge alleged in *Willis* was of the presence of drugs in the photograph albums, which were in W's luggage. "There was no question, as there is here, of a denial which went so far as to assert that she had no knowledge of any drugs whatsoever": *per* Evans L.J. The fact that Peters was asserting that he knew nothing about drugs at all (and not merely denying knowledge of the drugs found in the car) made the items found during the course of the search relevant and prima facie admissible. The Court regarded his replies as amounting to an assertion that he had no connection with any person who might have made him the victim of a trick and concluded that it was "from this" that the "necessary relevance arises" (82 D-E). It is submitted that the Court were correct in that analysis but the court went further and said described the judgement in *Willis* as being:

> "... clear authority for the proposition that, when knowledge is in issue, which carries with it the implication that the defendant is the 'innocent victim' of some other person who has concealed drugs in the defendant's luggage, or in his vehicle, then evidence showing that the defendant was connected with the kind of drugs inside the United Kingdom is relevant and admissible, subject to the court's power to exclude it on grounds of undue prejudice".

11–46 It is submitted that *Willis* is authority for just one proposition, namely, that evidence is admissible if it is relevant notwithstanding that the evidence may disclose an offence committed by the accused other than the offence with which he is charged. Unfortunately, the line of cases referred to above, seems to have developed quite independently of another spate of decisions concerning the admissibility of large sums of money found in the possession of an accused and which may be relevant evidence on a drug-trafficking charge: see below. In the final analysis, each case must be decided on its own facts. It is respectfully submitted that the Court of Appeal in Alexiou erred in describing *Willis* as a decision "of this Court, which is of course binding upon us". In fact, neither *Willis* nor any of the authorities cited above establishes new law. These cases are illustrative of existing principles and nothing more.

In *Sokialiois* [1993] Crim. L.R. 872, the Court applied the similar fact principle and not (surprisingly perhaps) the aforementioned line of cases.

> In *Sokialiois*, cocaine was posted in Holland to an address in Dover. S was in Holland on the day the drug was posted. X was arrested

when he went to Dover to recover it. S was arrested later: he was found in possession of a piece of paper and a diary that recorded the Dover address. S told officers "I don't deal in drugs. I don't even take drugs." A holdall belonging to S was recovered from an hotel. Cocaine was found in the holdall but this was not the subject of any charge. In evidence, S said that the documents and the drug in the holdall were planted.

Held: dismissing the appeal against conviction for the unlawful importation of the drug into Dover: the judge was correct to admit the evidence of the documents and the finding of cocaine in the holdall.

The Court of Appeal rejected the submission that the evidence went only to propensity. The evidence was relevant to rebut S's assertion when interviewed that he had no connection with the drug trade or drug taking. The court referred to *Boardman* [1975] A.C. 421 but do the facts of *Sokialiois* really justify the application of the "similar fact" principle or is the case not really a good example of the sort of considerations which were discussed in *Peters*? The court, on the facts of that case, also held in *Sokialiois* that it was not necessary to spell out to the jury the dangers of using evidence of "similar fact" as going merely to propensity because the Court concluded that the trial judge's discretion was "satisfactory" and yet, one of the hallmarks of another line of cases (from *Wright* to *Scott*, see below) is that where evidence is admitted of paraphernalia or money found in the possession of the accused, the judge should indeed "spell out" to the jury how that evidence is capable of being relevant and probative of an issue which the jury have to decide: see, for example, *Gordon* [1995] Cr. App. R. 61, *Nicholas* [1995] Crim. L. R. 942. 11–47

In *Nadiri* [1995] Crim. L. R. 889, N was charged with the unlawful importation of opium of which 317 grams was hidden within a dryer and 158 grams was concealed in a pouch. Both items were in a suitcase, which N had been carrying. N's appeal against conviction was allowed on the grounds that two items of evidence, namely (i) a photograph found in his luggage depicting a friend holding a cannabis cigarette and (ii) a positive result for the presence of cannabis in a sample of N's urine, was irrelevant to rebut (as a lie) N's account in interview that he did not know of the existence of the opium in the suitcase. The prosecution also relied on the similar fact principle by claiming that the urine test showed that N had only recently consumed cannabis but the facts were held to be far removed from those in *Sokialiois* and the occasion on which N's friend smoked cannabis was far removed from the importation of cannabis: (by contrast, see *Caceres-Moreira* [1995] Crim. L.R. 489). If the prosecution had put their case differently and contended that the result of the urine sample and photograph were relevant in the *Willis* sense, would the result have been different?

Again, in *Dellaway and Moriaty* (April 7, 2000), M complained that the judge wrongly admitted evidence of traces of cocaine found on a set of electronic scales at M's home, on the basis that it suggested he had some involvement with unlawful drugs of a different kind, which he denied, and which far outweighed any probative value it might have in relation to his knowledge of the importation of ecstasy tablets. The Court disagreed.

It is incumbent upon the judge to direct the jury as to the significance of the evidence and the relevance to the issues which the jury has to decide: *Esmieu* (February 20, 1998, CA).

(a) Evidence of money and drug paraphernalia

11–48 Evidence of money or drug paraphernalia is admissible in evidence if it is relevant and probative of any issue which the jury have to try notwithstanding that the evidence may suggest that the defendant has committed other, similar, offences: see *Wright* [1994] Crim.L.R. 55; but *cf. Batt* [1994] Crim.L.R. 592; *Gordon* [1995] 2 Cr.App.R. 61; *Dionne Morris* [1995] 2 Cr.App.R. 69; *Simms* [1995] Crim. L.R. 304; *Brown* [1995] Crim. L.R. 28; *Nicholas* [1995] Crim. L.R. 942; *Grant* [1996] Cr.App.R. 73; *Okusanya* [1995] Crim. L.R. 941; *Smith* [1995] Crim. L.R. 940; *Lucas* [1995] Crim. L.R. 400 *Halpin* [1996] Crim. L.R. 112; *Scott*, March 26, 1996, and see *Edwards* (July 29, 1997); *Wilkinson* (August 7, 1997); *Faal* (December 1, 1998); *Stockton* (January 27, 2000); and *McGinley and others* (July 10, 2000). Unfortunately, all of the above cases have been decided independently of another line of cases beginning with *Willis* (unreported, 1979) and see above para. 11–33.

In cases where the accused is charged with a drug trafficking offence (*e.g.* possession with intent to supply or unlawful importation) it frequently happens that the prosecution attempt to introduce evidence of drug paraphernalia, monies, drugs correspondence found in the possession of the accused, or to introduce evidence of an expensive life-style. When *Wright* was reported in 1994 the result was not regarded by practitioners as being particularly remarkable because although, in many cases, a person may intend to supply drugs which are in his possession as a one-off transaction (or because he is acting as custodian of the drug on behalf of another) there have been many cases where a person had drugs in his possession as stock-in-trade. Accordingly, large sums of money found in the possession of the accused have long been regarded as a possible hallmark of an intention to supply particularly if the money was kept with the drugs. The courts became accustomed to determining questions of admissibility of evidence (including cash) on an item-by-item basis and it was generally accepted that every case must be decided on its own facts. Accordingly, when *Batt* was decided it not only appeared to challenge the correctness of the reasoning in *Wright* but it was also viewed, in some quarters, as establishing a general principle against the admissibility of evidence if it suggested the commission of offences not included as counts on the indictment. The upshot has been a long string of decisions of the Court of Appeal since May 1994 (*Wright*). In *Lucas* the appellant was charged with two counts under section 170(2)(b) CEMA 1979 as well as a charge of possession with intent to supply. The trial judge ruled that evidence of money found in the appellant's possession was relevant only to the latter charge.

What, then, do all these cases really decide? In short, they have brought us back to first principles, namely: 11–49

(i) that evidence is admissible if relevant and probative of any issue that the jury has to determine;
(ii) evidence is not admissible if it merely demonstrates a propensity on the part of the defendant to commit the type of offence charged and the judge must be vigilant to ascertain why the evidence is said to be relevant by the party seeking to adduce it;
(iii) that the judge may exercise discretion to exclude evidence under section 78 or section 82(3) PACE 1984;
(iv) it is the duty of the trial judge to ensure that irrelevant evidence is excluded, particularly if its prejudicial effect outweighs its probative value (and this is so whether objection is taken to its admissibility or not) or in order to avoid the trial being swamped with superfluous material;
(v) that if the trial judge admits evidence of money or paraphernalia he is duty bound to spell out to the jury why the evidence is relevant, the issue to which the evidence is directed and to direct the jury to reject evidence which has no probative value although, in the last instance, it would obviously be better if the evidence were not admitted at all (see *Jardine* (February 8, 1999) and *Malik* (October 4, 1999);
(vi) Evidence of money is not "as a matter of principle inadmissible": *Nicholas*.

Most of the reported decisions of the Court of Appeal are concerned with large sums of cash found in the possession of the accused, or evidence of wealth, *i.e.* life-style (see *Halpin*). There have been relatively few case where the complaint is that the judge wrongly admitted evidence in respect of an article which may be regarded as the paraphernalia of the supplier, *e.g.* scales, razor-blades, poly-bags. The reason for this may be that items such as scales, are capable of defining themselves in terms of their purpose (and therefore questions of relevance and probative value are likely to be fairly straightforward) but the same cannot be said about money or lifestyle which may call for an explanation from the defendant and which may therefore introduce matters of a highly prejudicial nature (including the commission of offences, whether drug-related or not, which the jury are not required to try). It frequently happens that a defendant will seek to explain wealth as representing the fruits of a "cash business" in respect of which he kept no records, filed no tax returns and was not registered for VAT. Other defendants admit to defrauding the Department of Social Security and a few defendants are even prepared to admit that their income was derived from serious crime, *e.g.* robbery. At the time an objection is taken to the admissibility of cash or life-style, the judge will rarely know how the defence proposes to meet the evidence if it were to be admitted and, in any event, the judge cannot decide (even on a *voire dire*) whether the defendant's explanations, or any of them, are true because to do so would be to usurp the function of the jury. However, the judge is charged with the responsibility of managing the trial and part of that function includes ensuring that the evidence is "contained by the ring fence of relevance" (see *Gordon* [1995] Cr. App. R. 61, 67 F-G; *per* Henry L.J.). Henry L.J. went on to say, "the judge should ascertain in advance what the prosecution case is, and how the defence propose to meet it. He should not be too easily deterred by non-co-operation from the defence in this process." For the reasons given above there is a limit to this approach but the purpose is to see that trials are not "swamped with superfluous, irrelevant and eventually prejudicial issues". Thus in *Batt, Brown* and *Halpin* the Court displayed greater anxiety about admitting evidence of money or life-style than it displayed in respect of paraphernalia. Indeed, in *Brown*, the court said that the different considerations might apply to items such as scales as opposed to money found in the possession of the defendant. None of the cases has sought to suggest that *Batt* was wrongly decided but *Batt* has been sidelined more than once. In both *Nicholas* and *Okusanya*, the Court suggested that *Batt* should be regarded as a case strictly confined to its own facts. In two cases, (*Gordon* and *Nicholas*) the Court pointed out that in *Batt* the Recorder did not direct the jury as to the possible relevance of the money. This is perhaps the most persuasive basis for explaining the result in *Batt* and, if that analysis is valid, it puts *Batt* in line with *Gordon, Morris, Simms, Grant, Lucas* and *Halpin* all of which stress the obligation the judge has to give appropriate directions to the jury (and see *Jardine* (February 8, 1999) and *Malik* (October 4, 1999)). No two cases are the same and a judge has to tailor his directions to the needs of the case and the particular issues, which the jury has to determine: see *Okusanya*.

11–50 It is submitted that of the long list of decisions of the Court of Appeal profering guidance, *Gordon* should be regarded as the definitive authority because not only does it set out all the relevant principles of law but it also demonstrates how the principles should be applied in practice. Thus, Henry L.J. stated the relevant principles to be as follows:

1. The intention to supply must relate to the parcel of drugs that the appellant was found to be in possession of.
2. In order to be admissible, the evidence would have to be relevant to that intention.
3. To be relevant, that evidence would have to be logically probative of that intention, *i.e.* that the evidence made his intention to supply those drugs more or less probable.
4. Evidence of marginal relevance may and should be excluded if it would lead to a multiplicity of subsidiary issues.
5. It is the duty of the judge, whether objection is taken or not, to ensure that irrelevant evidence (particularly when it is prejudicial to the defence) be not received in court. Should such evidence have been received, then the judge has the special responsibility

to direct the jury either to disregard it or how to treat it, as the circumstances require. In *Gordon* the prosecution adduced the following items of evidence and the Court of Appeal dealt with them in the following way:

(i) Three savings books were found, dealing with accounts opened between 1984 and 1987. They were all in credit to a total sum of £10,500. These were active accounts and various credits and withdrawals were dealt with in the evidence. The Court held that this evidence was irrelevant and likely to confuse the real issue and should not have been admitted.

(ii) The appellant was found when arrested to be in possession of a Vodaphone registered in the name of his common-law wife who was at the club at the time of his arrest, when he passed the telephone over to her. The prosecution did not seek to trace any of the calls made on that telephone. The Court held that the possession and use of these items is "seen as part of the stereotype of not only drug dealers but also, for example, the young and upwardly mobile". The evidence should not have been admitted.

(iii) The appellant's home was searched for drug dealing paraphernalia, and the only item that might have been such was a test tube containing traces of bicarbonate of soda (apparently a substance used in the manufacture of crack cocaine). His common-law wife was to say that she had acquired this test tube to deal with urine samples when pregnant, and had cleaned it with bicarbonate of soda. The court held that this item was admissible as being capable of being probative of an intention to supply.

(iv) £4,200 cash was found at the appellant's home, approximately half of which was found in the pockets of various jackets. £2,000 was under the mattress and the police would not have found it but for the fact that the appellant told them it was there and showed them where it was. The Court held that this evidence was relevant and admissible.

(iv) Various documents were found relating to the ownership of the BMW, which the appellant was driving. This was registered in the name of a third party (who was to give evidence at the trial) and the suggestion was that that name was an alias the appellant used. Therefore, he was lying when he said that the car was not his but belonged to another. The Court held that this evidence was inadmissible.

(vi) When the appellant was being questioned as to his means, he had denied that he owned, or had any interest in, a house known as 19 Gascoyne Road. In fact, he inherited this property on the death of his mother some years earlier and lived partially off its rents. The contention of the prosecution was that he was concealing his wealth (because he could not account for it) but G said that the house had been lawfully acquired. This was held to be irrelevant and inadmissible because the drug dealer buying from his supplier is not going to get credit on the strength of the buyer claiming that he can offer his house as security.

11–51 However, by way of a contrast, consider *Wilkinson and Fraser* (August 7, 1997). In that case, the appellants appealed against their conviction for possessing a controlled drug with intent to supply it on the basis that the judge wrongly admitted evidence relating to a search at the appellants' premises, namely, the finding of a number of empty plastic bags, a pager, a mobile telephone, and £135 cash. In dismissing the appeal, the Court held that on the facts of this particular case the items were admissible as paraphernalia of drug dealing. The money was admissible in the context of the prosecution case based around the defendant's intentions and past actions in connection with a larger consignment of controlled drugs. The jury was entitled to take the view that the evidence demonstrated a current intention to supply.

In *Wright* [1994] Crim.L.R. 55, officers searched a car at Heathrow Airport and found packets of crack cocaine concealed inside it. W was arrested at Heathrow but denied that the car was anything to do with him. Enquiries revealed that W had hired the car three days earlier for cash. The trial judge ruled that a gold necklace (worth £9,000) and £16,000 in cash, found at W's address, was admissible in evidence. On appeal against conviction, Lord Justice Beldam observed that:

> "Substantial capital in hard cash is essential for someone who is minded to deal in these drugs, and so it comes about that those who carry on the trade are frequently found to have in their possession large amounts of cash, either because they have received it for sales already made, or because they need it to take advantage of any opportunity which may arise for the purchase of fresh supplies of the drug. Sometimes quantities of cash are concealed on the person; sometimes they are concealed in the home where it is thought that it will be safe from discovery.
>
> The question for decision is whether the finding of such a large amount of cash is a fact, which, if proved, makes it more probable that a person suspected of dealing in narcotic drugs, and who is found to be in possession of them, is in possession of them for the purpose of supplying them. In other words, does the fact of the possession of the large amount of cash tend to prove or render more probable the other facts the prosecution have to prove, that is that the drugs were in his possession for the purpose of supplying them to another?"

11–52 It may be said that the judgment is open to criticism in suggesting that the test is only whether the evidence "tends to prove or render more probable" the other facts which the prosecution have to prove. Although it might have been better if the words "render more probable" had been omitted, nevertheless the sense of the judgment is clear. It is the relevance and probative value of the evidence which is decisive of admissibility and much will depend on the facts of any given case.

In *Wright* it was said that:
"... supplying addictive narcotic drugs is a clandestine trade: high prices are demanded and have to be paid. These drugs are not supplied on credit. Substantial capital in hard cash is essential for someone who is minded to deal in these drugs." (*per* Beldam LJ).

These observations were made in the context of a case involving crack cocaine and with respect should not be viewed as expressing absolutes. Much will depend on (i) the amount of drug in the possession of the defendant, (ii) the value of the drug, (iii) whether the defendant is a user of the drug, and so on. The unlawful supply of any controlled drug (whether an addictive narcotic or not) is of course likely to be clandestine. Occasionally drugs are supplied on credit particularly where the amount of drug involved is small and the relationship between supplier and user is well established, but where the evidence suggests that a commercial enterprise was either afoot, or had taken place, the presence of a 'large amount of money (or paraphernalia) is likely to be significant for the reasons given by Lord Justice Beldam in *Wright*.

In *Batt* [1994] Crim.L.R. 592, the police found, in rabbit hutch **11–53** belonging to B, sufficient cannabis to make 3,000 cigarettes. A set of scales with traces of cannabis resin on them was found in the house as well as £150 found in an ornamental bottle. The prosecution contended that the cash was a "hallmark of intent to supply" and a "float". The Court of Appeal rejected the contention on the grounds that the money was the hallmark of a "propensity to supply generally or a hallmark of the fact that there has been a past supply" and that in the absence of a clear direction from the trial judge as to how the jury should treat the evidence of the money, the admission of the evidence was unfair and prejudicial. This case has been criticised (see the commentary [1994] Crim.L.R. 593) and described as being difficult to reconcile with *Wright*: see *Gordon* [1995] 2 Cr.App.R. 61 and *Dionne Morris* [1995] 2 Cr.App.R. 69. It has been said that where the Court of Appeal, in *Batt*, fell into error was in seeking to distinguish *Wright* on the grounds that the latter was a "drug trading case": see *Morris, ibid.* at 74 E-F. Morland J. said:

> "In our judgement, both cases were drug-trading cases despite the international dimension in *Wright* arising from the presence at Heathrow of the car containing cocaine. In *Batt*, whoever was the possessor of the cannabis was in possession as a commercial retailer. The evidence of the amount and nature of the cannabis in the rabbit hutch and the scales in the house established that."

This analysis is valid on the facts of *Batt* but it should not be overlooked **11–54** that scales are often employed by drug consumers as well as by suppliers. In *Batt*, the Court did not express a view as to the admissibility of the scales. The admission of the money formed the first ground of appeal and the Court did not go on to consider four other complaints. It is therefore unknown whether the admission of the scales involved a separate complaint. Clearly, the scales would be relevant if B had them for supplying the drug in question. The traces of cannabis resin on the scales would be consistent with the drug being supplied or measured for personal consumption but the probative value of evidence rarely depends on looking at the item in question in isolation: the cumulative effect of the evidence may be decisive, and see *Akram* [1995] Crim. L.R. 50 where the relevance of tinfoil was considered on a charge of possessing heroin with intent to supply.

In *Morris* [1995] Cr. App. R. 69, M was arrested at her parents' address. M dropped several bags containing money in excess of £5,000. Heroin was found in her bra. Further cash and a notebook containing names and figures, were found at the premises. The Court held that the judge should have spelt out the inferences which "he considered was capable of being drawn by the jury from the evidence which he was ruling admissible". This he failed to do and the conviction was quashed.

11–55 The Court went on to say that:

> "... *in our judgment evidence of large amounts of money in possession of a defendant or an extravagant lifestyle on his part, prima facie explicable only if derived from drug dealing, is admissible in cases of possession of drugs with intent to supply if it is of probative significance to an issue in the case.* The fact that a defendant gives an explanation for the possession of large sums of money does not of itself render such evidence inadmissible; the Crown may be able to rebut such an explanation ... if a judge decides that such evidence is admissible in law he must then decide whether or not to admit it in his discretion, having regard to its probative value and is prejudicial effect. If such evidence is admitted, it is incumbent upon the judge to spell out to the jury what its probative significance can be while making it clear to the jury that it is for them to decide whether it has or has not that probative significance. The judge must then warn the jury that, if they reach the conclusion that the defendant is the drug dealer this is not of itself either evidence of possession of drugs on particular occasion or a basis for disbelieving the defendant." [emphasis added]

The extent to which the trial judge will direct the jury as to the inferences that might be (or should not be) drawn from the evidence will depend on the facts of each case: *Stockton (Paul)* (January 27, 2000). In *Halpin* [1996] Crim. L.R. 112, the Court remarked that instances where evidence of lifestyle would be of probative significance "must, we would have thought, be extremely rare". The Court referred to a passage of Morland J. in *Morris* (cited in italics above) and said: "It may be we would prefer to say no more that the comment made in *Morris* went somewhat too far ...".

Cash as evidence of possession

In *Halpin*, H was convicted of two counts of possessing heroin with intent to supply. Police found heroin and £6, 460 in cash and the prosecution adduced evidence of a caravan bought in 1992 and lavish expenditure. The Court held that the cash and life-style could not have been relevant to the issue of possession and the judge was obliged to spell out the significance of such evidence. The reader may be puzzled as to why the court focused on the issue of possession when the appellant was convicted on two charges of possession with intent to supply. An explanation is not expressed in the judgment but presumably, the reason is that there was ample evidence that the drugs could not be for personal consumption and the appellant disputed being in possession of the drugs at all. Accordingly, if evidence of money and life-style stood any chance of being admitted it had to go to the issue of possession (and see *Scott*, NLP 26, March 21, 1996). However, how can money or life-style be probative of that issue? As the Court in *Brown* observed, money may not always be relevant, it will depend on the circumstances. In that case, the Court held that money, scales, 1.78 grams of cannabis in the refrigerator, plastic bags, a mobile phone and evidence that the appellant decamped from the scene on arrival of the police, were properly admitted in evidence as pointing to a possible inference that the appellant was in possession of 11.5 grams of cannabis (found in a pocket) with intent to supply. In *Nicholas* [1995] Crim.L.R. 942, evidence of £600 found on N was admitted in evidence to support a charge of possession of drugs (count 2). The evidence was not adduced to support a charge of possession with intent to supply (count 1) having regard to the decision in *Batt*. N was acquitted of possession but convicted on count 1. Nevertheless, the Court held that the evidence of money was, as a matter of law, admissible on count 1 in any event and dismissed the appeal. 11–56

The probative significance of money and wealth may be multi-faceted. 11–57
Evidence must not be adduced merely to show that the accused has a propensity to commit the crime charged although there have been many prosecutions pursued on the basis that a defendant has systematically sold drugs in order to finance their own drug consumption. Whether such an approach is permissible is not entirely clear. The similar fact rule is unlikely to apply (but see *Sokialiois* [1993] Crim. L.R. 872). Evidence as to propensity is forbidden but evidence of money generated from past supplying may be admissible if it is probative of future supplying, or indicates an ongoing trade in drugs: see *Lehaney* (June 11, 1996). The solution that presents itself to prosecutors is to decide with care how the case is put. Thus, it is probably not permissible to say "you have supplied drugs before; you need to sell drugs in order to finance your habit and therefore you are in possession of drugs again in order to supply all or part of them" (but see *Smith (Ivor)* [1995] Crim. L.R. 940). On the other hand the prosecutor may be permitted to adduce evidence of monies found in the possession of the defendant (or be able to quantify monies earned by him over the relevant

period) not to prove past dealing but to prove "on-going dealing in drugs": see *Grant* [1996] 1 Cr. App. R. 73. Care must be exercised to ensure that cross-examination as to a defendant's general financial position is relevant because, for example, it goes to "lifestyle"—that is to say, ". . . those cases where it is said that it can properly and safely be concluded by a jury that the only explanation for a person's lavish lifestyle is that they are engaged in some unlawful activity, the most obvious being trafficking in drugs" (*per* Lord Woolf C.J., in *McGinley* (July 10, 2000).

11–58 In *Edwards (Elroy)* (July 29, 1997), E was convicted of possessing of Class A drug with intent to supply. The police found in E's flat about 73 grams of crack cocaine, £1,000 cash, paraphernalia, and other items suggesting a good lifestyle. E denied that he had possessed the drug. It was submitted on appeal that evidence relating to cash and other items should have been excluded as irrelevant to the real issue, namely whether E had been in possession of the drugs. The judge directed the jury that "lifestyle" evidence did not go to the issue of possession. However, given that an intention to supply was a matter that the Crown had to prove, the evidence was potentially relevant to that issue: see *Morris* 2 Cr.App.R. 69; *Halpin*, June 22, 1995; *Richards*, February 24, 1997. The Court queried whether so-called "lifestyle" evidence was never relevant to possession.

The short answer is that cash, paraphernalia and lifestyle evidence may be relevant and admissible to prove the fact of possession, but each case must be carefully analysed on its facts. It is submitted that it is highly desirable that the tribunal's attention should not be deflected away from the essential issues that must be determined by a consideration of evidence that is of marginal significance or weight. In *Guney* (February 27, 1998), it was said that cash would often lack probative value but it might be relevant to the issue of knowledge where a defendant is charged with possession with intent to supply, and that different ingredients of the offence should not be artificially compartmentalised. *Guney* was applied in *Griffiths* (March 31, 1998) where D was prepared to admit that whoever possessed the controlled drug had the intention to supply it, but that the cash should be excluded as the only live issue was whether the accused was in possession of the drug. The Court of Appeal disagreed: and see *Edwards* [1998] Crim. L.R. 207. For two further examples, see *Sanchez* (October 14, 1999) and *Brown* (October 15, 1999).

Again, money and wealth may be probative not because it represents on-going drug dealing but because it demonstrates that the accused had the means to finance a drug trafficking venture, *e.g.* to buy a large consignment of drugs abroad and to pay for the costs of importing the drug.

In *Faal* (December 1, 1998) provides a further object lesson to prosecutors to consider carefully how a case should be put against an accused. In that case, the sum of £115 cash seized from F, at the time of his arrest, was admitted in evidence notwithstanding that the money was found four weeks after the last of three acts of supply alleged against him. The appellant denied that he was the person identified by police as being the man who appeared as the seller on video recordings. The seller gave his name as "Kareem". The appellant testified that he never used that name. The judge allowed the prosecution to adduce evidence in rebuttal of an occasion, prior to the alleged acts of supply, when the appellant spoke to an officer calling himself "Kareem". This dramatically altered the nature of the case against the appellant. The cash had no relevance to the three acts of supply that the jury had to consider, but the evidence came to support a much wider allegation. In short, the evidence and history of the trial rendered the conviction unsafe.

(b) Problems associated with possession with intent to supply

A charge of possession with intent to supply contrary to section 5(3) of the MDA 1971 can give rise to particular difficulties because the charge may be appropriate to cover four very different situations: (i) the defendant is in possession of the drug as part of his stock-in-trade of a business which has been trading for some time; (ii) the defendant was about to embark on the venture to supply for the first time; (iii) the defendant was in possession of the drug intending to distribute it to persons who each made a financial contribution to the pool and (iv) the defendant was in possession of the drug as a mere custodian intending that it should be kept safe and then returned. **11–59**

Money and paraphernalia, found in the defendant's possession may be relevant in one situation and not in another but it may not be until well into the trial that the judge is able to gauge for himself whether the evidence is relevant and probative. If objection is taken, by the defence, to money or paraphernalia being admitted in evidence, the defence will have to make a judgment as to whether to disclose explanations which the accused may be proposing to give about that evidence. Sometimes an explanation appears on the face of the prosecution papers but usually it does not or it is impossible to tell whether an explanation is credible. In *Morris*, evidence was admitted of money and a notebook found in M's possession at the time of her arrest by the time the judge summed the case up to the jury he seems to have indicated that the evidence was peripheral if not irrelevant. In *Gordon*, a simple case was "swamped with superfluous, irrelevant and eventually prejudicial issues". Each case will turn on its own facts. In *Evans (Martin)* (July 11, 1997), it was held that money in the possession of an accused, whether as cash sums or in accounts might be relevant to the issue as to whether drugs were intended for supply or not. The judge had ruled that the defendant's admission that he had over £6,000 in a bank account was admissible in evidence. The Court of Appeal quashed the conviction and substituted a conviction of simple possession, on the grounds that if the evidence was admissible at all it could only be as to past drug dealing and not current dealing. On the facts of the case, the evidence ought not to have been admitted.

Henry L.J. was therefore right to say that the judge "cannot in advance know what evidence is or will be prejudicial to the defendant" and he advised that the judge should "ascertain in advance what the prosecution **11–60** case is and how the defence propose to meet it". The first enquiry is unlikely to meet with resistance but the second enquiry is less straightforward although Henry L.J. added that the judge "should not be too easily deterred by non-co-operation from the defence in this process". From a judicial perspective, this statement is pragmatic but is does give rise to issues, beyond the scope of this book, as to how a trial should be managed and conducted. An increasing number of disputes as to the admissibility of evidence are being resolved by *voire dire* and it may be that the admissibility of money and paraphernalia could be dealt with in this fashion.

III. Evidence of Informers and Observation Posts

11–61 There has been much discussion as to the extent to which officers may be permitted not to give evidence that would or might disclose the identity of informers or the whereabouts of observation posts or matters relating to surveillance. The general rule, in relation to informers, is clear: a witness may not be asked, and he will not be allowed to disclose, the channels through which information has been obtained by the law enforcement agencies: *Marks v. Beyfus* (1890) 25 Q.B.D. 494, *Hallett* [1986] Crim.L.R. 462, and see *Savage v. Chief Constable of Hampshire* [1997] 2 All E.R. 631, but see *Reilly* [1994] Crim. L.R. 279 where the Court of Appeal quashed a conviction for an offence under section 170(2) CEMA because disclosure as to whether a particular person was an informer, or not, was vital: *cf. Pattemore* [1994] Crim. L.R. 836. This rule was extended in *Rankine* [1986] Q.B. 861 to observation posts in circumstances where disclosure will "embarrass [the officers'] sources of co-operation [and] imperil person or persons from whom they had co-operation into the affording of the vantage point".

It will be noted that the rule in *Rankine* is founded not upon the disclosure of the observation post or vehicle itself, but upon the need to protect the owner or occupier of the premises or the vehicle in question. The rule is therefore designed to protect individuals and not operational efficacy: see *Brown* (1982) 87 Cr.App.R. 52.

11–62 In each case ("informers" and "observation posts") there is an exception to the general rule, namely, where disclosure is necessary to avoid a miscarriage of justice (see *Rankine*, also *Slowcombe* [1991] Crim.L.R. 198 and see *Vaillencourt* [1993] Crim. L.R. 311); or where the evidence is necessary to show the innocence of the accused: *Marks v. Beyfus* (1890) (above); *D v. NSPCC* [1978] A.C. 171; *Rogers v. Home Secretary* [1973] A.C. 388, HL.

In *Johnson* [1988] 1 W.L.R. 1377 the Court of Appeal gave guidance on the evidence to be given during a *voire dire* to determine whether the information (albeit relevant) should be withheld or disclosed. The judge must then balance the interests of the defence and the interests of the prosecution as well as the interests of informers, owners or occupiers who may be affected by disclosure. In *Hewitt and Davis* (1992) 95 Crim.L.R. 81, submissions that the cases of *Johnson, Brown* and *Rankine* were wrongly decided, were rejected: and see *Brown, Robson and Wilson* (November 25, 1991, unreported) and see *Blake v. DPP* [1993] Crim. L.R. 283 and *Grimes* [1994] Crim. L.R. 213. For a relatively recent, but interesting, review of the rules relating to disclosure and the balancing exercise often required to be carried out by trial judges, see *Yirtici* (July 12, 1996) and *Yirtici No. 2* (July 18, 1997) and note the impact of *Johnson, Davis and Rowe* (March 29, 1999, CA); *Rowe and Davis* (2000) 30 EHRR 1; and *Smith* (December 5, 2000, CA).

C. PROVING PREMISES ARE USED FOR SUPPLYING

The presence of drugs on premises, particularly if separately wrapped; 11–63
the existence of drug paraphernalia consistent with the commercial supply of drugs; large sums of money; cutting agents; books and records may all be relied upon in appropriate cases to prove that premises are being used for the purposes of supplying drugs. The evidence, if relevant, may or may not go one step further and prove that the defendant himself was engaged in supplying: see *Morrison v. Smith*, 1983 S.C.C.R. 171.

The distinction between adducing evidence to prove (i) that the premises were used to supply drugs, and (ii) proving that the defendant himself was a supplier, may or may not be significant depending on one's interpretation of an unsatisfactory line of authority culminating in the decision of the House of Lords in *Kearley* (1992) 95 Cr.App.R. 88.

In a considerable number of drug trafficking prosecutions, the "high point" has been evidence of surveillance, carried out by police officers in respect of the number of visitors calling at the premises; the movement of such visitors; their conversations, and even details of telephone calls made to the occupiers enquiring about drugs.

In cases where it is not possible for the prosecution to call the visitors or telephone callers as witnesses, the question arises whether the observing police officers may give evidence of (i) the number of visitors arriving and leaving the premises, and (ii) statements made by callers enquiring about the purchase of drugs. The objection to the admissibility of such evidence is that it infringes the hearsay rule.

I. Proving Visits

Evidence of observation describing the movement of persons visiting or 11–64
leaving the premises is admissible if relevant and probative of any fact in issue in the proceedings. The hearsay rule has no application since the evidence is adduced to prove no more than the fact that the visits have taken place and not to implicitly assert that the visits were drug-related. Usually there will be other surrounding circumstances that may give such visits

probative significance, *e.g.* the presence of drugs, drug paraphernalia and cash on the premises.

II. Requests Made for Drugs

11–65 This has proved to be a far more difficult problem. Police may have overheard visitors or telephone callers enquiring whether drugs are available for sale and negotiating a price. The callers themselves may not be willing to give evidence of their association with the premises or with the accused.

The general rule is well established and clearly stated by the Privy Council in *Subramaniam v. Public Prosecutor* [1956] 1 W.L.R. 965, 969:

Evidence of a statement made to a witness by a person who is not called as a witness may or may not be hearsay. It is hearsay and inadmissible when the object of the evidence is to establish the truth of what is contained in the statement. It is not hearsay and is admissible when it is proposed to establish by evidence, not the truth of the statement, but the fact that it was made.

11–66 The distinction between a statement being admissible because it was made, but inadmissible as to its truth, is sometimes so fine as to be illogical. The significance of the statement being made often depends on the truth of its content. There will be cases where what matters is not what was said but how it was said. Thus, the fact that words were spoken in a distressed fashion may make conversation recorded by a third party admissible: *Ratten v. R.* [1972] A.C. 378. In that case it was said: "A question of hearsay only arises when the words spoken are relied on 'testimonially', *i.e.* as establishing some fact narrated by the words": *per* Lord Wilberforce at 387.

Similar reasoning is said to explain the decision in *Woodhouse v. Hall* (1980) 72 Cr.App.R. 39. In that case, the question was whether a massage parlour was in fact a brothel. Police officers were offered "hand relief" by the ladies at the premises. The Divisional Court held that the evidence of the officers as to what they had heard was admissible and did not infringe the hearsay rule. Donaldson L.J. (as he then was) said that the offers were not a matter of truth or falsity but a matter of what was really said. The evidence was held to be admissible to prove that the premises were in fact being used for immoral purposes.

11–67 With respect, it is difficult to see how the offers made by the ladies could have the significance attached to them by the Divisional Court without reference to their truth or falsity. If they were a joke, they could hardly prove that the premises were being used as a brothel.

In *Kearley* (1991) 93 Cr.App.R. 222, the Court of Appeal applied *Woodhouse v. Hall*. In *Kearley*, the appellant was convicted of possessing amphetamine with intent to supply it. Police raided the appellant's home. However, at the time of the raid the appellant was absent. A number of telephone calls had been made to his home which had been answered by the police in which the caller had enquired whether he could speak to "Chippie" (the appellant's nickname) and asked to be supplied with controlled drugs. The requests were therefore not spoken in the presence or hearing of the appellant and were not made by persons called as witnesses.

The Court of Appeal held that the requests were admissible (and were not hearsay) to prove that the premises were used to supply controlled drugs. The reasoning of *Woodhouse v. Hall* was applied in this regard. However, the Court of Appeal went further and held that the evidence was admissible to prove that the appellant himself was the supplier. The Court of Appeal held that if the evidence was admissible to prove the fact that the premises were used to supply drugs then it was admissible to prove that the appellant was the supplier.

Again, it is difficult to see how this latter step can be arrived at without 11–68 reference to the truth or falsity of the statements themselves. The makers of those utterances were not available for cross-examination.

The House of Lords ((1992) 95 Cr.App.R. 88), reversed the decision of the Court of Appeal in *Kearley* but the certified question was confined to whether the evidence may be added "for the purpose of inviting the jury to draw an inference from the fact that the words were spoken (namely that the defendant was a supplier of drugs)", (emphasis supplied).

It follows that the House of Lords was not invited to consider whether the fact that such requests were made was evidence that the premises were used for the purpose of supplying drugs.

A majority of their Lordships (Lord Griffiths and Lord Browne-Wilkinson dissented) held that the requests were inadmissible for the purposes set out in the certified question for two separate reasons. First, they were irrelevant. The requests went to the maker's state of mind but that was not an issue in the case. The content of the statements relied upon did not assert that the appellant had previously engaged in drug supplying to any of the callers in question. Secondly, the hearsay rule was infringed. The request was made in a form that contained an assertion that the premises were being used as a course of supply of drugs and that the supplier was the appellant. What the prosecution therefore sought to do was to rely on the requests as evidence of the truth of the proposition asserted.

It is submitted that the decision of the majority of their Lordships in the 11–69 House of Lords in *Kearley* is correct. Their Lordships regarded the facts in *Woodhouse v. Hall* as amounting to "original" and not hearsay evidence.

Ironically, perhaps, the decision of the Court of Appeal in *Kearley* sought to address some of the criticism levelled at another decision of that court in *Harry (D.)* (1988) 86 Cr.App.R. 105 in which it was held that evidence as to the content of telephone calls enquiring whether drugs were for sale, and asking for P by his nickname, was inadmissible on the grounds that the evidence was sought to be relied upon to establish some facts narrated by the words used. The sole question in *Harry* was whether the appellant could rely on the telephone calls to prove that the supplier of the drugs was his co-defendant and not himself. Lawton L.J. said (at 11):

"He was seeking to rely upon the contents of the telephone calls not to prove their purpose but to establish his case that it was the co-accused and not he who was doing the drug dealing on the premises."

11–70 In other words, if the appellant had sought to rely on the content of the calls to "prove their purpose", namely that the premises were being used to supply drugs, then the content would have been admissible: see *Subramaniam v. Public Prosecutor* [1956] 1 W.L.R. 965, 970; *Ratten* [1972] A.C. 378; *Woodhouse v. Hall* (above); *Davidson v. Quirke* (1923) N.Z.L.R. 552 and *McGregor v. Stokes* [1952] V.L.R. 347. In *Harry*, it was common ground that the premises were being so used and so that particular issue did not arise. In the opinion of the Court, the appellant sought to cross the line between what is admissible or inadmissible, by relying on the content of the conversations to show that the co-defendant was the supplier. The main criticism of this part of the decision in *Harry* is that the distinction drawn by the Court of Appeal in that case simply does not exist because the identity of the recipient of the calls is all part and parcel of the same purpose: see D.J. Birch's commentary on *Harry* [1987] Crim.L.R. 325.

Reform of the hearsay rules in criminal proceedings has been the subject of detailed scrutiny by the Law Commission (*Evidence in Criminal Proceedings: Hearsay and Related Topics*; Paper No. 138; 1995). The Commission point out that the callers' words in *Kearley* "were covered by the hearsay rule as being implied assertions" (para. 2.25). Their provisional conclusion is that the hearsay rule should be reformulated as follows (para. 9.36):

"... an assertion other than one made by a person while giving evidence in the proceedings is inadmissible as evidence of any fact or again that the person intended to assert" [see the definition of hearsay offered by Professor Cross, *Cross on Evidence*, 8th ed., p.46 on which the revised formula is based: and see *Sharp* [1988] 1 W.L.R. 7.]

11–71 The effect of the revised formula would be to exclude implied assertions (sometimes known as "inferred assertions") and to that extent, the decision in *Kearley* would be reversed. Putting the formula into practice may not be straightforward in many cases because the courts will be confronted with the problem of establishing whether there really was an "intention to assert" on the part of the maker of the statement.

In *Rothwell* (1994) 99 Cr. App. R. 388 R was convicted of offences of supplying heroin: Police observed R passing wraps to other persons. An officer testified that four of the recipients were known to him as heroin users. The defence submitted that the officers' evidence was hearsay and inadmissible.

Held: the officer did not have direct personal knowledge that the four persons were heroin users and therefore that part of his evidence should have been excluded. However, the proviso would be applied.

11–72 The Court of Appeal held that the evidence of the officer was potentially admissible "from the point of view of relevance" because it demonstrated the character of the transactions and was capable of rebutting an assertion that the transactions were either totally innocent or non-drug-related.

> In *Warner* (1993) 96 Cr. App. R. 324, police observed a number of visitors attending the address of one of the appellants from where it was alleged acts of supplying took place. The prosecution were permitted by the Court to introduce evidence of convictions for possessing or dealing in heroin in respect of eight visitors, under PACE, s.74. On appeal, it was submitted that the evidence of the visitors related solely to the state of mind of the persons attending the premises and was not relevant to the intentions of the appellants (see *Kearley*).
>
> *Held*: the evidence went to the character of the persons attending the house and therefore "no element of hearsay was involved". Accordingly, in *Rothwell*, the evidence of the officer fell into a similar category and again no element of hearsay was involved.

Presumably, the contention advanced on behalf of the appellants in both *Warner* and *Rothwell* was to the effect that evidence that the visitors had a history of drug use concealed an assertion that the appellants were present on the premises supplying or intending to supply drugs. In *Kearley* it was the conduct of the caller which gave rise to the implied assertions which were held to be inadmissible hearsay whereas, in *Warner* and *Rothwell*, the distinction appears to be that evidence as to the character of visitors is a matter of fact from which the character of the transaction in question can be inferred. This step does not involve an element of hearsay.

The fact that a person with whom the accused is associated is a user of controlled drugs or a drug trafficker may be established by proving convictions pursuant to PACE, s. 74 (*Warner*, and see *Aziz* [1996] 1 A.C. 41), or by direct personal knowledge of a third party. It was this obstacle that proved to be insurmountable in *Rothwell* because the officer relied upon information given to him by others (and general reputation) but the evidence offended the hearsay rule. Accordingly, the Court gave the following guidance (at 394): 11–73

> "Where the prosecution wish to lead evidence of this kind and objection is taken by the defence, the judge should inquire into the basis of the prosecution witness's evidence that the alleged recipient of the package from the defendant is a known user of the drug specified in the charge of unlawfully supplying the drug. If the basis turns out to be statements made to the witness by others, including the alleged recipient, then the evidence should not be admitted. If the prosecution witness's statement is based on the alleged recipient's convictions for possession of the specified drug, or, for example, observation of hypodermic needle marks on the alleged recipient's forearms, or on the fact that the prosecution witness had first hand knowledge of the alleged recipient being in possession of the drug, or receiving treatment for addiction to the drug, then the evidence is not hearsay and can be

admitted, subject to the Court's discretion, under section 78(1) of the 1984 Act. Convictions for possession of the drug specified in the charge will be admissible under section 74 of the Act, again subject to the judge's discretion under section 78.

In this second situation, the defence may well prefer that no reference to the convictions of the alleged recipient be made by the prosecution witness in his evidence in chief, so that prejudice to the defendant is minimised. No doubt the prosecution would assent to such a course, with the reservation that if the witness's statement were to be challenged in cross-examination the witness would then be able to refer to the conviction as forming the basis, or part of the basis, of his assertion." The trial judge relied on *Bryan* (unreported, November 8, 1984) . . . in which it was said that police officers "being on the streets and with their knowledge and meeting those having a drug problem . . . can give evidence of fact of what takes place on many occasions on the streets."

11–74 However, evidence of a suspicion that a person is a user or a dealer is not enough.

In *Coulson (Jason Lee)* (March 26, 1997) police stopped C shortly after he was seen to leave a house, and found him in possession of 4.31 grams of heroin in 13 wrapped packages. The trial judge declined to admit evidence that the police suspected that the occupier of the premises was a drug supplier. C's defence to a charge under section 5(3) was that the drug was for his consumption. The decision of the judge was correct. A suspicion was not evidence of a fact and an admission could only be made under section 10 of the Criminal Justice Act 1967. The appeal was allowed on other grounds.

The extent to which expert opinion is admissible, even if it incorporates elements of hearsay, it not straightforward but the reasoning of the Court in *Rothwell* may include the proposition that evidence that a visitor is a known drug user or supplier is not a matter of expert evidence at all and any person may give relevant evidence about facts of which they have direct personal knowledge and to this extent *Bryan* is not entirely helpful.

11–75 In Scotland, a rather different approach is taken. Thus, in *Forsyth v. H.M. Advocate*, 1992 S.L.T. 189, police officers observed two persons, whom the police knew had convictions for drug offences, in the company of the two defendants. It was held that there was a risk of unfairness in admitting the evidence because no notice had been given to the defence that the evidence was to be adduced. However, in *Craig v. H.M. Advocate*, 1993 S.L.T. 483 the High Court of Justiciary declined to uphold an appeal against convictions for offences committed under section 4(3)(b) and section 5(2) MDA where an officer was asked in evidence about his knowledge of names recorded in a notebook found at the defendant's house, and to state whether any of the names were known drug dealers. The defence complained that the evidence was speculative and should have been excluded because the officer could not say whether the names recorded were the same persons that he had in mind as drug dealers. The Court held that it was for the jury to determine what, if anything, they made of that evidence and whether the names or nicknames were the same persons that the officer had in mind or whether the names were mere coincidence. As *Rothwell* makes clear, in England and Wales the prosecution would need to satisfy the Court that the officer had direct personal knowledge that the persons in question were drug dealers. Speculative evidence is discouraged: see *Gordon* [1995] Cr. App. R. 61.

D. EXPERT EVIDENCE

I. General Note

In the ordinary way parol evidence is not admissible in respect of matters which are not within the personal knowledge of the witness: hearsay evidence is inadmissible. Usually a witness may not express an opinion or belief but there exists a necessary exception in respect of witnesses who are able to express a credible opinion, empirically based, on specialised topics of learning or knowledge. 11–76

It is important to bear in mind that evidence of an expert may fall into two categories. The first relates to findings of fact made or discovered by him, *e.g.* that a substance is a controlled drug of a particular description: see *Hunt* [1987] A.C. 352. The second relates to an expression of opinion as to the probable results or consequences flowing from facts found or proved. Thus an expert may give evidence as to the amount of heroin found in the body of the deceased at the time of the autopsy and that the drug found was the sole or substantial cause of death: *Clarke* (January 21, 1992, unreported, 4101/W3/91).

Objection is sometimes taken to the admissibility of a conclusion, which is said to be less than probable. The basis of the objection is that any such conclusion is inherently unreliable, speculative and therefore worthless or, put another way, that its prejudicial effect outweighs its probative value. In the author's experience some judges conduct a *voire dire* to determine admissibility and to seek clarification from the expert as to his findings and conclusions: and see *Ward* (1993) 96 Cr. App. R.1.

The duty of experts has been said to be the duty: 11–77

> "... to furnish the judge or jury with the necessary scientific criteria for testing the accuracy of their conclusions, so as to enable the judge or jury to form their own independent judgment by the application of these criteria to the facts proved in evidence": *Davie v. Edinburgh Magistrates*, 1953 S.C. 35, 40.

Laudable though these sentiments are, the performance of this duty is easier said than done. Some conclusions will depend on complicated tests, or a series of tests. The results may require interpretation by an expert, which, in turn may be difficult to explain to lay persons in a court. In practice, and where the conclusion or method of analysis is in dispute, the expert will tend to summarise techniques employed and to rely on models, photographs and diagrammatic representations to explain the basis for his findings and conclusions.

11–78 An interesting problem arose in *Matadeen and Peebles* in which his Honour Judge Dr Peter Jackson provided an interesting ruling, and one of practical importance (Southwark Crown Court, January 25, 2001):

> The defendants were charged with the unlawful possession of 10.155 grams of cocaine, and 51 ecstasy tablets, with intent to supply, contrary to section 5(3) Misuse of Drugs Act 1971. The defendants admitted possessing both substances for their own use. The prosecution called a member of the local drug squad (with at least three years' experience) competent to give expert evidence about the street price of controlled drugs, the "cutting" of cocaine, the "cutting agents" used, and the motifs found on Ecstasy tablets. Under cross-examination, the officer was asked about a user's typical rate of consumption of ecstasy tablets. In answer to the judge, the officer admitted that he was now "at the edge of his knowledge". The learned judge noted that the witness was based at the police station where other officers were conducting their investigation into the activities of the defendants.
>
> *Held*:
>
> (1) that, on the authorities, the officer was competent to give expert evidence in drug matters, but his expertise was at a low level, and probably limited to an area of London where he had spent the whole of his police service.
>
> (2) that, on the facts, the officer was not a competent witness regarding the consumption of Ecstasy tablets.
>
> (3) that, in any event, the fact that the officer came from the same police station as the investigating officers, undermined the appearance of fairness in the proceedings, when the officer purported to give independent expert evidence. The integrity of the officer was not in doubt but note *Gokal* (March 11, 1999, CA).
>
> (4) that, in the circumstances, the rights of the defendants under Article 6(1) had been breached, and the trial had been rendered unfair. The jury was discharged and a retrial ordered. The defendants were subsequently acquitted.

11–79 The ruling was founded on a concession, made by all counsel, that a police officer is competent to give expert evidence provided he has the necessary expertise, and he is impartial (for example, see *Bryan*, November 8, 1984, unreported, *Brown*, (May 19, 1988, unreported), and see *Barry (John)* (July 30, 1996)). However, in the submission of the defence, Article 6 provided an additional requirement namely, that the expert has *the appearance* of impartiality and independence. This requirement might well not exist if the expert is a police officer closely connected with the investigation. The learned judge accepted that submission. In the instant case, the officer had interviewed one of the defendants.

It would be very easy to brush this decision aside, as one decided on its own facts, but the ruling does raise important issues of principle as to the way expert evidence is traditionally obtained, and used, in our adversarial criminal justice process. Legitimate concerns have been voiced by a number of commentators (and judges) about the training, accreditation, and use, of persons holding themselves out as experts. The decision does, of course, leave a number of important questions unanswered. Would the proposed testimony of *any* police officer called by the prosecution to give expert evidence fall foul of Article 6(1) on the grounds that his very occupation would give the trial the appearance of unfairness? If the answer were "yes", the fall-out would be far reaching. For example, the evidence of an experienced road traffic officer concerning the cause of a motor vehicle accident would be susceptible to proper challenge under Article 6(1). What about experts (whether police officers or not) who tend to give evidence repeatedly for the prosecution or for the defence? Would their evidence also be challengeable under Article 6(1)? The ruling of the judge attempts to draw a line at the point where the "police expert" is closely connected with the investigation. At that point, his/her evidence might be challengeable under Article 6.

II. Qualifications of an Expert

As Bingham L.J. remarked in *Robb* (1991) 93 Cr.App.R. 161 a defendant could not fairly be asked to meet evidence of opinion given by "a quack, a charlatan, or even an enthusiastic amateur". 11–80

It is a matter for the Court to decide on the facts of a particular case whether a witness has sufficient "expertise" to give the evidence sought to be adduced. See *Bonython* (1984) 38 S.A.A.R. 45 for a useful summary of the relevant considerations, and see *Stockwell* (1993) 97 Cr. App. R. 260 and *Fenton* (April 23, 1998). There is no logical reason why an "enthusiastic amateur" should not be an expert, providing that he or she has the necessary expertise. Experienced members of the "drug squad" may give expert evidence as to the street value of a drug. In *Bryan*, (November 8, 1984, unreported; 3923B84) the Court of Appeal held that the evidence of a Drug Squad officer with experience of street dealing is admissible as to the fact of what happens on the street. He was therefore entitled to give evidence of the street value of drugs. However, this was not a matter for a pharmacist who would probably have less information concerning black market prices than a Drug Squad officer would. Wood J. said:

> "The view of this court is that police officers with their expertise of dealing with these problems, being on the streets and with their knowledge and meeting those having a drug problem and those pushing drugs, have a very wide experience and can give evidence of fact of what takes place on many occasions on the streets."

In *White v. H.M. Advocate*, 1986 S.C.C.R. 224, a Drug Squad officer was permitted to give evidence that (i) LSD was a social drug and not an addictive drug; (ii) that "trips" may be pleasant or awful; and (iii) that 25 squares of LSD would not be taken by a user within a fortnight.

Held: the evidence was rightly admitted "provided such a witness' qualification as a police officer and his experience in the Drug Squad are first established, such evidence is clearly competent.

11–81 In *Brown*, (May 19, 1988, unreported) officers observed B supplying packets of what appeared to be cannabis but none of the officers seized any of the packets. An officer of 20 years' experience gave evidence as to the description of cannabis and cannabis resin and its street value. The Court held, following Bryan, that this part of the officer's evidence was admissible but the officer also gave evidence about drugs recovered from persons other than B. This was not expert evidence and the Court held that it ought not to have been admitted because it "tended to put this particular defendant in a criminal scenario giving rise to the possibility that he might be convicted by association rather than admissible evidence". Evidence had also been given of a large number of other persons at the club doing "very much the same thing as Mr. Brown". That evidence was also held to be inadmissible:

> "The man who was being prosecuted on this occasion was the appellant Brown and the evidence which ought to have been admitted be it factual or of opinion, ought to have been limited to evidence which was relevant to Brown and Brown alone."

Again, in *Barry (John)* (July 30, 1996), a police officer gave expert evidence at the trial of his interpretation of a large quantity of handwritten notes that, on his analysis, were plainly referable to B's drug trafficking activities. The notes consisted of names, prices, abbreviations, and what purported to be references to items of clothing and footwear. The officer gave evidence that most of the values that purported to be prices could be shown to be consistent with drugs being purchased in particular quantities. In dismissing the appeal against conviction, the Court of Appeal held that it was appropriate for the jury to be given assistance by someone of the officer's knowledge and expertise of drug trafficking matters as to what the notes meant in order to avoid speculation and to rebut the defendant's explanation.

11–82 However, by contrast, in *Jeffries* (March 10, 1997), J was convicted of offences concerning the supply of amphetamines. In addition to the existence of amphetamine and paraphernalia at J's flat, police found lists. An officer testified that "in my opinion, the list . . . relates to the sale of drugs, and lists such as these are commonly found at the home addresses of drugs dealers". The judge rejected a submission that this evidence was inadmissible. The Court of Appeal held that although the witness had the expertise to give evidence of her knowledge of drug-related offences, including the value of drugs and the type of article one would expect to find in the possession of a drug dealer, her opinion that the list related to the sale of drugs was inadmissible: it amounted to an opinion that D was guilty of the offence with which he was charged, and the convictions were quashed.

Again, in *Squires v. CPS* (July 19, 1999, Divisional Court) S was convicted of possessing a piece of cannabis resin the size of a 10p coin. The substance was found in the jeans that S had been wearing at the time of the search. S denied knowledge of the existence of the substance. At the summary hearing, an officer testified that she was not a specialist drugs officer, but she had seen cannabis before during her five years' experience as a police officer. She found an unwrapped, brown, resinous substance that she "thought" was cannabis resin. The substance was not produced in court. Forbes J. said "the fact that the officer 'thought' that the substance was cannabis resin is not sufficient for the purposes of achieving the standard of proof required in a criminal case, whether the matter is considered at the end of the prosecution's case on a prima facie basis, or at the conclusion of the trial". And see *Watts (Peter)* (May 8, 2000, CA)

Where so-called "dealer lists" are admitted in evidence, the jury must be 11–83 carefully directed. Thus, in *Lovelock* (May 8, 1997) L was convicted of possession of controlled drugs with intent to supply. Among the items in D's possession was a document containing jottings of names and amounts. It was submitted that the judge failed to direct the jury adequately concerning the relevance of the document. The Court of Appeal stressed that if such material is to be admitted then there must be a careful direction about the relevance of the document, demonstrating future intent to supply drugs and not merely past drug dealings. The authorities dealing with sums of money in a defendant's possession were applicable to documentary evidence such as the sheet of jottings (and see *Chubb* (February 20, 1998).

An officer or forensic scientist may give evidence as to the methods by which drugs may be imported (*Wilson v. H.M. Advocate*, 1988 S.C.C.R. 384) or the hallmarks of a person in possession of drugs with intent to supply having regard to the quantity of drugs involved and the method adopted to prepare and package the drugs for supply: *McJimpsey v. H.M. Advocate*, 1995 G.W.D. 771.

Where the defence have obtained a report from an expert that contains 11–84 material adverse to the defendant's case, there is always a risk that the circumstances in which the report was obtained might result in the contents being used by the prosecution (normally by the prosecution calling the expert themselves). However, an interesting situation arose in *Coker* (December 8, 1997).

> In *Coker*, C was convicted of possessing 7.32 grams crack cocaine, with intent to supply. The drug was found in 10 small bags and when strip-searched, C was found to have a quantity of heroin on him. A police officer gave expert evidence that the total value of the cocaine and heroin was around £1,100. He agreed in cross-examination that the value of the cocaine might be only £200. In evidence, C said that

he was an addict and he purchased the cocaine for £200. An expert, instructed on C's behalf to prepare a report as to the value of the drugs, put the value at about £580 to £880. In the event, he was not called to give evidence. The prosecution were therefore granted leave to ask C in cross-examination (i) whether an expert report had been prepared for the defence; (ii) whether C agreed with the valuation of £580–£880. On appeal, it was submitted that the judge should not have permitted the questions to be asked. The Court of Appeal held that the first question was impermissible. Cases could arise where in order to obtain a full picture the jury might be told that the defence was in possession of expert advice. This could however be done by formal admission and this was not such a case. As to the second question, C was simply asked, against the background of the report, what he thought was the value of the cocaine. In the circumstances, the appeal would be dismissed.

Practitioners would be well advised to consider very carefully the implications of providing an expert with a copy of the accused's proof of evidence. An expert's report that contains conclusions based, even in part, on information derived from the accused's proof/statement (to his legal advisers) might give rise to arguments as to whether privilege has thus been waived.

In cases where an expert is called, it is important that the judge should make clear to the jury that they are not bound by the expert's opinion and that the issue is ultimately a matter for the jury to determine: see *Stockwell* (above), and see *Fitzpatrick (Gerald)* (February 11, 1999).

III. Sources of Information Used by Experts

11–85 Experts often give evidence of findings and conclusions even if the various tests employed (and results obtained) were carried out by laboratory technicians who are not called as supporting witnesses. Usually an expert will say that he supervised delegated tasks and so pre-empt objection that the evidence of an expert is founded on hearsay. However, expert knowledge is often empirically acquired and based on the researches of others. Accordingly, there is ample authority for the proposition that experts are entitled to rely on textbooks, materials and the experiments of others: see *Somers* [1963] 1 W.L.R. 1306.

Drug Squad officers are permitted (and have been for many years) to give evidence as to the street value and the rate and method of consumption of a particular drug: see *Bryan* (above). The source of the information may derive from data collated by the NCIS which, in turn, may have been derived from answers given by arrested persons to the police; see also *Patel* [1987] Crim.L.R. 839 and *Afzal*, *The Times*, June 25, 1991. The officer may well be able to add his own experiences to support the opinion he expresses. The complaint that such evidence infringes the hearsay rule has been advanced on a number of occasions at first instance but there is not one reported authority in which that complaint has been upheld and see *Wilson v. H.M. Advocate*, 1988 S.C.C.R. 38.

In *Wilson v. H.M. Advocate*, 1988 S.C.C.R. 384, Drug Squad officers and forensic scientists gave evidence that cannabis resin in the form of cannabis oil was commonly illegally imported into the United Kingdom from Morocco via Spain by putting it inside a condom or a balloon and secreting this capsule internally. The basis of this knowledge was acquired, in the course of their respective duties by attending seminars and by discussing drug enforcement questions with officers of the customs and excise.

Held: the submission that this evidence was hearsay and should not have been admitted was rejected. The Lord Justice-General said:

"... It appears to us that the evidence given by the drug squad officers and the forensic scientists could be described as simply disclosure of the received wisdom of persons concerned in drug enforcement, wisdom which they were bound to have picked up in various ways in order that they might perform their duties" ...
and see *Bryan*, (above)."

It will be noted that the Court did not deal head-on with the issue as to why the evidence was not inadmissible as being contrary to the hearsay rule. However, the answer to this question is already covered by authority. **11–86**

In *Abadom* [1983] 1 W.L.R. 126 fragments of glass were found embedded in the shoes of the appellant. One forensic expert ("X") gave evidence that the glass found on the shoes, and glass taken from a window at the scene of a robbery, were subjected to chemical analysis and were "similar on analysis". A second expert ("Y") measured the refractive index of both samples, which was found to be identical. "Y" concluded that the glass from the shoes originated from the window. He based his conclusion on the findings of himself, and "X", but also on statistics compiled by the Home Office Control Research Establishment, which showed that the refractive index in question occurred in only four per cent of all analyses, which had been made. On appeal it was argued that the evidence, founded on the Home Office data, was hearsay and therefore inadmissible.

Held: the evidence was not hearsay. In dismissing the appeal, the Court of Appeal explained the basis of admissibility in terms of cogency and the role of the expert.

Thus, it was said that the expert:

"... must be entitled to draw upon material produced by others in the field in which their expertise lies. Indeed, it is part of their duty to consider (such material) and not to draw conclusions merely on the basis of their own experience, which is inevitably likely to be more limited that the general body of information which may be available to them the statistical results of the work of others in the same field must inevitably form an important ingredient in the cogency or probative value of his own conclusion in the particular case."

11–87 The Court of Appeal made it plain that where an expert relies on the existence or non-existence of primary facts, which are basic to the conclusion reached by the expert, then those facts must be proved by admissible evidence. If "Y" had not himself determined the refractive index it would have been necessary to call the person who had done so before "Y" could have expressed any opinion based on their determination (see the judgment of Kerr L.J. at 52): and see *Jackson* [1996] 2 Cr. App. R. 420, and *English Exporters v. Eldonwall* [1973] Ch. 415; *Turner* [1975] 1 Q.B. 834; *Somers* [1963] 1 W.L.R. 1306; *Crayden* (1978) 67 Cr.App.R.1. In *Golizadeh* [1995] Crim. L.R. 232, it was held that in almost every case in which an expert gave evidence, he would rely on the work of assistants or on the result of machines. Where a machine is used so that an opinion is derived partly from the results of that equipment, the evidence is not hearsay because it still amounted to an expert opinion on data considered by the expert and by way of his expertise in interpreting the results of the analysis.

For the position in Scotland see *O'Brien v. H.M. Advocate*, 1996 S.C.C.R. 1177, where the rules appear to be less strict.

IV. Weight and Reliability

11–88 As has been mentioned above, whether a particular witness has the necessary "expertise" before he may be permitted to give evidence of an opinion, is a matter for the Court to determine on the facts of each case. Once that criterion is met then evidence of opinion may be admissible even if the expert relied on a technique which was accepted by the majority of professional opinion to be unreliable unless supplemented or verified by other methods: see *Robb* (1991) 93 Cr.App.R. 161. In that case, evidence was admitted of voice identification notwithstanding the questioned technique employed by the expert. Presumably the Court had in mind the general rule that relevant evidence which is more probative than prejudicial is admissible and that, thereafter, the weight to be attached to the evidence is a matter for the tribunal of fact and that it is open to the other party to the proceedings to adduce their own expert evidence in rebuttal.

To what extent inherently unreliable evidence can properly be said to be probative evidence at all has not been definitively decided by any appellate court. Plainly, evidence which is inherently unreliable, may be inadmissible because its prejudicial effect outweighs its probative value or because it ought to be excluded under section 78 of PACE 1984: see *Deenik* [1992] Crim.L.R. 578 where the evidence of a customs officer who recognised the voice of the appellant during his detention as being the person to whom the officer had spoken on the telephone during a covert operation, was admissible and would not be excluded under section 78 of PACE 1984.

Schedule 2 to the Misuse of Drugs Act 1971 deals with matters of a technical nature and the words employed in that Schedule must be given the meaning attributed to them by a person qualified to understand such words: see *Couzens* [1992] Crim. L.R. 822.

V. Evidence of Voice Recognition

In *Deenik*, above, the appellant was convicted of the unlawful importa- 11–89
tion of 500 kilograms of cannabis resin packed in boxes and concealed in a lorry. An undercover customs officer spoke on the telephone to a man she had never met called "Lloyd". The appellant was arrested in a telephone kiosk and taken to an office of Customs and Excise. The officer who made the call was also at that office and recognised the voice of the appellant as being the person she spoke to on the telephone. Objection was taken to the admissibility of the evidence of voice recognition at the premises of Customs and Excise. In dismissing the appeal, the Court of Appeal held that here was no justification for the exclusion of the evidence under section 78 of PACE 1984 on the facts of that case. What was done was not unfair and nothing else could be done to reduce the chance of error; and see *Gummerson* (November 27, 1998), *Vincent* (November 23, 1998) and *Robb* (above) in which it was held that evidence of voice recognition was admissible notwithstanding that the test carried out by the analyst was called into question as being unreliable. See also *Hookway* (February 1, 1999) in relation to facial mapping.

VI. Effect of a Drug

As to the admissibility of expert evidence on the effect of certain drugs 11–90
on an individual, see *Skirving; Grossman* [1985] Q.B. 819.

VII. Use of Tracker Dogs

The use of tracker dogs in the investigation of crime is a daily occurrence 11–91
and has been so for many years. In *Pieterson and Holloway* [1995] 2 Cr.App.R. 11 (and see the commentary [1995] Crim. L.R. 404) the Court of Appeal gave guidance as to the admissibility of tracker dog evidence. In that case, a robbery had taken place during which stolen property was placed into a holdall. A tracker dog picked up scent from the scene of the crime to a location where a strap was found and which was identified by a witness as being part of the holdall she had seen. The rest of the holdall, with H's name in it, was found at P's address. The Court of Appeal held that if a dog handler could establish that the dog had been properly trained and the dog's reactions over time suggested that it could serve as a reliable

pointer to the existence of a scent of a particular person, then the evidence might be admitted but a proper foundation had to be laid by evidence in detail establishing the reliability of the dog in question, and the judge was required to direct the jury to look with circumspection at evidence of tracker dogs having regard to the fact that the dog might not always be reliable and could not be cross-examined.

E. INTERVIEWS

I. Interviews Conducted by Customs Officers

11–92 Doubt has sometimes been expressed as to whether the Codes of Practice made under section 66 of PACE1984 apply to customs officers. It would be a startling result if they did not. In *Sanusi* [1992] Crim.L.R. 43 it was pointed out that section 67(9) of P.ACE 1984 had the effect of placing a duty upon customs officers to observe the provisions of the Codes of Practice although PACE (Application to Customs & Excise) Order 1985 (S.I. 1985 No. 1800) did not specifically apply section 66 of PACE 1984 to the activities of customs officers: see Schedule 1 to S.I. 1985 No. 1800. On the facts in *Sanusi* there was a breach of Code C: 3.1 and C: 3.2 in not informing S of his rights and the interview in question ought to have been excluded: see also *Twaites* (1991) 92 Cr.App.R. 106 and see now *Okafor* 99 Cr.App.R. 97. In *Bailey* (March 17, 1992, unreported; Croydon Crown Court) the Court excluded answers given by a suspect to customs officers in circumstances where a caution should have been administered under Code C: 10.1 (obviously the old caution at that time) but which was not.

The definition of an "interview" has undergone some modification in recent years and no doubt there will be a steady stream of decisions as a result of changes made by the Criminal Justice and Public Order Act 1994 and the Revised Codes of Practice which have followed; see PACE 1984 (Codes of Practice) (No. 3) Order 1995, S.I. 1995 No. 450, followed by other revisions, namely, S.I. 1997 No 1159 and S.I. 1999 No. 291.

11–93 In 1985, the original Codes of Practice merely said, by way of Code C: 12A, that the purpose of any interview was "to obtain from the person concerned his explanation of the facts and not necessarily to obtain an admission". Many thought this was a reasonably concise guide as to the nature of an interview and in *Absolam* (1989) 88 Cr. App. R. 332, the Court held that even one question and answer could constitute an interview: and see *Cox* (1993) 96 Cr. App. R. 464; *Weeks* [1993] Crim. L. R. 769 and *Ward* [1994] 98 Cr. App. R. 337; but see also *Cohen* [1993] Crim. L. R. 768. However, in 1990, the Codes provided a definition of an interview (Note 11A) which drew a distinction between (i) questioning in order to obtain information or his explanation of the facts or questions confined to the proper and effective conduct of a search and (ii) questioning a person regarding his involvement or suspected involvement in a criminal offence.

Questioning in the first category was an interview but questions falling into the second category would amount to an interview. This was not an easy distinction to apply in practice and was criticised for that reason. Accordingly the 1995 Revised Codes limit the definition of an interview to the questioning of a person regarding his involvement or suspected involvement in a criminal office: Code C:11.1A. It will be seen that the definition of an interview has moved from being a "note for guidance" to part of the Codes. Accordingly, Note 11A is now marked "Not Used". It would therefore seem that the existing case law, which explains and clarifies the meaning of an interview, is still relevant. Any questioning of a suspect regarding his suspected involvement in the alleged offence is likely to constitute an "interview": see *Millar* [1998] Crim.L.R. 209.

Following a decision to arrest a person he must not be interviewed about the offence except at a police station (Code 11.1) and this is obviously important to afford both the police and the suspect appropriate safeguards provided under PACE (*e.g.* legal advice and tape recorded interviews): see *Goddard* [1994] Crim. L. R. 46; *Weedesteyn* [1995] Crim. L. R. 238; and see *Cox* 96 Cr. App. R. 464; see also *Aspinall* (January 29, 1999). Of course, under sections 34, 36 and 37 of the CJPO Act 1994 an officer may now ask questions to seek an explanation from the suspect regarding his suspected involvement in the offence (s. 34) or as to objects and marks found on his person (s. 36) or regarding his presence at a particular place (s. 37) subject to the appropriate caution being administered (see Codes 10.1 and 10.5); and see *Bowes* (March 13, 1998); *Daniel* (April 3, 1998); and *Hart* (April 23, 1998).

What is not clear is the extent to which an officer is now permitted to ask questions away from the police station. Alternatively, must the officer defer any questioning until the suspect is brought to the police station? It should be noted that questioning, in pursuance of section 36 and section 37 of the CJPO Act 1994, follows an arrest. Code 11.1 states that a suspect must not be interviewed except at a police station (and note PACE, s.30). By contrast, section 34 and Code C: 10.1 apply at any time before being charged (or on being charged) and this may include a time before the suspect is arrested. It remains to be seen to what extent cases such as *Okafor* (see below) remain good law. In *Khan* [1993] Crim. L. R. 54 it was held that the police and customs should not think that even if they were justified in delaying taking a suspect to the police station, in order to obtain his assistance during a search, they were entitled to ask a lengthy series of questions that ought to be asked where the relevant statutory provisions and codes applied. *Khan* should be read in the light of *Okafor*, below, and see *Joseph* [1993] Crim. L. R. 206. See also *Raphaie* [1996] Crim.L.R. 812 and *Maynard* (April 2, 1998). 11–94

Where a customs officer had reason to suspect that an offence had been committed, he must either avoid asking questions in relation to the offence or he must follow the provisions of the Code of Practice and administer a caution: *Okafor* (1994) 99 Cr.App.R. 97; and see *Oni* [1992] Crim. L.R. 183 and *Shah* [1994] Crim. L.R. 125 which held that having regard to the wording of Code 10.1, there must be grounds for suspicion before the officer is required to caution a suspect: a mere hunch or sixth sense would not suffice; see also *T and L* (November 30, 2000). In *Nelson and Rose* [1998] 2 Cr. App. R. 399, it was held that the proper time to administer the caution was when, objectively viewed, there were grounds for suspicion, falling short of a prima facie case, that an offence had been committed by the suspect. There was no conflict between section 78(2) of CEMA 1979, and Code C:10.1.

As to when it becomes appropriate to charge the suspect and to cease questioning see *Ioannov* (December 11, 1998).

II. Failure to Make Contemporaneous Note

11–95 In *White* [1991] Crim.L.R. 779, W was charged with possessing a Class B drug with intent to supply. A short conversation took place at W's house when the premises were searched. A note of the conversation was not made until the officer arrived at the police station. It was submitted that there were three breaches of the 1985 Code to PACE namely (1) no time was entered recording the end of the interview: Code C: 11.3(b)(i) (now Code C: 11.5(b)); (2) there was no contemporaneous note of the interview: Code C: 11.3(b)(ii) (now C: 11.5(c)); (3) no reason for non-completion of the interview was recorded: Code C: 11.6 (now C: 11.9).
Held: that in all the circumstances, and despite the three breaches, it was not unfair to admit the interview and accordingly the arguments for its exclusion under section 78 of PACE 1984 were rejected.

III. Unfairness/Oppression/Agent Provocateur

(a) Evidence obtained by way of a trick

11–96 In *Cadette* [1995] Crim.L.R. 229, X arrived at Heathrow Airport and was found with cocaine concealed in her clothing. X was ultimately acquitted of being knowingly concerned in the fraudulent evasion on the prohibition on the importation of a controlled drug. However, C's telephone number was found on X who agreed with officers to contact C and their conversation was tape-recorded. In dismissing C's appeal against conviction for the unlawful importation of the drug, the Court of Appeal held that the mere fact that evidence was obtained by subterfuge did not automatically lead to its exclusion: officers were not required to fight their opponents with one hand tied behind their backs. There is indeed ample authority that some tricks are permissible, particularly if the defendant is merely detected doing what he would do anyway despite the trick, *e.g.* selling stolen jewellery to a shady jeweller: see *Christou and Wright* (1992) 95 Cr.App.R. 264, or mis-spelling a particular word in terms unique to the defendant: see *Voisin* [1918] 1 K.B. 53, or speak incautiously *Ali Hussain* (1965) 49 Cr.App.R. 230, even when they are at a police station and could be overheard: *Mills and Rose* (1962) 46 Cr.App.R. 336, and see *Stewart* (1970) 54 Cr.App.R. 210; *Jelen and Katz* (1990) 90 Cr.App.R. 456; *Bailey and Smith* (1993) 97 Cr.App.R. 365 and note *Latif and Shahzad* [1996] 1 All E.R. 353, where an importation of drugs from Pakistan to London was carefully managed by customs officers using undercover offices. See *Lawrence* (December 14, 1993) regarding a test purchase operation.

Although it may be convenient to ask whether "but for" the trick the offence would have been committed, it does not always follow that the answer is conclusive that the evidence should therefore be excluded because persons whose method of operating is to take advantage of opportunities presented to them could not be convicted by evidence-gathering techniques such as test purchase operations. See now *Att.-Gen.'s Ref. No. 3 of 2000* [2001] E.W.C.A. Crim. 1214. In any event it seems that different standards of conduct and detection practices exist in respect of law enforcement agencies on the one hand, and investigative journalists on the other: see *Hardwicke and Thwaites, The Times*, November 16, 2000. It should be noted that this area of the law must also be examined in the light ECHR/Human Rights Act 1998 jurisprudence. It seems that the crucial question is whether admitting agent provocateur evidence would compromise the fairness of the trial, for example, where the evidence was unreliable, or the evidence tainted in some other way: see *Bray* (July 31, 1998) and *Shannon, sub nom Alford, The Times*, October 11, 2000, and see *Teixeira de Castro v. Portugal* (1999) 28 E.H.R.R. 101. Note now *Att.-Gen.'s* Ref. No. 3 of 2000 [2001] E.W.C.A. Crim. 1214.

In *Khan* [1994] Crim. L.R. 830 an electronic listening device was applied 11–97
to the outside of B's house and a conversation involving K was covertly tape-recorded. The evidence of the recording was held to be admissible.

Some tricks may border on the grotesque and yet still not result in the evidence being excluded, *e.g.* by encouraging a family to falsely tell a suspect that an accomplice is in hospital and thereby identify the suspect leading to his arrest: *Maclean v. Kosten* [1993] Crim. L.R. 687.

However, if officers indulge in a trick the effect of which is to circumvent PACE and/or the Codes of Practice then a different result may follow: see *Bryce* (1992) 95 Cr.App.R. 320 and *Mason* (1988) 86 Cr.App.R. 349. Within those limits, every case depends on its own facts.

For a summary of the law in respect of alleged entrapment see *Farooq* [1995] Crim. L.R. 169; see A. Choo, "Halting Criminal Prosecutions", [1995] Crim. L.R. 864; and see "Australian Developments in Entrapment Cases" [1996] Crim. L.R. 137.

(b) Drug addict withdrawing in interview

The relationship between sections 76(2)(b), 78 and 82(3) has been the 11–98
subject of much attention by the courts and commentators alike: see *McGovern* (1991) 92 Cr.App.R. 228; *Everett* [1988] Crim.L.R. 826; *DPP v. Blake* [1989] 1 W.L.R. 432; *Goldenberg* (1989) 88 Cr.App.R. 285; *Rennie* (1982) 74 Cr.App.R. 207; and *Crampton* (1991) 92 Cr.App.R. 369.

For the purposes of section 76(2)(b), the cases seem to suggest a distinction, which the courts have not in fact expressly propounded, namely between words said and things done which are intrinsically likely to produce an untrue confession (*e.g.* threats), and mere circumstances "existing at the time" which fall outside the scope of section 76(2)(b) because the circumstances do not amount to "anything done" by the police within the meaning of that section.

> In *Crampton* (1991) 92 Cr.App.R. 369. The appellant, a heroin addict, made admissions during an interview in the police station 19 hours after his arrest in respect of an allegation that he conspired to supply heroin. The appellant complained at his trial that the admissions were made whilst experiencing withdrawal symptoms. The police relied on their own judgment to decide whether he was fit to be interviewed. They would not have interviewed the appellant if they had known he was withdrawing. After the interview, a doctor examined the appellant and concluded that he had been fit to be interviewed.
>
> *Held*: the argument that the confession should have been excluded under section 76(2)(b) or section 78 was rejected. Although the police had instigated the interview, the Court doubted whether the mere holding of an interview when the appellant was withdrawing from heroin, came within section 76(2)(b). The subsection seemed to postulate something said or done by the police, which was likely to induce an unreliable confession.

The Court observed that whether or not a drug addict was fit to be interviewed (in the sense that his answers could be relied upon as being true) was a matter for those present at the time subject to Note C: 9B. The judge on the *voire dire* had to decide whether the assessment of those present was correct. On the evidence, the appellant was fit to be interviewed at the relevant time.

11–99 It will be noted that in *Crampton* the Court of Appeal doubted whether the mere holding of an interview when C was withdrawing came within section 76(2)(b) but nevertheless the Court assumed, for the purposes of the appeal, that it did.

It is submitted that on a natural reading of section 76(2)(b) the interviewer must say or do something which, "in the circumstances existing at the time", was likely to render unreliable a confession made in consequence. In the ordinary way, merely putting elementary questions to a suspect, who in fact is withdrawing during interviews, falls outside the scope of section 76(2)(b). In *Goldenberg* (1989) 88 Cr.App.R. 285, G requested an interview during which he made a number of admissions although the evidence showed that he was withdrawing at the time. On those facts, nothing had been said or done by the interviewers within the terms of section 76(2)(b) to render a confession unreliable and the Court of Appeal so held. However, drawing the line between things "said" or "done", and mere circumstances prevailing at the time which fall outside section 76(2)(b) may be difficult to draw (see the commentary to *Crampton*

[1991] Crim.L.R. 277, 279). If officers instigate an interview knowing that the suspect is withdrawing then, it is submitted, the fact that questions are asked in such circumstances in consequence of which a confession follows, is enough to bring section 76(2)(b) into play: see *Everett* [1988] Crim.L.R. 826; *DPP v. Blake* [1989] 1 W.L.R. 432.

Even if "mere circumstances" fall outside the scope of section 76(2)(b), **11–100** it is of course open to the Court to exclude a confession made in those circumstances under section 78. The courts have yet to decide whether it must be shown, for the purposes of section 78, that the circumstances of the case are likely to render unreliable any confession or whether the Court is entitled to examine the truth of the confession in question. Ultimately, the test is "will the admission of the relevant evidence have such an effect on the fairness of the proceedings that the court ought not admit it?" *O 'Leary* (1988) 87 Cr.App.R. 387, CA.

Before section 76(2)(a) of PACE can apply, there must be at least oppression and a causal link or possible link, between the oppression and the confession: *Parker* [1995] Crim. L.R. 233.

F. TELEPHONE TAPPING

The position is now subject to the provisions of the Regulation of Invest- **11–101** igatory Powers Act 2000 ("RIPA"), which has replaced Interception of Communications Act 1985 as from October 2, 2000 (see S.I. 2000 No. 2543). Under the 1995 Act, there was much confusion as to the extent to which evidence relating to telephone intercepts could, or could not be, used in evidence. At the heart of the confusion was section 9 of the 1985 Act, now replaced by sections 17 and 18 of RIPA 2000. Much of what follows relates to the position prior to RIPA, but may still be relevant.

Preston (1994) 98 Cr. App. R. 405 disentangled a muddle which stemmed from the facts of *Preston* and *Effick*. In *Effick* (1994) 99 Cr. App. R. 312, HL, (1992) 95 Cr. App. R. 427, CA, E and M were convicted of offences of supplying controlled drugs. Part of the evidence against them consisted of tape recordings made by police who intercepted telephone calls made by the conspirators on cordless telephones. Objection was taken to the admissibility of the recordings on the grounds that they were inadmissible by virtue of section 9 of the Interception of Communications Act 1985 (or, as a fall-back position, under PACE, s.78). By section 1 of the 1985 Act it is an offence to intercept calls made as part of a "public telecommunications system" unless the intercept is authorised by warrant for, *inter alia*, "preventing or detecting serious crime" (s. 2) but evidence may not be adduced and no question may be asked in cross-examination to establish that an offence was committed contrary to section 1 or that a warrant had been issued (see s. 9). The appellant's original submission, before the trial judge, was that evidence of the calls would betray the existence of a warrant and should therefore be excluded, but the prosecutor announced that in fact no warrant had been issued. The defence switched tactics. If the use of a cordless telephone formed part of the public telecommunications systems (within the meaning of the Act) then the interception of the calls by the police may have involved the commission of an offence by them contrary to section 1 of the 1985 Act. The relevance of that point was to use it as a plank in support of the exclusion of the evidence under PACE, s.78, and to support the argument that section 9(1)(a) of the 1985 Act prohibits evidence being adduced if it suggests that an offence was committed under the Act. The Court of Appeal rejected the submission concluding that section 9 did not impose a complete embargo on evidence being admitted and it was not unfair to admit the evidence. They did not decide whether cordless phones were part of the public system or not.

11–102 Thus, in *Effick*, the prosecutor sought the admission of the evidence and the defence wanted the evidence excluded but in *Preston*, the parties reversed their arguments. In *Preston*, the defendants were convicted of a conspiracy to import controlled drugs. The prosecution introduced evidence of the fact that telephone calls were made between various parties but during the trial, it emerged that the defendants' telephones had been tapped. The defence pressed for disclosure of the content of the telephone calls but the prosecutor resisted disclosure. The House of Lords held that because a warrant may be issued to intercept telephone calls for "preventing" serious crime that was not the same consideration as disclosure in respect of the "prosecution" of serious crime. Although, under the 1985 Act, the defence cannot compel disclosure, nevertheless there is nothing in that Act which prevents the prosecution from disclosing information if they choose to do so. In this respect, the decision of the Court of Appeal in *Effick* is therefore consistent with the decision in *Preston* but, in the latter case, the House of Lords also held (in effect) that it was not open to the defence to argue that evidence of telephone calls should be excluded under PACE, s.78 unless the prosecution decide to disclose whether the calls had been intercepted and to disclosure details of the conversations. By reason of section 9, no reference should be made at the trial as to whether calls were intercepted.

In *Preston*, the House of Lords stated that the decision of the Court of Appeal in *Effick* should be overruled. Obviously, the decision is overruled as far as any limb of it conflicts with the ratio in *Preston* but there are significant aspects of the decision in *Effick*, which seem to have been accepted in *Preston* as being correct. First, there was agreement in both cases that section 9 of the 1985 Act does not automatically render inadmissible the contents of intercepts and secondly, both cases suggest that the prosecutor is entitled to adopt the stance of neither admitting nor denying that telephone calls were intercepted under the Act. In *Owen (Darren) and Stephen, The Times*, November 11, 1998, it was held that it is not appropriate to conduct a *voire dire* to determine whether O and S had consented to telephone calls from prison being intercepted. If consent had been given then no offence had been committed under section 1(1) of the 1985 Act. However, the defence, and the court, could not investigate whether consent had been given or not: to do so might suggest that an offence had been committed by an officer of the Crown (a suggestion prohibited by section 9 of that Act). In those circumstances, O and S contended that fairness demanded that evidence obtained as a result of the intercept be excluded. The Court of Appeal dismissed the appeals. There should not have been a *voire dire*—the evidence was admissible without further enquiry; and see *Bray* (June 26, (1998) and *Davies* (July 31, 1998).

Ironically, following the decision in *Preston*, the case of *Effick* was heard in the House of Lords (1994) Cr. App. R. 312, where it was held that the cordless telephones used in that case was a private system and therefore did not come within section 1(1) of the 1985 Act. The evidence was rightly admitted because section 9 of the Act had no application on the facts of that case (and see *Ahmed* [1995] Crim. L. R. 246). Also see *Morgans v. DPP* [2000] 2 W.L.R. 386 and see *R. v. P* (June 8, 2000). 11–103

Difficult issues arise where telephone calls made by inmates of a prison are intercepted and tape recorded by the prison authorities: see, for example, *Owen and Stephen* (November 6, 1998); see also *Taylor-Sabori* (September 25, 1998).

For background information, see the *Interception of Communication* (1957 Cmnd. 283); *Interception of Communication in Great Britain* (Cmnd 7873; 1980); the *Diplock Report* (Cmnd 8191; 1981) and the *Interception of Communication in the United Kingdom* (Cmnd 9438; 1985).

G. VIEW OF THE SCENE OF THE CRIME

In *Hunter* [1985] 1 W.L.R. 613 a ship's officer was tried for the unlawful importation of cannabis carried on his ship. At the judge's instigation a view of the *locus in quo* took place in the presence of the jury, the clerk of the court, counsel and solicitors and the witness under examination. The judge himself did not take part. The Court of Appeal quashed the conviction. The judge and jury had to be present throughout the giving of evidence: see *Tameshwar v. The Queen* [1957] A.C. 476. 11–104

Chapter 12
Powers of Police and Customs Officers

Recognising that much has been written by others concerning the powers of the police (but comparatively little concerning the powers of customs officers) what follows is intended only to be a summary of the most important powers, rights and duties conferred on officers insofar as they affect the investigation and prosecution of drug offences. The Police and Criminal Evidence Act 1984 (PACE) and the Drug Trafficking Act 1994 (DTA) have radically altered much of the earlier law, and therefore earlier authorities, to the extent that they may appear to be relevant, must be considered and applied with care. However, both PACE and the DTA do little to affect the powers exercisable under the Customs and Excise Management Act 1979 (CEMA). 12–01

Section 24 of the MDA, previously concerned with the powers of arrest under that enactment, has been totally repealed insofar as that section applies in England and Wales. That section still applies in Scotland. Accordingly, the duties, rights, powers and privileges conferred on police and customs officers are chiefly to be found in five statutes, namely:

(i) The Police and Criminal Evidence Act 1984.
(ii) The Misuse of Drugs Act 1971.
(iii) The Customs and Excise Management Act 1979.
(iv) The Drug Trafficking Act 1994
(v) The Criminal Justice (International Co-operation) Act 1990.

Citizens may also take certain steps in the prevention of crime—but very much at their peril. The overriding principle of our constitutional law is that no one in the United Kingdom may lay hands on another, or on his property, without his permission and without lawful justification. For this reason greater powers are given to police and to customs officers than to anyone else.

A. POWERS OF THE CITIZEN

I. Seizing a Controlled Drug

12–02 A citizen possesses no inherent right at common law to seize property under the control of another, but section 5(4) of the MDA provides a defence to a person charged with the unlawful possession of a controlled drug if he proves that he took possession of it for the purpose of preventing another from committing an offence in connection with the drug (s. 5(4)(a)), or that he took it for the purpose of giving it to a person lawfully entitled to take custody of it, for example a police officer or customs officer (see s. 5(4)(b) of the MDA). This defence only applies where the charge is one of possession.

II. A Citizen's Arrest

12–03 Under section 24(4) of PACE any person may arrest, without a warrant, anyone who is in the act of committing an arrestable offence, or anyone whom he has reasonable grounds for suspecting to be committing such an offence. Again, he may arrest, without a warrant, anyone who is guilty of the offence, or whom he has reasonable grounds for suspecting to be guilty of it: see section 24(5) of PACE Note that an offence must have been committed: *Selto* (1992) 95 Cr. App. R. 42, and see *Wrightman v. Lees* 1999 S.C.C.R. 664 where the Court said that common sense had to apply in a situation where the circumstances were strongly indicative of a crime having been committed.

Both subsections 24(4) and (5) follow the earlier law, so where no arrestable offence has in fact been committed, a private person who performs an arrest faces an action for false imprisonment: see *Walters v. W.H. Smith & Son Ltd* [1914] 1 K.B. 595 and *Beckwith v. Philby* (1872) 6 B. & C. 635; and see *Self*, 95 Cr. App. R. 42

An individual once arrested by another must be taken to a police station, by a constable, as soon as practicable: PACE, s.30(1).

There is no general power conferred by the law on a private person to effect a search of another.

B. POWERS OF THE POLICE

I. Arrests

12–04 Powers of arrest at least in England and Wales are conferred on constables by section 24 of PACE and include offences arising under the Customs and Excise Acts: see section 24(2) of PACE and section 1(1) of the CEMA. Note that an offence under section 170 of CEMA 1979 will, on a date to be appointed, be a "serious arrestable offence": see section 116 of PACE and section 72 of the Criminal Justice and Police Act 2001.

No warrant is needed where a constable has reasonable grounds for suspecting that an arrestable offence has been committed (s. 24(6) of PACE; and see *Chapman v. DPP*, 89 Cr. App. R. 190 D.C.). See *O'Hara v. Chief Constable of the RUC* [1997] A.C. 286, HL; and see *Hough v. Chief Constable of Staffordshire Police, The Times*, February 14, 2001. He may also arrest anyone who is, or is (on reasonable grounds) suspected to be, about to commit an arrestable offence (s. 24(7)). An arrest involves an act of compulsion so that a mere invitation to a person to accompany an officer to a police station is not an arrest: see *Alderson v. Booth* [1969] 2 Q.B. 216, *Wheatley v. Lodge* [1971] 1 W.L.R. 29 and *Inwood* [1973] 1 W.L.R. 647.

Reasonable suspicion is not the same as prima facie proof and may be based on the receipt of information which, at the trial, would in fact be inadmissible: see *Hussain v. Chong Fook Kam* [1970] A.C. 492 and *Dumbell v. Roberts* [1944] 1 All E.R. 326.

A person is to be told of the reason for the arrest at the time, or as soon as is practicable after the arrest: see PACE 1984, s.28(3) and *Christie v. Leachinsky* [1947] A.C. 573; and see *Wilson v. Chief Constable of Lancashire Constabulary, Daily Telegraph,* December 5, 2000.

II. Searches Without a Warrant

A constable who has reasonable grounds to suspect that any person is in possession of controlled drugs may stop and search that person and detain him for that purpose (s. 23(2)(a) of the MDA), or to search a vehicle or vessel in which the drug may be found (s. 23(2)(b) of the MDA). Section 23(2)(a) expressly authorises detention for the purpose of searching a suspect; it does not give the officer a general right to question him. But in *Green* [1982] Crim.L.R. 604, the Court of Appeal considered that a right to detain involved the right to ask questions, which were at least incidental to the exercise of that statutory power. 12–05

Furthermore, an officer has no right to stop a vehicle, or to search it simply because he suspects that the vehicle (and not the occupants) has been used in connection with a drugs offence.

> In *Littleford* [1978] Crim.L.R. 48 an officer stopped a vehicle and searched it and the occupants. The officer had been informed by radio that the car was suspected of being involved in drug trafficking.
>
> *Held*: the searches were illegal. The officer's suspicion was in connection with the vehicle and not the occupant.

By contrast, in *Campbell v. H.M. Advocate*, 1993 S.L.T. 245, officers acted on information received in respect of two persons using a hired car. The officers suspected that both men were in possession of a controlled drug. A roadblock was set up but when the car was stopped, the police noticed a third person occupying the rear seat. The officers had no suspicions regarding the third occupant until they saw him in the vehicle but the officers nevertheless detained and searched him (as well as the car) under MDA s.23(2). The Court held that where the officers' suspicion was not focused simply on the occupants, but also on the car that was used to convey drugs, there were sufficient grounds to suspect that the third occupant may also be in possession of drugs. *Littleford* was not referred to in the opinion of the Court: and see *McLeod v. Lowe*, 1993 S.L.T. 471.

12–06 In *Bett (Andrew Rae) v. Lees*, 1998 S.L.T. 1969, B was charged with possession of cannabis resin after he had been stopped and searched under section 23(2) of the Misuse of Drugs Act. B objected to the admission of evidence relating to the search on the grounds that the officers did not have reasonable grounds to suspect that he was in possession of controlled drugs. The Court refused B's appeal against conviction. B had been stopped by police after he cycled at night without lights; became agitated when officers spoke to him, and a radio check disclosed that B had two convictions for drug offences.

In *Barr (Stewart)*, 1997 S.L.T. 1007, B was seen by police acting suspiciously by a house known to police for its reputation for drug dealing. B ran from police but when apprehended he put something in his mouth. Despite repeated requests from the police to spit it out, he swallowed it. B was known to police as a drug user. The facts were sufficient to found a reasonable suspicion that B was in possession of a controlled drug for the purposes of section 23 of the Misuse of Drugs Act 1971 and the police were entitled to exercise their powers under section 23 of the Misuse of Drugs Act.

In *Stark v. Brown*, 1997 S.C.C.R. 382, S was seen by police close to property frequented by drug users and dealers. When confronted by police, S claimed that he was looking for a "bird". Police searched him and found him to be in possession of controlled drugs. At his trial, S objected to the admission of evidence relating to the search and what was discovered. The Court held that the sheriff was entitled to have regard to the officer's knowledge of the reputation of the premises where S was seen close by, his explanations and his behaviour.

In *French v. DPP* (November 27, 1996, Crown Office), F was convicted of obstructing police contrary to 51(3) of the Police Act 1964. F had been stopped and searched under section 23 of the Misuse of Drugs Act but neither gave evidence at the trial as to their reasons for doing so. F had been arrested by another officer who arrived at the scene after F had been stopped. It was impossible for the Court to establish whether the search was lawful, or the obstruction unlawful. The appeal was allowed.

12–07 By section 2(2) of PACE if a constable contemplates a search he must take reasonable steps to bring to the attention of the appropriate person the fact that he is a constable (if not in uniform) and, in any event, he must give his name, the name of the police station to which he is attached, the object of the search and his grounds for making the search (see s. 2(3) of PACE): *cf. Brazil v. Chief Constable of Surrey* [1983] 3 All E.R. 537 and *Lindley v. Rutter* [1981] Q.B. 128 and note the Code of Practice (1995) under A:2; A:3 and A:4.

An officer may also search an unattended vehicle but he must leave a notice inside the vehicle (if possible) of the fact that he has searched it and stating that an application for compensation may be made at the constable's police station: section 2(6) and (7) of PACE. The officer shall record details of a search: section 3(1) of PACE. A search of a car by Police under section 23(2)(b) of MDA 1971 allows for the removal of the car to a more convenient place to carry out the search: see *Nicholson v. H. M. Advocate* [2001] S.C.C.R. 13.

Where a person has been arrested, a constable may then search that person for anything which might be evidence relating to an offence (s. 32(2)(a)(ii) of PACE) providing that the constable has reasonable grounds to believe that the person may have concealed something on him relevant to an offence (s. 32(5)). Note also the application of the revised Codes of Practice: Police and Criminal Evidence Act 1984 (Codes of Practice) (No. 3) Order 1995 (S.I. 1995 No. 450); and revisions to the codes brought about by S.I. 1997 No. 1159; S.I. 1999 No.291.

Note that of course there may be a power of search under other statutory measures.

III. Search of Premises Without a Warrant

At common law there was no right vested in the police or anyone else to enter a private house without a warrant, no matter how serious the crime being investigated. The one exception was following a culprit in "hot pursuit": see *McLorie v. Oxford* [1982] Q.B. 1290, a decision reversed by section 18(1) of PACE. 12–08

If a person is arrested by police in any premises, and that person is a danger to himself or to others, the police are perfectly within their rights to search those premises but only for evidence relating to the offence for which he has been arrested (s. 32(2)(b) of PACE) and only to the extent that the search is reasonably required (s. 32(3)) but there must be reasonable grounds to believe that there is relevant evidence on the premises (s. 32(6)).

Irrespective of whether or not a person arrested is a danger to himself or to others, a constable, under section 18 of PACE, may enter and search any premises occupied or controlled by the person arrested if he has reasonable grounds for suspecting that on the premises there is evidence relating to that offence or indeed another similar offence. However, before invoking section 18, the constable needs the written authorisation of an officer of at least the rank of inspector unless (and this seems a curious addition to the section) the presence of the arrested party at the premises is "necessary for the effective investigation of the offence" (s. 18(5)) and see *Badham* [1987] Crim. L.R. 202. This would presumably include a person who had stashed drugs, and items relevant to the offence, and who would therefore be able to assist the police (if he wishes to do so) to find them.

The arrest must have been lawful: see R. *(on the application of Odewale) v. DPP* [2001] 2 Archbold News 2, DC. There are also limits on the extent to which an officer may enter force: see *Linehan v. DPP* [2000] Crim.L.R. 861.

IV. Searching for an Individual

12–09 In addition to these powers, a constable in uniform (s. 17(3) of PACE) may enter and search any premises—without a warrant—if the object of gaining entry is (*inter alia*) to execute a warrant of arrest, or to arrest a person for an arrestable offence (s. 17), providing there are reasonable grounds to believe that the person is on the premises (s. 17(2)(a)) and only if it is reasonably required for the purpose of finding the person concerned.

All former rules of common law, which emerged to give a constable power to enter premises without a warrant, are now abolished: section 17(5). It follows that section 17 is a codifying provision (cf. *Thomas v. Sawkins* [1935] 2 K.B. 249; *Davis v. Lisle* [1936] 2 K.B. 434; *Robson v. Hallett* [1967] 2 Q.B. 939). Parliament has now empowered officers not merely to enter premises in order to prevent the commission of an offence therein, but also to investigate crime generally.

V. Intimate Searches and Searches at Police Stations

12–10 Previous statutes and rules at common law affecting the ability of the police to search suspects at police stations and to carry out intimate searches have been abolished (section 53 of PACE).

Instead, a new set of principles has been enacted by section 55 of PACE as amended by the CJA 1988, Sched. 15, para. 99, and see Annex A of Code C. Thus, an intimate search is restricted to certain purposes only, *e.g.* where a Class A drug is concealed on the suspect and that he "was in possession of it with the appropriate criminal intent before his arrest"—a passage which may present some difficulties of application and construction (see s. 55(1)(b)). The definition of an "intimate search" is to be found in section 65 of PACE. Encouraging a suspect to spit out a package, which he put into his mouth, is not an "intimate search": see *Hughes, The Times*, November 12, 1993. The provisions are modified in relation to customs officers acting in respect of "assigned matters": see S.I. 1985 No. 1800.

12–11 An intimate search must be authorised in writing by an officer of at least the rank of superintendent (s. 55(1) and (3) (note that "superintendent" will be replaced by "inspector", if the Criminal Justice and Police Act 2001, s. 80(1) comes into force)) providing that he has reasonable grounds to believe that the Class A drug cannot be found without such a search (s. 55(2)) and that it is carried out by a registered medical practitioner or registered nurse ("practitioner if the Criminal Justice and Police Act 2001, s. 80(2) comes into force) (unless the superintendent (or "inspector", see s. 80(1) of CJPA 2001) thinks this impracticable): see subsections 55(4), (5) and (17) of PACE An intimate search for a Class A drug must not be carried out at a police station but at a hospital; or at the surgery of a general practitioner, or some other place used for medical purposes (see ss. 55(9) and (8)).

Again, intimate samples (*e.g.* blood, urine or a swab from a body orifice) may not be taken unless a person is reasonably suspected of having committed a "serious arrestable offence"—a term which is narrowly defined by the Act (see s. 116 of and Sched. 5 to PACE) but which includes an arrestable offence, aggravated by the happening of certain events listed in section 116(6), *e.g.* substantial financial gain to any person. Therefore, a person reasonably suspected of being a major drugs supplier who has substantially benefited financially as a result is liable to be a person from whom intimate samples may be taken subject to the requirements of section 62 (as amended). Other samples may be taken with the accused's consent. Note that a saliva sample is not an intimate one: see section 65 of PACE, as amended.

As to the position regarding the destruction of fingerprints and samples, see section 82(2) of the Criminal Justice and Police Act 2001 which replaced sections 64(1) and 64(2) as from May 11, 2001.

VI. Searches With a Warrant

Warrants may be obtained under a number of different enactments but three principal statutes are dealt with here. The first is section 23 of the MDA; the second is section 8 of PACE and the third is section 56 of the DTA 1994 (formerly s.28 of the DTOA). 12–12

(a) Warrants granted under section 23 of the MDA

Section 23 of the Misuse of Drugs Act provides as follows (as amended):

"(1) A constable or other person authorised in that behalf by a general or special order of the Secretary of State (or in Northern Ireland either of the Secretary of State or the Ministry of Home Affairs for Northern Ireland) shall, for the purposes of the execution of this Act, have power to enter the premises of a person carrying on business as a producer or supplier of any controlled drugs and to demand the production of and to inspect, any books or documents relating to dealings in any such drugs and to inspect any stocks of any such drugs.

(2) If a constable has reasonable grounds to suspect that any person is

in possession of a controlled drug in contravention of this Act or of any regulations made thereunder, the constable may—

(a) search that person, and detain him for the purpose of searching him;
(b) search any vehicle or vessel in which the constable suspects that the drug may be found, and for that purpose require the person in control of the vehicle or vessel to stop it;
(c) seize and detain, for the purposes of proceedings under this Act, anything found in the course of the search which appears to the constable to be evidence of an offence under this Act.

In this subsection "vessel" includes a hovercraft within the meaning of the Hovercraft Act 1968; and nothing in this subsection shall prejudice any power of search or any power to seize or detain property which is exercisable by a constable apart from this subsection.

(3) If a justice of the peace (or in Scotland a justice of the peace, a magistrate or a sheriff) is satisfied by information on oath that there is reasonable ground for suspecting—

(a) that any controlled drugs are, in contravention of this Act or of any regulations made thereunder, in the possession of a person on any premises; or
(b) that a document directly or indirectly relating to, or connected with, a transaction or dealing which was, or an intended transaction or dealing which would if carried out be, an offence under this Act, or in the case of a transaction or dealing carried out or intended to be carried out in a place outside the United Kingdom, an offence against the provisions of a corresponding law in force in that place, is in the possession of a person on any premises,

he may grant a warrant authorising any constable acting for the police area in which the premises are situated at any time or times within one month from the date of the warrant, to enter, if need be by force, the premises named in the warrant, and to search the premises and any person found therein and, if there is reasonable ground for suspecting that an offence under this Act has been committed in relation to any controlled drugs found on the premises or in the possession of any such persons, or that a document so found is such a document as is mentioned in paragraph (b) above, to seize and detain those drugs or that document, as the case may be.

(3A) The powers conferred by subsection (1) above shall be exercisable also for the purposes of the execution of Part II of the Criminal Justice (International Co-operation) Act 1990 or section 49 of the Drug Trafficking Act 1994, and subsection (3) above (excluding paragraph (a)) shall apply also to offences under section 12 or 13 of that Act of 1990, taking references in those provisions to controlled drugs as references to scheduled substances within the meaning of that Part.

(4) A person commits an offence if he—

(a) intentionally obstructs a person in the exercise of his powers under this section; or
(b) conceals from a person acting in the exercise of his powers under subsection (1) above any such books, documents, stocks or drugs as are mentioned in that subsection; or
(c) without reasonable excuse (proof of which shall lie on him) fails to produce any such books or documents as are so mentioned where their production is demanded by a person in the exercise of his powers under that subsection."

A justice of the peace is authorised by this section to grant a warrant authorising a constable to search premises at "any time or times" within one month from the date of the warrant. In *Brown (Frank) v. H.M. Advocate*, 1998 S.C.C.R. 356, the date on the warrant could refer back to the date of the information and thus, given that the warrant was marked "same day" and was preceded by a signed and dated information, the warrant was valid. 12–13

There must be reasonable cause to suspect that controlled drugs are in the possession of a person on any premises, or that documents exist in relation to a drugs transaction: and see *H.M. Advocate v. Rae*, 1992 S.C.C.R. 1 and see *Main v. Stainforth Lockhart*, 1993 S.C.C.R. 347.

The police may be entitled to search a visitor to premises under section 23(2) if he admits to police that he is in some way connected with dealing in drugs and an officer thus concludes that the person may be in possession of a controlled drug: *Gavin v. Normand*, 1995 S.L.T. 741; see *Stuart v. Crowe*, 1993 S.L.T. 439, and see *Ireland v. Russell*, 1995 S.L.T. 1348.

In *Don (Joanne)*, 1997 S.C.C.R. 449, D left a vehicle and entered a house whilst appearing to be concealing a bag. D left the house empty-handed. On the strength of that the police obtained a warrant under section 23(3). D sought suspension of the warrant on the basis that the officers had no reasonable grounds to suspect that the bag contained controlled drugs. The court held that D's complaint was well founded.

In *Hammond v. Howdle*, 1996 S.L.T. 1174, it was held that it is permissible for the warrant to say that one of its objects is to search "persons" on premises even if the police do not know who is going to be on premises at the time of the search. The Court said: 12–14

"What is required is that there should be reasonable grounds for suspecting that 'a person' on the premises concerned is in possession of controlled drugs. It is not necessary that a view should be formed as to precisely who that person may be. The name of the person is not important. . . . Nor is it important that in any other way the individual or individuals should be identified. The crucial point is the connection between controlled drugs and the premises, and the existence of a reasonable ground for suspecting that a person on the premises, whoever he or she may be, is in possession of the controlled drugs."

In *Adams* [1980] Q.B. 575, the Court of Appeal considered whether a warrant issued under section 3(1) of the Obscene Publications Act 1959 (OPA) authorised officers to search premises on more than one occasion. During the course of legal argument, section 3(1) was contrasted with section 23(3) of the MDA where the words "at any time or times within one month" might imply authorisation of a number of quite separate searches within that time. The Court considered section 23(3) of the MDA 1971 to "fortify, rather than found" their conclusion that the wording of section 3(1) of the OPA 1959 authorised only one search per warrant. (See also *Dickinson v. Brown* (1794) 1 Esp. 218; 170 E.R. 334 and s. 152(1) of the Licensing Act 1953.)

12–15 However, it is unlikely that Parliament intended to give police blanket authorisation to enter premises as often as they wish within the relevant time merely upon the grant of a warrant under section 23(3) of the MDA 1971.

In the absence of authority to the contrary, the words "time or times" may mean no more than that a justice of the peace is empowered to grant a warrant specifying multiple searches if the evidence given to him on oath justifies such a course. Any other construction would result in the total inability of the court granting the warrant to pre-empt a subsequent entry, search, and seizure within the operational period, which is not, on its merits, actually warranted.

By contrast, a search warrant granted under section 8 of PACE authorises an entry on one occasion only. If the main or only reason for being on premises is to detect offences under the MDA it is not essential that a warrant be obtained under section 23(3) of the MDA if entry is gained by virtue of another enactment: *Foster v. Attarde* (1986) 83 Cr.App.R. 214. It would seem that where a warrant is sought by police, both sections 15 and 16 must be satisfied.

Once a constable is authorised to enter premises by virtue of section 23 of the MDA he may use such force as is reasonably necessary to gain admission and to search the premises and any occupants but, in *King v. R.* [1969] 1 A.C. 304, the Privy Council held that a warrant, granted under similar Jamaican legislation, was unlawful if it did not expressly authorise the search of persons as well as premises.

12–16 Under section 16 of PACE 1984, and the Codes of Practice made under the Act, entry to the premises may be effected by the use of force or subterfuge before there is any requirement for a constable to identify himself by producing his warrant card or producing the search warrant as required by section 16(5). Both the Codes of Practice and, by implication, section 23 of the MDA, recognise that the use of force or subterfuge is permissible to gain entry. If the law were otherwise, then the whole object of section 16 of PACE and section 23 of the MDA 1971 would be frustrated: *Longman* (1989) 88 Cr.App.R. 148, CA.

In *Longman*, police officers obtained a warrant to enter L's premises to search for drugs pursuant to section 23 of the MDA 1971. The officers tricked L into opening the door and forced their way into the premises. They stated that they were police officers and that they had a warrant. L shouted to another man whom the police found about to administer cocaine to himself.

Held: on appeal, that a warrant was "produced" for the purposes of section 16(5)(b), (c) of PACE 1984 when the occupier of the premises was given an opportunity to inspect it. L obstructed the police under section 23 of the MDA 1971 and, by so doing, he had deprived himself of the opportunity of inspecting the warrant and the warrant card before he was arrested.

Again, in *Campbell v. Vannet*, 1997 S.C.C.R. 787, police saw C kneeling by a letter box to her front door receiving a package that they believed contained heroin. After the officers called on C to 'open the door', she fled to the bathroom. The police forced open the front door as well as the bathroom door where they saw C by the toilet with a brush in her hand. The Court held that the police were entitled to act as they did.

Any drugs or relevant documents found may accordingly be seized and retained by the police but the warrant must specify the information required: *R. v. Chief Constable of Lancashire, ex p. Parker and McGrath* [1993] Crim. L.R. 204. 12–17

In *Rollo v. H.M. Advocate*, 1996 S.C.C.R. 874, the defendant was convicted of being concerned in the supply of controlled drugs. The police obtained a warrant under section 23(3)(b) of the Misuse Of Drugs Act 1971. As a result of the search, the police obtained information that was stored on an electronic notepad. The defendant contended that the notepad was not a "document" for the purposes of the section or having regard to the terms of the warrant. It was further contended that the information obtained from the device was therefore inadmissible. The appeal was refused because the essence of the word "document" was the information recorded on it. It is immaterial that the information has to be processed by way of translation, or decoding, or a method of electronic retrieval. However, the terms of the section must be strictly met. The police are not empowered under section to recover other items which may be documents, but which are not related to or concerned with transactions or dealings contemplated by the subsection.

In *Baker* [1996] Crim. L.R. 55, the Court ordered the disclosure of the name of the "informer" in order to test the defendant's contention that, as a result of ill-feeling between B and the police station, a warrant under section 23 had been obtained without any information from a "real informer". The delay between the warrant being granted and executed exceeded two weeks. B's defence was that some 5 grams of cannabis resin had been planted. It is not clear whether the defence were also seeking to challenge the legality of the search at B's home address and that the evidence relating to the search should be excluded.

(b) Warrants granted under section 8 of PACE

12–18 The police also have power to apply to a justice of the peace for a search warrant in respect of premises under section 8 of PACE and note the safeguards provided by section 15 of PACE before a warrant may be issued. Although the granting of a warrant under this section is confined to cases where there is reasonable cause to believe that a "serious arrestable offence" has been committed, nevertheless this may include a major drugs supplier or a person concerned in the unlawful importation/exportation of controlled drugs where substantial gains are suspected to have been made.

Warrants granted under section 8 above may be executed by a constable: PACE, s.16(1). Again, entry may be effected within one month from the date of its issue: PACE, s.16(2) but with the qualification that the entry and search must be carried out at a reasonable hour unless the purpose of the search would be frustrated as a result.

(c) Warrants granted under section 56 of the DTA

12–19 By section 56(1), a constable may, for the purpose of an investigation into drug trafficking, apply to a circuit judge for a warrant in respect of specified premises authorising (by virtue of s. 256(2)) a constable to enter and search the premises if an order for the disclosure of material on premises under section 55 of that Act has not been complied with, or certain conditions stipulated in section 56(3) or section 56(4) are fulfilled. Where a constable has entered premises in the execution of a warrant issued under section 56(5), he may seize and retain any material, other than "items subject to legal privilege" (as defined by s. 10 of PACE) and "excluded material" (as defined by s. 11 of PACE) which is likely to be of substantial value to the investigation for the purpose for which the warrant was issued: see section 56(5) of the DTA.

References in the DTA to a "constable" include a person commissioned by the Commissioners of Customs and Excise: see section 63(1) of the DTA.

(d) Generally

12–20 Great care must be exercised in the application for warrants. Warrants must be obtained on a proper basis although the extent to which a justice is entitled to enquiry into the basis of the officer's suspicions before granting a warrant, is uncertain. In any event, it will not be easy to challenge the validity of a warrant that is granted because the presumption of regularity applies: see *A.F.P. Singh* (September 17, 1999). In *H.M. Advocate v. Rae*, 1992 S.C.C.R. 1, it was said that if a police officer gives evidence on oath that he has reasonable grounds for suspecting the presence of controlled drugs on premises, the justice is entitled to grant a warrant without further inquiry. However, there has been a human rights challenge in Scotland in respect of the procedure by which warrants under section 23(3) may be granted. Thus, in *Birse v. H.M. Advocate*, 2000 S.L.T. 869, it was said that officers who obtained a warrant on the grounds that strange recurring smells emanated from B's windows at his home address on Fridays and Saturdays, was a violation of his Convention rights under Article 8 of the ECHR. B further complained that no records were kept of the proceedings and the justice himself could not recall the particular case. It was held that the process by which warrants were granted was Convention-compliant. The purpose of the section was to ensure that an independent judicial figure decided whether to grant a warrant. It is submitted that the better view is that the justice is entitled to assess whether the request for a warrant is proper.

In *Rotherham Magistrates' Court, ex p. Todd* (February 16, 2000, Divisional Court) B was investigating an allegation that T was supplying counterfeit computer games. He was minded to apply for a warrant to search T's home address under section 28(3) of a Trade Description Act 1968. However, he also obtained information that T was supplying small amounts of cannabis. The police told B that they would be obtaining a warrant to search T's address under section 23 of the Misuse of Drugs Act and that B could simply enter and search the premises under the police warrant. This occurred: no drugs were found but some £3,000 worth of counterfeit discs was seized. The Divisional Court held that the search was unlawful—at least in respect of the seizure of the counterfeit articles. However, that did not make the evidence obtained as a result of the unlawful search inadmissible. The consequences of the unlawful conduct were a matter for the justices.

Although it is obviously desirable that warrants should be correctly drafted, nevertheless an inconsequential error or misspelling is unlikely to vitiate the warrant. 12–21

In *Atkinson* (1976) Crim.L.R. 307 police wished to search the defendant's flat. They thought that the number of the flat was "45" and accordingly obtained a warrant to search "Flat 45". In fact, the defendant lived at "Flat 30". Police entered Flat 30 and searched it. *Held*: the search could not be justified since a highly material particular, concerning the identity of the premises, had been misdescribed.

In *Whyte and others*, 1997 S.C.C.R. 461, a warrant to search premises granted under section 23 of the Misuse of Drugs Act 1971 was not invalid on the grounds that it was signed by officer H, who was examined by the magistrate, notwithstanding that the information had been supplied by officer B. The error was not in the circumstances fatal to the grant of the warrant.

On the other hand, there is abundant authority for the proposition that a general warrant expressing insufficient particulars is illegal at common law: see *Leach v. Money* (1765) 19 St.Tr. 1002, *Wilkes v. Wood* (1763) 19 St.Tr. 1153 and *Entick v. Carrington* (1765) 19 St.Tr. 1030. However, a suggestion that a court had insufficient grounds to justify granting a warrant will not be lightly entertained: see *Wyatt v. White* (1860) 5 H. & N. 371.

One object of present legislation seems to be to avoid putting goods into a more sacred category than persons: see Lord Denning M.R. in *Chic Fashions (West Wales) v. Jones* [1968] 2 Q.B. 299 and *Ghani v. Jones* [1970] 1 Q.B. 693.

VII. Seizure of Articles

12–22 Where Parliament has given a right to police to search persons and premises in connection with the purposes for which they have been authorised to carry out the search, there exists a corresponding right to seize relevant materials (see sections 8, 18, 32, 54 and 55 of PACE and section 23 of the MDA). However, there also exist general powers of seizure, conferred on the police by section 19(1) of PACE, which are exercisable by a constable who is lawfully on any premises. These powers are to seize anything which:

(i) has been obtained in consequence of the commission of an offence and which is in danger of being concealed, lost, damaged, altered, or destroyed; or
(ii) is evidence in respect of any offence; or
(iii) is evidence held by computer in respect of any offence and which may be destroyed, etc., if not seized.

The powers conferred by section 19 are additional to any other powers conferred under PACE: section 19(5). Items seized under section 19 may be retained for as long as is necessary in the circumstances: section 22(1).

In *Ghani v. Jones* [1970] 1 Q.B. 693 Lord Denning M.R. said, *obiter*, that seizure was not justified unless the police have reasonable grounds to believe that "the person in possession of it has himself committed the crime, or is an accessory or at any rate, his refusal must be quite unreasonable". However, an unreasonable refusal is not a sufficient reason for seizure under PACE.

Under Part 2 of the Criminal Justice and Police Act 2001, sections 50 to 53 give police (and customs officers (see section 67 of the Criminal Justice and Police Act 2001) additional powers of seizure from premises (s. 50) and persons (s. 51). As at September 2001, sections 50 to 70 were not in force. One object of those provisions is to deal with issues raised in *R. v. Chesterfield JJ., ex.p. Bramley* [2000] Q.B. 576, namely, the extent to which officers may remove items from premises in order to sift through the material elsewhere (*e.g.* at a police station) and retain items of value to the investigation but return irrelevant material to the person (or occupier of the premises) searched.

Officers also have to deal with other dilemmas in connection with a search. For example, items might be subject to the rules of legal privilege but a decision cannot be made as to the significance of the material unless it is removed, copied and considered. If the material is privileged, should it have been copied at all? Should the copies be returned or be destroyed? What is the position if privileged material is linked to other material that could lawfully be seized by police? Accordingly, by section 50(1), where an officer is authorised to search premises and finds material which he might be permitted to seize in law, then he should examine the material *on the premises* to decide whether he is entitled to seize all or part of that material, *provided* that it is "reasonably practicable" to do so. If it is not reasonably practicable to take that course, section 50(1) permits the officer to remove the material from the premises in order to determine whether he has power to seize it. That power exists even if the material contains other items that he would not be permitted to seize: section 50(2). Section 50(3) give some guidance as to the factors that should be taken into account when deciding whether it was "reasonably practicable" to sift material on premises, *e.g.* how long would that operation take? Similar powers exist under section 51 in respect of items found on the person (*e.g.* in the street). However, the exercise of powers under sections 50 and 51 are subject to written notice that sets out the items seized, the reasons for the seizure and other matters specified in section 52(1).

Provision is made in section 53 to ensure that seized material is sifted as soon as reasonably practicable after the search; that property to be retained or returned is separated; and that it is desirable to afford the person (from whom the property had been seized), or a person with an "interest in that property", the opportunity to be present during the examination: section 53(4). There are obligations to return items subject to legal privilege (s. 54), or "excluded and special procedure material" (s. 55). Sections 56, 57 and 58 provide officers with additional powers to "retain" property which has been seized (presumably lawfully seized) if that property was obtained "in consequence of the commission of an offence" (s. 56(2)(a)) or it is "evidence in relation to any offence" (s. 56(3)(a)) and it is necessary to retain the property in order to prevent it "being concealed, lost, altered or destroyed" (ss. 56(2)(b), 56(3)(b)). There is provision for the retention of property to the person with best title to it: see sections 58 and 59.

(a) Restoration of property seized

Where property has been seized by police an application for its restoration may be made to a magistrates' court under section 1 of the Police (Property) Act 1897. The application may be made either "by an officer of police or by a claimant of the property". Sections 21 and 22 of PACE deal with access and copying and retention of documents seized: see also section 22(5) and the Codes of Practice made under section 66 of PACE; and see *Webb v. Chief Constable of Merseyside* [2000] 2 W.L.R. 546. 12–23

However, section 22(5) does not apply to customs officers and there is no provision under the Customs and Excise Acts which corresponds to section 1 of the Police (Property) Act 1897.

In *Southampton Justices, ex p. Newman* (1989) 88 Cr.App.R. 202 the applicant had been arrested at home by customs officers and charged with conspiracy to import cannabis. Documents were lawfully seized under sections 17 and 19 of PACE. The applicant sought the restoration of certain documents, which he maintained were necessary for the preparation of his defence, under section 48 of the Magistrates' Court Act 1980. The Divisional Court refused the application. The words "taken from him" in section 48 of the 1980 Act applied only to property found on a person and not to property taken from the home of an arrested person: see *D'Eyncourt* (1888) 21 Q.B.D. 109 and *Arnell v. Harris* [1944] K.B. 60.

12–24 However, in *Southampton Justices, ibid.* the Divisional Court suggested that a magistrates' court could, in a case where the defendant had indicated that he required documents to prepare his defence, adjourn the case until the relevant documents had been delivered to the defendant in the interests of justice: *per* MacPherson J. (1989) 88 Cr.App.R. 202, 205.

Consider also *Gillilan v. Miller*, G.W.D., February 14, 1997, where G attempted to recover a mobile phone on the grounds that a search warrant granted under section 23 of the Misuse of Drugs Act related to controlled drugs and documents. The Court held that the police were nevertheless entitled to rely on their common law powers: and see *Tierney v. Allan*, 1989 S.C.C.R. 334.

Where money has been seized under section 23 which in fact belongs to a third party who has not been convicted of such an offence, the money must be restored to him, even if civil proceedings established (on a balance of probabilities) that the money was derived from drug trafficking: see *Webb v. Chief Constable of Merseyside* [2000] 2 W.L.R. 546.

C. POWERS OF CUSTOMS AND EXCISE

Introduction

12–25 The powers conferred on customs officials are extensive and deliberately widely drawn in response to the tasks that the Commissioners of Customs and Excise are expected to undertake. Most of the powers are conferred by the CEMA.

Section 1(1) of that Act defines an "officer" as a person commissioned by the Commissioners of Customs and Excise to be an officer. However, there is another class of "officer" which, by section 8(2), includes "any person, whether an officer or not" who is engaged in carrying out an "assigned matter" (see s. 1(1)), and shall therefore be deemed to be the "the proper officer". An officer falling within the latter category may be engaged by order of the Commissioners or simply engaged with their concurrence. Whether an officer is a "commissioned" officer or "engaged" under section 8(2), his powers are nevertheless identical: section 8(3).

Note that section 114 of the Police and Criminal Evidence Act 1984 deals with the application of that Act to the Customs and Excise 12–26

"114.—(1) [Amends the customs and excise Acts.]

(2) The Treasury may by order direct—

(a) that any provision of this Act which relates to investigations of offences conducted by police officers or to persons detained by the police shall apply, subject to such modifications as the order may specify, to investigations conducted by officers of Customs and Excise of offences which relate to assigned matters, as defined in section 1 of the Customs and Excise Management Act 1979, or to persons detained by officers of Customs and Excise; and

(b) that, in relation to investigations of offences conducted by officers of Customs and Excise—

(i) this Act shall have effect as if the following section were inserted after section 14—'Exception for Customs and Excise

14A. Material in the possession of a person who acquired or created it in the course of any trade, business, profession or other occupation or for the purpose of any paid or unpaid office and which relates to an assigned matter, as defined in section 1 of the Customs and Excise Management Act 1979, is neither excluded material nor special procedure material for the purposes of any enactment such as is mentioned in section 9(2) above'; and

(ii) section 55 above shall have effect as if it related only to things such as are mentioned in subsection (1)(a) of that section [*and*

(c) *that in relation to customs detention (as defined in any order made under this subsection) the Bail Act 1976 shall have effect as if references in it to a constable were references to an officer of Customs and Excise of such grade as may be specified in the order*].

(3) Nothing in any order under subsection (2) above shall be taken to limit any powers exercisable under section 164 of the Customs and Excise Management Act 1979.

(4) In this section "officers of Customs and Excise" means officers commissioned by the Commissioners of Customs and Excise under section 6(3) of the Customs and Excise Management Act 1979.

(5) [Identical to s. 113(13).]"

(Subs. (2)(c) is printed as prospectively inserted by the CIA 1988, s.150. As at September 10, 1999, section 150 had not been brought into force).

Pursuant to section 114(2) the Treasury have made the PACE Act 1984 (Application to Customs and Excise) Order 1985 (S.I. 1985 No. 1800), the

PACE Act 1984 (Application to Customs and Excise) Order 1987 (S.I. 1987 No. 439), the PACE Act 1984 (Application to Customs and Excise) (Amendment) Order 1995 (S.I. 1995 No. 3217) and the PACE Act 1984 (Application to Customs and Excise) (Amendment) Order 1996 (S.I. 1996 No. 1860). The 1987, 1995 and 1996 orders amend the 1985 order. The 1985 order applies to sections 56 and 58 of the 1984 Act (as amended by the Drug Trafficking Offences Act 1986, s.32: s.32(4) of the 1986 Act).

12–27

S.I. 1985 No. 1800

2.—(1) In this Order, unless the context otherwise requires—"the Act" means the Police and Criminal Evidence Act 1984;

"assigned matter" has the meaning given to it by section 1 of the Customs and Excise
Management Act 1979;
"the customs and excise Acts" has the meaning given to it by section 1 of the Customs and Excise Management Act 1979;
"customs office" means a place for the time being occupied by Her Majesty's Customs and Excise;
"officer" means a person commissioned by the Commissioners of Customs and Excise under section 6(3) of the Customs and Excise Management Act 1979.

(2) A person is in customs detention for the purpose of this Order if—

(a) he has been taken to a customs office after being arrested for an offence; or
(b) he is arrested at a customs office after attending voluntarily at the office or accompanying an officer to it,

and is detained there or is detained elsewhere in the charge of an officer, and nothing shall prevent a detained person from being transferred between customs detention and police detention.

3 (1) Subject to the modifications in paragraphs (2) and (3) of this article, in articles 4 to 12 below and in Schedule 2 to this Order, the provisions of the Act contained in Schedule 1 to this Order which relate to investigations of offences conducted by police officers or to persons detained by the police shall apply to investigations conducted by officers of Customs and Excise of offences which relate to assigned matters, and to persons detained by such officers.

(2) The Act shall have effect as if the words and phrases in Column 1 of Part 1 of Schedule 2 to this Order were replaced by the substitute words and phrases in Column 2 of that Part.

(3) Where in the Act any act or thing is to be done by a constable of a specified rank, that act or thing shall be done by an officer of at least the grade specified in Column 2 of Part 2 of Schedule 2 to this Order, and the Act shall be interpreted as if the substituted grade were specified in the Act.

4. Nothing in the application of the Act to Customs and Excise shall be construed as conferring upon an officer any power—

(a) to charge a person with any offence;
(b) to release a person on bail;
(c) to detain a person for an offence after he has been charged with that offence.

5.(1) Where in the Act a constable is given power to seize and retain any thing found upon a lawful search of person or premises, an officer shall have the same power notwithstanding that the thing found is not evidence of an offence in relation to an assigned matter.

(2) Nothing in the application of the Act to Customs and Excise shall be construed to prevent any thing lawfully seized by a person under any enactment from being accepted and retained by an officer.

(3) Section 21 of the Act (access and copying) shall not apply to any thing seized as liable to forfeiture under the Customs and Excise Act.

6. In its application by virtue of article 3 above the Act shall have effect as if the following section were inserted after section 14.

7. Section 18(1) of the Act shall be modified as follows—"18—(1) Subject to the following provisions of this section, an officer of Customs and Excise may enter and search any premises occupied or controlled by a person who is under arrest for any arrestable offence which relates to an assigned matter, as defined in section 1 of the Customs and Excise Management Act 1979, if he has reasonable grounds for suspecting that there is on the premises evidence, other than items subject to legal privilege, that relates—

(a) to that offence; or
(b) to some other arrestable offence which is connected with or similar to that offence.".

8. [Keeping of records (s.50)]

9(1) Section 55 of the Act shall have effect as if it related only to things such as are mentioned in subsection (1)(a) of that section.

(2) [Information to be included in Commissioners' annual report (s.55(15)]

10. Section 77(3) of the Act shall be modified to the extent that the definition of "independent person" shall, in addition to the persons mentioned therein, also include an officer or any other person acting under the authority of the Commissioners of Customs and Excise.

11. Where any provision of the Act as applied to Customs and Excise—

(a) confers a power on an officer, and
(b) does not provide that the power may only be exercised with the consent of some person other than an officer,

the officer may use reasonable force, if necessary, in the exercise of the power.

12. Section 24(6) of the Act shall apply without prejudice to section 138(1) of the Customs and Excise Management Act 1979, section 72(9) of the Value Added Tax Act 1994, section 20 of and paragraph 4 of Schedule 3 to the Criminal Justice (International Co-operation) Act 1990, or any other enactment, including any enactment contained in sub-

ordinate legislation, for the time being in force which confers upon officers of Customs and Excise the power to arrest or detain persons.

(Article 3)

SCHEDULE 1

12–28 PROVISIONS OF THE ACT APPLIED TO CUSTOMS AND EXCISE

Section 8	Section 36
Section 9 and Schedule 1	Section 37
Section 15	Section 39
Section 16	Section 40
Section 17(1) (b), (2), (4)	Section 41
Section 18 subject to the modification in article 7 hereof	Section 42
	Section 43
Section 19	Section 44
Section 20	Section 50 subject to the modification in article 8 hereof
Section 21 subject to the modification in article 5 hereof	Section 51(d)
Section 22(1) to (4)	Section 52
Section 24(6), subject to the modification in article 12 hereof (added by S.I. 1995 No. 3217)	Section 54
	Section 55 subject to the modifications in articles 5 and 9 hereof
Section 28	Section 56(1) to (9)
Section 29	Section 57(1) to (9)
Section 30(1) to (4) (a) and (5) to (11)	Section 58(1) to (11)
Section 31	Section 62
Section 32(1) to (9) subject to the modifications in article 5 hereof	Section 63
	Section 64(1) to (6)
Section 34(1) to (5)	Section 107 (*added* by S.I. 1987 No. 439)
Section 35	

I. Powers of Arrest

12–29 138.(1) Any person who has committed, or whom there are reasonable grounds to suspect of having committed, any offence for which he is liable to be arrested under the customs and excise Acts may be arrested by any officer or any member of Her Majesty's armed forces or coastguard at any time within 20 years from the date of the commission of the offence.

(2) Where it was not practicable to arrest any person so liable at the time of the commission of the offence, or where any such person having been then or subsequently arrested for that offence has escaped, he may be arrested by any officer or any member of Her Majesty's armed forces or coastguard at any time and may be proceeded against in like manner as if the offence had been committed at the date when he was finally arrested.

(3) Where any person who is a member of the crew of any ship in Her Majesty's employment or service is arrested by an officer for an offence under the customs and excise Acts, the commanding officer of the ship shall, if so required by the arresting officer, keep that person secured on board that ship until he can be brought before a court and shall then deliver him up to the proper officer.

(4) Where any person has been arrested by a person who is not an officer—

(a) by virtue of this section; or

(b) by virtue of section 24 of the Police and Criminal Evidence Act 1984 in its application to the customs and excise Acts,

the person arresting him shall give notice of the arrest to an officer at the most convenient office of customs and excise.

(This section is printed as amended by the PACE Act 1984, ss.26(1), 114(1), 119(1), (2), 120 and Sched. 6, Pt II, para. 37; the Finance Act 1988, s.11(1), (3); and the Police and Criminal Evidence (Northern Ireland) Order 1989 (S.I. 1989 No. 1341), art. 90(1).)

II. Powers of Search

The powers of stop and search under the CEMA are set out in Annex A 12–30
(see below) to the Police and Criminal Evidence Act 1984 (Codes of Practice) (No. 3) Order 1995 (S.I. 1995 No. 450); formerly to be found in the Police and Criminal Evidence Act 1984 (Codes of Practice) (No. 1) Order 1985 (S.I. 1985 No. 1937) and see S.I. 1990 No. 2580 and the revised Code A (S.I. 1997 No. 1159) and the further revision (S.I. 1999 No. 291) and para. 12–33.

There are a large number of activities carried out in respect of certain goods, which would entitle an officer to treat the goods as being liable to forfeiture. Controlled drugs unlawfully imported, or intended for export, fall into this category. Once liability to forfeiture arises a number of different powers come into effect.

Thus, by section 161(1) of the CEMA, an officer having a Writ of Assistance may enter any building or place where there are reasonable grounds to suspect that anything liable to forfeiture is kept or concealed. Entry may be made by day or by night. If the entry is to be made at night, the officer must be accompanied by a constable (s. 161(2)). Articles liable to forfeiture may be seized and detained (s. 161(1)(a)). In the exercise of these powers an officer may break open any window, door or container. He may forcefully remove any impediment (s. 161(1)(b)).

12–31 Additionally, the officer may apply to a justice of the peace for a search warrant, under section 161(3) of the CEMA (as amended by Sched. 6, para. 6 of PACE), which will entitle him to the same powers as if he had a Writ of Assistance. But whereas a Writ of Assistance runs for the duration of that writ and for a period of six months thereafter, a warrant must be executed within one month (see CEMA, s.161(6) and PACE, s.119(1), Sched. 6, para. 38). For completeness, section 161 reads as follows:

> "161(1) Without prejudice to any other power conferred by the Customs and Excise Acts 1979 but subject to subsection (2) below, where there are reasonable grounds to suspect that any thing liable to forfeiture under the customs and excise Acts is kept or concealed in any building or place, any officer having a writ of assistance may—
>
> (a) enter that building or place at any time, whether by day or night, on any day, and search for, seize, and detain or remove any such thing. and
>
> (b) so far as is reasonably necessary for the purpose of such entry, search, seizure, detention or removal, break open any door, window or container and force and remove any other impediment or obstruction.
>
> (2) No officer shall exercise the power of entry conferred on him by subsection (1) above by night unless he is accompanied by a constable.
>
> (3) Without prejudice to subsection (1) above or to any other power conferred by the Customs and Excise Acts 1979, if a justice of the peace is satisfied by information upon oath given by an officer that there are reasonable grounds to suspect that any thing liable to forfeiture under the customs and excise Acts is kept or concealed in any building or place, he may by warrant under his hand given on any day authorise any officer and any person accompanying an officer to enter and search the building or place named in the warrant within one month from that day.
>
> (4) An officer or other person so authorised shall thereupon have the like powers in relation to the building or place named in the warrant, subject to the like conditions as to entry by night, as if he were an officer having a writ of assistance and acting upon reasonable grounds of suspicion.
>
> (5) Where there are reasonable grounds to suspect that any still, vessel, utensil, spirits or materials for the manufacture of spirits is or are unlawfully kept or deposited in any building or place, subsections (3) and (4) above shall apply in relation to any constable as they would apply in relation to an officer.
>
> (6) A writ of assistance shall continue in force during the reign in which it is issued and for 6 months thereafter.

12–32 Where a person comes within a category of persons listed in section 164(4), *e.g.* any person who is within the dock area of a port, or who has landed from any ship or aircraft, he may be searched, providing that there are reasonable grounds to suspect that he is carrying any article (not just drugs) with respect to the importation or exportation of prohibited goods.

A person who is to be searched under section 164 may complain to the officer's superior or to a justice of the peace, who will decide whether or not a search is to take place: section 164(2) of the CEMA (as amended by the Finance Act 1984, s.8 and Sched. 4, para. 6; and the Finance Act 1988, s.10).

"164(1) Where there are reasonable grounds to suspect that any person to whom this section applies (referred to in this section as 'the suspect') is carrying any article—

(a) which is chargeable with any duty which has not been paid or secured; or

(b) with respect to the importation or exportation of which any prohibition or restriction is for the time being in force under or by virtue of any enactment,

an officer may exercise the powers conferred by subsection (2) below and, if the suspect is not under arrest, may detain him for so long as may be necessary for the exercise of those powers and (where applicable) the exercise of the rights conferred by subsection (3) below.

(2) The officer may require the suspect—

(a) to permit such a search of any article which he has with him; and

(b) subject to subsection (3) below, to submit to such searches of his person, whether rub-down, strip or intimate,

as the officer may consider necessary or expedient, but no such requirement may be imposed under paragraph (b) above without the officer informing the suspect of the effect of subsection (3) below.

(3) If the suspect is required to submit to a search of his person, he may require to be taken—

(a) except in the case of a rub-down search, before a justice of the peace or a superior of the officer concerned; and

(b) in the excepted case, 'before such a superior,

and the justice or superior shall consider the grounds for suspicion and direct accordingly whether the suspect is to submit to the search.

(3A) A rub-down or strip search shall not be carried out except by a person of the same sex as the suspect, and an intimate search shall not be carried out except by a suitably qualified person.

(4) This section applies to the following persons, namely—

(a) any person who is on board or has landed from any ship or aircraft,

(b) any person entering or about to leave the United Kingdom

(c) any person within the dock area of a port,

(d) any person at a customs and excise airport,

(e) any person in, entering or leaving any approved wharf or transit shed which is not in a port,

(ee) any person in, entering or leaving a free zone;

(f) in Northern Ireland, any person travelling from or to any place which is on or beyond the boundary.

(5) In this section—

'intimate search' means any search which involves a physical examination (that is, an examination which is more than simply a visual examination) of a person's body orifices;
'rub-down search' means any search which is neither an intimate search nor a strip search;
'strip search' means any search which is not an intimate search but which involves the removal of an article of clothing which—
(a) is being worn (wholly or partly) on the trunk; and
(b) is being so worn either next to the skin or next to an article of underwear;
'suitably qualified person' means a registered medical practitioner or a registered nurse.

(6) (Scotland.)

No woman or girl may be searched by a man (s. 164(3)) although there is nothing in section 164 to say that a male cannot be searched by a woman!

ANNEX A

12–33 Summary of Main Stop and Search Powers

POWER	OBJECT OF SEARCH	EXTENT OF SEARCH	WHERE EXERCISABLE
Unlawful articles general			
1. Public Stores Act 1875, s.6	HM Stores stolen or unlawfully obtained	Persons, vehicles and vessels	Anywhere where the constabulary powers are exercisable.
2. Firearms Act 1968, s.47	Firearms	Persons and vehicles	A public place, or anywhere in the case of reasonable suspicion of offences of carrying firearms with criminal intent or trespassing with firearms.
3. Misuse of Drugs Act 1971, s.23	Controlled drugs	Persons and vehicles	Anywhere

4. Customs and Excise Management Act 1979, s.163	Goods: Vehicles and vessels only (a) on which duty has not been paid; (b) being unlawfully removed, imported or exported; (c) otherwise liable to forfeiture to HM Customs and Excise		Anywhere
5. Aviation Security Act 1982, s.27(1)	Stolen or unlawfully obtained goods	Airport employees and vehicles carrying aircraft employees or aircraft or any vehicle in a cargo area whether or not carrying an employee	Any designated airport

It will be seen from the above table, that any vehicle or vessel may be stopped and searched by an officer, constable, coastguard or a member of the armed forces if there are reasonable grounds to suspect that the vehicle or vessel is carrying, *inter alia*, a controlled drug: section 163 (as amended by the CJA 1982, s. 38 and s. 46; and s. 10 of the Finance Act 1992). 12–34

"163.(1) Without prejudice to any other power conferred by the Customs and Excise Acts 1979, where there are reasonable grounds to suspect that any vehicle or vessel is or may be carrying any goods which are—

(a) chargeable with any duty which has not been paid or secured; or
(b) in the course of being unlawfully removed from or to any place; or
(c) otherwise liable to forfeiture under the customs and excise Acts,

any officer or constable or member of Her Majesty's armed forces or coastguard may stop and search that vehicle or vessel.

(2) If when so required by any such officer, constable or member the person in charge of any such vehicle or vessel refuses to stop or to permit the vehicle or vessel to be searched, he shall be liable on summary conviction tea penalty of level 3 on the standard scale.

(3) This section shall apply in relation to aircraft as it applies in relation to vehicles or vessels but the power to stop and search in subsection (1) above shall not be available in respect of aircraft which are airborne."

III. Searching at Will

12–35 Many of the powers conferred by the CEMA do not require an officer to have reasonable grounds to suspect the commission of any offence before he exercises those powers. Thus, by section 27 any officer and "any other officer duly engaged in the prevention of smuggling" may board any ship which is within the limits of a port, or any aircraft at a customs and excise airport, or a vehicle on an approved route, so that he may search it.

It is not clear which categories of person Parliament had in mind when referring to "any other person duly engaged in the prevention of smuggling" but this presumably includes a coastguard or police officers assigned to such a task.

Officers once on board are entitled to free access to every part of the ship, aircraft or vessel and may break open any place or container which is locked and of which the keys are withheld: section 28(1) of the CEMA. Any goods found concealed on board shall be liable to forfeiture: section 28(2).

12–36 Customs officers also have power by section 159 of CEMA 1979 (as amended by the Isle of Man Act 1979, s.13 and Sched.1; the Finance Act 1984, s.8 and Sched. 4; PACE 1984, s.114(1); and the Finance Act 1988, s.12(1)(a)), to examine and take account of goods and it is an offence to remove goods with intent to evade a prohibition or restriction imposed in respect of the goods, or with intent to defraud Her Majesty.

"159(1) Without prejudice to any other power conferred by the Customs and Excise Acts 1979, an officer may examine and take account of any goods—

(a) which are imported; or
(b) which are in a warehouse or Queen's warehouse; or
(bb) which are in a free zone; or
(c) which have been loaded into any ship or aircraft at any place in the United Kingdom or the Isle of Man; or
(d) which are entered for exportation or for use as stores; or
(e) which are brought to any place in the United Kingdom for exportation or for shipment for exportation or as stores; or
(f) in the case of which any claim for drawback, allowance, rebate, remission or repayment of duty is made;

and may for that purpose require any container to be opened or unpacked.

(2) Any examination of goods by an officer under the Customs and Excise Acts 1979 shall be made at such place as the Commissioners appoint for the purpose.

(3) In the case of such goods as the Commissioners may direct, and

subject to such conditions as they see fit to impose, an officer may permit goods to be skipped on the quay or bulked, sorted, lotted, packed or repacked before account is taken thereof.

(4) Any opening, unpacking, weighing, measuring, repacking, bulking, sorting, lotting, marking, numbering, loading, unloading, carrying or landing of goods or their containers for the purposes of, or incidental to, the examination by an officer, removal or warehousing thereof shall be done, and any facilities or assistance required for any such examination shall be provided, by or at the expense of the proprietor of the goods.

(5) If any imported goods which an officer has power under the Customs and Excise Acts 1979 to examine are without the authority of the proper officer removed from customs and excise charge before they have been examined, those goods shall be liable to forfeiture.

(6) If any goods falling within subsection (5) above are removed by a person with intent to defraud Her Majesty of any duty chargeable thereon or to evade any prohibition or restriction for the time being in force with respect thereto under or by virtue of any enactment, that person shall be guilty of an offence under this subsection and may be arrested.

(7) A person guilty of an offence under subsection (6) above shall be liable—

(a) on summary conviction, to a penalty of the prescribed sum or of three times the value of the goods, which ever is the greater, or to imprisonment for a term not exceeding 6 months, or to both; or

(b) on conviction on indictment, to a penalty of any amount, or to imprisonment for a term not exceeding 7 years, or to both.

(8) Without prejudice to the foregoing provisions of this section, where by this section or by or under any other provision of the Customs and Excise Acts 1979 an account is authorised or required to be taken of any goods for any purpose by an officer, the Commissioners may, with the consent of the proprietor of the goods, accept as the account of those goods for that purpose an account taken by such other person as may be approved in that behalf by both the Commissioners and the proprietor of the goods.

If goods have been loaded onto a vehicle for transportation through the Channel Tunnel, then section 159(1)(c) shall be construed accordingly, that is to say, for the words "loaded into a ship" read "loaded onto a vehicle": see the Channel Tunnel (Customs and Excise) Order 1990, art. 4, Sched., para. 24 (S.I. 1990 No. 2167). 12–37

A commander of an aircraft must allow an officer to board an aircraft and to inspect goods and documents therein: section 33. If an officer or a constable considers that an aircraft is likely to leave the United Kingdom from a place other than a customs and excise airport, then he may take such steps as appear to him to be necessary in order to prevent the flight: section 34. This seems to permit all manner of dramatic measures to be adopted (seemingly with impunity) if the officer sees fit.

An officer or constable who has reasonable cause to suspect that signals or messages in connection with a smuggling operation are being made or transmitted from a ship, aircraft, vehicle, house or place, may board or enter, as the case may be, and take such steps as are reasonably necessary to stop and prevent the sending of the signal or message: CEMA, section 84(5).

IV. Seizure of Articles and the Taking of Samples

12–38 An officer, constable, coastguard or any member of the armed forces may seize and detain anything liable to forfeiture under the Customs and Excise Acts: CEMA, section 139(1) (as amended by the CJA 1982, s.46.).

"139(1) Any thing liable to forfeiture under the customs and excise Acts may be seized or detained by any officer or constable or any member of Her Majesty's armed forces or coastguard.

(2) Where anything is seized or detained as liable to forfeiture under the customs and excise Acts by a person other than an officer, that person shall, subject to subsection (3) below, either—

(a) deliver that thing to the nearest convenient office of customs and excise; or

(b) if such delivery is not practicable, give to the Commissioners at the nearest convenient office of customs and excise notice in writing of the seizure or detention with full particulars of the thing seized or detained.

(3) Where the person seizing or detaining any thing as liable to forfeiture under the customs and excise Acts is a constable and that thing is or may be required for use in connection with any proceedings to be brought otherwise than under those Acts it may, subject to subsection (4) below, be retained in the custody of the police until either those proceedings are completed or it is decided that no such proceedings shall be brought.

(4) The following provisions apply in relation to things retained in the custody of the police by virtue of subsection (3). above, that is to say—

(a) notice in writing of the seizure or detention and of the intention to retain the thing in question in the custody of the police, together with full particulars as to that thing, shall be given to the Commissioners at the nearest convenient office of customs and excise;

(b) any officer shall be permitted to examine that thing and take account thereof at any time while it remains in the custody of the police;

(c) nothing in the Police (Property) Act 1897 shall apply in relation to that thing.

(5) Subject to subsections (3) and (4) above and to Schedule 3 to this Act, any thing seized or detained under the customs and excise Acts shall, pending the determination as to its forfeiture or disposal, be dealt with,

and, if condemned or deemed to have been condemned or forfeited, shall be disposed of in such manner as the Commissioners may direct.

(6) Schedule 3 to this Act shall have effect for the purpose of forfeitures, and of proceedings for the condemnation of any thing as being forfeited, under the customs and excise Acts.

(7) If any person, not being an officer, by whom any thing is seized or detained or who has custody thereof after its seizure or detention, fails to comply with any requirement of this section or with any direction of the Commissioners given thereunder, he shall be liable on summary conviction to a penalty of level 2 on the standard scale.

(8) Subsections (2) to (7) above shall apply in relation to any dutiable goods seized or detained by any person other than an officer notwithstanding that they were not so seized as liable to forfeiture under the customs and excise Acts."

Samples may be taken of any goods, which an officer is empowered to examine under the CEMA: section 160(1). See also the Channel Tunnel (Customs and Excise) Order 1990 (S.I. 1990 No. 2(67) and Schedule para. 20A inserted by S.I. 1993 No. 1813; and see Channel Tunnel (Miscellaneous Provisions) Order 1994 (S.I. 1994 No. 1405). Consider *R. v. Uxbridge JJ., ex p. Sofaer* 85 Cr.App.R. 367.

V. Detention of Persons

An officer, coastguard, or a member of the armed forces may arrest a person whom he has reasonable grounds to suspect has committed a drugs-related importation or exportation: CEMA, section 138. The power of arrest may be exercised within three years of the offence being committed: section 138(1). See also the Channel Tunnel (International Arrangements) Order 1993 (S.I. 1993 No. 1813) and the Channel Tunnel (Miscellaneous Provisions) Order 1994 (S.I. 1994 No. 1405). 12–39

D. WHO MAY INITIATE A PROSECUTION?

In *Ealing Justices, ex p. Dixon* [1990] 2 Q.B. 91, the Divisional Court held that a custody officer, in accepting a charge at a police station, did so on behalf of the police force irrespective of which law-enforcement body was in fact responsible for presenting the defendant to the custody officer, so that only the Director of Public Prosecutions might institute proceedings under section 6 of the Prosecution of Offences Act 1985. This meant that a customs officer who had been investigating an offence, arrested somebody without a warrant and took him to a police station to be charged by the custody officer under section 37 of PACE would thereby surrender the prosecution of the proceedings to the Director of Public Prosecutions. Such a conclusion would be inconsistent with section 145(1) of CEMA provides 12–40 that no proceedings for an offence under the Customs and Excise Acts should be instituted except by order of the Commissioners.

However, in *Stafford Justices, ex p. Commissioners of Customs & Excise* [1991] 2 Q.B. 339, the Divisional Court (Lord Justice Watkins and Mr. Justice Nolan) held that *Dixon* was wrongly decided. Proceedings could only be said to have been instituted on behalf of a police force when it was the police who had investigated, arrested, and brought the arrested person to the custody officer. Put shortly, a customs officer in investigating an offence lacked no essential power except that of charging the arrested person: see article 4 of the Police and Criminal Evidence Act 1984 (Application to Customs and Excise) Order (S.I. 1985 No. 1800).

12–41 Section 6 of the Prosecution of Offences Act 1985 plainly contemplates that persons other than the Director of Public Prosecutions may institute proceedings and prosecute. In *Stafford Justices, ex p. Customs and Excise Commissioners*, the applicant had been arrested in connection with an offence under section 24(1)(a) of the DTOA 1986 (now s.50(1)(a) of the DTA) and taken by a customs officer to a custody officer at a police station to be charged with that offence. The Divisional Court was prepared to accept that an offence under section 24 of the 1986 Act was an "assigned matter" for the purposes of section 1 and section 145(1) of the CEMA 1979. Although Parliament had conferred upon custody officers exclusive rights and duties in relation to charging arrested persons (see PACE 1984, s.37) there was no reason why others, including customs officers, should not be allowed to take advantage of that charging procedure without surrendering the prosecution of the offence to the Director of Public Prosecutions see *Akomolede* [1995] Crim. L.R. 161; and see *R. v. Croydon JJ, ex. p. Holmberg* [1992] Crim. L.R. 892.

E. ILLEGALLY OBTAINED EVIDENCE

12–42 It has long been a rule of law, although much criticised, that evidence adduced by unlawful or improper means (save in relation to involuntary confessions) and generally with regard to evidence obtained from the accused after the commission of the offence is admissible in evidence: see *Kuruma* [1955] A.C. 197, and *Maqsud Ali* (1966). The principal safeguard has always been the court's inherent discretion to exclude such evidence if its prejudicial effect outweighs its probative value: see *Sang* [1980] A.C. 402 and *Jeffery v. Black* [1978] Q.B. 490. A similar discretion has now been given statutory effect by section 78 of PACE which enables a court to disallow prosecution evidence if, having regard to the circumstances in which the evidence was obtained, its admissibility "would have such an adverse effect on the fairness of the proceedings". It is not yet clear whether section 78 has altered the earlier position, but it is of interest that the section makes reference to the effect on the fairness of the proceedings. In other words, it would seem that the Court is not merely concerned with whether admitting the evidence or not would be unfair to the accused, but also whether the evidence is so grossly prejudicial that it would be unreasonable to admit it. Accordingly, it is submitted that the words quoted were the draftsman's way of rewording the cliché that "justice must not only be done, but also be seen to be done". If, then, a reasonable bystander viewing the proceedings was to be heard to say that the evidence was obtained in circumstances so patently unfair that it would be an affront to our system of justice to admit it, then the judge (fulfilling the role of the bystander) ought to exclude it: but see *Christou and Wright*, [1992] 1 Q.B. 979; *H.M. Advocate v. Graham*, 1991 S.L.T. 416; *H.M. Advocate v. Harper*, 1989 S.C.C.R. 472 and *Weir v. Jessop*, 1992 S.L.T. 533 (a case of entrapment) and see *Latif* [1996] 1 All E.R. 353.

The matter must now be viewed in the light of the Human Rights Act 1998, developments in relation to the power of the courts to stay proceedings, and changes to the law in relation to the approach the Court of Appeal will take when faced with a submission that a conviction is 'unsafe' because the trial judge erred in admitting evidence obtained illegally or unfairly. The last matter was considered recently in *Togher and Others* (December 2000) when the Lord Chief Justice (Lord Woolf) departed from the decision in *R. v. Chalkley and Jeffries* [1998] 2 Cr App R 79, and said: 12–43

> "As a matter of first principles, we do not consider that either the use of the word 'unsafe' in the legislation or the previous cases compel an approach which does not correspond with that of the ECHR. The requirement of fairness in the criminal process has always been a common law tenet of the greatest importance. The common law approach has been enhanced by legislation and in particular, the Police and Criminal Evidence Act 1984 and the codes of practice made thereunder (sections 66 and 67). Fairness in both jurisdictions is not an abstract concept. Fairness is not concerned with technicalities. If a defendant has not had a fair trial and as a result of that injustice has occurred, it would be extremely unsatisfactory if the powers of this Court were not wide enough to rectify that injustice. If, contrary to our expectations, that has not previously been the position, then it seems to us that this is a defect in our procedures which is now capable of rectification under section 3 of the Human Rights Act 1998 ('the 1998 Act'). The 1998 Act requires primary legislation and subordinate legislation to be read and given effect to in a way which is compatible with Convention rights. Section 6(1) of the 1998 Act makes it unlawful for a public authority to act in a way which is incompatible with a Convention right and a court is a public authority for the purposes of section 6 (section 6(3)). The 1998 Act emphasises the desirability of taking a broader rather than a narrower approach as to what constitutes an unsafe conviction. In *R. v. Davis, Rowe and Johnson* (July 17, 2000, unreported), this Court acknowledged that there could still be a distinction between its approach and the approach of the

European Court of Human Rights. However, in the later case of *R. v. Francom* (July 31, 2000, unreported), this Court indicated, in a judgment which I gave on behalf of the Court, that we would expect, in the situation there being considered, that the approach of this Court applying the test of lack of safety would produce the same result as the approach of the ECHR applying the test of lack of fairness. We would suggest that, even if there was previously a difference of approach, that since the 1998 Act came into force, the circumstances in which there will be room for a different result before this Court and before the ECHR because of unfairness based on the respective tests we employ will be rare indeed. Applying the broader approach identified by Rose LJ, we consider that if a defendant has been denied a fair trial it will almost be inevitable that the conviction will be regarded as unsafe. For this reason we endorse the approach of Rose L.J. in *Mullen* and prefer the broader approach to the narrower approach supported by Auld LJ. Certainly, if it would be right to stop a prosecution on the basis that it was an abuse of process, this Court would be most unlikely to conclude that if there was a conviction despite this fact, the conviction should not be set aside."

However, the position has been made less clear as a result of other decisions of the Court of Appeal: *Blackwood* (March 10, 2000); *Bailey and Brewin* (March 15, 2001); and consider *Bhatti* (December 19, 2000).

F. OBSTRUCTION OF OFFICERS

I. Obstruction of Police Officers under the MDA

12–44 Section 23(4) of the MDA provides:

"A person commits an offence if he[—]

(a) intentionally obstructs a person in the exercise of his powers under this section; or
(b) conceals from a person acting in the exercise of his powers under subsection (1) above any such books, documents, stocks or drugs as are mentioned in that subsection; or
(c) without reasonable excuse (proof of which shall lie on him) fails to produce any such books or documents as are so mentioned where their production is demanded by a person in the exercise of his powers under that subsection."

Subsections (4)(b) and (c) apply only to commercial concerns which carry on business as producers or suppliers of controlled drugs.

Constables or other persons authorised by the Secretary of State may enter the business premises and inspect the companies' paperwork, stock or drugs. Accordingly, an offence will be committed if the relevant items are either concealed or not produced upon demand without a reasonable excuse.

The wording of section 23(4)(b) implies that an accused need only know that the documents, stock or drugs concealed relate to drug transactions and that an officer might wish to see them. However, section 23(4)(c) is absolute in the absence of a reasonable excuse that explains the reason why the documents concerned could not be physically produced when demanded, *e.g.* destroyed in a fire, or retained by a court for the purposes of pending litigation. The motives of the accused are immaterial. Thus, merely to protect the identity of a confidential client who is lawfully entitled to buy and possess the drugs would not be a defence or a reasonable excuse. 12–45

It is for the prosecution to prove that there has been an obstruction and be in a position to prove that the obstruction was not unlawful.

> In *French v. DPP* (November 27, 1996, Crown Office), F was convicted of obstructing police contrary to 51(3) of the Police Act 1964. F had been stopped and searched under section 23 of the Misuse of Drugs Act but neither gave evidence at the trial as to their reasons for doing so. F had been arrested by another officer who arrived at the scene after F had been stopped. It was impossible for the court to establish whether the search was lawful, or the obstruction unlawful. The appeal was allowed.

(a) Defining an intentional obstruction

In *Forde (J.)* (1985) 81 Cr.App.R. 19 the Court of Appeal held that an offence is committed once an act is done which, when viewed objectively, obstructed the officer in the execution of his powers under section 23 and was intended by an accused to obstruct. This principle probably explains the decision of the High Court in Scotland in *McDermott v. Scott*, 1993 G.W.D. 1747, in which it was held that there had been an obstruction of officers contrary to section 23(4)(a) by S and M who sat in their car and locked the doors after they were signalled to stop by police. The police produced their warrant cards and told the occupants of the car that they wished to carry out a search for controlled drugs. After waiting a short period of time, the police smashed a window in order to gain access. The fact that the police did not, it seems, ask S and M to open the doors, was irrelevant to the charge. 12–46

It would therefore appear that the words "intentionally obstructs" have the same meaning as "wilfully obstructs" found in other enactments and notably section 51(3) of the Police Act 1964. In *Hills v. Ellis* [1983] Q.B. 680 the Divisional Court, when considering section 51(3) of the Act, asked "what is meant by an 'intention to obstruct'"? and gave the following reply (*per* McCullough J.):

> "I would construe 'wilfully obstructs' as doing deliberate actions with the intention of bringing about a state of affairs which, objectively regarded, amounts to an obstruction . . . the fact that the defendant might not have called that state of affairs an obstruction is . . . immaterial"

12–47 What is an obstruction? The answer is an act calculated to make it more difficult for the police to carry out their duties: see *Rice v. Connolly* [1966] 2 Q.B. 414. Thus, to throw drugs away before the police can seize them is a classic example of obstruction under section 23. It is not necessary to prove a "hostile" motive in obstructing the officer: see *Willmott v. Atack* [1976] 3 W.L.R. 753 and *Green v. Moore* [1982] Q.B. 1044.

> In *Kelly* (November 19, 1984, unreported), the Court of Appeal held that an offence is committed under section 23(4)(a) if D knows that the officer is detaining, or trying to detain him, in order to search D for drugs. D's conduct when viewed objectively did obstruct the detention and search. D's conduct, viewed subjectively, was intended to obstruct.

The Court in *Kelly* accepted that there may be occasions where the obstructing act was performed before the constable had the opportunity to explain what he was doing. However, the existence of such a feature would not automatically excuse a defendant in circumstances where the reasons for the constable's conduct must have been obvious to the defendant.

12–48 The term "obstruct" as it appears in section 23 is capable of figurative use and is not limited to physical personal obstruction or restraint. Anything done by an accused with the intention of hindering officers in the exercise of their duty under the warrant issued is capable of bringing the accused within the scope of section 23.

> In *Gauld v. Normand*, 1997 S.L.T. 1025, the accused was observed by police officers leaving premises where, to the knowledge of police, drug dealing occurred. When the accused was approached by officers, she put something into her mouth and swallowed it. She was convicted of obstructing the police and she appealed on the basis that evidence leading to her arrest ought not to have been admitted because the police did not have reasonable grounds to suspect that she was in possession of controlled drugs. The appeal was refused because on the facts of the case, reasonable grounds to suspect did exist.

The obstruction must, of course, be intentional: *Carmichael v. Brannan*, 1986 S.L.T. 5. In that case, one defendant swallowed a substance, three defendants jumped from a veranda to avoid arrest, and all of them refused to open the door of the house to which the police sought to gain access. Lord Cameron rejected the argument that the swallowing of an unknown substance could not be construed as seeking to hide evidence of a crime.

He added that the article that was swallowed was in the possession of one of the men and that:

> "his person was liable to be searched, and it was clearly an object which could be comprised in the search and, if its character was or appeared to be of criminal character, liable to be taken possession of and taken for examination."

It follows that it is unnecessary for the prosecution to prove that what was disposed of was a controlled drug because frequently that would be impossible if the obstruction succeeded. Swallowing a substance is a classic way of obstructing officers under this provision: see also *Normand v. McCutheon*, 1993 S.C.C.R. 710 and *Dunne v. Normand* (November 18, 1992; commentary at 1993 S.C.C.R. 713). However, it is open to the Court to decide whether an accused had in fact swallowed a substance (and which would be an obstruction had he done so): in *Vannett v. Taylor (Stephen)*, 1998 S.C.C.R. 30, there was evidence that T raised his hand to his mouth but the sheriff declined to find that T had swallowed anything. He was not inevitably wrong and the appeal against his finding was refused. 12–49

However, it is necessary as a matter of evidence, to establish that the police officers were acting in the exercise of the powers given to them by the section having regard to the fact that under section 23(2) the officers must have reasonable ground to suspect that the person is in possession of controlled drugs whereas, under section 23(3) once a warrant has been issued pursuant to that provision, the officers may perform their statutory duties in connection with that warrant and it is an offence to obstruct them from doing so: see *Annan v. McIntosh*, 1993 S.C.C.R. 938; and see *Normand v. McCutcheon*, 1993 S.C.C.R. 709.

II. Obstruction of Customs Officers

By section 16(1) of the CEMA 1979: 12–50

"Any person who—

(a) obstructs [see *George* [1981] Crim.L.R. 185], hinders, molests or assaults any person duly engaged in the performance of any duty or the exercise of any power imposed or conferred on him by or under any enactment relating to an assigned matter, or any person acting in his aid; or

(b) does anything which impedes or is calculated to impede the carrying out of any search for any thing liable to forfeiture under any such enactment or the detention, seizure or removal of any such thing; or

(c) rescues, damages or destroys any thing so liable to forfeiture or does anything calculated to prevent the procuring or giving of evidence as to whether or not any thing is so liable to forfeiture; or

(d) prevents the detention of any person by a person duly engaged or acting as aforesaid or rescues any person so detained,

or who attempts to do any of the aforementioned things, shall be guilty of an offence under this section These provisions are really self-explanatory but go a great deal further than section 23 of the MDA."

Chapter 13
The Drug Trafficking Act 1994

This Chapter is divided into four sections:

(1) a practitioner's guide to the Drug Trafficking Act 1994;
(2) a practitioner's guide to confiscation under Part VI of the Criminal Justice Act 1988;
(3) the draft Proceeds of Crime Bill 2001;
(4) the Drug Trafficking Act 1994 —a detailed commentary.

(1)
A Practitioner's Guide to the Drug Trafficking Act 1994

Principal Reforms Introduced by the DTA 1994

13–01 (a) Removes the mandatory requirement (under the DTOA 1986) that a drug trafficking enquiry has to be conducted in every case where the offender is convicted of, or pleads guilty to, a drug trafficking offence;
(b) The Court is *required* to make the statutory assumptions under the DTA which may be rebuttable in two specified instances (see s.4);
(c) The standard of proof to be applied throughout the is the *civil* standard (see s.2(8));
(d) Confiscation orders can be enforced to payment of the full sum even if the defaulter has served a term of imprisonment in default (see s.9(5));
(e) Further proceedings can be taken within 6 years of a defendant's conviction in connection with confiscation orders and these include:
   (i) the power of the Court to consider embarking on confiscation proceedings when it had previously not done so through lack of evidence (see s.13);
   (ii) re-considering whether the defendant has *benefited* from drug trafficking in the light of new evidence, when the Court had previously decided that he had not so benefited (see s.14);
   (iii) in cases where a confiscation order has been made under the DTA, the Court is empowered to re-assess the *value* of the defendant's proceeds of drug trafficking in the light of new evidence (s. 15);
   (iv) the powers of the Court to make a downward variation of a confiscation order have been extended by enabling a

receiver (and not just the defendant) to make the necessary application to the High Court (see s.17);

(f) The High Court may confiscate the assets of the deceased or absconding defendant (see ss. 19–24);

(g) Offences created under the DTA now include:
- — the acquisition, possession or use of drug trafficking proceeds (see s.51);
- — failing to disclose knowledge or suspicion of money laundering activities (see s.52);
- — "tipping off" offences, *i.e.* divulging information likely to prejudice an investigation into drug money-laundering (see s.53).

A Conviction for a "drug trafficking offence" does *not* mean that there must be a DTA enquiry.

There are two stages: see *Klann* (July 13, 1999) 13–02

(1) establish whether the Court is to embark upon a drug trafficking enquiry. If the answer is "no"—proceed to sentence for the offence. If the answer is "yes" then:

(2) decide on the appropriate "time-table" for the purposes of (a) proceeding under the DTA and (b) sentencing the defendant:
   - (i) normally the Court must conduct the DTA enquiry *before* proceeding to sentence: see s.2(4) and s.2(5)
     but:
   - (ii) the Court may postpone a DTA hearing if:
     - (a) the Court requires more information in order to decide whether the defendant has "benefited" from drug trafficking *or* to determine the "amount to be recovered" under a confiscation order: see s.3(1)
       or
     - (b) where the defendant appeals against his conviction: see s.3(4)

Note: the Court need not postpone the entire DTA hearing. The Court could determine whether the defendant has "benefited" from drug trafficking and then postpone any remaining determinations: see s.3(1) and s.3(4).

Note: if the Court postpones a determination it MAY *proceed to sentence the defendant for the offence:* s.3(7). However, this could create difficulties if matters subsequently emerge during the DTA hearing, which should have been taken into account when sentencing for the offence.

Williams (March 24, 1998, CA)
Thompson (July 31, 1996, CA)

Who decides whether there is to be a DTA hearing?

The Court can only embark upon an enquiry under the Act if either:

(i) the prosecutor asks the Court to proceed: s.2(1)(a); or

(ii) the Court considers that it would be appropriate to do so: s.2(1)(b)

Note: if the prosecution ask the Court to proceed under the DTA it would seem that the Court has no power to override the wishes of the prosecutor unless the phrase "ask the Court", as it appears in section 2(1)(a), is construed to mean "applies for leave of the Court" to proceed under the Act. However, if that is what Parliament intended the effect of s.2(1)(a) to be, it would have been very easy for the draughtsman merely to have said so. May the Court penalise futile DTA hearings in costs?

Against whom may a confiscation order be made?

13–03 Confiscation orders may only be made against persons who appear before the Crown Court to be sentenced in respect of one or more "drug trafficking offences": s.1(3) of the 1994 Act.

The list of drug trafficking offences in s.1(3) of the 1994 Act broadly follows s.38(1) of the 1986 Act as amended by the Criminal Justice (International Co-operation) Act 1990, Sched.4, para.4(4) and by s.24(9) of the 1993 Act.

Note: the term "drug trafficking" is to be distinguished from "drug trafficking offences": see s.1(3). Not every "drug trafficking" activity amounts to a "drug trafficking offence".

> For example: an offence under section 8 of the Misuse of Drugs Act 1971 (permitting premises to be used for prohibited acts to take place therein) is not a "drug trafficking offence" even if drug trafficking did take place on the premises. The reason for omitting this offence is probably because the offence is wide enough to embrace persons who do not intend or desire that the prohibited activity should take place but they display an unwillingness to take the means available to them to prevent that activity: see *Thomas & Thompson* (1976) 63 Cr. App. R. 65. Also note, the proposal to include an offence under section 8 of the Misuse of Drugs Act 1971 as a "drug trafficking offence" (see the Proceeds of Crime Bill 2001). Similarly, the cultivation of cannabis under section 6 of the MDA 1971 is NOT a drug trafficking offence.

Postponing DTA hearings

13–04 The Court need not wait until a determination is made of the amount which may be recovered under a confiscation order before sentencing the defendant: see s.3(7) of the 1994 Act. Moreover, the Court is not prevented from imposing a fine, or making an order under s.27 of the 1971 Act or s.143 of the Powers of Criminal Courts (Sentencing) Act 2000, or any other monetary order, merely because a confiscation order is made beyond the 28-day period when the defendant was first sentenced for the offence before the Court: s.3(10).

The Court may:

(i) postpone making the determination for "such period as it may specify": s.3(1) and:

(ii) more than one postponement may be made in relation to the same case: s.3(2)
but

(iii) unless there are exceptional circumstances, the Court shall not postpone for a period longer than 6 months from the *date of conviction:* s.3(3)

Akpan (October 20, 1998, CA)
Cole (April 22, 1998)
Edwards (May 11th, 1999)
France (April 27, 1998)
Hussain (April 18, 2000)
Kelly (December 13, 1999)
Shergill [1999] 2 Cr. App. R(S) 341
Steele (December 14, 2000)
Tuegel (November 19, 1999)
Turberfield (May 11, 2000)
Ward (November 24, 1999)
Williams (March 24, 1998)
Zelzele (June 21, 1999) (leave to appeal)

(iv) again, unless there are exceptional circumstances, the Court shall not postpone for a period longer than 3 months after the date on which an appeal against conviction is determined: s.3(6) (and see *Rule 34 of the Crown Court Rules, SI 1994 No. 3153*).

Note: Where the defendant is convicted on more than one indictment (*e.g.* as a result of separate committals or separate trials ordered on severance of an indictment) the period of postponement runs from the last conviction for a drug trafficking offence: see s.3(11). This applies whether or not the convictions occurred at the same or different Crown Courts.

Is it wise for the Court to proceed to sentence before the DTA enquiry is concluded?

The answer to this question will no doubt depend, in part, on the length of the postponement but another consideration will be whether material emerges during the DTA enquiry which could either mitigate (or aggravate) the sentence: see *R. v. Ayensu and Ayensu* (1982) 4 Cr.App.R.(S) 248; *R. v. Bragason* [1988] Crim.L.R. 778; *R. v. Ralf* (1989) 11 Cr.App.R.(S) 121; *R. v. Harper* (1989) 11 Cr.App.R.(S) 240, *R. v. Saunders* (1991) 92 Cr.App.R. 6.; *R. v. Reeves (R.J.)* (1993) 5 Cr.App.R.(S) 292; *McNulty* (1994) 15 Cr.App.R.(S) 606 and see *Callan* (1994) 98 Cr.App.R. 467; see *Thompson* (July 31, 1996). 13–05

The structure of the DTA is designed to encourage the Crown Court to proceed to make its determinations under the Act i) without delay and ii) before sentencing the defendant: see s.2(4).

Note: If the Court does proceed to sentence, and postpones the DTA enquiry, then it must not make any financial order against the defendant: s.3(9). This is because the Court may determine that all of the defendant's assets are the proceeds of drug trafficking and it is the DTA which is the appropriate vehicle for recovering the proceeds of drug trafficking. Should a defendant have assets, which exceed the value of a confiscation order, the Court might then wish to order the defendant to pay costs or, to make some other financial order against him including the imposition of a fine. Section 3(10) permits this to be done within 28 days "beginning with the end of the specified period" (*i.e.* the period of postponement); see *Williams* (March 24, 1998).

Note: A postponement pending an appeal may be an attractive option if the DTA enquiry is likely to be difficult and protracted (and thus expensive) or if, in the opinion of the Crown Court, the appeal stands a good chance of succeeding. No doubt the Courts will be on their guard against parties seeking a postponement pending an appeal, if the real reason for seeking postponement is to put off the DTA hearing for the longest period permitted under the Act!

Who may apply for a postponement?

13–06 An application may be made by the prosecutor, or the defendant, or the Court may postpone of its own motion: s.3(5).

How is an application for a postponement to be made?

13–07 The procedure to be followed if an application is made under section 3(4) and 3(5) of the DTA is set out in Rule 35 of the Crown Court Rules: see the Crown Court (Amendment) (No. 2) Rules 1994 (S.I. 1994 No. 3153) which came into force as from February 3, 1995.

> "34.—(1) Where an application to the Crown Court is made by the defendant or the prosecutor under section 3(5)(a) of the Drug Trafficking Act 1994 asking the Court to exercise its powers under section 3(4) of that Act . . . such an application must be made in writing and a copy thereof must be served on the prosecutor or the defendant, as the case may be.
>
> (2) A party which is served with a copy of an application under paragraph (1) shall, within 28 days of the date of service, notify the applicant and the appropriate officer of the Crown Court, in writing, whether or not it proposes to oppose the application, giving its reasons for any such opposition.
>
> (3) After the expiry of the period referred to in paragraph (2), the Crown Court shall determine whether an application under paragraph (1) is to be dealt with—

(a) without a hearing, or
(b) at a hearing at which the parties may be represented."

Putting information before the Court

Statements tendered by the prosecution (s. 11)

13–08 Under the 1994 Act the procedure for the provision of information has been strengthened. The procedure applies *not only* to the usual situation where the Court proceeds under s.2, following a conviction for a drug trafficking offence, *but also* where the Court is asked to proceed under s.2 when it originally declined to do so (s.13(11)); *or* where the Court is asked to re-assess whether the defendant has benefited from drug trafficking (s.14(8)); *or* where the Court revises its assessment of the proceeds of any trafficking (s.15(3)); *or* where the defendant has died or absconded (s.19(6)(b)).

Where a prosecutor does not serve a "prosecutor's statement", the Court may order him to serve one (s.11(3)).

Statements served where the prosecutor initiates proceedings

13–09 Section 11(1) and (2) apply in cases where the prosecutor takes the initiative and asks the Court to proceed under section 2 with a view to the Court making a confiscation order:

"11.—(1) Where the prosecutor asks the Court to proceed under section 2 of this Act he shall give the Court, within such period as it may direct, a statement of matters which he considers relevant in connection with—
(a) determining whether the defendant has benefited from drug trafficking, or
(b) assessing the value of his proceeds of drug trafficking.
(2) In this section such a statement is referred to as a 'prosecutor's statement'."

Under the 1986 legislation it was not incumbent upon the prosecutor to serve, what used to be called a "section 3 statement", in every drug trafficking enquiry but section 11(1) of the DTA now places a duty on the prosecution to furnish the Court with a statement of matters relevant to only two determinations (i) whether the defendant has benefited from drug trafficking and (ii) the value of the benefit: see also rule 25A, Crown Court Rules 1982, as amended by the Crown Court Amendment Rules 1995 (S.I. 1995 No. 2618).

Note: s.11(1) does *not* require the prosecution to give details of all "realisable property" (see s.6(2) and (3)) or to calculate the "amount that might be realised" (*i.e.* the amount the defendant can truly deliver up: see s.6(1)).

At first sight, this might seem a surprising omission because in most cases the Court would wish to determine whether the defendant is able to pay back the full amount of the benefit he received or not. However it is probable that this omission was deliberate because it will be recalled that the scheme of the Act is intended to ensure that the Courts confiscate the full value of a defendant's proceeds of drug trafficking and that is the reason why section 5(1) begins by saying that the "amount to be recovered" under a confiscation order "shall be . . . the value of the defendant's proceeds of drug trafficking".

By virtue of s.5(3) the Court need only confiscate a lesser amount (or a nominal amount) if "the Court is satisfied" that the defendant is unable to pay back the full value of his proceeds. Usually it will be the defendant's task under s.5(3) to prove that he is worth less than the value of his proceeds and this will mean that he must satisfy the Court that he has been utterly frank about the extent of his assets and their value. Arguably, the persuasive burden always rests on the defendant: see *Barwick* (October 13, 2000)

Statements served when the court initiates proceedings

13–10 By section 11(3) it is provided that:

> "Where the Court proceeds under section 2 of this Act without the prosecutor having asked it to do so, it may require him to give it a prosecutor's statement, within such period as it may direct."

Note: there is one important difference between the scope and effect of this provision and s.11(1) and (2). Whereas the prosecutor is *obliged* to serve a "prosecutor's statement", if he asks the Court to embark upon confiscation proceedings (s. 11(1) and (2)), the Court is not obliged to order the prosecutor to prepare and to serve such a statement on the Court if it is the Court which initiates the enquiry.

The defence is entitled to know the case it has to meet and the prosecutor should at least identify at the outset (orally or in writing) those matters it regards as being relevant when determining whether the defendant has benefited from drug trafficking or assessing the value of his proceeds. No doubt this would normally be done at the stage at which the Court is considering whether it is appropriate for it to proceed under the Act (see s.2(1)) and it is submitted that it would be desirable for the prosecutor to specify those assets, which are said to be realisable under the Act.

Specifying the time for service of the prosecutor's statement

13–11 A "prosecutor's statement" (see s.11(2)) must be served "within such period as the Court may direct": see section 11(1) and (3).

The timetable will depend on the issues involved, whether enquiries are to be made, whether overseas enquiries are likely to be involved, and the amount of time which should be given to the defence to enable them to efficiently and effectively reply to the statement. Section 11(4)(a) allows the prosecutor to serve a further statement "at any time" and the Court need not wait for the prosecutor to take the initiative but may order the prosecutor to provide a further statement to be served on the Court within such period as it may direct: section 11(4)(b).

Proving matters contained in a prosecutor's statement

Matters may be included in the statement, which arose during the course of the trial of the offences before the Court: see *Comiskey* (1991) 93 Cr. App. R. 227. 13–12

The statement may also contain hearsay but this is subject to heavy qualification. Under the 1986 legislation it was generally understood that the prosecution should not include hearsay in the statement. In *Chrastny No. 2* [1991] 1 W.L.R. 1381, the Court of Appeal made it clear that the Court could only act on admissible evidence. Both under the DTOA, and under s.11 of the 1994 Act, the Court can ask the defendant to indicate the extent to which he accepts any allegation in the prosecutor's statement (see now s.11(5)). If the defendant accepts any allegation then it will be conclusive of the matters to which it relates (see s.11(7)). It may be difficult (on appeal) to go behind matters that had been agreed during the DTA confiscation proceedings: but see *Emmett* [1997] 3 W.L.R. 1119, HL, and see *Tredwen* [1994] Crim. L.R 388.

Where allegations contained in a prosecutor's statement are challenged then the defendant may be required, by the Court, to state his objection, and to give particulars of matters on which he proposes to rely (s.11(5)(b)). The prosecutor is then put on notice as to what he must do in order to prove the allegation by admissible evidence.

Defendant may be asked to reply to prosecutor's statement

By section 11(5) "where any prosecutor's statement has been given and the Court is satisfied that a copy of the statement has been served on the defendant, it may require the defendant (a) to indicate to it, within such period as it may direct, the extent to which he accepts each allegation in the statement; and (b) so far as he does not accept any such allegation, to give particulars of any matters on which he proposes to rely." 13–13

In the absence of such a direction, there is no obligation on the defendant to reply to the prosecutor's statement, but if is often wiser to do so if there is material that the Court will be asked to consider, *e.g.* documents, third party interests.

The effect on a defendant who fails to comply with directions given by the Court in respect of providing a proper response to the prosecutor's statement, is set out in section 11(8) which provides that "he may be treated for the purposes of this section as accepting every allegation in the prosecutor's statement in question apart from (a) any allegation in respect of which he has complied with the requirement and (b) any allegation that he has benefited from drug trafficking or that any payment or other reward was received by him in connection with drug trafficking carried on by him or another person."

By section 11 the defendant may be asked to state any matters on which he proposes to rely to refute an allegation contained in a statement tendered under section 11. The penalty, for failing to comply with s.11, is set out in subs. (8). The defendant may be treated as accepting every allegation in the prosecutor's statement apart from those stated in subs. (8) above.

Suppose that a defendant indicates to the Court that he does not accept a particular allegation in a statement tendered and served on him under section 11, and suppose that the defendant indicates to the Court a number of matters upon which he proposes to rely. Is the Court then bound to accept that he has complied with section 11(5) or, may the Court (believing that the accused could indicate a great deal more) treat him as having failed to meet the requirements of that subsection?

Provision of information by the defendant

13–14 By section 12, the Court is given broad powers to compel defendants to furnish information to the Court for making determinations under the Act. The defendant can be compelled to provide the relevant information at any stage of the confiscation proceedings.

This provision is a measure that is likely to have a considerable impact on the way confiscation determinations proceed under the Act. Restraint orders often include an order against the defendant to provide information disclosing the existence of all assets held by the defendant or by persons likely to be affected by the order. Such a disclosure order is usually followed by a clause granting the defendant limited protection from the material being used as evidence adduced by the prosecution in the proceedings pending against him. No doubt the Courts will be called upon to provide guidance as to grounds which do, or do not, amount to a "reasonable excuse" for a failure to comply with an order under it (see subs. (5); and see *Dechert v. Southwark Crown Court* [2001] E.W.H.C. Admin. 477).

Statements tendered by the defence

13–15 This aspect is now covered by section 11(9) and (10) of the 1994 Act but these provisions should also be read in conjunction with section 12 referred to above.

Note: that subsection 11(9) is limited purely to matters relevant to determining the amount that "might be realised" at the time the confiscation order is made. Unlike the preceding subsections, subs. 11(9) is not expressed to include matters that are relevant to determining whether the defendant has benefited from drug trafficking or assessing the value of his proceeds as a result.

Steps on the way to making an order

There are three determinations that the Court is likely to make under the Act:

I. Benefit

13–16 If the Court decides to embark on confiscation proceedings it must first decide whether the defendant has "benefited from drug trafficking": s.2(2):

(a) a person benefits from drug trafficking if he has at any time received any payment or other reward in connection with drug trafficking carried on by him or another: s.2(3)

(b) Formerly, the persuasive burden was on the prosecution to prove the fact that the defendant has benefited from drug trafficking to the criminal law standard of proof: see *R. v. Dickens* [1990] 2 Q.B. 102; *R. v. Enwezor* (1991) 93 Cr.App.R. 233. The persuasive burden remains on the prosecution but to the civil standard (see s.2(8) of the 1994 Act). Accordingly, *Dickens* and *Enwezor* are overruled on this point.

(c) the Court is *obliged* to make statutory assumptions under section 4 (and note in particular s.4(2) and (3)).

(d) The trigger for the making of assumptions, is set out in section 4, *e.g.*, the defendant HOLDS property at the time of his/her conviction, or property was RECEIVED by him in the 6-year period before proceedings were instituted.

(e) The making of assumptions is HRA/ECHR compliant

Phillips v. United Kingdom (Hudoc, 5.7.2001)
Benjafield (December 21, 2000)
Cf. McIntosh (October 13, 2000); reversed by the Privy Council (5.2.2001)
Consider: *Salabiaku v. France* 13 E.H.R.R. 379
Hoang v. France, September 25, 1992
Arman and Malik (May 9, 2000)
Brown (Paul) (December 18, 1997)
Danison v. United Kingdom (Hudoc, 7.9.1999; decision of the ECtHR)
Delaney and Hanrahan (May 14, 1999)
Elton v. United Kingdom (Hudoc, September 11, 1997)
HM Advocate v. McSalley (April 10, 2000)
Hussein (Ergin) (April 20, 1999)
Neal (Frederick) (September 30, 1998)

(f) the value of a drug seized by police/customs may be a benefit received by the defendant *but be careful:* it is usually better to look to the cost price of the drug if there is some evidence that the defendant was the purchaser or a joint purchaser of the substance in question:

Akengin (1995) 16 Cr. App. R. 499
Banks [1997] 2 Cr. App. R(S) 110
Berry (Paul) (14.7.99, CA)
Butler, 14 Cr. App. R.(S) 537
Dellaway (July 3, 2000)
DeSilva (May 14, 1996)
Dore [1997] 2 Cr. App. R. (S) 152
Lennie (unreported, April 1, 1993, CA)
Satchell [1996] 2 Cr. App. R. (S) 258
Thacker (1995) 16 Cr. App. R. 461

(g) the full value of "drug money" passing through the hands of a defendant will be his proceeds of drug trafficking:
Banks [1997] 2 Cr. App. R.(S) 110
Metcalfe [2001] E.W.C.A. 1343
Simons [1994] 98 Cr. App. R. 160
Simpson [1998] 2 Cr. App. R.(S) 111
Smith [1984] Cr. App. R.(S) 290

II. Assessing Value of the Proceeds

13–17 If the defendant has benefited from drug trafficking the Court goes on to determine the *value of the proceeds* of drug trafficking received by the defendant

Note: The defendants' proceeds of drug trafficking = the total value of payments or rewards received by the defendant in connection with drug trafficking carried on *by the defendant or by another* irrespective as to whether the drug trafficking occurred here or abroad: see s.4(1).

Note: the value of the defendant's proceeds is prima facie the "amount to be recovered" under the Act by way of a confiscation order: see section 5(1).

Note: the Court can again make statutory assumptions under section 4 of the DTA.

Note: Whereas, under the old law, the Court could make a "nil order", or "no order" (different courts seem to have had differing views about whether they should make a nil order or no order) now the Court is required to make a confiscation order for at least a "nominal amount" (s.5(3)(b)). Accordingly, if the Court wishes to make, literally, no order, then unless the prosecutor has asked the Court to proceed under s.2 of the 1994 Act, the Court should not embark upon confiscation proceedings at all.

Making the statutory assumptions

13–18 The statutory assumptions that the Court is now required to make, if it embarks upon a drug trafficking enquiry, are dealt with in section 4 of the DTA as follows:

"(3) The required assumptions are—
(a) that any property appearing to the Court—
(i) to have been held by the defendant at any time since his conviction, or
(ii) to have been transferred to him at any time since the beginning of the period of six years ending when the proceedings were instituted against him,
was received by him, at the earliest time at which he appears to the Court to have held it, as a payment or reward in connection with drug trafficking carried on by him;

(b) that any expenditure of his since the beginning of that period was met out of payments received by him in connection with drug trafficking carried on by him; and
(c) that, for the purpose of valuing any property received or assumed to have been received by him at any time as such a reward, he received the property free of any other interests in it.

(4) The Court shall not make any required assumption in relation to any particular property or expenditure if—
(a) that assumption **is shown to be incorrect** in the defendant's case; or
(b) the Court is satisfied that there would be **a serious risk of injustice** in the defendant's case if the assumption were to be made;

and where, by virtue of this subsection, the Court does not make one or more of the required assumptions, it shall state its reasons.

(5) Subsection (2) above does not apply if the only drug trafficking offence in respect of which the defendant appears before the Court to be sentenced is an offence under section 49, 50 or 51 of this Act."

Note: that s.4(2) does not apply if the only "drug trafficking offence" in respect of which the defendant appears before the Court to be sentenced is (for want of a better term) a money-laundering offence under ss.40,50 or 51 of this Act: see section 1(3). It is important to remember that the offences under ss. 40,50 and 51 are strictly speaking "drug trafficking offences" (see s.1(3)) but they are not, it would seem, regarded as being of a type that deserve the application of the draconian measures found in s.4(2)–(4). This approach is consistent with the law as it stood under the 1986 Act: see s.2(4) and s.24 of that Act, s.14 and, see Sched. 4, para.4(2) of the Criminal Justice (International Co-operation) Act 1990 (c.5) and s.16 of the 1993 Act. However, under the Proceeds of Crime Bill 2001, it is proposed that the statutory assumptions will apply in cases where a defendant is convicted of a money laundering offence.

The assumptions and their exceptions

If the Court makes any of the assumptions specified in s.4 then it will be made on the basis that the defendant has received a payment or reward in connection with drug-trafficking carried on by him and by no-one else: see s.4(2). 13–19

By virtue of subs. (4) the trial judge should not make any of the assumptions specified in subs. (3) if "any of the assumptions are shown to be incorrect in the defendant's case", or if "the Court is satisfied that there would be a serious risk of injustice in his case if the assumptions were to be made": subs. (4)(b). These are considered below.

First exception: if it is "shown to be incorrect"

13–20 Subsection (4)(a) follows the wording of s.2(2) of the 1986 Act. In *R. v. Dickens* [1990] 2 Q.B.102, it was held that the burden of proving an assumption to be incorrect falls on the defendant.

Second exception: serious risk of injustice

13–21 Would *any* risk of injustice (which is not merely fanciful) be regarded by the Courts as a "serious" one given the consequences that will flow from the making of an assumption?

See *Delaney* (May 14, 1999, CA).
See *Benjafield* (December 21, 2000)
And see *Croft, The Times*, July 6, 2000
See Performance and Innovation Unit Report *Recovering the Proceeds of Crime* (June, 2000);

A social injustice, *e.g.* hardship to wife and/or children is not sufficient. The ECtHR has held that a determination of third party interests (if any) is a matter for domestic courts: see *Danison* (September 7, 1999).

Even if the reasons stated by the Court, for not applying the assumptions under subs. (4)(b) are erroneous, that does not seem to entitle the prosecution to apply for re-assessment under s.13. It is not clear that the prosecutor would be entitled to seek judicial review of a judge's decision in the light of his stated reasons.

III. Assessing the "Amount that Might be Realised"

13–22 Frequently, the amount the defendant is able to pay (or is able to realise) is less than the full value of his proceeds of drug trafficking. This lower figure is termed the "amount that might be realised" and it is this figure, which becomes the "amount to be recovered under a confiscation order". *Almost always, if not always, it is for the defendant to satisfy the Court that he has insufficient assets to repay the full value of his benefit from drug trafficking:* see s.5(3) and

Atlan (February 20, 1997)
Barwick (October 13, 2000)
Carroll (1992) 13 Cr.App.R.(S.) 99
Comiskey (1991) 93 Cr.App.R.227
De Silva (May 14, 1996)
Ellington (May 6, 1999)
Ilsemann (1990) 12 Cr.App.R.(S) 398
Kataryn (July 17, 2000)
Klann (July 13, 1999)
Mullen (May 5, 2000)
Murray (November 29, 1996)

The "amount that might be realised" is the total value of "realisable property" held by the defendant *plus* the total value of gifts made by him that are "caught by the Act": *ss.5(3) 6(1)* and *s.8*.)

Note:

(a) The Court may be asked by the defendant (or the Court may act on its own motion; but see *Barwick*) to assess the "amount that may be realised" under s.5(3) as defined by s.6(1);

(b) The standard of proof to be applied under the DTA is the civil standard of proof (s.2(8));

(c) If the defendant fails to discharge the burden on him, or failed to raise the issue at all, then the Court may make a confiscation order for the *full amount* determined under steps (1) and (2) above: but see *Comiskey* (above) and *R. v. Keston* (1990) 12 Cr.App.R.(S.) 93 (referred to as "*Preston*" in [1990] Crim.L.R. 528). The law remains unchanged.

(d) Gifts: note that as the law presently stands, the value of a gift is part of the amount that might be realised even if the donee has disposed of the gift itself: see *Dickens*, and see *Wallace Duncan Smith* [1996] 2 Cr. App. R. 1.

Note: be very careful about agreeing a figure as to the value of the defendant's benefit/proceeds of drug trafficking or the value of his realisable assets because the figure *may* bind him in the Court of Appeal:

see *Naison-Naidoo* (March 29, 1994)
see *Tredwen* [1994] Crim. L.R. 388
see *Teale* (July 5, 1996)
see *Emmett* [1997] 3 W.L.R. 1119, HL
see *McKenzie (Kendrick)* (September 24, 1999)

Note: be careful about property which the defendant may think he has got at the time the order is made but which has already been forfeited under another enactment: *East* (unreported; 1994; boat carrying the drug forfeited under the CEMA 1979—no longer realisable.)

Enforcement of a confiscation order as a fine (s.9)

The Court treats the confiscation order as a fine and imposes a sentence of imprisonment in default. 13–23

Notwithstanding that the defendant served a sentence of imprisonment in default of payment of the confiscation order, a court may still proceed to enforce payment of the confiscation order: s.9

Note: Terms of imprisonment imposed in default are *maximum* terms—there are no minimum terms: *Szrajber* (1994) Cr. App. R.(S) 821; *French* (1995) 16 Cr. App. R. (S) 841; *Atlan* (February 20, 1997, CA); *Middelkoop* (October 25, 1996) and see (for application of the totality principle) *Taylor* (October 3, 1996), *Walpole* (June 19, 1997).

Note: property retained by police, which is found by the Court to be all or part of the defendant's benefit from drug trafficking, will also represent his realisable property.

Note: that the imposition of a term of imprisonment imposed in default of payment of a confiscation order is not a violation of Article 6 or 7 of the ECHR: *Arman* (May 9, 2000).

Note: There have been cases where the customs and excise have forfeited property under the CEMA 1979 and that property has been condemned long before the confiscation order was made, but the Court, when making the confiscation order, was unaware of that fact. The effect is that the forfeited property is no longer realisable and therefore (i) if the defendant's only asset is the property forfeited by the customs and excise then the confiscation order should be reduced in value, but (ii) if the defendant does have other legitimately acquired assets which would satisfy the order then he will be obliged to make full payment. This can produced harsh results, for example, D imports cannabis in a boat whereupon the vessel is forfeited by customs. The boat is worth £15,000 but it was not bought from the proceeds of drug trafficking. Nevertheless, D received a payment of £10,000 as a reward for his assistance in the venture. The Court learns that the value of D's interest in a house is worth £15,000. In those circumstances the Court may still make a confiscation order in the sum of £10,000: see the reference to *East* above; but see *Cadman Smith* (June 16, 2000).

Variation or discharge of a confiscation order

13–24 The powers of the Court in this regard have been substantially widened and strengthened under the 1994 Act, thus:

(a) formerly only a defendant could vary an order under s.14 of the 1986 Act (now s.17 of the 1994 Act), but now a receiver appointed under ss.26 or 29 of the 1994 Act may also apply under s.17(1) to vary or to discharge the confiscation order;

(b) third parties may now make representations to the Court at this stage: see s.17(5);

(c) a court now has power to:

  (i) make a confiscation order where the evidence did not, originally, justify the making of such an order: s.13(2);

  (ii) re-assess whether the defendant has benefited from drug trafficking: s.14;

  (iii) revise its assessment of the value of the defendant's proceeds of drug trafficking: s.15;

(d) the Court also has power to increase the amount which a defendant may be ordered to pay under a confiscation order: s.16 (which re-enacts s.16 of the Criminal Justice (International Co-operation) Act 1990); see *Tivnan* [1999] 1 Cr.App.R. (S) 92.

The Court of Appeal has advised judges to state the relevant findings at each stage of the proceedings, *per* Neill L.J. in *R. v. Johnson* [1991] 2 Q.B. 249 at p. 260. In addition, it is important for the judge to give a reasoned judgment: see *Guppy* (June 23, 2000).

(2) A Practitioner's Guide to Confiscation under Part VI of the CJA 1988

Relationship between confiscation under the CJA 1988 and sentence

- There is little doubt that a confiscation order is penal in nature notwithstanding that the Court must determine any question as to (i) whether a person has benefited from an offence or (ii) the amount to be recovered in his case, by applying the civil standard of proof (s.71(7A)).[1] That a confiscation order is a penalty appears to have been conceded in *Benjafield* (December 21, 2000). 13–25
- A confiscation order is *not* to be regarded as part of the sentence imposed in respect of the underlying offence [see s.72(5)], BUT:
  - (i) a confiscation order is a "sentence" for the purposes of an appeal against sentence;
  - (ii) The Court is probably entitled to have regard to the "totality principle" when considering the term of imprisonment to be imposed in default of payment;
  - (iii) Information gleaned from the confiscation proceedings might be taken into account by the sentencer but not in a manner which contravened the fundamental principle that the offender is only to be sentenced for the offences of which he had been convicted. Material coming to light in confiscation proceedings could be used to inform the Court of the seriousness of the offence: *Thompson and Smith* [1997] 1 Cr. App. R.(S) 289; *Harper* (1989) 11 Cr. App. R.(S) 240; and see *Andrews* [1997] 1 Cr. App. R.(S) 279; but see *Rogers* [2001] E.W.C.A. 1168.

[1] See s.27, CJA 1993; and see s.1(5), Proceeds of Crime Act 1995.

CJA Confiscation—a twin-track system

13–26 • Unlike the DTA 1994, the CJA provides two procedures by which the defendant's proceeds of criminal conduct may be calculated and a confiscation order made.

(i) The *standard procedure* (pursuant to s.71) enables the Court to recover from the defendant only the benefit he obtained in respect of the offences[2] for which he appears before the Court (including offences to be taken into consideration). Proceedings are initiated by the prosecution, upon written notice served on the Court, or by the Court of its motion. The Court cannot invoke any of the statutory assumptions under s.72AA unless the conditions of that section are satisfied.

Although the first procedure is sometimes described as calculating the "simple benefit", in fact s.71 is often appropriately applied in cases of serious fraud and the issues in the case may be far from simple.

(ii) The *extended procedure* (pursuant to s.71 and s.72AA) enables the Court to investigate and to calculate (with the aid of statutory assumptions) the defendant's benefit from criminal conduct over a much longer period of time. The defendant must have been convicted of at least one "qualifying offence" in the current proceedings *and* he must have been convicted of a further qualifying offence *either* in the same proceedings, *or* during the previous six years: **s.72AA(1) and (2).**

Note: it is widely believed that the assumptions apply only to property the defendant received, or in respect of his expenditure, in the six-year period before proceedings were instituted.[3] *This is not so*. The first assumption under s.72AA(4)(a)(i) is triggered by the mere fact that the defendant held the property in question "at the date of conviction" or "at any time between the date of conviction and determinations under the Act". The assumption is that the property was received by him as a result of, or in connection with, the commission of offences: see s.72AA(4)(a)(i).

It will be seen that section 72AA(4)(a)(i) is not limited to a six-year period. It is therefore immaterial that he acquired that property outside that period: *Brett, The Times*, October 13, 1997; and see *Bentham and Clark* (1997) 2 Cr. App. R. (S) 99, and *Chrastny No.2* (1991) 1 W.L.R. 1381.

Note: s.72AA(4)(a)(i) appears to be drafted to prevent offenders avoiding

[2] That is to say, "offences of a relevant description": s.71(1), s.71(1E), s.71(9)(c).

[3] For a decision that grappled with the meaning of the phrase "when the proceedings were instituted against him" (for the purposes of the DTOA 1986, see *Gooch (No.2), The Times*, July 15, 1998

the particularly draconian breadth of this provision, by disposing of their assets following a conviction.

Is s.72AA lost if D is convicted of a conspiracy rather than two substantive offences?

- Where a defendant, of previous good character, has been convicted on just one count (albeit that it is a "conduct crime"—*e.g.* conspiracy to defraud) the prosecutor will not be able to initiate confiscation proceedings under s.72AA. The position is different if the defendant stood convicted of two or more substantive offences, in respect of the same conduct. **13–27**

STANDARD PROCEDURE FOR MAKING A CONFISCATION ORDER IN THE CROWN COURT

I. Preliminary Matters

Step One—has the defendant been *convicted* in the Crown Court of an offence of a "relevant description"?

- The defendant must be *convicted* in the Crown Court of an offence of a "relevant description" (s.71 (1)). **13–28**
- A defendant committed by a magistrates' court to the Crown Court for sentence, is deemed to have been convicted in the Crown Court for the purposes of s.71, s.72 to s.74C of the CJA 1988 (s.71(9)(A) inserted by the Crime and Disorder Act 1998).[4] Section 71(9A) came into force on the September 30, 1998. See *Whellem* (June 11, 1989, unreported, C.A.), *Re F*, not followed (June 22, 1998, Jowitt J)[5], which examined the position before s.71(9)(A) was enacted.
- For the purposes of proceedings before the Crown Court, an offence "of a relevant description" means an offence to which Part VI of the CJA applies (**s.71(1E)**(a)). This, in turn, is defined by **s.71(9)** to mean:
  - (i) an offence listed in Sched.4 to the CJA (**s.71(9)(c)(i)**; *i.e.* mainly summary-only offences) or
  - (ii) An "indictable offence", other than a drug trafficking

[4] Where an offender is committed by a magistrates' court for sentence under section 38 or s.38A of the Magistrates' Court Act 1980, or s.56 of the CJA 1967, ss. 71, 72 to 74C will have effect "as if the offender had been convicted of the offence in the proceedings before the Crown Court and not in the proceedings before the magistrates' court".

[5] In *Whellem*, a confiscation order was quashed (but a compensation order was substituted) on the grounds that the appellant was not a person convicted in any proceedings before the Crown Court, having been committed for sentence to the Crown Court under the plea before venue procedure. The loophole has been plugged by s.71(9A).

offence, or an offence contrary to the Prevention of Terrorism Act 1989 (**s.71(9)(c)(ii)**).

- Accordingly, in practice, where a defendant is convicted of any indictable offence in the Crown Court (other than a drug trafficking, or a terrorism, offence) the confiscation provisions of s.71 CJA 1988 may be triggered.

Step Two—has the prosecutor empowered the Court to embark on confiscation proceedings?

13–29
- If the prosecutor invites the Court to embark on confiscation proceedings under the CJA 1988, ensure that he has put the Court on *written* notice that he considers that it would be appropriate for the Court to proceed under section 71. In a case where the defendant has two "qualifying offences", and the prosecuting advocate invites the Court to make any of the statutory assumptions under the CJA, check that he has included in the notice a written declaration that, in his opinion, it is appropriate for the provisions of s.72AA to be applied.

Step Three—if the prosecutor has not served a notice, can the Court initiate proceedings under section 71?

13–30
- Although the Proceeds of Crime Act 1995 removed the minimum benefit requirement of £10,000[6] nevertheless concern was expressed in Parliament[7] that confiscation proceedings should be cost-effective. However, in cases where there is evidence that the defendant has benefited by a substantial amount, the Court may enquire of the prosecutor whether confiscation proceedings have been considered and (depending on the circumstances of the case) to proceed under s.71 if there are reasonable grounds to suppose that the defendant has sufficient assets to pay a confiscation order. Note that the prosecution may be disinclined to initiate confiscation proceedings for reasons good or bad even if there is evidence that the defendant has obtained substantial sums as a result of his offending.

Step Four—can determinations under the CJA be postponed?

13–31
- The general rule is that confiscation proceedings should be heard and finalised before sentencing the offender: **s.71(1)**. However, in practice—particularly in cases of serious fraud—the parties will be unlikely to be in a position to furnish the Court with the information it needs to make appropriate determinations under the CJA.

[6] By the Proceeds of Crime Act.1995.
[7] When the PCA 1995 was debated as a Bill.

In those circumstances the Court may postpone making determinations under the Act for a period not exceeding 6 months—unless there are exceptional circumstances (**s.72A**).

Akpan (October 20, 1998, CA)
Cole (April 22, 1998)
Edwards (May 11, 1999)
France (April 27, 1998) [1999] 1 Cr.App.R(S) 85
Hussain (April 18, 2000)
Kelly (December 13, 1999)
Shergill [1999] 2 Cr. App. R.(S) 341
Steele (December 14, 2000)
Tuegel (November 19, 1999)
Turberfield (May 11, 2000)
Ward (November 24, 1999)
Williams (March 24, 1998)
Zelzele (June 21, 1999)

If the Court postpones the confiscation hearing, may it nevertheless proceed to sentence?

- Yes. **Section 72A(7)** gives the Court that power, BUT the Court must not (a) fine the defendant or (b) make any other financial orders (apart from a compensation order), or (c) make a forfeiture order under s.27 MDA 1971, or (d) a deprivation order under s.143 Powers of Criminal Courts (Sentencing) Act 2000 (**s.72A(9)**). This is because s.71, and s.72, place a duty on the Court to use the mechanism for making confiscation orders as the *primary method* by which the proceeds of criminal conduct are recovered; and see *Stuart and Bonnett* [1989] Crim L.R. 599.
- It is only after the amount to be recovered under a confiscation order is ascertained, that the Court can go on to consider (a) imposing any fine, or (b) making any other financial order (apart from a compensation order), or (c) making a forfeiture order under s.27 MDA 1971, or (d) a deprivation order under s. 143 PCC(S) Act 2000. If the making of a confiscation order is time-barred, the power to then make a compensation order also falls away: see *Dorrian* (October 19, 2000) [2001] Crim.L.R. 56.

Can the defendant be fined if the determinations were made more than 28 days after the defendant was sentenced for the offence?

- Yes. Until **s.72A(9A)** was inserted by the CJPOA 1994, problems 13–32
did arise in cases where confiscation proceedings were concluded 28 days after the defendant was sentenced for the underlying offence but the Court wished to fine him.[8] **S.72A(9A)** clarifies the position so that a court now has 28 days *from the end of the*

[8] That is to say beyond the time-limit permitted for varying sentence.

period of postponement to impose a fine or make any other order under **s.72(5)**.

Step Five—taking action to ensure that the Court has sufficient information to make the relevant determinations under the CJA

13–33
- The Court will usually have information from the following sources:
  - — evidence adduced during the trial;
  - — information contained in the prosecutor's statement: **s.73**;
  - — reply to the prosecutor's statement furnished by the defendant: **s.73(2)–(5)**;
  - — information obtained from the defendant by the Court: **s.73A**;
  - — reply to any statement furnished by the defendant: **s.73A(6), (7)**.
- The content of a prosecutor's statement is subject to Rules of the Crown Court. It is important that the statement should be carefully drafted and should set out clearly the basis on which the suggested benefit figure is calculated. It is also highly desirable—but not obligatory—that it should identify the assets held by the defendant at the time the statement was prepared. This is because the effect of s.71(6) is to require the Court to order the defendant to pay the value of the benefit OR the "amount that might be realised"—*whichever is the less*.[9]
- Note section 73A. This is a very powerful instrument in the hands of the Court to obtain information from the defendant regarding the extent of his wealth and the location of his assets: but see its limitations, *Dechart v. Southwark Crown Court* [2001] E.W.H.C. Admin 477.

II. The Confiscation Hearing

Step One—determining whether the defendant has benefited from "relevant criminal conduct" (s.71(1A) and s.71(1D))

13–34
- A two-step process is involved in determining the benefit figure. First, the Court must decide whether property (which is alleged to be a "benefit" obtained by the defendant from criminal conduct) really is a "benefit" for the purposes of the CJA. The next step is to value the benefit obtained. Those two steps—that are so easy to isolate in theory—are often difficult to separate in practice. It

[9] There is an exception where a victim of a relevant offence indicates that he has instituted, or intends to institute, civil proceedings (s.71(1C)). In such a case the court has a power to make a confiscation order in such sum as the court thinks fit.

frequently happens that problems associated with the value of a benefit is also a problem associated with the definition of a benefit.

(a) *How does the CJA 1988 define "benefit"?*[10]

- Section 71(4) states that "... *a person benefits from an offence if he obtains property as a result of or in connection with its commission and his benefit is the value of the property so obtained*". **13–35**
- Section 102(5) goes on to explain that the phrase "in connection with its commission" includes property obtained (or a pecuniary advantage derived) "both in that connection and in some other connection". It is submitted that the task of identifying property "obtained" as a result of, or in connection with, the defendant's offending, is a matter that should be approached in a practical manner having regard to the nature, and elements, of the offence. For a definition of "in connection with", see *Director of Public Prosecutions v. Jeffrey* (1992) 58 A. Crim. R. 310 (re the Confiscation of the Proceeds of Crime Act 1989 (Commonwealth)):

  > "... a substantial connection between the activity in question and the use of the property. It is not sufficient for there to be a mere accidental or incidental connection. The unlawful activity must be related to, or dependent upon, or could not have been committed without, or have resulted directly from, the use of the property": *per* Hunt CJ.

- The combined effect of s.71(4) and s.102(5) is that "benefit" is widely drawn and may catch property that the defendant obtains as an indirect consequence of the commission of the offence. Thus, the offender who (before confiscation proceedings have been concluded) sells his story to a newspaper for high reward, regarding his notorious crimes, might find that the Court includes the money paid to him as a benefit he obtained in connection with his offending. But the Court might need to go further and consider how much of his reward was due to his skill as an author.
  See *Randle and Pottle, The Independent*, March 26, 1991
  See *Cadman-Smith* (June 16, 2000)
- The standard of proof applicable to determine whether the defendant has benefited from any offence and the amount to be recovered, is the civil standard: **s.71(7A)**.
- The Court will *not* be entitled to invoke any of the statutory assumptions under s.72AA (unless the conditions, set out in that section, are met): see *Cadman-Smith* (June 16, 2000).
- The prosecution must prove some economic advantage or proceeds of criminal conduct: see *Causey* (October 18, 1999); see *Dimsey*

[10] The benefit must derive from "relevant criminal conduct"—that is to say any offence of "a relevant description" AND any other such offences of which he was convicted in the same proceedings AND offences to be taken into consideration: s.71(1D).

and Allen [2000] Cr.App.R.(S) 497; and see *Cadman-Smith* (June 16, 2000).

- In *Dimsey and Allen*, tax was evaded over a period of years but the appellant had thus been able to exploit the monies not paid to the Inland Revenue. In that sense he had "benefited" from the economic advantage he had obtained. However, in *Cadman*, the position was different because C imported a vast quantity of cigarettes (seized and forfeited by Customs). Although duty was payable, it was a hollow benefit to C, because the potential economic advantage had not by then been realised (*e.g.* by selling the cigarettes).
- Note that in *Cadman*, a boat was used to import the cigarettes. It seems that Cadman bought the boat. However, the purchase of the boat was held not to be a benefit. First, the assumptions did not apply. Secondly, the Court seems to have reasoned that the boat was not obtained "in connection with" the offence: but see *Randle and Pottle* and see *Osei* (1988) 10 Cr.App.R.(S) 289. Thirdly, the boat was not obtained "as a result of" the offence.

(b) *What is the position if the fraud taints* part *of the property obtained by the defendant?*

13–36

- Suppose a company, controlled by the defendant, received a substantial capital injection derived from frauds perpetrated by him. As a result, the company was rescued from financial ruin and continued to trade, successfully and honestly. On one analysis it may be said that the company's success was built on fraud and thus the value of that success represents the benefit he obtained "in connection" with the offences he committed. But would such a determination be consistent with the purpose of the legislation?
- There will often be more than one way to calculate the extent of the defendant's benefit within the definitions set out in s.71(4) and s.102(5): see *Danison*, unreported, December 11, 1997.

  Example

  D bought properties worth £3 million (true value) and sold them, at an inflated price, to fictitious individuals for £6 million (those transactions being financed by mortgages in the inflated sum). Is D's benefit £6 million, or £3 million (on the basis of the properties being repossessed)? After allowing for expenditure incurred in pursuing the criminal venture, D's net profit amounted to £2$\frac{1}{2}$ million. Is the benefit obtained therefore only £2$\frac{1}{2}$ million?
- The decision as to where the line should be drawn (to mark the limit of the defendant's benefit) is one that must be left to the good sense of the Court on the facts of each case.
- It is submitted that it is unlikely that a court would be criticised if, in the majority of cases, it treated the gross value of the property obtained as the benefit figure. However, in order to achieve a just and fair result, the Courts tend to look at the true benefit received

by the defendant from his offending. This might be no more than the value of the tax and duty evaded,[11] see *Martin and White* (1998) 2 Cr. App. R. 385, but the benefit figure should not be assessed on the basis of net profit: see *Banks* [1997] 2 Cr. App. R.(S) 110.

(c) *Using net profit—not to calculate the benefit—but to value the amount realisable*

- However (and it is important not to lose sight of the distinction) the Court would be entitled to take the net profit as the basis for calculating the assets that the defendant holds at the time of making a confiscation order—*i.e.* the value of the "amount that might be realised". It would then be up to the defendant to show that the asset he once held (represented by the net profit) was genuinely dissipated and lost. A hidden asset is still an asset in his hands. 13–37

  Example (drawn from the facts in Martin and White *(1998) 2 Cr. App. R.(S.) 385)*
  D was convicted of 2 offences of fraudulently evading duty on wines and beers, and 3 offences of fraudulently evading VAT. Total tax and duty evaded = £4.831 million. However, officer assessed sales by D of the goods inclusive of VAT at £7.448 million with an estimated total cost to D of the purchases of the goods (£4.216 million). This gave a profit in D's hands of £3.23 million.
  - The benefit figure was assessed by the judge to the value of the tax and duty evaded (*i.e.* £4.831 million)
  - In order to calculate the true figure of the "amount that might be realised" the Court looked at the profit D made by dealing in the goods (£3.23 million).
  - The Court of Appeal made further allowances in the determination of the "amount that might be realised" to reflect other expenses and costs and assessed the amount at £3 million.

(d) *Problems of valuation where D does not* personally *receive the full benefit*

- The question here is whether property, obtained as a result of a joint venture to commit the offence in question, is a benefit received by each of the participants (to the full value of the property)? Alternatively, must the Court apportion the value of the benefit obtained between the defendants convicted of the offence? 13–38
- In *Rees* (July 19, 1990, Auld J., Plymouth Crown Court), D pleaded guilty to three counts of obtaining property by deception. He had been charged jointly with two others. The value of the

[11] For a contrary view, see Mitchell, Taylor and Talbot, *Confiscation and the Proceeds of Crime*.

property obtained was £90,000. Auld J. held that the non-receipt of monies by the defendant and the absence of loss by the mortgage lenders were not relevant to the calculation of the benefit which the defendant had received.

- However, in *Gokal* (March 11, 1999, CA), the Court of Appeal declined to quash a confiscation order in the sum of approximately £2.9 million. The trial judge (Buxton J., as he then was) rejected the prosecution's argument that the defendant should be regarded as having obtained £548 million from BCCI for the Gulf Group (run by G and his family). He held that "the phrase 'if he obtains' in s.71(4) of the 1988 Act requires what can fairly be described as an obtaining by the defendant himself". The matter was further considered, at first instance, in *Saia, Tuegel, Martines* on April 20, 1999 and *Patel* (November 3, 1999); [2000] Crim.L.R. 201.

(e) *Does the "middleman" who momentarily holds property obtain a benefit?*

13–39 • Yes. A person obtains a benefit even if he holds it momentarily. The CJA 1988 is concerned with the *obtaining* of a benefit. It is immaterial that the defendant did not *retain* it: see *Simpson and others* [1998] 2 Cr. App. R.(S) 111, and see *Currey* (1995) Cr. App. R.(S) 420[12], *Simons* (1994) 98 Cr. App. R 100, and see *Metcalfe* [2001] E.W.C.A. Crim 1343.

(f) *Is property received by the defendant from another offender a "benefit"?*

13–40 • Unlike proceedings under the DTA (see s.2(3), DTA 1994), the Court can only look to the benefits obtained by the defendant as a result of *his* criminal conduct. Unless D is convicted of a money-laundering offence under the CJA, the fact that he obtained property that represents another person's criminal conduct will not be a benefit for the purposes of s.71, CJA.

Step Two—calculate the value of the benefit

13–41 • Frequently the value of the property obtained will be the value "to him" *when he obtained it* (adjusted to take into account changes in the value of money): **s.74(5)**. However, in respect of property which he obtained from his offending *and which he holds at the time of the confiscation hearing*, the value of the benefit will be the value to him at that time—whichever value is the greater: **s.74(6)**.

Step Three—determine "the amount that might be realised" (s.71(6)(b))

13–42 • Subject to one exception (s.71(1C)) the Court is required to

[12] And see the commentary in the Criminal Law Review, [1994] Crim. L.R. 960.

recover under a confiscation order either the value of the benefit, or the "amount that might be realised", whichever is the less (s.71(6)). The effect of the section is that the Court should determine the amount that might be realised in every case.

- However, almost always—if not always—the burden is on the defendant to prove that the amount that might be realised is less than the value of the benefit: see *Barwick* (October 13, 2000; [2001] Crim. L.R. 52; cf. *Kataryna* (17th July 2000)
- The Court is entitled to have regard to all the circumstances of the case—including the defendant's failure (or reluctance) to explain the whereabouts of his assets, or his failure to provide a satisfactory explanation for the "apparent" loss of his assets.
- It is important to perform "step three" for several reasons:
    - (i) Section 71(6) requires the Court to recover from the defendant either the value of the benefit, or the value of the amount that might be realised, whichever is the less;
    - (ii) By virtue of s.71(1C) the Court is given the power (but not the duty) to make a confiscation order in such amount "as the Court thinks fit", *if* a victim of the defendant's offending has instituted, or intends to institute, civil proceedings against the defendant. The Court can perform this task effectively if it calculates the amount capable of being recovered under a confiscation order, and the amount likely to be available to satisfy an order for the payment of damages in a civil action.
    - (iii) The Court must take account of the value of a confiscation order before imposing any fine on the offender, or making an order under s.143 of the Powers of the Criminal Courts (Sentencing) Act 2000 or s.27 MDA 1971;
    - (iv) The Court *is* empowered by s.72 to make a confiscation order and a compensation order against the defendant and to direct that any shortfall in the payment of a compensation order be met out of the amount recovered under a confiscation order (s.72(7)).

(a) *Do not confuse "realisable property" and the "amount that might be realised"*

- Unfortunately the expressions "realisable property" and the "amount that might be realisable" are often used interchangeably. "Realisable property" and "the amount that might be realised" are *not* the same (see *Dickens* (1990) 91 Cr. App. R. 164—a case that illustrates the distinction, at 172). 13–43
- *It cannot be over-emphasised that it is important to adhere closely to the wording of the CJA (particularly when judges giving reasons) in order to avoid confusion.*[13]

[13] See *Jeevan* (unreported, May 21, 1998) where it is submitted the court may have fallen into error for this reason.

(b) *Meaning of "Realisable Property"*

13–44
- "Realisable property" is crucial to the satisfaction of a confiscation order. The CJA gives the High Court a range of powers over realisable property (*e.g.* making a restraint order, or putting property into the hands of a receiver). The definition of "realisable property" is very broad. It means
  - (i) "any property held by the defendant" (s.74(1)(a)) and
  - (ii) "any property held by a person to whom the defendant has directly or indirectly make a gift caught by . . . this Act" (s.74(1)(b) and s.74(10); and see *Wallace Duncan Smith* [1996] 2 Cr. App. R. 1).
- "Realisable property" represents a pool of assets some or all of which a receiver may sell to satisfy a confiscation order (and to recover the value of a gift caught by the Act) but of course it does not follow that the third party loses the value of his or her interest in the property, and it does not mean that all of the property will necessarily be realised to satisfy a confiscation order.
- The defendant holds property if he holds *any* interest in it: s.102(7). A gift is caught by the Act if it was made by the defendant at any time after the commission of the offence[14] *and* the Court considers it appropriate in all the circumstances to take the gift into account: s.74(10). The Proceeds of Crime Bill 2001 removes this concession.
- To demonstrate the breadth of the meaning of "realisable property", consider two examples:
  - (i) X has a 10 per cent interest in a house owned in the names of X and Y. The *entire* house is potentially realisable—not just the 10 per cent interest in the property.
  - (ii) A gifts a car to B. B then sells the car and spends the proceeds on a world cruise. However, B owns other property worth £200,000. All of that property is realisable property—not just the value of the gift. The value of the gift is relevant to the calculation of the "amount that might be realised".
- The point to note is that realisable property is *identified* by the fact that the defendant has *any* interest in the property, or by the fact that he has made a relevant gift to a person who holds property. **Note:** that realisable property can include property that was lawfully acquired either by the defendant or by the recipient of a gift.
- In cases where the Customs and Excise have played a role in the investigation of the offence before the Court, it is not uncommon for that agency to forfeit property seized from the defendant that represents the instrumentalities of crime (notwithstanding that the defendant had not then been convicted of an offence). Unfortu-

[14] Or if more than one, the earliest of the offences to which the proceedings for the time being relate: s.74(10)(a).

nately it sometimes happens that, during the proceedings under the CJA 1988, the defendant is wholly unaware that the property has in fact been forfeited. Forfeited property should of course be excluded from the valuation of the defendant's "realisable property" and, consequently, the "amount that might be realised": see *Blower* (June 19, 1997, unreported, CA). However, if D has other assets, their value forms part of his realisable property, and D cannot offset the value of an instrumentality of crime forfeited under a different enactment.

(c) *Meaning of the "amount that might be realised"*

- Whereas "realisable property" represents a pool of property that can be sold, *e.g.* by a receiver, the "amount that might be realised" is an assessment of the *value* of the defendant's wealth as the CJA 1988 defines it (see s.74(3)). 13–45
- The calculation is as follows:
  - (i) Look at the "realisable property held *only* by the defendant. Focus only on the defendant's property at this stage.
  - (ii) Assess the value of the defendant's property. If the defendant owns property, in which nobody else enjoys an interest, the value is the market value (s.74(4)(b)). If there are third party interests in the property, the Court may assess the value of the defendant's beneficial interest (s.74(4)(a)(i)). Courts will often make a deduction for costs likely to be incurred in selling the property.
  - (iii) **Deduct** the value of any incumbrance on the defendant's beneficial interest in property (s.74(4)(a)(ii)). If the incumbrance is a sham (and the Court is satisfied about that) then its apparent value will be left out of account. Similarly, if the incumbrance cannot, or will not, be enforced, the Court is not obliged to take it into account: *Harvey* (July 31, 1998, CA)—see paragraph (e) below.
  - (iv) We now have the value of realisable property held by the defendant.
  - (v) **Deduct** "obligations having priority" (s.74(3)). These are few in number and the expression is defined in s.74(9). Debts that remain owing by the defendant as a result of holding property with a negative equity, do not have priority over the amount to be recovered under a confiscation order: see *Ghadami* [1998] 1 Cr. App. R.(S) 42; [1997] Crim. L.R. 606.
  - (vi) **Add** the *value* of gifts caught by the Act (note *Dickens* [1990] 2 Q.B. 102 and *Wallace Duncan Smith* [1996] 2 Cr.App.R. 1: see para. 13–48)—**Unless,** the Court concludes that it is not appropriate to take the gift into account. The Court has discretion in relation to gifts: see s.74A(10).

- Three of the above components of the calculation are examined in greater detail below.

(d) *Calculating the value of "realisable property" held by the defendant*

13–46
- This is governed by s.74(4) of the Act.
- It will often be necessary to value the defendant's beneficial interest in the property as well as those of third parties. Depending on the nature of the relationship between the parties (*e.g.* husband/wife; father/child; business partner/stranger) the issues involved may be complex; and see *Norris* (June 28, 2001, HL).
- Thus, (i) a voluntary payment by the defendant to another, or (ii) the payment by him (wholly or in part) for the purchase of property vested in the name of another alone, or in the joint names of the defendant and a third party, may amount to a "gift caught by the Act" (see s.74A(10)) or it might give rise to a resulting trust in favour of the defendant (in which case he has not made a gift, but the property forms part of his realisable property): see *Westdeutsche Landesbank v. Islington B.C.* [1996] A.C. 669; and see *Dyer v. Dyer* (1788) 2 Cox Eq. Cas. 92.
- Where property is held in joint names, the Court should start with the prima facie position as to where the beneficial interests lie and then to go on to find whether there are gifts caught by the Act which ought then to increase the value of the amount that might be realised: see *Buckman* [1997] 1 Cr. App. R.(S) 325; and see *Robson* (1991) 92 Cr. App. R. 2 (a DTOA decision but a useful illustration of the approach to be taken under the CJA 1988).
- Where a person contributes only part of the monies to the purchase price of property held in the name of another (or jointly with the defendant), a resulting trust will be presumed in his favour to the value of an equivalent proportion of the equitable interest.

  Midland Bank v. Cooke [1995] 4 All E. R. 562
  Pettitt v. Pettitt [1970] A.C. 777
  Gissing v. Gissing [1971] A.C. 886
  Tinsley v. Milligan [1993] 3 All E.R. 65
- Contributions to mortgage payments have been treated as contributions to the purchase price: *Cowcher v. Cowcher* [1972] 1 W.L.R. 425.
- There have been cases where the value of a discount in the purchase price of property has been treated as a contribution to the purchase price.

  Marsh v. Von Sternberg [1986] 1 F.L.R. 526
  Springette v. Defoe [1992] 2 F.L.R. 388
- Contributions to general household expenses may not be sufficient to give rise to a resulting trust in favour of the contributor.

  Burns v. Burns [1984] Ch. 317
- Is may be necessary to distinguish between a resulting and a con-

structive trust: see *Robson* (1991) 92 Cr. App. R. 1; (*Eves v. Eves* [1975] 1 W.L.R. 1338, considered).

(e) *Deducting the value of any incumbrance on the defendant's interest in property*

- This is part of the valuation of realisable property: s.74(4). 13–47

  Example 1:

  D is convicted of a conspiracy to defraud. The value of his benefit is £600,000. He owns a house worth £500,000 in his sole name but he claims that the house is subject to a "loan" of £400,000 secured by a charge on the house. The evidence establishes, on a balance of probabilities, that the so-called "loan" is a sham and a device (a) to conceal the fact that the purchase money came from the proceeds of his crime and (b) to retain the benefit by misleading the Court into believing that the incumbrance was genuine.

  Example 2:

  (taken from the facts in *Harvey* (1999) 1 Cr. App. R.(S) 354).

  The judge assesses D's benefit to the value of £600,000. His realisable property is a house valued at £432,500 (allowing for the costs of sale). D claims that the house is subject to a legal charge in respect of a so-called "mortgage loan" for £395,000 towards the purchase price of the house. The judge concludes that there was no real intention to enforce the loan and therefore the money advanced to D was a gift. The Court of Appeal held that the judge was correct in her determinations and that she was not bound to make a deduction in respect of the loan for the reasons she gave.
- If the claimed "incumbrance" is either a sham, or the lender does not intend to enforce a loan, or the agreement cannot be enforced, the Court is not obliged to make any deduction in respect of that item.
- Note possible application of the "presumption of exoneration": *Posener* (January 16, 2001).
- Where the market value is lower than the amount owing on a mortgage (negative equity), the difference cannot be deducted from the value of the "amount that might be realised": *Ghadami* [1998] 1 Cr. App. R.(S) 42; [1997] Crim. L.R. 606.

(f) *Calculate the value of a gift "caught by the Act"*

- Section 74(10) defines what is meant by a "gift caught by the Act". 13–48
  There are of course a number of ways in which the defendant can be held to have made a gift of property to another. Section 74(12) puts one situation beyond doubt: "where the defendant transfers property to another directly or indirectly for a consideration the

value of which is significantly less than the value of the consideration provided by the defendant".

- Gifts: note that as the law presently stands, the value of a gift is part of the amount that might be realised even if the donee has disposed of the gift itself: see *Dickens*; and see *Wallace Duncan Smith* [1996] 2 Cr. App. R. 1.

Step Four—making the confiscation order

13–49

- If the Court determines that the defendant has assets *the Court is under a duty* to order that the defendant pays either (a) the value of the benefit or (b) the amount that might be realised, whichever is the less. There is only *one exception* and that concerns the position of a victim, of the defendant's criminal conduct, who has initiated civil proceedings against the defendant (or who intends to do so) for loss and damage flowing from the offence: s.71(1C).

(a) *Position where a victim intends to bring civil proceedings*

13–50

- Where there is an identifiable victim who has, or who intends, to initiate civil proceedings against the defendant in respect of loss, injury, or damage, the Court is not obliged to make a confiscation order but it is empowered to do so *in such amount as the Court thinks fit:* s.71(1C).
- Of course, a victim may decide to initiate civil proceedings long after the date a confiscation order was made against the defendant. It seems that in such a case, it is open to the defendant to apply for leave to appeal to the Court of Appeal (Criminal Division)—albeit out of time—against the making of the confiscation order and that Court may quash or vary a confiscation order to take account of the value of the civil judgment: *Sorelli* (25.5.99, C.A.).

(b) *Ordering compensation to a victim and making a confiscation order*

13–51

- Even if the Court determines that the defendant has not benefited from relevant criminal conduct, it may go on to make a compensation order to a named victim under s.130 of the PCC(S)A 2000. Where the defendant has benefited from his offences, the Court is entitled to make a confiscation order and a compensation order: see *Mitchell and Mitchell* (November 23, 2000).
- Where the defendant has insufficient means to pay both the amount that could be recovered under a confiscation order and a compensation order, the Court may direct that any shortfall in the amount needed to satisfy a *compensation* order may be met out of the amount recoverable under the confiscation order: see s.72(7).

  Example:

  D's benefit from fraud is £$\frac{1}{2}$ million. The amount that might be realised is assessed at £200,000 and a confiscation order is made in that sum. A *compensation* order is made in the sum of £60,000. The Court directs under s.72(7) that so much of the compensation as will not be recoverable because of the insufficiency of the defendant's means, shall be paid out of any sums recovered under the confiscation order.

- For problems associated with the making of a compensation order and a confiscation order where the effect of the orders would be the enforced sale of the matrimonial home, see paragraph (c) below.

(c) *Is it open to the Court NOT to make a confiscation order if the only realisable asset is the defendant's matrimonial home?*

- There is only one situation that gives the Court a power (rather than a duty) to recover benefits under a confiscation order, and that concerns the position of a victim who has commenced civil proceedings against the defendant (or intends to do so): s.71(1C). Accordingly, it is difficult to see how the Court can (as a matter of discretion) leave the matrimonial home out of account. See: 13–52
  - *Judge and Woodridge* (1992) 13 Cr. App. R.(S) 685
  - *Crutchley and Tonks* (1994) 15 Cr. App. R.(S) 637
  - *Lee* (1996) 1 Cr. App. R.(S) 135; [1995] Crim. L.R. 960
  - *Gregory, The Times*, October 31, 1995 (judgment, October 19, 1995)
  - *Preston* [1990] Crim. L.R. 528—the same case is reported (1990) 12 Cr. App. R.(S) 93 in the name "*Keston*".
- Suppose D has made a gift of his interest in the matrimonial home to his spouse. By s.74(10) the Court retains discretion to leave out of account gifts caught by the Act. It is arguable that if the defendant made such a gift, the Court could hold that it would not be appropriate to take the gift into account on the grounds of family hardship. However, the exercise of discretion to achieve such a result might be considered to be undesirable in principle because it might be exploited by defendants seeking to avoid the consequences of their offending. [See *Bartlett*, (unreported, July 4, 1997) where a point was taken as to whether the sentencer exercised his discretion correctly in relation to a gift; and see *Lee* (1996) 1 Cr. App. R(S) 135; [1995] Crim. L.R.960.][15]
- A difficult sentencing problem arises if the effect of making a *compensation* order and a confiscation order, would be to enforce the sale of the matrimonial home. It is well established that the Courts are discouraged from making compensation orders if the defendant will be forced to sell the matrimonial home—especially if the consequence is that the defendant's family will be made homeless: see *Hackett* 10 Cr. App. R.(S) 388; *Holah* 11 Cr. App. R. (S) 282.

  It is open to the Court under the CJA (but not the DTA) to make a compensation order and a confiscation order, but there is

[15] For a further case in relation to the exercise of discretion (but which is not directly on the point in relation to s.74(10) see *Tighe* [1996] 1 Cr. App. R. (S) 314).

authority for the proposition that the Court is *not* bound to include the value of the defendant's interest in the matrimonial home if his means are insufficient to satisfy both orders: *Taigel* [1998] 1 Cr. App. R. (S) 328.

Step Five—impose the term of imprisonment in default of payment

13–53 • The date of commencement of the defendant's default sentence for non-payment of a confiscation order is the day on which he is released from custody: *R. v. City of London Justices, ex.p. Chapman* (1998) 162 J.P. 359; *The Times*, March 17, 1998.

Step Six—stipulate time to pay etc.

13–54 • It is desirable that the Court should specify a date for payment to be made under a confiscation order: see *R. v. City of London Justices, ex.p. Chapman, The Times*, March 17, 1998.

EXTENDED ASSESSMENT OF BENEFIT (WITH ASSUMPTIONS)—S.72AA

Step One—has the defendant been convicted of TWO "qualifying offences"?

13–55 • For the purposes of proceedings in the Crown Court, the defendant must be convicted of at least one offence "of a relevant description" in the Crown Court (usually an indictable offence). That offence must also be a "qualifying offence" (s.72AA(2)) which means:
  (a) That it must be an offence listed in Sched.4 to the CJA 1988, or an indictable offence,[16] and
  (b) The offence was committed after November 1, 1995,[1] and
  (c) The Court is satisfied that it is an offence from which the defendant has benefited.[18]

• Furthermore, the defendant must be convicted of another "qualifying offence" *either* in the same proceedings currently before the Court, *or* on an earlier occasion in the six years before he was charged (s.72AA(1)(c)).

Step Two—Has the Prosecutor initiated proceedings under s.72AA?

13–56 • The prosecutor must give *written* notice to the Court that he considers that it would be appropriate for the Court to proceed under

[16] This is the combined effect of s.72AA(2)(a) and s.71(9)(c).
[17] See s.72AA(2)(b).
[18] See s.72AA(c).

section 71. The prosecutor must also include a declaration, in that notice, that (in his opinion) it is appropriate for the provisions of section 72AA to be applied (**s.72AA(1)(b)**). **Note** that in the absence of such a declaration from the prosecutor, the Court has *no* power to direct of its own motion that it would be appropriate to apply the provisions of s.72AA. However, that does not mean that the Court is prevented from enquiring why such a declaration has not been included in the notice.[19]

Step Three—the prosecutor's statement

- By s.73(1A), in addition to the information that should appear in the statement for the purposes of standard confiscation proceedings under s.71, the statement must also set out all such information available to the prosecutor as may be relevant: **13–57**
  - (a) for the purposes of making assumptions under s.72AA(4), and
  - (b) for the purposes of *not* making assumptions in relation to:
    - (i) property received or expended by the defendant but which has been the subject of an earlier confiscation order (see s.72AA(5)(b)) or
    - (ii) where (for any other reason) there would be a serious risk of injustice in the defendant's case if the material disclosed by the prosecutor was not taken into account—*e.g.* matters relevant to possible double-counting errors.

Step Four—

- The Court must proceed in accordance with the steps required under s.71. If the Court is considering whether the defendant has (a) benefited from "relevant criminal conduct" and (b) assessing the value of his benefit, it MAY invoke any of the statutory assumptions (s.72AA(4)) **13–58**

What are the statutory assumptions?

- The assumptions appear in s.72AA(4). **13–59**
- The effect of making any of the assumptions is that the defendant has benefited from crimes in respect of which he was not convicted. But on one interpretation of s.72AA(4) it may be said that the subsection does not in fact attribute to the defendant an assumption that *he* committed the offence giving rise to the benefit—

[19] The reasoning behind this restriction appears to be a political one. The Government shoulders the responsibility for introducing and enforcing laws consistent with our international obligations. But a balance has to be struck between seizing assets and the amount of public money expended in that process.

merely that it is the property of somebody's offending. It will be seen that the first three assumptions in s.72AA(4) do *not* read "as a result of or in connection with offences *committed by him*" (see by contrast s.4(3), DTA 1994). If this interpretation is correct—and it may not be—it follows that even if the defendant persuaded the Court, on a balance of probabilities, that *he* was not committing offences at the time he received the property, *his failure* to prove that the property was not derived from the commission, by someone, of an indictable (or a schedule 4) offence[20] (see s.71(9)) might be sufficient to leave the assumption intact.

- **The first assumption:** *"that any property appearing to the Court . . . to be held by the defendant at the date of conviction or at any time in the period between that date and the determination in question" . . . was received by him, at the earliest time when he appears to the Court to have held it, as a result of or in connection with the commission of offences to which this Part of this Act applies"* (**s.72AA(4)(a)(i)**).
  - — The assumption is triggered solely by the fact that the defendant *held* the property at the relevant time—that is to say, he held "any" interest in the property (s.102(7)). The value of his benefit is the value of his interest in it (s.74(4)).
  - — The assumption is not expressed to be confined to offences presumed to have been committed in a six-year period before the defendant was charged. Accordingly it is immaterial that the defendant acquired the property long before the relevant six-year period: see *Brett, The Times*, October 13, 1997, and see *Bentham and Clark* (1998) and *Chrastny No.2* [1991] 1 W.L.R. 1385, at p. 1392.
  - — Section 72AA(4)(a)(i) appears to be drafted to prevent offenders avoiding the particularly draconian breadth of this provision, by disposing of their assets following a conviction.

- **The second assumption:** *"that any property appearing to the Court . . . to have been transferred to him at any time since the beginning of the relevant period . . . was received by him, at the earliest time when he appears to the Court to have held it, as a result of or in connection with the commission of offences to which this Part of this Act applies"* (**s.72AA(4)(a)(ii)**).
  - — This assumption embraces property that the defendant "held" in the relevant six-year period but which he no longer holds. Note that a defendant holds property if he has any interest in it (s.102(7)).

- **The third assumption:** *"that any expenditure of his since the beginning of the relevant period was met out of payments received by him as a result of or in connection with the commission of offences to which this Part of this Act applies"* (s.72AA(4)(b)).

[20] Other than drug trafficking or a terrorism offence.

— Note that this assumption is not actually concerned with what went out (expenditure), but with what came in (*i.e.* "payments received"). The obvious significance of expenditure is that it is evidence of what had been received. Clearly, the parties to the proceedings must be careful to ensure that there is no double-counting of receipts and expenditure.

- **The fourth assumption:** *"that, for the purposes of valuing any benefit which he had or which he is assumed to have had at any time, he received the benefit free of any other interests in it"* s.72AA(4)(c)).

Exercising discretion whether to invoke the assumptions or not

- The Court is not obliged to make statutory assumptions: s.72AA(3). 13–60
- The wording of s.72AA(3) appears to give the sentencer an unfettered discretion to make, or not to make, any of the statutory assumptions. The contrary view is that there must be some basic fact that entitles the Court to trigger the assumption. A similar problem arose under the DTOA 1986 (a problem removed by the DTA 1994). In *Redbourne* it was held that the Court should consider (as a precondition to invoking an assumption) whether there are reasonable grounds *to suspect* that the defendant has benefited from relevant criminal conduct in respect of the property that may be the subject of statutory assumptions.

  Redbourne (1993) 96 Cr. App. R. 201; [1992] 1 W.L.R. 1182

  Khan, Sakkaravej and Pamarapa (unreported, February 26, 1996)
- The prosecution do not have to establish prima facie proof that (i) the criminal activity involving the defendant, and (ii) that the proceeds, the subject of the confiscation proceedings, came from that criminal activity: see *Delaney and Hanrahan* (unreported, May 14, 1999) and *De Silva* (May 14, 1996).[21]

When assumptions must NOT be made

- Section 72AA(5) tells us that an assumption shall not be made IF: 13–61

  "(a) "that assumption, so far as it relates to that property or expenditure, is shown to be incorrect in the defendant's case;

  (b) that assumption, so far as it so relates, is shown to be correct in relation to an offence the defendant's benefit from which has been the subject of a previous confiscation order;

  (c) the Court is satisfied that there would (for any other reason) be a serious risk of injustice in the defendant's case if the assumption were to be made in relation to that property or expenditure."

[21] It is respectfully submitted that *Rose* (1993) 14 Cr. App. R. (S) 548 is not sound authority on this point.

- It will be seen that (a) and (c) broadly mirrors the DTA (s.4(4)). Section 72AA(5)(b) is clearly intended to ensure that property received or expended, and which was taken into account in making an earlier confiscation order, must be left out of account. An identical result is achieved under the DTA (but as part of the assessment of the proceeds of drug trafficking) under s.4(6) of that Act.

What amounts to a "serious risk of injustice" for the purposes of section 72AA(5)(c)?

13–62 • In *Delaney and Hanrahan* (unreported, May 14, 1999, CA), the Court remarked (*obiter*) that s.72AA(5)(c) may have been enacted to protect a defendant from errors of double counting. The Court said that subsection 5(c) must be read in conjunction with subsection 5(b). There is (arguably) further support for this view having regard to the duty placed on the prosecution by s.73(1A) to include in a prosecutor's statement (for the purposes of the s.72AA procedure) "all such information available to the prosecutor as may be relevant for the purposes of subsection (4) and 5(b) or (c) of (s.72AA). However, it is respectfully submitted that the words in parenthesis, namely, "for any other reason", require the Court to go further and not apply the assumption if (for any reason) the Court considers that the making of the assumption might give rise to injustice in the defendant's case. It may well be that the *usual* reason for not making an assumption by virtue of subsection 5(c) is the one mentioned by the Court in *Delaney*. See now *Benjafield* (December 21, 2000), *McIntosh* (February 5, 2001), and the Performance and Innovation Unit Report, *Recovering the Proceeds of Crime* (June 2000)

Step Five—determining the amount to be recovered

13–63 • It will be seen from s.71(1A) that the Court must determine whether the defendant has benefited from "relevant criminal conduct" and then (by s.71(1B) and s.71(6)) to recover the value of that benefit or the amount that might be realised. It will be recalled that "relevant criminal conduct" means the offences of which the defendant was convicted in the same proceedings and offences to be taken into consideration (s.71(1D)). However, where part of the benefit figure is calculated using assumptions, section 72AA(6) broadens the definition of "relevant criminal conduct" to include offences from which the defendant is assumed to have benefited.

- Where the Court has made any of the statutory assumptions (and which remain intact) the CJA creates a fiction, namely, that assumed benefits were obtained by the defendant as a result of offences for which he was convicted in the proceedings before the Crown Court (or which he has asked to be taken into consideration).

(3) The draft Proceeds of Crime Bill 2001

Introduction

13–64 The Proceeds of Crime Bill 2001 includes the following proposals (among many others):

- New *Assets Recovery Agency* [clause 1].
- Rules relating to confiscation set out mainly as one code.
- Confiscation for drug trafficking and other crimes put on a SIMILAR footing.
- A confiscation order may be made to recover benefits derived from the commission of the offence(s) of which the defendant falls to be sentenced. A confiscation order may go beyond the offences before the Court if the defendant has a "criminal lifestyle": clause 6(4)(a).
- "criminal lifestyle" has statutory meaning: (clause 75).
- There is one test for benefit, namely, "if he *obtains* property as a result of or in connection with . . . conduct": clauses 76(4); 76(7); 80
- Cases regarding "payments received" (in Drug Trafficking Act cases) may no longer be of much assistance.
- Would street value of drug obtained be included in the value of 'benefit'?
- Assumptions to be mandatory whether offence relates to drug trafficking or not; "drug trafficking offence" amended to include s.8 MDA offences: clause 88.
- Determining the "amount that might be realised" (if lower than benefit) to be restyled "the available amount": clause 10.
- An amount is available if it is "free": clause 10(1)(a) and clause 82.
- Property is "free" if it is not subject to a forfeiture order or confiscation order: clause 82.
- A court will no longer have the discretion to leave gifts out of account (currently Criminal Justice Act 1988 only).

- Time to pay will be immediate, unless court gives time to pay—then only for up to six months unless extended (maximum is one year) (clause 12).
- Rules relating to postponement radically changed: up to 2 years—unless that period is extended (clause 15).
- New power to discharge confiscation order if assets inadequate through no fault of defendant.
- New power for Justices Chief Executive, to apply to Crown Court for discharge of a confiscation order if the amount outstanding is under £50: clause 26.
- New power for prosecutors to ask the Crown Court to revise its calculation of the value of realisable assets available to the defendant to satisfy a confiscation order: clause 23.
- A right of appeal by the prosecution, to the Court of Appeal, against judge's ruling on a confiscation order: clause 32.
- A right of appeal by the prosecution, to the Court of Appeal, if judge declines to make confiscation order: clause 32(2).
- Power of the Court of Appeal to make determinations under clause 6.
- Power for prosecution/defence to appeal to the House of Lords at various stages.
- House of Lords may review a decision of the Court of Appeal and for the House of Lords to make determinations under clause 4.
- New power to order banks and building societies to pay money in an account, to enforcement authority, to satisfy a confiscation order: clause 67(5).
- Limited third party rights (not at confiscation stage it seems).
- Immunity for Insolvency Practitioners, who unwittingly interfere with restrained property: clause 417.
- Money laundering offences widened: clauses 321 to 329.
- *Mens rea* requirements modified for money laundering offences as to: see clauses 321 and 325.
- New scheme: civil recovery of property without conviction.
- New rules relating to taxation.
- Greater co-operation between agencies.

No power for magistrates to make confiscation orders

13–65 The power to make a confiscation order at first instance will normally be in the Crown Court. The magistrates will have no power to make a confiscation order once the defendant has been convicted of an offence—no matter how minor the offence. Instead, clause 70(1)(b) empowers the prosecutor to ask the Court to commit the defendant to the Crown Court "with a view to a confiscation order being considered". The reasoning may be that the prosecutor is best placed to make the decision as to whether it is desirable, or appropriate, for the Crown Court to embark on confiscation proceedings.

A number of factors are likely to influence the prosecutor's decision including the scale and nature of the offending and the amount likely to be recovered under a confiscation order. There may be public interest considerations too.

Once the prosecutor asks the magistrates' court to commit the defendant to the Crown Court for confiscation proceedings, it seems that the magistrates are *obliged to do so* by virtue of clause 70(2)(a). This is so irrespective as to whether the justices would have committed the defendant to the Crown Court for sentence in any event. If the Court would have done so, then it must make that fact clear in open court: clause 70(5). The reason for this is to ensure that the sentencer in the Crown Court is aware that the defendant falls to be sentenced as if he had been convicted on indictment: clause 71(2).

If the justices commit the defendant to the Crown Court *for confiscation proceedings*, the sentencing powers of the Crown Court are limited to those of the lower court: clause 71(3).

The scheme of Part II of the Proceeds of Crime Bill

Broadly stated, the Drug Trafficking Act, and Part VI of the Criminal Justice Act 1988, creates three discreet systems for making confiscation orders. 13–66

(1) The Drug Trafficking Act empowers the Crown Court to confiscate the proceeds a defendant's drug trafficking (benefits) but the criteria for "benefit" is whether the defendant "*received payments or rewards* in connection with drug trafficking carried on by him or by another".
(2) The standard benefit procedure under Part VI of the Criminal Justice Act 1988 enables the Court to determine "benefit" namely "*if he obtains property as a result of or in connection with its commission . . .*": section 71(4). No statutory assumptions may be made and less certain conditions are fulfilled.
(3) The extended benefit procedure under the Criminal Justice Act, Part VI, empowers the Court to determine benefit by reference to "property obtained" by the defendant and to make statutory assumptions if it wishes to do so (discretionary).

Under the Criminal Justice Act 1988, it was not easy to determine precisely what had been "obtained": see *Rees*, unreported, September 17, 1990; *Saia and others*, unreported, April 20, 1999 and *Gokal*, unreported, May 7th, 1997.

Meaning of "benefit" in Part II of the PCB

There is now one definition of benefit (regardless of the offence) and it is that "*a person benefits from conduct if the obtains property as a result of or in connection with the conduct*" (Clause 76). 13–67

It is likely that benefit based on "property obtained" will give rise to difficult problems of construction and application. The definition under

Part VI of the CJA 1988 is already problematic and current case law has not made the position entirely clear. Practitioners should also be aware that decisions made under earlier legislation will be of limited assistance to a court when construing provisions of the PCB because the scheme of confiscation under the Bill differs significantly from earlier enactments.

That said, Part II of the Bill does not treat all offenders in the same way, and it does not treat all offences equally either. This is because the Bill creates a twin track method of calculating benefit.

Twin-track "benefit" assessment

13–68 The Bill does not refer to "tracks" but the expression is used by the author to assist in explaining the effect of the system of confiscation under Part II of the Bill.

First track: the Court can recover the proceeds/benefit in respect of the offences for which the defendant falls to be sentenced. The Bill describes the defendant's conduct under this heading as "*particular criminal conduct*". The Court takes a global view of the defendant's conduct when looking at those offences (clause 9). No statutory assumptions can be invoked.

Second track: the Court can recover all the proceeds of crime received by the defendant during his entire criminal career. The Bill, somewhat clumsily, describes the defendant's conduct under this heading as "*general criminal conduct*" resulting from his "criminal lifestyle". Statutory assumptions (clause 11) will apply to lighten the task of the Court when assessing the value of the defendant's benefit.

> **Further explanation and comment:** It is only if the defendant has a "criminal lifestyle" that the Court is bound to apply the statutory assumptions. Yet, the value of the benefit is styled "general criminal conduct". It is difficult to see why it is necessary to have this bewildering array of 'conduct' terms. The Bill could simply provide that "the value of the defendant's benefit from his criminal lifestyle shall include property obtained as a result of all his criminal conduct irrespective as to whether the conduct occurred before or after the passing of this Act and irrespective as when the property was obtained": See clause 76.
>
> As for the statutory assumptions (clause 11), these broadly mirror the statutory assumptions under the Drug Trafficking Act 1994.
>
> The Court must deduct from the value of the defendant's "benefit", other confiscation orders made under the Proceeds of Crime Bill, or earlier asset recovery enactments: see clause 9(3). It is not clear why the value of property recovered under forfeiture orders, *e.g.* under section 27 MDA 1971, and section 143 of the Powers of the Criminal Courts (Sentencing) Act 2000 should not similarly be deducted at this stage (and see clause 82).

Which track applies?

The answer is that the Court must decide if the defendant has a "criminal lifestyle": clause 4(4)(a). If he has, the Court follows track two: if not, the Court follows track one. 13–69

The standard of proof, throughout, is the civil standard: clause 4(7). Clause 90 empowers the Secretary of State to make rules that correspond to the Civil Procedure Rules, which is sensible, but the rules of evidence will remain those applicable in criminal proceedings. Statutes such as the Civil Evidence Act 1995 can have no application to confiscation proceedings under Part II of the Bill.

How is "criminal lifestyle" defined?

"Criminal lifestyle" is defined by clause 75. *Be careful here*. The expression tends to imply that the defendant has followed a criminal way of life. That is broadly true of clauses 72(2)(d) and (e). Thus, a defendant will have a "criminal lifestyle" if: 13–70

(i) It is a drug trafficking offence: clause 75(2)(a).
(ii) It is a money laundering offence: clause 75(2)(b).
(iii) It is an offence specified in Regulations (this might include human trafficking, or arms trafficking). It follows that the Proceeds of Crime Bill does not treat all offences equally.
(iv) The defendant has been convicted of an offence from which he benefited AND at least THREE other offences in the same proceedings from which he has also benefited (clause 75(2)(d) and clause 75(3)(a)), or
(v) The defendant has been convicted of an offence from which he benefited AND he was convicted on at least *two other occasions* of an offence from which he has benefited (clause 75(2)(d) and clause 75(3)(b)), or
(vi) The defendant is convicted of an offence committed over a period of six months: clause 75(2)(e).

Note: it is very easy to misread clause 75(3)(a): it does NOT mean that the defendant must be convicted of three offences—*but four*—note the words "*other* offences".

Note: the defendant must be "convicted". This seems to exclude offences to be taken into consideration (see the wording of clause 76(3) for comparative purposes), or cautions, or out-of-court admissions of guilt.

Note: that (iii) above includes many "conduct crimes", such as conspiracy, fraudulent evasions *e.g.* under CEMA 1979, or perhaps any offence where the planning and execution of it exceeded six months.

Note: look carefully at the revised definition of "drug trafficking" (clause 88). It includes offences contrary to section 8 of the Misuse Of Drugs Act 1971 (allowing premises to be used for the production, supply, or even—it seems—the smoking of cannabis or prepared opium). The Independent

Inquiry into the Misuse of Drugs Act (Chaired by Viscountess Runciman, DBE) recommended that acts contrary to section 8(a) and (b) of the MDA 1971 (permitting the production and supply of controlled drugs) should be "drug trafficking offences" but that section 8(c) and (d) of the Misuse of Drugs Act 1971 should be repealed. The Government's response has been to widen the ambit of section 8(c) and (d) to embrace the use of any controlled drug section 38 of the Criminal Justice and Police Act 2001.

What is to be recovered under a confiscation order?

13–71 The proposed statutory formula is that the Court must assess the "recoverable amount" that is to say, "an amount equal to the defendant's *benefit*" [clause 8(1)] which is "the value of the property obtained" from his criminal conduct (clause 80).

How is the benefit calculated?

13–72 This again depends on whether the defendant has a "criminal lifestyle" or not. If he has a "criminal lifestyle" then the Court must apply the statutory assumptions: if has not, the Court cannot invoke the assumptions. In either situation, clause 9(2) states that the Court must "*(a) take account of conduct occurring up to the time it make its decision*" and "*(b) take account of property obtained up to that time*". This clause is liable to cause confusion particularly when read in conjunction with clause 11 (assumptions). Clearly, clause 9 is not a reverse onus provision but how much of the defendant's conduct and wealth is relevant in cases where the defendant is found NOT to have a "criminal lifestyle" (*i.e.* track one). The Government's "explanatory note" does not shed much light on the purpose of clause 9(2).

Clause 9 does little more than state the obvious. In order to determine whether the defendant has a criminal lifestyle or not the Court must take into account all relevant conduct—relevance would depend on whether the Court was assessing benefit under "track 1" or "track 2". It may be relevant to have regard to evidence that the defendant has (for example) no evidence of legitimate income, or that property in his possession remains unexplained.

The position of victims of crime and confiscation orders

13–73 Once the Court embarks on confiscation proceedings, it must confiscate the value of the benefit or the value of the defendant's available assets if less than that amount. There is one important exception to this mandatory regime and that concerns the position of victims of crime who have started, or intend to start, civil proceedings for loss or damage (clause 6(6)). In such a case, the Court has a power to make a confiscation order—it is not obliged to do so—and may therefore make a compensation order for all or part of the loss or damage suffered by the victim. This differs from the current scheme under Part VI of the Criminal Justice Act 1988.

It will be open to the Court to make both a confiscation order and a compensation order (clause 14(5)) but the assets available to the defendant may be insufficient to pay both. The position under Part VI of the CJA is preserved so that the Court may direct that where realised assets are insufficient to pay the full value of the compensation order, any shortfall must be paid out of sums recovered under the confiscation order: clause 14(6). This ensures that victims are compensated in preference to the satisfaction of the confiscation order. It is less clear whether it would be possible to make such orders in respect of drug trafficking cases where loss or damage has resulted from a particular investigation.

Defendant to prove amount available less than value of his benefit

Once the Court has determine benefit, it must proceed to make a confiscation order for that amount (clause 8(1)) unless the defendant proves that the "*available amount*" is less than the benefit recoverable: clause 8(2). The term "available amount" is defined by clause 8 to include the value of all "*free property*" held by the defendant, plus the value of all "*tainted gifts*". "Free property" means merely free of forfeiture orders: see clause 79, while "tainted gifts" is defined by clause 77. All "free property" held by the defendant and/or by a person holding a "tainted gift", is the defendant's "realisable property": clause 83. 13–74

Benefit problems

Why so many "conduct" terms?

Clause 76(4) states that a person "benefits from *conduct* if he obtains property as a result of all in connection with the conduct" [emphasis added]. 13–75

The point of interest here is the use of the word "conduct"—and not the expression "criminal conduct" or "general or particular conduct". It will be seen that clause 9 also refers to benefiting from 'conduct'. At first sight, it might be thought that the Government wishes to include conduct falling short of the commission of a substantive or inchoate offence, *e.g.* preparatory acts that nevertheless resulted in the defendant obtaining property. Examples might be hard to find.

However, clause 6(5) requires the Court to make a confiscation order IF the defendant has benefited "from the conduct referred to", *i.e.* conduct defined by clause 6(4)(b) as "*general conduct*" and clause 6(4)(c) "*particular conduct*". It does not matter where the conduct was performed provided it would constitute an offence by the laws of England and Wales: clause 76(1). It is therefore difficult to see how the Court can confiscate property that does not represent benefit from the defendant's *general* or *particular* "criminal conduct".

In the absence of a better explanation, the author suggests that clause

76(4) should read "a person benefits if he obtains property as a result of his general criminal conduct or his particular criminal conduct". Clause 76(7) should read, "The value of a person's benefit is the value of the property obtained." Similarly, clause 9 should make it clear that "conduct" means 'general' or 'particular' criminal conduct.

When is 'property obtained' a benefit?

13–76 In what circumstances can property be "obtained" so that it amounts to a benefit? That is to say, must the property be received by the defendant *personally*, or it is enough that he has caused the property to be obtained by a company (a separate legal entity) which he controls?

Again, is a benefit "obtained" if an empire is built on the back of an unlawful obtaining of the very small sum of money (the "fruits of the poisoned tree" approach)? Current case law here may be relevant.

The new scheme is bound to reopen the question as to whether the value of a drug seized by law enforcement agencies should be included as part of the defendant's benefit, and if so, what value is to be put on that benefit. Under the Proceeds of Crime Bill, all property "obtained" by the defendant "in connection with" the offence will be his benefit. However, what does 'obtain' mean? That question is answered by clause 84(2)(b): "*property is obtained by any person in the obtains an interest in it*".

> *Example:*
> Suppose a lorry driver knowingly imports five tonnes of cannabis into the United Kingdom for a reward of £10,000 to be paid on completion of the task, but he is arrested at Dover. The Court accepts that the street value is £18 million.

Has the driver obtained an £18 million benefit? The conclusion may not be easy to escape under the terms of the Bill. The lorry driver was in possession of the drugs. It is likely that a Court would have little difficulty in concluding that possession is a sufficient proprietary interest for the purpose of clause 84(2). The drugs were obtained in *connection with* the offence although they were not obtained *for the offence*. However, clause 4 does not define benefit in terms of obtaining "a reward", but merely that property was *obtained "in connection with"* the offence.

13–77 It might be argued that an interest in property means one capable of being enforced in law: that persons are expressly forbidden by statute to be in possession of controlled drugs (unless one of the exceptions apply), and therefore an unlawful possession is not an interest in property for the purposes of clause 84(2). Even if that argument is correct, it would not save the lorry driver who imports millions of pounds worth of cigarettes and alcohol into the country and fraudulently evades the payment of duty on those goods. Cigarettes and alcohol are dutiable goods but they may be possessed lawfully. Has the driver in that situation acquired an interest in the goods the full value of which he obtained "in connection with" the offence of 'evading duty'? This was one of the issues that confronted the

Court of Appeal in *Cadman Smith*, June 16, 2000, unreported. Leave to appeal to the House of Lords was refused by the Court of Appeal on December 20, 2000 (but granted by the House of Lords). That case, decided under Part VI of the Criminal Justice Act 1988, is illuminating.

> In November 1997, M carried out three trips to the continent to buy duty free cigarettes that were then unlawfully "smuggled" into the United Kingdom by boat. The boat was seized and a quantity of cigarettes recovered. His home was also searched and more cigarettes were found. M was then bailed. M then recruited C to buy another boat, which he did. M, R and C used the boat twice to smuggle more cigarettes to evade the payment of duty. However, for reasons that are not apparent, the prosecution alleged that the first trip was a "dry run"—which it was not—but the Court presumably felt obliged to deal with the case on the assumption that it was.
>
> On the second occasion, 1.25 million cigarettes were found on the boat. The duty evaded was £130,666.40. The boat was worth £55,000. The prosecution therefore alleged that the benefit figure was £185,666.40 (£55,000 + £130,666.40). A confiscation order was made against C for a lesser amount (on the basis of C's realisable assets).
>
> The Court quashed the confiscation order.
>
> The cigarettes (*i.e.* the subject of the second trip only) had not be retained and they had not been sold. He had not retained any sum from which he could be said to have benefited. He remained liable for the duty but the Court said, "it is . . . difficult to say that there has been a benefit in connection with the commission of the offence" (*Dimsey and Allen* [2000] Cr. App. R. (S) 497 distinguished).
>
> The boat was not obtained from the commission of the offence either and indeed that had been forfeited under a different enactment.

In *Cadman Smith*, the prosecution had not been able to rely on the statutory assumptions in respect of the value of the cigarettes or the boat. The prosecution argued ("although not with great conviction") that the cigarettes constituted property obtained as a benefit. The problem with that submission was that the Court went on to hold that liability to pay duty occurred the moment C crossed the entry of the harbour. It therefore seems, to this author, that the problem faced by the prosecution was that the cigarettes were not obtained *after* that moment, and were not obtained "as a result of or in connection with" the offence.

The case gives rise to difficult issues as to the scope of the phrase "in connection with" the commission of an offence. The reasoning of the Court appears to be that property (*e.g.* a boat) obtained as an instrument *to be used* for the commission of an offence, may not (for the purposes of section 71(4) CJA 1988) amount to property obtained "in connection with the commission of an offence".

Would a different result follow in respect of drug trafficking offences? 13–78
Possibly: each case will have to be decided by reference to the elements of

the offence charged. Where the allegation is that goods were imported/exported fraudulently and contrary to the evasion of the prohibition on importation/exportation, under section 170(2) of the Customs and Excise Management Act 1979, the offence is continuing and seems to be capable of commission when acts are performed in accordance with the intentions of the offender(s). An offence under section 170(2) of CEMA 1979, may be committed in respect of acts committed before, or after, the moment of importation. This is because an offence under section 170(2) can be committed in two ways (*i.e.* fraudulent evading the prohibition, or attempting to do so: see *Latif and Shahzad* [1996] 1 All E.R. 353, HL). An attempted fraudulent evasion is not charged under the Criminal Attempts Act 1981. Thus, even if drugs have been seized overseas, but were destined for this country, the smugglers may nevertheless be convicted under s.170(2), and that is so even if they were arrested overseas and extradited to the United Kingdom for trial. Alternatively, the prosecution might charge a conspiracy to evade section 170(2)). Both a conspiracy to evade a prohibition on importation/exportation, and the substantive offence under section 170(2), are wide in their scope.

It is therefore arguable that under Part II of the Proceeds of Crime Bill, property obtained in pursuance of a smuggling plan, was obtained "in connection with" the offence charged. Again, if Cadman Smith had been convicted of a conspiracy to evade the payment of duty, would the result in his case have been different on the basis that the cigarettes, and the boat, were obtained "in connection with" that offence? The Courts have not found the construction of section 71(4) of the 1988 Act easy. They will find the proper and just application of clause 76(4) no easier.

Postponed determinations

13–79 Current legislation has created a stream of cases flowing from decisions of the Crown Court either to postpone under the relevant enactment, or to adjourn proceedings as part of its inherent jurisdiction. Clause 15 introduces a new system. There is no requirement that the postponement is with a view to obtaining "further information" relevant to the making of any of the determinations under the Bill.

Clause 13 envisages that proceedings may be postponed for any reason on the application of the defendant, the prosecutor/Director, or the Court: clause 15 (6).

Confiscation proceedings may be postponed for a period not exceeding two years unless there are exceptional circumstances (clause 15 (2), 15(4) and 15(3)). This is a very long period indeed, and a recipe for procrastination on all sides. In the meantime, the defendant's assets (and those of innocent or tainted third parties) are likely to remain restrained or at least subject to restrictions. If proceedings are postponed, the Court may nevertheless proceed to sentence: clause 16.

Information supplied by prosecutor/Director

For the purposes of assisting the Court to decide whether the defendant has a criminal lifestyle, the prosecutor/Director MUST give the Court a "*Statement of Information*"—formerly a 'prosecutor's statement'. Although the content of a *Statement of Information* is likely to resemble most "prosecutor's statements" served under current legislation, there are also a number of significant differences. First, it seems likely that the new provisions will/should encourage a trend in favour of fuller, more detailed, statements setting out the defendant's criminal history (relevant to a decision as to whether he has a "criminal lifestyle"), *plus* property that has passed through his hands over the relevant period, and the value of that benefit. There is no obligation on the prosecutor/Director to identify the extent of a defendant's known assets, but it is likely that this would happen anyway—not least because assets found in the defendant's hands may well be relevant to the assessment of "benefit": see *Gokal*, unreported, March 16, 2001 (an object lesson). 13–80

The statement must also include matters relevant to the Court's decision as to whether to invoke the statutory assumptions, *or NOT do so* on the grounds that there exists a serious risk of injustice to do so.

Statements of Information are likely to include matters of belief/opinion, *e.g.* as to whether a defendant has a criminal lifestyle, or has benefited from general, or particular, criminal conduct. The statement is likely to contain hearsay but this is not a problem if the defendant accepts an allegation or fact. Areas in dispute will need to be proved during the course of confiscation proceedings in accordance with rules of evidence applicable in criminal proceedings.

The defendant will not be obliged to serve a response unless the Court exercises its discretion (clause 16) to require a response. A defendant who fails to comply with an order made under clause 16 may find that he is treated as having accepted every matter set out in the *Statement of Information* apart from any suggestion that he has benefited from criminal conduct: clause 18(3).

Where a defendant was not asked to serve a response, the prosecutor must be ready to prove the relevant matters set out in the Statement, but that does not mean that the defendant will be able to score technical points (*e.g.* as to admissibility of evidence) without risk of rebuke from the Court or an order for costs, if the proceedings are adjourned/postponed for further enquiries to be made.

Upward variation of "available about"

If the defendant proves to the Court that the assets in his hands fall below the value of his benefit, the Court must recover the lesser sum: clause 8(2) and (3). 13–81

Under current legislation the prosecutor can seek an upward variation of the "amount that might be realised" (now styled "available amount" and see *Tivnan* [1999] 1 C.A.R.(S) 92) because the value of property is greater than was first thought, or has subsequently increased in value. Clause 23 significantly alters the position. It will only be necessary for the prosecutor/ Director/receiver to request that the Crown Court makes "a new calculation". The Court must then do so, and if the value of the "available amount" has increased, the Court may make a revised confiscation order for such sum as it things "just" (clause 23(4)).

Downward variations

13–82 A defendant/receiver may apply to the Crown Court for a downward variation of the value of a confiscation order (clause 24). It is not clear whether the new provision would alter the current law in respect of "hidden assets" included in the value of the confiscation order. It is submitted that the current case law remains intact: *R v. C.*, November 18, 1997, unreported; *R v. W*, January 29, 1998, unreported; and see *Gokal v. SFO*, March 16, 2001, unreported.

Clauses 25 and 26 provide the Justices' Chief Executive with two new powers, namely, to apply to the Crown Court for the order to be discharged if (a) the amount outstanding is less than £1,000, and the defendant's assets are inadequate (through no thought of his) to pay the order (clause 25), or (b) the amount remaining to be paid is £50 or less (clause 26). Those statutory figures may be buried by the Secretary of State.

Enforcement

13–83 Unless the Court appoints the Director to be the enforcement authority, the magistrates' court will continue to enforce confiscation orders. Where, however, the Director has been appointed, clause 38 empowers him to apply to the Crown Court for the defendant to appear (by summons), and he fails to appear, the Crown Court may issue a warrant for his arrest, and he may be committed to prison (or detention) for defaulting to pay the confiscation order. Time served will be reduced in proportion to the amount that remains outstanding (expressed as a fraction of the original sum payable under the confiscation order): clause 36(7). Serving a term of imprisonment in default of payment of the confiscation order does not extinguished the debt: clause 39(5) and clause 87.

Appeals

13–84 The defendant may appeal the making of a confiscation order because a confiscation is a "sentence" for the purpose of the Criminal Appeal Act 1968 (as amended).

New provisions are included in the Bill relating to appeals that may be launched by the parties in the case, at various stages of the proceedings, to the Court of Appeal (with leave of that court: see clause 91) and to the House of Lords. Both of those tribunals will be able to make determinations under clause 6 of the Bill. Thus, if the prosecutor is aggrieved by any decision of the Crown Court, he may appeal to the Court of Appeal: clause 32.

An appeal will also lie to that Court, if the judge declines to make a confiscation order at all: clause 32. It would be unlikely that the Court of Appeal would grant leave unless the judge of the Crown Court exercised his discretion unreasonably—although whether it is now necessary to establish *Wednesbury* unreasonableness (since the enactment of the Human Rights Act) remains to be seen. It is unlikely that the provision will be used very often.

Challenging the decision to embark on confiscation proceedings

On what basis might the defendant be able to successfully challenge the decision of the prosecutor, or the Court, to embark on confiscation proceedings? Since *Benjafield*, December 12, 2000, this question seems important but the difficulty is that clause 6(3) and (4), and clause 70 (1) and (2), impose an obligation on the Court to initiate the confiscation process under the Proceeds of Crime Bill if the prosecutor asks it to do so. It will be almost impossible for the defendant to challenge a prosecutor's decision to proceed under the Proceeds of Crime Bill unless there is clear abuse of process, or *mala fides*. **13–85**

Appeals to the Court of Appeal

In the event of a successful appeal under clause 33(2), the Court of Appeal may itself proceed to make a confiscation order under clause 6 or it may remit the case to the Crown Court for a determination. **13–86**

Appeals lie to the Court of Appeal by the prosecutor/Director or by the defendant/third party in respect of any decision regarding—

- The making of a restraint order or charging order: clause 44;
- The appointment of a receiver: clause 65.

The Proceeds of Crime Bill makes it clear that the relevant Division of the Court of Appeal is the Criminal Division in respect of any matter arising in connection with proceedings under Part II of the Bill: clause 91. This is significant: the Government is no longer contending that confiscation proceedings are not penal in nature: see *Welch v. United Kingdom,* and *Benjafield* (where the point was conceded by the Crown).

Appeal to the House of Lords

An appeal will be available to the defendant, or to the prosecutor/Director, on appeal from a decision of the Court of Appeal under clauses 34, 45, 66 and see clause 92. **13–87**

They may be appeals to the House of Lords from the Court of Appeal in respect of:

- Restrained or charging orders: clause 45;
- The appointment of receivers: clause 66.

MONEY LAUNDERING OFFENCES AND THE PROCEEDS OF CRIME BILL 2001

General note

13–88 The purpose of Part VIII of the Proceeds of Crime Bill is to tighten up rules relating to money-laundering and to ensure that the laws of the United Kingdom fulfil our international obligations including the 1991 E.C. Money-laundering Directive, which is likely to be amended. United Kingdom law already exceeds the terms of the E.C. Directive—which is permissible.

Money laundering is occurring on a vast scale but the international response is not uniform. The money-laundering offences set out in Part VIII appear to resemble current offences, but there are significant differences between the old and new versions.

Confiscation orders and making statutory assumptions

13–89 Note that by section 4(5) of the Drug Trafficking Act, none of the statutory assumptions under the Act may be invoked if the only offence before the Court is a money-laundering offences under section was 49, 50, or section 56. Curiously, there appears to be no corresponding saving in Part VI of the Criminal Justice Act 1988. It is not clear why or how that has come about. However, under the Proceeds Of Crime Bill the point will no longer arise because the commission of any money-laundering offence will be treated as part of his "criminal lifestyle": see clause 75(1) and (2), and this attracts the making of the statutory assumptions (see clause 6 (4) (b) and clause 11). For those reasons, clause 85 does not include drug money laundering as a "drug trafficking offence": and see clause 75 (2) (a).

Concealing, transferring the proceeds of money laundering

13–90 Under the Drug Trafficking Act, section 49(1) it is an offence for a person to conceal, disguise, convert, transfer, or removed from the jurisdiction, his own of proceeds of drug trafficking. By section 49(2) it is an offence for another person to act similarly "knowing or having reasonable grounds to suspect that any property . . . . represents another person's proceeds of drug trafficking". The difference between subsections (1) and (2), is that in (2) it seems to be immaterial whether the property is actually the proceeds of drug trafficking. The defendant is to be judged on the facts as he knew, or suspected them, to be.

However, the scheme of clause 321 is different. It is an offence to conceal (etc.) "*criminal property*"—a term defined by clause 329 to mean any 'benefit' from criminal conduct where the defendant "*knows or suspects that it constitutes or represents such a benefit*". It does not matter who carried out the conduct or who benefited from it: clause 329(3). This is an improvement on the old law because the property must in fact represent someone's proceeds of criminal conduct. This fact will need to be established to the criminal standard of proof, but it will not be necessary for the prosecution to particularise the actual offence(s), or even the type of offences, to succeed under clause 321.

Entering into a (money laundering) arrangement

Clause 322 significantly streamlines its predecessor, namely, section 50 of the Drug Trafficking Act 1994. It is clear that the proposed offence is very widely drawn. It must be read in conjunction with clause 329. The defendant must know or suspect that (i) the arrangement will facilitate one or more of the forbidden activities and (ii) that the property is the proceeds of "criminal conduct". 13–91

Impact of this offence on lawyers

What impact might this offence have for lawyers? This is a difficult question to answer, as it is in relation to section 49 of the Drug Trafficking Act. If a lawyer (advising a client in respect of pending confiscation proceedings) is told by his client that he has assets that the prosecution have not discovered, would the lawyer be facilitating the retention of the benefit of criminal conduct if he took no action to persuade the client to come clean about his wealth? If the lawyer does advise the client to disclose, and the advice is ignored, then the lawyer has not concerned himself in an "arrangement" for the purposes of clause 322 (or section 49 of the Drug Trafficking Act). The grey area is where the lawyer 'shrugged his shoulders' or 'turned a blind eye' or, worse, advised the client "it is best to say nothing". The fact that the lawyer may be acting in the belief that his client is not obliged to incriminate himself, may not save the lawyer from prosecution under clause 322. Arguably, such a situation is not what clause 322 is designed to tackle. Clearly, a person must not be complicit in another person's scheme to money-launder, or to retain the proceeds of crime. 13–92

Acquisition, use and possession

Clause 323 significantly alters current law under section 51 of the Drug Trafficking Act 1994. It will no longer be necessary for the prosecution to show that the defendant knew the property represented another person's proceeds of drug trafficking. The *mens rea* has been extended to embrace a defendant's suspicion that it represented the proceeds of criminal conduct see clause 329(3)(b)). 13–93

It remains a defence for the accused to prove that he provided adequate consideration for the property. It seems that the provision of goods or services to another might constitute adequate consideration unless the property helps another person to carry out criminal conduct. The statutory defence exists to protect traders who know of a person's reputation for committing crimes. The defence is lost if the property (usually cash) supplied helps the recipient to "carry out criminal conduct": see clause 323(2)(d). This provision has its origins in section 14 (5) of the Criminal Justice (International Cooperation) Act 1990. It is not clear whether it must be proved that the defendant knew or believed or suspected that the property what be used for an unlawful purpose.

Failing to disclose suspicions

13–94 Failing to disclose knowledge or suspicion that another person is engaged in drug money laundering is an offence contrary to section 52 of the Drug Trafficking Act 1994. There is no corresponding obligation under the Criminal Justice Act 1988 to report suspicions of money laundering in respect of other crimes. The reasons for this are largely political and diplomatic, having regard to our international obligations at the time various United Kingdom statutory measures were introduced: see for example that terms of the United Nations Convention Against Illicit Traffic in Narcotics Drugs and Psychotropic Substances 1988; the Council of Europe Convention on Laundering, Search, Seizure and Confiscation of the Proceeds of Crime 1990; the *E.C. Money-Laundering Directive* (91/308/EEC) which is likely to be amended. There has been much resistance to the imposition of statutory coercive measures to report suspicious transactions—particularly from those contractually or professionally bound to maintain client confidentiality. Voluntary reporting schemes have been in existence for many years and they appear to have worked well. However, the scale of money-laundering is so great that the Government believes that more needs to be done to provide law enforcement agencies with the information they require to investigate serious crime more effectively.

Attempts to amend the 1991 E.C. Directive on money laundering have provoked a strong debate across Europe as to the extent to which persons (including lawyers) should be compelled to betray their clients—on suspicion. Developments in this are area are of the greatest importance to lawyers and such developments put the rules of legal professional privilege under tension.

Clause 324(8) affords quite wide protection to lawyers. It largely replicates the language employed in section 52(8) of the Drug Trafficking Act save that the phrase "[or] for the purpose of those proceedings" are omitted from clause 324(8)—perhaps because they were believed to be superfluous. The saving is wide enough to include information given to legal adviser by a potential witness, or by any person other than the client, provided the information relates to legal proceedings to have been initiated, or are contemplated.

Clause 324(6) is new. The Court must consider whether the defendant follows guidelines issued by a "supervisory authority" (and as approved by the Treasury).

Civil Recovery

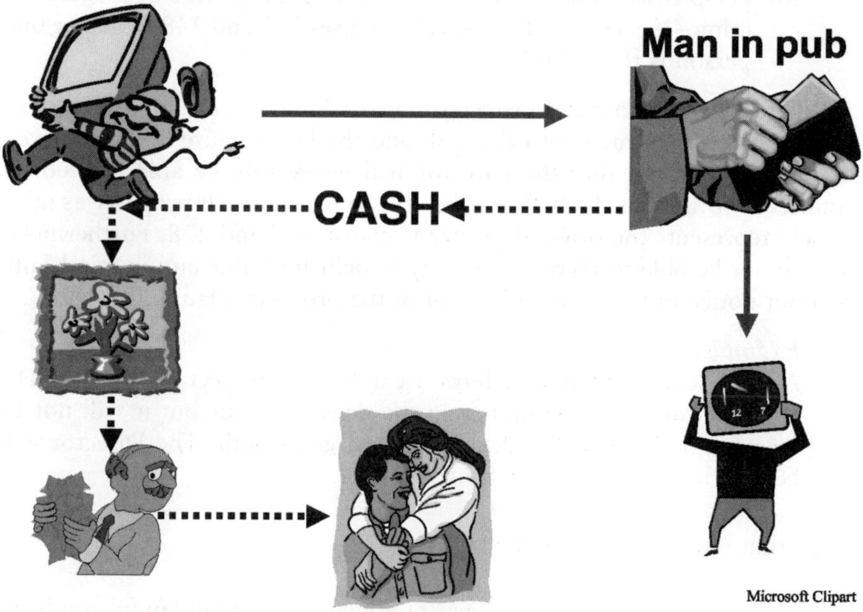

Microsoft Clipart

Introduction

The above diagram illustrates the mechanics of the proposed scheme including the notion that property, which represents the original property (obtained through criminal conduct), is treated as being the original property: clause 278. On one interpretation of Part 5, it seems that property in clause 278 can be of two types: "original property" and "property that represents original property", clause 278(1)(b) but on another interpretation it might be said that clause 278 creates a fiction so that converted property is deemed to be the "original property". Perhaps this matters little, but one wonders whether it is necessary to approach the problem of converted property in such a complicated manner. The Irish version of civil recovery seems far more straightforward: see the Proceeds of Crime Act 1996, the Disclosure for Taxation and Other Purposes Act 1996, and the Criminal Asset Bureau Act 1996. Has the Irish Government encountered problems tracing and recovering property under its legislation? 13–95

The scheme of a civil recovery (other than cash)

13–96 Proceedings under Part V will be taken in the High Court. They will be conducted by the Director of the Assets Recovery Agency (ARA). The Director will be empowered to move against three classes of persons:

(1) Persons who obtained property through unlawful conduct (clause 248(2)(a)); and
(2) Persons who obtained property from an offender (*e.g.* a car sold to be by the thief) (clause 302(3), and
(3) Persons who hold property that represent the original proceeds of crime—*i.e.* converted property (clauses 303 and 248) whether that person is the offender or another.

Where a person converts property, *e.g.*, cash into a boat, it will be open to the Director to trace both the cash and the boat: clause 303. However, that does not mean that the Director will necessarily be able to recover/confiscate both items: he will only be able to recover such property as most closely represents the original property: clause 277 and 278. Furthermore, he will not be able to recover property bought for value and in good faith without notice of the unlawful origin of the property: clause 306(1).

Example:
A thief steals money and buys a car from a respectable dealer. The Director can trace the money in the dealer's hands but it will not be recoverable because the dealer acted in good faith. The Director will be able to recover the car from the thief.

Steps that may be taken by the Director

13–97
1. Identifies property that was obtained through "unlawful conduct" (or that represents such conduct): see **clause 247(1)** and **clause 246**—including any profits which have accrued in respect of that property: **clause 305**. Note the requirement for dual criminality (clause 246(2)).
2. Establishes the history of property.
3. Identifies the persons in the chain of transactions.
4. Identifies:
   (a) Person(s) who obtained the property unlawfully (**clause 302**))—*and whether or not they disposed of it.*
   (b) And/or person(s) into whose hands the original item of property first passed (**clause 302**), and **clause 303**))—*and whether or not they disposed of it.*
   (c) And/or person(s) who subsequently acquire the original item of property (**clause 302**) and **clause 303**—*and whether or not they disposed of it.*
   (d) And/or the person(s) who did NOT receive the original (*e.g.* stolen) property but received converted property or mixed

property (**clause 303(3)**—and whether or not they then disposed of it.

(e) And/or persons who received the converted property after it was disposed of (*i.e.* persons in (c) above): **clause 303(3)**.

Note that where a person unlawfully obtains property (property 'A'), and converts it into other property (property 'B'), then **clause 303(2)** treats property 'B' as "original property"—as a result (a) to (e) run again.

Note that where that person goes on to convert property 'B' into property 'C', property 'C' is also treated by **clause 303(3)** as "original property" and so (a) to (e) also runs again.

5. Director decides which of those persons to join as Respondents: see clause 277. Property is not recoverable IF (in effect) it can be traced to persons entitled to retain it (or claim it), that is to say, they have not acquired it unlawfully, or they were unlawfully deprived of the goods, or have some other valid claim to the property, or they were bona fide purchasers for value without notice of the unlawful origin of the goods: **clause 280.**
6. Director obtains evidence to prove, to the civil standard, that the property was obtained through unlawful conduct (or represents such property): **clause 246, clause 246(3).** 13–98
7. Director obtains an **"Interim Receiving Order": clause 251.**

   Note:

   (a) Application is to the High Court.

   (b) Application may be made *ex parte*

   (c) There must be a "good arguable case" that property is recoverable (**clause 251 (5)**)

   (d) The Director must take reasonable steps to discover third party interests and to discover the identity of the parties: **clause 251(6)**.

   (e) The Director must nominate a suitable Interim Receiver.

   (f) The order may authorise the receiver to exercise powers set out in Schedule 3 and in accordance with the directions of the Court: **clause 252.**

   (g) There are restrictions on the disposal of property: **clause 255.**

   (h) The receiver has immunity from civil claims other than in tort for negligence: **clause 252(3)**.

   (i) The High Court may stay the proceedings or authorise their continuance on terms: **clause 256.**

   (j) The receiver must report on progress to the Director and to the Court: **clause 258.**
8. Director monitors the progress of the case:

   (a) Interim Receiving Order may be varied by the Court to exclude property either not recoverable or so much of property subject to an innocent third party interest: **clause 257.**

   (b) The High Court may release property for living, legal

expenses: **clause 255(3)**, perhaps subject to a full statement of assets and liabilities.

9. The respondent may be ordered to return property to the United Kingdom: **clause 253.**
10. The Director may nominate a trustee for civil recovery in anticipation of the High Court granting a recovery order: **clause 268.**
11. The Director may apply for a recovery order: **clause 267.** If the property is recoverable, the Court must make the order.
12. It is possible for innocent owners of a legal or a beneficial interest to obtain the entire interest, for value, payable to the trustee for civil recovery: **clauses 171 and 276.**

ECHR/HRA implications

13–99 Civil recovery does not involve an identified person being put on trial. The question as to whether or not Part V would be Convention compliant remains open. The Privy Council, in *McIntosh*, held that assumptions under the Drug Trafficking Act do not involve "criminal charges", for the purpose of Article 6. The Court of Appeal, in *Benjafield*, reached the opposite conclusion. But the ECtHR in *Phillips v. United Kingdom* (by a majority) preferred the reasons of the Privy Council in *McIntosh*.

However, there are notable differences between asset forfeiture triggered by the fact of conviction, and the proposed scheme for civil recovery under Part V of the PCB 2001. Part V does not involve any reverse onus clauses. Rules of evidence are largely within the appreciation of the domestic courts. It is by no means certain that the ECHR requires criminal charges to be proved beyond reasonable doubt: see *Goodman International and Goodman v. Italy* (1993) 16 E.H.R.R. CD 26: but see *Austria v. Italy* (1963) 6 Yearbook 740, and Starmer, *European Human Rights Law*, p. 276 . The Convention may require that the standard of proof should be high, *i.e.* a high probability that the property represents the proceeds of criminal conduct.

(4)
The Drug Trafficking Act 1994—a Detailed Commentary

A. INTRODUCTION

On July 8, 1986, by virtue of the Drug Trafficking Offences Act 1986 (c.32) (the "DTOA"), Parliament introduced sweeping and radical changes in the law to enable the Courts to recover the proceeds of drug trafficking. Sections 1(3), 2(1), 24, 34, 38 and 40 came into force on September 30,1986 (see the Drug Trafficking Offences Act 1986 (Commencement No. 1) Order 1986 (S.I. 1986 No. 1488) (c.53)), followed by sections 27 to 29, 31 and 33 (in force on December 30, 1986) and the remainder on January 12, 1987; see the Drug Trafficking Offences Act 1986 (Commencement No. 3) Order 1986 (S.I. 1986 No. 2145 (c.85)). 13–100

The 1986 Act was amended by the Criminal Justice (Scotland) Act 1987 (c.62), the Land Registration Act 1988 (c.3), the Criminal Justice Act 1988 (c.33), the Criminal Justice (International Co-operation) Act 1990 (c.5) (the "CJICA"); the Criminal Justice Act 1993 (c.36), Pt. II (the 1993 Act), and the Criminal Justice and Public Order Act 1994, Sched.9.

On November 3, 1994, the Drug Trafficking Act (the "DTA") received its Royal Assent. It consolidates the 1986 Act and certain provisions of the CJICA 1990 and came into force on February 3, 1995.

(a) What is the relevant date for the application of the DTA?

The DTA applies to persons charged with drug trafficking offences after February 3, 1995: see section 66(2). Note that the relevant date is the date when the offender was charged—not the date on which the offence was committed but there is one significant exception and that concerns the posi- 13–101 tion of a defendant who is charged with an offence committed prior to the DTA coming into force but who absconds either before his conviction or before the moment the Court decides if it is going to make a confiscation order against him. By virtue of section 19(3) and (4) the High Court is now entitled to exercise the powers of the Crown Court to make a confiscation order against an absconder (whether convicted or not). The relevant date for this purpose is the date the offence was committed and not the date on which the absconder was charged: see section 66(6). It is not entirely clear why there should be this exception. One reason may be that the legislature recognised that the powers vested in the High Court by virtue of section 19(3) and (4) were so unique, and of such consequence, that it would be inequitable not to put persons on notice of the Courts' extended powers of confiscation in this regard. However, where it is shown that an absconding defendant committed a drug trafficking offence after February 3, 1995, he may be presumed to have known of the full powers of the Court to confiscate assets in his absence. The ramifications of section 66 are considered in greater detail below (particularly in the light of the European Court decision in *Welch v. United Kingdom* (February 9, 1995) (1995) 20 E.H.R.R. 247).

(b) An historical sketch of our legislation

13–102 The law relating to asset forfeiture has changed a great deal in the last eight years and the scope of the DTA may be more clearly understood if put into an historical perspective. Before the DTOA was enacted, the Courts were equipped only with the statutory powers of forfeiture, the making of "deprivation" orders or "criminal bankruptcy" orders, and/or the imposition of fines. Save for criminal bankruptcy orders (which were abolished by the CJA 1988, s.170, and Sched.16; formerly ss. 39 and 40 of the Powers of the Criminal Courts Act 1973) these powers continue to exist, but they are very limited in scope. Thus, by section 27 of the Misuse of Drugs Act 1971, only those assets which directly relate to an offence committed by the accused, under that Act, may be forfeited: see *Morgan* [1977] Crim.L.R. 488, CA. In *Bowers* [1994] Crim.L.R. 230, B pleaded guilty to possessing cannabis resin with intent to supply and supplying the drug. He was the driver of a car stopped by police at a service area. B ordered his passenger to throw a quantity of resin out of the car. A forfeiture order, made under section 27 of the MDA, was upheld on appeal. Although the trial judge made a confiscation order under the DTOA it is clear that the evidence showed that the car was not purchased out of the proceeds of drug trafficking and thus it could not included as a benefit from drug trafficking: see also *Cadman-Smith* (a case decided under Part VI of the Criminal Justice Act 1988).

Choses in action and intangibles are not usually capable of being forfeited: see *Khan, Crawley* [1982] 1 W.L.R. 1405, CA.

Drug profits, originally received by the accused but then transferred to a third party, could not be seized. It was to meet such weaknesses in the law that the 1986 Act was enacted following recommendations contained in the Home Affairs Committee Fifth Report "Misuse of Hard Drugs—Interim Report" (HC 399, (1985)) which had approved the American policy of giving the Court "draconian powers" to strip drug dealers of the proceeds of drug trafficking even where their connection with drug trafficking offences was merely "probable".

It may be helpful at this stage to identify various landmarks on the way to the DTA being enacted: 13–103

(1) The United Kingdom signed the United Nations Convention Against Illicit Traffic in Narcotic Drugs and Psychotropic Substances 1988 and agreed to create offences in connection with the laundering and handling of the proceeds of drug trafficking (Art. 3) and to introduce measures to confiscate the proceeds of drug trafficking (Art. 5) whether they have been converted or not (Art. 5.6). The Convention permits Member States to place the burden of proving that assets were lawfully acquired, on the shoulders of the accused (see Art. 7). It is arguable that obligations that exist under some of these treaties may be in tension with the terms of the ECHR, but this is a matter yet to be explored by the Courts of the United Kingdom.

(2) The DTOA 1986 was enacted to recover drug trafficking proceeds (not just the profits) of persons convicted of a "drug trafficking offence" as defined by statute (see now section 1(3)). All payments and other rewards received by a defendant in connection with drug trafficking carried on by him or by another were his "proceeds" (s. 2(1) DTOA; now s.4(1) DTA) *i.e.* his "benefit" from drug trafficking (s. 1(3) DTOA; now s.2(3) DTA). Given that it is the defendant who is likely to be in the best position to explain the origin of property passing through his hands, the Courts were given a statutory discretion under the DTOA to assume that property held by the defendant since his conviction, or transferred to (or expended by) him, during the period of six years before being charged, represented the proceeds of drug trafficking. The DTOA made no specific provision as to the incidence of the burden or standard of proof, but the Courts held that it was for the prosecution to prove, to the criminal standard, that property received by the defendant was in connection with drug trafficking carried on by him: *Dickens* [1990] 2 Q.B. 102 and *Enwezor* (1991) 93 Cr. App. R. 233. The position changed under the Drug Trafficking Act 1994.

(3) The DTOA made it an offence to assist another to retain the benefit of that other's drug trafficking: (formerly s.24 DTOA; now s.50);

(4) The CJA 1988 abolished criminal bankruptcy orders (s.170, and Sched.16; formerly ss. 39 and 40 of the Powers of the Criminal Courts Act 1973);

(5) The loophole that allowed interest accrued by a defendant (on sums unpaid by him under a confiscation order) to escape confiscation, was filled by section 15 of the CJICA 1990 (now s.10 of the DTA): see the Report of the Home Office Working Party on Confiscation.

13–104 (6) The prosecution became entitled under s.16 CJICA 1990 (now s.16 DTA) to apply to the High Court for a certificate that the defendant's realisable property is greater than was thought at the time the confiscation order was made (or has subsequently increased): see now *Tivnan* as to the scope of section 16 of the Act.

(7) Section 14 of CJICA 1990 created a limited number of money laundering offences arising out of an accused's dealing in the process of drug trafficking (see now ss. 49 and 51);

(8) Following the Council of Europe Convention on Laundering, Search and Seizure and Confiscation of the Proceeds of Crime 1990 (Cm 2337) the United Kingdom agreed to introduce such legislation "as may be necessary" to confiscate not just the proceeds of drug trafficking, but also property and funds used or intended to be used to commit further offences (Art.2) and to create money-laundering offences in connection with drug trafficking (Art.6; note the reservation). Note that no agreement was reached that money laundering in respect of the proceeds of non-drug trafficking offences should be criminalised. Special investigative techniques may be employed including interception of telecommunications and access to computer systems (Art.4.2).

(9) In 1991, the United Kingdom ratified the United Nations Convention Against Illicit Traffic in Narcotic Drugs and Psychotropic Substances 1988 (which it was only able to do following the enactment of CJICA 1990) and agreed to create offences in connection with the laundering and handling of the proceeds of drug trafficking (Art.3).

(10) By virtue of the European Council Directive (91/308/EEC), the United Kingdom is required to ensure that money laundering is prohibited (Art. 2); that financial institutions examine with special attention transactions which they regard as particularly likely to be related to money laundering (Art.5) and to report facts which "might be an indication of money laundering" (Art.6) and that measures extend in whole or in part to "professions" which are "particularly likely to be used for money laundering purposes" (Art.12). Note that it is not a requirement of that Directive that money laundering should be criminalised—merely prohibited. However, it is important to note that by a statement annexed to the Directive, all Member States did agree to a commitment that money laundering would be made a criminal offence—at least in respect of drug trafficking offences.

13–105 (11) In May 1991, the Home Office Working Group in their Report on the Drug Trafficking Offences Act 1986 found that the 1986

Act had worked "reasonably well" (see para.1) but they made a number of recommendations designed to enhance the scope and effectiveness of the DTOA. Some of these recommendations were given statutory force by sections 7 to 15 (inclusive) of Part II of the 1993 Act.

(12) Parliament also used the 1993 Act to amend the DTOA by creating drug money-laundering offences. The DTOA was therefore re-modelled. If all the amendments had come into force, the DTOA would have brought about the following reforms in connection with the making of a confiscation order

(a) a drug trafficking inquiry would not be required in every case where the defendant is convicted of a drug trafficking offence;

(b) the making of statutory assumptions would no longer be discretionary: (see now section 4);

(c) the civil standard of proof would apply throughout the confiscation proceedings (see now s.2(8));

(d) a DTOA determination could be postponed following conviction but the Court could proceed to sentence the defendant;

(e) a receiver could apply for a downward variation of a confiscation order: (see now section 17);

(f) confiscation proceedings could be taken against an absconding defendant (whether convicted or not) or against a deceased but convicted defendant: (see now sections 19–24);

(g) the prosecutor could in certain circumstances apply to the Court to reconsider making a confiscation order; or to reconsider whether the defendant has benefited from drug trafficking; or to re-assess the value of his proceeds: (see now sections 13–15).

(13) The only provisions of the CJA 1993 which actually came into force were:

(a) s.16, on February 15, 1994 (acquisition, possession or use of proceeds of drug trafficking) introducing s.23A into the 1986 Act—now s.51 of this Act;

(b) s.17, on February 15,1994 which inserted corresponding provisions in s.42 of the Criminal Justice (Scotland) Act 1987;

(c) s.18, on April 1, 1994 (offences in connection with drug money laundering) which inserted s.26B (now s.52 of this Act) and s.26C (now s.53 of this Act) into the 1986 Act;

(d) s.19, which, on April 1, 1994, inserted similar provisions found in s.18 into s.43 of the Criminal Justice (Scotland) Act 1987;

(e) s.26, which on April 1, 1994, inserted s.31(2A) into the 1986 Act (disclosure of information etc. received in privileged circumstances) and which is now subs. (3) of s.58 of this Act.

(14) The Money Laundering Regulations 1993 (S.I. 1993 No.1933) came into force on April 1, 1994.

(15) The DTA 1994 consolidates the provisions of the DTOA as well as certain provisions of the CJICA 1990 and re-enacts (and brings into force) Part II of the CJA 1993.

(c) Why Part II, CJA 1993 was abandoned

13–106 When the 1993 Act was passed, a flurry of contributions from commentators soon followed anticipating that much of the Act (including the entirety of Part II) would be brought into force by April 1994, at the latest. This expectation was heightened when various provisions of the 1993 Act did come into force within that time-scale and the Money Laundering Regulations 1993 (S.I. 1993 No.1933) came into force on April 1, 1994. It was therefore logical to expect all or most of Part II of the Act to be brought into force at the same time.

However, according to a Home Office Circular (19/1994) the implementation of Parts II to IV of the 1993 Act proved to be more problematic than anticipated, and implementation was deferred until the summer of 1994. It would seem that no sooner had the ink of the 1993 Act dried, than the Government decided the time had come to consolidate various statutory powers in relation to the proceeds of drug trafficking and thus the DTA was enacted. Although no detailed explanation has officially been given by the Government for legislating in this fashion, it is not difficult to imagine what the reasons must have been. When, on October 22, 1992, the Criminal Justice Bill came before Parliament, it consisted of six parts and a total of 48 clauses, but by the date of Royal Assent (July 27, 1993) the Bill had expanded to seven parts with a total of 79 clauses. At a late stage in the Bill's progress through Parliament, substantial amendments were made to the Northern Ireland (Emergency Provisions) Act 1991 (c.24) and the Prevention of Terrorism (Temporary Provisions) Act 1989 (c.4). Many of those provisions were included in order to align the confiscation provisions, relating to the financing of terrorism, with the 1986 Act (as amended by the 1993 Act, Part II).

13–107 Money laundering offences relating to "criminal conduct"—that is to say, other than drug trafficking (see s.93A(7) of the CJA 1988 and s.29 of the 1993 Act) were added, by Part III of the 1993 Act, to the provisions of the Criminal Justice Act 1988 and again, those particular offences would have corresponded to offences under the 1986 Act (as amended).

What is often overlooked is that it is not just the Courts which have powers of forfeiture and confiscation: some powers are vested in the hands of particular law enforcement agencies, most notably the Commissioners of Customs and Excise (see ss. 139 to 144 and Sched. 3, of the Customs and Excise Management Act 1979 (c. 2)) albeit subject to the Courts performing a supervisory role. It follows that powers of forfeiture or confiscation are now to be found in an array of enactments and statutory instruments depending on (i) the agency or court seeking to exercise any of those powers, (ii) the relevant territorial jurisdiction of the agency or court in question, and (iii) the nature of the criminal activities complained of.

Not surprisingly, this confusing state of affairs prompted calls for the introduction of a single comprehensive code which could be applied throughout Britain (or even overseas): see the (Standing Committee B, col. 114, June 8, 1993, *per* Mr David Trimble). The call for codification has been supported by Lord Colville of Culross who, in relation to the legislation as it existed prior to the Drug Trafficking Act 1994, said that the:

> "Northern Ireland (Emergency Provisions) Act 1991 applies throughout the U.K.; the Courts will have to be prepared to exercise powers under the Drug Trafficking Offences Act 1986, the Criminal Justice Act 1988, Prevention of Terrorism (Temporary Provisions) Act 1989, Northern Ireland (Emergency Provisions) Act 1991, and the Criminal Justice Act 1993. Not only do some of the powers overlap, but also the codes are different in detail, as can be seen in Northern Ireland where the first two Acts mentioned above had their confiscation powers enacted by Order in Council. There is the additional dimension of the extension of these provisions to the Isle of Man, Jersey and Guernsey, which can be done to some, but not to a complete degree, by the U.K. government under Prevention of Terrorism (Temporary Provisions) Act 1989, s.28 (3) and Northern Ireland (Emergency Provisions) Act 1991, s.71(3). However, it can also be done by legislation in Tynwald; at the moment the Isle of Man is ahead of the field in that their Prevention of Terrorism Act 1990 has valuable provisions for reciprocal enforcement. In the Channel Islands, negotiations are still proceeding as to the extent of legislation to be presented to the respective States. It cannot be easy for any of them to keep up with the flow of legislative changes on the financial front and it is particularly important that they should be up-to-date in light of the facilities which would otherwise be available to terrorists in these off-shore market places. A U.K. codification would give them the opportunity to legislate on the basis of a single, comprehensive model."

Of all of these important measures, it is the drug trafficking legislation 13–108
that is the most draconian, and the most likely to be encountered by criminal law practitioners. It is therefore particularly important that the law in this area should be as compact and as comprehensible as possible. It seems that the Government reflected on the calls made by Lord Colville (and others) for codification, and hence the Drug Trafficking Bill was introduced in the Lords on May 25,1994. Unfortunately the Government, for reasons which are not entirely clear, kept the idea of introducing a consolidating Bill something of a secret until the Drug Trafficking Bill was on the point of being introduced into the House of Lords. One reason for this may be that the Government was uncertain as to whether there was going to be sufficient time to see the Bill through Parliament given that the Police and

Magistrates' Courts Bill and the Criminal Justice and Public Order Bill were already under detailed and protracted scrutiny. There may also have been some doubt as to whether the Drug Trafficking Bill was necessary or whether an attempt should be made to consolidate (or to codify) a range of other statutory provisions.

(d) The 1994 Act—a consolidation measure

13–109 It must be emphasised that the 1994 Act is, in essence, a consolidating measure but it will be seen that Parliament has taken the opportunity to rectify (and to modify) certain aspects of the previous legislation. For example, it was originally intended that amendments made by Part II of the CJA 1993 would apply if the drug trafficking offence, for which the defendant appears before the Crown Court to be sentenced, was committed after Part II came into force: see section 78(6) of the 1993 Act. However, if the offence was committed before that date, the old law would have applied even if the defendant had been charged or convicted of that offence many years after its commission so that two sets of rules would remain in existence for a very long time. Thus, an absconder who committed an offence in 1990, but who was not convicted of a drug trafficking offence until the year 2005 would expect the Court (under s.78(6) of the 1993 Act) to deal with him under the old law. No doubt, part of the thinking behind section 78(6) was to protect the interests of a defendant whose prosecution and/or trial was delayed through no fault of his or her own. On the other hand, as David Thomas Q.C. has pointed out (see "The Criminal Justice Act 1993" [1994] Crim.L.R.100), section 78(6) was probably enacted in deference to the principle against retroactive criminal legislation, but two sets of rules could cause confusion where, for example, the indictment includes two counts, one of which relates to an offence committed before the relevant date and the other after that date. To avoid this result, Parliament enacted section 66 of the 1994 Act which makes the date an accused is *charged* (or against whom proceedings have been instituted) the relevant date for the purposes of the DTA.

13–110 A second significant change relates to s.3(10) of the DTA, which enables proceedings to be postponed:

> "Where the Court has sentenced the defendant under subsection (7) above during the specified period it may, after the end of that period, vary the sentence by imposing a fine or making any such order as is mentioned in section 2(5)(b)(ii) or (iii) of this Act, so long as it does so within a period corresponding to that allowed by section 47(2) or (3) of the Supreme Court Act 1981 (time allowed for varying a sentence) but beginning with the end of the specified period."

The significance of the above provision is as follows. Under the DTA a court may, before the defendant is sentenced (*Ross*), postpone the drug trafficking enquiry for a period of up to six months after the date of conviction (or longer in exceptional cases): however, the Court may nevertheless proceed to sentence the defendant for the offence during the "specified period" (see s.3(7)). However, the Court cannot at that stage fine the defendant or make any monetary order against him or make any order under s.27 of the Misuse of Drugs Act 1971 (c.38) or s.143 of the Powers of Criminal Courts (Sentencing) Act 2000. What would happen if, two months after sentence is passed, the Court decided to make a confiscation order but wishes to order the defendant to pay costs or a fine out of his remaining assets, which were legitimately acquired? Would the Court be debarred from doing so? Without section 3(10) (the equivalent of which did not appear in the 1993 Act) it is possible that the Courts would have held that the moment of sentencing had passed and therefore the sentence could not be varied beyond the 28-day period permitted under the Supreme Court Act 1981. Alternatively, and in order to avoid this result, the Courts might have held that because a confiscation order is a sentence, the process of sentencing was not concluded until all the determinations had been made under the DTA. However, to put the matter beyond doubt, the Lord Chancellor moved (by way of amendment) what is now section 3(10) and said:

> "This amendment and Amendment No.2 (repealing Sched.9, para.26 of the Criminal Justice and Public Order Act 1994) are necessary to bring into the consolidation an amendment made to the Criminal Justice and Public Order Bill during its Committee stage in your Lordship's House. That amends section 1A of the Drug Trafficking Offences Act 1986, to remove a practical difficulty which may prevent the Court from passing certain kinds of sentences on a defendant after it has decided to exercise its power under section 1A to postpone making a determination under section 1 as to whether a defendant has benefited from drug trafficking or as to whether a defendant has benefited from drug trafficking or as to the amount to be recovered from him, so that further information can be obtained. The Joint Committee on Consolidation Bills was informed that the Government would move amendments in the same terms to this consolidation Bill.
>
> The second amendment to the third schedule is, as I have said, a consequential amendment to repeal the amending provision in the Criminal Justice and Public Order Bill which will be spent when the consolidation comes into force" (Hansard, HL, vol. 556, col. 992).

The DTA repeals and re-enacts most of the 1986 Act except for s.24(6) 13–111
(early release provisions); s.32 (authorisation of delay in notifying arrest, the Police and Criminal Evidence Act 1984 (c.60), s.65, as amended by Sched. l, para.8 of this Act); s.34 (inserting s.9A into the Misuse of Drugs Act 1971 relating to so-called "drug-kits"); s.40(1), (3)–(5) (short title, commencement and extent). The Act also consolidates Part III of the Criminal Justice (International Co-operation) Act 1990 (c.5) (drug trafficking money imported or exported in cash) as well as s.14 (concealing or transferring the proceeds of drug trafficking) in so far as s.14 of the 1990 Act applied to England and Wales (see s.68(7) of this Act) and a number of smaller amendments to ss.15(1),15(3), 23A (except Scotland), 30(2) and

(3), 31(2), and Sched. 4, para. 4 of the 1990 Act. Note that section 14 of the Criminal Justice (International Co-operation) Act 1990 still applies in Scotland.

Most of Part. II of the 1993 Act is repealed (and re-enacted in this Act) except for ss.17 and 19 (Scotland) and ss.20, 22, 24 and 26 insofar as those provisions relate to Scotland. Schedule 9, para.28 of the Criminal Justice and Public Order Act 1994 is now redundant (see s.3(10)) and is thus repealed by s.67, Sched.3 of this Act.

It will therefore be appreciated that this Act (which for the most part extends to England and Wales only (see s.68)) is not a codifying measure on the scale, or of the type, advocated by Lord Colville (see above).

13–112 Although codification of the laws of forfeiture and confiscation is a laudable objective, it will not be easy to attain it in practice, not least because major political and ideological differences exist (both domestically and internationally) as to the viability and validity of employing a variety of measures and devices designed to strip offenders of their ill-gotten benefits. Much of what is now being done, so far as drug trafficking and money laundering is concerned, is bound up with international obligations and agreements but the methods employed to confiscate assets differs considerably between nations. The Proceeds of Crime Bill 2001 is an attempt to codify a coherent system of asset recovery in both drug trafficking, and non-drug trafficking cases, both in Scotland and in England.

It will be seen from the above that our law has moved away from simple powers of forfeiture and enforcement to a system which is increasingly inquisitorial and which may involve a detailed examination of the defendant's financial position throughout his lifetime by virtue of a blend of powers which are in part civil, and in part criminal, in nature. An increasing number of prosecutions for a drug offence include evidence of a defendant's financial affairs—so much so, that it may seem as if the hearing is both a trial of the offence charged and a drug trafficking enquiry rolled into one. In such cases, care must be taken to ensure that material obtained from a defendant by way of a disclosure order (or during pre-trial proceedings under the DTA, *e.g.* a restraint order) is not introduced in evidence at the defendant's trial for the drug offence, contrary to an embargo imposed by the High Court.

(e) Combatting drug-trafficking and money laundering

(i) *Measuring the scale of drug trafficking by its proceeds*

13–113 No doubt, in the 1970s, the legislature hoped that drug use and drug trafficking could be controlled, or at least contained, by virtue of the provisions of the MDA 1971 (coupled with the CEMA 1979) which regulates the use and distribution of controlled substances by an administrative framework backed by coercive sanctions. Although drug trafficking has come to epitomise international crime on a grand scale, it has not monopolised it. International crime and money laundering, can be measured in terms of billions of pounds sterling.

In 1989, the National Drugs Intelligence Co-ordinator informed the Home Affairs Committee on Drug Trafficking and Related Serious Crime that at least £1,800 million (derived from drug trafficking) was circulating in the United Kingdom. The amount of money being laundered is now thought to be as high as £57 million a year from drug sales in America and Europe alone. The United Nations has estimated that the proceeds of drug trafficking, circulating the world economy, is between $200 billion to $400 billion. Despite our confiscation laws, the United Kingdom continues to be a major centre for money laundering. In 1989, the Home Office told the Committee that the 1986 Act has promoted drug traffickers to adopt greater sophistication in their efforts to launder the proceeds, so that money laundering is "probably the most organised aspect of drug trafficking": see the Home Affairs Committee 7th Report (1989). The Home Office indicated that although the evidence of links between organised crime and drug trafficking was largely anecdotal "there is an undoubted link between the two". The link is said to be evident between the drugs trade and the financing of wars and terrorism but usually the link is much more basic and symptomatic of general criminal activity committed by drug traffickers.

(ii) *International co-operation*

Because drug trafficking represents an international "common enemy", **13–114**
it has produced a much greater degree of co-operation (and unification of laws) between nations than might otherwise have been the case. If asset forfeiture, including "civil recovery" techniques, stand any chance of success in reducing international crime and drug trafficking, then there must be worldwide co-operation and comity of purpose. For this reason, many of the provisions of the 1986 Act (and subsequent legislation) are the product of intense diplomatic efforts resulting in several Treaties, Conventions, Bi-lateral Agreements and (now) European Directives: see the European Convention on Mutual Assistance 1957 (which the United Kingdom was not able to ratify until the enactment of the Criminal Justice (International Co-operation) Act 1990); the United Nations Convention Against Illicit Traffic In Narcotic Drugs and Psychotropic Substances 1988 (the Vienna Convention, ratified by the United Kingdom in 1991); the Council of Europe Convention on Laundering, Search, Seizure and Confiscation of the Proceeds of Crime 1990. See also the European Council Directive (91/308/EEC)

The arguments deployed in the fight against drug trafficking are now heard in the context of other areas of international and major crime. For example, the Financial Action Task Force (FATF) made a number of radical proposals in 1990 that went beyond those agreed at the 1988 United Nations Convention. FATF recommended that Member States should address their money-laundering provisions to various major crimes and not just drug trafficking. It also suggested that rules of secrecy or confidentiality applied by various financial institutions should be qualified so as to permit suspicious transactions to be reported to the authorities. It would seem that these proposals were already in Parliament's mind when the DTOA 1986 was being drafted (see Hansard, HL, vol. 474, col. 1094).

(iii) *Incremental teform adopted in England and Wales*

13–115 It is plain from the official Reports that Parliament has long regarded the 1986 Act as marking only the first step in the fight against organised crime by confiscating the proceeds of crime whether drug-related or not. Because other areas of the law in 1986 required extensive reform (*e.g.* extradition, banking and international co-operation in respect of the gathering and calling of evidence) the 1986 Act could not embrace every activity that was either linked (or akin) to drug trafficking and money laundering. Parliament was also mindful that the Criminal Justice Bill (now the Criminal Justice Act 1988) was being drafted but had to be considered by Parliament. Lord Harris of Greenwich explained the problem when he said:

> "... (I)t is an illusion to imagine that drug trafficking can be treated as an isolated crime ... we are confronted with the existence of highly sophisticated criminal syndicates. The operators move effectively from one form of serious crime to another; from drug trafficking to armed robbery, from counterfeit currency operations to large-scale fraud and then back again to drug trafficking." (Hansard, HL vol. 474, col. 1115).

It would seem that Parliament intended that the asset forfeiture provisions of Part VI of the Criminal Justice Act 1988 should be a far less severe piece of legislation than either the DTOA or the DTA. The climate changed with the passing of the Proceeds of Crime Act 1995, but the Drug Trafficking Act is still more draconian than the Criminal Justice Act 1988.

The DTOA was enacted following recommendations contained in the Home Affairs Committee Fifth Report "Misuse of Hard Drugs Interim Report" (HC 399 (1985)) which approved the American policy of giving the Court "draconian powers" to strip drug dealers of assets acquired during the course of their drug dealing "even where their connection with drug trafficking offences was merely probable".

13–116 This seemingly straightforward but important statement of policy conceals the extent of the power required to enforce it. Six points should thus be noted. First, the policy stems from the scale and nature of the illicit drug trade, often involving more than one jurisdiction and the laundering of substantial sums of money at home and abroad affecting a number of institutions or corporate bodies, many of whom may be totally innocent parties. Secondly, the policy is intended to "remove the profit motive by allowing the confiscation of all the trafficker's proceeds from drug trafficking, following conviction" (*per* Secretary of State, Home Office, Hansard, HC, vol. 222, col. 866). Thirdly, the policy is also intended to ensure that drug trafficking proceeds cannot be re-cycled to fund further drug trafficking. It is for this reason that Art.2 of the European Convention on Laundering, Search, Seizure and Confiscation of the Proceeds of Crime 1990 requires Member States to introduce measures to confiscate not just the proceeds of crime but also "instrumentalities", *i.e.* property used or intended to be used to commit a criminal offence (see Art.1). Fourth, the confiscation of assets, in circumstances where their connection with drug trafficking is "merely probable", is sometimes said to be justified by the first three objectives stated above. Fifth, a connection that need only be "probable", results in the application of the civil standard of proof in confiscation proceedings: see Article 5.7 of the Vienna Convention 1988. Sixth, the gleaning of information and "intelligence" is an essential task of law enforcement. By Article 4.2 of the European Convention (1990), measures are required to be introduced to permit the use of special investigative techniques facilitating the identification and tracing of proceeds and which may include "monitoring orders, observation, interception of telecommunications, access to computer systems and orders to produce specific documents". All of those techniques must be Human Rights Act 1998/ECHR compliant (and see, for example, the Regulation of Investigatory Powers Act 2000).

Some of these aforementioned points either cut across or challenge traditional principles and rules of procedure as they are normally applied in our criminal law. Nowhere has this been more apparent than the debate as to who should shoulder the burden of proof at various stages in the proceedings or what the appropriate standard of proof should be: see *Dickens* [1990] 2 Q.B.102; *Redbourne* [1992] 1 W.L.R.1182 and Rose [1993] 1 W.L.R.844; and "Making statutory assumptions under the Drug Trafficking Offences Act", *Archbold News*, Issue No. 5; May 28, 1993; see now s.2(8) of the DTA (formerly s.1(7A) of the Drug Trafficking Offences Act 1986 inserted by s.7(2) of the 1993 Act) and see *Benjafield* (December 2, 2000); and *McIntosh* (February 5, 2001); and *Salabiaku v. France* 13 E.H.R.R. 379; and *Phillips v. United Kingdom* (July 5, 2000); and see Lord Ackner, *Hansard*, HL, vol. 540, cols 744 and 749). Read also Dr Evan Bell, "ECHR and the Proceeds of Crime Legislation" [2000] Crim.L.R. 783.

(f) American influence on confiscation techniques

Developments in the United States have to some extent been mirrored elsewhere as a large number of countries have collaborated to combat drug trafficking and money laundering. 13–117

The American model was considered by the House of Lords in 1986 (Hansard, HL, vol. 474, col. 1112) when it was pointed out that American law was not confined to drug trafficking. The British Government was not then prepared to move in the direction of the American model although the then Parliamentary Under-Secretary had indicated that "there might be movement in the future" (Hansard, *ibid*).

American law draws a distinction between civil forfeiture and criminal forfeiture. The differences between the two are (as one would expect) differences of procedure and evidence, so that in civil proceedings the burden of proof is on a balance of probabilities whereas in criminal proceedings the property liable to forfeiture is generally required to be specified in the indictment: not so under the DTA. However, like English law, third parties have no locus in the criminal proceedings but must wait to be heard in ancillary proceedings after the forfeiture order had been made (18 USC §1963; 21 USC §853). Third parties who seek to be entitled to all or part of the forfeited property carry the burden of proving the existence of their right and that they come with clean hands. A punitive forfeiture may violate the excessive fines clause of the Eighth Amendment to the U.S. Constitution: see *U.S. v. Bajakajian* 1988, 524 U.S. 321.

Of particular interest are two concepts in American law. First, some statutory provisions enjoy a reduced standard of proof requiring the Government to prove only a "probable" cause to believe "that a substantial connection exists between the property to be forfeited" and the act, which contravenes the statute: *U.S. v. Four Million Dollars* [1985] 762 F.2d 895 (1985). In *Calero-Toledo v. Pearson Yacht Leasing* (1974) 416 U.S. 663, a yacht was forfeited where a cigarette containing cannabis was found on board and in circumstances where the owner of the vessel failed to prove that he was uninvolved in the offending conduct and that he had done all that he reasonably could to prevent the unlawful use of his property. Secondly, there is the "Relation-Back Doctrine" which is based on the fiction that illegally obtained property vests in the Government at the time the offence was committed (18 USC §981); and see *Bennis v. Michigan*, 1996 116 S.Ct. 994.

(g) Confiscation—penal or reparative in nature?

13–118 The answer to this question is not of mere academic interest. Understanding the philosophy that has persuaded successive governments to tackle crime through asset recovery, helps to explain how our legislation has developed, and explains some of the tensions and conflicts that exist in the case law, regarding the proper construction of confiscation statutes. In *Benjafield and others*, the Crown conceded that a confiscation order is a penal measure: but the concession was probably only made in the face of strong judicial opinion to that effect, particularly in the light of the decision of the European Court of Human Rights in *Welch* (1995) 20 E.H.R.R. 247. In *Welch*, the Government's position was quite the opposite, and the introduction of the civil standard of proof in confiscation proceedings (s. 2(8)), was a thinly disguised attempt to give *in personam*, value-confiscation, the appearance of being "civil", and not "criminal", in nature.

One view is that both the DTOA and the DTA were designed to be punitive in nature. The alternative view is that confiscation is reparative, or compensatory, (society being the victim) and thus the legislation is to be construed as if confiscation proceedings are part of the civil law.

However, if the legislation is truly only reparative and not penal, several consequences arguably follow:

(i) the appropriate standard of proof is the civil standard. This, of course, is now a reality by virtue of section 2(8) of the DTA;

(ii) evidence may be adduced and received in accordance with civil law principles. This is particularly relevant in respect of the rules relating to hearsay evidence and documents (for example, the Civil Evidence Act 1995 might apply). There is, as yet, no change to the practice adopted under the DTOA, namely, that the criminal law principles of evidence apply. The system remains adversarial;

(iii) the appropriate court is a court of civil jurisdiction. It is not without interest that even if the High Court is asked to make a confiscation order, in respect of the defendant who has died or absconded, the powers to be applied are those of "the Crown Court": see sections 19 to 23;

(iv) a confiscation order is not a penal order and therefore should not be regarded as a "sentence" for the purposes of an appeal to the Court of Appeal (Criminal Division): by contrast, see *Johnson* [1991] 2 Q.B. 249 and *Hayden* [1975] 1 W.L.R. 852 at 854 G. The DTA makes it plain that a confiscation order is a "sentence" for this purpose: see section 65 and para.2 to Sched.1;

(v) legal aid should be granted under a Civil Legal Aid Certificate;

(vi) if the DTA is not a penal enactment then a court is not constrained to resolve an ambiguity in favour "of the defendant": see *Chapman, The Times*, November 18, 1991 whereas, in fact, the opposite is the case;

(vii) A confiscation order would be by way of an *in rem* procedure (not dependent on establishing a conviction for a predicate offence).

The opinion that confiscation under the 1986 and 1994 Acts is reparative in nature was widely held within political and law enforcement circles. It is an opinion that has been expressed by the Home Office, the Central Confiscation Unit, and indeed, by the Government (see Hansard, HL, vol. 539, col. 1347; vol. 540, cols 1469, 1483) and note the arguments advanced by the Government in *Welch v. United Kingdom* (February 9, 1995). The judiciary was not united on the issue. *In Re Barretto* (1994) 99 Cr. App. R. 105, the Master of the Rolls regarded the making of a confiscation order as involving "broadly penal provisions inflicting the vengeance of society on those who have transgressed in this field" but he added: **13–119**

> "While it is also true that the Act of 1986 provides for drug traffickers to be stripped of their gains, it does not treat them as having forfeited their property rights. It puts them in much the same position as a defendant subject to a money judgement, but with a penalty for non-payment."

There is much in this brief passage that should not be overlooked. First, it explains the nature of a confiscation order. A confiscation order is not a forfeiture order but (what is sometimes styled) a "value order". In other words, the order does not necessarily compel the defendant (or a third party) to deliver up specified items of property to the Crown. It is an order to pay a sum of money. How that sum is paid is a matter for the defendant. For this reason a defendant is not treated as having forfeited his property rights.

13–120 On the other hand the potential reach of a confiscation order is likely to be much greater than a power of forfeiture because:

(a) a confiscation order relates to the value of the defendant's proceeds of drug trafficking and not to assets which have been identified by the Court as existing in the hands of the defendant at the time the order is made;
(b) the order does not have to relate to proceeds derived from the underlying offence or offences: the benefit may include property received by the defendant that is proved to be the proceeds of drug trafficking carried on by him, or "by another"—anywhere in the world (ss.2(2), (3),4(1), 5(1))—as well as receipts assumed to be in connection with drug trafficking carried on by the defendant himself see section 4(2), (5);
(c) the Court is able to confiscate proceeds even if they have been converted into other assets or transferred as gifts;
(d) the Court may be able to recover proceeds represented by assets held by the defendant overseas;
(e) Unlike civil judgments, unpaid confiscation orders carrying severe terms of imprisonment in default of payment (depending on the sum outstanding).

The argument has been advanced that once the conviction is proved, confiscation proceedings are merely ancillary to that fact and no further link exists with the conviction. That argument did not find favour with the members of the European Court in *Welch*, who turned the argument on its head by concluding that the "starting point in any assessment of the existence of a penalty is whether the measure in question is imposed following a conviction for a criminal offence" (para. 28) and that "prevention and reparation are . . . constituent elements of the very notion of punishment" (para. 30). The Court did not have to consider provisions (which are now in force) that empower the High Court to make a confiscation order in the case of a defendant who has absconded for at least two years and who has not been convicted of the drug trafficking offence with which he was charged: see section 19(3) to (6). A confiscation order is also a "sentence" for the purposes of any appeal. The European Court in *Welch* did not look at any one feature in isolation. Nevertheless, for the purpose of determining whether the making of a statutory assumption entails additional "criminal charges" for the purposes of Article 6(1) and 6(2) of the ECHR, a distinction has been drawn between provisions that relate to *culpability* and those that relate to *accountability*: see *Hussein* (April 20, 1999) and *Delaney* (May 14, 1999).

13–121 In *Re Thomas* [1992] 4 All E.R. 814, Leggatt L.J. appeared to suggest that a confiscation order may not be penal when he said (at 819 h):

"Confiscation is confined to the value of the defendant's proceeds of drug trafficking, whereas forfeiture extends to things used for the commission of crime, and is therefore punitive . . . a person does not by making reparation incur punishment."

Reliance has been placed on this passage by prosecutors in other cases as showing that the Act is not penal (see *Redbourne* (1993) 96 Cr. App. R. 201; and see *Welch* (1995) 20 E.H.R.R. 247 but *cf. Dickens*, above). However, the Court of Appeal in *Re Thomas* did not decide the point and there is much force in the observations of Sir David Croom-Johnson, in that case, when he described the 1986 Act as a "strange mixture of both criminal and civil jurisdiction" arising out of Parliament's aim to strip drug traffickers of the proceeds of their trade (at 820a/b). Thus, part of the Act is policed by the Crown Court and the remainder is administered by the High Court. The House of Lords in *Norris* (June 28, 2001) also drew a sharp distinction between the civil and criminal jurisdictions created by the Drug Trafficking Act.

When the 1993 Act was being debated as a Bill, both Houses of Parliament were divided as to whether confiscation proceedings were penal or reparative in nature. The Minister of State for the Home Office emphasised that the application of a civil standard of proof was always the Government's intention but that the 1986 Act did not make that intention sufficiently clear, resulting in the Courts applying a criminal standard of proof at certain stages of the proceedings (see *Dickens* [1990] 2 Q.B. 102 and Hansard, HL, vol. 539, cols 1350, 1383). Lord Ackner and Lord Brightman supported the view that the civil standard should apply (see Hansard HL, vol. 520, cols 1471, 1472) while Lord Williams of Mostyn (see Hansard HL, vol. 540, col. 741) pointed out that confiscation of assets involved a finding that the defendant had benefited from drug trafficking—a criminal activity. This issue is further developed below in respect of s.2(8) of the 1994 Act.

(h) The European Court of Human Rights: *Welch v. United Kingdom*

On February 9,1995, the European Court of Human Rights upheld a complaint, in the case of *Welch*, that confiscation orders made under the Drug Trafficking Offences Act 1986 (c.32) prior to that Act coming into force on January 12,1987, was in contravention of Article 7 of the European Convention on Human Rights which provides: 13–122

"Nor shall a heavier penalty be imposed than the one that was applicable at the time the criminal offence was committed."

(i) *To what extent is the DTOA/DTA retrospective?*

At the time, *Welch* was decided and reported, there was much speculation as to how far the reasoning of the European Court undermined the validity of English powers of confiscation under both the DTOA and the DTA. It seems to have been widely believed that the Court decided that the 13–123 retroactive effect of the legislation (particularly in so far as it relates to the making of the statutory assumptions) was contrary to Article 7. This is not what the Court decided and support for this view is to be found in *Taylor* [1996] Crim. L.R. 275; and see also *Danison* (September 7, 1999, ECtHR), *R.C. v. United Kingdom* (April 6, 1994) and *Hussein* (April 20, 1999). Part of the confusion stems from the ambiguous wording of paragraph 36 of the judgment, which reads:

> "The Court would stress, however, that this conclusion concerns only the retrospective application of the relevant legislation and does not call into question in any respect the powers of confiscation conferred on the Courts as a weapon in the fight against the scourge of drug trafficking."

In *Taylor*, the trial judge made a confiscation order in the sum of £15,311.729. Only about one-quarter of that sum arose from the offence in respect of which T had been convicted. The balance represented the proceeds of drug trafficking received by T between 1970 and 1979 and which resulted in his conviction for a drug trafficking offence in June 1986. In 1986, the DTOA was not in force and therefore a confiscation order could not be made. On appeal, T contended that the inclusion of proceeds generated before the Act came into force was a violation of Article 7.1. The Court of Appeal rejected that argument on the grounds (i) that the DTOA expressly permitted the Courts to confiscate the proceeds of drug trafficking at any time prior to the commencement of the Act, and (ii) *Welch* was to be distinguished because, in that case, the offence for which W appeared before the Court to be sentenced, was committed before the DTOA came into force. If the submission of the appellant had been upheld one consequence would have been that the statutory assumptions could not apply retrospectively. Despite the wording of section 2(3)(a)(ii) and section 2(3)(b) of the DTOA, the Court would only have been able to make assumptions over a full six-year period if the drug trafficking offence was committed after 1993 (*i.e.* 1987 + 6). Some practitioners have suggested that this is indeed the effect of the judgment of the European Court of Human Rights in *Welch*. Frankly, there is nothing in the judgment of the Court to support this view and indeed there are signs that suggest the opposite. At paragraph 35 of the judgment, the European Court held that the confiscation order amounted "in the circumstances of the present case to a penalty" (emphasis added) because "the applicant faced more far-reaching detriment . . . than that to which he was exposed at the time of the commission of the offences for which he was convicted ". It was this fact that proved to be decisive in *Welch*.

13–124 The European Court did not fully adopt the reasoning of the dissenting opinions delivered in the proceedings before the European Commission. Thus, in the opinion of Mr. Soyuer *et al*, it was said that ". . . such a penalty cannot, under the terms of the Article, be imposed retrospectively" and Mr. Shermers remarked that the confiscation of property "in excess of the amount which the authorities can prove to be obtained from crime is of a punitive character. That part of the confiscation, therefore, may not be retrospectively imposed." Note the words ". . . which the authorities can prove". In *Dickens*, it was held that the persuasive burden of proving that a defendant received a payment or reward in connection with drug trafficking remains on the prosecution but the burden is considerably lightened by the assumptions that the Court may make under the DTOA. However, this is not what Mr Schermers appears to have had in mind at all. He drew a distinction between the case where the underlying drug trafficking offence is proved by an assumption and the case where the prosecution must prove the commission of the offence unaided by an assumption. He concluded that confiscation in the former case "may not be retroactively imposed". It seems likely that the European Court of Human Rights will be called upon to consider this matter again.

(ii) *Confiscation order held to be penal*

In order to succeed the applicant had to show that the confiscation order was a "penalty" and it was the British Government's case that the 1986 Act was essentially reparative following the conviction for a drug trafficking offence. As we have seen, the argument is not new and, indeed, in *Redbourne* (1993) 96 Cr.App.R. 201 the prosecution conceded that if the 1986 Act is penal then it would be in breach of its international obligations, including Article 7(1) of the European Convention on Human Rights (but see *Re T* (1993) 96 Cr.App.R. 194, Leggatt L.J. at 200; and see *Benjafield* (December 2, 2000); and *Delaney and Hanrahan* (May 14, 1999, CA)). Various aspects of the 1986 legislation can be described as being civil in nature (*e.g.* the making of restraint orders, disclosure orders, etc.) and this remains the position under the DTA, but a confiscation order is quite clearly penal in character and the European Court unanimously so held for the following reasons. 13–125

- First, the Court had the power to make assumptions under s.2(3) of the DTOA (now section 4(3) of the DTA) that property held or transferred to the defendant within the relevant period represented the proceeds of his drug trafficking.
- Secondly, the legislation confiscates the proceeds (and not just the profits of drug trafficking) irrespective of whether there has been any personal enrichment (see *Simons* [1994] 98 Cr.App.R.100; *Simpson*, and *Metcalfe*). Accordingly, it was held that the order went beyond the notions of reparation and prevention into the realm of punishment.

An initial reading of the report of the Commission and the judgment of the Court may suggest that this conclusion proceeded solely on the basis that confiscation is punitive in practice if it is not limited to actual enrichment or profit. An argument along these lines was rejected by the majority of the Commission but it was accepted by the minority. In our jurisdiction the issues of reparation, restitution, or compensation, do not usually involve an arithmetic exercise to determine profit or miscellaneous expenses, and the position is no different in civil or criminal law. However, the real explanation for the Courts' conclusion on this point may be derived from the dissenting opinion of Mr Schermers who suggested that the DTOA was not merely concerned with taking back what was obtained illegally, but extended to monies which the prosecution could not prove to be obtained from crime (let alone drug trafficking) unless the Court applied the assumptions. This was a "punitive element" of a confiscation order. The Court may have reasoned that this element was punitive because the assumptions catch proceeds received by the defendant whether directly connected with the offence or not. Dr David Thomas Q.C. has suggested that if Welch had been convicted of his offences on the date on which they were committed it would have been open to the Crown Court to impose on him an unlimited fine and therefore the enactment of the DTOA did not expose Welch to a "heavier penalty" than the one that was applicable at the time the offence was committed. However, the extent to which the Courts have been entitled to use fines as a way of recovering ill-gotten gains is not clear or well defined. A fine must be kept in proportion to the nature and seriousness of the offence and, for over 20 years, the Crown Court has assessed the level of a fine by taking into account the means of the offender: see *King* (1970) 54 Cr. App. R. 362; *Jamieson* (1975) 60 Cr. App. R. 318, and *Deaga*, (October 10, 1975, unreported). In *Neville-O'Brien* (February 16, 1976, unreported) a fine of £10,000 imposed on a professional man who permitted his address to be used for the receipt of a consignment of cannabis posted from abroad, was reduced to £3,000 even though he earned £7,000 per year and had realised £15,000 from the sale of his house. The Court was influenced by the fact that the appellant had to live somewhere, a consideration that is not relevant to a determination under the DTA. There have been cases where the Court has used fines to recover from a defendant the profits derived from the commission of an offence but fines may not be used to recover the proceeds of crime not reflected by suitable counts on the indictment: see *Ayensu* [1982] 4 Cr. App. R. (S) 248.

- Thirdly, the DTOA by conferring such broad powers of confiscation on the Courts was also pursuing the aim of punishing the offender. The aims of prevention and reparation are elements of the notion of punishment.
- Fourthly, the judge was also empowered to determine the amount of imprisonment to be served in default of payment. The European Court went on to accept the proposition that the judge has a discretion, when fixing the amount of the order, to take into consideration the degree of culpability of the accused. The use of the word "culpability" in this context is misleading because the Court

can neither mitigate nor aggravate the amount to be recovered under a confiscation order to reflect the seriousness of the offence or the role played by the offender. It is clear that what the Court had in mind was the principle in *Porter* [1990] 1 W.L.R. 1260 by which the Court may apportion the benefit received in connection with a drug trafficking offence committed jointly. The Court of Appeal, in that case, was doing no more than estimating the value of the benefit received by each of the defendants. It used as a guide the roles played by each defendant to make that determination. In *Chrastny No.2* [1991] 1 W.L.R. 1381, a co-conspirator absconded but the Court of Appeal declined to reduce the value of the confiscation order made against C merely because C was less culpable than the Crown alleged her co-conspirator to have been.

- The European Court recognised that other factors may be taken into account when determining whether a provision is penal or not and these include the nature and purpose of the measure; its "characterisation under national law"; the procedures involved in implementing the measure and its severity" (para.28); and see Guy Stessens, *Money Laundering A New International Law Enforcement Model.*

(i) Is *Welch* binding on the United Kingdom in any event?

The strict answer is "no". Prior to the enactment of the Human Rights Act 1998, the European Convention on Human Rights was not adopted into English domestic law and thus it had the effect explained by Lord Donaldson M.R. in *Secretary of State for the Home Department, ex p. Brind* [1990] 2 W.L.R. 787, when he said, at 797: 13–126

"There have been a number of cases in which the European Convention on Human Rights has been introduced into the argument and has, accordingly, featured in the judgments. The convention is contained in an international treaty to which the United Kingdom is a party. The United Kingdom government can give effect to this treaty obligation in more than one way. It could, for example, 'domesticate' or 'patriate' the convention itself and there are many well-informed supporters of this course. Their view has not, as yet, prevailed. If it had done so, the convention would have been part of English domestic law. Alternatively, it can review English common and statute law with a view to amending it, if and in so far as it is inconsistent with the convention, at the same time seeking to ensure that all new statute law is consistent with it. This is the course that has in fact been adopted. Whether it has been wholly successful is a matter for the European Court of Human Rights in Strasbourg and not for the English courts. By contrast, the duty of the English courts is to decide disputes in accordance with English domestic law as it is, and not as it would be if full effect were given to this country's obligations under the treaty, assuming that there is any difference between the two.

It follows from this that in most cases the English courts will be wholly unconcerned with the terms of the convention. The sole exception is when the terms of primary legislation are fairly capable of bearing two or more meanings. In that situation various prima facie rules of construction have to be applied, such as that, in the absence of very clear words indicating the contrary, legislation is not retrospective or penal in effect. To these can be added, in appropriate cases, a presumption that Parliament has legislated in a manner consistent, rather than inconsistent, with the United Kingdom's treaty obligations."

Similar views were expressed by Diplock L.J. (as he then was) in *Salomon v. Customs and Excise Comrs* [1967] 2 Q.B. 116, 143; *Chundawadra v. Immigration Appeal Tribunal* [1988] Imm. A.R. 161, 173; *per* Lord Diplock in *Garland v. British Rail Engineering Ltd* [1983] 2 A.C. 751, 771, and see *Customs and Excise Commissioners v. Air Canada* [1991] 1 All E.R. 570, 584/585, *per* Purchas L.J.

The position now is that the Human Rights Act 1998 has adopted many of the articles of the ECHR but the jurisprudence of the Strasbourg court is something to be "taken into account" when a court is considering a convention issue.

(j) Are the provisions of the DTA more or less penal than under the DTOA?

13–127 The DTA is blandly described in the Preamble as an "act to consolidate the Drug Trafficking Offences Act 1986 and certain provisions of the Criminal Justice (International Co-operation) Act 1990". Technically speaking, the Drug Trafficking Act does consolidate earlier legislation, including Part II of the Criminal Justice Act 1993 (much of which did not come into force). However, because the Drug Trafficking Act re-enacted Part II, and brought those provisions into force, the effect was to radically overhaul the way in which drug trafficking confiscation proceedings are investigated and conducted, and to strengthen the Court's powers of enforcement in respect of the gathering and furnishing of information (relevant to confiscation proceedings) as well as ensuring the satisfaction (in full) of amounts payable under a confiscation order. On one view, the 1994 Act includes provisions which are now more favourable to the defendant (*e.g.*, the Court now has a discretion whether to embark upon a drug trafficking enquiry) but there are unquestionably other provisions, which are deliberately intended to be more draconian in nature than was the case under the 1986 Act. The mandatory application of the statutory assumptions under section 4 is one example and the application of the civil standard of proof (s.2(8)) is another.

For the purpose of making any of the statutory assumptions, it is of course true that the effect of an assumption once made, and not rebutted, is likely to be the same whether the standard of proof is phrased in terms of the civil or the criminal standard of proof but this is not necessarily so; see the result in *Enwezor* (1991) 93 Cr.App.R. 233. It is also true that the Court need not make an assumption under section 4 if to do so would give rise to a "serious risk of injustice in the defendant's case" (s.4(4)(b)) but this is not the same thing as vesting a discretion in the Court as to whether an assumption may be made or not. Furthermore, the mere fact that determinations are made by applying the so-called "civil" standard of proof does not necessarily mean that a confiscation order is not penal in nature. As the European Court remarked in *Welch*, it is necessary to look behind appearances. It is not just the Courts of England and Wales that have recognised confiscation orders as having a punitive character: several decisions of the Supreme Court of the United States of America have made similar observations concerning their legislation: see *Austin v. the United States* 125 F.ed 2d 441; *Alexander v. the United States* 125 F.ed 488.

(k) How successful have current confiscation laws proved to be?

The Government's short answer is that current confiscation laws have 13–128
not produced the results anticipated (and see the Performance and Innovation Unit Report, *Recovering the Proceeds of Crime*, June 2000). This has led the Government to publish the Proceeds of Crime Bill 2001—a consultation document at the moment—with a view to strengthening confiscation laws following a conviction for an offence, as well as introducing civil recovery (popularly known as 'confiscation without conviction').

Number of Confiscation Orders Made

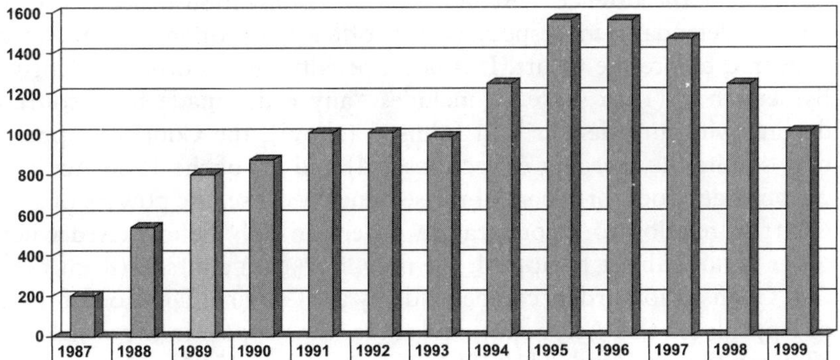

	1987	1988	1989	1990	1991	1992	1993	1994	1995	1996	1997	1998	1999
Number	203	539	802	871	1005	1002	983	1248	1562	1557	1466	1243	1009

The average confiscation for 1999 was £14,964. The amount of money recovered under confiscation orders made in Scotland is less than £1 million.

Value of Confiscation Orders

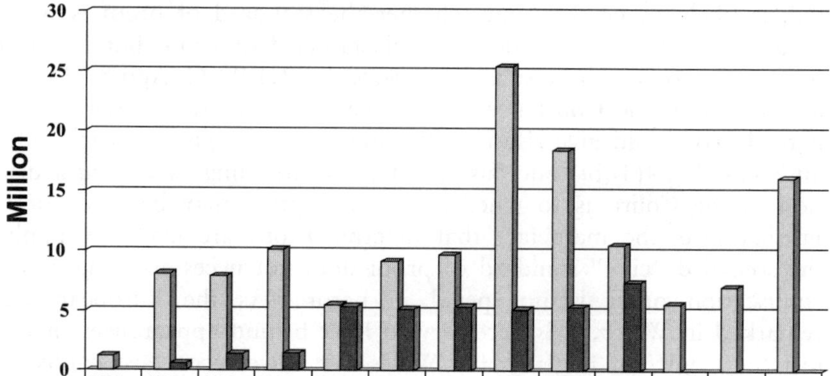

	1987	1988	1989	1990	1991	1992	1993	1994	1995	1996	1997	1998	1999
Confis.	1.2	8.1	7.9	10.1	5.5	9.1	9.7	25.4	18.4	10.5	5.6	7	16.1
Realised		0.6	1.37	1.45	5.38	5.18	5.38	5.13	5.34	7.41			

B. SENTENCING CONSIDERATIONS

(a) Is a confiscation order a sentence?

13–129 A confiscation order is a "sentence" for the purposes of section 50 of the Criminal Appeal Act 1968 (see para. 2 of Sched.1 to the DTA) but the powers now conferred upon the Courts (by virtue of ss. 3–15 of the DTA) to permit further proceedings to be taken in connection with confiscation orders within six years of a defendant's conviction, will no doubt fuel the debate as to whether the legislature regard the making of confiscation orders as amounting to a quasi-civil measure rather than a penal sanction, following conviction. Section 9 of the Criminal Appeal Act 1968 states that a person "may appeal to the Court of Appeal against any sentence passed on him for the offence". At first sight, a confiscation order is not passed on the defendant in respect of the offence, or offences, for which he appeared before the Court. It is not a penalty but an order of deprivation. By section 50(1), a sentence includes "any order made by a court when dealing with an offender". In Johnson (above), the Court of Appeal held that despite the wording of sections 2(4) and (5) of the 1986 Act a confiscation order does form part of the sentence because, the powers of the High Court in relation to a confiscation order can only be exercised where the order is not subject to appeal: see now s.29(1)(c) and s.41(8) of the 1994 Act. Confiscation orders can be made by the Criminal Division of the Court of Appeal: see this Act, s.9(6); and there was support in the words of Lord Widgery C.J. in *Hayden* [1975] 1 W.L.R. 852 at 854 G, when he said that an order for costs comes within the definition of "sentence" in s.50(1) of the Criminal Appeal Act 1968 because "it is an order which is contingent upon there having been a conviction and it is contingent on the person by whom the payment is to be made, having been convicted in that way": see *Neal* (September 30, 1998); and *Sorelli* (March 31, 1999).

(b) Factual findings in the DTA proceedings may influence the sentence

Upon an initial reading of section 2(5)(c), it might be thought that it is not just the amount of the order that should be left out of account for the purposes of sentencing, but also the factual findings made upon the evidence adduced during the DTA hearing. However, authorities decided under s.1(5)(c) of the DTOA (and which are still good law for present purposes) make it clear that some regard may be had to facts emerging from the DTA hearing if they rebut points raised in mitigation, *e.g.* that the offence represented an isolated incident. 13–130

The sentiments expressed in section 2(5)(c) are consistent with the general principles of sentencing in that an accused is entitled to be sentenced on the basis of what is proved or admitted (to the criminal standard of proof) in respect of the offences for which he falls to be sentenced: see *Ayensu and Ayensu* (1982) 4 Cr.App.R.(S) 248; *Ralf* (1989) 11 Cr.App.R.(S) 121; *Reeves (R.J.)* (1993) 5 Cr.App.R.(S) 292; *Bragason* [1988] Crim.L.R. 778; *McNulty* (1994) 15 Cr.App.R.(S) 606 and see *Callan* (1994) 98 Cr.App.R. 467; and the provisions of the Criminal Justice Act 1991 which tend to support that approach.

In *Harper* (1989) 11 Cr.App.R.(S) 240, the Court of Appeal seems to have encroached on this principle in holding that the sentencer may pay some regard to the evidence placed before him under the 1986 Act if it rebuts an assertion made in mitigation, *e.g.* that the offence represented an isolated incident. In *Saunders* [1991] 92 Cr.App.R. 6, Hutchison J. said (at 10):

> "... it would be absurd to say that if in the course of the Drug Trafficking Offences Act investigation the defendant, for example, admitted extensive drug trafficking, the sentencing judge should entirely disregard that in determining the appropriate sentence. He could and should take it into account in the manner indicated a moment ago."

The Court of Appeal in *Saunders* made two other important observations. The first is that the sentencer should be careful not to take into account factual matters of which the sentencer had not been satisfied beyond reasonable doubt, and this presumably remains the law notwithstanding s.2(8) of the 1994 Act: but see *McNulty* [1994] 15 Cr.App.R.(S) 606 and read the commentary to that case [1994] Crim.L.R. 385, 386. The second point is that the sentencer should not use the assumptions (under s.2(3) of the 1986 Act) to make a finding "adverse to the defendant in the realm of sentencing which he would not have made applying the ordinary burden of proof" (*per* Hutchison J. at 10): and see *Callan* (1994) 98 Cr.App.R. 467. Presumably, this remains the law notwithstanding s.4(2)–(5) of the 1994 Act.

The occasions on which sentence may properly take into account matters revealed under the DTA inquiry will be relatively few in comparison to the large number of cases coming before the Courts: and see *Thompson* [1997] 1 Cr. App. R.(S) 288.

C. THE PROCEDURE FOR MAKING CONFISCATION ORDERS

(a) Introduction

13–131 Politicians and laypersons are prone to speak about confiscation as being the means by which ill-gotten *gains* or *profits* are recovered by the State. In doing so, they misstate the true position. First, the Drug Trafficking Act does not directly confiscate the instrumentalities of crime or specific items of property: it is not a procedure *in rem*. For that reason, the Drug Trafficking Act is often described as "value confiscation", as opposed to "object confiscation" or "property confiscation". Secondly, the Drug Trafficking Act is concerned with recovering the *proceeds* of drug trafficking and not merely drug profits. The Court is not required to embark on an accountancy exercise to determine, for example, net profit, or to allow for expenses.

Four points should be borne in mind whenever the Court embarks upon a drug trafficking enquiry:

(i) what is to be confiscated are the proceeds of drug trafficking and not merely drug profits. A trafficker who receives £1,000 for the sale of a drug cannot seek to deduct the expenses he incurred in buying and transporting it: *Smith (Ian)* [1989] 1 W.L.R. 765. Broadly speaking his gross receipts are his proceeds.

(ii) the value of a confiscation order will not always mark the extent of the defendant's drug trafficking career, because the DTA catches all drug proceeds received by the defendant whether as a result of his drug trafficking or another's: see *Smith (Ian)* [1989] 1 W.L.R.765, and *Comiskey* (1991) 93 Cr.App.R. 227 (and note s.4(1)(a) and s.2(3) of the 1994 Act).

(iii) it is irrelevant whether the drug trafficking in question took place within the jurisdiction of the Courts of the United Kingdom, or abroad subject to a "corresponding law": see s.1(1), 1(2), 1(4) of the 1994 Act.

(iv) There was clear authority, for the purposes of the DTOA, that where it was shown that the defendant had benefited from drug trafficking, the Court was duty bound to follow the steps required by the DTOA and it was not permitted to use its powers of forfeiture under section 143 of the Powers of the Criminal Courts (Sentencing) Act 2000: *Stuart and Bonnett* (1989) 11 Cr.App.R.(S) 89. This is because the structure of the DTOA made it clear that the confiscation procedure under the Act was the primary method by which ill-gotten proceeds were to be recovered. This is no longer true under the DTA by virtue of s.2(1) of that Act. What is a judge to do if faced with a case where neither the prosecution nor the Court choose to proceed under the DTA, but the Court is nevertheless satisfied that the defendant was, at the time of his arrest, in possession of cash used for the purpose of committing or facilitating the commission of the offence? Is *Stuart and Bonnett* still relevant? It is submitted that it is in the sense that it should be taken as establishing a general rule of practice. However, the effect of section 2 is to afford the prosecutor a degree of discretion as to how best to proceed, *e.g.* whether by way of confiscation proceedings or by applying for a forfeiture order. Each case will turn on its own facts: see section 2(1)(b) which speaks of the Court's power to proceed under the Act if it is "appropriate" to do so.

The method by which a court is to determine the value of the defendant's **13–132**
proceeds of drug trafficking is one of the most controversial features of the 1986 and 1994 Acts. There will often be cases where an accused can be shown to have received property over a period of years but there exists little or no evidence to prove that the property represents the proceeds of drug trafficking. Accordingly, the 1986 Act created a number of far-reaching assumptions which the Court is now obliged to make unless the statutory exceptions apply: see section 4(2) and section 4(4). Inevitably, in complicated and hotly contested confiscation proceedings, much court time will be spent tracing funds and ascertaining the origin of property.

Before the Court may embark on a drug trafficking enquiry three basic conditions must be fulfilled:

(i) the offender must appear before the Crown Court to be sentenced for a "drug trafficking offence": section 2;

(ii) the Court must satisfy itself that it has jurisdiction to make a confiscation order;

(iii) the Court can only embark upon an enquiry under the Act if either the prosecutor asks the Court to do so or the Court of its own motion considers that it would be appropriate to do so: section 2(1). If the prosecution ask the Court to proceed under the DTA it would seem that the Court has no power (under this enactment) to override the wishes of thee prosecutor unless the phrase "ask the Court", as it appears in section 2(1)(a), is construed to mean "applies for leave of the Court" to proceed under the Act. However, if that is what Parliament intended should be the effect of section 2(1)(a) then it would have been very easy for the draughtsman merely to have said so.

(b) Persons to whom s.2 of the 1994 Act applies

Confiscation orders may only be made against persons who appear **13–133**
before the Crown Court to be sentenced in respect of one or more "drug trafficking offences", a classification which, by s.1(3) of the 1994 Act, means:

"(a) an offence under section 4(2) or (3) or 5(3) of the Misuse of Drugs

Act 1971 (production, supply and possession for supply of controlled drugs);

(b) an offence under section 20 of that Act (assisting in or inducing commission outside United Kingdom of offence punishable under a corresponding law);

(c) an offence under—

(i) section 50(2) or (3) of the Customs and Excise Management Act 1979 (improper importation),

(ii) section 68(2) of that Act (exportation), or

(iii) section 170 of that Act (fraudulent evasion), in connection with a prohibition or restriction on importation or exportation having effect by virtue of section 3 of the Misuse of Drugs Act 1971;

(d) an offence under section 12 of the Criminal Justice (International Co-operation) Act 1990 (manufacture or supply of substance specified in Schedule 2 to that Act);

(e) an offence under section 19 of that Act (using ship for illicit traffic in controlled drugs);

(f) an offence under section 49, 50 or 51 of this Act or section 14 of the Criminal Justice (International Co-operation) Act 1990 (which makes, in relation to Scotland and Northern Ireland, provision corresponding to section 49 of this Act);

(g) an offence under section 1 of the Criminal Law Act 1977 of conspiracy to commit any of the offences in paragraphs (a) to (f) above;

(h) an offence under section 1 of the Criminal Attempts Act 1981 of attempting to commit any of those offences; and

(i) an offence of inciting another person to commit any of those offences, whether under section 19 of the Misuse of Drugs Act 1971 or at common law;

and includes aiding, abetting, counselling or procuring the commission of any of the offences in paragraphs (a) to (f) above."

The content of s.1(3) of the 1994 Act broadly follows s.38(1) of the 1986 Act as amended by the Criminal Justice (International Co-operation) Act 1990, Sched.4, para.4(4) and by s.24(9) of the 1993 Act.

13–134 The payment or other reward must have been received in connection with "drug trafficking" carried on by the defendant or another: see section 4(1). Note that "drug trafficking" is defined by section 1(1) and section 1(2). The term "drug trafficking" is to be distinguished from "drug trafficking offences": see s.1(3). Not every "drug trafficking offence" amounts to "drug trafficking" for the purposes of section 1. A conspiracy is a "drug trafficking offence" but it is not "drug trafficking" under section 1. If B visits Jamaica and imports cannabis back into the United Kingdom then the airline ticket and hotel expenses (paid for by A) are "payments or other rewards" in connection with drug trafficking carried on by them see *Osei* (1988) 10 Cr. App. R. (S) 289. However, if B took fright in Jamaica and decided not to possess, let alone to import, cannabis then it would seem that neither the ticket nor the hotel expenses would fall within the meaning of section 2(3) because there had not been an activity performed by either A or B which amounted to "drug trafficking" under the Act: see *Johnson* [1991] 2 Q.B. 249.

An offence under section 8 of the Misuse of Drugs Act 1971 (permitting premises to be used for prohibited acts to take place therein) is not a "drug trafficking offence" even if drug trafficking took place on the premises. The probable reason for omitting that offence was because the offence is wide enough to embrace persons who do not intend or desire that the prohibited activity should take place but display an unwillingness to take the means available to them to prevent that activity: see *Thomas & Thompson* (1976) 63 Cr.App.R. 65. The position is set to change under proposed legislation currently before Parliament, *i.e.* the Proceeds of Crime Bill. Similarly, an offence under section 6 of the Misuse of Drugs Act 1971 (cultivating cannabis) is not a drug trafficking offence—but see section 4.

(c) Jurisdiction

Only the Crown Court is empowered to make a confiscation order under 13–135
s.2. Although the section applies in cases where the defendant is committed by the magistrates' court to the Crown Court for sentence pursuant to s.38 of the Magistrates' Courts Act 1980, it does not apply to juveniles who are committed to the Crown Court with a view to being sentenced to youth custody under s.37 of the Magistrates' Courts Act 1980 (as amended by the Criminal Justice Act 1991) or where the powers of the Court are limited to dealing with the defendant in a way in which a magistrates' court might have dealt with him in connection with the offence charged: (see the 1994 Act, s.2(7)(b)). Accordingly, s.2 does not apply to defendants who appeal to the Crown Court against their conviction and/or sentence in the magistrates' court. Furthermore, section 2 has no application where a defendant has been "previously . . . sentenced or otherwise dealt with in respect of his conviction for the offence or . . . any of the offences concerned": s.2(1). Section 2 therefore does not apply to persons who are in breach of a community service order or a suspended sentence of imprisonment. Note that where a defendant was committed to the Crown Court under s.38(2) on a mistaken view of the facts, the best course is for the defendant to be permitted to change his plea at the Crown Court: *Isleworth Crown Court, ex* p. *Buda* (October 19, 1999).

Note that the Court cannot initiate confiscation proceedings after the defendant has been sentenced: *Ross* (March 13, 2001). If the Court wishes to proceed to sentence before embarking on confiscation proceedings it must act in accordance with section 3 of the Drug Trafficking Act.

(d) Deciding whether to proceed under the Act

Section 2(1) of the 1994 Act provides as follows: 13–136

"2(1) Subject to subsection (7) below, where a defendant appears before the Crown Court to be sentenced in respect of one or more drug trafficking offences (and has not previously been sentenced or otherwise dealt with in respect of his conviction for the offence or, as the case may be, any of the offences concerned), then—

(a) if the prosecutor asks the Court to proceed under this section, or

(b) if the Court considers that, even though the prosecutor has not asked it to do so, it is appropriate for it to proceed under this section,

it shall act as follows. . . .

(2) the Court shall first determine whether the defendant has benefited from drug trafficking."

Section 2(1) of the Act represents the combined effect of s.1(l) of the 1986 Act as amended by s.7(1) of the 1993 Act.

Under the 1986 Act, whenever a defendant appeared before the Crown Court to be sentenced in respect of one or more "drug trafficking offences", the Court was obliged to embark upon a drug trafficking enquiry in every case. This is no longer so. Even under the old Act the Courts frequently made a "nil order" where it was evident that there was little or nothing to confiscate. This approach was pragmatic albeit not expressly part of the legislative framework of the DTOA. By s.2(1) of the Act, the Court need only embark upon confiscation proceedings if it is asked to do so by the prosecutor or when the Court considers that it is appropriate for it to proceed under the Act. The purpose of this provision (which originally appeared as s.7 of the 1993 Act amending s.1(1) of the 1986 Act) was described by the then Secretary of State for the Home Department (Kenneth Clarke):

"(the provision) relieves the Court from following the confiscation procedures . . . each time that it convicts a drug trafficker. Confiscation will take place only when notice is served on the Court by the prosecutor, or at the Court's discretion. This will filter out those cases in which there is obviously little or no benefit, or no realisable property. This does not mean that we are softening our approach to drug traffickers. The minor cases that do not attract a confiscation hearing under the new arrangements will continue to be dealt with severely by means of fines and forfeiture orders, as well as by imprisonment." (Hansard, HC, vol. 222, col. 866).

13–137 It will be seen that IF the Court embarks on confiscation proceedings (see s.2(1)) the Court's next step is to determine whether the defendant has benefited from drug trafficking: section 2(1). This may seem to be putting the issues in the wrong order: surely, it may be said, the Court should first decide whether the defendant has benefited from drug trafficking, and then (if the answer is in the affirmative) to start the confiscation process.

However, determining whether there has been a "benefit" will often be answered by an application of the statutory assumptions, and that step can only be taken if confiscation proceedings are underway. The initial step, of deciding whether to embark on confiscation proceedings, will often be based on a subjective assessment of the defendant's antecedents, his lifestyle or wealth, and the facts of the underlying offence(s) before the Court. The most obvious example is where the value of the benefits is likely to be small, the defendant clearly has no realisable assets (beyond the clothes he is wearing in the dock) and there is no material before the Court to suggest that any such assets are likely to be available in the foreseeable future: see para. 13–176.

Many drug traffickers are convicted of 'low level' dealing, or they are first time offenders, with no obvious signs of having benefited from drug trafficking. Many drug smugglers are couriers with, again, no outward signs of wealth. In such cases, confiscation may yield low value confiscation orders notwithstanding that the value of the drug carried is large. On the other hand, couriers of money (particularly cash) can find that their "benefit" is assessed in gigantic sums as a result of at least two Court of Appeal decisions (*Simons* (1994) 98 Cr.App.R. 160 and *Simpson* [1998] 2 Cr.App.R.(S.) 111) even though the reward was a fraction of the sum transported. Following the Court of Appeal's interpretation of section 16 of the Drug Trafficking Act (in *Tivnan* [1999] 1 Cr.App.R.(S.) 92), confiscation proceedings are often initiated, even if a nominal confiscation order is the end result, because the benefit figure is sufficiently high to justify the prosecution returning to court if the defendant acquires new wealth. Some will question the moral basis for calculating "benefit" on monies that merely passes through the hands of a defendant: others see a deterrent value in doing so.

Under the DTOA 1986, the Court had no choice but to follow the steps set out in the Act. Although the parties could "agree" a schedule of realisable assets and "admit" a benefit figure, it was the duty of the judge to ensure that the figures were realistic in the sense that they represented the extent of the defendant's proceeds of drug trafficking and assets: see *Atkinson* (1993) 14 Cr. App. R. (S) 182 and *Finch* [1992] Crim. L.R. 901. Accordingly, a defendant who gave considerable assistance to law enforcement agencies, could not be "rewarded" by way of a "concession" made by the prosecution not to confiscate assets under a confiscation order which would result in the loss of his home or prized motor vehicle. The Court was bound to confiscate such assets if it could. 13–138

Under the DTOA it theoretically possible for defendants to invite the prosecution not to embark on confiscation proceedings on the grounds that valuable assistance has or will be given to a law enforcement agency. The extent to which this happens (if at all) is unknown—for obvious reasons. Such arrangements can only be justified on the grounds of public interest, but a defendant has no guarantee that such an arrangement will be approved by the sentencing judge: the Drug Trafficking Act enquiry is ultimately the Court's enquiry, and the judge may initiate proceedings if he considers it appropriate to do so.

Note that although s.2(1)(a) allows the prosecutor to "ask" the Court to proceed under s.2, this courtesy belies the reality: once "asked" the Court is obliged to embark upon an enquiry. No doubt most prosecutors will be sensible in their approach—but it is not clear what control (even in costs) the Court has over decisions taken by prosecutors who compel a court to proceed under s.2 even if the Court believes the exercise is inappropriate.

In some jurisdictions, it is for the prosecutor, and not for the Court, to decide whether there should be confiscation/forfeiture proceedings. The justification for the rule is that the investigating authority will usually possess much more information, than the Court, to make that decision. That is not the approach in England and Wales. If asked, most people would probably say that they would prefer a judge to have the ultimate "say" as to whether there should be confiscation proceedings. Section 2 of the Drug Trafficking Act is perhaps a concession to that view—and no more than that—because (as stated above) although the judge may initiate proceedings, he has no power under the Drug Trafficking Act to decline to conduct such proceedings if the prosecutor asks him to do so. It is submitted that giving the judge discretion to determine whether there should be confiscation proceedings has much to commend it. The prosecution will usually exercise their discretion without seeking representations from the defendant or interested third parties. If the Court initiates confiscation proceedings, the matter has at least been canvassed in open court. The Proceeds of Crime Bill 2001 retains the power of the Courts, in England and Wales, to initiate confiscation proceedings, but the Bill also proposes that the prosecutor should be able to appeal to the Court of Appeal a decision of the Crown Court judge not to initiate confiscation proceedings. If that becomes law, it may be asked whether a defendant should not also be permitted to challenge the prosecutor's decision (or the Court's) to conduct such proceedings? What should be the test for determining whether the judge erred in the exercise of his discretion? Proportionality or *Wednesbury* unreasonableness?

13–139 In *Benjafield and others*, the Court of Appeal concluded that current confiscation laws are convention-compliant partly because a discretion exists as to whether confiscation proceedings should be initiated or not. The Court gave no guidance as to how the discretion should be exercised—a topic that may become the subject of further judicial opinion: see also *McIntosh* (February 5, 2001, PC) and now *Phillips v. United Kingdom* (July 5, 2001).

Many factors may influence the decision of the Court, or the prosecutor, not to embark on confiscation proceedings. Until relatively recently, the tendency was not to embark on confiscation proceedings unless the value of the benefit and/or realisable property, was high. There has also been a lack of warmth for such proceedings not just within the legal profession, but also within law enforcement agencies too. That is quickly changing. However, a major underlying problem has been the severe lack of financial and human resources, to investigate and to enforce confiscation laws. Although the Drug Trafficking Offences Act 1986 was enacted amidst much rhetoric as to its objectives, the resources were simply not there to realistically attain them. The number of trained financial investigators tasked to trace assets, and to pursue confiscation orders is still low. Financial investigation work is exacting, complex, time consuming, and expensive, and the results are far from guaranteed. Law enforcement agencies are faced with the prospect that officers trained by them may be lost to the private sector by offers of higher salaries and benefits. These problems have prompted some managers within law enforcement groups to ask "what is in it for us?" The Courts, too, are subject to budgetary constraints and heavy caseloads. Such difficulties are fuelling a debate as to the extent to which monies obtained from asset forfeiture/asset recovery should be ploughed back into enforcement. Some argue that law enforcement agencies need incentives to undertake such complex work; others argue that the public is looking for crime reduction rather than creative accountancy; others contend that law enforcement is already an "industry", and that confiscation of assets will only make that perspective worse (for some interesting reading see Guy Stessens, *Money Laundering; A New International Law Enforcement Model*; and Dorn *et al.*, *Regulating European Drug Problems*). Training for the judiciary, and for the legal profession, is now very much better than it was. There is greater awareness of confiscation issues, and there is no doubt that the number of confiscation proceedings is increasing.

(e) Postponing DTA hearings

It will be seen from section 2(1) of the Drug Trafficking Act that the procedure to be followed under the Act arises where a defendant appears before the Crown Court "*to be sentenced*". Thus, by section 2(4), the Court "shall, before sentencing . . . (the defendant) . . . determine . . . the amount to be recovered". The combined effect of those provisions is to require the Crown Court to embark on confiscation proceedings without delay, and before sentencing the defendant. It cannot be emphasised too strongly that there is no power to sentence the defendant first, and then to initiate confiscation proceedings: *Ross* (March 13, 2001). If the prosecutor, or the Court, initiates confiscation proceedings, that fact must be established before sentencing the defendant. The Court should proceed with the Drug Trafficking Act enquiry without delay *unless* an application has been granted under section 3 to postpone confiscation determinations. Only then may the Court proceed to sentence the defendant before conducting the confiscation hearing. Note "may" not "must". Under the DTOA the Court was obliged to embark upon a drug trafficking inquiry if, in the opinion of the judge, the case was a "benefit case" based on the evidence put before him or on the strength of a recital of the facts presented by counsel: *Dickens* (1990) 2 Q.B. 102. The Court could not sentence the defendant until all relevant determinations had been made under that Act: section 1(4). This ensured that the Courts did not make orders in respect of the defendant's property (*e.g.* a forfeiture order or a fine) other than by way of a confiscation order determined under the DTOA. A necessary consequence of that approach was that sentence was adjourned pending further inquiries, a pro- 13–140 cess that could take months in complex cases. The whole process was a costly and futile exercise if the underlying conviction was quashed on appeal. Not surprisingly, that approach attracted much criticism.

Section 3 of the DTA now permits a court to proceed to sentence if the Court decides to postpone the making of any determination under the Act: see section 3(7).

Section 3 of the DTA provides:

> "Where the Crown Court is acting under section 2 of this Act but considers that it requires further information before—
>
> (a) determining whether the defendant has benefited from drug trafficking, or
>
> (b) determining the amount to be recovered in his case by virtue of that section
>
> it may, for the purpose of enabling that information to be obtained, postpone making the determination for such period as it may specify.
>
> (2) More than one postponement may be made under subsection (1) above in relation to the same case.
>
> (3) Unless it is satisfied that there are exceptional circumstances, the Court shall not specify a period under subsection (1) above which—
>
> (a) by itself, or
>
> (b) where there have been one or more previous postponements under subsection (1) above or (4) below, when taken together with the earlier specified periods or periods,
>
> exceeds six months beginning with the date of conviction."

13–141 It will be seen that there are only two statutory grounds for making an application to postpone: (i) to obtain "further information" to assist the Court in making proper determinations under the Act (s. 3(1)), and (ii) where the defendant appeals against his conviction: section 3(4). Unless there are exceptional circumstances, the period of postponement to obtain further information should not exceed six months from the date of conviction, and in the case of an appeal against conviction, no postponement should be longer than three months from the disposal of the hearing of the appeal. It is unlikely that the Courts would be deterred from making a confiscation order merely because it learns that an appeal against conviction is pending (particularly where determinations under the DTA are likely to be straight-forward) but a postponement pending an appeal may be an attractive option if the DTA enquiry is likely to be difficult and protracted (and thus expensive) or if, in the opinion of the Crown Court, the appeal stands a good chance of succeeding. No doubt the Courts will be on their guard against parties who seek postponement pending an appeal, if the real reason for seeking that postponement is to put off the DTA hearing for the longest period permitted under the Act!

Confiscation and making other financial orders

13–142 If the Court does proceed to sentence, and postpones the DTA enquiry, it must not make any financial order against the defendant (s. 3(9) below).

The reason is obvious: the Court may determine that all of the defendant's assets are the proceeds of drug trafficking and it is the DTA that is the appropriate vehicle for recovering ill-gotten proceeds: see *Williams* (March 24, 1998). If a defendant has assets which exceed the value of a confiscation order the Court might wish (additionally) to order the defendant to pay costs or, to make some other financial order against him including the imposition of a fine: and see *Stuart and Bonnett* (1989) 11 Cr. App. R. (S) 89.

If the Court sentences the defendant before making a confiscation order it is conceivable, that without express statutory provision, the Court might be persuaded that it was debarred from making other financial orders and that the 28-day period for varying a sentence (permitted under s.47 of the Supreme Court Act 1981) should not be used as a tactical device to overcome that potential difficulty. In any event, s.47 of the 1981 Act would not be available if the DTA hearing was postponed for longer than 28 days. Accordingly, section 3(10) (the equivalent of which did not appear in the Criminal Justice Act 1993) puts the matter beyond doubt by granting the sentencing court the power to vary a sentence to include the imposition of a fine or other financial orders: see Hansard, HL, vol. 556, col. 992, as to the purpose of section 3(10). The Court must nevertheless continue to have regard to the overall effect of the sentences imposed (bearing in mind that a confiscation order is also a "sentence" for the purpose of s.50 of the Court of Appeal Act 1968).

Sections 3(9) to (11) provide: 13–143

"(9) In sentencing, or otherwise dealing with, the defendant in respect of the relevant offence or any of the relevant offences at any time during the specified period, the Court shall not—

(a) impose any fine on him; or
(b) make any such order as is mentioned in section 2(5)(b)(ii) (*i.e.* orders involving payment or (iii) of this Act (*i.e.* forfeiture or deportation orders).

(10) Where the Court has sentenced the defendant under subsection (7) above during the specified period it may, after the end of that period, vary the sentence by imposing a fine or making any such order as is mentioned in section 2(5)(b)(ii) or (iii) of this Act. so long as it does so within a period corresponding to that allowed by section 47(2) or (3) of the Supreme Court Act 1981 (time allowed for varying a sentence) but beginning with the end of the specified period.

(11) In this section—

"the date of conviction" means—

(a) the date on which the defendant was convicted; or
(b) where he appeared to be sentenced in respect of more than one conviction, and those convictions were not all on the same date, the date of the latest of those convictions; and

'the relevant offence' means the drug trafficking offence in respect of which the defendant appears (as mentioned in section 2(1) of this Act) before the Court;

and references to an appeal include references to an application under section 111 of the Magistrates' Courts Act 1980 (statement of case by magistrates' court)."

Newton *hearings and confiscation proceedings*

13–144 The basis of plea might be in dispute. Issues relevant to both a *Newton* hearing and Drug Trafficking Act proceedings, should be resolved prior to sentence either by conducting the confiscation inquiry and a *Newton* hearing in the same proceedings, or separately. If both sets of issues are dealt with in one hearing, it is important that the judge should ensure that he is applying the correct standard of proof in respect of all relevant matters that require a determination. Thirdly, (and this must not be overstated) matters may emerge during the Drug Trafficking Act enquiry that is relevant to the determination of the appropriate sentence for the underlying offence.
The most difficult question for the Court is not whether the hearing should be postponed, but whether the Court should proceed to sentence before making determinations under the Act. The answer to this question will no doubt depend, in part, on the length of the postponement, but another consideration will be whether material emerges during the DTA enquiry which could either mitigate (or aggravate) the sentence: see *Ayensu and Ayensu* (1982) 4 Cr.App.R.(S) 248; *Bragason* [1988] Crim.L.R. 778; *Ralf* (1989) 11 Cr.App.R.(S) 121; *Harper* (1989) 11 Cr.App.R.(S) 240, *Saunders* (1991) 92 Cr.App.R. 6.; *Reeves (R.J.)* (1993) 5 Cr.App.R.(S) 292; *McNulty* (1994) 15 Cr.App.R.(S) 606 and see *Callan* (1994) 98 Cr.App.R. 467. Maximum periods of imprisonment in default of payment of a confiscation order are imposed by the relevant provisions.

How is an application to be made?

13–145 The procedure to be followed if an application is made under section 3(4) and 3(5) of the DTA is set out in Rule 34 of the Crown Court Rules: see the Crown Court (Amendment) (No. 2) Rules 1994 (S.I. 1994 No. 3153) which came into force as from February 3, 1995:

"34.—(1) Where an application to the Crown Court is made by the defendant or the prosecutor under section 3(5)(a) of the Drug Trafficking Act 1994 asking the Court to exercise its powers under section 3(4) of that Act, or under section 72A(5)(a) of the Criminal Justice Act 1988 asking the Court to exercise its powers under section 72A(4) of that Act, such an application must be made in writing and a copy thereof must be served on the prosecutor or the defendant, as the case may be.

(2) A party which is served with a copy of an application under paragraph (1) shall, within 28 days of the date of service, notify the applicant and the appropriate officer of the Crown Court, in writing, whether or not it proposes to oppose the application, giving its reasons for any such opposition.

(3) After the expiry of the period referred to in paragraph (2), the

Crown Court shall determine whether an application under paragraph (1) is to be dealt with—

(a) without a hearing, or

(b) at a hearing at which the parties may be represented"

When does time begin to run?

It is perhaps surprising that section 3 should have generated so much case law or that it should have resulted in many confiscation orders being quashed or just not being made. On the other hand, there are powerful reasons why confiscation proceedings should not be allowed to drift. Frequently there will be good reason for delaying confiscation proceedings following a conviction. Confiscation can be an expensive, time consuming, exercise, and there is often is an incentive not to expend resources on any post conviction determination, unless and until there is a conviction. However, such an approach might mean that the trial itself is deprived of the benefit of admissible and probative evidence (*e.g.* lifestyle cases)—a fact not lost on the authors of the Performance and Innovation Unit Report, *Recovering the Proceeds of Crime*" (June 2000). A defendant should not be prejudiced in the presentation of his case caused by delay (*e.g.* because documents have been lost or witnesses are no longer traceable). On the other hand, it is often the defendant who seeks a lengthy adjournment or postponement of confiscation proceedings. It is for the defendant to rebut the statutory assumptions made under the Drug Trafficking Act, and it is also for him (usually) to satisfy the Court under section 5(3) that the value of the "amount that might be realised" figure is less than the value of the proceeds of his drug trafficking (*i.e.* his benefit). 13–146

The definitive authority on the issue of postponed determinations is *Steele and others* (December 14, 2000, CA). It is not a decision that entirely satisfies all commentators (notably Dr David Thomas Q.C. for the reasons he has set out in a series of commentaries to cases noted in the Criminal Law Review, and in *Archbold News*).

Section 3 is capable of several logical and reasonable interpretations. 13–147
Ultimately, the section requires a purposive construction that most closely reflects what Parliament probably had in mind. *Hansard* is of limited assistance because Parliament did not debate section 3 with the benefit of the range of situations that have in fact troubled the courts in practice. To assist the reader, a schedule of the majority of recent decisions pertaining to section 3 follows on page 484.

The periods of time expressed in section 3 run from the date of convic- 13–148
tion (section 3(3)) or from the date on which the appeal against conviction is disposed of (section 3(6)).

But what is the position if, on the first day of the DTA hearing (almost six months after the date of conviction) an application is made for the hearing to be adjourned "part heard" for further enquiries? Does that "adjournment" amount to a "postponement" for the purposes of section 3? It is submitted that it may well do so. Much will depend on the circumstances. The Court should look to the reality of the situation. If the Court has barely embarked

POSTPONED DETERMINATIONS SCHEDULE

Case	Act	Conviction	Sentence	Postponement	Adjournment	Con. Ord. Made	Result
HM Lord Adv. v. Donnelly (Oct. 11, 1996)	PC(S)A	Apr.18, 1996[1]	May 8, 1996		Oct. 10, 1996[2]		Adj. granted[3]
Cole (Apr. 22, 1998)	DTA	July 18, 1996	July 18, 1996	July 18, 1996	Jan. 2, 1997[4]	May 15, 1997	Upheld
France (April 27, 1998); [1999] 1 CAR(S) 85	DTA	July 1, 1996	July 1, 1996	July 1, 1996[5]	Dec. 11, 1996[6]	May 13, 1997	Upheld
Akpan (Oct. 20, 1998)	CJA	Nov. 18, 1996		Jan. 16, 1997[7]	June 27, 1997 [8]	Nov. 1997	Quashed
Abraham (Oct. 20, 1998)	CJA	Nov. 18, 1996	Jan. 16, 1997	Jan. 16, 1997	June 27, 1997	Sept. 23, 1997	Quashed
Shergill (Feb. 24, 1999); [1999] 2 CAR(S) 341	CJA	Oct. 18, 1996	June 4, 1997			Jan. 26, 1998	Quashed [9]
Edwards (May 11, 1999)	DTA	Oct. 30, 1997 July 22, 1998	Jan. 16, 1998 Quashed	July 15, 1998 [10]			
Tuegel and others (Nov. 19, 1999)	CJA	Feb. 13, 1998	Oct. 9, 1998	July 28, 1998 [11]	Oct. 1, 1998	Apr. 26, 1999	Upheld [12]
Ward (Nov. 24, 1999)	CJA	July 3, 1998	**Feb. 26, 1999**		July 3, 1998 [13]	**Feb. 26, 1999**	Quashed
Khan (Nov. 29, 1999); [2000] 2 CAR(S) 76	CJA	May 6, 1997[14]	May 23, 1997[15]	May 23, 1997?[16]	June 22, 1998[17]	Aug. 14, 1998	Quashed

[1] Prosecutor's statement lodged.
[2] Defendant sought an adjournment, which the Crown opposed on the basis that the adjourned date would fall outside the six-month period.
[3] Court held that (postponement provisions) do *not* apply where an allegation in prosecutor's statement is being challenged. Provisions do not interfere with the court's inherent powers to adjourn where necessary in the interests of justice. PC(S)A 1995, s.10 applies where the court is considering whether to make a confiscation order.
[4] **Judicial decision to extend period** for making confiscation order outside six-month period on grounds of judge's illness.
[5] Confiscation proceedings adjourned. The Court of Appeal said that confiscation proceedings were postponed on that date.
[6] Parties sought postponement (granted Feb. 12, 1997) having regard to the number of witnesses involved, etc. Therefore there was a judicial decision to postpone on the grounds of "exceptional circumstances".
[7] Sentence deferred.
[8] Judge ruled that he had jurisdiction to make confiscation orders.
[9] **No judicial decision that exceptional circumstances existed** to justify postponing proceedings beyond the six-month limit.
[10] Judge purported to retrospectively extend the postponed period.
[11] The judge expressly indicated that there were exceptional circumstances justifying an extension/postponement of confiscation proceedings given their complexity.
[12] The proceedings were postponed on July 28, 1998. Everyone consented to an adjournment to Oct. 1, 1998 (*i.e.* outside six-month period) given complexity of case.
[13] Confiscation proceedings and sentence, adjourned until Oct. 9, 1998, and adjourned again to Dec. 9, 1998, and then to Feb. 5, then to Feb. 26. It is questionable whether the fact of adjourning sentence and confiscation proceedings is automatically "a postponement".
[14] Khan pleaded guilty to different indictments in Apr. 1996, Oct. 1996, and May 1997.
[15] Judge directed that confiscation proceedings should be heard on another occasion. Arguably this was also the date of the first postponement.
[16] Judge directed that confiscation proceedings should be heard on another occasion. Arguably this was also the date of the first postponement.
[17] **Application (well outside six-month period) for extension of time**, on grounds of "exceptional circumstances".

POSTPONED DETERMINATIONS SCHEDULE *cont.*

Case	Act	Conviction	Sentence	Postponement	Adjournment	Con. Ord. Made	Result
Kelly (Dec. 14, 1999); [2000] 2 CAR(S) 129	DTA	Nov. 8, 1998	Dec. 11, 1998	May 9, 1999[18]	May 10, 1999[19]	July 26, 1999	Quashed[20]
Miranda (Feb. 15, 2000); [2000] CAR(S) 347	CJA	July 6, 1998[21]	**Apr. 1, 1999**	July 6, 1998?[22]	Oct. 1, 1998[23]	**Apr. 1, 1999**	Quashed[24]
Morgan (Mar. 23, 2000) [2000] Crim.L.R. 865	CJA	Mar. 4, 1999	**Sept. 28, 1999**	None	For sentence[25]	**Sept. 28, 1999**	Quashed[26]
Hussain and others (Apr. 18, 2000)	DTA	May 28, 1998	**Jan. 14, 1999**			**Jan. 14, 1999**	Quashed [27]
Turberfield (May 11, 2000)	CJA	July 24, 1998	**July 8, 1999**			**July 8, 1999**	Quashed[28]
Lingham (May 23, 2000); [2000] C.L.R. 696	DTA	June 5, 1998	July 6, 1998[29]	July 6, 1998?[30]	Nov. 20, 1998[31]	Aug. 5, 1999	Upheld[32]
Shevki (Dec. 14, 2000)	DTA	Nov. 12, 1997	Dec. 5, 1997[33]	Dec. 5, 1997[34]		June 12, 1998	Upheld
Steele (Dec 14, 2000)	CJA/DTA	Jan. 20, 1998	Mar. 4, 1998[35]	Mar. 4, 1998	Dec. 9, 1998	Aug. 24, 1999	Quashed[36]

18 Prosecuting counsel phoned judge at home inviting him to postpone hearing. Assumed by all parties that May 9 was one day late (*i.e.* from conviction).
19 Hearing in open court.
20 Too late. Prior to May 9, 1999, there had been **no judicial decision to postpone the confiscation proceedings.**
21 Miranda served with prosecutor's statement on that date.
22 Arguably, the proceedings were postponed from this date (following service of prosecutor's statement) but no application made for further adjournment outside six-month period.
23 Adjourned because judge was unavailable. A series of delays followed.
24 Confiscation proceedings began on July 6, but there was **no application to extend postponed period** for a period in excess of six months.
25 Adjourning for sentence, is not a postponement.
26 There had been **no judicial decision for a postponement**, and thus **no judicial decision to postpone outside the six-month period.**
27 Confiscation order made out of time. **Presumably no judicial order was made for postponing proceedings outside the six-month period.**
28 Notice under CJA 1988, s. 72(1) not given until Apr. 28, 1999. There was **no judicial decision to postpone beyond six-month period.**
29 Confiscation proceedings fixed for Nov. 23, 1998.
30 Arguably the proceedings were postponed on that date, given that confiscation proceedings were fixed for the Nov. 23, 1998.
31 Defendant changed solicitors on Nov. 18. Judge postponed confiscation proceedings on Nov. 20; change of solicitors constituted "exceptional circumstances".
32 There had been a **postponement for a period beyond six months** on the grounds that the change of solicitors constituted "exceptional circumstances".
33 Application made to postpone confiscation proceedings.
34 Judge postpones given exceptional circumstances.
35 Judge rules that as Steele had outstanding matters, the information required for a confiscation order was incomplete, amounting to "exceptional circumstances". The judge ordered a postponement until one month after conclusion of outstanding trial. That trial concluded on Nov. 13, 1998.
36 **No judicial order within one month of Nov. 13, 1998,** to extend period beyond Dec. 13, 1998.

on its task of making determinations under the Act, and a party seeks an adjournment, the reality is that the proceedings have been postponed.

It will be seen that the power to postpone or grant an extension of time (even where the defendant appeals against his conviction) is that of the Crown Court. The Court may order one, or several, postponements providing the total period does not exceed six months from the date of conviction: see subsections (3) and (11). Where the defendant is convicted on more than one indictment (*e.g.* as a result of separate committals or separate trials ordered on severance of an indictment) the period of postponement runs from the last conviction for a drug trafficking offence (see subs. (11) and Standing Committee B, May 27, 1993, col. 62). This applies whether or not the convictions occurred at the same or different Crown Courts.

Section 3 has been given three main meanings. The first is that there is a distinction between a "postponement" and an "adjournment"; that the legislature did not intend section 3 to replace the Court's inherent jurisdiction to manage its own affairs. Therefore, the Court is entitled (so the argument runs) to *adjourn* a Drug Trafficking Act hearing and/or to adjourn sentence, as it sees fit. Postponement, on the other hand, arises only where the Court requires "further information" and for no other reason. The second argument is a variation of the first, namely, that the Court may only postpone for "further information" but the provisions of section 3 replace the Court's usual powers to adjourn proceedings and establishes a timetable, which must be strictly adhered to. That timetable requires all determinations to be made, including the amount to be recovered under a confiscation order, within 6 months. The third meaning is a variation of the second, namely, that section 3 does indeed lay down a timetable for making determinations under the Act, but the Court is not required to conclude Drug Trafficking Act proceedings within six months, merely that the enquiry must be underway within that period. The Court retains the power to adjourn to another date (*e.g.* to resume proceedings) even if that results in a confiscation order being made outside the six-month period.

13–149 All three arguments seem to share the view that there must be a judicial decision, to postpone starting the Drug Trafficking Act hearing outside the six-month period, and only on the grounds that there are "exceptional circumstances" for extending the relevant period.

In Scotland the power to postpone confiscation proceedings exists under section 10 (1) of the Proceeds of Crime (Scotland) Act 1995, which reads

"If the Court considers—

(a) that it has some, but not sufficient, relevant information for the purpose of enabling it to come to a decision as to whether to make a confiscation order; or

(b) that it does not have sufficient relevant information to enable it to come to a decision as to the amount to be payable under the confiscation order,

it may, subject as the case may be to subsection (6) or (10) below, postpone that decision for a period not exceeding 6 months after the date of conviction for the purpose of enabling further information to be obtained."

It will be seen that there are some differences between section 10(1) (Scotland) and section 3(1) DTA (in England)—for example, section 10(1) refers to "some, but not sufficient, relevant information", and in Scotland, there appears to be no power to extend beyond six months in exceptional circumstances.

Section 9(6) of the Proceeds of Crime (Scotland) Act 1995, which is not replicated in the DTA, provides that "without prejudice to section 10(1)" where matters are in dispute, the Court shall consider those matters "at a hearing". Strictly speaking, the DTA does not make any provision for a hearing, and it does not lay down a statutory procedure for conducting one. However, determinations under the DTA can only be made following a hearing and therefore, in England, the practice is to conduct DTA enquiries in a fashion similar to trials on indictment. In England, it is also customary, for the trial judge to conduct confiscation proceedings. However, the Proceeds of Crime (Scotland) Act 1995 envisages that confiscation proceedings may be heard by a judge other than the trial judge. Thus, section 9(7) of that Act empowers the Court to "adjourn the hearing to date when the trial judge is available" if it would be "in interests of injustice to do so". It therefore seems that the Proceeds of Crime (Scotland) Act 1995, draws a distinction between an "adjournment" (section 9(6)) and a "postponed" determination (section 10(1)). Yet, section 9(6) is "without prejudice" to section 10(1).

In *H.M. Lord Advocate v. Donnelly*, G.W.D. November 29, 1996. D 13–150
was convicted on April 18th. Confiscation proceedings were fixed for October 1. D was granted an adjournment until January 6, 1997. The Crown complained that the judge had no power to extend the period beyond six months except in the event of an appeal against conviction. Thus in *Donnelly*, the prosecutor was making the submission often advanced by defending counsel in England. However, the Court rejected the submission, holding that section 10(1) only applied if the Court was considering making a confiscation order based on the evidence before it, and where the evidence was insufficient to make proper determinations. Section 10(1) had no application where allegations were merely being challenged by the defendant, or where the Crown took issue with the defendant. In such a case, the terms of section 9(6), applied. The time-limit specified in section 10(1) of the Proceeds of Crime (Scotland) Act 1995 did not apply to a hearing under section 9(6), and nothing in section 10(1) indicated a restriction on the Court's inherent power to adjourn where necessary in the interests of justice. The basis of D's application was that he required more time to prepare is case.

In England, it is open to either party to apply for a postponement beyond the a six-month period having regard to the complexity of the case, and the enquiries that the parties must make to obtain relevant information. It should be noted that in Scotland the power to postpone determinations has been in existence since 1987 (Criminal Justice (Scotland) Act 1987). In England, the power to postpone first appeared in the Criminal Justice Act 1993 (s. 8 (part)) but that provision was not brought into force until re-enacted in section 3 of the DTA. It seems unlikely that section 3 was enacted as a step towards the harmonisation of confiscation laws in England and Scotland.

In 1991, the Home Office Working Group On Confiscation recommended that "the Court should be empowered to defer decisions of confiscation for up to six months" on the grounds that:

> ". . . the working group was aware of anxiety over delays on sentencing which have been caused by the process of determining confiscation orders. Such delays may have a disturbing effect upon the organisation of court resources, and mean that the judge in passing sentence is cut off in time from the matters considered by the Court in deciding to convict."

13–151 No doubt, the Working Group was well aware of the position in Scotland but the object of section 3 is clearly to minimise the risk of injustice (both to the defence and to the prosecution) caused by delay. There is little purpose in enacting a statutory timetable if that timetable can be circumvented by the simple expedient of the Court exercising its inherent jurisdiction to "adjourn" proceedings—rather than "postponing" them. The fact that the judge is empowered to postpone determinations beyond the six-month period, in "exceptional circumstances", is a clear indication that Parliament intended that the judge should be charged with the task of managing confiscation proceedings, and that there should be a judicial decision on the merits of an application to postpone. In England, unlike Scotland, an application to postpone may exist at two levels: (1) postponing *within* the six-month period, and (2) postponing outside the six-month period where there are "exceptional circumstances". There will be cases where it is appropriate to grant a postponement beyond six months on the first application see section 3(3)(a).

It should also be noted, as the Court recognised in *Steele*, that although time begins to run from the date of conviction (s. 3), confiscation proceedings may be initiated from the moment the defendant appears to be sentenced for a drug trafficking offence (s. 2(1)). Frequently, that will be the moment the defendant has been convicted, but there are numerous cases where a defendant pleads guilty long before he appears before the Crown court to be sentenced: *Stuart v. Bonnett* [1987] 11 Cr. App. R. (S) 819. The distinction is confusing. Thus in *Cole*, Judge L.J. said "the power created by (section 3) is to postpone the determination not to date, but for a period". In *Steele*, Judge L.J. revisited the problem and compared section 3 with section 2 (1), and said:

> "There are of course occasions when the defendant's appearance before the Crown Court for sentence is delayed, sometimes for longer

than six months after conviction. The defendant may have been granted bail pending the preparation of reports, and absconded. The trial of his co-accused may be taking many months. In theory therefore, if time does not start to run until the appearance of the defendant before the Crown Court 'for sentence', it is arguable that even if this appearance were delayed for longer than six months after conviction, on the first occasion of an appearance 'for sentence', the judge could immediately decide that the confiscation proceedings should be postponed for the 'exceptional' reason that the defendant has not appeared for sentence until after the expiry of the six month period. Whatever the merits of this argument, there is an unbroken line of decisions of this court which leads us to the conclusion that it is now too late for orders for postponement to be made after the lapse of six months from conviction.

In any event, notwithstanding the opening words of s.2(1), whenever the Court is considering whether to postpone the determination, the date of conviction remains starkly relevant. The Court may not specify a period which 'exceeds six months beginning with the date of conviction', unless satisfied that the circumstances are 'exceptional'. In short, s.3(3), perhaps rather confusingly, but expressly, imposes its own discipline and this may serve to explain why it appears generally to have been assumed that for the purposes of postponed determinations time starts to run from the date of conviction, irrespective whether the legislation under immediate consideration is the 1994 Act or the 1988 Act, as amended. In our judgment, the opening words of s.3(1) refer to the provision for confiscation orders in s.2 generally rather than the specific words in s.2(1), 'where the defendant . . . appears to be sentenced'. Accordingly, where the Court anticipates that it will not be able to proceed under s.2(1) until after six months from the date of conviction, (for example, because a lengthy trial of co-accused will follow so that sentence will not arise until the end of that trial), the Court should decide there and then that any determination will be postponed until after the end of that trial, and such further period as may be anticipated for the completion of the investigation. There is nothing to preclude the Court from anticipating that the circumstances are or will remain 'exceptional' for more than six months after conviction, and to make an order accordingly, extending the period of postponement until after the conclusion of linked trials, as Hidden J. did in *R v. Steele*. In our judgment postponements in such circumstances would normally fall well within the 'exceptional circumstances' provision."

Judge L.J. reviewed a number of Court of Appeal decisions including *Miranda*, and *Lingham*, and reconciled them. The Court concluded: 13–152

"Confiscation orders should normally form part of the ordinary sentencing process. For lack of appropriate information, this will often be

> impractical. If the conditions in s.3(1) or s.3(4) are satisfied, and within six months of conviction, the Court may decide that the determination should be postponed. Unless the circumstances are exceptional this should not extend beyond six months after conviction. These decisions involve the Court's discretion, judicially exercised when the statutory conditions are present, taking full account of the preferred statutory sequence as well as the express direction in the statute that save in exceptional circumstances confiscation determinations should not be postponed for more than six months after conviction. So far as practicable, adjournments which would have the effect of postponing the determination beyond that period, or in exceptional cases, beyond the period envisaged when the decision to postpone was made, should be avoided. Nevertheless when the circumstances in an individual case compel an adjournment which would have this effect, then whether or not the information gathering process has been completed, it may be ordered, for example, to take account of illness on one side or the other, or the unavailability of the judge, without depriving a subsequent order for confiscation of its validity."

The conclusions of the Court in *Steele* are supported by the detail provided in the schedule (above). It will be seen that in many of the cases (at least until *Kelly*) the decision of the Court proceeded on the basis that time begins to run from the moment of conviction, and that a judicial decision is required to postpone proceedings outside the six-month period. Thus in *Cole*, a judge did postpone proceedings beyond the six-month period albeit on the grounds that the trial judge was unavailable through illness. Similarly, in *France*, the Court postponed confiscation proceedings beyond the six-month period having regard to the complexity of the case. In both cases, the making of the confiscation order was upheld. Of course, the decision in *Cole* could be criticised on the grounds that the reason for the postponement was "illness" and not—as required by section 3—"for further information. However, giving section 3 a purposive construction, it is clearly desirable for the trial judge to deal with determinations under the DTA. On one view, the knowledge of the trial judge is also relevant "information" the purposes of conducting a DTA hearing—which is, ultimately, the judges enquiry.

13–153 **Postponement—a judicial decision or can it be delegated?** In *Cole*, Judge L.J. said that at the decision to postpone outside the six-month period must be a judicial one. The reason being that the judge must decide whether the circumstances, are "exceptional, or not. Judge L.J. said:

> ". . . having studied the statutory code we do not consider that it was intended or drafted so as to preclude the listing officer making sensible arrangements for the conduct of Crown Court business, normally after discussion with the trial judge, if available, or the resident judge provided as we emphasise, that he or she does not purport to postpone the determination beyond his jurisdiction. Arranging a fresh date

> within the statutory period when the judge has already ordered a postponement is not. The only person with authority to order an extension of the statutory period is a judge of the Crown Court."

Earlier in the judgment Judge L.J. said:

> "subject to the statutory procedure in section 3 the ordinary administrative management of the Court's business remains unaffected. It is not without significant that section 3 uses the word 'postponement', a term of art, rather than the very well understood general word 'adjournment'. If it had been intended to interfere with the ordinary administration of court business . . . the legislation would have been differently and far more clearly worded."

It is submitted that Judge L.J. was not saying that despite section 3, the Court may exercise its usual power to adjourn sentencing and confiscation proceedings. He merely said that where a decision was required to postpone within the six-month period, the decision could be taken by the listing officer, normally after discussion with a judge, when the judge has already ordered a postponement. However, only a judge could order a postponed determination outside the six-month period. In *Steele*, Judge L.J., referred to what he had said in *Cole* and remarked:

> "the circumstances in which a postponement may be ordered are provided by . . . section 3 . . . which represents a concession to the requirements for a measure of sensible flexibility rather than a completely new sequence. . . . Nothing in (section 3) creates any express limitation on the Court's ordinary powers to control and manage his own process."

That passage does not fully deal with the issue as to the extent to which 13–154
the listing officer is entitled (on behalf of the Court) to manage the Court business under section 3. Judge L.J. continued:

> "The Court is required to make a positive decision postponing the determination. It does not follow from the fact that an order has not been made, when it might have been, that the order must have been postponed, or be deemed to have been postponed. Mere temporising, delay, or inaction, does not amount to postponement of a determination. In short, following an application from one side or the other, or as a result of the Court acting on its own initiative, for the purposes of section 3, a judicial decision is needed, and unless made within the permitted period (whether for postponement, or for an extension in 'exceptional circumstances') the jurisdiction to make the order for postponement lapses." (emphasis added).

Putting all those passages together, it is submitted that the position is that it is for the judge (preferably the trial judge) to make a judicial decision to postpone determinations under the Act. Only when that is done may a listing officer, after consulting the trial judge (or, if he is unavailable, the resident judge), set another date for the hearing (*e.g.* because of the volume of cases in the list, or the availability of judge/counsel/witnesses).

Consequences where there has not been a judicial decision to postpone

13–155 Applying the above, the result in *Shergill* was inevitable. There was no proper judicial decision that found exceptional circumstances justifying the postponement of determinations outside the six-month period.

It is not possible for a judge to seek to rescue the position by ruling that, had an application be made at the proper time, he would have found that there were exceptional circumstances justifying a postponed determination: *Edwards*; and see *Khan* and *Kelly*.

13–156 **Giving reasons for a postponement is to be preferred** In *Tuegal*, the Crown had applied for an extension of time outside the six-month period, which the defence did not "resist" and the judge indicated "his 'inclination' that there were special circumstances" (*per* Rose L.J.). The Court upheld the making of the confiscation order on the grounds that there had been a judicial decision to extend the period, and added:

> "there is no statutory obligation on the judge so to spell out his reasons, provided that he is satisfied that they exist; but clearly it avoids subsequent difficulties if a judge expressly spells out what the exceptional circumstances are".

There is a risk that, in failing to give reasons, the so-called "postponement" will be deemed to be "mere temporising, delay, or inaction" : note the words of Judge L.J. in *Steele* (see above). In *Kelly*, Laws L.J. said:

> "nothing is plainer than that postponement . . . is constituted . . . by a judicial decision, unless there is something wholly exceptional, the must be done in open court, *and reasons given for it*". (emphasis added)

The Court, in *Steele*, doubted whether Laws L.J. would have added those last few words had his attention been drawn to the remarks of Rose L.J. (cited above) in *Tuegal*. Judge L.J. added:

> ". . . the failure of the judge expressly to identify exceptional circumstances does not automatically vitiate his decision provided (1) they are indeed obvious. . . . And provided also that a judicial decision to postpone was made accordingly within the six-month period."

It will be noted that Laws L.J. said, in *Kelly*, that the decision should be made in open court—"unless there is something wholly exceptional". Obviously, the rules of natural justice must be adhered to. However, there is perhaps one exception to the usual requirement that a decision to postpone is to be made in open court—and that is where the parties apply in writing for a postponement, and the judge without a hearing concludes that there are exceptional circumstances justifying that course. This was the situation in *France*. It will be noted that even in that situation the judge must apply his mind as to whether there are "exceptional circumstances" justifying a postponement. It is not enough merely to say that the Court requires "further information": *Forde* (February 7, 2000).

In *Miranda* the Court said :

> ". . . postponement under section 72A (Criminal Justice Act 1988) was made here even though neither the Court nor the parties may have focused on that section . . . "

It is submitted that the Court should focus on the section.

Does "postponement" replace the power to "adjourn"? It has been argued that a judge is entitled to "adjourn" sentence and to "adjourn" confiscation proceedings as well. It will be seen from the schedule, that in at least five cases (*Ward, Miranda, Morgan, Hussain*, and *Turberfield*) the confiscation order was made on the same date as sentence was imposed for the offence. The argument runs that in such cases, section 3 is not engaged at all because that section applies only if the Court requires "further information". This is an attractive argument but (for the reasons expressed earlier) it does not address the concerns of the Legislature, or the Home Office Working Group On Confiscation, that delay—however caused—may result in distress, and injustice. It was to deal with those concerns that section 3 was enacted. 13–157

In *Kelly*, the defendant was convicted on the November 8, 1998, and sentenced on December 11. Before K was sentenced, prosecuting counsel indicated to the judge the Crown's intention to institute confiscation proceedings against K. On May 9, 1999, prosecuting counsel telephoned the judge at home asking that proceedings be postponed on the grounds of illness of a co-defendant. On May 10, the judge in open court confirmed the decision he had made on the May 9. The defendant complained that the decision, on May 10, was too late (beyond the six-month period). Proceedings had not been postponed on the December 11 (and no judicial decision had been involved) and the judge did not sit in open court on May 9.

It is to be noted that in *Kelly*, the reasons for not embarking on a DTA hearing, shortly after K was convicted, was because it was the "common understanding of all counsel that any question of confiscation orders should be dealt with and resolved after all outstanding trials". On one view, it could be said that the DTA determinations were not postponed for "further information" to be obtained, but that the Court merely adjourned proceedings until the conclusion of outstanding trials, and therefore there was no question of section 3 being engaged at all. This point was not advanced by the Crown, and it is difficult to see how it could have been, given that the prosecution and the judge asserted that there had been a postponement on the December 11 and on May 9. The prosecution contention was that section 3 was engaged and complied with. The Court of Appeal agreed with the first limb of the argument, but rejected the second limb. If section 3 did not apply—because the Court did not require further information—then it seems that the Court was not consciously exercising is usual power to adjourn either.

13–158 In *Miranda*, sentence and confiscation were dealt with on the same date, almost nine months after the date of Miranda's conviction. The case had to be decided under Part VI of the Criminal Justice Act 1988 (before that Act was amended by the Proceeds of Crime Act 1995). Thus in *Miranda's case*, the judge had a discretion (a) as to whether to initiate proceedings; (b) as to whether to make a confiscation order or not; and (c) whether to postpone determination for the purpose of obtaining further information pursuant to section 72A of the Criminal Justice Act 1988 (inserted into Pt VI of the Criminal Justice Act 1988, by the Criminal Justice Act 1993). The Crown argued that the first task of the judge was to decide whether he was going to embark on confiscation proceedings at all. He had not got as far as deciding whether he required further information and therefore section 72A did not apply. The Crown further argued that a distinction must be drawn between a postponement for further information, and a simple adjournment of sentencing, which of necessity involves adjourning the confiscation enquiry as well. The Court held that as soon as the Court began to inquire whether to make a confiscation order or not, it was acting under section 71 of the Criminal Justice Act 1988, and therefore time, for the purposes of section 72A (similar to section 3 of the DTA), ran from that moment. The Court took that first step on the day the defendant pleaded guilty. The Court did not adjourn sentencing the defendant with the coincidental effect of adjourning confiscation proceedings as well. The confiscation proceedings had to be adjourned for further determinations. No application had been made for a postponement beyond the six-month period and the confiscation order was quashed.

Example:
Suppose D pleads guilty to a drug trafficking offence. Under the DTA, the prosecution has a discretion as to whether or not to initiate confiscation proceedings against D. The case is adjourned for five months to enable the prosecution to decide whether it wishes the Court to hold a DTA hearing. In such a case, what the Court *cannot* do is to sentence D first, and then decide that it wishes to initiate confiscation proceedings: *Ross* (March 13, 2001). It can only sentence first, if it acts under section 2 of the Drug Trafficking Act, and postpones "making the determination" under section 3: see section 3(7). Assume now that, after a period of five months, the prosecution does ask the Court to proceed under section 2. The Court has one month to start making determinations under the Drug Trafficking Act. If the Court wishes to postpone making determinations to obtain further information then it must comply with section 3, but the clock started running from the date of D's conviction. If the Court postpones outside the six-month period (but not on the grounds that there are exceptional circumstances), then a confiscation order made beyond the six-month period will be time barred.

13–159 In *Miranda*, the Court appears to have accepted that section 72A (and thus section 3 of the DTA) has introduced a tight timetable that substantially cuts across the Court's usual power to adjourn. In *Lingham*, the Court of Appeal cited *Cole, France, Shergill*, and *Edwards*, and said that none of them "was a case in which the Court was considering the extent to which subsections (1) and (3) have replaced the Crown court's inherent powers or their ambit as we have done". The Court referred to *Ward* and said "... a two-judge court assumed the point had been considered in earlier cases, but it had not been". That may be so, but it is by no means obvious that the Court, in *Ward*, did make that assumption. The Court merely said that it was not persuaded that the Court in *Cole*, and in *Akpan*, overlooked the phrase "(postponing) for the purpose of enabling that information to be obtained", and thus the Court did not accept the Crown submission that an adjournment was the appropriate administrative step on the facts in that case.

In many of the judgments before *Miranda*, there may have been an underlying assumption that section 3 changes the usual order of things, and restricts the Court power to adjourn. In *Lingham*, L was convicted on June 5, 1998, and sentenced a month later. The DTA hearing was fixed for November 23—within the six-month period. However L changed his solicitors, and on November 20 the judge (concluding that there were exceptional circumstances) postponed the DTA hearing until April 12, 1999. It is submitted that November 20 is a crucial date that the reader should keep in mind. The November 20 was within the six-month period; there was a judicial decision to postpone the proceedings, and the circumstances for doing so were found by the judge to be exceptional. What happened thereafter was that in March, the judge was unavailable, and May 7 was fixed for the hearing. L submitted that the making of the determinations was time-barred. The judge rejected the submission. During the appeal, there appears to have been much discussion about the significance of the events in March when the DTA hearing was further postponed. However, the hearing was postponed outside the six-month period back in November. Section 3 does not tell us what should happen once proceedings are postponed beyond that period. Both in *Lingham* and in *Steele* (and some extent in *Cole*) the Court concluded that section 3 does not *entirely remove* the inherent powers of the Court to manage a DTA hearing: not entirely, but to a large extent section 3 does have that effect. In *Lingham* the Court of Appeal held that the decision of the Crown Court in March 1999, was not one to which section 3 applied save indirectly. It is submitted that *Lingham* is not authority for the proposition that the Court is free to adjourn both sentence and confiscation for a period longer than six months if it wishes to do so. If the judge had not made a judicial decision in November 1998 to postpone, for the exceptional reasons he gave, the result in *Lingham* would surely have been very different. As Judge L.J. said in *Steele*, the "preferred statutory sequence" is as set out in section 3. It is recognised that *Lingham* could be read as holding that the confiscation order was correctly made because section 3 did not apply at all: see *Archbold News*, March 12, 2001, p.5. Apart from the simplest of cases, it will be unusual for the Court to be in a position to make determinations immediately upon conviction without requiring further information. The expression "further information" should not be narrowly construed, and the parties should not seek to circumvent the statutory timetable, by cloaking applications as "adjournments".

13–160 **Must confiscation proceedings start or end within six months?** In *Lingham*, the Court had to consider whether the Court had to finalise the "amount to be recovered" under the Act within the six-month period. The Court answered that question in the negative. In earlier editions of this work, the answer was left open although it was suggested that adjournments, taking proceedings outside the six-month period, were probably "postponements" for the purposes of section 3. In *Lingham*, the Court said:

> "... the subsections nowhere say in terms that a determination of a confiscation application must be made within six months of confiscation, unless for exceptional reasons, further time is allowed. Nor do they say, in terms, that a determination must be made within six months of conviction unless, for exceptional reasons, further time is allowed because the Court considers it needs more information ... "

The problem here is that it cannot be assumed that the legislature drafted section 3 blessed with the foresight necessary to anticipate the range of situations the Courts have in fact considered. Section 3 does say, in terms, "make *the determination*". "The determination" can be (1) whether the defendant has benefited from drug trafficking, and (2) determining the "amount to be recovered". The amount to be recovered is the last determination the Court must make pursuant to section 2(4) and section 5 of the Act. It is not obvious whether Parliament intended that section 3 should mean that "making the determination may not be postponed beyond the six-month period save where more information is required and then only in exceptional circumstances" (meaning 1), or "the determination may not be delayed beyond the six-month period, when the purpose of the delay is to obtain more information and then, only in exceptional circumstances" (meaning 2). In *Lingham*, the Court preferred meaning 2.

13–161 However, it will be seen that section 3 does not use the phrase "the determination may not be delayed" but it does speak of "making the determination". It is therefore unsurprising that section 3 has not been easy to construe and some courts have, it is admitted, regarded the first meaning as being the correct one: see, for example *Cole*. In *Forde*, the Court said:

> "... section 72A lays down a strict timetable to be complied with and unless there are exceptional circumstances, the period of six months in total should not be exceeded between the date of conviction at the start, and the determination of the amount be recovered at the end."

There are, however, strong policy reasons to support the adoption of the second meaning for the reasons given by Judge L.J. in *Steele*:

> "Stripped to essentials, the fundamental question was whether the lim-

ited circumstances under which the postponement could be ordered under s3(1) (further information) carried with it a mandatory obligation on the Court to ensure that the confiscation proceedings were concluded immediately the required information was available. This approach would mean that in the ordinary case, once all the relevant information had been collected and was under consideration by the Court within the six month period, if the hearing went on rather longer than anticipated, an adjournment overnight to the day after the end of the six month period would be impermissible, or rather pointless, because time would lapse. An adjournment before the date fixed for hearing, or indeed part heard, for any of the many, sometimes compelling reasons, with which we are all familiar, would imperil the validity of the confiscation proceedings. The potential for and the advantages of deliberate mischief-making would multiply. In *Lingham*, focusing on the realities, it was held that the Crown Court had not been deprived of its 'inherent powers' over its own proceedings and was entitled to make its own decisions about when applications should be heard, and whether and in what circumstances adjournments should be ordered."

There will be cases where it is inappropriate to sentence first, and then to embark on confiscation proceedings. Where the Court wishes to consider making substantial financial orders, *e.g.* fines, or compensation, the better course is to sentence after confiscation determinations have been made: see *Williams* (March 24, 1998).

(f) Steps on the way to making an order

There are three determinations that the Court is likely to make under the Act: **13–162**

(i) *Benefit: has the defendant benefited from drug trafficking?*

(a) Formerly, the persuasive burden was on the prosecution to prove this issue to the criminal law standard of proof: see *Dickens* [1990] 2 Q.B. 102; *Enwezor* (1991) 93 Cr.App.R. 233. The persuasive burden remains on the prosecution but to the civil standard (see s.2(8) of the 1994 Act). Accordingly, *Dickens* and *Enwezor* are overruled on this point.
(b) The Court was empowered (but not obliged) to make any of the statutory assumptions contained in s.2(2) and (3) of the 1986 Act. The burden of rebuttal was on the defendant: see *Dickens* and *Enwezor*, above, and *Redbourne* (1992) 1 W.L.R. 1182, *Chandler* (May 21, 1993) and *Khan* (February 26, 1996); and see *Finch* 14 Cr.App.R.(S.) 226. The Court must now make the "required assumption" unless the statutory exceptions apply (see s.4(2)–(5) of the 1994 Act).

(ii) *Value of the proceeds*

13–163 If question (i) is answered affirmatively, then the Court proceeds to assess the value of the proceeds of drug trafficking received by the defendant because this is prima facie the "amount to be recovered" under the Act: see section 5(1). Whereas, under the old law, the Court could make a nil order, or no order (different courts seem to have had differing views about whether they should make a nil order or no order) now the Court is required to make a confiscation order for at least a "nominal amount" (s.5(3)(b)). Accordingly, if the Court wishes to make, literally, no order, then unless the prosecutor has asked the Court to proceed under s.2 of the 1994 Act, the Court should not embark upon confiscation proceedings at all.

(iii) *Amount that might be realised*

13–164 Frequently, the amount the defendant is able to pay (or is able to realise) is less than the full value of his proceeds of drug trafficking. This lower figure is termed the "amount that might be realised" and it is this figure that becomes the "amount to be recovered under a confiscation order".

The following points should be noted in determining the "amount to be recovered" and the "amount that might be realised":

(a) The value of the defendant's proceeds represents prima facie the "amount to be recovered" under a confiscation order: s.5(1).
(b) The persuasive burden of proving benefit remains on the prosecution but now only to the civil standard of proof (s.2(8)).
(c) Under the 1994 Act, the "required assumptions" must be made unless the statutory exceptions apply (s.4(2)–(5)).
(d) The Court can be asked (or decide of its volition) to assess the "amount that might be realised" under s.5(3) as defined by s.6(1), being the total value of realisable property held by the defendant plus the total value of gifts made by him and caught by the Act: ss.5(3), 6(1) and 8.
(e) Previously, if the defendant satisfied the Court on a balance of probabilities that the "amount that might be realised" was less than the "amount to be recovered" then the Court confiscated the lesser amount: see s.4(3) of the 1986 Act. See *Ilsemann* (1990) 12 Cr.App.R.(S) 398; *Comiskey* (1991) 93 Cr.App.R. 227; and *Carroll* (1992) 13 Cr.App.R.(S) 99. The judge issued a certificate recording that finding of fact: s.4(2) of the 1986 Act.

    This remains the position under the new procedure by virtue of s.5(3) and s.5(2) but the 1994 Act, like its predecessor, says nothing about the incidence of proof, presumably because the position is likely to be regarded as covered by authority: *e.g. Ilsemann* and *Comiskey* and *Barwick*, above.
(f) If the defendant fails to discharge the burden on him, or failed to raise the issue at all, then the Court may make a confiscation order for the full amount determined under steps (1) and (2) above: but

see *Comiskey* (above) and *Keston* (1990) 12 Cr.App.R.(S) 93 (wrongly referred to as "*Preston*" in [1990] Crim.L.R. 528).

(g) Enforcement of a confiscation order as a fine

The Court treats the confiscation order as a fine and imposes a sentence of imprisonment in default: section 9. Unlike the old law (under the 1986 Act) if the defendant serves a sentence of imprisonment in default, the Court may still proceed to enforce payment of the confiscation order: see section 9(5) and see the commentary to section 9 below. Terms of imprisonment imposed in default are maximum terms—there are no minimum terms: *Szrajber* (1994) Cr.App.R.(S) 821; *French* (1995) 16 Cr.App.R.(S) 841. In *Stuart and Bonnett* (1989) 11 Cr.App.R.(S) 89, the judge declined to make a confiscation order in the sum of £2,500 which was found in the defendant's possession at the time of his arrest on the grounds that to be obliged to impose a term of imprisonment in default of payment when the police already seized the money was "unnecessary and illogical". The Court of Appeal held that the Court had no option but to follow the steps under the (DTOA). Although it is easy to empathise with the judge, the fact is that a confiscation order, which would be immediately satisfied upon property being released by the police or customs and excise, should expose the defendant to no risk of serving any such default term. 13–165

It should be remembered that property retained by police, which is found by the Court to be all or part of the defendant's benefit from drug trafficking, will also represent his realisable property. There have been cases where the customs and excise forfeited property under the CEMA 1979 and which was condemned long before the confiscation order was made, but the Court when making the confiscation order was unaware of that fact. The effect is that the forfeited property is no longer realisable and therefore (i) if the defendant's only asset is the property forfeited by the customs and excise the confiscation order should be reduced in value, but (ii) if the defendant does have other legitimately acquired assets which would satisfy the order he will be obliged to make full payment. This can produced harsh results, for example, D imports cannabis in a boat whereupon the vessel is forfeited by customs. The boat is worth £15,000 and it was not bought from the proceeds of drug trafficking. Nevertheless, D received a payment of £10,000 as a reward for his assistance in the venture. The Court learns that the value of D's interest in a house is worth £15,000. In those circumstances, the Court may still make a confiscation order in the sum of £10,000 on the basis that D has sufficient realisable assets, *i.e.* the value of D's interest in the house. The boat is no longer realisable in D's hands and there is, as yet, no authority that would entitle D to set off the value of the boat against the sum due under the confiscation order.

Terms of imprisonment in default of payment are ECHR/HRA complaint: *Arman* (May 9, 2000).

(h) Application of the civil standard of proof

13–166 This is now dealt with by virtue of section 2(8) which provides that:

> "2(8) The standard of proof required to determine any question arising under this Act as to—
> (a) whether a person has benefited from drug trafficking, or
> (b) the amount to be recovered in his case by virtue of this section, shall be that applicable in civil proceedings."

The effect of s.2(8) is to overrule the decisions of *Dickens* [1990] 2 Q.B. 102 and *Enwezor* (1991) 93 Cr.App.R. 233 insofar as they held that the criminal standard of proof applied at any stage of the proceedings (Hansard, HL, vol. 539, col. 1383).

The Home Office Working Group in their Report on the Drug Trafficking Offences Act 1986 (1991) recommended that the civil standard of proof was the appropriate one. This seems to have been the Government's intention when the Drug Trafficking Offences Bill was introduced into the House of Lords. Lord Glenarthur (in proposing what became s.2 of the 1986 Act; now see s.4 of this Act) said:

> "The burden will remain on the prosecution, in the usual way, to prove beyond reasonable doubt that the defendant is guilty of the offence of which he is charged. *Once a person has been convicted* of a drug trafficking offence however, *the onus may be placed on him to show which, if any, of his assets were legitimately acquired*. . . . Such information is, however, very clearly within the knowledge of the offender. . . ." Hansard, HL vol. 472, col. 92. (emphasis added).

This approach is permitted by "Article 7 of the Vienna Convention 1988 which provides that "Each Party may consider ensuring that the onus of proof be reversed regarding the lawful origin of alleged proceeds or other property liable to confiscation, to the extent that such action is consistent with the principles of its domestic law and with the nature of the judicial and other proceedings"—but see Article 6.2 of the ECHR/Human Rights Act 1998.

13–167 The views of the Working Group are in marked contrast to the Home Affairs Committee who (in their 7th Report, Drug Trafficking and Related Serious Crime (1989)), accepted that a shift to the civil standard of proof would represent a "far reaching change in English criminal law" and required further evidence of its necessity. The National Drugs Intelligence Co-ordinator did not "appear to favour this solution" (para.8.2). The Home Office Affairs Committee recommended that the Home Office set up a Working Group whose membership consisted of representatives from the Home Office, H.M. Customs and Excise, the National Drugs Intelligence Unit, the Crown Prosecution Service and members representing the Association of Chief Police Officers. The views of the Criminal Bar Association were sought by the Home Office upon publication of the 1991 Report. For their part, the Criminal Bar Association expressed disquiet at such a shift.

The views of other interested parties and bodies were also sought by the Home Office. It is apparent that at least one judge endorsed the recommendation of the Working Group that the civil standard should apply to decide whether the defendant benefited from drug trafficking, and the amount of the benefit, and that the Court should make the assumptions in all cases unless they are rebutted by the defendant (Standing Committee B, June 8, 1993, col. 79). It is not clear to what extent this represented the views of the majority of the judiciary.

It is difficult to test objectively (rather than merely by anecdotal accounts) whether the criminal standard of proof made the task of confiscating drug proceeds more difficult in practice. Certainly, the result in *Enwezor* (1991) 93 Cr.App.R. 233 would have been different if the civil standard applied, but in the majority of cases, the task of the prosecution was "considerably lightened" by the assumption that the Court could make (see Lord Lane C.J. in *Dickens* [1990] 2 Q.B.102). That task is lightened further given the mandatory effect of s.4(2)–(5) of this Act. Note that an assumption made under s.4(3) of the 1994 Act proceeds on the basis that the payment or expenditure was received or made in connection with drug trafficking carried on by the defendant and by no one else. The making of an assumption results in a grave finding of fact and thus, given both the consequences of such a finding, as well as the stigma which it inevitably attracts, it is conceivable that the Courts will require a high degree of probability in any event. As Lord Ackner pointed out during the debates in respect of Part II of the 1993 Act, proof on the civil standard varies in its weight according to what has to be proved (Hansard, HL, vol. 540, col. 1472) and see the judgment of Denning L.J. in *Bater v. Bater* [1951] P.35, at 36–37, and see *Blyth v. Blyth (No. 2)* [1966] A.C. 643; and see also *Kebilene* [1999] 3 W.L.R. 972; and see the opinion of Lord Hope.

A proposed amendment to the Criminal Justice Bill, (now the 1993 Act) **13–168**
substituting the phrase "a balance of probabilities" in place of "the civil standard", was withdrawn (Hansard, HL, vol. 540, col. 1474). It may be said that the standard of proof is irrelevant if the Court makes any of the statutory assumptions because a fact assumed, and not rebutted, remains a fact proved. However, it will be recalled that by section 4(4)(b) of the Drug Trafficking Act, the Court is duty bound not to make a statutory assumption if the Court is satisfied that there would be a "serious risk of injustice in the defendant's case if the assumption were to be made". But what is meant by a "serious risk of injustice"? An assessment of the "risk" must depend to some extent on the standard of proof which the party making the allegation shoulders having regard to the nature of the allegations sought to be proved.

Note that the "amount to be recovered" is a term of art employed in s.2(4) and s.5(3) of this Act. That term is to be distinguished from the "amount that might be realised" which is another term of art—employed in ss.5(3) and 6(1). Given that the "amount to be recovered" could be assessed to be the "amount that might be realised" it follows that any question as to the standard of proof applicable to an assessment under s.5(3) is the civil standard by virtue of s.2(8).

(i) Variation or discharge of a confiscation order

13–169 In a proper case, the Court may vary or discharge the confiscation order. The powers of the Court in this regard have been substantially widened and strengthened under the 1994 Act, thus:

(a) formerly only a defendant could vary an order under s.14 of the 1986 Act (now s.17 of the 1994 Act), but now a receiver appointed under ss.26 or 29 of the 1994 Act may also apply under s.17(1) to vary or to discharge the confiscation order;
(b) third parties may now make representations to the Court in section 17 proceedings (certificates of inadequacy, s.17(5)) and where a receiver is empowered to realise property (s. 29(8));
(c) a court now has power to (i) make a confiscation order where, the evidence did not, originally, justify the making of such an order: s.13(2); (ii) re-assess whether the defendant has benefited from drug trafficking: s.14; and (iii) revise its assessment of the value of the defendant's proceeds of drug trafficking: s.15;
(d) the Court also has power to increase the amount which a defendant may be ordered to pay under a confiscation order: s.16 (which re-enacts s.16 of the Criminal Justice (International Co-operation) Act 1990).
The Court of Appeal has advised judges to state the relevant findings at each stage of the proceedings, *per* Neill L.J. in *Johnson* [1991] 2 Q.B. 249 at p. 260.

(j) Confiscating assets of the absconder or the deceased

13–170 In 1991 a Home Office Working Group made various recommendations regarding the application of the 1986 Act to persons charged with, or convicted of, a drug trafficking offence but who either died or absconded before a confiscation order could be made against them. A number of amendments were made to the 1986 Act by the CJA 1993, Pt II, to give effect to some of the recommendations, but in the event, none of those amendments came into force. They are now re-enacted in sections 19–24 of the 1994 Act. By virtue of those provisions the High Court may make a confiscation order in the case of a defendant (charged with a drug trafficking offence) who absconds for a period of two years—whether convicted or not—and a power of confiscation in the case of a defendant who is convicted of a drug trafficking offence but who dies before the Crown Court can make a confiscation order. For these purposes, no statutory assumptions may be made pursuant to s.4(2) of the Act (see s.19(6)(a)) and, in the case of an absconder, the Court shall not make a confiscation order unless it is satisfied that the prosecutor has taken reasonable steps to contact him (s.19(6)(c)). The Court may also hear representations from third parties who are "likely to be affected by the making of a confiscation order by the Court" (s.19(6)(d)); and see *Norris* (June 28, 2001, HL). If the High Court decides not to make a confiscation order in respect of an absconder, the prosecution are not entitled to re-open the matter under s.14 of the 1994 Act if they come into possession of evidence which had not been considered by the Court until the absconder returns: see s.19(9). Similarly, the High Court has no power to revise any assessment of the absconder's proceeds of drug trafficking whilst he remains an absconder: see ss.15 and 19(10). The defendant who ceases to be an absconder may apply for a variation of a confiscation order made under section 19 within a period of six years from the date the order was made: see s.21.

(k) Receivers; charging orders and compensation

Upon the making of a confiscation order, the prosecution may ask the High Court to appoint a receiver to realise assets that are held either by the defendant, or by persons to whom the defendant has directly or indirectly made a "gift" for the purposes of the Act: see ss.6 and 29; and see para. 13–318. Property realised by the receiver may then be applied towards satisfying the order: see ss.30 and 31. Special rules will apply in the case of any person (not just the defendant) who is adjudged to be bankrupt but who nevertheless holds "realisable property": see ss.32 and 33. Special rules also apply to companies which are in the process of being wound up but which possess realisable property: s.34. **13–171**

In order to avoid the risk that a defendant may be tempted to dispose of his assets before a court can confiscate them, the High Court is empowered, upon the application of the prosecutor, to grant a restraint order prohibiting any person from dealing with "realisable property" except as directed by the Court: ss.25 and 26. Furthermore, a receiver may be appointed to take possession of any realisable property and to manage or to deal otherwise with that property: s.26(7).

It is desirable, in cases where a confiscation order has not yet been made, to register a charge on the property to secure the payment of moneys to the Crown. The 1994 Act provides the necessary machinery for doing so by virtue of s.27 (see, formerly, s.9 of the 1986 Act). Accordingly, the High Court may, upon the application of the prosecutor, grant a charging order (ex parte if necessary) and may appoint a Receiver to take possession of the property: s.29.

If a defendant is aggrieved that the prosecution has detrimentally meddled in his financial affairs, and proceedings do not result in a conviction for a drug trafficking offence, he may apply to the High Court for an order of compensation to be paid to him: ss.18 and 22. For the purposes of s.18 there must be "serious default" on the part of a person concerned in the investigation or prosecution of the offence in question resulting in the loss but "the Court shall not order compensation to be paid in any case where it appears to the Court that the proceedings would have been instituted or continued even if the serious default had not occurred" (see s.18(3); formerly para.12 to Sched.5, Criminal Justice Act 1988 amending s.19 of the 1986 Act). It is no longer necessary to show that the loss is "substantial". The "amount of compensation shall be such as the High Court thinks just in all the circumstances of the case": s.18(4).

(l) Offences relevant to Part III and Part IV of the 1994 Act

13–172 For a detailed discussion of these offences, see para. 13–340. In summary, the relevant offences are now:

(a) Assisting another to retain the benefit of drug trafficking "knowing or suspecting" that the assisted person is a drug trafficker or someone who has benefited from drug trafficking: s.50, formerly s.24 of the 1986 Act;
(b) Prejudicing investigations: s.58, formerly s.31 of the 1986 Act;
(c) Concealing, disguising, transferring or removing the proceeds of drug trafficking the offence being committed by the trafficker himself: s.49(1), formerly s.14 of the Criminal Justice (International Co-operation) Act 1990;
(d) Concealing, disguising, transferring or removing the proceeds of drug trafficking the offence being committed by another who assists any person to avoid prosecution for a drug trafficking offence or the making or enforcement of a confiscation order: s.49(2);
(e) Acquisition, possession or use of proceeds of drug trafficking: s.51 of the 1994 Act (formerly s.23A of the 1986 Act inserted by s.16 of the 1993 Act);
(f) Failing to disclose knowledge of suspicion of money laundering: s.52;
(g) Disclosing information to another that is likely to prejudice an investigation or proposed investigation: s.53.

(m) Appeals—no power to remit to Crown Court

13–173 Note that where the Court of Appeal quashes a confiscation order, it has no power to remit the case back to the Crown Court for a rehearing: see *Guppy* (July 12, 2000).

(n) The Scottish approach

13–174 Most of the provisions of the DTOA 1986 did not apply to Scotland. A Bill to recover the proceeds of drug trafficking was considered by the Scottish Grand Committee and the First Scottish Standing Committee in 1987. Scotland proceeded to enact its own machinery for the confiscation of the proceeds of drug trafficking under the provisions of the Criminal Justice (Scotland) Act 1987. The 1987 Act operated in a very different way to the

DTOA. For example, the power to make a confiscation order was always discretionary in Scotland and if a confiscation order was made, it was for such amount as the Court considered appropriate.

Similarly, most of the provisions of Part I of the DTA 1994 (confiscation orders) do not extend to Scotland but Part II does do so (drug trafficking cash imported or exported). However, during 1995, the pace of legislative change in Scotland markedly increased. Following the Report of the Scottish Law Commission No.147, Part II of the Criminal Justice (Scotland) Act 1995 received its Royal Assent on July 19, 1995. Its purpose was to extend the powers of the Courts to the confiscation of the proceeds of crime other than drug trafficking or financial assistance for terrorism. But Part II was short-lived: its provisions have been consolidated by the Proceeds of Crime (Scotland) Act 1995 (c.43) which received Royal Assent on November 8, 1995. That Act does apply to drug trafficking offences and accordingly the machinery for making a confiscation order in Scotland is now to be found in that Act which came into force on April 1, 1996: see section 50(2).

The main provisions relating to the making of a confiscation order in Scotland may be summarised as follows: **13–175**

(1) the Court may embark on confiscation proceedings on the application of the prosecutor: section 1(1);
(2) the amount which the defendant can be ordered to pay under a confiscation order shall be "such sum as the Court thinks fit": section 1(1); and must not exceed either the value of the defendant's proceeds of drug trafficking or the "amount that might be realised" (if less): section 1(5);
(3) the standard of proof is the *criminal* standard of proof;
(4) all payments or rewards received by the defendant in connection with drug trafficking carried on by him or by another are his proceeds of drug trafficking: section 3(1);
(5) the Court may make statutory assumptions (note the discretion) except where they are shown to be incorrect in the defendant's case: section 3(2);
(6) statements relevant to the making of a confiscation order may be lodged by the prosecutor or by the defence: section 9;
(7) a determination under the Act may be postponed in order to obtain further information: section 10;
(8) if a confiscation order is made and it comes to light that the value of the defendant's proceeds of drug trafficking (or the amount that might be realised) is greater than first believed, the prosecutor may apply for a new confiscation order to be made: section 11;
(9) a confiscation order may be varied where the defendant's realisable property is inadequate to meet his payments under the order: section 12;
(10) interest may be added to the value of the confiscation order on sums unpaid: section 15;
(11) compensation may be awarded in certain cases: section 17.

Again, on April 1 1996, the Criminal Law (Consolidation) (Scotland) Act 1995 came into force; it creates offences that broadly mirror sections 50–53 of the DTA (offences in connection with the proceeds of drug trafficking; see sections 37–40 of the CL(C)(S)A 1995) and also creates the offence of prejudicing an investigation (see s.36 of the 1995 Act and compare with s.58 of the DTA).

D. BENEFIT

I. DETERMINATION OF "BENEFIT"

13–176 The Court must first determine whether the defendant has "benefited" from drug trafficking. If it is obvious that the defendant has obtained no benefit then nothing is to be gained by expending court time and money proceeding any further. The legislature may have originally contemplated that cases in which there was no discernible benefit would be weeded out speedily and expeditiously. It frequently happened that the prosecution indicated to the Court, upon conviction, that the defendant received no benefit or, even if he did, that his realisable assets were nil and the Court was invited to make a nil confiscation order.

In *Dickens* (1990) 2 Q.B. 102, Lord Lane C.J. said at 106:

> "... the judge has to make a preliminary assessment as to whether it is or is likely to be a 'benefit' case or not. No doubt the evidence from the trial, if there has been one, or from a recital of the facts if there has been a plea, will be enough for him to form such a preliminary assessment."

This approach did not always find favour with the judiciary on the grounds that it was for the Court to determine in every case whether the accused benefited from drug trafficking, and this the Court could only do if it was fully informed of the defendant's financial affairs during the relevant period.

13–177 The Home Office Working Group (1991) was unanimously in favour of the continuation of mandatory confiscation orders (para. 2.5) but suggested that the way in which the Court determines whether to invoke the assumptions should be reformed. They considered that one approach would be to provide that

> "once an individual had been convicted of drug trafficking, the Court should be required to assume that all property appearing to it to be in his possession (or which appears to have passed through his hands over the last six years etc.) represents the proceeds of drug trafficking. Only the application of the prosecutor could relieve the Court from the requirement to make these assumptions although the Court would retain the discretion to make the assumptions if it wished, even if the prosecutor recommended against. Once the

> assumptions had been made, it would be up to the defendant to seek to persuade the Court that the assumptions were inappropriate, either in regard to the whole of his property or specific items of it." (emphasis added; para. 2.6)

However, notwithstanding the view of the Home Office Working Group, it is plain that the amendments made by the 1993 Criminal Justice Act, and re-enacted in the 1994 Act, do not give effect to their proposals in either paras 2.5 or 2.6. The prosecutor has a limited discretion by virtue of s.2(1) as to whether to ask the Court to proceed under the Act but the prosecutor has no power to apply to "relieve the Court from the requirements to make (the) assumptions": see s.4(2). Furthermore, the effect of s.2(1) is exactly the opposite of the mandatory system for making confiscation orders recommended by the Home Office Working Group.

The Working Party also recommended that the Drug Trafficking Offences Act 1986 should be amended

> ". . . to ensure that the Court would make the assumptions in all cases, unless satisfied, from arguments produced by the defendant or any other information available to it, either during the trial or otherwise, that it would be inappropriate to do so. An example would be a minor or trivial case, such that confiscation proceedings would not, in the judge's view, be warranted. The judge would, of course, not apply the assumptions where it was obvious that they were incorrect. Where the Court concluded that the assumptions should not be applied, it would be required to state its reasons and those reasons would be subject to challenge in a higher court." (para. 2.8)

However, the recommendations of the Working Party do not seem to 13–178
have been accepted on this point because the making of assumptions are now mandatory (see s.4(2)) and may only be disapplied in two sets of circumstances, neither of which appear to be broad enough to entitle a judge not to make any of the assumptions merely because the procedure would not, in the judge's view, be warranted or would be unfair.

Thus, the Court must make the assumptions unless (i) the assumption in question is shown to be incorrect in the defendant's case (s.4(4)(a)), or (ii) the Court is satisfied that there would be a serious risk of injustice in his case if the assumption were to be made; s.4(4)(b). Note the phrase "serious risk". No statutory guidance is given as to the meaning of that phrase. Originally, the making of assumptions under section 2(3) of the 1986 Act was discretionary, but the discretion was deliberately removed, first by section 9 of the CJA 1993 (which did not come into force), and then by section 4(3) of the DTA. The statutory exceptions in s.4(4) are not free of difficulty. Who raises an issue under s.4(4)(a) or (b)? Would any risk of injustice (which is not merely fanciful) be regarded by the Courts as "serious", given the consequences that will flow from the making of an assumption? Even if the reasons stated for not applying the assumptions under s.4 of the 1994 Act are erroneous, that does not seem to entitle the prosecution to apply for re-assessment under s.14 of this Act nor is it clear that the prosecutor would be entitled to seek judicial review of a judge's decision in the light of his stated reasons. The draft Proceeds of Crime Bill 2001 includes proposals that will enable prosecutors to appeal a decision of a judge not to embark on confiscation proceedings, or in respect of any determination made by the judge. In *Delaney and Hanrahan* (May 14, 1999) the Court of Appeal did not express a concluded opinion as to the meaning of the equivalent provision of section 72AA (5)(c) of the Criminal Justice Act 1988, but thought that the provision "is concerned with protecting a defendant from a form of double counting". However, that view may be too restrictive and the authors of the Performance And Innovation Unit Report, *Recovering The Proceeds Of Crime* (June, 2000), were of the opinion that section 4(4)(b) offers wider protection than merely against the risk of double counting: see para. 13–215.

II. The Definition of Benefit

13–179 By section 2(3) of the Drug Trafficking Act:

> '. . . a person has benefited from drug trafficking if he has at any time (whether before or after the commencement of this Act) received any payment or other reward in connection with drug trafficking carried on by him or another person".

The phrase "benefited from drug trafficking" is a term which falls to be construed in accordance with s.2(3) (above), and see s.1(1) and (2) of the 1994 Act. A benefit has the following features:

(i) it must be a payment or other reward;
(ii) it must be received by a person;
(iii) the payment must be received in connection with drug trafficking;
(iv) the drug trafficking must have been carried on by the recipient or another;
(v) the recipient knew that the payment or reward was made "in connection with drug trafficking": *Richards* [1992] 2 All E.R. 573;

(a) Payment or other reward

(i) *Payment does not mean profit*

13–180 In *Smith* (1989) 89 Cr.App.R. 235 Lord Lane C.J. said:

> ". . . the words 'any payment' . . . must mean, indeed it is clear from the wording, any payment in money or in kind. It does not mean . . . net profit derived from the payment after the deduction of expenses, whether the expenses are those of purchase, travelling, entertainment or otherwise. The same consideration applies to the words 'other rewards'."

In other words, the Act is concerned with proceeds and not with profit: and see *Banks* [1997] 2 Cr. App. R.(S) 110. Confiscation under the Drug Trafficking Act is not confined to the recovery of ill-gotten gains or profit. The appellant complained, in *Smith*, that the judge erred in evaluating the extent of the appellant's proceeds by aggregating four payments of £2,500 received by him. The appellant contended that each sum received had been invested in purchasing the next consignment of drugs for sale so that the money had been "rolled over" by investment. The Court of Appeal noted that there was, in any event, no evidence of money being rolled over in this way but went on to say (*per* Lord Lane C.J.):

> "It seems to us that the section is deliberately worded so as to avoid the necessity, which the appellant's construction of the section would involve, of having to carry out an accountancy exercise which would be quite impossible in the circumstances of this case."

In *Smith*, counsel for the appellant ingeniously argued that the DTOA was concerned with profits on the basis, *inter alia*, of section 4(3) (now s.5(3)) which provides that the amount to be confiscated is the "amount that might be realised" at the time the confiscation order is made. Presumably, the submission was that the assets could only have been acquired with the profits, and not with gross proceeds, the bulk of which had been dissipated on expenditure. However, the Court of Appeal rejected that submission on the basis that (s.5(3)) is a mitigating provision in circumstances where the provisions of section 5(3) have been proved to the Court's satisfaction. In any event, the "amount that might be realised" may include assets which were in fact purchased with proceeds lawfully acquired: see *Chrastny (No. 2)* [1991] 1 W.L.R. 1385. The purpose of realising assets (whether lawfully acquired or not) is simply to pay off the confiscation order that represents some, if not all, of the defendant's proceeds of drug trafficking. A confiscation order is, after all, a value-order.

The decision of *Smith* was cited with approval by the Court of Appeal in *Comiskey* (1990) 12 Cr.App.R.(S) 562, 567. In *McDonald* (1990) 12 Cr.App.R.(S) 457, the appellant admitted receiving a total of £88,710.30 in respect of numerous drug transactions. He claimed that he spent about £78,840 and thus made a profit of just under £10,000. It was held that notwithstanding the expense incurred, the Court would assess the defendant's proceeds at the full amount of £88,710.30.

(ii) *"Other reward"*

The payment need not be received as a reward as such (*i.e.* in respect of a role performed by the recipient in a drug trafficking venture) but merely that it was received *in connection with* drug trafficking carried on by the recipient or another. **13–181**

> In *Osei* (1988) 10 Cr.App.R.(S) 289 the appellant pleaded guilty to the unlawful importation of Class A drugs at Heathrow Airport. The judge made a confiscation order in respect of £2,500, which was found

in her possession at the time of her arrest. The appellant claimed that she was a courier (which she was) and that the money was given to her by the organisers of the venture to show to immigration officers to enable her to pass through immigration.

Held: "payment" included not merely the courier's profit or fee but also a benefit of the type described by the appellant. The words "other reward" in (ss.2(3), 4(1) and (3) of the DTA) meant rewards in some form other than payment.

An airline ticket with a view to a free holiday would therefore be some "other reward". The ticket is "property" within the meaning of section 62(1), and when given to the courier, is a "transfer of property" for the purposes of section 62(5).

For a definition of "in connection with", see *Director of Public Prosecutions v. Jeffrey* (1992) 58 A Crim.R. 310 (re the Confiscation of the Proceeds of Crime Act 1989 (Commonwealth)):

> ". . . a substantial connection between the activity in question and the use of the property. It is not sufficient for there to be a mere accidental or incidental connection. The unlawful activity must be related to, or dependent upon, or could not have been committed without, or have resulted directly from, the use of the property." *per* Hunt C.J.

It follows that the Courts will usually be able to determine that a courier travelling from abroad has benefited from drug trafficking in most cases because the evidence frequently reveals that the cost of the courier's airline ticket and hotel expenses have been paid by another. For the purposes of section 4(3), the Court may make the assumption that any property transferred to the defendant during the relevant period was a payment or reward received in connection with drug trafficking.

Once it is shown that the defendant received the payment or reward, it is immaterial whether the payment was intended for the defendant's own use or not. In *Osei* (above), there was no evidence that the sum of £2,500 was in the appellant's hands to be disposed of as she would have wished. The cash was intended to satisfy immigration that she had sufficient funds to enable her to obtain leave to enter the United Kingdom. Even if it was arranged that the courier should bank the cash for the ultimate benefit of the instigator, the property is still caught by the wording of sections 2(3), 4(1) and 4(3) of the DTA.

(b) The value of the payment must be real

13–182 In *Johnson* (1991) 2 Q.B. 249 the appellant received a cheque for £6,750 which was credited to her bank account but debited six days later when it was dishonoured on presentation. Nonetheless, the judge included the value of the cheque when assessing the extent of the appellant's proceeds of drug trafficking. The judge was of course entitled to assume that the cheque represented a payment or reward in connection with drug trafficking (s.4(1)(a)) but that particular assumption was plainly shown to be incorrect once there was evidence that the cheque was dishonoured and therefore valueless. The appellant had bought a car for £6,000 of which £5,600 had been raised by way of a loan from a finance company. The appellant had paid the deposit of £400 and repaid £900 to the finance company.

Held: her payments/rewards amounted to £1,300 but the balance could not be said to be a payment or reward received "in connection with drug trafficking" because the origin of the money came from the finance company whose funds were in no way tainted.

(c) Can the value of a drug amount to a benefit?

This is a matter of considerable practical importance. Over the last few years, an increasing number of "prosecutor's statements" (made under s.11 of the DTA) included the street value of the drug seized as a benefit in the hands of the defendant. However, in recent months, the incidence of such claims appears to be in decline—and rightly so. If the value of the drug has any relevance at all, it will usually be the *cost* price of the drug, that is to say an expense incurred by the defendant (in the period of six years before he was charged) and which therefore engages the assumption that it was expenditure met out of the proceeds of drug trafficking received by him at some earlier time: section 4(3)(b). Occasionally, the street value might be relevant if, and only if, the drug was received by the defendant as a payment or reward in connection with drug trafficking carried on by him or by another. Thus, if D1 was permitted by D2 to retain half a kilogram of cannabis as a reward for "looking after" D2's drug, then the street value of that half a kilogram of cannabis might be the value of D1's benefit if (for example) D1 ordinarily bought cannabis in one gram deals so that the street value was the *value to him*. 13–183

The point is not straightforward, and policy considerations play some part in the interpretation of the expression "benefit from drug trafficking" in section 2 (3) of the Act.

As we shall see, the courier of the proceeds of drug money-laundering, will be saddled with the full value of the monies transported—as a benefit—even though the actual "payment or reward" received by him was a fraction of that sum: see *Simons* (1994) 98 Cr.App.R. 100 and *Simpson* [1998] 2 Cr.App.R.(S.) 111. Why it might be asked, should the position be different if the commodity is not "drug money", but drugs? The answer is influenced by policy considerations. At a practical level, legal tender does at least have a value capable of being readily ascertained. Controlled drugs unlawfully handled, attract prices determined by the forces of the illegal market. The economics of illegal drug markets are not well understood, and under researched. The lorry driver who delivers five tonnes of cannabis resin with a street value of over £20 million to "B" cannot sensibly be described as "benefiting" in that sum. It is unlikely that "B" (as a wholesaler) would buy the consignment for anything like that amount, and therefore the benefit to "B" should be the wholesale value and not the street value. The issue of the value of an illegally handled controlled drug as a benefit must be approached with great caution.

13–184 Most controlled drugs have a recognised medicinal value (save perhaps for drugs in Schedule 1 to the Misuse Of Drugs Regulations 1985) and may have a legitimate market value as well as a higher "black market" value. A controlled drug may properly be described as "property" for the purposes of the DTA (see s.62(1)). The value of the drug should not be treated as a benefit received, by the defendant, merely because he had been in possession or control of it. It is unlikely that the evidence will show that the defendant received the drug as a "payment or other reward" for his role in the unlawful venture. However, where the evidence shows that the defendant purchased the drug, then the monies used for that purpose may be a benefit if it can be proved (or assumed under s.4(3)(b)) that the money itself came from earlier drug trafficking. The fact that a defendant is in possession of drugs may be some evidence of an earlier benefit from drug trafficking, but clearly, this need not necessarily be so at all. Even if the drug was a payment or a reward in the defendant's hands, it will not be easy to determine the value of the benefit. There is then the separate question as to whether a drug can be "realisable property" for the purposes of the Act. In practice, the police will seize the drugs under section 23 of the MDA and apply for forfeiture under section 27 of the MDA—a step that should not be taken until proceedings under the DTA have been concluded (see s.2(4) of the DTA). Who holds the drugs between arrest and forfeiture?

There is already clear authority for the proposition that where the proceeds of drug trafficking have been rolled over into another illegal purchase of controlled drugs (which have been sold), the total value of the proceeds counts towards the determination of the benefit received: *Smith* (1989) 89 Cr.App.R. 235. It may be asked "if the proceeds of the sale can be included, then why should the value of drugs seized (and therefore not yet sold) not also be taken into account?"

What is the proper value of the benefit?

(i) *Value of the drug seized, as a benefit*

13–185 The issue as to whether the receipt of a controlled drug is capable of being a benefit was considered in *Butler* (1993) 14 C.A.R.(S) 537.

> In *Butler*, the defendant pleaded guilty to possessing a kilogram of cannabis with the street value of £8000. The judge found as a fact that this was a first offence and be had not been drug trafficking before. The judge made a confiscation order for £5110—the only benefit being the value of the drug itself.
>
> *Held:* the confiscation order was set aside.

In delivering the judgment of the Court, Popplewell J. said:

> "It is quite obvious that the drugs held by a drug trafficker may be a payment or other reward if drugs have been sold and further drugs

purchased. But in the instant case the judge took the view, having heard the evidence, that this was a first-time drug trafficking and that the drugs had been purchased on that single occasion. It is therefore impossible to say that the drugs themselves are 'any payment or other reward in connection with drug trafficking'."

The editor of the report noted that "where an offender purchases drugs for the purpose of drug trafficking, using funds obtained from other activities in order to do so, the drugs are not a payment or reward." The Court, in *Butler*, did not explain how the sale and subsequent purchase would amount to a benefit. Clearly if there is evidence D sold drugs for a particular sum, then the sale price would be a benefit without the Court applying any of the statutory assumptions. If the drug was not sold, the alternative basis would be to look to the cost price of the drug. If there is evidence that the defendant purchased the substance within the relevant six-year period, the Court must assume that his expenditure was met out of proceeds received in connection with his drug trafficking. Presumably, given the findings of fact made by the sentencer in *Butler*, the Court would have disapplied the assumption as having been "shown to be incorrect", *i.e.* on the grounds that there was no evidence of earlier drug trafficking: see (now) section 4(4)(a) of the DTA.

Butler is not authority for the proposition that the mere fact that drugs are held, or were received, by the defendant is sufficient to constitute a benefit for the purposes of the DTOA or the DTA. The matter was again considered in *Lennie* (April 1, unreported, 1993) although the facts were very different from *Butler. Lennie* was arrested by police in possession of two kilograms of amphetamine sulphate and £900 cash. L had just visited a farmhouse that was used as a laboratory for making amphetamine sulphate. One precursor chemical for the production of that drug is BMK. L bought 50 litres of BMK for £9,400. The money was derived from legitimate sources. BMK is not a controlled drug. There was no dispute that L benefited from drug trafficking in the sum of £7,900, made up as follows:

(1) sale of 10 litres of BMK to H for amphetamine production: £3,200 cash;
(2) sale of 15 litres of BMK to H in exchange for two kilos of amphetamine which L sold for £3,900;
(3) sale of 15 litres of BMK to H in exchange for two kilos of amphetamine—seized by police at the time of L.'s arrest as well as £800 cash.

However, the trial judge added £9,400 (expended by L on the purchase of the BMK) to the value of the benefit figure. In reducing the confiscation order by £9,400 (the price of BMK) the Court said: 13–186

"We consider it an unwarranted strain on the wording of the Act to regard goods received, at any rate in the first transaction, as a reward for the payment made to the vendor."

It is true that L's expenditure of £9,400, to buy BMK, would now be assumed to be expenditure derived from drug trafficking (section 4(3)(b)), but this assumption would surely have been displaced as "shown to be incorrect": section 4(4)(a). Item (1) above, namely the £3,200, was a benefit because it was a payment received "in connection with" drug trafficking carried on by L or "by another" (H). It was not necessary to apply any of the statutory assumptions: see section 4(1)(a). Item (2) was a benefit—not on the grounds that the drug was received by L as a reward—but because he sold it and thus received £3,900. Item (3) was also a benefit but only to the extent of £800 given by H to L for the BMK. The drug was not realised (that is to say sold) and it was not treated as a payment or reward received by L in connection with anyone's drug trafficking.

As the Court of Appeal rightly pointed out in *Akengin* (1995) 16 Cr. App. R (S) 499, cases exist where there is evidence that a defendant is given drugs as a payment or reward for his part in a drug trafficking venture. In such cases there is no logical reason why this form of payment should not be included in the assessment of the benefit, but it must be stressed that the drugs must be received by the defendant as a "a payment or other reward" in connection with drug trafficking. In *Akengin*, the Court of Appeal was required to consider whether the expenditure of some £54,600, for the purchase of 23.48 kilograms of heroin in Turkey, amounted to a "benefit" for the purposes of the what is now section 2(3) and section 4(1) of the DTA. The Court resolved the issue by holding (correctly on this point) that there was no evidence that A came into possession of the drug as a "payment or reward" for acting as a courier, or in respect of past services. Accordingly, the Court did not need to consider what would have been the proper basis for valuing the drug.

13–187 It is important to be mindful of the statutory assumptions under the 1994 Act. By section 4(3)(a), the Court is required to assume that property either "held" by the defendant since his conviction, or "transferred" to him in the six-year period prior to being charged, was received by him as a "*payment or reward*" in connection with drug trafficking carried on by him. Accordingly, drugs intended for re-sale, and not received as a payment or reward, cannot come within the scope of section 4(1) or 4(3)(a) and must therefore be left out of account when determining the extent of the defendant's benefit. It is inconceivable that 23.48 kilograms of heroin imported into the United Kingdom was intended to be a reward in Akengin's hands for his role in the smuggling venture: on the contrary, his role was designed to secure the onward transmission of the drug to others. Had the evidence been that A was given 23 grams of heroin in part-payment for his assistance, the position might have been different.

When considering this issue, it is also important to have regard to when it is alleged the defendant received the drugs as a payment or reward in connection with drug trafficking. Three time periods have to be considered.

13–188 **The drug is "held" as the defendant's property since conviction.** Property held by the defendant at any time since his conviction will be assumed to be payments or rewards received by him in connection with his drug trafficking (*i.e.* his proceeds): s.4(3)(a)(i). A controlled drug is "property" for the purpose of the Act but if it is seized by police and thus taken out of the defendant's possession before the DTA hearing, then it is no longer "held" by him (see *Thacker* (1995) 16 Cr.App.R.(S) 461). Note that the assumption under s.4(3)(a)(i) cannot apply.

In *Hayler* (May 9, 1994, unreported), the judge found that H had paid £217,000 for two imports of a controlled drug and treated that sum as a "benefit"—presumably on the basis that it was expenditure derived from drug trafficking. However, a substantial proportion of the drugs had been seized, and therefore H was not going to be able to realise any benefit. The Court of Appeal reduced the confiscation order from £200,000 to £20,000.

Even if there could be circumstances in which a defendant "held" drugs at the time of his conviction (notwithstanding that they were seized by police or customs) it is arguable that "held" for the purposes of section 4(3)(a)(i) and section 6(1) of the DTA means "lawfully held" *i.e.* that a person holds legal interest in the property (and see s.62(5)(a) which defines when property is "held"). Similarly, when section 62 is read as a whole, it is arguable that the word "interest", as it appears in the Act, means a legally enforceable interest, and it may be significant that section 62(3) refers to an interest as including a "right". If the defendant has an "interest" in the drug then it is likely to be derived from the defendant being in lawful possession of it at the relevant time. A person in unlawful possession of a drug enjoys no rights or interests in the property capable of being enforced in a court of law. Indeed, the MDA 1971 prohibits a person from being in possession except in the limited circumstances provided under the 1971 Act. Section 62(5)(b) defines a transfer of property as one which "transfers or grants" another "any interest in the property" (and see s.4(3)(a)(ii)). These are the concepts of civil law.

In an erudite commentary to *Thacker*, in the Criminal Law Review **13–189**
(1995), p.90, it is suggested, that drugs may continue to be "held" by a defendant if they are seized by police under section 23(2)(c) of the MDA 1971 and retained as an exhibit notwithstanding that they will probably be forfeited under section 27 of that Act after any confiscation order has been made. It is true, of course, that just because the police seize and detain articles found during the course of a search (and which may be used as evidence in the case) it does not follow that title vests in the police: seizure is not to be equated with forfeiture. It is for this reason that a defendant's lawfully acquired property (*e.g.* a passport) can be retained by the police as an exhibit and may then be returned to the defendant at the conclusion of the case (whether convicted or not): see s.23(2)(a) MDA 1971. However, if the property (seized under s.23) is a controlled drug, which the defendant was not entitled to have in his possession, then it is submitted that the reasoning in *Thacker* applies with equal force in that situation. Not only would such a defendant be powerless to compel the return of the drug, but also the police would be under a duty not to return it. The power of forfeiture, under section 27, is not contingent upon proving that the defendant

was in possession of the property in question at all. All that need be proved is that the property relates to the offence in respect of which the defendant was convicted. Section 27 is thus very different from section 143 of the Powers of the Criminal Courts (Sentencing) Act 2000 which does depend on proof that the defendant had the property in his possession (or on him, or was under his control) at the time it was seized when he was apprehended for the offence.

13–190 **The drug was transferred to the defendant within six years of being charged.** Where the prosecution prove (to the civil standard of proof) or establish a prima facie case that the drug was received by the defendant within the six-year period prior to being charged then, by section 4(3)(a)(ii), the Court is required to assume that it represents a payment or reward in connection with drug trafficking. However, it is an assumption that it is likely to be rebutted: see *Berry* (July 14, 1999). In *Akengin*, the Court remarked that the judge might have concluded that A was in possession of the heroin when it was purchased in Turkey although the evidence "was somewhat speculative". The mere fact that A may have been in possession of the heroin in Turkey is scant evidence to conclude that the defendant received the drug as a payment or reward for the purposes of section 4(3)(a)(ii).

13–191 **The drug was received outside the periods embraced by section 4(3).** Where property has been received by the defendant outside the six-year period and is no longer held by him at the time or since conviction, the burden will be on the prosecution to prove to the civil standard of proof (s.2(8)) that the property (i) represented the proceeds of drug trafficking carried on by him or by another and (ii) that (insofar as the property stemmed from another person's drug trafficking) it was received by the defendant as a "payment or reward" in connection with that activity. Again, valuing the benefit may be difficult.

(ii) *Monies expended to buy drugs as a "benefit"*

13–192 By section 4(3) of the DTA (formerly s.2(3)(a) DTOA) the Court is obliged to assume that any expenditure of the defendant within the relevant six years, was met out of payments received by him in connection with drug trafficking carried on by him. This would therefore include monies expended on the purchase of a controlled drug. Curiously, in *Akengin*, the Court of Appeal found that it was probable that the cost of the drug, (about £54,000) had come from the appellant's (and his confederates) profits of earlier drug trafficking. If it could have been shown that A paid £54,000 for the drug, then it was "expenditure" for the purposes of the legislation and thus the Court could have assumed that the monies came from the proceeds of earlier drug trafficking unless A showed that the expenditure was derived from another source: see *Butler* (1993) 14 Cr.App.R.(S) 537.

Akengin has been criticised (see (1995) Crim.L.R. 90). It will often be difficult for the Court to determine the extent to which a defendant contributed to the purchase price of the drug—if at all. There are cases in which it has been held that the Court should determine the value of the benefit received by each defendant in a joint enterprise and (in the absence of clear evidence) the sentencer may assume that the defendants shared equally: see *Porter* [1990] 1 W.L.R. 1260; but contrast with *Chrastny (No. 2)* [1991] 1 W.L.R. 1381. However, in those two cases the benefit was assessed (whether by making the statutory assumptions, or otherwise), and they are not directly on point as to how the Court should approach a case where participants in a joint enterprise make different financial contributions to the purchase price of the drug. It is submitted that section 4(3)(b) does require the Court to quantify the amount expended by the defendant because the subsection specifically refers to "expenditure of his". The point is not free of difficulty and it may be that the Court of Appeal in *Akengin* did not believe that it had sufficient evidence to be able to resolve the matter. In *Akengin*, the Court referred to *Porter*, *ibid.*, and remarked that the principle in that case should have been applied. This tends to suggest that the Court in *Akengin* did have, what is now section 4(3)(b), well in mind when considering the evidence in that case.

It should also be remembered that although the Court is required to 13–193 assume that any expenditure made by the defendant during the six-year period represents the proceeds of drug trafficking, it is for the prosecution to prove to the civil standard of proof (see s.2(8)) that the defendant did in fact make the relevant expenditure. Only when the judge is satisfied that there was an expenditure can the assumption under section 4(3)(b) have any application. The basis on which the defendant is to be sentenced for the drug trafficking offence (and which gave rise to the drug trafficking enquiry) may be a relevant consideration. In *Krishnamma* (April 28, 1994, unreported) K pleaded guilty to two offences of possession of a controlled drug with intent to supply. Police officers found the drug at K's home address and it was estimated that the purchase price of the drug was some £3,650. The judge sentenced K on the basis that he was keeping the drug "safely for somebody else" and that he was not going to sell the drug. In those circumstances, the Court of Appeal held that the Court should not have included the sum of £3,650 as a benefit from drug trafficking as to do so would be inconsistent with the basis on which the appellant was sentenced; and see *R. v. J* (July 7, 2000, CA).

Where there is evidence that a defendant has expended monies on drug purchases more than once, it is open to the Court to look to each item of expenditure as a benefit. However, what the Court cannot do is to take a figure that may properly be inferred to be expenditure and then apply a series of hypotheses for which there is no evidential basis. For example, one cannot take an item of expenditure, then treat it as net profit; then apply a hypothetical quantity and value of drugs that would generate that net profit: see *William (Errol)* (December 19, 2000).

(iii) *Valuing the drug/benefit*

A problem frequently encountered by the Courts is how the value of a 13–194 drug should be calculated. Two separate cases need to be considered under this heading.

Defendant buys the drug. The first situation is where the defendant buys the drug in question and the Court treats that figure as representing the benefit. Note that the situation considered here, is where D parts with money to buy drugs. If the Court accepts that D purchased drugs on credit, the value of that credit is not a benefit, because there has been no expenditure. Although the sum expended may reflect the market value of the drug at that time, it is important to remember that what is being regarded as a benefit is not, of course, the drug itself but the money paid to buy the drug on the basis that the money was derived from previous drug trafficking. That is the effect of an assumption made under section 4(3)(b). In *Taylor*, (March 15, 1994, unreported) the judge found that G and S made a joint purchase of drugs estimated at £279,350. The judge assumed that the drugs were financed from previous drug trafficking and apportioned G's expenditure/benefit as a 50 per cent share. This approach is of course consistent with the decision in *Porter*. The judge scaled down the figure to £75,000 and the Court of Appeal upheld that determination.

There may be evidence that the defendant expended a known amount of money to buy the drug (*e.g.* admissions in interview) or where information became known during an undercover operation. Of course, a defendant's answers in interview may involve a deliberate 'scaling down' of the true cost, but the Court might find it difficult to reject the defendant's account in the absence of other information. The Courts will apply common sense in relation to these matters. In *R. v. J* (July 7, 2000, CA), D pleaded guilty to conspiracy to supply a Class A drug, and a confiscation order was made in the sum of £22,890. D was found in possession of the drugs. He was dealt with on the basis that the drugs were entrusted to him. The Court of Appeal held that the normal assumption was that the drugs in a defendant's possession had been paid for by the defendant because there is no credit in the drugs trade. However, on the facts of the instant case, that assumption was shown to be incorrect (s. 4(4)(a))—*i.e.* to reflect the fact that D had not paid for the drugs entrusted to him. It is often said by the courts (and law enforcement officers) that there is no credit in the drugs trade. However, many defendants refute that claim, alleging that wholesaler-dealers agree to accept a percentage of the cost price of the drug upon successful (*i.e.* undetected) delivery of the consignment. Some defendants claim that they purchased drugs on a "sale or return" basis. Both claims maybe sceptically received by the Court—and understandably so—but illicit drug markets are not well understood and they are under-researched (*i.e.* objectively researched).

13–195 The Court can do no more than make a sensible, objective, assessment based on the information put before it including expert testimony. There are trained officers and civilians sufficiently qualified to speak about drug prices. "NCIS" have for many years maintained tables of drug values which reflect regional variations as well as prices likely to be paid in this country, and abroad, and at various points in the distribution chain. The voluntary organisation, "Release" also monitors drug values. The reader should be aware that there is authority (at first instance) for the proposition that an officer called as an expert witness, should not be part of the team investigating the defendant's conduct, and should be based away from that team: *Matadeen and Peebles* (Southwark Crown Court, January 25, 2001, His Honour Judge P. Jackson); but see *Gokal* (March 11, 1999). A valuation might need to reflect where the drug was purchased. If a consignment was purchased in the drug-producing country (and close to the source of production) the cost price is likely to be very much lower than if purchased from a "wholesaler" operating elsewhere.

In *Berry* (July 14, 1999), W was found by police to be in possession of cannabis with a street value of £34,055. B had supplied W with the drug. The judge ruled that the street value represented B's benefit notwithstanding that the Crown's case was that B was a wholesaler of the drug. What was the proper value? B did not "hold" the drug at the time of his conviction—he had supplied the substance—and therefore section 4(3)(a)(i) did not apply. The Court would have been able to treat the sale price obtained by B as the benefit, in which event, it was unnecssary to apply the assumptions: section 4(1)(a). The unknown fact was the value of the sale. Was it possible to put a value on the drug at the time B received it in the six-year period (*i.e.* under section 4(3)(a)(ii))? Given that B was a supplier, it would be inappropriate to conclude that B received the drug as a payment or reward. Accordingly, section 4(3)(a)(ii) did not apply. However, B presumably had to buy the drug, and that brought him within section 4(3)(b). Once again, the crucial question was "at what cost?" The Court referred to *Butler*, and *Dore* [1997] 2 Cr.App.R.(S.) 152. As the Court remarked, there is an obvious difference between the value of the proceeds of sale B received, and B's expenditure (the latter must have been significantly less). The prosecution was not entitled to look at what the drug might have realised at street level (*i.e.* prospective reward) because section 4(1)(a) is concerned with proceeds received—"the past tense is clearly used": *per* Tuckey L.J. The judge could not infer that B had received the street value of the drug. Doing the best it could, the Court discounted the street value by 20 per cent, to reach a figure closer to the wholesale cost. The Court emphasised that it was not suggesting that a 20 per cent discount was the way to reach a proper conclusion in other cases.

The decision of the Court of Appeal in *Berry* is to be welcomed. It is submitted that the approach taken by the Court was pragmatic and realistic: see *Fitzsimmons* (February 2, 2001).

Defendant is given drug as a reward. The second situation relates to drugs received by a defendant as an actual reward or payment in connection with drug trafficking. Determining the value of the drugs is much more complex because, in the ordinary way, one would begin by looking at the market value of the property in question. One solution is to assess its potential value if sold illegally. It is imprudent always to look to the street-value of the drug because that figure is usually based on the drug being broken down and sold in the smallest units encountered at street level. 13–196

Much may depend on the quality and quantity of the drug received by the defendant and his position and role in the enterprise. If the amount of the drug is small then its street value may be a meaningful basis upon which to determine its value in the hands of the defendant. If the amount of the drug is large, or substantial, then the defendant is unlikely to sell it in small units at street level. It will often be realistic to look to the "wholesale value" of the drug or to strike a balance between the wholesale price and street value.

Section 7(2) provides limited assistance:

> "Subject to section 8(2) of this Act, references in this Act to the value at any time referred to in subsection (3) below as 'the material time) of a gift caught by this Act or of *any payment or reward* are references to—
> (a) the value of the gift, *payment or reward to the recipient when he received it*, adjusted to take account of subsequent changes in the value of money, or
> (b) where subsection (3) below applies, the value there mentioned, whichever is the greater." (emphasis added)

The difficulty is quantifying the value *to the recipient* of the drug. If D intends to sell his 'reward', he may contemplate selling it in 1 gram deals, or wholesale. The latter is likely to be a figure significantly less than the street value. The value might therefore need to reflect D's intentions. By section 7(1) of the Act, the value of property (other than cash) is expressed to be its "market value". However, that provision only applies where a person (not necessarily the defendant) is "holding the property", *i.e.* at the time the confiscation order is made. It follows that section 7(1) is unlikely to be of any assistance: see *Thacker*, *ibid.*

(iv) *Value of the benefit if drug not realisable*

13–197 If D receives a car worth £8,000 as a payment for his role in a drug trafficking venture, that item is a benefit: section 4(1)(a). The value is the value to him (say £8,000): section 7(2). The Court can make a confiscation order in that sum, and the defendant knows that he can sell the car (which he still holds) to satisfy the order. However, where D obtains cannabis as a reward worth to him £8,000, but the drug is seized by police, the benefit will be assessed in the sum of £8,000. He is not allowed to possess the drug; the police have seized it, and therefore the drug is no longer realisable. Nevertheless, the defendant will be required to satisfy the order out of other property that he holds. It has been argued that such a result is objectionable, because the item representing the benefit, is no longer realisable by him. In *Satchell*, the Court said:

> ". . . if the drugs found in the appellant's possession are to be regarded as a benefit because of the assumption that they were acquired with money from drug trafficking, and if then a sum equivalent to the price paid for the drugs is the subject of a confiscation order, and the drugs themselves are then forfeited, the appellant will suffer, in a sense, double jeopardy. . . . "

The Court appears to have thought that the remedy exists in section 5(3)—formerly section 4(3) of the DTOA—namely, that "... the Court would be under a duty to take into account the fact that nothing could be realised from the proceeds of the drugs which were forfeited": and see *Barber* (December 15, 1995). In *Dore*, the Court of Appeal could not accept that reasoning. Doubtless, the Court in *Satchell* was seeking to mitigate the harshness of the DTA. However, the fact is that the provisions of both Acts are unforgiving. The trial judge in *Satchell* took the cost price of the drug as the value of the benefit. Section 5(3) empowers the Court to make a confiscation order for an amount less than the value of the benefit if the Court is satisfied that the "amount that might be realised" is less than the benefit figure. The "amount that might be realised" includes legitimately acquired property as well as the proceeds of drug trafficking. So where is the "double jeopardy" or "double recovery"? In substance, the position is no different from the case of the trafficker who obtained proceeds worth £10,000, and squandered the lot on high living, but he has assets which he obtained lawfully. Nevertheless, the property is realisable in the defendant's hands and will form part of the 'amount that might be realised' under the Drug Trafficking Act. The Courts have found no "sense of double jeopardy" in that situation: and see *Dellaway* (July 3, 2000). Why should it make any difference if the proceeds have not been "lost", or squandered, but forfeited?

The result can cause extreme hardship. If D uses a boat to smuggle cannabis into the United Kingdom and the boat is forfeited and condemned by virtue of the powers vested in the Commissioners of Customs and Excise, D will have to meet a confiscation order out of other property that he holds, and he cannot set off the value of the boat as property that he once held but which was forfeited by virtue of another enactment. **13–198**

In *Dore*, the Court of Appeal raised the interesting question as to whether drugs seized by police might remain "held" by the defendant within the meaning of section 62(5)(a) of the Drug Trafficking Act. The answer, suggested by the Court, was that the drugs would still be "without value" as realisable property:

> "That is because, by virtue of section 7(1) of the 1994 Act ... the value of the property is to be taken at its market value, and the market value *must be the market value if the property is sold lawfully*. In the case of drugs, it is obvious that the drugs cannot be sold lawfully and therefore they have no market value. ... " (emphasis added)

This was an ingenious attempt to deal with a particular problem that might arise in practice; and see *Haylor* (May 9, 1994). However, much will depend on the type of drug involved and the form in which it appeared at the time it was seized. Many controlled drugs have legitimate uses, *e.g.* temazepam, methadone and pethidine. There might be a legitimate market for them, although it is doubtful that they would be returned to that market. It is submitted that the short answer is that a controlled drug which a defendant is not permitted to have, is not realisable for precisely that reason. It is inconceivable that a defendant could compel the return of the property, which he is not entitled to have. There is perhaps one exception to the above. Suppose, for example, that a pharmacist was unlawfully dispensing/supplying a controlled drug from his pharmacy. The police seized the entire stock of that drug. It may be that the drug remains "held" by the pharmacist who would be legally entitled to return it for value to the manufacturer/distributor. The example is admittedly extremely unlikely to arise in practice.

13–199 **Does the value of the drug really matter?** There may be a temptation for legal practitioners to focus on the "amount that might be realised" rather than the value of the benefit—mistakenly believing that the latter figure is only of "academic importance" in cases where defendants have no assets. It is a temptation that must be resisted. The benefit figure represents a "ceiling"—a ceiling which can be raised in rare cases (see section 15)—but in any event section 16 (as interpreted by the Court of Appeal in *Tivnan* (April 27, 1998)), enables the prosecutor to return to court at any time in the defendant's lifetime, to recover the value of subsequently acquired assets to the full value of the benefit figure. Furthermore, it is usually for the defendant to prove that the amount that might be realised is less than the value of the benefit.

In *Butler* (1993) 14 Cr. App. R.(S) 537, the sentencer included the street value of the drug seized from the defendant as a benefit. The appellant did not pursue his complaint that the judge should have taken the cost value as the relevant sum—a complaint which Popplewell J said ". . . has, in our judgement, no merit". No reasons were given by the Court to support that conclusion. However, as the Court disposed of the appeal on the basis that it could not be said that B obtained the drug as a payment or reward in connection with drug trafficking, it was not necessary for the Court to give that aspect of the case detailed consideration.

(d) Payments "received" by a person

(i) *The "conduit" problem.*

13–200 It frequently happens that a chain of people will be involved in a drug trafficking venture each of whom receive a share of the proceeds. Suppose, for example, that A in Morocco sells cannabis (which he grew at no cost) to B for £1,000 who in turn sells it to C for £2,000 who imports it into the United Kingdom and sells it to D for £3,000. In each case the profit of A, B and C is £1,000 but the Act is not concerned with profits only "proceeds" and thus the benefit received by B and C is £2,000 and £3,000 respectively: see *Smith* (1989) 11 Cr.App.R.(S) 55.

The position would, of course, be the same if D received money from the sale of the drug and paid C £3,000, out of which C paid B £2,000, out of which B paid A £1,000. None of the parties in the chain can deduct trading expenses because that is an exercise designed to calculate profit. This is broadly stated, what occurred in *Simons* (1994) 98 Cr.App.R. 100.

> In *Simons* S was convicted of unlawfully importing phenobarbitone—a Class B controlled drug. S was a director of a pharmaceutical company, which shipped five consignments of the drug from Hong Kong to the United Kingdom. S received payments from X out of which he made payments to Y who had been instrumental in the shipping of the drugs.
>
> *Held:* the appeal against the judges' determination under the DTOA was dismissed. All payments received by a trafficker in that connection are his proceeds, not merely the amount he retained after payment to a third party. If there was a chain of contracts, each purchase price was a payment and this consequence could not be avoided by a middleman acting as a postman handing on a payment from the consignee to the consignor.

Clearly, it would be an onerous task if the Courts were required to embark on an accounting exercise to determine the profits, rather than the turnover, of the drug trafficker. The approach of the legislature is at least pragmatic albeit draconian. In *Simons* the Court of Appeal may have been anxious to avoid the difficulties which are likely to be encountered if the trial judge had to decide whether a defendant was just a middleman (acting as a postman) transferring a payment from one person to another, and accordingly the property which passed through his hands should not be taken into account as part of his proceeds of drug trafficking except for an amount which he charged as a commission, or a fee, for providing this postal service. It is well established that "payment" (for the purposes of s.2(3) and s.4) is not synonymous with "reward": it has a wider meaning so that a payment could be made "in some other way in connection with drug trafficking": *Osei* (1988) 10 Cr.App.R.(S) 289 at 283. **13–201**

However, the concept of "payment" suggests more than just a transient passing of property from one person to another. In common language, "benefit" connotes some advantage, profit, gain or entitlement to use the money or property in the hands of the recipient. It is clear from section 2(3) that a defendant does not "benefit" unless he has at least "received" the property as a payment or reward: see *Osei* (1988)10 Cr.App.R.(S) 289. The Court is now required to assume that property "held" by the defendant during the period specified in section 4(3) was "received by him" at the earliest time at which he appears to the Court to have "held it": section 4(3)(a).

It is submitted that the words "received" and "held", as they appear in the Act, import more than just a notional exercise of control over property coming into the hands of the defendant. Suppose that A, B, C, D and E are all convicted of a drug trafficking offence in respect of which A received £5,000 which he handed to B who in turn gave it to C who banked the money in one account whilst simultaneously transferring £5,000 to D in cash from another account, who then gave the cash to E who placed it in the boot of his car whereupon the police seized the cash from E at the time that all five persons were arrested. In truth, only £5,000 moved down the chain from A to E and that sum was recovered by the police. Assuming that each defendant has realisable assets in excess of £5,000, is the Court entitled to make a confiscation order against each of the five defendants on the basis that each "received" £5,000? If so, it is a staggering result that an Act, designed to deprive offenders of drug proceeds, can generate and seize £25,000 in this way. If all five defendants appear before the Court at the same time, and the £5,000 is before the Court, then it is easy for the Court to take a realistic course by holding that the monies were held jointly but, logically, a different result should not follow merely because the £5,000 was never found or if only some of the defendants appear before the Court. However, this is not how the legislation has been interpreted by the courts.

13–202 In *Simpson* [1998] 2 Cr.App.R.(S.) 111, S. made regular trips to Ireland with the proceeds of drug trafficking. F and L, brought £540,000 in cash to the hotel room where S was staying. He made four trips to Ireland carrying money to the value of £2½ million. He had been paid £25,000 to £30,000 for each trip. The judge assessed his benefit at about £3 million and made a confiscation order for £948,662.07. The complaint to the Court of Appeal was that the judge should have assessed benefit on the aggregate value of the rewards paid to the money launderers. The Court of Appeal dismissed the appeal holding that the words of the DTA should be given their "natural and ordinary meaning"—but then proceeded to say that the phrase "any payments or other rewards received in connection with drug trafficking" has been interpreted literally, notwithstanding that such an interpretation means that "there can be multiple recovery of the same sum that passes through the hands of successive dealers, regardless of the amount of profit made by the dealer or dealers, or whether any profit was made at all". It is, of course, true that S received "payments" in connection with drug trafficking. One issue is whether "payment" is qualified by the words "or other rewards"? The Court did not accept that the natural meaning of the definition of benefit led to a different result. The effect of this ruling is that very harsh results are likely to follow. The likely consequences are: (1) all monies passing through the defendant's hands will be his proceeds of drug trafficking carried on by another; and (2) the fact that he has transferred monies to others may constitute gifts "caught by the Act"; (3) such gifts—if they are gifts—will remain realisable in the defendant's hands irrespective as to whether the gift has been squandered (see *Dickens* (1990) 91 Cr.App.R. 164, and *Wallace Duncan Smith* [1996] 2 Cr.App.R. 1, but consider *Gokal* (March 16, 2001)); (4) the value of the benefit represents the ceiling that enables the prosecution to apply for a revised assessment of the value of realisable property held by the defendant at any time his life (see the effect of section 16 of the DTA as interpreted by the Court of Appeal in *Tivnan*); (5) the term of imprisonment in default of payment will of course be linked to the value of the confiscation order having regard to the value of the defendant's realisable property.

The problem that faced the Court in *Simpson* was the definition of benefit as interpreted by the Courts in earlier cases including *Osei, Smith*, and *Simons*; and see *Metcalfe* [2001] EWCA Crim 1343.

The meaning of benefit was reviewed by the Court of Appeal in *Banks*. 13–203
The Court pointed to four "insuperable objections" to the contention that the Court should look to the profits received by the trafficker, rather than his gross receipts, namely (1) the language of sections 2, 4, and 5 of the Act and the use of the words "proceeds"—not profits; (2) previous decisions of the Court of Appeal such as *Osei, Smith*, and *Simons*; (3) the fact that the provisions of the 1986 act have been re-enacted in the DTA 1994 without modification of the definition of benefit; (4) "proceeds" must have the same meaning throughout the DTA, see for example sections 49, 50, 51, and 52.

As far as the last point is concerned, the definition of "proceeds" is the same throughout the DTA but the *value* of the defendant's proceeds does not have to be the same value as another person's proceeds of drug trafficking. Section 4(1)(a) requires the Court to assess "his" (*i.e.* the defendant's proceeds) of drug trafficking. However, challenge to the decision in *Simons* has now passed into history, and the law is clearly established by the cases of *Banks, Simons*, and *Simpson*.

Earlier editions of this work have endeavoured to suggest one method by which thee harshness of the result in *Simons* could be avoided, namely, by apportioning a joint benefit between the defendants. However, the benefit would indeed have to be received "jointly". That is often not the case. It may be that *Porter* should be confined to cases where the court attempts to make a realistic assessment of a defendant's benefit where an offence was committed jointly.

> In *Porter* (1990) 1 W.L.R. 1260 P and R pleaded guilty to supplying cannabis resin and possessing resin with intent to supply. A confiscation order was made, jointly and severally, in the sum of £9,600 against both P and R. The venture was performed jointly and they had benefited jointly. However, the effect of a joint and several order meant that if either P or R failed to pay then the entire burden fell on to the other defendant. Both P and R owned a house in joint names which, when sold, left very little to discharge the confiscation order. The appellant contended that the order should not have been made jointly and severally.
>
> *Held:* the appeal would be allowed. Although there had been a joint venture, the DTOA did not contemplate the making of a joint order. The terms of (section 5(3)) envisaged that if the assets of the defendants differed, then the amount of the confiscation order could be adjusted to reflect their respective shares of the benefit received which, in the circumstances, would result in an order of £4,800 being made against each defendant separately.

Accordingly, in *Porter*, the Court allowed the appeal on the basis that in 13–204
assessing benefit, in accordance with section 2 of the DTA the Court must, as between co-defendants, determine the respective shares of any joint benefit that they may have received. If the defendants do not give or call evid-

ence as to their respective shares then the Court is entitled to assume that they were sharing equally. However, the evidence may demonstrate that they shared in varying proportions and a court may assess the proceeds of each defendant on that basis: and see *Newton* (May 21, 1998).

It will be appreciated that the Court is not obliged to hold that the benefit was shared equally, merely that the Court may do so. Evidence that the defendants benefited in unequal proportions may be derived from evidence that one defendant has greater assets than another (see section 4(1) and note the relevant assumptions under s.4(3)).

The *Porter* compromise is, by its nature, an imperfect solution to the problem: and see *Kaspers* (May 22, 1993). In the example given in para. 13–201, above, A, B, C and D have received no share whatsoever. On one analysis, their benefit should be assessed at "nil" but, if their benefit is truly nil, then it is artificial to say that they have "benefited" at all. In other words the benefit is not joint but a benefit received (ultimately) by E. One solution is to say that A, B, C and D did not "receive" a payment or reward for the purposes of either section 2(3) or section 4 but this result could only be achieved if the word "received" means more than mere.

By section 62(1), "property" includes money. The Court may assume that property "held" by the defendant or "transferred to him" during the relevant period was thus "received" by him at the earliest time at which he appears to have "held" it as a payment or reward in connection with drug trafficking carried on by him: section 4(3)(a). Property is "held" by any person if he holds any interest in it: section 62(5)(a).

13–205 Again, property is "transferred" by one person to another if the first person "transfers or grants to the other any interest in the property": section 62(5)(b). Accordingly, whether the property is "held" by the defendant, or "transferred to him", the property is not received by him for the purposes of section 4(3), unless he holds or acquires an interest in it. This seems to suggest that a mere transitory acquisition, or the receipt of property without any interest being vested in the defendant, is not sufficient for the purposes of the Act.

In *Porter* the Court did not favour a construction of the Act which allows the Courts to recover the same figure more than once in circumstances where several defendants participated in the same joint venture: and see *Viner and Long, The Times*, May 25, 1990, CA.

The same point seems to emerge from *Chrastny (No. 2)* [1991] 1 W.L.R. 1385 although the result in that case was rather more severe than in *Porter*. In *Chrastny (No. 2)*, C was convicted of conspiracy to supply cocaine, and supplying that drug, with a value in excess of £4 million. Her husband had absconded. They controlled assets worth over £2 million. She was ordered to pay a confiscation order in the sum of £2,676,627. The appellant argued that the Court should not find that the whole of the property held in joint names, and in their joint possession, was the proceeds of drug trafficking attributable to either defendant and that the value should be apportioned. The Court distinguished *Porter* and *Viner and Long, The Times*, May 25, 1990 on the basis that in those cases all the defendants were before the

Court whereas in *Chrastny (No. 2)* the husband had absconded. The appellant exercised sufficient control of the property to justify a finding that the value of her benefit was just over £2 million. If the appellant's husband were apprehended and convicted it would not be possible to make an order against him based on his possession of the same property.

Although the decision appears to be at variance with *Porter*, it is submitted that the two cases are reconcilable. What must not be overlooked is that in *Chrastny (No. 2)* the appellant's own benefit was assessed at over £2 million. On that basis the Court was entitled to look to see what assets were realisable at the time the order was made and to order the confiscation of that sum in accordance with (sections 5 and 6 of the Act). *Chrastny (No. 2)* is not authority for the proposition that the Court would be entitled to confiscate the same proceeds again if her husband were apprehended and convicted.

(e) Payment received in connection with drug trafficking

The payment or reward must have been received in connection with "drug trafficking" as defined by section 1(1) and section 1(2). The term "drug trafficking" is to be distinguished from "drug trafficking offences": see s.1(3). Not every "drug trafficking offence" amounts to "drug trafficking" for the purposes of section 1. This includes a conspiracy to import a controlled drug. Such a conspiracy is a "drug trafficking offence" but it is not "drug trafficking" under section 1. If B visits Jamaica and imports cannabis back into the United Kingdom then the airline ticket and hotel expenses (paid for by A) are "payments or other rewards" in connection with drug trafficking carried on by them. However, if B took fright in Jamaica and decided not to possess, let alone to import, cannabis then it would seem that neither the ticket nor the hotel expenses would fall within the meaning of section 2(3) because there had not been an activity performed by either A or B which amounted to "drug trafficking" under the Act: see *Johnson* (1991) 2 Q.B. 249. 13–206

In *Osei* (1988)10 Cr.App.R.(S) 289, (and see the commentary at (1988) Crim.L.R. 775) the appellant acted as a courier for the unlawful importation of Class A drugs. The sum of £2,500 found on her possession was (she claimed) to show to immigration officers to enable her to obtain leave to enter the United Kingdom. The Court held that "payment" meant any payment whether by way of reward or in some other way connected with drug trafficking. Presumably, the appellant had contended that the sum of £2,500 was wholly divorced from the drugs transaction and that the object was to fool the immigration officers into believing that she had sufficient funds to enter the country. On the facts in *Osei*, it is difficult to escape the conclusion that the attempt to circumvent immigration controls was part and parcel of the fraudulent evasion of the prohibition on importation of a controlled drug for the purposes of section 170(2) of the Customs and Excise Management Act 1979. However, the point remains that the payment or reward must have some connection with drug trafficking even if it was not exclusively connected with that activity and may (as in *Osei*) have had a dual purpose. Indeed, section 63(2) DTA seems to put that beyond doubt and provides that:

> "In this Act references to anything received in connection with drug trafficking include a reference to anything received both in that connection and in some other connection."

Where the payment is traceable to an innocent source, whose funds are not tainted, then the "connection" with drug trafficking is not made out. Indeed if an assumption is made prima facie under sections 4(2) and (3), then proof of an innocent source rebuts the assumption."

(f) Carried on by the recipient or another

13–207 As has been emphasised already, the defendant's benefits of drug trafficking are those payments or rewards which he received and it does not matter whether the drug trafficking activity was carried on by him or another. It is therefore unnecessary to establish that the defendant was a party to a conspiracy to commit a drug trafficking offence in respect of which the payment or reward was made: see the wording of section 2(3) and section 4(1)(a). However, by contrast, if the Court makes any of the assumptions set out in section 4(3)(a) or (b), the assumption will be made on the basis that the payment or reward was in connection with drug trafficking carried on by the defendant himself. The burden will therefore fall on to the defendant to show, on a balance of probabilities, that the origin of the payment or reward was from a source other than drug trafficking: see *Dickens* [1990] 2 Q.B. 102; *Comiskey* (1990) 12 Cr.App.R.(S) 562; *Enwezor* (1991) 93 Cr.App.R. 233.

(g) Knowledge of the origin of the proceeds

13–208 In *Richards* (1992) 2 All E.R. 572 R imported drugs into the United Kingdom concealed in a motor vessel. The co-accused was the prime mover in the venture. He lent £6,000 to R for the purchase of the boat. R denied knowing that, at the time, he received the monies, the boat was to be used for smuggling drugs.

Held: it must be shown that the accused knew that the payment or reward was made "in connection with drug trafficking."

The judge made no overt finding of fact as to R's knowledge when he received the £6,000 that the boat was to be used for drug smuggling.

The result is, perhaps, somewhat surprising since, both the 1986 Act and the DTA provide investigative procedures and therefore the question of knowledge does not arise as it may do if a criminal offence were being created. On the other hand, the reference to "or other reward", as that phrase appears in section 2(3), does tend to suggest that the defendant was aware of the origin of the property, because it is that knowledge which enables the defendant to perceive the payment as a "reward" and not a mere payment or gift.

(h) Burden of proof

The prosecution has the task of proving both the fact that the defendant has benefited from drug trafficking and the amount of such benefit: see *Dickens* [1990] 2 Q.B. 102 and *Enwezor* (1991) 93 Cr.App.R. 233. The evidence upon which that judgment is based will come in part from the trial and in part from statements tendered under section 11 and section 12 of the Act. The burden on the prosecution is lightened considerably by the assumptions that the Court must make under sections 4(2) and 4(3). Those assumptions can, of course, be rebutted by the defendant on a balance of probabilities but in so far as any of them survive they will, together with other evidence in the case, help the trial judge to determine whether a particular payment or reward was a benefit received by the defendant in connection with drug trafficking for the purposes of section 2(3) and section 4(1) of the Act. **13–209**

(i) Evidence by way of letters of request

Section 3(7) of the CJICA 1990 states that evidence obtained by virtue of a letter of request shall not (without consent of the relevant authority) be used for any purpose other than that specified in the letter . . . " **13–210**

Care must therefore be taken to ensure that if information is to be used in confiscation proceedings that this purpose is expressly permitted by the letter, or consent has been obtained from the proper authority, to do so. Unless the terms of section 3(7) are complied with, it seems that the material may not be used for the purpose of interviewing the defendant: see *Gooch* (June 26, 1998).

E. QUANTIFYING THE DEFENDANT'S PROCEEDS OF DRUG TRAFFICKING

I. Introduction

Section 4(1) of the DTA provides: **13–211**

(1) For the purposes of this Act—
- (a) any payments or other rewards received by a person at any time (whether before or after the commencement of this Act) in connection with drug trafficking carried on by him or another person are his proceeds of drug trafficking; and
- (b) the value of his proceeds of drug trafficking is the aggregate of the values of the payments or other rewards."

The second step is for the Court to assess the value of the defendant's proceeds of drug trafficking. Note the word "value". What has to be recovered prima facie is the value of the defendant's proceeds of drug trafficking (s.5) and not necessarily the value of tangible assets known to exist in the hands of the defendant.

The initial calculation involves aggregating all gross receipts received in connection with drug trafficking and then revaluing the total amount if necessary under section 7(2) to reflect inflation, profitable investment or market fluctuation. The severity of that calculation may be mitigated by the provisions of section 5(3), which provides that the amount to be recovered under the confiscation order is the amount that might be realised if that amount is less than the value of the defendant's proceeds of drug trafficking. The Court is concerned with "proceeds", not profit, and therefore the expense involved in buying, selling, transporting or distributing the drug is irrelevant and the Court can make no deduction in respect of drug proceeds reinvested in another purchase of drugs: see *Smith (Ian)* [1989] 1 W.L.R. 765; *McDonald* (1990) 12 Cr.App.R.(S) 457 and *Comiskey* (1991) 93 Cr.App.R. 227; *Simons* (1994) 98 Cr.App.R. 100.

13–212 A "payment" or "other reward" may be cash but it may also be a benefit in kind, *e.g.* an airline ticket: see *Osei* (1988) 10 Cr.App.R.(S) 289. A payment or reward may also be a "gift", a chose in action or another intangible: see section 62(1) of this Act. It does not matter when the payment or reward was received by the defendant. There is no time-limit as to how far back the prosecution may scan providing that the benefit relates to "drug trafficking" as defined by section 1(2) and (3). This is important because even if payments were received by a defendant from an activity which was not then prohibited by one of the enactments referred to in section 1(1) or (2), it is arguable that these payments should be excluded. Subject to this qualification, payments made before the commencement of the Act are included. The payment must actually be received by the defendant; presumably, an offer to advance a payment or reward cannot be taken into account; and similarly a payment that has been misdirected, (*i.e.* forwarded to another individual in error) cannot feature in the calculation. It does not matter whether the payment is in connection with the defendant's drug trafficking or someone else's: see s.4(1)(a).

The practical effect of section 4(1) may be summarised as follows. If the prosecution can prove that a payment or reward was received by the defendant at any time, and if it can be proved to be connected with drug trafficking, then such a payment represents the "proceeds" of drug trafficking for the purposes of the Act. Obviously, there will be many occasions when the prosecution cannot prove the link between a payment and a drug-trafficking offence—however suspicious the circumstances of its receipt may seem. Parliament therefore requires the Court to make certain "assumptions" concerning the origin of property received by the accused in the circumstances set out in section 4(3), and the Court may take into account any statement tendered by the prosecution as to any matters relevant "to the assessment of the value" of the defendant's proceeds of drug trafficking: section 11 (1).

Although the 1994 Act provides that a defendant may also tender a statement to the Crown Court (s.11(9)) it seems that the contents of that statement should be confined to matters relevant to determining "the amount that might be realised" rather than the value of any payments or rewards received by him. Acceptance of allegations contained in such a statement is to be conclusive of the matters to which it relates within the terms of section 11(9); and see para. 13–27.

II. Making the Statutory Assumptions

The statutory assumptions, which the Court is required to make if it embarks upon a drug trafficking enquiry, are dealt with in section 4 of the DTA as follows: **13–213**

"4(2) Subject to subsections (4) and (5) below, the Crown Court shall, for the purpose—

(a) of determining whether the defendant has benefited from drug trafficking, and

(b) if he has, of assessing the value of his proceeds of drug trafficking, make the required assumptions.

(3) The required assumptions are—

(a) that any property appearing to the Court—

(i) to have been held by the defendant at any time since his conviction, or

(ii) to have been transferred to him at any time since the beginning of the period of six years ending when the proceedings were instituted against him,

was received by him, at the earliest time at which he appears to the Court to have held it, as a payment or reward in connection with drug trafficking carried on by him;

(b) that any expenditure of his since the beginning of that period was met out of payments received by him in connection with drug trafficking carried on by him; and

(c) that, for the purpose of valuing any property received or assumed to have been received by him at any time as such a reward, he received the property free of any other interests in it.

(4) The Court shall not make any required assumption in relation to any particular property or expenditure if—

(a) that assumption is shown to be incorrect in the defendant's case; or

(b) the Court is satisfied that there would be a serious risk of injustice in the defendant's case if the assumption were to be made;

and where, by virtue of this subsection, the Court does not make one or more of the required assumptions, it shall state its reasons.

(5) Subsection (2) above does not apply if the only drug trafficking offence in respect of which the defendant appears before the Court to be sentenced is an offence under section 49, 50 or 51 of this Act."

13–214 Section 4 should be read in conjunction with s.2(8) (standard of proof). Members of Parliament sought clarification and evidence that amendments to what was then s.2 of the 1986 Act were necessary (Standing Committee B, May 27, 1993, col. 66). However, the Home Office did not maintain statistics on the number of cases in which assumptions had not been applied but the Minister of State for the Home Office referred to a "wealth of anecdotal evidence" that the previous provisions were unsatisfactory. The reasoning appears to have been that in cases where the prosecution cannot determine whether property passing through the defendant's hands was legitimately acquired or not, then the prosecution can progress no further because there is no obligation on the offender to account for such property given that s.11(8) specifically does not require the defendant to admit any allegation that property referred to in the statement represents the proceeds of drug trafficking. The 1994 Act, by s.12(2), empowers the Court to order the defendant to give it such information as may be specified in the order and if the defendant fails, without reasonable excuse, to comply with that order then the Court may draw such inference "as it considers appropriate" (s.12(5)): see para. 13–270. It is unclear whether section 12 empowers the court to ask the defendant whether or not he admits that the property represents the proceeds of drug trafficking and (in appropriate cases) to draw an adverse inference if he fails to answer the question. The scope of this section should be considered with the provisions of the HRA 1998 in mind.

Under the 1986 Act, s.2, the Courts enjoyed a discretion whether to invoke any of the statutory assumptions mentioned in s.2 (now s.4(3)) or not. Section 9 of the 1993 Act was enacted to remove this discretion from the Court, but that section was never brought into force. The substance of s.9 of the 1993 Act has been re-enacted in s.4(2)–(4). Note that s.4(2) does not apply if the only "drug trafficking offence" in respect of which the defendant appears before the Court to be sentenced is a money-laundering offence under ss.40, 50 or 51 of this Act (see s.1(3)). It is important to remember that the offences under ss. 40, 50 and 51 are strictly speaking "drug trafficking offences" (see s.1(3)) but they are not, it would seem, regarded as being of a type which deserve the application of the draconian measures found in s.4(2)–(4). This approach is consistent with the law as it stood under the 1986 Act: see s.2(4) and s.24 of that Act, s.14 and, see Sched. 4, para.4(2) of the Criminal Justice (International Co-operation) Act 1990 (c.5) and s.16 of the 1993 Act.

Furthermore, section 4(2) does not apply where a defendant has absconded or died and the High Court is being asked to exercise any of its powers under s.19 of this Act: see s.19(6)(a).

The application of the ECHR to drug confiscation orders made under the Drug Trafficking Act 1994 was considered by the Strasbourg Court in *Phillips v. United Kingdom* (July 5, 2001). That Court had the advantage of considering the decisions of the Scottish Court of Appeal and the Privy Council in *McIntosh v. H.M. Advocate* (October 13, 2000 and February 5, 2001, respectively), as well as the English Court of Appeal decision in *Benjafield and others* (December 21, 2000). Both the Scottish Court of

Appeal in *McIntosh* and the English Court of Appeal in *Benjafield* concluded that confiscation proceedings, particularly where the statutory assumptions were engaged, might involve the determination of a "criminal charge" against the defendant. In reaching that result, both Courts departed from (or distinguished) earlier decisions that had expressed, or implied, a contrary opinion: see *Delaney and Hanrahan* (May 14, 1999, CA); *Arman* (May 9, 2000, CA); *Brown* (December 18, 1997, CA); *Hussein* (April 20, 1999, CA); and (for Scottish decisions) see *H.M. Advocate v. McSalley* [2000] J.C. 485 and *H.M. Advocate v. Monaghan* (May 5, 2000).

On September 11, 1997, the European Commission declared as inadmissible and "manifestly unfounded" a complaint that the making of discretionary assumptions under the DTOA 1986 raised any issues regarding the presumption of innocence guaranteed by Article 6(2) of the ECHR: *Elton v. United Kingdom*. Similarly, the Privy Council, in *McIntosh*, rejected the submission that confiscation proceedings under Scottish legislation involved the making of a "criminal charge" against the defendant. In the light of the majority decision in *Phillips v. United Kingdom*, it seems highly probable that the House of Lords will support the reasoning of the Strasbourg Court in that case. The Court said:

> "... the right to be presumed innocent under Article 6(2) arises only in connection with the particular offence 'charged'. Once an accused has properly been proved guilty of that offence, Article 6(2) can have no application in relation to allegations made about the accused's character and conduct as part of the sentencing process, unless such accusations are of such a nature and degree as to amount to the bringing of a new 'charge' within the autonomous Convention meaning ... (see the *Engel and Others v the Netherlands* judgment of 8 June 1976 ..."

However, the above passage should also serve as an indication that the Strasbourg Court will almost certainly be asked to revisit the matter as ECHR jurisprudence develops. An unrebutted assumption made under section 4 of the Drug Trafficking Act does involve a finding that proceeds were received by the defendant "in connection with drug trafficking *carried on by him*" (s. 4(3)). True it is that the subsection refers to "drug trafficking" and not "drug trafficking offences [committed by him]", but such a distinction will surely not cut much ice with the defendant's neighbours. In *Phillips v. United Kingdom*, the Court remarked that criminal "charge" has an "autonomous Convention meaning", but what is that meaning? As the partly dissenting opinion of Judge Bratza and Judge Vaji makes clear, the scope of Article 6(2) has "undergone substantial development" in case law since *Engel v. The Netherlands* was decided. One might need to examine with greater care whether there is a link between Articles 6(1) and (2), and, if so, to examine the nature and quality of that link. Will different rules emerge depending on what is at stake, the "mischief", "evil", "scourge", sought to be tackled? In *Phillips v. United Kingdom*, the Court enquired whether the statutory assumptions "applied in the applicant's case" offended the basic principles of fairness inherent in Article 6(1). It held that there had been no violation for the following reasons:

> ". . . the system was not without safeguards. Thus, the assessment was carried out by a court with a judicial procedure including a public hearing, advance disclosure of the prosecution case and the opportunity for the applicant to adduce documentary and oral evidence. The court was empowered to make a confiscation order of a smaller amount if satisfied, on the balance of probabilities, that only a lesser sum could be realised. The principal safeguard, however, was that the assumption made by the 1994 Act could have been rebutted if the applicant had shown, again on the balance of probabilities, that he had acquired the property other than through drug trafficking. Furthermore, the judge had a discretion not to apply the assumption if he considered that applying it would give rise to a serious risk of injustice."

It is not clear whether the Court considered the meaning and scope of the phrase "serious risk of injustice". The Court did examine whether there had been a violation of Article 1 of Protocol No 1, and concluded that although a confiscation order amounted to an "interference with the applicant's rights to peaceful enjoyment of his possessions" nevertheless that interference was proportionate to the aims of the legislation. The Court left open the question whether issues relating to the amount that might be realised (where there is an allegation of hidden assets) complies with Article 6(1).

(a) The assumptions and their exceptions

13–215 If the Court makes any of the assumptions specified in s.4 then it will be made on the basis that the defendant has received a payment or reward in connection with drug-trafficking carried on by him and by no-one else: see s.4(2).

Although, the Court had a discretion whether or not to invoke any of the statutory assumptions the Drug Trafficking Offences Act 1986 (as originally drafted) did not indicate the circumstances in which it was appropriate to apply them: see *Redbourne* [1992] 1 W.L.R. 1182, *Rose* [1993] 1 W.L.R. 844, and see "Making Statutory Assumptions Under the Drug Trafficking Offences Act", *Archbold News*, Issue No. 5, May 28, 1993) and the *Report of the Home Office Working Group on the Drug Trafficking Offences Act 1986* (1991) at para. 2.6.

By virtue of subs. (4) the trial judge should not make any of the assumptions specified in subs. (3) if "any of the assumptions are shown to be incorrect in the defendant's case", or if "the Court is satisfied that there would be a serious risk of injustice in his case if the assumptions were to be made": subs. (4)(b). These are considered below.

(b) First exception if it is "shown to be incorrect"

Subsection (4)(a) follows the wording of s.2(2) of the 1986 Act. In *Dickens* [1990] 2 Q.B.102, it was held that the burden of proving an assumption to be incorrect falls on the defendant. With this proposition, the Home Office Working Group appears to have no quarrel (see para. 2.8 and para. 2.10(iv)). 13–216

One reading of s.4(4)(a) suggests that the burden need not necessarily be on the defendant if the words "is the defendant's case" are to be treated as being synonymous in meaning with the words "in the case against the defendant". It would have been very easy for the draftsman simply to have used the words "shown to be incorrect by the defendant". If the evidence in the case—no matter who adduces it—shows an assumption to be incorrect, then the Court may not make it.

In para. 2.10(iv) of their Report, the Home Office Working Group suggested that the onus should be on the defendant to rebut the assumption, but (somewhat inconsistently) they also suggested that the Court need not make the assumption if "for any other reason" it would not be appropriate to do so (para. 2.10(ii)).

In *Johnson* [1991] 2 Q.B.249 the appellant received a cheque for £6,750, which had been credited to her account. A few days later, the bank debited the account on the basis that the cheque was dishonoured on presentation. The Court was entitled to make the assumption that the appellant received a payment in connection with drug trafficking but the cheque was plainly of no value as it was dishonoured, and thus the assumption (if made) would be shown to be incorrect by proof (whoever adduced the evidence) that the cheque had no value. Again, a motorcar was bought by the appellant for £6,000 of which £5,600 was obtained by way of a loan from a finance house. The judge was entitled to make the assumption, prima facie, that she held the car and received it as a payment or reward in connection with drug trafficking carried on by her. However, there was no evidence that the money from the finance company was tainted and so the assumption would again be shown to be incorrect in the defendant's case; and see *R. v. J* (July 7, 2000, CA).

(c) Second exception: serious risk of injustice

Would any risk of injustice (which is not merely fanciful) be regarded by the Courts as a "serious" one given the consequences that will flow from the making of an assumption? Should the assessment of the "risk" be influenced by the fact that the civil standard of proof applies to proceedings under the Act? Even if the reasons stated by the Court, for not applying the assumptions under subs. (4)(b) are erroneous, that does not seem to entitle the prosecution to apply for re-assessment under s.13. It is not clear that the prosecutor would be entitled to seek judicial review of a judge's decision in the light of his stated reasons. In *Delaney and Hanrahan* (May 14, 1999) the Court of Appeal did not express a concluded opinion as to 13–217 the meaning of the equivalent provision of section 72AA(5)(c) of the Criminal Justice Act 1988, but thought that the provision "is concerned with protecting a defendant from a form of double counting". However, that view may be too restrictive and the authors of the Performance And Innovation Unit Report, *Recovering The Proceeds Of Crime* (June 2000), were of the opinion that section 4(4)(b) offers wider protection than merely against the risk of double counting:

> "The Courts have the discretion not to apply these statutory assumptions if they would lead to a serious risk of injustice."

> "Even with the consolidation, *the existing discretion of the Court can be invoked to disapply the assumptions in cases where use of them would be unjust.* But this discretion should be extended to protect human rights further by allowing the assumptions to be disapplied where their use would be unjust or *disproportionate* given the circumstances of the defendant." (para.8.15; emphasis added)

The Courts have yet to construe section 4(4)(b) as conferring a discretion and it seems that provision cannot be used to mitigate the harshness of the legislation: see *Croft, The Times*, November 16, 2000.

In *Danison* (September 7, 1999), the ECtHR ruled that the division of third party interests (if any) was a matter within the appreciation of the domestic courts. D's complaint that confiscation proceedings under the Criminal Justice Act 1988, Pt VI, would unjustly result in the home of his wife and child being confiscated, was rejected as manifestly ill-founded and therefore inadmissible.

(d) Weight attaching to an assumption

13–218 In *Redbourne* [1992] 1 W.L.R. 1182 the Court of Appeal also considered what effect the making of an assumption would have if it was not rebutted by or on behalf of the defendant. The short answer is that an assumed fact must be treated as being true. There would be little point in making an assumption if such a result were not to follow. The point is reinforced by the wording of subs. (4)(a), which includes a proviso in respect of the case where an assumption is shown to be "incorrect" in the defendant's case.

Although it was not expressly stated by the 1986 Act, there is clear authority for the proposition that the prosecution has the task of proving both the fact that the defendant has benefited from drug trafficking and the extent of that benefit: see *Dickens* [1990] 2 Q.B.102 and *Enwezor* (1991) 93 Cr.App.R. 233. The 1994 Act does not alter the earlier position as to the incidence of proof but the standard of proof is now on a balance of probabilities: s.2(8).

The following example demonstrates the relevant principles now to be applied. Suppose D is shown to have received a payment of £1,000 one year prior to proceedings being instituted against him for a drug trafficking offence. There is no direct evidence that D received the money in connection with drug trafficking but D was unemployed at the material time with no known sources of legitimate income. In those circumstances, it would be open to the judge to find as a fact that the sum was "transferred to (the defendant)" during the relevant period (s.4(3)(a)(ii)) and that he "held it" at that moment (see s.62(5)(b) (formerly s.38(10)) and s.62(5)(a) (formerly s.38(7))). That fact alone is enough to enable the Court to make the assumption under s.4(3)(a)(ii). Accordingly, the judge is required by statute to assume that the sum was "received" by the defendant as a payment or reward in connection with drug trafficking carried on by the defendant (s.4(3)(a)(ii)).

In *Enwezor* (above), the judge made a confiscation order of £20,000. A total of £11,000 had been paid into a building society account in the name of the appellant's sister. The appellant contended that the payments were made by various people coming from Nigeria and not (as alleged) by himself. The trial judge ruled that the payments into the account were gifts caught by the Act which represented the proceeds of drug trafficking and that the appellant had benefited by that amount. The judge said that "it is plain from the general tenor and working of the Act that the ordinary criminal burden and standard of proof is not applicable". He accordingly made his determination based on the civil standard of proof. The judge added that "if the criminal standard of proof had applied I would not have found against him". It was held, on appeal, that the judge was entitled to rely on the assumptions under s.2(2) and (3) of the 1986 Act (see now s.4(2)–(5)) but that the correct standard of proof was the criminal standard and that since the judge would have reached a different conclusion on that basis the appeal would be allowed. In the light of s.2(8) of the DTA, the result in *Enwezor* would now be different.

(e) Some ramifications of section 4(2)–(5)

Even if a defendant is convicted of supplying drugs over a very short period of time, the Court is required to assume that all property transferred to the defendant over the preceding six years (prior to the moment when proceedings were instituted against him) was a payment or reward made in connection with drug trafficking carried on by the defendant and moreover, that any expenditure made by the defendant over that period came out of the proceeds of drug trafficking. Where property is proved to have been received by an accused and where there is no evidence at all to suggest that when he received it, the accused (or the transferor) were engaged in drug trafficking, then such a lack of evidence may of itself be the best evidence to show that the "assumptions", which the Court can make under s.4(4)(a), are incorrect. 13–219

When an assumption is required to be made, the Court has no discretion but to make it. There is no room discretion but to make it. There is no room for the exercise of mercy: *Croft* (June 15, 2000); and see *Danison* (September 7, 1999, ECtHR).

(f) Periods of time embraced by section 4(3)

13–220 It was plainly the intention of Parliament that subsection 4(3) should embrace two very different periods of time. Obviously subsection 4(3)(a)(ii) relates to the six years ending when the proceedings were "instituted" against the defendant. By section 41(2), proceedings for an offence are instituted in England and Wales.:

> "(a) when a justice of the peace issues a summons or warrant under section 1 of the Magistrates' Courts Act 1980 (issue of summons to, or warrant for arrest of, accused) in respect of the offence;
> (b) when a person is charged with the offence after being taken into custody without a warrant;
> (c) when a bill of indictment is preferred under section 2 of the Administration of Justice (Miscellaneous Provisions) Act 1933 in a case falling within paragraph (b) of subsection (2) of that section (preferment by direction of the criminal division of the Court of Appeal or by direction, or with the consent, of a High Court judge);
>
> and where the application of this subsection would result in there being more than one time for the institution of proceedings, they shall be taken to have been instituted at the earliest of those times."

By contrast, section 4(3)(a)(i) relates to any property appearing to the Court ". . . to have been held by the defendant at any time since his conviction".

(i) *Property "held": when?*

13–221 However, subsection 4(a)(i) is so ambiguously drafted that it may be construed to apply either to payments received by the defendant at any time in his life and which he continues to hold since his conviction, or, it relates only to payments received and held by the defendant after his conviction. The ambiguity arises by virtue of the words "held by him since his conviction" in subsection 4(3)(a)(i).

(ii) *First interpretation*

13–222 The argument is that the draftsman did not (as he did in 4(3)(a)(ii)) use the words "transferred to him", or "received by him". Accordingly, it is said that section 4(3)(a)(i) was designed to apply to all property which was received by the defendant, at some time in his life and which he held at the time of his conviction and subsequently. The prosecution may not be able to show when the defendant actually received the property in question, but it may be possible to show when he "held" it and therefore, by section 4(3)(a), the Court may assume that the property was received "at the earliest time at which he appears to the Court to have held it" and, having made the assumption, that it was a payment or reward in connection with drug-trafficking.

(iii) *Second interpretation*

The second interpretation of section 4(3)(a)(i) (now redundant) is that the Court is only entitled to look to property received and held by the defendant literally since his conviction. Any assumption made by the Court will be on the basis that the proceeds resulted from the defendant's drug trafficking. As a matter of common sense (and for the reasons given by the Government; see above) it will be far more difficult, if not impossible, to rebut an assumption appertaining to payments received or paid before the six-year period. Records relating to a business, etc., which would otherwise support the defendant's contention that it was a payment or reward lawfully earned, may be lost or destroyed. Furthermore, witnesses may no longer be traceable or capable of supporting the legality of a given transaction. The statutory assumptions in subsection (3) were intended to embrace only a relatively short period of the defendant's career. In some cases, the proceeds of drug trafficking may be invested (*e.g.* abroad) and payments made to the defendant *after* his conviction for a drug-trafficking offence. There may be an appreciable delay between conviction and the making of a confiscation order. Because section 4(3)(a)(ii) only relates to payments received for a period of six years ending when the proceedings were instituted against the defendant, it follows that payments received after conviction would not be caught by that provision. Accordingly, section 4(3)(a)(i) was enacted. 13–223

One difficulty with this argument is that the Government introduced an amendment to clause 2 of the Drug Trafficking Offences Bill (now part of section 4(3)(a)(i)) which omitted the words "at the time of" and inserted the words which now appear "at any time since", *i.e.* his conviction.

(iv) *Which interpretation is correct?*

If section 4(3)(a)(i) really does catch property received by the defendant at any time, then why did the draftsmen use the words "at any time since his conviction?" A clue to the answer may be derived from Hansard when this provision first appeared in the Drug Trafficking Offences Bill in 1986 when Mr Mellor on behalf of the Government said: 13–224

> ". . . the Bill originally provided for the assumption that the trafficker's property was derived from drug trafficking applied to all assets that he held at the time of his conviction and all those that had been in his hands at any time during the previous five years". [Hansard, February 18, 1986; col. 207, 208]

The figure of five years was an "arbitrary decision" and was extended to six years, for reasons explained below, but what is perhaps not entirely clear is whether the Government intended that two very separate time periods should operate, or whether the Government contemplated that the assumptions would apply to property which the defendant either had or still has but (in either case) he would not be required to prove that his assets were from non-drug trafficking sources if he first came into possession of the property outside what is now the six-year period. The Government said that it arrived at the period of six years by answering this question:

> "... if a trafficker is asked to prove that his assets were not acquired as a result of drug trafficking, how long can we reasonably expect him to go back and for how long would he have kept the necessary records? For how long would he keep in touch with people who might be able to confirm what he said? ... However, it emerged ... that a recent Finance Act provided that VAT records, for example, should be kept for six years ... we invite the House to extend the period from five to six years. ... A longer period would increase the burden on the defence to an unacceptable extent, because many defendants who had had a legitimate income would not have the records many years later to prove that that was so. ... If the prosecution can prove differently, it should not be inhibited by the six-year limit." [Hansard, February 18, 1986; col. 207, 208]

13–225 There has been little appellate authority on this point but in *Chrastny No. 2* (1991) 1 W.L.R. 1385, the Court of Appeal appear to have had little doubt that the first construction is correct. Thus, Glidewell L.J., delivering the judgment of the Court, said:

> "The joint effect of s.2(2) and (3) (now s.4(2) and (3)) is that the assumption is to be made unless it is proved to be incorrect that any property held by the defendant at any time since, which obviously means after her conviction, was received as a payment or reward for drug trafficking. ... It follows in our view, therefore, that the defendant's proceeds of drug trafficking includes, certainly comprises, money and property received by her and property assumed to be received by her under the statutory assumption as a reward if at the time of her conviction she held an interest in that property. In other words, in our judgment, if at the time of her conviction, the defendant is in possession of property or has a sufficient control over it to be able to dispose of it, it can be assumed in the absence of contrary evidence to be her proceeds of drug trafficking. That is the test we have applied."

The consequences that flow from this construction are, at first sight, dramatic. Providing there exists prima facie evidence that the defendant held the relevant property at the time of (or since) his conviction, the Court will be required to assume (subject to the statutory exceptions) that it represents the proceeds of drug trafficking carried on by him: see *Brett* (June 20, 1997).

At first sight it would seem that (subject to one argument which is considered a little further on), section 4(3)(a)(i) applies to property acquired by the defendant at any time in his life including any property which he held since birth.

If the property can be shown to have been acquired by the defendant at birth then obviously the Court would have no difficulty in concluding that the assumption cannot be allowed to stand but the defendant may have greater difficulty rebutting the assumptions if he is asked to explain the origin of assets which he claims were acquired in the distant past, and long after the period he may reasonably be expected to preserve accounting records, or be in a position to call witnesses in support of his case.

Upon an initial reading of section 2(3), and section 4(3)(a)(i), it may be thought that the Court can travel through the entirety of a defendant's financial history no matter how long that is. However, it is arguable that there is a moment in history before which the Court cannot use its powers under the Act and that relates to the moment "drug trafficking" did not exist as a matter of law. This is because section 1(1) and (2) defines "drug trafficking" in the context of activities prohibited by various enactments. The earliest of these is specified to be the MDA 1971. Accordingly, when (for example) section 2(3) defines a benefit as being a payment or reward in connection with "drug trafficking" that appears to exclude conduct which precedes the prohibitions imposed by any of the relevant enactments referred to in section 1(1) and (2) even if the same conduct was outlawed under a different enactment. **13–226**

It will be seen from the wording of s.4(3), that the moment at which the defendant is to be assumed as having received the benefit is the earliest time the defendant appears to have "held" the property.

Thus, the prosecution may be able to demonstrate that the defendant held a yacht in 1978 and that he still had it in his possession at the time of his conviction. In fact, unbeknown to all but the defendant, he received the vessel as payment in kind for building work in 1970. On those facts, once the prosecution establish a prima facie case that the defendant "held" the yacht since 1978, the Court is required to assume it was a payment or reward in connection with drug trafficking carried on by him: section 4(3)(a)(i).

It will thus be presumed that the yacht was received as a benefit from drug trafficking carried on by him in 1978 and it will be up to the defendant to prove that he acquired the vessel in 1970 as a legitimate payment. Establishing when the property was "received" may have some relevance to valuation but it could also have some impact on sentence because, clearly, a defendant who is found to have benefited from drug trafficking on a regular basis over a period of 10 years, may find that this feature is reflected in the sentence. However, experience has shown that the Courts are mindful of the limitation of this exercise because the magnitude of the confiscation order may have more to say about the inability of the defendant to prove his case than it speaks about the defendant's true involvement in drug trafficking. This is particularly so under the DTA which applies a civil standard of proof throughout the legislation. Where a defendant, in mitigation, pleads that his supplying was only "social", and not commercial, it would be artificial if not absurd to overlook (in appropriate cases) the obvious inference from the DTA enquiry that the mitigation put forward cannot be true.

III. Other Issues Relevant to Quantifying Proceeds

(a) Evidential considerations

13–227 The defendant is of course entitled to call evidence during the hearing and he may seek an adjournment for that purpose. In *Nicholson* (1990) 12 Cr.App.R.(S) 58, the appellant pleaded guilty to various drug trafficking offences. Officers found £700 at the appellant's home address. The appellant wished to call witnesses to show that the money was not the proceeds of drug trafficking and applied for an adjournment for that purpose. The judge made remarks, which implied that, if the appellant persisted in his request, he might not get the maximum benefit from his plea of guilty whereupon the appellant proceeded without calling his witnesses. In the circumstances, the Court of Appeal held that the judge was putting unfair pressure on the appellant not to maintain his request for an adjournment and that justice was not seen to be done.

A curious state of affairs arose in *Jenkins* (1990) 12 Cr.App.R.(S) 582. Concern was expressed in the Court of Appeal that the appellant may not have been permitted to give evidence on his own behalf at all in order to rebut assumptions, which the trial judge was proposing to make. The transcript of the proceedings in the Crown Court did not make the position clear and therefore the Court of Appeal assumed in the appellant's favour. If the appellant had in truth been denied the opportunity to give evidence then this was manifestly irregular and the Court of Appeal in *Jenkins* made that clear. The trial judge also made an order for £12,000, whereas the prosecution in their statement under what was s.3 (now s.11) had only referred to £3,000. Again, it appears that the difference in computation was not fully explored, nor does it seem that the appellant was given an opportunity to give evidence on that issue. That, as the Court of Appeal remarked, was "another material irregularity". If the defendant fails to keep proper records, but he has acquired and spent large sums of money (the origin of which he is not able to explain), then he runs the risk that the Court will make findings adverse to him on the basis of the statutory assumptions under sections 4(2) and (3): see *Small* (1989) 88 Cr.App.R. 184.

13–228 It frequently happens that defendants do not give evidence in Drug Trafficking Act proceedings and do not adduce other evidence. There are no golden rules for practitioners as to whether a defendant should be called or not. The difficulty is that unless a defendant is called to give evidence, it will often be impossible to displace statutory assumptions or to persuade a court to impose a lesser amount under a confiscation order pursuant to section 5(3). Some defendants may feel that there is little point giving evidence on a DTA enquiry if their credibility has already been damaged or destroyed during a trial, or will be in DTA proceedings.

Sometimes it happens that a judge will conduct a *Newton* hearing and DTA proceedings simultaneously. There seems to be no authority for the proposition that he should not do so. Under the DTOA, the standard of proof was, originally, the criminal standard of proof. A judge will have to ensure that if DTA and *Newton* hearings are held simultaneously, that the correct standard of proof is applied in relation to each material finding of fact. In *Caine* (May 12, 1998) the Court of Appeal, on the facts of that case, held that it had not been necessary for the trial judge to hold a *Newton* hearing. In the event, he wrongly took into account (in confiscation proceedings) an adverse finding he had reached in the *Newton* hearing: and see *Marshall-Price* (March 22, 1994).

Note that the basis of plea may affect the basis for determining the value of the benefit from drug trafficking: *Krishnamma* (April 28, 1994); and see *Kearley* (May 8, 1996) where the quashing of counts on appeal to the House of Lords impacted on the validity of the confiscation order.

Where a defendant enters pleas of guilty to some counts on the indictment, but not others, it is highly desirable (if not essential) for counsel to agree a written basis of plea if the defendant intends to invite the Court to calculate his benefit from drug trafficking on a limited basis. If the Court agrees that verdicts of "not guilty" should be entered in respect of particular counts, (*e.g.* where the prosecution offer no evidence on those counts), then it may be that those verdicts are relevant in confiscation proceedings. On the other hand, if the prosecution merely leave counts on the file, the prosecution may well be entitled to adduce evidence in confiscation proceedings relating to those counts. This is because (i) determining benefit under the DTA is an exercise in accountability that often extends beyond the offences on the indictment (s. 4(1)), and (ii) the standard of proof in confiscation proceedings is the civil standard (s.2(8)): and see *Teale* (July 5, 1996, CA).

(b) Joint beneficiaries

Where two or more defendants have been engaged in a joint enterprise 13–229
to commit a drug trafficking offence but one defendant is shown to have received more payments during the relevant period than the other, the Court must determine the total value of the benefits received jointly and then determine the value of the benefit received by each of the defendants. In the absence of any evidence on the point, the sentencer may (but is not obliged) to assume that the defendants shared equally: see *Porter (Jeremy)* [1990] 1 W.L.R. 1260, but contrast that decision with *Chrastny (No. 2)* [1991] 1 W.L.R. 1381. There is nothing in the 1994 Act that alters the previous position; and see para. 13–203 and *Kaspers* (May 22, 1993).

(c) Assets held abroad

By s.62(2) (formerly s.38(3) of the 1986 Act), the 1994 Act applies to 13–230
property whether it is situated in England and Wales or elsewhere: *Hopes* (1989) 11 Cr.App.R.(S) 38. The Act applies to all unlawful drug trafficking ventures wherever they are carried out and the Act applies in respect of property held by the defendant anywhere in the world (see s.62(2) of the

1994 Act). The burden will therefore rest on the defendant to liquidate his assets or face the alternative of serving a consecutive sentence in default.

The approach adopted in *Hopes* appears to have differed from that in *Bragason* (1988) Crim.L.R. 778 where the Court assessed B's proceeds of drug trafficking at £15,000 but certified that the amount which might be realised from the assets which he held "in the jurisdiction" as nil. It is not clear whether the sentencer thought that it was necessary to assess the value of assets held by the defendant in England and Wales but, if he did, he was clearly in error (see also s.62(3)).

(d) Avoiding the double counting trap

13–231 It will be apparent from the above that great care must be exercised in the computation of items alleged to represent the benefits of drug trafficking. Double counting is a familiar error and very easily made. Suppose the prosecutor's schedule of D's bank account reveals that between 1991 and 1992 D deposited £15,000. He withdrew £1,250 by cheque on eight occasions during 1993. In 1994 D registered a car in his sole name and which was then worth £7,000. D has regularly supplied drugs commercially since 1986. The Court could assume that the deposits totalling £15,000 between 1991 and 1992 were the proceeds of drug trafficking (s. 4(3)(a)(ii). It could be inferred that the car was acquired by D at some time within the six-year period and that the value when he did so was approximately £7,000. His benefits at that point amounted to £15,000 and £7,000 = £22,000. However, further enquiries revealed that D paid £10,000 for the car in 1993 by way of the eight sums withdrawn from the account during 1993. Accordingly, the car did not represent a separate source of income after all and thus the sum of £7,000 should be ignored. This is a simple, and no doubt obvious example, but the room for error is much greater in cases involving a large number of bank accounts, assets and transactions.

Section 4(6) of the DTA provides that:

> "For the purpose of assessing the value of the defendant's proceeds of drug trafficking in a case where a confiscation order has previously been made against him, the Court shall leave out of account any of his proceeds of drug trafficking that are shown to the Court to have been taken into account in determining the amount to be recovered under that order."

This provision substantially re-enacts s.2(4) of the 1986 Act. It is clearly designed to protect a defendant from having the proceeds, which formed part of one confiscation order, being taken into account for the purpose of another confiscation order, *e.g.* where the defendant commits a subsequent drug trafficking offence. There is, however, one important qualification to this principle, which appears in s.15(8) of this Act. Under s.15(1) and (2), the Court may revise its assessment of the value of the defendant's proceeds of drug trafficking if there is evidence that satisfies the Court that the real value of those proceeds is higher than was thought to be the case at the time the original confiscation order was made. Obviously, the purpose of s.15 would be defeated if a defendant could pray in aid s.4(6) and thus s.15(8) ensures that the sums (which were properly taken into account when the confiscation order under review was made) are taken into account for the purposes of s.15. Note that similar considerations apply where a defendant ceases to be an absconder and applies for a variation of the amount of a confiscation order made in his absence: see s.21(4) below.

It is important to remember that the Court must not make any of the assumptions in section 4(3) if the only offence for which the defendant is to be sentenced is that of assisting a drug trafficker contrary to section 50 of the DTA.

F. ASSESSING THE AMOUNT THAT MIGHT BE REALISED

I. Introduction

(a) Nil Orders and Nominal Orders

In the ordinary way the amount to be recovered is the amount the Court assesses to be the defendant's proceeds of drug trafficking. This figure represents the ideal: and see *Klann* (July 13, 1999). However, the reality of the situation will often be that the defendant will not be able to pay the full amount and thus the Court will seek to confiscate the "amount that might be realised". Sometimes that figure is nil. 13–232

When the Drug Trafficking Offences Act 1986 was enacted, the prosecution could not apply to vary the order if assets held by the defendant (at the time the order was made) subsequently came to light or the value had subsequently increased. This was remedied by s.16 of the Criminal Justice (International Co-operation) Act 1990 (c.5), now s.16 of this Act. However, it will be seen that s.16 of this Act (like its predecessor) only applies where the defendant is ordered to pay "an amount" by way of a confiscation order but a "nil order" is not an "amount" for the purposes of s.16. Accordingly, assets that had been hidden at the time the "nil" confiscation order was made, but which subsequently surfaced, escaped the effect of s.16 of the Criminal Justice (International Co-operation) Act 1990. To defeat that abuse, s.5(3)(b) (originally enacted as s.7(3)(1) of the 1993 Act) now requires the Court to make a confiscation order for at least a "nominal amount".

(b) Confiscating a sum less than the benefit figure

The circumstances in which the Court can confiscate a lesser amount are very limited and the following points should be borne in mind. 13–233

First, there exists no provision under the 1994 Act for reducing the amount on grounds of personal hardship. Accordingly, no reduction can be made on the basis that the only realisable asset held by the defendant is the matrimonial home (but see *Keston* (1990) 12 Cr.App.R.(S) 93 where a contrary impression is given). On the other hand, it remains to be seen whether (by virtue of s.2(1)) decisions taken by prosecutors and by the Courts not to proceed under the 1994 Act are influenced by considerations of hardship, assistance given to police and so on.

Secondly, the Court must confiscate the full amount (being the defendant's proceeds of drug trafficking) unless it is satisfied that the lesser amount represents the "amount that might be realised" under s.5(3): see *Klann* (July 13, 1999). In those circumstances, the Court must make an order for the lesser amount. There is no halfway house.

Section 5(3) provides:

> "If the Court is satisfied that the amount that might be realised at the time the confiscation order is made [*(or) a 'determination is made'*] is less than the amount the Court assesses to be the value of his proceeds of drug trafficking, the amount to be recovered in the defendant's case under the confiscation order shall be:
> (a) the amount appearing to the Court to be the amount that might be so realised, or
> (b) a nominal amount, where it appears to the Court (on the information available to it at the time) that the amount that might be realised is nil."

Note that the words in italics have been inserted into s.5(3) merely for ease of reference. Where the Court revises its assessment of the defendant's proceeds of drug trafficking (under the provisions of s.15 of the 1994 Act) then s.5(3) shall have effect as if for "confiscation order is made" there were substituted "determination is made": see s.15(9)(b).

13–234 "The amount that might be realised" is defined by s.6(1). It is not the same thing as "realisable property" which is separately defined by s.6(2). However, in the majority of cases the practical effect is that the "amount that might be realised" under s.5 will be the value of the "realisable property", but this need not necessarily be so. In *Carroll* (1992) 13 Cr.App.R.(S) 99, the Court determined the value of the defendant's proceeds of drug trafficking at £39,692. His known assets amounted to £16,301 but the Court concluded that he had undisclosed assets and made a confiscation order of £30,000. The result implies that the Court was satisfied under section 5(3) that the "amount that might be realised" was £30,000 of which in excess of £13,000 represented "hidden assets", *i.e.* £30,000–£16,301). By definition, the "amount that might be realised" includes gifts caught by the Act (which did not feature in *Carroll*) and "realisable property" as defined by section 6(2). Accordingly, the Court's determination in *Carroll* is only valid if "hidden" assets may properly be included within the definition of "realisable property". It is submitted that if the Court in *Carroll* was not satisfied that the appellant only had assets worth £16,301, then the requirements of section 5(3) had not been fulfilled and the Court would have been entitled to make an order for the full amount. In the ordinary way, it is the defendant who knows the full extent of his "realisable property" and the burden under section 5(3) normally rests on him: see *Comiskey* (1990) 12 Cr.App.R.(S.) 562; *Ilsemann* (1990 12 Cr.App.R.(S.) 398; and *Barwick* (October 13, 2000).

Thirdly, any "realisable property" which forms part of the determination of the "amount that might be realised" under section 6(1) and section 5(3) need not, of itself, have been acquired with the proceeds of drug trafficking because the definition of "realisable property" in section 6(2) includes legitimately acquired property: *Chrastny (No. 2)* (1991) 1 W.L.R. 1385 and see *Currey* [1994] Crim. L.R. 960 (a case decided under the CJA 1988 but equally valid on this point). Thus, if X acquires a motor vehicle, the Court has to decide whether it represents the proceeds of drug trafficking. If it does not, then the vehicle must be left out of account in determining the value of the defendant's proceeds for the purposes of section 5(1): see, *e.g.* *Johnson* [1991] 2 Q.B. 249. However, the vehicle (lawfully acquired) will nevertheless be "realisable property" for the purposes of satisfying a confiscation order in respect of any proceeds of drug trafficking that the defendant did receive.

Fourthly, the burden will normally be on the defendant to satisfy the Court of the matters referred to in s.5(3), but it would seem that in appropriate cases the Court may, of its own volition, make a determination under that subsection: see *Keston* (1990) 12 Cr.App.R.(S) 93; *Comiskey* (1991) 93 Cr.App.R. 227; *R. v. Ilsemann* (1990) 12 Cr.App.R.(S) 398 and *Carroll* (1992) 13 Cr.App.R.(S) 99. The Court is not obliged to determine the extent of the defendant's realisable assets in every case where the Court proposes to make a confiscation order. This is because the Act places the burden on the defendant to satisfy the order or serve a consecutive sentence of imprisonment in default of payment: see *Ilsemann* (1990) 12 Cr.App.R. (S) 398, and see *Forrest* (October 11, 1993, unreported) and *Barwick*, above, which provide further support for the general proposition. 13–235

It should be remembered that property retained by police, which is found by the Court to be all or part of the defendant's benefit from drug trafficking, may also represent his realisable property. However, there have been cases where the customs and excise have forfeited property under the CEMA 1979 and that property has been condemned long before the confiscation order was made, but the Court when making the confiscation order was unaware of that fact. The effect is that the forfeited property is no longer realisable and therefore (i) if the defendant's only asset is the property forfeited by the customs and excise then the confiscation order should be reduced in value, but (ii) if the defendant does have other legitimately acquired assets which would satisfy the order then he will be obliged to make full payment. This can produced harsh results, for example, D imports cannabis in a boat whereupon the vessel is forfeited by customs. The boat is worth £15,000 and it was not bought from the proceeds of drug trafficking. Nevertheless, D received a payment of £10,000 as a reward for his assistance in the venture. The Court learns that the value of D's interest in a house is worth £15,000. In those circumstances, the Court may still make a confiscation order in the sum of £10,000 on the strength of D's interest in the house. The boat is no longer realisable but no provision exists by which the value of the boat can be used to offset the amount due under a confiscation order.

(c) Definition of "realisable property"

13–236 Section 6(2) provides:

> "In this Act, 'realisable property' means, subject to subsection (2) below—
>
> (a) any property held by the defendant; and
>
> (b) any property held by a person to whom the defendant has directly or indirectly made a gift caught by this Act."

"Realisable property" therefore includes property held by the defendant (s.6(2)(a)) but also gifts caught by the Act which are held by any person (s.6(2)(b)); and see *Walbrook and Glasgow* [1994] Crim.L.R. 613. Powers of the High Court are exercisable over "realisable property": see ss.26, 27 and 29. A controlled drug that is seized by police is no longer "held" by a defendant and is therefore not realisable property: see *Thacker* (1995) 16 Cr. App. R.(S) 461. In *Hayler* (unreported, May 9, 1994), the judge found that H had paid £217,000 for two imports of a controlled drug and treated that sum as a "benefit"—presumably on the basis that it was an expenditure derived from drug trafficking. However, a substantial proportion of the drugs had been seized, and therefore H was not going to be able to realise any benefit. The Court of Appeal reduced the confiscation order from £200,000 to £20,000.

Note that by section 62(5)(a) "property is held by any person if he holds any interest in it". Accordingly, if D has a one percent interest in property then all of the property is treated as being realisable. However, that does not mean that the Court can confiscate the fall value of the property because the Court may, pursuant to section 5(3), recover the "amount that might be realised" (section 6(1)) being the value of realisable property held by the defendant, less obligations having priority (s.6(1)), and the value of property is calculated by reference to the defendant's beneficial interest in the market value of the property (s.7(1)(a)) after the amount required to discharge any incumbrance has been deducted (s.7(1)(a)).

(d) Definition of the "amount that might be realised"

13–237 Section 6(1) (formerly 5(3) of the 1986 Act, as amended) provides:

> "For the purposes of this Act the amount that might be realised at the time a confiscation order is made against the defendant is:
>
> (a) the total of the values at that time of all the realisable property held by the defendant less

(b) where there are obligations having priority at that time the total amounts payable in pursuance of such obligations, together with the total of the values at that time of all gifts caught by this Act."

If the Court revises its assessment of the defendant's proceeds of drug trafficking (under s.15 of the 1994 Act) then s.6(1) shall have effect as if for "a confiscation order is made" there were substituted the words "of the determination": see s.15(9)(c).

Section 6(1) is concerned with values not limited to the value of realisable property. The draftsmen did not refer to "realisable property" in s.5 and this omission is deliberate. The Act contemplates a situation in which the defendant made gifts "caught" by the Act (as defined by s.8(1), formerly, s.5(9) of the 1986 Act), the value of which may be assessed for the purposes of ss.6(1) and 5, but which fall outside the strict definition of "realisable property" as set out in s.6(2).

The points referred to above were graphically demonstrated in *Dickens* [1990] 2 Q.B. 102. The appellant had been convicted of conspiracy to import cannabis and a confiscation order was made for £129,300 on the basis that the "amount which might be realised" was only £129,300. Included in that sum was the value of a Range Rover motor vehicle. That vehicle was acquired by D who then gave it to his wife. D had therefore made a gift to her and it was a gift caught by section 8. However, D's wife sold the vehicle for value to a solicitor who bought it in good faith. The Range Rover was therefore not a gift to him and it was not "realisable property" within the meaning of section 6(2). Accordingly, the appellant contended that the "amount that might be realised" should have been reduced by the value of the Range Rover.

This argument would have been valid if the phrase "amount that might 13–238
be realised" as it appears in section 5 is the same thing as "realisable property". In *Dickens* [1990] 2 Q.B. 102, the Court of Appeal referred to the fact that "realisable property" and "amount that might be realised" were separately defined under the Act and meant two very different things. Lord Lane C.J. said (at p.111):

"... the phrase 'realisable property' does not appear in section 4 of the Drug Trafficking Offences Act 1986 and in particular does not appear in section 4(3) (now s.5(3)). If Parliament had wished the confiscation order to be confined to the defendant's 'realisable property' as defined by section 5(1) (now s.6(2)), then it would undoubtedly have said so in section 4(3), which it did not. We have no doubt that that was deliberate and was designed to ensure that drug traffickers could not protect the assets they had acquired through drug trafficking by 'giving' those assets to others."

Accordingly, the judge was entitled to look at the value of the gift made by D to his wife. That gift was caught by the Act (s.5(9) of the 1986 Act—now s.8(1)) and its value fell within the definition of "the amount that might be realised" (now s.6(2) of this Act) for the purposes of what is now s.5(3) of this Act (formerly s.4(3)). The fact that the gift to the wife could no longer physically be realised was irrelevant: see *Wallace Duncan Smith*; but see also *Gokal* (March 16, 2001) and *Liverpool Magistrates' Court, exp. Ansen* [1998] 1 All E.R. 692.

Where a gift is "realisable" within the meaning of section 6(2), then the ramifications for the third party are potentially stark since he may be faced with an order from the High Court for the property to be delivered up to a Receiver appointed under section 29(1) of the Act. Third parties have no right to be heard (or to be legally represented) at the Crown Court in the confiscation proceedings respect of that part of the drug trafficking investigation that affects them. The answer is probably in the negative but there have been cases where the trial judge has permitted third parties to make representations.

(e) Who raises the issue under section 5(3) of the DTA?

13–239 In theory, the Court need only make two determinations before making a confiscation order: (see *Klann*, July 13, 1999), namely, (i) whether the defendant has benefited from drug trafficking, and (ii) to assess the value of the defendant's proceeds of drug trafficking.

In practice, the Court will often need to go on and assess the amount that might actually be realised under s.5(3) of this Act. However, the opening words, "If the Court is satisfied", pose the question as to whether the Court, of its own motion, should initiate the third stage or whether it is the defendant who must take the initiative and satisfy the Court on a balance of probabilities that a lesser amount should be confiscated. In *Johnson* (1991) 2 Q.B.249, Neill L.J. said (at 259):

> "It is only necessary to make a calculation in accordance with section 4(3) of the 1986 Act (now s.5(3) of the 1994 Act) if it appears that the amount that might be realised at the time that the confiscation order is made is less than the amount the Court assesses to be the value of the defendant's proceeds of drug trafficking. In the present case it is accepted on behalf of the appellant that her proceeds were not less than £1,300."

Those last few words imply that it is for the defendant to initiate a determination under section 5(3). In *Atlan*, (February 20, 1997) the Court said:

> ". . . the scheme of the 1986 Act was that, where there was no credible explanation from the defence for receipts and/or payments the Court might, if it considered it appropriate, make and act on the assumptions in section 2(2) and (3). As the judge observed in his ruling, 'Armand himself, if anyone, should be able to explain his own affairs'. If a defendant in a drug trafficking case is found to have conducted transactions involving very large sums of money, for which he has no adequate explanation or supporting documentation or other credible

evidence, it would be contrary to the legislative scheme to require the prosecution to investigate and produce evidence of the nature of the transactions, by following bank records or otherwise."

However, in *Keston* (1990) 12 Cr.App.R.(S) 93 (wrongly referred to as "*Preston*" in 1990] Crim.L.R. 528) the appellant had conceded that the sum of £17,000 was an appropriate sum for a confiscation order. It was also agreed that the sole realisable asset of the appellant was the matrimonial home where he lived with his wife and child. These facts were not made known to the trial judge. In the Court of Appeal, Pill J. said that had those facts been made known to the judge he might have taken a different course and, that having been referred to section 5(3), he might have made a very much lower confiscation order or possibly no order at all: "[t]here were other courses which he might have taken". 13–240

With respect, the judgment in *Keston* is not easy to understand. It can be read as implying that in every case the Court should determine "the amount that might be realised" under section 5(3). However, the judgment does not, in terms, go that far and such a statement would be at variance with *Johnson*[1991] 2 Q.B. 249, Comiskey (1990) 12 Cr.App.R.(S.) 562, *Ilsemann* (1990) 12 Cr.App.R.(S.) 398 and *Carroll* [1991] Crim.L.R. 720. In any event, there exists no discretion in the DTOA or the DTA to reduce the amount, which might be recovered by a confiscation order, on the grounds of personal hardship.

It is not apparent from the report in *Keston* what the Court had in mind when referring to "other courses" which the judge might have taken. By section 2(5), the Court must leave the order out of account in determining the appropriate sentence or other manner of dealing with the defendant. If the Court in *Keston* had in mind the possibility of combining a fine with a confiscation order then such a course, although technically possible, would be highly unusual because the confiscation order is the means by which the defendant is deprived of his assets and that sum may be sufficiently great to exhaust the defendant's means to pay a fine: see *Hedley* (1990) 90 Cr.App.R. 70.

In *Judge and Woodridge* (1992) 13 Cr.App.R(S) 685, a case decided under Part VI the Criminal Justice Act 1988, the Court said: 13–241

> ". . . (Counsel) invited us, as a plea of mercy, to exclude from the order for confiscation such figure as represents the matrimonial home, that being the home and not only of these two appellants but the three children who lived with them. We see no grounds upon which this court should, as an act of mercy, enable these appellants to benefit to a substantial financial extent from the result of their crime."

In *Dickens* [1990] 2 Q.B. 102 the Court of Appeal explained the mechanics of the Act in some detail, but determining the "amount that might be realised" was not a stage which the Court analysed in terms of the burden of proof or the requisite standard applicable or upon whom the burden was carried. The Court did remark that determining the "amount that might be realised" may overlap with the determination of the defendant's proceeds of drug trafficking and, indeed, Lord Lane C.J. said (at 105):

> "The provisions are intentionally draconian. Since the amount of those proceeds and the size of his realisable assets at the time of conviction are likely to be peculiarly within the defendant's knowledge, it is not surprising perhaps if essential burdens are cast upon him. . . . "

In *Comiskey* (1990) 12 Cr.App.R.(S) 562, the judge assessed the appellant's proceeds of drug trafficking at £250,000. In the judgment of the Court of Appeal, Tucker J. asked whether there was anything to cause the judge to be satisfied that the amount that might be realised was less than the value of the defendant's proceeds of drug trafficking in circumstances where the appellant did not give evidence during the drug trafficking enquiry or call evidence. Tucker J. said (at 567):

> "On whom is the duty laid of satisfying the Court that the amount that might be realised is less than the assessed value of the proceeds? There can be no doubt that the defendant is in an incomparably better position to do so since he (or she) alone knows what has become of the proceeds . . . there is no obligation on the Crown to satisfy the Court under section 4(3) . . . (now s.5(3))"

13–242 So, the burden is certainly not on the Crown to satisfy the Court under section 5(3), but the mere fact that the defendant is normally in a better position to shoulder the burden does not therefore preclude the Court, of its own motion, following the steps in section 5(3). This line of reasoning seems to be supported by another passage in the judgment of Tucker J. in *Comiskey* when he said (at 567):

> "The only remaining question is whether the Court itself ought to conclude as a matter of common sense that the amount that might be realised must be less than the value of the proceeds by reason of the expenses that must necessarily have been involved in the operation . . . draconian though the provisions of the Act may be, the Court . . . cannot ignore the fact that some expenses must have been incurred."

The Court of Appeal therefore reduced the amount of the order in *Comiskey* from £250,000 to £200,000.

Much of the reasoning in *Comiskey* is sound and the guidance helpful but it is doubtful whether section 5(3) permits any deduction for operational expenses. When the Court referred to expenses involved in "the operation", it is not entirely clear what "operation" the Court had in mind. If that was intended to be a reference to the drug trafficking activities carried on by the defendant, in respect of which payments were received and invested, then allowing for expenses incurred is just the sort of accounting exercise which the Court of Appeal in *Smith* [1989] 1 W.L.R. 765, and *Comiskey* itself, said should not take place. If, by "operation", the Court was referring to expenses incurred in acquiring realisable property (*e.g.* conveyancing fees; stamp duty, etc.) then, again, it is difficult to see how such an exercise (even on a common sense basis) is consistent with the draconian provisions of the Act. However, that said, there is no doubt that there is much force in the suggestion that section 5(3) envisages that either the defendant or the Court itself may carry out a determination under section 5(3). Each case must depend on its own facts as to who should take the initiative.

In *Ilsemann* (1990) 12 Cr.App.R. (S) 398 the Court of Appeal again made it plain that the Court is not obliged to make a determination under section 5(3) unless the defendant raises the issue evidentially.

> In *Ilsemann*, the trial judge made a confiscation order in the sum of £396,385 as representing the defendant's proceeds of drug trafficking. The prosecution submitted a schedule showing that the realisable assets known to the prosecution were only £214,637. The appellant agreed both figures. He did not give, or call, evidence and argued that the Court could only confiscate those assets known to exist and which the prosecution could prove existed.
>
> *Held:* on appeal, that it was for the defendant to satisfy the Court that the lesser figure was all that was realisable. The appellant had not sought to challenge the larger figure.

As Lord Lane C.J. in *Dickens* [1990] 2 Q.B. 102 remarked, the extent 13–243
of the defendant's realisable assets is likely to be peculiarly within the defendant's knowledge and (*per* Tucker J. in *Comiskey*) "the object of the Act is to oblige a defendant to reveal this information so as to enable the Court to make an effective order"; and see *Wallbrook and Glasgow* (1992) 13 Cr.App.R.(S.) 685 and *Lee* [1996] 1 Cr.App.R.(S.) 135. It is therefore usually not enough for the defendant merely to sit back and rely on the facts put forward by the prosecution. If the prosecution in *Ilsemann* had admitted that the lower figure represented the extent of the defendant's assets as being the "amount that might be realised" then it is submitted that the Court, armed with that admission, can say that it is satisfied that the requirements of section 5(3) have been satisfied even if the defendant did not formally give evidence in support of that admission. The latter course would be unnecessary. However, in *Ilsemann*, the issue as to whether the defendant had hidden assets was very much at large. Similarly, in *Carroll* [1991] Crim.L.R. 72, the judge made a confiscation order for £30,000. The appellant's proceeds of drug trafficking were assessed at £39,692 but the prosecution could only prove assets worth £16,301. The judge heard evidence from the appellant but concluded that he had undisclosed assets. He made a confiscation order for £30,000. The Court of Appeal held that the judge was correct in his determination. The appellant had failed to discharge the burden on him to satisfy the Court that the "amount that might be realised" was less than the "value of his proceeds".

In an interesting commentary to *Robson* [1991] Crim.L.R. 222 the learned commentator said:

> "If the prosecution are trying to establish that the defendant has an

interest in a property, in order to allow the Court to make assumptions for the purpose of assessing the value of his proceeds of drug trafficking *Dickens* [1990] Crim.L.R. 603 establishes that the prosecution must prove the existence of his interest to the criminal standard; but if the defendant is attempting to establish that some other party has an interest in a house of which he appears to be the owner, in order to reduce 'the amount that might be realised' under section 5(4)(a)(ii) (see now s.7) it seems that the burden of proof will be on the defendant (see *Ilsemann* (1990) 12 Cr.App.R. (S) 398) presumably to the civil standard."

It is respectfully submitted that this analysis is not complete in that *Dickens* is authority for the proposition that the prosecution need only adduce prima facie evidence that the defendant "held" an interest in property for the purposes of the Act. *Bear in mind that the prosecution is no longer required to prove, to the criminal standard of proof,* that property held by the defendant, at the material time, was a payment or reward in connection with drug trafficking carried on by him or another: section 4(1) (and, if appropriate, s.4(3)) and see s.2(8).

13–244 In *Dickens* [1990] 2 Q.B. 102 the Court of Appeal remarked that determining the "amount that might be realised" may overlap with the determination of the defendant's proceeds of drug trafficking. In *Comiskey* (above), Tucker J. asked whether there was anything to cause the judge to be satisfied that the amount that might be realised was less than the value of the defendant's proceeds of drug trafficking in circumstances where the appellant did not give evidence during the 1986 Act enquiry or call evidence.

If a judge scales down an estimated figure of the benefit received by a defendant, that does not mean that the judge is also required to scale down the value of the defendant's realisable assets. This was the rather odd contention advanced on behalf of one of the appellants in *Taylor*, (March 15, 1994, unreported) where the judge found that G and S made a joint purchase of drugs estimated at £279,350. The judge assumed that the drugs were financed from previous drug trafficking and apportioned G's expenditure/benefit as a 50 per cent share. This approach is of course consistent with the decision in *Porter*. The judge scaled down the figure to £75,000 and the Court of Appeal upheld that determination. The Court rejected an argument that the judge should have found that the realisable property "was a much lower figure and so have arrived at an award in the light of that finding". The value of a defendant's realisable assets includes legitimately acquired property, which may have to be liquidated in order to satisfy the confiscation order: see *Rose and Murray* (November 29, 1996). In any event, the duty of satisfying the judge under section 5(3) was on the defendant in question.

The authorities decided under the 1986 Act are still relevant for these purposes and therefore seem to show that either the defendant or the Court may take the initiative to make a determination under ss.5(3) and 6(2).

Each case depends on its own facts. What has not been conclusively decided is whether the defendant carries merely an evidential burden under s.5(3) or whether he must go on and discharge the persuasive burden as well.

(f) Evidential or persuasive burden under section 5(3)

In *Barwick*, October 13, 2000, a case under the Criminal Justice Act 1988, Part VI, the Court expressed the view that the words of section 73(6) of that Act: 13–245

> "... clearly indicate that the burden is on the defendant to satisfy the Court that the amount that might be realised is less, his being the interest in doing so".

The Court added that

> "... it is likely than an offender may take steps to make the proceeds of crime difficult to trace. Once it is proved that he has received the benefit, *it is pragmatic, and entirely fair to the defendant, to place upon him the onus of showing to the civil standard* that he no longer has the proceeds or that their extent or value has diminished." (emphasis added)

This is not a straightforward issue. As a general rule it is the defendant who shoulders the burden of satisfying the Court of the matters set out in section 5(3), but there is a case for saying that the Court may of its own motion make such a determination: see *Comiskey* (1990) 12 Cr.App.R.(S) 562; *Keston* (1990) 12 Cr.App.R.(S) 93.

In *Ilsemann* [1991] Crim.L.R. 141., Taylor L.J. said:

> "It is accepted that that subsection (what is now s.5(3) Drug Trafficking Act) puts the burden upon the defence to satisfy the Court that the amount that might be realised is less than the amount of the value of the proceeds".

The commentary to that case (1991) Crim.L.R. 141, at p.142 states that the decision:

> "... makes it plain that the Court does not need to embark on the third stage of the investigation (s.5(3)) ... except *at the invitation of the defendant*. If the defendant does not attempt to show that his available resources are insufficient to allow him to meet a confiscation order in the amount, which has been determined to be the 'value of his proceeds', the Court can make a confiscation order for that amount. The Act in effect *puts an evidential burden on the defendant on this issue: it is still not clear who has the persuasive burden on what may be a difficult and complex issue of fact* relating to the determination of the amount that might be realised—such as whether a particular transaction was a disposal of assets for full value, or a disposal for less than full value, in which case the property concerned would be a gift caught

by the Act to the extent to which it was disposed of for less than full value." (emphasis added)

13–246 In *Ilsemann*, the Court was not prepared to accept that the appellant had no hidden assets and therefore, on the facts of that particular case, the appellant's only course would have been to have given evidence in support of his contention that the lesser figure was appropriate. It follows that the defendant has at least an evidential burden, but once raised, does he also have the persuasive burden?

The prosecution in *Ilsemann* could only prove realisable assets of £214,637. The appellant did not give evidence. Had he gone into the witness box and merely said that he had no hidden assets, would the Court then be obliged to accept that blanket assertion in the absence of any evidence to the contrary?

Again, can the Court make even an educated guess as to the extent of the defendant's hidden assets (as seems to have occurred in *Carroll* [1991] Crim.L.R. 720) and stipulate an amount for the purposes of section 5 as being the amount which may be recovered? Does the burden fall on the defendant to show that a transfer of property was not a gift but was a disposal for full value? (See *Enwezor* (1991) 93 Cr.App.R. 233.)

In endeavouring to answer these questions it is, perhaps, not very helpful to analyse the problem merely in terms of whether the defendant carries an evidential or persuasive burden. This is because the DTA operates in a way that is rare in the criminal law by virtue of the assumptions, which the Court is now required to make (adverse to the defendant's interests) under the Act. Prima facie, the Court is obliged to recover the amount that the Court assesses to be the value of the defendant's proceeds of drug trafficking having regard to any assumptions that the Court makes under section 4. The Court need not proceed to determine the "amount that might be realised" under section 5(3) unless the defendant raises the issue and this he can only realistically do by giving evidence or adducing other evidence. Ultimately, the Court must satisfy itself of the matters set out in section 5(3), on all the available evidence, before it is entitled to substitute the lesser figure.

13–247 In other words, once the Court has determined the amount to be recovered under a confiscation order (being the proceeds of the defendant's drug trafficking), the presumption is that the defendant has sufficient assets to satisfy the order and that this presumption can only be displaced if the Court is satisfied to the contrary under section 5(3). The result in *Ilsemann*, above, is consistent with that view although a rather more liberal approach appears to have been taken in *Carroll* and *Comiskey* (1990) 12 Cr.App.R.(S) 562 where some "allowance" was made in the final determination of the amount to be confiscated.

In *Phillips v. United Kingdom* (July 5, 2001), the ECtHR said that:

"Whilst the Court considers that an issue relating to the fairness of the procedure *might arise in circumstances where the amount of a confiscation order was based on the value of assumed hidden assets,* this was far from being the case as regards the present applicant." (emphasis added).

The Court therefore left open the question whether the procedure under section 5(3) complies with Article 6(1). The answer probably is that much will depend on the facts of a given case. However, gifts caught by the Act and dissipated might arguably fall foul of Article 6(2) if they are nevertheless included as being part of the amount that might be realised in the defendant's case. Were a judge to take the view that he has little choice but to include certain items as representing "realisable property", notwithstanding that they are highly unlikely to be realised, he might be able to mitigate the harshness of the result by imposing a much lower term of imprisonment in default of payment than would otherwise be the case: and consider *Hill* (October 14, 1996, CA).

In practice the net effect is that the defendant will generally have the task of discharging not only the evidential burden but also the persuasive burden and see *Murray* (November 29, 1996); and *Mullen*, May 5, 2000). On first principles, evidence of any witness (including a defendant) which is unchallenged, is to be accepted as representing the truth of the matter. In *Johnson* [1991] 2 Q.B. 249, the Court of Appeal seems to have followed this approach: see *McDonald* (1990) 12 Cr.App.R.(S) 457.

If the Court makes a confiscation order and later discovers that assets are available to the Court which were originally unknown, then the Court may vary the order under section 47 of the Supreme Court Act 1981 within the relevant time-limit: see *Miller* (1991) 92 Cr.App.R. 191 and see section 16 (formerly s.16 of the Criminal Justice (International Co-operation) Act 1990, s.16).

In *Dickens* [1990] 2 Q.B. 102 a witness, called by the prosecution, testifies that D had claimed owning two boats which were lying in southern Spain and showed the witness photographs of those two boats. D denied any interest in them. On appeal, the appellant argued that the prosecution should have made further enquiries as to the existence or non-existence of these boats, and that in the absence of such enquiries, the burden of disproving the alleged connection no longer rested on the defendant. The Court rejected that argument. There was evidence on which the judge was entitled to conclude, as he did, that the boats were held by the appellant and that their values must be included in the proceeds of drug trafficking and in the amount that might be realised at the time of the confiscation order. **13–248**

The appellant's argument seems to have been advanced on the basis that he had discharged the evidential burden and that the task of discharging the persuasive burden shifted to the prosecution. The Court of Appeal, without actually deciding the point, resolved the argument by concluding that the trial judge was entitled to find as he did based on the evidence already put before him. Certainly, the defendant is not to be denied the right to give evidence: see *Jenkins* (1990) 12 Cr.App.R.(S) 582.

Where co-defendants are involved, who shared a joint benefit and may even own assets jointly, the provisions of section 5(3) highlight the importance of quantifying the extent of a particular defendant's benefit and then tailoring the confiscation order to his actual means: see: *Porter* (1990) 1 W.L.R. 1260 and *Robson* (1991) 92 Cr.App.R. 1.

II. Quantifying the Amount That Might be Realised

13–249 The "amount that might be realised" is defined by s.6(1) of the 1994 Act (formerly, s.5(3) of the 1986 Act, as amended):

> "For the purposes of this Act the amount that might be realised at the time a confiscation order is made against the defendant is—
> (a) the total of the values at that time of all the realisable property held by the defendant, less
> (b) where there are obligations having priority at that time the total amounts payable in pursuance of such obligations, together with the total of the values at that time of all gifts caught by this Act."

Note that if the Court revises its assessment of the defendant's proceeds of drug trafficking (under s.15 of the 1994 Act) then s.6(1) shall have effect as if for "a confiscation order is made" there were substituted the words "of the determination": see s.15(9)(c).

The calculation therefore involves the sum of the value of "realisable property" (defined by s.6(2)) plus the value of gifts caught by the Act (see s.8(1): formerly s.5(9)) but excluding the total value of payments made in pursuance of obligations "having priority". Such obligations are specified in s.6(4) of the 1994 Act (formerly, s.5(7) of the 1986 Act as amended by s.12 of the 1993 Act) as follows:

> "For the purposes of subsection (1) above, an obligation has priority at any time if it is an obligation of the defendant
> (a) to pay an amount due in respect of a fine, or other order of a court, imposed or made on conviction of any offence, where the fine was imposed or order made before the confiscation order [*(or) "determination"*], or
> (b) to pay any sum which would be included among the preferential debts (within the meaning given by section 386 of the Insolvency Act 1986) in the defendant's bankruptcy commencing on the date of the confiscation order or winding up under an order of the Court made on that date."

Note that the italicised words within the square brackets have been added to s.6(4)(a) for ease of reference. Where a court revises its assessment of the value of the defendant's proceeds of drug trafficking under s.15 of the 1994 Act, ss.5(2), 6(4) and 11(9)(a) are to be read as if for the words "confiscation order" there were substituted "determination": see s.15(9).

(a) "Obligations having priority": section 6(1) and (4)

"Obligations having priority" is defined by ss.6(1) and 6(4) as follows: 13–250

"6(1) For the purposes of this Act the amount that might be realised at the time a confiscation order is made against the defendant is—

(a) the total of the values at that time of all the realisable property held by the defendant, less

(b) where there are obligations having priority at that time, the total amount payable in pursuance of such obligations together with the total of the values at that time of all gifts caught by this Act.

(4) For the purposes of subsection (1) above, an obligation has priority at any time if it is an obligation of the defendant—

(a) to pay an amount due in respect of a fine, or other order of a court, imposed or made on conviction of an offence, where the fine was imposed or the order was made before the confiscation order; or

(b) to pay any sum which would be included among the preferential debts (within the meaning given by section 386 of the Insolvency Act 1986) in the defendant's bankruptcy commencing on the date of the confiscation order or winding up under an order of the Court made on that date."

In *McDonald* (1990) 12 Cr.App.R.(S) 457, the appellant's proceeds of drug trafficking were assessed at £88,710,30. His realisable assets amounted to £870 cash and a flat in Bath worth £50,000 as its marketable value. However, the flat was subject to an outstanding mortgage of £18,000. The trial judge declined to deduct the mortgage on the basis that the debt was not an obligation having priority under section 6(1) and s.6(4). It was correctly conceded in the Court of Appeal that the judge erred in that regard. However, two loans that were provided by relatives towards payment of the deposit when purchasing the flat, were to be disregarded in computing the amount under section 5. Although not apparent from the report these loans may have been found to have been informal in nature which did fall with the category of an "obligation having priority" within the meaning of section 6(4); and see *Ghadami* [1998] 1 Cr.App.R.(S.) 42.

(b) Valuation and re-valuations

Provisions dealing with the revaluation of property and gifts to take 13–251
account of changes in the value of money, successful investment and so on, are to be found in section 7(1)–(3) (formerly, s.5(4)–(6) of the 1986 Act) and provide that:

"7.—(1) Subject to the following provisions of this section and to section 8 of this Act, for the purposes of this Act the value of property (other than cash) in relation to any person holding the property is the market value of the property, except that, where any other person holds an interest in the property, the value is—

(a) the market value of the first-mentioned person's beneficial interest in the property, less

(b) the amount required to discharge any incumbrance (other than a charging order) on that interest.

(2) Subject to section 8(2) of this Act, references in this Act to the value at any time (referred to in subsection (3) below as 'the material time') of a gift caught by this Act or of any payment or reward are references to—

(a) the value of the gift, payment or reward to the recipient when he received it, adjusted to take account of subsequent changes in the value of money, or

(b) where subsection (3) below applies, the value there mentioned, whichever is the greater.

(3) Subject to section 8(2) of this Act, if at the material time the recipient holds—

(a) the property which he received (not being cash), or

(b) property which, in whole or in part, directly or indirectly represent his hands the property which he received, the value referred to in subsection (2)(b) above is the value to him at material time of the property mentioned in paragraph (a) above or, as case may be, of the property mentioned in paragraph (b) above so far as represents the property which he received, but disregarding in either any charging order."

The obvious importance of putting before the Court up-to-date and accurate information regarding values and expenses cannot be too strongly emphasised if a fair order is to be made: *Lemmon* (1992) 13 Cr.App.R.(S) 66.

It is not necessary that the assets must be proved to be the proceeds of drug trafficking for the purposes of ss. 5(3) and 6(1) except in the case of gifts made more than six years prior to the institution of proceedings against him (see s.6(2)(b)): see *Chrastny (No. 2)* [1991] 1 W.L.R. 1385 and see *Chapman, The Times,* November 18, 1991. This section is also discussed under "Gifts".

(c) Establishing an interest in property

13–252 Realisable property also includes a beneficial interest created under a resulting or constructive trust: see *Robson* (1991) 92 Cr.App.R.1; see also *Eves v. Eves* [1975] 1 W.L.R.1338 and *Grant v. Edwards* [1986] Ch. 638. In both of those latter cases, the Court concluded that a beneficial interest was conferred in circumstances where the beneficiary had acted to her detriment. Accordingly, in Robson, the Court reduced the confiscation order to £1,490.

An interesting exercise in valuation appeared in *Chapman, The Times,*

November 18, 1991. In that case, a confiscation order was made against C in the sum of £3,120,015.36. The problem concerned the value of a house bought by C's wife to whom C had made a gift of £58,000. The wife bought the house for £78,000 and used the gift as part payment. The balance of £20,000 she obtained by way of mortgage. By the date of the confiscation order the house was worth £150,000. The trial judge assessed the updated value of the wife's gift as £58,000/£78,000 × £150,000 = £111,538. On appeal, C contended that the judge erroneously failed to take into account the mortgage debt of £20,353.32 outstanding at the time of the order. By section 7(1), where any person (other than the defendant) holds an interest in property then the value is the market value less the amount required to discharge an incumbrance: section 7(1)(a). With some reservation, the Court of Appeal held that the appropriate formula was (£150,000–£20,353.32) × 58/78 = £96,403. Effect must be given to section 7(1) and bearing in mind that the provisions of the Act were penal, they should be construed, if there was any doubt, in favour of the appellant.

As has been said, "the amount that might be realised", as defined by section 6(1), includes "realisable property", being property held by the defendant or a person to whom the defendant has made a gift caught by the Act (ss.6(2) and 8). Property is held by any person if he holds any interest in it (s.62(5)(a)) and, again, property is transferred by one person to another if the first person transfers or grants to the other any interests in the property (s.62(5)(b)). It follows that the Court must be satisfied that the defendant held an interest in property at the relevant time for the purposes of determining the benefit (and the extent of that benefit) pursuant to sections 2(2), 5(1), 4(1) and 4(3) as well as determining the "amount that might be realised" under section 5(3). It is for the prosecution to put before the Court prima facie evidence that property has been held by the defendant before the Court may make any of the assumptions under section 4(3) of the DTA: *Dickens* [1990] 2 Q.B. 102.

Deciding whether the defendant held an interest in property may sometimes be a difficult matter, which can only be resolved by an application of the civil law. There is no doubt that realisable property also includes a beneficial interest created under a resulting or constructive trust: see *Robson* (1991) 92 Cr.App.R. 1. 13–253

In that case, R pleaded guilty to several drug trafficking offences. The trial judge assessed R's benefit as £8,750 but determined the full extent of R's proceeds of drug trafficking at £18,361, being the amount that might also be realised under a confiscation order. The judge accordingly made an order in that sum. In calculating the sum of £18,361 the judge took into account the sum of £1,490 found at R's house. The judge also had to resolve whether a house in Cambridge was also realisable property. He found that it was and that the appellant had a 60 per cent interest and his mother had a 40 per cent interest in that house. The house was worth £72,500 at the time the order was made. It had been bought in 1987 for £39,500 in the mother's name. She had paid the deposit of £2,500 as well as the legal costs and expenses. She also contributed £3,000 towards improvements. R lived in the house from September 1987 until November 1988 together with a number of lodgers who had paid a total of £3,000 to R but which was used by the mother to discharge the mortgage. The mother never lived in the house and R paid outgoings on the property. R referred to the house as "his house".

The Court of Appeal held that on those facts there was neither a constructive nor resulting trust that vested in R a beneficial interest in the house because the evidence did not disclose a common intention that R should acquire such an interest and there was no finding that R acted to his detriment. Furthermore, the evidence did not show that R had made a contribution to the cost of capital acquisition for there to be a resulting trust. The outgoings were not referable to the purchase of the property and the appellant's assertion that the house was "his" afforded no proper basis for inferring a common intention that R held a beneficial interest. The Court was referred to *Eves v. Eves* [1975] 1 W.L.R. 1338 and *Grant v. Edwards* [1986] Ch. 638. In both of those cases, the Court concluded that a beneficial interest was conferred in circumstances where the beneficiary had acted to her detriment. Accordingly, in *Robson*, the Court reduced the confiscation order to £1,490.

13–254 It frequently happens that defendants assert that property is wholly or partly owned by a third party, for example, a spouse. Neither the DTOA nor the DTA made express provision for third parties to be legally represented during the making of determinations at the Crown Court. This state of affairs has sometimes been said to be unfair and that the legislation is seriously deficient in that regard. Strictly speaking the DTA does not make any provision for a hearing to be conducted at the Crown Court. The Proceeds of Crime (Scotland) Act 1995 does make express provision for a hearing. It is arguable that the Courts in England could develop their own rules of procedure to enable third parties to be heard in confiscation proceedings and to be legally represented if they wish. Some judges do permit third parties to be heard but this tends to be the exception rather than the rule. However, there is another way for a third party to be heard and that is for the defendant to call him or her. This frequently happens. It is good practice for legal practitioners to advise a third party to seek independent legal advice (*i.e.* independent of the defendants legal advisers) about their position and to receive advice as to whether it is advisable for the third party to give evidence at all (either on confiscation proceedings or at the enforcement stage). Views differ as to *when* it is usually desirable to call a third party in confiscation proceedings that have not be concluded. The divergence of views has become wider as a result of the decision of Latham J in *Re N (Norris)* (March 31, 1999). In that case, N's husband was convicted of a drug trafficking offence. The judge sought to determine the value of his realisable property including a house in which N was then living. The property was in N's name but the judge concluded that the property was her husband's realisable property. N gave evidence at her husbands DTA enquiry before the Crown Court judge. He rejected her evidence. A receiver was appointed and N again asserted her claim that she had an interest in the property. At the hearing in the High Court, regarding the appointment of a receiver, objection was taken to N raising the issue again. Latham J. upheld the complaint and his judgment was upheld in the Court of Appeal. However, in the House of Lords the decision was reversed (June 28, 2001). The interests of the third party are not identical to those of the defendant.

Some practitioners have expressed the firm opinion that it is prudent *not* to call a third party during the course of DTA proceedings, but to do so at the enforcement stage. With deference to those who hold that view, there is another. It is submitted that a blanket policy not to call a third party (who is prepared to give evidence) is unwise. First, the structure of the DTA is to resolve issues, and to make determinations, at the Crown Court stage. Secondly, if the judge proceeds to determine the amount that might be realised under the DTA, he should value the property in respect of which the defendant holds a beneficial interest. The judge may of course hear from the defendant about the alleged existence of a third party interest, and there may be some documents to assist the judge, but the judge is not going to be assisted any further if the defendant—for tactical reasons—chooses not to call the third party. Thirdly, a tactical decision not to call the third party in the confiscation proceedings rests on an assumption that there will be a subsequent occasion when that party could give evidence, or be able to claim an interest. This is an unwarranted assumption. The burden of paying a confiscation order is on the defendant. It sometimes happens that a receiver is not appointed to sell property. The defendant is coerced into realising his assets, and paying the order. If he fails to do so he faces being committed to prison in default of payment (which does not extinguish the debt). Even if there are ancillary enforcement proceedings in the High Court, or County Court, it should be assumed that a judge there will be more likely to accept the testimony of the third party than a judge sitting at the Crown Court. It is submitted that the decision not to call a third party at Drug Trafficking Act proceedings in the Crown Court, for tactical reasons, is one that should only be done—if at all—after fully explaining the implications of taking that course to the defendant. The decision ultimately should be that of the defendant and the third party (having sought independent legal advice). 13–255

In *Castro* (May 28, 1999), the judge made a confiscation order in the sum of £28,394.81 which the judge found represented the value of the realisable assets of himself "and his wife". C appealed on the grounds that the judge should not have taken into account assets in the name of C's wife and which the Crown could not prove were the property of the defendant ("C"). C contended that the word "defendant" in the DTA referred to the defendant alone and it was wrong for the judge to interpret the statutory provisions as in compassing C's wife. A confiscation order is an order *in personam*, and the judge did not apply the gift provisions. The Court of Appeal dismissed the appeal. It is submitted that is important to view this case as one that turns on its facts. It is for the judge to decide whether property was received and/or is held by a defendant or not. It would have been preferable if the Court had given specific attention to the gift provisions. These obviously apply where, at some stage, the defendant held an interest in the property and then transferred it without any (or sufficient) consideration and where the presumption of advancement does not apply. Gifts "caught by the Act" remain realisable in the defendant's hands.

13–256 In *Ellington* (May 6, 1999) police searched E's room and found £3510 in a drawer in the locked master bedroom normally used by his mother. In confiscation proceedings, E agreed that he had access to the cash in his mother's bedroom, and it seems his mother left the money there so that E could use it while she was away in Jamaica. The judge was under the impression that it was agreed that E had a beneficial interest in the money in the drawer. However, that was not E's case. E said he only had a limited right to use the money. The Court held that it was clear that when E did use sums of money from the drawer, he had an interest in those sums, but there was no factual basis upon which it could be found that he had a beneficial interest, or a right in the balance of the sum in the drawer. Clearly, each case will turn on its own facts.

Although property purports to be held in the name of another, or in joint names, it is open to the Court to find as a fact that the property is held entirely by the defendant and that the arrangement is a "sham": *Sehmi* (February 2, 1999) and see *Castro* (above).

In *Buckman* [1997] 1 C.A.R.(S) 325, the Court said:

> "The correct approach in a case of this type, where property is held in joint names, is for the Court to start with the prima facie position as to where the beneficial interests lie and then to go on to find whether there are gifts caught by the Act which ought then to increase the realisable value of the property within the meaning of section 6 of the Act."

(d) Value of the drug as "property"

13–257 This topic has already been considered insofar it is relates to the value of drugs as a benefit received by the defendant: see para. 13–183. But it is important to bear in mind that we are now dealing with whether the drugs, found in the defendants possession at the time of his arrest, can be taken into account as forming part of his realisable assets (*i.e.* the third determination under section 5(3) of the Act).

Logically, there is no valid reason why the drugs themselves should not be regarded as "property" as defined by section 62(1). However, there are two fundamental reasons why controlled drugs, unlawfully in the defendant's possession, cannot be taken into account for the purposes of section 5(3). First, the "amount that might be realised" under section 5(3) includes "realisable property" (s.6(1)(a)) and that includes "property held by the defendant" (s.6(2)(a)) but, drugs seized by the police or by customs and excise at the time of his arrest, are no longer "held" by him: see *Thacker* (1995) 16 Cr.App.R.(S) 461. In an erudite commentary to this case in the

Criminal Law Review (1995), p.90, it is suggested that the position might be different if the drugs were seized by police under section 23(2) of the MDA 1971 and which are retained by police as an exhibit. It is true, of course, that section 23(2) does not destroy a defendant's (or a third party's) legitimate rights and interest in the property (*e.g.* a passport used as an exhibit remains the holders' document), but if a controlled drug is seized from a defendant under section 23(2), he would have no legal right to compel the return of a drug which he is not allowed to have under the MDA 1971 and the police would have a duty not to return it. Accordingly, the reasoning in *Thacker* applies with equal force in this situation; and see *Hayler* (May 9, 1994). It may make no difference if the drugs were removed from the defendant in an unlawful way (*e.g.* by way of a defective search warrant) because the defendant is forbidden to possess the drug in any event (see s.5 of the MDA 1971).

Secondly, it will be very difficult to quantify the appropriate value of the drug. Most drugs are relatively cheap to cultivate, manufacture or to buy in the country of origin. The so-called "street-value", can be relevant to sentence but it will usually bear no relation to the value of that drug at the moment the defendant received it. In any event, it is inconceivable to think that the drug (even if it is "property") could truly be regarded as "realisable" given the illicit nature of the substance or the unlawful activity contemplated by the defendant. Not all controlled drugs are illegal *per se*. Indeed many have a legitimate purpose in proper hands including heroin, cocaine, amphetamine and many Class B and C drugs (*e.g.* Temazepam). There will therefore be cases where drugs seized in the hands of a drug trafficker could be used legitimately and have a commercial value. Such cases are, however, likely to be rare and valuation is likely to be a difficult exercise. The better course is to ignore the value of the drugs seized in all but the most exceptional cases (but see the commentary to *Stuart and Bonnett* [1989] Crim.L.R. 599 and (1989) 11 Cr. App. R.(S) 89.

(e) Actual value of property

There is authority for the proposition that when determining the amount 13–258
to be realised, the combined effect of sections 6(2) (and 6(1)) is that the Court should look at the true value of property held by the defendant and/or a donee of a gift caught by the Act: *Comiskey* (1990) 12 Cr.App.R.(S) 562, 568.

If by "actual property", the Court of Appeal meant no more than actual values assessed in accordance with the express provisions of the Act then the judgment is without complaint. However, in *Comiskey* the Court went on to say that:

> ". . . the Court cannot close its eyes to the obvious and cannot ignore the fact that some expenses must have been incurred. There can be no question of carrying out an accounting exercise, but it does not seem

to us that some acknowledgment ought to be made of the realities of the situation."

The Court, in the light of those remarks, reduced the order from £250,000 to £200,000. The intention of the Court was laudable but unhappily, the provisions of the Act, strictly construed and applied, do not permit such an exercise. It is not plain from the judgment what expenses the Court had in mind or even what the activity or operation was that incurred expense. Given that the Court could not carry out an accounting exercise, it is not clear upon what basis the discount of £50,000 was made—presumably, it was (at best) an informed estimate or (more likely) a guess.

Where property is ascertained, the obvious importance of putting before the Court up-to-date information as to value cannot be too strongly emphasised if an erroneous and over optimistic valuation is to be avoided: *Lemmon*]1991] Crim.L.R. 791. It is not clear whether the prosecution or the defendant has the burden of proving the correct value of the property. If the defendant contends that the "amount that might be realised" under section 5(3) is less than the value of property alleged by the prosecution, then it seems that it is for the defendant to prove the lower valuation: see *Ilsemann* (1990) 12 Cr.App.R.(S) 398; *Comiskey* (1990) 12 Cr.App.R.(S) 562; *Carroll* [1991] Crim.L.R. 720.

(f) Increase in realisable property

13–259 If the judge makes a confiscation order on the basis that the amount that might be realised is less than the amount assessed to be the value of his proceeds of drug trafficking then, on the application of either the prosecutor or the receiver, an application may be made to the High Court for a certificate of the amount that might actually be realised: see section 16 of the DTA (and see *Tivnan* [1999] 1 Cr.App.R.(S.).

G. EVIDENCE

I. May the Judge Rely on Evidence Heard at the Trial?

13–260 There is authority for the proposition that the judge is entitled to rely on the evidence given during the trial of the drug trafficking offence and that the prosecution is not obliged to call or recall that evidence again during the drug trafficking investigation: see *Jenkins* (1990) 12 Cr.App.R.(S) 582 but see *Rose* (1993) 97 Cr.App.R. 257. However, a confiscation order is a "sentence" (see s.65 and para.2 to Sched.1) and it is also a penal order (see *Welch* (1995) 20 E.H.R.R. 247). It is submitted that the ordinary rules of criminal procedure and evidence are to be applied just as strictly for the purposes of the drug trafficking enquiry as for the trial of the offence itself. This was obviously the view of the Court of Appeal in *Rose* (1993) 97

Cr.App.R. 257. In that case, R pleaded guilty but evidence was given by a co-defendant, G, during the latter's trial regarding money transferred under a bond. After a ten-day drug trafficking enquiry, the trial judge made a finding that R had benefited from the bond based on the evidence given by G. The Court of Appeal found no basis for that finding because, in referring to G's evidence:

> "This was inadmissible evidence upon the drug trafficking enquiry . . . only the evidence in the 10-day enquiry was admissible against the appellant."

It is submitted that the Court, in *Rose*, was correct on this point. In *Chrastny (No.2)* [1991] 1 W.L.R. 1385, the Court gave some thought as to whether evidence which is inadmissible in the trial of the offence, is necessarily admissible on the drug trafficking hearing. Thus, Glidewell L.J. remarked (at 1391E):

> "For our part, we do have some doubt whether evidence which would not be admissible, if the prosecution were for an offence other than conspiracies, is therefore also admissible in relation to proceedings for confiscation under the (1986 Act) . . . but we do not think it necessary at this stage to resolve that question."

Of course, there will be cases where the evidence relied upon for the purpose of the drug trafficking enquiry is essentially the same as that adduced at the trial. Much court time would be wasted if the same evidence had to be called all over again. However, the solution to this problem rests with the proper management of the drug trafficking hearing, by the Court, using the provisions of sections 11 and 12 of the DTA appropriately. The salient parts of the prosecution case should be embodied in the prosecutor's statement and it is desirable that the defendant's financial career should be reduced into schedule format. The defendant may then be asked under section 11(5) to specify which allegations he accepts or to give particulars of any matters on which he proposes to rely to answer allegations which he disputes. Usually, the drug trafficking hearing is narrowed down to relatively few live issues. 13–261

The prosecution may rely on and call evidence in respect of any statement or notice served by them in accordance with s.11 of the 1994 Act. As the Court of Appeal in *Comiskey* (1991) 93 Cr.App.R. 227 remarked:

> "Section 3 of the Act (the fore-runner to s.11 DTA) provides convenient and effective machinery for ascertaining matters relevant to the Courts' determination of the amount to be paid under a confiscation order. It is very desirable that those responsible for the prosecution of offences should make full use of this."

The Court also pointed out the desirability, in appropriate cases, of inviting the defendant to indicate to what extent he accepts the Crown's allegations or, if he does not do so, to indicate any matters he proposes to rely on (see now s.11(5)). Previously, a statement made out of court by a person not called as a witness could not be admitted, except in accordance with established principles of admissibility at common law or under statute: see *Chrastny (No. 2)* [1991] 1 W.L.R. 1381. However, material (including hearsay) may be included in the prosecutor's statement (s.11). If the allegation is accepted then the information may be presented in such fashion as "the Court may direct", see s.11(10).

Section 11(11) affords a most important safeguard, namely, that no admission made by the defendant in response to a prosecutor's statement, to the effect that he has benefited from drug trafficking, or that the drug trafficking was carried on by him, is admissible "in any proceedings for an offence". This provision seems to be wide enough to protect not just the defendant who makes the admission, but also other persons who may be incriminated by it. However, the protection is limited to proceedings for "an offence". It is not clear whether this provision prevents the Court taking an admission made by the defendant into account for the purposes of sentence.

II. Statements Tendered by Prosecution (s.11)

13–262 Putting the relevant party to "strict proof" of their case will often result in the contents of any statement tendered to the other side not being admitted for a variety of reasons, *e.g.* the statement infringes the hearsay rule. Where, for example, a prosecutor is in possession of information alleging that on certain dates valuable property was transferred to the accused, he may seek to embody those allegations in a statement which he can then serve on the defence by way of s.9 of the Criminal Justice Act 1967 (c.80), in the hope that the statement will be accepted. In fact, if put to strict proof, the prosecutor might find that he cannot prove the contents at all.

Under the 1994, Act the procedure for the provision of information has been strengthened. The procedure applies not only to the usual situation where the Court proceeds under s.2, following a conviction for a drug trafficking offence, but also where the Court is asked to proceed under s.2 when it originally declined to do so (s.13(11)); or where the Court is asked to re-assess whether the defendant has benefited from drug trafficking (s.14(8)); or where the Court revises its assessment of the proceeds of any trafficking (s.15(3)); or where the defendant has died or absconded (s.19(6)(b))

Where a prosecutor does not serve a "prosecutor's statement", the Court may order him to serve one (s.11(3)).

(a) Statements served where the prosecutor initiates proceedings

13–263 Section 11(1) and (2) apply in cases where the prosecutor takes the initiative and asks the Court to proceed under section 2 with a view to the Court making a confiscation order:

"11(1) Where the prosecutor asks the Court to proceed under section 2 of this Act he shall give the Court, within such period as it may direct, a statement of matters which he considers relevant in connection with—

(a) determining whether the defendant has benefited from drug trafficking, or

(b) assessing the value of his proceeds of drug trafficking.

(2) In this section such a statement is referred to as a 'prosecutor's statement'."

Under the 1986 legislation it was not incumbent upon the prosecutor to serve, what used to be called a "section 3 statement" in every drug trafficking enquiry but section 11(1) of the DTA now places a duty on the prosecution to furnish the Court with a statement of matters relevant to only two determinations (i) whether the defendant has benefited from drug trafficking and (ii) the value of the benefit. It will be seen that s.11(1) does not require the prosecution to give details of all "realisable property" (see s.6(2) and (3)) or to calculate the "amount that might be realised" (*i.e.* the amount the defendant can truly deliver up: see s.6(1)) and see the Crown Court Rules, r.25A. At first sight, this might seem a serious omission because in most cases the Court would wish to determine whether the defendant is able to pay back the full amount of the benefit he received or not. However it is probable that the omission was deliberate because it will be recalled that the scheme of the Act is designed to ensure that the Courts confiscate the full value of a defendant's proceeds of drug trafficking. That is the reason why section 5(1) begins by saying that the amount to be recovered under a confiscation order "shall be . . . the value of the defendant's proceeds of drug trafficking".

By virtue of s.5(3), the Court need only confiscate a lesser amount (or a nominal amount) if "the Court is satisfied" that the defendant is unable to pay back the full value of his proceeds. In theory then, the Court may assume that the defendant has sufficient assets to satisfy the confiscation order. It is also not uncommon to find that the prosecution allege (and the Court accepts) that the defendant has "hidden assets".

Usually it will be the defendant's task under s.5(3) to prove that he is worth less than the value of his proceeds and this will mean that he must satisfy the Court that he has been utterly frank about the extent of his assets and their value. In practice, the Courts are realistic in their approach and it will be rare indeed for the Court not to make its own enquiries as to the amount that might be realised under a confiscation order. Most judges are not prepared to stand on theory and to assume that sufficient assets exist to meet the full amount unless the defendant proves the contrary. This is not a concession to ameliorate the harshness of the Act but a recognition that a confiscation order can be costly to enforce and that a receiver can only begin to liquidate assets, which are known to exist, and, just as important, he knows where they are (but note *Barwick*)

The Courts are therefore assisted if the statement served under section 11 does deal with matters relevant to any determination that the Court may make under section 5(3) and it is to be hoped that most prosecutors will resist the temptation to say that whether a defendant has sufficient assets to meet the full value of his benefit is an area peculiarly within the knowledge of the defendant and thus not address the issue adequately or at all.

(b) Statements served when the Court initiates proceedings

13–264 By section 11(3), it is provided that:

> "Where the Court proceeds under section 2 of this Act without the prosecutor having asked it to do so, it may require him to give it a prosecutor's statement, within such period as it may direct."

It will be seen that whereas the prosecutor is obliged to serve a "prosecutor's statement", if he asks the Court to embark upon confiscation proceedings (s.11(1) and (2)), the Court is not obliged to order the prosecutor to prepare and to serve such a statement on the Court if it is the Court which initiates the enquiry. Usually, the Court would make such an order in all but the most straightforward of cases. By giving the Court a discretion under s.11(3), time and resources will be saved if the parties are able to proceed under the Act without a prosecutor's statement. However, the defence is entitled to know the case it has to meet and the prosecutor should at least identify at the outset (orally or in writing) those matters it regards as being relevant when determining whether the defendant has benefited from drug trafficking or assessing the value of his proceeds. No doubt, this would normally be done at the stage at which the Court is considering whether it is appropriate for it to proceed under the Act (see s.2(1)) and it is submitted that it would be desirable for the prosecutor to specify those assets that are said to be realisable under the Act.

However, the extent to which the prosecutor is able to prepare a full or adequate analysis of the defendant's financial position for the purposes of section 11, depends in part on the way the defendant has conducted his affairs. Thus, in *Small* (1989) 88 Cr.App.R. 184, the Court of Appeal remarked:

> "... (the applicant) had kept no records, and he had spent considerable sums of money in the recent past. In most cases, it is to be expected that there would be a fuller analysis of a defendant's financial affairs and of the amount that might be realised from them. In this case, the applicants attitude, his unreliability and lack of records made that impossible."

(c) Specifying the time for service of the statement

13–265 A "prosecutor's statement" (see s.11(2)) must be served "within such period as the Court may direct": see section 11(1) and (3). Clearly much will depend on the issues involved; the number and nature of the enquiries to be made, whether overseas enquiries are likely to be involved and the amount of time which should be given to the defence to enable them to efficiently and effectively reply to the statement. Section 11(4)(a) allows the prosecutor to serve a further statement "at any time" and the Court need not wait for the prosecutor to take the initiative but may order the prosecutor to provide a further statement to be served on the Court within such period as it may direct: section 11(4)(b).

Further statements may be required in order to deal with matters raised by the defence, or by the Court, or they may be required in order to clarify or to rectify matters raised in earlier statements. There does not seem to be a limit imposed on the number of further statements which could be served under this provision unless the phrase "a further such statement" is to be construed as meaning literally just one further statement—which would be absurd. The prosecutor may serve a further statement either before or during the hearing of the drug trafficking enquiry. Such a facility is clearly desirable in cases where some adjustment or amendment has to be made in respect of previous statements or where new facts or issues emerge which need to be brought to the attention of the Court. It is clearly desirable that statements are served within a reasonable period. Where a determination is postponed (as is likely to be the case) under section 3 of the Act, then the maximum period permitted is six months from the date of conviction unless there are "exceptional circumstances" and it is by no means obvious that the Courts would be inclined to treat the late service of a statement as amounting to "exceptional circumstances". The answer may be said to depend on the meaning of the phrase "making the determination" as it appears in section 3. Although that phrase could define the moment the Court proceeds to follow the steps mentioned in section 2 of the Act (*i.e.* usually the first day of the DTA hearing) the alternative and better view is that it "includes all" stages of the proceedings until the very moment the Court states its findings of fact in respect of any of the determinations made under the Act (and see, in this context, s.5(2) concerning certificates issued under that section).

(d) Proving matters contained in a statement

The Crown Court Rules (S.I. 1995 No. 2618) provide as follows: 13–266

"25A(1) When, in any proceedings in respect of a drug trafficking offence . . . the prosecutor or the defendant tenders to the Crown Court any statement or other document under section 11 of the Drug Trafficking Act 1994 . . . he must serve a copy thereof as soon as practicable to the defendant or the prosecutor, as the case may be.

(2) Any statement tendered to the Crown Court by the prosecutor under section 11(1) of the said Act of 1994 . . . shall include the following particulars, namely:

(a) the name of the defendant;
(b) the name of the person by whom the statement is made and the date on which it was made;

(c) where the statement is not tendered immediately after the defendant has been convicted, the date on which and the place where the relevant conviction occurred;

(d) such information known to the prosecutor as is relevant to the determination as to whether or not the defendant has benefited from drug trafficking . . . and to the assessment of the value of his proceeds of drug trafficking. . . .

(3) Where, in accordance with section 11(7) of the said Act of 1994 . . . the defendant indicates the extent to which he accepts any allegation contained within the prosecutor's statement, he must indicate the same in writing to the prosecutor, and serve a copy of that reply on the appropriate officer of the Crown Court.

(4) Expressions used in this rule shall have the same meanings as in the said Act of 1994. . . ."

The "prosecutor's statement" should contain matters relevant to determining whether the defendant has benefited from drug trafficking and the value of that benefit. The statement will usually begin with a summary of the salient features of the prosecution case including a description of the charge or charges; the extent of the defendant's criminality, *e.g.* in terms of the number of importations or acts of supply; the amount of drug involved (purity, street value and so on); followed by a resume of the defendant's background including his financial history including a detailed analysis of his property (including money) passing through his hands during the six years prior to being charged, as well as a history of all the property held by him at any time since his conviction irrespective of when that property was acquired (see section 4(3)(a)(i) and see *Chrastny No. 2* [1991] 1 W.L.R. 1381). It may be necessary to include schedules relating, for example, to the number of bank or building society accounts obtained or held in the relevant period. The statement should also endeavour to specify those items and calculations which come under different headings for the purposes of making an accurate determination, *e.g.* items falling within the category of property "held" since conviction (s.4(3)(a)(i)); items "received" or "expended" within the preceding six years (s.4(3)(a)(ii) and 4(3)(b)); items representing the proceeds of drug trafficking received by the defendant at any time in his life (s.2(3)) and so on.

13–267 Matters may be included in the statement which arose during the course of the trial of the offences before the Court: see *Comiskey* (1991) 93 Cr. App. R. 227.

The statement may also contain hearsay but this is subject to heavy qualification. Under the 1986 legislation, it was generally understood that the prosecution should not include hearsay in the statement. Indeed, in *Chrastny No. 2* [1991] 1 W.L.R. 1381, the Court of Appeal made it clear that the Court could only act on admissible evidence. Both under the DTOA, and under s.11 of the 1994 Act, the Court can ask the defendant to indicate the extent to which he accepts any allegation in the prosecutor's statement (see now s.11(5)). If the defendant accepts any allegation then it will be conclusive of the matters to which it relates (see s.11(7)) and this will be so for the purposes of an appeal against the making of a confiscation order: *Tredwen* (1994) Crim. LR 388 but, *cf. Emmett* (February 16, unreported). As Dr. David Thomas Q.C. has pointed out, in his commentary to *Tredwen*, the DTA now provides several ways in which the prosecution can reopen various determinations but "none of these procedures will assist the defendant". The case of *Tredwen* demonstrates the care that defendants must exercise in the preparation of their replies to a prosecutor's statement: and see *McKenzie* (September 24, 1999).

However, where allegations are challenged then the defendant may be required by the Court to state his objection and to give particulars of matters on which he proposes to rely (s.11(5)(b)). The prosecutor is then put on notice as to what he must do in order to prove the allegation by admissible evidence.

(e) Effect of non-compliance with court directions

By section 11(5), it is provided that: 13–268

> "Where any prosecutor's statement has been given and the Court is satisfied that a copy of the statement has been served on the defendant, it may require the defendant—
> (a) to indicate to it, within such period as it may direct, the extent to which he accepts each allegation in the statement; and
> (b) so far as he does not accept any such allegation, to give particulars of any matters on which he proposes to rely."

The effect on a defendant who fails to comply with directions given by the Court in respect of providing a proper response to the prosecutor's statement, is set out in section 11(8) which provides that:

> "If the defendant fails in any respect to comply with a requirement under subsection (5) above he may be treated for the purposes of this section as accepting every allegation in the prosecutor's statement in question apart from—
> (a) any allegation in respect of which he has complied with the requirement and
> (b) any allegation that he has benefited from drug trafficking or that any payment or other reward was received by him in connection with drug trafficking carried on by him or another person."

By section 11, the defendant may be asked to state any matters on which he proposes to rely to refute an allegation contained in a statement tendered under section 11. The penalty, for failing to comply with s.11, is set out in subs. (8). The defendant may be treated as accepting every allegation in the prosecutor's statement in question apart from those stated in subs. (8) above.

Although it is obvious, from the wording of subs. (8)(b), that the legislature was not prepared to go so far as to say that a defendant's non- 13–269 compliance with the requirements of subs. (5) should be construed as an admission either that he benefited from drug trafficking, or that any payment or reward received by him represents the proceeds of that activity, the reality of the situation is that once the prosecution has established that the defendant has received property, the Court may be required to apply the statutory assumption that the payment was received in connection with drug trafficking by virtue of s.4(2)–(5).

Suppose that a defendant indicates to the Court that he does not accept a particular allegation in a statement tendered and served on him under section 11, and suppose that the defendant replies in very general terms. Is the Court then bound to accept that he has complied with section 11(5) or, may the Court (believing that the accused could indicate a great deal more) treat him as having failed to meet the requirements of that subsection? Although any Court must be very slow to conclude that an accused has failed to comply with section 11(5), nevertheless, where a defendant is clearly demonstrated to be obstructive or less than forthcoming, there exists no good reason why the Court should be prevented from treating his conduct as a constructive failure to meet the requirements of section 11(5).

(f) Provision of information by the defendant—section 12

13–270 The Court is now given much greater powers by virtue of section 12 to compel defendants to furnish information to the Courts for the purposes of making determinations under the Act and provides:

"This section applies where—

(a) the prosecutor has asked the Court to proceed under section 2 of this Act; or

(b) no such request has been made but the Court is nevertheless proceeding, or considering whether to proceed, under section 2.

(2) For the purpose of obtaining information to assist it in carrying out its functions, the Court may at any time order the defendant to give it such information as may be specified in the order.

(3) An order under subsection (2) above may require all, or any specified part, of the required information to be given to the Court in such manner, and before such date, as may be specified in the order.

(4) Crown Court Rules may make provision as to the maximum or minimum period that may be allowed under subsection (3) above.

(5) If the defendant fails, without reasonable excuse, to comply with any order under this section, the Court may draw such inference from that failure as it considers appropriate.

(6) Where the prosecutor accepts to any extent any allegation made by the defendant in giving to the Court information required by an order under this section, the Court may treat that acceptance as conclusive of the matters to which it relates.

(7) For the purposes of this section, an allegation may be accepted in

such manner as may be prescribed by Crown Court Rules or as the Court may direct."

This was originally introduced into the drug trafficking legislation by s.10(5) of the 1993 Act but that particular meaure was not brought into force. It is a measure that is likely to have a considerable impact on the way confiscation determinations proceed under the Act. Restraint orders often include an order requiring the defendant to provide information disclosing the existence of all assets held by the defendant or by persons likely to be affected by the order. Such a disclosure order usually contains a clause that affords the defendant limited protection from the material being used as evidence adduced by the prosecution in the proceedings pending against him. Section 12 does not expressly provide a similar protection. The extent to which the sentencer will employ this section in the management of a drug trafficking enquiry is not yet apparent. Once a decision has been made to initiate confiscation proceedings there seems to be nothing to prevent the Court making orders under section 12 before a prosecutor's statement is served. However, that does not mean that the Court has an unbridled power to investigate the defendant's financial affairs and history. As Dr Evan Bell has pointed out, orders disclosing personal financial information probably do constitute an interference with that person's private life, so that Article 8 of the Human Rights Act 1998 is engaged: see "The ECHR and the Proceeds of Crime Legislation" [2000] Crim.L.R. 783 at 792. Such orders might also embrace third parties who have an interest in property held by the defendant. Their rights must be respected and protected. Orders made under section 12 should not be used as "fishing expeditions" but should, it is submitted, be capable of being justified as a proportionate and legitimate enquiry in pursuance of a proper aim, namely, the enforcement of the Drug Trafficking Act 1994. No doubt, the Courts will be called upon to provide guidance as to grounds that do, or do not, amount to a "reasonable excuse" for a failure to comply with an order under it (see subs. (5)). For an interesting example of the limitations of section 12, see *Dechert v. Southwark Crown Court* [2001] E.W.H.C. Admin. 477.

III. Statement Tendered by the Defence

This aspect is now covered by section 11(9) and (10) of the 1994 Act but these provisions should also be read in conjunction with section 12 referred to above. By section 11(9) and (10), it is provided that: **13–271**

"(9) Where—

(a) there is given to the Crown Court by the defendant a statement as to any matters relevant to determining the amount that might be realised at the time the confiscation order is made, and

(b) the prosecutor accepts to any extent any allegation in the statement, the Court may, for the purposes of that determination, treat the acceptance by the prosecutor as conclusive of the matters to which it relates.

(10) An allegation may be accepted, or particulars of any matter may be given, for the purposes of this section in such manner as may be prescribed by rules of court or as the Court may direct."

It will be seen that subsection 11(9) is limited purely to matters relevant to determining the amount that "might be realised" at the time the confiscation order is made. Unlike the preceding subsections, subsection 11(9) is not expressed to include matters that are relevant to determining whether the defendant has benefited from drug trafficking or assessing the value of his proceeds as a result.

IV. Use of Admissions in a Trial for an Offence

13–272 Section 11(11) (formerly section 3(6)) provides an accused with a crucial safeguard, namely that:

> "No acceptance by the defendant under this section that any payment or other reward was received by him in connection with drug trafficking carried on by him or another shall be admissible in evidence in any proceedings for an offence."

Accordingly, no admission made by the defendant (in order to comply with s.11) to the effect that he has benefited from drug trafficking, or that the drug trafficking was carried on by him, is admissible "in any proceedings for an offence". Thus where, for example, a defendant is accused of supplying drugs over a period of two weeks but he accepts (for the purposes of proceedings under the DTA) that he has received property in connection with drug trafficking over the preceding six years, it is not open to the prosecutor to use that admission to initiate fresh proceedings, or to support the charge alleged, or to support an application to add a count alleging the supplying of drugs over the longer period to which the admission relates. Section 11(11) seems to be wide enough to protect not just the defendant who make the admission, but also other persons who may be incriminated by it. However, the protection is limited to proceedings for "an offence" and it does not go far enough to prevent the Court from taking into account (for the purpose of sentencing the defendant) any admission he made under section 11, *e.g.* that demonstrates that the offence was not a "one-off" or out of character.

In *Re T. (Restraint Order)*, *The Times*, May 19, 1992, the Court of Appeal held that section 3 of the DTOA (now s.11) enabled the Crown Court to make orders which were or might be akin to disclosure orders (and see *Re O. (Restraint Order)* [1991] 2 Q.B. 520). It was said that section 3 of the DTOA was designed to prevent the defendant from refusing to answer an allegation that an asset was received as a payment or reward for drug trafficking on the ground of self-incrimination. Applying the same reasoning under the 1994 Act, self-incrimination is therefore no ground for failing to comply with a Crown Court order under section 11.

H. GIFTS

As has been explained above, the purpose of the DTA is to confiscate the defendant's proceeds (and not just the profit) of drug trafficking. The "amount to be recovered" (a term defined by s.5(1)) is the full value of those proceeds and thus a confiscation order can be made in that sum unless the Court is persuaded to order a lesser amount being the "amount that might be realised" (another term of art defined by s.5(3)). 13–273

The burden is therefore on the defendant to pay the order or serve a term of imprisonment in default (s.9). This means that the defendant will be expected to use his best endeavours to liquidate his assets. However, it frequently happens that gifts are made to third parties which represent the proceeds of drug trafficking and these may be gifts properly so-called (*i.e.* in the sense that the defendant does not claim any further interest in them and parts with the property without receiving any, or adequate, consideration). Occasionally, a transfer of property will be cloaked as a gift when in truth the defendant expects the return of all or part of the asset. The problem is that it is the defendant rather than the prosecutor who will normally be in a better position to know the true position.

Without the benefit of the powers under the DTA, it would be difficult, if not impossible, to recover property that is held by a third party whether described as a gift or otherwise. If D receives a vase worth £1,000 as a reward in connection with drug trafficking, which he then sells to T for £1,000 cash, there is no difficulty because the £1,000 (if banked and saved) will be part of the defendant's "realisable assets" but if the vase is transferred to T for no consideration then it is a "gift caught by the Act" (s. 8) and a number of consequences follow. If the Court decided that D's benefit was £1,000 then it could order him to pay that sum (s. 5(1)). If the gift was, truly, a sham transfer then the defendant would be coerced by the Act to get the vase back in order to sell it to pay off the order.

If D claimed that he was not worth £1,000 then the Court would embark upon a determination under section 5(3) *i.e.* "the amount that might be realised", and that term is defined by section 6(1) to include "realisable property held by the defendant" and the value of gifts "caught by this Act" (s.6(1)) and, for the reasons given above, the vase was such a gift (s. 8). It should be noted that a gift caught by the Act is also "realisable property" (s. 8(2). Accordingly, D must try to realise the asset if he can in order to avoid serving a term of imprisonment in default. D's burden may be lightened if the prosecutor applies to the High Court or the County Court for the appointment of a receiver (s.29) and the Court may order the holder of the gift to make such payment (which may represent the full value of the gift) to the receiver as the Court directs under section 29(6) or the

Court may empower the receiver to realise its value in some other way (s.29(5)) or it may order the person holding the property to deliver it up to the receiver (s.29(4)).

It will be seen that it is the prosecutor who can apply to the Court for a receiver to be appointed. The defendant has no such power under the DTA.

(a) Definition of gift

13–274 Section 8(1) reads:

"A gift (including a gift made before the commencement of s.1 of this Act) is caught by this Act if:

- (a) it was made by the defendant at any time since the beginning of the period of six years ending when the proceedings were instituted against him, or
- (b) it was made by the defendant at any time and was a gift of property:
  - (i) received by the defendant in connection with drug trafficking carried on by him or another, or
  - (ii) which in whole or in part directly or indirectly represented in the defendant's hands property received by him in that connection."

It is therefore plain that where it can be shown that the defendant made a gift at any time in his career then it will be caught by the Act if it was received by him in connection with, or represents the proceeds of, drug trafficking. No such qualifications or restrictions operate in respect of gifts made by the defendant during the six-year period ending when proceedings were instituted against him: see section 8(1)(a). Accordingly, it is submitted that all gifts made by the defendant during the relevant six-year period are caught by the Act irrespective as to whether the prosecution can prove that they represent the proceeds of drug trafficking or not. The case law in relation to gifts is not as developed as one might have expected. Are transfers of money out of the jurisdiction to third parties "gifts caught by the Act"?

It is tempting to construe section 8(1) in conjunction with the assumptions the Court may make pursuant to sections 4(2) and (3), but such an approach is liable only to mislead, not least because section 4 and section 8 are concerned with two very different stages in the determination of a confiscation order. Section 8 applies only after the Court has assessed the value of the defendant's proceeds of drug trafficking by making, if necessary, any of the statutory assumptions for that purpose. Gifts "caught by the Act" are included as part of the defendant's "realisable property" (s.6(2)) and the value of all gifts caught by the Act is to be included in any calculation of the "amount that might be realised for the purposes of ss.5(3) and 6(1). This is so irrespective as to whether or not the donee has disposed of the gift: see *Dickens* and see *Wallace Duncan Smith* [1996] 2 Cr.App.R.1; but see *Gokal* (March 16, 2001) and *Liverpool Magistrates'*

Court, ex p. Ansen [1998] 1 All E.R. 692; and consider *McCarthy* (January 22, 1998).

A gift is expressly caught by the Act if it is made by the defendant, but it is not clear what the position would be if the gift was in fact made by a person other than the defendant, *e.g.* by his wife. Presumably, where a person can be demonstrated to have acted on behalf of the defendant, then the Courts would have little difficulty in holding that the acts performed were in reality those of the defendant himself.

In the ordinary way a "gift" of property relates to a transfer of property, **13–275** to another, free of any consideration. However, the Act anticipates cases where the defendant transfers property to another for a consideration far less than the actual value of the property. Accordingly, section 8(2) provides:

"For the purposes of this Act—

(a) the circumstances in which the defendant is to be treated as making a gift include those where he transfers property to another person directly or indirectly for a consideration the value of which is significantly less than the value of the consideration provided by the defendant, and

(b) in those circumstances, the provisions of subsection (1) above and of section 7 of this Act shall apply as if the defendant had made a gift of such share in the property as bears to the whole property the same proportion as the difference between the values referred to in paragraph (a) above bears to the value of the consideration provided by the defendant."

It follows that where property is sold to another for a consideration, which substantially reflects its true value, then the property sold is not realisable. Instead, the Court will look to the payment received by the defendant, as a result of the sale, and confiscate that sum, or the property it represents, if it has been converted. Obviously, if the defendant does not invest or re-invest the proceeds of sale but chooses to squander the proceeds instead, then the extent of the defendant's "realisable property" is diminished as a result. Section 8(2)(b) is explained below.

By section 62(5)(b), property is transferred by one person to another "if the first person transfers or grants to the other any interest in the property."

(b) Valuing the gift

The DTA makes special provision in connection with the valuation of **13–276** gifts. Obviously, a gift of property made by a defendant in, for example, 1978, will now be worth a great deal more once inflation is taken into account. Accordingly, section 7(2) provides for an adjustment of the value of a gift as follows:

"Subject to section 8(2) of this Act, references in this Act to the value at any time referred to in subsection (3) below as 'the material time') of a gift caught by this Act or of any payment or reward are references to—

(a) the value of the gift, payment or reward to the recipient when he received it, adjusted to take account of subsequent changes in the value of money, or

(b) where subsection (3) below applies, the value there mentioned, whichever is the greater."

Section 7(3) is concerned with the value of the gift as assessed by the recipient himself. For example, if an antique vase (being the proceeds of drug trafficking) is sold to the recipient for £1,200 when, in fact, according to expert opinion it was only worth £800, the Act takes the higher figure as representing the value of the gift. Section 7(3) reads as follows:

"Subject to section 8(2) of this Act, if at the material time the recipient holds—

(a) the property which he received (not being cash), or

(b) property, which in whole or in part, directly or indirectly represents the property that he received,

the value referred to in subsection (2)(b) above is the value to him at material time of the property mentioned in paragraph (a) above or, as the case may be, of the property mentioned in paragraph (b) above so far as it represents the property which he received, but disregarding in either case any charging order."

(c) Valuation under section 8(2)(b)

13–277 As we have seen, the defendant may transfer property for a consideration significantly less than its actual value. The DTA will treat that transfer as a gift: section 8(2)(a). Obviously the property, once in the hands of the recipient may increase in value. Therefore, by section 8(2)(b) the value of the property so transferred is calculated as follows:

"In those circumstances, the provisions of subsection (1) above and of section 7 of this Act shall apply as if the defendant had made a gift of such share in the property as bears to the whole property the same proportion as the difference between the values referred to in paragraph (a) above bears to the value of the consideration provided by the defendant."

Where a defendant pays £1,500 for a rare vase which he then sells to another for £500 the defendant has thus made a gift which is caught by the Act: see s.8(2)(a). The difference between the price paid by the defendant and then received by him is £1,000 and thus the value of the share of the gift is 2:1 (see subs. (2)(b)). This ratio is important for the purposes of s.7(2) of the Act because the appropriate value of the gift is its adjusted value to take account of any changes in the value of money: see s.7(2)(a). Thus, if the vase (by the date of determination under s.2) was worth £3,000 then the value of the gift would be £2,000.

(d) Knowledge that a gift represents drug proceeds

As originally drafted, the DTOA did not create any offences designed to punish those who acquired property (as a gift or otherwise) knowing or suspecting its drug trafficking history. 13–278

The DTA includes a number of money-laundering offences (see ss. 49 and 53) and, in the context of gifts, it is as well to be mindful of section 51 of the Act which should be read and compared with its forerunner s.14(3) of the Criminal Justice (International Co-operation) Act 1990 (c.5) because the intention of both provisions was to deal with property coming into the hands of another which represents in whole, or in part, directly or indirectly, the proceeds of drug trafficking. The offence under s.14(3) of the 1990 Act was narrower in the sense that it was confined to property which had been "acquired", presumably in the sense that the recipient acquired an interest in the property or was held by the recipient on more than a merely temporary or short-term basis. By contrast, section 51 includes any acquisition, but the section also includes the possession or use of that property.

I. Enforcing a Confiscation Order

Broadly stated, there are two ways in which a confiscation order may be enforced. The first method is by treating such an order as a fine: a defendant who is tempted not to pay the fine faces the prospect of a consecutive sentence of imprisonment in default. The second method is by the appointment of a Receiver who will (if necessary) seize, realise and manage the defendant's realisable property. 13–279

I. Treating the Confiscation Order as a Fine

Section 9(1) of the DTA sets out the general principles to be applied: 13–280

> "Where the Crown Court orders the defendant to pay any amount under section 2 of this Act, sections 139(1) to (4) and 140(1) to (3) of the Powers of Criminal Courts (Sentencing) Act 2000 (powers of Crown Court in relation to fines and enforcement of Crown Court fines) shall have effect as if that amount were a fine imposed on him by the Crown Court."

The Powers of the Criminal Courts (Sentencing) Act 2000, section 139 provides the powers of the Court in relation to the payment of fines. When a confiscation order is made, the Court must make an order fixing a term of imprisonment in default under section 139(2) albeit that a failure to do so does not invalidate the confiscation order: *Ellis* [1996] 2 Cr.App.R.(S) 403. Section 139(4) sets out the maximum periods of imprisonment, which are to be imposed in default, as follows:

Over £50, not exceeding £200	7 days
Over £200, not exceeding £400	14 days
Over £500, not exceeding £1,000	28 days
Over £1,000, not exceeding £2,000	45 days
Over £2,500, not exceeding £5,000	3 months
Over £5,000, not exceeding £10,000	6 months
Over £10,000, not exceeding £20,000	12 months
Over £20,000, not exceeding £50,000	18 months
Over £50,000, not exceeding £100,000	2 years
Over £100,000, not exceeding £250,00	3 years
Over £250,000, not exceeding £1 million	5 years
Over £1 million	10 years

It will be noted that section 139 provides maximum terms of imprisonment: there are no minimum terms and therefore the judge does have a discretion below the maximum term permitted and it will frequently happen that the Court will fix the term approximately half-way between the maximum of the band in question and the maximum term of the band immediately below. Thus, in *Szrajber* (1994) Cr.App.R.(S) 821, Latham J. said:

> "Normally the Court is likely to determine that the appropriate period in default will fall between the maximum for the band immediately below that which was being considered, and the band itself. In the present case the sum in question (£407,188) is the band of £250,000 to £1 million for which the appropriate maximum is five years' imprisonment. The band next below it, which is £100,000 to £250,000 has a maximum of three years, so one would normally expect that the sentence would be between three and five years and would of course be determined in the exercise of the Court's discretion by reference to the amount which was in fact in question in the particular case."

13–281 In *French* (1995) 16 Cr. App. R. (S) 841, Hobhouse L.J. gave further guidance as to how the Courts should approach this problem in the context of the nature of the order which the Court is seeking to enforce:

> "The overriding policy of the Drug Trafficking Offences Act 1986 is to ensure that those who have engaged in drug trafficking do not retain the benefits of their activities. A wide range of powers is given to the Courts and the relevant authorities to assist in achieving that end. One power (which is directed to ensuring or obtaining as far as possible the co-operation of the relevant individual) is the power to impose a period of imprisonment in default of compliance with the order.
>
> It is to be borne in mind that there is a scheme under the Act whereby orders may be reviewed and whereby the period in default falls to be reduced if the order has been partially complied with. However, the hypothesis on which the order in default has to be made is that there is a wilful and total refusal to comply with the order. It postulates that the relevant person may be preferring to serve an additional period of imprisonment rather than comply with the financial

order. It is not the role of the Courts to encourage a defendant in any way in his non-compliance with the order. The period of imprisonment in default which is imposed should be such, within the maxima permitted, as to make it completely clear to the defendant that he has nothing to gain by failing to comply with the order."

Accordingly, the judge is required to consider the circumstances of the case including its overall seriousness, and to fix a term that will act as a deterrent to the defendant against failing to comply with the confiscation order. In *Taylor* [1996] Crim.L.R. 275, the trial judge made a confiscation order in the sum of £15,311,729 but imposed a term of only four years' imprisonment in default. The value of the order is not decisive for the reasons given by Latham J. in *Szrajber*:

"... it is not necessarily appropriate to approach the case on a simple arithmetical basis, in other words providing a sort of ladder up the scale from three years to five years dependent on where within the band the confiscation order lies, otherwise Parliament would presumably have indicated that that was the way to do it by rather clearer definition in the scaling process."

Except for section 9(5) of the Drug Trafficking Act, the new provisions broadly repeat section 6 of the 1986 Act: and see *Elliott* (August 14, 2000).

Defendants often complain that their failure to discharge the burden on them under section 5(3) of the Drug Trafficking Act has led, or will lead, to the default term being executed. Where a judge believes that the "amount that might be realised" is likely to be unrealised in practice, it is open to him to impose a lesser term of imprisonment in default of payment.

The Court is also entitled to have regard to the totality of the sentence imposed when assessing the length of the term of imprisonment to be passed in default of payment of the confiscation order: *Cukovic* (1996) 1 Cr.App.R.(S.) 131, and see *Walpole* (June 19, 1997). In *Walpole*, a default term was quite exceptionally reduced below the normal band, that is to say the term was reduced from eight years' imprisonment to four years' imprisonment: and see *Atlan* (February 20, 1997); *Middlekoop* (October 25, 1996; *Andrews* (July 29, 1996). It should be carefully noted that if the Court fails to impose a term of imprisonment in default of payment, a magistrate has no power to commit the defendant prison for non-payment of the confiscation order: see *R v. Greenwich JJ. ex p. Dixon* (July 30, 1988); and see *Martins v. Liverpool City Magistrates' Court* (October 17, 1997).

Note that the imposition of a term of imprisonment in default of payment of a confiscation order is not a violation of Articles 6 and 7 of the ECHR: *Arman* (May 9, 2000).

(a) Time to Pay

It is very important that defendants ask for time to pay, for otherwise, the payment of a confiscation order arises from the moment the order is 13–282 made. In the *City of London Justices ex.p. Chapman* (March 5, 1998) the Divisional Court advised judges that it would be better to set a specific date by which sums under a confiscation order have to be paid.

(b) Effect of confiscation order over other debts

13–283 A confiscation order takes priority over an unsecured debt. The Court has no power to take unsecured debts into account when assessing the amount of a defendant's realisable assets: see *Re W, The Times*, November 15, 1990.

II. Committing a Defaulter into Custody

13–284 In the event of commitment for default of payment, it must be served consecutively to any sentence of imprisonment (or detention) imposed for the drug trafficking offence itself: see section 9(2).

Commitment to prison is a measure of last resort but unlike a fine (or indeed a confiscation order under the old law) the defaulter can no longer serve a term of imprisonment in default of payment and expect to be released from his obligations to satisfy the confiscation order. This is the result of section 9(5) (originally inserted into the 1986 Act by s.13 of the 1993 Act but which did not come into force). The plain purpose of the 1986 Act was that a person convicted of a drug trafficking offence should be deprived of his proceeds of drug trafficking by way of a confiscation order to the extent that he was in possession of adequate resources to satisfy the order. A magistrate should not issue a warrant of commitment unless s/he has considered all other methods of enforcing payment: see *Harrow Justices, ex.p. D.P.P.* (1991) 1 W.L.R. 395.

Under the 1986 Act, the practical consequences flowing from the defendant's commitment to prison were threefold. First, the period to be served in default of payment, relieved the defendant of the requirement to satisfy that proportion of the order that remained outstanding. The defendant therefore effectively "served" his way out of paying the order and so defeated the primary purpose of the Act. Secondly, a warrant, once issued, cannot be withdrawn by the magistrates' court: see *Newport Pagnell Justices, ex. p. Smith* (1988) 152 J.P. 475. Thirdly, proceedings for the purposes of the 1986 Act were "concluded" upon the defendant serving a term of imprisonment in default of payment: s.38(12) as amended by Sched.5, para.16 of the Criminal Justice Act 1988. Although this result must have been part of the Government's strategy at the time, it was quickly criticised as enabling drug traffickers to keep their ill-gotten gains for purposes lawful or unlawful.

Following the Seventh Report of the Home Office Affairs Committee on Drug Trafficking and Related Serious Crime (1989), the Home Office Working Group (1991) expressed concern that trafficking could obstruct the satisfaction of a confiscation order by shifting funds. Once he had served a term of imprisonment in default, his property would not be liable to confiscation wherever it was situated. The Group therefore recommended that a term of imprisonment served in default should not expunge what ought to be regarded as a "debt" (para.3.11). Accordingly, what is now subs. (5) has been introduced into the legislation to give effect to that proposal (derived from s.13(1) of the 1993 Act which inserted s.6(7) into the 1986 Act).

Section 38(12) of the 1986 Act has now been replaced by s.41 of the DTA 1994. Powers conferred on the High Court in respect of the making of a restraint or charging order, or the realisation of property by the appointment of a receiver, are only exercisable where proceedings are not concluded: see ss.25–31 and 41(3), below. **13–285**

Even where monies had actually been taken from the defendant at the time of his arrest, it was a mandatory requirement of s.6 of the 1986 Act that a term of imprisonment be imposed in default of payment of the sums confiscated: see *Popple* (1993) 14 Cr.App.R.(S) 60. This is because Customs and Excise officers, for example, did not have power to pay money in satisfaction of a confiscation order without first obtaining the defendant's consent or applying to a magistrates' court for a distress warrant.

By s.9(2) of the 1994 Act, a term of imprisonment (or detention) ordered to be served in default of payment, shall run after the defendant has served any sentences of imprisonment which were imposed in respect of the offences for which he appeared at the Crown Court.

Thus, a warrant of commitment may be issued under section 9(2) of the DTA that provides that:

> "Where:
> (a) a warrant of commitment is issued for a default in payment of an amount ordered to be paid under section 2 of this Act in respect of an offence or offences, and
> (b) at the time the warrant is issued, the defendant is liable to serve a term of custody in respect of the offence or offences,
>
> the term of imprisonment or of detention under section 108 of the 2000 Act (detention of persons aged 18 to 20 for default) to be served in default of payment of the amount shall not begin to run until after the term mentioned in paragraph (b) above."

By section 9(3) of the DTA:

> "The reference in subsection (2) above to the term of custody which the defendant is liable to serve in respect of the offence or offences is a reference to the term of imprisonment, or detention in a young offender institution, which he is liable to serve in respect of the offence or offences—and for the purposes of this subsection—
> (a) consecutive terms and terms which are wholly or partly concurrent shall be treated as a single term, and
> (b) there shall be disregarded—
>   (i) any sentence suspended under section 118(1) of the 2000

Act (power to suspend sentence of imprisonment) which has not taken effect at the time the warrant is issued;

(ii) in the case of a sentence of imprisonment passed with an order under section 47(1) of the Criminal Law Act 1977 (sentences of imprisonment partly served and partly suspended) any part of the sentence which the defendant has not at that time been required to serve in prison; and

(iii) any term of imprisonment or detention fixed under section 139(2) of the 2000 Act (term to be served in default of payment of fine etc) for which a warrant of commitment has not been issued at that time."

13–286 Since confiscation orders are enforced as fines imposed on defendants by the Crown Court, the 1994 Act (like its predecessor) employs the machinery created by the Powers of Criminal Courts (Sentencing) Act 2000 and the Magistrates' Courts Act 1980 (c. 43) for the collection of sums due under confiscation orders. Thus by s.139(1)(a) of the 2000 Act, the Crown Court may allow time for the payment of the amount due or it may direct payment by instalment but it must fix a term of imprisonment in default of payment (s.139(2) of the 2000 Act).

Although there exists a line of cases in which the Court of Appeal have held that a term of imprisonment imposed for an offence, plus any term imposed in default term of payment of a fine, should not constitute an excessive sentence when viewed globally (see *Michael and others* (1984) 6 Cr.App.R.(S) 379 and *Chatt* (1984) 6 Cr.App.R.(S) 75) nevertheless it seems that different considerations apply where the Court is concerned with terms imposed in default of the payment of a confiscation order because the purpose of the default term is to encourage or to coerce payment of the sum due under the order; see *Garner and others* (1985), 7 Cr. App. R. (S) 285. In any event, the table of default terms of imprisonment in s.31 (3A) of the 1973 Act are maximum terms only and, in the ordinary way, the Court would be likely to determine that the appropriate term would fall between the maximum of the band being considered and the maximum of the band immediately below but much would depend on the facts of the case: see *Szrajber*, 15 Cr.App.R.(S) 821 and *French* (1995) 16 Cr. App. R. (S) 841 and see *Taylor* [1996] Crim.L.R. 275.

13–287 In *Harrow Justices, ex p. DPP* (above) the Divisional Court suggested that the magistrates should keep in mind a number of points when exercising their discretion whether or not to issue a warrant of commitment, including that:

"(1) The object of the confiscation order was to divest the defaulter of money or other realisable assets.

(2) It was not a matter of choice for the defaulter to buy his way out of such an order by serving the term of imprisonment imposed in default.

(3) The mere fact of a confiscation order was evidence that when it

was made there were realisable assets available to meet the requirements of the order.

(4) Even if at the date when justices had to consider the question of enforcement, the value of realisable assets was less than at the date of the confiscation order, it was open to the defaulter to apply for a certificate of inadequacy under (section 17 of the Drug Trafficking Act) which would lead to a reduction in the amount of the original order.

(5) Given the inter partes nature of the procedure leading to a confiscation order, the prosecution would probably have had information available which would be relevant for the justices' consideration. More compellingly, the prosecution would have had a legitimate interest in being heard before the justices came to a decision.

(6) Given the purposes of (the legislation) it was incumbent on justices to consider all methods of enforcement short of issuing a warrant of commitment in a (DTA) case before doing so."

On the facts of that particular case, the Court granted certiorari to quash a decision to commit D to prison, in circumstances where magistrates had made no enquiry into D's means but merely relied on the fact that he was at the time serving a prison sentence. Given that a defendant can no longer "serve-out" his obligation to pay the sum due under a confiscation order, it remains to be seen whether there will be a greater readiness to issue a warrant of commitment.

Sometimes there are very lengthy periods of delay between the date when time to pay has expired and enforcement proceedings are instituted. However because a defendant carries the burden of paying the confiscation order, he cannot easily complain (if at all) that delay in bringing enforcement proceedings against him amounts to an abuse of the process of the Court: see *Chichester J.J. ex. p. Crowther* (October 14, 1998).

It should also be noted that it is not necessary for magistrates to conduct a means inquiry before committing a defendant to prison for failing to pay a confiscation order: *R. v. Hasting & Rother J.J. ex. p. Ariscombe* (February 5, 1998).

In *Re Peracha* (March 31, 1998), it was contended that section 16 of the DTOA (now s.9(2) of the Drug Trafficking Act) should be construed so that the word "liable" in that section, means "susceptible, exposed or open to" and not "bound or obliged" to serve a term of custody in default of payment. In order to succeed in the submission, P contended that *Chapman* (s.3.98) was wrongly decided. In *Peracha*, the Divisional Court disagreed. Lord Justice Rose said: 13–288

> "For my part, I see no reason to regard *Chapman* having been wrongly decided. On the contrary, agree with those passages in the judgments of Mr Justice Gage and Mr Justice Pill which I have cited in relation to the construction of section 6; that is to say, 'liable' in section 6 means, 'presently liable'.

The history of the legislation, insofar as it provides any assistance, to my mind suggests that the words 'liable to serve' which appear in section 6(3) should, if anything, be given a restricted meaning, because they are no longer immediately preceded by the word 'serving'.

In any event, for my part, I am satisfied that 'liable' means 'bound to serve', and not 'exposed to the risk of serving'. There is a separate regime for sentences for substantive offences and default terms imposed if confiscation orders are not complied with. This is demonstrated, to my mind, both by the definition of sentence of imprisonment in the 1967 Act, which is repeated in the 1991 Criminal Justice Act section 51, and by the separate regime which is provided in the 1991 Act for default terms as compared with sentences of imprisonment.

To my mind, it would be absurd to suppose that in the draconian provisions in relation to drug trafficking, Parliament intended that a person, subject to a default term, should be able to avoid serving that term by taking advantage of a period of liberty stretching to months or, as in the present case, to years, in order to abscond either in this country or abroad. If this were the case, there would, as it seems to me, never be any practical purpose in a Court making an order for committal in default, for it would not have the effect of encouraging regurgitation of drug profits. There is, as it seems to me, no reason, by virtue of the principle *expressio unius est exclusio* alterius, to regard the three particular sentences referred to in section 6(2) and section 6(3)(b) as being exhaustive. As I have indicated, I accept what Lord Justice Pill said in *Chapman* this aspect of the case. The purpose of section 6, to my mind, as Mr Talbot submits, is to ensure that a term of committal for default is not served concurrently with a sentence for the substantive offence. Accordingly, I would reject Mr Williams' submissions on the construction of the section."

It should be noted that a defendant can also be ordered to return to England property held in another jurisdiction, for example, monies held in an account overseas. The defendant is liable to be imprisoned for contempt if he wilfully refuses to comply with such an order and no question of double jeopardy arises: *Re S* (May 20, 1999), affirmed by the Divisional Court on the December 20, 1999 (*CPS v. Scarlett*).

III. Confiscation Where Defendant Dies or Absconds

13–289 Prior to the DTA, where a defendant either died or absconded before a confiscation order was made, the Court was powerless to proceed to make a confiscation order. An indication of the sort of problems that can arise where a defendant absconds was demonstrated in *Chrastny (No. 2)* [1991] 1 W.L.R. 1385. In that case, the Court had to determine whether property held jointly between husband and wife (both of whom had been jointly charged with a drug trafficking offence) was "realisable" for the purposes of s.4(3) of the 1986 Act (now s.5(3). above), in circumstances where the wife had been convicted but where the husband had absconded. The Court held that if the husband were to be apprehended, tried and convicted, then the Court could not include in any confiscation order against him, property realised to satisfy the order payable by his wife because the property was no longer under his control: *per* Glidewell L.J. at 1394. The Home Office Working Group on Confiscation identified three situations to which different considerations may apply but which originally fell outside the ambit of the 1986 Act namely (1) death after conviction but before a confiscation order is made, (2) the defendant absconds after conviction but before the order is made, and (3) the defendant either dies or absconds before conviction.

The High Court now has power, by virtue of ss.19–24 of the 1994 Act, to make a confiscation order in the case of the defendant (charged with a drug trafficking offence) who absconds for a period of two years—whether convicted or not—and there is now a power of confiscation in the case of a defendant who is convicted of a drug trafficking offence but who dies before the Crown Court can make a confiscation order. See the Criminal Procedure Rules sc 115.2B

For these purposes, no statutory assumptions may be made pursuant to s.4(2) of the Act (see s.19(6)(a)) and, in the case of an absconder, the Court shall not make a confiscation order unless it is satisfied that the prosecutor has taken reasonable steps to contact him (s.19(6)(c)). The Court may also hear representations from third parties who are "likely to be affected by the making of a confiscation order by the Court" (s.19(6)(d)). If the High Court decides not to make a confiscation order in respect of an absconder, the prosecution are not entitled to re-open the matter under s.14 of the 1994 Act if they come into possession of evidence which had not been considered by the Court until the absconder returns: s.19(9). Similarly, the High Court has no power to revise any assessment of the absconder's proceeds of drug trafficking whilst he remains an absconder: see ss.15 and 19(10). The defendant who ceases to be an absconder may apply for a variation of a confiscation order made under s.19 within a period of six years from the date the order was made: see s.21.

(a) Death or absconding after conviction

The Working Group, in their Report on the Drug Trafficking Offences Act 1986 (1991), saw no reason to distinguish between the defendant who dies, or who absconds, after being convicted of a drug trafficking offence and they believed that it should be possible to make confiscation orders in each case (para.5.6). The 1994 Act broadly follows that approach. When reading s.19, it is important to group subss. (1) and (2) together, and to read subss. (3) and (4) together. The reason is that subss. (1) and (2) apply to defendants who have been convicted of a drug trafficking offence but the defendants have either died or absconded. By contrast, subss. (3) and (4) only relate to defendants who have absconded. Sections 19(3) and (4) have 13–290 no application to defendants who have died before they were able to appear for the trial.

Whichever category is appropriate, it is only the High Court (exercising the powers of the Crown Court) that can make a confiscation order under this section.

Where a defendant absconds, whether convicted (s.19(1)) or not (s.19(3)), the High Court cannot be asked by the prosecutor to make a confiscation order under s.19 until at least two years after the date on which the defendant absconded: see section 19(5). It is not clear what the position would be if a defendant inexplicably went "missing", *e.g.* after a boating trip in mysterious circumstances pending the drug trafficking enquiry, but after conviction. Would the Court treat him as having "absconded" or must the Court wait seven years until he could be presumed dead? Note the obligation imposed on the prosecution by subs. (6). Note that the statutory assumptions do not apply: subs. (6)(a).

Where an absconder returns, the High Court may cancel the confiscation order if there has been undue delay on the part of the prosecution in pursuing proceedings under s.19(4) of the 1994 Act: see s.23(2). This provision codifies s.19B(1)–(3) of the 1986 Act inserted by s.15 of the 1993 Act.

(b) Defendant dies or absconds before conviction

13–291 The Working Group sought views as to whether the Courts should be empowered to commence proceedings against persons who died or absconded prior to conviction (para. 5.9) but Parliament clearly took the view that it would be too drastic a step to extend the provisions of s.19 to those who died and who could never answer the indictment which they faced.

Where an absconder is acquitted (whether in his absence or otherwise), the Court by which the defendant was acquitted (*e.g.* the Crown Court) may cancel the confiscation order: s.22(1) and (2), and the defendant may apply for compensation if he has suffered loss as is just in all the circumstances of the case: s.22.

Note the power of the High Court to vary confiscation orders upon the application of the defendant, which was made under s.19: see s.21.

IV. Appointment and Powers of a Receiver

13–292 "29.—(1) Where a confiscation order—

(a) has been made under this Act,
(b) is not satisfied, and
(c) is not subject to appeal, the High Court or a county court may, on an application by the prosecutor, exercise the powers conferred by subsections (2) to (6) below.

(2) The Court may appoint a receiver in respect of realisable property.

(3) The Court may empower a receiver appointed under subsection (2)

above, under section 26 of this Act or in pursuance of a charging order—
(a) to enforce any charge imposed under section 27 of this Act on realisable property or on interest or dividends payable in respect of such property; and
(b) in relation to any realisable property other than property for the time being subject to a charge under section 27 of this Act, to take possession of the property subject to such conditions or exceptions as may be specified by the Court.

(4) The Court may order any person having possession of realisable property to give possession of it to any such receiver.

(5) The Court may empower any such receiver to realise any realisable property in such manner as the Court may direct.

(6) The Court may—
(a) order any person holding an interest in realisable property to make to the receiver such payment as it may direct in respect of any beneficial interest held by the defendant or, as the case may be, the recipient of a gift caught by this Act; and
(b) on the payment being made, by order transfer, grant or extinguish any interest in the property.

(7) Subsections (4) to (6) above do not apply to property for the time being subject to a charge under section 27 of this Act or section 9 of the Drug Trafficking Offences Act 1986.

(8) The Court shall not in respect of any property exercise the powers conferred by subsection (3)(a), (5) or (6) above unless a reasonable opportunity has been given for persons holding any interest in the property to make representations to the Court."

Note also the Criminal Procedure Rules (see for example sc 115.7).

Once a confiscation order has been made which is not subject to appeal **13–293**
and which has not been satisfied, the High Court may, on the application of the prosecutor, appoint a receiver to realise any realisable property (subs. (S)) with a view to satisfying the confiscation order (s.31(2)) and to apply the property so realised on the defendant's behalf towards the satisfaction of the order (s.30(1)). A reasonable opportunity must be given for persons holding any interest in the property to make representations to the Court (subs. (8)). Sums remaining in the hands of the receiver after the satisfaction of a confiscation order must be distributed among the holders of property in such proportions as the Court shall direct (s.30(3)). The material powers conferred on a receiver are set out in this section (formerly, s.11 of the 1986 Act, as amended by s.13(8) of the 1993 Act). Note that by subs.(1)(c), a receiver cannot be appointed if the order is subject to appeal. Again, by subs.(1)(b), a receiver can only be appointed if the confiscation order "is not satisfied". By s.41(3) (formerly. s.38(12) of the 1986 Act) proceedings in England and Wales for an offence are concluded on the occurrence of one of the events set out in that section. The powers of the High Court or the receiver must be exercised within the framework set out in s.31.

It must be noted that by section 29(1)(c) a receiver cannot be appointed if the order is subject to appeal. An order is expressed, pursuant to section 41(8) to be subject to appeal:

> "... until (disregarding any power of a court to grant leave to appeal out of time) there is no further possibility of an appeal on which the order could be varied or set aside."

Again, by section 29(1)(b), a receiver can be appointed if "the confiscation order is "not satisfied" which, by section 41(6) and (7) means:

> "(6) A confiscation order is satisfied when no amount is due under it.
>
> (7) For the purposes of this section as it applies to sections 32 and 33 of this Act, a confiscation order is also satisfied when the defendant in respect of whom it was made has served a term of imprisonment or detention in default of payment of the amount due under the order."

13–294 The Powers of the High Court or the receiver must be exercised within the framework set out in section 31 which (insofar as it is material) provides:

> "(1) The following provisions apply to the powers conferred—
>
> (a) on the High Court or a county court by sections 26 to 30 of this Act, or
>
> (b) on a receiver appointed under section 26 or 29 of this Act or in pursuance of a charging order.
>
> (2) Subject to the following provisions of this section, the powers shall be exercised with a view to making available for satisfying the confiscation order or, as the case may be, any confiscation order that may be made in the defendant's case, the value for the time being of realisable property held by any person, by means of the realisation of such property.
>
> (3) In the case of realisable property held by a person to whom the defendant has directly or indirectly made a gift caught by this Act, the powers shall be exercised with a view to realising no more than the value for the time being of the gift.
>
> (4) The powers shall be exercised with a view to allowing any person other than the defendant or the recipient of any such gift to retain or recover the value of any property held by him.
>
> (5) In exercising the powers, no account shall be taken of any obligations of the defendant or of the recipient of any such gift which conflict with the obligation to satisfy the confiscation order. It will be seen that the principal object is to satisfy the confiscation order notwithstanding any obligation which the defendant or the recipient may have which conflicts with the satisfaction of the order."

V. The Application of Proceeds of Realisation

13–295 The application of proceeds of realisation and other sums is explained in section 30 which provides:

"30(1) The following sums in the hands of a receiver appointed under section 26 or 29 of this Act or in pursuance of a charging order, that is—

(a) the proceeds of the enforcement of any charge imposed under section 27 of this Act
(b) the proceeds of the realisation, other than by the enforcement of such a charge, of any property under section 26 or 29 of this Act, and
(c) any other sums, being property held by the defendant shall be applied, subject to subsection (2) below, on the defendant's behalf towards the satisfaction of the confiscation order.

(2) Before any such sums are so applied they shall be applied—

(a) first, in payment of such expenses incurred by a person acting as an insolvency practitioner as are payable under section 35(3) of this Act; and
(b) second, in making such payments (if any) as the High Court or a county court may direct.

(3) If, after the amount payable under the confiscation order has been fully paid, any such sums remain in the hands of such a receiver as is mentioned in subsection (1) above, the receiver shall distribute those sums—

(a) among such of those who held property which has been realised under this Act, and
(b) in such proportions, as the High Court or a county court may direct after giving a reasonable opportunity for such persons to make representations to the Court.

(4) The receipt of any sum by a justices' clerk on account of an amount payable under a confiscation order shall reduce the amount so payable, but the justices' clerk shall apply the money received for the purposes specified in this section and in the order so specified.

(5) The justices' clerk shall first pay any expenses incurred by a person acting as an insolvency practitioner and payable under section 35(3) of this Act but not already paid under subsection (2) above.

(6) If the money was paid to the justices' clerk by a receiver appointed under section 26 or 29 of this Act or in pursuance of a charging order the justices' clerk shall next pay the receiver's remuneration and expenses.

(7) After making—

(a) any payment required by subsection (5) above, and
(b) in a case to which subsection (6) above applies, any payment required by that subsection the justices' clerk shall reimburse any amount paid under section 36(2) of this Act.

(8) Any balance in the hands of the justices' clerk after he has made all payments required by the preceding provisions of this section shall be treated for the purposes of section 61 of the Justices of the Peace Act 1979 (application of fines, etc.) as if it were a fine imposed by a magistrates' court.

(9) In this section 'justices' clerk' has the same meaning as in the Justices of the Peace Act 1979."

By subs. (1), what was s.12(1) of the 1986 Act has been reorganised into the form, which now appears, but the overall effect of this section is to consolidate the provisions of s.12 of the 1986 Act as amended by Sched. 5, of the Criminal Justice Act 1988. The provisions are largely self-explanatory. Expenses incurred by the receiver will be met out of realised property.

Note also the terms of the Criminal Procedure Rules sc 115.8. Where a receiver has fully paid the amount payable under a confiscation order and any sums remain in his hands, "he shall make an application to the Court for directions in accordance with CPR Part 23, as to the distribution of such sums": *per* sc 115.8(3).

J. VARIATION OF A CONFISCATION ORDER

I. Variation by the Defendant or by the Receiver

(a) Variation by the defendant

(i) *Variation of a confiscation order*

13–296 A downward variation of a confiscation order is to be carefully distinguished from an appeal against the making of an order. Where a defendant complains that the Court erred in the determination of the order, *e.g.* in the assessment of his proceeds of drug trafficking, then his appropriate course is to appeal against the making of the order because such an order is a sentence for the purposes of ss.9 and 11 of the Criminal Appeal Act 1968, see *Johnson* [1991] 2 Q.B. 249.

However, an application for the downward variation of a confiscation order under section 17 of the Act, proceeds on the footing that the confiscation order was correctly determined by the trial judge, but the value of the defendant's realisable assets have subsequently decreased, or been destroyed, or dissipated, so that the defendant's assets are now inadequate to satisfy the making of an order.

It cannot be emphasised too strongly that hearings under section 17 proceed on the basis that at the time the confiscation order was made, the defendant had sufficient realisable assets to satisfy the order. It is not a proper basis, for an application under section 17, to contend that the defendant never had sufficient assets when the confiscation order was made. The defendant cannot use the s.17 procedure as an avenue of appeal against the making of the order: see *The Matter of T* (February 1, 1996) and *Gokal* (April 18, 2000). The decision *in "T" (Taylor)*, was confirmed on appeal on the June 25, 1996.

Thus, section 17(1) provides:

"17(1) If, on an application made in respect of a confiscation order by—

(a) the defendant, or
(b) a receiver appointed under section 26 or 29 of this Act or in pursuance of a charging order,

the High Court is satisfied that the realisable property is inadequate for the payment of any amount remaining to be recovered under the confiscation order, the Court shall issue a certificate to that effect, giving the Court's reasons."

Note that the High Court can do no more than issue a certificate and give its reasons for doing. It cannot vary the order under this section. Clearly if the defendant has been adjudged, bankrupt then the Court must take into account the extent to which his property will be distributed amongst his creditors. The Court must also guard against the manipulative defendant who has taken steps to prevent the Court seizing his assets. To this end, section 17(2) provides: 13–297

"For the purposes of subsection (1) above—
(a) in the case of realisable property held by a person who has been adjudged bankrupt or whose estate has been sequestrated the Court shall take into account the extent to which any property held by him may be distributed among creditors, and
(b) the Court may disregard any inadequacy in the realisable property which appears to the Court to be attributable wholly or partly to anything done by the defendant for the purpose of preserving any property held by a person to whom the defendant had directly or indirectly made a gift caught by this Act from any risk of realisation under this Act."

By subs.(3), where a certificate has been issued under subs.(1), the person who applied it "may apply to the Crown Court for the amount to be recovered under the order to be reduced". The powers of the Crown Court are set out in subs. (4).

"The Crown Court shall, on an application under subsection (3) above—
(a) substitute for the amount to be recovered under the order such lesser amount as the Court thinks just in all the circumstances of the case; and
(b) substitute for the term of imprisonment or of detention fixed under subsection (2) of section 139 of the Powers of Criminal Courts (Sentencing) Act 2000 in respect of the amount to be recovered under the order a shorter term determined in accordance with that section (as it has effect by virtue of section 9 of this Act) in respect of the lesser amount."

It would seem that the Crown Court is obliged to substitute a lesser amount but the actual figure is entirely a matter for the Court to decide. Even if the High Court were to quantify the amount by which the realisable property is inadequate to satisfy the order, the Crown Court is not obliged to vary the order to that extent but must substitute a lesser amount "as the Court thinks just in all the circumstances of the case": subs. (4)(a).

13–298 Formerly under s.14 of the DTOA, only the defendant could apply for a variation of a confiscation order. Two major changes have been introduced into section 17. First, the application may be either made by the defendant or by a receiver appointed under s.26 or s.29, below. Secondly, section 17(5) now addresses the concern expressed by members of the judiciary (among others) in respect of the interests of third parties who seemed (under the 1986 Act as originally drafted) not to have any *locus standi* in confiscation proceedings before the Crown Court. By contrast, third party representation was always expressly catered for in the 1986 Act in respect of High Court proceedings where property was sought to be realised by the receiver (see s.11(8) of the 1986 Act, now s.29(8)). Since 1988, third parties have had a right to apply to vary or to discharge a charging order: s.9(8) of the 1986 Act, Sched. 5 of the Criminal Justice Act 1988, and see now s.27(8), below.

When applying for an order under section 17 of the Act, it is important to have regard to Order 115 of the Civil Procedure Rules which provides that the defendant may apply by summons for a certificate under section 17: see Rule 9(1), and that the summons shall be served with any supporting evidence not less than 7 days before the date fixed for the hearing of the summons on the prosecutor and on the receiver, where one has been appointed in the matter: Rule 9(2).

Normally the evidence is served by way of an affidavit sworn by the applicant and should set out a brief history of the matter and the applicant's present financial position. The Court is obliged to give its reasons for issuing a certificate of inadequacy (see s.17(1)) but there is authority, under a similar provision of the CJA 1988 (s.83), that when considering whether to grant a certificate the judge was obliged only to assess the amount of realisable property at the date of the application and he was not concerned with the reasons why the assets had declined in value since the confiscation order was made: *Re C (confiscation order) The Times*, November 1, 1994.

II. Variation by the Prosecution

13–299 Where, at the time the confiscation order was made, the Court was satisfied that the amount that might be realised was less than the amount assessed to be the value of the defendant's proceeds of drug trafficking, and thus made a confiscation order for the lesser amount under section 5(3), the prosecutor may to apply to the High Court for a variation of the original order if it transpires that the defendant's realisable assets are greater than first thought. This increase may arise in two ways: first, by virtue of previously hidden assets being discovered or secondly, by virtue of changes in the value of the property in question.

As originally drafted, the DTOA did not enable the prosecution to apply for a variation of the original order in such circumstances or at all. By an ingenious route, the prosecution in *Miller* (1991) 92 Cr.App.R. 191 successfully applied for a variation of the order by invoking the provisions of s.47 of the Supreme Court Act 1981 (c.54) in circumstances where further assets, held by the defendant at the time the order was made, were discovered. This route might not be appropriate in all cases and, in any event, the procedure is subject to time-limits (normally 28 days): see also *Onwuka* (1992) 95 Cr.App.R. 47.

In 1990, Parliament enacted the Criminal Justice (International Co-operation) Act 1990 (c.5) and took the opportunity to amend the law to take account of this problem but its application was held not be retrospective: see *Re Barretto* (1994) 99 Cr. App. R. 105. Parliament did not, technically speaking, amend the 1986 Act itself but, by s.16 of the 1990 Act, the prosecution became entitled to apply for a variation in the limited circumstances specified in s.16 and which has been re-enacted in the form it now appears in s.16 of the DTA 1994:

> "(1) This section applies where, by virtue of section 5(3) of this Act, the amount which a person is ordered to pay by a confiscation order is less than the amount assessed to be the value of his proceeds of drug trafficking.
>
> (2) If, on an application made in accordance with subsection (3) below, the High Court is satisfied that the amount that might be realised in the case of the person in question is greater than the amount taken into account in making the confiscation order (whether it was greater than was thought when the order was made or has subsequently increased) the Court shall issue a certificate to that effect, giving the Court's reasons.
>
> (3) An application under subsection (2) above may be made either by the prosecutor or by a receiver appointed in relation to the realisable property of the person in question under section 26 or 29 of this Act or in pursuance of a charging order.
>
> (4) Where a certificate has been issued under subsection (2) above the prosecutor may apply to the Crown Court for an increase in the amount to be recovered under the confiscation order; and on that application the Court may—
>
> (a) substitute for that amount such amount (not exceeding the amount assessed as the value referred to in subsection (1) above) as appears to the Court to be appropriate having regard to the amount now shown to be realisable; and
>
> (b) increase the term of imprisonment or detention fixed in respect of the confiscation order under subsection (2) of section 139 of the Powers of Criminal Courts (Sentencing) Act 2000 (as it has effect by virtue of section 9 of this Act) if the effect of the substitution is to increase the maximum period applicable in relation to the order under subsection (4) of that section."

Note that the terms of imprisonment in default are maximum terms: see *Szrajber*, 15 Cr App.R.(S) 821 and *French* (1995) 16 Cr. App. R. (S) 841.

Similar amendments were made to Scottish law by s.17 of the 1990 Act (see section 1(1)(b) of the Criminal Justice (Scotland) Act 1987 (c. 41)).

13–300 It will be seen from the wording of this section that the High Court is itself empowered to vary the order. It can do no more than certify that the facts set out in subs. (2) exist and leave it to the Crown Court to substitute an amount that is "appropriate" (subs.(4)(a)) and to increase the default period accordingly (subs.(4)(b)). Furthermore, an application made under this section is subject to a ceiling, namely, the amount which the Crown Court assessed to be the proceeds of the defendant's drug trafficking. That figure will often be calculated on the basis of what was believed to be the defendant's financial position, over the relevant period, at the time the original order was made. The Home Office Working Group on Confiscation suggested that the Crown Court should be empowered to make a fresh order based on a reassessment of the extent of the defendant's benefit.

Under both s.17 (formerly s.14 of the 1986 Act) and s.16 it is necessary to go to the High Court first and not straight to the Crown Court. It is not clear why the legislature thought this route to be desirable or necessary. An initial reaction is that the provisions were intended to confer upon the High Court a supervisory role and thus safeguard the interests of persons likely to be affected by a successful application, but the terms of ss.16 and 17 impose a mandatory obligation on the High Court to issue a certificate upon making the requisite findings of fact for the purposes of ss.16(2) and 17. Of these two sections, neither gives any indication or guidance as to the burden or standard of proof.

Before the decision in *Tivnan* [1999] 1 Cr.App.R.(S.) 92, there was uncertainty as to whether section 16 applies to property, which comes into the possession of the defendant after the confiscation order is made. The argument was based on the history of section 16. When the DTOA was passed, there was provision for a defendant to apply for a downward variation of a confiscation order where the value of his realisable assets was inadequate to satisfy the amount owing under a confiscation order. That might be because the defendant dissipated the property, or because the value of the property had decreased. However, an application under section 17 proceeds on the basis that the defendant had the assets at the time the confiscation order was made and therefore a defendant cannot use the section 17 procedure to say that he never had the assets at all. That would be to use the procedure as an avenue for appealing the making of the original confiscation order. However, under the DTOA the prosecution could not go back to court for an upward variation of the value of the realisable assets if the value increased after the order was made. To address the problem, section 16 (formerly section 16 of the Criminal Justice (International Co-operation) Act 1990) was enacted.

It will be seen that section 16(2) states that the Court must be satisfied that the amount that might be realised is greater than the amount taken into account, when the order was made, for one of two reasons: (1) the value is greater than first thought when the order was made, or (2) the value has subsequently increased. It is not entirely clear whether Parliament applied its mind to cases where defendants acquired assets after the making of a confiscation order.

In *Barretto*, Schieman J. (as he then was) in the light of an article written by Philip Taylor (N.J.L. May 14, 1993) saw force in the point that section 16 did not apply to assets acquired after the making of a confiscation order. A different view had been expressed by Turner J. in *Re C* (February 3, 1995), but *Barretto* was not cited in *Re C*. **13–301**

In *Tivnan* [1999] 1 Cr.App.R.(S.) 92, the Court declined to follow *Barretto* and gave five reasons for doing so. First, section 16 contains no words of limitation of time. True, but such words would be superfluous if the section was intended to relate to the value of the defendants' assets that existed at the time the confiscation order was made. Secondly, section 16 is expressed in the present tense: but that will be so if one is looking at the current value of property shown to exist at the time the confiscation order was made, but in respect of which the value has subsequently increased. Thirdly, the marginal note reads "increase in realisable property"—which perhaps merely begs the question whether the section was intended to relate to assets in existence when the confiscation order was made. Fourthly, section 16 includes no reasons why the realisable property might increase, for example, concealment, subsequent acquisition or another reason. That is true, but the "amount that might be realised" is a term of art, defined by section 6, that, again arguably, relates to the *value* of property assessed at the time the confiscation order is made. Finally, serving a term of imprisonment does not extinguish the debt under a confiscation order. That, too, is correct but that does not shed much light on the construction of section 16.

However, despite all of the above, there are policy considerations too. A drug trafficker who enjoys "counting his money" and investing it, risks a confiscation order being made to the full value of his proceeds of drug trafficking: he will be stripped of his wealth. By contrast, a trafficker who squanders his proceeds on the high life, so that he has almost nothing left by the date of his conviction, may find that his benefit figure is substantial, but the value of the confiscation order is low because his realisable assets are insufficient to pay the full value of the order. Has crime paid in his case? It was partly to deal with that issue, and the terms of Article 5.1 and 6(c) of the 1988 Vienna Convention, that the Court of Appeal in *Tivnan* reached the decision it did. There are other practical, and related policy issues. Unlike other provisions of the DTA, for example section 13, 14, and 15, that are subject to time-limits, section 16, as interpreted in *Tivnan*, is not. Time-limits were introduced into sections 13, 14 and 15, to avoid the risk that a person might be hounded years after he committed the predicate offence. In theory, a defendant whose benefit is £1 million, with realisable assets of £100,000 may find that years after his conviction, the prosecution apply to recover £900,000 of his winnings in a £1 million jackpot that he was lucky enough to win. There are concerns that the Court's interpretation of section 16 may make rehabilitation more difficult in some cases or stifle proper ambition (*i.e.* a reluctance to become a high earner lest subsequently acquired assets are realised many years later by the State). *Tivnan* may place a heavy burden on law-enforcement agencies, and lawyers, to keep records and case papers for very many years. Some of these issues might need to be addressed by Parliament in subsequent legislation.

K. RESTRAINT AND CHARGING ORDERS

I. INTRODUCTION

13–302 The primary objective of Part I of the DTA is the recovery of the proceeds of drug trafficking. Stiff terms of imprisonment are imposed upon defaulters. However, committal to prison is a course of last resort, but it is no longer self-defeating because the period served in default will not now relieve the defendant of the requirement to satisfy that proportion of the order which remains outstanding, to enjoy the benefit of his assets upon release: see s.41(6) and see *Harrow Justices, ex p. DPP* [1991] 1 W.L.R. 395. Accordingly, the powers conferred on the High Court in respect of realisable property continue to apply even if a term has been served in default.

Under the DTA, the Courts do not have to wait to see if the convicted defendant will default before taking action to realise his property. The High Court (or a receiver appointed by that Court) may order any person having possession of "realisable property" to deliver it up to a receiver s.26(7)(b), who may realise that property as directed by the Court (s.26(11)).

Once a person learns that proceedings for a drug trafficking offence may be instituted against him then the temptation to dissipate, or to conceal, his assets will be very strong.

In civil law, an injunction may be granted to restrain the defendant from disposing of assets to defeat the interests of the plaintiff should he be successful in the action: *Mareva Compania Naviera S.A. v. International Bulk Carriers S.A.* (1980) 1 All E.R. 213, CA. Restraint orders made under the DTA (see s.26), are intended to achieve a similar result. They have been described as closely analogous to the *Mareva* injunction. Indeed Lord Donaldson M.R. has graphically described the statutory jurisdiction as the "Drugs Act Mareva": *Re Peters* [1988] 3 All E.R. 46, 51e. However a restraint order does not have the same effect as a freezing order: see *Re R (Restraint Order)* [1990] Q.B. 307.

The broad scheme involved in making protective orders is to prevent a defendant from rendering any confiscation order nugatory by disposing of his assets before his conviction. This point is reinforced by section 31(2), which provides that powers exercisable by the High Court or receiver (including powers under s.26) shall be exercised with a view to satisfying the confiscation order by realising the value of realisable property held by any person.

13–303 To make the disposal of property more difficult, the Act empowers the

High Court to make a charging order on realisable property for securing payment to the Crown: section 27. The effect of a charging order is the same as a general equitable charge and enforceable in the same courts: section 28(3).

In the ordinary way proceedings under sections 26 and 27 of the 1994 Act are exercisable where proceedings have been "instructed" in England and Wales (see s.41(2)) against the defendant for a "drug trafficking offence" (see s.1(3)) or an application has been made by the "prosecutor" (see s.25(4)(b)) to the Crown Court for the purposes of:

(i) inviting the Court to consider making a confiscation order when it had previously not done so: section 13;
(ii) re-assessing whether the defendant has benefited from drug trafficking: section 14;
(iii) revising the assessment of the extent of a defendant's benefit from drug trafficking: section 15;
(iv) increasing the amount that might be realised under the order: section 16.

The powers under s.26 and 27 are also exercisable in connection with proceedings taken in the High Court where the defendant either died or absconded (see s.25(1) and s.19).

It will be seen from the terms of section 25(1) set out below, that a number of conditions must be satisfied before the Court has jurisdiction to entertain any application for the making of a restraint or charging order.

(a) Cases in which restraint orders and charging orders may be made

Section 25 of the 1994 Act sets out the relevant framework for the making of restraint and charging orders as follows: 13–304

"25(1) The powers conferred on the High Court by sections 26(1) and 27(1) of this Act are exercisable where—

(a) proceedings have been instituted in England and Wales against the defendant for a drug trafficking offence or an application has been made by the prosecutor in respect of the defendant under section 13, 14, 15, 16 or 19 of this Act
(b) the proceedings have not, or the application has not, been concluded; and
(c) the Court is satisfied that there is reasonable cause to believe—
    (i) in the case of an application under section 15 or 16 of this Act, that the Court will be satisfied as mentioned in section 15(4) or, as the case may be, 16(2) of this Act, or
    (ii) in any other case, that the defendant has benefited from drug trafficking

(3) The powers mentioned in subsection (1) above are also exercisable where—

(a) the Court is satisfied that, whether by the laying of an information or otherwise, a person is to be charged with a drug trafficking offence or that an application of a kind mentioned in subsection (1)(a) above is to be made in respect of the defendant; and

(b) the Court is also satisfied as mentioned in subsection (1)(c) above."

As originally drafted the circumstances in which proceedings for a drug trafficking offence were to be treated as "concluded" were relatively straightforward because the machinery for varying a confiscation was limited only to an application made by the defendant under s.14 (s.38(12) of the 1986 Act).

Not only will proceedings now not be concluded upon serving a sentence in default of payment (s.9(5), above) but the ability of the prosecution to seek a re-determination of issues under s.2, above, over a period of six years from the date of the relevant conviction or determination (see ss.13, 14 and 15, above) means that the machinery necessary to enforce the satisfaction of the order had to be re-defined. Thus: (a) the powers of the High Court in which restraint and charging orders may be made under ss.26(1) and 27(1) are extended to applications brought by the prosecutor under s.16 (defendant who has died or absconded) and ss.13, 14 and 15 (re-determination under s.2); (b) the same powers exist even if any such applications are to be made (subs. (3) as amended) subject to the safeguards set out in subs. (5); (c) restraint orders under s.26 may be varied or discharged: s.26(5); (d) similarly, changing orders may be varied or discharged: s.27(7); (e) powers under s.29 may be exercised where an order is not satisfied; and (f) the circumstances in respect of proceedings for "drug trafficking offences", which can be said to be "concluded", are re-defined: s.41(3). Note that section 25(3) should also be read in conjunction with s.25(5)

Exceptions are provided by s.25(2) thus:

"The Court shall not exercise those powers by virtue of subsection (1) above if it is satisfied—

(a) that there has been undue delay in continuing the proceedings or application in question; or

(b) that the prosecutor does not intend to proceed."

(b) Undue delay: s.25(2)(a)

13–305 Restraint and charging orders can inflict considerable hardship and financial damage on persons affected by them. It is often overlooked that it is not just the defendant on trial for the drug trafficking offence who can be made the subject of such orders but anybody who has any interest in the property affected. In complex cases, these orders will often endure for periods exceeding a year (if not two) particularly in cases where there is an appeal pending or where the defendant has absconded (see now s.25(1)(a) and s.19). Whilst it would always have been open to parties affected by an order to complain that undue delay in proceedings with the prosecution amounted to "an abuse of process", section 25(2)(a) makes that course unnecessary and, in certain respects, the matters to be established under this provision are less onerous than an abuse of process argument.

If the Court upholds a complaint under s.25(2)(a) the result would not necessarily be fatal to the prosecution of the drug trafficking offence: it just means that a restraint or charging order cannot be made because the High Court no longer has jurisdiction to proceed under s.26 or s.27. It follows that no question of "staying" the proceedings arises.

(c) The prosecutor does not intend to proceed

By s.25(2), the High Court shall not exercise powers under s.26 or s.27 if the prosecutor "does not intend to proceed". The first question is: proceed with what? At first sight, it may be thought that the use of the phase "to proceed" is a reference to the proceedings brought by the prosecutor in the High Court. However, when s.25(2)(b) is read in the context of the whole section it would seem that what is being referred to is either the proceedings for a drug trafficking offence or one of the applications mentioned in s.25(1). Whatever the phrase means, it would be a surprising result if the Court continued to make an order under s.26 or s.27 once the prosecutor decided to abandon or not to pursue prosecution or one of the aforementioned applications. The result is less obvious if s.25(2)(b) includes or is intended to refer to the proceedings before the High Court because a court is usually entitled to determine its own rules of procedure and, given that the Crown Court initiate confiscation proceedings under s.2(1) of the Act, then without s.25(2) it would not be an unwarranted result for a court to hold that (once seized of jurisdiction) it may proceed under ss.26 or 27 (if in its view it is appropriate to do so) irrespective of the views of the prosecutor which maybe misguided or even influenced by considerations which the Court regards as inappropriate in the circumstances (*e.g.* budgetary constraints). However, s.25(2)(a) ensures that the prosecutor retains control over the decision whether to proceed or not.

Given that applications under sections 26 and 27 may be made *ex parte* (and prior to charge), the property of a prospective defendant (and innocent third parties affected by the orders) can be hit by surprise. Accordingly, the Act permits an application for the discharge of variation of a restraint or charging order by persons affected by such orders: see section 26(7) and s.27(7) and see *Re R (Restraint Order)* [1990] 2 Q.B. 307 and C.P. Rules 115).

It should be carefully noted that an application for a restraint order cannot be made (and the powers exercisable thereunder shall not have effect) in relation to property subject to a charging order made under section 27. The reason for this is that the powers of the High Court, and the receiver appointed by the Court to manage or otherwise deal with the property are extensive: see s.26(3) and ss.29(3), (4), (5) and (6).

II. Restraint Orders

(a) Effect of a restraint order

13–306 Section 26 of the DTA empowers the High Court to make restraint orders for the purposes of Part I of the DTA. The section substantially reproduces section 8 of the 1986 Act (as amended by the Criminal Justice Act 1988, Sched. 5 and, so far as subs. (7) is concerned, by s.24(1) of the 1993 Act).

It has been said that a restraint order is closely analogous to a Mareva injunction in civil proceedings and it is designed to prevent a person (not just the defendant) dealing with, or disposing of property, which may be made the subject of a confiscation order when the defendant appears before the Crown Court to be sentenced in respect of one or more drug trafficking offences: see *Re Peters* [1988] 3 All E.R. 46.

A restraint order has the effect of freezing all the realisable property from the moment the order is made. It prohibits any person from "dealing" with any realisable property (see s.26(1). Accordingly, the defendant is prevented from petitioning for his own bankruptcy. It also prevents him from making an application to the County Court for an interim order (under s. 252 of the Insolvency Act 1986) preventing the institution of proceedings against him, or his property, where the defendant intends to make a proposal to his creditors for a composition in satisfaction of his debts or a scheme or arrangements of his affairs which involves the realisable property caught by the restraint order: *Re M, The Times*, April 17, 1991, and see sections 32(2) and (3) of the 1994 Act. Where the Court makes a restraint order it may discharge that order if proceedings for the offence are not instituted, or if an application for a restraint order is not made within a reasonable time: s.25(5), above. Compensation may be paid if "a person who held property which was realisable property" (see s.18(1)) has suffered loss in consequence of an order under s.26 of the Act: see s.18(2), above.

It should also be noted that restraint orders are normally coupled with a disclosure order as a means of identifying and ascertaining the whereabouts and value of assets affected by the restraint order. Disclosure orders are dealt with below: *Re O (Restraint Order)* [1991] 1 All E.R. 330 and *Re T (Restraint Order), The Times,* May 19, 1992. Such orders should be coupled with a condition to give effect to the common law rule against self-incrimination.

Section 26(1) provides as follows:

> "The High Court may by order (in this Act referred to as a 'restraint order') prohibit any person from dealing with any realisable property, subject to such conditions and exceptions as may be specified in the order."

Section 26 is of no effect in relation to any property for the time being subject to a charge under section 27: see section 26(3).

(b) When may a restraint order be made?

The powers are exercisable by the High Court or by a receiver appointed by the Court under section 26(7) where proceedings have actually been instituted against a defendant or, where a person is to be charged with a drug trafficking offence: section 25(1) and (3) In either case it will be seen that there must exist reasonable cause to believe that the accused has benefited from drug trafficking: s.25(1)(c)(ii) and section 25(3)(b). The Court is obliged to discharge the order if the proceedings in respect of the offence are not instituted within a reasonable time: see s.25(5) which should be read in conjunction with s.25(3). Note that s.25(3) relates to the period before any decision is taken to prosecute the defendant or to make one of the applications referred to in s.25(1). 13–307

(c) Applying for an order

Section 26(4) is largely self-explanatory: 13–308

"A restraint order:
- (a) may be made only on an application by the prosecutor,
- (b) may be made on an ex parte application to a judge in chambers, and
- (c) shall provide for notice to be given to persons affected by the order."

Note the Criminal Procedure Rules sc 115.3. Note that the application must be supported by a witness statement or affidavit (usually by the former). There must be full and frank disclosure: *Re a Defendant, The Independent,* April 2, 1987.

The importance of giving notice was emphasised in *Re R (Restraint Order)* [1990] 2 Q.B. 307. Otton J. (as he then was), delivering the judgment of the Divisional Court, said "it is, in my view, incumbent on the commissioners, or any other body which is exercising the powers granted under the restraint procedure, to consider carefully who should be informed".

In that case, the applicants were landlords who let industrial premises to T who installed plant and machinery. T fell in arrears with his rent and was subsequently charged with a drug trafficking offence. The landlords attempted to distrain on the plant and machinery unaware of the existence of a restraint order, under section 8. They organised an auction but cancelled it upon being informed of the order. They incurred costs and a loss of rent as a result of the delay in being able to forfeit the lease. Notwithstanding that a restraint order was analogous to a Mareva injunction, the Court had no jurisdiction either under the DTOA, or its inherent jurisdiction, to grant an indemnity as against the Customs and Excise Commissioners for the loss and costs incurred.

(d) Property affected by the order

13–309 Section 26(2) provides:

"A restraint order may apply:

(a) to all realisable property held by a specified person, whether the property is described in the order or not, and

(b) to realisable property held by a specified person, being property transferred to him after the making of the order."

The order therefore relates only to property that is "realisable" within the meaning of section 6(2) and (3) of the DTOA Accordingly, gifts caught by the Act (see s.8) are included. The order must specify the person holding the property. This is clearly important because notice must be given to the persons so specified: (s.26(4)(c)).

For clarity, it is desirable that the order should particularise the property affected by the order but this is not strictly speaking essential. Thus, the order may be drafted in the following form:

> "The Defendants be restrained whether by themselves, their servants or agents or otherwise until further order for removing from the jurisdiction of the Court or from otherwise disposing of, diminishing or otherwise in any way dealing with money, goods, property or other assets whatever within or without the jurisdiction That all the defendants be restrained from in any way howsoever dealing with ( ) That (Mr. X) be restrained in any way howsoever from dealing with bank account number ( ) held at the (Bank). . . . "

"Realisable property" includes property whether it is situated in England and Wales or abroad: see sections 6 and 62(2), and accordingly the restraint order may similarly embrace property within or without the jurisdiction (see the draft order above).

(e) Prohibit "dealing with" realisable property

13–310 The purpose of a restraint order is to prohibit persons affected by the order from "dealing with" any realisable property subject to such conditions and exceptions as may be specified in the order: section 26(1). By section 26(8), "dealing with property", held by any person, includes:

"(a) where a debt is owed to that person, making a payment in reduction of the amount of the debt, and

(b) removing the property from Great Britain".

The purpose of section 26(8)(a) is to preserve the value of property. It will be seen that section 26(8) is merely inclusory, and it does not offer a comprehensive definition of the phrase "dealing with" as it appears in section 26(1). Conventional restraint orders include a prohibition against the "disposing of" or "diminishing of" assets within or without the jurisdiction and it is plain that both activities describe an act of "dealing" for the purposes of section 26(1). Less clear, perhaps, are accountancy exercises used to determine the financial position or standing of an individual or corporate body. In *Re K (Restraint Order)* [1990] 2 Q.B. 298, F made large payments into two deposit accounts. She also obtained an overdraft from the bank on condition that the bank had a right to "combine and consolidate" all her accounts. F gave her two brothers a mandate over the overdraft account. F and her two brothers were charged with a drug trafficking offence but only one brother was convicted. There was a credit balance in her deposit accounts of £639,541.87 but an overdrawn balance of £337,585.59 on the overdraft account. The Crown Prosecution Service sought and obtained a restraint order in respect of the sums then held in the two deposit accounts. The Bank of India applied to the High Court for a variation of that order so as to permit the accounts to be combined and consolidated. The balance remaining therefore would be £301,956.28.

During the course of argument, the bank made two concessions: first, that the monies deposited in the two deposit accounts were a gift from the convicted brother; and secondly, that all monies deposited were the proceeds of drug trafficking. Nevertheless, the bank contended, (1) that the right of a bank to combine and to consolidate accounts arose by operation of law and not by agreement and was a right *sui generis*; (2) that the DTOA does not extinguish or diminish the inherent right of the bank to combine accounts; (3) the right to combine accounts is a means of establishing the true indebtedness of the customer to the bank and the bank to the customer; it is merely an accounting procedure.

Otton J. upheld the submissions of the bank. There is a presumption that a statute does not alter vested rights. Nothing in the DTOA, so ruled Otton J., alters vested rights or extinguishes or diminishes them. Otton J. referred to section 13(4) of the DTOA, now s.31(4), which provides that powers under, *inter alia*, section 8 shall be exercised with a view to allowing any person other than the defendant (or the recipient of a gift caught by the DTA) to retain or recover the value of property held by him. This would appear to cover a lien.

As stated above, the purpose of section 26(8)(a) is to preserve the value 13–311
of property. However, section 26(8)(a) does not impose a complete embargo on the payment of debts to third parties because the Court under section 26 may permit payments in certain circumstances. The circumstances in which the value of realisable property may be diminished by the Courts permitting payments to be made to innocent third parties, *e.g.* in respect of expenses, are not easy to categorise.

In *Re Peters* [1988] 3 All E.R. 46, a strongly constituted Court of Appeal (Civil Division) held that the jurisdiction to make or to vary a restraint order under the DTOA was analogous to that under the Mareva jurisdiction; its purpose being to strike a balance before trial between preserving a defendant's assets to satisfy a possible confiscation order if he were convicted, and meeting his reasonable requirements meanwhile. In other words, the primary objective of the order is to prevent an accused rendering any confiscation order nugatory by disposing of his assets before conviction, but the defendant is entitled to maintain himself and his family, within reasonable limits, from the resources available to him. In striking a balance between the interests of the Court, and the defendant, the Court will have regard to all the circumstances of the case. In *Re Peters* (above), the Court of Appeal said that the anticipatory discharge of liabilities which could be expected to arise only after he had been acquitted or convicted was wholly contrary to section 13(2) (now s.31(2)) and the underlying purpose of the protective provisions of the Act. By "anticipatory discharge of liabilities", the Court seems to have had in mind expenditure which a defendant would wish to make at some time in the future but which would go beyond his reasonable requirements. This would, therefore, include items of expenditure on luxury goods, the provision of a holiday and so on. Mann L.J. said (at 52): "In my experience a restraint order does not, and properly does not, prevent the meeting of ordinary and reasonable expenditure."

13–312 In *Re Peters* McNeill J. varied a restraint order to enable P to comply with a consent order, made in matrimonial proceedings, that the defendant pay to his son (a minor) £25,000 in respect of school fees and maintenance until he reached the age of 18. The lump sum to the son was in settlement of the claim for periodical payments, lump sum and property adjustment orders. P's assets were assessed at £95,000 and his proceeds of drug trafficking were said to be about £540,000. On appeal, the Court of Appeal ruled in favour of the Commissioners of Customs and Excise. The sum of £25,000 amounted to a discharge of future liabilities and was not consonant with the purpose of section 8. As far as there was a conflict between the Court order in the divorce proceedings, and the restraint order, it should have been resolved in favour of the restraint order. It is not clear whether the Commissioners had agreed that the payment of the £25,000 would be a "gift caught by the Act" as defined by section 5(9) of the DTOA (now s.8 of the Drug Trafficking Act 1994). Counsel for the son contended that it was not a gift at all, and in this respect, the Court of Appeal agreed, because the payment was in satisfaction of future liabilities.

Again, it is not clear in *Re Peters*, above, whether the Commissioners contended that the Court, in exercising its powers (*inter alia* under s.26) should ignore any obligations of the defendant in the terms of section 31(5).

In exercising those powers, no account shall be taken of any obligations of the defendant or of the recipient of any such gift which conflict with the obligation to satisfy the confiscation order The Court of Appeal, in considering section 31(5), was inclined to accept the contention of the son that section 31(5) presupposed the existence of a confiscation order. Although convicted of a drug trafficking offence, the father had yet to be sentenced, or a confiscation order made, at the date judgment in *Re Peters* was delivered.

Note that the Court has an inherent jurisdiction to make ancillary orders to ensure that the order is effective: *DPP v. Scarlett* [2000] 1 W.L.R. 515.

(f) Legal expenses

In *Re P; Re W, The Times,* April 11, 1990, CA the Court of Appeal considered variations of restraint orders to allow the payment of legal expenses. It will be seen that the combined effect of CPR r.115.4(1) and section 26(1), (see above) is to exempt both legal and living expenses of the defendant from property subject to a restraint order. Indeed, in *Re Peters* (1988) 3 All E.R. 46, Nolan J. had previously varied a restraint order on those grounds. However, in *Re P ; Re W.* the question arose as to whether the judge was correct to order that the solicitors' legal costs should be taxed at the conclusion of the trial on an indemnity basis. The Court had no difficulty in holding that such a course was not wrong in principle, even if taxation could result in some delay in pronouncing sentence. The decision on the point is plainly right being consonant with the purpose expressed in section 31(2): and see *Re L* (June 10, 1996). 13–313

In *Re P; Re W* (above), the applicants also submitted that the restraint order should have contained a maximum figure for legal costs. This was normal practice in the case of *Mareva* applications: see *PCW (Underwriting Agencies) Ltd v. Dixon* (1983) 2 All E.R. 158. The Court of Appeal did not find this matter straightforward, and indeed, suggested that in future cases, judges might think it desirable to include such a maximum figure for legal expenses. However, the judge had a discretion in the matter and the Court of Appeal would not lightly interfere with the exercise of that discretion.

Restraint orders usually contain a standard clause that reads something along the following lines:

> "This order does not prohibit the defendant from spending £x a week towards his ordinary living expenses as long as he is not in prison and also £x on legal advice and representation. But before spending any money the defendant must tell the [prosecuting agency] where the money is to come from.
>
> The defendant may spend further money on legal expenses actually, reasonably and properly incurred in these proceedings and the criminal proceedings to which these proceedings are ancillary:
> PROVIDED THAT:—
> Before any monies are released for this purpose the defendant shall notify the [prosecuting agency] in writing of (a) the source of the fund to be used to pay the said costs, (b) the general nature of the costs incurred, (c) the time spent and by whom (whether partner, assistant solicitor or otherwise) in incurring the said costs, (d) the hourly rate applicable to the costs incurred and in the event that the [prosecuting agency] consider the claim to be in respect of costs that have not actually, reasonably, or properly been incurred then the entitlement to draw such costs be restricted to 65 per cent the amount claimed and the whole claim for costs then be subject to assessment on an indemnity basis in accordance with CPR, Pt 48 but without the provisions of 48.8(2)(a) and (b) applying."

There are tensions here. On the one hand, the assets (pre-trial) are those of the unconvicted defendant, and without lawful justification or excuse, he must surely be entitled to continue to use them for legitimate purposes: see Article 1 of Protocol No 1 of the ECHR. It is not the object of confiscation proceedings to manage the defendant's affairs in such a way that the Crown is enriched. On the other hand, the Court is entitled to take steps to ensure that the defendant does not frustrate the aims of the confiscation legislation. That may mean that a receiver and/or a manager is appointed in respect of the defendant's assets, or limits are placed on the movement of assets (including the amount payable to lawyers). Where a receiver and a manager have been appointed (pre-trial), they are under an obligation to use their best endeavours to ensure that they act responsibly, and if possible, not to act to the defendant's detriment. Getting the balance right is exceedingly difficult, but there have been cases where legal fees have largely exhausted, or totally exhausted, a defendant's realisable property: see *Dechert v. Southwark Crown Court* [2001] EWHC Admin 477.

In *Customs & Excise Commissioners v. Norris* [1991] 2 Q.B. 293, the question of legal costs arose again but on this occasion the question was whether the applicant should be allowed access to funds held by him in order to prosecute the appeal. Having regard to section 26(1), CPR r.115.4(1), and the authorities discussed above, it is hardly surprising that the Court of Appeal (Civil Division) answered the question affirmatively. The principal argument of the Commissioners was that the full value of the defendant's realisable property would be diminished if the application succeeded (contrary to s.31(2)), and that the defendant's appeal could be funded, either by the defendant's family (as was the case at trial) or by legal aid. The Court of Appeal swiftly rejected both alternatives. First, there was no obligation on the family to fund the appeal, nor should they be forced to do so, and secondly, it would be an odd position if the Court forced somebody to qualify for legal aid who would not otherwise qualify.

(i) *Power to sell assets of the unconvicted defendant*

13–314 The powers of a receiver are set out in section 29 (see above). In the matter of *Piper* (July 23, 1999), the Court examined the circumstances in which a receiver appointed under section 26 of the DTA should be empowered to sell an unconvicted defendant's assets before trial, and the approach to be adopted towards such sales. There are clear human rights issues connected with this matter. On the one hand, where a confiscation order may be made against a defendant, it is desirable to try to ensure that the value of assets that he holds and which might be included as his realisable property to satisfy the order, is maintained or preserved. On the other hand, there must be restrictions on the extent to which the State can limit the freedom of an unconvicted defendant to conduct his own affairs. In *Piper*, a restraint order was served on Piper and the prosecutor appointed a receiver. Piper recognised that for practical reasons, the receiver would need to sell the majority of listed assets but he strongly objected to the sale of three horses including one that was the family's "much loved pet". The receiver had been appointed with a general power to sell any of the assets. In the Court of Appeal (Civil Division) it was said that the legislative steer, that "the value of the realisable property shall be maintained in order that it may be available to satisfy any confiscation order", says more about whether particular expenditure should be permitted than whether particular assets should be retained or sold (*per* Simon Brown L.J.). The Court said that section 31(2) dealt with two different situations: (1) an interim restraint order, and (2) where a confiscation order has been made in respect of a convicted defendant. In *Piper*, the defendant was unconvicted. The Court explained the position as follows:

> "the provision, in short, is not be read as a requirement upon the Court in all cases to appoint a receiver with full powers of sale and for the receiver then immediately to realise all assets. Rather the Court and receiver are directed (at which ever stage the question arises) to seek to preserve the present value of the defendant assets. But plainly that cannot be the only relevant consideration, least of all before the defendant comes to be tried and whilst, therefore, he is to be presumed innocent. Rather, as *Peters* makes clear, a balance has to be struck between on the one hand, preserving the worth of the defendant's reliable property against a possibility that he may be convicted if a confiscation order may be made against him, and on the other hand allowing him meantime to continue the ordinary course of his life. The problem in *Peters* was in deciding just what expenses are reasonable, the point at which expenditure becomes dissipation. The difficulty in the present type of case is to decide whether certain assets ought properly to be retained so that the defendant may continue to enjoy them, not merely to the limited extent possible whilst in custody awaiting trial but in future were he ultimately to be acquitted and a restraint order and receivership accordingly discharged. It is at this stage that I would return to what I have already suggested is the central policy underlying this legislation—Parliament's desire to strip criminals of their present assets to the extent of their past criminal profits. The Act is designed essentially to impoverish defendants, not to enrich the Crown. That this is so, indeed, is arguably evident even from the language of section 31(2) itself. In a case like the present (and no doubt the great majority of cases) where the assumed proceeds of crime far exceed the defendant's realisable assets, the amount of the confiscation order will be dictated by the latter not the former. The subsection speaks only of "satisfying the confiscation order", not of producing assets equivalent to past criminal gains. Even assuming, therefore, that a defendant holds depreciating assets, I see no great compulsion to require their sale, even before any confiscation order comes to be made."

In saying that, the Court was anxious that its judgment should not be a charter for niggling defendants. Nevertheless, there is a balancing exercise involved:

"As it seems to me however, it is one thing to say that the receiver and manager has power to deal with property in the course of carrying on business, another to say that he or she is thereby empowered without more to realise the business in its entirety. Selling ice creams . . . is not the same as selling the ice cream van itself. The first involves the sale of assets in the ordinary course of the business: the other the disposal of the essential assets without which the business cannot be carried on. . . . The Court's interim power under section 26(7)(ii)—the power to direct a receiver, appointed to take possession of realisable property, 'to manage or otherwise deal with' that property—ought to be restrictively construed. I have the greatest doubts whether the Court could properly confer on a receiver appointed under section 26(7) broad discretion without any further direction whatever to sell all the defendant's property, least of all upon an application made ex parte."

(g) Variation of a restraint order

13–315 Section 26(5) and (6) provides

"(5) A restraint order—

(a) may be discharged or varied in relation to any property—and

(b) shall be discharged on the conclusion of the proceedings or of the application in question.

(6) An application for the discharge or variation of a restraint order may be made by any person affected by it."

Many of the cases concerning the matter which the High Court has to consider when hearing an application under this provision have been discussed: see *Re Peters* (1988) Q.B. 871, *Re P; Re W, The Times*, April 11, 1990.

III. Disclosure Orders

13–316 Nothing was expressed stated in either the DTOA or the corresponding provisions in the CJA 1988, which empowered the High Court to compel a defendant to swear an affidavit disclosing the nature, whereabouts and value of assets held by persons affected by the restraint order and note now the provisions of section 11 which entitles the Court to require a defendant to provide information to it relevant to the making of determinations under the Act. However, disclosure orders are normally sought in all cases in which restraint orders are made. In *Re O (Disclosure Order)* [1991] 1 All E.R. 330 the appellants were required to swear an affidavit in the following terms:

". . . disclosing the full value of any salary, money, goods or other assets whatsoever within and without the jurisdiction identifying with full particularity the nature of all such assets, their whereabouts and whether the same be held in their own names or jointly with some other person or persons or by nominees or otherwise howsoever on their behalf. . . ."

In *Re O (Disclosure Order)*, above the question was raised whether the Court has any jurisdiction to make such an order. A similar question arose in *A. J. Bekhor & Co. Ltd v. Bilton* [1981] 2 W.L.R. 565 in the context of Mareva injunctions where orders for the disclosure of assets are frequently made. The Court of Appeal (Civil Division) in *Bekhor* upheld the validity of disclosure orders as being inherent in the power granted by what is now section 37 of the Supreme Court Act 1981 "to make all such ancillary orders as appear to the Court to be just and convenient to ensure that the exercise of the Mareva jurisdiction is effective for its purpose", *per* Ackner L.J. at 576.

In *Re O*, the same Court held that the High Court must have been intended to have power to render effective a restraint order. The decision in *Re O* was concerned with section 77 of the CJA 1988 but the Court remarked that the jurisdiction to make restraint orders under the DTOA is mirrored by that under the CJA 1988 and (*obiter*) that "a decision in relation to one Act will apply equally to the other", *per* Lord Donaldson M.R. at 527. See also *Re T (Restraint Order), The Times*, May 19, 1992 in which *Re O* was followed in the context or orders made under section 26 of the DTA.

For the reasons set out below, a disclosure order should contain an appropriate condition to give effect to the rule against self-incrimination: see *Re O (Disclosure Order)*, above. Indeed, in *Re C (Restraint orders: identification), The Times*, April, 21, 1995, Ognall J. has made it abundantly plain that "the line of authority demonstrated quite conclusively that the Courts would not countenance any inroads into the privilege of refusing to incriminate oneself unless either it was required by statute that the privilege took second place to a wider public interest or that there was some adequate protection afforded as of the kind envisaged by the letter adduced in *AT & T Istel v. Tully* (1993) A.C. 45. Accordingly, Ognall J. held that defendants subject to a restraint order but ordered to disclose their assets and all individuals with whom he had financial dealings, were entitled to be protected from the possibility that the police might collect evidence from such individuals for use against him.

The reader should be aware of the offences created by sections 49–53 (drug-money laundering).

(a) **Rule against self-incrimination**

Section 11(11) of the 1994 Act expressly provides that acceptance by the defendant of any allegation, made by the prosecution in a section 3 statement, that the defendant received a payment or reward in connection with drug trafficking, shall not be admissible in criminal proceedings for an offence. This is consistent with the common law rule against self-incrimination. Thus, no man shall be compelled to comply with an order 13–317 which might to incriminate him: see *Lamb v. Munster* (1982) 10 Q.B.D. 110.

In *Re O (Disclosure Order)* (1991) 1 All E.R. 330 it was held that nothing in section 77 of the CJA 1988 (and therefore s.26 of the DTA) abrogates the common law rule. Although this might tend to frustrate the purpose of a disclosure order, the solution was to impose conditions on the use which may be made of the affidavits sworn in compliance with the order. The Court of Appeal suggested that an "appropriate condition", which should be inserted in all disclosure orders, would read:

> "No disclosure made in compliance with this order shall be used as evidence in the prosecution of an offence alleged to have been committed by the person required to make that disclosure or by any spouse of that person": *per* Lord Donaldson M.R. at 336.

The Court suggested that such a condition was "preferable" to the giving of an undertaking merely limiting the class of person to whom the disclosed information could be given and the purposes for which it could be used: *per* Lord Donaldson M.R. at 336, and see *Re T, The Times*, May 19, 1992.

Furthermore, in *Re C (Restraint orders: identification) The Times,* April, 21, 1995, an order was made in the following terms to prevent evidence being gathered from individuals who are identified by the defendant:

> "... and no use shall be made in any such prosecution against (the defendant) of evidence obtained as a direct result of such disclosure".

The use of a condition against self-incrimination, in the context of restraint orders made under section 77 of the CJA 1988 (and the corresponding provisions of the DTA) relates to a "special case" where although technically civil, the proceedings were ultimately bound up with criminal proceedings. Accordingly, the use of such a condition is not appropriate in the context of a civil action and the order cannot be used as a substitute for the privilege against self-incrimination: see *A T & T Istel Ltd v. Tully, The Times*, November 18, 1991; *Re O (Disclosure Order)* (above); *Att.-Gen. v. Times Newspapers Ltd* [1991] 2 W.L.R. 994 distinguished: and *Rank Film Distributors Ltd. v. Video Information Centre* [1982] A.C. 380.

IV. Appointment of a Receiver

13–318 Clearly, it will often be desirable, particularly in complicated cases where assets are not easily seized, to employ the services of a receiver. Accordingly, section 26(7) provides:

> "Where the High Court has made a restraint order, the High Court or a county court—
> (a) may at any time appoint a receiver—
> (i) to take possession of any realisable property, and
> (ii) in accordance with the Court's directions, to manage or

otherwise deal with any property in respect of which he is appointed subject to such exceptions and conditions as may be specified by the Court; and

(b) may require any person having possession of property in respect of which a receiver is appointed under this section to give possession of it to the receiver."

In cases where a receiver has been appointed under this section, the Court must exercise its powers in accordance with the provisions of section 29 (Realisation of Property); section 30 (Application of Proceeds of Realisation) and section 31 (Exercise of Powers of High Court or Receiver). Each of those sections has been quoted above (in so far as they are material) save for section 29(3), which provides:

"The Court may empower a receiver appointed under subsection (2) above, under section 26 of this Act or in pursuance of a charging order:

(a) to enforce any charge imposed under section 27 of this Act on realisable property or on interest or dividends payable in respect of such property, and

(b) in relation to any realisable property other than property for the time being subject to a charge under section 27 of this Act, to take possession of the property subject to such conditions or exceptions as may be specified by the Court."

In *Re M* (1992) 1 A.E.R. 537, it was held that an interim order made under section 252 of the Insolvency Act 1986 precluding the institution of bankruptcy or other proceedings against a debtor, or his property, did not affect the rights of the prosecution to make an application under (what is now section 26(7)) for the appointment of a receiver in respect of a defendant's realisable property, provided that a restraint order had been made against the defendant before the commencement of proceedings under section 252 of the 1986 Act. Otten J. (as he then was) said:

"the property to which the restraint order applies is no longer to be considered a part of the defendant's estate. He holds only notional title to such property. All dealings with such property might be held in abeyance until such time as the defendant is acquitted or a confiscation order is made and satisfied."

(a) Protection of receivers

Section 36 provides: 13–319

"(1) Where a receiver appointed under section 26 or 29 of this Act or in pursuance of a charging order—

(a) takes any action in relation to property which is not realisable property, being action which he would be entitled to take if it were such property, and

(b) believes, and has reasonable grounds for believing, that he is entitled to take that action in relation to that property,

he shall not be liable to any person in respect of any loss or damage resulting from his action except in so far as the loss or damage is caused by his negligence.

(2) Any amount due in respect of the remuneration and expenses of a receiver so appointed shall, if no sum is available to be applied in payment of it under section 30(6) of this Act, be paid by the prosecutor or, in a case where proceedings for a drug trafficking offence are not instituted, by the person on whose application the receiver was appointed.

(b) A defendant cannot appoint a receiver

13–320 In *Re M, The Times*, April 17, 1991, Otton J. (as he then was) described as "unthinkable" the fact that an application could be entertained by the High Court for an appointment of a receiver by or on behalf of the defendant to preserve assets intended for the satisfaction of a confiscation order. Otton J. ruled that an appointment of a receiver could only be made by the prosecutor given that an application for a restraint order could, similarly, only be made by the prosecutor.

(c) Consent of the receiver needed to sell

13–321 Where a person has an interest in property, but wishes to take possession or to sell that property, the consent of the receiver or the Court should be obtained. In *Re M, The Times*, May 20, 1991, a restraint order was made against M whose property included a restaurant. Valuers had advised the receiver that the restaurant should be sold as soon as possible. However, two mortgagees had interests in that property and they expressed a wish to take possession and to sell the property. The Divisional Court held that because the property was under the Court's restraint the mortgagees were affected by that restraint and accordingly the mortgagees could not attempt to take possession or to sell without the consent of the Receiver or the Court.

V. Charging Orders

13–322 Where a person is about to be charged, or has been charged, in connection with a drug trafficking offence, the High Court upon the application of the prosecutor (*ex parte* if necessary), may make a charging order under section 27 in respect of certain assets (chiefly land, securities and trusts) held by, or on behalf of that person. The powers exercisable by the Court under section 27 must comply with the requirements of sections 29, 30 and 31. Section 27 re-enacts much of s.9 of the 1986 Act (as amended by s.13(7) of the 1993 Act in respect of what is now s.27(7), and by Sched. 5 to the Criminal Justice Act 1988). Where the Court makes a charging order it may discharge that order if proceedings for the offence are not instituted, or if an application for a restraint order is not made within a reasonable time: s.25(5). Compensation may be paid if "a person who held property which was realisable property" (see s.18(1)) has suffered loss in consequence of an order under s.27 of the Act: s.18(2), above.

By section 27(2) a "charging order" is defined as:

> ". . . an order made under this section imposing on any such realisable property as may be specified in the order a charge for securing the payment of money to the Crown".

Not all assets may be the subject of a charging order. Indeed, by section 27(4) and subject to subsection (6), a charge may be imposed by a charging order only on:

> "(a) any interest in realisable property which is an interest held beneficially by the defendant or by a person to whom the defendant has directly or indirectly made a gift caught by this Act and is an interest—
> (i) in any asset of a kind mentioned in subsection (5) below; or
> (ii) under any trust, or
> (b) any interest in realisable property held by a person as trustee of a trust ("the relevant trust") if the interest is in such an asset or is an interest under another trust and a charge may by virtue of paragraph (a) above be imposed by a charging order on the whole beneficial interest under the relevant trust."

The assets referred to in subsection 27(4) are expressed by section 27(5) thus: 13–323

> "The assets referred to in subsection (4) above are—
> (a) land in England and Wales; or
> (b) securities of any of the following kinds—
> (i) government stock,
> (ii) stock of any body (other than a building society) incorporated within England and Wales,
> (iii) stock of any body incorporated outside England and Wales or of any country or territory outside the United Kingdom, being stock registered in a register kept at any place within England, and
> (iv) units of any unit trust in respect of which a register of the unit holders is kept at any place within England and Wales."

The Secretary of State may amend this list: see section 28(5).

Section 27(6) allows the High Court to extend the charge to include any interest or dividend payable in respect of the assets listed in section 27(5)(b), above.

The High Court may discharge or vary the charging order and it must do so if either the proceedings for the offence are concluded or if the value of the amount secured by the charge is paid into court: section 27(7). Where a charging order has been protected by an entry registered under the Land Charges Act 1972 or the Land Registration Act 1925 an order, discharging the charging order under section 27(7), may direct that the registered entry be cancelled: section 28(4).

VI. Compensation

13–324 Where persons hold realisable property in connection with proceedings instituted against any person which do not result in his conviction, it is open to them to apply for compensation under section 18 provides:

"If proceedings are instituted against a person for any drug trafficking offence or offences and either—

(a) the proceedings do not result in his conviction for any drug trafficking offence, or

(b) he is convicted of one or more drug trafficking offences but—

(i) the conviction or convictions concerned are quashed, or

(ii) he is pardoned by Her Majesty in respect of the conviction or convictions concerned,

the High Court may, on an application by a person who held property which was realisable property, order compensation to be paid to the applicant if having regard to all the circumstances, it considers it appropriate to make such an order."

However, quite considerable hurdles are placed in the path of the party seeking compensation under this section. Thus, by section 18(2):

"(2) The High Court shall not order compensation to be paid in any case unless the Court is satisfied—

(a) that there has been some serious default on the part of a person concerned in the investigation or prosecution of the offence or offences concerned, being a person mentioned in subsection (5) below; and

(b) that the applicant has suffered loss in consequence of anything done in relation to the property by or in pursuance of—

(i) an order of the High Court or a county court under sections 26 to 29 of this Act, or

(ii) an order of the Court of Session under section 11 (as applied by subsection (6) of that section), 27 or 28 of the Criminal Justice (Scotland) Act 1987 (inhibition and arrestment of property affected by restraint order and recognition and enforcement of orders under this Act)."

The persons, mentioned in section 18(2)(a), are listed in section 18(5): 13–325

"Compensation payable under this section shall be paid—
(a) where the person in default was, or was acting as, a member of a police force, out of the police fund out of which the expenses of that police force are met
(b) where the person in default was a member of the Crown Prosecution Service or was acting on behalf of the service, by the Director of Public Prosecutions; and
(c) where the person in default was an officer within the meaning of the Customs and Excise Management Act 1979 by the Commissioners of Customs and Excise."

By subsection (4) the amount of compensation payable under section 18 "shall be such as the High Court thinks just in all the circumstances of the case".

Given the wording of section 18(2) it follows that very few cases are likely to succeed under this section. Proving some serious default on the part of a person concerned in the investigation or prosecution, is difficult enough but establishing that the proceedings would not have been instituted or continued had it not been for that default, is unlikely to be successful in all but the rarest and clearest of cases. It is not necessary to prove that the loss was substantial: see s.18(2)(b).

L. FURTHER PROCEEDINGS IN CONNECTION WITH CONFISCATION ORDERS

(a) Introduction

As originally drafted, the 1986 Act allowed a defendant to apply for a downward variation of the confiscation order but it did not give the Court a power to vary or to re-assess the amount to be recovered under a confiscation order if assets (or evidence relevant to determinations made under the Act) come to light after the making of an order. Reform in this area has been piecemeal, which aggravates an already confused and difficult area of the law. 13–326

There are three determinations which a court will normally make if it embarks upon a drug trafficking enquiry under s.2 of the 1994 Act. First, whether the defendant has benefited from drug trafficking at all. Secondly, the amount which represents the total proceeds of the defendant's drug trafficking. Thirdly, the "amount that might be realised" under what are now sections 5(3) and 6(2) of this Act.

The Criminal Justice (International Co-operation) Act 1990 (c.5) amended the law in respect of the third determination but it did not touch the first two determinations (and see para. 4.1 of the Working Group Report (1991)). Reforms introduced by ss.13, 14 and 15 address the problems associated with the first two determinations. Thus:

(a) Section 13 empowers the Crown Court to embark upon a drug trafficking enquiry when it had earlier declined to do so. This provision is particularly significant given that by s.2(1) a court may not be asked by the prosecutor to proceed under s.2 in every case.
(b) By s.14, the Court that did embark upon an enquiry but nevertheless concluded that there was no benefit received by the defendant, can now reassess that determination if new evidence becomes available.
(c) By s.15, the Court may re-assess the value of the defendant's proceeds of drug trafficking if new evidence becomes known. Prosecutors will be anxious to keep this figure under review because it represents the maximum that can be recovered under a confiscation order. Accordingly, where the prosecutor successfully applies to the Crown Court for an increased confiscation order on the basis that there were more realisable assets in existence than at first known (*i.e.* under s.16 below, formerly s.16 of the Criminal Justice (International Co-operation) Act 1990) it follows that the new order cannot exceed the amount originally determined to be the value of the defendant's proceeds of drug trafficking.

Common to each of these new provisions is a six-year time-limit which runs from the date of the defendant's last conviction for a drug trafficking offence in respect of which he appeared before the Crown Court to be sentenced at the time the confiscation order was made.

These provisions have been attacked as "hounding" a man who has been convicted (Hansard, HL, vol. 539, col. 1357) and it is perhaps to this end that s.13(4) was enacted but even where a court is required to make a determination under s.14 or s.15, the Court is not entitled to rely on any of the statutory assumptions under s.2 (and similarly in respect of s.13). Furthermore, under both s.13 and s.15 the Court appears to be entitled to mitigate the amount to be confiscated as is "just in all the circumstances" (see s.13(5) and s.15(12)). As far as the author is aware, these provisions have only been invoked in one case (and that case has yet to be heard).

(b) Reconsideration of the making of an order

13–327 Where the Court did not originally embark upon a drug trafficking enquiry under the DTA because, for example, there seemed little point in doing so or because there was insufficient evidence to justify proceeding under the Act, it is open to the prosecution to return to court under section 13 and to invite the Court to reconsider its decision in the light of fresh evidence. It is not enough for the prosecutor to say that the evidence, or the significance of it, was overlooked: he must go to court armed with evidence that was "not available to him" when confiscation proceedings were originally considered by the Court: section 13(2)(a). Thus, section 13 of the 1994 Act, provides:

"(1) This section applies where the defendant has appeared before the Crown Court to be sentenced in respect of one or more drug trafficking offences but the Court has not proceeded under section 2 of this Act.

(2) If the prosecutor has evidence—

(a) which was not available to him when the defendant appeared to be sentenced (and accordingly was not considered by the Court), but

(b) which the prosecutor believes would have led the Court to determine that the defendant had benefited from drug trafficking if—

(i) the prosecutor had asked the Court to proceed under section 2 of this Act, and

(ii) the evidence had been considered by the Court,

he may apply to the Crown Court for it to consider the evidence."

At this stage, the prosecutor can do no more than invite the Court to consider the evidence. He cannot insist that the Court embarks upon a DTA hearing even though he would have been able to have done so, pursuant to section 2(1)(a), if he had the same evidence available to him originally. A further safeguard is afforded by section 13(3) which makes it clear that it is for the Court to decide, having considered all the evidence, whether it is appropriate to proceed under section 2 in the light of the new information. For this purpose, the Court must have regard to "all the circumstances of the case": section 13(4). Undue delay on the part of the prosecution in obtaining the evidence, or putting the material before the Court, is likely to be taken into account notwithstanding that there exists a statutory time-limit of six years (from the date of conviction) for making an application under section 13. The Court is obliged to have regard to—but not necessarily to leave out of account—any fines imposed on the defendant in respect of the "offences in question" (s.13(6)). Presumably, the Court should also have regard to other financial orders made against the defendant upon being sentenced, including costs and forfeiture orders.

The Court may take into account payments or rewards received by the defendant "on or after the date of conviction" but the prosecution cannot rely on the statutory assumptions (s.13(9)). Accordingly, the prosecution must prove (to the civil standard (s.2(8))) that the defendant (a) received the payment; (b) received it in connection with drug trafficking carried on by him or by another; and (c) that the drug trafficking activity occurred before the date of conviction: see subss. (8) and (12). The likely reasoning behind this approach is that the conviction should be seen as marking the end of the defendant's drug trafficking career, for confiscation purposes, and that the use of the assumptions is justified where payments are received up and until the moment of conviction. Clearly, this is not a complete answer because the assumptions will also apply where property is "held" by the defendant at any time since his conviction but, even in this situation, it is likely that property coming 13–328 into the defendant's possession after conviction was the result of drug trafficking carried on prior to that date.

Where a determination is made under s.2(4), the Court is only obliged to order a payment that is "just" in all the circumstances. It is not bound to confiscate the full extent of the defendant's proceeds of drug trafficking (or the amount that might be realised): section 13(5). No application may be entertained after the end of the period of six years from the date of the defendant's conviction: section 13(10).

(c) Re-assessment of whether defendant has benefited

13–329 Much of section 14 is self-explanatory and provides that:

"(1) This section applies where the Court has made a determination under section 2(2) of this Act ('the section 2(2) determination') that the defendant has not benefited from drug trafficking.

(2) If the prosecutor has evidence—

(a) which was not considered by the Court in making the section 2(2) determination, but

(b) which the prosecutor believes would have led the Court to determine that the defendant had benefited from drug trafficking if it had been considered by the Court, he may apply to the Crown Court for it to consider that evidence.

(3) If, having considered the evidence the Court is satisfied that it would have determined that the defendant had benefited from drug trafficking if that evidence had been available to it, the Court—

(a) shall make

(i) a fresh determination under subsection (2) of section 2 of this Act and

(ii) a determination under subsection (4) of that section of the amount to be recovered by virtue of that section; and

(b) may make an order under that section.

(4) Where the Court is proceeding under section 2 of this Act by virtue of this section, subsection (4) of that section shall have effect as if the words "before sentencing or otherwise dealing with him in respect of the offence or, as the case may be, any of the offences concerned" were omitted.

(5) The Court may take into account any payment or other reward received by the defendant on or after the date of the section 2(2) determination, but only if the prosecutor shows that it was received by the defendant in connection with drug trafficking carried on by the defendant or another person on or before that date.

(6) In considering under this section any evidence which relates to any payment or reward to which subsection (5) above applies, the Court shall not make the assumptions which would otherwise be required by section 4 of this Act.

(7) No application shall be entertained by the Court under this section if it is made after the end of the period of six years beginning with the date of conviction; and in this subsection, "the date of conviction" has the same meaning as in section 13 of this Act.

(8) Sections 11 and 12 of this Act shall apply where the prosecutor makes an application under this section as they apply where the prosecutor asks the Court to proceed under section 2 of this Act."

By subs. (2), the Court appears to be required to form an opinion based on hindsight, *i.e.* that it "would have" determined that the defendant had benefited from drug trafficking if the evidence which ultimately came to light had been available to it. Payments received by the defendant after the date on which the Court originally concluded he received no benefit may be taken into account, but the prosecution will not be able to rely on the statutory assumptions.

(d) Revised assessment of proceeds

Section 15 of the DTA provides as follows: 13–330

"(1) This section applies where the Court has made a determination under subsection (4) of section 2 of this Act of the amount to be recovered in a particular case by virtue of that section ('the current section 2(4) determination').

(2) Where the prosecutor is of the opinion that the real value of the defendant's proceeds of drug trafficking was greater than their assessed value, the prosecutor may apply to the Crown Court for the evidence on which the prosecutor has formed his opinion to be considered by the Court.

(3) Sections 11 and 12 of this Act shall apply where the prosecutor makes such an application as they apply where the prosecutor asks the Court to proceed under section 2 of this Act, but subject (in the case of section 11) to subsection (9)(a) below.

(4) If, having considered the evidence, the Court is satisfied that the real value of the defendant's proceeds of drug trafficking is greater than their assessed value (whether because the real value at the time of the current section 2(4) determination was higher than was thought or because the value of the proceeds in question has subsequently increased), the Court shall make a fresh determination under subsection (4) of section 2 of this Act of the amount to be recovered by virtue of that section.

(5) In subsections (2) and (4) above—
'assessed value' means the value of the defendant's proceeds of drug trafficking as assessed by the Court in accordance with section 5(1 of this Act; and
'real value' means the value of the defendant's proceeds of drug trafficking which took place—

(a) in the period by reference to which the current section 2(4) determination was made, or
(b) in any earlier period.

(6) Where the Court is proceeding under section 2 of this Act by virtue of this section, subsection (4) of that section shall have effect as if the words 'before sentencing or otherwise dealing with him in respect of the offence or, as the case may be, any of the offences concerned' were omitted.

(7) Any determination under section 2(4) of this Act by virtue of this section shall be by reference to the amount that might be realised at the time when the determination is made.

13–331 (8) In the case of any determination under section 2(4) of this Act by virtue of this section, section 4(6) of this Act shall not apply in relation to any of the defendant's proceeds of drug trafficking taken into account in respect of the current section 2(4) determination.

(9) In relation to any such determination by virtue of this section—
(a) sections 5(2), 6(4) and 11(9)(a) of this Act shall have effect as if for 'confiscation order' there were substituted "determination";
(b) section 5(3) shall have effect as if for 'confiscation order is made' there were substituted 'determination is made', and
(c) section 6(1) of this Act shall have effect as if for 'a confiscation order is made against the defendant' there were substituted 'of the determination'.

(10) The Court may take into account any payment or other reward received by the defendant on or after the date of the current section 2(4) determination, but only if the prosecutor shows that it was received by the defendant in connection with drug trafficking carried on by the defendant or another person on or before that date.

(11) In considering under this section any evidence which relates to any payment or reward to which subsection (10) above applies, the Court shall not make the assumptions which would otherwise be required by section 4 of this Act.

(12) If, as a result of making the fresh determination required by subsection (4) above, the amount to be recovered exceeds the amount set by the current section 2(4) determination, the Court may substitute for the amount to be recovered under the confiscation order which was made by reference to the current section 2(4) determination such greater amount as it thinks just in all the circumstances of the case.

(13) Where the Court varies a confiscation order under subsection (12) above it shall substitute for the term of imprisonment or of detention fixed under section 139(2) of the Powers of Criminal Courts (Sentencing) Act 2000 in respect of the amount to be recovered under the order a longer term determined in accordance with that section (as it has effect by virtue of section 9 of this Act) in respect of the greater amount substituted under subsection (12) above.

(14) Subsection (13) above shall apply only if the effect of the substitu-

tion is to increase the maximum period applicable in relation to the order under section 139(4) of the 2000 Act.

(15) No application shall be entertained by the Court under this section if it is made after the end of the period of six years beginning with the date of conviction; and in this subsection 'the date of conviction' has the same meaning as in section 13 of this Act.

There appears to be a difference of scope in the ambit of these provisions when subs. (2) (formerly, s.5C(2) of the 1986 Act inserted by s.12 of the 1993 Act) is contrasted with subs. (4). Subsection (2) seems to look to the "real value" of the proceeds of drug trafficking (as they should have been assessed at the time the order was made) but the conclusion, which the Court is actually entitled to make under subs. (4), includes any increased value of the proceeds in question. Nevertheless, the governing provision is subs. (4). The Court therefore looks at the current value of the proceeds plus any payments received by the defendant on, or after, that date which were the fruits of drug trafficking carried on by the defendant or another before that moment (subs. (10)). The prosecution cannot rely on the statutory assumptions (subs. (11)). However, the "amount to be recovered", under a fresh confiscation order, is prima facie the "amount that might be realised" (see ss. 5(3), 6(2) and 15(7)). It follows that if the defendant's finances have improved by the date of the subsequent determination, it is the higher figure, which is relevant. Given that the Court is being asked to make a fresh confiscation order it follows that section 4(6) must be disregarded and that is what s.15(8) is designed to achieve. Even if, prima facie, the "amount to be recovered" (being the "amount that might be realised") is greater than it was originally assessed to be, nevertheless, the Court need only order such greater amount as it thinks just in all the circumstances of the case. 13–332

(e) How is an application made under sections 13, 14 or 15 of the DTA?

The procedure is set out in Rule 35 of the Crown Court Rules (S.I. 1995 No. 2618) that now provide as follows: 13–333

"(1) Where the prosecutor makes an application under section 13, 14 or 15 of the Drug Trafficking Act 1994 . . . such an application must be in writing and a copy thereof must be served on the defendant.

(2) The application must include the following particulars, namely—

(a) the name of the defendant;
(b) the date on which and the place where the relevant conviction occurred;
(c) the date on which and the place where any relevant confiscation order was made;
(d) the grounds on which the application is made;
(e) an indication of the evidence available to support the application. . . . "

M. DRUG-MONEY LAUNDERING OFFENCES

I. Introduction

(a) The scale of the problem

13–334 In 1989 the National Drugs Intelligence Co-ordinator informed the Home Affairs Committee on Drug Trafficking and Related Serious Crime that at least £1,800 million (derived from drug trafficking) was circulating in the United Kingdom. The amount of money being laundered is thought to be £57 million a year, from drug sales, in America and Europe alone. Despite the 1986 Act, the United Kingdom continues to be a major centre for money laundering. In the same year, the Home Office told the Committee that the 1986 Act has promoted drug traffickers to adopt greater sophistication in their efforts to launder the proceeds, so that money laundering is "probably the most organised aspect of drug trafficking": see the Home Affairs Committee 7th Report (1989). The Home Office indicated that although the evidence of links between organised crime and drug trafficking was largely anecdotal "there is an undoubted link between the two". The link is said to be evident between the drugs trade and the financing of wars and terrorism but usually the link is much more basic and symptomatic of general criminal activity committed by drug traffickers. There was much in the 1993 Act, and now this Act, which represents the views and the concerns of the legislature when the Drug Trafficking Offences Bill was being debated. It is plain from the Official Reports that Parliament regarded the 1986 Act as marking only the first step in the fight against organised crime and not solely against drug trafficking. The extent to which other areas of the law in 1986 required reform (*e.g.* extradition, banking and international co-operation in respect of the gathering and calling of evidence) meant that the 1986 Act could not embrace every activity that was either linked (or akin) to drug trafficking and money laundering. Parliament was also mindful that the Criminal Justice Bill (now the Criminal Justice Act 1988) was being drafted but had to be considered by Parliament. Lord Harris of Greenwich explained the problem when he said

> "... (I)t is an illusion to imagine that drug trafficking can be treated as an isolated crime ... we are confronted with the existence of highly sophisticated criminal syndicates. The operators move effectively from one form of serious crime to another; from drug trafficking to armed robbery, from counterfeit currency operations to large-scale fraud and then back again to drug trafficking." (Hansard, HL, vol. 474, col. 1115).

13–335 The object of money laundering is to transfer the proceeds of crime through the financial sector so that it re-emerges back into legitimate commercial or financial concerns controlled or directed by the participants in the criminal enterprise.

The object of money laundering is to convert the proceeds of crime through the legitimate commercial and financial markets so that it re-emerges back into the hands of the participants in the criminal enterprise. Anti-money laundering legislation is designed to frustrate that process, but the debate as to whether it is necessary or desirable to criminalise that activity tends to revolve around the following points:

(i) criminal acts often generate ill-gotten proceeds and wealth ("dirty money"). That might be achieved by creating a chain of bogus transactions, companies, and using false identities. Money laundering often sees that process being reversed: "dirty money" is converted into "clean money". Frequently, the result is achieved using persons and agencies acting lawfully. The money, laundered in this way, may itself be used legitimately, and taxes properly paid.

(ii) Those who assist in the money laundering process are usually persons who have not participated in the predicate offence that generated the proceeds. Indeed such persons would ordinarily be styled "law abiding": there is no general legal duty to report suspicions of criminal activity to police.

(iii) Many criminal activities involve the use of the so-called "black market" economy. Much money laundering is achieved using legitimate markets.

(iv) Some offences may lead to property and money being taken out of circulation for very long periods of time. Money laundering takes money, that would otherwise be hidden "under the mattress" and puts it back into circulation. Monies invested may generate income which is taxed. It is not unknown for money launderers to overstate income/turnover (as a method by which ill-gotten monies are filtered back into circulation) and pay taxes on inflated sums. The predicate offence will often generate income that is obviously not declared to the Inland Revenue.

(v) Money laundering, carried out in a State where the predicate offence was not committed, will often not violate the laws of that State. The predicate offence may not comply with the test for "dual criminality" (*e.g.* a fiscal/taxation offence).

(vi) Proving that a person knew, or believed, that wealth was derived from a particular activity (*e.g.* drug trafficking) will often be difficult to prove unless the sum of money involved, or the number of transactions, or the circumstances of the transactions, make the origin of the monies obvious.

However, combating crime—particularly organised crime—is now an international objective, with many States shifting towards a common position on ways of targeting offenders who are often beyond their reach.

Organised crime exploits the three elements of business, supply, demand

and profit, and the law enforcement agencies (while traditionally deployed to tackle the first two elements) are devoting more resources to tackling the profit element for two reasons; (a) funds removed from circulation cannot be re-used to finance further criminal enterprises, and (b) it removes the incentive to commit crime.

(b) International action

13–336 Given that drug trafficking and money laundering operate on an international scale, many of the provisions of the 1986 Act (and subsequent legislation) are the product of diplomatic efforts and rooted in several Treaties, Conventions, Bi-lateral Agreements and (now) European Directives: see the European Convention on Mutual Assistance 1957 (which the United Kingdom was not able to ratify until the enactment of the Criminal Justice (International Co-operation) Act 1990); the United Nations Convention Against Illicit Traffic In Narcotic Drugs and Psychotropic Substances 1988 (the Vienna Convention, ratified by the United Kingdom in 1991); the Council of Europe Convention on Laundering, Search, Seizure and Confiscation of the Proceeds of Crime 1990; and see the European Council Directive (91/308/EEC).

The Financial Action Task Force (FATF) made a number of radical proposals in 1990, which went beyond those agreed at the 1988 United Nations Convention. FATF recommended that Member States should address their money laundering provisions to various major crimes and not just drug trafficking. It also suggested that rules of secrecy or confidentiality held by various financial institutions should be qualified so as to permit suspicious transactions to be reported to the authorities.

These proposals were already in Parliament's mind in 1986 (see Hansard, HL, vol. 474, col. 1094); and s.50 of the Drug Trafficking Act 1994 (formerly s.24 of the 1986 Act) makes it an offence to assist another to retain the benefit of drug trafficking in circumstances where the defendant knew or even suspected that the assisted person has benefited from drug trafficking. Section 50 does not impose an obligation to disclose a suspicion but where a person or body (*e.g.* a bank) discloses suspicions to the authorities he will have the protections afforded to him by s.50(3) (*e.g.* against breach of contract) and he may continue to act for the person under suspicion (*e.g.* without closing his bank account) within the limits set out in s.50(3) (see also the Wilton Park Paper 65, 1993, HMSO).

13–337 The U.S.A. has been developing powerful anti-money laundering laws over the last 25 to 30 years. The Bank Secrecy Act 1970 (U.S., 31 USC) applies to financial institutions and businesses that accept large sums of cash. A "financial institution" is very broadly defined: see *U.S. v. Rigdon* (1989) 874 F.2d 774 and *U.S. v. Clines* (1992) 958 F.2d 578. The Bank Secrecy Act 1970 requires businesses and individuals to submit Currency Transaction Reports (CTRs) as well as various reports of currency instruments, foreign bank accounts, and cash payments over U.S. $10,000 in a trade or business. Businesses and their employees may be required to lodge Criminal Referral Forms (CRFs) in respect of any "known or suspected criminal violation committed against (or through) a bank" used to facilitate a criminal transaction. Failure to file a CRF may result in so-called civil penalties being assessed against the institution, its officers or employees. Data and intelligence gleaned from these records are collated on a database utilised by FINCEN (Financial Crimes Enforcement Network). The Anti-Abuse Act 1988 (U.S.) includes a requirement upon the Secretary to the Treasury to negotiate with other countries to ensure that they have adequate records on international currency transactions, which might be taken as a requirement for mandatory reporting along United States lines. The question as to what happens to all this information is a matter of growing concern and debate. The Money Laundering Control Act (1986; 18 USC, see §981, 982), creates a number of offences in respect of the knowing participation by any person in transactions with persons who derive their money from specified unlawful activities, *e.g.* drug trafficking. Forfeiture, under U.S. legislation, is permitted under the Bank Secrecy Act 1970, the Money Laundering Control Act 1986 (18 USC), the Comprehensive Drug Abuse Prevention and Control Act, the Controlled Substances Act (21 USC §853, 881), the Racketeer-Influenced and Corrupt Organisations Act (RICO; 18 USC §1961–1968) and the Continuing Criminal Enterprise statutes.

British legislation is rapidly being modified to increase the powers of investigation and to set in place an intelligence-gathering network. Thus, our law, by virtue of Part III of the DTA, imposes a duty on persons to report (in effect to police) transactions and other information based on a suspicion held (or which ought reasonable to have been held) relevant to a possible contravention of the drug trafficking legislation. A system of reporting, based on suspicion, is controversial but follows recent developments in American law. From the mid 1980s, financial institutions within the United States have been required to complete a Criminal Referral Form (CRF) if an employee reasonably suspects money laundering or the commission of a criminal offence (Code of Federal Regulations; s.21.11; title 12). The Crime Control Act 1990 (§1517) amended the Bank Secrecy Act 1970 (31 USC §5318) by requiring "any director, officer, employee, or agent of any financial institution" to report any relevant suspicious transactions. Following complaints from the financial sector that this provision was proving to be unduly onerous, section 1517 of the Crime Control Act (U.S.) has since been amended so that a person making the report has immunity from criminal or civil liability. This is an important feature and the amendment is designed to encourage reporting without the informer fearing civil liability from customers: see *Ricci v. Key Bancshares of Maine Inc.* (768 F.2d 456).

English legislation imposes a similar duty to report suspicions relating to drug money laundering—but the duty applies to all persons—and not just those working for financial institutions. It is not at all clear to what extent persons making a report are protected from civil actions in the event of the 13–338 information being incorrect. It is concerns of this type that have, to some extent, led to calls for a reconsideration of a suspicion-based system of reporting.

As we have seen, the American system is bolstered by a bureaucratic structure, which requires persons engaged in any business to report information that meets specified objective criteria. It is then a matter for the law enforcement agencies to determine what significance is to be attached to the information provided. Despite the colossal amount of paper-work generated by this system (which is transferred to FINCEN) the information is processed and collated within days—a feat which cannot yet be accomplished in this country without further resources being provided in terms of labour and technology. Critics of the suspicion-based system of reporting, point out that an administrative system avoids placing individuals in the embarrassing, invidious and precarious position of evaluating whether the information they have obtained is enough to generate a suspicion that drug trafficking has occurred or not.

There is some evidence that certain legitimate businesses turn customers away if they fear that the transaction might lead to questions being asked concerning the circumstances of it. In law, such action hardly affords a defence and it may demonstrate "wilful blindness", but no doubt the perception is that proving wilful blindness is one thing but committing oneself to a transaction likely to be reduced to writing is to expose the business to an enquiry later to be regretted. Obviously reactions of this sort is not what law-enforcers wish to see happening because the "problem" merely moves somewhere else and valuable information is lost and the money is driven further underground and is laundered.

Developments in the U.S. have to some extent been mirrored elsewhere as a large number of countries have collaborated to combat drug trafficking and money laundering. These two activities now have to be seen in the context of each other.

13–339 The American model was considered by the House of Lords in 1986 (Hansard, HL, vol. 474, col. 1112) when it was pointed out that American law was not confined to drug trafficking. The British Government was not then prepared to move in the direction of the American model although the then Parliamentary Under-Secretary had indicated that "there might be movement in the future" (Hansard, *ibid*).

Significantly, Article 5(1) of the Vienna Convention 1988 provides that each party is to adopt such measures as may be necessary to enable confiscation of "(a) the proceeds derived from offences established in accordance with article 3, paragraph 1, or property the value of which corresponds to that of such proceeds" while Article 5(3) requires each party to empower its courts to order that bank, financial or commercial records be made available or seized. Provision for the reversal of the burden of proof is made by Article 7: "each Party may consider ensuring that the onus of proof be reversed regarding the lawful origin of alleged proceeds or other property liable to confiscation, to the extent that such action is consistent with the principles of its domestic law and with the nature of the judicial and other proceedings".

Article 3 of the 1988 Convention also requires member states to make the concealment or disguising of the proceeds of drug trafficking an offence without reference (as appeared in s.24 of the 1986 Act) to "facilitating" or "assisting" the drug trafficker. Article 3 also requires the creation of an offence of handling the proceeds of drug trafficking.

Accordingly, the Home Affairs Committee in their Seventh Report (Vol I, session 1988–89) recommended that English law be amended so that the United Kingdom could ratify Article 3. The U.S. authorities made representations to the Home Affairs Committee that the United Kingdom should introduce money-laundering measures similar to those already operating in the U.S. The 1994 Act suggests that the Government are moving in that direction but the severity of American law should not be underestimated both in terms of the draconian effect of their law and the vigorous way it is enforced with very heavy penalties for non-compliance: see also the European Council Directive 91/308/EEC (O.J. L166/77).

II. Offences Relevant to Part III and part IV of the 1994 Act

The relevant offences are now: 13–340

(a) Assisting another to retain the benefit of drug trafficking "knowing or suspecting" that the assisted person is a drug trafficker or someone who has benefited from drug trafficking: s.50, formerly s.24 of the 1986 Act;
(b) Prejudicing investigations: s.58, formerly s.31 of the 1986 Act;
(c) Concealing, disguising, transferring or removing the proceeds of drug trafficking; the offence being committed by the trafficker himself: s.49(1), formerly s.14 of the Criminal Justice (International Co-operation) Act 1990;
(d) Concealing, disguising, transferring or removing the proceeds of drug trafficking; the offence being committed by another who assists any person to avoid prosecution for a drug trafficking offence or the making or enforcement of a confiscation order: s.49(2);
(e) Acquisition, possession or use of proceeds of drug trafficking: s.51 of the 1994 Act (formerly s.23A of the 1986 Act inserted by s.16 of the 1993 Act);
(f) Failing to disclose knowledge of suspicion of money laundering: s.52;
(g) Disclosing information to another, which is likely to prejudice an investigation or proposed investigation: s.53.

A table of money laundering offences follows on page 632.

MONEY LAUNDERING OFFENCES—CRIB SHEET

Act	*Actus*	Result	*Mens rea*	Statutory defence
DTA, s.9(1)(a) (CJA, s. 93C) *Causey* (Oct. 18, 1999)	• **Conceals or disguises** D's own proceeds of drug trafficking. (14 years on indictment.)		• To avoid drug trafficking prosecution. • To avoid the making of C.order. • To avoid enforcement of a C.order.	
DTA, s. 49(1)(b)	• **Converts, transfers** D's own proceeds of drug trafficking. • **Removes from the jurisdiction** D's own proceeds of drug trafficking.		• To avoid drug trafficking prosecution. • To avoid the making of C.order. • To avoid enforcement of a C.order	
DTA, s. 49(2)(a)	• **Conceals or disguises** property.[1] (14 years on indictment.)		• Knowing OR • Having reasonable grounds to suspect the property represents another person's proceeds of drug trafficking.	
DTA, s. 49(2)(b)	• **Converts, transfers** property. • **Removes from the jurisdiction** property: *El-Kurd* (July 26, 2000).		• Knowing OR • Having reasonable grounds to suspect the property represents another person's proceeds of drug trafficking.	

[1] It is arguable that it is not necessary for prosecution to prove that the property in fact represents the proceeds of drug trafficking. However, that would put a third party in a worse position than the trafficker who conceals his own lawfully acquired property.

MONEY LAUNDERING OFFENCES—CRIB SHEET *cont.*

Act	*Actus*	Result	*Mens rea*	Statutory defence
DTA, s.50(1)(a) (CJA, s .93A)	• **Enters into** an arrangement. • **Concerned in** an arrangement: *McMaster* (Oct. 8, 1998).	Retention or control of A's proceeds of drug trafficking is facilitated.	• Knows • Suspects A carries on, OR has carried on, OR has benefited from drug trafficking	
DTA, s. 50(1)(b)	• **Enters into** an arrangement. • **Concerned in** an arrangement. (14 years on indictment.)	• A's proceeds of drug trafficking USED **to place funds** at A's disposal. • A's proceeds USED to **invest in property** for A's benefit.	• Knows • Suspects 7 A carries on, OR has carried on, OR has benefited from drug trafficking: *Colle* (1992) 95 Cr.App.R. 67; *Butt* (Nov. 16, 1998); serious misdirection: judge thought the defendant had to prove D did not know of A's career.	• D did not **know** or **suspect** that arrangement related to drug trafficking. • D did not **know** or **suspect** his acts led to the forbidden results. • Intended to disclose **to the police** D's suspicions [2] in accordance with s. 50(3)(b).[3]
DTA, s. 51(1) (CJA, s. 93B)	• Acquires, or USES, or • Has possession of another person's proceeds of drug trafficking. (14 years imprisonment.)		• KNOWS drug trafficking origins of the property: *Gibson* (Feb. 23, 2000)—burden of proving defence rests with defendant.	• Gave "adequate consideration". • Intended to disclose a suspicion or belief in relation to the property as per s. 50(5).[4]

[2] Note that disclosure protection appears to relate to "funds and investments" derived from drug trafficking (s .50(3)). It is not clear why s. 50(3) does not expressly extend the protection to disclosures of suspicions relating to ANY property.

[3] There must be a "reasonable excuse" for not doing so.

[4] There must be a "reasonable excuse" for not making the disclosure.

MONEY LAUNDERING OFFENCES—CRIB SHEET *cont.*

Act	*Actus*	Result	*Mens rea*	Statutory defence
DTA, s. 52(1)(a) (Not mirrored in the CJA.)	• **Failing to disclose** information to the police as soon as reasonably practicable. • The information, material, came to attention of D. • The information came to D *in the course of his trade, profession, business, or employment.* (Five years on indictment.)		• Knows • Suspects 7 another person is engaged in "drug money laundering".[5]	• Reasonable excuse for not disclosing the information (s. 52(3)). • D disclosed information to an "appropriate person" in accordance with employer's procedure. • Limited protection for lawyers.[6]
DTA, s. 53(1) (CJA, s. 93D)	• **Disclosure** of information, to another person 7 where constable is acting, or proposing to act, in connection with an investigation being conducted, or about to be conducted, into drug money laundering. (Five years, on indictment.)	Likely to prejudice the investigation or Proposed inquiry.	• Knows • Suspects that constable is so acting.	• Limited protection for legal advisors. • Prove D did not know or suspect that disclosure was likely to be prejudicial. • Immunity if acting so as to enforce the DTA, or related legislation.
DTA, s. 53(2)	• Discloses to another the fact that disclosure has been made under DTA, ss.50, 51, 52.	• Likely to prejudice the investigation or • Proposed inquiry.	• Knows • Suspects that disclosure has been made	As above.

[5] That is to say, an offence contrary to ss. 49, 50, 51, or one that would be such an offence if done in England or Wales (s .52(7)).

[6] Privilege does not exist if the information is "communicated or given with a view to furthering any criminal purpose". What does that phrase mean? Whose view? If the information is given to a legal adviser, by a person who keeps to the unlawful purpose secret, does that destroy the privilege? Or, must the legal adviser also know of the criminal purpose?

MONEY LAUNDERING OFFENCES—CRIB SHEET *cont.*

Act	*Actus*	Result	*Mens rea*	Statutory defence
DTA, s. 53(3)	• Discloses the fact that a disclosure has been made to [an MLRO] under DTA, ss. 50(5), 51(8), 52(5).	• Likely to prejudice the investigation or • Proposed inquiry.	• Knows • Suspects disclosure has been made.	• Limited protection for legal advisors. • Prove D did not know or suspect that disclosure was likely to be prejudicial. • Immunity if acting so as to enforce the DTA or related legislation.

(a) Assisting drug traffickers

13–341 By section 50:

"(1) Subject to subsection (3) below, if a person enters into or is otherwise concerned in an arrangement whereby:

(a) the retention or control by or on behalf of another (call him "A") of A's proceeds of drug trafficking is facilitated (whether by concealment, removal from the jurisdiction, transfer to nominees or otherwise), or

(b) A's proceeds of drug trafficking:

(i) are used to secure that funds are placed at A's disposal, or

(ii) are used for A's benefit to acquire property by way of investment,

knowing or suspecting that A is a person who carries on or has carried on drug trafficking or has benefited from drug trafficking, he is guilty of an offence.

(2) In this section, references to any person's proceeds of drug trafficking include a reference to any property which in whole or in part directly or indirectly represented in his hands his proceeds of drug trafficking."

The offence is designed to prohibit the "laundering" of drug money. It is triable either way and punishable on conviction on indictment, to imprisonment for a term not exceeding 14 years or to a fine or to both (s.54(1)(b) and, on summary conviction, to a term of imprisonment not exceeding six months or to a fine not exceeding the statutory maximum or to both (s.54(1)(a)). An offence under section 50 falls within Part II of Schedule 1 to the Criminal Justice Act 1982 so that offenders will not be eligible for early release: see s.65 and para. 7 to Sched.1 of the 1994 Act and see the 1990 Act, s.31(1) and Sched.4, para.3 amending Part II of Sched.1 to the Criminal Justice Act 1982 (c.48), and note the observations of the Home Secretary, Hansard, HL, vol. 514, col. 902. It is also a "serious arrestable offence" for the purposes of section 116 of the Police and Criminal Evidence Act 1984: see para. 9 to Sched. 1 of the 1994 Act.

The *mens rea* of the offence is either knowing or suspecting that "A" is a person who carried on, or has carried on drug trafficking, or has benefited from someone else's drug trafficking. The burden of proving those matters rests on the prosecution, see *Colle* (1992) 95 Cr.App.R. 67; and see *Butt* (November 16, 1998) where the jury were misdirected as to the burden of proof. However, it would seem that it is not necessary for the prosecution to prove that the defendant knew or suspected that he had in fact entered into, or was otherwise concerned in, any of the arrangements specified in subsection 24(1). The prosecution need do no more than to prove, as a fact, that the defendant entered into or was concerned in an arrangement as defined by section 50(1)(a) or (b). Thus where D provides a false reference in the name of B, (being an alias for A), the fact that D did not know the reference was to be used by A to conceal A's proceeds of drug trafficking is irrelevant. By providing a false reference, D became concerned in an arrangement (albeit organised by others). The prosecution do not have to identify an individual who was engaged in drug trafficking, or to prove a conviction or to prove specific acts of drug trafficking: see *Sabharwal* (February 12, 2001). Section 50(1) does not preface the phrase "enters into" or "concerned" with the word "knowingly."

To reinforce the point, section 50(4) provides statutory defences but the legislature has shifted the burden of proof to the accused to prove, by section 50(4), (and see *Colle*, above): 13–342

"(4) In proceedings against a person for an offence under this section, it is a defence to prove—

(a) that he did not know or suspect that the arrangement related to any person's proceeds of drug trafficking;

(b) that he did not know or suspect that by the arrangement the retention or control by or on behalf of A of any property was facilitated or, as the case may be, that by the arrangement any property was used as mentioned in subsection (1)(b) above; or that—

(i) he intended to disclose to a constable such a suspicion, belief or matter as is mentioned in subsection (3) above in relation to the arrangement, but

(ii) there is reasonable excuse for his failure to make any such disclosure in the manner mentioned in paragraph (b)(i) or (ii) of that subsection."

When reading the case of *Colle*, as it is reported in (1992) 95 Cr.App.R. 67, it should be noted that a small but important typographical error has appeared in the head-note, namely, that section 24(4) did not read "for the defence" but "a defence" and the section is correctly reproduced in the judgement at 71. The point is important because the complaint was that section 24(4) did not read "for the defence to prove".

The words in section 50(1)(a) are not limited to 'concealment'. What is being facilitated is retention or control, and therefore the terms of section 50(1)(a) are "opt to cover facilitation, by conversion" of sterling without reference to what the purpose or reason for that conversion was: *McMaster* (October 8, 1998).

Not only does the Act prohibit the laundering of drug monies, it also seeks to encourage the relaying of information concerning the movement of monies to the police, even if that information was originally given to a party who was contractually bound to treat it as confidential.

Thus, section 50(3) provides: 13–343

"Where a person discloses to a constable a suspicion or belief that any funds or investments are derived from or used in connection with drug trafficking, or discloses to a constable any matter on which such a suspicion or belief is based—

(a) the disclosure shall not be treated as a breach of any restriction upon the disclosure of information imposed by statute or otherwise; and

(b) if he does any act in contravention of subsection (1) above and the disclosure relates to the arrangement concerned, he does not commit an offence under this section if—
  (i) the disclosure is made before he does the act concerned and the act is done with the consent of the constable; or
  (ii) the disclosure is made after he does the act, but is made on his initiative and as soon as it is reasonable for him to make it."

Accordingly, a banker who holds money on behalf of A, suspecting that A has benefited from drug trafficking will not be in breach of contract if he discloses his suspicion to a constable (s.50(3)(a) and he will be protected by the provisions of subs.50(3)(b)(i) or 50(3)(b)(ii)). Solicitors representing alleged drug traffickers may find that they are put in a similarly difficult position.

It should be noted that the expression "drug trafficking" is a term defined by section 1(1) and is to be contrasted with the definition of a "drug trafficking offence" (defined by s.1(3)). Not every activity that is described as "drug trafficking" under the Act is necessarily a "drug trafficking offence".

"(1) In this Act 'drug trafficking' means, subject to subsection (2) below, doing or being concerned in any of the following, whether in England and Wales or elsewhere—
  (a) producing or supplying a controlled drug where the production or supply contravenes section 4(1) of the Misuse of Drugs Act 1971 or a corresponding law;
  (b) transporting or storing a controlled drug where possession of the drug contravenes section 5(1) of that Act or a corresponding law;
  (c) importing or exporting a controlled drug where the importation or exportation is prohibited by section 3(1) of that Act or a corresponding law;
  (d) manufacturing or supplying a scheduled substance within the meaning of section 12 of the Criminal Justice (International Co-operation) Act 1990 where the manufacture or supply is an offence under that section or would be such an offence if it took place in England and Wales;
  (e) using any ship for illicit traffic in controlled drugs in circumstances which amount to the commission of an offence under section 19 of that Act;
  (f) conduct which is an offence under section 49 of this Act or which would be such an offence if it took place in England and Wales;
  (g) acquiring, having possession of or using property in circumstances which amount to the commission of an offence under section 51 of this Act or which would amount to such an offence if it took place in England and Wales.

(2) 'Drug trafficking' also includes a person doing the following,

whether in England and Wales or elsewhere, that is to say, entering into or being otherwise concerned in an arrangement whereby—

(a) the retention or control by or on behalf of another person of the other person's proceeds of drug trafficking is facilitated, or

(b) the proceeds of drug trafficking by another person are used to secure that funds are placed at the other person's disposal or are used for the other person's benefit to acquire property by way of investment.

(3) . . .

(4) In this section, 'corresponding law' has the same meaning as in the Misuse of Drugs Act 1971.

(b) Concealing or transferring the proceeds of drug trafficking

By section 49(1): 13–344

"A person is guilty of an offence if he—

(a) conceals or disguises any property which is, or in whole or in part directly or indirectly represents, his proceeds of drug trafficking, or

(b) converts or transfers that property or removes it from the jurisdiction, for the purpose of avoiding prosecution for a drug trafficking offence or the making or enforcement in his case of a confiscation order.

(2) A person is guilty of an offence if, knowing or having reasonable grounds to suspect that any property is, or in whole or in part directly or indirectly represents, another person's proceeds of drug trafficking, he—

(a) conceals or disguises that property, or

(b) converts or transfers that property or removes it from the jurisdiction, for the purpose of assisting any person to avoid prosecution for a drug trafficking offence or the making or enforcement of a confiscation order.

(3) In subsections (1)(a) and (2)(a) above the references to concealing or disguising any property include references to concealing or disguising its nature, source, location, disposition, movement or ownership or any rights with respect to it."

Several sets of offences were created in s.14 of the Criminal Justice (International Co-operation) Act 1990 (c. 5) to give legislative effect to the provisions of Article 3 of the 1988 Vienna Convention against Illicit Traffic in Narcotic Drugs and Psychotropic Substances. By s.14(1)(a) of the 1990 Act, it was made an offence to conceal or to disguise property that represented the proceeds of drug trafficking. This offence has been retained and is now to be found in subs. (l)(a). The second offence was that of converting, transferring or removing such property: s.14 (l)(b) of the 1990 Act. This offence is re-enacted in subs. (l)(b). Note that both of these offences relate to the activities of the drug trafficker himself.

By contrast, s.14(2) of the 1990 Act created similar offences but these relate to the same activities committed by a person other than the trafficker himself. These offences have also been re-enacted as subs. (2). The third offence under s.14(3) of the 1990 Act was aimed at those who receive gifts knowing or having reasonable grounds to suspect that the gift represented the proceeds of another's drug trafficking. However, the 1993 Act inserted s.23A into the 1986 Act which made it an offence knowingly to acquire, use or to be in possession of the proceeds of drug trafficking (now re-enacted in s.51, below) and thus s.14(3) of the 1990 Act was repealed by Sched.6, Part. 1 of the 1993 Act.

Offences under ss.49, 50 and 51 are "drug trafficking offences". However, none of these offences entitles the Courts to make any of the "assumptions" under s.4(2), above: see s.4(5). This is to preserve the distinction between money-laundering offences and more serious drug trafficking offences (see the Home Secretary, Hansard, HL vol. 514, col. 902).

13–345 There are an increasing number of cases where the evidence discloses that the defendant handled substantial sums of money but the evidence may be insufficient to prove that it came from drug trafficking. In other cases, the evidence may be capable of proving that the money came from both drug trafficking and other types of criminal offences.

> In *El Kurd* (July 26, 2000), the prosecution charged four conspiracies—two alleged an agreement to contravene s.49, DTA and two alleged an agreement to contravene the mirror offence in s.93C(2), CJA 1988. E was the proprietor of a Bureau de Change. Sums in excess of £70 million were laundered through that facility. E appealed on the basis that the jury could not be sure that the money represented the proceeds of drug trafficking, or other criminal activity: in short, the jury had to speculate between two possibilities.
>
> The Court of Appeal dismissed the appeal.

The essence of the Court's reasons for doing so is that the evidence against E was overwhelming; that this was not an "either/or" case; and that the jury could be sure that E laundered the proceeds of both types of offending and it was unnecessary for the prosecution to prove that all the money represented one activity or the other. *El Kurd* is best viewed as a decision on its facts. However, the Court expressed its concern that "Parliament has created this dichotomy" but saw "good reason for there to be a separate regime for dealing with drug trafficking offences".

At the conclusion of the Court's reasons for dismissing the appeal it added:

> ". . . the appropriate course to take, when confronted with problems in relation to the provenance of the proceeds in relation to which it is said that the defendant has carried out the activity of money laundering, is by way of a compendious court of conspiracy which would avoid the necessity for any choice to have to be made, so that in a case such as the present, if the jury were satisfied . . . that the proceeds were

> the proceeds of illicit activity, the jury should be provided with the opportunity to conclude that the conspiracy was a conspiracy by the conspirators to launder money illicit obtained, whether it be by way of drug trafficking or other criminal activity."

The advice of the Court may be sound, but that is not a foregone conclusion. It is true that the penalty under both enactments for a money laundering offence is 14 years' imprisonment and therefore the point that arose in *Siracusa* and *Courtie* does not arise. However, it remains to be seen whether complications arise where different alleged conspirators advance different explanations regarding their belief as to the nature of the agreement.

The Courts cannot use the offence of conspiracy to legislate. Parliament brought the "dichotomy" about. If the evidence discloses that laundered money represents the proceeds of *both* drug-trafficking and other criminal acts, then a compendious count is appropriate. Such a charge might also be appropriate if two or more persons agreed to launder both the proceeds of drug trafficking and non-drug trafficking offences. Even if the money came from legitimate sources, the fact that the conspiracy was impossible to perform affords no defence. However, suppose A, B, C and D are charged on a compendious count of conspiracy to money-launder, but the evidence shows that A and C agreed to launder the proceeds of drug trafficking, while B and D believed the money was derived from fraudulent transactions on the Stock Exchange. Suppose also that there is insufficient evidence to prove that any of the proceeds were in fact derived from drug trafficking, but there is evidence to prove that much of it did indeed flow from fraudulent transactions on the Stock Exchange. It is submitted that the safer course would be to include separate counts on the indictment under the Drug Trafficking Act, and the Criminal Justice Act 1988, that would avoid cases collapsing (or being aborted) on the grounds that a compendious charge is bad for duplicity.

In *El-Kurd*, the Court of Appeal referred to the 1988 Vienna Convention, 13–346
the Council of Europe Convention on Laundering, Tracing, Seizure and Confiscation of the Proceeds of Drug Trafficking 1990 (sometimes referred to as the "Strasbourg Convention"), and the 1991 E.C. Money Laundering Directive. It is true that the 1988 Vienna Convention requires Member States to enforce, mainly by penal means, the money laundering of the proceeds of drug trafficking, but there was no agreement to criminalise money laundering in respect of non-drug trafficking offences. The criminalisation of money laundering in respect of most, if not all, criminal offences had been opposed on a number of grounds. How narrow should the mesh of the net be? Which offences should be predicate offences for money laundering offences? Would the police be required to act as collectors on behalf of the revenue? Would there be a real risk of "double-jeopardy" if penalties were imposed for the commission of a predicate offence and then additional penalties were imposed for laundering the proceeds of that offence? Is the principle of "double-jeopardy" really engaged at all? Even if it is, does that matter?

It will be seen that the 1991 Money Laundering Directive does not require Member States to criminalise money laundering, but by Article 2, it does require Member States to prohibit that activity. Article 14 requires each Member State to take "*appropriate measures* to ensure full application of all the provisions" of the Directive and to determine "*penalties* for infringement" (emphasis added). However, the penalties may be civil in nature: they need not be contingent upon a conviction. That is not to say that a civil penalty may not amount to a "criminal charge" for the purposes of Article 6 of the ECHR. It will also be seen that the 1991 Directive applies to drug-related crimes specified in Article 3(1)(a) of the 1988 Vienna Convention. The Directive applies to other activities "designated . . . for the purposes of the Directive".

So much for the terms of the Directive. However, it is important to note that, by a statement annexed to the Directive, all Member States did agree to a commitment that money laundering would be made a criminal offence—at least in respect of drug trafficking offences. Following a European Council meeting held in Dublin in December 1996, an Action Plan to Combat Organised Crime was adopted by the Council in April 28, 1997. The plan called for the 1991 Directive to be widened to all offences connected with serious crime and should include professions other than financial institutions, *e.g.* legal advisers. This particular recommendation has caused pan-European concern among lawyers. It follows that at three levels (U.N., E.U. and domestic), the clear trend is towards the criminalisation of money laundering in respect of all criminal conduct, and to confiscate the proceeds and the instrumentalities of all such offences. It is important to note that there is growing pressure for lawyers to report suspicious transactions, and for the concept of legal professional privilege to be weakened (see E.C. Doc. 599 PC 0352; see the Common Position E.C. No 5/2001; and see the Draft Report of the Committee on Citizen's Freedoms and Rights, (JHA), September 26, 2000; and note the 2nd Protocol to the Convention on the Protection of the E.C. Financial Interests, on the basis of K.3 E.U. (O.J. C221; July 19, 1997). This is being met with strong resistance from lawyers who regard privilege as the "anvil" of their profession. It should also be noted that Article 15 of the 1991 Directive states, "Member States may adopt or retain in force stricter provisions in the field covered by the Directive to prevent money laundering". During a recent Crown Court trial, a submission was advanced to the trial judge that money laundering offences under the Criminal Justice Act 1988 (as amended) were invalid as being beyond the scope of the 1991 Directive. This ingenious argument was doomed to fail. Quite apart from Article 15—the effect of which is clear—the argument cannot alter the fact that Parliament retains a large measure of sovereignty to legislate as it pleases. The Appellate Committee of the House of Lords cannot disapply clear provisions in a statute—let alone a judge at first instance. Even a statute incompatible with the Human Rights Act 1998 would not produce that result.

(c) Acquisition, possession or use of proceeds

By section 51, it is provided that: 13–347

"(1) A person is guilty of an offence if, knowing that any property is, or in whole or in part directly or indirectly represents, another person's proceeds of drug trafficking, he acquires or uses that property or has possession

(2) It is a defence to a charge of committing an offence under this section that the person charged acquired or used the property or had possession of it for adequate consideration.

(3) For the purposes of subsection (2) above—

(a) a person acquires property for inadequate consideration if the value of the consideration is significantly less than the value of the property; and

(b) a person uses or has possession of property for inadequate consideration if the value of the consideration is significantly less than the value of his use or possession of the property.

(4) The provision for any person of services or goods which are of assistance to him in drug trafficking shall not be treated as consideration for the purposes of subsection (2) above.

(5) Where a person discloses to a constable a suspicion or belief that any property is, or in whole or in part directly or indirectly represents, another person's proceeds of drug trafficking, or discloses to a constable any matter on which such a suspicion or belief is based—

(a) the disclosure shall not be treated as a breach of any restriction upon the disclosure of information imposed by statute or otherwise, and

(b) if he does any act in relation to the property in contravention of subsection (1) above, he does not commit an offence under this section if—

(i) the disclosure is made before he does the act concerned and the act is done with the consent of the constable; or

(ii) the disclosure is made after he does the act, but is made on his initiative and as soon as it is reasonable for him to make it.

(6) For the purposes of this section, having possession of any property shall be taken to be doing an act in relation to it.

(7) In proceedings against a person for an offence under this section, it is a defence to prove that—

(a) he intended to disclose to a constable such a suspicion, belief or matter as is mentioned in subsection (S) above, but

(b) there is reasonable excuse for his failure to make any such disclosure in the manner mentioned in paragraph (b)(i) or (ii) of that subsection.

(8) In the case of a person who was in employment at the time in question, subsections (5) and (7) above shall have effect in relation to

disclosures, and intended disclosures, to the appropriate person in accordance with the procedure established by his employer for the making of such disclosures as they have effect in relation to disclosures, and intended disclosures, to a constable.

(9) No constable or other person shall be guilty of an offence under this section in respect of anything done by him in the course of acting in connection with the enforcement, or intended enforcement, of any provision of this Act or of any other enactment relating to drug trafficking or the proceeds of drug trafficking."

This section should be read and compared with s.14(3) of the Criminal Justice (International Co-operation) Act 1990 (c.5) since both were drafted to deal with property coming into the hands of another which represents in whole, or in part, directly or indirectly, the proceeds of drug trafficking.

13–348 The offence under s.14(3) of the 1990 Act was narrower in the sense that it was confined to property which had been "acquired", presumably in the sense that the recipient acquired an interest in the property or was held by the recipient on more than a merely temporary or short-terms basis. By contrast, this section includes any acquisition, but the section also includes the possession or use of that property. Presumably, the defendant (in order to be in possession) must know that he has it (see *Warner v. Metropolitan Police Commissioner* [1969] 2 A.C. 256) and this seems to be supported by s.51(6) which appears to define possession in terms of "doing an act in relation to" the property. This may mean no more than that a person exercises control over the property in question. An essential exemption is given by subs. (9) to persons who deal with the property in connection with the investigation, detection or judicial process relating to drug trafficking matters by virtue of any enactment.

On the other hand, this section is narrower than s.14(3) of the 1990 Act in terms of the *mens rea* required to be proved. Under s.14(3) it was enough if a defendant acquired property "knowing or having reasonable grounds to suspect" its drug trafficking origins. The objective element does not appear in s.S1 and what is required is actual knowledge; suspicion is not enough.

The offence created by section 51(1) is very widely drawn. It is not clear whether legal advisers (whether prosecuting or defending) are included in this provision. Under s.14(3) of the 1990 Act, the burden was on the prosecution to prove that the defendant acquired the property for "no or inadequate consideration" but this last ingredient is omitted from s.51. However, by section 51(2), it remains a defence if the defendant provided "adequate consideration". Until the case of *Gibson* (February 23, 2000), it was not entirely clear whether the defendant shoulders the burden of proving that particular defence or whether he need do no more than "raise the issue" so that it will be for the prosecution to negate the defence. However, it is now clear that the defendant shoulders the burden of proving the defence: consider *Lambert* (July 7, 2001, HL). It will be for the jury to decide whether the consideration provided is in fact "adequate" having regard to subs. (3) but it is likely that it will fall to the Courts to decide what that phrase means. Subsection (3) provides two instances where consideration is "inadequate" but is subs. (3) a closed category? If a person pays an excessive price for the property is the consideration to be regarded as being "adequate"? By s.62(1), "property" includes money. If services are provided in consideration for a substantial sum of drug money, how is it to be determined that the value of the service was not worth what was claimed or charged? (see Hansard, HC, vol. 222, col. 907, Sir Ivan Lawrence Q.C.). In the majority of cases, issues as to value may be resolved with expert help.

The upshot of s.51 seems to be that it will be lawful to use a drug traf- 13–349
ficker's villa or motor vehicle providing an adequate sum is paid for it—but it will be an offence if he pays too little or nothing. It seems that knowledge of the origins of the property will not taint the consideration nor will it negate the defence.

The effect of section 51(4) is to exclude persons who provide goods or services to another so long as the goods or services supplied were not of "assistance to him in drug trafficking". If the goods or services are of assistance to him then subs. (4) creates a fiction and deems the supply not to be adequate consideration. Subsection (4) is intended to protect tradespeople who are paid for goods and services from the proceeds of drug trafficking (see Standing Committee B, June 8, 1993, col. 93). It is not clear whether the defendant must know or intend that the goods or services supplied "are of assistance to him in drug trafficking" for the purposes of subs. (4).

Subsections (5) and (7) follow the model provided by s.24(3) of the 1986 Act, which is designed to protect persons from any action for breach of contract, confidence or a duty arising out of their obligations to their clients. This protection is particularly relevant to those employed in the financial sector.

Both subs. (5) and s.50(3) refer to the disclosure of "suspicions". In this context note the terms and scope of section 52 and see the commentary that follows.

(d) Failure to disclose knowledge or suspicion

Section 52(1) provides: 13–350

"(a) he knows or suspects that another person is engaged in drug money laundering,

(b) the information, or other matter, on which that knowledge or suspicion is based came to his attention in the course of his trade, profession, business or employment, and

(c) he does not disclose the information or other matter to a constable as soon as is reasonably practicable after it comes to his attention.

(2) Subsection (1) above does not make it an offence for a professional

legal adviser to fail to disclose any information or other matter which has come to him in privileged circumstances.

(3) It is a defence to a charge of committing an offence under this section that the person charged had a reasonable excuse for not disclosing the information or other matter in question.

(4) Where a person discloses to a constable—

(a) his suspicion or belief that another person is engaged in drug money laundering, or

(b) any information or other matter on which that suspicion or belief is based,

the disclosure shall not be treated as a breach of any restriction imposed by statute or otherwise.

(5) Without prejudice to subsection (3) or (4) above, in the case of a person who was in employment at the time in question, it is a defence to a charge of committing an offence under this section that he disclosed the information or other matter in question to the appropriate person in accordance with the procedure established by his employer for the making of such disclosures.

(6) A disclosure to which subsection (5) above applies shall not be treated as a breach of any restriction imposed by statute or otherwise.

(7) In this section "drug money laundering" means doing any act—

(a) which constitutes an offence under section 49, 50 or 51 of this Act; or

(b) in the case of an act done otherwise than in England and Wales, which would constitute such an offence if done in England and Wales;

and for the purposes of this subsection, having possession of any property shall be taken to be doing an act in relation to it.

(8) For the purposes of this section, any information or other matter comes to a professional legal adviser in privileged circumstances if it is communicated, or given, to him—

(a) by, or by a representative of, a client of his in connection with the giving by the adviser of legal advice to the client;

(b) by, or by a representative of, a person seeking legal advice from the adviser; or

(c) by any person—

(i) in contemplation of, or in connection with, legal proceedings; and

(ii) for the purpose of those proceedings.

(9) No information or other matter shall be treated as coming to a professional legal adviser in privileged circumstances if it is communicated or given with a view to furthering any criminal purpose."

13–351 This section creates an offence new to English law. Although s.50 and s.51 both include provisions to protect those who disclose their suspicions concerning drug trafficking carried on by another, in neither provision is there an actual obligation to make a disclosure. By contrast, s.52

makes it an offence to fail to disclose to a constable (or to an "appropriate person": see subs. (5)) as soon as reasonably practicable, knowledge or even a suspicion that a person is engaged in drug money laundering, where that knowledge or suspicion is gained in the course of a person's employment. Protection is afforded to legal advisers who give legal advice on a "privileged occasion" as defined by subs. (8) but not if information is received or given to further "any criminal purpose"—not just drug trafficking (subs. (1)).

The history of this offence has its roots in American law. When the 1986 Act was being debated as a Bill, Lord Denning moved an amendment (No. 30, subsequently withdrawn; see Hansard. HL, vol. 472, col. 1185) which proposed that the Secretary of State be empowered to draw up a scheme requiring banks and financial institutions to report to various authorities any deposit of, or a transaction in, currency exceeding a certain sum. This, in turn, was modelled on the American Bank Secrecy Act reported.

Following publication of the Guidance Notes on Money Laundering for Banks and Building Societies, on December 10, 1990, the number of suspicious transactions reported amounted to some 12,000 cases without mandatory legislation (Hansard, HL, vol. 539, cols 1373, 1385). The Home Affairs Committee had previously expressed concern that financial institutions would adopt an approach that was too passive and which would require the Government to "take the initiative" (para. 8 of their Seventh Report, 1988–89). In the light of agreements reached by the Council of Europe Convention on Laundering, Tracing, Seizure and Confiscation of Proceeds of Crime (1990) and the Council Directive 91/308/EEC, s.52 was enacted.

By Article 6 of that Directive, Member States are required to ensure that credit and financial institutions, their directors and employees co-operate fully with the authorities by informing them of "any fact which might be an indication of money laundering". Such institutions are required to "refrain from carrying out transactions which they know or suspect to be related to money laundering until they have appraised the authorities": see Article 7.

By Article 9, a disclosure in good faith to the authorities "shall not constitute a breach of any restriction on disclosure of information imposed by contract or by any legislative, regulatory or administrative provision". The provisions of that Directive are to extend in whole, or in part, to professions and various undertakings "likely to be used for money laundering purposes": Article 12. Section 52 is not, by itself, as extensive in its scope as the Directive permits since it is limited to drug money laundering only. The reasons for including a mere suspicion in this provision are essentially the same as those relevant to s.51: see the General Note to that section. 13–352

There would seem to be two reasons why disclosure based on "suspicion" is said to be relevant. First, disclosure based on any higher standard would present individuals with a difficult issue of fact to resolve. How much information does an individual need to form a belief that ought to be disclosed? (see Hansard, HL, vol. 474, col. 1114). Critics of this approach would question why it is necessary for reporting to be opinion-based at all. Part of the answer may be found in the second reason, namely, that law enforcement agencies act on suspicion and accordingly a lot of intelligence could be lost if all that could be disclosed were beliefs or where the system of reporting was restricted to material that came within clearly defined parameters. The Government consider that it would be "up to the policemen, the professionals, the investigators to decide whether or not (the suspicion) was true" (*per* Earl Ferrers, Hansard, HL, vol. 540, col. 753). Potentially, section 52 can put persons who have the duty to decide whether to make a report, in a difficult, embarrassing or even perilous position. Confidentiality and discretion are two vital ingredients for ensuring confidence and trust between a customer and a financial institution. There is some evidence that potential customers of a business are turned away (*e.g.* those presenting or offering large sums of cash) rather than commit staff to what is likely to be a documented transaction and thus expose them to the risk of prosecution on the grounds that they "turned a blind eye" if the cash transpired to be drug money. It may be said that this is a good thing, and to be encouraged, but it means that the law enforcement agencies may lose the information that they want if the offender takes more elaborate steps to launder the money or he becomes more deeply immersed in the black market. By contrast, the American system of reporting transactions and information is much more clearly defined and reporting is less opinion-based. Various documents must be completed and submitted to the appropriate organisation in respect of particular transactions. The amount of paperwork involved is colossal and the system would be pointless if processing the information were protracted or inefficient. The American system is reputedly efficient, and the information is processed within days, due largely to a substantial investment in technology and labour. This country does not yet have the resources to adopt the American model.

(e) **Tipping-off**

13–353 By section 53(1) a person is guilty of an offence if—

"(a) he knows or suspects that a constable is acting, or is proposing to act, in connection with an investigation which is being, or is about to be, conducted into drug money laundering, and

(b) he discloses to any other person information or any other matter which is likely to prejudice that investigation or proposed investigation.

(2) A person is guilty of an offence if—

(a) he knows or suspects that a disclosure has been made to a constable under section 50, 51 or 52 of this Act ('the disclosure'), and

(b) he discloses to any other person information or any other matter which is likely to prejudice any investigation which might be conducted following the disclosure.

(3) A person is guilty of an offence if—

(a) he knows or suspects that a disclosure of a kind mentioned in section 50(5), 51(8) or 52(5) of this Act ('the disclosure') has been made, and

(b) he discloses to any person information or any other matter which is likely to prejudice any investigation which might be conducted following the disclosure.

(4) Nothing in subsections (1) to (3) above makes it an offence for a professional legal adviser to disclose any information or other matter—

(a) to, or to a representative of, a client of his in connection with the giving by the adviser of legal advice to the client; or

(b) to any person—

(i) in contemplation of, or in connection with, legal proceedings; and

(ii) for the purpose of those proceedings.

(5) Subsection (4) above does not apply in relation to any information or other matter which is disclosed with a view to furthering any criminal purpose.

(6) In proceedings against a person for an offence under subsection (1), (2) or (3) above, it is a defence to prove that he did not know or suspect that the disclosure was likely to be prejudicial in the way mentioned in that subsection.

(7) No constable or other person shall be guilty of an offence under this section in respect of anything done by him in the course of acting in connection with the enforcement, or intended enforcement, of any provision of this Act or of any other enactment relating to drug trafficking or the proceeds of drug trafficking.

(8) In this section "drug money laundering" has the same meaning as in section 52 of this Act.

This section creates three offences. First, it is an offence for a defendant who knows or suspects that an investigation into drug money laundering is being conducted (or is about to be) to divulge that fact, or other information, which is likely to prejudice such an investigation: subs. (1). Secondly, if a disclosure of a suspicion (or information) has been lawfully disclosed to a constable (*e.g.* by a bank) under s.51, s.50 or s.52 then it is an offence to disclose to another information which is likely to prejudice an investigation which might be conducted on the basis of the original disclosure: subs. (2). The third offence is similar to that created by subs. (2), but involves the original disclosure being made to an "appropriate person" (*e.g.* an employer). There is an exemption in the case of legal advisers (within the terms of subss. (4) and (5)). It is a defence to each of the three offences if the defendant proves that he did not know or suspect that the disclosure was likely to be prejudicial: subs. (6).

(f) Offence of prejudicing an investigation

13–354 Section 58 provides:

"(1) Where, in relation to an investigation into drug trafficking—

(a) an order under section 55 of this Act has been made or has been applied for and has not been refused; or

(b) a warrant under section 56 of this Act has been issued,

a person is guilty of an offence if, knowing or suspecting that the investigation is taking place, he makes any disclosure which is likely to prejudice the investigation.

(2) In proceedings against a person for an offence under this section, it is a defence to prove—

(a) that he did not know or suspect that the disclosure was likely to prejudice the investigation; or

(b) that he had lawful authority or reasonable excuse for making the disclosure.

(3) Nothing in subsection (1) above makes it an offence for a professional legal adviser to disclose any information or other matter—

(a) to, or to a representative of a client of his in connection with the giving by the adviser of legal advice to the client; or

(b) to any person—

(i) in contemplation of, or in connection with, legal proceedings; and

(ii) for the purpose of those proceedings.

(4) Subsection (3) above does not apply in relation to any information or other matter which is disclosed with a view to furthering any criminal purpose.

(5) A person guilty of an offence under this section shall be liable—

(a) on summary conviction, to imprisonment for a term not exceeding six months or to a fine not exceeding the statutory maximum or to both; and

(b) on conviction on indictment, to imprisonment for a term not exceeding five years or to a fine or to both."

13–355 Section 31(1) of the 1986 Act provided:

"Where, in relation to an investigation into drug trafficking, an order under section 27 of this Act has been made or has been applied for and has not been refused or a warrant under section 28 of this Act has been issued, a person who, knowing or suspecting that the investigation is taking place, makes any disclosure which is likely to prejudice the investigation is guilty of an offence It will be seen that s.58 broadly re-enacts s.31(1) of the 1986 Act. Section 58(3) was originally inserted into s.31 by s.26 of the 1993 Act. Section 55, above, is concerned with the making of material available to a constable or an officer of customs and excise relevant to an investigation into drug trafficking."

An offence under s.58 can only be committed if an order under s.55 has been made or applied for, or a warrant (authorising a search) has been issued under s.56. The prosecution must prove that the accused knew or suspected that the investigation was taking place, but it is not necessary for the prosecution to prove either that he knew or suspected that any of the steps mentioned in subs. (1) had in fact been taken, or that he knew or suspected that the disclosure was likely to prejudice the investigation.

III. Investigations Into Drug Trafficking

Notwithstanding the fact that the police or the customs and excise may **13–356** have insufficient evidence to arrest or charge an individual in connection with a drug trafficking offence, nevertheless, by section 55(1) a constable may, for the purpose of an investigation into drug trafficking, apply to a circuit judge for an order under section 55(2) requiring the person who appears to be in possession of particular material, or material of a particular description to either produce it to a constable for him to take away, or to give a constable access to it for a period of seven days unless a longer or shorter period is deemed to be appropriate by order of the Court: section 55(3).

(a) Section 55(1), (2) and (3) of the DTA

Section 55(1)(2) and (3) (reflecting amendments made by s.70(2) and **13–357** Sched. 2 to the Criminal Justice (Scotland) Act 1987) provides as follows:

"(1) A constable may, for the purpose of an investigation into drug trafficking, apply to a Circuit judge for an order under subsection (2) below in relation to particular material or material of a particular description.

(2) If on such an application the judge is satisfied that the conditions in subsection (4) below are fulfilled, he may make an order that the person who appears to him to be in possession of the material to which the application relates shall—

(a) produce it to a constable for him to take away, or

(b) give a constable access to it, within such period as the order may specify.

This subsection has effect subject to section 59(11) of this Act.

(3) The period to be specified in an order under subsection (2) above shall be seven days unless it appears to the judge that a longer or shorter period would be appropriate in the particular circumstances of the application."

Section 59(11) of the Act is concerned with the disclosure of information held by government departments. Accordingly, by section 59(11) an order granted under section 55(2) may require an officer of the department (whether named in the order or not) to comply with the order, and "such an order shall be served as if the proceedings were civil proceedings against the defendant".

(b) Section 55(4)

13–358 No order may be made under section 55(1) unless the conditions in subsection (4) are fulfilled. These are:

The conditions referred to in subsection (2) above are—

> "(a) that there are reasonable grounds for suspecting that a specified person has carried on or has benefited from drug trafficking;
> (b) that there are reasonable grounds for suspecting that the material to which the application relates—
> (i) is likely to be of substantial value (whether by itself or together with other material) to the investigation for the purpose of which the application is made; and
> (ii) does not consist of or include items subject to legal privilege or excluded material; and
> (c) that there are reasonable grounds for believing that it is in the public interest, having regard—
> (i) to the benefit likely to accrue to the investigation if the material is obtained, and
> (ii) to the circumstances under which the person in possession of the material holds it
>
> that the material should be produced or that access to it should be given."

In *R. v. Southwark Crown Court, ex p. Bowles* [1998] 2 C.A.R. 187 it was held that s.93H of the CJA 1988 (which broadly mirrors s.55, DTA), is concerned with an investigation into the proceeds of crime to assist the authorities to obtain information which may enable an application to be brought for a restraint order or a confiscation order, and did not involve the investigation of criminal offences which should be pursued by means of s.9 of, and Sched. 1 to PACE 1984: and see the judgment of Simon Brown L.J. (1997) 1 C.A.R. 436. It seems probable that s.55 carries identical limitations.

13–359 It will be noted that the order may be made against any individual (named in the order) who appears to be in possession of the material to which the application relates: see section 55(2). It is not necessary to show that he is suspected of having benefited from drug trafficking or that he is suspected of having committed any offence. An order of a circuit judge under section 55 will have effect as if it were an order of the Crown Court (s.55(8)). However, the section expressly refers to a "circuit judge" and not "the Crown Court". Accordingly, a recorder, or an assistant recorder has no jurisdiction to make an order under section 55: see *Central Criminal Court, ex p. Francis and Francis* [1989] A.C. 346.

By section 55(10)(a) an order under subsection (2) shall "not confer any right to production of, or access to, items subject to legal privilege or excluded material". "Items subject to legal privilege" and "excluded material" have the same meanings as in PACE: see section 57(2) of the DTA.

(c) Section 10 of PACE: "legal privilege"

By section 10 of PACE: 13–360

"(1) Subject to subsection (2) below, in this Act 'items subject to legal privilege' means—

(a) communications between a professional legal adviser and his client or any person representing his client made in connection with the giving of legal advice to the client;

(b) communications between a professional legal adviser and his client or any person representing his client or between such an adviser or his client or any such representative and any other person made in connection with or in contemplation of legal proceedings and for the purposes of such proceedings; and

(c) items enclosed with or referred to in such communications and made—

(i) in connection with the giving of legal advice; or

(ii) in connection with or in contemplation of legal proceedings and for the purposes of such proceedings,

when they are in the possession of a person who is entitled to possession of them.

(2) Items held with the intention of furthering a criminal purpose are not items subject to legal privilege."

Note that in *R. v. Central Criminal Court, ex p. Francis and Francis (a Firm)* [1989] A.C. 346, the majority of the House of Lords interpreted section 10(2) of PACE as leaving the rule in *Cox and Railton* (1884) 14 Q.B.D. 153 unaffected. This provision has given rise to difficulty because the question is: whose intention is relevant for the purposes of the section—the legal adviser, the client or a third party? In *Francis and Francis*, the House of Lords held that it could relate to any of the three and they rejected the argument that the intention in section 10 was that of the person holding the items. This topic is discussed in greater detail below.

In *Southampton Crown Court, ex p. J and P* [1993] Crim. L.R. 962, the 13–361
Divisional Court quashed warrants issued under section 9 of PACE to search the offices of a firm of solicitors. The Court gave the following guidance (as reported in the Crim. L.R. 962, at 964) thus:

"There was a need to balance the competing interests of the investigation of crime and the confidentiality of communications between solicitor and client. A judge must be given information upon which he could reasonably infer that material was not privileged. It might not be possible to satisfy a judge that there were reasonable grounds for believing that every document in a file, or every file in a category, were not legally privileged. If an investigation was relatively narrow, it should be possible to exclude privileged material with some precision."

On the facts in that case, the Divisional Court held that the judge should have considered whether any of the material was privileged and, if so, whether privilege had been lost by section 10(2) or waived. The judge should have considered if it was practicable to exclude files or correspondence unconnected with the client's affairs and he should also have considered the possibility of excluding from his property, transaction files, correspondence with persons other than the client or those representing the client and see *R. v. Inner London Sessions Crown Court, ex p. Baines & Baines* [1988] 1 Q.B. 579; and see *Manchester Crown Court, ex.p. R* [1999] 2 All E.R. 267.

(d) Section 11 of PACE: "excluded material"

13–362 So far as "excluded material" is concerned, section 11 of PACE reads:

"(1) Subject to the following provisions of this section, in this Act "excluded material" means—

(a) personal records which a person has acquired or created in the course of any trade, business, profession or other occupation or for the purposes of any paid or unpaid office and which he holds in confidence;
(b) human tissue or tissue fluid which has been taken for the purposes of diagnosis or medical treatment and which a person holds in confidence;
(c) journalistic material which a person holds in confidence and which consists—
 (i) of documents, or
 (ii) or records other than documents.

(2) A person holds material other than journalistic material in confidence for the purposes of this section if he holds it subject—

(a) to an express or implied undertaking to hold it in confidence; or
(b) to a restriction on disclosure or an obligation of secrecy contained in any enactment, including an enactment contained in an Act passed after this Act.

(3) A person holds journalistic material in confidence for the purposes of this section if—

(a) he holds it subject to such an undertaking, restriction or obligation; and
(b) it has been continuously held (by one or more persons) subject to such an undertaking, restriction or obligation since it was first acquired or created for the purposes of journalism."

(e) Section 13 of PACE: "journalistic material"

By section 13 of PACE "journalistic material" means: 13–363

"(1) Subject to subsection (2) below, in this Act 'journalistic material' means material acquired or created for the purposes of journalism.

(2) Material is only journalistic material for the purposes of this Act if it is in the possession of a person who acquired or created it for the purposes of journalism

(3) A person who receives material from someone who intends that the recipient shall use it for the purposes of journalism is to be taken to have acquired it for those purposes."

IV. Privilege and the Position of the Solicitor

In *Central Criminal Court, ex p. Francis and Francis* [1989] A.C. 346 13–364
an order was made under section 27 of the DTOA (now section 55) against a firm of solicitors, requiring them to give the police access to material in their possession relating to the affairs of one of their clients, Mrs. G, who was acquiring property with the proceeds of drug trafficking on the part of D.

The solicitors contended that the material was subject to legal privilege and therefore the order should not have been made. For other cases regarding legal professional privilege, see *Sidu and Takhor* (May 7, 1996) and *Derby JJ., ex p. B* [1995] 3 W.L.R. 681. It will be recalled that an order under section 55(2) shall not confer any right to production of, or access to, "items subject to legal privilege" (s.55(10)) as defined by section 57(2) and section 10 of PACE. However, by section 10(2), "items held with the intention of furthering a criminal purpose are not items subject to legal privilege".

The case was argued on three important assumptions: (1) that D intended to further a criminal purpose of concealing his proceeds of drug trafficking by acquiring property for Mrs G; (2) that Mrs G was innocent of complicity; (3) that the solicitors acted with propriety and with no suspicion of any illegality affecting the transaction.

The House of Lords had to rule on the proper construction of section 10(2). The key question was "to whose intention does subsection (2) refer?" Does the intention have to rest with the holder of the material (*e.g.* the solicitor) or with the client (Mrs G), or, is it enough that the intention is that of a third party who has not in fact received any legal advice (*e.g.* D)? By a majority (Lord Bridge and Lord Oliver dissenting), the House of Lords concluded that the "intention of furthering a criminal purpose" cannot be restricted to the intention of the person who actually has the items in his possession. In other words, it is enough to show that the client or even a third party had the necessary intention. Accordingly, the validity of the order was upheld.

The basis upon which the majority arrived at their conclusion is persuasive but not free of difficulty for the reasons given principally by Lord Bridge.

(a) **Solicitor and client**

13–365 In order to understand the various opinions expressed in *Francis' case*, it is important to have regard to the common law rule laid down in *Cox and Railton* (1884) 14 Q.B.D. 153 which held that the protection of legal professional privilege excludes communications made by a client to his solicitor with the intention of furthering a criminal purpose and that the "client must either conspire with his solicitor or deceive him": *per* Stephen J. at 168. This neat phrase embraces the situation of a solicitor, acting in good faith, who is unaware of any illegality intended by the client. Put shortly, the majority held that section 10(1) and (2) reflected the common law position. Lord Bridge and Lord Oliver disagreed. Lord Bridge saw no sound basis for making the assumption that in section 10, Parliament set out to reproduce in the form of a statutory code, every aspect of the common law relating to legal professional privilege, and that if "true codification had been intended, something more elaborate would clearly be required" (at 781 b-c). Indeed, Lord Oliver could see good reason why Parliament, would wish to restrict the denial of legal privilege on the basis that a solicitor should not be put in a position where the correctness of his decision depends on an intention of which he knows nothing (at 794 g-h).

(b) **Solicitor, client and third party**

13–366 In *Francis' case* [1988] 3 All E.R. 775, HL, it was assumed that both the client and the solicitor acted in good faith. The question therefore arose as to whether it could properly be said that, at common law, a criminal intent on the part of a stranger destroys what is, after all, the privilege of the client. Neither Lord Bridge (at 785 f-h) nor Lord Oliver (at 793 g-h) could find any authority in the common law to answer that question affirmatively. In their opinion if the majority is right then, "it is breaking new ground" (*per* Lord Oliver, at 793 h). However, Lord Goff relied on a passage in the judgment delivered by Stephen J. in *Cox* when he said that:

> "The reason on which the rule is said to rest cannot include the case of communications . . . intended to further any criminal purpose, for the protection of such communications cannot possibly be otherwise than injurious to the interests of justice . . . "

Lord Goff regarded as immaterial to that exception, whether it is the client himself, or a third party who is using the client as his innocent tool, who has the criminal intention (at 799 f-j). The Divisional Court, in *Francis' case* [1988] 1 All E.R. 677, also seems to have had in contemplation the client who is "the innocent instrument or beneficiary of the third party's criminal purpose" (*per* Lloyd L.J. at 682).

An order under s.55(2) of the 1994 Act will override any obligation as to secrecy or other restrictions upon the disclosure of information imposed by statute or otherwise (s.55(10)(b)), and may be made in relation to material in the possession of an authorised government department (s.55(10)(c)).

Where the material to which an application under section 55(2) relates, consists of information contained in a computer, then the data must be produced in a form in which it can be taken away and in which it is both visible and legible: section 55(9)(a).

Where an order is made under section 55(2)(b) then the constable may order any person who appears to the Court to be entitled to grant entry to the premises, to allow a constable to enter the premises to obtain access to the material.

V. Authority for Search

By s.56 of the DTA a constable may, for the purpose of an investigation into drug trafficking, apply to a circuit judge for a warrant in relation to specified premises, authorising (by virtue of subsection (2)): 13–367

"... a constable to enter and search the premises if the judge is satisfied—

(a) that an order made under section 55 of this Act in relation to material on the premises has not been complied with;

(b) that the conditions in subsection (3) below are fulfilled; or

(c) that the conditions in subsection (4) below are fulfilled."

By section 28(3) the conditions referred to in subsection (2)(b) are:

"(a) that there are reasonable grounds for suspecting that a specified person has carried on or has benefited from drug trafficking;

(b) that the conditions in subsection (4)(b) and (c) of section 55 of this Act are fulfilled in relation to any material on the premises; and

(c) that it would not be appropriate to make an order under that section in relation to the material because—

(i) it is not practicable to communicate with any person entitled to produce the material;

(ii) it is not practicable to communicate with any person entitled to grant access to the material or entitled to grant entry to the premises on which the material is situated; or

(iii) the investigation for the purpose of which the application is made might be seriously prejudiced unless a constable could secure immediate access to the material."

Again, by section 56(4) the conditions referred to in subsection 28(2)(c) are: 13–368

"(a) that there are reasonable grounds for suspecting that a specified person has carried on or has benefited from drug trafficking;

(b) that there are reasonable grounds for suspecting that there is on the premises material relating to the specified person or to drug trafficking which is likely to be of substantial value (whether by itself or together with other material) to the investigation for the purpose of which the application is made, but that the material cannot at the time of the application be particularised; and

(c) that—

(i) it is not practicable to communicate with any person entitled to rant entry to the premises;

(ii) entry to the premises will not be granted unless a warrant is produced; or

(iii) the investigation for the purpose of which the application is made might be seriously prejudiced unless a constable arriving at the premises could secure immediate entry to them."

A constable who enters premises in the execution of a warrant issued under section 56 may seize and retain any material other than items subject to "legal privilege" and "excluded material" (see s.57(2) of the Act and ss.10, 11 and 13 of PACE) which is likely to be of "substantial value" to the investigation for the purposes of which the warrant was issued: see section 56(5).

VI. Disclosure of Information Held by Government Departments

13–369 By section 59, the High Court may, on the application of the prosecutor, order material in the possession of an authorised government department to be produced to the Court within a period specified by the Court. Note the Criminal Procedure Rules and in particular, see sc 115.11.

The material must first have been submitted to an officer of the relevant department either by the defendant or by a person who has at any time held realisable property (s.59(3)(a)); secondly, the material must have been made by an officer of that department in relation to the defendant or such a person (s.59(3)(b)); or thirdly, the material is correspondence which passed between an officer of the relevant department and the defendant or such a person (s.59(3)(c)).

No order may be made under section 59(1) unless the conditions specified in section 25 are satisfied (s.59(2)), and no material may be produced under section 59(1) unless it appears to the High Court that the material is likely to contain information that would facilitate the exercise of the powers conferred on the Court by virtue of sections 26 to 29 of the Act or, alternatively, on a receiver appointed under section 26 or 29 of the Act or in pursuance of a charging order: see section 59(4).

The Court may order the disclosure of the material produced by the relevant government department to any member of the police force (s.59(8)(a)); the Crown Prosecution Service (s.59(8)(b)), or an officer within the meaning of the Customs and Excise Management Act 1979 (s.59(8)(c)).

However, the Court must not disclose any part of the material unless a reasonable opportunity has been given for an officer of the department to make representations to the Court and it appears to the Court that the material is likely to be of substantial value in exercising "functions" relating to drug trafficking: see section 59(5).

The expression "authorised government department", as it appears in section 59, means a government department which is an authorised department for the purposes of the Crown Proceedings Act 1947: see section 59(10).

N. DRUG CASH IMPORTED OR EXPORTED

I. Introduction

In recent years it has been the experience of the Customs and Excise that large sums of cash are being exported from and imported into the United Kingdom. There currently exist no exchange control regulations in this country so that cash imported may be changed into foreign currency, which is then exported. Neither the officers of Customs and Excise, nor the police, have any powers to seize the cash to investigate its origins if there are reasonable grounds for suspecting that the cash directly or indirectly represents the proceeds of someone's drug trafficking. As a result of complaints expressed in evidence by American and British law enforcement officers to the Home Affairs Select Committee (see the 7th Report 1989, vol. I, para. 87) Parliament enacted Part III of the Criminal Justice (International Co-operation) Act 1990 (c. 5), ss.25–29 now ss.42, 43, 46, 47 and 48 of this Act. The 1990 and 1994 Acts represent a seamless webb of legislative authority: see *R. v. Dover J.J., ex.p. Webb* (March 18, 1998). 13–370

The Metropolitan Police also complained that the abolition of exchange controls has been exploited by drug traffickers (see para.87 of the 7th Report). The Home Affairs Committee has therefore recommended that the law be changed to: (i) require anyone importing or exporting cash over a limit set by H.M. Customs to declare it; (ii) make illegal the import or export of proceeds of drug trafficking or other serious crimes and; (iii) allow customs officers to retain cash entering or leaving the country which they know or suspect arises from the proceeds of such crime.

This approach has found favour with the Customs and Excise with the consequent assumption of the powers, which may be required by Article 5 of the 1988 Vienna Convention (see para. 88 of the 7th Report). These recommendations have not become law. Section 42 of this Act (formerly s.25 of the Criminal Justice (International Co-operation) Act 1990) is limited to the cash suspected to represent a person's proceeds of drug trafficking but not where it may relate to other criminal acts. It is debatable whether the Home Affairs Committee's original proposals would run contrary to existing laws concerning the free movement of capital and the

E.C. Capital Liberalisation Directive. The Home Affairs Committee has suggested that requiring a declaration of cash over a pre-set limit would not require primary legislation but could be achieved by an order issued under s.1 of the Import, Export and Customs Powers (Defence) Act 1939 (c.69).

II. Summary of the Position

13–371 The effect of Part II of the DTA is draconian. The general scheme is as follows. Where a customs officer, or a constable, has reasonable grounds for suspecting that "cash" imported or exported (being £10,000 or more) directly or indirectly represents the proceeds of drug trafficking, the officer may seize that cash (s.42(1), formerly s.25(1) of the Criminal Justice (International Co-operation) Act 1990) and detain it for up to 48 hours without the need to make any application to a court. After 48 hours, the officer must either return the cash or apply to a justice of the peace (or in Scotland the sheriff) for an order permitting its continued detention on the grounds set out in s.42(2). A procedural error to use the right form to detain the cash will not render the detention order a nullity: *Luton Justices, ex. p. Abecasis* (2000) 164 J.P. 265.

The order cannot endure longer than three months (s. 42(3); formerly s.25(3)), but further orders can be made by the Court provided the total period of detention does not exceed two years from the date of the first order (s.42(3)). It should be noted that these powers may be exercised even if no criminal proceedings have been instituted (or even contemplated) against any person for a drug trafficking offence in connection with the money seized. Where proceedings are instituted (s.42(7), formerly s.25(6) of the 1990 Act), or where application is made to forfeit the money on the basis that it represents drug proceeds (s.43(1), formerly s.26(1) of the 1990 Act), the cash is not to be released until the relevant proceedings have been concluded (and so overrides the two-year restriction set out in s.42(3)). If forfeiture is applied for, the prosecutor need only prove that the cash represents the proceeds of drug trafficking to the civil standard: see *Best* (May 23, 1995, unreported, DC). This was at variance with the position under the 1986 Act: see *Dickens* [1991] 2 Q.B.102 and *Enwezor* (1991) 93 Cr.App.R. 233, but see now s.2(8), above.

13–372 The person from whom the cash was seized, or any person on whose behalf the cash was being exported or imported, may apply to the magistrates' court (or in Scotland the sheriff) for the money to be released on the basis that there are no reasonable grounds for suspecting that it directly or indirectly represents any persons proceeds of drug trafficking or is intended by any person for use in drug trafficking: see s.42(6); 42(2) and 42(1) and see *Thomas* (January 20, 1995; unreported, DC). Clearly in this instance, the burden is on the applicant (presumably to the civil standard). Notice may be required to be given, made by rules of court, to persons affected by the order (s.46(1), formerly s.28(1) of the 1990 Act).

The money must be held in an interest-bearing account (payable to the Crown if forfeited or to the person entitled to possession if released), unless the money was released within 48 hours of its seizure: s.42(8), formerly s.27 of the 1990 Act. The Divisional Court has emphasised that it is important that these provisions be complied with strictly: *Uxbridge Magistrates' Court, ex p. Henry* [1994] Crim. L.R. 581, applied in *Walsh v. Commissioners of Customs and Excise* [2001] EWHC Admin 426.

It should be noted that "exported" has an extended meaning and includes cash "being brought to any place in the United Kingdom for the purpose of being exported": s.48(1), formerly s.29(1) of the 1990 Act.

III. The Previous Position

Reference has already been made to the reasons why Part II of the DTA was enacted. However, in several cases, the Commissioners of Customs and Excise have achieved a similar result (seizure, detention and forfeiture) by an ingenious if not complicated route through the CEMA 1979. Under the 1979 Act, a number of offences and events entitle the Commissioners to seize the goods in question, which are then liable to forfeiture. Under the 1979 Act "goods" includes "money". 13–373

Thus, to take an example, section 78(2) of the CEMA 1979 provides:

> "Any person entering or leaving the United Kingdom shall answer such questions as the proper officer may put to him with respect to his baggage and any thing contained therein or carried with him, and shall, if required by the proper officer, produce that baggage and any such thing for examination at such place as the Commissioner may direct."

Note the words "shall answer" in section 78(2). The consequences of a failure to comply with section 78(2) appear in section 167(1) of the CEMA, which provides that:

> "If any person either knowingly or recklessly—
>
> (a) makes or signs, or causes to be made or signed, or delivers or causes to be delivered to the Commissioners or an officer, any declaration, notice, certificate or other document whatsoever; or
>
> (b) makes any statement in answer to any question put to him by an officer which he is required by or under any enactment to answer,
>
> being a document or statement produced or made for any purpose of any assigned matter, which is untrue in any material particular, he shall be guilty of an offence under this subsection and may be detained; and

any goods in relation to which the document or statement was made shall be liable to forfeiture."

13–374 Accordingly, if an officer asks a passenger at the airport the question "are you taking anything out of England?" or "do you have anything which you have obtained in the United Kingdom?" and the passenger replies in the negative, then the argument is that section 167(1) of the CEMA is contravened if in truth the passenger is exporting £50,000 which he obtained in the United Kingdom. Identifying the "assigned matter" (defined by s.1 of the CEMA 1979), for the purposes of section 167(1) may prove difficult, but it now includes the investigation of any offence under Part III of the DTA: see sections 60(4) and (6). By section 139(1) of the CEMA 1979, the Commissioners may seize or detain "anything liable to forfeiture" and invoke condemnation proceedings for the forfeiture of the cash under section 139(6) and Schedule 3 to the CEMA 1979. The validity of this route has not been the subject of any reported decision of a superior court and a number of difficult issues arise. The relationship between section 78 and section 167(1) is not clear. There is an obligation to answer questions put to a person entering or leaving the United Kingdom in respect of his baggage and "anything" carried with him, but must the question be directed to goods which are "prohibited, restricted or dutiable" under the 1979 Act or may the questions be general? It is startling that a person who answers the question "are you taking goods out of England?" negatively, commits an offence under section 167(1) if he knows he has in his pockets a wallet containing £300. Is an officer of Customs and Excise entitled to seize the £300? Furthermore, is forfeiture contingent upon a conviction or is it enough to prove that an offence has been committed albeit that the offender was not in fact prosecuted?

In *Lucien* (*The Times*, March 3, 1995) the Divisional Court held that the words "anything carried with a person entering or leaving the United Kingdom" as they appear in section 78(2) of the CEMA 1979, mean "carried by sea, air or train". Cocaine had been found in L's shoes by customs officers who intercepted him after he boarded a train having recently arrived in the United Kingdom. L contended that the evidence of what had been discovered should have been admitted in evidence because the shoes were neither part of L's baggage nor "carried with him". The Court dismissed the appeal on the ground that section 78(2) included carriage by train. The decision is plainly right on the facts in that case but the decision has the potential for raising some interesting questions as to when a person may properly be described as "entering" or "leaving" the United Kingdom for the purposes of the section. If L had been followed on the train to Victoria Station, in London, would he still be "entering the United Kingdom"? There is no doubt that the shoes worn by him upon his arrival at Gatwick Airport came within section 78(2) as being a "thing . . . carried with him". It is a pedantic argument to limit the word "carried" as being synonymous with being physically "held by hand".

IV. General Power of Seizure and Detention

Section 42(1) of the DTA (formerly section 25(1) of CJICA 1990) provides: 13–375

"(1) A customs officer or constable may seize and, in accordance with this section, detain any cash which is being imported into or exported from the United Kingdom if—

(a) its amount is not less than the prescribed sum; and

(b) he has reasonable grounds for suspecting that it directly or indirectly represents any person's proceeds of drug trafficking, or is intended by any person for use in drug trafficking."

Several matters should be carefully noted about this provision. First, the proceedings are civil in nature and therefore the civil standard of proof applies throughout: see *Best* (May 23, 1995, unreported, DC). Furthermore, the rules of evidence are those applicable in civil proceedings and thus the Civil Evidence Act 1995 applies. Secondly, the officer must have reasonable grounds for this suspicion. Each case must, of course, be decided on its own facts. The officer would be entitled to take into account a number of features including, for example, whether the cash was concealed; explanations offered by persons who have an interest in the cash; the fact that the cash was being exported to a place known to be a centre for illicit drug trafficking (see *Bassick* and *Osbourne*, March 22, 1993, unreported, DC); the amount of cash that was being transported; whether traces of a controlled drug were detected on part or all of the cash (see *Thomas*, January 20, 1995, unreported, DC). Thirdly, cash may be seized or detained if the money is intended "by any person" for use in drug trafficking: see s.42(1)(b). It is not necessary for the officer to suspect that the person carrying the cash had been engaged in drug trafficking or intended to use the cash for that purpose: see *Thomas* (January 20, 1995, DC).

Because proceedings (under what were ss. 25 and 26 of CJICA) are civil, legal aid, on a criminal legal aid certificate, is not available for the purpose of opposing an application for the detention of cash or for the purposes of applying for the cash to be released: see *Crawley Justices, ex p. Ohakwe* (1994) Crim. L.R. 936.

V. Period of Detention and Continued Detention

(a) Power of detention

Section 42(2) of the DTA provides: 13–376

"(2) Cash seized by virtue of this section shall not be detained for more than 48 hours unless its continued detention is authorised by an order made by a justice of the peace or in Scotland the sheriff; and no such order shall be made unless the justice or, as the case may be, the sheriff is satisfied—

(a) that there are reasonable grounds for the suspicion mentioned in subsection (1) above; and

(b) that continued detention of the cash is justified while its origin or derivation is further investigated or consideration is given to the institution (whether in the United Kingdom or elsewhere) of criminal proceedings against any person for an offence with which the cash is connected."

See para. 13–372 and note *Walsh v. Commissioners of Customs and Excise* [2001] EWHC Admin. 426; and *R. v. Uxbridge JJ., exp. Henry* [1994] Crim.L.R. 581.

Section 42(3) of the Act provides:

"(3) Any order under subsection (2) above shall authorise the continued detention of the cash to which it relates for such period, not exceeding three months beginning with the date of the order, as may be specified in the order; and a magistrates' court or in Scotland the sheriff, if satisfied as to the matters mentioned in that subsection, may thereafter from time to time by order authorise the further detention of the cash but so that—

(a) no period of detention specified in such an order shall exceed three months beginning with the date of the order; and

(b) the total period of detention shall not exceed two years from the date of the order under subsection (2) above."

(b) Making the application

13–377 By section 42(5) of the DTA:

"(5) Any application for an order under subsection (2) or (3) above shall be made—

(a) by the Commissioners of Customs and Excise or a constable if made to a justice or magistrates' court; and

(b) by a procurator fiscal if made to the sheriff."

The fact that there as been a deficit in the process by which the application is made, for example, an inappropriate form was used, will probably not render the detention of cash unlawful: see *Luton JJ., ex. p. Abecasis* (2000) 164 J.P. 265.

(c) Application for release

13–378 Either the prosecutor or an interested party may apply for the money to be released in the circumstances set out in section 42(6) of the Act below:

"(6) At any time while cash is detained by virtue of the preceding provisions of this section—

(a) a magistrates' court or in Scotland the sheriff may direct its release if satisfied—

(i) on an application made by the person from whom it was

seized or a person by or on whose behalf it was being imported or exported, that there are no, or are no longer any, such grounds for its detention as are mentioned in subsection (2) above; or

(ii) on an application made by any other person, that detention of the cash is not for that or any other reason justified; and

(b) a customs officer or constable, or in Scotland a procurator fiscal, may release the cash if satisfied that its detention is no longer justified, but shall first notify the justice, magistrates' court or sheriff under whose order it is being detained."

A party who seeks the release of cash, seized under s.42, has two possible routes pursuant to s.42(6). First, he may attempt to persuade a customs officer (or a police officer) to release the cash. The officer can only do so if he is satisfied that its detention is no longer justified and he informs the Court that he proposes to release the money. The Court therefore performs a supervisory role. However, the usual route for the release of cash is by way of an application to the Magistrates' Court (or to the Sheriff in Scotland) under s.42(6)(a). If the applicant is either the person from whom the cash was seized, or a person on whose behalf the cash was being exported or imported, he must establish that there are no longer "grounds for its detention". The grounds for detention are "reasonable grounds for suspecting" that the cash "directly or indirectly represents any person's proceeds of drug trafficking, or is intended by any person for use in drug trafficking": see the combined effect of s.42(2) and s.42(1). Note the use of the phrases "any person's proceeds" and "intended by any person". It is not necessary that the applicant intended to use the cash in drug trafficking. It is important to bear in mind that the magistrates are constrained to apply the test laid down by the section, namely, that there are no longer reasonable grounds for holding a suspicion mentioned in section 42(2) and (1) above: see *Customs and Excise Commissioners v. Shah* (1999) 163 JP 759.

In *Thomas*, (January 20, 1995, unreported, DC) F was stopped at Dover in a motor vehicle. Approximately £78,000 in cash was found in a holdall on the back seat of the car. Part of the money was supplied by R.

Held: an appeal, by case stated, against the forfeiture of the cash was dismissed.

After referring to what is now s.42(5)—formerly s.25(5) CJICA—Kennedy L.J. observed:

"It may be thought unjust that if a man advances money to another for what the first man believes to be a normal business venture but the intention of the second man is that the money shall be used for drug trafficking, the money becomes liable for forfeiture under (s.43) but, in my judgement, that is what the plain words of the statute provide."

13–379 It will be seen that section 42(6)(a) empowers a magistrates' court to release detained cash if *inter alia*, there are no grounds for its detention "as mentioned in subsection (2)". When one looks at subsection (2) it refers to the existence of "reasonable grounds *for the suspicion* mentioned in subsection (1). . . ." When one then goes to subsection (1) the *grounds for suspicion* are that the cash directly or indirectly represents *any* persons proceeds of drug trafficking or is intended by any person for use in drug trafficking. Accordingly, and put shortly, where a person applies for the release of detained cash under section 42(6) the burden is on him to show that there are no grounds *for those suspicions*, or any other reason, that justifies detention.

In *Commissioners of Customs & Excise v. Shah* (June 18, 1999) the Justices ordered the release of cash on the grounds that they were not satisfied on the balance of probabilities that the money was the proceeds of drug trafficking. The Divisional Court quashed the order on the grounds that the Justices applied the wrong test, and reversed the burden of proof. The Justices heard a great deal of evidence and it may be that they concluded that if a claim for forfeiture under section 43 would have failed, the sooner the money was returned the better. However, section 42(6) did not empower the Court to jump to that stage or to make such a finding.

(d) When the money must not be released

13–380 There are two relevant circumstances as set out in section 42(7) below:

"If at a time when any cash is being detained by virtue of the preceding provisions of this section—

(a) an application for its forfeiture is made under section 43 of this Act, or

(b) proceedings are instituted (whether in the United Kingdom or elsewhere) against any person for an offence with which the cash is connected, the cash shall not be released until any proceedings pursuant to the application or, as the case may be, the proceedings for that offence have been concluded."

(e) Forfeiture under Part II

13–381 Section 43 of the 1994 Act provides:

"(1) A magistrates' court or in Scotland the sheriff may order the forfeiture of any cash which has been seized under section 42 of this Act if satisfied, on an application made while the cash is detained under that section, that the cash directly or indirectly represents any person's proceeds of drug trafficking, or is intended by any person for use in drug trafficking.

(2) Any application for an order under this section shall be made—
(a) by the Commissioners of Customs and Excise or a constable if made to a magistrates' court; and
(b) by a procurator fiscal if made to the sheriff.

(3) The standard of proof in proceedings on an application under this section shall be that applicable to civil proceedings; and an order may be made under this section whether or not proceedings are brought against any person for an offence with which the cash in question is connected.

(4) Proceedings on an application under this section to the sheriff shall be civil proceedings."

Note that it is not necessary to establish that the person who carried the money (or even the person who supplied the money) intended that the cash should be used in drug trafficking for the purposes of s.43: see *Thomas* (January 20, 1995, unreported, DC); and see *Pruijsen v. HMCE* (October 18, 1999).

The Court is entitled to look at all the surrounding circumstances including explanations given by those who, for example, intended to use the cash or carried it; the circumstances in which the cash was transported; the lack or presence of traces of a controlled drug on the cash (see *Thomas*) or the fact that the cash was destined for a centre known for illicit drug trafficking: see *Bassick*, March 22, 1993, unreported, DC).

The fact that the person in possession of the cash has been acquitted of drug trafficking charges does not necessarily preclude the circumstances relating to the criminal matter, being used in forfeiture proceedings: *HMCE v. Thorp* (November 28, 1996).

(f) Appeals

Section 44 of the Drug Trafficking Act provides: 13–382

"(1) This section applies where an order for the forfeiture of cash ('the forfeiture order') is made under section 43 of this Act by a magistrates' court.

(2) Any party to the proceedings in which the forfeiture order is made (other than the applicant for the order) may, before the end of the period of 30 days beginning with the date on which it is made, appeal to the Crown Court or, in Northern Ireland, to a county court.

(3) An appeal under this section shall be by way of a rehearing.

(4) On an application made by the appellant to a magistrates' court at any time, that court may order the release of so much of the cash to which the forfeiture order relates as it considers appropriate to enable him to meet his legal expenses in connection with the appeal.

(5) The Court hearing an appeal under this section may make such order as it considers appropriate.

(6) If it upholds the appeal, the Court may order the release of the cash, or (as the case may be) the remaining cash, together with any accrued interest.

(7) Subsection (3) of section 43 of this Act applies in relation to a rehearing on an appeal under this section as it applies to proceedings under that section".

(g) Practitioners Beware

13–383 Note that the time-limit is 30 days, beginning on the day the forfeiture order is made. Appeal is to the Crown Court. There is no power to extend the period for an appeal: *West London JJ., ex. p. Lamai* (July 6, 2000). An application may be made for the release of forfeited cash to meet reasonable legal expenses (s.44(4)) but the DTA does not make any other express provision for the release of monies to meet legal expenses: see *Commissioners of C & E v. Harris* (January 29, 1999).

Magistrates' Courts (Detention and Forfeiture of Drug Trafficking Cash) Rules 1991

(S.I. 1991 No. 1923 and amended by S.I. 1994 No. 3154)
Citation, Commencement and Interpretation

1(1) Citation and commencement.
(2) In these Rules—
(a) "the Act" means the Criminal Justice (International Co-operation) Act 1990; and
(b) any reference to a form is a reference to a form set out in the Schedule to these Rules or a form to the like effect.

Application for continued detention of seized cash

2.(1) An application for an order under section 25(2) of the Act for continued detention of cash seized under section 25(1) thereof shall be made in writing in Form A to a justice of the peace who ordinarily acts for the petty sessions area in which the cash was seized.

(2) a copy of the written application under paragraph (1) above shall be given by the applicant the person from whom the cash was seized

Hearing of application for continued detention of seized cash

3.(1) A justice of the peace considering an application under section 25(2) of the Act shall require the matters contained in it to be sworn by the applicant under oath, may require the applicant to answer any questions under oath, and may require any statement in response by the from whom the cash was seized to be made under oath.

(2) The justice shall record or cause to be recorded in writing the substance of any statements made under oath which are not already recorded in the written application.

Unattended parcels etc.

4. In rules 2, 3 and 8 of these Rules, references to the person from whom the cash was seized include references to the sender and the intended recipient, where known, of a letter, parcel, container or other means of unattended dispatch, but a justice of the peace shall not decline to

hear an application in such a case solely on the ground that it has not been proved that the sender or intended recipient has received a copy of the written application under rule 2(2) of these Rules.

Order for continued detention of seized cash

5.(1) An order made by a justice of the peace under section 25(2) of the Act shall be in Form B.

(2) Notice of any order mentioned in paragraph (1) above shall be given forthwith by the applicant to any person appearing to him to be affected by it and such notice shall be in the form set out in Form B and shall be accompanied by a copy of the said order.

Notice of order for continued detention of seized cash

6. Where, in accordance with an order made under section 25(2) of the Act, the applicant gives notice to any person affected by the order, the applicant shall notify the clerk of the magistrates' court to which any application under section 25(3) or (5) would, in accordance with rule 7(1) and (2) of these Rules, be made of the names and addresses of the persons so notified.

Subsequent applications

7.(1) An application under section 25(3) of the Act for further deten- 13–384
tion of cash shall be in Form C and shall be sent to the clerk to the justices for the petty sessions area in which the seizure was made.

(2) An application under section 25(5) of the Act for the release of detained cash shall be made in writing to the clerk of the said magistrates' court, and shall specify the grounds on which it is made.

(3) The clerk of the magistrates' court who receives an application in accordance with paragraph (1) or (2) above shall fix a date for the hearing of the application, shall notify the applicant thereof and shall notify any persons to whom notice of the order for continued detention has been given of the application and of the date fixed for the hearing.

(4) If the Court is satisfied that an order for further detention of cash should be made under section 25(3) of the Act, it shall endorse the order for continued detention accordingly, and a copy of the order so endorsed shall be given by the clerk of the Court to any persons to whom notice of the order for continued detention has been given.

Direction for release of cash

8. A direction under section 25(5)(a) of the Act for the release of detained cash shall be in Form D, and shall provide for the release of the cash within 7 days of the date of the making of the direction or such longer period as with the agreement of the person from whom the cash was seized may be specified in the notice.

Forfeiture

9.(1) An application for forfeiture of cash under section 26 of the Act shall be in Form E and shall be addressed to the clerk of the magistrates' court referred to in rule 7(1) of these Rules.

(2) The clerk of the magistrates' court who receives such an application shall fix a date for the hearing, shall notify the applicant thereof, and shall notify any persons to whom notice of an order for continued detention has been given of the application and of the date fixed for the hearing.

Appeal against order forfeiting cash

9A.(1) An application under section 44(4) of the Drug Trafficking Act 1994 for the release of cash to meet the appellant's legal expenses shall be made in writing and shall contain the name and address of the solicitor instructed by the appellant and the amount requested to be released, together with any evidence in support of the application.

(2) A copy of the written application under paragraph (1) above shall be served by the appellant on the complainant.

(3) The clerk of the magistrates' court who receives such an application shall fix a date for the hearing of the application, shall notify the appellant thereof, and shall notify any persons to whom notice of forfeiture was given.

(4) A direction for the release of cash under section 44(4) of the Drug Trafficking Act 1994 shall be in Form F.

Joinder

10. At any hearing under section 25(3) or (5) of the Act, or under section 26 thereof, or on the application of any person affected by an order for continued or further detention, the Court may, if it thinks fit, order that such person be joined as a party to the proceedings and, if the Court so orders, otherwise than at such a hearing, the clerk of the magistrates' court shall give notice to the other parties.

Notice

11. Any notice or copy of any order required to be given to any person under the foregoing provisions of these Rules may be given by post to his last known address.

Procedure at hearings

12.(1) At the hearing of an application under section 25(3) or (5) of the Act, or under section 26 thereof or under section 44 of the Drug Trafficking Act 1994 any person to whom notice of the application has been given may attend and be heard on the question whether a further order should be made, an existing order should be discharged, or a forfeiture order should be made, as the case may be, but the fact that any such person does not attend shall not prevent the Court from hearing the application.

(2) Subject to the foregoing provisions of these Rules, proceedings on such an application shall be regulated in the same manner as proceedings on a complaint, and accordingly for the purposes of this rule the application shall be deemed to be a complaint, the applicant to be a complainant, the respondents to be defendants, and any notice given by the clerk to a magistrates' court under rule 7(3) or 9(2) of these Rules to be a summons; but nothing in this rule shall be construed as enabling a warrant of arrest to be issued for failure to appear in answer to any such notice.

Chapter 14
Powers of Forfeiture

A. STATUTORY POWERS (OTHER THAN UNDER THE DTA)

I. General Note

For the purposes of the DTOA, there was very clear authority that where it was shown that the defendant benefited from drug trafficking, the Court was duty bound to follow the steps required by the DTOA and it was not permitted to use its powers of forfeiture under what was s.43 of the Powers of the Criminal Courts Act 1973 (now s.143 of the Powers of Criminal Courts (Sentencing) Act 2000): *Stuart and Bonnett* (1989) 11 Cr. App. R.(S) 89. This is because s.1(5) of the DTOA made it clear that s.43 of the 1973 Act was subordinate to the provisions of the DTOA. Of course, it should be noted that the DTOA had to be applied in every case where the defendant was convicted of a drug trafficking offence. This is no longer true under the DTA by virtue of s.2(1) of that Act and perhaps it could be argued that a judge may be faced with a case where neither the prosecution nor the Court choose to proceed under the DTA but the Court is nevertheless satisfied that the defendant was, for example, in possession of cash at the time of his arrest, which was used for the purposes of committing or facilitating the commission of the offence. **14–01**

It may be asked: is *Stuart and Bonnett* still relevant? It is submitted that it is to the extent that the decision should be taken as establishing a general rule of practice. However, the effect of section 2 is to afford the prosecutor a degree of discretion as to how best to proceed, *e.g.* whether by way of confiscation proceedings or by applying for a forfeiture order. Each case will turn on its own facts: and see section 2(1)(b) which speaks of the Court's power to proceed under the Act if "appropriate" to do so.

II. Forfeiture under the CEMA 1979

Reference has already been made to the fact that, under the Customs & Excise Management Act 1979, the Commissioners have broad powers of **14–02** forfeiture in relation to many activities embraced by the Customs and Excise Acts (see Chap. 2). Anything liable to forfeiture under those Acts may be seized or detained by any officer, constable, member of Her Majesty's armed forces, or a coastguard (s.139(1) of the CEMA) and dealt with in accordance with section 139 of and Schedule 3 to the 1979 Act.

Thus, goods improperly imported may be forfeited under section 49(1). By section 88 ships, aircraft and vehicles which are constructed, altered or fitted in any manner for the purpose of concealing "goods" (including stores and baggage: s.1(1)) may be forfeited. A ship under 250 tons may be forfeited if any part of its cargo is thrown overboard, or is staved, or destroyed to prevent seizure (s.89). A ship over 250 tons (s.142) may have other penalties imposed under section 143: see *Att.-Gen. v. Hunter* [1949] 2 K.B. 111.

Forfeiture proceedings under the Customs and Excise Acts are *in rem*: see *Denton v. John Lister Ltd* [1971] 3 All E.R. 669, a case decided in respect of s.44 of the Customs and Excise Act 1952 and which was concerned with the forfeiture of goods. The principles applied in that case are pertinent to a consideration of corresponding or similar provisions under the 1979 Act.

14–03 Not all of the powers of forfeiture available to customs and excise are dependant on proving that the carrier of the offending material knew of its existence or played some part in the forbidden activity. Thus, in *Customs and Excise Commissioners v. Air Canada* [1991] 1 All E.R. 570, the commissioners seized a large commercial aircraft owned and operated by Air Canada. The aircraft landed at Heathrow, having arrived from Bombay, but when the cargo was unloaded, officers found a substantial amount of cannabis resin in a container. The commissioners seized the aircraft pursuant to sections 139(1) and 141(1) of the CEMA 1979 on the grounds that it was used for the carriage of goods "liable to forfeiture". The aircraft was returned to the airline upon payment by the latter in the sum of £50,000 (see para.16 of Sched.3 to the CEMA 1979) but the airline gave notice under para.3 of Sched.3 that the aircraft was not liable to forfeiture. The question arose as to whether the commissioners had to prove that Air Canada knew or ought to have known that goods liable to forfeiture were being carried on the aircraft. At first instance, that question was answered affirmatively, but on appeal, it was held that liability was absolute and that proof of *mens rea* was not required because sections 139(1) and 141(1) did not create criminal offences and that proceedings brought in respect of those provisions were *in rem*. In so deciding, the Court of Appeal (Civil Division) drew support from *Lord Advocate v. Crookshanks* (1888) 15 R. 995, decided under s.202 of the Customs Consolidation Act 1876 which employed the words "made use of in the importation, landing of prohibited goods". That case concerned the forfeiture of a horse and cab used for carrying tobacco that was prohibited. The Court said the "mere fact that the cab and horse have been used in the particular manner referred to in the statute is a sufficient ground for forfeiture " and concluded that the statute was "very strict". *Lord Advocate v. Crookshanks* was followed in

De Keyser v. British Railway Traffic and Electric Co. Ltd [1936] 1 K.B. 224 in which Lord Hewart remarked:

> "... they did not know of the wrongful use for which the lorry was being employed. That circumstance was wholly irrelevant to the proceedings before the justices. It did not affect the purpose for which the lorry had been used."

The forerunner to section 141(1) CEMA 1979 was section 277(1) of the Customs and Excise Act 1952 and which was relevant in *Customs and Excise Commissioners v. Jack Bradley (Accrington) Ltd* [1959] 1 Q.B. 219. Although that case was decided on very different facts, the Court in *Jack Bradley* considered the phrase "which has been used for the carriage of the goods liable to forfeiture" and concluded that it meant "where use has been made of the vehicle to carry" *i.e.* to carry the offending goods. It therefore provided peripheral support for the Commissioners' contention in Air Canada, because the section omits the word "knowingly". 14–04

The airline relied, *inter alia*, on Article 6 of the Convention on Human Rights and Article 1 of the Protocol (Paris, 1952; Cmd 9221) which provides: "Every natural or legal person is entitled to the peaceful enjoyment of his possessions" but this argument failed because, at that time, the European Convention on Human Rights was not part of English domestic law: see *R v. Secretary of State for the Home Dept, ex p. Brind* [1990] 2 W.L.R. 787, at 797, *per* Lord Donaldson M.R. who said:

> "There have been a number of cases in which the European Convention on Human Rights has been introduced into the argument and has, accordingly, featured in the judgments The convention is contained in an international treaty to which the United Kingdom is a party The United Kingdom government can give effect to this treaty obligation in more than one way.... It could, for example, 'domesticate' or 'patriate' the convention itself and there are many well-informed supporters of this course. Their view has not, as yet, prevailed. If it had done so, the convention would have been part of English domestic law. Alternatively, it can review English common and statute law with a view to amending it, if and in so far as it is inconsistent with the convention, at the same time seeking to ensure that all new statute law is consistent with it. This is the course which has in fact been adopted. Whether it has been wholly successful is a matter for the European Court of Human Rights in Strasbourg and not for the English courts. By contrast, the duty of the English courts is to decide disputes in accordance with English domestic law as it is, and not as it would be if full effect were given to this country's obligations under the treaty, assuming that there is any difference between the two.
>
> It follows from this that in most cases the English courts will be wholly unconcerned with the terms of the convention. The sole exception is when the terms of primary legislation are fairly capable of bearing two or more meanings In that situation various prima facie rules

of construction have to be applied, such as that, in the absence of very clear words indicating the contrary, legislation is not retrospective or penal in effect. To these can be added, in appropriate cases, a presumption that Parliament has legislated in a manner consistent, rather than inconsistent, with the United Kingdom's treaty obligations."

14–05 Similar views were expressed by Diplock L.J. in *Salomon v. Customs and Excise Commissioners* [1967] 2 Q.B. 116 at 143, and see *Chundawadra v. Immigration Appeal Tribunal* [1988] Imm. A.R. 161 at 173 and *Garland v. British Rail Engineering Ltd* [l983] 2 A.C. 751 at 771.

Notwithstanding the passing of the Human Rights Act 1998, it is very doubtful that the Strasbourg jurisprudence will alter current case law. Air Canada pursued their complaints before the European Court of Human Rights (*Air Canada v. United Kingdom*, Series A, No. 316, (*The Times*, May 13, 1995). The Court held that the conduct of the Commissioners did not violate Article 1 of Protocol I because seizure of the aircraft did not involve a transfer of ownership and Air Canada did not lose ownership. Furthermore, on the facts of the instant case, there had been no violation of Art.6 (right to a fair trial). It is also doubtful whether forfeiture provisions of CEMA 1979 involve a "criminal charge" for the purposes of Article 6: see *Agosi v. United Kingdom* 1986, ECHR, Series A, No. 108; and see *Phillips v. United Kingdom* (5th July 2001). See also *Goldsmith v. H.M. Commissioners for Customs and Excise* [2001] EWHC Admin 265. In that case, G's car was stopped at the port of Dover and found to contain 26 kilograms of hand-rolling tobacco and other items. Under the Excise Duties (Personal Reliefs) Order 1992, as amended by SI 1999 No. 1617, the Commissioners may require a person to satisfy them that such goods are not being held or used for a commercial purpose. G contended that Article 6(2) of the ECHR applied and that the application of the reverse onus provision was contrary to Article 6(2). The Court had some sympathy with G, because "whether the proceedings are criminal or civil, the fact that his goods are, in accordance with our domestic law, forfeited, contains an innuendo . . . that [the appellant] has evaded the duty which he should have paid". Nevertheless, the Court was clear that G was in the best position to know whether the goods imported were for personal or commercial use, and in any event, the presumption was capable of being rebutted. The Court held that the statutory requirements were reasonable in the circumstances, and in any event, the condemnation and forfeiture provisions in CEMA 1979 are not ones to which Article 6(2) applies (the Court cited The Queen on the application of *McCann v. Manchester Crown Court and the Chief Constable of Greater Manchester*, March 1, 2001).

III. Forfeiture under the MDA 1971

14–06 Section 27 of the Misuse of Drugs Act 1971, as amended by the Criminal Justice Act 1988, s.70, the Criminal Justice (International Co-operation) Act 1990, and s.65(1) of the Drug Trafficking Act 1994, provides:

"(1) Subject to subsection (2) below, the Court by or before which a person is convicted of an offence under this Act or a drug trafficking offence, as defined in section 1(3) of the Drug Trafficking Act 1994 or an offence to which section 1 of the Criminal Justice (Scotland) Act 1987 relates, may order anything shown to the satisfaction of the Court to relate to the offence, to be forfeited and either destroyed or dealt with in such other manner as the Court may order.

"(2) The Court shall not order anything to be forfeited under this section, where a person claiming to be the owner of or otherwise interested in it applies to be heard by the Court, unless an opportunity has been given to him to show cause why the order should not be made."

An order under section 27 must be made within 28 days after passing sentence and cannot be varied, or rescinded, or made after that period: see *Menocal* [1980] A.C. 598."

Section 27 will only apply to things shown "to relate to the offence". *As originally drafted*, property sought to be forfeited under section 27 had to relate to an offence created under the M.D.A. 1971 alone. Accordingly, a conspiracy to contravene an offence under that Act was excluded because the MDA 1971 created no statutory conspiracies: *Cuthbertson* [1981] A.C. 470. The ambit of section 27 has been widened considerably to include a "drug trafficking offence" as defined by the Drug Trafficking Act 1994, or section 1 of the Criminal Justice (Scotland) Act 1987; see now s.49(5) Proceeds of Crime (Scotland) Act 1995. A "drug trafficking offence" includes an offence of conspiring, inciting or attempting to commit specified offences under the MDA.

Only tangible things can be forfeited under section 27 of the MDA and not choses in action: see *Cuthbertson* (above); *Beard* [1974] 1 W.L.R. 1549; *Khan* [1982] 1 W.L.R. 1405 and *Pearce* [1996] Crim.L.R. 442. In other words, the property sought to be forfeited must relate to the transaction, which is covered by an appropriate charge, or count on the indictment. In *Cuthbertson*, T and C had transferred a considerable portion of their shares in the profits to various bank accounts in Switzerland and France. Assets representing their proceeds of drug trafficking were traced and amounted to about £3/4m. The judge made a forfeiture order under section 27 for that amount. The House of Lords held that it was necessary to connect the specific thing sought to be forfeited with the particular substantive offence to which it related. As Lord Diplock observed (at 406 f-g), orders of forfeiture under section 27 were not intended by Parliament to serve "as a means of stripping the drug trafficker of the total profits of their unlawful enterprises". 14–07

The decision in *Cuthbertson* has been criticised in academic circles but it is submitted that Lord Scarman correctly described section 27 as being concerned "not with restitution, compensation or the redress of illegal enrichment but with forfeiture": *Cuthbertson* [1981] A.C. 470, 486; and note by contrast the sweeping effect of the DTA 1994. In *Pearce* [1996] Crim.L.R. 442, the Court regarded itself bound by earlier decisions. In that case, P pleaded guilty to producing a controlled drug, namely, cannabis. P bought a house in which he installed an elaborate system for the cultivation of cannabis. The trial judge ordered that the house be forfeited under section 27 of the Misuse of Drugs Act 1971. The Court of Appeal quashed the order. It should be noted that cultivating cannabis contrary to section 6 of the Misuse of Drugs Act is not a "drug trafficking offence" for the purposes of the Drug Trafficking Act 1994, but producing cannabis by cultivation contrary to section 4 of the Misuse of Drugs Act, is such an offence. It is submitted that the decision of the Court in *Pearce* is, in any event, sensible. Where the allegation is that the defendant has benefited from drug trafficking, and realisable property consists of land (in respect of which there might well be third party interests), the most appropriate mechanism for investigating the matter is under the Drug Trafficking Act 1994.

Where money is seized by police *in specie, e.g.* in the form of banknotes, and then put into a bank account by police for safe keeping, the money so seized is sufficiently tangible for the purposes of section 27. The relevant moment is the moment of seizure: see *Marland* (1985) 82 Cr.App.R. 134.

(a) The tangible item must relate to the offence

14–08 In *Cuthbertson*, the House of Lords emphasised the importance of ensuring that the tangible items relate to the offence and see *Beard* [1974] 1 W.L.R. 1549; *Khan* [1982] 1 W.L.R. 1405 and *Pearce, The Times*, February 22, 1996. In *Haggard v. Mason* [1976] 1 W.L.R. 187, the Court of Appeal quashed an order under section 27 which related to the sum of £146 found in the defendant's possession. He had been convicted of offering to supply another with LSD. The £146 represented the remaining proceeds of M's illegal dealings, which were not the subject of a separate charge. Accordingly, the money did not "relate" to the offences. Similar considerations resulted in a forfeiture order being quashed in the case of *Ribeyre* (1982) 4 Cr.App.R.(S) 165, where R admitted that £700 was the proceeds of drug sales but the receipt of the money was not reflected by a suitable count on the indictment (R having pleaded guilty to possessing cocaine with intent to supply it) and the £700 did not relate to that purpose. Judges in other cases have fallen into the same trap: see *Morgan* [1977] Crim.L.R. 488; *Cox* [1987] Crim.L.R. 141; *Llewellyn* (1985) 7 Cr.App.R.(S) 225; *Boothe* (1987) 9 Cr.App.R.(S) 8; *Simms* (1987) 9 Cr.App.R.(S) 417; *O'Farrell* (1988) 10 Cr.App.R.(S) 74; *Askew* [1987] Crim.L.R. 584; *Neville* [1987] Crim.L.R. 585; and see *Griffiths* (October 15, 1996).

In *Bowers* [1994] Crim. L.R. 230, B pleaded guilty to possessing cannabis resin with intent to supply and supplying the drug. He was the driver of a car stopped by police at a service area. B ordered his passenger to throw a quantity of resin out of the car. A forfeiture order was made under section 27 of the MDA. B appealed against the making of the order on the grounds that the car had been purchased with money obtained from his mother but the car was registered in his name and used by him. The Court upheld the order. It would have been a surprising result if the Court of Appeal had reached a different conclusion because, although the requirements under s.27 of the MDA and s.143 of the Powers of Criminal Courts (Sentencing) Act 2000 differ to some extent, there is clear authority that an order under section 143 can be made if a vehicle is used to carry controlled drugs illegally: see *Boothe* (1987) 9 Cr. App. R.(S) 8. In *Bowers*, the Court also made a confiscation order under the DTOA but it is clear that the evidence showed that the car was not purchased out of the proceeds of drug trafficking and thus it could not be included as a benefit from drug trafficking.

By contrast, in *Griffiths*, above, an order was quashed that forfeited a tobacco pipe, an Oriental pipe, floodlights and infrared lamps. None of those items was shown to be linked to the smoking of cannabis or the offence charged (producing cannabis).

In *Maidstone Crown Court, ex p. Gill* [1986] 1 W.L.R. 1405, a forfeiture order under section 27 had to be quashed in respect of a motor car which related to a charge to which the accused had pleaded not guilty and the matter was "left on the file". **14–09**

(b) Orders made against non-defendants

Section 27(2) gives the owner of goods, or an interested party in it, the right to have the opportunity of being heard before an order is made.

Where the evidence is that such parties were put on notice, or should have been, that the item in question was going to be used for some illegal purpose, then it might be proper for a judge to make a forfeiture order: *Maidstone Crown Court, ex p. Gill*, but see *Churcher* (1986) 8 Cr.App.R.(S) 94, below.

(c) Opportunity to give evidence

In *Churcher* (1986) 8 Cr.App.R.(S) 94, the Court of Appeal observed that the Court was under a duty to give the defendant a proper opportunity to put material before it, in order to demonstrate that the requirements of the section were not fulfilled. The facts in *Churcher* related to two sums of money found in the possession of the appellant. He pleaded guilty to a variety of drug trafficking offences. On similar facts, a court today would endeavour to confiscate such moneys under the DTA. **14–10**

IV. Forfeiture under the Powers of Criminal Courts (Sentencing) Act 2000

"143.—(1) Where a person is convicted of an offence and the Court by or before which he is convicted is satisfied that any property which has been lawfully seized from him, or which was in his possession or under **14–11** his control at the time when he was apprehended for the offence or when a summons in respect of it was issued—

(a) has been used for the purpose of committing, or facilitating the commission of, any offence, or

(b) was intended by him to be used for that purpose,

the Court may (subject to subsection (5) below) make an order under this section in respect of that property.

(2) Where a person is convicted of an offence and the offence, or an offence which the Court has taken into consideration in determining his sentence, consists of unlawful possession of property which—

(a) has been lawfully seized from him, or

(b) was in his possession or under his control at the time when he was apprehended for the offence of which he has been convicted or when a summons in respect of that offence was issued,

the Court may (subject to subsection (5) below) make an order under this section in respect of that property.

(3) An order under this section shall operate to deprive the offender of his rights, if any, in the property to which it relates, and the property shall (if not already in their possession) be taken into the possession of the police.

(4) Any power conferred on a court by subsection (1) or (2) above may be exercised—

(a) whether or not the Court also deals with the offender in any other way in respect of the offence of which he has been convicted; and

(b) without regard to any restrictions on forfeiture in any enactment contained in an Act passed before 29th July 1988.

(5) In considering whether to make an order under this section in respect of any property, a court shall have regard—

(a) to the value of the property; and

(b) to the likely financial and other effects on the offender of the making of the order (taken together with any other order that the Court contemplates making).

(6) Where a person commits an offence to which this subsection applies by—

(a) driving, attempting to drive, or being in charge of a vehicle, or

(b) *failing* to comply with a requirement made under section 7 of the Road Traffic Act 1988 (failure to provide a specimen for analysis or laboratory test) in the course of an investigation into whether the offender had committed an offence while driving, attempting to drive or being in charge of a vehicle, or

(c) *failing*, as the driver of a vehicle, to comply with subsection (2) or (3) of section 170 of the Road Traffic Act 1988 (duty to stop and give information or report accident),

the vehicle shall be regarded for the purposes of subsection (1) above (and section 144(1) (b) below) as used for the purpose of committing the offence (and for the purpose of committing any offence of aiding, abetting, counselling or procuring the commission of the offence).

(7) Subsection (6) above applies to—

(a) an offence under the Road Traffic Act 1988 which is punishable with imprisonment;

(b) an offence of manslaughter, and

(c) an offence under section 35 of the Offences Against the Person Act 1861 (wanton and furious driving).

(8) Facilitating the commission of an offence shall be taken for the purposes of subsection (1) above to include the taking of any steps after it has been committed for the purpose of disposing of any property to which it relates or of avoiding apprehension or detection.

Property which is in possession of police by virtue of section 143 14–12

144.—(1) The Police (Property) Act 1897 shall apply, with the following modifications, to property which is in the possession of the police by virtue of section 143 above—

(a) no application shall be made under section 1(1) of that Act by any claimant of the property after the end of six months from the date on which the order in respect of the property was made under section 143 above; and

(b) no such application shall succeed unless the claimant satisfies the Court either—

(i) that he had not consented to the offender having possession of the property or

(ii) where an order is made under subsection (1) of section 143 above, that he did not know, and had no reason to suspect, that the property was likely to be used for the purpose mentioned in that subsection.

(2) In relation to property which is in the possession of the police by virtue of section 143 above, the power to make regulations under section 2 of the Police (Property) Act 1897 (disposal of property in cases where the owner of the property has not been ascertained and no order of a competent court has been made with respect to it) shall, subject to subsection (3) below, include power to make regulations for disposal (including disposal by vesting in the relevant authority) in cases where no application by a claimant of the property has been made within the period specified in subsection (1)(a) above or no such application has succeeded.

(3) The regulations may not provide for the vesting in the relevant authority of property in relation to which an order has been made under section 145 below (court order as to application of proceeds of forfeited property).

(4) Nothing in subsection (2A) (a) or (3) of section 2 of the Police (Property) Act 1897 limits the power to make regulations under that section by virtue of subsection (2) above.

(5) In this section "relevant authority" has the meaning given by section 2(2B) of the Police (Property) Act 1897.

14–13 Application of proceeds of forfeited property

145.—(1) Where a court makes an order under section 143 above in a case where—

(a) the offender has been convicted of an offence which has resulted in a person suffering personal injury, loss or damage, or
(b) any such offence is taken into consideration by the Court in determining sentence,

the Court may also make an order that any proceeds which arise from the disposal of the property and which do not exceed a sum specified by the Court shall be paid to that person.

(2) The Court may make an order under this section only if it is satisfied that but for the inadequacy of the offender's means it would have made a compensation order under which the offender would have been required to pay compensation of an amount not less than the specified amount.

(3) An order under this section has no effect—

(a) before the end of the period specified in section 144(1) (a) above; or
(b) if a successful application under section 1(1) of the Police (Property) Act 1897 has been made."

14–14 In *Boothe* (1987) 9 Cr.App.R.(S) 8:

> B was convicted of possessing a drug intending to supply it and unlawfully possessing a drug. Officers, by chance, stopped B's motor car and found packages of cocaine. £1,489 was found in his possession. B was not a regular full-time dealer.
>
> Held: (1) the forfeiture of his motor car under what was section 43 of the Powers of Criminal Courts Act 1973 was valid.
>
> *Held:* (2) the forfeiture of the money under M.D.A., s.27 must be quashed.

It was contended in *Boothe* that the motor car was not essential for the commission of the offence (see *Lidster* [1976] Crim.L.R. 80). The Court had no difficulty in concluding that the use of the car was an "integral part" of the offence as it was being used to transport packages of cocaine: but see *Brown* (February 28, 1974; unreported).

It follows from the above that a tenuous connection between the item and the commission of the offence is not enough: see *Jones* (October 10, 1985, unreported).

If, as in *Boothe*, money found in the possession of the accused cannot be forfeited under section 27 of the MDA, the Court may be able to justify an order under section 143(1)(b) of the PCC(S)A 2000 if it can be shown, for example, that the money was intended to be used by the defendant to increase his stock-in-trade (*i.e.* to buy additional drugs in order to supply them) and provided that the defendant either pleads guilty, or is convicted of an offence which reflects his intention. However, the matter is not clear: see *Tarpy* (February 8, 1985, unreported).

It should be noted that section 143 is confined to property used or facilitating the commission of an offence (or intended to be so used) by the person convicted. It does not apply in cases where someone other than the defendant intended to (or did) use the property: *Slater* [1986] 1 W.L.R. 1340; but see *Coleville-Scott* [1990] 1 W.L.R. 958. There should also be evidence to justify forfeiture: see *Pemberton* 4 Cr. App. R.(S) 328. A very useful case, as to the scope and application of section 143 (formerly s.43 PCCA1973), is *Kurt* (May 13, 1999), and the reader may find the following passages from the judgment of the Court useful. That case concerned money, found by police, in the possession of the accused: 14–15

> "Although the argument was confined to the ambit of section 43 of the 1973 Act, three grounds were advanced in support of the appeal against the forfeiture order.
>
> First, the cash found by the police was no longer available, and the subject matter of the order which formed part of the assets of the client account of the applicant's solicitors was no longer tangible property within the meaning of section 43.
>
> Second, the order for forfeiture was disproportionate, having regard to the totality of sentence for a single offence of simple possession of a Class A drug.
>
> Third, there was no sufficient evidence that this money was to be used by the appellant to commit or facilitate the commission of an offence in the future and given that the case proceeded on the basis of a plea of guilty to simple possession only, on the admissible evidence the judge should not have made any such finding. Indeed to do so amounted to a collateral attack on the verdict of not guilty entered on count 1, and the decision by the Crown not to proceed with the allegation of possession with intent to supply on count 2. We shall consider these submissions in the order in which they were advanced.
>
> The actual cash found by the police in the appellant's car is no longer available for his solicitors to hand back to the police. Compliance with the forfeiture order would require them to draw a cheque on their client account for the requisite amount. According to the submission for the appellant the property referred to in section 43(1) is limited to tangible property: it does not extend to a chose in action in a mixed fund. Reliance was placed on *R v. Cuthbertson* [1981] AC 470 where, at page 483, Lord Diplock said:
>
> > 'One limitation on the subject matter of an order for forfeiture is that it must be something tangible.'
>
> In *Cuthbertson* the House of Lords was considering the question of forfeiture in the context of a conspiracy to contravene the provisions of the Misuse of Drugs Act 1971, and in particular, whether or not conspiracy was an 'offence' within section 27(1) of the Act by which the Court was empowered to make an order for forfeiture of 'anything

shown . . . to relate to the offence.' On analysis conspiracy was found not to be such an offence. Lord Diplock commented:

> 'Where it is possible to identify something tangible which can fairly be said to relate to any such transaction, such as the drugs involved, apparatus for making them, vehicles used for transporting them, or cash ready to be, or having just been, handed over for them, then if it is desired to forfeit it, the transaction must be made the subject of a charge of the substantive offence.'

In the present case, the cash found in the car was undoubtedly in the appellant's possession or under his control when he was apprehended. It was also lawfully seized from him. At that time it was tangible property, cash. As its language shows, section 43(1) of the 1973 Act is concerned with the moment when the property is seized, or the appellant is apprehended. The power to make the order does not depend on what may subsequently have become of the property, and in particular on the continued safe keeping of the cash itself in a secure place, available for physical production when an order for forfeiture is made.

Having reached these conclusions without the advantage of the decision of this Court in *R v. Marland* [1986] 82 Cr App R 134, we were fortified by the observations of Lord Lane CJ when considering an identical problem:

14–16 'The next ground is that the money which the police seized in cash . . . having been taken by the police, was then put into a deposit account. . . . So that it might earn interest pending the outcome of the proceedings. It is now submitted that that money, when paid into the bank, ceased to be a tangible asset to which Lord Diplock referred, and itself became a chose in action, and therefore . . . was not properly the subject of forfeiture for the reason which Lord Diplock in his speech gave. We reject that argument. Lord Diplock was dealing with things which were tangible at the time when the defendant was arrested and his property seized by the police. The fact that cash seized in specie (in the shape of bank notes or Dutch guilders) is put into a bank account for safe custody to earn interest rather than kept in the police station safe, or kept in a safe deposit box, does not, in our judgment, put it beyond the reach of forfeiture. The moment to consider is the moment of seizure. Unlike the accounts in the building society with which [we] have already dealt, this money was certainly something tangible when seized by the police.

An order for forfeiture is not precluded by sensible arrangements of the kind used to ensure the preservation of the fund (earning interest) in a bank account. The effect of the order for forfeiture is to deprive the appellant of his rights in that fund, and at present we can see no proper basis on which the appellant's solicitors may refuse to hand over an appropriate cheque to the police. Certainly their client has no further right of any kind in the fund. The second ground of appeal concerns proportionality. The appellant's case at interview was that none of the money found by the police in the car belonged to him. In his defence statement his case had developed and he now claimed that he owned the money in the briefcase. The judge found that the money (all of it) was intended for use in the commission of crime. On the facts of this case we can see no disproportion in the making of an order which deprived the offender of any rights he may have enjoyed in funds which were either not his at all, or largely not his, and which were plainly to be used to finance major drug dealing transactions.

We can now come to the third, and final, ground. We were invited to consider that there is some uncertainty whether section 43(1)(a)(i) of the 1973 Act is to be read as if the words 'by him' appear after the words 'any offence'. *R v. Slater* [1986] 8 Cr App R(S) 217 and *R v. Neville* (1987) 9 Cr App R(S) 222 suggest that this paragraph does not apply when the property was used by someone other than the offender to commit or facilitate the commission of an offence. *R v. Coleville-Scott* [1990] 12 Cr App R(S) 238 leads to the conclusion that the power to make an order under paragraph (a)(i) also arises when the property was used by someone other than the offender to facilitate the commission of an offence by the offender himself.

These authorities are binding on us. Although we have some doubts whether the Court in *Slater and Neville* considered all the practical ramifications of section 43(1)(a), they require no further analysis, or discussion. Paragraphs (a)(i) and (a)(ii) of section 43(1) of the 1973 Act are not mutually exclusive. Therefore the power to make a forfeiture order arises not only where the money, or property, 'has been used' (that is, in the past), but also where, at the time of seizure, the defendant intends that it should be used at some future, even if unspecified, date to commit or facilitate the commission of an offence. It also follows from the statutory language, that the offence so facilitated or intended to be facilitated is not confined to the specific offence of which the defendant has actually been convicted.

Accordingly, although the defendant was acquitted of any criminal involvement arising from the vast amount of heroin found in his hotel bedroom, it was in our judgment open to the judge to conclude from all the circumstances, but in particular from what the appellant himself said to the police about the money, that the cash in his possession was intended by him to facilitate the purchase of a large quantity of heroin. The fact that others might also have been involved in the intended transaction did not put him outside the ambit of section 43(a). Therefore, notwithstanding the verdict of not guilty entered on count 1, following the appellant's conviction on count 2 it was open to the judge to reach the conclusion that he did. This did not constitute a collateral attack on the verdict entered on count 1, nor any failure by the judge properly to deal with the case on the basis of the plea to count 2. ccordingly the appeal against the forfeiture order is dismissed." [emphasis added]

14–17 If, during the course of the trial or plea in mitigation, the defence make it plain that the prosecution case on possession is not accepted, it is essential that the trial judge holds an inquiry and (if necessary) hears evidence: see *Braker* (March 19, 1985, unreported).

Forfeiture orders, under section 143, should not be used as a method of ordering that the proceeds of sale be used to meet a compensation order which is not otherwise enforceable: see *Jarvis* (February 5, 1985, unreported).

It has also been held that there has to be a degree of proportionality when a forfeiture order is made between the value of the property ordered to be forfeited, and the value of the property derived from the predicate offence: see *Hammond* [2001] EWCA Crim 1046.

Chapter 15
Sentencing

A. MAXIMUM SENTENCES FOR OFFENCES UNDER THE MDA 1971

By section 25 of the MDA, the maximum sentences, which may be imposed in respect of any of the offences under the Act, are set out in Schedule 4, which has been amended by the following enactments: 15–01

(a) sections 27 and 28 of, and Schedule 5 to the Criminal Law Act 1977;
(b) sections 32(2) and 32(3) of, and Schedule 7 to the Magistrates' Courts Act 1980;
(c) section 46 of the Criminal Justice Act 1982;
(d) the Controlled Drugs (Penalties) Act 1985;
(e) the Criminal Justice and Public Order Act 1994, s.157(2) and (4) and Part II to Sched. 8.

For ease of reference, Schedule 4 to the MDA is set out at the end of this Chapter.

In the ordinary way, by section 32(2) of the Magistrates' Courts Act 1980, offences triable either way, and which are not specified in Schedule 1 to that Act, carry a maximum fine on summary conviction of the "prescribed sum", *i.e.* £5,000 (see s.17(2)(c) and para.6 to Sched.12 of the CJA 1991 and note the Criminal Justice Act 1991 (Commencement No.3) Order, S.I. 1992 No. 333).

For reasons which are not entirely easy to understand, section 32(5) of the 1980 Act provides that section 32(2) does not apply (on summary conviction) in respect of an offence under section 5(2) of the MDA if that offence involves a Class B or Class C drug. Moreover, section 32(2) does not apply to an offence under sections 4(2), 4(3), 5(3), 8, 12(6) or section 13(3) if the controlled drug involved falls within Class C. Accordingly, the appropriate penalties are set out in Schedule 5 to the Criminal Law Act 1977 as amended by Schedule 7 to the 1980 Act. 15–02

The Controlled Drugs (Penalties) Act 1985 increased, from 14 years' imprisonment to life imprisonment, the maximum sentences in respect of offences under sections 4(2), 4(3) or 5(3) of the MDA which involve a Class A drug.

B. MAXIMUM SENTENCES FOR OFFENCES UNDER THE CEMA 1979

15–03 By Schedule 1 to the CEMA, where a person is convicted of an offence contrary to section 50 (unlawful importation) or section 68 (unlawful exportation) or section 170 (fraudulent evasion), and where the offence involves a Class A or Class B drug, then he shall be liable, on summary conviction to either:

(i) a penalty of the "prescribed sum" (*i.e.* £5,000: see S.I. 1992 No. 333); or
(ii) of three times the value of the goods, whichever is the greater; or
(iii) to imprisonment for a term not exceeding six months; or
(iv) to both.

On conviction on indictment, he shall be liable to either:

(i) a penalty "of any amount"; or
(ii) imprisonment for a term not exceeding 14 years in the case of Class B drugs; or
(iii) life imprisonment where the goods are a Class A drug (see the Controlled Drugs (Penalties) Act 1985; or
(iv) to both.

15–04 Cases involving a Class C drug attract lesser penalties, namely (*per* paragraph 2 of Schedule 1 to the CEMA 1979):

"(a) on summary conviction in Great Britain, to a penalty of three times the value of the goods or level 5 on the standard scale whichever is the greater, or to imprisonment for a term not exceeding three months, or to both;
(b) on summary conviction in Northern Ireland, to a penalty of three times the value of the goods or level 3 on the standard scale whichever is the greater, or to imprisonment for a term not exceeding six months, or to both;
(c) on conviction on indictment, to a penalty of any amount, or to imprisonment for a term not exceeding five years, or to both."

I. Valuation

15–05 It may seem strange that the Court can order three times the value of drugs in the context of an illicit trade. How is the value to be assessed? The answer, which is not entirely satisfactory, is that the Court may look to the "black market" value of the drugs as well as the legitimate value.

This answer is the combined product of section 171(3) of the CEMA 1979 and the decision of the Divisional Court in *Byrne v. Low* [1972] 3 All E.R. 526.

Section 171(3) reads as follows:

> "Where a penalty for an offence under any enactment relating to an assigned matter is required to be fixed by reference to the value of any goods, that value shall be taken as the price which those goods might reasonably be expected to have fetched, after payment of any duty or tax chargeable thereon, if they had been sold in the open market at or about the date of the commission of the offence for which the penalty is imposed."

Accordingly, the value is the value of the drugs "if they had been sold in the open market". If one construes the words "open market" literally, then section 171(3) can have no application since drugs unlawfully imported cannot "openly" be marketed. If sold, their price can only be at the black market value.

This problem was considered in *Byrne v. Low* [1972] 3 All E.R. 526. 15–06

> B unlawfully imported prohibited goods, namely indecent articles. The invoice price of the goods was approximately £2,235. The magistrates sentenced B to a fine of £3,000 which was varied, on appeal to quarter sessions, to £100 on the basis that since the importation was prohibited there was no "open market" for them.

The Divisional Court allowed the appeal. Lord Widgery C.J. held (at 529) that a court is not "restricted by the distinction between the so-called black market and white market". He said (at 529 a-b):

> "What is being sought is the price which a willing seller would accept from a willing buyer for those goods as landed at the port or airport at which they were originally landed."

The Court thought that the invoice price could be a very good guide to the open market value "and may well be the conclusive and only guide".

II. Assessing the Street Value of a Drug

This topic is now of less relevance since the decision of the Court of Appeal in *Aranguren* (1994) 99 Cr. App. R. 347; see below. However, where the drug is relatively small, the street value of that drug may afford the sentencer some guidance as to the gravity of the offence. 15–07

Of course, drug transactions are rarely committed to paper in intelligible form. Accordingly, evidence of the value of a given substance will normally be given to the Court by an expert, normally a police officer who has had many years' experience in dealing with drug offences. His information will be obtained from a variety of sources: prisoners or suspects may speak of the value; the officer may have been personally engaged in undercover drug operations during the course of which he has negotiated a price, or he may refer to records kept by NCIS at New Scotland Yard, which collates information concerning drug activities nation-wide. The tables produced by the Unit are elaborate and frequently updated. Values are expressed by region and will reflect a variety of important factors, including the purity of the drug. The voluntary organisation, Release also gathers information relating to values and use.

In *Afzal, The Times*, June 25, 1991, the Court of Appeal remarked that prosecuting counsel should take great care to ensure that correct figures in respect of the street value of the drug were placed before the Court. Accordingly, where the appellants thought they were importing heroin of reasonable quality which in fact had a purity as low as one per cent, then the Court would be entitled to have regard to what the appellants thought they had done but some reduction was required because the *actus reus* was not as serious as in cases where the level of purity was higher with greater devastating consequences.

In so far as the street value of a drug is relevant to sentence, two points should be borne in mind. The street value of a drug should not be slavishly followed by the Courts as being the only relevant criterion for the purposes of applying the sentencing guideline expressed in *Aramah* (1983) 76 Cr.App.R. 190 and *Bilinski* (1988) 86 Cr.App.R. 146. Secondly, street values vary as monetary values and market forces vary.

The reader is invited to read Chapter 11 in relation to expert evidence.

C. SENTENCING GUIDELINES

I. INTRODUCTION

15–08 Sentencing attitudes quickly change and it would be idle to pretend that sentencing decisions do not reflect attitude "swings" over the years. Thus, in *Pandit* [1974] Crim.L.R. 60, a 35-year-old man, with no previous convictions, was sentenced to 18 months' imprisonment after he pleaded guilty to the importation of 27.5 grams of cannabis for his own use. His sentence was upheld on appeal. Again, in *Daher* (1969) 53 Cr.App.R. 490, a sentence of three years' imprisonment was upheld where D unlawfully imported approximately five kilograms of cannabis resin in the false bottom of a suitcase. The defendant was then aged 19, of good character and had been recruited as a drugs runner in the Lebanon. Such cases are rightly to be regarded as being out of line with current sentencing policy.

During the 1970s and the early 1980s, the Courts of the United Kingdom were experiencing a then unprecedented number of drug trafficking cases, including importations, coming before them. Courts that were local to busy airports and seaports developed their own routines and procedures for the management of such cases and, to some extent, they established their own sentencing tariffs to take account of matters of particular concern in their area. Regional variations in sentencing could be explained for many different reasons, *e.g.* prevalence or the type and Class of drug involved. The United Kingdom has long been the staging-post for the onward transmission of drugs to other countries by virtue of our geographical position in the world, and it is usually not possible to tell whether a drug imported is intended for "home" consumption or not. Some routes are more popular with smugglers in respect of one Class, or type, of drug than another, or one method of importing a drug is prevalent in one area but not in another. Countries differed (and still do) in their response to drug trafficking.

(a) Guidelines to determine the parameters of sentencing

There is no doubt that sentencing guidelines have proved to be of considerable assistance to practitioners and judges: they assist judges to set appropriate tariffs according to law; practitioners may more easily explain sentencing policy to clients; and guidelines promote consistency in sentencing. However, as the commentary to the decision of the Court of Appeal in *Hurley* [1997] Crim.L.R. 840 demonstrates, some concern was expressed as to the way cases were selected for providing guidelines, and more importantly, whether the procedure for putting information before the Court of Appeal in guideline cases was adequate. Occasionally, the parties (acting adversarially of course) called such witnesses as they were minded to call in the hearing of a guideline case: see *Hurley* [1998] 1 Cr.App.R.(S.) 299, and *Aranguren* (1994) 99 Cr.App.R. 347, for just two examples. It should not be forgotten that in *Aramah* it was the Court that took the initiative in framing guidelines. 15–09

Now, however, the Sentencing Advisory Panel exists (Chairman Professor Martin Wasik) (see s.80, Crime and Disorder Act 1998). The Court of Appeal would now seek the assistance of SAP if it wished to give sentencing guidelines of a general nature, as required under section 81(2) of that Act. There are signs that SAP will be more proactive in sentencing matters, commissioning research, and consulting generally. The Police Foundation Independent Inquiry had much to say about the sentencing of offenders in drug cases, and recognised the invaluable role that SAP is likely to play in future "drug" guideline cases (March, 2000 Chapter 4, para.41, recommendation 23, and see overview):

> "With regard to all trafficking offences, we believe that much would be gained by statutory sentencing guidelines and we hope that the new Sentencing Advisory Panel will so advise the Court of Appeal. Such guidelines should incorporate the aggravating factors to which we believe the Courts should have consistent regard in their sentencing. Key aggravating factors which should be included are: the involvement of an organised criminal group; the use of violence or firearms; the use of children or young persons in trafficking activities; supply to minors; the commission of the offence in the vicinity of schools, psychiatric facilities or prisons; and public nuisance elements in the offence."

15–10 Accordingly, although Parliament will continue to set sentencing maxima, it will be the Court of Appeal that frames guidelines—after receiving assistance from SAP. Nevertheless, it will remain open to the Courts to "tweak" existing guidelines or to deal with particular aspects of sentencing that give effect to existing law: and see *Twisse* (November 7, 2000).

By 1982, the Court of Appeal in *Aramah* (1982) 76 Cr. App. R. 190 decided that the time had come to give some guidance as to the level of sentences that could reasonably be imposed for drug offences principally in connection with offences of drug smuggling (s.3 MDA and s.170 CEMA); supplying a controlled drug (s.4 MDA); and possession with intent to supply a controlled drug (s.5 (3) MDA) where the drug involved was either of Class A (*e.g.* heroin and cocaine) or Class B cannabis.

However, the guidelines given in 1982 were based on two very different criteria depending on whether the drug was Class A (*i.e.* by its street value) or cannabis (by its weight). In *Marintinez* (1984) 6 Cr. App. R. (S) 364, it was made clear that the *Aramah* guidelines did not distinguish between different drugs in Class A. The Court of Appeal suggested that the probable reason for the different approaches in respect of the two types of drug could be explained on the grounds that cannabis is not normally adulterated before it is used or sold whereas many powdered drugs will be reduced in purity by the addition of other materials (which may or may not be inert) before being sold or used: *Aranguren* (1994) 99 Cr. App. R. 347.

15–11 The guidelines were modified in *Bilinski* (1988) 86 Cr. App. R. 146 but only in relation to consignments of Class A drugs worth £100,000 or more and this was done to reflect the increase in the maximum sentence permitted for trafficking in such drugs namely, life imprisonment: see the Controlled Drugs (Penalties) Act 1985. In any event, in *Gilmore, The Times*, May 21, 1986 the Court of Appeal felt that "the time had come" when it was necessary to move up the level of sentencing for such offences. May L.J. expressed the same view in *Ansari* (1985) 7 Cr.App.R.(S) 312, CA and again in *Obliyaei* (October 14, 1985; unreported) although, in both cases, the Court of Appeal felt constrained to apply the guidelines in *Aramah*. *Satvir Singh* (1988) 10 Cr. App. R(S) 402 modified the tariff, suggested in *Aramah*, that the starting point for any supply of a Class A drug should seldom be less than three years' imprisonment to five years' imprisonment: and see *Samuels* (1990) 12 Cr. App. R (S) 118 and, more recently, *Twisse*.

The Court in *Bilinski* made no other changes to the guidelines in *Aramah*. However, at the time *Bilinski* was decided, confusion arose as to whether the sentences suggested in *Aramah*, in so far as they related to drugs in Class B, were too low: see, for example, *Beaumont* [1987] Crim.L.R. 786, a case concerning the supply of cannabis. Since that time, a line of cases repeated that the sentencing guidelines expressed in *Aramah* (1983) 76 Cr.App.R. 190 remained the same, notwithstanding increased penalties in respect of Class A drugs under the Controlled Drugs (Penalties) Act 1985: see *Daly* (1988) 9 Cr.App.R.(S) 519 but note the reservations expressed in *Fleming* (1989) 89 Cr.App.R. 225 and see *Ronchetti* [1998] 2 Cr.App.R.(S.) 100.

(b) Guidelines given to declare the courts' domestic and international policy

Apart from giving guidance to practitioners and sentencers, the decision in *Aramah* served another function which was to demonstrate this country's commitment to tackling, through the medium of law enforcement, what was already regarded as an international problem. Thus, Lord Lane C.J. said: 15–12

> "Consequently, anything which the Courts of this country can do by way of deterrent sentences on those found guilty of crimes involving these Class A drugs should be done."

The attitude of the British courts towards sentencing in respect of drug trafficking offences is not dissimilar to that of the Australian courts. In *McCarthy v. The Queen* (1988) 38 A. Crim.R. 407 it was held that those who deal in heroin in substantial quantities must expect to be treated harshly. It is not relevant to argue that the sentence imposed results in a release date similar to that which would apply, had life imprisonment been imposed: *Wong* (1988) 39 A.Crim.R. 1 (New South Wales Court of Criminal Appeal). The effectiveness of current sentencing practice has been much debated, but it is a topic beyond the scope of this book. However, see the Police Foundation Independent Inquiry Report (March, 2000) as an introduction to this topic.

(c) Sentencing and Article 6 of the Human Rights Act 1998/ECHR

It is well established that a defendant is to be sentenced on the basis of what is proved or admitted (*e.g.* by way of offences to be taken into consideration). Despite some doubts expressed in the mid 1990s, it is now clear that this principle means that a defendant ought not to be sentenced on the basis of specimen or sample counts on the indictment. There should be appropriate counts on the indictment, and in sufficient number, to enable the sentencer to impose the proper penalties on the defendant: see *Barry* (July 30, 1996, unreported, CA, disapproving *Clark* [1996] 2 Cr. App. R.(S) 282) but see now *Canavan and Kidd* [1998] 1 Cr. App. R.(S) 243, *Brown* [2000] 1 Cr. App. R.(S) 300, *Djahit* [1999] 2 Cr. App. R.(S) 142, and *Twisse* (November 7, 2000). In *Twisse*, it was suggested that if the prosecution can prove that a defendant has been acting as a supplier over a substantial period of time, it can put the Court in a position to sentence properly by (i) charging a number of offences of supplying or possession of drugs at different dates; or (ii) by charging the defendant with conspiracy to supply over a prescribed period; or (iii) by charging him with being concerned in the supply of a controlled drug over a specified time, contrary to section 4(3)(b) of the Misuse of Drugs Act 1971. However, with respect, the third of those options, may or may not be well founded. There is as yet no clear definitive statement as to whether section 4(3)(b) is an "activity" offence or not. Note that the Government has rejected the 15–13

Independent Inquiry's recommendation that there should be an offence of "dealing". The Inquiry said:

> "... We see the need to strengthen the law's armoury against supply by creating a new offence of *dealing which would allow the Courts to sentence for a course of conduct rather than only for an isolated act of supply*. We also found a need for change in the offences relating to premises, paraphernalia, the cultivation of cannabis and the regulations relating to the therapeutic use of cannabis. In each case our aim has been to enhance the law's capacity to reduce harm where those who use drugs are concerned, and to concentrate in line with the national strategy on those who produce, process, distribute and sell them." [emphasis added]

II. What is the Legal Status of a Guideline Case?

15–14 It has been said by one commentator that *Aramah* constitutes "a restatement of existing sentencing policy and a convenient source of reference rather that a change of direction" [1983] Crim. L.R. 273. There is some truth in that statement but the decision in *Aramah* came as a surprise to many practitioners who had become accustomed to witnessing sentencing tariffs evolving, rather than being set out, in respect of a range of offences of a particular class. Although, in reality, the Court did provide "guidelines" this is not a description which was used by Lord Lane C.J. who said no more than that the Court thought it "may be of assistance if they made "some general observations".

By contrast, in *Aranguren* (1994) 99 Cr. App. R. 347, which is now the leading case on sentencing tariffs for Class A drugs in powdered form, the present Lord Chief Justice described *Aramah* as having "laid down" sentencing guidelines. In reality, that may be so but at the time that *Aramah* was decided there was some uncertainty as to the status of sentencing guidelines in English law. They have long been regarded by the Courts as being more than just persuasive but, occasionally, they have been described by commentators, as being *obiter*. Whatever term is applied, cases decided after *Aramah* emphasised that sentencing guidelines are not to be thought of as "laying down" rigid rules, to be applied strictly in every case (see *Nicholas, The Times*, April 23, 1986; and *Brown*, unreported, 1986) and that a sense of proportion is necessary in the application of the guidelines to sentencing problems: *Morris, The Times*, November 22, 1988. There is nothing in *Aranguren* which modifies that perspective and indeed, the Lord Chief Justice stressed that:

> "There are, of course, other important factors for the sentencing judge to consider such as the role played by the individual defendant, whether he has previously been convicted of drugs offences and, by way of mitigation, whether he has pleaded guilty or rendered assistance to the prosecuting authority."

In *Aranguren*, counsel on behalf of some of the appellants may have had this topic in mind because he argued that the revised guidelines should apply only to future cases and not to the cases then being considered. The Court disagreed and held that their duty "is to see whether by [the revised guidelines] the sentences passed were either wrong in principle or manifestly excessive" (at 352). Perhaps, as seems likely, the argument on behalf of the appellant Aranguren was, that a decision by the Court to dismiss his appeal against a sentence of eight years' imprisonment for the unlawful importation of cocaine on the basis of the revised guidelines put him in a worse position than if the guidelines in *Aramah* remained valid. However, as the Court pointed out, one of the problems of using street values as the sentencing criteria, is that if the price of a single "deal" is reduced or increased by market forces, then the value of a large consignment of the drug will show a marked change in value and thus the sentence is determined partly by market forces rather than by the culpability of the offender. The Court recognised that measuring street values is often difficult and imprecise and that the "effect of this imprecision is that prosecution figures for average price may be challenged and where this occurs, the judicial response may vary" (at 351). Consider also the guidance given by the Court of Appeal in *Graham* (January 12, 1999) in relation to the application of the guidelines. 15–15

By contrast, in Scotland, there is no tariff in sentencing and accordingly cases such as *Aramah* and *Aranguren* are of persuasive effect only: see *Kenmure v. Lowe*, 1990 S.C.C.R. 367 and Robert Shiels, "Controlled Drugs and Assistance to the Authorities", 1991 S.L.T. 187.

III. Sentencing Guidelines for Cocaine (Salt) and Heroin in Excess of 500 Grams

The leading guideline case now is *Aranguren* (1994) 99 Cr. App. R. 347. That case was decided by the Court of Appeal on June, 20 1994 but it has been reported in the name of *Aroyewumi and others* in the Criminal Law Review [1994] Crim. L.R. 695. The Court of Appeal had to consider five appeals against sentences of imprisonment for offences of being knowingly concerned in the importation of cocaine and (in the case of "Gould") possessing cocaine with intent to supply it. *Aranguren* revised the guidelines for Class A drugs by expressing them in terms of the weight of a drug (assuming 100 per cent purity) rather than street value. It was in *Patel* [1987] Crim. L.R. 838 that reform of the guidelines was suggested. In *Patel*, the Court remarked that the use of street values as an aid to sentencing was to be approached with caution but, provided such values were used as a rough yardstick, there was no reason why the Courts should not measure the length of sentence to some degree by it. The case of *Patel* reinforced the observations made in *Afzal* (above) as to the importance of putting before the Court reliable figures and information: see also Kay, "Aramah and Street Value of Drugs" [1987] Crim.L.R. 814. These difficulties are 15–16 removed if the relevant criteria for sentencing can be determined by weight rather than by street value. Accordingly, the Court held that for the yardsticks established in *Bilinski*, there should be substituted the following:

(i) a sentence of 10 years' imprisonment and upwards would be appropriate where the weight of the drug at 100 per cent purity was of the order of 500 grams or more, but

(ii) where the weight was five kilograms or more (at 100 per cent purity) then sentences of 14 years or higher were appropriate.

15–17 In *Aranguren* (1994) 99 Cr. App. R. 347, the Court of Appeal looked to see if the revised guidelines were broadly in line with sentences imposed under *Aramah* and *Bilinski* and held that they are:

> "To check the suggested figures, we have compared the sentences they would support with the sentences actually passed in reported cases where the weight and purity of the drug is quoted. We are satisfied that the figures suggested would support sentences in line with those reported. To take, for example, the guideline case of *Bilinski*, the seizure was 3.306 kilograms of heroin, 90 per cent pure. Its street value was said to be £600,000. The equivalent weight of 100 per cent pure heroin would have been 2.73 kilograms. £100,000 worth of 100 per cent pure drug would therefore have been 2.73/6 kilograms = 455 grams, approaching half a kilogram. It was said in *Bilinski* (at p.149) that 'a term of 12 years or thereabouts would have been appropriate . . . in the absence of any mitigating factors'. £1 million worth would be 2.73/6 × 10 kilograms = 4.55 kilograms or approaching five kilograms."

(a) Making the conversion to 100 per cent purity

15–18 The formula to be applied is merely actual weight x actual % = weight @ 100%. Unfortunately, this is not verified if the calculation made in *Aranguren* is used as an example because, using the figures published in the law reports, 3.306 x 90 per cent does not equate with 2.73. However, this is easily explained: there is a typographical error in the reports: the actual weight in *Bilinski* was 3.035 kilograms and that produces the results referred to in the judgment in *Aranguren*.

(b) Points to note

15–19 *Aranguren* is only concerned with Class A drugs. It does not alter the previous position in respect of Class B drugs.

Aranguren does not apply to any case involving tablets, or units or doses (*e.g.* LSD, see now *Hurley* [1998] 1 Cr.App.R.(S.) 299 for sentencing guidance in relation to that drug).

Aramah and *Bilinski* will continue to provide some assistance when considering offences of supplying, possession and possession with intent to supply, contrary to the MDA 1971 where the amount of a Class A drug involved is significantly less than 500 grams.

It is clear that the Court in *Aranguren* was not seeking to introduce an arithmetic formula so that the length of sentence was in direct proportion to the weight of the drug seized. In order that some sense of proportion in sentencing is maintained, previous sentencing decisions including *Aramah* and *Bilinski* should be considered.

It makes no difference whether the drug was intended for exportation: *Powell, The Times*, October 5, 2000.

Aranguren is relevant to drug trafficking cases other than importation/ exportation offences. It is likely that the Court focused on importation cases, in order to identify the appropriate benchmark. A factor, relevant to sentence, is the closeness of the offender to the source of the production or importation of the drug. To express the same point in another way, it is relevant to ascertain an offender's place in the chain of distribution of the drug: see *Satvir Singh* (1988) 10 Cr. App. R.(S) 402. 15–20

Purity analysis is essential for sentencing purposes in cases that involve cocaine, heroin or amphetamine in excess of 500 grams: see *Morris* (July 14, 2000).

IV. Sentencing Guidelines for Class A Drugs—Less Than 500 Grams

(a) Supplying heroin—*Aramah* guidelines

"The sentence will largely depend on the degree of involvement, the amount of trafficking and the value of drug being handled", (*per* Lord Lane C.J.: *Aramah* (1983) 76 Cr.App.R. 190, 192). A sentence of less than five years would seldom be justified: see *Satvir Singh* (1988) 10 Cr. App. R.(S) 402. The nearer the source of supply the defendant was shown to be, the heavier would be the sentence. The matter was again considered in *Djahit* [1999] 2 Cr. App. R.(S) 142, and more recently in *Twisse* (November 7, 2000). In that case, the Court looked at a wide range of reported cases dealing with all Class A drugs and the sentences imposed over a period extending from 1988 to date. Lord Justice Kennedy said: 15–21

> "All indicate a sentencing bracket, on the hypothesis put forward by Hooper J, of between 5 and 7 years: in other words, as the judge said, an offender may expect about 6 years' imprisonment, which can be increased or mitigated in the way he outlined."

Purity analysis is necessary if the Court is being invited to sentence on the basis that the defendant is close to the source of supply or if it is alleged by the prosecution that the defendant is a wholesaler of the drug: see *Morris* (July 14, 2000).

(b) Simple possession of heroin—*Aramah* guidelines

15–22 "It is at this level that the circumstances of the individual offender become of much greater importance. Indeed the possible variety of considerations is so wide, including often those of a medical nature, that it is impossible to lay down any practical guidelines. . . . The maximum penalty for simple possession of Class A drugs is seven years' imprisonment and a fine, and there will be very many cases where deprivation of liberty is both appropriate and expedient". (*per* Lord Lane C.J., *Aramah*, above, 193.)

V. Sentencing Guidelines for Ecstacy

15–23 In *Aranguren* (1994) 16 Cr. App. R. (S) 211, the Court of Appeal declined to provide guidelines for Ecstasy until it heard further evidence and argument. Ecstasy may appear in powdered form but the drug is usually encountered as tablets or capsules. Strictly speaking, there is no such drug as Ecstasy but it is the label used to describe at least three substances

(i) MDMA (*i.e.* "3, 4 Methylene-dioxy-N- methylamphetamine";
(ii) MDEA (*i.e.* "3,4 Methyene-Dioxy-Ethyl-Amphetamine") and
iii) MDA (*i.e.* "3, 4 Methylene-Dioxy-Amphetamine". Ecstasy has been controlled since 1977: see the MDA 1971 (Modification) Order 1977, S.I. 1977 No. 1243 which inserted sub-paragraph (c) in to the list of Class A drugs in Part 1; para. 1 of Sched. 2 of the 1971 Act and see *Couzens and Frankel* [1992] Crim. L.R. 822.

In *Warren and Beeley* [1996] 1 Cr. App. R. (S) 233, the Court of Appeal heard evidence as to the nature, uses and effects of Ecstasy. Although tablets and capsules vary in the content of the active constituent (between 75 milligrams to 125 milligrams) the Court took an average of 100 milligrams per tablet. Thus 10,000 tablets (at 100 milligrams of Ecstasy per tablet) contains 1 kilogram of the drug. This was an important step because the *Arunguren* guidelines are expressed in terms of 500 grams (10 years+) and 5,000 grams (*i.e.* 5 kilograms; 14 years+). Accordingly, the Court of Appeal in *Warren and Beeley* held that the tariff in regard to offences concerning Ecstasy could be maintained substantially at the same levels as in relation to other Class A drugs: thus,

- for 5,000 or more tablets the sentence would be in the order of 10 years' imprisonment and upwards;
- for 50,000 or more tablets the sentence would be in the order of 14 years' imprisonment and upwards. The Court emphasised that the criteria are by way of guidance only and that the quantity of the tablets or the weight is only one factor to be considered in deciding the appropriate sentence. The "role of the offender, his plea, any assistance he may have given to the authorities are some, but not all, of the other considerations which the Court will have to weigh." *per* Lord Taylor C.J. (at 237).

If the analysis reveals a substantially different content of the drug in any given case "then the weight of the constituent will be a determinative factor" (237). It follows that the sentencer, and practitioners, should ensure that the Court is provided with a sufficiently clear analyst's report in order that the Court may carry out its task in accordance with the guidelines: see, however, *Morris* (July 14, 2000). Where a judge passes a sentence on the basis of a misapprehension of his powers he is at liberty to vary the sentence within the period permitted by statute: and see *Hadley* [1995] Crim. L.R. 86. 15–24

It should also be noted that there is nothing wrong with random sampling to determine the purity of the drug in question. It is unnecessary to examine all the drugs. However, it is submitted that it is important for the analyst to approach this matter in a scientific, logical manner: and see *Carnegie v Findlay*, 2000 S.C.C.R. 873.

VI. Guidelines in Respect of LSD

Guidelines were given in *Hurley* [1998] 1 Cr. App. R.(S) 299 as to the appropriate level of sentencing in cases involving LSD. In the 1960s, LSD was used for strong psychedelic experiences whereas in recent years that seems not to be the case. Thus, the quantity of LSD per dosage unit seems now to be much lower than it was in the 1960s. The guidelines of the Court of Appeal are based on the quantity of LSD in the unit rather than the sheer number of units recovered. Street value is only a factor to be taken into account—if at all. 15–25

- 25,000 units @ 50 micrograms: 10 years' imprisonment
- 250,000 units @ 50 micrograms: 14 years' imprisonment and upwards

Again, adjustment may be made where purity more or less than 50 micrograms. The role played by the offender will obviously be highly relevant.

In *Morris, The Times*, August 4, 2000, the Court of Appeal said that weight of the drug could generally be assessed by reference to the number of units on an assumption that each unit contained 50 micrograms of LSD. Analysis would not normally be desirable or necessary where the defendant was in possession of a small amount of the drug for personal use or for supply to a limited number of persons.

VII. Guidelines in Respect of Opium

In *Mashaollahi* [2001] 1 Cr. App. R. 106 the Court of Appeal gave guidance following recommendations made to it by the Sentencing Advisory Panel set up under the 1998 Crime and Disorder Act. The guidelines are as follows: 15–26

- 40 kilograms or more: 14 years' imprisonment and upwards

- 10 kilograms or more: 10 years' imprisonment and upwards
- if to be converted into heroin or morphine assume 10 units of average purity to make 1 unit of heroin or morphine

VIII. Guidelines for Amphetamine

15–27 In *Wijs* [1998] 2 Cr. App. R. 436, the Court of Appeal gave the following guidance:

• up to 500 grams:	up to 2 years' imprisonment
• 500 grams to 2.5 kilograms:	2 to 4 years' imprisonment
• 2.5 kilograms to 10 kilograms:	4 to 7 years' imprisonment
• 10 kilograms to 15 kilograms:	7 to 10 years' imprisonment
• 15 kilograms and over:	up to 14 years' imprisonment

The Court opined that the penalty for importing a controlled drug would usually be higher than for possession with intent to supply it. However, it is submitted that it is better to look to the role played by the defendant whether a defendant is charged under the Misuse of Drugs Act or CEMA 1979 may depend on which law enforcement agency has investigated the matter.

IX. Guidelines in Respect of Cannabis

15–28 Cannabis was singled out by the Court of Appeal in *Aramah* as being the drug most likely to be exercising the minds of the Courts.

(a) Importation

• Massive quantities:	10 years
• Over 20 kilograms:	3 to 6 years
• Up to 20 kilograms:	18 months to 3 years

(b) Supply

• Massive quantities:	10 years
• Other cases:	1 to 4 years

In *Ronchetti and others* [1998] 2 Cr. App. R.(S) 100, the Court of Appeal gave guidance to sentencers "by way of addendum" to *Aramah*, where the amount of the drug was in the order of 100 kilograms:

• 100 kilograms:	7 to 8 years' imprisonment
• 500 kilograms or more:	10 years' imprisonment
• "larger importations":	will attract a higher starting point.

15–29 The guidelines are expressed on the basis that the defendant contested the case and that s/he played more than a subordinate role. In *Ronchetti*, the Court did not distinguish between cannabis (herbal) and cannabis resin. It did say that the fact that a court might one day have to deal with an even greater quantity of the drug was not by itself a reason for not imposing the maximum sentence where those at the top of an organisation are before the Court.

(c) **Possession—*Aramah* guidelines**

• Small amounts/personal use:	Fines
• Persistent flouting:	Possible custodial

D. GENERAL PRINCIPLES OF SENTENCING

A detailed schedule of recent sentencing appears in the schedule at Appendix 2. Previous editions of this book have set out detailed case summaries of earlier cases but the schedule no longer makes this necessary. In any event, it is important to bear in mind that sentencing cases more than ten years old are of less value because there have been many developments in sentencing law and practice over that time, for example, the Criminal Justice Acts of 1991 and 1993; the Crime (Sentences) Act 1997; and now the Powers of the Criminal Courts (Sentencing) Act 2000 (as amended); and the Criminal Justice and Court Services Act 2000. **15–30**

The most important consideration in applying sentencing guidelines in cases of unlawful drug smuggling has been said to be the defendant's position in the drug smuggling venture: see *Hussain, The Times*, June 27, 1990. Substantial credit should be given in appropriate cases in respect of pleas of guilty or co-operation with the authorities.

It is not always appropriate to assess the seriousness of the offence by reference solely to the quantity of drugs involved. Some regard should be given to the method of importation, the degree of organisation and the difficulty of detection: *Kouadio, The Times*, February 21, 1991. It is not valid mitigation that the defendant was in transit to another country and that the drug was not intended for distribution in the United Kingdom: see *Gasper* (1988) 10 Cr.App.R.(S) 173. **15–31**

Similarly, where a defendant produces a controlled drug by experimental means in this country, the trial judge is entitled to take into account the fact that the purpose of the experiment was to produce the drug on a large scale in another country: see *Couzens, The Times*, April 17, 1992. The fact that production of the drug would be lawful by the laws of that other country is irrelevant if the drug is to be unlawfully distributed elsewhere.

As far as mitigation is concerned, it was said in *Aramah* (1983) 76 Cr.App.R. 190 that a confession of guilt coupled with considerable assistance to the police could properly be marked by a substantial reduction in what would otherwise be the proper sentence and this appears to have been endorsed in *Aranguren* and *Warren and Beeley*.

(a) The value of citing sentencing decisions

15–32 As the Court of Appeal has remarked on several occasions, yardsticks for the purposes of sentencing provide guidance only and must not be seen as laying down rigid rules to be applied strictly in every case: see *Nicholas, The Times*, April 23, 1986, *per* Lord Lane C.J. and *Brown* (June 16, 1986, unreported, 769B86).

For this reason, the extent to which "guideline" cases and other sentencing authorities may properly be cited has yet to be satisfactorily resolved. The author once heard Lord Widgery C.J. severely castigate counsel for citing such authorities to the Court on the grounds that each case had to be decided on its own facts. In *De Havilland* (1983) 5 Cr.App.R.(S) 109 (at 114), Dunn L.J. fired "a warning shot" regarding the increasing practice of citing sentencing decisions of the Court of Appeal when he said:

> ". . . the appropriate sentence is a matter for the discretion of the sentencing judge. It follows that decisions on sentencing are not binding authorities. . . . Indeed they could not be, since the circumstances of the offence and of the offender present an almost infinite variety from case to case. Occasionally this Court suggests guidelines for sentences. . . . But the sentencer retains his discretion within the guidelines, or even to depart from them if the particular circumstances of the case justify departure."

By contrast, in *McEvilly, The Times*, November 4, 1986, CA, Lord Lane C.J. expressed the view that public money expended on unnecessary sentencing appeals might have been avoided if *Current Sentencing Practice* (Sweet & Maxwell, loose-leaf edition) had been drawn to the trial judge's attention. It is submitted that there can be nothing improper in the citation of "guideline" cases but the value in citing other sentencing cases must be a matter of professional judgment.

It is plain that both the Court of Appeal, and judges of the Crown Court, are assisted in their task if sentencing decisions are cited in a sensible and appropriate fashion.

(b) The Courts' attitude towards couriers

15–33 In *Aramah* (1983) 76 Cr.App.R. 190, the Court of Appeal remarked that the good character of a courier, as he usually was, is of less importance than the good character of a defendant in other cases. In the judgment of the Court, the reason why this should be is that drug-smuggling organisers deliberately recruit persons who will exercise the sympathy of the Court. Thus, students, the sick, and the elderly were (and are) often employed as couriers. They are vulnerable to suggestion and vulnerable to the offer of quick profit. The Court was concerned that such smugglers would also believe that the Courts might be moved to misplaced sympathy in their cases. Similar considerations had been voiced a year earlier by Lawton L.J.

in *Hamouda* (1982) 4 Cr.App.R.(S) 137; see also *Anderson* [1981] Crim.L.R. 270.

It is a fact that many couriers are extremely vulnerable. Many of them are from overseas, often astonishingly uneducated, poor, naive and frequently have never travelled beyond their own region let alone to another country. They are therefore easy targets for the smuggler. Furthermore, they are expendable. They are easy targets for the officers of Customs and Excise who quickly spot a bewildered, nervous and sometimes plainly inept visitor. By imposing deterrent sentences on couriers, the Courts in this country, and elsewhere, hope that the "word will be spread" and so deter others from acting as couriers. However, achieving success in that way perhaps depends on the making of too many assumptions which, given the vulnerability of the type of person being considered, cannot realistically be made. Having said that, the Courts are undoubtedly put in a very difficult position. For a discussion as to the effectiveness of current sentencing practice see the Police Foundation Independent Inquiry Report (March, 2000), and see Green, *Drugs, Trafficking and Criminal Policy* (Waterside Press, 1998), and *Drug Couriers* (Quartet Books, 1996).

(c) *Newton* hearings/factual basis for sentence

It has to be remembered that a courier may not always know precisely what he is carrying. He may be told that it is something prohibited from importation into England but he does not always appreciate what the substance is, *e.g.* cannabis or heroin. Although narcotics are expensive to buy in the United Kingdom, drugs such as heroin and cannabis are astonishingly cheap to buy in the producing country and it would be idle to suppose that some organisers do not think it tactically advantageous to keep the courier "in the dark" as to the precise substance he will be asked to carry. For the purposes of a charge under the CEMA it does not matter what the defendant believes the goods to be so long as he knew them to be prohibited from importation: see *Hussain* [1969] 2 Q.B. 567, and *Hennessey* (1978) 68 Cr.App.R. 419. Again, for the purposes of a charge under the MDA, his ignorance (subject to section 28 of the Act) as to the quality of the thing, will afford him no defence. But a mistaken belief that the offending drug is of a different kind from that which he had been told it was is a mitigating factor: see *Ghandi* (1986) 8 Cr.App.R.(S) 391, and similarly, a mistaken belief that the goods imported were of a totally different character, *e.g.* pornographic videos, is also a mitigating factor: see *Ellis* (1987) 84 Cr.App.R. 235, 248; and see *White (Eileen)* [1999] 1 Cr. App. R.(S) 325. 15–34

However, in *Bilinski* (1988) 86 Cr.App.R. 146, B pleaded guilty to importing 3.036 kilograms of heroin. He claimed that he believed the packages contained cannabis although a book found in his possession seemed to relate to the topic of heroin. He was sentenced to 12 years' imprisonment. The trial judge had taken the view that the appellant's belief was irrelevant and therefore declined to hear evidence about it in accordance with the principles set out in *Newton* (1982) 4 Cr.App.R.(S)388. The Court of Appeal held that the appellant's belief was relevant to sentence and that the man who believed he was importing cannabis was less culpable than the man who knew it to be heroin. However, to what extent such a belief mitigated the sentence would depend on the facts in each case including the degree of care exercised by a defendant. In *Bilinski*, the mitigating effect of B's belief (if held) was small but the appeal was allowed on that and other grounds.

15–35 If a defendant's story is patently false then the judge is entitled to reject it without hearing evidence: see *Hawkins* (1985) 7 Cr.App.R.(S) 351 and *Bilinski* (ibid.). The decision of *Mackenzie* (1985) 7 Cr.App.R.(S) 441, which suggested a contrary proposition, may no longer be good law and see *Broderick* [1994] Crim. L.R. 139.

Furthermore, the calling of evidence if disbelieved, or if it only repeated an absurd and spurious explanation given by a defendant, may considerably nullify any discount to be gained from a plea of guilty: see *Walton* [1987] Crim.L.R. 512; *Stevens* (1986) 8 Cr.App.R.(S) 297; *Jauncey* (1986) 8 Cr.App.R.(S) 401 and *Mackenzie* (above).

If the trial judge does accept the defendant's explanation, the next question is to what extent is the sentencer bound to sentence the defendant on his explanation?

A mistaken belief as to the type of goods imported or handled is only a mitigating consideration. It does not entitle the defendant to be sentenced on that basis as such at all. The defendant's mistake may and probably will result in the sentence being reduced depending on the facts of the case (including the degree of care exercised by him). The discount may be substantial or it may be negligible: see *Bilinski* (above).

15–36 Not every contentious issue raised during mitigation is a suitable matter for inquiry by the trial judge: see *Long and Jones* (May 12, 1998). So where a defendant with many previous convictions alleges that he has changed his lifestyle and reformed himself, a *Newton* hearing is not appropriate: *Odey* (1984) 6 Cr.App.R.(S) 318, CA. But where a defendant claims that he imported a large quantity of drugs for his own consumption then this is just the sort of case where a judge should hold a *Newton* hearing unless the suggestion is so absurd that it can be rejected out of hand: *Meah and Marlow* (1991) 92 Cr.App.R. 254. In that case, Meah unlawfully imported 150 packets of heroin (136 grams of 37 per cent purity worth £16,930) of which almost 70 packets had been swallowed. Marlow unlawfully imported 71 packets of heroin (worth £6,806) of which 32 packets had been swallowed. In each case, the appellants claimed that the drugs were intended for personal consumption. In neither case did the judge hold a *Newton* hearing. In reducing Meah's sentence from six years to three years, and Marlow's sentence from four years to two years, the Court of Appeal held that in having declined to hold a *Newton* hearing, the judge had to sentence on the basis that he had accepted that these large quantities of the drugs were intended for personal consumption.

If a judge does think it right to sentence on the basis that drugs have been brought in for a man's personal consumption, it will still be a serious offence and, if the quantity is substantial, the result may well be immediate imprisonment for a substantial period The reader should also be mindful of the observations of the Court of Appeal in *Mohun* [1992] Crim.L.R. 598 and *Beswick* [1996] Crim. L.R. 62. In *Myers* [1996] Crim. L.R. 62, the Court of Appeal endorsed the practice of reducing to writing the basis on which a plea of guilty is tendered and accepted.

E. FACTORS THAT MIGHT AFFECT SENTENCE

The defence version must be accepted unless the judge, or the jury, is sure that it is wrong and the Court of Appeal will not interfere with the finding unless, for example, no reasonable tribunal could have reached that result: see *Ahmed* [1985] Crim.L.R. 250, CA (Parker L.J.). 15–37

Curiously, in *Hall* (October 19, 1984, unreported), Lincoln J. remarked that where the sentence is likely to be the same whichever version is accepted, it is undesirable that the trial judge should be seen to be adopting the prosecution version. If Lincoln J. meant no more than that the benefit of the doubt should be resolved in favour of the accused, then clearly there can be no complaint, but any tribunal, which is required to resolve conflicting versions, should not be slow to express frankly the version it accepts or rejects. This is so even where the judge considers that the sentence is likely to be the same.

(a) Personal circumstances of the defendant

There is a substantial deterrent element to sentences imposed in respect of drug trafficking offences. The personal considerations of an accused are secondary: see *Aramah* (1983) 76 Cr.App.R. 190. A graphic example of just how "secondary" these considerations can be appears in *Stark* [1992] Crim.L.R. 384. A sentence of four years' imprisonment was upheld for the unlawful importation of heroin worth £2,500. The appellant, who had been HIV positive, developed AIDS. His life expectancy was said to be no better than 12 months. The appellant said he wished to die in dignity. The Court of Appeal dismissed the appeal. There was a risk that the appellant would resort again to drug trafficking but, in any event, the Court said "It is not for the Court to manipulate the sentence to achieve a desirable social end": *per* Jowitt J. 15–38

The result in *Stark* is supported by other authority: see *Herasymenko* (unreported) and *Aramah*, *ibid*. However, the approach of the Courts has not been consistent in this regard. In *Saunders* (1992, unreported) the Court of Appeal reduced the sentence on the appellant convicted of offences of dishonesty (in relation to the "Guinness Affair") having regard to the appellant's physical and mental condition. The position of the Courts is now more flexible and health is not infrequently taken into account: see *Appleby* (May 22,

1996); *Bernard* (May 24, 1996); *Marchesi* (March 13, 1998); *Higgins* (December 10, 1998) and *Farrington* (February 12, 1999).

It is no mitigation to say that a certain drug (*e.g.* cannabis) is part of one's religion: see *Daudi* (1982) 4 Cr.App.R.(S) 306.

(b) No challenge by prosecution

15–39 Where an explanation is put forward by the defendant, which explanation the prosecution then choose not to challenge, the judge may consider it appropriate to sentence on that basis. Thus in *Lawless* [1981] Crim.L.R. 845, L pleaded guilty to possessing 960 grams of cannabis resin with intent to supply. He claimed that he bought the drug on behalf of a syndicate of five or six persons, and not with a view to resale. The prosecution did not challenge this version. The Court of Appeal reduced his sentence of two years' imprisonment so as to allow his immediate release (after having served nearly 12 months), on the grounds that the case could not be safely treated as a commercial venture.

Of course, if the trial judge feels uneasy about the matter he may, of his own volition, assess the defendant's version in accordance with the principles set out in *Newton*, above.

(c) Acceptance of pleas

15–40 When a defendant pleads guilty to "lesser counts", he is entitled to be sentenced on that basis. So where, in *Lawrence* (1981) 3 Cr.App.R.(S) 49, the appellant pleaded guilty to one count of cultivating cannabis plants and two counts of possessing cannabis resin, but pleaded not guilty to a further count of possessing a controlled drug with intent to supply (these being accepted by the Court), the judge was bound to deal with the appellant purely on the basis that the drugs were for his own consumption; and see *Long and Jones* (May 12, 1998).

In England and Wales, it would seem to be settled that a court may proceed to try an accused for an offence alleging possession of a controlled drug, with intent to supply it, contrary to section 5(3) of the MDA notwithstanding the fact that the accused has already entered a plea of guilty to simple possession of the same drug contrary to section 5(2): see *Bebbington* (1978) 67 Cr.App.R. 285, CA. If an accused is convicted of the section 5(3) offence, no separate penalty should be imposed for the lesser offence.

An admission by the accused to simple possession assists the prosecution to prove an essential element of an offence charged under section 5(3). If the prosecution, or the Court, anticipate the basis upon which a plea to simple possession is to be tendered (usually that the drug was intended for personal consumption) and that basis is not acceptable to the prosecution, or to the Court, then the Court need not accept such a plea, but proceed to try the accused on both counts.

In Scotland, an accused cannot be found guilty of more than one offence arising out of the same *species facti: Kyle v. H.M. Advocate*, 1988 S.L.T.

601. Accordingly, the Crown cannot competently pursue a charge of possession with intent to supply, in circumstances where the accused had entered a plea of guilty to simple possession on a basis inconsistent with the prosecution case, *e.g.* possession for personal use: *Mattison v. H.M. Advocate*, 1992 S.L.T. 197.

The defence must make the basis of plea clear: *Tolera* [1999] 1 Cr.App.R. 29; *Aldridge* (June 29, 1998).

(d) Specimen counts, etc.

The position is now governed by the decisions of the Court of Appeal in *Canavan and Kidd* [1998] 1 Cr. App. R.(S) 243, *Brown* [2000] 1 Cr. App. R.(S) 300, *Djahit* [1999] 2 Cr. App. R.(S) 142, and *Twisse* (November 7, 2000). Decisions such as *Barry* (July 30, 1996, unreported, CA, disapproving *Clark* [1996] 2 Cr. App. R.(S) 282) that are inconsistent with *Canavan*, should not be followed, or at least, if applied at all, applied carefully. 15–41

In *Ayensu* (1982) 4 Cr.App.R.(S) 248, the appellants pleaded guilty to one count of unlawfully importing 46.87 grams of cannabis. Their passports showed that they had made frequent trips between Ghana and the United Kingdom. They admitted to customs officers that they had smuggled cannabis into the United Kingdom on other occasions. A count alleging a conspiracy to import drugs was not pursued. Their counsel submitted that the plea represented the whole of their admissions. The Court of Appeal held that it was the task of the Crown Court to sentence on the basis of the particular offence. The Court could not take into account matters which were hotly contested, or the alleged admissions given to the customs officers.

Ayensu is in accord with the decision of *O'Conner* (1981) 3 Cr.App.R.(S) 225 but not, it would seem, with *Russen* (1981) 3 Cr.App.R.(S) 134 where the Court remarked that:

> "... the Court is perfectly entitled to look at a man's statement in order to discover if the incident in question is an isolated incident or not. When it appears perfectly clear from the statement that the event in question is not an isolated incident, the Court is entitled to take that into account when sentencing."

It is submitted that *Ayensu* and *O'Conner* are to be preferred.

(e) Assistance to law enforcement

This has long since been regarded as a powerful mitigating factor: see *Aramah* (1983) 76 Cr.App.R. 140. An immediate confession of guilt coupled with considerable assistance to the police or customs should therefore be marked by a substantial reduction in what would otherwise be the "proper sentence": see *Afzal, The Times,* October 14, 1989, *Sinfield*, 2 Cr. App. R.(S) 258, and see *Rose and others* 2 Cr. App. R.(S) 239. In *Yaman* (January 14, 1992; unreported), the Court of Appeal reduced the appel- 15–42 lant's sentence in respect of a conspiracy to supply three kilograms of heroin from 13 years' to 10 years' imprisonment after he had given "quite considerable assistance to police". Glidewell L.J. remarked "that fact does earn him the support of those concerned to stamp out this terrible trade". There is no set discount for co-operating with the police. All factors should be taken together in order to calculate the appropriate discount: *Sehitoglu and others* [1998] 1 Cr. App. R.(S) 89.

The Court will therefore take into account the extent of the assistance given and it should not overlook the degree of danger which can attach to such assistance being given.

15–43 In *Sivan* (1988) 87 Cr.App.R. 407 the Court gave guidance as to how the facts of any assistance given should be furnished to the Court in cases where the defendant was an informer:

> "First, it was advisable . . . that there should be before the Court a letter from a senior officer . . . unconnected with the case, who had examined all the facts and was able to certify that the facts were as reported by the officers conducting the investigation, that is, facts relating to the assistance rendered by the defendant.
>
> Second, . . . there had to be a statement in writing from the officer in charge of the investigation setting out those facts.
>
> Third, it was advisable in the more important cases that the officer in charge of the investigation should be available to give evidence if necessary, whether in court or in the judge's room as the situation might demand."

Additional guidance has been given by the Court of Appeal in *A and B* (April 23, 1998). See also: *Debbag* (1991) 12 Cr.App.R.(S) 733; *R. v. X* [1994] Crim. L.R. 469; *R v. C* (April 2, 1996); *Taylor* (June 10, 1996) and Robert Shiels, "Controlled Drugs and Assistance to the Authorities", 1991 S.L.T. 187.

(f) Social supplying

15–44 The presence of a commercial motive, even if the drugs were to be supplied to friends, is an aggravating feature. The fact that a person supplies other drug users or addicts is something of a "double-edged sword". In *Guiney* (1985) 7 Cr.App.R.(S) 200, a sentence of six years' imprisonment was reduced to four years where G had supplied other addicts with heroin. G was a "small-time supplier". See also *Hyams* (1983) 5 Cr.App.R.(S) 312 and *Gee* (1984) 6 Cr.App.R.(S) 86.

(g) Proceeds used to feed the addiction of the offender rather than profiteering

15–45 In *Leaver*, (*The Times*, March 14, 1989) it was held that there was no mitigation in asserting that the proceeds of supply were to enable the supplier to obtain for himself what he needed to feed his own addiction rather than to make a profit: and see *Lawrence* (*The Times*, December 1, 1988).

(h) Importing drugs intending to re-export them

There is in fact no mitigation at all in the argument that the drugs were merely in transit to another country, or were not intended for distribution in the United Kingdom: see *Mbelu* (1981) 3 Cr.App.R.(S) 157 and *Winter* [1973] Crim.L.R. 63, CA. 15–46

The drug trade is an international business carried on to the detriment of citizens of all civilised countries. Accordingly, this country owes a duty to other civilised countries to deter the trade: *per* Griffiths L.J. in *Otjen* (1981) 3 Cr.App.R.(S) 186, and see *Chukwu* (May 10, 1984, unreported, 1433C84).

(i) Is police entrapment mitigation?

In *Sang* [1980] A.C. 402, the House of Lords held that although a trial judge had no discretion, except in the case of confessions, to refuse to admit evidence merely because it had been improperly obtained, nevertheless, it could be a significant factor in mitigation. Lord Fraser of Tullybelton said (at 446 A-B.): 15–47

> "The degree of guilt may be modified by the inducement and that can appropriately be reflected in the sentence: see *Birtles* [1969] 1 W.L.R. 1047 and *Browning v. J.W.H. Watson (Rochester) Ltd* where Lord Goddard C.J. pointed out that the Court could even grant an absolute discharge in such circumstances."

Consequently, in *Petfield* (unreported, 407E86) Kennedy J. accepted that there had been police entrapment, which led to P and C possessing 1.78 kilograms of cannabis and 27.62 grams of amphetamine, with intent to supply it. The judge took account of it and sentenced P and C to 21 months' imprisonment and 12 months' imprisonment respectively.

Each case will of course depend on its own facts. It is well known that many drug operations, particularly elaborately planned ventures, are successfully prosecuted as a result of police or Customs and Excise "undercover" work. This may include an officer posing as an interested purchaser of narcotics in order to ascertain who the suppliers, or importers, are in a distribution network. Such work is sometimes dangerous and without it, many serious cases would go undetected. Is it therefore to be said that, in every case, entrapment is a significant mitigating factor? 15–48

In *Underhill* (1979) 1 Cr.App.R.(S) 270, it is submitted that the Court of Appeal took a realistic view. The appellant was encouraged to sell a quantity of drug to a police officer who, on one view of the facts, instigated the offence. But the Court declined to treat this feature as mitigation on the grounds that the appellant was, in any event, ready to sell the drugs to anybody who was willing to pay the price. The Court suggested that one would have to inquire whether the offence, or one like it, would have been committed notwithstanding the involvement of police and, secondly, whether investigating officers "crossed the line" between legitimate infiltration of criminal activities and conduct which could "fairly be condemned as illegitimate instigation".

15–49 In *Beaumont* [1987] Crim.L.R. 786 B pleaded guilty to being concerned in the supply of cannabis. Undercover agents asked B if she knew anyone who would supply them with cannabis. B suggested her father and took the agents to meet him whereupon he produced a quantity of cannabis and was arrested along with B. B was sentenced to two years' imprisonment. The judge ignored the entrapment aspect. B was also pregnant.

Held: the trial judge was wrong to ignore entrapment and the sentence would be reduced to 12 months of which six months would be suspended.

It is not clear from the report whether B was a person of previous good character or not, or whether the prosecution alleged that she had been concerned in the supply of cannabis on other occasions. Clearly, where a person of good character is entrapped, and there is no reason to believe that the offence would have been committed but for the instigation of the officers, or agents, then the entrapment must be quite substantial mitigation. However, on the facts of *Beaumont*, it is obvious that the appellant's father was ready and willing to sell cannabis and B undoubtedly acted in concert with him. Unfortunately, it is not apparent from the report whether the Court applied the principles expressed in *Underhill* (1979) 1 Cr.App.R.(S) 270 and therefore *Beaumont*, as reported, should be treated with caution: see also *Chapman* (1989) 11 Cr.App.R.(S) 222; *Mackey* [1992] Crim.L.R. 602, and more recently, *Mayeri* [1999] 1 Cr. App. R.(S) 304, and *Springer* [1999] 1 Cr. App. R.(S) 217. By contrast, see *Tonnessen* (February 2, 1998).

(j) Personal Use

15–50 Clearly, the fact that the drugs were intended for personal consumption is a mitigating factor but offenders, even if they are of previous good character, are in great danger of receiving an immediate custodial sentence. Where the amount involved is appreciable then such a result is almost inevitable. Thus, in *Keech (Walter)* (1984) 6 Cr.App.R.(S) 402, K, a famous television personality, pleaded guilty to the unlawful importation of 36.7 grams of cocaine (worth £4,500) that was contained in a shaving cream can. K obviously knew the risks involved and took careful steps to evade the prohibition on importation. His appeal, against an immediate sentence of nine months' imprisonment, was dismissed.

A defendant who makes real effort at rehabilitation may be afforded some credit in mitigation: see *Hatcher* (April 24, 1998).

F. RECENT SENTENCING STRATEGIES

I. Drug Treatment and Testing Orders

There is now provision for courts to make Drug Treatment and Testing Orders ("DTTOs")—provided arrangements are in place to give effect to them. The purpose of the DTTO is to give an offender the support s/he needs to control/eliminate his or her drug misuse, to prevent re-offending, and to enable the Court to monitor progress by requiring the offender to undergo tests for illicit drug use. The DTTO has its origins in the Crime and Disorder Act 1998 but the relevant provisions are now set out in sections 52 to 58 of the Powers of Criminal Courts (Sentencing) Act 2000. The DTTO is intended, by the Government, to replace what are now "community rehabilitation orders" (formerly "probation orders") with a condition of treatment, but the extent to which a court can make a DTTO, *and* a 'community rehabilitation order' with conditions (other than for treatment), remains unclear. It will be interesting to see how courts use the new power and what they will do in cases where the defendant has both a drug and a drink problem. The Government argue that the DTTO will offer greater powers to the Courts to tackle an offender's drug use than under the previous legislation. The Government also make the point that DTTOs will be well resourced. Others take the view that nothing would be lost by having an array of powers so that a court is free to make a DTTO, and/or a probation order coupled with conditions, as it sees fit. 15–51

It seems that those aged between 24 and 29 years are proving to be the most responsive to treatment.

The history of the DTTO may be useful. It is proposed to adhere to the old terminology as it was used when various statutory measures were introduced. By section 2(1) of the Powers of the Criminal Courts Act 1973 ("PCCA"), the Court was given the power to make a probation order in the following circumstances:

> "Where a court by or before which a person of or over the age of seventeen years of age is convicted of an offence (not being an offence the sentence for which is fixed by law) is of the opinion that having regard to the circumstances, including the nature of the offence and the character of the offender, it is expedient to do so, the Court *may, instead of sentencing him, make a probation order*, that is to say, an order *requiring him to be under the supervision of a probation officer* for a period to be specified in the order of not less than one year nor more than three years." [emphasis added]

It will be seen that originally section 2(1) gave the Court the power to impose a probation order "instead of sentencing him". 15–52

The Courts were given limited powers under section 2 to impose conditions to the making of a probation order. The power was to require:

> "*an offender to comply* during the whole or any part of the probation

> period *with such requirements as the Court . . . considers necessary* for securing the good conduct of the offender or for preventing a repetition by him of the same offence or the commission of other offences." [emphasis added]

By section 2(3) a court was empowered to impose a condition of residence namely in "an approved probation hostel, an approved probation home or any other institution. . . ." There was no power *under section 2* to make conditions as to mental treatment but this was expressly catered for under section 3 of the PCCA 1973.

15–53 The Criminal Justice Act 1991 made substantial amendments to the PCCA 1973 in respect of a court's power to make a probation order.

First, section 8 of the CJA 1991 substituted a revised section 2 into the PCCA. Thus, the substituted wording of the revised section 2 of the PCCA provided that:

> "*Where a court* . . . [in respect of a person of or over 16] . . . is convicted of an offence . . . [other than one fixed by law, *e.g.* murder] . . . *is of the opinion* that the *supervision of the offender* by a probation officer *is desirable* in the interests of (a) securing the rehabilitation of the offender or (b) protecting the public from harm from him or preventing the commission by him of further offences, *the Court may make a probation order* . . . requiring him to be under the supervision of a probation officer for a period . . . of not less than six months nor more than three years."

Section 2(6) read "an offender . . . shall keep in touch with the probation officer responsible for his supervision in accordance with such instructions as he may . . . be given by that officer. . . . "

It will be recalled that section 3 of the PCCA dealt with treatment for a mental condition and section 4 required attendance at day training centres. However, by section 9 of the CJA 1991, section 3 was revised to read:

> ". . . a probation order may in addition require the offender to comply during the whole or any part of the probation period with such requirements as the Court, having regard to the circumstances of the case considers desirable in the interest of (a) securing the rehabilitation of the offender or (b) protecting the public from harm from him or preventing the commission by him of further offences".

15–54 The Criminal Justice Act 1991 also inserted Schedule 1A in the PCCA 1973 (Part II to Sch.1 of the CJA 1991). Schedule 1A gave the Courts new powers to impose conditions as to residence (para.1); requirements as to activities (para.2); requirements as to attendance at probation centres (para.3); requirements for sexual offender (para.4); requirements for treatment for a mental condition *and requirements as to treatment for drug or alcohol dependency* (para.6).

Paragraph 6(1)(a) of Sched. 1A stated that the paragraph applied where a court was proposing to make a probation order, and the Court was satisfied that "*the offender is dependent on drugs or alcohol*". In other words the conditions of para. 6(1)(a) had to be satisfied before the Court could go on to impose conditions of treatment or residence for the purpose of receiving treatment.

However, paragraph 34 to Schedule 8 of the CDA 1998 *amended* para. 6(1) of Sched. 1A of the Powers of Criminal Courts (Sentencing) Act 2000, and therefore para. 6(1) of the Sched. 1A read as follows: 15–55

> "Subject to sub-paragraph (1A) below this paragraph applies where a court proposing to make a probation order is satisfied—
> (a) that the offender is *dependent on drugs or alcohol*;
> (b) that his dependency caused or contributed to the offence in respect of which the order is proposed to be made; and
> (c) that his dependency is such as requires and may be susceptible to treatment.
>
> (1A) If the Court has been notified by the Secretary of State that arrangements for implementing orders under section 61 of the Crime and Disorder Act 1998 (drug treatment and testing orders) are available in the area proposed to be specified in the probation order, and the notice has not been withdrawn, *this paragraph shall have effect as if the words 'drugs or', in each place where they occur, were omitted.*"

What effect did those words have? The answer seems to be that *if* the Court received notification that DTTO arrangements were in place in its area, *then para. 6(1) of Sched. 1A did not apply in respect of drug dependency but only alcohol dependency*. Note that only paragraph 6 was disapplied—*not* the entirety of Sched. 1A. 15–56

The position now is that sections 41 and 42 of the Powers of Criminal Courts (Sentencing) Act 2000, replicate the provisions of section 2, and 3 of the 1973 Powers of Criminal Courts Act, and Schedule 2 replicates Schedule 1A (as amended). Provisions relating to the making, enforcement, and monitoring of DTTO's are dealt with in sections 52 to 58 of the PCCA 2000. Accordingly, although the position is not as clear as it should be, it seems that a court is entitled to make a DTTO, *and* to make a probation order subject to conditions *other than those* provided by *para.* 6 to Sched. 2 (but which continue to apply to those dependent on alcohol).

DTTOs have been the subject of pilot studies and an 18-month evaluation conducted by South Bank University: see Research Findings No. 128 (2000), and see the Home Office Research Study 212 (DTTO's Final Evaluation Report, October, 2000). The scheme has now been "rolled-out" nationally. The South Bank team were unable to "portray the pilot programmes as unequivocally successful" (Final Report, p. 87), but, then, how is success to be measured? The researchers concluded that drug-dependent offenders can be successfully coerced into treatment as they pass through the criminal justice process. They also found that the best schemes "rely for their effectiveness on local 'champions' who are heavily committed to the enterprise"—a statement that is perhaps unsurprising. The evaluation is upbeat, noting that the amount of crime prevented "will be substantial"

(Research Findings 128). However, concern has been voiced about the targeting of persons suitable for assessment for a DTTO. The aim of DTTOs is to prevent further offending and therefore "the vast majority of suitable candidates will be convicted of acquisitive crimes" (*Guidance For Practitioners Involved in DTTO Pilots*, Circular 50/1999). Research suggests that a small group of problem drug-users may commit offences in a considerable number. There is also a tendency to target those aged 18 and over, partly because those aged between 24 to 29 appear to be particularly susceptible to treatment programmes, but partly because there exist complex rules relating to offenders under that age. Concern has also been voiced as to the lack of research to critically compare DTTOs with non-coercive approaches (see Substance Misuse Faculty Newsletter (June, 2001), "DTTOs, the new answer to drug problems?").

(a) General provisions for making a DTTO

15–57 The general provisions for making a DTTO are set out below:

"52(1) Where a person aged 16 or over is convicted of an offence, the Court by or before which he is convicted may (subject to sections 34 to 36 above) make an order which—

- (a) has effect for a period specified in the order of not less than six months nor more than three years ('the treatment and testing period'); and
- (b) includes the requirements and provisions mentioned in sections 53 and 54 below;

but this section does not apply in relation to an offence committed before 30th September 1998.

(2) An order under subsection (1) above is in this Act referred to as a 'drug treatment and testing order'.

(3) A court shall not make a drug treatment and testing order in respect of an offender unless it is satisfied—

- (a) that he is dependent on or has a propensity to misuse drugs; and
- (b) that his dependency or propensity is such as requires and may be susceptible to treatment.

(4) For the purpose of ascertaining for the purposes of subsection (3) above whether the offender has any drug in his body, the Court may by order require him to provide samples of such description as it may specify; but the Court shall not make such an order unless the offender expresses his willingness to comply with its requirements.

(5) A court shall not make a drug treatment and testing order unless it has been notified by the Secretary of State that arrangements for implementing such orders are available in the area proposed to be specified in the order under section 54(1) below and the notice has not been withdrawn.

(6) Before making a drug treatment and testing order, the Court shall explain to the offender in ordinary language—

(a) the effect of the order and of the requirements proposed to be included in it;
(b) the consequences which may follow (under Part II of Schedule 3 to this Act) if he fails to comply with any of those requirements;
(c) that the order will be periodically reviewed at intervals as provided for in the order (by virtue of section 54(6) below); and
(d) that the order may be reviewed (under Parts III and IV of Schedule 3) on the application either of the offender or of the responsible officer;

and 'responsible officer' here has the meaning given by section 54(3) below.

(7) A court shall not make a drug treatment and testing order unless the offender expresses his willingness to comply with its requirements."

(b) The treatment and testing requirements

This is dealt with by section 53 of the Powers of Criminal Courts (Sentencing) Act 2000 which provides: 15–58

"(1) A drug treatment and testing order shall include a requirement ('the treatment requirement') that the offender shall submit, during the whole of the treatment and testing period, to treatment by or under the direction of a specified person having the necessary qualifications or experience ('the treatment provider') with a view to the reduction or elimination of the offender's dependency on or propensity to misuse drugs.

(2) The required treatment for any particular period shall be—
(a) treatment as a resident in such institution or place as may be specified in the order; or
(b) treatment as a non-resident in or at such institution or place, and at such intervals, as may be so specified;

but the nature of the treatment shall not be specified in the order except as mentioned in paragraph (a) or (b) above.

(3) A court shall not make a drug treatment and testing order unless it is satisfied that arrangements have been or can be made for the treatment intended to be specified in the order (including arrangements for the reception of the offender where he is to be required to submit to treatment as a resident).

(4) A drug treatment and testing order shall include a requirement ('the testing requirement') that, for the purpose of ascertaining whether he has any drug in his body during the treatment and testing period, the offender shall during that period, at such times or in such circumstances as may (subject to the provisions of the order) be determined by the treatment provider, provide samples of such description as may be so determined.

(5) The testing requirement shall specify for each month the minimum number of occasions on which samples are to be provided."

(c) Supervision and reviews of DTTOs

15–59 There is provision pursuant to section 54 of the Powers of Criminal Courts (Sentencing) Act 2000 to supervise and review DTTO's as follows:

"54(1) A drug treatment and testing order shall include a provision specifying the petty sessions area in which it appears to the Court making the order that the offender resides or will reside.

(2) A drug treatment and testing order shall provide that, for the treatment and testing period, the offender shall be under the supervision of a probation officer appointed for or assigned to the petty sessions area specified in the order.

(3) In this Act 'responsible officer', in relation to an offender who is subject to a drug treatment and testing order, means the probation officer responsible for his supervision.

(4) A drug treatment and testing order shall—

(a) require the offender to keep in touch with the responsible officer in accordance with such instructions as he may from time to time be given by that officer, and to notify him of any change of address; and

(b) provide that the results of the tests carried out on the samples provided by the offender in pursuance of the testing requirement shall be communicated to the responsible officer.

(5) Supervision by the responsible officer shall be carried out to such extent only as may be necessary for the purpose of enabling him—

(a) to report on the offender's progress to the Court responsible for the order;

(b) to report to that court any failure by the offender to comply with the requirements of the order; and

(c) to determine whether the circumstances are such that he should apply to that court for the revocation or amendment of the order.

(6) A drug treatment and testing order shall—

(a) provide for the order to be reviewed periodically at intervals of not less than one month;

(b) provide for each review of the order to be made, subject to section 55(6) below, at a hearing held for the purpose by the Court responsible for the order (a 'review hearing');

(c) require the offender to attend each review hearing;

(d) provide for the responsible officer to make to the Court responsible for the order, before each review, a report in writing on the offender's progress under the order; and

(e) provide for each such report to include the test results communicated to the responsible officer under subsection (4)(b) above and the views of the treatment provider as to the treatment and testing of the offender.

(7) In this section references to the Court responsible for a drug treatment and testing order are references to—

(a) where a court is specified in the order in accordance with subsection (8) below, that court;

(b) in any other case, the Court by which the order is made.

(8) Where the area specified in a drug treatment and testing order made by a magistrates' court is not the area for which the Court acts, the Court may, if it thinks fit, include in the order provision specifying for the purposes of subsection (7) above a magistrates' court which acts for the area specified in the order.

(9) Where a drug treatment and testing order has been made on an appeal brought from the Crown Court or from the criminal division of the Court of Appeal, for the purposes of subsection (7)(b) above it shall be deemed to have been made by the Crown Court."

(d) Periodic reviews; amending DTTOs; review hearings

Section 55 of the Powers of Criminal Courts (Sentencing) Act 2000 also empowers the Court to conduct periodic reviews and to deal with orders that are not having the desired effect: 15–60

"55.—(1) At a review hearing (within the meaning given by subsection (6) of section 54 above) the Court may, after considering the responsible officer's report referred to in that subsection, amend any requirement or provision of the drug treatment and testing order.

(2) The Court—

(a) shall not amend the treatment or testing requirement unless the offender expresses his willingness to comply with the requirement as amended;

(b) shall not amend any provision of the order so as to reduce the treatment and testing period below the minimum specified in section 52(1) above, or to increase it above the maximum so specified; and

(c) except with the consent of the offender, shall not amend any requirement or provision of the order while an appeal against the order is pending.

(3) If the offender fails to express his willingness to comply with the treatment or testing requirement as proposed to be amended by the Court, the Court may—

(a) revoke the order; and

(b) deal with him, for the offence in respect of which the order was made, in any way in which it could deal with him if he had just been convicted by the Court of the offence.

(4) In dealing with the offender under subsection (3)(b) above, the Court—

(a) shall take into account the extent to which the offender has complied with the requirements of the order; and

(b) may impose a custodial sentence (where the order was made in respect of an offence punishable with such a sentence) notwithstanding anything in section 79(2) below.

(5) Where the order was made by a magistrates' court in the case of an offender under 18 years of age in respect of an offence triable only on indictment in the case of an adult, any powers exercisable under subsection (3)(b) above in respect of the offender after he attains the sage of 18 shall be powers to do either or both of the following—

(a) to impose a fine not exceeding £5,000 for the offence in respect of which the order was made;

(b) to deal with the offender for that offence in any way in which the Court could deal with him if it had just convicted him of an offence punishable with imprisonment for a term not exceeding six months.

(6) If at a review hearing the Court, after considering the responsible officer's report, is of the opinion that the offender's progress under the order is satisfactory, the Court may so amend the order as to provide for each subsequent review to be made by the Court without a hearing.

(7) If at a review without a hearing the Court, after considering the responsible officer's report, is of the opinion that the offenders progress under the order is no longer satisfactory, the Court may require the offender to attend a hearing of the Court at a specified time and place.

(8) At that hearing the Court, after considering that report may—

(a) exercise the powers conferred by this section as if the hearing were a review hearing; and

(b) so amend the order as to provide for each subsequent review to be made at a review hearing.

(9) In this section any reference to the Court, in relation to review without a hearing, shall be construed—

(a) in the case of the Crown Court, as a reference to a judge of the Court;

(b) in the case of a magistrates' court, as a reference to a justice of the peace acting for the commission area for which the Court acts."

II. Minimum Sentences for Third Drug Trafficking Offence

15–61 "110(1) This section applies where—

(a) a person is convicted of a class A drug trafficking offence committed after 30th September 1997;

(b) at the time when that offence was committed, he was 18 or over and had been convicted in any part of the United Kingdom of two other class A drug trafficking offences; and

(c) one of those other offences was committed after he had been convicted of the other.

(2) The Court shall impose an appropriate custodial sentence for a term of at least seven years except where the Court is of the opinion that there are particular circumstances which—

(a) relate to any of the offences or to the offender; and
(b) would make it unjust to do so in all the circumstances.

(3) Where the Court does not impose such a sentence, it shall state in open court that it is of that opinion and what the particular circumstances are.

(4) Where—

(a) a person is charged with a class A drug trafficking offence (which, apart from this subsection, would be triable either way), and
(b) the circumstances are such that, if he were convicted of the offence, he could be sentenced for it under subsection (2) above,

the offence shall be triable only on indictment.

(5) In this section 'class A drug trafficking offence' means a drug trafficking offence committed in respect of a class A drug; and for this purpose— 'class A drug' has the same meaning as in the Misuse of Drugs Act 1971; 'drug trafficking offence' means a drug trafficking offence within the meaning of the Drug Trafficking Act 1994, the Proceeds of Crime (Scotland) Act 1995 or the Proceeds of Crime (Northern Ireland) Order 1996.

(6) In this section 'an appropriate custodial sentence' means—

(a) in relation to a person who is 21 or over when convicted of the offence mentioned in subsection (1)(a) above, a sentence of imprisonment;
(b) in relation to a person who is under 21 at that time, a sentence of detention in a young offender institution."

This section first appeared in section 3 of the Crime (Sentences) Act 1997. The value of it, or otherwise, as a sentencing tool has been much debated. The supply of any Class A drug is a serious matter, but the provisions of section 110 Powers of Criminal Courts (Sentencing) Act 2000, demonstrate the importance of ensuring that drugs are appropriately classified in Schedule 2 to the Misuse of Drugs Act 1971: see the Independent Inquiry Report regarding that topic. Where the offender is aged 18 or more, and has on two previous occasions been convicted of a Class A "drug trafficking offence" (as defined by the Drug Trafficking Act 1994), the Court is required to sentence him to a minimum term of seven years' imprisonment unless there are "particular circumstances" that warrant the imposition of a lesser term. The Court must give its reasons in open court for imposing a lesser term. It seems that it is not enough to say that the term would (apart from the section) be regarded as "manifestly excessive" *Harvey*, 1 Cr.App.R.(S) 368, but the Court might need to reconsider that issue in the light of the Human Rights Act 1998. 15–62

It is perhaps regrettable that section 110 does not alert the reader to the provisions of section 152 and in particular section 152(3) which empowers a court to impose a term of not less than 80 per cent of the sentence it is otherwise required to impose where the defendant has indicated an intention to plead guilty: see *Brown (Sebert)* [2000] 2 Cr. App. R.(S) 435.

The definition of a "drug trafficking offence" under the Drug Trafficking Act does not include the offence of permitting premises to be used for an activity set out in section 8(a) to (d) of the Misuse of Drugs Act 1971, or cultivating cannabis contrary to section 6 of the Misuse of Drugs Act.

III Drug Abstinence Orders

15–63 The following provision is inserted into the Powers of Criminal Courts (Sentencing) Act 2000 by section 47 of the Criminal Justice and Court Services Act 2000. The provision came into force on the July 2, 2001: see S.I. 2001 No. 2232.

"58A(1) Where a person aged 18 or over is convicted of an offence, the Court by or before which he is convicted may (subject to sections 34 to 36 above) make an order which requires the offender—

(a) to abstain from misusing specified Class A drugs; and
(b) to provide, when instructed to do so by the responsible officer, any sample mentioned in the instruction for the purpose of ascertaining whether he has any specified Class A drug in his body.

(2) An order under subsection (1) above is in this Act referred to as a 'drug abstinence order'.

(3) The Court shall not make a drug abstinence order in respect of an offender unless—

(a) in the opinion of the Court, the offender is dependent on, or has a propensity to misuse, specified Class A drugs; and
(b) the offence in question is a trigger offence or, in the opinion of the Court, the misuse by the offender of any specified Class A drug caused or contributed to the offence in question.

(4) A drug abstinence order shall provide that, for the period for which the order has effect, the offender shall be under the supervision of a person, being a person of a description specified in an order made by the Secretary of State.

(5) In this Act, 'responsible officer', in relation to an offender who is subject to a drug abstinence order, means the person who is responsible for his supervision.

(6) The function of giving instructions for the purposes of subsection (1)(b) above shall be exercised in accordance with guidance given from time to time by the Secretary of State.

(7) A drug abstinence order shall have effect for a period specified in the order of not less than six months nor more than three years.

(8) The Secretary of State may make rules for regulating the provision of samples in pursuance of such instructions.

(9) A court shall not make a drug abstinence order unless the Court

has been notified by the Secretary of State that arrangements for implementing such orders are available in the area proposed to be specified in the order under section 54(1) above (as applied by section 58B(2) below) and the notice has not been withdrawn."

Supplementary requirements to the making of a drug abstinence order

"58B(1) Before making a drug abstinence order, the Court shall explain to the offender in ordinary language— 15–64

(a) the effect of the order and of the requirements proposed to be included in it;
(b) the consequences which may follow (under Part II of Schedule 3 to this Act) if he fails to comply with any of those requirements; and
(c) that the order may be reviewed (under Parts III and IV of that Schedule) on the application either of the offender or of the responsible officer.

(2) Section 54 above (except subsections (2), (3) and (6)) and section 57 above (except subsections (2), (3A) and (4)(b)) shall apply for the purposes of section 58A above and this section as if references to drug treatment and testing orders were references to drug abstinence orders.

(3) Schedule 3 to this Act (which makes provision for dealing with failures to comply with the requirements of certain community orders, for revoking such orders with or without the substitution of other sentences and for amending such orders) shall have effect so far as relating to drug abstinence orders."

IV. Pre-sentence Drug Testing

Section 48 of the Criminal Justice and Court Services Act 2000 inserted section 36A into the Powers of Criminal Courts (Sentencing) Act 2000. This provision came into force on July 2, 2001: see S.I. 2001 No. 2232. 15–65

"36A(1) Where a person aged 18 or over is convicted of an offence and the Court is considering passing a community sentence, it may make an order under subsection (2) below for the purpose of ascertaining whether the offender has any specified Class A drug in his body.

(2) The order shall require the offender to provide, in accordance with the order, samples of any description specified in the order.

(3) If it is proved to the satisfaction of the Court that the offender has, without reasonable excuse, failed to comply with the order it may impose on him a fine of an amount not exceeding level 4.

In this subsection, 'level 4' means the amount which, in relation to a fine for a summary offence, is level 4 on the standard scale.

(4) The Court shall not make an order under subsection (2) above

unless it has been notified by the Secretary of State that the power to make such orders is exercisable by the Court and the notice has not been withdrawn."

V. Drug Abstinence Requirements for "Community Sentences"

15–66 By section 49 of the Criminal Justice and Court Services Act 2000, section 42 of the Powers of Criminal Courts (Sentencing) Act 2000, is amended to include provisions for the making of drug abstinence requirements:

"In section 42 of the Powers of Criminal Courts (Sentencing) Act 2000 . . . in subsection (2)—

(a) after 'above' there is inserted—'(a)'

(b) at the end there is inserted—

'(b) subject to subsections (2D) and (2F) below, the order shall, if the first set of conditions is satisfied, include a drug abstinence requirement and may include such a requirement if the second set of conditions is satisfied.'

(2A) For the purposes of this Part of this Act, a drug abstinence requirement is a requirement for the offender—

(a) to abstain from misusing specified Class A drugs; and

(b) to provide, when instructed to do so by the responsible officer, any sample mentioned in the instruction for the purpose of ascertaining whether he has any specified Class A drug in his body.

(2B) The first set of conditions is—

(a) that the offender was aged 18 or over on the date of his conviction for the offence;

(b) that, in the opinion of the Court, the offender is dependent on or has a propensity to misuse specified Class A drugs; and

(c) that the offence is a trigger offence.

(2C) The second set of conditions is—

(a) that the offender was aged 18 or over on the date of his conviction for the offence; and

(b) that, in the opinion of the Court—

(i) the offender is dependent on or has a propensity to misuse specified Class A drugs; and

(ii) the misuse by the offender of any specified Class A drug caused or contributed to the offence.

(2D) The order may not include a drug abstinence requirement if—(a) the community rehabilitation order includes any requirement in respect of drugs under paragraph 6 of Schedule 2 to this Act; or (b) the community sentence includes a drug treatment and testing order or a drug abstinence order.

(2E) The function of giving instructions for the purposes of subsection (2A)(b) above shall be exercised in accordance with guidance given from time to time by the Secretary of State; and the Secretary of State may make rules for regulating the provision of samples in pursuance of such instructions.

(2F) The Court shall not include a drug abstinence requirement in the order unless the Court has been notified by the Secretary of State that arrangements for implementing such requirements are available in the area proposed to be specified under section 41(3) above and the notice has not been withdrawn."

(2) In section 47 of that Act (obligations of person subject to community punishment order), after subsection (3) there is inserted—"(3A) Subject to subsection (3B) below, the community punishment order shall, if the set of conditions in section 42(2B) above is satisfied, include a drug abstinence requirement and may include such a requirement if the set of conditions in section 42(2C) above is satisfied.

(3B) The order may not include a drug abstinence requirement if the community sentence includes a drug treatment and testing order or a drug abstinence order.

(3C) Subsections (2E) and (2F) of section 42 above apply for the purposes of this section as they apply for the purposes of that.'"

This provision came into force on July 2, 2001: see S.I. 2001 No. 2232. The Criminal Justice (Specified Class A Drugs) Order 2001 (S.I. 2001 No. 1816), made under the Criminal Justice and Court Services Act 2000, s. 70, specifies diamorphine (heroin) and cocaine as "specified Class A drugs" for the purposes of pre-sentence drug testing, drug abstinence requirements and orders, and testing person in police stations.

VI. Testing Persons in Police Detention

By section 57(1) of the Criminal Justice and Court Services Act 2000, the Police and Criminal Evidence Act 1984 is amended in accordance with subsections (2): 15–67

"(2) After section 63A there is inserted—"Testing for presence of Class A drugs 63B(1) A sample of urine or a non-intimate sample may be taken from a person in police detention for the purpose of ascertaining whether he has any specified Class A drug in his body if the following conditions are met.

(2) The first condition is—

(a) that the person concerned has been charged with a trigger offence; or

(b) that the person concerned has been charged with an offence and a police officer of at least the rank of inspector, who has reasonable grounds for suspecting that the misuse by that person of any specified Class A drug caused or contributed to the offence, has authorised the sample to be taken.

(3) The second condition is that the person concerned has attained the age of 18.

(4) The third condition is that a police officer has requested the person concerned to give the sample.

(5) Before requesting the person concerned to give a sample, an officer must—

(a) warn him that if, when so requested, he fails without good cause to do so he may be liable to prosecution, and

(b) in a case within subsection (2)(b) above, inform him of the giving of the authorisation and of the grounds in question.

(6) A sample may be taken under this section only by a person prescribed by regulations made by the Secretary of State by statutory instrument.

No regulations shall be made under this subsection unless a draft has been laid before, and approved by resolution of, each House of Parliament.

(7) Information obtained from a sample taken under this section may be disclosed—

(a) for the purpose of informing any decision about granting bail in criminal proceedings (within the meaning of the Bail Act 1976) to the person concerned;

(b) where the person concerned is in police detention or is remanded in or committed to custody by an order of a court or has been granted such bail, for the purpose of informing any decision about his supervision;

(c) where the person concerned is convicted of an offence, for the purpose of informing any decision about the appropriate sentence to be passed by a court and any decision about his supervision or release;

(d) for the purpose of ensuring that appropriate advice and treatment is made available to the person concerned.

(8) A person who fails without good cause to give any sample which may be taken from him under this section shall be guilty of an offence.

15–68 By section 57(1) of the Criminal Justice and Court Services Act 2000, the Police and Criminal Evidence Act 1984 is also amended to make additional provision for the testing of the presence of Class A drugs:

"63C.—(1) A person guilty of an offence under section 63B above shall be liable on summary conviction to imprisonment for a term not exceeding three months, or to a fine not exceeding level 4 on the standard scale, or to both.

(2) A police officer may give an authorisation under section 63B above orally or in writing but, if he gives it orally, he shall confirm it in writing as soon as is practicable.

(3) If a sample is taken under section 63B above by virtue of an authorisation, the authorisation and the grounds for the suspicion shall be recorded as soon as is practicable after the sample is taken.

(4) If the sample is taken from a person detained at a police station, the matters required to be recorded by subsection (3) above shall be recorded in his custody record.

(5) Subsections (11) and (12) of section 62 above apply for the purposes of section 63B above as they do for the purposes of that section; and section 63B above does not prejudice the generality of sections 62 and 63 above.

(6) In section 63B above— 'Class A drug'' and ''misuse'' have the same meanings as in the Misuse of Drugs Act 1971;
'specified' (in relation to a Class A drug) and 'trigger offence' have the same meanings as in Part III of the Criminal Justice and Court Services Act 2000.''

This provision came into force on July 2, 2001 in Nottinghamshire, Staffordshire, and the Metropolitan Police District.

VII. Right to bail: Relevance of Drug Misuse

By section 58 of the Criminal Justice and Court Services Act 2000, section 4 of the Bail Act 1976 (general right to bail), is amended by inserting after subsection (8) 15–69

''(9) In taking any decisions required by Part I or II of Schedule 1 to this Act, the considerations to which the Court is to have regard include, so far as relevant, any misuse of controlled drugs by the defendant ('controlled drugs' and 'misuse' having the same meanings as in the Misuse of Drugs Act 1971).''

Chapter 16
A General Guide to Drug Misuse

Frequently the Courts are asked to draw inferences of fact from "the surrounding circumstances" of the case. Yet, in a high proportion of cases involving drugs, the relevant circumstances will display a way of life that is often totally alien to the majority of the population. Therefore, without some knowledge of drug misuse, it is no easy matter to find, let alone accurately interpret, the necessary hallmarks that point the way to the truth. It is important to remember that many of the reasons for drug-taking, coupled with the methods of drug use and abuse, are as various as they are personal and liable to change as quickly as fashion and personal techniques bend with current market forces, medical and public influences or other social or delinquent trends. **16–01**

Accordingly, this Chapter is included to provide a few basic facts and principles applicable to the types of drugs under consideration, the methods of their misuse and their consequential effects. The information is provided for guidance only and is therefore necessarily descriptive. Astonishingly, courts often find themselves trying drug cases with little or no scientific help. The importance of adducing sound expert evidence (except in obviously straightforward cases) cannot be too strongly emphasised.

Having regard to the above, little is to be gained by describing every controlled drug. Instead, the main categories have been defined by their "type", *e.g.* opiates, hallucinogenics and so on. Within each category or "type", only the most popularly abused drugs are described. Nevertheless they serve as useful examples of other drugs of the same class.

A. TYPES OF DRUG

I. Opiates

These are some of the most dangerous drugs abused. They include heroin, opium, morphine, DF 118, methadone (physeptone), dipipanone (diconal), and pethidine. All were developed as pain relievers of varying **16–02** degrees of strength. All share the fact that they are physically and psychologically addictive. Tolerance can develop alarmingly and it is not uncommon to find heroin addicts who consume up to half a gram of heroin per day in order to fight off the effects of withdrawal.

(a) Heroin

16–03 Towards the end of the nineteenth century, diamorphine hydrochloride, a derivative of morphine, was synthetically produced to serve as a powerful pain reliever. Termed "heroin" in 1899 (from the Greek, "hero"), the drug was recognised as having the ability to inflate the personality. Today, heroin is widely misued.

All heroin must be imported, the majority of which now comes from Afghanistan via the Balkan and "Silk Road" routes. In its purified form the drug will be a white powder, otherwise it will assume a brown or beige appearance. When put into soluble form, it is then capable of being injected (*i.e.* "mainlined"), but this practice has several very dangerous aspects. First, a host of diseases including hepatitis and HIV may be transmitted by the use of unclean needles. Secondly, heroin is often "cut" with an inert substance in order to reduce the level of purity. Depending on the integrity of the dealer, many substances are used to dilute the drug, *e.g.* lactose or paracetamol. There have been rare instances of despicable dealers adulterating the drug with patently harmful materials such as Vim, Plaster of Paris and talcum powder, which devastate the arteries and damage various organs. Since 1988 the addition of phenobarbitone to heroin has become more frequent. This makes the treatment of heroin abuse more difficult. The reasons for "cutting" the drug are dealt with elsewhere, (see para. 16–32, below). (It is worth noting that as heroin has become more plentiful and a greater number of "suppliers" are competing on the black market, the practice of cutting the drug with bad substances seems to be declining.) Thirdly, the rate of absorption is instantaneous but tolerance may develop more quickly.

16–04 The perils of injecting the substance have caused other methods of consumption to increase in popularity, particularly smoking the drug, colloquially referred to as "chasing the dragon". This involves putting heroin onto a piece of silver foil which is held over a small flame. The vapour/smoke is inhaled through a tube, *e.g.* a milk-shake straw or a roll of paper. Occasionally, heroin is inhaled or "snorted". The rate of absorption is slower by reason of the mucous membranes which restrict the penetration of the drug into the blood-stream.

Over the last ten years the price of heroin, in real terms, has fallen, while its purity has increased from between 20 per cent to 50 per cent with an average of about 39 per cent. "Fixes" can be bought in "deals" costing as little as £5 or £10 representing approximately one-eighth of a gram. There are regional differences, *e.g.* £40–£60 in Liverpool, £80–£100 in Birmingham (NCIS; H.O. Statistics, 2000). A "deal" or "fold" is often a strip of paper measuring approximately four inches square, wrapped to form a sachet. Since heroin is being imported in ever greater quantities it is now easier for a user to acquire "bulk purchases" at a much reduced price, an important point to bear in mind when considering an allegation of possession with intent to supply the drug contrary to section 5(3) of the MDA. Per kilogram, heroin may cost between £16,000 and £20,000, depending on purity (50 per cent to 90 per cent). Most heroin had been of Turkish or Iranian origin, but this picture is shifting with international events. Over 2,340 kg of heroin was seized in 1999 (351 kg in 1989).

According to the BBC Drugwatch Survey 1985, most users will receive their first supply from a friend and then resort to a known dealer for a constant supply.

(b) Opium

The unripe seed capsules of the opium poppy (*Papaver somniferum L*) are cut to release a brown liquid. Once dried and removed from the capsules, the result is a narcotic used as a sedative and intoxicant. Opium may be raw, prepared or medicinal. (See: definitions in Part IV of Schedule 2.) Almost 38 kg of opium was seized in 1999. 16–05

(c) Morphine

There are many alkaloids of the opium poppy of which morphine is the most valuable. Aptly named "morphine" after "Morpheus", the God of Dreams and the Son of Sleep, it is highly addictive both physically and psychologically. Tolerance also develops. It is not a popular drug with drug abusers since it produces very unpleasant side-effects. 16–06

(d) Methadone and DF 118

One widely used technique in the treatment of heroin addiction is the substitution of methadone (physeptone) or DF 118 (dihydrocodeine) for heroin. The advantages are that these drugs block the effects of withdrawal and cause less dependence than heroin. It follows that by adopting a course of substitution, using drugs that are progressively less addictive, the addict is hopefully "weaned" off his or her addiction. The technique is not without its critics because it would not be correct to describe either methadone or DF 118 as a "safe" drug. Both are synthetic pain relievers but are also addictive. The effects and side-effects of DF 118 are less severe than those of methadone. For that reason DF 118 is a Class B controlled drug while methadone is Class A. 16–07

(e) Dipipanone (Diconal)

This is another narcotic pain reliever capable of causing morphine-type 16–08
dependence. Diconals ("dikes") contain dipipanone and cyclizine hydro-

chloride (an antihistamine). Only the former is controlled by the MDA 1971 (Class A).

II. Psychotropic/Hallucinogenic Drugs

16–09 All such drugs are very potent and include LSD, "angel dust", DMT (dimethyltryptamine) and psilocin (from the so-called "magic mushroom"). All produce mind-bending, psychedelic effects and loosely mimic psychosis. They are not thought to be addictive but mentally disturbing experiences may be encountered causing, in extreme cases, actual mental breakdown.

(a) Lysergic Acid Diethylamide (LSD)

16–10 First synthesised in 1938 in the Sandoz Laboratories in Basle, LSD is one of the most powerful hallucinogens known to man. It has been used, clinically, to treat acute alcoholics. Psychotherapists originally expressed considerable interest in the drug, but tests produced few favourable results and interest in it fell away when it was realised that the artificial effect of LSD on the mind differed from schizophrenia and so could not be used by psychiatrists to effectively understand, let alone treat, that type of mental disorder. The drug is difficult to detect being colourless, tasteless and odourless, but a minute quantity produces a colossal effect. Tracing the "factories" has proved to be a monumental task involving a great deal of police time. Impregnated onto "dots" of paper, small tablets, or lumps of sugar, LSD is usually taken by mouth but can also be "snorted" or injected. Effects of the drug are unpredictable. Many cases have been reported of users engaging in bizarre conduct as they enacted their experiences, including attempts to "fly", with occasionally fatal results. Perhaps the most invidious aspect of the drug is its ability to cause "flashbacks" or "ghosts", even months after the last dose in which the user resumes his psychotropic experiences.

Anecdotally, LSD was widely used in the 1960s and early 1970s, but it is not clear whether most users voluntarily repeated the experience after their first "trip". There were signs in the early 1990s that use of LSD was gaining popularity and seizures of the drug increased to 540,000 doses in 1992. However, interest appears to have waned, probably because most users did not enjoy the experience. This was despite the fact that the amount of LSD per "tab" has been very much lower in the last 10 years (50μg to 60μg) compared with the amount typically consumed in the 1960s to produce a "cosmic effect". The reason appears to be that latter-day LSD users sought a caffeine-type effect, *e.g.* at dances. Over 67,000 doses were seized in 1999 (compared with 164,000 doses in 1997). The street price of LSD in 1999 ranged between £2 and £5 per unit—or less. LSD has a short shelf life: supplies that cannot be sold at typical prices may be heavily discounted.

(b) Psilocin

The mushroom, *psilocybe mexicana*, had been used by the Aztecs in some of their religious ceremonies. Today, it is better known as one of the "magic mushrooms". The active constituent is psilocin which was first synthesised by Hoffman in the 1950s. The mushroom itself is probably not controlled. When picked and chewed, the effect is mildly hallucinogenic. If the drug is extracted then it is classified as a Class A substance. 16–11

III. Cocaine

In the 1980s cocaine was labelled the "rich man's speed". This is not new. Cocaine has always been expensive to abuse. What is new is the extent to which the drug has swollen in popularity in the last few years: see *Martinez* (1984) 6 Cr.App.R.(S) 364. Cocaine has been with us for over 100 years, being an alkaloid obtained from the leaves of the coca plant, which grows in abundance in South America, particularly Bolivia. When the leaves are dried and then chewed with powdered lime, the substance stimulates the nervous system and reduces the desire to eat. For centuries, the leaves have been used in this way by the natives of the Andes. 16–12

Formerly used as a local anaesthetic (particularly by dentists), cocaine had been used in many preparations including chewing gum and "Coca-Cola", hence the name, although cocaine has long since been removed from the product. Although the drug was abused by certain elements of the Victorian middle-classes, it was last significantly abused in Britain in the 1920s. Today, cocaine is used to a very limited extent in practical medicine by reason of its dangers and addictive quality. Both coca and cocaine are controlled by the MDA as Class A drugs.

All cocaine is imported, mainly from South America, and usually takes the form of a white powder. The drug in its salt form is administered by running a "line" of the substance along a flat surface, *e.g.* a sheet of glass/mirror and then sniffed through a tube of rolled up paper. The once popular method of injecting cocaine under the skin has declined.

Cocaine may appear in a salt form (cocaine hydrochloride) or in base form and indeed these two forms also exist in respect of heroin and amphetamine. The distinction between the base and salt forms is emphasised below. The average purity of the salt of cocaine *seized by police* in 1999 was about 62 per cent. The average United Kingdom price of cocaine in that year, was about £63 per gram and £20,000 to £22,000 per kilo (distributor value).

(a) Crack cocaine

"Crack" is not new but its production has been simplified in recent years. 16–13
"Crack" is still cocaine but it is "free base cocaine" and not a salt.

The base form of a drug appears as a wax or an oil. It may be converted into a salt by treating it with an acid. If hydrochloric acid is applied to cocaine then the base can be converted into cocaine hydrochloride (or diamorphine hydrochloride, if applied to heroin). Cocaine base is normally referred to merely as "cocaine". It is controlled in Part I, paragraph 1 of Schedule 2 to the 1971 Act. The salt is controlled by paragraph 4 of that Part of the Schedule.

Similarly, the salt form of a drug may be converted into base by using alkali (*e.g.* sodium bicarbonate or ammonia). This cycle (*i.e.* salt base salt base) may be repeated and indeed this may assist purification.

Cocaine base is waxy, melts and vaporises readily and is therefore preferable for smoking. It is insoluble in water and therefore unsuitable for injecting. By contrast, the salt of cocaine appears as crystals. It does not vaporise easily but it is soluble in water and may therefore be injected.

16–14 It follows from the above that base cocaine is required if it is to be smoked. "Crack" is merely a dried form of base cocaine. If base cocaine is not available then the salt must be converted into base. One method is to mix the salt with alkali and water. Ether may be added to the mixture. The cocaine base dissolves in ether but ether repels water. Accordingly the ether layer is removed and the water discarded. The ether evaporates and the free base cocaine remains. This process is highly dangerous because ether is inflammable.

A second method is to mix the salt of cocaine with an alkali (*e.g.* baking powder) and water. The mixture is boiled and the base melts and separates. The water is removed. Alternatively, if baking powder and salt is moistened with water and heated in a microwave oven, "crack" may be produced.

Converting a drug from salt to base or vice versa is an act of production for the purposes of section 4 of the 1971 Act: see *Russell* (1992) 94 Cr.App.R. 351; *Greensmith* [1983] 1 W.L.R. 1124. The average purity of "crack" cocaine seized by police in 1999 was about 81 per cent. A "rock" of crack (0.2 grams) may cost between £10 to £25 but there are regional differences, and many factors affect price. Some 16 kilograms of crack cocaine were seized in 1999 (33 kilograms in 1997).

IV. Amphetamines

16–15 These are stimulants used in medicinal preparations for a wide range of purposes, including the alleviation of depression, treating alcoholism, slimming aids or simply to maintain a state of alertness. Their effects are not dissimilar to adrenalin. Subsequently the user will experience a mood "trough" and other possible effects, *e.g.* nausea, dizziness and weakness.

Abusers may administer amphetamines by injection but they are mainly taken by mouth or sniffed. The effect of the drug is enhanced by injection but tolerance will develop more quickly. The MDA has controlled many amphetamines including amphetamine sulphate, methyl phenidate (Ritalin), dexamphetamine (Dexedrine) and chlorphentermine (used as a slimming drug).

The popularity of amphetamine has risen considerably in recent years. The street level purity was typically six per cent several years ago, but purity appears to have increased in recent years to about 13 per cent. Cost ranges from £5 to £15 per gram. The United Kingdom average is £10 per gram, and the average distributor cost is between £1,000 and £2,000, per kilo and retails between £10 and £15 per gram. Caffeine and glucose are popular cutting agents but other agents include aspirin and boric acid. Amphetamine often appears in tablet or capsule form. Relatively little methylamphetamine ("ice") has been seized. Methylamphetamine is a hydrochloride salt suitable for smoking. It is a Class B drug.

(a) Ecstasy

Ecstasy" (MDMA, MDEA or MDA) is a Class A drug, being a deriv- 16–16
ative of amphetamine. It is normally sold in capsule or tablet form and retails between £10 and £20 per unit. In 1990 there was evidence that Ecstasy was declining in popularity as it competed with an increased consumption of LSD. However, 1991 saw a substantial increase in the consumption of Ecstasy Reports suggest that up to half a million people have used the drug, a significant number of whom have not used drugs before. In at least one European country this drug has been lawfully administered under strictly controlled conditions for the purposes of psychotherapy. The doses given are low and only occasionally repeated over a long time scale.

Reports in the press have occasionally described serious side effects of the drug, and Ecstasy-related deaths tend to attract much publicity, but such reports must be viewed with caution because there have been a disturbing number of cases where Ecstasy has been mixed with other drugs such as LSD. Occasionally, the substance may be described as "Ecstasy" when in fact it is a mixture of amphetamine and ketamine ("Special K": controlled under the Medicines Act 1968). The average United Kingdom price of Ecstasy is £11 per dose, but prices range between £5 to £15 per dose. Many factors affect price. Ecstasy can also be "stacked", *i.e.* taken back-to-back. Some users report taking two to five doses of the drug during a "session". There have been rare instances of users taking very many more in the same period.

V. Mood Enhancers/Cannabis

All narcotics will have an effect on mood but cannabis is renowned for 16–17
creating effects of relaxation, timelessness, changes of perspective and apparent "happiness" or "distress". There is much evidence that cannabis will accentuate pre-existing moods of happiness or tension which may, in turn, be linked to the prevailing environment. It is probable that the drug is not addictive and the evidence of physical or mental harm resulting from its use is equivocal.

In certain African countries, and in the West Indies, cannabis is regularly used and may even form part of the sub-culture. Some people use it as a medicine, *e.g.* for colds, some will fry their fish in the oil, others will smoke the herb or make tea from it, or sprinkle the herb into soups. Others even bake with it. Its use in the United Kingdom is, on average, less exotic, being principally smoked.

16–18 Cannabis is grown in many parts of the world, *e.g.* Morocco, Thailand and India. The active constituent of cannabis is THC (tetrahydracannabinol). Extracted in its purest form, *i.e.* pure THC, the drug is controlled as a Class A drug. Not all of the plant contains THC, therefore not all of it will be controlled. Section 37(1) of the MDA (as amended by section 52 of the Criminal Law Act 1977) defined "cannabis" as meaning:

> "any plant of the genus *Cannabis* or any part of any such plant except that it does not include cannabis resin or any of the following products after separation from the rest of the plant, namely
>
> (a) mature stalks of any such plant
> (b) fibre produced from mature stalk or any such plant
> (c) seed of any such plant Although it is not illegal to possess the seeds, it is an offence to sow them in order to cultivate the plant: see section 6 MDA."

The most popular forms of cannabis are:

(i) cannabis oil: can be very potent;
(ii) cannabis resin: less concentrated than oil and extracted from the leaves;
(iii) herbal cannabis: weaker than resin; produced from the dried leaves, flowering and fruiting tops of the plant. When smoked, cannabis produces a sweet, distinctive smell.

The average United Kingdom cost of cannabis, per ounce, for 1999 was £89 (herbal) and £100 (resin). The average United Kingdom distributor price per kilogram (in 1999) was £1,500 to £2,000.

VI. Sedatives (Hypnosedatives)/Barbiturates

16–19 These drugs are the opposite of amphetamines. They all depress the operation of the brain. In large doses they will act as sleeping drugs (hypnotics); in small doses they will tranquillise. The drugs may be a barbiturate (*e.g.* barbitone or phenobarbitone) or non-barbiturate for example, chloral hydrate (known as a "Mickey Finn" when combined with alcohol), chlormethiazole (Heminevrin), or methaqualone. In 1971, methaqualone (a sedative) was classified as a Class C drug but all barbiturates escaped control, notwithstanding abundant evidence of widespread abuse and psychological dependence. However, the real peril of methaqualone was not in its use as a sedative, but as a powerful hypnotic when combined with diphenhydramine (an antihistamine). If taken with alcohol the effects are pronounced. "Mandrax" was the trade name of a substance that contained both these drugs. It has now been withdrawn in the light of widespread abuse as an hypnotic.

(a) Barbituric acid

Barbituric acid was discovered on St. Barbara's Day in 1869. Since then the acid has been combined to form several salts and esters (*i.e.* the barbiturates). Barbitone, barbitone sodium and phenobarbitone are long term sedatives. All substances containing 5,5 disubstituted barbituric acid are now controlled (Class B). As from April 1, 1986 other sedatives are controlled, including: 16–20

(a) Glutethimide (Doriden) (Class B).
(b) Ethchlorvynol (Class C).
(c) Nitrazepam (Mogadon) (Class C).
(d) Methyprylone (Noludar) (Class C).

(b) Tranquilisers

Some of these drugs are also subject to control, including (as from April 1, 1986): 16–21

(a) Chlordiazepoxide (Librium) (Class C).
(b) Clobazam (Frisium) (Class C).
(c) Clonazepam (Rivotril) (Class C).
(d) Diazepam (Valium) (Class C).
(e) Flurazepam (Dalmane) (Class C).
(f) Meprobamate (Equanil) (Class C).
(g) Oxazepam (Serenid-D) (Class C).
(h) Temazepam (Normison) (Class C).
(i) Triazolam (Halcion) (Class C).

All sedatives are highly addictive, particularly psychologically, and tolerance is liable to develop. When combined regularly with alcohol there is a marked increase in the risk of overdosing, since alcohol is also a depressant. To a person physically dependant on a sedative, the symptoms of the sudden withdrawal can be most unpleasant, including fear, sickness and delirium.

VII. Slimming Drugs

Certain drugs are designed to encourage the loss of appetite or to "burn up energy". They may ostensibly accentuate the level of one's "awareness". The effects are therefore similar to amphetamine and indeed many slimming drugs contain amphetamine as an active ingredient. We have seen 16–22 that amphetamine is controlled (Class B) and examples of other "slimmers" are:

(a) Phenmetrazine (Class B).
(b) Dexamphetamine (Class B).
(c) Benzphetamine (Class C).
(d) Chlorphentermine (Class C).
[Dexamphetamine is omitted from paragraph 1(a) of Part II of Schedule 2 to the MDA, but it is still included in Part II by virtue of paragraph 2, being a stereoisomeric form of amphetamine: see S.I. 1985 No. 1995.]

VIII. Solvents

16–23 In the last few years an alarming number of individuals, predominantly teenagers, have indulged in the highly dangerous practice of "sniffing" solvents, *e.g.* glues. The glue is often put into a bag, the top of which is shaped to cover the nose and mouth. The vapours released are then inhaled. Many other toxic substances are abused, ranging from typewriter correction fluid to nail varnish remover. It is the relative ease and inexpensive involved in obtaining these substances which find favour with the teenage abuser, rather than the "satisfaction" derived from the abuse.

In attempting to control the abuse of solvents, Parliament has been faced with a major practical problem. One option would be to control the chemical ingredient concerned under the MDA but this would adversely affect commerce and the everyday lives of millions of non-abusers. The alternative was to restrict the supply of certain solvents to persons likely to be affected. Parliament opted for the latter course which led to the passing of the Intoxicating Substances (Supply) Act 1985.

B. THE CONSUMPTION FACTORS

I. Administration

16–24 By section 37(2) MDA 1971 the misuse of a drug involves:

> "... misusing it by taking it; and the reference to the taking of a drug is a reference to the taking of it by a human being by way of any form of self-administration, whether or not involving assistance by another".

Drugs are principally taken by injection, by mouth and by inhalation into the lungs or the nostrils. Injections may be intravenous, *e.g.* heroin, intramuscular, *e.g.* heroin, if slow absorption is intended (rarely done and dangerous) or subcutaneous (under the skin), *e.g.* cocaine. Different methods of administration determine different rates of absorption of the drug into the bloodstream. Intravenous injection produces a near-instant effect. Other methods are much slower.

II. Dosage

Assessing the amount of the drug to administer involves a very complex interaction between first, the rate of absorption; secondly, the rate at which the drug is destroyed/eliminated by the body; and thirdly, the desired effect. Dosage will also depend on many personal factors including the level of personal tolerance to the drug. An addict may consume heroin at a rate which might well kill a normal individual. 16–25

III. Drug Metabolism

The body keeps certain drugs inactive until a chemical conversion has taken place or until it can be excreted. In this way, the body keeps certain substances "in storage" until needed or eliminated from the body altogether. 16–26

IV. Destruction and Disposal

If the level of absorption exceeds the rate at which the body gets rid of the drug then there will be a build up of that drug in the body. Depending on the drug and the amount consumed, it may be a matter of hours or months, before the drug is totally removed or destroyed by the body. 16–27

V. Addiction

Dependence may be physical, in which event tolerance develops. The body therefore needs the drug in order to prevent the effects of withdrawal if the regular administration of the substance is suddenly halted or interrupted. Alternatively, dependence may be psychological, resulting in a "craving" for the drug. Curing both forms of addiction is very difficult. Indeed treatment can only be successful if the addict displays a determined resolve to rid himself of the habit. 16–28

VI. Synergistics: the Drug Cocktail

A combination of several drugs may have no more effect than if only one drug had been taken. Where the effect of any combination is greater than if only one drug had been taken, the drugs are said to act synergistically. If the effect produced is less, then they are said to act antagonistically. Sometimes addicts will mix a "cocktail" in order to mimic the effects of a substance that they would prefer to use, *e.g.* heroin, but 16–29 which may be in short supply. Alternatively, the cocktail may be intended to produce a totally different experience, may be the product of an "experiment", or is intended to defeat certain side effects, *e.g.* depression, sickness or trembling.

It should come as no surprise to find that drug dealers have jumped on the band-wagon and now retail ready-made cocktails. Nevertheless, this is a fairly recent development but a most disturbing one. Heroin, imported from Pakistan for example, has occasionally been found to contain phenobarbitone and methaqualone. The amount of heroin in the product may be no higher than 30–35 per cent but, given the presence of the other drugs, the effect is largely similar to heroin of greater purity. The user may be totally unaware of the additives. If tolerance develops the user will therefore be unwittingly addicted to the additive(s) as well as to the heroin. He will be deterred from buying elsewhere since other supplies may not contain, say, phenobarbitone (to which he is now addicted), and will experience withdrawal symptoms in consequence. Furthermore, the user wishing to cure his addiction will find the task far more difficult, since treatment must now attack addiction to more than one substance.

It follows that dealers peddling this type of concoction can only expect the Courts to administer harsh penalties.

VII. Other "Drug" Terms

16–30 It will be seen from the various Schedules to the MDA and the current Regulations that drugs are specified as "controlled" in paragraph 1 of Parts I, II or III of Schedule 2 to the MDA. However, the Schedules also refer to the "stereoisomeric forms", the "esters", the "ethers" and the "salts" of various controlled drugs. These terms are not defined by the MDA, being terms of science. Without a reasonable knowledge of chemistry, merely defining these terms is not very helpful. Nevertheless, if only to serve as an indication, here they are:

> Isomers consist of at least two compounds which are structurally different but molecularly identical. Since they differ structurally, the compounds will have different chemical and physical properties. However, where the structures of the compounds are asymmetrically similar then they may be optically stereoisomeric: their chemical and physical properties are the same.
>
> Esters are combinations of alcohol and acid forming organic chemicals. They often produce an appealing fragrance. Common ether is made up of carbon, hydrogen and oxygen, but ethers is a generic term embracing compounds made by the interaction of alcohols and acids. Expressed very generally, a salt is the resultant combination of a metal atom with other non-metal atoms, *e.g.* chloride and sulphate.

C. THE TOOLS OF "THE TRADE" AND OTHER HALLMARKS

Proving possession of a drug is relatively easy. Proving allegations of supplying, possession with intent to supply, permitting premises to be used for smoking cannabis, etc., frequently involves asking the Courts to draw safe inferences from the surrounding circumstances. When assessing the relevance and the significance of certain facts, the following points should be borne in mind: 16–31

(i) The quantity bought by a drug user will depend on his means and the state of the black market.

(ii) A bulk purchase will be very much cheaper. A large quantity of drug divided up into several small "lots", "doses", "deals" or "folds", may indicate an intent to supply but may either have been acquired in that form or may have been divided up by the user in order to regulate his intake.

(iii) The place where the drug was found is clearly relevant and may be highly significant. Thus a large quantity of drug that would still be consistent with personal use, might well be inconsistent with that purpose if the drug had been found in the suspect's pocket at a public house, place of work, or at school.

(iv) Unexplained "profits" in the hands of a suspect is frequently a powerful indication that clinches allegations of supplying. "Following the money" is therefore an invaluable line of enquiry which is frequently neglected. However, it is an item that must also be examined with care, for it is only too easy to make false assumptions. Where large "profits" received by the defendant are totally unaccounted for and not consistent with the known legitimate activities of the individual concerned, then that fact will clearly be relevant to charges of supplying or trafficking in controlled drugs. Again, where the cost of buying the drug, said to be for personal use, exceeds the user's income, then that fact will also be relevant to an allegation of supply or possession with intent to supply because it may indicate that small quantities were sold by the user in order to feed his addiction.

Of course, monies may have been acquired by other illegal activities, *e.g.* theft, prostitution, in which case the suspect will be most reluctant to admit those offences which may explain the existence of large sums of money in his possession which have not been invested with a financial institution. Secondly, there is always the possibility of "hidden income", *i.e.* credit, that would substantially account for the difference. Many drug suppliers sell drugs on credit. Courts and law enforcement agencies are prone to say that there is no credit in the drug trade, but there are no fixed "rules". The economics and structure of drug markets are not fully understood, although research is improving. Again, arrears of rent and other debts must 16–32 be put into the calculation since one might discover that had it not been for the drug habit the bills would otherwise have been paid.

(v) Scales used for measuring minute quantities, *e.g.* milligrams and grams, may be equivocal if the suspect is a user of drugs who, typically, must measure his own supply in such small amounts.

(vi) Razor blades, panes of glass or mirrors bearing traces of the drug, straws, tubes or rolls of paper, squares of silver foil, pipes, may all be consistent with personal use but may also be consistent with supplying (save for the pipe) if other features are present, *e.g.* a very large quantity of drug.

(vii) Cutting agents. These are used to dilute certain drugs, especially heroin. The existence of a large quantity of drug coupled with a separate finding of a familiar cutting agent may be indicative of supply. Such a view may be reinforced if the drug is also found to be mixed with that agent. There are three reasons why the drug may be cut. First, to maximise profits if cut for the purpose of supply. Secondly, to reduce the purity, from the addict's point of view, if a lesser dose is required, or in order to enforce an "economy" by padding out the quantity, and thirdly, with a view to adding another active substance to achieve a desired effect. In recent years the practice of cutting the drug with "rubbish", *i.e.* a harmful additive such as cleaning powder, seems to be on the decline. This is probably not because suppliers have become more scrupulous, but simply because it makes good commercial sense given that there is now much more heroin on the illicit market, sold by many more dealers. Since competition is tougher, there is a disincentive to supply "bad" heroin.

(viii) The existence of a large number of strips of paper (perhaps torn from a magazine), or a number of small plastic "bank bags", may also suggest supplying.

(ix) An exceptionally large number of casual acquaintances visiting the suspect's home for apparently unsociably short periods of time, may indicate supplying if other tools of the trade, etc., are found at the address.

(x) Abbreviated records or calculations for which no reasonable explanation is given may suggest supply but might also be a record of sums owed to various drug creditors. This is another feature which must be examined with particular care.

(xi) A suspect, found in possession of a drug, who is not himself a user of that drug. Such a finding of fact is totally inconsistent with personal use and therefore the suspect is either holding the drug on behalf of another, *e.g.* as a mere bailee, or is an outright supplier.

(xii) Telephone "billing" evidence has proved to be a powerful (sometimes compelling) source of evidence against traffickers, as it may establish the existence and extent of a network. The frequency of telephone calls between phones may also be powerful evidence.

D. THE STATUTORY BODIES

I. THE ADVISORY COUNCIL

The Advisory Council created by section 1 of the MDA, is entrusted with the responsibility of keeping under review the situation in the United Kingdom with respect to drugs which are being abused, or are likely to be abused, or may have harmful effects sufficient to constitute "a social problem". It must therefore monitor the current situation, promote research (s.1(2)(e)) and, above all, advise the government on measures: 16–33

(i) which ought to be taken to prevent drug misuse;
(ii) to deal with resultant social problems;
(iii) to restrict/supervise the supply of dangerous drugs;
(iv) to facilitate treatment;
(v) to promote co-operation between the community and the professions;
(vi) to educate the public.

It is apparent that the Advisory Council needs to pool the knowledge of many different disciplines. Accordingly, the Council consists of at least 20 members, including practitioners from the fields of medicine, dentistry, veterinary medicine and pharmacy. Other members must have wide and recent experience of social problems connected with drug misuse.

It has already been noted how important it is that the law should be as certain as possible while being flexible enough to adjust to social and medical opinion. With every change of Government there may also be a change of policy or direction. Nevertheless, continuity is substantially maintained through the Advisory Council by virtue of section 31(3) of the MDA which provides:

> "The Secretary of State shall not make any regulations under this Act except after consultation with the Advisory Council."

Again, the Advisory Council must be consulted before draft Orders in Council, intended to amend the classes of controlled drugs in Schedule 2 of the MDA, are laid before Parliament; see section 2(5), or before an Order is made under section 7(4) (restricting the use of certain drugs to research purposes only; or prohibiting a practitioner, pharmacist, etc., from manufacturing, supplying or administering certain drugs other than by licence): see section 7(5).

II. TRIBUNALS

Where a practitioner is suspected of being in breach of certain provisions of the MDA, or is, in fact, in breach of any of them, the Secretary of State may contemplate issuing a direction to that practitioner not to prescribe, administer or supply drugs specified in the direction. In order to investigate 16–34 the matter, the Secretary of State should refer the case to a tribunal who shall report on it to the Secretary of State: section 14(1) of the MDA If the tribunal finds the case "proved" it may indicate, in its report, the controlled drugs which it considers should be specified in the direction: section 14(4).

The tribunal consists of five persons. The chairman, who is a barrister or solicitor of at least seven years' standing, is appointed by the Lord Chancellor. The remaining members are all drawn from the practitioner's profession. Proceedings are normally heard in private unless the respondent, *i.e.* the practitioner, successfully applies to the tribunal for a public hearing: see Schedule 3 of the MDA.

The Lord Chancellor may regulate the rules of procedure to be followed and the rules of evidence to be observed. All parties may be legally represented.

III. Advisory Bodies

16–35 If the tribunal finds the case proved, and the Secretary of State notifies the respondent of his intention to give a direction prohibiting the respondent prescribing, administering or supplying certain drugs, then the respondent may within 28 days make representations in reply. If representations are made the case is then referred by the Secretary of State to an advisory body consisting of three persons chaired by a Queen's Counsel appointed by the Lord Chancellor. The respondent may be legally represented. The task of the advisory bodies, as the name implies, to advise the Secretary of State: see section 14(6) and (7) of the MDA. Their findings are not binding on the Secretary of State.

IV. Professional Panel

16–36 The above procedure can be protracted. The Secretary of State may consider that prompt and decisive measures are required. Accordingly, by section 15(1), where the Secretary of State considers that a practitioner has been prescribing irresponsibly, hence the need for rapid action, he may give temporary directions to the practitioner. In order to protect the interests and rights of the respondent, the Secretary of State must first refer the case to a professional panel which in turn, must afford the respondent the right to be heard. The Secretary of State may not give temporary directions unless the panel confirms that the information available "affords reasonable grounds" for thinking that the respondent has been prescribing controlled drugs irresponsibly: see sections 15(2)(a) and (b).

The panel consists of a chairman and two members all of whom are drawn from the ranks of the respondent's profession. The respondent is entitled to be legally represented.

Appendix 1
Schedule 2 to the Misuse of Drugs Act 1971

Part 1 CLASS A DRUGS

1. The following substances and products, namely:

(a)[1] Acetorphine
Alfentanil[2]
Allylprodine
Alphameprodine
Alphamethadol
Alphaprodine
Anileridine
Benzethidine
Benzylmorphine (3-benzylmorphine)
Betacetylmethadol
Betameprodine
Betamethadol
Betaprodine
Bezitramide
Cannabinol, except where contained in cannabis or cannabis resin
Cannabinol derivatives
Carfentanil[3]
Clonitazene
Coca leaf
Cocaine
Desomorphine
Dextromoramide
Diamorphine
Diampromide
Diethylthiambutene
Difenoxin (1-(3-cyano-3,3-diphenylpropyl)-4-phenylpiperidine-4-carboxylic acid)[4]
Dihydrocodeinone O-carboxymethyloxime

Dihydromorphine
Dimenoxadole
Dimepheptanol
Dimethylthiambutene
Dioxaphetyl butyrate
Diphenoxylate
Dipipanone
Dronabinol
Drotebanol (3,4- dimethyoxy- 17- methylmorphinan-6β, 14-diol)[5]
Ecgonine, and any derivative of ecgonine which is convertible to ecgonine or to cocaine
Ethylmethylthiambutene
Eticyclidine[6]
Etonitazene
Etorphine
Etoxeridine
Etryptamine[88]
Fentanyl
Furethidine
Hydrocodone
Hydromorphinol
Hydromorphone
Hydroxypethidine
Isomethadone
Levomethorphan
Levomoramide
Levophenacylmorphan
Levorphanol
Lofentanil[7]
Lysergamine
Lysergide and other N-alkyl derivatives of lysergamide
Mescaline
Metazocine
Methadone
Methadyl acetate
Methyldesorphine
Methyldihydromorphine (6-methyldihydromorphine)
Metopon
Morpheridine
Morphine
Morphine methobromide, morphine
N-oxide and other pentavalent nitrogen morphine derivatives
Myrophine
[Nicodicodine (6-nicotinoyldi-hydrocodeine][8]
Nicomorphine (3,6-dinicorinoylmorphine)
Noracymethadol

Norlevorphanol
Normethadone
Normorphine
Norpipanone
Opium, whether raw, prepared or medicinal
Oxycodone
Oxymorphone
Pethidine
Phenadoxone
Phenampromide
Phenazocine
Phencyclidine[9]
Phenomorphan
Phenoperidine
Piminodine
Piritramide
Poppy-straw and concentrate of poppy-straw
Properidine (1-methyl-4-phenyl-piperidine-4-carboxylic acid isopropyl ester)
Psilocin
Racemethorphan
Rolicyclidine[10]
Sufentanil[11]
Tenocylidine[12]
Thebacon
Thebaine
Tilidate[13]
Trimeperidine
4-Bromo-2,5-dimethoxy-α-methylphenethylamine[14]
4-Cyano-2-dimethyllamino-4, 4-diphenylbutane
4-Cyano-1-methyl-4-phenylperidine
N, N-Diethyltryptamine
N, N-Dimethyltryptamine
2,5 Dimethethoxy-α-4-Diemethylphenethylamine
N-Hydroxy-tenamphetamine[15]
1-Methyl-4-phenylpiperidine-4-carboxylic acid
2-Methyl-3-morpholino-1, 1-diphenylpropanecarboxylic
4-Methyl-aminorex 16
4-Phenylpiperidine-4-carboxylic acid ethyl ester

(b) any compound (not being a compound for the time being specified in sub-paragraph (a) above) structurally derived from tryptamine or from a ring-hydroxy tryptamine by substitution at the nitrogen atom of the sidechain with one or more alkyl substituents but no other substituent;[17]

(c) any compound (not being methoxyphenamine or a compound for the time being specified in sub-paragraph (a) above) structurally derived from phenethylamine, an N-alkylphenethylamine, α-methylphenethylamine, an N-alkyl-αmethylphenethylamine, α-ethylphenethylamine, or an N-alkyl-α-ethylphenethylamine by substitution in the ring, to any extent with alkyl, alkoxy, alkylenedioxy or halide substituents, whether or not further substituted in the ring by one or more other univalent substitutions.[18]

(d)[19] any compound (not being a compound for the time being specified in sub-paragraph (a) above) structurally derived from fentanyl by modification in any of the following ways, that is to say:

(i) by replacement of the phenyl portion of the phenethyl group by any heteromonocycle whether or not further substituted in the heterocycle;

(ii) by substitution in the phenethyl group with alkyl, alkenyl, alkoxy, hydroxy, halogeno, haloalkyl, amino or nitro groups;

(iii) by substitution in the piperidine ring with alkyl, alkenyl groups;

(iv) by substitution in the aniline ring with alkyl, alkoxy, alkylenedioxy, halogeno or haloalkyl groups;

(v) by substitution at the 4-position of the piperidine ring with any alkoxycarbonyl or alkoxyalkyl or acyloxy group;

(vi) by replacement of the N-propionyl group by another acyl group.

(e)[20] any compound (not being a compound for the time being specified in sub-paragraph (a) above) structurally derived from pethidine by modification in any of the following ways, that is to say,

(i) by replacement of the 1-methyl group by an acyl, alkyl whether or not unsaturated, benzyl or phenethyl group, whether or not further substituted;

(ii) by substitution in the piperidine ring with alkyl or alkenyl groups or with a propano bridge, whether or not further substituted;

(iii) by substitution in the 4-phenyl ring with alkyl, alkoxy, aryloxy, halogeno or haloalkyl groups;

(iv) by replacement of the 4-ethoxycarbonyl by any other alkoxycarbonyl or any alkoxylakyl or acyloxy group;

(v) by formation of an N-oxide or of a quaternary base.

2. Any stereoisomeric form of a substance for the time being specified in paragraph 1 above not being dextromethorphan or dextrophan.

3. Any ester or ether of a substance for the time being specified in paragraph 1 or 2 above not being a substance for the time being specified in Part II of this Schedule.[21]

4. Any salt of a substance for the time being specified in any of paragraphs 1 to 3 above.

5. Any preparation of other product containing a substance or product for the time being specified in any of paragraphs 1 to 4 above.

6. Any preparation designed for administration by injection which includes a substance or product for the time being specified in any of paragraphs 1 to 3 of Part II of this Schedule.

PART II CLASS B DRUGS

1. The following substances and products, namely:

(a)[22] Acetyldihydrocodeine
Amphetamine
Cannabis and cannabis resin
Codeine
[Dexamphetamine][23]
Dihydrocodeine
Ethylmorphine (3-ethylmorphine)
Glutethimide[24]
Lefetamine[25]
Mecloqualone[26]
Methaqualone[27]
Methcathinone[89]
Methylamphetamine
Methylphenidate
Methylphenobarbitone[28]
Nicocodine
Nicodicodine (6-nicotinoyldihydrocodeine)[29]
Norcodeine
Pentazocine[30]
Phenmetrazine
Pholcodine
Propiram[31]
Zipeprol[90]

(b) any 5,5 disubstituted barbituric acid.[32]

2. Any stereoisomeric form of a substance for the time being specified in paragraph 1 of this part of this Schedule.

3. Any salt of a substance for the time being specified in any of paragraph 1 or 2 of this Part of this Schedule.

4. Any preparation or other product containing a substance or product for the time being specified in any of paragraphs 1 to 3 of this Part of this Schedule, not being a preparation falling within paragraph 6 of Part I of this Schedule.

PART III CLASS C DRUGS

1. The following substances, namely:

(a)[87] Alprazolam[33]
Aminorex[91]
Benzphetamine

Bromezepam[34]
Brotizolam[92]
Buprenorphine[35]
Camezepam[36]
Cathine[37]
Cathinone[38]
Chlordiazeproxide[39]
Chlorphentermine
Clobazam[40]
Clonazepam[41]
Clorazepic acid[42]
Clotiazepam[43]
Cloxazolam[44]
Delorazepam[45]
Dextropropoxyphene[46]
Diazepam[47]
Diethylpropion[48]
Estazolam[49]
Ethchlorvynol[50]
Ethinamate[51]
Ethyl loflazate[52]
Fencamfamin[53]
Fenethylline[54]
Fenproporex[55]
Fludiazepam[56]
Flunitrazepam[57]
Halezepam[58]
Haloxazolam[59]
Ketazolam[60]
Loprazolam[61]
Lorazepam[62]
Lormetezepam[63]
Mazindol[64]
Medezepam[65]
Mefenorex[66]
Mephentermine
Meprobamate[67]
Mesocarb[93]
[Methaqualone][68]
Methyprylone[69]
Midazolam[70]
Nimetezepam[71]
Nitrazepam[72a]
Nordezepam[72]
Oxazepam[73]
Oxazolam[74]
Pemoline[75]

Phendimetrazine
Phentermine[76]
Pinazepam[77]
Pipradol
Prazepam[78]
[Prolintane][79]
[Prophylhexedrine][80]
Pyrovalerone[81]
Temazepam[82]
Tetrazepam[83]
Triazolam[84]
N-Ethylamphetamine[85]
(b)[88] Atemestane
Bolandriol
Bolasterone
Bolazine
Boldenone
Bolmantalate
Calusterone
4-chloromethandienone
Clostebol
Drostanolone
Enestebol
Epitiostanol
Ethyloestrenol
Fluoxymesterone
Formebolone
Furazabol
Mebolazine
Mepitiostane
Mesabolone
Mestanolone
Mesterolone
Methandienone
Metheneolone
Methyltestosterone
Metribolone
Mibolerone
Nandrolone
Norbolestone
Norclostebol
Norethandrolone
Norethandrolone
Ovandrotone
Oxabolone
Oxadrolone
Oxandrolone

Oxymesterone
Oxymetholone
Prasterone
Propetandrol
Quinbolone
Roxibolone
Silandrone
Stanolone
Stenbolone
Testosterone
thimesterone
Trenbolone

(c) any compound (not being Trilostane or a compound for the time being specified in sub-paragraph (b) above) structurally derived from 17-hydroxyandrostan-3-one or from 17-hydroxyestran-3-one by modification in any of the following ways, that is to say,
  (i) by further substitution at position 17 by a methyl or ethyl group;
  (ii) by substitution to any extent at one or more of positions 1, 2, 4, 6, 7, 9, 11 or 16, but at no other position;
  (iii) by unsaturation in the carbocyclic ring system to any extent, provided that there are no more than two ethylenic bonds in any one carbocyclic ring;
  (iv) by fusion of ring A with a heterocyclic system;

(d) any substance which is an ester or ether (or, where more than one hydroxyl function is available, both an ester and an ether) of a substance specified in sub-paragraph (b) or described in sub-paragraph (c) above;

(e) Chorionic Gonadotrophin (HCG)
Clenbuterol
Non-human chorionic gonadrophin
Somatotropin
Somatrem
Somatopin

2. Any stereoisometric form of a substance for the time being specified in paragraph 1 of this part of this Schedule not being phenylpropanolamine.[86]

3. Any salt of a substance for the time being specified in any of paragraph 1 or 2 of this Part of this Schedule.

4. Any preparation or other product containing a substance for the time being specified in any of paragraphs 1 to 3 of this Part of this Schedule.

[1] The letter "(a)" was added by S.I. 1977 No. 1243, art. 3(a).
[2] Inserted by S.I. 1984 No. 859, art. 2(2)(a).
[3] Inserted by S.I. 1986 No. 2230, art. 2(2)(a).
[4] Inserted by S.I. 1975 No. 421, art. 3(a).
[5] Inserted by S.I. 1973 No. 771, art. 2(a).
[6] Inserted by S.I. 1984 No. 859, art. 2(2)(b).
[7] Inserted by S.I. No. 2230, art. 2(2)(a).
[8] Inserted by S.I. 1973 No. 771, art. 2(a).

[9] Inserted by S.I. 1979 No. 299, art. 2.
[10] Inserted by S.I. No. 859, art. 2(2)(c).
[11] Inserted by S.I. 1983 No. 765, art. 2(a).
[12] Inserted by S.I. 859, art. 2(2)(d).
[13] Inserted by S.I. 1975 No. 765, art. 2(a).
[14] Inserted by S.I. 1975 No. 421, art. 3(b).
[15] Inserted by S.I. 2589.
[16] Inserted by S.I. 2589.
[17] Sub-paragraph (b) was inserted by S.I. 1977 No. 1243, art. 3(b).
[18] Paragraph (c) was added by S.I. 1977 No. 1243, art. 3(c).
[19] The entire paragraph was inserted by S.I. 1986 No. 2230, art. 2(2)(b).
[20] The entire paragraph was inserted by S.I. 1986 No. 2230, art. 2(2)(b).
[21] The words "not being a substance for the time being specified in Part II of this Schedule" were added by S.I. 1973 No. 771, art. 2(b).
[22] The letter "(a)" was inserted by S.I. 1984 No. 859, art. 2(3)(a).
[23] Omitted by S.I. 1985 No. 1995, art. 2(2)(a), the reason being that the drug is a stereoisomeric form of amphetamine and is included in Part II by way of paragraph 2.
[24] Inserted by S.I. 1995 No. 859, art. 2(2)(b).
[25] Inserted by S.I. 1995 No. 859, art. 2(2)(b).
[26] Inserted by S.I. 1984 No. 859, art. 2(3)(b).
[27] Moved from Class C to Class B by S.I. 1984 No. 859, paras 2(3)(b), 2(4)(b).
[28] Inserted by S.I. 1984 No. 859, art. 2(3)(c) following concern regarding barbiturate abuse.
[29] Inserted by S.I. 1973 No. 771, art. 2(c).
[30] Inserted by S.I. 1985, No. 1995, art. 2(2)(c).
[31] Inserted by S.I. 1973 No. 771, art. 2(c).
[32] Inserted by S.I. 1984 No. 859, art. 2(3)(d) following concern regarding the misuse of barbiturates (whether intentionally abused or not).
[33] Inserted by S.I. 1985 No. 1995, art. 2(3).
[34] Inserted by S.I. 1985 No. 1995, art. 2(3).
[35] Inserted by S.I. 1989 No. 1340, art. 2(a).
[36] Inserted by S.I. 1985 No. 1995, art. 2(3).
[37] Inserted by S.I. 1986 No. 2230, art. 2(3)(a).
[38] Inserted by S.I. 1986 No. 2230, art. 2(3)(a).
[39] Inserted by S.I. 1985 No. 1995, art. 2(3).
[40] Inserted by S.I. 1985 No. 1995, art. 2(3)(c).
[41] Inserted by S.I. 1985 No. 1995, art. 2(3)(c).
[42] Inserted by S.I. 1985 No. 1995, art. 2(3)(c).
[43] Inserted by S.I. 1985 No. 1995, art. 2(3)(c).
[44] Inserted by S.I. 1985 No. 1995, art. 2(3)(c).
[45] Inserted by S.I. 1985 No. 1995, art. 2(3)(c).
[46] Inserted by S.I. 1983 No. 765, art. 2(b).
[47] Inserted by S.I. 1985 No. 1995, art. 2(3)(d).
[48] Inserted by S.I. 1984 No. 859, art. 2(4).
[49] Inserted by S.I. 1985 No. 1995, art. 2(3)(e).
[50] Inserted by S.I. 1985 No. 1995, art. 2(3)(e).
[51] Inserted by S.I. 1985 No. 1995, art. 2(3)(e).
[52] Inserted by S.I. 1985 No. 1995, art. 2(3)(e).
[53] This drug was originally included in Part III but subsequently omitted by S.I. 1973 No. 771, art. 2(d) and re-inserted by S.I. 1986, No. 2230, art. 2(3)(b).
[54] Inserted by S.I. 1986 No. 2230, art. 2(3)(b).
[55] Inserted by S.I. 1986 No. 2230, art. 2(3)(b).
[56] Inserted by S.I. 1985 No. 1995, art. 2(3)(e).
[57] Inserted by S.I. 1985 No. 1995, art. 2(3)(e).
[58] Inserted by S.I. 1985 No. 1995, art. 2(3)(e).
[59] Inserted by S.I. 1985 No. 1995, art. 2(3)(e).
[60] Inserted by S.I. 1985 No. 1995, art. 2(3)(e).
[61] Inserted by S.I. 1985 No. 1995, art. 2(3)(e).
[62] Inserted by S.I. 1985 No. 1995, art. 2(3)(e).
[63] Inserted by S.I. 1985 No. 1995, art. 2(3)(e).
[64] Inserted by S.I. 1985 No. 1995, art. 2(3)(e).
[65] Inserted by S.I. 1985 No. 1995, art. 2(3)(e)
[66] Inserted by S.I. 1985 No. 1995, art. 2(3)(c).

[67] Inserted by S.I. 1985 No. 1995, art. 2(3)(f).
[68] Moved from Class C to Class B by S.I. 1984 No. 859, paras 2(4)(b); 2(3)(b).
[69] Inserted by S.I. 1985 No. 1995, art. 2(3)(f).
[70] Inserted by S.I. 1990 No. 2589.
[71] Inserted by S.I. 1985 No. 1995, art. 2(3)(f).
[72] Inserted by S.I. 1985 No. 1995, art. 2(3)(f).
[72a] Inserted by S.I. 1985 No. 1995, art. 2(3)(f).
[73] Inserted by S.I. 1985 No. 1995, art. 2(3)(f).
[74] Inserted by S.I. 1985 No. 1995, art. 2(3)(f).
[75] This drug was originally included as a Class C drug and then omitted by S.I. 1973 No. 771, art. 2(d) but re-inserted by S.I. 1989 No. 1340, art. 2(b).
[76] This substance was originally included as a Class C drug and then omitted by S.I. 1973 No. 771, art. 2(d) but re-inserted by S.I. 1989 No. 1340, art. 2(b).
[77] Inserted by S.I. 1985 No. 1995, art. 2(3)(g).
[78] Inserted by S.I. 1985 No. 1995, art. 2(3)(h).
[79] Omitted by S.I. 1973 No. 771, art. 2(d).
[80] Originally inserted by S.I. 1986 No. 2230, art. 2(3)(d) and then omitted by S.I. 1995 No. 1966, art. 2
[81] Inserted by S.I. 1986 No. 2230, art. 2(3)(d).
[82] Inserted by S.I. 1985 No. 1995, art. 2(3)(h).
[83] Inserted by S.I. 1985 No. 1995, art. 2(3)(h).
[84] Inserted by S.I. 1985 No. 1995, art. 2(3)(h).
[85] Inserted by S.I. 1986 No. 2230, art. 2(3)(e).
[86] ". . . not being phenylpropanolamine" was added by S.I. 1986 No. 2230, art. 2(4).
[87] Inserted (b) to (e) inclusive by S.I. 1996 No. 1300, art. 2(2)(a).
[88] Inserted by S.I. 1998 No. 750, art. 2(2).
[89] Inserted by S.I. 1998 No. 750, art. 2(2)(a).
[90] Inserted by S.I. 1998 No. 750, art. 2(2)(b).
[91] Inserted by S.I. 1998 No. 750, art. 2(2)(a).
[92] Inserted by S.I. 1998 No. 750, art. 2(2)(b).
[93] Inserted by S.I. 1998 No. 750, art. 2(2)(c).

APPENDIX 2—SENTENCING AND RESULTS

Amphetamine and cannabis

OFFENCE	NAME	REFERENCE	WEIGHT/VALUE	FEATURE	PLEA	AT TRIAL	ON APPEAL
possession with intent	*Cocks*	(1992) 13 Cr.App.R.(S.) 166	7.10g.(amph.) + 2.82g.(can.)	personal consumption	G	12 months	3 months
possession with intent	*Rigby* [19 years]	(1992) 13 Cr.App.R.(S.) 111	77g (amph.) + 21.9 (resin)		G	200 hrs CSO	upheld

Amphetamine

OFFENCE	NAME	REFERENCE	WEIGHT/VALUE	FEATURE	PLEA	AT TRIAL	ON APPEAL
attempting to import	*Purcell*	[1996] 1 Cr.App.R.(S.) 190	1.96kg — innocuous material	believed material amph.	G	3 years	2 years
attempting to produce	*Richard*	(1994) 15 Cr.App.R.(S.) 249	intention to make 1kg	psychiatric disorder	G	3 years	2 years
conspiracy to produce	*Chapman & Denton*	(1989) 11 Cr.App.R. (S.) 222	X met D via C	entrapment as mitigation	G	4 years (each)	33 months & 3 years
conspiracy to produce	*King*	(1993) 14 Cr.App.R.(S.) 252	scale = £5–£10 million	large scale production	G	10 years	upheld
conspiracy to produce	*Morgan*	(1985) 7 Cr.App.R.(S.) 443	large scale production planned	large scale production	NG	6 & 8 years	upheld
conspiracy to produce	*Murphy and Others*	(1994) 15 Cr.App.R.(S.) 329	substantial amount	sophisticated venture	NG	5 years	upheld
conspiracy to produce	*Shaw*	(1986) 8 Cr.App.R.(S.) 16	112 litres (BMK) + Amm. For.	case analogous to importing	NG	10 years	upheld
conspiracy to produce	*Taylor* [19 years]	(1991) 12 Cr.App.R.(S.) 665	unsuccessful production	D acted as laboratory assistant	G	2 years YOI	12 months YOI
importation	*Coughlan*	(1995) 16 Cr.App.R.(S.) 519	12kg (29%)	central role in venture	NG	12 years	9 years

APPENDIX 2—SENTENCING AND RESULTS *cont.*

OFFENCE	NAME	REFERENCE	WEIGHT/VALUE	FEATURE	PLEA	AT TRIAL	ON APPEAL
importation	*Fitzgerald*	(1994) 15 Cr.App.R.(S.) 236	33.1kg	Ds = principal players	NG	11 years	upheld
importation	*Rimmer*	[1999] 1 Cr.App.R.(S.) 234	32kg (100%)		G	6 years	upheld
importation	*Wijs and others*	*The Times*, May 21, 1998		substantial amounts			
possession'	*Lyth*	(1995) 16 Cr.App.R. (S.) 68	7,500	D acted as "minder"	G	4 years	2 years
possession with intent	*Hole*	(1991) 12 Cr.App.R.(S.) 766	6 oz. worth £2,000 +	young; just started to deal	G	6 months	upheld
possession with intent	*Lyth*	(1995) 16 Cr.App.R. (S.) 68	value = £7,500	custodian; safe-eeping	G	4 years	2 years
possession with intent	*Morley*	(1994) 15 Cr.App.R.(S.) 86	10kg (1%)	courier; subordinate role.	G	4 years	3 years
possession with intent	*Oliver*	[1997] 1 Cr.App.R.(S.) 125	209.6g (8%)	life-threatening condition	G	18 months	suspended
possession with intent	*Porter (Michael)*	[1999] 2 Cr.App.R.(S.) 205	4,063 tablets	substance not controlled	G	30 months	12 months
supplying	*Ettridge*	(1994) 15 Cr.App.R.(S.) 688	200gs (9%); 32gs (4%)	considerable frankness	G	2 years	upheld
supplying	*Falshaw*	(1993) 14 Cr.App.R.(S.) 749	2kg supplied to co-def.	organiser of venture	G	7 years	4 years
supplying	*Hung*	November 13, 1995	sold drug to undercover officer (x 3)	small-time drug dealer	21 months	upheld	
supplying	*Martin*	(1994) 15 Cr.App.R.(S.) 612	240,000 pills made	assisted police/ frankness	G	7 years	6 years

APPENDIX 2—SENTENCING AND RESULTS *cont.*

Cannabis

OFFENCE	NAME	REFERENCE	WEIGHT/VALUE	FEATURE	PLEA	AT TRIAL	ON APPEAL
attempted importation	*Sturt*	(1993) 14 Cr.App.R.(S.) 440	217kg; seized in Spain	organiser in venture	NG	9 years	upheld
being concerned in	*Brown (Lorenzo)*	[2000] 1 Cr.App.R.(S.) 300	profit £25K; dealt over 33 months	whether an "activity" offence?	42 months	18 months	
conspiracy to import	*Att.-Gen. Ref. No. 36 of 1999*	[2000] 2 Cr.App.R.(S.) 303	400kg	D played a principal role.	NG	7 years	9 years
conspiracy to import	*Rescorl*	(1993) 14 Cr.App.R.(S.) 522	320kg	prime mover	G	9 years	upheld
conspiracy to supply	*Att.-Gen. Ref. No. 19 of 1997*	[1998] 1 Cr.App.R.(S.) 164	17kg in barn + 195kg in van	allowance for double jeopardy	G	4½ years; 3½ years	7 years; 6 years
conspiracy to supply	*Att.-Gen. Ref. No.53 of 1997*	March 16, 1998	20kg	good character time on remand		240 hours CSO	upheld
conspiracy to supply	*Chisholm and others*	[1999] 1 Cr.App.R.(S.) 443	large amounts of can. + amph.	imported drugs to supply	G	11 years	10 years
cultivating cannabis	*Blackham*	[1997] 2 Cr.App.R.(S.) 275	75 plants; sophiscated methods	not commercial	G	2 years	1 year
cultivating cannabis	*Booth*	[1997] 2 Cr.App.R.(S.) 67	capacity to grow 12kg p.a.	hydroponic methods used.	G	4 years	upheld
cultivating cannabis	*Evans*	[2000] 1 Cr.App.R.(S.) 107	21 plants; harvested leaves	hydroponics; personal use	G	12 months	9 months
cultivating cannabis	*Mineham*	[1997] 1 Cr.App.R.(S.) 268	320g + 1,800g (fruiting tops)	commercial; *Newton* hearing	G	4 years	3 years
cultivating cannabis	*Peters (Duncan)*	[1999] 2 Cr.App.R(S.) 334	37 plants + 28 seedlings + 13.6g	person use; medicinal use	G	9 months	6 months
drugs on high seas	*Maguire*	[1997] 1 Cr.App.R.(S.) 130	1850kg to Holland	U.K. sentence relevant	NG	9 years	upheld

APPENDIX 2—SENTENCING AND RESULTS *cont.*

OFFENCE	NAME	REFERENCE	WEIGHT/VALUE	FEATURE	PLEA	AT TRIAL	ON APPEAL
drugs on high seas	*Wagenaar and Pronk*	[1997] 1 Cr.App.R.(S.) 178	17.5 tonnes	to Holland; lower penalty?	NG	12 & 9 years	upheld
importation	*Adewoye*	(1988) 10 Cr.App.R.(S.) 226	3.37kg	more than a mere courier	G	24 months	18 months
importation	*Aramah*	(1982) 4 Cr.App.R.(S.) 407	59kg; £130,000	similar previous conviction	NG	6 years	upheld
importation	*Astbury*	[1997] 2 Cr.App.R(S.) 93	1100g (herbal) + 20g (resin)	for personal use	G	9 months	3 months
importation	*Bernard*	*The Times*, July 2, 1996	27.7kg	63 years; medical condition		5 years	3 ½ years
importation	*Bisset*	[2000] 2 Cr.App.R(S.) 397	1,151kg	strong evidence	G	11 years	upheld
importation	*Blyth*	[1996] 1 Cr.App.R(S.) 388	16kg in suitcase = £56,000	good character; 3 earlier trips	G	2 years	upheld
importation	*Elder*	(1994) 15 Cr.App.R.(S.) 514	200g (resin); 700g (herbal)	personal use	G	9 months susp.	180 hrs CSO
importation	*Fishleigh and others*	[1996] 2 Cr.App.R.(S.) 283	worth £13 million	not at top of organisation	G	12½ years	9 years
importation	*Frank*	[1992] Crim. LR. 378	19.93kg=£65,000	drugs carried in car	G	2 years. 9 months	2 years
importation	*Frazer*	[1998] 1 Cr.App.R(S.) 287	36kg in suitcase	2 convictions — like offences.	G	6 years	upheld
importation	*Golder*	[2000] 1 Cr.App.R(S.) 59	141kg	lorry driver	G	7 years	5 ½ years
importation	*Harris*	(1989) 11 Cr.App.R.(S.) 169	6.02kg	intended to sell the drug	G	3 years	18 months
importation	*Klitkze*	(1995) 16 Cr.App.R.(S.) 445	15.29kg (herbal)	co-operation; guilty plea	G	4 years	3 years
importation	*Otjen*	(1981) 3 Cr.App.R.(S.) 216	3.84kg = £6,000 in 1981	drug destined for Holland	G	30 months	upheld

APPENDIX 2—SENTENCING AND RESULTS *cont.*

OFFENCE	NAME	REFERENCE	WEIGHT/VALUE	FEATURE	PLEA	AT TRIAL	ON APPEAL
importation	*Roberts (Karl)*	[2000] 1 Cr.App.R(S.) 569	19.3kg	in custody ($2\frac{1}{2}$ months) other offences	G	42 months	37 months
importation	*Ronchetti*	*The Times*, December 9, 1997	600kg	guidelines	G	12 years	10 years
importation	*Royle and Pollitt*	[1997] 1 Cr.App.R.(S.) 184	1,609kg = £5.5 million	imported by boat	G	13 & 7 years	upheld
importation	*Vickers*	[1999] 2 Cr.App.R.(S.) 216	700kg of cannabis resin	lorry driver	NG	10 years	upheld
importation	*Watson*	(1988) 10 Cr.App.R.(S.) 256	12kg (W carried 7.4Kg)	courier acting with another	G	4 years	2 years
permitting premises	*Morrison*	[1996] 1 Cr.App.R(S.) 263	young persons 14/15 smoking	did not encourage smoking	G	12 months	upheld
possession	*Hughes*	[1999] 2 Cr.App.R.(S.) 329	1.35g	found in pocket by police		80 hrs CSO	40 hrs CSO
possession	*Jensen*	unreported, May 5, 1993	14g found in two blocks	drug on prisoner	G	12 months	3 months
possession with intent	*Black* [19 years]	(1992) 13 Cr.App.R.(S.) 262	29.6g	whether custody justified	NG	6 months YOI	3 months YOI
possession with intent	*Caunter* [20 years]	unreported, February 23, 1993	2g	supplying for two weeks	G	12 months YOI	3 months YOI
possession with intent	*Cook*	(1991) 12 Cr.App.R.(S.) 374	631g	lied during DTOA enquiry	G	3 years	2 years
possession with intent	*Cunnington*	[1999] 2 Cr.App.R.(S.) 261	15kg (in car) + 5kg (at home)	four previous offences	G	5 years	4 years
possession with intent	*Daley*	(1989) 11 Cr.App.R.(S.) 243	450g	retail dealing	G	30 months	upheld
possession with intent	*Doyle*	[1998] 1 Cr.App.R(S.) 79	8.7g (resin) + 10.4g (herbal)	intended for serving prisoner	G	18 months	12 months

APPENDIX 2—SENTENCING AND RESULTS *cont.*

OFFENCE	NAME	REFERENCE	WEIGHT/VALUE	FEATURE	PLEA	AT TRIAL	ON APPEAL
possession with intent	*Doyle*	[1996] 1 Cr.App.R.(S.) 449	380g	keeping most "for another"	G	12 months	6 months
possession with intent	*Farooqi*	[1999] 1 Cr.App.R.(S.) 379	1.91g	intended for serving prisoner	G	12 months	upheld
possession with intent	*Freeder*	[2000] 1 Cr.App.R(S.)	48kg under seat in car	courier; previous drug offender		7 years	5 years
possession with intent	*Freeman*	[1997] 2 Cr.App.R(S.) 224	5.5g to serving prisoner	medical condition	G	21 months	15 months
possession with intent	*Friend*	(1993) 14 Cr.App.R.(S.) 77	58g; £2,000 cash seized	small-time; knew buyers	G	12 months	upheld
possession with intent	*Fyffe*	(1994) 15 Cr.App.R.(S.) 13	19kg	courier	G	4 years	2 years
possession with intent	*Netts*	[1997] 2 Cr.App.R.(S.) 117	94kg = £250,000	found in car in London.	NG	7 years	5 years
possession with intent	*Oliver and Scott*	unreported, November 18, 1993	215kg	very limited role in venture	G	2 years	12 months
possession with intent	*Robbins*	unreported, December 17, 1992	4 oz.	supply to friends	G	9 months	3 months
possession with intent	*Sanderman*	(1989) 11 Cr.App.R.(S.) 226	80g	retail dealing	G	2 years	upheld
premises	*Chamberlain*	[1998] 1 Cr.App.R(S.) 49	542 plants; hydroponic system	prevalence of activity	G	4½ years	upheld
production	*Bennett*	[1998] 1 Cr.App.R(S.) 429	87 plants; 2.41kg of leaf	no sophisticated growing	G	12 months	6 months
production	*Blake and Owen*	[1997] 1 Cr.App.R(S.) 394	534 cannabis plants; £96K	NG		8 years	6 years
production	*Case*	(1992) 13 Cr.App.R.(S.) 20	3 plants + some cannabis	whether custody justified	G	3 months	upheld

APPENDIX 2—SENTENCING AND RESULTS *cont.*

OFFENCE	NAME	REFERENCE	WEIGHT/VALUE	FEATURE	PLEA	AT TRIAL	ON APPEAL
production	*Challis*	[1996] 2 Cr.App.R.(S.) 425	est. yield = 2.1 to 12kg p.a.	to share with landlords	G	5 years	2 years
production	*Dibden*	[2000] 1 Cr.App.R(S.) 64	estimated 400g from harvest	for sale to friends	G	12 months	upheld
production	*Lyall*	(1995) 16 Cr.App.R.(S.) 600	possible harvest = 3Kg	carefully planned venture	G	42 months	upheld
production	*Marsland*	(1994) 15 Cr.App.R.(S.) 665	22 mature plants + 55 others	personal use	G	18 months	9 months
production	*Snow*	(1988) 10 Cr.App.R.(S.) 93	112 plants	unmarketable harvest	G	4 years	2 years
production and supply	*Davy*	[1997] 1 Cr.App.R(S.) 17	32 plants; 616g; £590 found	D declined community sentence	G	12 months	upheld
production and supply	*Roberts*	[1998] 1 Cr.App.R(S.) 155	4 plants; 10.74g + 3g	sold small amounts to friends	G	6 months YOI	2 months YOI
supplying	*Alexis*	December 7, 1995	1.6g	small-time dealer; drug CRO		12 months	upheld
supplying	*Badley*	July 22, 1996	small amount; taken into prison	single mother; relevance of		9 months	upheld
supplying	*Barton*	[1997] 1 Cr.App.R.(S.) 140	7.2g	supply to a serving prisoner	NG	30 months	15 months
supplying	*Beaumont*	(1987) 9 Cr.App.R.(S.) 342	U.S. airbase	entrapment; mitigation	G	2 years	1 year part susp.
supplying	*Elder*	(1991) 12 Cr.App.R.(S.) 337	31g intended for sale	worked at bottom of market	G	30 months	21 months
supplying	*Fantom*	February 2, 1999		supp. to 17-year-old for months	G	3 years	2 years
supplying	*Finkhouse*	(1991) 12 Cr.App.R.(S.) 17	23 small portions	5/8ths supplied in 4 weeks	G	2 years	15 months part susp.

APPENDIX 2—SENTENCING AND RESULTS *cont.*

OFFENCE	NAME	REFERENCE	WEIGHT/VALUE	FEATURE	PLEA	AT TRIAL	ON APPEAL
supplying	*Kitching*	[2000] 2 Cr.App.R(S.) 194	small amounts	cleaner at school; to pupils		2 years	18 months
supplying	*Luke*	[1999] 1 Cr.App.R.(S.) 389	6.83g to friend + 84.68g to share	social supply	G	9 months	4 months
supplying	*Nolan*	(1992) 13 Cr.App.R.(S.) 144	14g bought as a pool	supply to school children	G	4 years	30 months
supplying	*Peck*	November 16, 1995		supplied over 9 months	G	9 months	upheld
supplying	*Savage*	(1993) 14 Cr.App.R.(S.) 409	small quantity	supplied to prisoner	NG	6 months	upheld
supplying	*Steventon*	(1992) 13 Cr.App.R.(S.) 127	730g resin	retailer of drug over 3 months	G	3 years	2 years
supplying	*Vickers*	(1993) 14 Cr.App.R.(S.) 317	reefer cigarette	given to 12-year-old to smoke	G	30 months	9 months
supplying	*Weeks*	(1993) 14 Cr.App.R.(S.) 94	supplied 3g	supplying outside pub	NG	12 months	6 months

Cannabis and ecstasy

OFFENCE	NAME	REFERENCE	WEIGHT/VALUE	FEATURE	PLEA	AT TRIAL	ON APPEAL
supplying	*Clarke*	December 19, 1996	breached CSO	G	15 months	8 months	

Cocaine

OFFENCE	NAME	REFERENCE	WEIGHT/VALUE	FEATURE	PLEA	AT TRIAL	ON APPEAL
conspiracy to import	*R. v. X*	[1994] Crim. L.R. 469	major conspiracy	assistance — post-conviction	NG	16 years	upheld
conspiracy to import	*Richardson*	(1994) 15 Cr.App.R.(S.) 876	44kg + 144kg	massive importations	NG	25 years	upheld
importation	*Aranguren*	(1995) 16 Cr.App.R.(S.) 211	521.525g (100%)	courier — "swallower"	G	8 years	upheld

APPENDIX 2—SENTENCING AND RESULTS *cont.*

OFFENCE	NAME	REFERENCE	WEIGHT/VALUE	FEATURE	PLEA	AT TRIAL	ON APPEAL
importation	*Aroyewumi*	(1995) 16 Cr.App.R.(S.) 211	1.01kg (100%)	a "meeter" — vulnerable	NG	10 years	upheld
importation	*Ashley* [20 years]	(1993) 14 Cr.App.R.(S.) 581	926g; £186,000	courier; *mens rea* cannabis	G	10 years YOI	7 years YOI
importation	*Bell*	(1995) 16 Cr.App.R.(S.) 93	387g	more than a mere courier	NG	8 years	upheld
importation	*Bristol (Kenturah)*	[1998] 1 Cr.App.R(S.) 47	1.5kg (85%) = 1275g (100%)	18 years old at time of offence	NG	10 years YOI	8 years YOI
importation	*Broderick*	[1994] Crim. L.R. 139	59 packages; swallower	factual basis for sentence	G	6 years	upheld
importation	*De Brito*	[2000]2 Cr.App.R(S.) 255	2 packs (5.59 + 4.94 (100%))	own use; mail intercepted	G	2 years	upheld
importation	*Garcia*	(1992) 13 Cr.App.R.(S.) 583	5.33kg + 1.44kg = £600,000	major operator	G	14 years	upheld
importation	*Griffiths*	[1996] 1 Cr.App.R(S.) 444	6.71kg (100%)	cooperation (continuing)	G	8 years	4 ½ years
importation	*Guy*	[1999] 2 Cr.App.R.(S.) 24	2.29kg (100%)	became prosecution witness	G	8 years	5 years
importation	*Littlefield*	(1995) 16 Cr.App.R.(S.) 211	12.14kg (100%)	more than a mere courier	NG	15 years	upheld
importation	*McLean*	(1994) 15 Cr.App.R.(S.) 706	288g (85%)	personal use	G	6 years	5 years
importation	*Nwoko*	(1995) 16 Cr.App.R.(S.) 612	at least 222g (70%)	liable to be sentenced abroad	G	5 years	upheld
importation	*Radjabi-Tari*	(1991) 12 Cr.App.R.(S.) 375	989g (85%); £122,000	imported by post	G	9 years	upheld
importation	*Roberts*	(1989) 11 Cr.App.R.(S.) 575	194,000	found in luggage	NG	11 years	upheld

APPENDIX 2—SENTENCING AND RESULTS *cont.*

OFFENCE	NAME	REFERENCE	WEIGHT/VALUE	FEATURE	PLEA	AT TRIAL	ON APPEAL
importation	*Salandy de Four*	[1996] 2 Cr.App.R.(S.) 106	13.5kg (at 100%)	two importations involved	NG	25 years	20 years
importation	*Scamaronie*	(1992) 13 Cr.App.R.(S.) 702	20kg (95%) = £4 million	prime mover in venture	G	20 years	upheld
importation	*Serdeiro*	[1996] 1 Cr.App.R(S.) 251	20kg value over £3 million;	courier; important role	NG	18 years	upheld
importation	*Valencia-Cardenas*	(1992) 13 Cr.App.R.(S.) 678	694g (85%); £130,000	courier — "swallower"	G	10 years	8 years
importation	*White*	[1999] 1 Cr.App.R.(S.) 325	386g (100%)	belief drug "cannabis"	G	6 $\frac{1}{2}$ years	5 $\frac{1}{2}$ years
importation (× 2)	*Salandy*	[1996] 2 Cr.App.R(S.) 106	9.9kg + 5.7kg	16 + 9 years consec.; organiser	NG	25 years	13 years
offering to supply	*Prince*	[1999] 2 Cr.App.R(S.) 419	actually paracetamol	D knew drug not controlled	G	18 months +	term reduced
possession	*Beveridge*	(1993) 14 Cr.App.R.(S.) 211	173mg	personal use		6 months	upheld
possession with intent	*Conwap*	[2000] 1 Cr.App.R(S.) 284	$\frac{1}{28}$g (96% pure)	girlfriend supplying inmate	G	4 years	upheld
possession with intent	*Iqbal (Zahir)*	[2000] 2 Cr.App.R(S.) 119	crack; 3.59g (80%)	supply to undercover officer	G	4 $\frac{1}{2}$ years	upheld
possession with intent	*Milton*	[1996] 1 Cr.App.R.(S.) 281	1.56g (24% purity)	to share with girlfriend	G	2 years	1 year
possession with intent	*Samuels*	(1991) 12 Cr.App.R.(S.) 18	13.96g (52%)	applied *Satvir Singh* (1988)	NG	7 years	5 years
supplying	*Cargill*	[1999] 2 Cr.App.R.(S.) 72	crack; 1.4g (×3); + 11 rocks	supplied to undercover officers	G	6 years	5 years

APPENDIX 2—SENTENCING AND RESULTS *cont.*

OFFENCE	NAME	REFERENCE	WEIGHT/VALUE	FEATURE	PLEA	AT TRIAL	ON APPEAL
supplying	*Mitchell*	(1989) 11 Cr.App.R.(S.) 562	8.43g; £2,270 found	supplying for 6 months	G	3 years	upheld
supplying	*Mulvey*	unreported, 5 May, 1994	2.34g; £200	believed drug was "cannabis".	G	9 months	2 months
Cocaine and amphetamine							
OFFENCE	NAME	REFERENCE	WEIGHT/VALUE	FEATURE	PLEA	AT TRIAL	ON APPEAL
importation	*Brougham*	[1996] 2 Cr.App.R.(S.) 88	cocaine = 6kg (100%)	1/2kg of amph. (20%)	G	15 years	12 years
Cocaine and heroin							
OFFENCE	NAME	REFERENCE	WEIGHT/VALUE	FEATURE	PLEA	AT TRIAL	ON APPEAL
supplying	*Williams (Derek)*	[2000] 2 Cr.App.R(S.) 308	supplies to visitors to house	W supplied to known users	G	6 ½ years	?
cocaine/crack							
OFFENCE	NAME	REFERENCE	WEIGHT/VALUE	FEATURE	PLEA	AT TRIAL	ON APPEAL
premises	*Bradley*	[1997] 1 Cr.App.R(S.) 59	crack sold from premises	no profit; no corruption	G	4 years	2 years
cocaine; ecstasy							
OFFENCE	NAME	REFERENCE	WEIGHT/VALUE	FEATURE	PLEA	AT TRIAL	ON APPEAL
supplying	*Day*	[2000] 2 Cr.App.R(S.) 312	£50 cocaine; 8 Es; 37.7g can.	test purchase operation	G	5 ½ years	4 years
Crack and Ecstasy							
OFFENCE	NAME	REFERENCE	WEIGHT/VALUE	FEATURE	PLEA	AT TRIAL	ON APPEAL
possession	*Cox [18 years]*	(1994) 15 Cr.App.R.(S.) 216	1.5gs (crack) + 16 tablets	D — history of drug abuse	G	18 month YOI	3 month YOI

APPENDIX 2—SENTENCING AND RESULTS *cont.*

Crack cocaine

OFFENCE	NAME	REFERENCE	WEIGHT/VALUE	FEATURE	PLEA	AT TRIAL	ON APPEAL
possession	*Scarlett*	(1995) 16 Cr.App.R.(S.) 745	7 pieces = 1.69g	sentencing factors discussed	NG	6 months	upheld
possession with intent	*Frankson*	[1996] 2 Cr.App.R.(S.) 366	44g of crack	disparity with co-defendant	NG	7 years, proper	5 years
supplying	*Edwards*	(1992) 13 Cr.App.R.(S.) 356	small amount (× 2)	previous good character	G	4 years	upheld
supplying	*Howard*	[1996] 2 Cr.App.R.(S.) 273	4 "deals" over two weeks	sold to undercover officer	G	5 years	4 years
supplying	*Virgo*	[1996] 2 Cr.App.R.(S.) 443	211 millig	sold to undercover officer	G	5 years	4 years

Diazepam

OFFENCE	NAME	REFERENCE	WEIGHT/VALUE	FEATURE	PLEA	AT TRIAL	ON APPEAL
driving whilst unfit	*King*	[2000] 1 Cr.App.R(S.) 105		diazepam and barbiturate trace	G	6 months	4 months
possession with intent	*Holloway*	(1995) 16 Cr.App.R.(S.)	86 tablets	smuggled into prison	G	3 months	upheld

Ecstasy

OFFENCE	NAME	REFERENCE	WEIGHT/VALUE	FEATURE	PLEA	AT TRIAL	ON APPEAL
conspiracy to import	*Ellis and Avis*	[2000] 1 Cr.App.R(S.) 38	88,000 tablets (100%)	drug seized in Belgium		18 year; 22 year	16 years
exportation	*Powell*	*The Times*, October 5, 2000	9,245 tablets; by post to USA	previously exported amph.	G	10 years	upheld
importation	*Bayley*	(1995) 16 Cr.App.R.(S.) 605	58kg	assisted in organising offence	NG	15 years	upheld
importation	*Beeley*	[1996] 1 Cr.App.R.(S.) 233	1,585 tablets = 158g	courier, in debt, threatened	G	7 years	6 years

APPENDIX 2—SENTENCING AND RESULTS *cont.*

OFFENCE	NAME	REFERENCE	WEIGHT/VALUE	FEATURE	PLEA	AT TRIAL	ON APPEAL
importation	*Main and Johnson*	[1997] 2 Cr.App.R.(S.) 63	295kg; 1.3 million tablets	over 1.3 million tablets	NG	24 years	upheld
importation	*Warren*	[1996] 1 Cr.App.R.(S.) 233	1,011 tablets = 100g	courier, belief drug cannabis	G	6 years	5 years
offering to supply	*Chambers (Mark)*	[1999] 1 Cr.App.R.(S.) 262		actually decongestant pills	G	18 months	12 months
offering to supply	*Skidmore*	[1997] 1 Cr.App.R.(S.) 15	50 tablets	to sell at nightclub	G	2 years	upheld
possession	*Myers*	*The Times*, June 22, 1995	14 tablets	social; *Newton* hearing	G	18 months	12 months
possession with intent	*Allery*	(1993) 14 Cr.App.R.(S.) 699	19 pills + more at home	whether drug dangerous	NG	5 years	upheld
possession with intent	*Asquith [19 years.]*	(1995) 16 Cr.App.R.(S.) 453	48 tablets	dispensing/profit	G	3 years YOI	upheld
possession with intent	*Broom*	(1993) 14 Cr.App.R.(S.) 677	190 tablets worth £3,900	to sell; named supplier	G	3 years	upheld
possession with intent	*Bryant*	(1993) 14 Cr.App.R.(S.) 707	unspecified amount	disparity	G	4 years	3 years
possession with intent	*Burton*	(1993) 14 Cr.App.R.(S.) 716	1470 pills (£22,000–28,000)	totality principle	G	6 years	varied
possession with intent	*Busby*	[2000] 1 Cr.App.R(S.) 279	14 Ecstasy; 4 amph. tablets	to share with friends; club	G	9 months	6 months
possession with intent	*Byearne*	[1996] 2 Cr.App.R(S.) 34	18 tablets	minder for friends in a club	G	2 years	12 months
possession with intent	*Forsdick*	[1996] 1 Cr.App.R(S.) 300	21 tablets to share with friends	18 years old at time of offence	G	$2\frac{1}{2}$ years YOI	18 months YOI
possession with intent	*Gass*	[2000] 1 Cr.App.R(S.) 475	25 tablets; club	flawed *Newton* hearing	G	3 years	2 years

APPENDIX 2—SENTENCING AND RESULTS *cont.*

OFFENCE	NAME	REFERENCE	WEIGHT/VALUE	FEATURE	PLEA	AT TRIAL	ON APPEAL
possession with intent	*Harris*	[1998] 1 Cr.App.R(S.) 38	705 tablets in seven bags	H said he was a "minder"	G	5 years	4 years
possession with intent	*Harvey*	[1997] 2 Cr.App.R(S.) 306	900 tablets	D a "warehouseman"	G	5 years	3½ years
possession with intent	*Jones*	(1994) 15 Cr.App.R.(S.) 856	273/4 tablets	outside "rave" premises	NG	4 years	upheld
possession with intent	*Kempley*	unreported, February 14, 1994	134 tablets = £1,800	in envelope; in appl. Poss.	NG	5 years	upheld
possession with intent	*McLaughlin*	(1995) 16 Cr.App.R.(S.) 357	1,000 tablets	passenger/minor role	G	5 years	4 years
possession with intent	*McPhail*	August 20, 1996	238 tablets	purity rather than street value		7 years	5 years
possession with intent	*Mitchell*	[1996] 2 Cr.App.R.(S.) 369	25 tablets	to sell to friends	G	3 years YOI	upheld
possession with intent	*Paparella*	[1996] 2 Cr.App.R.(S.) 165	46 tablets	found with £436	G	3½ years	upheld
possession with intent	*Pettet*	[1998] 1 Cr.App.R(S.) 399		collected drug in car	G	12 m YOI	upheld
possession with intent	*Robertson*	[2000] 1 Cr.App.R(S.) 514	28 tablets, divided up into wraps	social group; not for profit	G	18 months	12 months
possession with intent	*Spalding*	(1995) 16 Cr.App.R.(S.) 803	54 tablets	'minding' drug for dealer	G	30 months	18 months
possession with intent	*Veeraswamy*	(1993) 14 Cr.App.R.(S.) 680	50 tablets	exceptional hardship	G	5 years	3 years
supplying	*Bull*	[2000] 2 Cr.App.R(S.) 195	2 tablets to friend	heart failure; death; no profit	G	18 months	9 months
supplying	*Catterall* [20 years]	(1993) 14 Cr.App.R.(S.) 724	small amount	parent informed police	G	4 years YOI	2 years YOI

APPENDIX 2—SENTENCING AND RESULTS *cont.*

OFFENCE	NAME	REFERENCE	WEIGHT/VALUE	FEATURE	PLEA	AT TRIAL	ON APPEAL
supplying	*Mayeri*	[1999] 1 Cr.App.R.(S.) 304	four transactions	sold to undercover officer	G	2 years	upheld
supplying	*McLellan*	(1994) 15 Cr.App.R.(S.) 351	supplied 1 tablet	supplied from her home	G	3 years	2 years
supplying	*Sharpe*	May 1, 1997	actually 1/2gram of amph.	persistent requests by officer		18 months	12 months
supplying	*Thompson* [20 years]	[1997] Cr.App.R.(S.) 223	tablets sold in night-club	£495 on defendant; 20 years	G	5 years. YOI	4 years YOI
supplying	*Wakeman*	[1999] 1 Cr.App.R.(S.) 222	1g cocaine + 4gr cannabis	supply to friends	G	2 years	18 months

Ecstasy and amphetamine

OFFENCE	NAME	REFERENCE	WEIGHT/VALUE	FEATURE	PLEA	AT TRIAL	ON APPEAL
importation	*Tattenhove*	[1996] 2 Cr.App.R.(S.) 91	493,620 tablets +146.5kg (amph.)	more than mere courier	NG	25 years	20 years
possession with intent	*McPhail*	[1997] 1 Cr.App.R.(S.) 321	238 tablets (E) + 125g (amph.)	purity of drug important	G	7 years	5 years
supplying	*Foggarty*	[1997] 1 Cr.App.R(S.) 238	sold 20–30 tablets (E) 20 wraps (amph.)	value sold = £4,000	G	7 years	5 years

Ecstasy and LSD

OFFENCE	NAME	REFERENCE	WEIGHT/VALUE	FEATURE	PLEA	AT TRIAL	ON APPEAL
possession with intent	*Kingham*	(1995) 16 Cr.App.R.(S.) 399	199 tablets; 79 LSD	party use / no profit	G	4 years	3 years

APPENDIX 2—SENTENCING AND RESULTS *cont.*

Ephedrine and K

OFFENCE	NAME	REFERENCE	WEIGHT/VALUE	FEATURE	PLEA	AT TRIAL	ON APPEAL
offering to supply	*Kramer*	[1997] 2 Cr.App.R.(S.) 82	34 tablets	to be sold as Es at a club	G	12 months YOI	upheld

Heroin

OFFENCE	NAME	REFERENCE	WEIGHT/VALUE	FEATURE	PLEA	AT TRIAL	ON APPEAL
being concerned in supply	*Mackey and Shaw*	(1993) 14 Cr.App.R.(S.) 53	1kg. (61%) = £150,000	entrapment; mitigation	G	7 year. [Shaw]	6 years
conspiracy to supply	*Att.-Gen. Ref. No.* 64 of 1997	[1999] 1 Cr.App.R.(S.) 237	1485g (100%)	minders	G	30 months	6 years
conspiracy to supply	*A-G Ref No: 16 1991*	(1992) 13 Cr.App.R.(S.) 653	2oz. per day for 6 months	wholesaler	NG	7 years	10 years
conspiracy to supply	*Brocklesby (David)*	[1999] 1 Cr.App.R.(S.) 80	heroin and cocaine	used violence against others	NG	21year(D); 22(P)	upheld
conspiracy to supply	*Sehitoglu and Ozakan*	[1998] 1 Cr.App.R(S.) 89	24kg (pure)		G	15 years (Sehitoglu); 25 years (Ozakan)	8 years (Sehitoglu); 18 years (Ozakan)
importation	*Abayomi*	unreported, December 16, 1993	303g	curse of abuse not abated	G	7½ years	upheld
importation	*Afzal and Arshad*	(1992) 13 Cr.App.R.(S.) 145	1236g (1%); unsaleable	believed drug of aver purity	G	12 year + 8 year	8 year + 5 year
importation	*Daniel*	[1995] 16 Cr. App.R(S.) 960	643.5g (100%)	courier; ill children	G	9 years	upheld
importation	*Faluade*	(1989) 11 Cr.App.R.(S.) 156	210g. (35%) = £22,000	courier	G	4½ years	upheld
importation	*Hurst*	(1989) 11 Cr.App.R.(S.) 365	1kg (60%) = £126,000	some assistance to officer	G	11 years	upheld

APPENDIX 2—SENTENCING AND RESULTS *cont.*

OFFENCE	NAME	REFERENCE	WEIGHT/VALUE	FEATURE	PLEA	AT TRIAL	ON APPEAL
importation	*Kavusturan*	unreported, March 4, 1993	240kg = £33 million	assistance given	NG	18 years	13 years
importation	*Kayar*	[1998] 2 Cr.App.R.(S.) 355	10.3kg = £1.6, million	organiser		20 years	16 years
importation	*Latif and Shahzad*	(1994) 15 Cr.App.R.(S.) 864	20kg	alleged entrapment	NG	20 years	upheld
importation	*Meah*	(1991) 12 Cr.App.R.(S.) 461	136g (37%)	personal use	G	6 years	3 years
importation	*Middelkoop*	[1997] 1 Cr.App.R.(S.) 423	90 kg (65%)		NG	20 years	16 years
importation	*Mouzulukwe*	[1996] 2 Cr.App.R.(S.) 48	38gs (100%) in 31 packs	drug destined for USA	NG	6 years	upheld
importation	*Nweke*	(1989) 11 Cr.App.R.(S.) 500	172g. (25%) = £15,480	twice imported cannabis	G	6 years	upheld
importation	*Ogburu and Okoroha*	*The Times*, October 14, 1992	value = £36,000	liable to be sentenced abroad		5 & 11 years	upheld
importation	*Patel and Varshney*	(1995) 16 Cr.App.R(S.) 267	two counts; 563g (100%)	low purity 2%–4%		15 & 9 years	12 & 8 years
importation	*Telli*	[1997] 1 Cr.App.R.(S.) 423	90 kg (65%)	exportations also involved	G	20 years	18 years
importation	*Varshney*	(1995) 16 Cr.App.R.(S.) 267	310–316g (100%)	low purity/*mens rea*	NG	9 years	8 years
possession	*Gallagher*	(1991) 12 Cr.App.R.(S.) 224	3.3g (33%)	personal use	G	12 months	6 months
possession	*Lutzo*	(1989) 11 Cr.App.R.(S.) 495	283 mg (44%)	personal use	G	12 months	6 months
possession	*Roberts*	[1997] 2 Cr.App.R.(S.) 187	0.188g; 34 years old	D a serving prisoner	G	15 months	upheld

APPENDIX 2—SENTENCING AND RESULTS *cont.*

OFFENCE	NAME	REFERENCE	WEIGHT/VALUE	FEATURE	PLEA	AT TRIAL	ON APPEAL
possession with intent	*Appleton*	[1999] 2 Cr.App.R.(S.) 289		custodian of drug	G	5 years	upheld
possession with intent	*Arif*	(1994) 15 Cr.App.R.(S.) 895	213.42g (100% purity)	'minder'	G	6 years	4½ years
possession with intent	*Batt (Jeanne)*	[1999] 2 Cr.App.R.(S.) 223	4.9g to serving prisoner	mental health; sucide risk	NG	3 years	2 years susp.
possession with intent	*Black (Craig)*	[2000] 2 Cr.App.R(S.) 41	13.6g (48%); for inmate	B instigated supply to him		12 years	6 years
possession with intent	*Djahit*	[1999] 2 Cr.App.R.(S.) 142	21.497g	purity not established	G	6 years	4 years
possession with intent	*Giunta*	[2000] 1 Cr.App.R(S.) 365	120.9g heroin + can., Es, temaz.	supply to known users	G	5 years	upheld
possession with intent	*Hamilton*	[2000] 1 Cr.App.R(S.) 91	6.02g	girlfriend, supply to inmate	G	2 years	upheld
possession with intent	*Lane*	(1989) 11 Cr.App.R.(S.) 547	9g = £1,000	sold to friends for 1 year	G	6 years	upheld
possession with intent	*McHugh*	unreported, 2 November, 1992	0.58g	visitor; supply to inmate	G	9 months	upheld
possession with intent	*Smythe (Scott Lee)*	[2000] 1 Cr.App.R(S.) 547	1.82g	social group; not profit	G	4½ years	2 years
possession with intent	*Stark*	(1993) 13 Cr.App.R.(S.) 548	1.03g + 26g = £2,500	AIDS; terminal	G	4 years.	upheld
premises for supply	*Fitzpatrick*	[2001] 1 Cr.App.R.(S.) 6	heroin and money exchanged	period of months; no profit	G	4½ years	3½ years
supply / manslaughter	*Clarke*	(1992) 13 Cr.App.R.(S.) 552	C injected deceased (X)	social users; C helped X	G	3year (supply)	upheld [??]
supplying	*Ashford*	[2000] 1 Cr.App.R(S.) 389	heroin to X; X died	heroin not cause of death	G	3 years	2 years

APPENDIX 2—SENTENCING AND RESULTS *cont.*

OFFENCE	NAME	REFERENCE	WEIGHT/VALUE	FEATURE	PLEA	AT TRIAL	ON APPEAL
supplying	*Ball*	*The Times*, December 1, 1997	sold small quantities	to undercover officer; rehabilitation	G	5½ years	upheld
supplying	*Harvey (Winston)*	[2000] 1 Cr.App.R(S.) 368	small amounts (2 to undercover officer)	previous Class A offences		7 years	upheld
supplying	*Lucas (Andrew)*	[1999] 1 Cr.App.R.(S.) 78	some to girlfriend (user) who died	girl requested heroin	G	5 years	3 years
supplying	*O'Brien*	(1994) 15 Cr.App.R.(S.) 556	£30 vial of heroin shared	social supply; death of user	G	5 years	3 years
supplying	*Robb and Akram*	[1996] 2 Cr.App.R.(S.) 414	494g. (36%) = 169g (100%)	agreed to supply undercover officer	NG	10 years	7 years
supplying	*Springer (Robert)*	[1999] 1 Cr.App.R.(S.) 217	1.5g supplied to undercover officer	3 counts; info. re supplying	G	4 years	upheld
supplying	*Tonnessen*	*The Times*, March 3, 1998	deal supplied to journalists	entrapment	G	12 months	6 months
supplying	*Weeks (David)*	[1999] 2 Cr.App.R.(S.) 16	9 counts; 1.04g	dealt over 2½ months	G	7 years	5 years

Heroin and LSD

OFFENCE	NAME	REFERENCE	WEIGHT/VALUE	FEATURE	PLEA	AT TRIAL	ON APPEAL
supplying	*Wiggins*	(1994) 15 Cr.App.R.(S.) 558	small amounts	sold to teenagers	G	3 years YOI	30 months YOI

Heroin and cannabis

OFFENCE	NAME	REFERENCE	WEIGHT/VALUE	FEATURE	PLEA	AT TRIAL	ON APPEAL
supplying	*Young*	[2000] 2 Cr.App.R(S.) 248	10.7g heroin + 25.9g can.	intended supply to inmate	G	2½ years	upheld

Heroin and crack

OFFENCE	NAME	REFERENCE	WEIGHT/VALUE	FEATURE	PLEA	AT TRIAL	ON APPEAL
possession with intent	*Jones*	[1996] 2 Cr.App.R.(S.) 134	7.4g (heroin) + 5.3g (crack)	selling for 2 weeks	G	4½ years	upheld

APPENDIX 2—SENTENCING AND RESULTS *cont.*

OFFENCE	NAME	REFERENCE	WEIGHT/VALUE	FEATURE	PLEA	AT TRIAL	ON APPEAL
Heroin and methadone							
OFFENCE	NAME	REFERENCE	WEIGHT/VALUE	FEATURE	PLEA	AT TRIAL	ON APPEAL
possession with intent	*Prince*	[1996] 1 Cr.App.R(S.) 335	491 mg (27%)	drug for prisoner; ill-health	G	5 years	upheld
Heroin and cocaine							
OFFENCE	NAME	REFERENCE	WEIGHT/VALUE	FEATURE	PLEA	AT TRIAL	ON APPEAL
possession with intent	*Morris (Harold)*	*The Times*, August 4, 2000		purity % not always needed		5 years	upheld
LSD							
OFFENCE	NAME	REFERENCE	WEIGHT/VALUE	FEATURE	PLEA	AT TRIAL	ON APPEAL
conspiracy to import	*Att.-Gen.'s Ref.* No. 3–5 of 1992	(1993) 14 Cr.App.R.(S.) 191	19,000 tablets (£60–£100,000)	major importation	G	30 months	5 & 4 years
possession	*Campbell*	(1992) 13 Cr.App.R.(S.) 630	impregnated strip of card	acquitted on s.5(3)	NG	18 months	12 months
possession with intent	*Andrews [20 years]*	(1992) 13 Cr.App.R.(S.) 504	20 doses	sold to friends; no profit	G	18 months YOI	upheld
possession with intent	*Hurley*	*The Times*, August 5, 1997	280,000 units (31 micrograms)		G	14 years	10 years
LSD oth Class A							
OFFENCE	NAME	REFERENCE	WEIGHT/VALUE	FEATURE	PLEA	AT TRIAL	ON APPEAL
supplying	*Chesterton*	[1997] 2 Cr.App.R(S.) 297		juvenile offenders to pupils	G	3 year YOI	upheld
Methylamphetamine							
OFFENCE	NAME	REFERENCE	WEIGHT/VALUE	FEATURE	PLEA	AT TRIAL	ON APPEAL
conspiracy to produce	*Popple*	(1993) 14 Cr.App.R.(S.) 60	seized = £2 million; capacity = £20 million	imposition of max. term?	G	14 years	12 years

APPENDIX 2—SENTENCING AND RESULTS *cont.*

OFFENCE	NAME	REFERENCE	WEIGHT/VALUE	FEATURE	PLEA	AT TRIAL	ON APPEAL
Opium							
OFFENCE	NAME	REFERENCE	WEIGHT/VALUE	FEATURE	PLEA	AT TRIAL	ON APPEAL
possession with intent	*Mashollahi*	*The Times*, August 4, 2000		guidelines given	G	14 years	9 years
Steroids							
OFFENCE	NAME	REFERENCE	WEIGHT/VALUE	FEATURE	PLEA	AT TRIAL	ON APPEAL
possession with intent	*Wilson (Paul)*	[1998] 1 Cr.App.R(S.) 364	value = £84,000	medicines	G	15 months	upheld
production w/o licence	*Yanko*	[1996] 1 Cr.App.R(S.) 217	trade mark offences	cooperated with police	G	3 years 7 months	2 years 10 months
prohibited sale	*Wileman*	[1997] 2 Cr.App.R.(S.) 326	worth some £31,000	PoM; large amount	G	9 months	6 months
variety of drugs							
OFFENCE	NAME	REFERENCE	WEIGHT/VALUE	FEATURE	PLEA	AT TRIAL	ON APPEAL
possession with intent	*Wilson*	unreported, May 26, 1994	value = £71,000 [5 counts]	incinerator operator stealing drug	G	8 years	leave refused

INDEX